Principles of
International Taxation

Principles of International Taxation

Sixth Edition

Lynne Oats PhD
Professor of Taxation and Accounting,
University of Exeter

Angharad Miller PhD, FCA, CTA
Senior Lecturer in Taxation, Bournemouth University

Emer Mulligan PhD, AITI
Lecturer in Taxation and Finance,
National University of Ireland, Galway

Bloomsbury Professional

Bloomsbury Professional

An imprint of Bloomsbury Publishing Plc

Bloomsbury Professional Ltd	Bloomsbury Publishing Plc
41–43 Boltro Road	50 Bedford Square
Haywards Heath	London
RH16 1BJ	WC1B 3DP
UK	UK

www.bloomsbury.com

**BLOOMSBURY and the Diana logo are trademarks of
Bloomsbury Publishing Plc**

British Library Cataloguing-in-Publication Data

A catalogue record for this book is available from the British Library.

ISBN:	PB:	978 1 52650 169 1
	ePDF:	978 1 52650 171 4
	ePub:	978 1 52650 170 7

Typeset by Compuscript Ltd, Shannon
Printed and bound by CPI Group (UK) Ltd, Croydon, CR0 4YY

To find out more about our authors and books visit
www.bloomsburyprofessional.com. Here you will find extracts, author information,
details of forthcoming events and the option to sign up for our newsletters

Preface

The principal aim of this book is to present the topic in an accessible manner to those who are fairly new to international taxation or, indeed, are new to taxation in any guise. It will be useful for university students, for those preparing for professional qualifications, and for practitioners generally.

Angharad Miller and I first embarked on this project in 2006, at her instigation, with the aim of producing a text to underpin an introductory course in international taxation on a wide range of undergraduate and postgraduate degree programmes. The book also aims to be useful to practitioners and policymakers who want to get back to basics and examine what lies beneath the current complexities of international tax rules, or perhaps to acquire a broader understanding of the principles. The book does not provide a comprehensive legal reference work on the topic, since others have done this already, but rather a solid foundation in the principles and policies of international taxation in generic terms, as well as an introduction to some UK-specific rules. To achieve this, the book blends theory, policy and practical application for each of the topics under discussion. Additional reading is suggested within each chapter. This is drawn from a wide range of sources including, but not limited to, legal texts, and practitioner and academic journal articles.

This is the last edition of the book that Angharad will be actively involved in, and in this edition we are joined by Emer Mulligan, from the National University of Ireland, Galway.

This book examines international tax principles primarily from the viewpoint of a multinational group of companies. However, where appropriate, the concerns of the tax authorities are addressed, and wherever possible we have advanced the reasoning behind the various anti-avoidance measures affecting international groups. The international taxation of high net worth individuals and trusts is not covered in this book, although we devote two chapters to the taxation of expatriate staff.

The sixth edition updates all the chapters and, throughout the book, new text examines developments in light of the OECD BEPS Project work. Rather than attempt to summarize the BEPS Project separately, BEPS recommendations are integrated into each chapter, setting out the main recommendations, and offering some explanation and comment on these. The BEPS material includes events subsequent to the release of the final reports in October 2015 up to June 2017.

As with the previous edition, we have borne in mind the requirements of students preparing for the Advanced Diploma in International Tax (ADIT) as offered by the Chartered Institute of Taxation. These students may find the 'Further study' sections which we have appended to certain chapters to include more complex or detailed issues very useful, but students on more general courses of study could be advised that these sections are optional reading.

The first chapter is a brief introduction to taxation, including the different forms that taxation may take and how tax systems are designed and administered, which can be skipped by those with some basic level of understanding of taxation in general. Chapters 2 to 6 are designed to introduce some key issues in international taxation, globalization, residence, source, double taxation and an introduction to double tax treaties. Chapters 7 to 12 consider what happens when one moves from doing business *with* another country to doing business *in* another country, and examine key features of the operation of double tax treaties. Chapters 13 to 19 examine the way in which differences in tax systems can be exploited by taxpayers to minimize global tax liabilities, and the measures adopted by governments to combat perceived tax avoidance. In Chapters 20 to 22, we examine respectively: the influence of the European Union on direct taxation; indirect taxes, particularly VAT; and tax and development.

Lynne Oats
June 2017

Contents

Abbreviations

AEOI	Automatic exchange of information
AOA	Authorized OECD approach
APA	Advance pricing agreement
ATAD	Anti-Tax Avoidance Directive
B2B	Business-to-business
B2C	Business-to-consumer
BEPS	Base erosion and profit shifting (BEPS Project)
CA	English Court of Appeal (from which appeal lies to the UK Supreme Court, and formerly to the UK House of Lords)
CAFC	Court of Appeals for the Federal Circuit (from which appeal lies to the US Supreme Court)
CbCR	Country-by-country reporting
CCCTB	Common consolidated corporate tax base
CCTB	Common corporate tax base
CEN	Capital export neutrality
CFC	Controlled foreign company
CIN	Capital import neutrality
CJEU	Court of Justice of the EU (formerly European Court of Justice (ECJ))
CON	Capital ownership neutrality
CPM	Comparable profits method
CPR	Civil Procedure Rules (rules that govern civil litigation procedure in England and Wales)
CRA	Canada Revenue Agency
CRS	Common Reporting Standard
DAC	Directive on Administrative Cooperation in the Field of Taxation
DTA	Double Taxation Agreement
DTT	Double Tax Treaty
EBIT	Earnings before interest and tax
EBITA	Earnings before interest, tax and amortization
EBITDA	Earnings before interest, tax, depreciation and amortization
EC	European Commission
EEA	European Economic Area (consisting of the EU plus Iceland, Liechtenstein and Norway)
EFTA	European Free Trade Area (Iceland, Liechtenstein, Norway and Switzerland)
EIOR	Exchange of information on request
EU	European Union (formerly the European Community)
FATCA	Foreign Account Tax Compliance Act
FDI	Foreign direct investment
FTT	Financial transaction tax
G8	Group of 8

G20	Group of 20
GAAR	General anti-avoidance rule
GATS	General Agreement on Trade in Services
GATT	General Agreement on Tariffs and Trade
GST	Goods and services tax
HL	UK House of Lords (replaced by UK Supreme Court)
HMRC	Her Majesty's Revenue & Customs
HNWI	High net worth individual
HST	Home state taxation
IFRS	International Financial Reporting Standards
IGA	Inter-governmental agreement
IMF	International Monetary Fund
IRS	Internal Revenue Service (the US tax authority)
LOB	Limitation on benefits
MAP	Mutual agreement procedure
MCAA	Multilateral Competent Authority Agreement
MFN	Most favoured nation
MLI	Multilateral instrument
MNC	Multinational company
MNE	Multinational enterprise
MTC	Model Tax Convention (Treaty)
NICs	National Insurance Contributions
NN	National neutrality
NON	National ownership neutrality
OECD	Organisation for Economic Co-operation and Development
OVDP	Offshore voluntary disclosure program (or facility)
PAC	Public Accounts Committee
PE	Permanent establishment
R&D	Research and development
SAAR	Specific anti-avoidance rule
SPV	Special purpose vehicle
SRT	Statutory resident test
TAAR	Targeted anti-avoidance rule
TIEA	Tax information exchange agreement
TNMM	Transactional net margin method
TRIPs	Trade-Related Aspects of Intellectual Property Rights (administered by the WTO)
UN	United Nations
VAT	Value added tax
WIPO	World Intellectual Property Organization
WTO	World Trade Organization (administers TRIPs)

Glossary

Administrative costs	Public sector or government costs incurred in administering the tax legislation and regulations.
Alienation	Used in connection with the disposal of assets. The term includes sale, exchange, gift and other means by which a taxpaying entity or individual divests itself of an asset.
Alternative minimum tax	A special base level tax, usually computed as a percentage of gross income, imposed to combat tax minimization by high income earners. Used in the US.
Anti-avoidance measures	Measures to combat the avoidance of tax are found in taxation legislation as well as double tax treaties. They may be targeted at specific activities or, in some cases, a generic rule is used that disregards transactions entered into for tax avoidance purposes.
Arbitrage	Taking advantage of inconsistencies between different countries' tax rules to achieve a more favourable result than would have resulted from investing in a single jurisdiction.
Arbitration	The settling of disputes by an independent person or group of persons. In international tax, the term is often used in connection with the settling of transfer pricing disputes by a group of persons somewhat independent of the taxpayer and tax authority.
Arm's-length principle	This term refers to unrelated parties dealing with each other wholly independently. Where parties to an agreement are related in some way, it may be that the price is not that which would apply if they were not so related. Tax legislation and double tax treaties often give the government power to substitute an arm's length price, for tax purposes, for the actual price used between related parties.
Average tax rate	This is derived by dividing taxable income by tax payable. It is sometimes referred to as the effective tax rate.

Beneficial owner | In common law countries the term is used to mean the persons who ultimately enjoy the benefit of an asset. Beneficial and legal ownership may be with different parties, for example in trust or agency relationships.

BEPS | Base erosion and profit shifting: practices of multinational enterprises aimed at avoiding tax through exploiting differences in tax systems to achieve double non-taxation and through planning so as to have taxable profits located in low tax countries.

Bi-lateral | Involving two states; for instance, a double tax treaty is a bi-lateral agreement.

Branch profits tax | Many countries subject the profits of branches of foreign companies to an additional tax, so that they are treated in the same way as subsidiaries which generally pay withholding tax on profits distributed as dividends.

Broad based consumption tax | A generic term to describe consumption tax that applies to a broad range of goods and services, as distinct from narrow based which target specific items.

Capital export neutrality | This is where investors in the capital exporting country are subject to the same effective tax rate on income from domestic investment and income from foreign investment; that is, the decision whether to invest at home or abroad is tax neutral.

Capital import neutrality | This is a term used by economists to describe the position where domestic and foreign investors receive the same after-tax rate of return on similar investments in that market.

Capital gains (losses) | These arise (are realized) on the disposal of assets and are the change in value of the asset between purchase and sale.

Civil law | Body of law based primarily on statutes rather than judicial decisions.

Classical system | The classical system of company tax involves taxation of companies as separate entities, and no allowance is given to shareholders in receipt of dividend income for company tax paid.

Common law	Legal system based on the common law of England, although different jurisdictions have developed differently, so it cannot be assumed that all common law countries have the same approach to the law.
Company tax	A tax on company income. Its tax base is corporate profits, which are generally different from the profits reported for other purposes, such as under financial reporting rules. Also referred to as corporation tax.
Competent authority	Under double tax agreements, both countries appoint a representative, such as the Ministry of Finance, to try to resolve disputes that arise from the operation of the treaty. The UK's competent authority is HMRC.
Compliance costs	Costs incurred by taxpayers or third parties in meeting the requirements laid on them by the tax rules and regulations.
Consumption tax	A tax levied on the purchase of goods and services. Value added tax, goods and services tax, retail sales tax, and manufacture sales tax are examples of consumption taxes.
Controlled foreign company (CFC)	This term is used in the context of legislation aimed at preventing tax deferral by using companies in low tax jurisdictions, where the company involved is controlled by the country with the CFC legislation.
Customs duties	Taxes on goods imported into a country.
Death duties	Taxes imposed on property transferred on the death of the owner. Also referred to as inheritance taxes, estate duty, succession tax.
Depreciation	The allowable portion of the cost of the depreciable assets that are used up during an income-generating activity that can be included in the cost of production.
Developing country	In this book, the term is used to denote any country classified as other than 'high income' by the World Bank. Thus the term includes low income, lower middle income and upper middle income states.
Direct taxes	Taxes which cannot be shifted from the legal taxpayer to the ultimate consumer of the good or service. Personal and company income taxes, payroll taxes and property taxes are usually considered to be direct taxes.

Dividends	Distribution of profits by a company to its shareholders.
Domestic law	A state's own national laws.
Domicile	A person's domicile is his or her permanent home, the place to which he or she always intends to return.
Double non-taxation	This can arise where a transaction involves more than one country and, typically, the payment leg of the transaction produces a deduction against taxable profits in the first country, but the receipt leg of the transaction is not taxed in the second country.
Double taxation	This arises when the same activity is taxed more than once, as in the case of taxation of distribution of corporate profits under a classical system of company tax.
Effective rate of tax	The actual tax payable on the profits before taxation as shown in the financial accounts.
Energy tax	Taxes on fossil fuels with a view to reducing emissions of carbon dioxide and other greenhouse gases.
Entity characterization	The process of determining whether a commercial entity is to be recognized for tax purposes or whether the transactions which it enters into are to be treated as entered into by the individuals who have an interest in the entity.
Evasion	The illegal or fraudulent arrangement of affairs to eliminate or reduce tax liability.
Excise tax	A tax on the production of a particular good or services. It may be either a fixed rate (for example, dollars per kilo) or ad valorem (varying according to the value, for example, X% per dollar). Cigarettes, alcohol and petrol are among the goods most commonly subjected to an excise tax or duty.
Exemptions	Tax rules will often provide exemptions for particular people, items or transactions which would otherwise be taxed.
Force of attraction	Under this 'rule', permanent establishments are taxed not only on income and property directly attributable to them, but also on all other income earned from sources in the country where the permanent establishment is located.

Foreign direct investment	Investment into a state by a non-resident, such as the setting up of a factory as opposed to mere financial investment. The term can refer to investment either via setting up a foreign subsidiary or via a branch.
Foreign tax credit	A system for the relief of double taxation so that foreign sourced income of residents is taxed in the home country but then credit is allowed for foreign tax paid on that income.
Free capital	The amount of non-interest-bearing capital (typically, share capital) that a branch or subsidiary might be expected to have if it was an independent enterprise.
Gift duty	A gift is a gratuitous transfer of property during the donor's lifetime. Many countries levy a gift tax on such transfers by reference to the value of the gift.
Immovable property	This term generally covers land and buildings.
Incidence of tax	The legal incidence is the point where tax is legally assessed. The effective or economic incidence refers to the ultimate bearer of the tax.
Income	This is a difficult concept to define, but it generally encompasses employment income, business profits, rental income and interest.
Income taxes	Income tax is a direct tax, usually imposed annually on the income of individuals and other entities such as companies.
Indirect taxes	Taxes which can be shifted from the legal taxpayer to the economic taxpayer. Consumption taxes are usually deliberately designed to be indirect taxes.
Integration	In connection with company and personal income taxes, this refers to the process of taxing all company income at the individual's level using personal income tax rates.
Intellectual property	Literary, dramatic, musical and scientific works are intellectual property which is protected by copyright, patent, registered design, or trademark. Payments for the use of intellectual property are referred to as royalties.

Jurisdiction	The authority to make law and to enforce it within a defined geographical area.
Know-how	Technical information necessary to reproduce a product or process.
Land tax	A tax assessed on the value of land, usually the annual rental value, and may be with or without buildings.
Letter box company	A company which has complied only with the bare essentials for registration in a particular country, it really only exists on paper and does not actually conduct any activities.
Limitation on benefits	A tax treaty provision with the aim of preventing treaty shopping, which limits treaty benefits (for example, reduced rates of withholding tax) to those who meet specified criteria.
Manufacturer's sales tax	A single-stage sales tax that is collected at the manufacturing level of the production/ distribution process.
Marginal tax rate	The rate applicable to the last unit of the tax base.
Most favoured nation clause	A provision often found in double tax treaties whereby, typically, one state promises to reduce the rate of withholding tax charged under the treaty if, in future, it concludes a new treaty with any other state under which it charges a lower rate of withholding tax.
Multinational enterprise	Company or group of companies with business establishments in two or more countries.
Neutrality	A principle which states that taxes should not affect the economic decisions of consumers or producers.
OECD	The Organisation for Economic Co-operation and Development is an organization composed of representatives of the industrialized countries in Europe, the US, Japan, Canada, Australia and New Zealand. It was founded in 1961 and provides economic research and statistics and offers a forum for discussing and co-ordinating policies of common interest.

Opaque entity	An entity, such as a partnership which is viewed as a taxable person in its own right, independently of its members. The opposite would be 'transparent' where a state does not recognize the partnership for tax purposes at all but only the individual partners are recognized as taxpayers.
Partnership	An association of two or more persons. In some countries, partnerships are treated as separate entities for tax purposes, but in others they are not.
Payroll tax	A tax on the payroll or sums paid to employees.
Permanent establishment	This term is used in double tax agreements to determine whether a non-resident has sufficient presence in a country to justify being taxed on the business profits that it earns there.
Personal taxes	This term includes all taxes paid by individuals, income, payroll, consumption and wealth taxes.
Poll tax	A per capita tax, or a tax per head of population, normally a fixed amount and not in common use.
Portfolio investment	A holding of shares in a company which is a small proportion of the total shares, usually less than 10 per cent.
Profit shifting	The allocation of income and expenses between related organizations to reduce overall worldwide tax liability.
Progressive tax	A tax by which the ratio of tax paid to income is higher for high income individuals than for low income ones. A progressive tax rate has a marginal rate which is always in excess of the average rate of tax.
Property tax	A tax imposed on property ownership.
Regressive tax	A tax by which the ratio of tax paid to income is lower for high income earners than for low income earners. The average rate of tax falls as income rises. Consumption taxes are often viewed as regressive, as consumption is a larger share of income for the poor.

Residence	This is a common basis for the imposition of taxes, sometimes, but not always, defined in tax legislation.
Royalties	Payments for the use of, or the right to use, intellectual property.
Schedular tax system	Where income from different sources is taxed separately (for example, business profits, employment income and property income).
Special purpose vehicle	A legal entity set up to undertake a limited and specific transaction or set of transactions. Often used in treaty shopping.
State	A geographical area with a government and the capacity to enter into relations with other states. A sovereign state is not dependent on any other state or under the control of any other state. The term 'country' is often used interchangeably with 'state', but 'country' strictly only refers to the geographic area involved and could also refer to a non-sovereign state without the power to make law and enter into treaties.
Taxable income	The amount on which income tax is levied, usually defined by statute.
Tax base	The object to which the tax applies (for example, income, consumption or wealth).
Tax expenditure	This is revenue forgone by a government as a result of special provisions of the tax legislation which, for example, grant preferential tax rates or exclude certain items from the tax base.
Tax havens	Countries with very low or even nil tax rates on some or all forms of income.
Tax incentives	Special provisions to promote a particular activity, such as investment in particular activities or geographical regions.
Tax incidence	The ultimate distribution of the tax burden. The initial payer of the tax may be able to shift the burden of the tax to others (see Direct taxes and Indirect taxes).
Tax shelter	A provision of the tax legislation which allows individuals to reduce or eliminate tax liabilities, a form of tax expenditure.
Tax sparing	A special category of double tax relief in tax treaties to prevent tax incentives from being overridden by the treaty partner.

Tax treaty	A treaty between nations concerning the tax treatment of income of each country's citizens and corporations which is generated in the other country.
Thin capitalization	A company is said to be 'thinly capitalized' when it has a high ratio of debt to equity.
Transparent entity	An entity which is disregarded for tax purposes, the relevant taxpayers being the members of the entity. Some states treat bodies such as partnerships and certain types of company in this way.
Treaty override	This occurs where a state gives priority to its national laws over its treaty with another state. Override can be intentional or non-intentional.
Treaty shopping	A tax minimization (or avoidance) activity that entails setting up structures or arrangements in order to take advantage of a tax treaty with a third country, other than the country of residence and the country of investment of the taxpayer.
Underlying tax	Tax on the profits of a company which pays dividends to a non-resident shareholder, which may be allowed as a credit under some systems of double tax relief.
Unilateral	One sided; for instance, double tax relief granted by a state in the absence of a double tax treaty with a state which has already charged tax on an income receipt would be unilateral relief.
Value added tax	VAT is levied on goods and services based on their increase in value as they move through the cycle from production to consumption. It is a form of multi-stage consumption tax.
Wealth taxes	Taxes based on the ownership of wealth, which include taxes on real property, estate taxes and annual wealth taxes.
Withholding tax	A tax payable at the source where it is a final tax, ie a third party is charged with the task of deducting tax from certain payments and remitting it to the government.

Table of Statutes

Table of Statutory Instruments

Table of European Legislation

Table of Cases

V

W

X

Chapter 1

Introduction to Taxation

BASICS

1.1 The purpose of this chapter is to provide a brief overview of tax systems, the component parts of tax systems, and the operational practices and procedures of tax systems. It is designed for those who are new to taxation and have not previously considered how national tax systems work. In this regard, this chapter lays the foundation for the remainder of this book, which deals with international tax. One key point to remember is that while there is considerable difference in detail between the tax systems of different countries, many foundational issues and approaches are common to all jurisdictions, including the reasons for levying taxes and their component parts.

For readers who have not previously thought about these issues, this chapter provides some basic definitions and introduces some concepts that will be referred to in the remainder of this book, as well as other reference works. It also points to some further reading for those not familiar with the wealth of scholarship and practical guidance available on the subject of taxation.

> 'For the impositions that are laid on the people by the sovereign power are nothing else but the wages due to them that hold to public sword, to defend private men in the exercise of their several trades and callings.'

Thomas Hobbes, *Leviathan* (1651)

Governments all have, to some extent, a commitment to provide services for the population, for example a legal system, defence, health services, as well as infrastructure such as roads. To fund this public expenditure, they must obtain funds; borrowing is a possibility but revenue is most usually obtained through taxation. Taxation is therefore required to finance public spending. It is a system of compulsory levies or exactions imposed for this purpose on a variety of taxpaying subjects, but it may also be imposed for other social and economic objectives.

Today we find enormous diversity in the types of tax systems used by governments around the world. The range of taxes used and the complexity of the rules used to impose them vary from country to country and can often be correlated with the stage of development of the country in question.

The purpose of this chapter is to introduce you to some of the different types of taxes that can be levied by government, the different forms these types of taxes may take and some of the criteria by which taxes and tax systems can be evaluated. The focus here is on domestic tax systems, and the next chapter will consider questions arising when two domestic tax systems interact, ie international taxation.

WHY GOVERNMENTS LEVY TAXES

1.2   There are generally considered to be three categories of government function that result in the need to impose taxes: the provision of public goods, the distribution of resources, and economic stabilization.

The term 'public goods' refers to goods and services that are not provided by the private market, usually because it is not efficient for them to do so. They are things that people need or want in their society, and so the government is left with the job of supplying them. Examples are protection of property rights through the police force and the legal system, utilities such as power, roads and street lights. These are often things that people are not prepared to pay for directly, and so the government must supply them free of charge, and therefore needs to raise revenue to fund the cost of provision.

Taxes are not just used to raise funds for the provision of public goods, however, they are also used for distributive purposes. This means removing resources from the private sector and directing them according to perceived needs, eg through social services, to even out the distribution of wealth in the economy. The tax system can be used as a direct redistribution mechanism, by not collecting it from people intended to benefit from a particular concession rather than collecting it and giving it back in the form of a subsidy. This is often referred to as a tax expenditure (see para **1.14** below) that is, it is revenue forgone by the government in order to achieve a particular economic or social objective.

The final purpose for which taxes are imposed is economic stabilization. In any modern economy there will be fluctuations in employment rates, inflation rates, currency exchange rates and so on. Governments are able to use taxation as a mechanism for controlling, or at least influencing, these fluctuations.

It is important that the tax system be flexible in order to allow governments to influence the economy. This is one reason why tax systems often contain a mixture of different kinds of taxation, rather than relying on just one, as different forms of taxation influence the economy in different ways and some are more responsive to change than others.

ELEMENTS OF TAXES

1.3   Every tax has three essential elements: a base, a rate of tax and someone to pay it, a taxpayer.

The tax base is the subject of the tax; it is the 'thing' which is being taxed. There are generally four main bases of taxation: consumption taxes on what we spend; wealth taxes on what we own; income and profit taxes on what we earn; and poll, or head, taxes, on ourselves as human beings.

The rate of a given tax is extremely important in evaluating its impact. Taxes are usually discussed in terms of their average and marginal rates. The average rate of tax is found by dividing the total tax liability by the amount of the tax base. The marginal rate of tax is the rate the taxpayer will pay on an additional unit of the base.

A proportional, or a flat, rate is one where the average rate is equal to the marginal rate, which means that for each extra unit of the base, the rate stays the same. For example, many countries levy a profits tax on companies at a single flat rate which stays the same regardless of the level of the taxable profits.

A progressive rate on the other hand has an average rate less than the marginal rate, ie the larger the base, the higher the rate. In many countries, personal income tax is a progressive tax, although there has been a worldwide trend in recent years to reduce the degree of progression by having fewer steps in the rate scale.

It is conceivable, but not common, to have a regressive rate scale where the average rate of tax actually falls as the tax base increases its value, hence the marginal rate is always less than the average rate of tax. Very few taxes actually have truly regressive rates, however sometimes flat rate taxes such as consumption taxes are referred to as being regressive as to income since the *proportion* of income paid out as tax decreases as the level of income increases. This happens because consumption taxes are only levied on income which is spent: poorer taxpayers might need to spend their whole income, whilst wealthier taxpayers do not.

Finally, any tax must have someone to pay it, a taxpayer, and a discussion of the concept of 'taxpayer' usually leads to the distinction between the impact and the incidence of taxation. The legal taxpayer is the one who is named in the legislation as being responsible for paying the tax; he or she bears the impact of the tax. The economic taxpayer is the one who actually ends up parting with the cash at the end of the day; he or she bears the incidence or burden of the tax. Using this distinction, taxes can be broadly split into two types, direct and indirect. As a broad generalization, direct tax is one where the legal taxpayer cannot pass on the incidence of the tax; there is no mechanism for building the tax into prices charged to other persons for goods or services. Under a direct tax, the legal taxpayer must bear its burden, for example a departure tax imposed on people leaving a country and income tax for employees. With indirect taxes, however, the incidence is shifted to another person, for example a consumption tax, which is usually specifically designed to be paid by the seller of the goods and services but then passed on to the consumer.

In considering the taxpayer, one must also consider what form the taxpayer or tax unit will take. Will only individuals be liable for the tax, or can the family unit share the liability, and if so how does the government define 'family'? How will the government treat other entities such as companies and trusts and partnerships?

3

EVALUATING TAXES AND TAX SYSTEMS

1.4   How then does a government decide what mix of taxes to use in designing, or reforming, a tax system? There are a number of commonly accepted criteria by which taxes and tax systems can be evaluated, although they are described differently in the various books dealing with taxes in different countries. For the purposes of this introduction to taxes generally, two key criteria will be discussed, namely equity and economic efficiency. Other criteria, such as convenience, simplicity and flexibility, are beyond the scope of this book which focuses on international taxation, although it should be noted that most countries agree that excessive complexity is not a desirable feature of a tax or tax system.

Equity

1.5   In the context of taxes, the term equity can be equated to fairness and it is possible to say that a good tax is a fair tax. In this regard, perceptions of fairness are as important as, if not more important than, actual fairness, as it is generally accepted that where a taxpaying population believes a tax or tax system to be fair, then they are more likely to comply with the rules and not attempt to evade payment. In terms of individual taxpayers, it is common to say that a fair or equitable tax is one that is levied in accordance with the taxpayer's ability to pay, that is, the economic resources that they have available to them. Horizontal equity dictates that where two persons have the same ability to pay, then they should bear the same tax burden. Vertical equity on the other hand, suggests that where one taxpayer has a greater ability to pay, then they should bear a higher tax burden; it is this principle which is used to justify a progressive tax rate that increases as the tax base increases. Measuring ability to pay can, however, be problematic and raises questions such as what economic resources should be taken into account in evaluating a person's ability to pay?

An alternative mechanism for ensuring that the distribution of the tax burden is equitable is referred to as the 'benefit principle' which suggests that taxes should be levied in line with some relationship to the usage of government services. The problem with this approach is, however, that some benefits cannot be attributed to specific taxpayers, and some are difficult to measure.

Economic efficiency

1.6   The principle of economic efficiency is also referred to as neutrality. This principle states that a tax should not interfere with decision making, for example decisions whether to work or not work, to spend or save, to invest in one product or another. Ideally taxes should be neutral so that rational business and commercial decisions can be made without the influence of the tax consequences flowing from them. In practice, however, neutrality is difficult to achieve and often governments will want deliberately to interfere with people's choices to ensure that certain behaviour is encouraged or discouraged.

There is a large body of research that examines the notion of 'optimal' taxation which entails designing taxes and tax systems that minimize their excess burden. The concept of excess burden refers to the economic distortions that arise in response to taxes over and above the actual monetary transfer from the private sector to government.

TYPES OF TAXES

1.7   This section considers briefly each of the basic types of taxes and explores the different variations in the way in which they are constructed and administered.

Consumption taxes

1.8   Consumption-based taxation involves the consumer being taxed on his or her spending on goods and services. There are a number of different forms of consumption tax. Some are levied on the producers of goods, others on retailers, others again on both. Most consumption taxes are designed so that they are built in to pricing structures and so passed on to the ultimate consumer of the goods and/or services.

> 'The best taxes are such as are levied on consumptions, especially those on luxury; because such taxes are least felt by the people. They seem, in some measure, voluntary; since a man may chuse (sic) how far he will use the commodity which is taxed. They pay gradually and insensibly: they naturally produce sobriety and frugality, if judiciously imposed, and being confounded with the natural price of the commodity, they are scarcely perceived by the consumers.'

> David Hume, *Of Taxes* (1752)

The taxation of consumption is historically the oldest form of taxation. Indirect consumption taxes were levied in ancient times and still form a significant portion of tax revenue in most systems. They are indirect taxes, purposely designed to be passed on through the chain of persons handling the goods or services from initial creation or production to the final consumer. This means that the person who has the legal liability for the tax and is therefore initially responsible for its payment, does not bear the incidence of the tax; he or she builds it into the price received for the product and thereby recoups it from the purchaser. In this way the tax is passed on from purchaser to purchaser until it finally reaches the end consumer who can pass it on no further. It is the end consumer who bears the incidence of an indirect consumption tax.

The base on which the consumption tax is levied may be broad or narrow. A broad-based consumption tax is one that is imposed on a wide range of goods and services with few exemptions.

Most governments impose a variety of narrow-based consumption taxes on various items of consumption expenditure. Common examples include alcohol and tobacco. Usually these taxes are imposed as a revenue-raising exercise, although in some instances they may be an attempt to influence consumer spending patterns for some reason, for example 'vice' taxes to discourage certain undesirable activities. These taxes are sometimes imposed irrespective of whether there is also a broad-based consumption tax in operation. Broadly based and narrowly based consumption taxes need not be mutually exclusive.

A number of questions arise in the context of the rate structure. Will it be a single flat rate or a system of multiple or progressive rates? Will the same rate apply to all goods and services or will some categories be given a lower or higher rate than the basic rate used? In many countries, some categories of goods, particularly exports, are allocated a zero rate. Luxuries are often allocated a higher than normal rate. The advantages of a single rate tax with a very broad base include greater revenue-raising potential and simplicity, neutrality towards consumers and different types of business, and reduced administrative costs for government and compliance costs for traders.

Consumption taxes may be single stage, imposed at only one point in the production to consumption cycle, or multi-stage, imposed more than once. A single stage tax has some advantages, however problems arise, for example where the tax is imposed at a stage before that of final consumption, say at the manufacture level, because the value added to the goods beyond that stage, that is at the retail level, is ignored. This means that many services that are retail only by nature are not taxed if only a manufacture sales tax is used.

The most common form of consumption tax in recent years is a multiple stage tax, usually modelled on the European style value added tax (VAT) which is imposed at each stage of production or distribution of a good or service, on the value added at that stage. The administrative burden of a value added tax can be higher than with a single stage sales tax since there are a greater number of taxpayers and points of collection, but it may also be less prone to avoidance since it is collected in increments at each stage of the process.

VAT was first proposed in Germany in 1919 and in the USA in 1921 as a substitute for company tax. It was advocated in Japan in 1949 and introduced in France in 1955. Real growth in the acceptance of VAT did not occur, however, until the formation of the European Community following its adoption by Denmark in 1967, Germany and the Netherlands in 1969, Luxembourg in 1970, Belgium in 1971, Ireland in 1972 and the UK in 1973. More recent versions of this form of consumption tax have been named 'goods and services' taxes (GST), as in Canada in 1991 and Australia in 1999.

A retail sales tax is imposed at the point of sale to the final consumer. A retail sales tax theoretically raises the same revenue as a value added tax given the same rate, but is paid at one stage rather than progressively over the life of the goods. It therefore has fewer taxing points than a value added tax and lower compliance costs overall. Arguably a retail sales tax is less robust than a VAT/ GST model in the absence of the checks and balances that the invoice and credit system affords.

Wealth taxes

1.9   A wealth tax may comprise an annual levy on wealth, or a tax on the transfer of wealth such as death and gift duties. Wealth taxes are generally not imposed for their revenue-raising capabilities, but rather for the purposes of equity and efficiency. In terms of equity, wealth taxes are justified on the basis that to effectively treat persons with equal capacities to pay equally, wealth must be taken into account. The ownership of wealth gives rise to status and prestige, improved access to credit, security and should therefore be taken into account in assessing taxable capacity. Another argument for the imposition of a wealth tax is as a double check for the administration of income and capital gains taxes through the information provided in regular wealth tax returns. Problematic aspects of wealth taxes are usually associated with valuation. Whether a wealth tax is imposed annually, or only at some point of realization of the assets, for example on death, valuations are essential and for assets that do not have an established market, these can be difficult to obtain.

Land and property taxes can be viewed as forms of wealth taxes and are usually imposed on an annual basis in respect of the value of the land in question. Land and property have a fixed geographical location which cannot be transferred, and therefore provide a stable and readily identifiable tax base for subordinate governments. Land and property taxes are favoured sources of revenue for local government authorities for this reason.

Personal income tax

1.10   Income tax is levied on a taxpayer's income. For this purpose income can include a variety of things like salary and wages, rental received from leasing property and the proceeds of business operations. Income tax systems usually provide for a variety of deductions so that the result, which is subject to the tax, is a net amount often referred to as taxable income.

Taxes on personal income and business profits are major revenue sources for most industrialized nations; they also play a growing role in the tax structures of many developing nations. A number of design issues arise in relation to income taxes that lead to considerable variation worldwide. For example, should the rate of tax be progressive, and if so to what maximum rate and with how many intervals? The general trend has been for a lowering of maximum rates, certainly compared to the 1970s when some countries imposed very high rates on high income earners leading to concerns about the disincentive effects on labour provision as well as tax avoidance and evasion. The more intervals or points at which the rate changes, the smoother the progression, which arguably lessens the likelihood of taxpayers behaving aberrantly around the thresholds, but at the cost of increased complexity. There are also questions as to what is the appropriate unit for income tax, eg the individual, married couple or family? Countries that choose to levy income tax on an individual basis, combined with a progressive tax rate scale then face potential problems with 'income splitting', that is, artificially transferring income to family members so as to reduce the overall tax liability.

7

The design of an income tax system also requires decisions about the nature of the tax base. Should particular forms of income, transactions or activities be exempt from the tax, for example to encourage particular activities? What items of expenditure should be deductible in determining the tax base, for example private expenditure such as mortgage interest on private residences? How should the distinction between income and capital be dealt with? For many countries this last question is addressed through the imposition of a separate capital gains tax that recognizes the different nature of capital receipts.

Capital gains

1.11   Capital gains can be defined as the profit resulting from the increase in value of assets that are not part of the owner's stock in trade (inventory) or assets that he or she regularly sells. They usually arise on the sale or realization of property, tangible and intangible, and are usually distinguished from income receipts. Whether or not a government chooses to include capital gains in the income tax base depends largely on how concerned it is with the comprehensiveness of the tax base.

Some governments opt to have a separate capital gains tax, such as in the UK. Others choose to include capital gains within the income tax system, although often with some form of concessional treatment either in calculating the amount of the gain or in applying the rate of tax to that gain, or both as in the UK and Australia.

Some countries such as Hong Kong, Korea and Singapore choose not to tax capital gains at all. This can lead to substantial definition problems in deciding when a profit is of an income nature and therefore subject to income tax, and when it is of a capital nature and therefore not taxed. In such jurisdictions, there are usually extensive rules concerning whether a transaction is in the nature of a trading rather than a capital transaction. Factors such as motive, frequency of transactions, length of ownership, source of financing etc, will often provide indications of whether an activity is a trading activity and therefore more appropriately taxed as income. One possible consequence of not taxing capital gains is increased likelihood of tax-avoidance activity to circumvent the distinction between income and capital receipts.

Two particular issues arise in the context of taxing capital gains. One is the point at which capital gains should be recognized for tax purposes. In most systems this will be on realization, although from the point of view of establishing a comprehensive income tax base, arguably increases in the value of assets should be recognized and taxed annually even without realization occurring. Realization is usually adopted as the trigger point for capital gains tax for pragmatic purposes, and because of the valuation problems that arise as discussed earlier in the context of wealth taxes. The second problem is what to do with inflationary gains? There are various mechanisms that can be adopted to remove the inflation component of a capital gain from the tax net, including indexation mechanisms as used in the UK for corporations, or the more simple approach of using a lower rate of tax than for income receipts in recognition of the period of time over which capital gains accrue.

Corporation tax

1.12   In most countries, a company or corporation is a separate legal entity. This means that it has an existence independent of its ultimate owners, the shareholders. Companies own assets, make profits and incur liabilities in their own right and usually the shareholder has no direct right to those assets or profits. The rights of the shareholder are to have the company managed on their behalf by the directors, and to receive a share of the profits periodically by way of dividend.

Treating companies as taxpayers separate from their shareholders allows governments to impose an income tax on them directly. Another alternative is to treat them as being only 'conduits' through which profits flow to the shareholders. Using this view of the company and shareholder relationship allows governments to levy tax only on the shareholders and not the company in the first instance. In actual fact, many countries adopt a combination of the two approaches by way of a compromise.

Under what is commonly known as the 'classical' or 'separate' system of taxing companies, the company is treated as a taxable entity separate from its shareholders. The classical system of company taxation operates so that corporate profits are charged with corporation tax, in some countries referred to as corporate income tax, at the corporate level whether or not they are distributed to shareholders, and then again in the hands of the shareholder when those profits are distributed by way of dividend. This can be viewed as 'over-taxation' of distributed profits and may result in a number of undesirable economic effects.

At the other end of the scale, a full integration system adopts the view that the company is a mere conduit and company income is taxed in the hands of the shareholder on an attribution basis. In this way company tax, if it is imposed on the company in the first instance, becomes merely a prepayment of individual income tax. The company in this model is viewed as not being separate from its shareholders, the view is that the company is owned and controlled by the shareholders and is not a separate taxable entity. Proponents of the full integration model point out that ability to pay can only be related to natural persons and if income is the best measure of ability to pay, then horizontal equity demands an all-inclusive definition of income.

Partial integration is a compromise approach between the separate and conduit views of companies and their shareholders. It usually consists of allowing some relief from the dual levels of taxation in respect of distributed profits. Partial integration may take a number of different forms as follows:

- Dividend deduction. Here companies are allowed to deduct dividend distributions in calculating their taxable income.

- Split-rate system. Under a split-rate system, a lower rate of tax is applied to distributed profits than to retained profits, therefore reducing the incentive for companies to retain profits.

- Dividend exemption. Under a dividend exemption scheme, the company pays tax as a separate entity on all of its profits in the first instance.

When those profits are distributed to shareholders as dividends, they are exempt in the hands of the shareholder recipients.

- Dividend imputation. Has become the most common form of relief from the double taxation of company profit distributions. It involves taxing the company in the first instance, usually at a flat rate of tax, and then including in the shareholder's taxable income not only the amount of dividend actually received, but also the company tax attributable to that dividend. This process is referred to as 'grossing up'. When the shareholder's liability is calculated, a credit or rebate is allowed for the company tax on the dividend. In this way, the progressivity (if any) of the individual income tax rate scale is maintained.

It is common, particularly in an international business context, for operations conducted through companies to comprise a group of companies with common ownership. One of the questions that arises in the design of a system of company tax is whether to treat companies that are members of a group as separate entities for taxation purposes or to treat the group as one single taxpayer. Very few countries allow for group consolidation of total profits for taxation purposes. Usually some form of concession is allowed, however, for intra-group transactions and the transfer of losses between group members.

THE FLAT TAX DEBATE

1.13   The idea behind a flat tax is that a progressive system of income tax rates is a disincentive to extra work, savings and reinvestment, whereas if the tax was imposed at a low, flat rate, people would have more incentive to work and invest which would then benefit the whole economy. It can be argued that tax revenues will increase at a steeper rate when the tax rate is low. A point is then reached, however, where the government is obtaining the maximum possible revenue from a given tax rate. After this point, if the tax rate increases, the government gets a decreasing amount of revenue, because there is less incentive to work harder or invest, and more incentive to avoid paying taxes.

In a 1985 book by Hall and Rabushka called *The Flat Tax*, published in the US, a new system of flat taxes was proposed. Under this system, wages and salaries would be taxed at a low flat rate after a personal allowance. Business income would be taxed on:

- total revenue from sales;

- fewer inputs purchased from other businesses (which are taxed in the hands of those other businesses);

- less wages and pensions paid to workers (which are taxed in the hands of the employees);

- fewer purchases of plant and equipment (so that investment is not discouraged by the tax system); and

- under this model, savings and investment income is not taxed at all.

There is some evidence that a flat tax works well, but so far it has only been tried in either tax haven countries such as Hong Kong and Jersey, or transitional economies such as Estonia and Russia. No developed country has yet tried a flat tax, despite its obvious attractions. Owens (2013) provides a summary of the pros and cons of flat taxes, and concludes that any debate over flat taxes will be dominated by concerns about progressivity.

TAX EXPENDITURES

1.14 Tax expenditures can be thought of as 'negative revenue'; they are tax revenue deliberately foregone by the government in order to achieve a particular purpose, for example, encouraging a particular industry or activity. In some respects, tax expenditures can be thought of in the same way as public expenditure. They are variously described as 'tax breaks', 'tax concessions', 'tax reliefs', 'tax subsidies' or even 'tax aids'. The term was first coined in the late 1960s by Stanley Surrey in the US. In practice, tax expenditures are defined as deviations from a tax norm, or benchmark that result in a reduced tax liability for a specific group of taxpayers or a specific type of activity. Difficulties arise, however, in identifying the benchmark, which involves taking a view about the tax base, the rate structure and the tax unit and necessarily involves some judgment. The Organisation for Economic Co-operation and Development (OECD) (2010) describes three broad approaches to identifying a benchmark:

1 A conceptual approach – using a 'normal' tax system based on theoretical concepts of income, consumption or value added.

2 A reference law approach – using a country's own laws to define the benchmark.

3 An expenditure subsidy approach – categorizing as tax expenditures only those concessions that are analogous to subsidies.

The objectives of tax expenditures can vary. Some are introduced to more closely align tax burdens to ability to pay. This could include a zero-rate band for an income tax, allowances linked to marital status and family circumstances and the exemption from VAT of necessities. Some tax concessions are introduced to change behaviour, for economic reasons such as tax-favoured savings and investment vehicles or reliefs for pension contributions, or social reasons such as relief for health care and education expenses or charitable donations.

Some tax expenditures are designed to create administrative efficiencies, for example, exemption of financial services from VAT.

Tax expenditures may also take a number of different forms, for example:

● exemption of certain types of income from liability to income tax; or

● additional income tax deductions for certain types of expenditure such as research and development.

Burton and Sadiq (2012) note that tax expenditures are significant 'by virtue of their number, distribution, impact upon the fiscal position of states, constitutional significance, impact upon public administration in general and tax administration in particular and also because of their relevance to the legitimacy of democratic governments'. A European Commission workshop held in October 2013 considered various aspects of the rationale for business tax expenditures, as well as how tax expenditures are reported and analysed in various jurisdictions. The reform of tax expenditures appears to offer the prospects for improved revenue raising, but the distributional impacts need to be carefully considered.[1]

The use of tax expenditures in tax policy is a matter for considerable debate and disagreement, as is their role in terms of tax competition in an international sphere.

For example, the most traditional form of tax incentive used to attract foreign investment, particularly by developing countries, is a tax holiday, which is usually an exemption from income tax for a number of years commencing from the date on which an enterprise begins operations. Tax holidays are usually subject to conditions in respect of geographical location or type of industry. They are an important factor, therefore, in the location decision of a business. Such incentives are discussed in more detail in Chapter 22.

---

1 For a report from the EC Conference, see Bauger, L (2014) *The Use of tax expenditures in times of fiscal consolidation*, European Economy Economic Papers, No 523.

COMPLIANCE AND ADMINISTRATIVE COSTS OF TAXATION

1.15 Every tax entails compliance costs, which are the costs incurred by the taxpayer in meeting the requirements of the legislation. These include the cost of engaging tax advisers to assist them in fulfilling their obligations under the legislation as well as suggesting how to minimize tax liabilities, legitimately or otherwise. Administrative costs are costs to the government of administering the tax system. Because compliance costs are borne by the taxpaying population, they tend to be more hidden than administrative costs. They are also notoriously difficult to quantify. From studies that have been conducted in various countries, however, it is known that compliance costs are not consistent; they vary considerably across different parts of the taxpaying population and are often more onerous and disproportionate for smaller taxpayers than large taxpayers, for example a small business conducted by a sole trader compared to a multinational group of companies.

Some types of tax are more onerous in terms of compliance and administrative costs than others, and this then becomes an important factor in the design of a tax system, ie the various taxes that will make up a tax system and the particular forms that those taxes will take.

The publication *Paying Taxes*, produced jointly by PwC and the World Bank, has been produced annually since 2004 and provides some interesting insights into country and regional differences in the way taxes are administered and the compliance burden imposed on taxpayers. The most recent publication in 2017[1] reveals an overall downward trend in the total taxes borne and the compliance burden measured in terms of time to comply and the number of payments required. The 2017 publication includes for the first time a 'post filing index' that attempts to measure compliance costs associated with events occurring subsequent to filing of returns, eg audits.

---

1   See www.pwc.com/gx/en/paying-taxes/pdf/pwc-paying-taxes-2017.pdf.

TAX COMPLIANCE

1.16   Tax compliance is a major concern of the tax authority, whose job it is to ensure that maximum revenue is collected from the tax system. There has been a considerable increase in the volume of research into tax compliance in recent years, which recognizes that the traditional 'deterrence' model does not explain taxpayer behaviour. The deterrence model assumes that taxpayers pay their taxes because they are afraid of being detected, so that they are motivated by the threat of penalties and the likelihood of detection. Studies of taxpayer attitudes towards compliance now show that levels of compliance are generally higher than would be predicted under the deterrence model. Recognition that there are other factors at work has led to more research drawing on behavioural psychology, and links between compliance and the impact of factors such as occupational groupings, gender and level of education are being explored (see Kirchler, 2007, for example).

Much of the research into tax compliance deals with compliance by individual taxpayers. Much less has been done in respect of corporations, and in particular large corporations, although some revenue authorities, such as HMRC in the UK, are beginning to invest in such research to obtain a better understanding of the way corporate taxpayers behave.[1]

Compliance with tax rules by large business has been the focus of considerable attention in recent years also. In the UK, the tax authority has recently published a consultation document entitled 'Improving Large Business Compliance',[2] which proposes a more explicit link between corporate governance and tax strategy through a named executive officer taking responsibility for signing off the tax strategy. It also proposes a voluntary code of practice for large businesses, reflecting the increasing importance of reputational risk management in the area of tax compliance for large companies.

---

1   For example, see the Large Business Panel Survey conducted by HMRC over a period of time to elicit views about the relationship between large business and HMRC.
2   Available   at: www.gov.uk/government/consultations/improving-large-business-tax-compliance.

TAX ADMINISTRATION

1.17   In recent years there has been a significant shift in the way tax systems are administered. From a traditional approach, commonly referred to as 'command and control', there is a move towards more 'responsive' regulation.

This reflects concerns that the way in which taxpayers respond to the tax system, in terms of their willingness to pay tax, is influenced by the approach adopted by the revenue authority. Several tax administrations have adopted a 'compliance pyramid', which tries to match taxpayer behaviour to administrative responses. The pyramid shape reflects the assumed dispersion of taxpayer behaviour across society. At the base of the pyramid are the majority of taxpayers who are willing to comply with the tax system and need only education and support from the revenue authority to be able to do so. At the top of the pyramid is a small grouping of taxpayers who refuse to engage with the tax system, and the administrative response to this group takes the form of punitive sanctions. This approach was pioneered by the Australian Taxation Office and has been subsequently adopted by a number of other countries including New Zealand and the UK.

Certainly the way in which the tax system is administered is an important part of any country's tax 'culture'. Even the most carefully designed tax system can fail to achieve its goals if it is poorly administered, or if the taxpayer population lacks respect for the tax authority. Kirchler (2007) has developed a model called the 'slippery slope' that builds on the notion of the compliance pyramid by including a further dimension – that of trust in the tax authority. He posits that maximum voluntary compliance can be achieved if taxpayers understand their obligations and have positive attitudes towards the government and the need for paying taxes. If trust in the authorities is weak, however, and/or the power of the tax authority is low, then taxpayers will look for ways to avoid or evade their taxpaying obligations (see also Kirchler et al, 2014, and for a discussion of recent developments in Australia, see Langham & Paulsen, 2015 and Whait, 2015).

TAX AVOIDANCE AND EVASION

1.18   The term 'tax avoidance' usually refers to working within the law, or exploiting the law in order to minimize tax liability, in a way not intended by the government. It usually entails taking steps to arrange the taxpayer's affairs before a tax liability arises in such a way that less tax is paid than would otherwise be paid. Tax avoidance can be contrasted with tax evasion where a taxpayer does not pay a tax liability that has already arisen, for example by not declaring all income in an income tax return. Tax avoidance is sometimes subdivided into acceptable and unacceptable avoidance, to distinguish activities that comprise using the tax law to best advantage to minimize tax liabilities (acceptable) from those activities which were not envisaged when the law was put in place, ie that go against Parliament's intention (unacceptable). Unacceptable tax avoidance and tax evasion can be grouped together and labelled as 'non-compliance', that is a failure to comply with the requirements of the tax system, although the former is *ex ante* (ie steps taken before a tax liability crystallizes) and the latter is *ex post* (after a liability arises).

Some commentators suggest that there is a phenomenon called 'tax aversion' (McCaffrey, 1994) such that people think differently about taxes than other forms of costs or expenditures and are prepared to go to greater lengths to avoid paying them. Fennell and Fennell (2003) note that if people are averse to taxes over and above the actual financial losses involved, it is likely that they will 'spend more time and money on tax avoidance than a purely economic analysis predicts'. This may explain why the tax shelter, or tax avoidance, industry is such big business in many jurisdictions (see Braithwaite, 2005), although this has certainly diminished in more recent years.

Many jurisdictions have some form of general anti-avoidance rule, which gives the tax authority discretion to cancel tax benefits where transactions are entered into purely for tax purposes. Some also have specific rules designed to combat particular forms of tax avoidance. The success or otherwise of a general anti-avoidance provision will depend largely on the attitudes of the courts or other appeal bodies in upholding the revenue authority's right to collect the correct amount of tax. It should also be remembered that the prevalence of tax avoidance in any country will probably be related to cultural values and norms, which will influence the extent to which it is tolerated.

In 2008, the OECD published its *Study into the Role of Tax Intermediaries*, following an investigation by a study team headed up by representatives from the UK's revenue authority (HMRC) into the role of intermediaries who act on behalf of taxpayers in their dealings with tax authorities, for example, accountants, lawyers and banking institutions, particularly in relation to tax minimization arrangements. The study recommends that revenue authorities need to develop good relations with tax intermediaries in order to assist in combating tax avoidance. The report noted that several countries have recently introduced special rules requiring taxpayers and their advisers to disclose certain types of arrangements that are viewed as unacceptable tax avoidance, sometimes in advance of tax returns being filed.[1]

In recent years, largely as a result of the Financial Crisis in 2008, there has been increasing attention brought to bear by both governments and the wider public on the question of tax avoidance and evasion. Some jurisdictions, including the UK, have introduced new general anti-avoidance rules to attempt to bring tax avoidance in its most aggressive forms, under control. Alvarrenga (2013) suggests that given recent experiences and commonality in approaches, very slowly and over many years it is conceivable that a harmonized approach to countering tax avoidance may emerge.

There have also been significant protests by tax campaigners, most notably against large multinational corporations. A useful summary of recent debates in relation to responsible tax practice by companies has been published by ActionAid[2] and which reviews 45 sources of recommendations published since 2005. The ActionAid report observes significant differences of opinion as to what constitutes 'good' practice. The most difficult issue is how to distinguish acceptable and unacceptable tax practice. Few of the sources examined deal with wider corporate stakeholders, such as customers; and few consider the particular concerns of developing countries. This will be dealt with in more detail in Chapter 19, where the activities of specific companies named in public campaigns will be examined.

Chapters 17 and 19 deal with specific areas of tax avoidance law aimed at multinational groups.

---

1   For a comparison of the disclosure rules in the US and the UK, see Granwell and McGonigle (2006).
2   ActionAid (2015) *Responsible Tax Practice by Companies*. Available at: www.actionaid.org. uk/sites/default/files/publications/responsible_tax_practice.pdf.

TAX POLICY

1.19   Tax policy refers to the approach of a government to the design and implementation of its tax system, including the tax mix or choice of different forms of taxation as well as their individual design features. It entails decisions also about the goals of the tax system and the priorities to be given to the different criteria discussed earlier such as equity and efficiency, which are not always compatible. Choices need to be made also about the overall objectives of the tax system and social and economic priorities that the tax system needs to support.

A 2010 study by the OECD examines the link between the design of tax structures and the desire for economic growth, about which there has been heightened attention in the wake of the Financial Crisis. The different forms of taxation are evaluated with respect to their capacity to stimulate or hinder economic growth, with the conclusion that a growth-oriented reform would seek to shift the burden from income taxes to consumption or property taxes.

In designing national tax systems, governments do not, however, act alone and studies such as that of the OECD referred to above are influential in the diffusion of ideas across national borders. Increasingly tax systems interact with one another and together with increased co-operation between revenue authorities and tax policy experts; there is evidence of considerable copying of the tax policies adopted in other countries.

LeBlanc et al (2013)[1] evaluate the changes in tax policy among OECD members in the five years subsequent to the advent of the Financial Crisis. They observe a number of changes as follows.

Corporate income tax has been the most cyclical post-2008 crisis, and is also sensitive to a variety of structural economic changes that have been taking place, including the growing interconnectedness via global value changes as well as the increasing importance of intangibles. Because of the importance of business to the economic recovery, several countries have reduced corporate tax rates and/or introduced new incentives for research and development activity. Corporate income tax has, of course, also featured prominently in public debates in many countries, in particular its international dimensions which are considered throughout this book.

Reform options are more limited in relation to personal income tax. Some countries have attempted to incentivize employers to take on new employees in response to increased unemployment. Another trend is to increase the top rate of income tax, to be seen to be compelling wealthier taxpayers to visibly contribute to economic recovery.

In many countries, rates of broad-based consumption taxes, notably VAT, have been increased. In addition, several countries have targeted the financial sector with punitive taxes such as banking levies to correct their alleged undertaxation. Countries shifting from income/profits taxes to consumption taxes include Hungary, Israel, Chile, the Czech Republic and the UK.

A 2016 study by Ernst and Young[2] has collected data from tax policy professionals in 38 jurisdictions and finds that the broad base, low tax trend in business taxes continues, but is accompanied by expectations of an increase in the overall corporate income tax burden. The report observes the strong link between tax policy and politics which is influencing tax design in many countries, with Greece being a prominent European Union (EU) example. Transfer pricing changes are forecast to be the main issue leading to a higher tax burden (see Chapters 13 and 14).

Clearly the recession and its aftermath have affected tax policy, creating a need for increased revenue collection, but with recipients of tax expenditures lobbying to retain them. There is also evidence of reduced tolerance to tax evasion and aggressive tax avoidance. It is important to remember that tax and politics are intertwined, which goes some way to explain the differences between the tax policies adopted in different countries (Zolt, 2014).

---

1   LeBlanc, P, Matthews, S and Mellbye, K (2013) 'The Tax Policy Landscape Five Years after the Crisis', *OECD Taxation Working Papers*, No 17.
2   EY (2016) *The Outlook fSheor Global Tax Policy in 2016*. Available at: www.ey.com/Publication/vwLUAssets/ey-the-outlook-for-global-tax-policy-in-2016/$FILE/ey-the-outlook-for-global-tax-policy-in-2016.pdf.

COMPARATIVE TAXATION

1.20   It is extremely difficult to compare the taxes in use in different countries for a variety of reasons, not least differing economics, social and institutional frameworks. It is common to make judgements about a country's taxes by reference to the rates that are imposed. But care must be taken in making such judgements, because the rate, as we have just seen, is only one feature of a tax, and the coverage in terms of extent of the base and definition of the taxpayer are possibly even more important. This is particularly important in the context of corporate tax rates, where judgements are frequently made by reference to the headline rate, yet there are significant differences in terms of how corporate profits are determined for tax purposes.

SUMMARY

1.21   In this chapter we have examined the question of why governments need to impose taxes, and what forms of taxes are available to them. In designing a tax system, any government will generally use a range of different forms of taxation. In evaluating taxes, and weighing them up against one another in designing a tax system, a number of different criteria or principles have been developed. The most important criteria from the perspective of this book are equity and economic efficiency. Tax policy is complicated and has come under pressure and scrutiny in the wake of the financial crisis of 2008. Comparative taxation is difficult, because of the extent of variations in political, legal and cultural systems across the world. The most significant differences are to be found when comparing modern liberal democracies with developing countries.

FURTHER READING

ActionAid (2015) *Responsible Tax Practice by Companies*. Available at: www. actionaid.org.uk/sites/default/files/publications/responsible_tax_practice.pdf.

Alvarrenga, C (2013) 'Preventing Tax Avoidance: Is there convergence in the way countries counter tax avoidance?', *Bulletin for International Taxation*, July 2013.

Bauger, L (2014) 'The use of tax expenditures in times of fiscal consolidation', *European Economy Economic Papers*, No 523).

Braithwaite, J (2005) *Markets in Vice, Markets in Virtue*, Oxford University Press.

Braithwaite, V (2003) *Taxing Democracy: Understanding Tax Avoidance and Evasion*, Ashgate.

Burton, M and Sadiq, K (2012) *Tax Expenditure Management: A Critical Assessment*, Cambridge University Press.

Cnossen, S (1989) 'Value Added Tax: Key to a Better Tax Mix', *Australian Tax Forum*, Vol 6, No 3, pp 265–81.

Ernst & Young (2016) *The Outlook for Global Tax Policy in 2015*. Available at: www.ey.com/Publication/vwLUAssets/ey-the-outlook-for-global-tax-policy-in-2016/$FILE/ey-the-outlook-for-global-tax-policy-in-2016.pdf.

Fennell, C C and Fennell, L A (2003) 'Fear and Greed in Tax Policy: A Qualitative Research Agenda', *Washington University Journal of Law and Policy*, Vol 13, p 75.

Granwell, A and McGonigle, S (2006), 'US Tax Shelters: A UK Reprise', *British Tax Review* 2006, No 2, pp 170–208.

HMRC (2015) *Improving Large Business Compliance*. Available at: www.gov. uk/government/consultations/improving-large-business-tax-compliance.

Institute for Fiscal Studies (2010) *Dimensions of Tax Design*, Oxford University Press. Available at: www.ifs.org.uk/mirrleesReview.

James, S and Nobes, C (2008) *The Economics of Taxation*, 8th edn, Fiscal Publications.

Kirchler, E (2007) *The Economic Psychology of Tax Behaviour*, Cambridge University Press.

Kirchler, E, Kogler, C and Muehlbacher, S (2014) 'Cooperative tax compliance: from deterrence to deference', *Current Directions in Psychological Schience*, Vol 23(2), 87092.

Langham, J and Paulsen, N (2015) 'Effective engagement: Building a relationship of cooperation and trust within the community', *eJournal of Tax Research*, Vol 13(1), pp 378–402.

LeBlanc, P, Matthews, S and Mellbye, K (2013) 'The Tax Policy Landscape Five Years after the Crisis', *OECD Taxation Working Papers*, No 17.

McCaffrey, E J (1990) 'The Holy Grail of Tax Simplification', *Wisconsin Law Review*, Vol 5, pp 1267–1322.

McCaffrey, E J (1994) 'Cognitive Theory and Tax', *UCLA Law Review*, Vol 41, p 1861.

Mumford, A (2002) *Taxing Culture: Towards a Theory of Tax Collection Law*, Ashgate.

OECD (1979) *The Taxation of Net Wealth, Capital Transfers and Capital Gains of Individuals*.

OECD (2008) *Study into the Role of Tax Intermediaries*.

OECD (2010) *Tax Policy Reform and Economic Growth*.

OECD (2010) *Choosing a Broad Base – Low Rate Approach to Taxation*.

Owens, J (2013) 'Flat taxes Myths and Realities', *Bulletin for International Taxation*, December 2013, pp 679–670.

PwC & World Bank (2015) *Paying Taxes 2015*. Available at: www.pwc.com/gx/en/paying-taxes/download.jhtml.

Sandford, C (1995) *Taxing Wealth, from More Key Issues in Tax Reform*, Fiscal Publications.

Thuronyi, V (2003) *Comparative Tax Law*, Kluwer Law International.

Whait, R B (2015) 'Let's talk about compliance: Building understanding and relationships through discourse', *eJournal of Tax Research*, Vol 13(1), pp 130–157.

Zolt, E (2014) 'Politics and Taxation: An Introduction', *Tax Law Review*, Vol 67, 453–470.

Chapter 2

Introduction to International Taxation

BASICS

2.1 The essence of the subject of international taxation is the issue of whether, and to what extent, a country has the right to tax an individual or a company. In legal terminology, what is its jurisdiction to tax? This is a matter of public international law. A study of international taxation requires familiarization with both domestic taxation laws of individual countries and international tax law. There is no international 'tax system' as such; each country has its own domestic system that has often been developed over a long period of time. A country's domestic laws will provide for how it intends to tax its residents, and also what types of receipt or activity it wishes to bring into the tax net.

In moving from thinking about tax in the context of a single jurisdiction, to thinking about tax in a global context, a number of new conceptual issues come to the fore. We need to expand our understanding of 'equity' to embrace internation equity, and consider how to attach taxing rights to particular geographical locations.

These issues have become particularly controversial in recent years in the case of allocation of corporate profits, and the OECD's work on base erosion and profit shifting (BEPS) is proving to be a catalyst for quite wide-ranging change in that particular area.

HISTORY

2.2 The liberalization of the world economy has been in progress since at least the end of World War II, at a seemingly accelerating pace. The current taxation systems of most countries, certainly OECD members, are largely the product of policies that were developed in the first half of the twentieth century when there was less cross-border trade. There is truth in the old adage that an old tax is a good tax, and taxes can be notoriously difficult to displace once they are enacted, along with supporting regulatory mechanisms. Taxes that are appropriate in the context of a national, or domestic, environment, however, do not necessarily function well when we enter the world of significant cross-border activity, and much of the complexity that is found in current tax systems stems from the need to interact with other tax systems in a global environment.

Tax systems that have evolved differently in different countries, each with their own peculiarities, become something entirely different when they interface with other tax systems in the international marketplace. This creates opportunities for taxpayers, and scope to play one tax system off against another in the quest to minimize worldwide tax burdens. On the other hand it provides a threat to national governments who have to take action to prevent capital flight and loss of tax revenue.

The 1960s saw considerable removal of trade barriers as well as barriers between national capital markets[1] and alongside this was an increase in tax evasion. The period also saw a significant increase in corporate activities across national boundaries. By establishing parts of activities in different locations, multinational entities can take advantage of the differences between national tax systems.

Globalization, then, means that a nation's tax policy no longer stands alone, but must be robust enough to withstand competition from other countries. We return to the question of tax competition in Chapter 16. It was in the 1960s that the US started to pass anti-avoidance legislation to prevent multinationals using foreign affiliates to reduce the amount of tax paid in the US. Other countries soon followed suit and today we even see developing countries enacting rules similar to those developed in the US to prevent international tax avoidance, for example in dealing with transfer pricing (see Chapter 13).

As a result of the increased complexity in tax policies, rules and administration, we are starting to see greater co-operation among nations, as well as changes in tax policies to make tax systems more robust in the global era. There has also been movement towards common tax policies, for example the worldwide trend towards reducing the corporation tax rate from an OECD average of 50 per cent in the early 1980s to between 25 per cent and 30 per cent at present. In order to understand these developments, which will be examined in greater detail in later chapters, this chapter introduces some key concepts.

---

1   Although now a bit dated, Grenshell (2005) provides a very good overview of the impact of globalization on tax systems. See also Roxan (2012).

JURISDICTION TO TAX AND PUBLIC INTERNATIONAL LAW

2.3   International tax law, according to Qureshi (1994) consists of customary international law and international agreements. It covers the right of a state to tax, tax treaties and dispute settlement where it is unclear what the respective taxing rights of two states are. It may extend to protocols for exchange of information on taxpayers.

The sources of international tax law are difficult to pinpoint, as public international law is often a matter of acceptance and interpretation by the countries affected. In summary, there are certain international agreements which constitute international law and the rest is merely customary. Agreements include the Vienna Convention on the Law of Treaties, the Treaty of Rome (which is binding on the members but subject to the principle of subsidiarity). There is a worldwide network of bilateral double tax treaties and a few multilateral ones. The customary parts of international public law are more difficult to pin down but will include the legal principles commonly adopted by the Western world.

The question is: what determines the right of a country to levy tax on a person or company? What connection, if any, between the taxpayer and the taxing authority is necessary? Most countries use the principles of source and residence outlined below.

In this book, we will mainly focus on the international tax issues involving corporations, although many of the matters examined will be equally relevant to individuals.

ESSENTIAL CONCEPTS IN INTERNATIONAL TAXATION

2.4   Which individuals and firms does a country have the right to tax? The answer to this question depends on the geographical boundaries of the country and the identification of the individuals and firms operating within those boundaries as either tax resident or not tax resident. The concept of tax residence is often quite different from the concept of residence for other purposes. Even where a company is not a tax resident of a particular country, it may nevertheless be earning profits there, using the facilities and infrastructure of that country. It can then be said that the company's profits are 'sourced' in that country, which may also then give that country a right to tax those profits. The extent of a country's right to tax is known as its tax jurisdiction.

Two key principles are therefore in common use around the world to determine the extent of a country's tax jurisdiction; residence and source.

A country may reserve the right to tax its residents on their worldwide income and gains. Note that the concept of tax residence may differ from physical residence. We will examine this concept at some length in Chapter 3 with respect to individuals and Chapter 4 with respect to corporations.

A country will usually wish to tax all income and gains arising within its jurisdiction. This extends the right to tax which a country already has under the residence principle. As we noted earlier, individuals or corporations who are not tax resident in a country may nevertheless carry out business there, or own sources of income there. Under the source principle, a country reserves the right to tax not only the worldwide income and gains of its tax residents, but also the income and gains of non-residents arising within its borders.

Issues in international taxation arise whenever a person resident in one country has the right to income or gains arising in another country. From a country perspective, the countries concerned will wish to ensure that they are collecting the tax to which they believe they are entitled. From a taxpayer perspective, this situation may lead to double taxation. Hence the two countries will probably have to come to an agreement regarding which of them has the right to tax international income flows. Many countries have entered into bilateral treaties, referred to as double tax treaties, which aim, inter alia, to define which country a taxpayer will be considered to be resident of for tax purposes and how taxes on different types of income and capital are to be divided between the two countries. In this regard, one of the most influential bodies in the development of a network of bilateral treaties, has been the OECD which in 1963 produced a Model Double Tax Convention which now forms the basis for most bilateral treaties. We consider the nature of double tax treaties and in particular the OECD Model in more detail in Chapters 7, 8 and 9.

A country's tax base may therefore be defined in terms of:

● The persons who are liable to pay tax (eg individuals only, individuals and corporations, individuals and trustees and corporations, etc).

● The types of income and capital on which tax must be paid. For instance, a typical tax base might include:

— Income taxes on earnings.

— Income taxes on investment income.

— Income/corporation taxes on profits of corporations.

— Capital taxes on capital profits.

— Capital taxes on inheritances.

— Indirect taxes on purchases of goods and services.

— Capital taxes on holdings of property and wealth.

If the tax base is reduced through tax planning, tax avoidance or tax planning activities, we say that the tax base is being eroded. This 'base erosion' also occurs if a government has to give tax deductions for payments made by its residents to non-residents, whom it cannot tax, even if there has been no tax-planning, avoidance or evasion activity.

Protecting the tax base from erosion is one of the objectives of any government, and in a world of globalization this is becoming increasingly difficult. This issue has become particularly acute in recent years following the Financial Crisis. The work of the OECD on BEPS (see below), and the acceleration of the timeline for completion of this work as a result of public and political pressure, is indicative of the increased urgency on this important issue.

There is considerable current debate about which principle should have primacy in the allocation of taxing rights between countries, the residence principle or the source principle. This is a complex issue and views have changed over the years since the start of the twentieth century when international tax rules were beginning to be developed. Views also differ between developed nations and developing nations. We return to this question in the context of tax competition in Chapter 16 and development in Chapter 22.

Federal systems and local-level taxes

2.5   The principles set out above have been described in relation to national tax systems. However, they can apply equally when considering the taxing rights of different parts of the same country. Some countries have multi-tier tax systems where the federal government collects taxes and the internal divisions of the country also have their own tax systems. The prime example of this is the US but Canada, Australia and Switzerland, to name but a few, also operate taxes at the sub-national (state) level. These sub-national tax systems may consist of taxes on income, profits and gains and may rival the national (federal) system in complexity, or they may be more limited. In the US, Alaska, Florida, Nevada, South Dakota, Texas, Washington and Wyoming do not levy direct income taxes on individuals but only sales taxes. Other states confine themselves to levying taxes on sales, whilst others have complex income taxes. A few states limit their taxation of income to dividends and interest only (New Hampshire and Tennessee). The US state taxes are generally only a few per cent and they are deductible for tax purposes from income chargeable to US federal taxation, thus avoiding double taxation. In addition to federal and state taxes, certain US cities (eg New York) also levy their own income tax, thus making their residents subject to no fewer than three income tax systems. Note that those states which do not levy a personal income tax at state level usually do levy state income tax on corporations. Nearly all the states levy sales taxes and although there is no sales tax or VAT at the federal level, sales taxes are sometimes also levied at county and municipal level. This prevalence of sales tax at the local level is often cited as one of the principal reasons why the US remains the major economy in the world not to operate VAT.

Tax policy makers have much to learn from the operation of these sub-national tax systems. Issues which the supra-national tax policy makers grapple with, such as artificial shifting of profits to low-level tax countries and which country has the right to tax a particular company have often been dealt with successfully in state-level tax systems. This is not to say that the solutions adopted between the states are always suitable for adoption between separate nations, but they at least provide evidence of the pros and cons of certain policies.[1]

In our study of double tax relief we are not usually concerned with sub-national taxes. This is for two reasons:

- As stated above, sub-national taxes are normally tax deductible when computing tax at the federal (national) level, thus any potential double taxation to which they give rise has already been dealt with.

- Following on from this first reason, double taxation treaties (mainly bilateral agreements under which two countries decide how double taxation arising from the interface of their tax systems is to be relieved) normally exclude sub-national taxes from their provisions. In any case, double tax treaties normally only deal with the taxation of income, gains and capital, not sales or other indirect taxes.

However, tax planners cannot afford to ignore sub-national taxes. A multinational company may find that it has a liability to pay, say, US state taxes but not US federal taxation. If the profits on which the state taxation is levied are also taxed in another country where the multinational is resident, this may give rise to unrelieved double taxation. The tax treaty between the home country and the US is unlikely to be of any help because the state taxes in question are likely to be sales taxes, and even if they are income taxes, they will not be covered by the double tax treaty. Whether or not there is any double tax relief will depend upon whether the home country allows tax relief for the foreign sub-national taxes in its national (domestic) law.

---

1   In recent years there has been renewed interest in this as a result of concerns over the continued efficacy of the arm's length principle as a mechanism for allocating profits for tax purposes between jurisdictions. This issue is covered in more detail Chapter 13.

Tax principles in an international environment

2.6   In Chapter 1 we considered two main criteria against which individual taxes, and a composite tax system, can be evaluated, namely equity and efficiency. In now considering what happens when national tax systems must interact with those of other nations, we need to reconsider these criteria.

Instead of thinking of equity in terms of individuals' ability to pay taxes, in a global context the issue becomes one of inter-nation equity. How should tax revenues be divided between the various countries in which taxpayers do business or otherwise earn taxable profits? This question takes us to the issue of what gives the state the right to levy taxes – that is, what gives it jurisdiction to tax, residence of a taxpayer or the source of the taxable income or profits, or both? There is no easy answer to this question and some national tax policies will reflect a desire to give residence primacy over source, and others vice versa.

Economic efficiency, or neutrality, also takes on a different layer of meaning in the context of the interaction between two or more national tax systems. It will be recalled that generally the principle of economic efficiency or neutrality (see para **1.6**) suggests that taxes should not interfere with decision making, a neutral tax is one which leaves a pre-tax decision unchanged post tax, so that taxes do not impinge on choices about savings and investment for example. In the 1960s, Peggy Musgrave (then Peggy Richman) gave prominence to three notions of neutrality in her book The Taxation of Foreign Investment Income: An Economic Analysis. These three notions are national neutrality, capital export neutrality and capital import neutrality. Their focus is on the overall rate of tax which applies when taxpayers earn profits in more than one country and both source country and residence country taxes are taken into account.

National neutrality (NN) is insular, in that it focuses on ensuring that the domestic fisc does not lose when residents invest overseas. It is concerned with equalising the after-tax rate of return on foreign investments with the pre-tax return on domestic investments by treating foreign taxes paid in the same way as other business expenses. The overriding concern is national welfare, rather than global welfare.

The other two forms of neutrality popularized by Musgrave are, on the other hand, concerned with worldwide welfare and are premised on the assumption that foreign investment is matched by an equivalent reduction in domestic investment.

Capital export neutrality (CEN) is concerned with neutrality in the location of investment. Under this principle, a tax system should be designed so that it is neutral regarding outflows of capital, so that the total of domestic and foreign taxes does not leave a capital exporter worse off than if the investment had all been in the home country. One criticism of CEN is that it underestimates, or even ignores, the link between taxes in a country and the level of government benefits provided by that country. There may be good reasons to invest in a particular location, notwithstanding higher tax rates, if the level of government support is high (Hines 2009). Government support in this context could include, for example, strong infrastructure and a sound regulatory environment.

Capital import neutrality (CIN) on the other hand, is concerned with neutrality in the source of investment and from a government's point of view means that domestic companies should be protected from a higher tax burden in a foreign market than taxpayers from other countries operating in that same market (ie all firms of all nations pay the same rate of tax).[1]

Policies to achieve capital export neutrality and capital import neutrality will not necessarily be consistent, but for both, the focus is on the overall rate of tax. For capital export neutrality it is the domestic rate that is most important, for capital import neutrality it is the foreign tax rate that is most important.

In recent years, the focus of attention has shifted to another international norm, developed by Desai and Hines (2003), which is concerned with how ownership of businesses is allocated across countries, with the emphasis on productivity.

National ownership neutrality (NON) suggests that the amount of tax paid by a business should not depend on the identity, or location, of its owners. Therefore, decisions such as how to structure foreign investment (eg as foreign direct investment or otherwise), should not be influenced by tax considerations.

Capital ownership neutrality (CON) suggests that tax systems should not distort asset ownership on a worldwide basis; which should be such that productivity is maximized. 'Efficient allocation of capital ownership means that it is impossible to increase productivity by reallocating assets between owners'.[2] NON and CON, in emphasising ownership patterns, are based on a transaction cost economics approach. The importance of ownership is demonstrated by Desai and Hines (2003), who find by examining patterns of ownership of US multinationals, including corporate inversions (see Chapter 11) where the location of the parent company is shifted to another jurisdiction, that decisions are significantly affected by home country tax incentives. NON and CON thus highlight the distortion of international ownership patterns leading to inefficiencies, such as those arising from the pursuit of CEN.

In a discussion of technology and knowledge transfer, Margalioth (2011) observes that the emergence of NON and CON welfare norms have changed the academic debate and highlighted the need for more detailed analysis of international tax policy. It is important to recognize that these concepts relate to the economics of taxation. There are, of course, other ways of thinking about taxation. Roxan (2013) reminds us that tax is also a legal construct as a mechanism for regulating the allocation of power. It is also a social issue, concerned with the impact of taxation on particular groups in society, or on one society *vis à vis* another in an international context. Tax is also a political issue, and at times political concerns override those of economics, law and social policy.[3] The political aspects of international tax have come to the fore recently in the work of the OECD BEPS Project – discussed at para **2.13** below.

---

1   For an examination of the misunderstandings between economists and non-economists as to the significance of CIN, see Knoll (2009).
2   Hines, J (2009) 'Reconsidering the Taxation of Foreign Income', *Tax Law Review* 62, pp 269–299, at p 277.
3   See Lamb et al (2005) and Oats (2012) for alternative ways of thinking about and researching taxation.

TAX PLANNING IN MULTINATIONAL ENTERPRISES

2.7   Multinational enterprises (MNEs) usually consist of groups of companies or other business entities which are resident in a number of different countries, but which are under common control. Multinational enterprises can also consist of partnerships and other business forms where the partners are resident in different countries. They typically seek to exploit differences in the tax systems in the various countries within which they operate. The aim of such planning is to minimize the global tax bill, and thereby maximising global after-tax profits. Scholes et al. (2015) maintain that investment strategies and financial policies within firms are linked through taxes. Tax rules reflect before-tax rates of return on assets. These differ, however, because different types of assets are taxed differently, or similar assets in different jurisdictions may be taxed differently. 'Effective tax planning considers the role of taxes when implementing the decision rule of maximising after-tax returns' (Scholes et al, p 20) and may or may not include tax minimization strategies. 'To avoid operating at a competitive disadvantage, managers must understand how changes in tax rules influence the behaviour of their customers, employees, suppliers and competitors' (Scholes et al, p 22).

Firms, whether MNEs or not, spend huge amounts of money on tax-planning activities and on complying with the tax rules and regulations. Mills, Erikson and Maydew (1998) estimate that large corporations save on average $4 for every $1 spent on tax-planning activities. 'Thus, not only is tax planning a big business, but returns to investment in tax planning can be large' (Scholes et al, p 25). Note that Scholes et al (2015) is a US publication and contains considerable detail which is only relevant to the US context and not elsewhere. The introductory chapters, however, provide some interesting insights into the tax-planning process generally. Yancey & Cravens (1998) similarly examine international tax planning, albeit also with a US focus.

Planning techniques include the use of tax havens, the use of specially targeted tax regimes by countries which are not obviously tax havens and the manipulation of internal transfer prices to transfer profits into low-tax jurisdictions away from higher tax ones. These issues will all be examined in more detail in later chapters.

MNEs may seek to exploit differences not only in tax rates but also in the way tax profits are computed – for example, by claiming a tax deduction in one country for an item of expenditure which is being paid to a fellow group member in another country, whose tax system does not count the receipt as taxable income. A variation on this theme is to finance an overseas subsidiary through hybrid financial instruments. The aim of such planning is to have the return on capital paid by the subsidiary treated as (tax deductible) interest, but have the receipt of the return on capital treated as a return of capital and therefore not taxable. Even a halfway house such as having the payment classed as interest but the receipt classed as a taxable dividend is preferable to perfectly symmetrical treatment.

A country must weigh up the costs of losing tax revenue through such planning against the risk of migration of MNEs if it unilaterally enacts anti-avoidance tax legislation aimed at the MNE.

A group that operates in two or more countries will be faced with a bewildering array of tax rules and regulations, different methods of calculating profits, special incentives and concessions. When choosing a location for a new business venture or investment, the tax regime is important and even for existing offshore activities, needs to be constantly monitored for changes and developments. Tax is, however, only one of a range of factors that must be taken into account when choosing a new business location. Other factors include:

- proximity to markets;

- proximity to raw materials;

- availability of a suitable labour pool at suitable cost;

- political stability;

- climate;

- transport links;

- availability of government incentives; and

- governmental regulations and restrictions.

It is generally agreed that tax should not drive business strategy and should only be considered once a location is determined as being suitable in other respects. Physical factors will be especially important in manufacturing location decisions. Choosing a location primarily on the basis of the tax regime is not advisable, as tax reliefs can be withdrawn at short notice by governments.

Arguably, businesses such as financial and internet-based services which involve little physical and human capital are better placed to take advantage of attractive tax regimes than manufacturing businesses, due to the relative ease with which operations can be moved from country to country. There is indirect evidence, both econometric and from surveys, which suggests that taxes do influence firms' location decisions (Bond et al (2000), p 31). Other factors are obviously key, as mentioned above, but in situations where these factors are broadly similar, tax becomes a more important and differentiating factor. Devereux & Griffiths (1998) found that the location decisions of US multinationals within Europe are influenced by the average effective tax rate applicable.

The relationship between tax systems and location decisions includes decisions about individual assets of businesses, and in this regard, intangible assets are particularly mobile. Margalioth (2011) notes that the current international tax system unintentionally motivates the transfer of knowledge through, for example, licensing of intangibles in particular jurisdictions allowing for profit shifting. Ensuing knowledge transfer, however, is arguably positive in global welfare terms, however whether this is also to the benefit of national interests is a more difficult question. In a panel study of European data, Dischinger and Riedel (2011) analyse the correlation between the location of intangibles within multinational companies and find evidence of a significant bias of intangible property holdings towards affiliates based in a country with a low corporation tax rate relative to other group locations. For a series of papers dealing with the issue of mobility and taxes, see *National Tax Journal*, Vol 63(4).

The tax planning activities of MNEs have come under intense scrutiny in the past two years, largely as a result of media attention that has fuelled public debate in a number of countries, most notably the UK, Ireland, France and the US. There have been attacks on the tax strategies of named large corporations, which in some cases, for example, Starbucks, has led to considerable reputational damage. In Chapter 19, the activities of these named large MNEs will be examined more closely to demonstrate how the concepts introduced in intervening chapters are mobilized in practice. As mentioned earlier, one significant consequence of the publicity surrounding the activities of large MNEs is pressure to re-examine some of the key issues in the allocation of taxing rights between countries.

TAX ADMINISTRATION

2.8   Increased globalization puts considerable pressure on tax administrations (Revenue Authorities) and we are seeing increasing levels of co-operation and sharing of best practice among them. The OECD issues regularly comparative information about practices, and performance across a number of advanced and emerging economies. The latest publication[1] released in 2015 includes 56 countries including all OECD, EU and G20 members. The European Commission (EC) brings together representatives from Member State tax administrations under a risk-management platform, which meets annually to share experiences.

As early as 2000, Tanzi, talked of 'fiscal termites'; factors that threaten the integrity of tax systems, and most of which relate to the internationalization of tax. These are:

1   electronic commerce and transactions;

2   electronic money;

3   intra-company trade;

4   offshore financial centres and tax havens;

5   derivatives and hedge funds;

6   inability to tax financial capital;

7   growing foreign activities; and

8   foreign shopping.

Braithwaite (2005) argues that fiscal termites lead to 'moral termites', a decline in tax morality that is demonstrated by, for example, the relocation of many sports stars to more convivial tax jurisdictions. This apparent decline in tax morality represents another problem for tax authorities to deal with, and leads to a need for greater co-operation between tax authorities.

The economic crisis led to increased pressure on tax administrations to ensure the maximum amount of revenue is collected. In many countries this has been translated into new campaigns to close the 'tax gap', ie the difference between the amount theoretically collectable under the tax law and that which is actually collected. The tax gap is the result of a number of factors, such as non-payment, tax evasion and disagreements about the application of the law. In many countries, serious attempts are made to measure the tax gap, an extremely difficult task, so as to provide a strategic focus and benchmark for evaluating improved tax authority performance.[2]

Recent developments in the area of co-operation between tax authorities in combating aggressive tax avoidance include the formation of the Joint International Tax Shelter Information Centre (JITSIC), based in Washington and London and entailing information sharing between the US, UK, Australia, Canada and Japan. This body has been rebranded in 2014 as the Joint International Taskforce on Shared Intelligence and Collaboration and now includes 37 members.[3]

Another development is the Seoul Declaration, which emerged in 2006 from the OECD's Forum on Tax Administration and outlines the challenges faced by tax administrations around the world. It notes the increase in international non-compliance and aims to promote better co-operation internationally to counter it. The EU promotes mechanisms to encourage cooperation between Member State tax authorities, not only in terms of tax collection, but also tax policy. The specific international tax issues in relation to companies in the EU are covered in Chapter 20.

---

1   Available at: www.oecd.org/ctp/administration/tax-administration-23077727.htm.
2   For example, information about the UK tax gap can be found at: www.hmrc.gov.uk/statistics/tax-gaps.htm.
3   See www.oecd.org/tax/forum-on-tax-administration/jitsic/.

ROLE OF SUPRANATIONAL ORGANIZATIONS

2.9   Several supranational organizations[1] have emerged and developed in the last century with the aim of encouraging international trade whilst providing a level playing field for their member countries in terms of their ability to attract MNEs to invest in their countries. The most active organization in the field of international taxation is the OECD (see: www.oecd.org). The OECD has long been particularly active in promoting the adoption of double tax treaties and has been active in recent years in establishing principles for the taxation of international money flows resulting from the digital economy. We examine the digital economy in more detail in the context of corporate income taxes in Chapter 9 and in the context of consumption taxes in Chapter 21.

As noted above, the EU is also active, particularly in promoting harmonization of the tax systems of its member countries. In Chapter 20 we consider actions taken by the EU towards harmonization, as well as key decisions of the European Court of Justice (CJEU) which has considerable influence on the tax rules adopted by Member States.

The United Nations' (UN) role includes, for example, promoting measures to ensure that developing countries get their fair share of the tax on profits of multinational companies operating within their borders. We consider the role of the UN in offering alternatives to the OECD model tax treaty[2] to protect the interests of developing countries in Chapter 7.

The International Monetary Fund (IMF) also plays a role in the international tax arena, primarily through providing technical assistance to countries in developing their tax policy and practice, and mainly to low and middle income countries.

The Group of 20 (G20) and its subset, the Group of 7 (G7, formerly G8), provide a forum for international cooperation on economic and financial issues facing the member countries. The G20 was first established in 1999, in the aftermath of the 1997 financial crisis, with a meeting of finance ministers and central bank governors. In 2008, the first meeting of G20 leaders took place in Washington DC, at which leaders agreed to an action plan to stabilize the global economy, and summit meetings have been held each year subsequently. The G8[3] was formed earlier in 1975, and comprises heads of state of the governments of the major industrial democracies, and became the G7 in 2014 with the removal of Russia from the Group.

The interrelationship between these various supranational organizations is complex and they are increasingly becoming interlinked. For example, the OECD presented a report to G20 leaders in advance of the 2013 St Petersburg meeting outlining progress of the Global Forum on Transparency and Information Exchange as well as the BEPS work discussed at para **2.13** below.[4]

In April 2016, a Platform for Collaboration on Tax was launched as a joint initiative by the IMF, OECD and World Bank Group. A jointly developed concept note[5] describes the aims of the Platform as to provide a structured and transparent framework for:

1. Producing concrete joint outputs and deliverables under an agreed work plan ... [which] may cover a variety of domestic and international tax matters.

2.   Strengthening dynamic interactions between standard setting, capacity building and technical assistance …

3.   Sharing information on activities more systematically, including on country-level activities.

A number of 'toolkits' are envisaged dealing with issues such as transfer pricing, tax treaty negotiations, supply chain restructuring and assessment of BEPS risks. In June 2017, a toolkit for addressing difficulties in accessing comparables for transfer pricing purposes was published[6] to help developing countries, particularly in relation to mineral product pricing.

---

1   For a discussion of the role of networks of international experts in developing national tax policies, see Christians (2009).
2   *The Model Tax Convention on Income and on Capital.*
3   The University of Toronto hosts a G8 research group. Available at: www.g8.utoronto.ca/what_is_g8.html.
4   OECD (2013) *Secretary General Report to the G20 Leaders.* Available at: www.oecd.org/tax/SG-report-G20-Leaders-StPetersburg.pdf.
5   Available at: www.oecd.org/ctp/concept-note-platform-for-collaboration-on-tax.pdf.
6   Available at www.oecd.org/tax/pct-delivers-toolkit-to-help-developing-countries-address-lack-of-comparables-for-transfer-pricing-analyses.htm.

CROSS-BORDER ENFORCEMENT OF TAXES

2.10   Historically, the general principle in international law has been that a country will not assist in the collection of taxes charged by another country. Quite why this principle, sometimes referred to as the Revenue Rule, should have become so entrenched is not known but Baker (2002), writing with reference to the position in the US, puts forward the opinion that perhaps it is because the collection of tax is an act of sovereignty and no sovereign state allows another state to exercise its sovereignty on its territory. This is the view taken by the UN Group of Experts.[1]

Considering other possibilities, Baker concludes that the principle definitely exists even if we are not sure why.

However, cooperation in the collection of taxes of other countries is now widespread, if limited, via:

●   Provisions in the thousands of bilateral double tax treaties which exist. Most double tax treaties contain provisions on the exchange of information for tax purposes and a few contain provisions for assistance in the collection of the tax revenues of the other contracting state.

●   Agreements which are essentially one-sided whereby one country agrees to provide information to another country to enable that country to enforce its taxes. Why a country should give such assistance on a unilateral basis is an interesting question: the countries concerned are usually low-tax countries which have been put under pressure to do so by the OECD. This is discussed further in Chapter 16.

- The EU Mutual Assistance for the Recovery of Tax Claims Directive[2] and the Directive on Administrative Cooperation in the Field of Taxation.[3]

- The 1988 Council of Europe/OECD Convention on Mutual Administrative Assistance in Tax Matters.[4]

The EU and OECD multilateral measures generally include:

- The requirement to exchange information, automatically (eg lists of interest payments by banks), spontaneously, where one state passes information to the other state which it thinks would be of interest to it without being asked and upon request.

- The right to permit tax officials from one country to visit the other country to carry out investigations.

- Recovery of tax claims: where one state actually collects the tax due to the other state and then hands it over. This is the most problematic form of assistance as one state may not understand or agree with the taxes which it is being asked to collect and there may be issues concerning the human rights of the taxpayer.

- Measures of conservancy, such as freezing the assets of the taxpayer or even seizing them, to ensure that the tax claims of the other state can actually be met.

---

1 See *Report of the Tenth Meeting of the Ad Hoc Group of Experts on International Cooperation in Tax Matters*, Geneva, 10–14 September 2001. UN ST/SG/AC,8/2001/L.2. Available at: http://unpan1.un.org/intradoc/groups/public/documents/UN/UNPAN001659.pdf.
2 Council Directive 2010/24/EU.
3 Council Directive 2011/16/EU.
4 Available at: http://www.oecd.org/ctp/exchange-of-tax-information/ENG-Amended-Convention.pdf.

PRIVATE INTERNATIONAL LAW AND TAXATION

2.11   Private, as opposed to public, international law refers to matters not directly involving the state itself. In the UK the distinction between public and private international law is somewhat hazy, but in the tax field, private international law (or conflict of laws, as it is sometimes referred to) generally governs questions as to which country's laws are relevant to a particular taxpayer. Whether an enterprise is a partnership or a corporation may well affect which country's tax laws are in point. If one country considers the enterprise to be a partnership, it may well wish to apply its tax laws to the individual partners. If another country considers that same enterprise to be a corporation with strong links to that country, it may well wish to tax the enterprise under its laws as a corporation.

RECOGNITION OF FOREIGN LEGAL ENTITIES

2.12   The way in which an enterprise is recognized (or 'characterized') for tax purposes can have a dramatic effect on its tax treatment, both in terms of the amount of tax paid and to which state that tax is paid. Different states have different rules for determining whether a legal entity is to be considered 'transparent' or 'opaque' for tax purposes. If an entity is considered to be transparent, then a state will wish to tax the individuals or other persons who make up that entity. In the case of a partnership, this would mean that the individual partners would find themselves potentially liable to tax in the state in which they were tax resident. On the other hand, if an entity is considered to be 'opaque' for tax purposes, then it will primarily be taxable in the state in which it is established. This can give rise to double taxation. Take the case of an entity which is established under the laws of State A, but whose individual partners are tax resident in State B. If State A considers an entity to be opaque, but State B considers it to be transparent, then the profits or income could be taxed in both states. There might not be any double tax relief: if State B does not recognize the entity itself then it might not give any relief for tax suffered at the entity level when assessing the individual partners to tax.

In practice this is a matter which gives rise to considerable uncertainty in international taxation. First, it is necessary to understand the commercial law of a country to determine how an entity will be viewed and only then can the tax consequences be considered. Because of the level of detail in domestic laws needed to determine how an entity is viewed, double tax treaties do not normally deal with this matter. Therefore, before a taxpayer can decide how a treaty will apply, or even if it will apply at all, that taxpayer must first ascertain how he/it will be viewed by each of the parties to the treaty. Entity characterization is considered in more detail in Chapter 11.

THE OECD'S BEPS PROJECT

2.13   The OECD's BEPS Project is concerned with the problems of base erosion and profit shifting by MNEs. Although we have not yet covered the details of the mechanisms by which multinationals' profits are taxed, the following is an outline of the BEPS Project and its progress to date. The concepts dealt with briefly here will be explained further in later chapters.

The base erosion problem

2.14   Base erosion refers to a reduction of the amount of profits which a country can tax. The tax base of a country is defined as the persons and the profits that a country is permitted to tax. For instance, the corporation tax base of the UK is the profits and gains of companies resident in the UK (after double tax relief) and the profits of non-resident companies from trading in the UK through a permanent establishment (PE).

Base erosion refers to the reduction of the number of companies and/or amount of profits that a country can tax. If a company moves its residence to a different country or causes its profits to arise in a different country (eg by transferring its intellectual property (IP) to another country so that the royalties go there) then the ability of the original country to collect corporation tax will be diminished, ie the tax base has reduced or completely eroded. If a payment is made to a non-resident, but the UK government has to grant a tax deduction for it, then that payment is a 'base eroding payment'. Base erosion results from either companies themselves (or all, or part, of their profits) ceasing to be taxable in the country.

The profit-shifting problem

2.15   In addition to tax planning strategies aimed at achieving double non-taxation – so that profits are not taxed anywhere at all – MNEs also engage in planning activity aimed at attributing *tax* profits to lower tax jurisdictions, now commonly, although not accurately, referred to as profit shifting. It is important to note here that we are not talking about the profits of companies as reported to external parties, ie the accounting profits, but the profits as determined under the tax code as forming the tax base for a particular country. Sometimes these lower tax countries will be well recognized as tax havens, but frequently they are countries which offer low tax regimes alongside their normal corporation tax systems. This can be achieved by, for example, having a special rule by which royalty income is very lightly taxed. Many countries not immediately identifiable as tax havens have these favourable tax rules – eg Luxembourg and the Netherlands – and even the UK now taxes certain royalties very lightly due to its 'patent box' rules.[1] Tax havens are discussed in Chapter 16.

Base erosion and profit shifting activity therefore frequently overlap: shifting tax profits to a lower tax country will erode the tax base of the country from which the profits are being shifted.

In 2012, the G20[2] group of finance ministers and central bank governors requested that the OECD produce a report and an action plan to combat BEPS, which was endorsed at its July 2013 meeting. In its communique[3] the G20 finance ministers made the following statements:

- effective taxation of mobile income is a key challenge;

- profits should be taxed where functions driving the profits are performed and where value is created;

- G20 member countries should ensure that international and domestic laws do not permit or encourage artificial profit shifting to low-tax jurisdictions;

- there should be a new single global standard for automatic exchange of information; and

- all countries should join the Multilateral Convention on Mutual Administrative Assistance in Tax Matters.

The OECD produced its report *Addressing Base Erosion and Profit Shifting* (BEPS Report) in February 2013. This important Report is a response to widespread and critical press coverage of the practices of MNEs in avoiding taxes.

It sets out the main ways in which MNEs are known to take advantage of differing international tax rules and how they interconnect to reduce their global tax liabilities. These are summarized at para **2.18**.

---

1   Corporation Taxes Act 2010 (CTA 2010), Pt 8A.
2   The members of the G20 group of countries are: Argentina, Australia, Brazil, Canada, China, European Union, France, Germany, India, Indonesia, Italy, Japan, Mexico, Russia, Saudi Arabia, South Africa, South Korea, Turkey, United Kingdom, and the United States of America.
3   Available at: www.financialtransparency.org/wp-content/uploads/2013/07/Final_Communique_FM_July_ENG.pdf?c5e598.

GLOBALIZATION OF BUSINESS AND THE NON-GLOBALIZATION OF TAX AUTHORITIES

2.16   In Chapter 19 you will find three case studies that demonstrate how MNEs adopt specific planning strategies. In all three case studies the strategies depend on the individual subsidiary companies within a MNE acting in a very coordinated way, under the direction of the parent company. However, this direction does not amount to 'effective management' or 'central management and control', so it does not usually alter the tax residence of the subsidiaries. Typically, MNEs operate so-called 'matrix management' systems. This means that in addition to managers in a particular country, reporting to the managing director of their particular subsidiary company, they also report to people in the headquarters of the MNE. The people based at the headquarters have an important role in coordinating and directing staff in the group's subsidiaries around the world. MNEs have also become highly vertically-integrated, so that companies within the Group deal with everything from the supply of raw materials through research and development (R&D), production, assembly, and sale to end customers.

Instead of production being carried out in one country only, it is now common for production to be broken down into several stages, and for those stages to be carried out in different countries by different subsidiaries in a way which minimizes costs and taxes. Thus, although on paper and in legal terms, the various subsidiaries in the different countries are separate, in operational practice, they are run as a single organization. The OECD BEPS Report describes this as 'unprecedented interconnectedness at all levels'.[1]

This is in contrast with how a tax authority operates: taking HMRC as an example, the UK tax authority operates almost exclusively in the English language. Its rights to information about what is happening in a MNE are mainly limited to the UK subsidiaries only. A MNE which might have subsidiary companies in 50 countries is being taxed by 50 different tax authorities, none of whom necessarily have intelligence about what the other authorities are doing, or what information they hold about the MNE. Compared to the ease with which the different subsidiaries in a MNE can communicate and coordinate their activities so as to pay the least tax, the tax authorities can only cooperate in a very limited, very slow, and very cumbersome manner. They are constrained by the need to use the medium of tax information exchange agreements, or the procedures laid down in the mutual assistance articles of double tax treaties (DTTs). It should also be remembered that tax authorities are not working towards a collective 'group' result; they each have their own agendas, capabilities and needs around tax collection.

1   OECD *BEPS Report*, p 28.

What makes BEPS activity possible?

2.17   Apart from the gulf in the level of coordination between different parts of a MNE, and the different tax authorities which attempt to tax its profits, there are certain features of the international tax system that permit BEPS activity.

Branch structures can be exploited, particularly if one country (eg the UK) exempts from tax the income earned by foreign branches of a resident company. The country where the branch is located might not think there is a taxable entity (permanent establishment (PE)), and so might not tax the branch profits (see Chapter 9 which explains PEs further). Alternatively, it might only charge a very low rate of tax. Some countries even permit the branch to reduce its taxable profits by interest not actually paid.

Different tax systems classify payments and receipts differently, giving rise to tax arbitrage as discussed in Chapters 11 and 12. Typically, one country might classify a payment by a subsidiary to a foreign holding company as interest, so that it reduces taxable profits. However, when it reaches the holding company, that country might classify it as a dividend, and exempt it from tax. So there is a tax deduction not matched by a tax receipt. The profits used to pay the 'interest' have not been taxed anywhere: 'double non-taxation'. Differences in recognition of hybrid entities are also exploited.

The BEPS Report also voices concerns that MNEs are taking advantage of tax treaties where this was not intended by the countries involved. Typically, such activity would involve the use of a special purpose vehicle (SPV) that would be tax resident in one of the countries, and therefore able to take advantage of its double tax treaties to obtain treaty benefits such as low rates of, or exemption from, withholding tax. This type of activity is examined in more detail in Chapter 15. Withholding taxes on interest can also be avoided by making payments in respect of derivatives instead of paying interest.

The other major type of BEPS activity concerns the group's transfer prices, as discussed in Chapter 13. In a closely coordinated MNE, there will be many transactions between its subsidiaries in different countries for which it is very difficult for the tax authority to evaluate what the arm's-length price should have been. This is usually because there are no comparable transactions outside the group. Intangibles, and payments for their use, are particularly hard to value and the MNE will always be at an advantage over the tax authorities in arguments as to what the arm's-length rate of royalty payments, or sales proceeds ought to be. The OECD's *Transfer Pricing Guidelines* place a heavy emphasis on looking at where risks are borne to justify the levels of internal prices charged or borne by the group members. However, it can often be very difficult in practice to say exactly where risk is being borne, or how much a particular subsidiary ought to be compensated for bearing it. The *Transfer Pricing Guidelines* look at contractual allocations of risk, but these might not reflect the reality of the distribution of risk within an MNE.

Main targets of BEPS

2.18 The OECD 2013 Report identifies a number of 'key pressure areas' that it considers are permitting BEPS activity:

- International mismatches in entity classification and financial instrument characterization (ie the use of hybrid instruments and hybrid entities, which we look at in Chapter 11).

- The application of treaty concepts (eg the PE definitions) to profits derived from the delivery of digital goods and services – is it still reasonable to assume that profits from this type of activity are necessarily associated with physical premises in a particular country, a concept that was developed for manufacturing trades?

- The tax treatment of related party debt-financing, captive insurance, and other intergroup financial transactions.

- Transfer pricing, particularly with respect to intangibles, and the artificial splitting of ownership of assets within a MNE.

- The effectiveness of anti-avoidance measures (eg general anti-avoidance rules, CFC legislation and thin capitalization rules).

- The availability of 'harmful preferential regimes', eg recognized tax havens, and other countries which routinely act as tax havens in some respects, eg Luxembourg.

Evidence of base erosion and profit shifting

2.19 The 2013 OECD Report provides an overview of available data that provides an indication of the scale of the BEPS problem. Some indicators are:

- The amount of investment being made cross-border through SPVs. For example, in 2011, 81 per cent (US$2,625 billion) of inward equity investment into the Netherlands was made through SPVs, and about 75 per cent of outward equity investment (US$ 3.023 billion). Luxembourg, another popular centre for offshore investment, also saw significant flows of equity funds being made via SPVs.

- A marked difference between the effective tax rates (ETRs)[1] suffered by companies, and the published statutory rates may also indicate tax avoidance activity. However, the OECD's review of the available studies concluded that ETRs did not provide definite evidence of BEPS. This is largely due to the inadequacies of the accounting and other publicly available data on which the ETR studies are based.

- The relative amounts of the profits of a MNE that are reported as arising in the residence country and those arising offshore. Studies appear
  to show that if domestic tax rates are significantly higher than those
  in countries where other group companies are located, then profits
  tend to be shifted abroad. This appears to be achieved through transfer pricing practices rather than through a shifting of commercial activity: profit margins of group companies in lower tax locations tend to
  increase, whilst those in the higher tax locations decrease.[2] In particular,
  it appears that much of the profit shifting relates to income from R&D
  based intangibles. Given that it is very difficult to establish the proper
  arm's-length price for transactions involving the use of such intangibles, as noted in Chapter 13, this is hardly surprising. Again it should
  be noted that such studies are generally based on publicly available
  accounting profit data that may not be adequate to capture the shifting of
  taxable profits.

- A mismatch between the locations where foreign affiliates have their
  employees (and thus, presumably, where there operations really are)
  and the locations in which these affiliates report their profits as arising.
  For instance, Clausing (2011)[3] found that Bermuda, Switzerland,
  Luxembourg and Singapore all featured in the top ten locations for the
  reporting of gross profits, but none of these countries were in the top 10
  in terms of number of employees.

- An improbable percentage of the national GDP of certain countries
  accounted for by the profits of US controlled foreign corporations (subsidiaries): for instance, a study carried out by the US Department of the
  Treasury found that: in 2008, profits of subsidiaries of US companies
  accounted for 645.7 per cent of Bermuda's GDP. In other words, US
  subsidiaries accounted for more than six times the GDP produced in
  Bermuda itself, either by Bermudan firms or (more likely) subsidiaries of non-US companies. The figure for Luxembourg, an EU Member
  State, was 18.2 per cent and for the UK 1.3 per cent.

There is a remarkable level of uncertainty about the quantitative measurement
of BEPS and one of the most difficult aspects of the BEPS Project is to develop
indicators to show its scale and economic impact. In April 2015 Working Party
No 2 of the Committee on Fiscal Affairs released a discussion draft[4] containing an initial assessment of currently available data, and making some recommendations for indicators of the scale and economic effects of BEPS. A public
consultation meeting was then held on 18 May 2015.[5]

Currently available data has considerable limitations and one of the aims of
this part of the BEPS Project is to identify new types of tools and data that
could be collected going forward to make the task of monitoring BEPS easier.
The OECD draft acknowledges that no single indicator can provide a complete
picture of the existence and scale of BEPS. It suggests that a 'dashboard' of
indicators may be possible for monitoring purposes.

Some commentators are very critical of the approaches proposed to measure
BEPS. Robillard,[6] for example, suggests that because every proposed indicator

is formulaic in nature, the alleged existence of BEPS is diagnosed by reference to a global apportionment of an MNE's profits, which runs counter to the commitment to the separate accounting, and arms-length principles that underpin the current system. This aspect is discussed further in Chapter 13.

---

1 In simple terms the effective tax rate is tax currently payable and deferred tax expense/net income before tax.
2 Grubert, H (2012), *Foreign Taxes and the Growing Share of U.S. Multination Company Income Abroad: Profits, Not Sales, Are Being Globalized*, Office of Tax Analysis Working Paper No 103, February 2012. Available at: www.treasury.gov/resource-center/tax-policy/taxanalysis/Documents/OTA-W2012-103-Multinational-Income-Globalized-.
3 Clausing, K A (2011), *The Revenue Effects of Multinational Firm Income Shifting*, Tax Notes, 28 March 2011, pp 1580–1586.
4 See www.oecd.org/ctp/tax-policy/discussion-draft-action-11-data-analysis.pdf.
5 Public comments on the action 11 discussion draft are available at: www.oecd.org/tax/tax-policy/public-comments-beps-action-11-data-analysis.htm.
6 Robillard, R (2015) 'Finding its way on a foggy moonless night: Measuring BEPS', *Tax Notes International*, Vol 78(9) pp 823–827.

Why the hurry with the Action Plan?

2.20   The publication of the OECD's BEPS Report was speedily followed in July 2013 by an Action Plan.[1] This consists of a list of 15 actions and deadlines for their achievement.

The 15 actions, together with a progress update, are given below in Table 2.1.

The short deadlines in the OECD's Action Plan reflect concerns that, in the absence of international developments to counter BEPS, countries will take the law into their own hands. A good example would be the introduction in the UK in 2015 of a new tax to capture profits 'artificially' diverted from the UK, dubbed the 'Google tax' (see Chapter 19.) This would mean a unilateral approach to a multilateral problem. Worse, it would mean that, in all probability, each country would try to adopt different solutions without coordinating their laws with those of other countries. It is precisely this kind of development of legal and tax systems which has enabled BEPS behaviour to flourish in the first place.

The BEPS Action Plan could also be viewed as an act of protection by the OECD of its role as the developer and coordinator of what passes for the world's international tax system.[2]

To some extent, the OECD's work on the exchange of information for tax purposes has lost impetus as a result of the introduction by the US of its Foreign Account Tax Compliance Act (FATCA) legislation (see Chapter 18). Unlike the OECD's work on information exchange, FATCA is likely be highly effective in forcing financial intermediaries to act as tax intermediaries, and supply a stream of valuable information to the US government about the foreign income of its residents. This is because FATCA contains a significant threat: that payments to financial intermediaries, whether in the US or anywhere else in the world, will be subject to a 30 per cent US withholding tax if the FATCA rules are not complied with. Contrast this with the threat of not complying with the OECD's regime on information exchange: a possible blacklisting as an uncooperative tax haven. Whilst the threat is real, the consequences are vague, and lack a clearly defined target. Of course, the type of tax mischief that FATCA seeks to address is different to the type of tax avoidance activity implicit in BEPS. Nevertheless, FATCA has shown that it is possible for a single country to impose its anti-avoidance legislation on the rest of the world.

Another threat to the OECD's position is the EU's development of legislation to counter BEPS within the EU. As with the work on discouraging tax competition, and the work on exchange of information, this would see duplication of effort and a set of parallel rules to be negotiated by MNEs, large and small. The EU's proposal for a system of formulary apportionment is still alive, although struggling to find acceptance,[3] notwithstanding its 2015 and 2017 reinvigoration.

One of the criticisms of the BEPS Project is that it is being developed by developed countries for the benefit of developed countries, and the needs of developing countries are not being given due attention. To overcome these concerns, developing countries have been invited to participate, and over 80 non-OECD/G20 countries were consulted in the first year of the Project. Their input has been reflected in the 2014 deliverables work, and a dedicated two-part Report was delivered to the G20 Finance Ministers in Cairns in September 2014.[4] The impact of BEPS on developing countries will be further considered in Chapter 22.

---

1   As discussed in Corwin (2014). For a discussion of the corporate tax avoidance debate that has escalated since the inception of the BEPS Project, see Berg & Davidson (2017). For a discussion of BEPS more broadly, see Christians (2017).
2   See   http://ec.europa.eu/taxation_customs/business/company-tax/anti-tax-avoidance-package_en.
3   The Common Consolidated Corporation Tax Base (CCCTB) – see Chapter 20.
4   Available at: www.oecd.org/tax/tax-global/part-1-of-report-to-g20-dwg-on-the-impact-of-beps-in-low-income-countries.pdf.

Implementing BEPS measures

2.21   Following release of the final reports on the 15 BEPS actions (see Table 2.1 below), the focus of attention has shifted to implementing the new rules, monitoring progress and capacity building for those countries with less well-developed tax systems and/or tax administrations.

An 'Inclusive Framework' has been established by the OECD to collaborate on the implementation of BEPS. Members of the inclusive framework, which includes several developing countries,[1] aim to develop monitoring mechanisms in relation to four minimum standards that have been developed, specifically Actions 5, 6, 13 and 14.

Table 2.1 Summary of the BEPS Action Plan

	Action	**Output**	**Status**
1	Address the tax challenges of the digital economy	Report identifying issues raised by the digital economy and possible actions to address them	Interim report September 2014 Final report October 2015
2	Neutralize the effects of hybrid mismatch arrangements	Changes to the Model Tax Convention Recommendations regarding the design of domestic rules	Interim report September 2014 Final report October 2015 Discussion draft August 2016: comments received 19 September 2016
3	Strengthen the CFC rules	Recommendations regarding the design of domestic rules	Final report October 2015
4	Limit base erosion via interest deductions and other financial payments	Recommendations regarding the design of domestic rules Changes to the *Transfer Pricing Guidelines*	Final report October 2015 Updated report December 2016
5	Counter harmful tax practices more effectively, taking into account transparency and substance	Finalize review of member country regimes	Interim report September 2014 Final report October 2015 Exchange on tax rulings July 2016 Peer review documents February 2017
6	Prevent treaty abuse (in particular, clarify that tax treaties are not intended to be used to generate double non-taxation)	Changes to the Model Tax Convention and Recommendations regarding the design of domestic rules	Interim report September 2014 Final report October 2015 Discussion draft pension funds February 2016 Discussion draft non-CIV funds March 2016

	Action	Output	Status
7	Prevent the artificial avoidance of PE status	Changes to the Model Tax Convention	Final report October 2015 Discussion draft July 2016 Comments on discussion draft September 2016
8	Assure that transfer pricing outcomes are in line with value creation: intangibles		
9	Assure that transfer pricing outcomes are in line with value creation: risks and capital	Changes to the *Transfer Pricing Guidelines* and possibly to the Model Tax Convention	Interim report November 2014 Final report October 2015 Discussion draft Chapter IX Transfer Pricing Guidelines July 2016
10	Assure that transfer pricing outcomes are in line with value creation: other high-risk transactions		
11	Establish methodologies to collect and analyse data on BEPS and the actions to address it	Recommendations regarding data to be collected and methodologies to analyse them	Final report October 2015
12	Require taxpayers to disclose their aggressive tax planning arrangements	Recommendations regarding the design of domestic rules	Final report October 2015
13	Re-examine transfer pricing documentation	Changes to *Transfer Pricing Guidelines* and Recommendations regarding the design of domestic rules	Interim report September 2014 Final report October 2015 CbCR User Guide March 2016 Peer review documents February 2017 Guidance on implementation April 2017

	Action	Output	Status
14	Make dispute resolution mechanisms more effective	Changes to the Model Tax Convention	Final report October 2015 Peer review documents October 2016
15	Develop a multilateral instrument	Report identifying relevant public international law and tax issues	Interim report September 2014
		Develop a multilateral instrument	Final report October 2015 Discussion draft: MLI May 2016 MLI November 2016

Most of the BEPS package was due to be circulated to the G20[2] in September 2015, and the deadline was largely met, although final recommendations on a number of matters were postponed pending the publication by the United States of the latest version of the United States Model Tax Convention. The deadlines for delivery of the BEPS actions are extremely ambitious, and although final reports have been delivered on schedule, implementation of the recommendations by the OECD members is likely to take some time yet. Implementation by individual countries can be expected to be patchy, notwithstanding the proposal for a multilateral instrument in Action 15. For a view from the US on the opportunities that the BEPS Project brings, see Corwin (2014).[3]

---

1   See www.oecd.org/tax/beps/inclusive-framework-on-beps-composition.pdf for a list of countries as at April 2017.
2   Available at: www.g20.org/news/20130906/782776427.html.
3   Corwin, M.S. (2014) 'Sense and Sensibility: The policy and politics of BEPS', *Tax Notes*, 6 October 2014. Note this pre-dates current debates in the US about international tax reform.

TAX CERTAINTY

2.22   At the G20 summit in Hangzhou, China in September 2016, leaders requested that the OECD and IMF work on issues of tax certainty. Heightened uncertainty has arisen for a variety of reasons, including the emergence and spread of new business models, concerns over aggressive tax planning, the fragmented system of international tax rules and disparate responses to the BEPS proposals. A report published in March 2017[1] explores the nature of tax uncertainty and its effect on business decision making. The report makes recommendations to policy makers in the form of a list of practical 'tools' to enhance tax certainty, including effective dispute resolution and simplified withholding tax collection and treaty relief procedures.

---

1   See: www.oecd.org/tax/g20-report-on-tax-certainty.htm.

SUMMARY

2.23   Since individual countries define their tax jurisdictions in slightly different terms, these jurisdictions often overlap. Potentially, this can result in taxpayers being liable for tax in two or more countries on the same income or profits. International law, usually in the form of bilateral double tax treaties, seeks to alleviate this problem. The form and content of international law is strongly influenced by supra-national bodies such as the OECD.

One of the key issues in international tax is the question of jurisdiction, which arises through residence and source. The way in which these concepts interact causes potential problems and there is much debate about which one is more important in terms of the allocation of taxing rights between nation states. Principles guiding the development of international tax policy include capital export neutrality and capital import neutrality. Much of the focus of current international tax policy development stems from the need to control the tax-planning activities of multinational groups of companies, who have considerable choice available to them as to where to locate their activities so as to potentially achieve tax savings.

The OECD BEPS Project represents a bold attempt to correct perceived problems in the current international tax system. The speed with which decisions are being taken in terms of defining the problems, and recommending solutions is unprecedented, and threatens to cause considerable disruption in the next few years. One response to this is increasing attention to the need for certainty in international tax.

FURTHER READING

Baker, P (2002) 'Changing the Norm on Cross-border Enforcement of Tax Debts', *Intertax*, 30 (6/7).

Berg, C & Davidson, S (2017) 'Stop this Greed: The Tax-Avoidance Political Campaign in the OECD and Australia', *Econ Journal Watch* 14(1) 77–102.

Bond, S, Chennels, L, Devereux, M, Gammie, M and Troup, E (2000) *Corporate Tax Harmonisation in Europe: A Guide to the Debate*, Institute for Fiscal Studies.

Braithwaite, J (2005) *Markets in Vice, Markets in Virtue*, Oxford University Press.

Christians, A (2010) 'Networks, Norms and National Tax Policy', 9 *Wash U. Global Stud. L Rev*.

Christians, A (2017, forthcoming) 'BEPS and the New International Tax Order', *Brigham Young University Law Review*.

Corwin, M S (2014) 'Sense and Sensibility: The policy and politics of BEPS', *Tax Notes*, October 6, 2014.

Desai, M and Hines, J (2003) 'Evaluating International Tax Reform', *National Tax Journal*, pp 56, 487.

Desai, M and Hines, J (2004) 'Old Rules and New Realities: Corporate Tax Policy in an International Tax Setting', *National Tax Journal*, Vol 57(4), pp 937–960.

Devereux, M and Griffiths, R (1998) 'Taxes and the Location of Production: Evidence from a Panel of US Multinationals', *Journal of Public Economics*, Vol 68, pp 335–67.

Dischinger, M and Riedel, N (2011) 'Corporate Taxes and the Location of Intangible Assets within Multinational Firms', *Journal of Public Economics*, Vol 95, pp 691–707.

Elgood, T, Paroissien, I, Quimby, L (2005) 'Managing Global Risk for Multinationals', 16 *Journal of International Taxation* 22.

European Commission (2006) *Risk Management Guide for Tax Administrations*.

Fitzgerald, V (2002) 'International Tax Co-operation and Capital Mobility', *Oxford Development Studies*, Vol 30, Issue 3, pp 251–266. Available at: www2. qeh.ox.ac.uk/research/qehwp-list2.html?jor_res_cat=1.

Grenshell, P (2005) 'Globalisation and the Transformation of the Tax State', *European Review*, Vol 13, Supp No 1, pp 53–71.

Hines, J (2009) 'Reconsidering the Taxation of Foreign Income', *Tax Law Review* 62, pp 269–299.

International Monetary Fund (2013) 'Issues in International Taxation and the role of the IMF'. Available at: www.imf.org/external/np/pp/eng/2013/062813. pdf.

Kane, M A (2006) 'Ownership Neutrality, Ownership Distortions and International Tax Welfare Benchmarks', *Virginia Tax Review*, pp 26, 53.

Knoll, M S (2009) 'Reconsidering International Tax Neutrality', *Institute for Law and Economics*, Research Paper No 09–16.

Margalioth, Y (2011) 'Taxing Multinationals: Policy Analysis with a Focus on Technology', *British Tax Review*.

Pinto, D (2002) 'Through the World's Eye: Governance in a Globalised World', *E-Law, Murdoch University Electronic Journal of Law*, Vol 9, No 3. Available at: www.murdoch.edu.au/elaw/issues/v9n3/pinto93.html.

Qureshi, A F (1994) *The Public International Law of Taxation*, Graham & Trotman Ltd.

Robillard, R (2015) 'Finding its way on a foggy moonless night: Measuring BEPS', *Tax Notes International*, Vol 78(9), pp 823–827.

Roin, J A (2007) 'The Economic Underpinnings of International Taxation', in *Research Handbook in International Economic Law* Guzman and Sykes (eds) Edward Elgar, Cheltenham UK and Northampton MA, USA.

Roxan, I (2012) 'Limits to Globalisation: Some Implications for Taxation, Tax Policy, and the Developing World', LSE Law, Society and Economy Working Paper, 3/2012.

Scholes, M, Wolfsen, M A, Erikson, M, Hanlon, M, Maydew, E L and Shevlin, T (2015) *Taxes and Business Strategy: A Planning Approach*, 5th edn, Prentice Hall Inc.

Sharman, J C (2013) 'Seeing like the OECD on Tax', *New Political Economy*, Vol 17(1), pp 17–33.

Tanzi, V (2000) 'Globalization, Technological Developments and the Work of Fiscal Termites', Washington DC, IMF Working Paper WP/00/181.

Wilson G P (1993) 'The Role of Taxes in Location and Sourcing Decisions', Chapter 6 in A Giovannini, R Glenn Hubbard, J Slemrod (eds) *Studies in International Taxation*, National Bureau of Economic Research, University of Chicago Press.

Yancey, W F and Cravens, K S (1998) 'A Framework for International Tax Planning for Managers', *Journal of International Accounting Auditing and Taxation*, Vol 7(2), pp 251–272.

Chapter 3

The Right to Tax Individuals

BASICS

3.1   As noted in Chapter 2, if an individual is classed as tax resident in a particular country then that country usually has the right to tax them on their worldwide income. However, they may also be taxed in other countries according to the source principle if he or she has sources of income arising in other countries. If this gives rise to potential double taxation of the same income then usually the country of residence will give double tax relief. The manner in which this relief is calculated will be covered later in Chapters 5 and 6.

Every country has its own detailed rules as to exactly what constitutes tax residence for an individual. Residence status normally implies liability to a country's taxes on worldwide income and gains. The most common approaches to determining the tax residence of individuals are tests of physical presence, and examination of the individual's economic and social circumstances. Domicile may also be relevant.

There are three principal approaches to individual residence for tax purposes as follows: the amount of time spent in a country, the extent of personal connections with a country, and using a residence concept from another branch of law, for example, citizenship.

Due to the variety of rules adopted by different countries, dual residence is often possible but, where a person appears resident in two countries, the double tax treaty (DTT) between those two countries often provides a means of fixing tax residence in one country only.

The tax issues that arise in the case of individuals working overseas is considered in Chapter 8.

INTRODUCTION

3.2   Whilst there are often similarities across countries – for instance, many countries will consider an individual to be tax resident if they are present there for more than 183 days in a particular year or if a person has close social and economic ties with it – the differences in definitions of residence can lead to a person being potentially regarded as simultaneously tax resident in more than one country. Where this happens, it is necessary to refer to the DTT, if one exists, between the two countries concerned. The Article on residence in the

OECD Model Convention on Double Taxation aims to help decide in which of the two competing countries a person is resident and this provision in the treaty is referred to as a 'tie breaker' clause. The Article also gives a general flavour of the nature of tax residence for individuals.

Extracts from Article 4 of the OECD Model Tax Convention on Income and Capital (2014)

'1   For the purposes of this Convention, the term 'resident of a Contracting State' means any person who, under the laws of that State, is liable to tax therein by reason of his domicile, residence ...

2   Where by reason of the provisions of paragraph 1 an individual is a resident of both Contracting States, then his status shall be determined as follows:

(a)   he shall be deemed to be a resident only of the State in which he has a permanent home available to him; if he has a permanent home available to him in both States, he shall be deemed to be a resident only of the State with which his personal and economic relations are closer (centre of vital interests);

(b)   if the State in which he has his centre of vital interests cannot be determined, or if he has not a permanent home available to him in either State, he shall be deemed to be a resident only of the State in which he has an habitual abode;

(c)   if he has an habitual abode in both States or in neither or them, he shall be deemed to be a resident only of the State of which he is a national;

(d)   if he is a national of both States or of neither of them, the competent authorities of the Contracting States shall settle the question by mutual agreement.'

Note that nationality plays a minor role in this OECD tie-breaker provision. Note also that there is no reference to the number of days in each tax year spent in any country, and yet as we will see below, the number of days of physical presence in a country is used by several jurisdictions to determine tax residence of individual taxpayers.

APPROACHES TO DETERMINING TAX

3.3   Thuronyi (1998) identifies three principal approaches that are discussed below.

According to time spent in a particular country

3.4   Most countries determine tax residence according to the number of days spent in a country in any given period or consecutive periods. Most countries use the calendar year, but some use a different period: for example, the UK uses the tax year, which runs from 6 April to the following 5 April. Other countries look for a 183-day period in any 12 months. This approach is fairly objective and, in most cases, enables a person's tax residence to be determined quite easily. If the tax year is used, this approach is open to the taxpayer being present for nearly a year, spending just under six months in the country in each of two consecutive tax years. For this reason, time-based systems often contain averaging provisions as well as a 183-day rule. Such rules are usually laid down in statute law and often used in conjunction with the next approach. In countries with land borders and a culture of cross-border employment (eg Switzerland/ Liechtenstein) a person living in one country and working in another might be considered resident in both. The mechanical nature of a time-based test tends to lead to unsatisfactory results, which is why it is often used in conjunction with one of the other approaches to determining residence.

According to a person's connections with a particular country

3.5   This approach considers tax residence as a personal attribute. It is usually enshrined in case law as it is impossible to legislate with regard to every single person. All the facts relating to a person's residence status are considered together, with no criterion being regarded as definitive. The Netherlands, which makes no mention of time limits in determining the residency status of individuals, places high reliance, however, on personal and economic ties to determine the facts and circumstances of the taxpayer. This approach does not lend itself to being laid down in statute law and decisions are taken based on case law precedent and tax authority interpretations and accepted practices. The criteria used are generally those listed in Article 4 of the Model Tax Convention. Paragraph 2 of Article 4 of the Model Convention takes this approach particularly with regard to establishing a person's 'centre of vital interests'.

According to residence rules adopted for other civil law purposes

3.6   Using this approach, a country might determine that anyone with citizenship status, or perhaps the right to work there, should be considered tax resident. This may be simpler than having different rules for different purposes, although in practice the only major economic power to use this type of test is the US, which bases its residence test on US citizenship.

CONSEQUENCES OF TAX RESIDENCE

3.7   The normal consequence of tax residence is that once the fact of tax residence is established, the country concerned has the right to tax the individual on his worldwide income. Whether a country enforces this right depends on the type of double tax relief system employed (see Chapter 5). Broadly, a country may operate a credit system, whereby credit is given against tax liabilities in the residence country for taxes suffered elsewhere, or it may operate an exemption system (sometimes referred to as a territorial system) whereby foreign income is not subject to tax in the residence country. All this applies equally to capital gains.

Most countries apply the same tax rates to resident and non-resident taxpayers, although some choose to subject non-residents to a higher rate and/or deny them the benefit of a particular concession, for example, zero rate bands or other entitlements.

Often, special rules will apply to temporary residents so as to limit the tax base to particular categories such as employment income and domestic sourced investment income. In Japan, for example, residents who do not intend to live permanently in Japan and do not stay for more than five years are treated as temporary residents and are taxed on Japanese-sourced income and foreign sourced income that is remitted to Japan, unlike residents who are taxed on worldwide income and non-residents who are only taxed on Japanese sourced income.

Most countries reserve the right to tax all income arising within their borders, whether it accrues to tax-resident individuals or to non-residents, using the source principle. However, the UK, for example, does not generally apply this principle to the capital gains on disposal of UK property by non-residents, with the exception, from April 2015 onwards, of gains on UK residential property. Thus a non-resident earning income in the UK would pay UK tax on that income, but a non-resident disposing of a chargeable capital asset other than UK residential property, in the UK would *not* pay UK capital gains tax on that sale.

In some countries, the tax consequences depend on a taxpayer's domicile as well as place of residence. The concept of domicile may be used as part of the process of determining which country the taxpayer is attached to for tax purposes.

Domicile is not a concept specific to taxation, but one which determines by which country's laws an individual is bound. An individual must always have a domicile but may only have one domicile at a time. For most people, their domicile will be that of the country where they were born and where they continue to live. This is known as a domicile of origin. It is possible for a person to change their domicile of origin to a domicile of choice once they attain the age of 16. Before the age of 16 a child's domicile is that of the adult on whom they are legally dependent (domicile of dependency).

Treatment of split year residence also varies. In some countries, the taxpayer is treated as resident for the whole year once certain conditions are met, and the timing of arrival and departure have no other effects. Other countries take into account arrival and departure and modify, for example, tax-free thresholds and other entitlements accordingly.

COMPARATIVE APPROACHES TO DETERMINING THE RESIDENCE OF INDIVIDUALS

3.8 The short survey that follows deals with the residence of an individual according to a country's domestic law. Bear in mind that under their double tax treaties with each other, most countries have special rules for individuals working abroad. These are discussed in Chapter 8.

Canada

3.9   Under Canadian law, an individual is resident in Canada if, in fact, he resides in Canada under the criteria established by the case law. Further, under the Income Tax Act, a reference to a person resident in Canada includes a person who was 'ordinarily resident'. It has never been clear precisely what the word 'ordinarily' adds to the word 'resident'. Some UK cases have interpreted 'ordinarily resident' as being slightly broader than 'resident', but the only substantial Canadian authority on the subject merely contrasts 'ordinarily resident' with 'casually resident'.

The Canada Revenue Agency (CRA) has published an Interpretation Bulletin setting out its administrative practices with respect to the factors for determining whether an individual has ceased to reside in Canada or has established residence in Canada. The CRA takes the approach that residence status in any particular case must be determined on the specific facts under consideration. However, an individual will be considered to continue residence if the individual fails to sever what are considered significant ties with Canada. In the CRA's view, the significant residential ties are the location of a dwelling or dwellings, the location of a spouse, and any dependants, personal property such as a car or furniture and social ties. There is no particular length of absence from Canada that establishes non-residence. Instead, the focus is on the number and type of the individual's residential ties with Canada and the individual's intention to sever those ties. In addition to the significant ties, secondary ties with Canada include medical insurance arrangements, Canadian driving licence, Canadian bank or credit cards and immigration or work status. Interpretation Bulletins do not have the force of law, but are intended to reflect administrative practice.

United States

3.10   Citizens and resident aliens of the USA are taxable on their worldwide income regardless of the length of any absence from the US. It is therefore possible to be considered tax resident in both the US and another country.

Individual tax residents to the US include citizens and resident aliens. A resident alien satisfies either the 'green card test' (see below) or the substantial presence test for the calendar year. If neither test is satisfied, an individual may be able to choose to be treated as a tax resident for part of the year under certain conditions.

Green card test

3.11   An individual is resident for tax purposes if he/she is a lawful permanent resident of the US at any time during the calendar year. Lawful permanent residency is awarded to individuals given the privilege, according to the immigration laws, of residing permanently in the US as an immigrant. This is generally recognized by the issuance of an alien registration card also known as a green card.

Substantial presence test

3.12   To meet this test of residency the individual must be physically present in the US on at least:

- 31 days during the current year; and

- 183 days during the three-year period that includes the current year and the two years immediately before that, counting:

  — all the days present in the current year; and

  — 1/3 of the days present in the first year; and

  — 1/6 of the days present in the second year before the current year.

Dual-status aliens

3.13   An individual can be both a US non-resident alien and a resident alien during the same tax year. This usually occurs in the year of arrival and departure from the US.

An individual can choose to be treated as a US resident for part of a tax year not satisfied by the green card test or the substantial presence test if one of the tests will be satisfied the following tax year. This choice is available when:

- the individual is present in the US for at least 31 days in a row, and

- the individual is present in the US for at least 75 per cent of the number of days beginning with the first day of the 31-day period and ending with the last day of that tax year (five days of absence is disregarded as *de minimis*).

A dual-status alien can choose to be treated as US resident for the entire year if all of the following apply:

- they were non-resident aliens at the beginning of the year;

- they were resident aliens at the end of the year;

- they married a US citizen or resident alien at the end of the year; and

- their spouse joins them in making the choice.

An election can be made to treat a non-resident spouse as a US resident when the other spouse is a US citizen or resident alien. This includes the situation where one spouse is non-resident at the beginning of the year and resident at the end of the year, while the other spouse is non-resident at the end of the same year.

Germany

3.14   The 'residence' of an individual is established either by place of residence or a customary place of abode. Citizenship is not relevant in determining German jurisdiction to tax an individual's income. The 'residence' of an individual is defined as the place where the individual occupies a residence under circumstances that indicate an intention to remain and not merely to use the residence temporarily. An individual may have more than one residence, and if an individual has residences within, as well as outside Germany, he or she is considered to be a resident of Germany for German income tax purposes. No distinction is made between first and second residences. Intent is established only by external and recognizable facts and not by declared or undeclared intention. Some of the more important factors in this respect are whether an individual moving to Germany brings family, and whether the apartment or house that he or she owns or leases is furnished and equipped for his use elsewhere. Customary abode means residence for six months or more, disregarding short interruptions.

Japan

3.15   A distinction on the basis of citizenship is made for the purposes of differentiating between 'permanent' and 'non-permanent' residents.

A non-permanent resident is an individual who has come to Japan with the intention of having his domicile (JUSHO) in Japan for one year or more but who does not intend to reside in Japan permanently. Non-Japanese citizens who come to Japan for employment or to engage in business are generally presumed to be non-permanent residents from the moment of arrival, unless there is clear evidence (such as an employment contract) that the period of stay will be less than one year. If a non-permanent resident remains in Japan for five years out of the last ten years, he or she then becomes a permanent resident of Japan for tax purposes. A non-permanent resident is subject to Japanese tax at the standard progressive rates, but only on his or her Japanese-domestic source income and on income from sources outside Japan only to the extent that such foreign source income is paid in Japan or is remitted to Japan.

A permanent resident is an individual who intends to reside permanently in Japan. A Japanese citizen returning to Japan from abroad is presumed to intend to reside permanently in Japan and, absent special circumstances, is considered to be a permanent resident for tax purposes from the moment of his return. A non-Japanese citizen who has resided in Japan for more than five years is considered to be a permanent resident for tax purposes.

India

3.16   Liability to tax under the Income Tax Act 1961 depends upon a taxpayer's residence status and is not affected by the taxpayer's nationality or domicile. An individual is regarded as resident in India in any tax year if he or she:

(a) is in India for a period or periods amounting to 182 days or more in a tax year; or

(b) is in India for an aggregate period of 60 days or more in a tax year and has been in India for an aggregate period of 365 days or more in the four tax years preceding that tax year. In the case of an individual who is a citizen of India who leaves India in any previous year as a member of the crew of an Indian ship or for the purpose of employment outside India or an individual who is a citizen of India, or a person of Indian origin, who, being outside India, comes on a visit in any previous year the period is extended from 60 days to 182 days.

An individual is regarded as 'resident but not ordinarily resident' (NOR) in India in any tax year even though qualifying as a resident on one or both of the bases referred to above in (a) and (b), if he or she:

● has been a non-resident of India in nine out of the ten tax years preceding that tax year; or

● has during the seven tax years preceding that year, been in India for a period or periods amounting to 729 days or less.

The consequence of NOR status is that there is no liability to Indian tax on income arising outside India unless derived from a business controlled in India or from a profession set up there.

This brief overview of several countries' approaches to the residence of individuals demonstrates the complexities that may arise when these regimes interact. Details of the UK's approach can be found in the 'Further study' section at the end of this chapter.

FURTHER READING

Australian Tax Office (2006) Chapter 10. International Tax Arrangements (useful summary of rules used by several countries to establish tax residence). Available in *International Comparison of Australia's Taxes* at: http://comparativetaxation.treasury.gov.au/content/report/downloads/12_Chapter_10.pdf.

Chamberlain, E (2011) 'Carrot and Stick' (feature on the UK domicile and remittance basis rules), *Taxation*, 4, August 2011, 12.

Finney, M (2015) 'The hangman's noose and non-doms', *Tax Journal*, Issue 1271, 6.

Golding, J (2005) 'Flying the Nest', *Taxation*, 23 June 2005, p 327.

Gordon, K (2011) 'A Good StaRT' (feature on proposed UK statutory residence test), *Taxation*, 7 July 2011, p 10.

HM Revenue & Customs (2013) 'RDR3 – RDR3 Guidance Note: Statutory Residence Test (SRT)'. Available at: http://search2.hmrc.gov.uk/kb5/hmrc/forms/view.page?record=FhT41sOFA5E&formId=7361.

Kamal, S (2011) *Individual Tax Residence*, Sweet & Maxwell.

Kessler, J (2011) *Taxation of Foreign Domiciliaries*, 10th edn, 2011/12, Keyhaven Publications.

McKie, S 'Squeezing the Pips (critique of new domicile regime in the UK)', *Taxation*, 24 April 2008, p 415.

Schwarz, J (2013) *Booth & Schwarz: Residence, Domicile and UK Taxation*, 17th edn, Bloomsbury Professional.

Thuronyi, V (1998) Part IV of Chapter 18; International Aspects of Income Tax in *Tax Law Design and Drafting*, Vol 2, IMF 1998. Available at: www.imf.org/external/pubs/nft/1998/tlaw/eng/ch18.pdf.

Tolley's Offshore Tax Planning, 'Chapter 32; Emigration of Individuals', *Tolley's Offshore Tax Planning*, 'Part B Section 1; Territorial Limits of UK Income Tax and CGT', LexisNexis, Butterworths.

Truman, M (2005) 'Wise Guidance?', *Taxation*, 1 September 2005, p 593.

FURTHER STUDY

The United Kingdom's approach to determining the tax residence of individuals

3.17   In the next sections, we take an in-depth look at the way in which the concepts of residence and domicile are used in the UK. The position in the UK is complex partly because the UK has only recently introduced a statutory rule for the determination of residence. The Finance Act 2013 contains the new statutory residence test that applies, subject to transitional rules, from 6 April 2013.

Attempts to reform the UK's previous archaic system of establishing the tax residence of individuals had been going on for some time. In the Committee debates on the Finance Act 2008, in which the Liberal Democrats sought (unsuccessfully) to introduce a statutory residence test, the UK's system was referred to as:

> 'a hotchpotch of legislation, case law, guidance and established practice, some of which has a firm legal basis and some of which is for the purposes of guidance only'

(Finance Bill Committee, 19 June 2008).

The Finance Act 2013 Statutory Resident Test (SRT) replaced all the previous case law, legislation and HMRC guidance on the tax residence of individuals. It applies to income tax and to capital gains tax and, in more limited circumstances, to inheritance tax and corporation tax. Individuals are categorized by the SRT into one of four categories:

- UK residents;

- UK non-residents;

- UK residents for part of the year only;

- temporary non-residents.

The new rules have three components:[1]

1. An automatic UK test – an individual will be a UK tax resident if they:

    — are present in the UK for at least 183 days in a tax year; or

    — have a home in the UK for more than 90 days, spend at least 30 separate days in that home, there are 91 consecutive days during which they don't have an overseas home or if they do, they spend fewer than 30 separate days in each of them; or

    — work full time in the UK for a period of 365 days with no significant breaks.

2. An automatic overseas test – individuals meeting certain conditions will be non-resident for UK tax purpose. The conditions are that the taxpayer was:

    — resident in the UK in one of more of the previous three tax years, and present for fewer than 16 days in the current tax year; or

    — not resident in the UK for the previous three tax years and not present in the UK for fewer than 46 days in the current tax year; or

    — left the UK to carry out full time work overseas, provided they are present in the UK for fewer than 91 days in the tax year and fewer than 31 days are spent working in the UK in the tax year.

3. A 'sufficient UK ties' test – which looks at the ties the individual has to the UK and specifies the number of days they can spend in the UK without becoming tax resident. The ties are:

    — UK resident family;

    — available accommodation in the UK;

    — substantive work in the UK;

    — UK presence in the previous tax years (more than 90 days in the UK in either of the previous two tax years);

    — more time in the UK than in any other single country.

The 'sufficient ties' test is used if the first two tests – the automatic UK tests and automatic overseas test – do not give a conclusive result.

---

1   There are also rules concerning whether persons were non-resident in the UK in the year of death.

How days are counted

3.18   Because arguments arose under the UK's old rules as to what counts as a day in the UK, the new system contains specific rules. A day when the individual is present in the UK at midnight counts as a day in the UK.[1] There are special rules to stop a person with a least three UK ties and who has been resident in the UK during the last three years from playing this system by arriving in the UK and departing on the same day if they do this on at least 30 days in the tax year. Each tax year is considered separately: there is no averaging of days spent in the UK over a number of years, as in the old system.

A day 'at home' means a day on which a person is present there for some or all of the day. Even a fleeting visit would be counted. It is not even necessary for the person to ever actually live there (but a home – 'available accommodation' – in the context of the 'sufficient ties' test must be a home where the individuals actually lives for at least some of the year.)

---

1   But exceptions are made for transit passengers and for cases where a person is only still in the UK at midnight due to exceptional circumstances which are beyond their control such as natural disasters or life-threatening illness.

'Home' and 'available accommodation'

3.19   The automatic tests for either non-residence or for residence use the concept of 'home', whereas the 'sufficient UK ties' test uses the concept of 'available accommodation'. According to HMRC, the difference between a 'home' and 'available accommodation' is that available accommodation 'can be transient and does not require the degree of stability of permanence that a home does'.[1]

---

1   HMRC RDR3 at Annexe A, para A27.

When is a house a home?

3.20   When does a house (or, for that matter, a flat, camper van, boat or 'structure of any kind') become a home for the purpose of the automatic non-resident/resident tests? This is a tricky question, not dealt with in the new legislation. Instead, in the guidance notes on the new system (HMRC's 2013 'RDR3' publication), HMRC sets out many pages of explanation and examples. The place must be capable of being used as a home, even if it is temporarily unavailable and the individual must actually use it as a home at some point. HMRC will look for evidence that a person was actually living there, for example: payment of utility bills; possession of a local parking permit; presence there of family, etc, are just a few of a long list of factors that would suggest it was your home. HMRC give several examples, including the following:

> 'Aneta moved from Poland to the UK and completed the purchase of her new house on 1 June. Whilst it was empty she stayed with friends, until her belongings arrived. These were moved in by the removal firm on 15 June.

Aneta stayed in her new home overnight that night. However, as she had arranged to have some extensive refurbishment done to her bathrooms and kitchen, she stayed in a local hotel and with colleagues whilst the main works were carried out. She moved into her home on a permanent basis on 15 July.

For SRT purposes we would consider that the house became Aneta's home from 15 June.'[1]

---

1   HMRC RDR3 at Annexe A Example A7.

When is accommodation 'available accommodation'?

3.21   There will be a tie to the UK – an 'accommodation tie' – if accommodation is available to a person for a continuous period of at least 91 days during the tax year and the individual uses that accommodation for at least one night during the tax year. As with the definition of 'home', there is no requirement to own the home or have a lease on it. HMRC gives the following example:

'Peter left the UK last year to travel the world. He let his UK property on a two-year lease and has no rights to use the property. Peter has no home in the UK.

Before leaving the UK, Peter agreed with his cousin that he could stay with her on any occasion he was in the UK. This is more than a casual offer; Peter's cousin is fully prepared to put Peter up for several months at a time should he need it. He made two visits to the UK this year, each for ten days, and stayed with her. Peter has an accommodation tie this year.'[1]

So even if a person does not have a home in the UK, they could still have an accommodation tie. However, HMRC states that casual offers to 'stay with us any time' from friends and family will not be an accommodation tie unless it can be shown that they really mean that you can stay with them for 91 days at a time in a single tax year.

Short gaps (of less than 16 days) in the availability of accommodation are ignored in considering whether it is available for the 91-day continuous period.

An accommodation tie can arise through staying at UK hotels. If, say, a contractor who is not resident in the UK undertakes a big contract in the UK and stays in UK hotels, then if the same hotel is used throughout, the 91-day period could be exceeded, due to the short gaps rule. Obvious planning would be to change hotels now and then.

To take account of normal family visiting, you are allowed to stay with very close relatives for up to 16 nights a year without it being considered an accommodation tie.

---

1   HMRC RDR3 at Annexe A, Example A13.

Five 'sufficient ties' test

3.22   This test is only applied where neither the automatic resident or auto-matic non-resident tests give a conclusive answer.

The test works in conjunction with a count of the number of days a person is in the UK. There are five 'ties' and the longer a person spends in the UK, the fewer ties are required in order for that person to be considered UK resident. The test is applied differently according to whether or not the person has, in the previous three years, been resident in the UK.

Table 3.1 and 3.2

Person was resident in UK in at least one of previous three tax years: Ties applicable: all 5

Days present in the UK	Residence status
Fewer than 16	Non-resident regardless of whether have any ties with the UK
16–45 days	Resident if have 4 or more ties
46–90 days	Resident if have 3 or more ties
91–120 days	Resident if have 2 or more ties
More than 120 days	Resident if have 1 or more ties

Person was NOT resident in UK in any of previous three tax years: Ties applicable: family, accommodation, work, 90-day

Days present in the UK	Residence status
Fewer than 46	Non-resident regardless of whether have any ties with the UK
46–90 days	Resident if have all 4 applicable ties
91–120 days	Resident if have 3 or more applicable ties
121–182 days	Resident if have 2 or more applicable ties
183 or more days	Resident regardless of UK ties

The family tie

3.23   This looks at the residence status of a person's close family: spouse, civil partner, and anyone with whom the person cohabits as husband/wife/civil partner. It does not matter where the family home is.

It also looks at the residence of a person's minor children, unless the parent sees the child on less than 61 days during the tax year. If the child is not be resident in the UK if time spent at school was disregarded, and that child is in the UK out-side of term-time for less than 21 days a year, the child would not give rise to a family tie. Thus having a child at a UK boarding school who goes home (outside the UK) for most of the school holidays would not usually give rise to a family tie. Non-UK parents may need to think carefully before agreeing to requests from their children for long visits to their UK school friends during the holidays.

The co-habitation aspect of the family tie rules is problematic as it is difficult to prove whether or not people are living together in a husband/wife/civil partner relationship or as 'just friends', particularly in the era of 'friends with benefits'.

The accommodation tie

3.24   This is discussed at para **3.21** above.

The work tie

3.25   Briefly, a work tie arises where a person works in the UK for 40 or more days a tax year, whether continuously or not. A working day is defined as a day when at least three hours' work is done. This may well catch many project workers.

The 90-day tie

3.26   This looks at the days spent in the UK in the two previous tax years. If the person spent 90 days in the UK in either or both of the two previous years, there is a 90-day tie.

The country tie

3.27   If the country in which the person spent the greatest number of days in a tax year was the UK, then there is a country tie. A day in a particular country means the person was in that country at the end of the day. Thus a person could travel widely and spend time in many countries during the tax year, with only a few days spent in the UK, but still have a country tie. No doubt the advice to persons who travel a lot and are worried about this test, it would be pertinent for them to ensure they are airborne when midnight comes.

For reasons unknown, the separate states of the US count as separate locations as do separate states, cantons or territories of all countries.

The split-year rules

3.28   The basic rule is that a person is either resident or not resident for the entire tax year. However, as in the previous system of determining residence, there are special rules for the year when an individual comes to or leaves the UK. Under the new rules, there are eight possible instances where split-year treatment might apply, so that a person is only taxed as if they were tax resident for the part of the year they are in the UK.

Split-year treatment will mainly apply to persons leaving, or coming to, the UK to work, but may also apply where a person moves from or arrives in the UK other than for work, but with an air of permanence, measured according to whether they cease to have a home in the UK or start to have one. Split-year treatment for persons leaving the UK to work abroad is considered in the 'Further study' section of Chapter 8.

If the move overseas is other than for work, then split-year treatment will only be available if the person ceases to have a home in the UK at some point in the tax year and once they leave they return for less than 16 days in that year. They must also show that they intend to live abroad more or less permanently by evidencing links with the new country within 6 months of leaving the UK. They must not be UK resident in the following tax year.

Different rules apply to persons arriving in the UK. Such a person must not have been resident in the UK in the previous tax year. If they only had one home, that must not have been in the UK. They must not have had sufficient UK ties (the number of ties deemed 'sufficient' will vary according to how long they spend in the UK in the year of arrival and the time-driven ties are scaled down according to the length of time in the UK).

Capital gains arising in the overseas part of the year will generally not be chargeable to UK tax, although there are complex rules.

Temporary non-residence – capital gains

3.29   Because non-residents are not liable to UK capital gains tax, even on assets located within the UK, people might be tempted to move out of the UK temporarily, sell the asset concerned and then resume their UK tax residence. As with the previous UK system, capital gains realized during a period of temporary non-residence in the UK, will be taxed when that person resumes UK residence. To realize capital gains free of UK tax, a person must realize the gain during a period of non-residence which amounts to at least five years. The pre-2013 system required a period of absence of five complete tax years, but the new system appears slightly more generous. At the time of writing, no detailed guidance is available from HMRC.

United Kingdom's system of determining residence of individuals prior to 6 April 2013

3.30   Because residence status in the current year depends partly on residence status in the previous two or three years, the old UK rules on residence will continue to be relevant until 2018. Residence in any of the previous three years is determined according to the rules in force during the year in question. For example, an individual wanting to be classed as non-resident in the UK for the tax year ending on 5 April 2017, will have to show that he was not resident in the UK for the three years ending 5 April 2016, 2015 and 2014. However, in deciding whether or not he was resident in the year ending 5 April 2016, he would also have to look back three years, to the tax years ending 5 April 2015, 5 April 2014 and 5 April 2013. The UK's old residence rules applied for the year ending 5 April 2013. So establishing his residence status for the year ending 5 April 2017 would mean having to consider the SRT for most of the years involved, but also using the old UK rules in respect of the year ending

5 April 2013. Thus tax advisers in the UK are facing several years of having to understand both the old and new systems in detail. The following paragraphs set out the old UK system.

United Kingdom's concepts of 'residence' and 'ordinary residence' (applicable for tax years ending 5 April 2013 and earlier)

3.31   Prior to the introduction of the statutory residence test in 2013, there are effectively two degrees of residence status in the UK. Simple 'residence' is normally used with respect to persons coming to the UK temporarily (but for more than 183 days in a tax year). Such persons will usually have been tax resident somewhere else immediately before they arrive in the UK. Such persons are often foreign nationals but may include UK nationals who have been living outside the UK for some considerable period of time.

The term 'ordinary residence' applied to those who have been tax resident in the UK for a number of years. Typically, a person born and brought up in the UK will be 'ordinarily resident'. However, a foreign national arriving in the UK for the first time may also be deemed ordinarily resident from the day of his arrival if his intention is to remain in the UK for a number of years.

The main practical effect of the difference was that 'ordinary residence' is a more adhesive concept. It is far more difficult to shed UK 'ordinary residence' status than it is to shed simple 'residence' status. Thus a person who is ordinarily resident may find himself still considered fully liable to UK tax on his worldwide income even if he is absent from the UK for a period of some years. The concept of ordinary residence has not been carried through to the statutory residence test.

The previous non-statutory guidance, HMRC6, which replaced IR20, went into great detail in order to specify the circumstances in which a person would be regarded as resident and also when he will be regarded as ordinarily resident.

A '91-day test' referred to earlier was recently considered by the Special Commissioners.[1] In that case, the Commissioners looked very closely at the pattern of Mr Gaines-Cooper's life, in particular the pattern of presence in the UK compared with that overseas, using the patterns of presence in the UK as part of the evidence of his habits and lifestyle in order to determine that he had in fact been continuously resident in the UK and the '91-day test' was not relevant in his situation. They did not apply the IR20 91-day test as such, but rather looked carefully at the pattern of visits he made to the UK over a number of years in order to establish whether he possessed the quality of residence in the UK for those years. However, the method used by the Commissioners to measure his visits to the UK differed from the practice adopted in IR20 at the time, of ignoring both the day of arrival and the day of departure. The Commissioners chose to count a day when he was in the UK at midnight as a day in the UK. This was partly because of the extraordinary lifestyle of Mr Gaines-Cooper which involved him spending around 150 days each year in the air and his habit of visiting his family in the UK by arriving in the UK one day and leaving the next. IR20 was subsequently amended to include as a day in the

UK any day when the taxpayer is present at midnight. This is not surprising, given that IR20 (now HMRC6) represents HMRC's working practices which are adopted in the light of case law.

In 2010, the Court of Appeal found in favour of HMRC, and the subsequent appeal was heard in the Supreme Court on 7–8 July 2011. The majority decision, handed down on 19 October 2011, went in favour of HMRC.[2] Lord Wilson, delivering the leading judgment, observed that IR20 was not clear in relation to the means by which a taxpayer becomes non-resident, ie the extent of the break in the pattern of life in the UK, leaving the taxpayer nothing on which to rely. Further, the majority view was that the appellants were unable to show that HMRC had adopted a settled practice giving rise to a legitimate expectation. Commentators have noted that the most important lesson from this case is that taxpayers need to be extremely cautious in relying on HMRC guidance that is poorly drafted.

---

1 *Robert Gaines-Cooper v HMRC* SpC 568.
2 *R (on the application of Davies) v Revenue and Customs Comrs; R (on the application of Gaines-Cooper) v Revenue and Customs Comrs* [2011] UKSC 47.

United Kingdom's statute and case law applicable to tax years ending 5 April 2013 and earlier

3.32   Prior to the Finance Act 2013, there was little statute law concerning the tax residence of individuals. The Income Tax Act (ITA) 2007, Part 14, Chapter 2 deals with residence of individuals but consists of only a few sections:

Income Tax Act 2007, s 829: residence of individuals temporarily abroad

3.33

'(1) This section applies if–

(a) an individual has left the United Kingdom for the purpose only of occasional residence abroad, and

(b) at the time of leaving the individual was both UK resident and ordinarily UK resident.

(2) Treat the individual as UK resident for the purpose of determining the individual's liability for income tax for any tax year during the whole or a part of which the individual remains outside the United Kingdom for the purpose only of occasional residence abroad.'

Thus a person who has been ordinarily resident in the UK will be unable to escape UK taxation on his worldwide income unless he leaves the UK for something more than 'occasional residence' abroad. This was examined closely in the cases of *Rogers v IRC* and in *Reed v Clark* (see para **3.38** below). The example below illustrates the difficulties in shedding ordinary residence status. Note that the UK tax year runs from 6 April to the following 5 April.

Example 3.1

Jim and his wife, Kay have been resident and ordinary resident in the UK all their lives. After watching too many programmes about other people transforming their lives by moving to other countries and finding their perfect home there, they decide to move to Spain. They leave the UK on 18 July XX01, having put their house on the market and having put most of their possessions into storage. On their arrival in Spain, they rent temporary accommodation whilst they search out their dream house. They return to the UK for 28 days over Christmas to stay with relatives.

They return to the UK several times during the tax year XX02/XX03 for family weddings and other visits, spending 88 days in the UK in total. By May XX03 they have still not sold their house in the UK, meaning that they have still been unable to buy their dream home in Spain.

Jim and Kay claimed that they ceased to be resident and ordinarily resident in the UK from 18 July XX01. The practice of the UK HMRC would be to look at their case and determine whether there is sufficient evidence to support this claim, taking into account the extent to which Jim and Kay still have ties with the UK and the quality of the evidence supporting their stated intention to live in Spain long term. It is quite possible that a decision would be deferred and that HMRC would apply its policy of continuing to treat them as ordinarily resident in the UK until they had actually been non-resident for three complete tax years. (At that stage, provided they did pass the non-residence test, any tax paid since 18 July XX01 on the basis of UK residence would be repaid.)

Their case will be reviewed following the end of each complete tax year for which they are absent from the UK. This first review will be undertaken following the end of the tax year XX02/XX03. The 90-day test will be applied on a pro rata basis:

Table 3.3

Visits to UK between 18 July
XX01 and 5 April XX03
Total days in this period

$$\frac{28 + 88}{265 + 365} = \frac{116}{630} = 67 \text{ days per annum average}$$

As their visits to the UK average less than 91 days per annum they have not worsened their chances of achieving non-resident status. However, they still own a house in the UK and still do not own a property in Spain. Home ownership is by no means the only factor taken into account: if they have found employment in Spain or set up a business there and can prove they have forged other economic and social links there this will strengthen their case.

By 5 April XX05, provided their visits back to the UK have continued to average less than 91 days per tax year and visits in any one tax year amount to less than 183 days, they will be regarded as not resident or ordinarily resident, regardless of any ties with the UK or with Spain. At this point they should receive a tax refund from HMRC. In the period since they left the UK they may well have been taxed in Spain as well, although under the terms of the

UK/Spain DTT it is unlikely that they will have been considered tax resident in both countries. They will have been given double tax relief for any tax suffered in Spain on income which has been taxed in the UK in the meantime. Spain may wish to review the situation with a view to considering them tax resident in Spain since 18 July XX01. Thus Jim and Kay will face the complications of dealing with two tax authorities until their tax residence status is finally settled.

Shepherd v IRC

3.34   A real life case[1] on the subject of whether a person had shed his UK residence and ordinary residence concerned an airline pilot who flew long haul flights, all of which started or finished in the UK. In October 1998, in anticipation of his retirement, he rented a flat in Cyprus and argued that he ceased to be resident in the UK from that date. HMRC had declined to apply ESC A11 so that he was considered tax resident in the UK for the whole of 1998/1999 without that tax year being split. HMRC contended that he was still resident in the UK for the tax year 1999/2000 and this is what the arguments were about. This case is important partly because it contains a good summary of the case law to date on the UK tax residence of individuals.

Mr Shepherd had a house in Wokingham which he shared with his estranged wife (it was reported that he had had an affair with an air stewardess). He was away for most of the days in any particular year and when back in the UK, either stayed at his house in Wokingham or went on sporting trips. He was due to retire in April 2000. He was granted an immigration permit by the Cypriot authorities in February 2000. In February 1999, Mr Shepherd had forged various links in Cyprus: he joined a sailing club and a gliding club, but did not give up his membership of similar UK clubs. He was a keen amateur radio ham and moved all his equipment to Cyprus. Between renting the flat in Cyprus and the date of his retirement, he spent some of his days off in the UK and some in Cyprus, as well as various holidays and trips elsewhere. His wife sometimes used the Cyprus flat, usually when Mr Shepherd was not there. On his retirement, the house in Wokingham was retained. Mr Shepherd remained on the UK electoral roll until 2000.

When he retired on 5 April 2002, his pension was paid into a bank account he had opened in Cyprus, although he maintained his UK bank accounts. Because of his family circumstances, he continued to pay the bills in connection with the marital home, continued to use it as a correspondence address and continued to vote in UK elections. He set off in June 2000 to sail around the world in his yacht, and this cruise lasted until October 2002. He took breaks from it to visit relatives in the UK. In November 2002, he bought an apartment in Cyprus. Mr Shepherd argued that he had been resident in Cyprus for the tax year 1999/2000 and had commuted to the UK to work. He was unable to convince the Special Commissioners of Income Tax that he had ceased to be ordinarily resident in the UK for 1999/2000. The Cypriot authorities declined to tax him on his earnings, saying that they were the earnings of an alien individual from the rendering of salaried services outside Cyprus. He had lived in

Cyprus for only 68 days between October 1998 and 31 December 1999. He was not accepted by the Cypriot authorities as tax resident there until 1 January 2000.

Even though he only stayed in the UK house as a visitor from that time on, HMRC considered that there was no distinct break in his circumstances. He had remained in the UK for a settled purpose – his employment. Rather like Mr Levene (see below) he continued to come back to the UK to attend to his employment duties and to maintain contact with family and friends. He had only been in the UK for 80 days but this was not conclusive. The courts agreed with HMRC, taking into account:

- his past and present habits of life;
- the regularity and length of his visits to the UK;
- his ties with the UK; and
- the temporary nature of his attachments abroad.

Summing up, Lewison J, at page 1841, agreed with the judgment of the Special Commissioner:

> 'I have come to the conclusion that at least until 5 April 2000 he continued to be resident and ordinarily resident in the United Kingdom. He dwelt permanently here and this was where he had his settled or usual abode and so he was resident here. He resided here continuously as part of his everyday life; his residence here was part of the regular and habitual pattern of his mode of life and it persisted despite temporary voluntary absences to fly in the course of his employment, or to go to Cyprus, or to go sailing, or to visit Europe; his residence here also had a settled purpose and so I also conclude that the appellant was ordinarily resident here.'

---

1 *Shepherd v IRC* [2006] STC 1821.

R & C Comrs v Grace[1]

3.35   A more recent case, again concerning an airline pilot, examined whether ICTA 1988, s 336 provided an exemption from UK residence for an individual if he would otherwise be held to be resident in the UK. If an individual was not in the UK for some temporary purpose, then s 336 would not apply at all and could not be used to help the person avoid being considered resident in the UK. The term 'temporary' was held not to relate to the number of days spent in the UK, but rather to the purpose of the time spent in the UK. As in *Shepherd*, the taxpayer was a British Airways long-haul pilot, operating out of Heathrow and Gatwick airports and he had a house near Gatwick airport. Following marital problems, he decided to return to his native South Africa in 1997 and commute to work in the UK. He bought a property there, kept a car there and joined two flying clubs there, becoming an active member. His links with the UK, post 1997, were that he kept his house and a car and remained on the electoral roll. His postal address remained in the UK and in 2005 he spent money replacing the windows and doors. His salary continued to be paid into his UK bank account. He had no contacts with family in the UK.

As in *Gaines-Cooper* there was much discussion of the way in which the number of days he spent in the UK ought to be counted. The taxpayer's figures, excluding days of arrival and departure came to no more than 71 days per tax year, but using different assumptions, the courts were able to double these figures. Typically, he spent the two or three rest days between flights in the UK but on his longer breaks of 13 to 15 days, he would go to South Africa. In the five years under examination, he had only spent three consecutive periods of more than seven days in the UK, but had spent 60 such periods in South Africa. The taxpayer argued that the periods of two to three days before and after flights were for a merely temporary purpose and that he had not spent more than 183 days in the tax year in question in the UK. The Special Commissioner agreed with him, but in the High Court, Lewison J (who also gave judgment in *Shepherd*) found that presence in the UK in fulfilment of duties to be performed under a permanent contract of employment could not be considered to be a temporary purpose. Therefore, the taxpayer could not rely on what is now ITA 2007, s 831 (see below) to deem him not resident in the UK. Lewison J also rejected the proposition that a person could have only one permanent residence at a time. Mr Grace, the taxpayer, had never lost his UK residence. The case is unusual in that decisions of lower courts in cases concerning residence, which is a matter of fact, are rarely overturned by a higher court, but in this case, the High Court found that the Special Commissioner had made an error of law in her interpretation of the meaning of 'temporary'.

The Court of Appeal subsequently decided that the High Court was wrong in finding for HMRC and should have sent the case back to the Tax Tribunal. This was done and the January 2011 decision of the First-tier Tax Tribunal[2] was that, although Mr Grace was neither domiciled in the UK nor a UK citizen, he was nonetheless tax resident.

---

1   [2009] STC 213.
2   [2011] UKFTT 36 (TC).

Income Tax Act 2007, s 831: foreign income of individuals in the United Kingdom for temporary purpose

3.36

'(1) Subsection (2) applies in relation to an individual if–

    (a)   the individual is in the United Kingdom for some temporary purpose only and with no view to establishing the individual's residence in the United Kingdom, and

    (b)   in the tax year in question the individual has not actually resided in the United Kingdom at one or several times for a total period equal to 183 days (or more).

In determining whether an individual is within paragraph (a) ignore any living accommodation available in the United Kingdom for the individual's use.'

Subsection (2A) then goes on to set out the rules concerning the types of income which are affected by this section which are, broadly, pension and social security income and foreign income. Section 832 contains equivalent rules relating to employment income. Section 831 forms the basis of the 183-day presence test and replaces a six-month test which was open to different interpretations, with HMRC once unsuccessfully attempting to argue that six months meant six lunar months.[1]

Case law involving this section has mainly centred around the duality of the test in s (1)(a) – that a person must be in the UK temporarily *and* with no intention to establish tax residence here.

---

1 *Wilkie v CIR* (1951) 32 TC 495.

Taxation of Chargeable Gains Act 1992, s 9

3.37   This section deals with the residency aspects of capital gains tax which applied until 6 April 2013. Capital gains tax is covered by the new statutory residence test. Section 9 states that for the purposes of capital gains tax, the terms 'resident' and 'ordinary resident' have the same meanings as in the Income Tax Acts and that disputes as to domicile or ordinary residence relating to capital gains will be dealt with in the same way as disputes relating to income tax liabilities. Subsection (3) is worth noting:

'(3) Subject to … An individual who is in the United Kingdom for some temporary purpose only and not with any view or intent to establish his residence in the United Kingdom shall be charged to capital gains tax on chargeable gains accruing in any year of assessment if and only if the period (or the sum of the periods) for which he is resident in the United Kingdom in that year of assessment exceeds 6 months.'

Note that this means that a non-resident will not be charged to UK capital gains tax on the disposal of UK or foreign assets. This led to the practice of individuals leaving the UK for long enough to shed their ordinary residence status, disposing of capital assets without incurring liability to UK capital gains tax and then, in a later tax year, resuming UK tax residence. Per IR20 (and then HMRC6), three complete tax years' absence were normally required to shed ordinary residence status unless there was strong evidence at the date of departure to suggest that a person is making changes in their life consistent with losing UK ordinary residence. This practice led to the introduction of subs 10A, which is too long to reproduce here. The gist of this section, entitled 'temporary non-residents' is as follows:

●   where a person who has been either resident or ordinarily resident in the UK for four out of the seven years of assessment immediately preceding his departure from the UK;

- makes a disposal of a capital asset acquired whilst so resident;

- and then resumes UK residence or ordinary residence;

- and there are fewer than five full years of assessment falling between the year of departure and the year of return,

then all the capital gains made whilst absent from the UK are treated as taxable in the tax year of return to the UK.

Effectively, the period required to establish non-residence for the purposes of taxation on capital gains on UK assets acquired whilst UK resident was five full tax years, rather than three.

Example 3.2

Joe, who has always lived in the UK, decides to move to Canada, departing the UK on 30 June XX06 and intending to return on 30 June XX11. On 7 July XX06 he disposes of a portfolio of UK quoted shares, making a capital gain of £50,000. On 30 May XX10 he disposes of a holiday home in the UK bought in XX00 making a capital gain of £150,000. On 31 July XX10 he disposes of a property in France bought in XX08 making a capital gain of £100,000.

Following the *Fulford-Dobson* case, it is possible that HMRC would refuse to allow Joe the benefit of ESC D2. Thus the gain made on 7 July may well be charged to UK capital gains tax. He would have to show that the timing of the sale was not effected with tax avoidance as the motive.

The gain on the holiday home in May XX10 is made during a year in which he is not resident or ordinarily resident in the UK and in the first instance there is no charge to UK capital gains tax. However, only four full tax years have elapsed between the date of departure from the UK and the return date. Joe left the UK in XX06/7 and returned in XX11/12. He was absent for the tax years XX07/8 to XX10/11 inclusive. The gain on the holiday home would be charged to UK capital gains tax in the tax year in which he returns, XX11/12, because he was absent for fewer than five years of assessment.

He will not be taxed on the gain on the French house, as this was acquired after he became non-resident, provided that the house was not acquired with monies from the sale of other assets on which less than full UK capital gains tax was paid, due to tax reliefs.

United Kingdom tax residence – the older underlying case law

3.38   As explained above, case law currently provides the foundation in UK law for the largely time-driven rules set out in IR20 (now HMRC6), although new statutory tests for the taxation of individuals are under consideration at the time of writing. Several of the key cases date back to the early part of the last century.

The leading case of *Levene v IRC*[1] concerned a man who had been ordinarily resident in the UK until 1919 but who had sold his house in the UK and gone to live abroad, mainly in Monaco. He continued to visit the UK in the five years following, for periods of around 20 weeks every year. The Inland Revenue (as it then was) contended that despite being present in the UK for less than six months in any tax year, he nevertheless remained ordinarily resident. If he had been present for more than six months then he would have been caught by the provisions of what is now ITA 2007, s 831.

The case is important in that the judiciary attempted to define 'residence'. Per Sargant LJ:

> 'the residence which makes a person chargeable depends not on mere presence in the United Kingdom (unless that is six months in all), but on the quality of the presence in relation to the objects and intentions of the person sought to be made chargeable.'

The court sought to establish whether Mr Levene had left the UK merely for 'occasional residence' abroad. Under what is now ITA 2007, s 829, 'occasional residence' abroad would be insufficient for him to shed his UK ordinary resident status. The court examined the pattern of visits to the UK and the reasons for his movements. It was established that he tended to leave the UK as winter approached, for health reasons, but spend the warmer months in the UK 'to attend the calls of interest, of friendship and of piety'. The dictionary definition of the word 'reside' was considered: 'to dwell permanently or for a considerable time, to have one's settled or usual abode, to live in or at a particular place'. Although considered sound, this definition did not help very much in this case, as Mr Levene had no fixed abode anywhere, having sold his house in the UK and lived in a series of hotels. However, it was concluded that his residence abroad, when considered in conjunction with his previous full-time residence in the UK and his continued presence here for up to five months of the year, was only 'occasional residence' abroad. Thus, under the provisions of what is now ITA 2007 s 829, he continued to be fully taxable in the UK as he remained ordinarily resident.

In the case of *Lysaght v IRC*,[2] Mr Lysaght, an Irish resident, was held to be resident and ordinarily resident in the UK on account of regular business meetings in the UK. These meetings required visits of approximately one week each month, leading to total days spent in the UK for the three years under consideration of 101, 94 and 84 days respectively. He also visited for 48 days in a further six-month period which was also under consideration. This may be considered to be the origin of the IR20 'more than 91 days per year over four years' rules. It would be misleading to think that the court was unduly influenced by the duration of his visits. According to Viscount Sumner, 'grammatically, the word 'resident' indicates a quality of the person charged'. However, the regularity of the visits was certainly significant with Viscount Sumner describing 'ordinary residence' as 'the regular order of a man's life, adopted voluntarily and for settled purposes'.

The nature of 'occasional residence abroad' was also examined in *Reed v Clark*.[3] This case concerned a pop musician, Dave Clark, who had just sold his back catalogue and realized a large sum of trading profits. Under the tax rules then existing, he would have been liable to tax on these profits in the tax year following that in which the profits were made. He arranged to spend that entire tax year in the US, leaving on 3 April 1978, and argued that he had ceased to be ordinarily resident in the UK for that tax year. He returned after the end of the tax year (on 2 May 1979), without having sold his London flat in the meantime. However, he was able to show that he had established a settled way of life in the US; he had stayed long term in rented houses rather than hotels and had concluded several business deals in the US. A key question was whether a person could be considered to be resident in the UK for a tax year during which they had not set foot in the UK, or whether such an absence could still be considered to be merely 'occasional residence' abroad. This question was not new; it had been discussed at length in *Rogers v IRC*.[4] Captain Rodgers, a master mariner, had been away from the UK at sea for a whole tax year, but his wife and family lived in Scotland and he had no other place of abode. At page 226, 'He is not the least bit less a resident in Great Britain because the exigencies of his business have happened to carry him away for a somewhat longer time than usual during this particular voyage'. However, in the case of Dave Clark, 'he established himself (in the US) in a way which would make him resident and ordinarily resident there under UK tax rules'.[5] Clark won his case notwithstanding that there was clearly a tax-avoidance motive in his absence from the UK.

1   13 TC 486.
2   13 TC 511.
3   [1985] STC 323.
4   (1879) 1 TC 225.
5   Special Commissioners at 541.

CONCEPT OF DOMICILE

3.39   Domicile still plays a part in establishing liability to UK taxation, for example, and, in particular, liability to inheritance tax but also liability to income tax, even under the new statutory residence test.[1] Most tax disputes concerning domicile centre around whether a person's entire estate is liable to UK inheritance tax (if UK domiciled), or merely his UK assets (if domiciled elsewhere). From an income tax perspective, the main reason for wishing to establish that a person's domicile is outside the UK is that any foreign income or proceeds of sales of foreign assets will only become liable to UK income tax if actually remitted to the UK. A UK domicile will also affect the liability to UK income tax on earnings from a non-UK employer and this is explored in Chapter 8. It is quite possible for a person to be tax resident in the UK whilst being domiciled in another country.

The main reason a person would want to establish a change of domicile from the UK to another country is to escape UK inheritance tax on non-UK assets.

1   The effect of a non-UK domicile status on liability to UK income tax mainly concerns remuneration and is considered in Chapter 8.

Establishing a domicile of choice

3.40   There is no statute law concerning the definition of domicile. A change of domicile must be proven by the taxpayer. Factors associated with domicile must be evidenced with respect to the new country, for instance:

- In which country does the person own property?

- In which country are the person's family and friends mainly?

- Under which country's law is the person's will drawn up?

- Where is the person's main bank account and investments?

- Where does the person intend to retire?

- Where does the person intend to be buried?

A leading case on establishment of a change of domicile is *IRC v Bullock*[1] which concerned Group Captain Bullock. His domicile of origin was in Nova Scotia but he lived in the UK for more than 40 years, during which time he would have been regarded as resident and ordinarily resident in the UK for tax purposes. However, he managed to successfully defend the challenge from the Inland Revenue that he had acquired a domicile of choice in the UK. Important factors in his victory included evidence that his English wife refused to live in Canada (possibly because she would have had to share a house with her father-in-law whom she disliked), and that he had made his will under Nova Scotia law, in which he stated that he intended to return to Canada when his wife eventually died. Lesser factors included his refusal to acquire British nationality or to vote in UK elections and that he continued to take Canadian newspapers.

Interestingly, *Gaines-Cooper* (see para **3.31** above) was predominantly a domicile case, but the Commissioners felt that there could be no acquisition of a domicile of choice in circumstances where a taxpayer had failed to shed his UK tax residence.[2]

The UK is open to accusations of acting as a tax haven to wealthy individuals who are domiciled abroad, possibly in a conventional tax haven. This is because it is extremely difficult to establish exactly when and if foreign income has been remitted to the UK. The problem is that income, once earned, produces interest or can be spent on assets which are then sold, so that characterization of sums arriving in the UK is difficult. Apart from this it is difficult for HMRC to track all flows of funds into the UK to such persons, regardless of their character as income (taxable) or capital (not taxable).

---

1   [1976] STC 409.
2   For a fascinating look into the Gaines-Cooper domicile debate, see: www.robertgainescooper. com.

Deemed domicile

3.41   For the purposes of inheritance tax only, a person is deemed to retain his UK domicile for a period of three years after he has shed it for all other purposes.[1] This is an anti-avoidance measure to make it harder for a person to avoid liability to UK inheritance tax on non-UK assets by changing his or her domicile. A further application for the concept of deemed domicile is found in the Inheritance Tax Act 1984, s 267(1)(b) which states that a person will be deemed to be domiciled in the UK for inheritance tax purposes if he has been resident in the UK for 17 out of the last 20 years of assessment, ending with the year of assessment in which the purported liability arises (probably the tax year in which the person dies). Thus, if this law (which only applies to persons becoming resident in the UK on or after 1974) had applied to Group Captain Bullock, he would have continued to have enjoyed the benefit of the remittance basis on his non-UK income for income tax purposes, but had he died whilst in the UK his worldwide assets would have been subject to UK inheritance tax.

---

1   Inheritance Tax Act 1984, s 267(1)(a) and (3).

REMITTANCE-BASED CHARGE

3.42   Taxpayers who were resident but not ordinarily resident in the UK were, prior to 6 April 2008, only taxed on non-UK sourced income as and when remitted to the UK. Those not domiciled in the UK could claim the remittance basis for overseas capital gains. A change effective from 6 April 2008 now requires taxpayers to make an annual claim to apply the remittance basis, unless the unremitted overseas income does not exceed £2,000. Taxpayers with more than £2,000 in foreign, unremitted income or gains in a tax year are now required to make a claim to have the remittance basis applied; otherwise UK tax will be payable on worldwide income irrespective of remittance or otherwise. In addition, a new remittance-based charge has been introduced such that taxpayers who are aged 18 years or more and have been resident in the UK for at least seven of the previous nine tax years, are required to pay a charge of £30,000 in order to use the remittance basis. The £30,000 charge is not pro-rated for the first year of application. In addition, taxpayers using the remittance basis will lose their entitlement to the personal allowance for income tax and the annual exemption for capital gains tax (both of which operate as tax-free thresholds). The £30,000 charge effectively becomes an advance payment for nominated foreign income and gains that remain unremitted, so that if they are remitted in future, no further UK tax will be payable. The decision whether it is worthwhile to pay the £30,000 charge will depend on a number of factors and will arguably require greater reliance on professional advice on a year-by-year basis. About 5,400 individuals paid the charge in the tax year 2008/9 which indicates that the remittance basis rules apply to a tiny minority of persons living in the UK.

From April 2012, the annual charge was increased to £50,000 for those who have been resident in the UK for at least 12 of the last 14 years, enabling non-domiciles to remit overseas income and capital gains tax free to the UK for the purposes of commercial investment in UK businesses, and simplifying the remittance-basis rules. From April 2015, the charge became £60,000 for the 12-out-of-14-years category and a new category of 17-out-of-20-years will attract a remittance-based charge of £90,000. The 2015 increases are estimated to impact on approximately 5,000 non-domiciled individuals who choose to pay tax on the remittance basis.

From April 2017, it is planned that those who have been resident for more than 15 tax years will no longer be able to use the remittance basis, and will become deemed UK domiciled.

Chapter 4

The Right to Tax Companies

BASICS

4.1   As noted in Chapter 2 a country's jurisdiction to tax is determined largely by a taxpayer's residence status. Typically, under the residence principle, a country has the right to tax the worldwide income of a company which is tax resident.

The law on company residence was first developed in the UK and the principles so developed form the basis for international tax law on company residence. Whilst most countries consider companies incorporated in their jurisdiction to be tax resident, additional tests are usually necessary. Many countries also look at the place where the company's central management and control is located. The principle of 'place of effective management' is used as a tie-breaker test for the purposes of applying the provisions of a double tax treaty (DTT) where the two countries that are party to the treaty each claim the right to tax a particular company using different approaches to company residence.

Not all countries take advantage of the right to tax the worldwide income of companies based on residence, opting instead to apply the principle of territoriality. This means that they only tax their resident companies on profits earned in the country of residence, rather than on the worldwide profits.

INTRODUCTION

4.2   In the previous chapter we examined the residency rules as they apply to individual taxpayers. Here we consider the position of companies. A company might not trade solely in the country where it is resident; indeed increasingly companies of all sizes are operating across country boundaries. In this case, a company may be liable to tax in two countries on the same profits. The country of source, ie the country where the profits are earned, will generally have the primary taxing rights over those profits. If the country of residence exercises its right to tax the company's worldwide income then it will usually have to give double tax relief for the tax charged in the country of source. The principles governing the rights of a country to tax companies which are not its tax residents are examined in Chapter 9.

Before examining the tax residence of companies, it should be noted that the residence of a company for tax purposes can be different from its residence for the purposes of suit (ie the country in which it may be sued). Case law on residence for the purposes of suit turns on whether a company has carried on its business at a fixed place for more than a minimum period of time, or whether an agent in the foreign country makes contracts for the foreign company. Whilst this is very similar to the tests used to establish a taxable presence in another country (see Chapter 9), there is an important difference in that a company, for the purposes of suit, may commonly be considered to be resident in more than one country. For instance, a debt will be recoverable according to the situs of the debt ie the country in which it is primarily payable.[1] However, as discussed in Oliver (1996) the tests of tax residence are sometimes used in determining residence for the purposes of suit and in fact the test of residence for suit appears to be closely based on the tests for company residence.

---

1   See *Jabbour v Custodian of Absentee's Property of State of Israel* [1954] 1 All ER 145.

APPROACHES TO DETERMINING TAX RESIDENCE

4.3   There are two basic approaches to determining the residence of companies for tax purposes, the legal approach and the economic approach:

● Under the legal approach, tax residence is determined according to the country of incorporation/registry in the commercial register. It is concerned with the legal form of the incorporation process.

● Under the economic (or commercial connection) approach, tax residence is determined according to one or more of these factors:

— place of management;

— principal business location; or

— tax residence of shareholders (not widely used).

Many countries use a combination of these two approaches.

Most of the early case law which established the economic approach to company residence is UK law, simply because the UK was one of the first countries to industrialize and to experience widespread expansion abroad of its enterprises. The test developed under UK law is the 'central management and control' test. Some of these cases date back more than a century, from the period in history when British businesses first started to earn significant amounts of profits abroad. This expansion in overseas trade was happening when the UK was establishing its tax system. Because these two sets of circumstances occurred earlier in the UK than in most other countries, the UK concept forms the basis of the international standard of 'place of effective management'. This is why it is appropriate to consider these old UK tax cases briefly.

Prior to 1988 the UK used only the 'central management and control' test to determine a company's residence. This reliance on case law led to many arguments, many nuances and suspected flouting of the law. There were no absolute rules and the outcome of an argument over tax residency depended on the facts of each situation. These facts never quite matched those in the legal cases upon which the law was founded. The increasing internationalization and sophistication of business led to a change in the UK law so that post 1988 all UK-registered companies are considered UK tax resident. However, the UK has retained the economic approach as well so that for non-UK registered companies the test of the location of 'central management and control' still applies. In the next section, we will examine a few of the tax cases in which the concept of 'central management and control' was developed in the UK.

'Central management and control' – the case law basis

4.4   One of the first tax cases to be heard was *Calcutta Jute Mills v Nicholson*[1] in 1876. The background to the case was that India did not charge any significant amounts of tax to British firms operating there, as India was at that time under British rule. However, if the company was found to be tax resident in the UK as opposed to India, its Indian income would have been taxable in the UK under the *residence* principle. The company had a director in India who ostensibly exercised control of the company but the Board of Directors held their meetings in London and:

> 'from that office would issue all the orders to the managing director in Calcutta. No doubt, until he received orders to the contrary, he would have full power and discretion to do what he liked in Calcutta; but at any moment from this Head Office, they might have revoked his authority, or altered any arrangement which he had made connected with the working of the company.'

In other words, for all his powers the director was still just a delegate. The decision was that the company was tax resident in the UK. Delegated authority was insufficient to constitute central management and control.

---

1   (1876) 1 TC 83.

The De Beers *case*

4.5   *De Beers Consolidated Mines Limited v Howe*[1] a case dating from 1905 is still considered by many to be the leading case on central management and control. The company was fabulously wealthy, being the world's major diamond miners and brokers and the case concerned disputed tax assessments of around £3 million, in 1905 money. The company was registered in the Colony of the Cape of Good Hope (now part of South Africa). Directors' meetings were held both in Kimberley (South Africa) and in London and under the company's constitution at least four of the directors had to reside in London. There were 19 directors altogether. Eleven of these were resident in the UK, two were itinerant between London and Kimberley (a considerable undertaking in the days before air travel), four, plus the chairman, Cecil Rhodes,[2] were resident in South Africa and the other had a home in both countries. The directors' meetings held in London were attended by more directors than those held in Kimberley.

However, the courts examined not just the frequency and composition of directors' meetings but, importantly, the nature of the decisions taken in each location. The company's residence would be determined by looking at the relative strategic importance to the company of decisions taken in each place. Decisions concerning the raising of capital (£3.5 million of debentures was issued in 1888) and decisions designed to control the global market for diamonds and hence the price were taken in London. Decisions concerning the mining activities themselves were generally taken in Kimberley. The courts also heard that the Kimberley directors were to some extent answerable to the London directors but not vice versa. The decisions taken by the London directors were those which most amounted to central management and control:[3]

> 'the Directors' Meetings in London are the meetings where the real control is always exercised in practically all the important business of the Company except the mining operations. London has always controlled the negotiation of the contracts with the Diamond Syndicates, has determined policy in the disposal of diamonds and other assets, the working and development of mines, the application of profits and the appointment of directors.'

The company was held to be UK tax resident.

1   5 TC 198.
2   Who went on to found Rhodesia, now Zimbabwe.
3   5 TC at p 213.

Bullock v Unit Construction: *company residence as fact*

4.6   The question of company residence is one of fact. This was illustrated in *Bullock v Unit Construction Co Ltd*,[1] according to Lord Radcliffe's summary of the case: 'a company is resident where its central management and control abide ... where its real business is carried on'.

Rather unusually, in this particular case the taxpayer was arguing that companies *were* resident in the UK. The case concerned a UK-resident subsidiary of Alfred Booth & Co Ltd, a UK-resident parent company. This subsidiary made certain payments to three fellow subsidiaries in Kenya and claimed these as allowable business expenses in arriving at its UK taxable profits. However, these payments would only have been allowed for tax purposes if the three subsidiaries to which they were made were resident in the UK, not Kenya. They were incorporated in Kenya and their Articles of Association expressly stated that management and control rested with the directors and also required directors' meetings to be held outside the UK. Presumably this had been done with the intention of protecting the company from any future accusation of residence outside Kenya.

It was found as a fact that due to trading difficulties at the material times the boards of directors of the Kenyan subsidiaries were standing aside in all matters of importance and also many matters of minor importance affecting the central management and control and that real control of them was being exercised by the Board of Alfred Booth & Co Ltd in London. Hence all the subsidiaries physically located in Kenya were in fact UK tax resident.

---

1   (1959) 38 TC 712.

Role of the shareholders in determining central management and control

4.7   The central management and control test is a dual test: control by itself is insufficient. The case of *The Gramophone and Typewriter Ltd v Stanley*[1] confirmed that a controlling interest does not amount to central management and control:

> 'the individual corporator does not carry on the business of the corporation. He is only entitled to the profits of that business to a certain extent, fixed and ascertained in a certain way depending on the constitution of the corporation and his holding in it. This legal proposition that the legal corporator cannot be held to be wholly or partly carrying on the business of the corporation is not weakened by the fact that the extent of his interest in it entitles him to exercise a greater or less amount of control over the manner in which that business is carried on. Such control is inseparable from his position as a corporator and is a wholly different thing both in fact and in law from carrying on the business himself .... The extent but not the nature of his power is changed by the magnitude of his holding.'[2]

In other words, directors can manage and control; shareholders can merely control the directors.

---

1   [1908] 2 KB 89.
2   At p 98.

Importance of finance and dividend policy

4.8   Raising finance is central to the implementation of policies, as seen in *De Beers*. In *The American Thread Company v Joyce*,[1] seasonal purchases of cotton needed to be made by the New York office each year resulting in a number of large transactions each year, but the financing decisions as to how much to spend were made in Manchester rather than the US. In this case, dividend policy was also formulated in the UK and the American board of directors was expected to implement the policy without alteration at the shareholders' meetings which were held in the US.

> 'The whole purse strings in the sense of money coming in by borrowing are kept most zealously at Manchester, and by means of those purse strings they are able to control and do control the policy of the Company.'[2]

The company was held to be UK resident. The reasoning behind this is that if a UK board of directors has control of borrowing then it probably has central management and control. In *Bullock v Unit Construction Co Ltd* referred to above, the bank overdraft of the Kenyan subsidiaries was negotiated by the London directors of Alfred Booth & Co Ltd who also sometimes imposed overdraft limits within the ceiling allowed by the banks.

The authorization of major capital expenditure may also indicate central management and control. For instance, in *The New Zealand Shipping Co Limited v Stephens*[3] the London board had the sole duty of constructing and acquiring ships that were by far the most important item of expenditure.

---

1   (1906) TC 61.
2   Above, p 29.
3   (1907) 20 TLR 167, CA.

More recent case law on central management and control

R v Dimsey[1]

4.9   The *Dimsey* case concerned a UK businessman, Mr A, who wished to arrange sanctions-busting deals between a German supplier and a South African customer in the avionics industry. Due to the apartheid regime which existed in South Africa at that time many companies operated trade and other economic sanctions against South Africa. Mr A introduced Mr C to the German supplier and Mr C then brokered the deals. Dimsey, who ran a financial services business in Jersey, was asked by Mr C to form two companies to deal with the South African contracts in such matters as paying commission to Mr A, who collected this in person from Jersey under arrangements made by Dimsey. The shares in the two companies were beneficially owned by, and the companies were controlled by Mr C. Dimsey, acting on instructions from Mr C, also signed contracts with the South African customer on behalf of the two Jersey companies. The German supplier usually dealt with Mr C, but also dealt with Dimsey, apparently under a misconception that Dimsey was Mr C's accountant. (In fact, he was merely an acquaintance who happened to carry out some administrative work in relation to Mr C's Jersey bank accounts.) The South African company dealt with both the UK intermediary and with Dimsey. Questions put forward in the case to determine the place of central management and control of each of the Jersey companies included:

- What did the business of the company consist of?

- What role was played by each individual in the running of that business?

- Where did the people running the business carry it on?

- Where did they hold their meetings and make their decisions?

- Where were the contracts discussed?

- Where were telephone calls made from and where was correspondence sent?

- Where was the administrative work of the company conducted?

- Where were the records kept?

- Where were the company bank accounts held, and from where were instructions sent to those banks?

Although the decision was that Mr C was the linchpin of the whole series of transactions and that the companies were therefore managed and controlled from the UK, the judge (in this criminal justice case) was criticized for this rather mechanical approach to establishing company residence. The tests just outlined centre upon management of the company, whereas the true test is a dual one of central management and control. Control was clearly in the UK.

Dimsey not only failed to disclose to HMRC that the two companies incorporated in Jersey, of which he was an officer, were managed and controlled from the UK as he should have done, but he also participated in activities designed to cover up the true nature of Mr C's dealings when he was being investigated by HMRC. Mainly for this reason, Dimsey was found guilty of conspiring to cheat the public revenue, a criminal offence.

---

1   [2001] UKHL 46, [2001] STC 1520.

Wood v Holden[1]

4.10   *Wood v Holden* again concerned a question of company residence connected with the use by individuals of tax havens, in this case the British Virgin Islands. The taxpayers were shareholders who sought to avoid a capital gains tax liability of about £12 million. They entered into a complicated scheme involving companies in several countries and Swiss trustees. The scheme involved a company incorporated in the British Virgin Islands transferring shares worth about £23 million to a Netherlands company. So long as both were non-UK resident, the gain made by the Netherlands company when it sold the shares on to the eventual outside purchaser could not be attributed back to the UK taxpayers.[2] The courts decided to examine the tax residence of the Netherlands company in some detail. Although the directors of the Netherlands company were trustees resident in Amsterdam, the documentation for the sale was prepared by UK accountants according to a tax saving scheme devised by UK accountants. Crucially though, the documents were signed by the Netherlands directors who appeared to have been, formally at least, consulted on the transactions. This differed from the circumstances in *Bullock* where the Kenyan directors stood aside in all matters, not even 'rubber stamping' decisions taken by the parent company in London. The fact that the directors of the Netherlands company acted to facilitate a plan involving several parties in several countries did not affect their residence status:

> 'when companies are established in overseas jurisdictions in order to carry through some element in a wider scheme or business structure the idea for which originated with the parent company, their directors customarily do fall in with the overall plan: but the companies do not thereby fail to be resident in their own jurisdictions.'[3]

HMRC argued that the directors in Amsterdam had insufficient information on which to base informed decisions but although they argued that the Netherlands company was not resident in the Netherlands they were unable to point to a location in the UK at which it might have been resident. There was no evidence to suggest that either the UK individual taxpayers concerned or the firm of UK professional accountants had exercised central management and control. HMRC were not helped in this case by the fact that the only way they could have imposed a tax charge on the UK-resident taxpayers was to argue that the other company used, the British Virgin Islands one which was operated along very similar lines to the Netherlands company, was definitely not UK tax resident. The Netherlands company was held to be tax resident in the Netherlands.

The gist of the reasoning in *Wood v Holden* was summed up in *Re the Trevor Smallwood Trust; Smallwood and Another v Revenue and Customs Commissioners.*[4]

'A distinction must be drawn between directors being dictated to by an outsider, and directors taking the decision pursuant to a tax scheme devised by an outsider who gives advice to and influences the board.'[5]

---

1   (2005) STC 789.
2   Under TCGA 1992, s 13.
3   [2005] STC 789 at p 838 (para 51).
4   [2008] STC (SCD) 629.
5   At p 653.

News Datacom

4.11   *News Datacom Ltd and Another v Atkinson (Inspector of Taxes)*[1] concerned a joint venture company (NDSP, owned as to 60 per cent by News International Plc group of companies and 40 per cent by minorities) set up to pursue the commercial applications of certain mathematical codes used for encryption and smartcard technology and in particular, the Videocrypt system used by satellite TV companies such as BSkyB. The brains of the operation (the minority shareholders) were based in Israel, whilst the 60 per cent shareholder and financier was a UK-resident company. The ultimate UK holding company of NDSP was News International Plc and it was decided that the News International group should buy out the 40 per cent minority holdings in NDSP. The mechanics by which this was achieved were that NDSP transferred most of its assets to a new UK tax-resident subsidiary of NDSP, NDL, which NDSP then sold to News International Plc. Under TCGA 1992, s 178, NDL faced a charge to tax on a deemed capital gain by reason of having left a group of companies (NDSP and NDL) within six years of having received capital assets from a group company (NDSP) at no gain/no loss, under the provisions of TCGA 1992, s 171. However, for NDSP and NDL to be considered a group of companies, both would have needed to be UK resident. Note that NDSP was not in the wider UK capital gains group of News International because only 60 per cent was held by News International, rather than the required minimum of 75 per cent. The case centred on the issue of whether NDSP was indeed UK resident. Several important questions on the interpretation of the concept of 'central management and control' were examined in this case including:

- Was the location of the meetings of the board of directors the sole criterion by which to determine the location of central management and control?

- Should the matters dealt with at board meetings be a factor in determining residence?

- Was there evidence that the authority of the board had been usurped?

- What was the balance of power between different members of the board?

All but one of the board meetings were held outside the UK during the period in question. It was held to be significant that at the one UK meeting, only matters of good corporate housekeeping were dealt with, rather than matters of strategic importance to the company's trade. For instance, at that meeting, it was decided to reduce the number of directors needed for a quorum from four to two. The nature of matter dealt with at board meetings is the crucial factor in determining whether the board of directors is the centre of management and control, not the fact or location of board meetings per se. Board meetings are not the sole criterion by which the location of central management and control are to be established. This was one of the points argued by HMRC, but in the event, the evidence pointed towards management and control being exercised outside of board meetings, rather in the US and Israel, so victory on this point did not assist HMRC. It must be remembered at all times that company residence is a matter of fact.

For a period of around 15 months, the board of directors did not meet formally, although there was evidence that it was only the directors who made decisions of strategic importance during this period, albeit on an informal basis. The existence of an executive committee which met in London on five out of nine occasions was not held to have affected the status of the board of directors as the organ of central management and control, as the executive committee dealt only with day-to-day operational issues. There was no evidence that the authority of the board had been usurped, even though it had failed to meet formally for a lengthy period. During the period when the board failed to meet, the Commissioners took note of the fact that an extremely important contract had been negotiated on behalf of the company by directors of NDSP operating mainly in the US. Even the fact that one of the UK-resident directors had formally signed the contract was not held to indicate strategic management and control in the UK, because there was evidence that the UK director had not been instrumental in the negotiations and the contract had been signed in the US.

The strategic importance of the board was reinforced by the fact that one of the directors appointed by the minority (who was not himself UK resident but reported as resident in France/Switzerland/Israel) was the brains behind the operation and was in effective control to the extent that he was able to defraud the company to the tune of around £28 million without the rest of the board or anyone else noticing. (He was later caught.) Further evidence of the location of the strategic management and control of the company was that prior to acquiring the whole of NDSP's business, the 60 per cent shareholder (the one with the UK connection) felt it necessary to have a full due diligence investigation carried out into the affairs of NDSP, which was essentially being run by one of the minority directors (the fraudster) in Israel. There was no evidence that the authority of the board had been usurped, in contrast with the situation in *Bullock v Unit Construction*.

For most of the period in question, only one or two out of the eight directors were UK residents. Although one of these held the title of chief executive officer, the Commissioners found as a fact that the functions fulfilled by him were more administrative than operational and that one of the non-UK directors based in Israel was able to run rings around him.

For all these reasons, NDSP was held not to be tax resident in the UK.

---

1 [2006] STC (SCD) 732.

Legal consequences of tax residence

4.12   In the UK a finding of the lower courts on company residence cannot be appealed against, provided there was evidence to support the finding and HMRC had not misdirected themselves in law. Not surprisingly then, no case on company residence has ever been finally overturned on its journey through the UK courts.

However, the cases examined so far illustrate that determining company residence solely by reference to the place of central management and control is difficult and uncertain; indeed, this has become more complex with the increasing use of technologies/digital communications to conduct business across borders (see para **4.16** onwards below). This has led to the increasing use of the legal approach whereby tax residence follows the country of legal registration of a company.

Summary – how to find the place of 'central management and control'

4.13   It is not necessarily the same as 'day-to-day' management and control. Strong indications are:

- where its governing body meets;
- where the decision to carry out operations emanates from;
- where strategic control is exercised; and
- where the fundamental policies are conceived and adopted as opposed to the place where they are carried out.

The key appears to be to find the group of persons who decide the what, where, when and how of a company's activities.

Comparative approaches to company residence

4.14   Different countries around the world interpret 'central management and control' differently – some countries take it to mean the policy-making, some the operational management (eg Switzerland), some the legal head office, and yet others rely on where the board meetings are held.

Domestic law in selected countries

4.15   The US uses a purely formal approach to company residence for tax purposes. All corporations organized under the laws of the US or one of the federal states are treated as 'domestic'. All other corporations are 'foreign' – even if all their commercial and economic activities are linked to the US. Thus the US relies exclusively on the legal concept of tax residence. This rigid approach has led to the widespread practice of corporate inversions (see Chapter 11), whereby a US holding company incorporates a new subsidiary outside the US (probably in a tax haven) which takes over the role of holding company. Bermuda is a popular location.

China uses the formal test: if a company is established under Chinese law then it will be resident there. However, it also uses place of effective management for companies established outside China.

Russia uses the legal test only so that companies established under Russian law will be considered resident. It does not use the concept of central management and control or any similar test.

Italy uses the tests of incorporation, central management and control or main business purpose. Company residence was recently the subject of a criminal prosecution against the designers, Dolce and Gabbana who were accused of running a Luxembourg company from Italy. They transferred ownership of their trademarks to a Luxembourg company (which was subject to a low rate of tax in Luxembourg). However, the Italian authorities argued although employees of the company took turns in performing mere secretarial functions in Luxembourg and the Board of Directors apparently met there, the trademarks were, in fact, being managed from Italy. Therefore the company was resident in Italy. Dolce and Gabbana were accused of trying to establish a fictitious foreign corporate residence (the Italian concept of *esterovestizione*). They had continued to receive royalties (about €1 billion in all) in respect of the trademarks transferred, through a complicated chain of companies. The designers, Dolce and Gabbana were sentenced to one year and eight months in prison for the crime of fraud against the state, although it is uncertain whether the sentence will be enforced. As in the case of *Laerstate BV v HMRC*,[1] much of the evidence against the defendants was in the form of emails, which strongly suggested that management and control was in Italy.

Japan also adopts a formal test. There, a resident corporation is one that has its headquarters or 'principal office' in Japan. Note that all corporations incorporated in Japan must have their headquarters in Japan so that in practice this is not so different from the US system.

Australia uses a number of tests of corporate residence for tax purposes. If a company is incorporated in Australia it will be tax resident there. However, doing business in Australia (having management there is deemed to be 'doing business' there) and a majority of voting power held by Australian shareholders also results in tax residency. (But note that there is nothing to stop Australian-resident companies and individuals from holding their shares in a potentially resident corporation through non-resident intermediaries.) Australia also uses the central management and control test. Most Commonwealth countries, having to some extent inherited a UK-style tax system, use the test of central management and control, sometimes supplemented by an incorporation test.

The Australian Taxation Office released a draft taxation ruling[2] in April 2017 setting out its views on the central management and control test. The draft ruling confirms that the concept relates to high-level decision making and not day-to-day management, and will not necessarily be where legal power or authority is located.

In Ireland since 1999, all Irish incorporated companies are regarded as Irish resident in the first instance, but may avail of a 'treaty exemption' or a 'trading exemption', with the latter exemption being removed from January 2015 (see below). However, even if a company could avail of either of these exemptions, it would still be deemed tax resident in Ireland based on being centrally managed and controlled in Ireland. Ireland has come under criticism in recent years arising from its corporate tax regime, which saw it in particular being a party to arrangements whereby some companies were deemed 'stateless', thereby avoiding a tax liability in any country. This arose due to a mismatch between different countries' residence rules. Consequently, Ireland amended its residency rules such that, with effect from January 2015, a company incorporated in Ireland will be considered to be tax resident in Ireland if it is not considered to be resident elsewhere. Effectively, the 'trading exemption' referred to above was removed.

The position in the Netherlands is similar to that in the UK. Formal incorporation in Netherlands results in tax residence. Case law is used to determine the location of central management and control of foreign incorporated companies. The concept used is that of 'effective management' which is slightly different to the UK idea of strategic management. Also, if a company's principal activity is in the Netherlands, the company will be deemed tax resident there.

New Zealand applies the test of incorporation but also considers the location of the head office, which it defines as the centre of administrative management and from which the company's operations are directed and carried on. If the head office is outside New Zealand, a company may still be considered resident there if its centre of management is located there. 'Centre of management' broadly means that the entire company is managed out of New Zealand but this is taken as day-to-day management and not necessarily strategic management. It also considers whether the directors exercise control of the company in New Zealand.

In Singapore, the place of incorporation is not important. However, if management and control are exercised in Singapore, then even if the company's operations take place elsewhere the company will be considered tax resident.

India introduced in 2015 a new 'place of effective management' test in place of its long-standing 'control and management' test. Under the old rule, Indian tax residence required that control and management be 'wholly' situated in India. The new test defines place of effective management as 'a place where key management and commercial decisions that are necessary for the conduct of business of an entity as a whole are, in substance made'. Ironically, this brings India into line with the OECD MTC tie-breaker test, at a point where this is about to be removed following BEPS Action 6 recommendations (see para **4.17** below).

Surinam has perhaps the most complicated system of all which takes into account each of the following:

- central management;

- statutory seat;

- place where business conducted;

- place where shareholders' general meetings held; and

- place where books and records maintained.

---

1   (2009) UKFTT 209.
2   TR 2017/D2.

Effect of digital communications

4.16   We might ask whether concepts developed before the age of the international telephone and even before the wireless telegraph, which was invented in 1895 by Marconi, are still appropriate in today's world. The *De Beers* case concerned profits earned before Orville and Wilbur Wright had made the first successful flight ever in 1903. The contrast with the current availability of international communications by telephone, email, videophone, video conferencing and the ubiquity of air travel is sharp. It is perfectly possible for a company to be genuinely managed and controlled from several countries simultaneously. The OECD considered these issues in a Discussion Paper published in 2001, which was followed up by a Discussion Draft suggesting changes to the place of effective management concept (OECD, 2003). However, the OECD Model Convention as it stands at July 2010 does not reflect the proposals contained in these documents.

The 2001 Discussion Draft (OECD, 2001) considered the impact of technology such as videoconferencing and other electronic means of communication such that it is no longer necessary for a group of persons (such as the board of directors) to be physically in the same place in order to hold discussions and make decisions. The Discussion Draft raised the possibility that the place of effective management may be located in several countries at the same time or even be peripatetic. Alternative tie-breaker tests were considered: place of incorporation, place of residence of the directors (or shareholders) or the place where the enterprise's economic links are strongest. Only this last suggestion was thought worthy of further investigation, but in the event even this appears to have fallen off the agenda mainly because it has been seen as too difficult to apply in practice. It seems that, as long as the issue of dual residence remains a relatively rare occurrence, it will have to be dealt with on a case-by-case basis, making use of the mutual agreement procedures laid down in tax treaties, so that each case is discussed individually by the tax authorities of the countries involved.

COMPANY RESIDENCE AND DOUBLE TAX TREATIES: THE TIE-BREAKER TESTS

4.17   The OECD does not define company tax residence: that is a matter for each country under its domestic laws. Article 4 of the OECD's Model Tax Convention (see Chapter 7) provides that a person (which includes a company) will be considered resident for the purposes of a tax treaty if it is 'liable to tax therein by reason of his domicile, place of management or any criterion of a similar nature'. However, as can be seen from the international comparisons outlined above, it is quite possible that a company will be resident under the domestic law of each of the countries that have entered into a bilateral DTT with each other. For instance, Company X might be managed and controlled in Country A but incorporated in Country B. If Country B defines company residence as companies which are managed and controlled in Country A, and Country B defines residence as companies which are incorporated in Country B, then Company X is legally resident in both of the Countries. However, for a DTT to operate, only one of the countries can be designated as the country of tax residence. This is because the treaties are set up so that one country is the country of residence, and the other country is the country where foreign income arises. For this reason, the OECD provides rules to decide which of the two countries will be treated as the country of residence. This is only for the purposes of applying the treaty. It does not necessarily mean that the company stops being a resident of one of the two countries under domestic laws. We call these rules 'tie-breakers'.

If, after applying the tie-breaker tests in respect of the treaty between Countries A and B, it is decided that Company X will be treated as if it was resident solely in Country A, then this leaves a rather messy legal situation: Company X is treated as tax resident in Country A for the purposes of the Country A–Country B DTT, but still resident in Country B as well for all other tax purposes. Some countries (eg the UK) deal with this by deeming a company resident in a country other than the UK for the purpose of any of the UK's tax treaties to be not resident in the UK for all other UK tax purposes as well.

The tiebreaker test historically used by the OECD is that the country in which the company has its place of effective management will be considered, for treaty purposes only, as the country of residence. This rule also applies to other legal persons, such as trusts. The OECD, as part of its work on base erosion and profit shifting (BEPS – see Chapter 2), is about to abandon 'place of effective management' as the sole tie-breaker test in the OECD Model Tax Convention, because the view is that it has allowed too much tax avoidance by companies who set themselves up as deliberately dual resident. Nevertheless, the test is widely used in existing tax treaties, and it will be some years or even decades before all existing treaties are changed to remove it as the sole criterion for determining company residence for treaty purposes.. For this reason, we will look in some detail at the test.

In the Commentary to the OECD Model Tax Convention (which we will examine in more detail in Chapter 7) the OECD defines the place of effective management as follows:

> 'the place where key management and commercial decisions that are necessary for the conduct of the entity's business are in substance made. All relevant facts and circumstances must be examined to determine the place of effective management. An entity may have more than one place of management but it can have only one place of effective management at any one time'.[1]

The Commentary underwent some changes in 2008: prior to this, instead of just stating that all relevant facts and circumstances must be examined, there was a statement that the place of effective management would ordinarily be the place where the most senior person or group of persons (eg a board of directors) makes its decisions, the place where the actions to be taken by the entity as a whole are determined. Between 2001 and 2008, several documents discussing changes to the interpretation of 'place of effective management' were published by the OECD,[2] some of which put forward much more detailed suggestions for guidance on interpretation. There were suggestions for additions to the Commentary dealing with situations where, for instance, board decisions were made in substance in one country but finalized in another.

A hierarchy of tests similar to those used to determine the residence of individuals was also proposed. However, it seems that the OECD has decided that the circumstances in which questions as to company residence can arise are so varied, and at the same time relatively rare, that general guidance only is required. The place of board meetings is not mentioned in the 2014 Commentary except in the context of states which decide not to incorporate a tie-breaker test at all, but rather to deal with questions of dual residence on a case-by-case basis. States not using a tie-breaker clause at all are encouraged to take account of the location of the meetings of the board of directors, and the place where the senior executives carry on their activities amongst other factors.

There is some debate as to whether 'place of effective management' and 'central management and control' can really be distinguished. If there is a distinction, it is that the place of effective management test tends to place more weight on the day-to-day running of a company's affairs. However, this is not a hard and fast rule, as illustrated by the following extract from a document presented to the Committee on Foreign Relations of the US Senate,[3] explaining some proposed amendments (known as a Protocol) to the US/Sweden DTT.

The extract concerns the requirements for eligibility of a company to enjoy the benefits of the treaty:

> 'The second alternative requirement determines whether the company's primary place of management and control is in the treaty country where it is a resident. A company … may claim treaty benefits if its primary place of management and control is in the treaty country of which it is a resident. A company's primary place of management is located in the treaty country in which the company is a resident only if the executive officers and senior management employees exercise day-to-day responsibility for more of the strategic, financial and operational policy decision making for the company (including its direct and indirect subsidiaries) in the residence country than in any other country, and the staffs conduct more of the day-to-day activities necessary for preparing and making those decisions in that country than in any other country.
>
> … the management and control test should be distinguished from the "place of effective management" test which is used by many countries and in the OECD model to establish residence. The place of effective management test has often been interpreted to mean the place where the board of directors meets. Under the proposed protocol, however, the primary place of management and control test looks to where day-to-day responsibility for the management of the company (and its subsidiaries) is exercised.'

Note that management and control is interpreted here as meaning day-to-day management, albeit including 'day-to-day' responsibility for strategic decisions. It forms an interesting contrast to the principles laid down, say, in *American Thread*.

The distinction between the concept of 'central management and control' and the place of effective management was examined in a UK Special Commissioners decision in 2008, *Re the Trevor Smallwood Trust; Smallwood and Another v Revenue and Customs Commissioners*.[4] This case concerned the residence of a trust central to a tax-avoidance scheme, referred to as the 'round the world' scheme, which took advantage of a provision in the UK–Mauritius DTT. Under the domestic law of the UK and of Mauritius, the trustee was resident in both places and so the tie-breaker under the treaty, place of effective management, had to be brought into play. 'Place of effective management' is the most common tie-breaker in DDTs for all taxable persons except individuals, and so *Smallwood* also is of relevance to company residence, even though it involved a trust rather than a company.

In *Smallwood*, the Special Commissioners defined 'central management and control' as being a test carried out by a single country. The fact that central management and control may be split between several countries does not prevent each of them from determining that a company is resident on the basis that central management, and control is found in each. Central management and control is not a tie-breaker test, and it may well exist in more than one country, leading to dual residence. However, 'place of effective management' is designed as a tie-breaker, and the term 'effective' when used elsewhere in a treaty context, means 'real', eg the term 'effectively connected' in Article 9 of the Model Convention means 'in reality, connected'.

The *Smallwood* case centred around a plan developed by KPMG, Bristol, and a UK private client fund manager (Morgan Stanley Quilter) to sell off some shares in a manner designed to avoid UK tax by having the gain taxable in Mauritius only (that did not tax capital gains). Summing up, the Special Commissioners said:

> 'We conclude that the state in which the real top level management, or the realistic, positive management of the trust, or the place where key management and commercial decisions that were necessary for the conduct of the trust's business were in substance made, and the place where the actions to be taken by the entity as a whole were, *in fact*, determined between 19 December 2000 and 2 March 2001 was the United Kingdom.'[5]

In July 2010, the Court of Appeal by majority upheld an appeal from HMRC.[6] Each judge found that the trustees were resident in both jurisdictions, and so the tie-breaker 'place of effective management' was of critical importance. Patten, LJ, dissenting, considered that the place of effective management at the time of the disposal was decisive, but the majority disagreed, finding in support of the Commissioners that the trust had its place of effective management in the UK. Hughes LJ said it was incorrect to take a snapshot at the time of the disposal, rather an examination of the whole of the relevant fiscal year was required. In December 2010, the taxpayer was refused leave to appeal to the Supreme Court, and there is some suggestion that this decision leaves the question of residence of SPVs in some doubt.

To reiterate, it is expected that changes will be made to the OECD Model as a result of the work on BEPS (Action 6) to remove the reference to place of effective management as the sole tie-breaker test. It is expected to be replaced with a requirement that the two states involved reach agreement, having regard to other factors as well as the place of effective management. This is as a result of a number of tax avoidance cases involving dual-resident companies, which are considered to be best dealt with on a case-by-case basis. The BEPS Action 15 Multilateral Convention deals with the question by placing the decision in the hands of the competent authorities of the contracting states.

---

1   Para 24 of the *Commentary on the OECD Model Tax Convention on Income and on Capital*, July 2005 Condensed Version.
2   See, for instance, OECD, 'Place of Effective Management Concept: Suggestion for Changes to the OECD Model Tax Convention', Technical Advisory Group on Monitoring the Application of Existing Treaty Norms for the Taxation of Business Profits, Discussion Draft, 27 May 2003.
3   'Explanation of proposed protocol to the income tax treaty between the United States and Sweden', 26 January, 2006 JCX-1-06. Available at: www.house.gov/jct/x-1-06.pdf.
4   [2008] STC (SCD) 629.
5   Above at p 681.
6   *HMRC v Smallwood and Another* [2010] EWCA Civ 778.

FURTHER READING

Avery Jones, J F '2008 OECD Model: Place of Effective Management – What One Can Learn from the History', *Bulletin for International Taxation* 2009, Vol 63, No 5.

Hughes, D 'The Determination of UK Corporate Residence: *LaerstateBV*', *European Taxation* 2010, Vol 50, No 2/3.

Langston, R (2012) 'Analysis Back to Basics: Corporate Tax Residence, *Tax Journal*, 17 February 2012.

Lawrence, D '*Smallwood v Revenue and Customs Commissioners*: Part 1 – A Mauritian Mission Explained', *Private Client Business* 2011, 1, 7–11.

Lawrence, D '*Smallwood*: Part 2 – Poetic Justice?' *Private Client Business* 2011, 2, 77–82.

Maisto, G (2009) *Residence of Companies under Tax Treaties and EC Law* IBFD. (NB this book includes useful analyses of the approach to company tax residence in a range of countries.)

Nathan, A (2005) 'Determining company residence after *Wood v Holden*'. Available at: www.taxbar.com/documents/Company_Residence_Wood_v_Holden_AN_000.pdf.

OECD (2001) 'The Impact of the Communications Revolution on the Application of "Place of Effective Management" as a Tie Breaker Rule', Discussion paper from the Technical Advisory Group on monitoring the application of existing treaty norms for the taxation of business profits'. Available at: www.oecd.org/dataoecd/46/27/1923328.pdf.

OECD (2003) 'Place of Effective Management Concept: Suggestions for Changes to the OECD Model Tax Convention', Discussion Draft 27 May 2003. Available at: www.oecd.org/dataoecd/24/17/2956428.pdf.

OECD (2008) *Commentary on Art 4, Para 3 to Model Tax Convention on Income and Capital*, July 2008 Condensed Version.

Oliver, J D B (1996) 'Company Residence – Four Cases', *British Tax Review*, No 5, 1996.

Schwarz, J (2013) *Booth & Schwarz: Residence, Domicile and UK Taxation*, 15th edn, Bloomsbury Professional.

Chapter 5

The Double Tax Problem

BASICS

5.1   Double taxation arises mainly due to the overlap of the residence principle and the source principle. Companies that are tax resident in Country A may operate partly in Country B, thus being fully taxable on worldwide income in Country A, and taxable on income derived from Country B in Country B as well. This is juridical double taxation.

The two main systems in use for relieving double taxation are the credit system and the exemption system, although many variations are found on both systems. The credit system gives credit for foreign tax on foreign income against the home country tax liability on that income. The exemption system means that the home country does not tax income which has already been taxed abroad.

It is considered good practice for a country to adopt a method of double tax relief which ensures both capital export neutrality, and capital import neutrality. If these conditions prevail then the working of the economy is relatively unaffected by the issue of double taxation because residents gain no advantage from having foreign income, and non-residents face the same tax burden as residents. If tax neutrality is present then tax is not a deciding factor in the decision as to whether to trade abroad or at home.

When a country decides to give double tax relief it is effectively giving up the right to tax, in full, certain income of its residents. The total amount of taxable income and gains in a country is known as its tax base. The choice of the system of double taxation relief can determine the extent to which a country is able to preserve its tax base. Although simpler to operate than the credit system, use of a basic exemption system is likely to lead to a country's residents transferring their mobile, income-producing assets, eg savings and intellectual property (IP) to tax havens. To prevent this, many countries combine an exemption system for foreign direct investment (FDI) with a credit system for portfolio income, known as exemption with participation. There are several variations on the credit system, mainly affecting the extent to which pooling of foreign income and related tax credits is permitted, both across different income sources and different time periods.

Turnover taxes such as VAT are not normally covered by double tax relief credit systems. The types of taxes most often credited are withholding taxes and foreign corporation taxes. Withholding taxes are taxes on the payment of income from the foreign country, borne by the home country investor. Foreign dividends sometimes attract a further amount of double tax relief as well as relief for foreign withholding taxes. Relief for foreign corporation taxes (suffered by the company paying the dividend on the profits out of which dividends have been paid, ie an underlying tax) may be available to corporate (but not individual) shareholders where the investment is in the nature of FDI. To be considered FDI as opposed to merely a portfolio holding, the minimum shareholding is normally 10 per cent.

HISTORICAL CONTEXT

5.2   Many of the systems of double tax relief that are in place today were developed following the First World War, when many countries began to levy income/profits taxes for the first time, and/or increase the rates of tax. This made the problem of double taxation more pressing; but because each country at the time was developing its own tax system independently, there emerged a difference in approach to relieving international double taxation. In Central Europe, a number of treaties were negotiated to relieve international double taxation, through an exemption mechanism (ie the country in which the taxpayer is resident does not attempt to tax profits earned outside of that country). A different approach, however, was developing in the British Empire and in the US: a credit mechanism where the country of the taxpayer's residence taxes all profits or income wherever in the world it was earned, but then gives a credit for any foreign tax paid. In this chapter we will examine this issue, first by considering more closely the nature of the double tax problem and the theoretical ways of relieving it, and then by looking more closely at the two most common methods now in use, exemption and credit.

Increasingly, countries are moving towards territorial (also known exemption) systems. The US is one country, however, that has chosen to retain a credit system, and we will look more closely at the US system in Chapter 6. For an overview of the historical origins of the debate over credit *v* exemption, see Avery Jones (2012).

THE BASIC PROBLEM

5.3   Whenever a company or an individual undertakes activities in another country, they will be dealing with more than one set of tax rules and therefore there will be the potential for international double taxation. The term double taxation refers to being exposed to tax more than once on the same profit or income. There are two types of double taxation, economic and juridical.

Economic double taxation is a broad term that covers any situation where an amount of income is taxed twice. For example, it occurs when a single country taxes the same income twice, as in the case of the taxation of corporate profits. After being subject to this corporation tax, when the post-tax profits are distributed to shareholders in the form of dividends, the shareholders are subject to income tax in part or in full on the dividend they receive. However, this form of double taxation is not the subject of this chapter. We are concerned with international double taxation, which is a narrower, legal form, technically known as juridical double taxation.

Juridical double taxation occurs where more than one country attempts to tax the same income. It arises specifically because of a 'jurisdictional' conflict in the rules that are used to determine residence and/or source. Sometimes it will occur because different countries use different rules for the attribution of tax residence. So, for instance, one country may use place of incorporation, and the other country uses effective management and control, and both then claim jurisdiction over the same company. It could also occur if two countries have different rules about how to determine the source of income.

Most commonly, however, juridical double taxation occurs because a company or an individual has a source of income in a country other than the country of residence. The home country often taxes the income using the *residence principle*, and the foreign country taxes the income using the *source principle*.

Example 5.1

Jones Ltd (a company resident in the country of Ponstantia) has a subsidiary (Pire Ltd) in the country of Ruritania. Ponstantia's tax system is such that it will charge the worldwide income of Jones Ltd to tax (using the *residence* principle). Thus any dividends received by Jones Ltd from Pire Ltd will be fully subject to Ponstantian tax.

Ruritania normally charges non-residents to tax on their income from sources within its jurisdiction.

Jones Ltd will therefore have a liability to Ruritanian tax on dividends paid to it by Pire Ltd by reason of the *source* principle. Shares in Pire Ltd are considered a source of Ruritanian income (dividends from a Ruritanian company) belonging to a non-resident of Ruritania (Jones Ltd).

Thus the profits used to pay the dividend will have suffered tax twice: Ponstantian tax – on the *residence* basis and Ruritanian tax – on the *source* basis.

DOUBLE TAX RELIEF

5.4   This is the term normally applied where the country of residence acts to prevent or reduce the extent to which its residents are taxed more than once on the same income. There are many different systems of double tax relief. Mechanisms for the relief of double taxation are often set out in double tax treaties (DTTs). These are bilateral (or less commonly, multilateral) agreements between pairs of countries in which the two countries set out how they will eliminate double taxation on their residents with respect to income or gains derived in the other country. These are governed by international law and are considered in further detail in Chapter 7.

In addition to the use of double tax treaties, most countries normally set out provisions for unilaterally relieving double taxation on their residents in their domestic law. This ensures that relief for double taxation is available to cover income received from countries with which there is no double tax treaty.

There are three main methods by which countries may give relief for double taxation:

- *Exemption method*: under this method, the country of residence does not tax the foreign income of its tax residents. Foreign income is said to be *exempt*.

- *Credit method*: here, the income earned from the overseas country is taxed in the country of residence. The foreign tax paid is then credited against the tax on the income charged by the country of residence. Thus the country of residence gives credit for the foreign tax suffered.

- *Deduction method*: under the deduction method, foreign taxes are treated as an expense of doing business. The country of residence taxes the foreign income, but allows a deduction from the foreign income for any foreign taxes paid.

Consider the following Example 5.2, that compares the three methods:

Example 5.2

A company resident in Country A, where the rate of corporation tax is 30 per cent, has a branch in Country B. The Country B branch pays Country B profits tax on its profits at the rate of 35 per cent. The following Table 5.1 demonstrates how different methods for alleviating double taxation impact on the effective tax rate.

Table 5.1

	No relief	Deduction	Exemption	Credit
Country B branch profits	1000	1000	1000	1000
Country B tax @ 35%	350	350	350	350
Net after-tax profits	650	650	650	650
Country A tax on 1000 @ 30%	300	–	–	300
Country A tax on 650 @ 30%	–	195	–	–
Credit for Country B tax	–	–	–	(300)*
Total tax paid	650	545	350	350
Effective tax rate (total tax/ profits before tax)	65%	54.5%	35%	35%

Notes: *the credit for foreign taxes cannot normally exceed the amount of tax on the income charged by the country of residence: this is explained in the following sections.

Where there is no relief from double taxation, the company must pay full tax in both Country A and Country B, which makes the investment in Country B expensive compared to only doing business in Country A. If the company only earns income in Country A, its maximum tax rate would be only 30 per cent. The deduction method provides some relief from double taxation, reducing the effective tax rate from 65 per cent to 54.5 per cent. This method was used by a number of countries in the early part of the twentieth century when tax rates were quite low. As the century progressed, however, and rates of tax increased, the deduction method declined in popularity because the alternative exemption and credit methods provided greater relief from double taxation. Because the deduction method does not fully relieve double taxation, it favours domestic investment, indeed it is based on the notion of national neutrality discussed in Chapter 2. Some countries still use it in conjunction with the other methods as an optional system (as in the UK) which can be of benefit where perhaps a taxpayer has accumulated losses and cannot benefit from the other systems. Most countries now use either the exemption or credit methods, which are recommended by the OECD. For the rest of this chapter, then, we will focus on these two methods.

In Example 5.2, the rate of tax in Country B (the foreign, or host, country) was higher than that in Country A (the residence, or home, country), and under this situation, the total tax paid under the exemption method was the same as that using the credit method. So where the foreign tax rate is higher, the credit and exemption methods produce the same net tax liability. There is effectively no tax on the foreign income at all, in the country of residence under either method. What happens, then, when the foreign tax rate is lower than that in the taxpayer's country of residence?

Example 5.3

A company resident in Country A, where the rate of corporation tax is 30 per cent, has a branch in Country C. The Country C branch pays Country C profits tax on its profits at the rate of 20 per cent. How do the exemption and credit methods compare in this situation?

Table 5.2

	Exemption	Credit
Country C branch profits	1000	1000
Country C tax @ 20%	200	200
Net after-tax profits	800	800
Country A tax on 1000 @ 30%	–	300
Credit for Country C tax	–	(200)
Balance due to Country A		100
Total tax paid	200	300
Effective tax rate	20%	30%

Now it is possible to say that where the foreign tax rate is lower than the domestic tax rate, the exemption method will give greater relief. This may be good from the taxpayer's point of view, but what about the government of the country of the taxpayer's residence, in this case Country A? In both Examples 5.2 and 5.3, the exemption method meant that Country A did not collect any tax on the foreign profits.

Credit method – limitation on amount of credit

5.5   In Example 5.3 where the foreign tax rate was lower than the domestic rate, the credit method allowed Country A still to collect some tax at the rate of 30 per cent. However, in Example 5.2, where the foreign tax rate was higher than the domestic rate, the credit method resulted in Country A giving a tax credit of only 300 when the foreign tax suffered was 350. If Country A had given a credit of 350 it would have subsidized the investment in Country B by protecting the taxpayer from the 35 per cent rate of tax in Country B. That would be referred to as '*full credit*' because the country of the taxpayer's residence allows credit for all the foreign tax paid by the taxpayer. Since this reduces the tax take of the home country when the foreign tax rate is higher than the domestic rate, the OECD recommends '*ordinary credit*'. This is the method most countries using a credit method will adopt, and it places a limit on the amount of foreign tax that can be credited. The limit is the amount of tax that would have been paid if the profits were earned at home instead of overseas.

Using the 'full credit' method and assuming that the company also has profits earned at home in Country A of 500, the credit method calculations in Example 5.2 would look like this:

Table 5.2 cont.

	Country B Income	Country A Income	Total
Profits	1000	500	1500
Country A tax at 30%	300	150	450
Credit for Country B tax	(300)	(50)	(350)
Country A tax payable	0	100	100
Country B tax payable	350	0	350
Total tax paid	350	100	450
Effective tax rate	35%	20%	30%

As the tax credit for Country B tax of 350 is more than the Country A liability on the same profits, the excess credit (350–300 = 50) has been set against Country A profits, reducing the Country A tax payable on these profits from 150 to 50. Country A has given up tax of 50 on Country A profits, because of Country B's high tax rate. Country A is thus subsidizing Country B.

So, instead of allowing credit for the full amount of foreign tax paid, Country A limits the credit to 30 per cent, the rate applicable to domestic profits, as shown in Example 5.2. The taxpayer is disadvantaged in that it now pays more tax by earning profits overseas than it would if it had earned them at home (350 as opposed to 300) but the government of Country A is no longer 'out of pocket' beyond the amount of domestic tax foregone on the Country B profits.

Exemption 'with progression'

5.6   Some countries apply a single rate of corporation tax whilst others use a rate band, or bracket system similar to the UK income tax rate band system. Under a rate band system (a 'progressive' system), a company's profits are allocated into several rate bands for corporation tax purposes. What if, in Country A, there were two rates of tax on company profits, 30 per cent for profits below 100,000, and then 40 per cent above that limit? Assume that the amount of branch profits, were they taxable in Country A, would be sufficient to move the company from one tax bracket to the next. Let us assume that the company has Country A profits of exactly 100,000 and foreign branch profits of 20,000. In other words, without the branch profits it would just be taxed at 30 per cent, but with the branch profits, 100,000 of profits would be taxed at 30 per cent and the remaining 20,000 of profits would be taxed at 40 per cent. It means that the amount of tax foregone is even more, ie it is even more costly to the government of Country A. To overcome this, the OECD recommends a variation on the exemption method which is referred to as *exemption with progression*. Effectively, the foreign profits are treated as being exempt, however they are still taken into account in deciding what rate of domestic tax will apply to the rest of the taxpayer's profits – they 'use up' all or part of the lower rate bands.

Example 5.4 Exemption with progression

Table 5.3

Country A tax if all income taxed in Country A: 100,000 @ 30% + 20,000 @ 40%	38,000
Country A tax forgone if Country B income is simply exempted: 20,000 @ 40%	8000
Applying 'exemption with progression': Country A income taxed at 30%: 100,000–20,000 = 80,000	
80,000 @ 30%	24,000
Remainder (100,000–80,000 = 20,000) @ 40%	8000
Total Country A tax on Country A income	32,000
Reduction in Country A tax foregone by applying exemption with progression 38,000–32,000	6000

Choosing between methods of double tax relief

5.7   When choosing which method, or combination of methods to employ, a country will need to consider the following factors:

- capital export neutrality;

- protection of its tax base; and

- the costs to the state and to taxpayers of the method adopted.

Capital export neutrality

5.8   Capital export neutrality is the main reason for a country to try to prevent double taxation of business profits. The concept of neutrality is concerned with whether or not a tax is distortionary. As we saw in Chapter 1, it can be argued that a 'good' tax is one that does not influence a taxpayer's commercial decisions. In Chapter 2 it was noted that capital export neutrality will exist when there is no incentive or disincentive for resident investors to invest at home rather than abroad. This is achieved when a company's total worldwide tax liability is the same whether it is paying tax solely to its home government or to both the home and foreign governments. The next two examples further demonstrate the difference between full credit and ordinary credit.

Example 5.5 Capital export neutrality – using the credit method

A Baldevian company is considering expanding by setting up a new factory either in the country of Baldevia or the country of Morania.

Baldevia has an effective corporation tax rate of 30 per cent.

Morania has an effective corporation tax rate of 40 per cent.

Table 5.4

Profits from present activity	1000
Anticipated profits from new factory	200
Profit before tax	1200

Worldwide tax if new factory is set up in Baldevia:

1200 @ 30%	360

Moranian tax if new factory is set up in Morania:

Moranian tax on Moranian income: 200 @ 40%	80

	Baldevian income of 1000	Moranian income of 200	Total of 1200	
Baldevian tax:	300	60	360	
Double tax relief (using ordinary credit method – see para **5.5** above)		–60	–60	
Total Baldevian tax	300	0	300	300
Worldwide tax if new factory is set up in Morania			360	380

Thus setting up in Morania would expose the company to an increase of 20 (380–360) corporation tax. Capital export neutrality is not present and there is a disincentive to set up the new factory abroad.

Capital export neutrality is desirable as it permits the expansion of a country's businesses into overseas markets without a tax penalty, thus encouraging exports, bolstering a country's foreign earnings and contributing towards the health of the country's economy. Perfect capital export neutrality would be achieved if every country had the same tax system so that the after-tax return is the same no matter where in the world a company is taxed.

Capital export neutrality is more difficult to achieve when foreign tax rates are generally higher than the domestic tax rate. It can only be achieved if the country of residence is prepared to operate a system of *full* credit. The application of the credit method used so far in Example 5.5 is *ordinary* credit. Example 5.6 reworks Example 5.4 but using a system of *full* credit, whereby credit for foreign taxes is given not only against residence country tax on foreign income, but also against residence country tax on domestic income.

Example 5.6 Capital export neutrality: 'full credit'

A Baldevian company is considering expanding by setting up a new factory either in Baldevia or Morania.

Baldevia has an effective corporation tax rate of 30 per cent.

Morania has an effective corporation tax rate of 40 per cent.

Profits from present activity	1000
Anticipated profits from new factory	200
Profit before tax	1200

Tax if new factory is set up in Morania using *full* credit method:

Moranian tax on Moranian income: 200 @ 40% = 80

Baldevian tax:	Baldevian income of 1000	Moranian income of 200	Total of 1200
Baldevian tax @ 30%	300	60	360
Double tax relief (using *full* credit method)	–20	–60	60
Total Baldevian tax	280	0	280
Add Moranian tax			80
Wordwide tax if new factory is set up in Morania			360

Thus the tax liability is the same as if all the income had been earned in Baldevia.

The credit method is broadly capital export neutral in that all taxpayers in the state of residence are taxed initially at the state's normal tax rates. However, note that there may still be important differences between the tax position of an exporting firm and a firm operating exclusively in the home country:

●   The overall global tax liability for the exporting firm may be higher due to the adoption of 'ordinary credit' rules which restrict double tax relief for foreign tax in excess of domestic taxes.

●   The timing of tax payments will differ as foreign dividends will generally be taxed when received in the residence country, rather than when the profits used to pay those dividends are earned.

As noted in Chapter 2, the corollary of capital export neutrality is capital import neutrality – consumers should be indifferent as to whether they buy imports or home-grown products. If the home country tax rates are higher than foreign tax rates then imports will be cheaper than domestically produced items. Capital import neutrality requires that firms operating in a particular country suffer the same worldwide tax on their profits arising in that country, whether they are resident in that country or whether they are resident elsewhere. It is considered that capital import neutrality can only be attained where a country and all its major trading partners have essentially the same tax system and the same rates.

Protecting the domestic tax base

5.9   In Chapter 2 we defined the tax base as being the individuals and companies resident in a country, and the type of income or profits earned in a country. Which of the two main methods of dealing with the double tax problem best protects the tax base?

The exemption method eliminates foreign income (and possibly capital gains as well) of resident individuals and corporations from the tax base altogether. The principal danger of the exemption method to a country's tax base is that its residents will move mobile capital into other countries. Thus there is a tax incentive to deposit cash into foreign bank accounts and to invest in foreign rather than domestic companies so that interest and dividend payments and capital gains on sale of shares are exempt in the country of tax residence. Naturally the foreign country will be one where the rates of tax are lower than the country of tax residence. Thus the exemption method, in its simple form, can be said to encourage the legal use of tax havens. This ignores any conditions that may be attached to the exemption, which we will examine later in the chapter.

The credit method taxes foreign income, so keeping it within the tax base. However, if a country's taxes are generally lower than in countries from which its residents derive income and gains, then the credit method will still not result in any tax revenue for the home country on the foreign income and gains of its residents. The credit method does not encourage the use of tax havens, as if the taxes paid abroad are lower than domestic taxes on the foreign income there is home country tax to pay. The credit method therefore affords more protection to the domestic tax base than the exemption method.

Relative complexity of methods

5.10   One of the differences between the two methods relates to their complexity. In its simple form the exemption method is very easy to operate, presenting few administrative costs to the country of residence. The taxpayer only has to account to one tax authority for the tax on the foreign income. However, because of the problem of flight of mobile capital to low-tax countries, many countries operate variants of the basic exemption method. A common variant applied to foreign dividend income is the 'exemption with activity clause' which only allows the exemption method to be operated in respect of dividend income from foreign direct investment (where the taxpayer may be said to 'participate' in the management of the foreign company from which dividends are received). Income and gains from foreign portfolio investment are subject to a separate system of double tax relief by credit.

Running such a dual system of double tax relief introduces complexity to the system, which you will recall from Chapter 1 is generally thought to be undesirable:

- The tax authority has to administer two systems of double tax relief.

- All foreign income and gains must be characterized as either foreign direct investment or portfolio investment to determine which method of double tax relief is appropriate. This inevitably leads to lengthy and expensive disputes.

- When making investment decisions the taxpayer may be uncertain as to which method will operate with respect to a particular source of income, leading to a need for advance rulings from the tax authority.

Another variant often adopted is exemption with progression: as already noted, this may be used where a country has a progressive tax rate structure. Although foreign income is exempt from domestic taxes, it is taken into account when working out the rate of tax on domestic income. The foreign income is allocated against the lower bands of income so that domestic income becomes taxable at the higher rates. Exemption systems often incorporate both an activity clause (sometimes referred to as 'exemption with participation') and progression.

The credit method is inherently more complex than the simple version of the exemption system as it requires a computation of tax on foreign income in the country of residence. All foreign taxes must be examined to determine if they qualify for double tax relief/foreign tax credit, ie whether or not they are 'creditable'.

There is often considerable difficulty in establishing the amount of the foreign tax credit. The credit consists of the foreign tax *paid* on the foreign income. It is not sufficient simply to apply the headline rate of foreign tax to the gross foreign income. This requirement means that the foreign tax liability must be known with certainty before the home country will grant the double tax relief. Any delay in establishing the amount of overseas tax paid results in a delay in finalizing the tax position in the country of residence. In practice, tax authorities may allow a degree of relief on a provisional basis, but this tends to be at their discretion.

Foreign dividends in particular present problems in determining the amount of the foreign tax credit. Under most legal systems, dividends may be paid from a company's accumulated distributable profits. If these profits have accumulated over several years, then they will have been subjected to tax at different rates. It is therefore necessary in a credit method for double tax relief to have rules to establish the exact source (ie company profits used to pay the dividends), in terms of the country in which they were earned and the period during which they were earned.

QUALIFYING FOREIGN TAX

5.11 We now consider the types of foreign tax which a country may consider acceptable for the purposes of reducing the domestic tax liabilities of its residents. These are sometimes known as 'creditable taxes'.

There are two types of taxes that may be credited in connection with foreign dividends:

- Direct taxes on the foreign shareholder: withholding taxes.

- Indirect taxes on income suffered by the foreign shareholder/head office – usually the foreign corporation tax.

Most countries using the credit system will publish lists of 'creditable' taxes.

Generally speaking, countries do not give double tax relief for turnover taxes, such as sales taxes or for indirect taxes. Often such relief is not necessary as the GATT (General Agreement on Tariffs and Trade) permits the indirect taxes on exports to be rebated where these can be ascertained with accuracy. For instance, exports from EU countries to non-EU countries do not carry VAT.

Unfortunately, the definition of what is or is not a sales tax differs from country to country. Thus the characterization of a foreign tax is crucial in determining whether double tax relief will be available in the home country. Such disputes are often referred to as treaty characterization problems. There is a large body of tax law on this issue.

Double tax relief will usually be available for capital taxes such as foreign capital gains taxes or inheritance taxes.

WITHHOLDING TAXES

5.12 These represent the tax liabilities due under the source principle and are commonly levied on non-residents. They are also frequently levied on residents, as a mechanism for ensuring tax compliance. Although a country is legally permitted to levy taxation on non-residents under the source principle, there are practical difficulties in collecting this tax directly from foreign persons. For instance, if a Ruritanian company has a UK-resident shareholder then it will not be practical for the Ruritanian government to insist that the UK shareholder files a Ruritanian tax return and makes payment of the tax due on a dividend from the Ruritanian company. If the UK shareholder fails to comply there is little the Ruritanian government can do in a cost-effective manner to enforce the tax liability.

Therefore the Ruritanian tax due under the source principle will probably be deducted from the total dividend payment and paid over to the Ruritanian government by the Ruritanian company so that the UK shareholder receives the dividend net of Ruritanian source taxation. This is known as a withholding tax as the source taxation is withheld from the total payment. The Ruritanian company is under the jurisdiction of the Ruritanian government, so that the withholding requirement is legally enforceable.

Typically the withholding tax settles the liability of the UK shareholder under Ruritanian tax law without the need for him to submit a Ruritanian tax return. It is normally levied at a fairly low rate, the maximum usually being the basic rate of income tax. Double tax treaties usually state that both countries involved (Ruritania and UK) may tax dividends from Ruritania. Ruritania takes a slice of tax via a withholding tax and the UK charges its normal rate, giving relief by the credit method for the Ruritanian withholding tax.

Example 5.7 Withholding tax

Jones Ltd, a Ponstantian resident company, holds 1000 shares (5 per cent of the issued share capital) in Jurum Inc, a company resident in Ruritania. Jurum Inc has declared a dividend of £0.1 per share. Jones Ltd is due a dividend of

£100. Ruritania levies a withholding tax of 5 per cent on dividends paid to non-resident shareholders.

Table 5.5

	£
Total dividend due to Jones Ltd	100
Payment received by Jones Ltd from Jurum Inc	95
Payment sent by Jurum Inc to the Ruritanian tax authority (the withholding tax	5
Jones Ltd's Ponstantian tax liability:	
Total dividend due from Jurum Inc	100
Ponstantian tax at 30%	30
Deduct: double tax relief for Ruritanian withholding tax	−5
Ponstantian tax payable	25
Total tax suffered by Jones Ltd: Ruritanian	5
Ponstania	25
	30

Note that in Example 5.7, capital export neutrality is present.

A country may grant double tax relief for foreign corporation taxes against the domestic tax liability of resident shareholders on dividends from a foreign company in circumstances where the resident shareholder holds a significant percentage of the shares in the foreign company. This recognizes the fact that the dividend represents profits which have been subject to the foreign corporation tax.

An important distinction is made in international taxation between what may be termed 'portfolio investment' and 'foreign direct investment'.

Portfolio investment is the term used where a shareholder owns only a very small percentage of the total shares in a company. The holding may be part of a portfolio of similar small shareholdings. Private individuals will typically hold shares in this manner so as to spread their total investment across many companies, reducing the risk of losses if any one of the companies performs badly.

Foreign direct investment is the term used for a significant shareholding in a foreign company, typically 10 per cent or more. In these circumstances the shareholder is able to exercise some degree of control and influence over the affairs of the company and runs the risk of significant financial loss if the company performs badly.

Where there is foreign direct investment, as opposed to portfolio investment most countries will allow the foreign corporation taxes suffered on the foreign profits out of which the dividend has been paid to be set against the home country tax liability in addition to any withholding tax. In other words, the shareholder can claim a double tax credit for foreign corporation tax paid by the company which paid the dividend. These foreign corporation taxes are sometimes referred to as 'underlying tax'.

Example 5.8

Assume the same facts as in Example 5.7 except that Jones Ltd now owns 10,000 shares (50 per cent of the issued share capital) in Jurum Inc. The effective rate of corporation tax in Ruritania is now assumed to be 20 per cent.

Table 5.6

	£
Payment received by Jones Ltd from Jurum Inc	950
Payment sent by Jurum Inc to the Ruritanian tax authority (the withholding tax)	50
	1000
Dividend gross of withholding tax	1000
Ruritanian corporation tax suffered on profits after tax of 1000	
$1000 \times (20 \div 80)$	250
Profits before tax used to pay the dividend of £1000	1250
Total creditable Ruritanian taxes:	
Withholding tax	50
Ruritanian corporation tax (the underlying tax)	250
	300
Ponstantian tax computation:	
Ponstantian tax at 30% on a gross dividend of £1250	375
Deducted double tax relief:	−300
Residual Ponstantian tax liability	75
Total taxes on profits of 1250:	
Ruritanian taxes	300
Ponstantian tax	75
	375

Where a company has a branch in a foreign country the profits of that branch will usually be taxed in the foreign country under the source principle on an accruals basis. Usually, the foreign country will charge the branch profits to corporation tax. Some, but not all, countries also levy a withholding tax when the profits are repatriated to the head office country. This is known as a 'branch profits tax' and is used so that the source country collects both corporation tax and withholding tax regardless of whether the foreign investor chooses to invest via a subsidiary or via a branch.

Chapter 6 expands on the issues raised in this chapter and considers how double tax relief systems work in operational practice.

FURTHER READING

Avery Jones, J (2012) 'Avoiding Double Taxation: Credit versus Exemption – The Origins', *Bulletin for International Taxation*, February 2012, pp 67–76.

Brinker, T M and Sherman W R (2005) 'International Double Taxation: The Basics', *Journal of International Taxation*, 16.

Dickescheid, T (2004) 'Exemption v Credit Method', *International Tax and Public Finance*, 11, 721–739.

Gravelle, J G (2004) 'Issues in International Tax Policy', *National Tax Journal*, September 2004, 57, 3, p 773.

OECD (2015) *Articles 23A and 23B. Commentary on Model Tax Convention on Income and Capital*, July 2010 Condensed Version.

Weichenrieder, A (1996) 'Fighting International Tax Avoidance: The Case of Germany', *Fiscal Studies*, Vol 17, pp 37–58.

Chapter 6

Double Tax Relief in Practice

BASICS

6.1   Chapter 5 contains a broad outline of the main issues and choices in systems of double tax relief. There we discussed the two main forms of double tax relief, the credit and exemption methods at a basic level, and acknowledged the deduction method as an alternative, but a less-used method. The actual practice of double tax relief is very complicated for several reasons:

- Nearly all countries adopt hybrid systems of double tax relief. The most commonly encountered type of system uses the exemption method for income from foreign direct investment (FDI), eg branch profits or dividends from trading subsidiaries. However, because the exemption method exposes the residence country to excessive loss of revenues, many countries then employ the credit method for income classed as passive income, eg interest, certain royalties, and dividends from minority holdings.

- Each country operates its own version of exemption or credit with its own detailed rules. Countries which use the credit method do so in a manner which incorporates many variations in the way in which the foreign tax credit can be used, and the extent to which it can be used. Where the credit method is used to grant double tax relief on foreign dividends received by resident corporations, the rules tend to be particularly complex. Countries which operate progressive tax rate structures often allocate the exempt foreign income to the lower tax rate bands, the 'exemption with progression' system which was briefly outlined in Chapter 5.

- Countries will normally insist on the methods used in their domestic laws also being used by them under any DTTs which they enter into. However, sometimes differences exist, either as part of the treaty negotiation process or because, subsequent to entering into the treaty, the country changes the method(s) of double tax relief used under its domestic law. For instance, many of the UK's treaties specify the credit method for all income, whereas in practice, the exemption method would be applied to foreign dividends received by UK corporate taxpayers.

Even systems which advertise themselves as using the credit method may, in practice, have results which are closer to the exemption method. If foreign income is not taxed until repatriated, eg until a dividend from a subsidiary is paid to a resident parent company, then the indefinite deferral of such income means that it is effectively exempt. This is a particular problem faced by the US with its credit system.

This chapter contains a good deal of material on the UK tax system, because the UK's system of double tax relief for companies has been subject to considerable and ongoing revision over the past decade, making it an excellent case study of alternative systems of double tax relief. The UK introduced the exemption method for the foreign dividends of UK companies in 2009 in order to improve the competitiveness of the UK as a location for holding companies, and to ensure compliance with EU non-discrimination rules. Although the exemption can apply to all foreign dividends, regardless of whether the foreign shareholding represents foreign direct investment (FDI) or portfolio investment, there are complex anti-avoidance rules governing this area. The UK has also introduced an option for double tax relief by the exemption method for the profits of foreign branches.

WHO USES WHAT?

6.2   Of the 32 countries that submitted reports to the International Fiscal Association in 2011 (see Blanluet and Durand, 2011), 11 countries reported systems based mainly on the credit method whilst 8 reported mainly the use of the exemption method. The remaining 13 countries reported a hybrid approach. The reports generally put forward a view that the credit method was less likely to facilitate tax avoidance. However, the administrative burden (and therefore cost) was significant compared with the exemption method, yet the credit method was thought unlikely to yield higher tax revenues. There is considerable ongoing discussion in the US as to whether a system of double tax relief by exemption for foreign dividends should be adopted.[1]

Historically, the UK operated a series of complex versions of the credit method for corporation tax purposes, but since 2009 it has used an exemption (territorial) system for two important classes of foreign income earned by UK corporations, ie foreign dividends and branch profits. Other foreign income of UK companies, and other types of UK taxpayers are still granted double tax relief under the credit method.

---

1   See: *US Joint Committee on Taxation, Present Law and Background related to proposals to reform the taxation of income of multinational enterprises*, July 2014. Available at: www.jct. gov/publications.html?func=startdown&id=4656.

VARIATIONS ON THE CREDIT METHOD

6.3   Credit methods in practice are much more complicated than was depicted in Chapter 5. Countries which use the credit method each have particular rules within their domestic law as to:

●   How the foreign tax credit is to be calculated.

- Whether there are any limits on the amount of foreign tax credit in relation to the amount of domestic taxation.

- Whether credit is given merely for foreign withholding taxes, or whether it extends to relief for foreign corporation taxes on the profits used to pay dividends.

- Whether tax credits from lower tier companies can be recognized: for instance, where Company 1 in Country A owns Company 2 in Country B, which in turn owns Company 3 in Country C – if no tax is payable in Country B, and so no double tax relief is claimable there, can the tax credit arising from the tax paid in Country C be set against the tax liability in Country A?

- Whether unused foreign tax credits can be used in previous or future tax years or whether they can be used by other companies in the same corporate group as the recipient.

- Whether tax credits may be set against domestic tax liabilities on foreign income other than that which gave rise to the foreign tax credit. This is known as pooling and there are two main types. With 'onshore pooling', high foreign tax credits on some sources of overseas income can be offset against residual home country taxation on other foreign sources of income. This is the most favourable system of ordinary or normal credit for the taxpayer. Under a system of 'offshore pooling' a multinational group may route its dividends from overseas subsidiaries through an intermediate holding company, which then pays a single dividend to the ultimate parent company. If the parent country tax authority does not permit onshore pooling, this strategy achieves pooling offshore. The lack of any facility for onshore pooling can be circumvented by the parent company only having one immediate source of foreign income: a dividend from the offshore intermediate holding company. Provided the tax authority in the parent company's country recognizes the tax credits attaching to the dividends from each of the subsidiaries further down the shareholding chain, the dividend from the intermediate holding company is paid carrying a tax credit representing the average rate of tax suffered on the dividends paid by lower tier companies to the intermediate holding company. Note that to avoid additional tax liabilities the intermediate holding company would be located in a country such as the Netherlands, which operates a double tax system of exemption with participation.

- Which foreign taxes may be credited at all.

Before considering the exemption system in more detail, we first consider some examples of credit systems in operation.

Credit relief in the US

6.4   The US is one of the very few countries that continues to use a credit system of double tax relief. Citizens, resident aliens and domestic corporations of the US may credit against US income tax any 'qualified' foreign taxes paid or accrued to a foreign country. Taxpayers may choose each year between taking a credit against US tax or a deduction against US taxable income for the foreign income taxes.

The foreign tax credit is computed separately for two different categories of income. This is known as the 'separate baskets' system:

● the passive income basket: interest, certain dividends, rents and other items of investment income;

● the general basket: everything else, including some dividends from companies in which the US corporate shareholder owns more than 10 per cent of the capital. Dividends from controlled foreign companies (where US persons collectively own 50 per cent of the vote or value of the paying company and each of those US persons owns at least 10 per cent) may also fall into the general basket. To decide which basket they fall into, a 'look-through' rule is used. Broadly, if the dividend is paid by the controlled foreign company out of trading income then the dividend can be treated as active, rather than passive, income. This treatment would also apply to interest, rents and royalties received, provided they were paid to the US recipient out of trading income. Where the 50 per cent ownership rule is not met, but a US shareholder owns at least 10 per cent of the foreign company, the look-through rule can still be applied to dividends, and possibly to royalties, if certain conditions are met.

The overhead expenses of the US parent company, such as R&D, interest, administrative expenditure, which relate to each of the income categories are deducted from the foreign income before computation of the US tax which is attributable to that category of income. Then, within these categories of foreign income (passive and active), cross-crediting of foreign tax credits is permitted. This means that excess foreign tax credits on one source of foreign active income can be offset against residual US tax liability on another source of foreign active income, ie where the foreign tax credit is less than the US tax. This effectively permits averaging of foreign tax rates within the two baskets.

The rationale for separating out income in this way is that it is easier for a US firm to position the assets giving rise to investment income in a low tax country, because passive investment assets tend to be financial assets and are therefore mobile. On the other hand, income from foreign direct investment, such as dividends from manufacturing subsidiaries and branches, is likely to be positioned in the country best suited to the investment by reference to more general (non-tax) commercial factors. It is therefore likely to have suffered substantial amounts of foreign tax. Without the separate baskets, the total foreign income and total foreign tax credits would be amalgamated and, effectively, the high tax credits on the foreign direct investment income would offset the low foreign tax credits on the foreign passive investment income.

However, if any passive investment income has suffered high rates of foreign tax (for US companies, an effective rate of 35 per cent or more on the foreign income) then it is transferred across to the general basket (this is known as the 'high tax kickout'[1]).

The credit for each category is the lesser of: (1) the amount of foreign taxes paid or accrued with respect to that category; or (2) the US tax on the foreign income in that category. The following formula is used to determine the credit:

$$\frac{\text{Total taxable income within the separate category from all sources}}{\text{Total taxable income}} \times \text{US income tax} = \begin{array}{l}\text{Maximum credit} \\ \text{for that category of} \\ \text{income}\end{array}$$

The taxpayer aggregates net income and net losses within each category from all sources outside the US and calculates that category's separate foreign tax credit limitation.

A US corporation is deemed to have paid, and may claim a credit for, a portion of the foreign taxes paid or accrued by a foreign corporation in which it holds at least 10 per cent of the voting stock (first-tier corporation). This is the credit for 'underlying tax'. A domestic corporation is also deemed to have paid a portion of the taxes paid or accrued by a foreign second- through sixth-tier corporation in certain cases.

If foreign taxes paid or accrued exceed the amount that may be credited for the tax year, the excess is carried back one year and forward ten years.

A foreign levy (ie a payment required from a person by a foreign country) qualifies as a creditable foreign tax, ie one for which double tax relief will be given, only if: (1) it is a tax; and (2) its predominant character is that of an income tax in the US sense.

---

1   Tax Reform Act 1986, s 904(d)(2)(A)(iii)(III) and s 904(d)(2)(F).

Problems with the credit method

6.5   A live issue in the US in 2017 is the fact that US-based multinational groups will go to great lengths to avoid repatriation of their foreign income. Rather than have their foreign subsidiaries pay dividends to the US, profits are allowed to accumulate and recirculate outside the US. The reason given for this is usually that the US corporate tax rate of 35 per cent is higher than that levied by most other countries, so that repatriating profits to the US via dividends would result in additional tax payable for the multinational group. We will see in Chapter 19 how some of the big multinationals such as Apple Corporation avoid repatriation of profits to the US. However, the reasons for the lack of repatriation of foreign profits may be more complex than this, as discussed in the next paragraph.

There is much discussion as to whether the US ought to move to an exemption method for active income: the consensus appears to be that, rather than reducing the US tax bill for US companies with foreign income, such a change would actually increase US tax payable. For an overview of the possibilities for US international tax reform, see Kadet (2013). Intuitively, one might think that the US retains the credit method because it would collect less tax if it switched to an exemption method. However, a study by Grubert and Altshuler (2013) estimated that total US tax revenue would increase by about $1 billion if the US adopted the exemption method for foreign dividend income. This is because foreign dividends from non-portfolio holdings (ie where in excess of 10 per cent of shares in the paying company are held) are treated as active income. These dividends often carry not only withholding tax credits but also credits for the foreign corporation tax suffered on the foreign profits out of which the dividends were paid. This means that foreign dividends often carry tax credits in excess of 35 per cent, the US domestic rate. The excess foreign tax credits are then set against other foreign income in the 'active income basket', such as royalties, and so there is little or no US tax paid on the receipt of foreign royalties either. If dividends were exempted, it is highly likely that there would be some US tax to pay on foreign royalty receipts, which would only carry a foreign tax credit for foreign withholding tax, probably at a rate of no more than 10 per cent.

The US government has tried many strategies to collect tax on the foreign earnings of US-based multinationals. It is not only the potential residual US tax revenues that are at stake, but the fact that the US would like the inflow of funds so that they can be reinvested at least partially in the US: it is estimated that up to $2.1 trillion[1] of funds are being held outside the US by US-based multinationals. In the past, it has offered 'repatriation holidays' which involve allowing US shareholder companies to take dividends from their foreign subsidiaries which are then subject to a lower than usual rate of US tax, for a limited period. These have met with limited success. Possibly, one important reason for the lack of repatriation of foreign earnings is the fact that once repatriated, even at little, or no US tax costs, future earnings generated from the reinvestment of foreign earnings would likely be subject to US tax, at the 35 per cent rate. The 2004 repatriation holiday[2] gave US corporate shareholders a tax deduction equal to 85 per cent of the increase in foreign earning repatriation, an effective tax rate of 5.25 per cent, with a proportional allowance of foreign tax credits. However, despite measures to try to ensure that the money was invested in wealth-creating activities, and not merely paid to the parent companies as dividends, it proved impossible to impose restrictions on its use, and Gravelle (2015) reports that studies have found that most of the repatriated funds were used for share repurchases (the equivalent of dividend payments), acquisitions of other firms, or debt reduction. None of these uses represented increased investment, or economic stimulus, and thus the object of the repatriation holiday was not met. In any case, repatriation holidays result in reduced tax revenues for the US Government: although there might be an increase in the early days, at least some of the foreign earnings of overseas subsidiaries which are repatriated under a holiday would have been repatriated anyway, at normal tax rates. A 2014 proposal for another repatriation holiday was shelved partly because the projections were that although it would produce tax revenues of $30 billion in the first three years of operation, it would go on to lose the US Government $148 billion over the next eight years (Gravelle 2015). As with any tax amnesty, repatriation holidays also have the effect of deterring US taxpayers from repatriating foreign earnings outside a repatriation holiday in anticipation that another one will be along soon.

---

1   This estimate is probably not reliable but is often cited by pundits writing on this subject. It originates in a paper by Credit Suisse: Zion D, Gomatan R and Graziano R (2015) 'Parking A-Lot Overseas', Credit Suisse, 21 March 2015.
2   The American Jobs Creation Act of 2004 (P.L. 108–357).

Obama's 2016 budget proposals

6.6   In his February 2015 Budget for 2016, President Obama proposed a 19 per cent minimum tax on foreign earnings on an ongoing basis. Even more controversially, the Budget proposed a 14 per cent one-time tax on deemed repatriations – that is, on accumulated non-repatriated earnings of foreign affiliates of US corporate shareholders. This proposal goes hand in hand with a plan to switch from the credit method to the exemption method for foreign dividends.

Much of the estimated $2.1 trillion of unrepatriated assets is believed to be in cash (of firms studied by Credit Suisse in their 2015 report, companies accounting for $1.5 trillion out of the $2.1 trillion indicated that 45 per cent of the relevant assets were in cash).

As it would be unpalatable to impose a tax on unrepatriated assets other than cash (because such assets might well consist of productive assets such as plant and machinery which would never, in practice, be liquidated to provide repatriatable cash) the chances of this one-time tax on deemed repatriations becoming law appear slim. Gravelle (2015) advances a number of other arguments concerning the effects of tax credits and repatriations which would be made anyway, concluding that this one-time tax on deemed repatriations would be unlikely to result in any net revenue gain.

Exemption for the US?

6.7   The real problem faced by the US is not that it is losing out on tax revenues through non-repatriation of foreign earnings – indeed, in some cases, after double tax credits are given, little US tax liability remains – but that for-eign earnings are not being reinvested in the US, and are thus not contributing to the wealth of the US economy. The US Government wants foreign earnings to be remitted to, and reinvested in the US, even if it cannot effectively tax them. The credit method hampers this aim because US-based multinationals do not want to pay even a small percentage of residual US tax after foreign tax credits have been applied. Why increase your global tax liability if you do not need to? Moving to an exemption system for active income (including dividends from non-portfolio shareholdings) would remove this disincentive to repatriate. However, such a move would appear to sanction the tax planning non-repatriation practiced by US-based multinationals in the past. Thus, various plans to move to an exemption system, but to first impose a one-time tax on deemed repatriation of accumulated foreign earnings, have been put forward in the US over the last decade or so. None of these have gained any traction in the legislature. This seems to be because the proponents of the various plans produce wildly differing estimates of their costs and benefits. Additionally, changing the existing US tax code is very political, with recent government administrations not being in a position to wield sufficient political support across the Houses for US corporate tax reform (despite what appears to be a general consensus within US political corridors that reform is needed). The main difficulty though, is that none of them address the root cause of the reluctance of US-based multinationals to pay US taxes on their worldwide profits: the 35 per cent rate of corporation tax.

In the context of recent proposals to shift to a destination cash flow tax system, Fleming et al (2017) ask the question 'What should Congress do with the $2.4 trillion to $2.6 trillion of profits that US multinational corporations have earned primarily in low-tax foreign countries that have been accumulated offshore and not yet borne a US tax?'. The authors explore options for a transition solution and recommend treating foreign earning accumulations as taxed to shareholders under controlled foreign corporation (CFC) rules, effectively at 10%.

The current US administration under President Trump has just recently published a very brief plan for 'historic' tax reform which includes plans to significantly reduce the US corporate tax rate to 15%, introduce a one-time tax on trillions of dollars overseas, and a territorial tax system. Details of this plan have yet to be revealed and such significant tax reform will be a challenge again politically.

Credit relief in China

6.8   Foreign taxes may only be credited against Chinese tax on a particular source of income if the foreign tax was suffered in the same country as that in which the income arose (but not necessarily from exactly the same source within that country). The system is illustrated below:

Example 6.1

		Income	Tax rate		Tax
Taxable income from China		400	25%		100
Branch income: Country A	80		40%	32	
Interest income: Country A	75		15%	11.25	
		155			43.25

	Income	Tax rate		Tax
Country B: interest income	200	20%	40	
Country B: royalty income	125	10%	12.5	
Country B: rental income	120	5%	6	
	445			58.5
	1000			201.75

Global taxable income:	1000
Credit for Country A tax suffered is limited to	
$1000 \times 25\% \times 155/1000$	38.75
Credit for Country B tax suffered is limited to	
$1000 \times 25\% \times 445/1000$	111.25
Credit claimable:	
Country A: lesser of 38.75 or 43.25	38.75
Country B: lesser of 111.25 or 58.5	58.50
Total double tax credit	97.25
Corporation tax computation	
Global taxable income	1000
Chinese tax at 25%	250
Deduct: double tax credit	–97.25
Chinese tax payable	152.75

Source: Adapted from Gao, Ma, Zhou (2011)

Credit for underlying foreign corporation taxes is available. Unused tax credits can be carried forward for a maximum of five years. Tax credits from lower-tier companies may be claimed providing that the claimant company owns, directly or indirectly, at least 20 per cent of the company which paid the foreign tax. The 20 per cent may be calculated by looking at companies which are up to three tiers below the Chinese company: in Figure 6.1, we assume that all the companies pay at the maximum possible dividend so that the Chinese company receives a dividend from the Singapore company which is sourced from the dividend received by the Singapore company from Thailand and thus partly also from Vietnam and India. Although the Chinese company owns 40.96 per cent of the Indian company, it will not be able to claim any double tax relief in respect of Indian corporation tax suffered by the Indian company because it is in the fourth tier.

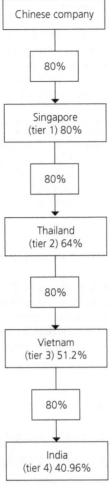

Figure 6.1

When might a double tax credit be refused?

6.9   There are a number of situations in which a taxpayer might be refused a credit for foreign tax paid which include the following:

● *Grossing-up*: It is very common for a recipient of payments subject to withholding tax (WHT) to insist on 'grossing up' so that the amount received by the recipient is the same as it would have been in the absence of WHT. This effectively passes the burden of the WHT back on to the payer. The recipient's tax authority might take the view that no foreign tax has been paid by the recipient and therefore no tax credit is due.

- *Non-recognition of the taxpayer:* Mr X, resident in Ruritania, is a partner in the firm of X & Y. Ruritania treats partnerships as transparent: it does not recognize partnerships for tax purposes, but taxes each partner individually on their share of partnership income. The partnership suffers WHT in Inistania on income earned there. The Ruritanian tax authorities might refuse a double tax credit on the basis that the taxpayer which suffered the WHT was the partnership, X & Y, rather than Mr X personally.

- *Non-recognition of the tax suffered:* Company A, resident in Ruritania, suffers WHT on the remittance of branch profits from its branch in Inistania. The WHT is levied by the local government rather than by the national government of Inistania. The DTT between Ruritania and Inistania only gives relief for national taxes, not local taxes. Company A would not be able to claim double tax relief under the treaty.

VARIATIONS ON THE EXEMPTION METHOD

6.10 As noted in Chapter 5, it is practically unheard of for a country to operate a pure exemption system. Such a system would only be feasible if there were absolutely no tax incentives to move income and capital producing assets out of the country to a lower tax jurisdiction. There are two main variations: exemption with progression and exemption with participation. Many systems incorporate both elements.

Exemption with participation

6.11 This is sometimes referred to as exemption with activity clause.

For example, Orville Ltd has the following foreign income:

Example 6.2

Table 6.1

Interest on Cayman Islands bank account	10,000
Royalties from purchased copyrights	5,000
Dividend from 100% subsidiary Wright Inc	50,000
Dividend from 9% holding Emerald Inc	50,000
Profits from US factory (US branch income)	30,000

A distinction must be made between the income to be regarded as active income (and therefore exempt) and the income to be regarded as passive income (and therefore subject to the credit method). The problem is that what is passive income for one taxpayer may be active income for another. For many companies, interest on a Cayman Islands bank account would be passive income but for an international bank it may well be considered as trading (active) income. The royalty income is probably passive income. The dividend from Wright Inc might be either passive or active income, depending on the activities of Wright Inc. If it is a manufacturing company with no investment income then the dividend would be considered active income. However, if all Wright Inc's income was from portfolio dividends (passive income) then the dividend paid by Wright Inc would probably also be considered passive income. Whether the dividend from Emerald Inc is considered passive or active would depend on the make-up of Emerald Inc's own income or there might be a minimum shareholding imposed by the tax authority in Orville's country which Orville Ltd needs to attain before the dividend could be considered active income. Typically, exemption systems set the bar at a 10 per cent shareholding. Finally, the profits from the US factory would almost certainly be regarded as active income and therefore exempt. We must conclude that any exemption system other than a pure exemption system is going to be susceptible to income characterization disputes.

Exemption with progression

6.12

Example 6.3

Jangles Inc is tax resident in Inistania which operates a double tax system of exemption with progression. The corporation tax rates in Inistania are:

Table 6.2 Inistanian corporation tax rates

Profits 0–50,000	10%
Profits 50,000–200,000	20%
Profits 200,000+	25%

Jangles Inc has the following income for the year:

Inistanian trading income	150,000
Dividends from 100% subsidiary in Ruritania: gross amount	70,000
(Ruritanian tax was 30,000)	220,000

Table 6.3 Liability of Jangles Inc to Inistanian tax

On Ruritanian dividend	nil	
On Inistanian trading income:		
At 10%:	nil	
At 20%: (200,000–70,000)	130,000	26,000
At 30%	20,000	6,000
Total	150,000	32,000

Thus the Ruritanian dividend has not been taxed but it has 'used up' all of the 10 per cent rate band and has pushed 20,000 of the Inistanian income into the 30 per cent bracket. The value of double tax relief under exemption with progression is thus limited.

EXEMPTION METHOD IN PRACTICE

6.13   The exemption method is used by countries which are said to operate a 'territorial' system of taxation. Such systems are found in Hong Kong, the Netherlands, France and Belgium. Germany operates the exemption principle in its double tax treaties. The following extract from the Germany–India Double Tax Treaty (DTT) provides a good example of the elements which often appear in an exemption method. German domestic law provides for the exemption method to be used but where a country, such as Germany, has an extensive network of double tax treaties, the domestic law will not be used in many cases. The precise combination of exemption and credit that a country will use in dealings with another country are set out in the DTT with that other country. Double tax treaties are considered in Chapter 7 but a key point to note at this stage is that a tax treaty can only improve a taxpayer's position, not make it worse. Thus, if German domestic law produces a better result for the taxpayer than the tax treaty, domestic law would apply. The language of tax treaties is often difficult for the lay person to follow and so each clause is analysed (in italics).

'Extract from Article 23 Germany–India Double Tax Treaty of 19 June 1995:

'Relief from double taxation

1.   Tax shall be determined in the case of a resident of the Federal Republic of Germany[1] as follows:

   (a)   Unless foreign tax credit is to be allowed under subparagraph (b), there shall be exempted from German tax any item of income arising in the Republic of India and any item of capital situated within the Republic of India, which, according to this Agreement, may be taxed in the Republic of India. The Federal Republic of Germany, however, retains the right to take into account in the determination of its rate of tax the items of income and capital so exempted.

   [Germany uses the exemption method for income which India may tax but the credit method will apply to some items. Germany will use exemption with progression.]

   In the case of dividends exemption shall apply only to such dividends as are paid to a company (not including partnerships) being a resident of the Federal Republic of Germany by a company being a resident of the Republic of India at least 10 per cent of the capital of which is owned directly by the German company.

There shall be exempted from taxes on capital any sharehold-ing the dividends of which are exempted or, if paid, would be exempted, according to the immediately foregoing sentence.

[Only certain dividends are exempt: these are dividends paid to a company which owns at least 10% of the capital of the German pay-ing company. Such shareholdings also enjoy exemption from German taxes on capital.]

    (b)   Subject to the provisions of German tax law regarding credit for foreign tax, there shall be allowed as a credit against German tax payable in respect of the following items of income arising in the Republic of India and the items of capital situated there the Indian tax paid under the laws of the Republic of India and in accordance with this Agree-ment on:

[There now follows a list of items to which the credit method will be applied:]

      (i)   dividends not dealt with in sub-paragraph (a);

The credit method is applied to dividends where the shareholder owns less than 10% of the paying company.

      (ii)   interest;

      (iii)   royalties and fees for technical services;

The credit method is used for these.

      (iv)   income in the meaning of paragraph 4 of Article 13;

The credit method is used for certain capital gains.

      (v)   directors' fees;

      (vi)   income of artistes and sportspersons;

      (vii)   income taxes and periodic taxes on capital.

The credit method is used for these.

    (c)   For the purpose of credit referred to in letter (ii) of sub-paragraph (b) the Indian tax shall be deemed to be 10 per cent of the gross amount of the interest, if the Indian tax is reduced to a lower rate or totally waived according to domestic law, irrespective of the amount of tax actually paid.

[Because India is a developing country, Germany has agreed to give a credit which assumes Indian withholding tax on interest paid to German residents was 10% minimum, even if the actual rate paid was lower. This is an example of 'tax sparing'.]

    (d)   The provisions of sub-paragraph (c) shall apply for the first 12 fiscal years for which this Agreement is effective.

[This clause puts a time limit on the interest tax credit concession.]

(e) Notwithstanding the provisions of sub-paragraph (a) items of income dealt with in Articles 7 and 10 and gains derived from the alienation of the business property of a permanent establishment as well as the items of capital underlying such income shall be exempted from German tax only if the resident of the Federal Republic of Germany can prove that the receipts of the permanent establishment or company are derived exclusively or almost exclusively from active operations.

In the case of items of income dealt with in Article 10 and the items of capital underlying such income the exemption shall apply even if the dividends are derived from holdings in other companies being residents of the Republic of India which carry on active operations and in which the company which last made a distribution has a holding of more than 25 per cent.

Active operations are the following: producing or selling goods or merchandise, giving technical advice or rendering engineering services, or doing banking or insurance business, within the Republic of India. If this is not proved, only the credit procedure as per sub-paragraph (b) shall apply.'

[This part contains a specific "activity clause": the exemption method will not apply to certain income and gains unless they derive exclusively or almost exclusively from "active operation", meaning trading rather than investment. If the clause applies, the credit method will be used instead. It applies to income from a permanent establishment (broadly speaking, a branch: see Chapter 9), dividends, capital gains on the alienation of the business property of a permanent establishment and items of capital underlying such income.

The exemption method will also apply to dividends from Indian holding companies where lower-tier companies are carrying on active operations and where the stake of the holding company in the active company is at least 25%. "Active operations" are defined as producing or selling goods, giving technical advice or rendering engineering services or doing banking or insurance business within India. The purpose of this clause is to prevent German residents taking unfair advantage of the exemption method to site investments in low-tax countries. In the past, Germany has suffered from treaty partner countries lowering their taxes substantially (eg Ireland, via the Irish Financial Services Centre special tax rates) so that German residents enjoyed very low taxes on earnings from substantial shareholdings in the treaty partner country and complete exemption from tax on the dividends in Germany. In the Irish example, Germany was forced to alter its domestic law and override the treaty provisions, which is technically illegal in international law.]

This treaty also contains some provisions which allow Germany to apply the credit method rather than exemption in certain circumstances. Broadly, where Germany and India each insist on a different characterization of the same income or insist on attributing it to different persons (eg to a partnership as a taxable entity or to an individual partner), and the mutual agreement procedure set out in the treaty for the resolution of disputes has been exhausted, Germany will apply the credit method if the different characterizations/attributions of the income would give rise either to double taxation or to no taxation at all. It is more likely that this provision would be used in the case of no taxation in India. Germany reserves the right to specify items of income to which this rule will be applied and must notify India through diplomatic channels. If it does so, then India may re-characterize the income so as to achieve consistency with the German characterization.

Under the terms of this particular DTT, Germany will use a combination of exemption and credit methods. It will use both exemption with progression and exemption with activity clause. There is a general presumption that a dividend from a holding of 10 per cent or more in the Indian paying company is active income.

---

1   Note that this treaty now applies to the former German Democratic Republic (which was also known as East Germany).

FROM CREDIT TO EXEMPTION METHOD: JAPAN

6.14   As at 2015, Japan has a corporation tax rate of 25.5 per cent and corporations are also subject to enterprise and municipal taxes, bringing their total rate of tax up to about 36 per cent. The Japanese Government is keen that multinationals should repatriate their foreign earnings to Japan to assist economic growth. Japan changed to the exemption method for foreign dividends in 2009. Dividends from foreign subsidiaries are 95 per cent exempt from Japanese tax provided the shareholder company holds at least 25 per cent of the overseas company. However, capital gains on the sale of shares are still taxed. Japan retains the credit method for all other types of income. Although considered to be largely successful, Japan reduced its national corporation tax rate in April 2015 to 23.9 per cent, in April 2016 to 23.4 per cent, and the rate is scheduled to be reduced to 23.2 per cent from April 2018. Problems have also arisen with the exemption method as it appears that some dividends being paid to Japanese parent companies are tax deductible in the subsidiary's country, leading to double non-taxation of profits. There are plans to remove the exemption for such dividends, in line with the OECD's recommendations under BEPS Action 2 (see Chapter 11).

FROM CREDIT TO EXEMPTION METHOD – THE 2009 UK TAX REFORMS

6.15   Between 2000 and 2009 the UK operated a highly complex variant of the credit method. The Finance Act 2009 introduced a hybrid system of exemption and credit. This move was prompted partly by the incompatibility with the previous UK double tax relief system, and the UK's obligations as a Member State of the EU (see Chapter 20). The objection at the EU level to the UK's former system was that dividends received by UK companies from EU companies were treated less favourably for UK tax purposes than dividends from UK companies.

The move to the partial adoption of the exemption method was a major reform and in the following sections, the reasons for the reform are considered and the partial exemption system is outlined.

Background: the FII case[1]

6.16   The facts of this landmark case were concerned primarily with the system of taxation of dividends and subsequent payment of corporation tax which was operated by the UK up to 1999 (advance corporation tax). The principles established in the case are directly relevant to the subsequent UK system of taxation of dividends and the case prompted a complete overhaul of the UK's system of double tax relief of the foreign profits of companies. Broadly speaking, the system which operated in the UK prior to 1999, and the system which replaced it, both treated dividends received by UK companies from other UK companies more favourably for tax purposes than dividends received from foreign companies. The UK, under its domestic law, until 2009, permitted foreign tax paid on profits used to pay dividends (ie underlying tax) to be credited against UK corporation tax on the dividends where the recipient company held at least 10 per cent of the capital of the paying company. However, where less than 10 per cent of the paying company was held, only foreign withholding tax could be claimed as a double tax credit, usually leaving a significant liability to UK corporation tax on the dividend. In contrast, dividends received by a UK company from another UK company did not suffer any UK corporation tax in the hands of the recipient company. As explained in more detail in Chapter 20, one of the rules with which Member States of the EU must comply is that a person should not be disadvantaged by investing or operating in one EU Member State as opposed to another (an application of the so-called 'freedom of establishment' principle). In the *FII* case, a group of UK corporate taxpayers complained that they were disadvantaged by receiving dividends from payers resident in other EU Member States rather than from UK payers.

By the time the case was heard, the worst of this disadvantage had passed with the demise of the advance corporation tax system (under which amounts of corporation tax were payable whenever a dividend was paid, irrespective of whether there were sufficient taxable profits to give rise to such a liability) and the convergence of rates of corporation tax throughout the EU. In practice, by the mid-2000s, a UK company receiving a dividend from a paying company elsewhere in the EU in which it held a stake of at least 10 per cent was quite unlikely to have any liability to UK tax. The combination of the tax credit for both withholding tax and underlying foreign corporation tax and the fact that the UK rate of corporation tax was roughly on a par with effective rates in EU Member States meant that the total foreign tax credit (withholding tax and underlying corporation tax) usually equalled or exceeded the UK tax liability. The Court of Justice of the EU (the CJEU) held that a system of double tax relief which might in *theory* discriminate against dividends received from EU paying companies but which *in practice* did not, was not a breach of the UK's obligations as an EU Member State. However, where the UK recipient company owned less than 10 per cent in the paying company, the UK's system for granting double tax relief in respect of dividends paid to UK companies by EU companies was in breach of EU obligations, as the tax credit for foreign withholding tax only was usually lower than the UK liability, leaving UK tax payable.

---

1   C-446/04 *Test Claimants in the FII Group Litigation v IRC* case [2007] STC 326.

Anti-tax haven complication

6.17   The UK faced another problem apart from this CJEU decision: the old system of double tax relief by credit contained an important mechanism to protect the UK from the misuse of tax havens by UK companies. This is explained in the 'Further study' section of this chapter. Around the same time as the *FII* case, the UK's anti-tax haven legislation in general came under attack from the CJEU (see Chapter 20 for more details). It became clear that the UK was going to have to revise both its system of double tax relief for companies *and* its system of protecting against abuse of tax havens by UK companies. Attempting such a wide-ranging reform of the taxation of foreign income resulted in a drawn out process.

Credit method as a disincentive to locate a holding company in the UK

6.18   The drawbacks of the UK's credit method, particularly for UK companies, were typical of the drawbacks of credit systems of double tax relief in general. The credit method, as it applied to UK companies until 2009, was a highly complex system. Often, highly complex calculations had to be carried out, at considerable expense, only for it to become apparent that there was no UK tax liability on the foreign income. Tax liabilities of UK holding companies could not be finalized until the double tax computations had been completed. To complete the double tax computation, the final amounts of foreign taxes on the foreign income had to be known, so that UK holding companies were at the mercy of foreign tax administrations, some of which took many years to agree tax liabilities. Some, but not all, UK holding companies were able to enter into agreements with HMRC to use provisional amounts of foreign taxes in the calculations. These factors meant that there was a high level of uncertainty for UK holding companies as to what the final amount of the UK tax liabilities would be. Anecdotal evidence suggests that multinationals based in the UK had to spend large amounts on tax planning and implementing and maintaining complex group structures in order to minimize their UK tax liabilities on foreign income. Uncertainty in a tax regime is a very off-putting characteristic for multinationals when considering the location of their holding companies. The complexity and uncertainty inherent in the UK's credit method of double tax relief, combined with the uncertainty created by the need to reform the system of both double tax relief and anti-tax haven legislation led, in part, to the high-profile departure of a number of multinational holding companies from the UK during 2008.[1]

All these disadvantages had to be set alongside the fact that the UK's corporation tax rates were, by 2008, on a par with those in most other developed countries, apart from the US. This meant that the foreign tax credits available on foreign dividends (for withholding taxes and for underlying foreign corporation taxes) usually resulted in little, or no residual UK corporation tax on foreign dividends. Hence, the move to exemption for foreign dividends was, broadly speaking, revenue neutral.

The 'Further study' section of this chapter contains more detail of how the UK rules operate in relation to dividends and foreign branches.

---

1   See, for example, Smith D, O'Connell, D and Day, I 'Corporate bale out' [sic], *The Sunday Times*, 31 August 2008, p 5.

FURTHER READING

Altshuler, R, Shay, S, Toder, E (2015) 'Lessons the United States can Learn from Other Countries' Territorial Systems for Taxing Income of Multinational Corporations' Tax Policy Center, Urban Institute and Brookings Institution. Available at: www.taxpolicycenter.org/publications/lessons-united-states-can-learn-other-countries-territorial-systems-taxing-income/full.

Avi-Yonah, Reuven S (2008), 'Back to the Future? The Potential Revival of Territoriality' (19 July 2008). University of Michigan Law & Economics, Olin Working Paper No 08-012; University of Michigan Public Law Working Paper No 114. Available at SSRN: http://ssrn.com/abstract=1185423.

Blanluet, G and Durand, P J (2011) 'General Report' in *Cahiers de Droit Fiscal International Vol 96b Key Practical Issues to Eliminate Double Taxation of Business Income*, International Fiscal Association.

Fleming, C C, Jr , Peroni, R J, Shay, S E (2008) 'Some Perspectives from the United State on the Worldwide Taxation v. Territorial Taxation Debate', 3, *Journal of the Australasian Teachers Association*, 35. Available at: www.business.unsw.edu.au/About.../1_JATTA_vol3_no2.pdf.

Fleming, C C, Jr , Peroni, R J, Shay, S E (2009) 'Worse than Exemption', 59, *Emory Law Journal*, 79, 2009–2010.

Fleming, J C, Peroni, R J, Shay, S E (2016) 'Two Cheers for the Foreign Tax Credit, Even in the BEPS Era', *Tulane Law Review* 91(1).

Fleming, J C, Peroni, R J, Shay, S E (2017) 'Getting from Here to There: The Transition Tax Issue', *Tax Notes*, March 27, 2017, p 69.

Gao, S, Hongxiang, M, Huaishi, Z (2011) 'China' in *Cahiers de Droit Fiscal International Vol 96b Key Practical Issues to Eliminate Double Taxation of Business Income*, International Fiscal Association.

Graetz, M J, Oosterhuis, P W (2001) 'Structuring an Exemption System for Foreign Income of US Corporations', *National Tax Journal*, Vol LIV, No 4.

Gravelle, J (2015) 'Statement of Jane G Gravelle, Senior Specialist in Economic Policy, Congressional Research Service, before the House Ways and Means Committee on Select Revenue Measures. United States House of Representatives', June 24 2015 on 'Repatriation of Earnings as a Source of Funding for the Highway Trust Fund'. Available at: https://waysand-means.house.gov/wp-content/uploads/2015/06/2015-06–24-SRM-Gravelle-Testimony.pdf.

Grubert, H (2009) 'MNC Dividends, Tax Holidays and the Burden of the Repatriation Tax: Recent Evidence'. Available at: www.sbs.ox.ac.uk/centres/tax/Documents/Grubert%20mondayMNC%20Dividends%20and%20the%20Burden%20of%20the%20Repatriation%20Tax-2009.doc.

HMRC (2001) *Large Business Taxation – The Government's Strategy and Corporate Tax Reforms*, HMRC Consultation Document, Oct 2001.

HMRC (2008) (2) *Technical Note*. Available at: www.hm-treasury.gov.uk/d/foreignprofits_technicalnote210708.pdf.

Joint Committee on Taxation (US Senate). *Economic Efficiency and Structural Analysis of Alternative US Tax Policies for Foreign Direct Investment.* Senate Committee on Finance, 26 June 2008. Available at: www.house.gov/jct/x-55-08.pdf.

Kadet, J M (2012) 'U.S. International Tax Reform: What Form Should it Take?', *Tax Notes International*, January 2012.

Kofler, G (2012) 'Indirect Credit versus Exemption: Double Taxation Relief for Intercompany Distributions', 66, *Bulletin for International Taxation*, 2.

Lokken, L, Kitamura, Y (2010) 'A Comparative Study of Double Tax Relief in the United States and Japan', *Northwestern Journal of International Law and Business*, Summer 2010, Vol 30, Issue 3, pp 621–646.

Ludicke, J (2010) 'Exemption and Tax Credit in German Tax Treaties – Policy and Reality', *Bulletin for International Taxation*, 2010, Vol 64, No 12.

Matheson, T, Perry, V, Veung, C (2013) 'Territorial vs. Worldwide Corporate Taxation: Implications for Developing Countries', IMF Working Paper WP/13/205. Available at: www.imf.org/external/pubs/ft/wp/2013/wp13205.pdf.

Munro, A (2009) 'Staking the Territory', *Tax Journal*, Issue 963, p 9, 12 January 2009.

Pintaro, A (2010) 'Should the United States Exempt Foreign-Source Income Similar to Foreign Business Partners?', *Illinois Business Law Journal*, 5 April 2010. Available at: www.law.illinois.edu/bljournal/post/2010/04/05/

Should-the-United-States-Exempt-Foreign-Source-Income-Similar-to-Foreign-Business-Partners.aspx.

Sanger, S (2009) 'Foreign Profits Reform – a "Sliding Doors" Moment?', *Tax Journal*, Issue 995, p 5, 7 September 2009.

Simons Direct Tax Service, Binder 9, International, Division F2, LexisNexis Butterworths, 2006.

Sotos, D J, Glunt, P J, Willis, B M (2012) 'The Separate Limitation of Code Sec 914(d)(6)', 38, *International Tax Journal*, 27.

US Joint Committee on Taxation, *Present Law and Background related to proposals to reform the taxation of income of multinational enterprises*, July 2014. Available at: www.jct.gov/publications.html?func=startdown&id=4656.

Walker, L (2010) 'Analysis – Case Study – UK Holding Company: Pros and Cons', 1 November 2010, *Tax Journal*, Issue 1051, p 22.

FURTHER STUDY

UK EXEMPTION SYSTEM FOR FOREIGN DIVIDENDS

6.19   Although focusing on the UK system, this section provides an overview of a system of exemption for foreign dividends, and illustrates the type of issues faced by any country when operating a system of double tax relief by exemption for foreign dividends. In this first part, the basics are covered; the second part (para **6.23** onwards) goes into additional detail.

To address the problems associated with the credit system and to make the UK a more attractive location for foreign businesses, the most important source of foreign income by far for UK companies – dividends – is normally exempt from UK tax. The UK introduced its exemption system in the Finance Act 2009 (s 34 and Sch 14), with effect from 1 July 2009. Most dividends received by UK companies from both UK and foreign paying companies are exempt:

1   Distributions where the recipient controls more than 50 per cent of the paying company. (The definition of 'distributions' is considered at para **6.21** below.)

2   Distributions on non-redeemable ordinary shares, even where the recipient does not control the payer.

3   Distributions from portfolio holdings: of 10 per cent or less.

4   Dividends (as opposed to distributions), the payment of which had no significant tax-reduction motives.

5   Dividends (as opposed to distributions) in respect of shares accounted for as liabilities, eg certain redeemable preference shares.

Dividends will often fall into more than one of these categories. Dividends not exempt will generally attract double tax relief under the credit method. The most common categories of dividends not exempt are:

- certain dividends paid by companies located in tax havens;

- dividends which are tax deductible for the payer;

- dividends, the payment of which had the main purpose of securing a tax advantage (a number of schemes which it is anticipated might be used by taxpayers are set out);

- interest payments treated as dividends because the amount or terms on which the interest is paid are not at arm's length.[1]

Many commentators noted that this was a wide-ranging and generous reform, requiring no minimum shareholding in order to benefit from the exemption. The UK government's own estimates put the cost of the reform at around £600 million, which takes into account not only the loss of tax revenue from foreign dividends but also the effect of tax planning which UK-based multinationals would be likely to enter into.[2] It might be observed that the UK's neighbour, the Irish Republic, played a large part in prompting and accelerating this reform through its long-term adoption of a 12.5 per cent corporation tax rate and its reputation for a stable and low compliance cost corporation tax system with (in 2009) no anti-tax haven rules. It might also be noted that the reform was designed to enable the UK to compete effectively with Luxembourg as a location for international holding companies as, like Luxembourg, the UK now has a comprehensive participation regime for large and medium-sized companies, covering both the capital gains on the sale of shares (the 'substantial shareholding exemption') and the dividends.

Note that exemption only applies to dividends received by companies and, in certain circumstances, to profits of foreign branches. The credit method applies to other forms of foreign income (eg foreign interest, royalties and capital gains).

---

1   ICTA 1988, s 209(2)(d), rewritten as Clause 946E of the Draft Corporation Tax Bill, brought into the Corporation Tax Act 2009 via the Finance Bill 2009.
2   See HMRC 2008 (1) Technical Note of July 2008.

Rules for small companies[1]

6.20   Distributions received by small companies may also be exempt but different rules apply. The main difference between the main regime and the regime for small companies is that distributions received by small companies can only be exempt if received from a payer resident in a country with which the UK has a full DTT. In particular, the DTT must include a non-discrimination clause which follows Article 24 of the OECD Model Tax Convention. Thus, a small company will not be exempt from UK tax on dividends received from, for example, the Channel Islands. Apart from this requirement, three other basic rules must be satisfied:

- The distribution must fall into at least one of the five classes of exempt distribution and must not be caught by any of the anti-avoidance rules which attach to the dividend exemption regime.

- The dividend must not be a payment that would be treated as interest (under s 209(d) or (e)).

- No person (the payer or otherwise) must have obtained a tax deduction in respect of, or by reference to, the dividend.

Small companies are defined in s 931S as one with a staff headcount of less than 50 people and either turnover not exceeding €10 million or a balance sheet total not exceeding €10 million.[2]

Dividends in respect of which exemption is granted, whether UK or foreign, are not treated as franked investment income and therefore do not enter into calculations establishing whether or not a company qualifies for the reduced rate of corporation tax for small companies.

---

1   CTA 2009, ss 931B and 931C.
2   Note that this is the EU definition of a small enterprise as per Commission Recommendation 2003/361/EC of 6 May 2003.

Exempt payments

6.21   Whilst the most common form of exempt payment will be periodic dividends paid out of profits, the exemption is for the whole class of payments known in the UK as 'distributions'[1] but with some exceptions. Thus it is necessary to be aware of the types of payment which are classified as distributions and to which of these types the exemption from UK tax will apply. The following types of payment are distributions:

1   dividends (whether paid in cash or in other forms of asset) paid out of either income or capital profits (such as profits on the sale of a fixed asset);

2   any other distribution made out of the assets of the company in respect of shares, other than amounts representing repayment of capital or amounts equal to new consideration received by the company from the shareholder;

3   the issue of redeemable share capital and securities for no consideration;

4   interest paid which exceeds a commercial rate of return;

5   interest on certain specified securities;[2]

6   transfers of assets by subsidiaries to a parent at below market value, but it does not apply to transfers by subsidiary companies to parent companies or to transfers between UK companies which are not connected, neither of which is a 51 per cent subsidiary of a non-resident company;

7   bonus issues of shares or securities following a repayment of share capital; and

8   benefits in kind paid to shareholders in 'close' companies (mainly benefits paid to shareholders who are not employees in family companies).

Out of this list, the types of distribution which do not enjoy the exemption from UK tax are those which are considered to represent payments of interest (types 4 and 5 above). The reason for characterizing these payments as distributions in the first place was to ensure that they are not tax deductible for the payer (interest is deductible whereas distributions are not). However, now that distributions are largely exempt, there would be a tax advantage in a foreign subsidiary overpaying interest to a UK parent because the foreign subsidiary might get a deduction for the interest, reducing its overseas tax liability, whilst the UK parent would receive the interest tax-free under the dividend exemption. This is why the dividend exemption does not extend to these payments.

Distributions on a winding up of a company are treated as a disposal of the shares rather than an income distribution and thus do not enjoy the exemption.

Capital distributions, which include repayment of share capital up to the amount originally invested, distributions in the course of a liquidation and payments on the purchase by a company of its own shares are treated as exempt. A measure of certainty as to whether the exemption will definitely apply to a particular payment from a foreign company may be obtained by applying to HMRC for a clearance.

Further detail on the UK exemption system is given in the 'Further study' section of this chapter.

---

1   The various types are listed in CTA 2010, s 1000.

2   These types of securities are, broadly, convertible securities, those where the interest is dependent on the results of the company, those which are linked to shares in the company and those classed as equity notes. Equity notes are securities with no redemption date or with a redemption period in excess of 50 years.

UK exemption for profits of foreign branches

6.22   Having introduced exemption for foreign dividends, but not for returns on other forms of foreign investment, the Finance Act 2009 reforms left UK companies in the position that, if they invested abroad via a subsidiary, the return on the investment (ie the dividends) would be exempt from tax in the UK. However, if they decided to invest via a foreign branch, the branch profits were still liable to UK corporation tax on an arising basis (ie in the year they were earned), irrespective of whether they were remitted back to the UK. A fundamental concept in tax systems is that taxes should be neutral: they should not unduly influence business decisions. The discrepancy in the treatment of foreign dividends and foreign branch profits has been addressed in the Finance Act 2011 by the introduction of a system of exemption for foreign branch profits.

As with dividends, the UK government is anxious that businesses do not gain any unfair tax advantages. A big difference between having a foreign subsidiary and a foreign branch is that, if a foreign subsidiary makes losses, those losses cannot usually be offset against any UK taxable profits. However, because a branch is part of the UK company, branch losses can be used to reduce taxable profits of the UK company. For instance, if a branch makes losses in the early years of its existence, those losses would be used to reduce the taxable profits of the UK company, or other companies in its UK corporate group. HMRC would be content with this situation because, when the branch moves into profit, those profits would be liable to tax in the UK and the branch losses made in previous years would not be available to reduce them, as the losses had previously been offset against other profits of the UK company/UK corporate group. However, if foreign branch profits are exempt from taxation in the UK, HMRC would be in a position of giving relief for branch losses but unable to tax branch profits. One solution to this would be to say that foreign branch profits are exempt and foreign branch losses may not be set against any UK taxable profits. This would be very unpopular with UK companies, as the ability to offset foreign branch losses against UK profits in the early years of the foreign branch operation may make the difference between the foreign branch being a viable business proposition or not. The system for the granting of double tax relief by exemption for profits of foreign branches of UK companies is therefore as follows:

- The UK company must make an election if it wishes foreign branch profits to be exempt. If no election is made, double tax relief for branch profits continues to be granted using the credit method.

- The election must apply to all the company's foreign branches, including any which are set up in the future.

- The election is irrevocable: you cannot revert to the credit method if your branches start to make losses.

- The election must be made in the accounting period before the period in which it is to take effect. This means that companies cannot adopt a 'wait and see' approach, making the election only if the branch turns out to be profitable.

- If the foreign branch made any losses in the six years prior to making the election and UK tax relief was granted for those losses, then even after the election takes effect, foreign branch profits continue to be taxed in the UK until the amount so taxed is equal to the amount of the branch losses relieved in the UK in the previous six years.

- If the branch made large losses in the six years prior to making the election (more than £50 million) and UK tax relief was given for the losses, then the rule is that branch profits after the election continue to be taxable in the UK up to an amount which equals:

  — the losses for which UK tax relief was given, plus

  — any losses incurred after the exemption regime took effect, for which no UK relief was given.

These rules also apply to non-UK profits of non-UK companies – eg in situations where a non-UK company has a foreign branch in the UK and the UK branch has operations in a third country, the profits of which are attributable to the UK branch.

Once again, a key point to note is that the exemption system is rarely simple in practice.

The UK exemption for foreign dividends received by companies: additional detail

6.23   The categories of exempt dividends are analysed below. Remember that a payment may fall into more than one of these categories.

Distributions from controlled companies[1]

6.24   A controlled company is one where the parent owns more than 50 per cent. The term has a particular meaning in connection with companies resident in countries where the tax is significantly less than in the UK. Unless such companies can be shown to be established there for non-tax purposes, or unless their profits are small, the UK parent is taxed on its proportionate share of the foreign company's profits, whether or not a dividend is paid (see Chapter 15 for more detail on this). The controlled foreign companies legislation thus acts so as to tax the foreign profits as if they had been earned by the UK parent, or to leave them out of UK tax if the foreign subsidiary is established other than for the purpose of saving tax. If the parent company in the UK has suffered a charge under the controlled foreign companies (CFC) legislation in respect of the foreign subsidiary's profits, then it would be double taxation to tax those profits again when they are sent to the UK in the form of a dividend. If the foreign company is exempt from the legislation because it is set up for a non-tax purpose, there is no reason to deny the new foreign dividend exemption when a dividend is paid to the UK. Either way, dividends from controlled foreign companies ought to be exempt. Under the previous system of double tax relief by credit, the UK permitted an additional foreign tax credit against dividends from controlled foreign companies based on any UK tax charge the parent had previously suffered on those profits under the CFC legislation.

---

1   CTA 2009, s 931E.

Distributions in respect of non-redeemable ordinary shares[1]

6.25   This is the main category. Ordinary shares are defined as shares carrying no present or future preferential rights as to dividends or the company's assets on a winding-up compared with other shares issued by the company.[2] Preferential rights are not defined but the guidance issued by HMRC simply indicates that preferential rights will be present where a shareholder's entitlement to payments exceeds that of other shareholders. Care will need to be taken where a company has more than one class of shares. Note that there is no reference in the definition to voting rights, which usually have to be considered in identifying shares which are not ordinary shares.

Although the concept of ordinary shares may seem simple enough in the context of UK companies, it is important to appreciate that different countries have different rules and customs as to the types of shares which a company might issue, if indeed a company issues shares at all. Identifying a non-preferential ordinary share in a UK company might be easy but identifying this type of share in a foreign company might not be. In practice, it is going to be essential to correctly characterize the types of shareholdings in respect of which dividends are paid to a UK corporate shareholder. HMRC mention the example of a Delaware limited liability company which would not issue share capital, but rather would issue certificates of interest in the company. Such certificates, depending on their terms, might be considered analogous to ordinary shares. Other common types of company without share capital are the German GmbH and the Italian SRL which have quotas rather than shares. Because of the practical difficulty UK companies are likely to face in determining whether their investments in foreign companies may be treated as if they are ordinary shares, HMRC have agreed to offer advice, under the terms of HMRC Code of Practice 10. Under this Code of Practice, they have agreed, inter alia, to advise on the interpretation of legislation passed in the last four Finance Acts.[3]

---

1   CTA 2009, s 931F.
2   CTA 2009, s 931U.
3   HMRC has also indicated that Customs Business Brief 54/07 may be used to determine whether or not the entity paying a dividend has ordinary share capital.

Distributions in respect of portfolio holdings (holdings of less than 10 per cent)

6.26   In accordance with the decision of the ECJ in the *FII GLO* case, that it is not in accordance with the TFEU that dividends paid by UK companies to other UK companies should be exempt from tax whilst those from companies within the EEA were not, the dividend exemption extends to dividends paid in respect of shareholdings irrespective of size. The exemption in respect of portfolio dividends extends to dividends paid not just on ordinary shares but on any type of share. The main requirement is that the UK shareholding holds less than 10 per cent of the share capital of the same class as the shares in respect of which the distribution is made.

It is perfectly possible for a UK company to own both ordinary shares and preference shares in an overseas company. A UK company owning 40 per cent of the ordinary share capital and, say, 6 per cent of its preference share capital would be entitled to exemption on dividends from both shareholdings. The 10 per cent threshold is measured only by reference to the class of shares out of which the dividend is paid, so for the purpose of this leg of the exemption, the 40 per cent holding in the ordinary share capital does not matter: the preference dividend would be exempt because less than 10 per cent of the preference shares are owned.

Dividends derived from transactions not designed to reduce tax[1]

6.27   This is another very wide class of exempt dividends, into which most foreign dividends (dividends only, not other types of distribution) will fall: so long as the profits out of which the dividend was paid do not arise due to transactions designed to avoid tax in the UK, they will be exempt.

To be exempt under this heading, a dividend must be paid in respect of 'relevant profits'. These are defined as any profits available for distribution at the time that the dividend is paid, other than profits that reflect the results of a transaction(s) which achieved a reduction in UK tax and this was the purpose (or one of the main purposes) of the transaction(s). To interpret this class of exempt dividends, we need to be able to interpret this 'purpose' test. The wording makes it clear that it is only reductions in UK tax, as opposed to foreign taxes, which are important. The 'purpose' test is similar to the motive already in use for determining whether or not a UK company should be exempt from an apportionment of the profits of a controlled foreign company, where none of the other available exemptions apply.[2] Applying that test would indicate that the 'purpose' test would be failed even if the company receiving the dividend did not itself enjoy a reduction in UK tax. Neither is it necessary that the reduction in taxes be enjoyed in the same period as that in which the dividend is paid.

Example 6.4

UK Plc sells assets liable to capital gains tax at an arm's-length price to a foreign subsidiary and makes a gain, which is covered by capital losses brought forward. The foreign subsidiary, resident in a territory which would not tax the gain, sells the property to another group company, which obtains a tax deduction for the expenditure. The gain is then paid to the UK in the form of a dividend.

---

1   CTA 2009, s 931H.
2   CTA 2010, s 1064.

Dividends in respect of shares accounted for as liabilities[1]

6.28   This last head of exemption briefly states that a dividend will be exempt if paid in respect of a share which would normally be treated as a loan, but is not so treated merely because the investing company does not hold the share for a so-called 'unallowable purpose'. 'Unallowable purpose' is just one of six conditions, all of which must be met for a share to be treated as a loan. In practical terms, this exemption will apply to shareholdings which are accounted for under GAAP as a loan, and on which the return is not reclassified for tax purposes as disguised interest only by virtue of the fact that it was not set up for an unallowable purpose (ie to obtain a tax advantage). An example would be a redeemable preference share, which is a type of security commonly issued for its commercial rather than for its tax advantages.

---

1   CTA 2009, s 931I.

Anti-avoidance rules for the dividend exemption

6.29   Even if a dividend falls under one of more of these five heads of exemption, it will still not enjoy the exemption if it falls foul of the set of eight anti-avoidance rules specifically designed to protect the dividend exemption regime from abuse.

Rule 1 – manipulating the controlled company exemption

6.30   This applies where the only possible head of exemption for a dividend is the controlled company distribution exemption and the dividend is paid as part of a scheme where the main, or one of the main purpose(s) is to ensure that the dividend enjoys the exemption for controlled company distributions. If the paying company has profits which are not vulnerable to a CFC charge on the shareholder as well as those which are, the dividend, if this rule applies, is treated as coming out of the profits susceptible to a CFC charge (ie to the disadvantage of the UK shareholder so that the dividend is not exempt). Vulnerable ('pre-control') profits are those which arise in the foreign company at a time before the UK dividend recipient owned more than 50 per cent of the payer or could be said jointly to control the company using the joint venture rules (see Chapter 15). This anti-avoidance rule only applies to profits arising in periods of account ending after 28 June 2009 or earlier.

Rule 2 – quasi-preference shares

6.31   This rule (CTA 2009, s 931K) limits the application of the very wide exemption for dividends paid on non-redeemable ordinary shares by identifying shares which are 'quasi-preference' shares. It is designed to catch changes in rights following the issue of shares. This rule is aimed at arrangements whereby, for instance, one shareholder agrees to waive the dividend in favour of another shareholder. For the rule to apply, this would have to be done as part of a scheme designed to save tax. A possible scenario would be where an overseas company in a low-tax regime (but not a CFC) is held by a UK company and also by subsidiaries of that UK company which are resident in high-tax countries, which do not operate a dividend exemption regime. The UK dividend exemption could, absent this rule, be manipulated so as to achieve a tax-deductible transfer of profits from the other shareholders to the UK company. The non-UK shareholders, having made tax-deductible payments to the overseas affiliate, could waive their dividends in favour of the UK company, so that the service payments made by them save tax in their home countries at high rates and result in the overseas subsidiary paying a large dividend to the UK company which would be exempt (see Figure 6.2).

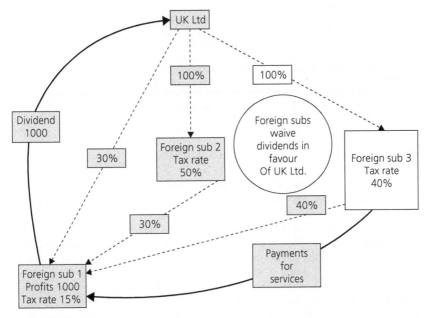

Figure 6.2

Rule 3 – manipulating the exemption for portfolio dividends

6.32   Where a group has a foreign shareholding, the dividends on which could only be exempt in the UK by virtue of the exemption under s 931G for dividends paid on portfolio holdings, it would be tempting to disperse the holding over enough UK group companies so that each held less than 10 per cent of the foreign company.

The rule operates by simply aggregating the shareholdings of all connected companies.[1]

If dividend exemption would be available under any of the other four headings, then it will be given.

---

1   The section refers to 'relevant persons'. These in turn are defined at CTA 2009, s 931T as per ICTA 1988, s 839:
   '(5) A company is connected with another company–
   (a) if the same person has control of both, or a person has control of one and persons connected with him, or he and persons connected with him, have control of the other; or
   (b) if a group of two or more persons has control of each company, and the groups either consist of the same persons or could be regarded as consisting of the same persons by treating (in one or more cases) a member of either group as replaced by a person with whom he is connected.
   (6) A company is connected with another person if that person has control of it or if that person and persons connected with him together have control of it.

(7) Any two or more persons acting together to secure or exercise control of a company shall be treated in relation to that company as connected with one another and with any person acting on the directions of any of them to secure or exercise control of the company.

(8) In this section–

'company' includes any body corporate or unincorporated association, but does not include a partnership, and this section shall apply in relation to any unit trust scheme as if the scheme were a company and as if the rights of the unit holders were shares in the company;

'control' shall be construed in accordance with section 416; and

'relative' means brother, sister, ancestor or lineal descendant.

In relation to any period during which section 470(2) has effect the reference above to a unit trust scheme shall be construed as a reference to a unit trust scheme within the meaning of the Prevention of Fraud (Investments) Act 1958 or the Prevention of Fraud (Investments) Act (Northern Ireland) 1940.'

Rule 4 – schemes in the nature of loan relationships

6.33   This rule turns existing anti-avoidance wisdom on its head: prior to dividend exemption, anti-avoidance provisions generally aimed to ensure that funding which was essentially equity could not be passed off for tax purposes as debt, thus generating a tax-deductible interest payment rather than a non-deductible dividend. Now that most dividends are exempt, anti-avoidance provisions are needed to prevent the recipient of a payment passing it off as an exempt dividend when it is economically more akin to taxable interest.[1] Section 931M does just this. For the rule to apply, there must be a tax-avoidance motive and the payer and the recipient must be connected companies. Note that, confusingly, a different definition of control is used in this section than elsewhere.[2]

Note that this anti-avoidance rule will not be invoked if the distribution qualifies for exemption under the controlled company exemption (s 931E).

---

1   Payments which are economically equivalent to interest are defined in CTA 2009, s 931M(5). The most common case will be where it is reasonable to assume that the return on the funding has been computed by reference to the time value of money and by reference to commercial rates of interest. Also, there is no likelihood that the return will not be paid from year to year.

2   The definition in CTA 2009, s 472 is used – rather than merely measuring voting control and other metrics, there is a more organic definition, that a company is controlled by a person if that person is able to secure that the affairs of the company are conducted in accordance with that person's wishes, either by means of holding shares, voting power or resulting from any powers conferred by the articles of association or any other document regulating the company or any other company.

Rule 5 – schemes involving distributions for which deductions are given

6.34   This rule disapplies the dividend exemption in the UK if the payment was tax deductible in the payer's tax computation. It goes further than the simple case (certain payments of interest taxed as dividends in the hands of the recipient are caught under the basic rules) as it also disapplies the exemption where the deduction might not be given to the paying company but to a connected company. It is enough that a tax deduction is given by reference to the amount of the dividend paid. HMRC give as an example the case where there is a manufactured payment akin to a dividend, but not where the payment can be shown to have been made for commercial purposes as, for example, in the case of payments for cross-border stock lending.

Rule 6 – schemes involving payments for distributions

6.35   If a payment is made (or income given up) in return for the receipt of a distribution, either by the recipient company or a connected company, the exemption will not apply. The rule only applies where the distribution arrangements were part of a scheme to secure a tax advantage. The company receiving the distribution must have incurred a liability to make the payment, the consideration for the liability being the right to receive the distribution. Where a payment is made, the rule will only apply if the payment is one of a certain type of payments (so-called 'annual payments').

Rule 7 – schemes involving payments not on arm's-length terms

6.36   This is a particularly convoluted rule. It seems to be aimed at situations where companies are not dealing with each other on arm's-length terms, but in a manner which does not bring them within the ambit of the transfer pricing rules. HMRC's guidance gives the example of five unconnected companies each with an interest in an insurance company. The five companies pay more than the market rate for insurance and, in return, the insurance company pays them an inflated dividend. This would not come under the terms of the transfer pricing regime because the insurance company is not connected to its shareholders; nor are they within the 'acting together' rules.

Rule 8 – schemes involving diversion of trade income

6.37   This rule tackles possible abuses by taxpayers for whom distributions may constitute a trading receipt, normally financial traders. Such taxpayers are required to offset attributable expenses against foreign dividend income before applying double tax relief. The rule operates to prevent such firms from entering into schemes designed to give the income the appearance of investment income, thus leaving the expenses to be offset against income liable to UK tax.

Special types of company

6.38   In general, where a special tax regime applies to a particular type of company, mainly banks and insurance companies, those special rules will continue to apply and take precedence over the dividend exemption.

What happens to distributions which are not exempt?

6.39   The credit method is applied. Foreign withholding tax suffered on the distribution and any underlying corporation tax on profits used to pay the distribution (providing the recipient holds at least 10 per cent of the payer) may be deducted from UK tax on the distribution.

No onshore pooling is permitted. Offshore pooling is restricted by the mixer cap so that foreign taxes are limited to those which would have arisen if the UK rate had been applied. The mixer cap prevents income which has suffered high rates of foreign tax being aggregated with income which has suffered lower rates.

UK dividend exemption: as complicated as the credit method?

6.40   This brief summary of the UK 2009 rules introducing the exemption method for foreign dividends received by UK companies serves to illustrate the point that the exemption method is not necessarily simpler than the credit method. The UK rules are aimed at preventing companies from taking advantage of the rules to obtain double tax relief by exemption where it was not intended (eg for receipts which are really foreign interest rather than dividends). What is, in essence, a simple concept (ie foreign dividend exemption), is in reality a highly complex piece of tax legislation with which UK holding companies must comply, which is a time-consuming and costly process. A danger is that the central aim of introducing the exemption for foreign dividends (ie to improve the competitiveness of the UK as a location for international holding companies), is impeded by the sheer complexity of the rules. The UK's dividend exemption is actually very generous, giving exemption for foreign dividends regardless of the percentage of shares held in the foreign company. Experience to date suggests that, in spite of the high level of anti-avoidance rules, most foreign dividends received by UK companies are being granted exemption.

Chapter 7

Double Tax Treaties

BASICS

7.1   Double tax treaties (DTTs) are instruments of international law, and most are governed by the Vienna Convention on the Law of Treaties, whilst their text is usually based on the Model Tax Convention (MTC) provided by the OECD. The provisions of treaties normally override any conflicting provisions in a state's domestic law. Double tax treaties are usually bilateral, between two taxing states (the Contracting States). In the context of DTTs, we therefore refer to 'states' rather than to 'countries'. No two states have the same tax system. They will, for example, have different definitions of what constitutes tax residence, different interpretations of the source principle and may have adopted different systems of giving double tax relief. One state might tax an amount of income according to the source principle and another state might tax the same amount of income according to the residence principle. Thus, if a taxpayer operating in two states relies solely on the domestic tax law of those two states they may well find themselves subject to double taxation. By entering into a DTT, two states aim to minimize the extent to which a taxpayer will be subject to double taxation. Double tax treaties provide a consistent, common and logical basis by which pairs of states can divide up between themselves the taxing rights over persons who have a tax connection with both states, whether by reason of tax residence or because of the existence of a source of income. They can only improve a taxpayer's position over that which would result from the application of a state's domestic law – they can never increase a taxpayer's liabilities.

The chief purposes of DTTs are to:

- provide a means of settling, upon a uniform basis, the most common problems which arise in the field of international juridical taxation (per the OECD's introduction to its Model Tax Convention, hereafter 'OECD MTC');

- prevent evasion of tax, by making provision for exchange of information between tax authorities and for assistance in collection of the tax debts owed to the treaty partner;

- protect taxpayers against double taxation, direct or indirect, to a greater extent than the protection offered under domestic law;

- prevent tax from discouraging the free flow of international trade and investment and the transfer of technology;

- prevent discrimination between taxpayers; and

- provide a measure of fiscal and legal certainty in international operations. An individual or enterprise considering investing in a foreign state can obtain an indication of the way in which the investment, be it financial, manufacturing, sales or otherwise, will be subject to tax in that state.

Tax treaties are, in the main, bilateral agreements under which a pair of states, referred to as the 'Contracting States', will decide how their tax systems will interact, so as to ensure that residents of each state get the double tax relief to which they are entitled. Without tax treaties, differences in the two tax systems involved, and even differences in the interpretation of tax terms within those systems, could mean that both states are entitled to tax the same income. For instance, State A might state that it considers every person with a State A passport to be tax resident. State B might have a different rule, say that every person spending more than six months of the year in State B is tax resident. Hence a person possessing a State A passport who spent more than six months of the year in State B would find themselves considered tax resident (and thus possibly taxable on their worldwide income) in *both* states. All tax treaties therefore contain a clause whereby the two states agree how they will interpret tax residence, to limit the circumstances in which a person can find themselves dually resident and hence fully liable to tax in both states. Besides the key function of providing relief for double taxation, a tax treaty will have provisions aimed at preventing tax avoidance. These can take the form of specific rules, say to prevent the income of a partnership ending up not being taxable anywhere at all, or more generally there will usually be a provision for the exchange of tax information between the contracting states. One other extremely important function of tax treaties is that they provide a mechanism whereby two states can interact in a relatively informal way so that double tax disputes and problem situations can be dealt with directly by the tax authorities of the two states rather than having to go through the normal diplomatic channels. All DTTs provide for a 'mutual agreement procedure' between the two tax authorities.

The OECD MTC awards priority in taxing rights to the state of source. The state of residence usually agrees either to give credit for tax paid in the state of source or to operate exemption from tax. The benefits of using the OECD MTC are that it provides common rules of interpretation via the extensive Commentary, aids the negotiation of new treaties, and provides a measure of certainty for multinational enterprises in planning their tax affairs. It also provides a useful means of reducing tax evasion and avoidance by means of exchange of information clauses.

The definition of a source of taxable income/profits is dealt with at some length in the OECD's Commentary on the MTC. Another major subject dealt with by the MTC is the control of transfer prices between related enterprises. The articles most commonly consulted are probably those which give the maximum possible withholding tax rates on dividends, interest and royalties, although it must always be remembered that if no withholding tax is charged under domestic law, or a lower rate is charged, then the rates given in the DDT will not, in practice, apply. The Article that often gives rise to legal disputes is the 'non-discrimination' article whereby the Contracting States agree to treat each other's taxpayers without discrimination.

There are several model DTTs besides the OECD MTC. The UN Model is commonly used in DTTs where at least one of the parties is a developing state, and awards greater taxing rights to the source state. The US uses its own model. All other model treaties are largely based on the OECD MTC.

The interpretation of DTTs needs to be approached in a purposive manner, which may not be the correct approach to the interpretation of a state's domestic law. A broad interpretation of the words used in a treaty is appropriate, rather than any narrow meaning adopted in interpretation of the same word when used in the domestic law. The Vienna Convention lays down the ground rules for treaty interpretation generally. Treaties are assumed to have been entered into in good faith, on the understanding that a state will keep its promises made under the DTT. The OECD Commentary is an acceptable aid to interpretation.

A state cannot renege on a treaty by, for instance, a newly elected government asserting that the previous incumbents had no authority or were not competent to enter into the treaty. The incumbent head of state and ministers are regarded as fully competent to enter into treaties on behalf of the state.

The OECD MTC will be significantly updated following the OECD's BEPS Project, but at the time of writing, the changes agreed upon as part of the BEPS Project have not yet been incorporated into an official version of the Model. To facilitate speedier action on implementation of the BEPS recommendations, a new Multilateral Instrument (MLI) has been devised which has the effect of automatically updating bilateral treaties entered into by signatories. The MLI is discussed in more detail at para **7.12** below.

RELATIONSHIP OF DOUBLE TAX TREATIES TO DOMESTIC LAW

7.2   Treaties are governed by international law rather than by domestic laws, usually under the Vienna Convention on the Law of Treaties (1980). This Convention lays down rules for matters such as the territorial scope of treaties, general rules of interpretation, breaching of treaties and for dealing with a fundamental change in the circumstances of one of the states.

The general rule is that the provisions contained within treaties override those of domestic tax law. Where domestic law overrules treaty provisions this is known as 'treaty override' and is a controversial area. It may be intentional, which, if it takes the form of newly enacted domestic law, is frowned upon, or unintentional, such as a domestic court decision which fails to use the treaty definitions or departs in some other way from the Vienna Convention rules for interpretation of treaties. This may be by mistake, through ignorance or deliberate if there is too much tax revenue at stake.

It should be noted that some states specifically provide that subsequent changes in domestic law will, if they contradict the treaty, override the treaty. This is sometimes referred to as the *lex posterior* rule. It is followed by the US where there is a clear intent to override treaties expressed in the statute concerned.

This is clearly unsatisfactory from the point of view of that state's treaty partners. The central tenet of the Vienna Convention is that treaties are concluded 'in good faith' and there is a presumption that a state will not want to override its treaties.

How easily treaty provisions can be overridden by domestic law is a function of the way that a state's constitution incorporates treaties into its lexis. Generally, if, as in the UK, a parliamentary statute is required to give effect to a treaty then subsequent domestic law may override the treaty.

Tax treaties versus domestic law

7.3   An important point is that treaties cannot, of themselves, impose tax liabilities where none exist under domestic law. They can only reduce or eliminate domestic tax liabilities. Thus, if a treaty between State A and State B provides that there is to be a maximum of 10 per cent withholding tax on dividends, State A can only charge a withholding tax at all if its domestic law provides for withholding tax on dividends. If it does not, then whatever the rate specified in the treaty, State A would not charge any withholding tax. If State B provided for a withholding tax on dividends at 5 per cent, then it would still only charge 5 per cent, even though the maximum rate in the treaty is stated at 10 per cent. The rates of withholding tax stated in treaties are always the maximum possible rates, not necessarily the rates that will actually be applied in practice.

Treaty override: revoking treaty promises

7.4   Treaty override can occur either *deliberately* or *accidentally*. Deliberate treaty override occurs where:

● a state deliberately enacts domestic legislation that contradicts one or more of its DTTs, removing treaty benefits; or

● a state passes legislation that does not mention DTTs but which has the effect of removing or restricting treaty benefits.

Accidental treaty override typically occurs if a state makes changes to its domestic laws, or interpretations of those laws which restrict treaty benefits, even where this was not a direct intention. The same thing can happen with decisions of the domestic courts.

Despite the fact that a state ought not to override its DTTs, under the laws of the Vienna Convention on the Law of Treaties, there is not much that a treaty partner can do about it – short of terminating the treaty. This is a very drastic course of action. Treaty override is considered bad practice internationally because it reduces the certainty of tax treatment that DTTs provide to taxpayers. A state with a reputation for treaty override might find it difficult to negotiate new DTTs.

This topic is considered in more depth at para **7.55**.

Tax treaties and EU law

7.5 Until fairly recently, EU law relating to taxation was concerned mostly with VAT and duties, and so relatively little work has been done on the relationship between treaty law (ie the provisions of DTTs which are effective in a state's domestic law) and EU law. VAT and duties are not covered by DTTs except for provisions concerning non-discrimination against non-residents and provisions for the exchange of information between states. Within the EU there is a network of more than 300 bilateral DTTs which exist alongside EU law. It is worth stating that EU law for tax purposes normally takes the form of Directives and the decisions of the Court of Justice of the European Union (CJEU). The relationship between this EU law and the domestic laws of the Member States is complex but in general, Member States are required to incorporate the provisions of the Directives into their domestic laws and to follow the decisions of the CJEU. The lack of co-ordination between treaty law within the EU and EU law itself is not surprising as they have different objectives: the former is to allocate taxing rights between a pair of states, and the latter is to help to establish the EU Single Market.

What is established beyond all doubt is that Member States of the EU are at liberty to develop and enforce their own rules in the sphere of direct taxation. In *Gilly*[1] the CJEU stated:

> 'The Member States are competent to determine the criteria for taxation on income and wealth with a view to eliminating double taxation – by means inter alia, of international agreements – and have concluded many bilateral conventions based, in particular, on the Model Tax Conventions on income and wealth tax drawn up by the OECD.'[2]

In the case of *Saint Gobain*[3] the principle was established that it is up to the individual EU Member States to determine the connecting factors (residence, etc) for the purposes of allocating powers of taxation. However, the rights afforded to taxpayers under the Treaty on the Functioning of the European Union (TFEU), and in particular under Article 49, the freedom to establish anywhere in the EU without hindrance (ie without suffering less favourable tax treatment than if the person had remained taxable purely in the State where resident) cannot be subordinated to the provisions of a DTT. Where there is a conflict between EU law and the provisions of a DTT, the EU law will prevail. This was made explicit by the ECJ in the famous *Avoir Fiscal*[4] case in which it was stated: 'the rights conferred by Article 43 of the Treaty are unconditional and a Member State cannot make respect for them subject to the contents of an agreement concluded with another Member State.'[5]

In the *Avoir Fiscal* case, the taxpayer was resident in another Member State and under the terms of the DTT, received tax treatment which was more onerous than that received by taxpayers who were French residents. There is a distinction to be made between the allocation of powers of taxation and the exercise of those powers. The first is a matter for the individual Member States, but in the second, the principles set down in the Treaty on the Functioning of the EU (TFEU) must be followed. In other words, Member States are free to decide *who* has the right to tax, but not *how* to tax if this results, broadly, in discrimination against the foreign taxpayer if that taxpayer is a resident of a fellow EU Member State.

---

1   Case C-336/96 *Mr and Mrs Robert Gilly v Directeur des services fiscaux du Bas-Rhin* [1998] All ER (EC) 826.
2   At para 24.
3   Case C-307/97 *Compagnie de Saint-Gobain SA, branch Germany* [2000] STC 854.
4   Case C-270/83 *Commission v France* [1986] ECR 273. The Article number refers to an earlier version of the Treaty.
5   Above fn 4, at para 5.

Relationship between double tax treaties and EU law

7.6   There is no direct relationship as such, but the Parent/Subsidiary Directive[1] and the Interest and Royalties Directive[2] in particular contain provisions regarding withholding taxes on dividends, interest and royalties which must be enacted in the domestic law of all EU Member States unless a Member State specifically obtains permission to omit or vary them. The effect of this is that it is now frequently the case that the domestic law of an EU Member State will provide for withholding tax rates on certain types of dividend, interest and royalty payments which are lower than those provided for in its DTTs with other Member States. Even where domestic law has not been amended in line with a Directive, taxpayers, in some circumstances, have the right to rely on the Directive rather than on the corresponding domestic law. Thus an EU Member State might charge a 20 per cent withholding tax rate on interest in its domestic law which would apply to payments of interest to non-EU resident recipients, or EU-resident recipients not covered by the Interest and Royalties Directive. Then there could well be a DTT with a fellow EU Member State providing for a maximum withholding tax rate of 10 per cent. Finally, domestic law for certain EU recipients qualifying under the Interest and Royalties Directive would exempt certain interest payments from withholding tax altogether. Hence great care is needed when determining the correct rate of withholding tax on payments made between EU enterprises.

---

1   90/435/EC, updated by 2003/123/EC.
2   2003/49/EC.

STAGES IN THE LIFE OF A DOUBLE TAX TREATY

7.7   It may take many years from the start of negotiations between two states to the date when a tax treaty into which they enter comes into effect. Sometimes treaties progress to the final stages but are never brought into use, perhaps because in the time it has taken to negotiate the treaty, the domestic tax laws of the two states have changed significantly and the states are forced to 'go back to the drawing board'. However, the key stages are as follows.

Signing

7.8   The date of signature is the date by which the treaty is generally referred to (eg 'The Norway–Russia Income and Capital Tax Treaty of 26 March 1996'). At this stage, the negotiators for the two states will be satisfied with the wording of the treaty. The treaty then needs to be ratified by each state so that it becomes legally binding. Ratification is the process by which the treaty is adopted as law. The procedures for ratification differ from state to state: in the UK it is the Foreign and Commonwealth Office which is responsible for negotiating treaties under Royal Prerogative. Treaties are signed by the Queen, which constitutes ratification. However, Parliament is given 21 days' notice of impending ratification. The date when the treaty becomes legally binding is known as 'entry into force'.

Entry into force

7.9   A treaty will normally enter into force when each of the states has 'ratified' it. This means that the state has adopted the provisions of the treaty into its domestic law. This can be done directly, whereby a state's constitution provides that a treaty will automatically become part of domestic law once it has been approved by the appropriate officials. Alternatively, a new treaty may need specific approval from the government or the monarch. When the appropriate procedures have been completed in each contracting state, the states exchange 'instruments of ratification'. This triggers the 'entry into force' of a treaty, making it legally binding on both states. Frequently one state will pass on to the other state its instrument of ratification well before it receives one back from this other state. Completing the exchange brings the provisions of the treaty into effect for taxpayers, but only in accordance with a formula laid out in the treaty, not immediately. The US operates rather differently: a treaty will become operative as if it were domestic law once it has been approved by the Senate and instruments of ratification exchanged.

Effective date

7.10   For instance, the 1996 Norway–Russia Treaty entered into force on 20 December 2002. However, the terms of the treaty could not be used by Norwegian taxpayers until the start of the 'year next following that in which the Convention enters into force' (Article 29). This would be 1 January 2003. There was a slightly different rule for Russian taxpayers.

Protocols to double tax treaties

7.11   Once the negotiators have done their work and the treaty has been signed, it then needs approval, either from specific government officials or from the governments themselves. At this stage, those in a position to grant approval of the treaty may insist upon additions and clarifications to the treaty before they will agree to ratify it. For instance, one reason why there was such a long gap between signature and entry into force of the 1996 Norway–Russia Treaty was because Norway insisted upon including in the treaty (via the Protocol) lengthy additional provisions concerning the taxation of offshore oil and gas profits. These later additions and clarifications are never consolidated into the main treaty, even by the various treaty updating services. This type of Protocol is known as a 'contemporaneous' protocol.

A DTT can be updated from time to time by mutual agreement of the two states. The updates are contained in documents known as subsequent protocols, which are subject to the same adoption processes as the original treaty and which are referred to by the year in which they were signed. The major treaty databases offer versions of DTTs which incorporate the contents of subsequent protocols (but not the contemporaneous protocol) into the main treaty for ease of reference. Thus, even when using a 'consolidated' version of a treaty it is always necessary to check for further provisions contained in any contemporaneous protocol.

Besides protocols, clarifications to a treaty can be provided via an exchange of diplomatic notes, often done at the date the treaty is signed. Occasionally, lengthier clarifications and worked examples of the effect of certain articles are contained in Memoranda of Understanding which accompany the treaty and provide evidence of the way in which the two states have agreed to interpret certain of the provisions in the treaty.

The Multilateral Instrument – BEPS Action 15

7.12   The Model Tax Treaties are frequently altered and updated in order to respond to developments in international trading patterns, and the tax practices of multinational groups of companies, as well as to make them more useful in dealing with tax evasion and avoidance. These updates, however, can take years to agree upon. Once the updates are incorporated into the Model Tax Treaties, they have no effect unless and until; countries update actual tax treaties to include the new material. Negotiating changes to an existing tax treaty can take years, because during the negotiation process, requests for inclusion of new material by one of the Contracting States are likely to be met with counter-requests by the other Contracting State for the inclusion (or removal) of other material. Add to this, the fact that many countries have over 100 DTTs. For these reasons, it takes many years for changes to the Model Tax Conventions to be incorporated into existing treaties. Many treaties are not updated at all.

The OECD's BEPS Project will result in many changes to the OECD MTC, some of them quite extensive. If the only way that existing treaties can be updated is via the existing cumbersome mechanism of treaty-by-treaty renegotiation, then it will be many years before the OECD's BEPS work which has resulted in changes to the OECD MTC has any effect in practice. In order to solve this problem, Action 15 of BEPS has developed a new mechanism for the updating of existing treaties. This mechanism will consist of a multilateral legal instrument (MLI; effectively a multilateral treaty). The countries which sign up to it are likely to agree to automatically update their bilateral treaties with each other (without engaging in a lengthy negotiation process) whenever the OECD MTC changes. At the time of writing, more than 100 countries have concluded negotiations on a MLI and a signing ceremony will be held in June 2017 in Paris.

To illustrate the benefits of such a multilateral instrument, and how it might work in practice, we will look at a group of ten countries, A–J, who each have a full tax treaty with each other. Some of the treaties are quite old (eg concluded before 1980), whilst others are more recent. Some of the countries are OECD members, whilst some are not. Of those which are OECD members, some agree with the whole of the content of the OECD MTC, whilst others have a few reservations about certain aspects of it. In total, there are 45 bilateral DTTs to consider.

Table 7.1 Example of the benefits of a multilateral instrument: involving 45 bilateral DTTs

	A	B	C	D	E	F	G	H	I	J
A		1	2	3	4	5	6	7	8	9
B			10	11	12	13	14	15	16	17
C				18	19	20	21	22	23	24
D					25	26	27	28	29	30
E						31	32	33	34	35
F							36	37	38	39
G								40	41	42
H									43	44
I										45
J										

The first point is a purely practical one. None of the countries have enough trained treaty negotiators to negotiate updates to multiple treaties concurrently.

The MLI is worded to the effect that, whenever the OECD MTC is changed, Countries A–J will all automatically update their treaties with each other. There are still administrative and legal formalities to be completed, but the time-consuming and costly negotiation stage of updating is largely bypassed.

The treaty negotiators will still have a significant job of work as some of the treaties (eg numbers 25 and 26 in Table 7.1 above) might have been negotiated in the 1980s, and might not have been updated since then. Since the 1980s, there have been many changes to the OECD MTC. If, in 2017, the OECD introduces a change into, say, paragraph 5 of Article 25 (which provides for binding arbitration in the case of disputes), then because this paragraph was only added to the OECD MTC in 2008, those treaties will not contain paragraph 5 of Article 25. Countries D, E and F will have to negotiate on whether to ignore the 2017 change, or whether to update treaties 25 and 26 to now incorporate paragraph 5 of Article 25.

One of the countries, eg Country J, might feel very strongly that it cannot accept the proposed changes to Article 5 on the definition of dependent agents (see Chapter 9). Despite having signed the MLI, it might refuse to update its treaties to reflect the changes. Whilst this would be a clear breach of Country J's obligations under the MLI, and not in accordance with its obligations under the Vienna Convention, it could still happen.

Country G may have always insisted on negotiating its treaties with a particular form of words defining what is meant by 'a dividend'. If, in future, the OECD amends part of the definition in Article 10 of the OECD MTC, because of the significant difference in wording in Country G's current treaties, and the OECD MTC amendments before the change; it might prove impossible to import the OECD's updated wording into Country G's treaties. Country G would have to negotiate with the rest of the signatories to the MLI as to how, or whether, its treaties should be reworded to conform to the latest version of the OECD MTC.

DEVELOPMENT OF DOUBLE TAX TREATIES

7.13   The first DTT that applied to income taxes was entered into between Prussia and Austria–Hungary in 1899, and this treaty shaped developments before the First World War. Harris (1996) provides an excellent commentary on treaty development with particular reference to company and shareholder taxation. For a broader and more comprehensive analysis, refer to Picciotto (1992).

The League of Nations Financial Committee was prevailed upon by the International Chamber of Commerce in 1919/20 to examine the question of international double taxation, and produced a report in 1923 as the basis for the first Model Tax Convention in 1928. Some of the questions addressed were:

- Which state has priority in taxing:

  — state of source?

  — state of residence?

- Should this differ depending on the type of income?

The Committee arrived at three important decisions that form the basis of the rules governing a state's jurisdiction to tax today:

- Profits of a permanent establishment (PE) of a foreign taxpayer (eg a foreign branch) could be taxed by the host state.

- Tax residence depended on the place of centre of management.

- Subsidiaries were to be treated as separate entities for tax purposes rather than as an integral part of the parent company.

At this point in history, although the basic rules had been laid down for the taxation of persons with income in more than one state, the use of formal tax treaties was still rare. Then, as international trade developed a new problem emerged – the transfer price problem. Realizing that the profits of branches and subsidiaries were liable to taxation in the states in which they operated, multinational companies began artificially to manipulate their internal pricing policies. They did this so that, whilst not affecting the overall profit of the company or group of companies, those profits arose principally in states with low taxation. The Carroll Report to the League of Nations, 1933 dealt in particular with this problem. Transfer pricing is covered in more detail in Chapter 13.

This led to the 1935 Draft Convention for the Allocation of Business Income between States for the Purposes of Taxation which was the forerunner of today's tax treaties. The artificial internal transfer-pricing practices were attacked. Under this Draft Convention, enterprises with establishments in more than one state would be required to attribute to each establishment: 'the net business income which it might be expected to derive if it were an independent enterprise engaged in the same or similar activities under the same or similar conditions' (Draft Convention, 1935).

Following the adoption of the Carroll Report, many states around the world entered into DTTs. The US was particularly active, as was the Netherlands. However, the UK resisted entering into tax treaties until it concluded the UK–US Treaty in 1945, which then paved the way for many more treaties. It was not until 1953 – to encourage more agreements – that the UK introduced unilateral double tax relief.

This difference in attitude towards the development of tax treaties reflects the wider historical differences between the UK, and states such as the US. For the first half of the twentieth century, the UK had been involved mainly in outward investment, principally with states forming part of the British Empire. As the UK had considerable influence over governments in those states, it was able to secure very low, or even the absence of, taxation by those states on the source principle. The UK retained the right to tax residents investing abroad on their worldwide income without giving relief for double taxation. Whilst trade was mainly with ex-Empire states, such double taxation was low but by the mid-twentieth century the position was changing. The volume of trade by UK companies with the US occasioned by the Second World War made it imperative that the UK at last started to give relief for double taxation and enter into DTTs.

THE OECD MODEL TAX CONVENTION

7.14   In the 1950s, the OECD was founded and took over the work of developing a model tax treaty. One of the principal aims of the OECD is to promote trade between its member nations. An important facet of its work is to assist in removing barriers to trade posed by taxation issues. It amended the 1935 model to take account of developments since that time and in 1963 published a draft Model Tax Convention on Income and Capital which has served as the model for double tax agreements between developed nations since then. By 1994, there were 225 treaties which are primarily based on the OECD MTC.

The OECD MTC is not binding upon any state but is usually used as the template for bilateral treaties, with the OECD's detailed Commentary on each of the Articles being used as supplementary data to aid interpretation. Nearly all treaties are based on the OECD MTC, except the US's treaties, which use an alternative model (the US Model Income Tax Convention, which is broadly similar to the OECD MTC in many respects). The United Nations has adapted the OECD MTC for use between developed and developing countries, producing the UN Model. The OECD MTC has been very widely used for a long time. The particular advantages of using an internationally accepted model include:

- common rules of interpretation;

- a major aid to treaty negotiation – in terms of what should be included and also in terms of setting boundaries (eg for upper limits on rates of withholding taxes); and

- certainty for multinational enterprises resident in a state using the OECD MTC as to the uniformity of treatment regarding double taxation in all states in which they do business (although individual treaties may vary, such variations in the treaties concluded by a single state are usually small).

A major advantage of using the OECD MTC is the existence of the well-established and well-respected Commentary. This provides a valuable tool of interpretation which has widespread international acceptance amongst states which are not OECD members. The importance of the Commentary is considered further in the next section.

The OECD MTC is divided into broad chapters, and then each chapter is sub-divided into a number of articles which contain specific rules.

Table 7.2 OECD MTC Articles

Articles	Provisions
1–5	Definitions: including who may benefit from the treaty, residents, taxable presence of business enterprises.
6–21	These rules classify and allocate different types of income to one or other or both of the states concerned for tax purposes.
22	Rights to tax capital.
23	Methods of double tax relief.
24–31	Administrative and anti-avoidance provisions.

The Commentary is a detailed document, the 'condensed' version of which runs to about 400 A4-size pages. Besides the authoritative interpretative material, the Commentary sets out the reservations which OECD members have expressed with respect to each article. These reservations contain details of alternative treatments which particular states intend to apply, matters where particular states do not agree with the OECD interpretations and details of additional provisions which particular states intend to include in future treaties. For instance, Canada announces in the 'reservations' on Article 12 (royalties) that it intends to continue to charge a withholding tax of 10 per cent on certain royalty payments. Advance knowledge of such state positions is a useful tool for treaty negotiators. Besides lists of 'reservations' on each article, there is also a list of 'observations' on each article in which the individual OECD states can put forward their views on matters dealt with in the Commentary or add small amounts of supplementary material. States which are not full OECD members, but which have 'observer status', can also record observations.

The current version of the OECD MTC dates back to 1963, but it has been updated on several occasions, the most recent being July 2008, July 2010 and July 2014. The main matters dealt with in the 2008 update were:

- some clarifications on the tie-breaker test for company residence in the Commentary and an alternate test for use where the contracting states wish to retain flexibility in the case of apparently dual-residence companies (or other types of enterprises);

- an extension of the definition of a permanent establishment (PE) (branches, etc) to include the case where an enterprise provides services in the other state without having a fixed place of business there;

- revisions to the Commentary to incorporate the work of the OECD on the attribution of profits to PEs;

- provisions for real estate investment trusts;

- clarifications to the Commentary on the definition of royalties;

- clarification as to how the non-discrimination principles are to apply; and

- the mutual agreement procedure (whereby disputes can be dealt with) is strengthened by a requirement for mandatory binding arbitration in some cases.

The 2010 changes include:

- provisions relating to collective investment vehicles;

- entitlement to treaty benefits for state-owned entities such as sovereign wealth funds;

- revision to the definition of 'employer'; and

- implementation of the 2008 Report on attribution of profits for PEs.

The 2014 changes include:

- changes to the text of Article 26 (exchange of information);

- clarification of the meaning of 'beneficial owner' in Articles 10–12;

- the application of Article 17 (sportspersons and entertainers);

- treaty issues with emissions permits and credits; and

- the tax treaty treatment of termination payments paid to employees.

As already noted, significant further changes are expected following completion of the BEPS Project. The 2014 update does not include any of the changes brought about via the various BEPS actions.

The real importance of the OECD MTC is that it lends a degree of certainty to the tax implications of international business, which makes international expansion less risky for enterprises. If two states have entered into a DTT based on the OECD MTC, then an enterprise which is resident in one state can have a reasonable degree of certainty as to how it will be treated for tax purposes if it expands its operations into the other state. Because of the existence of the detailed Commentary and the recognition of the Commentary as an authoritative source of interpretation of the DTT, the enterprise can be reasonably certain not only of the broad principles of double tax relief which the home state and the destination state will use, but also how those principles might be interpreted in particular situations. There is also the comfort that should double taxation occur, the taxpayer has the right, under the DTT, to require the two tax authorities to consult together in situations not expressly covered by the treaty to ensure that the enterprise is not subject to double taxation.

The US Model Income Tax Convention

7.15 The US uses an alternative model (the 2016 US Model Income Tax Convention). This model is based on the OECD MTC but with some important differences. Being the leading world economy, the US is in a powerful negotiating position to insist upon its own model. Perhaps surprisingly, it only has around 50 treaties, significantly less than the number concluded by the UK and the Netherlands. This cautious approach is also evident in the content of its treaties: the US places great emphasis on 'limitation of benefits' with respect to its treaties (see Chapter 15) and does not enter into 'tax-sparing' agreements in its treaties. Neither is the exemption method of double tax relief permitted, only the credit method. This contrasts with the OECD MTC which permits either.

Another feature of the US Model is the 'saving clause', Article 1.4, which preserves for the US the right to tax its residents and citizens even if they now reside in another contracting state. This right extends for varying periods, often up to 10 years after US citizenship is abandoned. In other words, the US reserves the right to continue to tax its residents, citizens and former citizens as if the treaty did not exist so that they do not pay less tax in overall terms than if they were solely resident in, and fully liable to tax in, the US.

> **'Article 1.4 US Model**
>
> Except to the extent provided in paragraph 5, this Convention shall not affect the taxation by a Contracting State of its residents (as determined under Article 4 (Resident)) and its citizens. Notwithstanding the other provisions of this Convention, a former citizen or former long-term resident of a Contracting State may, for the period of ten years following the loss of such status, be taxed in accordance with the laws of that Contracting State.'

Although technically usable by both parties to a treaty, the saving clause is mainly to the advantage of the US and is evidence of the strength of the bargaining position of the US when entering into treaties. Taken together with the extensive Article on limitation of treaty benefits, the US goes to great lengths to prevent its treaties from being used for the purpose of tax avoidance. Treaties based on the OECD MTC do not automatically contain a specific limitation of benefits clause. Besides the limitations of benefits clause, the US often employs a 'later in time' rule which means that a federal law passed subsequent to the ratification of a treaty will override the treaty, in violation of the Vienna Convention.

BEPS Action 6 proposes a savings clause for the OECD MTC, despite the fact that few countries apart from the US have adopted it. The OECD savings clause will be simpler than that in the US Model.

The US Model also reflects the US approach to determining company tax residence, stating that residence shall be determined by reference to place of incorporation rather than place of effective management. In general, US treaties tend to be far more detailed than those of other states as the US seeks to preserve within the treaty the effects of much of its highly complex domestic tax law.

The US Model contains lengthy provisions aimed at limiting treaty benefits to residents of US and the other Contracting State. The 2016 update contains a number of significant amendments to tighten up the rules on the persons to whom the US will grant benefits under its treaties. These are discussed in more detail in Chapter 15.

The Commentary on the OECD MTC is used as a principal and authoritative tool of interpretation of treaties based on the US Model. Additionally, for many US treaties, the US Treasury Department publishes a 'Technical Explanation' of that treaty. The Technical Explanation is based on the negotiations which led up to the signing of the treaty and seeks to explain the purpose of each article from the US viewpoint and, in some detail, how each article dovetails with US domestic tax law, the Internal Revenue Code. Although very useful and containing many helpful examples, they are not an authoritative means of interpreting the US treaties because they are prepared unilaterally by the US Treasury Department rather than bilaterally by the contracting states. They tend to be very short on detail as to how the treaty in question interacts with the domestic law of the other state. Also, as the US is normally the dominant partner in the treaty process, the material in the technical explanations is very much the US view. However, in a few cases, the treaty partner will formally indicate assent to the explanations given by the US.

UN Model Tax Convention

7.16   The UN Model Tax Convention (UN MTC) developed in 1980, favours capital importing states as opposed to capital exporting states and was developed for use between a developing state and a developed state. Although it is based on the OECD MTC, more scope is afforded for the taxation of the foreign investor by the source state. The UN MTC is designed to aid developing states to tax a larger part of the overseas investor's income than the other two Models. It permits double tax relief by exemption and includes tax-sparing clauses (see below). It permits withholding tax to be levied on royalty payments leaving the state whereas the latest versions of the other two Models do not. One of the most useful features of the UN MTC is the enhanced rights it affords to developing states to tax a part of the profits of multinational companies. An updated version of the UN MTC was published in 2011. The Model was previously updated in 2001. Whilst the UN MTC has its own commentary, this quotes extensively from the commentary on the OECD MTC.

The main differences between the OECD and the UN MTCs are:

- The UN MTC provides for an additional form of PE in the text of Article 5: the services PE (see Chapter 10).

- The UN MTC permits withholding tax on royalties.

- The UN MTC retains a separate article dealing with income from professions: 'independent personal services'. To some extent this replicates the provisions of Article 5, but it provides a time-threshold which many countries consider useful.

- The UN MTC will, from 2016 onwards, contain a separate article permitting withholding tax to be charged on fees paid to non-residents for technical services.

- The UN MTC awards the primary taxing rights over 'other income' to the country in which that income arises, rather than the country where the owner is tax resident.

ALLOCATING THE RIGHT TO TAX

7.17   The rules dealing with the allocation of taxing rights between the two Contracting States in DTTs are referred to as 'distributive rules' and there are five of them:

1   rules for certain activities such as businesses, agriculture and forestry;

2   rules for income from certain types of assets such as dividends from shares, interest on loans, royalties paid for the use of intellectual property and rent from immovable property;

3   rules which refer to capital gains;

4   rules which refer to the status of the taxpayer involved, such as artistes, sportsmen and students; and

5   a residual rule for income which does not fall under any of the previous four categories.

The way in which the rules work is to nominate which state is to tax the relevant type of income, or in some cases give priority to one state without giving it exclusive rights (ie by permitting the state from which income is being paid to levy a withholding tax on the foreign taxpayer). It should be remembered that a double tax agreement cannot create a right to tax which does not already exist under the state's own domestic tax laws. In other words, a DTT can only improve a taxpayer's situation, not worsen it. Some categories of income can only be taxed in the state in which the taxpayer is a resident. Others may be fully taxed by both states, in which case there are rules for relieving any double taxation that arises.

All DTTs are different. The differences may appear slight to the casual reader but a treaty cannot be properly interpreted without a thorough examination of its exact wording. A number of general rules are set out below, but these are *only* general, and some treaties will not adhere to them.

Some categories of income may only be taxed in the state of the taxpayer's residence. The types of income and capital covered by this principle are usually:

- business profits – unless there is a PE in the other state – see below;
- royalty income;
- capital and capital gains – unless specified;
- income from independent personal services where there is no fixed base in the source state;
- private pensions; and
- certain foreign government salaries and pensions.

In some cases, income may be taxed by both of the contracting states, with the residence state giving double tax relief for tax levied by the source state. The types of income to which this principle applies are usually:

- business profits from a PE (eg a branch);
- dividends and interest;
- income earned by sportsmen and artistes; and
- income and capital gains from immovable property (eg rentals received on property) owned by a resident of one state, in the other state.

Note that there are special provisions for income and gains from international transport undertakings, and special rules for students.

MAIN ARTICLES IN THE OECD'S MODEL TAX CONVENTION

7.18   In this section, the individual articles of the MTC are considered. It is important to note that the OECD Commentary on each article can run to dozens of pages, so the sections below provide only brief summaries of the substance of each article. The main variations between the OECD and the UN and US Models are briefly summarized and commonly encountered variations in tax treaties are also discussed. It would be a good idea to consult the OECD MTC alongside studying the sections below.

Note also that some changes are anticipated to the text of the MTC following the OECD's BEPS Project and that extensive changes to the Commentary are expected for the same reason. At the time of writing, these changes are public in the Final Reports on the various BEPS actions, but have not been published as part of the text of the MTC and its Commentary. The BEPS changes will be highlighted as we proceed through the various articles.

Article 1: Persons covered

7.19   Typical wording would be: 'This Convention shall apply to persons who are residents of one or both of the Contracting States.'

This article sets out the scope of the treaty (the Convention), ie the persons to whom it applies. Invariably, the treaty is to apply to persons who are residents of one of the contracting states. Although the OECD Commentary considers the problem of ensuring that only residents of the two states manage to benefit under the treaty, provisions limiting the benefits of the treaty to either specific persons, or in particular ways where it is suspected that a person in a third state may be trying to take advantage of the treaty are normally contained either in a separate 'limitation of benefits' article, or in the articles dealing with the vulnerable types of income, typically dividends, interest and royalties.

Article 2: Taxes covered

7.20   This article sets out the taxes to be covered either in general terms (income, periodic taxes on capital, wages and salaries, etc) or in specific terms by giving a list of taxes. Often both approaches are used. The problem with lengthy lists of specific taxes is that they may quickly become out of date. Hence Article 2 invariably contains a provision that the treaty is to apply to any substantially similar taxes which replace those on this list. The procedure for notifying the other state of these replacement taxes is normally set out. Typical wording for this provision is:

> 'The Convention shall apply also to any identical or substantially similar taxes that are imposed after the date of signature of the Convention in addition to, or in place of, the existing taxes. The competent authorities of the Contracting States shall notify each other of any significant changes that have been made in their taxation laws.'

A treaty may cover all taxes: income, periodic taxes on capital such as an annual wealth tax, gains, inheritances but it is more likely that the double taxation of inheritances and estates will be dealt with in a separate treaty. Treaties do not normally cover indirect taxes. Local taxes are sometimes covered but only if this is specifically indicated.

Article 3: General definitions

7.21   Para 1 of this article lays down the definitions of some fundamental terms, such as 'person', 'company' and 'enterprise'. However, para 2 goes on to state that any terms not defined in the MTC are to have the meaning from the domestic law of the states, unless the context otherwise requires. This inevitably gives rise to difficulties where terms not defined in a treaty have different meanings in the domestic laws of the two states which are party to the treaty. The domestic law in point is the law as at the time the treaty is being applied, not that in existence at the time the treaty was entered into, if different. This is the normal method of treaty interpretation in this respect and is known as the 'ambulatory' approach (as opposed to the 'static' approach). Typical wording of such a provision is:

> 'As regards the application of this Convention at any time by a Contracting State, any term not defined therein shall, unless the context otherwise requires, have the meaning that it has at that time under the law of that State for the purposes of the taxes to which this Convention applies, any meaning under the applicable tax laws of that State prevailing over a meaning given to the term under other laws of that State.'

The tax authorities of the two states can use the mutual agreement procedure, as provided for in Article 25, in order to establish agreed definitions of certain terms. See para **7.53** below for further commentary on definitions.

Article 4: Resident

7.22   Article 4 lays down provisions for determining the residence of individuals and other entities. The first paragraph sets out the possibilities for each state to consider a person (individual or legal entity) resident. For treaties to work, one of the states must be designated as the residence state and the other as the source state. It is quite possible, however,, for a taxpayer to be tax resident in both of the states under their domestic laws. Where this is the case, Article 4 provides a set of rules for deciding in which one of the two states, for treaty purposes only, the taxpayer is to be considered resident.

The usefulness of this article thus lies in the tie-breaker clauses it contains, which aim to prevent a taxpayer from being considered resident in both of the contracting states. The concept of tax residence for individuals and companies is considered in detail in Chapters 3 and 4 respectively. Most treaties contain a standard series of tie-breaker tests for individuals. Many treaties contain a tie-breaker test for companies, usually (but not always) the place of 'effective management'. The test in US treaties, where it exists, is normally the place of legal incorporation, reflecting US domestic law. Even this varies from treaty to treaty, as there can be a problem with companies moving their place of legal incorporation in order to benefit under a particular tax treaty. In some more recent treaties, the US has adopted the place where the company was created as the tie-breaker test, rather than where the company is presently legally incorporated. The tie-breaker test for companies (and other entities) is usually worded as follows:

> 'Where by reason of the provisions of paragraph 1 a person other than an individual is a resident of both Contracting States, then it shall be deemed to be a resident only of the State in which its place of effective management is situated.'

If a treaty does not contain this tie-breaker test, then there is often a requirement that the tax authorities of the two states must use the mutual agreement
procedure (Article 25) to reach agreement as to a single state where the taxpayer is to be considered resident for treaty purposes. The wording of these
requirements is crucial. If the article is worded so that the tax authorities 'must'
decide upon a single state of residence, then a company can only be resident
for treaty purposes in one of the states. If the wording is that the tax authorities
'shall endeavour to' agree on a single state of residence, then the position is
much more difficult. This wording leaves the way open for the tax authorities
to fail to agree upon a single state of residence. In this case, a company could
find itself considered resident by both of the states. As the treaty is based upon
the idea of allocating taxing rights between the two states, they would both
have the right to tax a dual-resident company. This is obviously untenable and
the usual requirement in cases of dual residence is for the two tax authorities
to reach mutual agreement on how they will use the tax treaty with reference
to the dual-resident company on a case-by-case basis. Some treaties are more
prescriptive and state that a dual-resident company cannot benefit from the
articles in the treaty which deal directly with the issue of allocating taxing
rights (Articles 5–23). Benefit is denied, because the operation of these articles
depends on one state being designated as the residence state and the other as
the source state. The only benefits which the company can enjoy under the
treaty would be the principle of non-discrimination (Article 24) and the right
to have the mutual agreement procedure used (Article 25). So, from a treaty
point of view, dual residence is a 'bad thing' although there may well be other
tax advantages which compensate, such as the right to set off the same loss in
both states, effectively using it twice.

Articles 5 and 7: Taxation of business profits

7.23   The concept of a permanent establishment (PE) is very important for
the taxation by the host state of the business profits of non-residents.

Article 7 states that: 'profits of an enterprise of State A shall be taxable only
in State A unless the enterprise carries on business in State B through a
"permanent establishment" situated therein'.

Articles 5 and 7 deal essentially with the taxation of foreign branches. It is
important to understand that Articles 5 and 7 do not normally apply to foreign subsidiaries. Typically, they will apply, for example, where a company,
White Ltd, resident in State A has a branch in State B. Thus White Ltd is a
non-resident as far as State B is concerned and resident in State A. State B can
only tax the profits arising in the branch located in State B. State A can tax the
entire profits of White Ltd: those earned in State A and in State B. By contrast,
if White Ltd has a subsidiary company, Grey Ltd, which is located in and tax
resident in State B, State B could tax all of the profits of Grey Ltd.

The ground rules for deciding how much of the total profits of the enterprise are
attributable to the 'permanent establishment' are laid down in Article 7. What
Article 5 does is to decide whether a PE exists at all. Without a PE located

in State B, State B has no right at all to tax the profits made by an enterprise resident in State A.

Article 5 determines when a source of business profits will be deemed to arise in the state in which the taxpayer is not resident. The general rule in Article 7 is that business profits are taxable by the state in which the taxpayer is resident only, unless there is a source of profits in the other state.

A PE as defined in Article 5, broadly includes a:

- place of management;
- branch;
- office;
- factory;
- workshop;
- mine, oil well, etc; and
- buildings and construction sites lasting more than 12 months.

The UN Model also deems a PE to exist where the non-resident provides services in the other state, even without a fixed place of business. All the Models deem profits from contracts concluded on behalf of a non-resident by an agent to be treated as if they arise from a PE in some circumstances.

We will examine the concept of PEs and the attribution of profits to them in detail in Chapter 9.

Article 6: Income from immovable property

7.24   Income from immovable property, for example rent from office buildings or from land used for agriculture, may be taxed in the state in which that property is located. Article 6(1) gives the right to tax income from immovable property to the state of source since there is obviously a very close economic connection between the source of this type of income and the state in which it is located. Usually the definition of 'immovable property' includes land and buildings, agricultural equipment and livestock. It also includes payments indirectly connected with immovable property, for instance payments for the right to work mineral deposits as well as more obvious types of income from property such as rent.

Article 8: International transport

7.25   As it would be impracticable to try to work out exactly where the profits of an international transport enterprise, operating in many states, are earned, the general rule is that these profits are only taxed by the state in which the international transport enterprise is resident. There are special rules to prevent an enterprise from avoiding any tax at all by operating from a ship located in international waters.

Article 9: Associated enterprises

7.26   Where the operations in each state are controlled by the same party, or for example are part of the same enterprise or corporate group, it would be easy to manipulate the pricing of transactions between them so as to achieve the best overall tax result by maximizing group profits in lower tax countries.

To tackle this potential abuse, both Article 7 (business profits) and Article 9 (associated enterprises) allow for the profits to be computed as though the two parties were unconnected. Note that Article 7 is used for determining the split of profits between a head office and branch, whereas Article 9 normally applies to transactions between separate companies in the same group.

If one state makes an upwards adjustment to the profits of an enterprise, then Article 9 may provide for the other state to make a corresponding downwards adjustment. However, this adjustment is to taxable profits, not the tax itself, so an enterprise suffering transfer-pricing adjustments will probably still be worse off even if a corresponding adjustment is made as invariably it will be the state with the higher tax rate that makes the upwards adjustment. Even if there is no specific provision for a corresponding downwards adjustment to taxable profits, this will normally be addressed by the mutual agreement procedure provided for in Article 25 so that double taxation is avoided. In the case of states which are Member States of the EU, the EU Arbitration Convention will apply.

Most states have detailed laws designed to help determine whether multinational companies/groups of companies are fixing their transfer prices to take advantage of lower tax rates in one of the states. The US has very detailed legislation – the 'S482 code'. We will consider the problem of transfer pricing further in Chapter 13.

Article 10: Dividends

7.27   The OECD MTC provides that dividends may be taxed in both states – that is, in the state of *source* (where the company paying the dividend is tax resident) and also in the state where the shareholder is *resident*. In practice, it is difficult to make non-resident shareholders fill in tax returns and pay tax annually, so common practice is to require companies only to pay their foreign shareholders their dividends after they have acted as tax collectors and deducted a flat rate of tax. The paying company sends the dividend (minus tax) to the foreign shareholder, and the tax to its own state's tax authority. This is the form of tax known as 'withholding tax':

- The charge in the source state normally takes the form of a withholding tax and the maximum charge allowed is 15 per cent. The UK's treaties, in common with many, often have rates lower than 15 per cent. However, there is no withholding tax on dividends under UK domestic law and therefore, whatever, the UK's treaties say, the UK will not charge withholding taxes on dividends. The provisions are there to enable the UK's treaty partners to charge withholding tax on UK residents.

● The state where the shareholder is resident then taxes the gross amount of dividend, but allows a credit for the foreign tax already paid. Alternatively, it may exempt the dividend from taxation.

Article 10 of the OECD MTC is reproduced below with explanations in italics:

'DIVIDENDS

1. Dividends paid by a company which is a resident of a Contracting State to a resident of the other Contracting State may be taxed in that other State.

   [*This normally means that the State where the shareholder is resident can tax the dividends. The shareholder should include the dividend on his or her income tax return, gross of any withholding tax charged.*]

2. However, such dividends may also be taxed in the Contracting State of which the company paying the dividends is a resident and according to the laws of that State, but if the beneficial owner of the dividends is a resident of the other Contracting State, the tax so charged shall not exceed:

   (a) 5 per cent of the gross amount of the dividends if the beneficial owner is a company (other than a partnership) which holds directly at least 25 per cent of the capital of the company paying the dividends;

   (b) 15 per cent of the gross amount of the dividends in all other cases.

   [*This means that the State in which the paying company is resident can also tax the dividends. The tax charged will be a percentage of the gross amount of the dividend, and takes the form of a withholding tax. For instance, if White Ltd, resident in State A, pays a dividend to its 100 per cent holding company in State B, then para 2(a) means that White Ltd will send 5 per cent of the gross amount of the dividend to the tax authority in State A and will only send 95 per cent of the dividend to the shareholder.*]

   The competent authorities of the Contracting States shall by mutual agreement settle the mode of application of these limitations.

   This paragraph shall not affect the taxation of the company in respect of the profits out of which the dividends are paid.' [*In other words, the withholding tax is the liability of the shareholders, not the paying company. All the paying company is doing is to act as a tax collector.*]

Most treaties insist that the 'beneficial owner' of the dividends must be resident in the state to which the dividend is paid, and in older treaties there might be a requirement that the recipient is actually the same person as the beneficial owner. This is to stop persons in third states benefiting from the reduced rate of withholding tax charged under the treaty in situations where the shareholder is a company artificially set up to receive the dividends and which is obliged to pay the dividend straight on to a person in a third state. The concept of beneficial ownership is explored further in Chapter 15. The requirement for beneficial ownership also appears in Article 11 (Interest) and Article 12 (Royalties).

Example 7.1 Applying Article 10

Assume Parent Co, resident in State A, has a subsidiary, Sub Co, resident in State B. Sub Co wishes to pay a dividend of £500 gross to Parent Co. State A levies corporation tax at 30 per cent and uses the credit method of double tax relief. We could restate Article 10 as follows:

> 'Dividends paid by Sub Co which is a resident of State B to Parent Co, a resident of State A may be taxed in State A (at 30% with double tax relief for any State B tax).
>
> However, such dividends may also be taxed in State B, where Sub Co is resident, but if the beneficial owner, Parent Co, is a resident of State A (which it is), the tax charged by State B shall not exceed 5%, provided Parent Co is a company holding at least 25% of the capital of Sub Co.'

First, the domestic tax law of State B should be checked – unless State B charges withholding taxes on payments of dividends to foreign shareholders under its domestic law, then whatever the treaty says, it cannot charge withholding tax under the treaty. We will assume that under its domestic law, State B would charge a withholding tax of 20 per cent on payments of dividends to foreign shareholders. Next, the tax law of State A needs to be checked. Does State A, under its domestic law, charge tax on foreign dividends received by companies resident in State A? If not, then it will not tax the dividend received from State B, whatever the treaty says. We will assume that State A charges tax on foreign dividends under its domestic law.

Hence the taxes on the dividend of £500 will be:

Table 7.3

	£	Total Tax £
Tax in State B:		
Gross dividend	500	
Less tax at 5% (withholding tax)	–25	25
Paid to Parent Co	475	
Tax in State A		
Dividend from Sub Co *before* State B tax	500	
State B corporation tax at 30%	–150	
Less: double tax relief:	25	
Final State A tax	125	125
Total taxes		150

Both State A and State B have taxed the dividend.

In the case of dividends paid between companies resident in EU Member States, domestic law in the Member States, as amended by the EU Parent Subsidiary Directive provides that, from 1 January 2009, where there is a minimum shareholding of 10 per cent in the paying company, no withholding tax may be charged to a corporate shareholder.

The treaty rates are the *maximum* rates that may be charged but they will only apply where they are lower than the domestic rates.

Besides dealing with the rate of withholding tax, Article 10 deals with the occasions on which withholding tax would not be charged. Article 10, para 4 states:

> 'The provisions of paragraphs 1 and 2 shall not apply if the beneficial owner of the dividends, being a resident of a Contracting State, carries on business in the other Contracting State of which the company paying the dividends is a resident through a permanent establishment situated therein and the holding in respect of which the dividends are paid is effectively connected with such permanent establishment. In such case the provisions of Article 7 shall apply.'

Paragraphs 1–2 deal with taxation in the shareholder's state and withholding tax in the state where the paying company is resident. Paragraph 4 may be illustrated (see Figure 7.1):

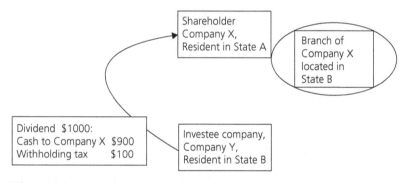

Figure 7.1

Example 7.2

Say Company X in State A has a PE (a branch) in State B. Company X owns a shareholding in Company Y which is resident in State B which pays a dividend. The company's trade consists of the manufacture of wooden garden furniture and also bamboo garden furniture. The bamboo furniture is produced by the branch in State B. Company X has purchased all the shares in Company Y, a company resident in State B which is a supplier of bamboo. The internal accounts of Company X show the following allocation of assets between the head office in State A and the branch in State B:

Table 7.4

	Head office in State A	Branch in State B	Total
	$	$	$
Premises	150,000	100,000	250,000
Financial assets:			
Shares in Company Y	0	40,000	40,000
Net current assets	30,000	20,000	50,000
Total	180,000	160,000	340,000

In this example (see Figure 7.2), because Company Y's trade is closely linked to the activities of the branch of Company X which is located in State B, the shares in Company Y are allocated to the branch for internal accounting purposes by Company X. The shareholding forms part of the assets of the branch, rather than the head office.

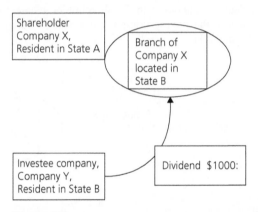

Figure 7.2

The dividend is regarded as being paid from a source within State B to a recipient within State B. Because the dividend has not left the state, State B would not charge withholding tax, but would be entitled to tax the PE (the branch) of the taxpayer in State B on the full amount of the dividend. This treatment would probably be favourable to Company X as, if the dividend is treated as part of the profits of the branch, the tax will be computed on net profits after expenses, whereas the withholding tax is computed on the gross amount of the dividend. Depending on the exact rules for double tax relief, the taxpayer might also be liable to tax on the dividend in State A and so State A would have to give double tax relief on the full State B corporation tax suffered by Company X on the dividend, rather than on withholding tax. Whether State A would also give a double tax credit for corporation tax suffered by Company Y in State B on the profits used to pay the dividend would depend on the exact provisions of the DTT between State A and State B.

Paragraph 5 of Article 10 deals with the situation where a company paying a dividend derives some of its income from the state in which the shareholder is resident. This may be illustrated as follows (see Figure 7.3):

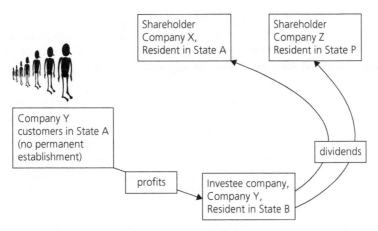

Figure 7.3

The rule in paragraph 5 forbids State A from charging any tax on the dividends paid by Company Y which are not paid to a resident of State A. Thus State A is only permitted to tax the dividend paid to Company X, even though the dividend paid to Company Z might be derived wholly or partly from the profits which Company Y made from its customers in State A. Paragraph 5 also explains that if Company Z had a PE located in State A and Z's shareholding in Company Y formed part of Company Z's assets allocated in its internal accounts to its branch in State A, then State A *would* be entitled to tax Company Z on the dividend it received from Company Y.

Article 10 also contains a definition of what is meant by the term 'dividend'. In essence, dividends are defined as income from shares and have the key attribute of being payments which represent a participation in the profits of the paying state. In states such as Germany or Austria where entities other than companies are treated in a similar way to companies for tax purposes, dividends may include certain payments to 'sleeping partners' in silent partnerships and may include the return on certain loans where the amount of interest depends on the profitability of the borrower.

Article 11: Interest

7.28 The OECD Commentary defines interest as being generally 'remuneration on money lent' and is distinguished from dividends as not generally being subject to double taxation, ie it is not generally taxed both in the hands of the debtor and in the hands of the creditor. Like dividends, however, interest may be taxed in both states if the recipient is the beneficial owner, although withholding tax deducted at source must not exceed 10 per cent, per the 2010 version of the MTC. In practice, rates of up to 15 per cent are common, particularly in older treaties. The source state is identified as the state of residence of the payer.

A two-tier structure is quite common, with interest payable to the government of one of the states being exempt from withholding tax. Often, interest on export-related loans which are guaranteed by the state is also exempt, as is interest on credit sale agreements for the purchase of plant and machinery. Other interest may be subject to withholding tax.

As with dividends, there is a rule dealing with the situation where an enterprise resident in State A has a PE in State B and the enterprise receives interest from a payer in State B which relates to an investment or other loan which forms part of the assets of the PE as opposed to the head office. Such interest would form part of the income of the PE and thus would be taxed in full by State B under Article 7. Thus the taxpayer would suffer corporation tax or income tax on a net basis in State B rather than withholding tax. Double tax relief will be granted by State A.

There is also a rule (in para 6) dealing with interest payments on loans which form part of the liabilities of a PE, rather than of the head office. If a taxpayer resident in State A has a PE in State B and the borrowings form part of the taxpayer's liabilities allocated to the PE in State B, then the borrower need not deduct any State A withholding tax on payments of interest to a recipient in State B. This is despite the fact that a State A taxpayer has made a payment of interest to a State B taxpayer. The logic for this is that the interest has not crossed any border: it was paid on a borrowing located in State B to a taxpayer resident in State B. State B will give a tax deduction for the interest paid (to the PE) and can charge tax on the interest receipt because the interest is paid to a lender taxable within State B. This is illustrated below (see Figure 7.4):

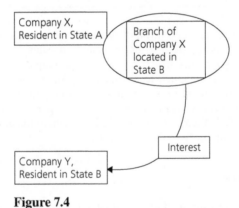

Figure 7.4

Interest is normally defined very widely, often according to the domestic law of the two states, but the definition usually excludes amounts treated as dividends.

Scope exists to attack 'thin capitalization' as well as interest at other than commercial rates. A company, usually a wholly-owned subsidiary, would be considered to be thinly capitalized where the proportion of debt capital to equity capital is large. The risk associated with such a capital structure means that it is rarely found except where the loan holder is the parent company or other group company. The tax advantage of this structure is that the return on debt capital is interest, which is usually deductible from taxable profits, whereas dividends, the return on equity capital, are not. This is examined further in Chapter 11. Article 11 deals with the matter by stating that where there is a special relationship between the payer and the recipient and the amount of interest is in excess of what might be expected between an independent borrower and lender, the excess will not enjoy the treaty withholding tax rate. Either the higher domestic rate will apply to the excess, or the excess might be treated as a dividend.

Article 12: Royalties

7.29   Article 12(1) gives exclusive taxation to the state of residence of the beneficial owner of the royalty. Thus the OECD MTC does not permit any withholding tax to be charged. However, many treaties entered into before the most recent OECD MTC, and those based on the UN MTC, still permit withholding tax to be charged. Sometimes only certain types of payment carry withholding tax with others (commonly literary and artistic copyright payments) being exempt.

The term 'royalty' in this context is defined in Article 12(2) to mean payments received as consideration for the use of, or right to use, any copyright, patent, trade mark, design or model, plan, secret formula or process or for information concerning industrial, commercial or scientific experience. Sometimes international plant and equipment leasing payments are covered: in this case, the definition would include the wording: 'or for the right to use industrial, commercial or scientific equipment'. Although not in the 2008 version of the OECD MTC, this provision is in widespread use in existing treaties and many OECD members have expressed in the 'reservations' to Article 12 their intention to continue to include leasing payments as royalties in future treaties.

The nature of payments in respect of computer software is a difficult area. Are they royalties or not? The pure intellectual property in question is the computer program itself and this is what is normally protected by copyright. However, there is a spectrum of possible transfers of computer software, ranging from the outright transfer of the software itself to a limited right to use the software. If a payment is in respect of rights to use the copyright in a program, (eg by reproducing it and distributing it) then such a payment would be considered as a royalty. Other payments, however, only give a user the right to operate the program, possibly by making a copy of it which runs on a personal computer. Whether paying for the right to make a personal copy of a computer program constitutes a payment in respect of copyright or not depends on the domestic law of a state but the OECD view is that where a consumer pays for a copy of a computer program to use on one or more personal computers, this is not a royalty payment but a simple sale of a product. Whether the program is transferred to the consumer electronically or via a physical medium is irrelevant.

Payments for music, film and other digital downloads by consumers are not considered to be royalties, because although the payment covers the right to make a copy of the song or film, it does not confer the right to reproduce it further. The payment is essential to enable the consumer to acquire the data.

Capital gains on intangibles are sometimes subject to withholding tax under Article 11, particularly if they are, in reality, 'up front' royalties, that is, if they are lump sums which are worked out according to the expected future usage of the intangible, or if the amount is dependent on any future sale of the intangible by the buyer.

In actual treaties, where one of the treaty partners is a developing state, it is common to find fees for technical services included in Article 12 rather than under Article 7 (business profits). As technical services are usually provided to the developing state, this gives that state the right to levy a withholding tax on the gross amount of the technical fees charged to its residents, rather than just on the profits attributable to those technical fees which are made by the foreign provider. This has two advantages for the developing state. First, the amount of tax will probably be higher as it is based on the gross amount of the fees, and secondly there is very little scope for the foreign provider to minimize his exposure to tax in the developing state by attributing only a small amount of profits to the fees. The practice of 'grossing up' of fees is common and shifts the burden of the withholding tax onto the taxpayer.

As with dividends and interest, there is a rule dealing with the situation where an enterprise resident in State A has a PE in State B and the enterprise receives royalties from a payer in State B which relates to an intangible asset which forms part of the assets of the PE as opposed to the head office. Such royalties would form part of the income of the PE and thus would be taxed in full by State B under Article 7. Thus the taxpayer would suffer full taxation in State B rather than merely withholding tax. Double tax relief will be granted by State A.

Although not found in the MTC, many existing treaties contain a rule dealing with royalty payments in connection with intangibles which are used by the PE, rather than by the head office. This is equivalent to the rule in paragraph 5 of Article 11 (Interest). If a taxpayer resident in State A has a PE in State B which uses intangibles in State B and pays royalties to a recipient in State B, then State A will not charge any withholding tax, despite the fact that a State A taxpayer has made a payment of royalties to a State B taxpayer. The logic for this is that the royalties have not crossed any border. Currently, Belgium, Canada, the Czech Republic, Mexico, France and the Slovak Republic have stated in the 'reservations' to Article 12 that they intend to continue to include such a provision in future treaties.

Article 13: Capital gains

7.30   The taxation of capital gains varies from state to state: in some they are taxed in the same way as ordinary income, in others they are given special treatment and in yet others they may not be taxed at all. The OECD MTC does not attempt to deal with these different approaches and does not specify what kind of tax it applies to. The basic rule is that capital gains are taxable only in the state in which the taxpayer is resident. This does not mean that the state where the taxpayer is resident *must* tax the gains: it simply means that only that state has the right to tax the gains. A good number of states choose not to tax capital gains even though their treaties give them the right to do so. As with any treaty provision, this article cannot create a tax liability where none would otherwise have existed.

Article 13 refers to 'alienation' of property. This term is used in connection with events giving rise to capital gains. It will include normal disposals of assets, for example by sale, and also events such as exchange of assets, expropriation, gifts and the passing of assets to another on death. Not all states levy tax in all these situations, but the meaning of the term 'alienation' is sufficiently wide to give them the right to do so if their domestic law provides for a charge to tax in a particular situation.

Two provisions are found in most tax treaties:

- First, a state is permitted to tax gains from the alienation (eg sale) of immovable property (land and buildings) situated in that state. This is because of the very close link between the gain and the state in which the property is located.

- Second, gains on alienation of movable property forming part of the assets of a PE may be taxed by the state where the PE is situated, including gains from the alienation of the PE, whether or not as part of the alienation of the whole enterprise. Thus, for example, the sale of a wholly-owned company resident in State A and owned by a resident of State A could give rise to a tax charge in State B if that company has a PE in State B.

Gains on the alienation of ships or aircraft used in international traffic businesses are invariably taxable only in the state in which the place of effective management is located. This is sensible in that an international transport firm will have assets located around the world, with the locations of those ships and aircraft changing daily. In the absence of this rule, an international transport firm could find itself liable to a capital gains tax charge in whatever state the ship or aircraft happened to be at the time the sale took place.

Apart from these basic provisions, treaties often include more detailed provisions dealing with the indirect holding of immovable property. The OECD MTC only includes one: a rule that gains on the alienation of shares which derive more than 50 per cent of their value directly or indirectly from immovable property situated in the other state may be taxed in the other state. This would result in a tax on gains from sales of shares in property companies. Many variations on this rule are found in practice. Some treaties make an exception if the company is publicly quoted. Some do not explicitly state the percentage of value to be represented by immovable property in the other state. This rule is illustrated below (see Figure 7.5):

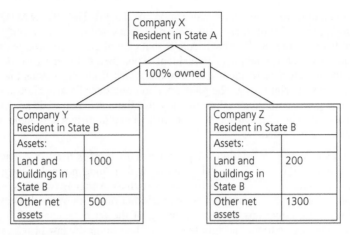

Figure 7.5

If Company X sells its shares in Company Y at a gain, that gain may be taxed by State B. It may also be taxed in State A, which would then give double tax relief for the State B tax. However, if the shares in Company Z were sold at a gain, only State A would be entitled to tax that gain. The reason for this rule is that the value of the shares in Company Y is closely linked to the value of the land and buildings owned by that company in State B and therefore State B is awarded taxing rights over the gain on the sale of the shares.

Some treaties may include a provision that gains on the sale of shares in any company, whether or not it owns immovable property, can be taxed by the state in which the company is resident if the alienation is made out of a holding in the company amounting, typically, to 25 per cent or more of the voting power in the company.

Some treaties have provisions which specifically preserve the benefits of deferral of tax on gains which would be granted by the state in which the taxpayer is resident (eg gains made in the course of a group reorganization where there is no change in the ultimate ownership).

Provisions relating to individuals who switch their residence from one contracting state to the other are frequently found in Canadian, Austrian and US treaties (but not exclusively so). For instance, the 1980 Canada–Austria Treaty contains, inter alia, these rules:

●   Where an individual changes residence from one state (either of which he is a national or of which he has been a resident for at least 10 years) to the other, (say from Canada to Austria) then using this as an example, Canada retains the right to tax any gains made in the five years following the change of residence. Austria retains the same right regarding individuals who move to Canada.

●   If an individual changes his tax residence, say from Canada to Austria, and if Canada makes an exit charge on the capital gains accrued as at the date of the change, then the individual can elect in Austria to be treated as having sold and repurchased the property in question as at the date of change of residence. In other words, if one state imposes a capital gains exit charge, the other state will permit an uplift in the base cost of the assets involved.

Each of these rules has a different purpose. The first is an anti-avoidance measure, whereas the second is a means of preventing double taxation.

Finally, notice that there are no instructions whatsoever as to how a gain should be computed. This is left entirely up to the individual states, who will normally apply their domestic rules.

Article 14: Independent personal services

7.31 Article 14 was deleted in the 2000 version of the OECD MTC, but it still appears in many existing treaties and is also still included in the UN MTC. The OECD considered that there was duplication in the rules and that the taxation of sole traders and partnerships could be dealt with adequately under Article 5 (PE) and Article 7 (business profits).

However, many existing treaties incorporate a parallel set of rules to those set out in Article 5 and Article 7 for use in the case of professional services such as those provided by unincorporated persons: typically doctors, lawyers, engineers, architects, dentists and accountants. Also included would be income from literary, artistic, educational, teaching or independent scientific activity (but not royalty income, which would be dealt with under Article 12). Income of sole practitioners and partners is typically covered. Rather than looking for a PE, the article looks for a 'fixed base' which would probably be an office in the other state in regular use by the professional person. The income attributable to activities carried out in the fixed base located in the other state may be taxed by the other state. Some treaties, often those based on the UN MTC, include an alternative test – even where there is no fixed base, the other state may tax the professional if he is present there for at least 183 days in the tax year.

The UN MTC continues to include Article 14, although there is an alternative formulation for states wishing to include provisions dealing with independent personal services in Article 5.

Article 15: Income from employment

7.32 The operation of the source principle means that, technically speaking, any remuneration in respect of work carried out in a state is taxable in that state, even if it is over a small number of days. Paragraph 1 of Article 15 sets out this rule – if the employment is exercised in State A, then State A may tax the wages or salary from the work done in State A.

However, the main purpose of this article is to prevent remuneration from short-term assignments being taxed in the state in which the assignment is carried out. If the employer is not taxable in a state, because it is neither resident there nor has a PE there then it will not receive any tax deduction in that state for wages and salaries paid. Therefore, to tax remuneration of the employees would mean that the state where the short-term assignment is carried out would tax the employee without giving any tax deduction to the employer.

Besides preserving symmetry in taxation in this way, the exemption from tax, in the visited state, of income from short-term assignments provides significant administrative savings, both for employees and for the tax authorities who would otherwise need to try and keep track of all foreigners being paid for work done within their state, no matter how short the assignment.

There is relatively little variation in the way that the OECD MTC is used in practice. The basic rule is that the source state has the right to tax remuneration from any employment exercised within it. Then the exemption for short-term assignments is set out. The maximum length of the assignment in order for exemption from source state taxation to apply is 183 days. There is some variation in exactly how the 183 days is determined – it may be 183 days in any calendar year, or in the tax period in question, or in any 12-month period commencing or ending in the tax period in question. The current wording in the OECD MTC is '183 days in any twelve-month period commencing or ending in the fiscal year concerned'. This wording is designed to prevent manipulation of the rules by, for instance, a worker being posted abroad for an 11-month period with the timing arranged so that he was present in the other state for five and a half months in one year and five and a half months in the next, thus not breaking the 183-day in any year rule. Exact measurement of the 183 days is also subject to interpretation – do days of arrival and departure count? Normally the rules of domestic law are used to decide. The 183-day period is an aggregate period, so that shorter assignments will be added together.

Two other conditions must be fulfilled for the source state to exempt the remuneration from a short-term assignment: the remuneration must not be paid by, or on behalf of, an employer resident in the state to which the employee is posted; nor must it be borne by a PE which the employer has in the state to which the employee is posted. Otherwise, the visited state would be giving a tax deduction for the remuneration to the employer without taxing the employee.

Example 7.3

Paula is tax resident in the UK and employed by Brown Ltd, a UK company with a South African subsidiary. She is sent to work on a project being carried out partly in the UK and partly in South Africa. In the South African tax year which ended on 28 February 20X1 she had made three visits to South Africa of ten days each. All her wages were paid by her UK employer and were not recharged to the South African subsidiary. Brown Ltd did not have a PE in South Africa. Thus although she had earned wages for work performed in South Africa, she had spent fewer than 183 days in South Africa and her wages were not tax deductible for any person against South African taxable income. The effect of the UK–South Africa Treaty is that South Africa would not seek to charge tax on the portion of her wages relating to the work done in South Africa.

Employee stock options

7.33   The treatment of employee stock options is not expressly dealt with and can be difficult as entitlement to the benefit taxable as a result of the option may have accrued partly whilst the employee was working temporarily in one of the states but there may be no taxable event, such as exercise of the option until the employee returns to the other state. A state is permitted to tax that part of the taxable benefit that can be related to the portion of the entitlement period spent working in that state. The Commentary on Article 15 deals with stock options at some length. For a discussion of how employee stock options are dealt with, see Chapter 8.

Article 16: Directors' fees

7.34   The general rule is that directors' fees can be taxed in the state in which the company is resident, as well as that in which the director is resident. Broadly, the reason for this rule is that the fortunes of the director and the company are very closely linked. Thus a director resident in the Netherlands who is a director of a German company might find himself taxable in Germany on his directors' fees. Germany would be able to tax the full amount, even if none of the directors' duties were carried out in Germany, with the Netherlands having to provide double tax relief. The US Model takes a more lenient view, only permitting the state where the company is resident to tax the director on remuneration for duties carried out in that state rather than on his total remuneration.

Many treaties distinguish between true directors' fees and payments for work of a routine administrative nature, with the latter being treated as income from employment in the normal way.

Article 17: Entertainers and sportspersons

7.35   Entertainers and sportspersons are recognized as being a special category because they often perform in many different states and can earn very large sums of money in a matter of days or weeks rather than the six months which is the usual threshold for Articles 5, 7 and 14. Using the source principle, each state in which they perform is entitled to tax the income generated by that performance. In the interests of simplicity, we might expect that the OECD would recommend that they be taxable in the state where they are resident only but in fact, because the earnings are potentially very high, the OECD MTC provides that they may be taxed by the source state. Often, the artiste or sportsperson will not be paid directly by the venue in which he or she performs, but the earnings will be paid to a management company (often a 'one man' company, wholly owned by the artiste and with only one employee – the artiste). In these cases the usual rule is that the source principle still applies so that the state in which the performance takes place retains the right to tax the income. Usually this means that the performer suffers withholding tax on the fee in the state where the performance takes place. This withholding tax might be on the gross amount of the fee or it might be charged on the net amount after deduction of expenses. It might be a final withholding tax (ie the amount of the withholding tax is fixed at a percentage of the income and no refund is possible should it turn out that normal source state income tax on the net profit would have been a smaller figure). If it is a non-final withholding tax, then the artiste or sportsperson has the opportunity to make a tax return in the state in which the performance took place and to calculate normal income tax on the net income after expenses. If the withholding tax deducted exceeds the tax as calculated on the net income, then the host state will make a tax refund.

Two common exceptions are found:

- where the artiste or sportsperson is substantially supported out of public funds in the state where he is resident, only the state where he is resident may tax the income; and

- where the performance takes place under a programme of cultural exchange between the two contracting states, again, the income is only taxable in the state of residence, not where the performance takes place.

Note that the 2014 update to the MTC makes a number of clarifications to the scope and application of Article 17.

Article 18: Pensions

7.36   The basic rule is that pensions from past employment are only to be taxed in the state where the recipient is resident. In practice, there are many exceptions to this. Many treaties provide that social security pensions, the amount of which may be dependent on a person's past employment record, are only to be taxed by the state which pays the pension. Some states adopt their own rules entirely: for instance, Canadian treaties usually state that pensions in respect of past employment may be taxed by the state from which they are paid. If the state where the recipient is resident also taxes them, as is probably the case, then the residence state will have to give double tax relief.

Some treaties contain other rules – there may be a difference in the treatment of periodic and lump sum pensions, with lump sums typically being taxable in the state from which they are paid. More recent US treaties contain provisions protecting the right of expatriates to deductions against their taxable income in the state in which they are working for pension contributions made to pension schemes in their home state. Provisions dealing specifically with alimony and child support are common.

Payments made post-termination of employment

7.37   In the 2014 update, material was added dealing with payments, such as non-competition payments, made following the termination of employment, or payments with respect to unused holidays. There is a risk that such payments could be treated differently in the state where the person was working, and the state where the person is normally resident. States should look for the true nature of the payments to decide whether they are within Article 15 (employment) or Article 18 (pensions).

Article 19: Government service

7.38   This article contains provisions covering the taxation of government and local authority employees. The basic rule is that only the state paying the remuneration can charge tax, even if the recipient is resident in the other state. Pensions are taxable only where the recipient is resident provided he is also a national of that state.

Article 20: Students

7.39   Students who go abroad to study may well be present for long enough in the visited state to become tax resident there. This would normally mean that they would find themselves taxable in the visited state on their worldwide income, including income from their home state. The basic rule is that students are not taxed in the visited state on payments which they receive from outside that state (eg from their home state). Such payments must be for the purpose of their maintenance, education or training.

Many treaties extend the rules so that students may be able to work in the visited state for a certain period, or earn remuneration up to certain limits without becoming taxable there. Provisions for business trainees are common, although there is usually a limit on the period for which the favourable treatment will apply, often a year.

Indian treaties tend to have very detailed rules for students, with provisions whereby the visited state will exempt from tax all manner of grants, scholarships and allowances, even if they arise in the visited state. US treaties often cover three separate categories – students, general business trainees or students sponsored by their employer and then government-sponsored trainees. US treaties often also contain a clause so that the same individual cannot claim treaty benefits as a student and then, immediately afterwards, as a teacher.

The 2010 OECD MTC does not contain any specific rule for teachers and researchers, but many existing treaties provide that a teacher or researcher may go to work in the other state for up to two years and, even though technically tax resident in the visited state, remain taxable only in the home state. This favourable treatment normally only applies to researchers if they are engaged in publicly funded research, rather than, say, working for a pharmaceutical company which has exclusive rights to the fruits of their labours.

Article 21: Other income

7.40   This rather innocuously titled article covers all the types of income which might otherwise not be covered by the preceding articles. The types of income dealt with might include income from non-competition agreements, gambling winnings, income from certain types of financial instruments which falls neither under the heading of dividends nor interest (in practice, an important use of this article), perhaps punitive damages and any income which does not fall clearly into any other category.

Not all treaties include this article, although most do.

The usual rule is that 'other income' may only be taxed in the state where the owner is resident, although the UN MTC and the treaties concluded by certain states, such as Australia, Canada, Mexico and New Zealand, insist that other income is to be taxed in the state in which it arises. Some treaties which take this position only allow the state of source to impose a withholding tax, typically at a maximum of 15 per cent.

Article 22: Capital

7.41   This is a rather puzzling article to those used to a tax regime (such as the UK or the US) which does not impose periodic wealth taxes. Many states, such as France and India, impose an annual tax on the stock of a person's wealth, so that the taxpayer might be charged tax of, say, 2 per cent of his total worth each year. No disposals are necessary, as with capital gains tax, to trigger liability and nor is it necessary that the assets being taxed should have produced any income. It is a tax on a person's 'balance sheet' value.

Sometimes, the tax extends to annual local taxes on immovable property. Normally the types of asset which can be taxed are those covered by Article 6 (income from immovable property) and Article 13 (capital gains).

The article does not appear in all treaties. Where neither party to the treaty imposes this type of tax in their domestic tax systems, there is no point. However, sometimes, treaty negotiators include it 'just in case'. It is common in cases where one treaty partner imposes this type of tax and the other does not for the article to be included and worded reciprocally, so that the partner which does not currently charge the tax has the right to do so in the future with respect to residents of the other state. This would not be done, though, unless that state changed its domestic law so that this became a general feature of its domestic tax system, as a treaty cannot create a tax liability where none would otherwise exist, and neither may a state discriminate against residents of its treaty partner, as compared with its own residents (Article 24 (non-discrimination)).

Article 23: Double tax relief

7.42   You will recall that in Chapters 5 and 6 we saw a detailed explanation of the different types of double tax relief that can be used. The OECD MTC offers a choice of credit relief, where the state of tax residence taxes the income from abroad, but gives credit for foreign tax paid on that income, and relief by exemption where either the source state or more usually the state of tax residence will exempt the foreign income from taxation altogether.

The contracting states will then choose which method to use, which is a matter of negotiation between them.

In this article, each state will set out, in broad terms, the method it will use to relieve double taxation. Each state is free to adopt a different method to the other, and indeed it is rare to find a treaty where both states will use the same method. A state might set out in this article that it will use different methods for different types of income. For instance, it is quite common for a state to set out in its treaties that it will exempt dividends received from the other state if they are paid on shareholdings representing more than 10 per cent of the capital of the paying company. Other dividends might be given double tax relief via the credit method. Other common exceptions where a state specifies the exemption method in its treaties are that interest and royalties will also be given double tax relief via the credit method. The detail of the double tax relief will, however, be governed by domestic law.

Tax sparing

7.43 Double tax treaties with developing states which are based on the UN Model often contain 'tax sparing' provisions. This means that State A will give credit for tax in State B (the developing state), even where no tax has actually been paid in State B. This preserves the usefulness to an investor in State A of any tax incentives offered to it by State B. In the absence of tax-sparing provisions, the only result of a reduction in tax in State B would be an increase in tax in State A due to a lower or non-existent State B tax credit. Tax-sparing provisions can be worded so that they refer to tax exemptions given under particular statutes (usually to do with encouraging foreign inward investment). This is typical of Indian treaties. Alternatively, the provisions might state that, in our example, State A will allow a certain percentage of gross dividend, interest or royalty income as a credit, even if no withholding tax has been charged by State B. This is common in Chinese tax treaties, many of which date from the early 1980s and are still based on the UN MTC. Sometimes a time limit is placed on the provisions, typically ten years from the date of the treaty, and in other cases the provision is open-ended.

US treaties – the 'saving clause'

7.44 US treaties have a unique problem to deal with in the double tax relief article – because the US reserves the right, through the 'saving clause' (Article 1, para 4 of the US model), to charge full US taxes on its residents and on individuals who are, or have been, US citizens. A US citizen tax resident outside the US in State X may find that they have been subject to full residence-based taxation in both the US and in State X. The US wishes to achieve the effect that the individual pays the same amount of tax worldwide as if he were merely resident in the US. State X is normally in the position of giving a credit to its residents for tax suffered overseas, but does not see why it should concede a very large tax credit just because the US has insisted on taxing the individual as if he were still resident in the US. Therefore State X will usually only agree to grant the tax credit up to the amount of tax that would be paid if the US did not impose extra tax charges on the grounds of the individual's US citizenship, in other words, the normal amount of tax the US would charge to a non-resident who was *not* a US citizen. At this point the individual is suffering a high combined tax liability – full US residence-based tax plus residual tax (after the tax credit for 'normal' US tax) in State X. The solution usually adopted is for the US to reduce the tax it charges to the non-resident on the basis of citizenship by granting, in turn, a credit for the tax suffered State X. The amount of the credit will be limited to the amount needed to bring the US citizen's global tax bill back down to what it would have been had the individual been both a US citizen and a US tax resident. The problem with this solution is that it involves treating income arising in State X as if it had arisen in the US and so lengthy provisions are needed to ensure that the income can be treated as arising out of a source in the technically correct state: so called 're-sourcing' rules.

Article 24: Non-discrimination

7.45   The purpose of this article is to prevent discrimination against foreign taxpayers. State A may not subject a national of State B to any taxation or connected procedures which are in addition to, or more burdensome than those to which, in the same circumstances, it subjects its own nationals. Notably, this article is expressed in terms of 'nationals' rather than residents, which arguably is a wider concept. This means that all nationals of each contracting state are entitled to invoke the non-discrimination article against the other contracting state even if they do not fall within the definition of resident for tax purposes (ie they could even be a tax resident of a third state). Thus, states are permitted to discriminate on grounds of residence but not nationality. However, where residence status has no bearing on the treatment in question, states are not permitted to discriminate on the grounds of residence alone. The Commentary gives several examples illustrating these principles.

This article is the one that generates the greatest number of international tax law disputes and the most contentious phrase is 'in the same circumstances'.

There is nothing to stop a state from negotiating exceptions from the principle of non-discrimination. For instance, India commonly insists upon the right to discriminate against the PEs of foreign enterprises by subjecting their profits to a higher rate of tax than that applied to the profits of Indian enterprises. Poland, in some of its treaties, reserves the right to discriminate in favour of its formerly state-owned enterprises. More commonly, states which operate a branch profits tax usually reserve the right to charge this tax in the non-discrimination article.

Many treaties extend the principle of non-discrimination to all taxes, not just those specifically covered by the treaty.

Article 25: Mutual agreement procedure

7.46   Article 25 of the OECD MTC is designed to provide a procedure for resolving difficulties in the application of the treaty. It provides that the competent authorities of each state must attempt to resolve the situation of a taxpayer who is taxed other than in accordance with the provisions of the treaty, for example in relation to the attribution of profits to a PE, or where the treaty has been misapplied, perhaps in the determination of residence. Instances of double taxation not eliminated by any specific article in the treaty can also be dealt with using the mutual agreement procedure (MAP). This procedure is for the protection of the taxpayer and is initiated by the taxpayer, without interfering with any other remedies available to them under domestic laws. There does not need to be any double taxation in order to invoke the procedure, the only requirement is that the taxation in dispute has been imposed in contravention of the treaty. For example, State A may tax a particular class of income that the Convention allocates rights to tax to State B, although State B may not in fact tax it, for example due to a gap in its domestic tax laws. The more common situations in which the MAP is invoked are:

- Where profits have been attributed to a PE, determining the proportion of head office expenses and overheads which can be deducted from the profits of the PE.

- Establishing the amount of any reciprocal adjustment in the case of transfer-pricing adjustments: where State A has made an upwards adjustment to the profits of an enterprise under Article 9, Article 9 may or may not require the treaty partner, State B, to make corresponding downwards adjustment to the taxable profits of the related person resident in State B with whom the transactions in question were made. If no reciprocal adjustment, or an incomplete reciprocal adjustment is made, then some profits will have been taxed by both State A and State B. As the aim of the treaty is to eliminate double taxation, the mutual agreement procedure provides a framework for negotiation between the two tax authorities. They may also take into account so-called 'secondary adjustments', which are rarely addressed in the treaty. If one state makes an upwards adjustment of taxable profits and the other makes an exactly equal corresponding downwards adjustment, then the tax revenues of the two states might still be different to what they would have been had arm's-length pricing been applied in the first place. This is because higher profits in the state where the upwards adjustment took place might well have given rise to higher dividends or interest payments, on which withholding taxes might have been chargeable. So even though the state making the upwards adjustment has retrieved the tax deficit on the enterprise resident there, it has still not retrieved any deficit in withholding taxes. Whether it makes a secondary upwards adjustment to make good this deficit in withholding tax receipts depends on whether this is provided for in domestic law. If it does so, then double taxation will result which will not necessarily be relieved by the normal treaty article on elimination of double taxation and it may be necessary to invoke the mutual agreement procedure.

- Establishing the amount of any interest and royalty payments that are to be regarded as 'excessive' because of the special relationship between payer and recipient, and which thus do not qualify for treaty withholding rates.

- Establishing a single state of tax residence, where the tie-breaker clauses in Article 4 have failed, or where the treaty does not include any tie-breaker clauses.

- Deciding whether a PE exists or not.

- Deciding whether an employee has breached the 183-day limit set out in Article 15 so that he does not qualify for exemption from tax in the visited state.

There are some conditions attached to the MAP. To be admissible, objections must be presented to the competent authority of the state of residence of the taxpayer concerned within three years of first being notified of the action that is at the heart of the dispute. The OECD Commentary discusses at length the point from which the time limit should be considered to start running. The time limit is designed to protect tax authorities from late objections. Not all treaties include a time limit for bringing claims, and in those that do, the time limit varies.

The MAP is also used in cases where there is no disgruntled taxpayer bringing a case. It is used to agree on definitions of terms which are not expressly defined anywhere in the treaty. It can also be used to reach agreement as to whether a new tax is covered by the treaty, or whether any change in a state's domestic law affects the treaty. There may be situations where a person is not, strictly speaking, covered by the treaty, but is nevertheless subjected to double taxation by both State A and State B, for instance, where a company resident in State C has a PE in both State A and State B and both State A and State B consider that the same item of profits of the company is attributable to the PE in their territory, thus both taxing that profit.

The complaint is first considered by the 'competent authority' of the state in which the complainant is a national and may be resolved unilaterally, or in consultation with the 'competent authority' of the other contracting state. The 'competent authority' of a state is generally the Ministry of Finance, or the subdivision which has particular responsibility for tax matters (eg in the case of the UK, HMRC, and in the case of the US, the IRS). Cases brought under this article are sometimes referred to as 'competent authority procedures'.

The MAP is particularly valuable to taxpayers because it provides a mechanism for the tax authorities of each state to communicate with each other without having to go through diplomatic channels: they may simply write, email, telephone, or even meet face to face. Some treaties specifically permit an oral exchange of views. Some provide for a joint commission, to which the taxpayer may make representations, assisted by counsel if desired.

Newer treaties contain a provision which either requires the contracting states, or offers them the opportunity, to enter into a binding arbitration process. There may or may not be a time limit whereby if agreement has not been reached, the arbitration process is triggered. The 2008 version of the MTC puts this at two years. Note that Member States of the EU are, in any case, bound by the provisions of the EU Arbitration Convention, so that even if there is not express requirement or provision for arbitration in a treaty between EU

Member States, arbitration may nonetheless take place. Arbitration is possible under treaty where one or both contracting states are not members of the EU even where that treaty makes no provision for arbitration, as the tax authorities may decide, by mutual agreement, to enter into arbitration. Typically, an arbitration board will consist of senior members of each tax authority who have not so far been involved in the case.

A significant practical problem with the use of the MAP is that it can take a long time. It is not unusual for a MAP to take between eight and ten years to be concluded and binding arbitration can speed up the resolution of disputes considerably.

Article 26: Exchange of information

7.47   One of the more sensitive issues that will arise when two states negotiate a double tax treaty is that of the extent to which they will exchange information with each other about the tax affairs of their residents. Article 26(1) provides that the tax administrators of the treaty parties shall exchange such information as is *foreseeably relevant* for carrying out:

● the provisions of the double tax agreement (DTA); or

● the provisions of domestic law of the contracting states concerning taxes covered by the double tax agreement insofar as this is not contrary to the agreement.

The term 'foreseeably relevant' is important – it gives a high degree of flexibility to treaty partners in the type of information that may be requested, whilst at the same time discouraging speculative enquiries, where one state may have vague suspicions concerning its taxpayer but no real evidence that tax liabilities are not being met. The Commentary on Article 26 gives some useful examples of the type of information that might typically be exchanged:

● Information concerning the amount of royalty transmitted by a taxpayer in State A to a taxpayer in State B.

● Information required to establish the proper allocation of taxable profits between associated companies (transfer-pricing information), or the allocation of profits between a head office operation and its branch. The power to exchange information in this respect is quite wide. State A could legitimately ask State B for information on prices charged by suppliers in State B (who have no other connection with State A and are not State A taxpayers). State A would want this information so that it could cross-check prices being charged for similar products by State A taxpayer companies, to help establish whether their intragroup pricing is such as would be charged by unconnected parties. (See Chapter 13 on transfer pricing.)

● Where a person works abroad, information about the amount of earnings in each state.

The 2014 update to the MTC confirms that the term 'foreseeably relevant' does not encompass so-called 'fishing expeditions', ie speculative enquiries.

These are defined as 'speculative requests that have no apparent nexus to an open inquiry or investigation'. However, it is not necessary that names, and addresses of specific taxpayers are included in the request, so long there is enough information to identify the taxpayer concerned. 'Group requests' are particularly troublesome, and so the new Commentary clarifies that where the request concerns a group of taxpayers who are not individually identified, the following details must be given:

- A detailed description of the relevant group, eg account holders of a specific type at a specific financial institution.

- The specific facts and circumstances that have led to the request, eg a discovery that a State A resident taxpayer had held an account at that financial institution, and there are grounds for believing that other taxpayers resident in State A also had similar, undisclosed, accounts.

- An explanation of the applicable law, eg the requirement to disclose all foreign income on the tax return.

- Why there is reason to believe that the taxpayers in the group have not complied with that law, supported by a clear factual basis.

Another change included in the 2014 update is that the information exchanged may be used for non-tax purposes; if that is allowed under the domestic laws of both of the states concerned.

The Treaty is silent as to how the exchange of information should proceed: it is up to the treaty partners to decide the mechanics. The OECD commentary contemplates that information may be exchanged:

- *automatically* – where the revenue authorities arrange for the routine exchange of certain classes of information at regular intervals;

- *on request* – where the state requesting the information has something particular that it wants to know; or

- *spontaneously* – where information is supplied to a treaty partner without them having to ask for it first.

In practice, this article is very useful to the two tax administrations. There is a general principle that states will not enforce the tax claims of other states. Generally, this is known in international law as the 'Revenue Rule'. A leading authority on this subject states: 'English courts have no jurisdiction to entertain an action ... for the enforcement, either directly or indirectly, of a penal, revenue or other public law of a foreign State.'[1]

The authority for this statement is the decision of the English courts in *Government of India v Taylor*,[2] a case in which the Indian government tried to enforce a claim for unpaid Indian taxes against a UK company which had been trading in India. The principal way in which one state can assist another to enforce its own tax claims against its own residents is to supply information to the other state which makes enforcement of domestic tax law possible. For instance, if State A agrees to supply State B with details of interest paid on bank deposits in State A to residents of State B, then State B can pursue its residents for income tax payable under the domestic laws of State B.

It may be necessary for a state to amend its domestic laws in order to permit it to gather information requested by the treaty partner where the information is not required to establish any domestic tax liability. The UK found it necessary to amend its laws in this respect[3] to enable it to fulfil its obligations regarding information exchange under its tax treaties.

The wording of exchange of information articles in current treaties varies somewhat. Some treaties restrict the exchange of information to that which is necessary for the operation of the treaty itself, whereas many more extend the provision to information necessary for the operation of the treaty and of the domestic laws of the two states. Some go further and make specific reference to information needed to combat fraud and tax evasion. Relatively few treaties currently use the latest wording of information which is 'foreseeably relevant'. It should be noted that many states have entered into separate arrangements for the exchange of information and mutual assistance in tax matters. An important multilateral treaty in this respect is the Council of Europe–OECD Mutual Assistance Treaty 1988 entered into by over 60 countries, including all the G20 countries, almost all the OECD countries, Brazil, Russia, India and China and some major financial centres including Switzerland. The 2011 EU Directive on Administrative Co-operation in the Field of Taxation[4] covers all taxes except VAT and excise duties and improves upon the previous Directive by setting up common procedures, forms, formats of claims and channels for exchange of information. Tax officials of the requesting state are permitted active participation in inspections and administrative enquiries. Importantly, banking secrecy may not be invoked as a reason for failing to supply information. The Directive goes much further than Article 26 of the OECD MTC in that, from 1 January 2014, it provides for the automatic exchange of information between EU Member States on income from employment, directors, fees, pensions, ownership of and income from immovable property and income from certain life assurance products.

A large number of bilateral exchange of information treaties also exist, although most exchange of Information treaties are made between states which may potentially be used as tax havens and what might best be described as their 'customer states' (eg the UK and the British Virgin Islands). Many of these treaties flowed out of the OECD's work on 'harmful tax competition' which is discussed in Chapter 16. Finally, along with 'le weekend' and 'le sandwich', readers may be interested to know that another English/American phrase has entered the French language – several of the information exchange articles in Swiss treaties, including those with Norway and Austria, specifically forbid the mounting of 'fishing expeditions' by the treaty partner. In broad terms, they must have specific grounds for suspicion when requesting particular information, rather than asking for information just to see if there is any evidence of tax evasion by their taxpayers.

---

1 Dicey and Morris, The Conflict of Laws, 13th edn, 2000, p 89, quoted in P Baker, Ch 21, Transnational Enforcement of Tax Liabilities in International Corporate Tax Planning, 2002, Tolley LexisNexis.
2 [1955] AC 491.
3 TMA 1970, s 20ff.
4 Council Directive 2011/16/EU.

Article 27: Assistance in the collection of taxes

7.48   Subject to the remark in the previous paragraph that states do not, in general, enforce each other's tax claims, the Model Tax Convention does offer a model for an Article whereby the two Contracting States may lend assistance to each other in the collection of revenue claims. This is a recent development, first appearing in the 2002 version of the Model Tax Convention. However, the Commentary acknowledges that in some states, national law, policy or administrative considerations may not allow or justify this type of assistance. The type of assistance envisaged is administrative in nature.

In general, these provisions are more common between states which are close neighbours and which have a history of co-operation. They are relatively common in treaties between EU Member States. Where there are common land borders and a significant number of workers live in one state and work in the other, such provisions are very useful. The extent of the provisions varies – in some treaties, the requesting state must have exhausted all means available to it before asking the treaty partner for help, others do not contain this requirement. The range of matters covered also varies; in some treaties, assistance is given with the collection of tax-related interest and penalties, in others, not.

The UK has not traditionally included such provisions in its tax treaties but some recently concluded treaties (eg UK–Netherlands Treaty 2008) include this article. There are some provisions under the limitations of benefits clauses in certain tax treaties (discussed in Chapter 18), notably the 2001 UK–US Treaty for some administrative assistance in collecting tax technically due to the other state. The main driver behind this particular provision is not that the UK wishes to assist the US with collection of US taxes, but merely to ensure that only persons properly entitled to relief from US tax under treaty actually get such relief. This type of restricted administrative assistance article is common in US treaties.

The Council of Europe–OECD Mutual Assistance Treaty 1988 also covers assistance in the collection of taxes, although these clauses are optional. Within the EU, the 2010 Directive on Mutual Assistance for the Recovery of Claims Relating to Taxes, Duties and Other Measures[1] provides for a common standard of mutual assistance.

See Chapter 2 for a more general discussion on assistance in collection of other states' taxes, and Chapter 18 for multilateral agreements on mutual assistance in tax matters.

---

1   Council Directive 2010/24 EU.

LIMITATION OF BENEFITS CLAUSES

7.49   US treaties invariably contain a separate 'limitation of benefits' article, but separate articles are relatively rare in treaties not involving the US. These are usually inserted to prevent the practice of 'treaty shopping' whereby companies or individuals may try to manipulate their tax-residency status so as to benefit from particular tax treaties. Of particular interest in this respect is the use of various types of holding company structure. These provisions are examined in detail in Chapter 15 along with the relevant BEPS-related changes.

'MOST FAVOURED NATION' ARTICLES

7.50   'Most favoured nation' clauses, referred to as MFN clauses, are sometimes written into treaties to ensure that a contracting state continues to give the 'best deal' possible to its treaty partner. Suppose State A and State B enter into a double tax treaty which provides for a maximum rate of withholding tax of 15 per cent on dividends. State A might subsequently enter into a new tax treaty with State C which provides for a maximum withholding tax of only 5 per cent on dividends. State A is thus extending more favourable treatment to residents of State C than it is extending to residents of State B. State B might be rather aggrieved by this. An MFN clause could be inserted at the time of negotiation into the treaty between States A and B to the effect that should either State A or State B subsequently enter into a treaty with a third state which provides for more favourable treatment than that permitted under the treaty between State A and State B, then the State A–State B Treaty will be amended to provide treatment at least as favourable as that afforded by the new treaty with State C.

An example of an MFN clause taken from Article 12 of the 1996 Czech Republic–Belgium Treaty is given below. Article 12 of the treaty provided for a withholding tax rate of 10 per cent on literary and artistic royalties:

> 'If in the event that, after the signing of this Convention, the Czech Republic signs with a third State an Agreement which limits the taxation of royalties arising in the Czech Republic to a rate lower, including exemption, than the rate provided for in sub-paragraphs (a) or (b) of paragraph 2 of Article 12 of the Convention, as the case may be, that lower rate or exemption will automatically be applicable for the purposes of this Convention from the date of which the Agreement between the Czech Republic and that third State will have effect.'

> (Para 1 of the contemporaneous Protocol, adding to Article 12.)

In the event, the Czech Republic entered into a double tax treaty with Austria which became effective on 1 January 2008 which provided for a rate of only 5 per cent on all royalties. Thus, from 1 January 2008, the maximum rate to be applied to any royalty, including literary and artistic royalties under the Czech–Belgian Treaty was reduced to 5 per cent. Notice that this particular clause provides for the *automatic* application of the new rate. Some MFN clauses merely provide that if a more favourable treaty is entered into by one of the treaty partners, then negotiations to amend the treaty will be triggered.

One lesson from this is that it is insufficient merely to glance at the treaty to determine the withholding tax rates. Users need to check first whether any MFN clause is present and then need to check whether, where such a clause exists, it has been triggered. MFN clauses only appear in a relatively small number of treaties.

There is a school of thought that the bilateral DTTs entered into by a Member State of the EU can favour one fellow Member State over another in a manner which is contrary to the EC Treaty. Thus a taxpayer resident in that Member State investing in a Member State with an inferior tax treaty could argue that freedom to establish within the EU under Article 43 of the EC Treaty has been denied to that taxpayer, and that the taxpayer should be granted the best treatment afforded under *any* of the taxpayer's home state's tax treaties with other EU Member States. This is the argument that, within the EU, in order to avoid discrimination and thus restriction of freedom of establishment, MFN treatment must be considered implicit in all of a state's DTTs with fellow Member States. The argument has failed, so far.

INTERPRETATION OF TAX TREATIES

7.51   Treaties are governed by public international law as opposed to domestic law. This gives rise to problems of interpretation. The interpretation of treaties is key to their success in dealing with issues of double taxation. The fact that tax treaties generally have two main purposes: the settling of common problems which arise in the field of international juridical taxation, such as double taxation, and the prevention of tax evasion, means that the interpretation of tax treaties can be more complex than the interpretation of other types of international treaties.

Tax treaties may need to be interpreted in a number of contexts:

- In settling the tax liability of a resident taxpayer, for instance, through the granting of double tax relief in accordance with the treaty. In such a case, a judge will inevitably have to have recourse to principles of domestic law.

- In determining in which of the two Contracting States an amount of income or gains is primarily taxable; for instance, in determining the profits attributable to a PE the tax authority of the residence state may well have to consult with the tax authority of the source state.

- In acting in a capacity as an independent arbitrator, for instance, as a member of a commission set up under the auspices of the EU Arbitration Convention to settle a transfer-pricing dispute.

The broad rules of Articles 31–33 of the Vienna Convention on the Law of Treaties must be applied, whether or not this is done in conjunction with the application of principles of domestic law. The Vienna Convention covers the territorial scope of conventions, provides general rules of interpretation and covers the position when there is a breach of treaty obligations.

Different states approach matters of legal interpretation in different ways. There are three main approaches:

- *Objective approach* – using the 'ordinary' meanings of words. This is prone to problems of translation and other cultural differences.

- *Subjective approach* – where the intentions of the parties are examined. However, these may not be recorded or, even if they are, interpreting intentions can be problematic.

- *Teleological approach* – which looks at the aims and objectives of the treaty.

In practice, most states will construe a tax treaty liberally – where an interpretation based on the narrow meaning of certain words would give a result at odds with the intention of the treaty (which is to relieve double taxation) then a broader interpretation will usually be allowed.

This is consistent with Article 31 of the Vienna Convention which provides that treaties must be interpreted by the parties 'in good faith', so that a broad interpretation is to be favoured over a narrow, literal interpretation of treaty wording if that is what is required to achieve an outcome consistent with the overall aims of the treaty.

Articles 31–33 of the Vienna Convention are key to treaty interpretation:

'**Article 31**

General rule of interpretation

1. A treaty shall be interpreted in good faith in accordance with the ordinary meaning to be given to the terms of the treaty in their context and in the light of its object and purpose.

2. The context for the purpose of the interpretation of a treaty shall comprise, in addition to the text, including its preamble and annexes:

    (a) any agreement relating to the treaty which was made between all the parties in connection with the conclusion of the treaty;

    (b) any instrument which was made by one or more parties in connection with the conclusion of the treaty and accepted by the other parties as an instrument related to the treaty.

3. There shall be taken into account, together with the context:

    (a) any subsequent agreement between the parties regarding the interpretation of the treaty or the application of its provisions;

    (b) any subsequent practice in the application of the treaty which establishes the agreement of the parties regarding its interpretation;

    (c) any relevant rules of international law applicable in the relations between the parties.

4. A special meaning shall be given to a term if it is established that the parties so intended.

Article 32

Supplementary means of interpretation

Recourse may be had to supplementary means of interpretation, including the preparatory work of the treaty and the circumstances of its conclusion, in order to confirm the meaning resulting from the application of Article 31, or to determine the meaning when the interpretation according to Article 31:

(a)   leaves the meaning ambiguous or obscure; or

(b)   leads to a result which is manifestly absurd or unreasonable.

Article 33

Interpretation of treaties authenticated in two or more languages

1   When a treaty has been authenticated in two or more languages, the text is equally authoritative in each language, unless the treaty provides or the parties agree that, in the case of divergence, a particular text shall prevail.

2   A version of the treaty in a language other than one of those in which the text was authenticated shall be considered an authentic text only if the treaty so provides or the parties so agree.

3   The terms of the treaty are presumed to have the same meaning in each authentic text.

4   Except where a particular text prevails in accordance with paragraph 1, when a comparison of the authentic texts discloses a difference of meaning which the application of Articles 31 and 32 does not remove, the meaning which best reconciles the texts, having regard to the object and purpose of the treaty, shall be adopted.'

A common mistake is to try to interpret treaties using the same principles of statutory interpretation as are applied to domestic law. However, as noted earlier, treaties are governed by international law such as the Vienna Convention. Unlike the extremely detailed provisions of most domestic tax law, treaties are 'purposive' and their interpretation must be agreed between the two contracting states. In the UK, courts have generally reserved the use of an overtly purposive approach for cases involving aggressive tax-avoidance schemes. In civil law states, such as Germany, the interpretation of domestic statute law does not call for a purposive approach. Thus, in the interpretation of domestic tax law, a literal approach is usually employed. Furthermore, words used in domestic law sometimes acquire a special tax meaning, such as the UK use of the phrase 'beneficial ownership' to denote a particular situation in trust and estate law. These special meanings are sometimes open to challenge, for instance, as in *McNiven v Westmoreland Investments*[1] where Lord Hoffmann famously decreed that 'paid means paid' in the context of determining whether there could be a deduction for interest accrued.

States may not use any material prepared unilaterally to aid interpretation but only the text of the treaty itself, the preamble, the annexes and any other material prepared on a bilateral basis such as protocols, memoranda of understanding which were agreed upon by both parties at the time the treaty was concluded. So all interpretative materials must be contemporaneous with the signing of the treaty, unless concluded with the other contracting state subsequently by mutual agreement.

Each treaty must be construed individually. The fact that the tax authorities in State A construed a certain term in a certain way in the treaty between State A and State B does not mean that the term must be construed identically in the treaty between State A and State C. Having said that, it is highly likely that a state will strive for a certain amount of consistency in the interpretation of its treaties, as one of the key benefits of tax treaties is the degree of certainty which they provide for international business in cross-border tax matters.

Court cases are a useful aid to treaty interpretation, particularly if a case is recognized as having international fiscal significance. Good examples are the cases on the meaning of the term 'beneficial ownership'[2] where the *Indofood* case has been accepted as providing an international fiscal meaning of the term which is widely used in tax treaties but rarely specifically defined in them.

Treaties will usually define important terms such as 'person', 'enterprise' and 'permanent establishment' within the text, but the MTC also provides at Article 3(2) some general rules of definition – that terms not specifically defined within the text should have the meaning that they have at the time the treaty was concluded under the tax law of the state concerned. However, if the context so requires, it may have to be given a different meaning. This does leave open the possibility that a particular term might have a different meaning in each of the two states, which is where Memoranda of Agreement, exchange of letters, etc may be needed.

The UK approach to the interpretation of tax treaties was summed up in the case of *IRC v Commerzbank AG*.[3] A UK judge ought to:

- look first for a clear meaning of the words, using a purposive approach;

- bear in mind that the language of a treaty differs from the legal language found in domestic law and not necessarily use domestic legal precedent or technical rules;

- bear in mind the 'in good faith' principle;

- where appropriate, use supplementary means and *travaux préparatoires*; and

- bear in mind the reputation of foreign courts when relying on their judgments.

In developing these principles, the Court in *Commerzbank* referred back to the judgment in *Fothergill v Monarch Airlines*[4] to the effect that:

'the language of an international convention has not been chosen by an English parliamentary draftsman. It is neither couched in the conventional English legislative idiom nor designed to be construed exclusively by English judges. It is addressed to a much wider and more varied judicial audience than is an Act of Parliament which deals with purely domestic law. It should be interpreted ... unconstrained by technical rules of English law, or by English legal precedent, but on broad principles of general acceptation'.

More recently, in *Memec Plc v CIR*:[5] 'Mr Venables rightly cautioned us against interpreting the convention as though it had been drafted in Lincoln's Inn.' In *Memec*, the court looked for assistance in interpretation of the UK German treaty in decisions of the German courts concerning the Germany–Switzerland Treaty.

---

1   *McNiven (Inspector of Taxes) v Westmoreland Investments Ltd* [2001] STC 237.
2   *Indofood International Finance Ltd v JP Morgan Chase Bank NA* [2006] EWCA Civ 158, (2006) 8 ITLR 653, [2006] STC 1195.
3   [1990] STC 285.
4   [1981] AC 251.
5   [1998] STC 754.

Significance of the OECD Commentary

7.52   Article 32 of the Vienna Convention provides that recourse may be had to supplementary means of interpretation, including the preparatory work (*travaux préparatoires* – that are the official record of negotiations) and the circumstances of its conclusion. Use of such materials may be invaluable in casting light on the context in which particular provisions were agreed upon and the object and purposes of particular provisions. Article 32 provides a practical means of applying the general rules of interpretation set out in Article 31. *Travaux préparatoires* are not generally available to the public.

Every version of the OECD MTC from the 1963 draft through to the 2010 version has been published with a detailed commentary expanding upon each provision contained in the Model. It is generally accepted that the OECD Commentary and reports of the OECD Committee on Fiscal Affairs may be used to help interpret treaties and are sometimes expressly referred to within tax treaties. The Commentary is a key source of interpretation. It is used in this manner not only to interpret the treaties based directly on the OECD MTC, but also those which follow the US or UN Models, where appropriate. This is because the US and UN Models are essentially adaptations of the OECD MTC. The OECD Commentary is widely used in the process of treaty interpretation by courts around the world and its existence is a principal benefit of basing a treaty on the OECD MTC. The first use of the Commentary in a UK tax case was in *Sun Life Assurance of Canada v Pearson*[1] in which the judge said: 'the views of the experts who sat on the Fiscal Committee on the Regulation of Double Taxation are entitled to very great weight'. In that case, the judge also stated that any doubts he had were dispelled by the Commentary.

The Model itself and the Commentary are the work of the Committee on Fiscal Affairs (CFA) of the OECD, which is composed of senior government officials drawn from the OECD members. All play an active role in formulating and implementing tax policies in their respective states. There is frequent consultation with business and with other international and regional tax organizations. The Commentary thus sets out the informed intentions of the OECD when formulating the articles of the Model. Its currency as an official aid to interpretation is sometimes questioned, but there is ample evidence of its widespread acceptance. The OECD itself, upon adopting the 1992 version of the Model, stated that OECD members should ensure that their future treaties conformed to the OECD MTC as interpreted by the Commentaries and later recommended that the tax authorities in the OECD member states should follow the commentaries when applying and interpreting the provisions of their bilateral conventions which are based upon the OECD MTC (Baker (2002) at A-06). Baker also cites examples of the Commentaries having been referred to as an aid to interpretation by the courts in Austria, Australia, Belgium, Canada, Denmark, Germany, Japan, Malaysia, the Netherlands, New Zealand, Spain, Sweden, Switzerland and the US.

One practical issue that arises is that once a treaty has been concluded, the CFA may well revise its Commentary relating to particular provisions. Should that treaty be interpreted by reference to the relevant Commentary as it read at the date the treaty was concluded, or at the date that the need for interpretation arises? In *Commerzbank*[2] the question of interpretation of double tax treaties was considered in depth. The guidance regarding use of OECD Commentary material written subsequent to the signing of the treaty is that subsequent Commentaries have persuasive value only. However, the OECD itself, in the Introduction to the 2008 version of the Model Convention confirms its advice that, providing the provision in question in the double tax treaty being interpreted is substantially the same as that in the current version of the Model Convention, then the most recent version of the Commentary on that provision should be used by the parties. The existing provisions are to be interpreted in the spirit of the revised Commentary. The justification for using the most up-to-date version of the Commentary is that this best reflects the consensus of the OECD as to interpretation. More recently, the Special Commissioners in *Trevor Smallwood Trust v R & C Commrs*[3] noted that 'our view is that the negotiators on both sides could be expected to have the Commentary in front of them'. Interestingly, this case concerned a DTT in which one of the Contracting States was not a member of the OECD. The *Smallwood* case confirmed that the correct version of the Commentary to use was the one contemporaneous with the facts at issue rather than the one in force at the date the treaty in question was signed: this is known as the 'ambulatory principle'.

Despite the overwhelming acceptance of the Commentaries as a valid means of interpretation by the courts in many states, their legal status remains unclear. It is unfortunate that there is no direct reference to the Commentaries in the Vienna Convention as this omission leaves the way clear for their detractors to argue that they fall within Article 32 only, and thus have less influence than if they were included under Article 31. However, their widespread acceptance by the courts perhaps renders this a point of mainly academic interest. The Commentaries are now updated from time to time separately from the Model Convention itself.

However, the Technical Explanations prepared by the US Department of the Treasury in connection with treaties made between the US and other states would not be acceptable as means of interpretation as they are prepared unilaterally by the US and represent the US view of the meaning of the treaty. Where the treaty partner publicly declares its recognition of the Technical Explanation as a valid explanation of the treaty, the situation alters so that it *does* become acceptable as a means of interpretation (eg as with the Technical Explanation to the Fifth Protocol to the US–Canada Treaty).

---

1   [1984] BTC 223.
2   *IRC v Commerzbank AG* [1990] STC 285.
3   [2008] STC (SCD) 629.

What definitions should be used?

7.53   Treaties will define certain common terms in a broad manner. This is provided for at Article 3 of the Model Convention. However, not all terms are defined and even where a definition is given, this may be interpreted differently by the parties to the treaty due to, say, cultural or linguistic differences. Invariably, the terms used in the treaty have well-developed definitions in the domestic law of each state and these definitions might be quite different from one another. Article 3(2) of the OECD MTC deals with terms not defined in the treaty itself:

> 'As regards the application of the Convention at any time by a Contracting State, any term not defined therein shall, unless the context otherwise requires, have the meaning that it has at that time under the law of that State for the purposes of the taxes to which the Convention applies, any meaning under the applicable tax laws of that State prevailing over a meaning given to the term under other laws of that State.'

The mutual agreement procedure provided for in Article 25 will often be used to agree upon a common definition of a term. Generally, the rule is that the term be given the meaning which it has in the domestic tax law of the states. For instance, the term 'distribution' in a non-tax context might mean the spacing of a range of figures in statistics or the dishing out of mashed potato to a line of schoolchildren at dinner time. In the tax sense though, the UK meaning is a distribution of profits which would include, but not be limited to, a cash dividend. What if, following the conclusion of the treaty, the UK alters its tax definition of the term 'distribution'? Should the treaty be interpreted using the definition in place at the date the treaty was concluded, or the meaning at the date the treaty falls to be interpreted using the term? The consensus is that, as with the Commentaries themselves, an ambulatory approach should be used, so that the most up-to-date meaning is used. The caveat 'unless the context requires otherwise' is discussed in the Commentary on Article 3. The context in which a term is defined is to be determined by the intention of the contracting states when signing the Convention as well as the meaning given to the term in the legislation of the other state. The Commentary does not help when it comes to deciding what alternative meaning to that used in domestic tax law ought to be used, given that the context requires a different meaning. There is no general answer to this question: it is a matter for negotiation between the two states.

Some Brazilian cases illustrate the difficulties that can arise where terms used in double tax treaties do not match up with domestic law. In *Federal Union (National Treasury) v Copesul – CIA/Petroquímica do Sul*[1] a Brazilian case, the point at issue was whether or not services fees were business profits, such that they could only be taxed by Brazil if the recipient had a PE there. Otherwise they would be vulnerable to Brazilian withholding tax by virtue of the 'other income' article in the relevant tax treaty. The case concerned a German company providing repair services and a Canadian company providing coating services, on machinery and components respectively which were owned by the Brazilian company. Crucially, all the services were performed in Germany and Canada. The logic for the argument that the fees for the services were not business profits stemmed from the Brazilian domestic law definition of business profits. The relevant treaties did not define what was meant by business profits, so that the meaning of the phrase within the domestic law of Brazil had to be considered. This definition states that 'business profits' are 'net income' after all deductions and additions required by tax law. 'Net income' is defined as gross income minus all related costs and expenses of the period. Hence, the argument was that service fees, being a gross payment, could not be 'business profits' but were instead 'revenues'. The taxpayer countered this argument by stating that the service fees entered into their computations of business profits. The taxpayer argued that the term 'business profits' meant all income derived from business activities, apart from those specifically mentioned in articles of the relevant treaty other than the business profits article. The upper court agreed with the taxpayer and decided that it was incorrect to construe the term 'business profits' by reference to its narrow meaning within the Brazilian tax code.

However, the Brazilian courts appear to have been inconsistent in their approach: in a case decided nearly at the same time, *PCI do Brasil LTDA v Federal Union (National Treasury)*[2] a different second level Brazilian court decided that, in connection with the Brazil-France treaty, which also lacks a definition of 'profits', the levy of withholding tax on payments of technical service fees would be possible. The grounds for this decision were that the service fees should be classed as revenue rather than profits so that Article 21 (Other Income) rather than Article 7 (Business Profits) of the treaty was in point.

The Brazilian tax authority was only able to take the positions on services just described because the double tax treaties concerned did not specifically state that services income was taxable under Article 7. Thus Brazil was able to assert that the term should be construed according to its domestic law, as directed by Article 3(2) of the Model Tax Conventions.

---

1   12 ITLR 150, Brazil No 2002.71.00.006530–5/RS.
2   Federal Court of the 2nd Region, Case 2002.51.01002701-0 of 16 March 2010. Note that the Brazil-Finland treaty of 1996 does not contain the protocol found in most Brazilian tax treaties which provides that technical services fees are to be treated in the same way as royalties.

The 'competent authority' process

7.54   As noted earlier (para **7.46**) the mutual agreement article provides a mechanism whereby the two states can consult directly without having to go through formal diplomatic channels. Generally, the principal use of Article 25 is the resolution of more factual disputes, such as the need for and the quantification of transfer-pricing disputes. Paragraph (3), though, specifically addresses the matter of treaty interpretation.

Article 25(3) of the OECD MTC reads:

> 'The competent authorities of the Contracting States shall endeavour to resolve by mutual agreement any difficulties or doubts arising as to the interpretation or application of the Convention. They may also consult together for the elimination of double taxation in cases not provided for in the Convention.'

The Commentary on this paragraph observes that the competent authorities (eg HMRC in the UK) can:

●   complete or clarify the definition of terms where these have been ambiguously or incompletely defined in the treaty itself; and

●   in cases where domestic laws have been altered, but without affecting the substance of the treaty, they can deal with any difficulties which emerge from the changes to domestic tax laws.

As already noted, a major drawback with the mutual agreement procedure has been the length of time, and consequent expense, it takes for agreement to be reached. In 2007, the OECD produced a report 'Improving the Resolution of Tax Treaty Disputes'[1] which deals, inter alia, with formal processes of arbitration to be adopted in cases of dispute and provides an Annexe to be added to the Commentary on Article 25. This contains the following statement on the general approach to treaty interpretation under an arbitration procedure:

> '14. Applicable Legal Principles. The arbitrators shall decide the issues submitted to arbitration in accordance with the applicable provisions of the treaty and, subject to these provisions, of those of the domestic laws of the Contracting States. Issues of treaty interpretation will be decided by the arbitrators in light of the principles of interpretation incorporated in Articles 31 to 34 of the *Vienna Convention on the Law of Treaties*, having regard to the Commentaries of the OECD MTC Tax Convention as periodically amended, as explained in paragraphs 28 to 36.1 of the Introduction to the OECD MTC Tax Convention.' (*Source*: OECD (2007) at p 16.)

The OECD notes that whilst there has been little experience to date with the use of Article 25(3) to resolve difficulties in treaty interpretation, it may be more widely used in future, given the far-reaching changes to the interpretation of Article 7 which were adopted by the OECD in 2008. (See Chapter 9 for a full discussion.) This is because the changes to the interpretation of Article 7 relate to the attribution of profits to branches (PEs). As branches are not residents of a state in which their profits are subject to tax on the source principle, they might not be able to use the mutual agreement procedures laid down in paras 1 and 2 of Article 25, which are only open to residents. Thus, a resident of a third state suffering double taxation through having PEs in each of the two Contracting States might only be able to rely on para 3.

---

1   OECD (2007) 'Improving the Resolution of Tax Treaty Disputes' Report adopted by the Committee on Fiscal Affairs, February 2007.

DOUBLE TAX TREATY OVERRIDE – FURTHER DETAILED CONSIDERATION

7.55   Treaty override refers to the situation where a state has entered into a DTT but at a later date passes a domestic law which has the effect that taxpayers are denied the benefits of one or more of the treaty provisions.

Example 7.4

For instance, in a worst case scenario, the states of Ruritania and Inistania might enter into a DTT in 2009 that states that they will not charge any withholding tax on payments of royalties to a patent owner who is tax resident in the other state.

Subsequently in 2011, Inistania realizes that this is far too expensive, in that it is foregoing more tax revenue than anticipated. Inistania enacts a domestic law imposing a withholding tax of 25 per cent on payments of royalties to residents of Ruritania. Inistania has thus deliberately overridden the terms of the DTT with Ruritania.

Treaty override can happen intentionally or unintentionally. Referring back to the observation that states enter into DTTs in good faith, a state will usually try to undo or amend the domestic provisions that have given rise to unintentional treaty override. Likewise, where a domestic court reaches a decision which is not in accordance with a relevant DTT, the state will often correct the situation by passing a new statute so that the court decision does not affect treaty rights of its residents in the future.

Article 18 of the Vienna Convention reads:

'A State is obliged to refrain from acts which would defeat the object and purpose of a treaty when:

(a) it has signed the treaty or has exchanged instruments constituting the treaty subject to ratification, acceptance or approval, until it shall have made its intention clear not to become a party to the treaty; or

(b) it has expressed its consent to be bound by the treaty, pending the entry into force of the treaty and provided that such entry into force is not unduly delayed.'

Article 26 of the Vienna Convention contains the *pacta sunt servanda* principle: 'every treaty in force is binding upon the parties and must be performed by them in good faith'.

A complex question arises when a treaty has been overridden intentionally. Can the taxpayer still rely on the treaty? This depends on the comparative status of treaty law and domestic law. Baker (2002) analyses the position in terms of whether the state perpetrating the treaty override is a common law state (eg the UK) or a civil law state (eg Germany).

In common law jurisdictions, treaty law has the same status as domestic law and therefore, using the general principle that a later law overrides an earlier law, the treaty override is usually effective. There may, of course, be protection for treaty law built into the domestic legal system, as in Australia and Canada.

In some civil law states, treaty law is accorded a higher status than domestic law, and thus cannot be overridden. What can the treaty partner do when the other party to the treaty deliberately overrides it? It can terminate the treaty, but this is rather a drastic step, and would entail denying its residents all those benefits under the treaty which are still effective. If the two states have fallen out with each other this badly, the prospects for negotiating a replacement treaty are also slim. Often it is the dominant partner in the treaty pairing that will indulge in treaty override: the US (a common law state) has overridden its treaties on numerous occasions.[1] (Note that the US has not ratified (ie brought into US law) the Vienna Convention, although it became a signatory in 1970.) This does not mean that the US ignores the provisions of the Vienna Convention; it considers them to be a summary of customary international law, so that it will normally be bound by the principles contained in the Vienna Convention. Alternatives to terminating the treaty available to the injured party are to enter into arbitration, possibly under the terms of the DTT itself, or to refer to the International Court of Justice (ICJ). The OECD (1989) issued a report[2] exhorting states not to override their treaties, and this was widely believed to be firmly targeted at the US.

The OECD report on treaty override in 1989 is still relevant to the topic today (OECD, 1989). Table 7.5 below contains some useful examples of treaty override.

Table 7.5 Examples of treaty override

Facts	*Material breach of obligations?*	*Possible remedies*
State A introduces a new, final, withholding tax on royalties. State A's treaties provide that royalties paid to residents of treaty partner states are exempt from withholding tax.	Material breach	Protest then consider repeal

Facts	*Material breach of obligations?*	*Possible remedies*
State B taxes gains on the sale of real estate. State A taxpayers have started to avoid this tax by holding their real estate through a company and selling the shares in the company. The treaty permits State B to tax gains of State A residents only if they arise from sales of real estate, not shares. State B changes its laws so that gains on sales of shares in companies used to hold real estate are taxable in State B.	The purpose of State B's new law is to stop improper use of its treaty – tax avoidance. This is not necessarily a treaty override as it might be covered under the Commentary on Article 1 on improper use of treaties.	State B could ask State A whether it agrees that the new law is justified by improper use of the treaty or it could ask State A for Article 13 (capital gains) to be amended. However, if State A disagrees, State A could terminate the treaty.

(*Source: Report on Tax Treaty Override* (OECD, 1989).)

---

1 See Baker (2002) at para F.04 for some examples.
2 *Report on Tax Treaty Override*, OECD Committee on Fiscal Affairs, 1989.

Does the UK ever override its treaties?

7.56   Whether or not the UK is capable of overriding its treaties is unclear. Technically, being a common law state, it ought to be able to do so. However, the Taxation (International and Other Provisions) Act 2010, s 6 provides that a DTT is to be given effect 'notwithstanding anything in any other enactment'. The question arises as to whether this means any law extant at the date the treaty comes into effect, or whether it means that no domestic legislation past or future, can constrain the effectiveness of the tax treaty.

Working on the general UK constitutional principle that Parliament cannot bind its successors, it would seem that it is possible for subsequent domestic law to override the provisions of a treaty. Thus, so long as the legislators make it clear that a new provision in domestic law is expressly designed to override a treaty provision (eg by stating that s 6 is not to apply), then override is possible. Without a clear reference that s 6 is not to apply, the new provision would be interpreted using the general rule that UK statutes should not be interpreted in such a way as to produce a breach of international law (ie to override a treaty).

There have been very few instances of the UK attempting to deliberately override the provisions of its DTTs. The case of controlled foreign companies (CFCs) legislation is sometimes cited as an example of treaty override, but as the discussion of this topic in Chapter 17 will indicate, this is not so. Where a taxpayer is relying on the provisions of a treaty in the course of a scheme of tax avoidance, there is more sympathy for the idea of overriding the treaty provisions.

In the cases of *Padmore*[1] a UK-resident individual who was a partner in a partnership that dealt with patents, was considered opaque and resident in Jersey. This Jersey partnership acquired a share in a UK partnership that operated out of London, was considered resident in the UK and which paid UK income tax. Mr Padmore claimed that the part of the profits of the London partnership which were attributed to him ought to have been exempt from UK tax under the terms of the then UK–Jersey Double Tax Agreement (DTA). In the first case which Mr Padmore brought, he won. However, following that decision, s 62 of the Finance Act (No 2) 1987 was enacted, that overturned the court's decision for future income.

Mr Padmore returned to court once more, arguing that a DTT could not be overridden by subsequent domestic legislation. By the time the case reached court, s 62 of the Finance Act (No 2) 1987 had been consolidated into ICTA 1988. As often happens, some pruning and rationalization of the wording of the legislation was undertaken as part of the consolidation process. Mr Padmore argued that the consolidated version of s 62 did not unequivocally state that it was intended to override the UK–Jersey DTT, and therefore had to be interpreted as being subsidiary to the terms of the UK–Jersey Treaty. The provisions in the Finance Act (No 2) 1987 were supplemented by provisions preventing the new rules from applying prior to certain dates. These happened to be the dates of Mr Padmore's first court case. By the time his first case had reached the High Court, s 62 had already been enacted, and these additional conditions were needed so as not to prejudice his case.

In the second *Padmore* case, the courts held that the intention of the legislators was perfectly clear, and the intention was to override the terms of the UK–Jersey Treaty (as well as any other treaties, where the same point concerning foreign controlled partnerships applied). Therefore Mr Padmore could not continue to rely on the UK–Jersey Treaty. To sum up, treaty override in the UK is only possible where it is the clear intention of the legislator to achieve it.

---

1   *Padmore v Inland Revenue Commissioners* [1989] STC 493 and *Padmore v Inland Revenue Commissioners (No 2)* [2001] STC 280.

Remedies available if a state overrides its treaties

7.57   If a state overrides its DTT then the treaty partner state can require that the treaty be repealed. This is a very drastic step, as it would deprive residents of the wronged state not only of the treaty benefits lost due to the override, but *all* of the benefits of the treaty. Normally, the wronged state would file an official protest in writing – upon learning of the possibility of treaty override – setting out the details, and insisting that the partner state complies with its treaty obligations. If this does not work, then full or partial repeal is the only option remaining. Whether repeal is possible depends on how serious the override is. Only 'material breaches' treaty obligations give the wronged state the right to invoke the breach of obligations as a ground for terminating the DTT.

Tax treaty override by the United States

7.58   The US has a long history of overriding its tax treaties. Section 7852(d) of the US Tax Code reads:

'For purposes of determining the relationship between the provision of a treaty and any law of the United States affecting revenue, neither the treaty nor the law shall have preferential status by reason of its being a treaty or a law.'

The most recent example is the Foreign Account Tax Compliance Act (FATCA, which is examined in Chapter 18). This imposes US withholding taxes at 30 per cent on payments to foreign financial institutions even where the relevant DTTs clearly state that payments are to be either free of withholding tax, or to carry withholding tax at a lower rate.

LIMITATIONS ON THE USE OF DOUBLE TAX TREATIES BY TAX AUTHORITIES

7.59   The purpose of DTTs is to allocate the right to tax the same source of income between the two contracting states. They cannot therefore increase a state's right to tax. For instance, if a DTT states that the source state may tax dividends and so may the residence state, then if one of them does not routinely levy taxes on dividends, or if one of them allows special domestic tax reliefs against dividend income such that no domestic tax is payable, then the treaty does not authorize that state to start charging tax.

There are a number of exceptions to this, which are broadly connected with tax avoidance and evasion. Article 9 allows states to compute profits on transactions between related parties on the 'arm's-length basis' which may well increase the tax burden on the company involved. Where a taxpayer seeks to evade tax, Article 26, which provides for exchange of information, may lead to an increased tax liability. However, it should be noted that these provisions usually help to enforce domestic law rather than supplement it.

USE OF MULTILATERAL TREATIES

7.60   It might have been expected that a natural development in tax treaties, given the move towards global trading, would have been the development of multilateral tax treaties (ie treaties concluded between larger groups of states). Bilateral treaties remain the norm, however. To date the Nordic states have concluded a multilateral convention with the aim of reducing the scope for avoidance and establishing uniformity of tax treatment. An important feature is the zero withholding tax. The other main multilateral agreement is the CARICOM (Caribbean) Agreement 1994. An important feature of this agreement is the predominance of the source principle.

Although not a double tax treaty, the importance of EU Directives must not be overlooked: both the Parent/Subsidiary Directive and the Merger Directive have amongst their effects the prevention of double taxation. These are considered in Chapter 20.

UK TREATY PRACTICES

7.61   The UK's DTTs generally follow the OECD MTC, although when concluding treaties with developing states, the UK sometimes agrees to treaty provisions which give greater taxing rights to the host state, such as a definition of a PE which does not involve a fixed place of business, or a provision which permits withholding tax to be levied on royalties and/or technical fees. Although treaty negotiations are not publicly reported, it is likely that such provisions are included as part of a general bargaining process whereby other provisions are inserted at the insistence of the UK.

Because the UK uses a fiscal year commencing on 5 April for individuals and trusts and a financial year commencing on 1 April for bodies corporate, the commencement dates of the treaties are often split, with the UK commencement dates differing from those of the treaty partner.

The UK's use of the remittance basis of taxation (as discussed in Chapter 3) for certain individuals sometimes results in an additional provision, often under the heading 'Miscellaneous Rules'. The purpose of the provision is to permit the treaty partner to tax in full income which, although paid to a UK resident, is not remitted to the UK and therefore not taxed by the UK. Typical wording is:

> 'Where under any provision of this Convention any income is relieved from tax in a Contracting State and, under the law in force in the other Contracting State a person, in respect of that income, is subject to tax by reference to the amount thereof which is remitted to or received in that other Contracting State and not by reference to the full amount thereof, then the relief to be allowed under this Convention in the first-mentioned Contracting State shall apply only to so much of the income as is taxed in the other Contracting State.'

For instance, if Mr A, a UK-resident individual, domiciled in Guernsey, was due a dividend from a US company, but the dividend was paid into an account maintained by the UK individual in, say, Guernsey, then the US domestic withholding tax rate of 30 per cent would be applied, because the UK would not tax the individual on the dividend unless and until Mr A remits the dividend to the UK. The US would rely on Article 1, paragraph 7 of the UK–US Income Tax Treaty 2001 which contains this provision.

Most UK treaties contain tie-breaker rules for determining residence for treaty purposes, although a few minor treaties do not contain a tie-breaker rule for individuals.[1]

The UK does not consider that a website is capable of constituting a PE and also considers that a computer server located in the UK is not, of itself, a PE, whether owned or rented by a foreign resident.[2]

Although the UK does not levy a withholding tax on dividends, its treaties contain a variety of approaches to allocation taxing rights over dividends. Many UK treaties provide for withholding tax, usually with two possible rates which include a lower rate for participation dividends (where the beneficial owner is a company owning more than a specified minimum percentage of the equity in the paying company). Some treaties, eg UK–Malaysia Treaty 1996, include a 'subject to tax' clause which could cause problems in the light of the Finance Act 2009 provisions exempting most corporate recipients of dividends from UK taxation. Because the dividends are not subject to tax in the UK, the treaty partner does not have to apply the treaty rates of withholding tax but may apply its domestic rate instead. In the case of some treaty partners potentially affected by the UK's dividend exemption, such as Malaysia and Kuwait, there would not be any withholding tax anyway, as those states do not charge withholding tax on dividends under their domestic law.

Students studying UK double tax treaties are often puzzled by lengthy and complex provisions in the dividend articles which do not seem to bear any relation to the UK's domestic position of not charging withholding tax or granting tax credits to corporate shareholders. For instance, the UK–Italy Treaty 1988 contains extensive provisions regarding the entitlement of certain Italian shareholders to UK tax credits. This relates to the 'half-tax credit' system employed in the UK in treaties negotiated at a time when the UK had quite different domestic rules concerning the taxation of dividends to the current rules. In some cases, a very small percentage of the dividend could be claimed as a refund by the foreign shareholder, but the costs of doing the calculations and making the claim are likely to outweigh the benefits. It is important to bear in mind that tax treaties often endure for far longer (20 years is not at all uncommon) than the domestic tax laws on which they are based so that when reading a treaty it should be remembered that current domestic law will, if more favourable to the taxpayer, be applied, rather than the obsolete treaty provisions.

Although most UK treaties do not contain US-style limitation of benefits (treaty shopping) provisions (see Chapter 15), they often contain general anti-avoidance clauses in the dividends, interest and royalties articles which typically read:

> 'The provisions of this Article shall not apply if it was the main purpose or one of the main purposes of any person concerned with the creation or assignment of the shares or other rights in respect of which the dividend is paid to take advantage of this Article by means of that creation or assignment.' (Article 11.6, UK–France Treaty 2008)

Such provision would prevent treaty rates of withholding tax being enjoyed by an entity set up in a treaty partner state for the receipt of payments from the UK by a person resident in a non-treaty state.

Some UK treaties extend the benefit of UK personal allowances to individuals resident in, or nationals of treaty partner states.[3] However, in some cases, there is an exclusion of individuals whose income in the treaty partner state consists only of dividends, interest and royalties. Without this exclusion, the UK would incur a significant administrative burden on refunding withholding tax where charged.

---

1 Antigua, Isle of Man, Jersey, Myanmar, Belize, St Kitts, Brunei, Kiribati, Sierra Leone, Gambia, Malawi, Solomon Islands, Greece, Montserrat, Tuvalu.
2 Revenue Press Release 11 April 2010.
3 Residents of Austria, Barbados, Belgium, Burma (now Myanmar), Falkland Islands, Faroe Islands, Fiji, Finland, France, Germany, Indonesia, Irish Republic, Kenya, Luxembourg, Mauritius, Namibia, Netherlands, Norway, Portugal, Singapore, South Africa, Swaziland, Sweden, Switzerland and Zambia, nationals of Bulgaria, Faroe Islands, France, Germany, Israel and South Africa and individuals both resident in and nationals of China, Denmark, Egypt, Hungary, Italy, Ivory Coast, Japan, Korea, Philippines, Poland, Romania, Spain, Sudan, Thailand, Tunisia, Turkey, and, where treaties are still recognized by the UK, successor states to the USSR and Yugoslavia.

FURTHER READING

Arnold, B (2010) 'The Interpretation of Tax Treaties: Myth and Reality', *Bulletin for International Taxation*, 2010 Vol 64, No 1.

Arnold, B (2010) 'An Introduction to the 2010 Update of the OECD Model Tax Convention', *Bulletin for International Taxation*, 2011, Vol 65, No 1.

Arnold, B (2011) 'United Nations – Tax Treaty News: An Overview of the UN Model (2011)', *Bulletin for International Taxation*, Vol 66, No 10.

Avi Yonah, R (2005) 'All of a Piece Throughout: The Four Ages of US International Taxation', *Virginia Tax Review*, Vol 25, pp 313–337.

Baker, P (2002/2011) *Double Taxation Conventions: a Manual on the OECD Model Tax Convention on Income and on Capital*, Sweet and Maxwell.

Barret, E (2014) 'The changes introduced by the 2014 Update to the OECD Model Tax convention', 10, *Bulletin for International Taxation*, 68.

Brauner, Y (2016) 'Treaties in the Aftermath of BEPS', *Brooklyn Journal of International Law*, 41(3), 974.

Christians, A (2016) 'Kill Switches in the IS Model Tax Treaty', *Brooklyn Journal of International Law*, 41(3), 1043.

Christians, A (2016) 'While Parliament Sleeps: Tax Treaty Practice in Canada', *Journal of Parliamentary and Political Law*, 10, 15.

De Pietro, C (2015) 'Tax Treaty Override and the Need for Coordination between Legal Systems: Safeguarding the Effectiveness of international law', 7, *World Tax Journal*.

Gassner, W, Lang, M, Lechner, E (1997) eds, *Tax Treaties and EC Law*, Kluwer Law International.

Harris, P A (1996) *Corporate/Shareholder Income Taxation and Allocating Taxing Rights between Countries: a Comparison of Imputation Systems*, International Bureau of Fiscal Documentation.

Lang, M (2010) *Introduction to the Law of Double Tax Conventions*, IBFD.

Maisto, G (2005) 'The Observations on the OECD Commentaries in the Interpretation of Tax Treaties', *Bulletin for International Taxation*, January 2005.

OECD (1989) 'Tax Treaty Override', Report R(8,) available as part of the full version of the OECD Model Tax Convention on Income and on Capital (2012).

OECD (2014) Articles of the Model Tax Convention on Income and Capital. Available at: www.oecd.org.

OECD (2014) Model Tax Convention on Income and on Capital Condensed version – July 2014 (includes the Commentary). Available at: www.keepeek. com/Digital-Asset-Management/oecd/taxation/model-tax-convention-on-income-and-on-capital-condensed-version-2014_mtc_cond-2014-en#page1.

OECD (2015) 'Developing a Multilateral Instrument to Modify Bilateral Tax Treaties', Action 15 – 2015 Final Report.

Picciotto, S (1992) *International Business Taxation*, Butterworths.

Schwarz, J (2015) *Schwarz on Tax Treaties*, 4th edn CCH, London.

Shelton, N (2004) *Interpretation and Application of Tax Treaties*, 1st edn Bloomsbury Professional, London.

US Treasury United States Model Income Tax Convention 2016. Available at: www.treasury.gov/resource-center/tax-policy/treaties/Documents/Treaty-US%20Model-2016.pdf.

Vann, R J (1998) 'International Aspects of Income Tax', Chapter 18 in V Thuronyi, *Tax Law Design and Drafting*, IMF. Available at: www.imf.org/external/pubs/nft/1998/tlaw/eng/index.htm.

Vann, R J (2004) 'The New Australia–UK Tax Treaty', *British Tax Review*, 2004, 3, pp 194–233.

Yaffar, A L (2012) 'United Nations – An Introduction to the Updated UN Model (2011)', *Bulletin for International Taxation*, Vol 66, No 11.

Chapter 8

Internationally Mobile Employees

BASICS

8.1   When companies expand their operations abroad it is common practice to send experienced employees to manage or work in the new foreign branch or subsidiary. Established multinational enterprises (MNEs) will routinely second specialist staff between their various offices and locations around the world for various periods of time. It is vital that both the employer and the employee understand the personal tax and the social security implications of temporary assignments abroad.

When an employee works in another country, they may or may not become tax resident there, which has implications for the way in which remuneration will be taxed. If the employee remains a resident of the home country, a tax liability may nonetheless arise in the host country by virtue of the source principle. If the employee becomes tax resident in the host country, there may still be a liability in the country of previous residence for other sources of income.

Most countries have special rules for individuals going abroad for the purpose of employment, broadly following the provisions of the OECD MTC. Many countries also have rules to accommodate short-term assignments so as not to create an additional tax liability that might impede international movement of labour.

The general rule is that an employee working abroad will be taxed on employment income in the country where the work is actually being performed. Article 15 of the OECD MTC provides that where an individual works for fewer than 183 days in a tax period in a foreign country, that individual should only be taxed in the country where they are tax resident, subject to certain requirements. The main requirement is that the visited country has not given any tax deduction for the employee's earnings. This saves the administrative trouble of collecting tax in the visited country on earnings from very short visits. The Commentary on Article 15 discusses ways of combating abuse of the Article 15 exemption from host country taxation on remuneration from short secondments.

Special rules apply to company directors such that physical presence is not required to confer taxing rights on the state of source, ie the state in which the company paying the director's fees is resident.

INTRODUCTION

8.2 In Chapter 3 we examined the concept of tax residence for individual taxpayers. This chapter starts by considering the general principles governing the taxation of employees temporarily working abroad. In practice the position of any employee working abroad is highly dependent on the domestic laws of the residence country and the visited country. The 'Further study' section of this chapter analyses the UK tax treatment of outbound and inbound employees. Whilst the UK rules are, of course, particular to the UK, they give an insight into the level of detail in a tax system with respect to internationally mobile workers and the types of tax-planning issues which arise.

If a firm is planning to expand its operations overseas it would be common for it to send some of its employees overseas to supervise the setting up of the new venture and to run it in the initial stages. The success of a new overseas venture can easily be influenced by the quality of personnel located in the new country and so it is important that key employees are not dissuaded from accepting the overseas posting for personal tax reasons. In some cases, there will be tax savings for such employees which will constitute an incentive to accept the posting. The application of the rules considered below is not limited to employment within the same company or group of companies; they apply to any person going to work abroad under a contract of employment.

When employees are posted overseas, they are exposed to two tax systems: that of the home country and that of the visited, (sometimes referred to as work or host) country. Two main possibilities arise, whereby the employee may:

- Remain taxable in the home country without becoming tax resident in the other country. Using the source principle, a country is entitled to tax any income which has its source in the country. Earnings from even short postings abroad could therefore be liable to tax in the visited country. However, most countries disregard short working visits, either in their domestic tax law, their DTTs or both.

- Cease to be tax resident in the home country but become tax resident in the visited country. In this case, the employee would remain taxable in the home country on any income which has its source in the home country, such as property rental income.

It is unlikely (although not impossible) that the employee could become resident in both countries for tax purposes, or in neither of them due to the way in which double tax treaties are worded and to differences in the definition of the tax year. It is never enough just to consider whether an employee will cease to be resident in the home country – the employee's residence status in the visited country must always be examined as well. Every country has its own detailed rules as to how it will apply the general principles. Some countries offer favourable tax regimes to foreign expatriates in order to make their country more attractive to MNEs looking to expand their operations and to attract expert staff. For instance, the Netherlands offers the '30 per cent ruling' to visiting employees who have specific know-how which is not generally available in the Netherlands. Such employees would have specific educational and professional qualifications, at least two and a half years' experience and be highly paid. Under this special regime, 30 per cent of the salary is considered tax free in the Netherlands, with further deductions available for school fees.[1] A regime such as this one is highly attractive to an expatriate if they are able to shed their tax residence (and thus, liability to tax on the earnings from the Netherlands secondment) in their home country.

---

1   IBFD Country Survey, Netherlands.

GENERAL PRINCIPLES

8.3   We discussed the notion of residence for individual taxpayers in Chapter 3. Some taxpayers exhibit features of both residents and non-residents, specifically those who are present in a country for more than half the year, but without the intention of remaining there permanently. Many countries accommodate such 'temporary residents' or 'expatriates' with special rules by limiting the extent to which they are taxed, so as not to impede the international mobility of labour. This may entail only taxing employment income and perhaps locally sourced investment income. In relation to social security contributions, temporary residents may or may not be treated differently in terms of level of contribution and entitlement to benefits.

ARTICLE 15 OF THE OECD MODEL

8.4   As we saw in Chapter 7, Article 15 of the OECD MTC deals specifically with the issue of employees working abroad, and broadly provides that the employee will not be taxed by the foreign country provided the employee is present in the foreign country for less than 183 days in any 12-month period and he is being paid by an employer not resident in the foreign country. His or her remuneration must not be borne by any PE the employer may have in the foreign country for this relief to apply. For example, for UK employees posted abroad for short periods, the effect of the relevant DTT is often to exempt the foreign earnings from foreign tax, leaving them subject to UK tax only.

The purpose of these rules is to ensure symmetry in taxation. If the employer is not taxable in a state, because it is neither resident there nor has a permanent establishment there, then it will not receive any tax deduction in that state for wages and salaries paid. Wages and salaries paid by the employer in respect of short-term employment postings of employees to that state are correspondingly exempted from tax in that state in the hands of the employee. If the employment is exercised in the visited state for more than 183 days in the tax year, then the situation changes and the employee is taxable in the visited state, despite the fact that the person paying the remuneration might not obtain a tax deduction in that state. However, the rules ensure that where the overseas posting is short term, the tax position is kept as simple as possible.

The way in which the 183 days are counted is important. The Commentary on the OECD MTC tells us that the only way of counting the 183-day period which is consistent with the application of Article 15 is the 'days of physical presence' method. This means that the days of arrival and departure are counted, as are parts of days. Non-working days forming part of the tour of duty also count whether they occur before, after, or during the period of overseas duties. The only exception is that days of sickness should not be counted where they prevent the individual from leaving the visited state.

The rules are open to manipulation, as discussed in the next paragraph.

International hiring out of labour

8.5   Some double tax treaties amend the rules set out above to try to prevent a particular misuse of the rules. For instance, Article 15, para 2 of the Canada–Norway DTT of 12 July 2002 contains this provision:

'2.   ... Remuneration derived by a resident of a Contracting State in respect of an employment exercised in the other Contracting State shall be taxable only in the first-mentioned State if:

(a)   the recipient is present in that other State for a period or periods not exceeding in the aggregate 183 days in any period of twelve months commencing or ending in the fiscal year concerned;

(b)   the remuneration is paid by, or on behalf of, an employer who is a resident of the State of which the recipient is a resident, and whose activity does not consist of the hiring out of labour; and

(c)   the remuneration is not borne by a permanent establishment or a fixed base which the employer has in that other State.'

'Hiring out of labour' describes the situation where an employee who is, say, a Canadian resident, is hired by a Canadian-resident employer to perform work in say, Norway. Applying Article 15, Canada would be the 'first-mentioned State'. The provisions will apply where, in broad economic terms, the person for whom the work is performed is someone other than the legal employer, say a Norwegian firm. In this example, it could be that the Canadian firm might not bear responsibility for the employee's work, might leave the Norwegian client firm to instruct the worker, or the work might be performed at a place which is under the control of the Norwegian client. Other indicators of where the provisions might apply are where tools and materials are provided by the Norwegian client, or where the Canadian firm receives fees from the Norwegian client based on the salary or wages paid to the employee. In other words, in economic terms, the real employer, sometimes referred to as the 'economic employer' is the Norwegian firm, with the Canadian firm acting in a labour agency role.[1]

The advantage to the Norwegian firm of this arrangement is that, in the absence of provisions such as found here, the salary or wages paid to the employee could be free of Norwegian employee and employer taxes provided the three conditions set out above, and in particular the 'less than 183 days' are met. The OECD Commentary defines 'international hiring out of labour' as the situation where:

- the employee provides services in the course of an employment to a person other than the employer, and that person supervises, directs or controls the manner in which the services are performed; and

- those services constitute an integral part of the business activities carried on by that person.

If these conditions are met, the short-term exemption from tax in the country where the work is performed contained in para 2 will not be available. The effect will be that all of the wages and salaries for work performed will be taxable in the state where it is performed. Not all countries include such provisions in their double tax treaties, but they are common in Norwegian treaties, presumably because of the large number of foreign workers employed in the North Sea oil industry.

The Commentary on Article 15 suggests a list of factors which may be relevant in determining the true economic employer:

- Which company enjoys the benefit and bears the risks in relation to the work done by the employee?

- Who has the authority to instruct the individual as to how the work should be performed?

- Who controls and has responsibility for the place at which the work is performed?

- Is the remuneration directly recharged to the organization for whom the services are performed?

- Who provides the tools and materials necessary for the work?

- Who determines the number and qualifications of the individuals who perform the work?

- Who has the right to select the individual who will perform the work and to terminate the involvement of that individual?

- Who can impose disciplinary sanctions on the worker?

- Who determines the worker's holidays and work schedule?

A recent UK Tax Tribunal case[2] found that a Croatian resident employed by a Cypriot company and whose services were contracted to a UK company was liable to UK tax.

---

1   For a comprehensive discussion of this issue together with examples, see Dzurdż & Pötgens (2014) 'Cross Border Short-Term Employment', *Bulletin for International Taxation*, August 2014.
2   *Mr Tomislav Kljun v HMRC* TC/2010/04825.

International hiring out of labour – UK position

8.6   Although the UK does not generally insist on specific 'hiring out of labour' provisions in its DTTs (see para **8.5** above), HMRC is known to adopt a rather narrow interpretation of the Article 15 provisions.[1] In particular, the UK will look closely at the purported employment arrangements where a worker is seconded to the UK to work for someone other than the formal employer. For instance, Company A in Ruritania might send an employee to work in the UK for one of its UK clients, Company X. HMRC might consider that the 'economic employer' is really Company X so that the para 2 exemption would not be granted. The employee would be viewed as working for Company X. Because Company X is indirectly claiming a tax deduction in respect of the employee (in the form of fees charged to it by Company A), para 2 would not apply and UK tax would be payable on the salary. It would then be up to the employee to claim double tax relief in his country of residence, Ruritania. If there was a dispute between HMRC and the tax authority in Ruritania as to the true economic employer then the mutual agreement procedure provisions of the UK–Ruritania DTT would have to be used to settle it.

HMRC is known to operate a '60-day rule', whereby it will not assert that the economic employer is a UK company if the foreign employee is in the UK for less than 60 days in the tax year.[2]

---

1   See *Revenue Tax Bulletin*, June 1995, p 220.
2   *Tax Bulletin*, October 1996, p 358 and December 2003, pp 1069–1071.

International hiring out of labour – China

8.7   According to Yang (2015), there are more than 600,000 foreign workers in China, including some 110,000 from the US. The Chinese rules relating to foreign workers distinguish between ordinary employees and managers, and generally treats foreign workers more favourably than domestic workers. Distinction is also made between ordinary income and investment income, and whether the wages are taxable in China depends on whether they are earned in China and paid by a Chinese employer, although the legislation is not clear on the question of source.[1] Employees who work in China for less than 90 days are treated as temporary visitors, and therefore not liable for Chinese income tax. Once a worker has lived in China for more than five years, they are taxed on worldwide incomes.[2]

---

1   See Yang J (2015) 'The Taxation of Foreigners Working in China', *Bulletin for International Taxation*, Vol 69(9).
2   See Webster, et al (2014) 'Taxation of Personal Services in China', *Bulletin for International Taxation*, December 2014.

INTERNATIONAL SHIP, BOAT AND AIRCRAFT CREW

8.8   Paragraph 3 of Article 15 deals specifically with remuneration of crews of ships or aircraft operated in international traffic, or boats engaged in inland waterways transport. The rule provides for tax in the contracting state in which the place of effective management of the enterprise concerned is located, consistent with Article 8. Also consistent with Article 8, however, states are able to agree to confer taxing rights on the state of the enterprise operating the ships, boats or aircraft, on the assumption that domestic law facilitates this.

REMUNERATING INTERNATIONALLY MOBILE EMPLOYEES

8.9   Remuneration packages for internationally mobile employees can be complex and the way in which they are taxed is complicated by timing issues. Cash bonuses, for example, may depend on meeting a number of conditions and may not be paid until after the international assignment is complete. It could also be the case that a bonus is received while working overseas based on work previously performed in the home country. The tax consequences in the host country may be determined by the date on which entitlement to the bonus becomes unconditional or by the date of receipt by the employee. These dates may occur while the employee is tax resident in the host country, or after the assignment is finished. Mismatches between home and host country rules in relation to taxation of bonuses raise the potential for double taxation. Similarly, deferred compensation arrangements can create difficulties for the employee and/or the employer. These various forms of remuneration can create 'trailing' income issues for personal income tax purposes, as well as complexities for social security and pension entitlements.

SHARE INCENTIVES

8.10   Employees are often granted stock options, whereby they are granted the right to buy shares in their company at a future date but at today's price. If, by the date they are entitled to buy the shares (ie to 'exercise' the option) the share price has increased, then the employee is able to buy the shares at below the current market price and sell them immediately at the current market price. The difference between the price paid by the employee and the current market price is often subjected to income tax. Even if there is no income tax, there will be a taxable capital gain if the employee subsequently sells the shares which were bought cheaply. The treatment of employee stock options can be difficult as entitlement to the taxable benefit as a result of the option may have accrued partly whilst the employee was working temporarily in one state but there may be no taxable event, such as exercise of the option until the employee returns to his or her home state. A state is permitted to tax that part of the taxable benefit that can be related to the portion of the entitlement period spent working in that state. The entitlement period would be the period between the date the employee was granted the right to buy the shares in the future, and the date on which he/she can actually buy the shares.

Most DTTs do not set out specific rules as to how income and gains from stock options should be taxed where an employee has been working in both of the states concerned. However, the OECD Commentary on Article 15 of the MTC offers some guidance. Determining the extent to which an employee stock option benefit is derived from employment exercised in a particular state has to be done on a case-by-case basis, taking into account all relevant facts and circumstances. Whether a period of employment would be considered in allocating taxing rights between two states would depend on whether the entitlement to exercise the stock option was contingent upon continuing employment during that period. If an option was granted with a right to exercise, say, in three years' time, regardless of continuing employment then time elapsing between grant and exercise would not count towards an apportionment of the taxing rights over the benefit in the absence of any other factors.

Periods of employment before the option was granted may be considered in the apportionment of taxing rights if the grant of the option was contingent upon a minimum period of employment or attainment of performance objectives.

Once the option is exercised, any further benefit to the employee, normally in the form of a capital gain on a disposal of the shares at a profit, will be dealt with under Article 13 of the relevant DTT and so probably only taxable in the state where he or she is resident. If the shares do not vest irrevocably on exercise of the option (eg because they are liable to forfeiture upon certain conditions) then the increase in value of the shares until they do vest irrevocably will also be dealt with as employment income and subject to the same considerations as the benefit arising between grant and exercise.

The method of apportioning stock option benefits recommended by the OECD is by reference to the proportion of the number of days during which the employment was exercised in one state to the total number of days of employment from which the entitlement to the stock option benefits were derived. Thus if an employee was required to work for an employer for 520 days in total during a particular time period to qualify for the benefits of the stock option and was sent to work in the other state for 260 days out of that period, then half of the stock option benefits would be taxable in each state.

DIRECTORS' REMUNERATION

8.11   Article 16 of the OECD Model deals with the specific situation of company directors, who may otherwise be dealt with under Article 14 (as it existed prior to 2000) or Article 15, depending on the terms of the engagement. As we saw in Chapter 7, Article 16 attributes taxing rights to the state of residence of the company, without removing the right of the recipient's state of residence to also tax the remuneration. Any residual double taxation is then dealt with by Articles 23A or B. Unlike either Articles 14 (as was) or 15, Article 16 does not require physical presence and was described in the 1963 OECD Commentary as a special provision to Article 15, rather than an exception.[1]

Article 16 only has application to the fees and other similar payments received in the capacity as a board member, and not if they are in respect of other functions performed for the company.

The OECD commentary observes that many of the issues discussed in relation to stock options granted to employees (see para **8.9** above) also arise in respect of stock options granted to board members. To the extent to which such stock options are attributable to board membership, and not granted to the taxpayer in some other capacity, the state of source will have the right to tax that part that corresponds to director's fees or similar payments.

The UN MTC adopts similar terms to that of the OECD, but in addition has a second paragraph that expressly refers to remuneration paid to 'top-level' managerial positions. This refers to a 'limited group of positions that involve primary responsibility for the general direction of the company, apart from the activities of directors'.[2] Taxing rights are conferred on the state of the company's residence for this category of remuneration.

---

1   See De Jaegher (2013) for a thorough commentary on Article 16 with particular reference to the Germany–Belgium Treaty.
2   Lennard, M (2009) 'The UN Model Tax Convention as Compared with the OECD Model Tax Convention – Current Points of Difference and Recent Developments', *Asia Pacific Tax Journal*, January/February 2009, pp 4–11.

Tax equalization arrangements

8.12   Many employers operate tax equalization arrangements which have the effect of ensuring that the net pay after tax of an employee is the same wherever they happen to be posted. Whether this benefits the employee or not depends on whether the employee is sent to a country with a higher tax burden than the home country. If the tax burden is lower than that in the home country, then the employer will be the party which benefits from the arrangement. Although these arrangements may be costly for the employer in terms of both the employee tax burden assumed and the compliance work performed or paid for on behalf of the employee, the benefits are increased employee motivation through the certain knowledge of what the after-tax pay will be.

The first step is usually to work out what the tax and social security liability would be if the employee were to remain in the home country, known as the hypothetical tax liability (or 'hypo tax'). Any special allowances, such as a cost of living supplement or danger money, are added to this to give the total net pay to be received by the employee. This total net pay must then be grossed up to take account of the actual tax and social security liabilities in the destination country. This actual foreign tax will be borne by the employer. The employer will normally arrange for the tax return to be filed in the destination country so that the employee need not get involved. However, it should be remembered that, because this service is provided to the employee by the employer, it may constitute a taxable benefit in kind. In the UK, tax equalization arrangements are not recommended for statutory company directors because the nature of the arrangements is that the employee is effectively being made an interest-free loan in years where the true tax liability exceeds the equalized tax liability. Such loans are illegal in the UK.

A further complication which arises is that, because the employer meets the foreign tax liability of the employee, this in itself constitutes a benefit in kind which may be taxable in the destination country. Also, in circumstances where the home country currency (eg the pound sterling) is depreciating against other currencies, the employer also stands to incur exchange losses where the employee is promised a guaranteed level of after-tax pay designated in the home country currency.

Tax equalization arrangements are quite common but they are expensive in tax terms and represent quite a heavy administrative burden for the employer.

FURTHER READING

DeJaeger, C (2013) 'International Taxation of Directors' Fees: Article 16 of the OECD Model or How to Reconcile Disagreement among Neighbours', *World Tax Journal*, June 2013, pp 215–268.

Dziurdź, K (2013) 'Article 15 of the OECD Model: The 183-day Rule and the Meaning of "Borne by a Permanent Establishment"', *Bulletin for International Taxation*, March 2013, pp 124–127.

Dziurdź & Pötgens (2014) 'Cross Border Short-Term Employment', *Bulletin for International Taxation*, August 2014, pp 404–414.

Finney, M (2008) 'Offshore Access', *Taxation*, 27 November 2008, 567.

Gething, H, Shiers, R (2011) 'Analysis – The Proposed Statutory Residence Test', *Tax Journal*, Issue 1083, 18, p 1, July 2011.

HMRC (2005) *Tax Edition Special Bulletin 2005* (concerned with NICs on share incentives for internationally mobile employees). Available at: www. hmrc.gov.uk.

HMRC (2011) *Statutory Definition of Tax Residence: a Consultation*, June 2011.

HMRC (2013) *RDR1 Guidance Note: Statutory Residence Test*. Available at: http://search2.hmrc.gov.uk/kb5/hmrc/forms/view.page?record=FhT41sOFA5E&formId=7361.

HMRC (2013) *RDR4 (on Overseas Workday Relief)*. Available at: http://search2.hmrc.gov.uk/kb5/hmrc/forms/view.page?record=hiOFWzoaVm4&formId=7362.

Ingle, M (2006) 'Income Tax on Share Benefits for Mobile Employees', *Tax Journal*, Issue 825, p 9, 20 February 2006.

Lennard, M (2009) 'The UN Model Tax Convention as Compared with the OECD Model Tax Convention – Current Points of Difference and Recent Developments', *Asia Pacific Tax Journal*, January/February 2009, pp 4–11.

OECD (2010) Art 15. *Commentary on Model Tax Convention on Income and Capital*, July 2010, Condensed Version.

Sullivan, A (2014) *Tolley's Expatriate Tax Planning 2014–2015*, LexisNexis.

Webster, M, Guo, Y M and O'Connell, A (2014) 'Taxation of Personal Services in China', *Bulletin for International Taxation*, December 2014.

Yang, J (2015) 'The Taxation of Foreigners Working in China', *Bulletin for International Taxation*, Vol 69(9).

FURTHER STUDY

Tax position of UK residents going to work abroad

8.13   Whilst the principles of taxation of residents working abroad may not appear too complex, the detailed rules are frequently very complex indeed. The following sections attempt a flavour of the tax regime for individuals either leaving the UK for work or coming to the UK for work. This regime was drastically overhauled by the Finance Act 2013 as part of the UK's general overhaul of its rather antiquated system of determining tax residence. However, whereas the former system relied on case law and HMRC guidance and was sometimes lacking in detail (eg as to what constitutes 'full-time' work), the new rules are set out in detailed legislation, and HMRC's interpretations of the way the new rules will operate are set out in even more detailed HMRC guidance notes.

Individuals leaving the UK for work

8.14   The UK adopted a new statutory test for residence effective from 6 April 2013 which has largely codified the rules previously outlined in the HMRC6 guidance as discussed in Chapter 3. The 'automatic overseas test' looks at the nature and duration of overseas full-time employment to determine residency status. An individual working outside the UK will be non-resident for UK tax purposes if he or she passes any of the three automatic overseas tests:

- *Automatic overseas test 1*: Resident in the UK for at least one of the three preceding tax years, and spends fewer than 16 days in the UK in the current year.

- *Automatic overseas test 2*: Not resident in the UK during any of the three preceding tax years, and spends fewer than 46 days in the UK in the current tax year

- *Automatic overseas test 3*: Works full-time overseas during the tax year without any significant breaks from the overseas work; and

  — spends fewer than 91 days in the UK during the tax year; and

  — the number of days on which he or she works for more than three hours a day in the UK is less than 31.

(There are special rules for workers in the travel and transport industries, such as airline cabin crew, and automatic overseas test 3 does not apply to them.)

'Work' is defined in detail. Time spent working will include:

- Time spent travelling back from full-time employment overseas to the UK for temporary work purposes, eg to attend a meeting or training course.

- Being on-call or stand-by, if this is part of the normal duties and if time on stand-by is paid.

- Overseas work includes work done whilst travelling to, or from the UK (but special rules apply to transport and travel industry employees).

The employment must be full-time and the meaning of 'full-time' is set out in great detail but the intention of the rules is that full-time equates to an average of 35 hours per week, averaged over the number of weeks spent abroad. Where a person works both in the UK and abroad on the same day, the foreign work does not count if more than three hours was spent working in the UK on that day. There are special rules for counting the length of the period spent abroad: adjustments may be needed if there is more than one overseas employment with a gap in between. Days when the employee was sick, injured or on annual leave, or parenting leave, are also left out of the calculation, so long as HMRC considers the length of leave to be reasonable. The extreme complexity and detail of these rules may be attributed to an over-reaction to cases which have appeared before the UK courts in recent years, notably *Derek William Hankinson v Revenue and Customs Commrs*.[1] HMRC gives two examples of the way the rules work in RDR3 but they are too long to reproduce here.[2]

---

1 [2009] UKFTT 384 (TC).
2 RDR3 para 1.10 onwards.

Split-year treatment for employees starting or finishing an overseas assignment

8.15   It will usually be the case that a new overseas job or secondment starts or finishes other than on 5 April in a year. This means that employees will often fail automatic overseas test 3. In these cases, the employee will normally be taxed as if non-resident for the portion of the year spent abroad. As mentioned in Chapter 3, there are eight cases where this split-year treatment is given, and some of these relate specially to individuals working abroad. Individuals may well qualify under more than one of the eight cases.

Individuals starting to work abroad

8.16   These individuals will usually fall under Case 1. Split-year treatment will be afforded if the individual:

- is UK resident for the tax year before the overseas employment is taken into consideration;

- has been UK resident for the previous year (whether or not that was a split-year);

- will be non-UK resident in the following tax year by reason of meeting the third automatic overseas test; and

- satisfies the overseas work criteria:

  — works full-time overseas during a 'relevant period'. Broadly, this is the part of the tax year from the date the overseas employment commences;

  — has no 'significant break' from work during that period;

  — does not work for more than three hours a day in the UK, on more than a permitted number of days; and

  — spends no more than the permitted number of days in the UK during the relevant period.

The permitted number of days depends on the size of the portion of the tax year spent working overseas. For instance, an individual leaving the UK to work overseas between 6 and 30 April in a tax year would be permitted to spend up to 90 days in the tax year during the relevant period in the UK without jeopardizing the individual's split-year treatment. However, an individual leaving the UK in December would only be permitted up to 30 days.

Treatment in the year of return to the UK

8.17   Split-year treatment may also be available for this tax year. The rules work along similar lines (but in reverse) to those used to determine whether split-year treatment can be given in the year of departure.

Split year treatment for persons coming to the UK for full-time work

8.18   Rules which broadly mirror those for persons leaving the UK for full-time work are applied in determining whether a person who becomes tax resident through working full-time in the UK can be given split-year treatment in the year of arrival. Such a person must not have 'sufficient UK ties' with the UK before their arrival to start work. 'Sufficient UK ties' are discussed in Chapter 3 and consider a person's connections to the UK through family, existence of available accommodation, work, length of time spent in the UK, and whether the UK is the country in which the person spent the most number of days during the tax year. So a person arriving in the UK to work who already has a house or other accommodation here, or who has close family here might not be given split-year treatment, but might instead be treated as tax resident for the whole year.

Split year treatment for accompanying spouses/partners

8.19   Cases 2 and 7 of the eight cases provides that accompanying spouses/ partners of those going to work abroad full-time (or returning to the UK) may also be granted split-year treatment. As discussed in Chapter 3, the definition of partner includes anyone with whom the person going to work overseas lives with, as husband and wife, or as civil partner.

Tax treatment of employees who have a foreign domicile

8.20   Subject to the split-year rules, if an individual is resident in the UK he will be liable to UK tax on all his worldwide earnings. A special relief, overseas workday relief, is available, however, for:

- non-domiciled individuals;

- who are tax resident in the UK; and

- claim the remittance basis (see Chapter 3); and

- who have an employment in which the duties are carried out wholly or partly outside the UK and;

- in a year which is either:

  — the first tax year immediately following three consecutive tax years during which he was not UK resident; or

  — one of the next two tax years after such a year.

Thus, the relief is only available for the first three years of UK residence. For this relief, the residence of the employer is not important.

Additional relief

8.21   If an individual is UK resident, but not UK domiciled, claims the remittance basis *and* the salary earned is in respect of a contract of employment with a non-UK employer, the duties of which are performed wholly outside the UK, then the earnings from the employment are only taxable in the UK if remitted to the UK.

Travelling expenses

8.22   The rules concerning deductibility of travelling expenses are more generous for employees working abroad than for other employees. Deductions will be allowed, either from earnings, or in the usual case where the employer has reimbursed the travel expenses, from the amount of taxable travel expenses. In all cases, if the travel expenditure was only partly incurred for the purposes of the employment only a partial deduction is allowed. ITEPA 2003, s 341 provides that a deduction for travel expenses at the start and finish of the overseas employment will be allowed if:

- the duties are performed wholly outside the UK;

- the employee is resident in the UK; and

- (in the case of a non-resident employer) if the employee is UK domiciled.

If these conditions are met, and the employment is carried out in more than one overseas location, then ITEPA 2003, s 342 also permits a deduction for travel between the different overseas locations.

In both cases, if the expenses are only partly incurred in connection with the employment then only a partial deduction is permitted.

In addition, ITEPA 2003, s 370 permits a deduction for travel costs to and from the UK where the absence from the UK is wholly and exclusively for the purpose of performing the duties of one or more employments, or to where the duties of an employment have to be performed partly abroad. There is no limit to the number of journeys allowed.

Family visits

8.23 A deduction is also allowed in respect of travel expenses between the UK and the place of employment for family members (spouse and children) provided that the employee is absent from the UK for a continuous period of at least 60 days for the purpose of performing the duties of one or more employments. The deduction is limited to two outward and two inward journeys per person per tax year (ITEPA 2003, s 371).

Non-domiciled employees

8.24 The reliefs for travel expenses are similar to those described above, but only apply where the person was either not resident in the UK in the two tax years before the tax year of arrival in the UK or had not set foot in the UK during the two-year period immediately preceding the arrival date. The deductions can only be claimed for a five-year period starting with the date of first arrival in the UK for the employment.

Special deduction for seafarers

8.25 Seafarers who are away from the UK for a period of at least 365 days, but not for a complete tax year (and who would thus remain ordinarily resident) can claim a special deduction of 100 per cent of the emoluments relating to the period abroad. There are complex rules regarding how separate periods of absence may be strung together. Oil rig workers do not count as seafarers.

NICs for employees going to work abroad

8.26   The rules for national insurance contributions (NICs) are extremely complex and are not affected by the UK's statutory residence test. The position varies depending on where the employment and the employer are located.

UK employers sending employees to another EEA country (or Switzerland) for fewer than 24 months: UK NICs continue to be paid. There will be no need to pay social security contributions in the destination country. In certain circumstances, the period can be extended to five years.

UK employers sending employees to another EEA country for more than 24 months: contributions will have to be paid in the destination country unless the UK has a special agreement with that country, eg the agreement with Germany which provides for home country social security contributions only for secondments of up to five years.

If a person goes to another EEA country to work for a foreign employer then contributions will be due in the destination country rather than in the UK, although voluntary contributions may still be paid in the UK, eg to protect pension rights.

Mobile workers, who normally work in more than one EEA state but pursue a substantial part of their activities in the state where they are tax resident pay NICs only in the tax residence state. In this context, 'substantial' is taken to mean 25 per cent of working time or remuneration.

In addition to these special rules for EEA countries, the UK has bilateral social security agreements with a number of other countries including the US. These agreements sometimes permit the continuance of UK contributions rather than destination country contributions.

If a UK ordinarily resident employee is sent to a country by an employer with a place of business in the UK which is neither an EEA country nor one with which the UK has a bilateral agreement then UK NICs must continue to be paid for the first 52 weeks of employment in the destination country. This only applies to employees who are ordinarily resident in the UK and who were resident in the UK immediately before starting the secondment abroad. The destination country may also require payment of social security contributions.

NICs for employees coming to work in the UK

8.27   Generally speaking, mirror image treatment applies. There will be no liability to UK NICs for the first 52 weeks. In the case of US workers, this period is extended further by bilateral agreement as US workers must normally continue to pay US social security contributions despite being posted abroad for several years.

Personal tax planning for employees posted abroad

8.28   It is common for an employee posted abroad for a significant length of time to let out their UK property. Because any rent arises from a UK source it remains taxable in the UK regardless of the residence or domicile status of the recipient. To ensure that tax liabilities are properly paid, the UK insists that either the letting agent or the tenant deducts income tax at the basic rate from the rentals paid and accounts for this tax to HMRC. This is known as the non-resident landlord scheme and usually applies to persons living outside the UK who have living accommodation available to them in another country for a period of at least six months. It is then up to the home owner to submit a UK tax return declaring the rent received. As the personal allowance continues to be available to British citizens regardless of their residence status, this may absorb the rent and a tax repayment will then be due.

It is possible to obtain approval to receive rents without deduction of tax at source, provided an application has been made on the correct form and that either the taxpayer's tax affairs are up to date, there is unlikely to be any tax liability, or the person has never had a UK tax liability.

The UK tax liability on interest from UK sources and on dividends from UK companies will be limited to the tax deducted at source per the Income Tax Act 2007, s 811. However, the personal allowance will be set against this income, leaving any rental income from a UK property more exposed to UK tax. Depending on the amounts involved, it may be worth transferring deposits to a low-tax jurisdiction, although if the individual has become tax resident in the country of employment, that country might expect to tax the employee's worldwide income.

For high net worth individuals (HNWIs) an offshore company might be considered. The employee would set up a company in a low-tax jurisdiction and transfer to it his income producing assets. The capital gains tax position needs to be closely examined to avoid exposure to a UK capital gains tax charge on the disposals to the company on the employee's return to the UK.

Pensions: deductions for contributions

8.29   The UK will generally allow deductions for pension contributions paid by employees seconded to the UK in to pension schemes in the home country. This is specifically provided for on a reciprocal basis in some DTTs. The UK operates a scheme of migrant member relief so that relief for contributions will be given where an individual:

- is resident in the UK for the period of the claim;

- has relevant UK taxable earnings in the period;

- has been a member of the relevant pension scheme prior to arrival in the UK;

- has been entitled to tax relief for contributions abroad within ten years prior to arrival in the UK; and

- has been notified by the scheme manager that information concerning benefit crystallization events (usually benefit payments but they include other events) will be given to HMRC.

The scheme needs to be a 'qualifying overseas pension scheme' which broadly means that it should be established outside the UK, formally regulated, open to residents of the country where it is established and approved or otherwise recognized in that country.

Chapter 9

Permanent Establishments

BASICS

9.1   This chapter is concerned with whether a state can tax any of the business profits of a non-resident enterprise (an individual, a company or a partnership). The term 'permanent establishment' (PE) usually refers to a foreign branch, although it can have a much wider meaning.

Two articles in the OECD's Model Tax Convention are particularly relevant to this topic: Article 5 deals with the definition of a permanent establishment, and Article 7 lays down the basic rule that a state can only tax the business profits of a non-resident if that non-resident has a permanent establishment there. It then deals with how to decide how much of the non-resident enterprise's profits can be taxed.

The state where the PE is located can only tax the net profits (revenue minus tax deductible expenses) of the PE. It cannot levy a withholding tax.

The non-resident enterprise normally has to register for corporation tax with the state in which the PE is located, and make a corporation tax return there in respect of the profits attributable to the PE.

There are several types of PE:

- An actual PE: the test for this is whether the non-resident enterprise has a fixed place of business in another state from which its business is wholly or partly carried on.

- A deemed PE: although the non-resident might not have any fixed place of business in another state, there might be someone in another state who is making contracts in its name, ie doing business on its behalf. This is usually known as an 'agency PE'.

- Some double tax treaties (DTTs) identify a further type of deemed PE: a 'services PE'. This usually arises where the non-resident enterprise sends staff to another state to provide services to customers for a period exceeding six months.

The type of activities carried on in the foreign state is important: the activities of an enterprise can be broken down into 'core activities' – ones which are central to its operations, and activities which are 'preparatory or auxiliary' to its core operations. If the only activities carried out in the foreign state are ones that are preparatory or auxiliary to the enterprise's core activities, then there will not be a PE, even if the non-resident has a fixed place of business, or an agent in the foreign state.

The OECD has been reviewing the PE rules as part of the BEPS Project. Action 1 looks at whether the concept of PE is suitable for modern business models which make extensive use of the Internet. Action 7 deals with instances where taxpayers are artificially avoiding having PEs.

A subsidiary company is not normally a PE of its parent company, although this is not impossible – Figure 9.1 illustrates the difference between a company having a PE and a company having an overseas subsidiary.

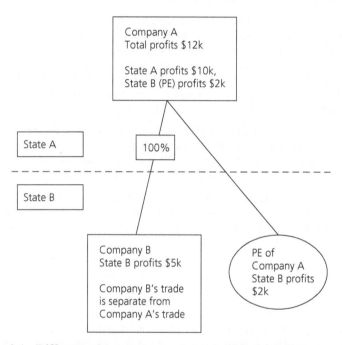

Figure 9.1: Difference between a company having a PE and a company having an overseas subsidiary

Company A, tax resident in State A, has total worldwide trading profits of $12k. It makes $10k of these profits in State A and $2k in State B. How much of the profits can the two States (A&B) tax?

- State B can tax $2k of the profits of Company A, assuming it can show that Company A has a PE there.

- State B can tax all the profits of Company B, because Company B is tax resident in State B.

- State A has the right to tax all of the $12k profits of Company A. If it does so, it will have to give double tax relief for tax charged on the $2k of profits that have also been taxed by State B (the source state). If State A gives double tax relief by exemption method, it would only tax $10k.

- State A cannot tax any of the profits of Company B.

GENERAL INTRODUCTION

9.2   The PE concept evolved in the 1920s, based on a concept of economic allegiance that requires a threshold level of presence to be reached before source state taxation rights are triggered.

A PE is usually part and parcel of the same corporate entity as the head office. This leads to particular difficulties in determining the allocation of total company profits to different parts of the same company located in different states (as in Chapter 7, we refer to 'states' rather than 'countries'). Once it has been established that a permanent establishment exists, the profits of the PE must be arrived at by employing the fiction that it is a separate legal entity. Many of the issues dealt with in Chapter 13 on transfer pricing are relevant here.

It is crucial to the taxing rights of the states concerned that the existence of a PE is identified. If a PE exists through which the foreign resident entity carries on business, then the state where the PE is located may tax the profits of the entity that are attributable to the PE using the source principle.

The term 'permanent establishment' will normally be defined in a state's domestic law[1] and the domestic law definition will be used in cases where there is no double tax treaty (DTT) with the state of residence of the foreign entity.

---

1   In the UK, the Finance Act 2003, s 148.

9.3   Article 5 of the OECD Model deals with the question of whether or not a PE exists. Where a DTT exists between the state where the PE is located and the state where the head office of the entity is located, the tax treaty definition of PE will override the domestic law provisions. The main rules of the OECD Model, Article 5 are briefly summarized in Figure 9.2 below.

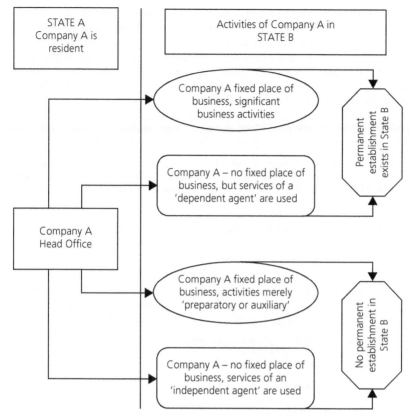

Figure 9.2: Summary of main rules in the OECD Model, Article 5

If Company A is found to have a PE in State B, then State B can tax the profits of Company A which are attributable to that PE. State B would be exercising its taxing rights under the *source* principle. However, if Company A had a subsidiary company which was resident in State B, then this would not normally mean that Company A has a PE in State B. The usual form of a PE is a branch. However, in some circumstances, a PE can arise through the activities of an agent, the provision of services with no fixed place of business or the presence of a subsidiary company. These other types of PE are discussed later in the chapter, along with details of some possible new types of PE proposed by the OECD as part of the BEPS Project.

The OECD Commentary on the Model Tax Convention on Article 5 (PE article) goes into some detail as to how the existence of a PE is to be ascertained. Because the Commentary is an accepted tool of interpretation of the MTC, its provisions will be examined in some detail here. In 2011 and 2012, the OECD issued discussion drafts aimed at clarifying the definition of a PE and detailing some suggested changes of wording to the Commentary[1] (the 2011 and 2012 Discussion Drafts). The UN MTC contains some extensions to the OECD definitions of a PE which are of great importance to developing states and those doing business with them and these will also be examined. This chapter will first examine the three broad categories of PE: a fixed place of business, the provision of services and the existence of a dependent agent, and then will go on to consider some key issues in the attribution of profits to the PE. Proposed changes to the definition of a PE contained in the OECD's BEPS Project are examined along the way.

---

1   OECD Ctr. For Tax Policy and Admin., *Interpretation and Application of Article 5 (Permanent Establishment) of the OECD Model Tax Convention Public Discussion Draft: 12 October 2011 to 10 February 2012* (2011).
See also International Bureau for Fiscal Documentation, Interpretation and Application of Article 5 (Permanent Establishment) of the OECD Model Tax Convention. Response from IBFD Research Staff (IBFD, 2012). Available at: http://www.oecd.org/tax/taxtreaties/49782184.pdf.

A 'FIXED PLACE OF BUSINESS'

9.4   Paragraphs 1–3 of Article 5 of the 2014 OECD Model read as follows:

'1. For the purposes of this Convention, the term "permanent establishment" means a fixed place of business through which the business of an enterprise is wholly or partly carried on.

2. The term "PE" includes especially:

(a) a place of management,

(b) a branch,

(c) an office,

(d) a factory,

(e) a workshop, and

(f) a mine, an oil or gas well, a quarry or any other place of extraction of natural resources.

3. A building site or construction or installation project constitutes a PE only if it lasts more than twelve months.'

The first part of the definition of the term 'PE' stipulates that it means a fixed place of business. Note that a physical presence appears to be required, which must be fixed. There are three basic requirements for a 'fixed place of business' to exist:

● there must be a place of business: premises, or possibly just machinery or equipment which is not moved around;

● this place of business must be fixed: established at a distinct place, with a certain degree of permanence; and

● the business of the enterprise must be wholly or partly carried on there: the business of the enterprise must be conducted from this place by persons who are dependent on the enterprise: generally this means personnel.

What is meant by 'fixed'?

9.5   According to the OECD Commentary, fixed means established at a distinct place with a certain degree of permanence, however, it could be a pitch in a marketplace, or even part of the premises of another enterprise. There is no requirement that premises exist, or if they do, that they be owned by the enterprise. The Commentary offers the example of an employee of Company A, based in State A, who is allowed to use an office at the premises of Company B, based in State B, on a long-term basis. This could create a PE for Company A in State B if the arrangement persists for long enough and if the employee is carrying out activities which are more than merely 'preparatory or auxiliary' (see para **9.14**). The minimum requirement would seem to be that the enterprise has a certain amount of space at its disposal. It does not even have to have the legal right to occupy that space. Thus a trader in State A who illegally sets up a roadside stall just across the border in State B would have a PE in State B.

A case which considered whether there was a fixed place of business is *Toronto Blue Jays Baseball Club and Another v Ontario (Minister of Finance).*[1] In this case, the time spent at the premises was considered as well as what happened in them. Although this case concerned liability under the Ontario Employer Health Tax it is relevant because the persons liable under this tax are employees who report for work 'at a PE' in Ontario. The definition of PE for this purpose is very similar to the OECD definition, which is extensively referred to in the case report. About half of the games played by the sportsmen in question were 'away' games, played outside Ontario. At a typical away game, the teams would be provided with a dressing room, a coaches' room and a training room. The taxpayer (the Toronto Blue Jays Baseball Club) claimed a refund of half of its liability under the Ontario Employer Health Tax on the grounds that the remuneration paid to the players related to duties carried out at away locations, which should be viewed as 'PEs'. Thus, to the extent that the players reported for work at PEs outside Ontario, they were not reporting for work at PEs *inside* Ontario.

The taxpayers lost the argument mainly on the grounds that the locker rooms, etc used by players at away matches did not constitute 'fixed places of business'. None of the vital functions of sports businesses were carried on there – the making of contracts, the selling of tickets, the licensing of concessions, the negotiation of sponsorships and advertising or the sale of media rights. The connection of the teams with the away venues was considered too transitory for them to constitute a PE. The away team locker rooms, etc – were not 'at the disposal' of the teams to the extent required by the OECD Commentary on Article 5, the use of the facilities being similar to the type of use expected of a hotel room.

The OECD considers that to be fixed, a place of business must be at a specific geographic point. However, if the PE consists of mechanical equipment only, then there is no requirement for it to be fixed to the soil.

---

1   (2005) Docket: C41861, Ontario Court of Appeal reported at 7 ITLR 591.

Duration of presence

9.6   As to how long a period is needed before there is a sufficient degree of permanency and hence a fixed place of business can be said to exist, the OECD Commentary does not give a specific period. It just makes the observation that many states have found that six months is a suitable time limit before a PE can arise. This continuing failure of the OECD to set out a time limit is a cause of uncertainty for businesses wanting to expand abroad. The Commentary offers a few examples: for instance, a non-resident painter and decorator who is contracted to redecorate a large office building and is present there for three days a week for two years would be considered to have a PE in that office building. However, there are problems with this example which are considered further later in this chapter.

The uncertainty is compounded by the OECD's statement in the Commentary that a PE can arise in a state even if a foreign enterprise is trading there for a very short period of time. The OECD revisited the issue in its 2012 Discussion Draft and offer two examples of this. First, if a foreign enterprise is carrying on its trade in another state for a short period of time in a particular year, but it does so on a recurrent basis. The example given is of an enterprise carrying on drilling operations at a remote Arctic location. Weather and sea conditions are severe, so that the drilling can only take place for about three months a year, but the enterprise expects to keep coming back for five seasons. The recurrent nature of the business would justify the Arctic state in claiming that a PE arises there for the whole five-year period. However, obvious problems exist with this example: what if the enterprise withdraws from operations before the five years are up? Would it still have a PE in the first few years? On the other hand, if a 'wait and see' approach is taken, then enterprises might find that they are being charged tax on a retrospective basis by foreign states based upon the actual pattern of their trading operations over an indeterminate number of past years. It would be very hard to plan for the tax liabilities that might arise.

Example 9.1

Another example deals with 'pop-up' businesses: Sally, who is tax resident in Ruritania, hears that her parents, who live in the state of Inistania, have rented out their home to a film company for a period of four months. Realizing that her parent's house is in the middle of nowhere, and that there will be many hungry mouths to feed, Sally rushes to Inistania to set up a cafe in her mother's (presumably very large) kitchen. When filming finishes, Sally packs up and returns to her normal (non-catering) job in Ruritania. The point is that the film catering business only ever existed in Inistania and only for those four months. In these circumstances, the OECD considers that Sally could have a PE in Inistania. If she made a living as a film caterer, travelling to different international locations, then she probably would not have a PE in Inistania.

Fixed place of business: whose business is being carried on there?

9.7   It has become common for MNEs with manufacturing operations in relatively high tax states to reduce the taxable profits arising from the manufacturing operations by reducing the profitability of the manufacturing subsidiary. This is usually done by changing the status of the manufacturing subsidiary from a 'fully fledged manufacturer/distributor' to a 'contract manufacturer'. A fully fledged manufacturer would be expected to do its own purchasing, find its own customers, make what it wants, how it wants and when it wants. On the other hand, a contract manufacturer would typically only have responsibility for the manufacturing itself. Another group company would buy the raw materials, send them to the contract manufacturer for incorporation into the finished product and would then buy all the output from the contract manufacturer. A contract manufacturer performs very few business functions and bears very little risk. Consequently, multinational groups can justify the fact that very little profit is made by them.

The question which arises is whether the contract manufacturer really has a trade of its own at all, or whether it is acting merely as a PE of the parent company. If a state can prove that it is really the parent company's trade that is being carried on at the fixed premises of the contract manufacturer, then that state can tax not only the small profits of the contract manufacturer but also a portion of the profits of the parent company.

In its 2012 Discussion Draft, the OECD considered the following example: see Figure 9.3.

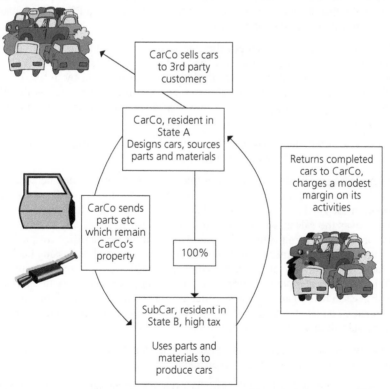

Figure 9.3: Example considered in the OECD 2012 Discussion Draft

The OECD considers that in this situation, SubCar is carrying on its own trade, not that of CarCo, despite the close relationship of the two. This would be the case even if SubCar was formerly a fully-fledged manufacturer. Therefore, the premises of SubCar, in State B, are not a fixed place of business of CarCo and so CarCo does not have a PE in State B. State B can only tax the (small) profits of SubCar – it cannot tax any of the profits of CarCo. It is likely that the tax rate is higher in State B than in State A. By adopting this business model, the CarCo group of companies will reduce its global tax liability.

Fixed place of business: the premises of agents

9.8   Two important cases on whether a PE exists which give useful guidance on the question of whether there is a fixed place of business are *American Income Life Insurance Company v Canada*[1] and *Knights of Columbus v R*.[2] The essential question in both these Canadian cases was whether the activities of agents of a US insurance enterprise gave rise to a PE in Canada. The cases were hard fought by the Canadian tax authorities because these two US insurance enterprises sold large amounts of insurance cover in Canada. In the *American Income* case, the tax assessments, including interest and penalties, totalled some C$13 million. Yet despite the volume of business implied by this figure, the insurance companies insisted they did not have a PE in Canada and therefore Canada could not tax them.

The cases considered at length the question as to whether the premises of the Canadian agents constituted a 'fixed place of business' of the US enterprises and they provide valuable insights into what is meant by 'a fixed place of business'. The principle which emerges from these two cases is that the foreign enterprise must have some power of disposition over the premises in question.

These Canadian decisions can be contrasted with the case of *Universal Furniture Ind AB v Government of Norway*.[3]

In this case, a Swedish company employed a Norwegian sales person. The salesman operated one day per week from his home and spent the rest of the week on the road soliciting orders. The taxpayer company had no ownership rights over the salesman's home and neither did it pay him any expenses for use of his home as an office. The salesman used his home office for planning his itinerary of customer visits, making telephone calls and discussing business issues with his employer. These activities were held to constitute core activities of the taxpayer company (as opposed to being merely preparatory or auxiliary, as discussed below) and the home office was deemed to be a PE of the taxpayer company. The result was that profits arising from the contracts made as a result of the salesman's activities were taxable in Sweden.

The key distinction between this case and the Canadian cases is that the salesman was an employee rather than an agent.

In its 2012 Discussion Draft the OECD gave further guidance of when the use of home as office might constitute a fixed place of business. Where employees work from home, the OECD considers it unlikely that the employee's home could be considered a fixed place of business through which the business of the employer is partly carried on unless no office accommodation is provided for that employee at the employer's premises in circumstances where the employee could not fulfil his/her role without office facilities. In many cases, the activities carried out from the employees home would be merely auxiliary or preparatory and thus excluded from the definition of a PE (see para **9.14** below).

1   2008 TCC 306 Tax Court of Canada, reported at 11 ITLR 52.
2   2008 TCC 307 Tax Court of Canada, Ottawa, reported at 10 ITLR 827.
3   Case No 99-00421A Stavanger County Court 19 November 1999.

Fixed place of business – is it 'at the disposal' of the foreign enterprise?

9.9   It is not necessary for the foreign enterprise to legally own or lease the foreign premises. It is quite possible that a fixed place of business for a foreign enterprise could be the premises of a resident enterprise. Once it has been established that a fixed place exists, it is necessary to consider whether the enterprise is carrying on its business there: 'through which the business of an enterprise is wholly or partly carried on' is a key phrase in para 1 of Article 5. The Commentary interprets this to mean that the premises, which do not belong to the foreign enterprise, are 'at the disposal of' the foreign enterprise. However, there are serious problems in deciding when premises are 'at the disposal of' a foreign firm.

In the case of *R v Dudney,*[1] Mr Dudney, a US resident, was contracted to provide services to a client in Canada. The work involved staff training and installation of new systems. He carried out this work at the client's premises, using the client's equipment. He was given office accommodation, but was moved around from time to time, and only had access to the office accommodation during the client's normal business hours. He was only allowed to use the client's telephone on that client's business. The contracts lasted for 300 days in one year and 40 days in the next. He claimed exemption from Canadian income tax on the grounds that US individuals providing personal services in Canada were only so liable if they operated in Canada from a 'fixed base'. Although the relevant DTT did not define this term, it was held to be analogous to 'permanent establishment'. Despite the length of the contract, the terms on which he was permitted to operate in Canada were such that he did not have a 'fixed base' and thus his firm had no PE in Canada.

The OECD members are divided on whether or not the decision in Dudney was good law. Were the premises of his client 'at his disposal'?

The OECD's 2012 Discussion Draft attempts to define when premises will be 'at the disposal of' a foreign enterprise. It does this by stating that a foreign enterprise must have 'the effective power to use' the premises and be there for a sufficiently long period of time. However, we then have to know what is meant by 'the effective power to use'. The Discussion Draft defines this as when an enterprise is allowed to use a specific location that belongs to another enterprise ... and performs its business activities at that location on a continuous basis during an extended period of time. But as we have just seen, the OECD refuses to define any time period. Intermittent or incidental use of the premises of another enterprise is not sufficient for a PE to arise.

The case of *Société France Touristik Service*[2] is a nice illustration of the requirement for a fixed place of business, through which the business of an enterprise is wholly or partly carried on. The case concerned a German company based in Munich, which specialized in block-booking hotel rooms in Paris for German tour operators. It had no premises in France, nor any person capable of binding it in contract there. An unconnected travel agency in Paris made office space available to the German company from time to time which was used by a manager of the German firm when he visited. It was hardly ever used as a correspondence address. The German manager owned a couple of flats in Paris and stayed in these during his visits. The lack of formal accommodation at the disposal of the German company and the lack of evidence that any business of the company was conducted from any Parisian address led the court to decide that there was no PE in France. The German company had no legal interest in any premises in Paris, nor could it be proved that the company's business was being carried on in Paris in premises owned by anyone else.

---

1   Docket No A-707-98, Court of Appeal, Canada, 20 January 2000, reported at 2 ITLR 627.
2   (1998) Case no 95-1188, Administrative Court of Appeal, France, reported at 1 ITLR 857.

Fixed place of business: computer servers

9.10   The OECD has always accepted that it is technically possible for a PE to consist only of machinery, without the need for the presence of any personnel, although the PE concept was clearly designed with the idea of a foreign factory or sales outlet in mind. In other words, the PE concept is funded on the expectation of foreign premises and personnel. The practice of enterprises establishing international computer networks which necessitate having computer servers located in different countries which became widespread towards the end of the 1990s prompted much debate about whether a machine on its own, located in a foreign country, could constitute a PE.

The OECD updated the Commentary on its Model Tax Convention to give its interpretation of situations where a computer server could, by itself, give rise to a PE. In order to decide each case, it is necessary to examine the business functions performed by the server which hosts the website.

To be considered a PE, the server would have to be owned by the foreign firm. Renting space on someone else's machine would not possibly constitute a 'fixed establishment'. There must be an actual piece of machinery: merely having your website hosted on someone else's server in a foreign state would not give you a PE there.

If the functions are merely 'auxiliary', that is, they consist, for example, of merely collecting the customer's contact details or relaying details of an order to the home country for acceptance then it is unlikely that the server can constitute a PE. However, where the server performs substantial business functions such as offering goods for sale, taking the customer's credit card details, electronically verifying these, initiating download of, say, a computer game to the customer's computer, then there probably is a PE. There are many problems inherent in the notion that a machine could constitute a PE, not least the question of whether it is 'fixed'. Whilst there is no requirement that a machine be physically bolted to the floor, how long a machine stays in one place is problematic. There are also problems of discovery.

In the light of these problems, many states have decided not to try to track down servers owned by foreign firms that are located in their territories. For instance, the UK HMRC released the following statement in 2002:

> 'In the UK we take the view that a website of itself is not a PE. And we take the view that a server is insufficient of itself to constitute a PE of a business that is conducting e-commerce through a website on the server. We take that view regardless of whether the server is owned, rented or otherwise at the disposal of the business.'[1]

In direct contrast to the current OECD position on computer servers and PEs, it is interesting to note a CJEU decision that, for the purposes of EU VAT, services can only be supplied from locations where a business has human and technical resources permanently present. This was the decision in *Gunter Berkholz v Finanzamt Hamburg-Mitte-Altstadt*[2] a case concerning whether gaming machines on board North Sea ferries could constitute a 'fixed establishment' which is broadly the VAT equivalent of a PE. The CJEU was asked to rule on the relevant criteria for a fixed establishment and decided that:

> 'An installation for carrying on a commercial activity, such as the operation of gaming machines, on board a ship sailing on the high seas outside the national territory, may be regarded as a fixed establishment within the meaning of that provision only if the establishment entails the permanent presence of both the human and technical resources necessary for the provision of those services.'

---

1 HMRC News Release 11 April 2002: Electronic Commerce: Tax Status of Websites and Servers.
2 Case C-168/84 ECJ, 6 June 1985.

CONSTRUCTION SITES

9.11   Paragraph 3 of Article 5 states that a building site or construction, or installation project constitutes a PE only if it lasts more than 12 months. Although a building/construction/installation site would not be a permanent place of business for a non-resident construction firm, construction sites are big business, and the amounts that can be earned in a fairly short space of time by foreign construction firms are large. Paragraph 3 gives the state where the construction site is located the right to tax the profits made by non-residents from the construction activity.

The time limit varies in individual DTTs. The UN Model Tax Convention has a limit of 183 days rather than 12 months. The shorter the time period stated, the more opportunity there is for the state in which the construction takes place to tax the profits from it.

There have always been some difficulties with the interpretation of the construction PE rule. When does the time limit run from and what brings it to an end? What if the same foreign construction firm has multiple sites in a state in the same time period? When are multiple construction sites considered separate sites, and when must they be treated as a single site? Does it make any difference if sub-contractors are used?

One construction site or several sites?

9.12   If a non-resident has several construction sites in a state, the 12-month threshold must be applied to each of them separately. Thus a non-resident construction firm might argue that it has several construction sites running consecutively in a state, none lasting for more than 12 months, but the aggregate time for which all the sites operate amounts to 36 months. If the host state accepts that the sites are separate, there would be no PE, and the host state could not charge tax. If they were amalgamated, the host state could charge tax on the profits attributable to all the sites.

Alternatively, a non-resident construction firm might have two sites running concurrently, each commencing on the same date. Site A runs for 11 months and Site B for 13 months. If they are considered to be separate sites, the host state can only tax the profits from Site B. If they are considered to be connected projects, the host state can tax the profits from both of them.

The general rule is that, to be connected, the sites must constitute a coherent whole, commercially and geographically, with respect to the non-resident construction firm. This is a general rule used for deciding whether separate activities of non-residents should be considered separately or together for the purpose of deciding whether all, or any of them constitute a PE (Commentary on Article 5 at para 5.1).

Example 9.2

A non-resident construction firm, Company A, is contracted to build a row of three houses in Acacia Avenue in State X by Developer A in the year 20X0. Construction starts in January 20X0 and is finished by October 20X0. Company A is also contracted with Developer B to build another four houses in Acacia Avenue. Construction on these starts in June 20X0 and finishes in May 20X1.

Taken separately, neither of the contracts would give rise to a PE in State X, as construction activities on each one last for less than 12 months. However, the aggregate period during which Company A is building houses in Acacia Avenue is 17 months. If the two contracts are considered to be separate, Company A has no PE in State X and does not have to pay corporation tax in State X on any of the profits from the construction of the houses. However, if the two contracts are considered to be connected, then there is a PE and corporation tax would be due to State X. The Commentary indicates that in this example, the two contracts are connected and thus there would be a PE. Although it might be argued that there is only geographic coherence to the activities, not commercial coherence (because there are different customers) the OECD's view is that a building site should be viewed as a single unit.

In this situation, it would be open to Company A to form a new subsidiary company, Company B, and have one of the customers contract with the new subsidiary. In this way, the PE rules would be applied separately to Company A and Company B, even though they are part of the same group and neither of them would have a PE. This kind of planning is tackled in BEPS Action 7.

Construction PEs and BEPS Action 7

9.13 The BEPS Action 7 Discussion Drafts[1] focussed on the issue of artificial splitting up of contracts in order to avoid having a construction site for more than 12 months. A foreign construction firm might argue that it has two, separate construction projects in a state, each lasting for less than 12 months and so no PE exists. It might go further and divide up the construction projects between separate group companies.

The Final Report on Action 7 concludes that the 'principal purposes test' developed under Action 6 (treaty abuse) that is set out in Article 7 of the Multilateral Instrument (MLI) would apply. It reads as follows:

'7. Notwithstanding the other provisions of this Convention, a benefit under this Convention shall not be granted in respect of an item of income or capital if it is reasonable to conclude, having regard to all relevant facts and circumstances, that obtaining that benefit was one of the principal purposes of any arrangement or transaction that resulted directly or indirectly in that benefit, unless it is established that granting that benefit in these circumstances would be in accordance with the object and purpose of the relevant provisions of this Convention.'

In Example 9.2 at para **9.12** above if it could be shown that the principal purpose of having the contract split between Company A and Company B was to avoid a construction PE in State X, then if the DTT between State X and the State where Companies A and B are resident includes the new Article 10, State X could use the new rule to treat both Company A and Company B as having a PE.

Not all countries will want to, or be able to insert the new Article 10 into their treaties. For these countries, an alternative proposal offered by the OECD is to insert a specific rule in Article 5 to deal with this type of planning: under this rule, if Company A and Company B are 'closely related' (see para **9.31** below for a definition of 'closely related') and they carry on 'connected activities' at the same building/construction/installation site during different periods of time, each lasting between 30 days and 12 months, then the various time periods can be added together to decide whether the time threshold has been breached. 'Connected activities' are identified according to the facts of each case, but indicators are:

- contracts with the same person or related persons;

- whether the activities could all have been covered by a single contract in the absence of tax planning;

- the nature of the work: same work indicates connected activities; and

- same employees working on the different contracts.

---

1   OECD Ctr. for Tax Policy and Admin., *Public Discussion Draft: BEPS Action 7: Preventing the Artificial Avoidance of PE Status: 31 October 2014 to 9 January 2010* (OECD 2014). OECD Centre for Tax Policy and Administration, *New Discussion Draft on Action 7 (Prevent the Artificial Avoidance of PE Status) 15 May 2015* (2015).

'PREPARATORY OR AUXILIARY' ACTIVITIES

9.14   Having a fixed place of business from which a foreign enterprise is partly carrying on its business exists does not automatically mean that the foreign enterprise has a PE. There are a currently a number of specific exceptions from the definition of PE, set out in para 4 of Article 5. However, Action 7 of the BEPS Action Plan has resulted in an overall limitation on these exceptions. This is discussed further in para **9.15** below:

'Article 5, para 4 of the Model

Notwithstanding the preceding provisions of this Article, the term "permanent establishment" shall be deemed not to include:

(a)   the use of facilities solely for the purpose of storage, display or delivery of goods or merchandise belonging to the enterprise;

(b)   the maintenance of a stock of goods or merchandise belonging to the enterprise solely for the purpose of storage, display or delivery;

(c)   the maintenance of a stock of goods or merchandise belonging to the enterprise solely for the purpose of processing by another enterprise;

(d)   the maintenance of a fixed place of business solely for the purpose of purchasing goods or merchandise or of collecting information, for the enterprise;

(e)   the maintenance of a fixed place of business solely for the purpose of carrying on, for the enterprise, any other activity of a *preparatory or auxiliary character*;

(f)   the maintenance of a fixed place of business solely for any combination of activities mentioned in subparagraphs (*a*) to (*e*), provided that the overall activity of the fixed place of business resulting from this combination is of a preparatory or auxiliary character.

Provided that such activity or, in the case of subparagraph f: the overall activity of the fixed place of business, is of a preparatory or auxiliary character'.

(Words in *italics* added in October 2015 – following BEPS Action 7.)

Paragraph 4 of the Model gives an important exception to the PE rule, whereby a fixed place of business will *not* constitute a PE provided the activities being carried out in it are merely preparatory or auxiliary to the firm's main business. All the business activities listed in para 4 of Article 5 would historically have been considered preparatory or auxiliary in nature. Examples of activities which are merely preparatory or auxiliary would be advertising or the supply of information for scientific research. They contribute to the profits of the enterprise but have been considered remote from the actual realization of such profits.

Any activity which can be regarded as management, even if only in respect of part of the enterprise, cannot be regarded as preparatory or auxiliary. According to para 24 of the Commentary on Article 5, the decisive criterion is whether or not the activity of the fixed place of business in itself forms an essential and significant part of the activity of the enterprise as a whole.

If a fixed place of business is used merely to provide advertising services for the whole company, that would be preparatory and auxiliary and there would be no PE. However, if the fixed place of business also provided advertising services for third parties, then that would constitute a PE. The same principle applies to any functions which could be considered preparatory or auxiliary.

Not all states agree that a fixed place of business from which a combination of these activities are performed can be excluded from the definition of a PE. Italy, in particular, takes a strict view, substituting for sub-paras (e) and (f) above merely the following sub-para:

'(e)   The maintenance of a fixed place of business solely for the purpose of carrying on any other activity of a preparatory or auxiliary character (including advertising and scientific research).'

(*Source*: Article 5 of the Italy–Czech Republic Income Tax Treaty of 1984.)

Treaties which use this wording usually also restrict the activities of an agent which are not viewed as constituting a PE to the mere purchase of goods for the enterprise. This follows the 1963 version of the OECD MTC.

There have always been disputes as to whether or not an activity or, more likely, a combination of activities, is merely preparatory or auxiliary. Relatively few cases have been heard on this point, but there was a German case[1] where a German newspaper had editorial offices in several other states. Germany uses the exemption method of double taxation relief in domestic law and under its treaties so that if profits were allocated to the foreign editorial offices then, given the high rates of tax in Germany relative to those charged in other states at that time (the early 1980s) the global tax bill would be reduced. The activities of the foreign editorial offices were examined. Because the editorial offices did more than solely collect information but also translated, wrote messages, reports and commentary, their activities were more than preparatory or auxiliary. The wording in para 4 of Article 5 which is 'solely' means that the provisions must be interpreted narrowly. Further, it is necessary to look at the overall business activity of an enterprise. Activities which are core activities cannot be regarded as merely preparatory or auxiliary and so the taxpayer lost the case also on the grounds that collecting information and providing news stories was the core activity of a newspaper.

---

1   Case IR 292/81 21 January 1985 (name of taxpayer not disclosed).

Changes as a result of BEPS Action 7

9.15   Action 7 of the BEPS Action Plan[1] reads:

'ACTION 7 – Prevent the Artificial Avoidance of PE Status

Develop changes to the definition of PE to prevent the artificial avoidance of PE status in relation to BEPS, including through the use of commissionaire arrangements and the specific activity exemptions. Work on these issues will also address related profit attribution issues.'

The Final Report on Action 7[2] proposes a key change to the paragraph 4 exemptions from PE status. Each of the exemptions will be made subject to the requirement that the activities in question (listed in subparagraphs (a)–(f)) are preparatory or auxiliary in nature, either alone or taken together.

---

1   OECD Ctr. For Tax Policy and Admin., *Action Plan on Base Erosion and Profit Shifting* (2013).
2   OECD (2015)(2) Action 7: 2015 *Final Report – Preventing the Artificial Avoidance of Permanent Establishment Status*, 5 October 2015.

Definition of 'preparatory or auxiliary' activities

9.16   As this definition will assume increased importance, a better definition is needed. The Action 7 Final Report introduces new material for the Commentary that includes a definition. Activities of an enterprise can be split up into 'core activities' and those that are merely preparatory or auxiliary. If core activity is defined, then any activities that are not core activities will be preparatory or auxiliary. The OECD proposes the following:

●   it is necessary to decide which activities constitute the essential and significant parts of the activity of the enterprise as a whole (in other words, identify the 'core' activities);

● preparatory activities will often be relatively short term; and

● auxiliary activities are those that support the core activities. Carrying them out does not usually require a significant proportion of the assets or employees of the enterprise.

The 'anti-fragmentation' rule

9.17   An anti-fragmentation rule is required because there will only be a PE if the types of activities undertaken at a fixed place of business or by a dependent agent, listed in paragraph 4, are more than preparatory or auxiliary in relation to the core business functions of a non-resident enterprise, either separately or taken together. The fewer functions undertaken at any single fixed place of business, the more likely it is that the functions being performed at any single fixed place of business will be preparatory or auxiliary. To avoid having a PE, a non-resident enterprise might be tempted to set up several separate fixed places of business (possibly, separate subsidiaries) in another state, and scatter the functions of, say, warehousing, purchasing, information gathering and so on, around the various places.

To combat this type of planning, the Action 7 Final Report introduces a new 'anti-fragmentation' rule to be inserted at the end of paragraph 4.

'4.1.   Paragraph 4 shall not apply to a fixed place of business that is used or maintained by an enterprise if the same enterprise or a closely related associated enterprise carries on business activities at the same place or at another place in the same Contracting State and

a)   that place or other place constitutes a permanent establishment for the enterprise or the closely related associated enterprise under the provisions of this Article, or

b)   the overall activity resulting from the combination of the activities carried on by the two enterprises at the same place, or by the same enterprise or closely related associated enterprises at the two places, is not of a preparatory or auxiliary character,

provided that the business activities carried on by the two enterprises at the same place, or by the same enterprise or closely related associated enterprises at the two places, constitute complementary functions that are part of a cohesive business operation.'[1]

The following Figure 9.4 is based on an example intended for new Commentary on paragraph 4, supplied by the OECD in the Final Report on Action 7.

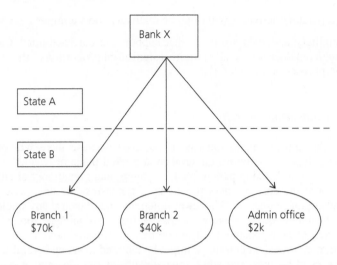

Figure 9.4: Based on an example intended for new Commentary on paragraph 4 (OECD, Final Report on Action 7)

Notes: the monetary amounts are the profits of Bank X attributable to each of its locations in State B. Bank X's total profits are £500k.

Bank X, tax resident in State A, has several branches in State B. It also has an administration office in State B in which staff perform initial screening checks on loan applications made by clients at the State B branches. The applications are forwarded to Bank X in State A after the initial checking. Before any changes to Article 5, the activities of the administration office in State B would have been considered to be preparatory or auxiliary in nature. Thus, the administration office would not have been treated as a PE of Bank X and State B could not tax any profits arising from the activities carried out in the administration office. State B could only tax the profits arising from Branch 1 and Branch 2, which are definitely PEs.

However, once the anti-fragmentation rule is added into the DTT between State A and State B, this would change because:

- the administration office is a fixed place of business used by Bank X and;

- Bank X (the 'same enterprise') carries on business activities in State B (the 'same enterprise', carrying on business activities at 'another place in the same contracting State'); and

- the business activities carried on by Bank X (the 'same enterprise' at two places (the administrative office and either of the branches) constitutes complementary functions that are part of a cohesive business operation.

Therefore, if the rule applies, State B will be able to tax profits of Bank X amounting to $112k ($70k+$40k+$2k). Without the rule, it would only be able to tax profits of $110k.

---

1   Para 41 of the 2015 Discussion Draft on Action 7.

9.18 Would the anti-fragmentation rule apply to business models such as those used by Amazon? No, taking the relationship between the two group companies involved in the sale of goods to UK customers, the following business model is employed by Amazon:

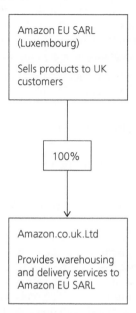

Figure 9.5: Based on an example intended for new Commentary on paragraph 4 (OECD, Final Report on Action 7)

Using this business model, most of the profits on sales to the UK customer are attributed to the Luxembourg company. This company then pays the UK company a modest fee for its warehousing and delivery services. The anti-fragmentation rule will only apply if a non-resident business (Amazon EU SARL) has a fixed place of business in the UK. Assuming it is careful to avoid this, the rule would not apply.

The UK can tax the profits of the UK subsidiary in full, but they are very small. Simply by fragmenting its activities between separate group companies – having a separate subsidiary in the UK – the Amazon group has protected itself against having to pay UK tax on the vast majority of its profits from sales to UK customers.

PE ARISING FROM THE USE OF AGENTS

9.19 Article 5 of the OECD Model contains two ways in which a foreign enterprise can be found to have a PE in a state: either it:

• has a fixed place of business there; or

- it uses the services of a particular type of agent, who is tax resident in that state.

When first starting to trade in another state it is very common to use agents to secure sales rather than to set up a new shop or business premises staffed by the firm's own employees. An agent is a person who acts on behalf of the principal (the foreign enterprise in this case). A PE can be deemed to exist by virtue of the activities of an agent even though the foreign enterprise has no premises or other fixed place of business or employees in the state.

Changes to these rules have been made as a result of BEPS Action 7 (Prevent the Artificial Avoidance of PE Status). The changes are discussed in para **9.27** below.

The existing (as at July 2015) and the proposed new wordings are given in Table 9.1 below.

Table 9.1 BEPS Action 7 (Prevent the Artificial Avoidance of PE Status): amendments

	Old wording (as at July 2015)	*New wording (as proposed in BEPS Action 7 work)*
Para 5	Notwithstanding the provisions of paragraphs 1 and 2, where a person – other than an agent of an independent status to whom paragraph 6 applies – is acting on behalf of an enterprise and has, and habitually exercises, in a contracting State an authority to conclude contracts in the name of the enterprise, that enterprise shall be deemed to have a permanent establishment in that State in respect of any activities which that person undertakes for the enterprise, unless the activities of such person are limited to those mentioned in paragraph 4 which, if exercised through a fixed place of business, would not make this fixed place of business a permanent establishment under the provisions of that paragraph.	Notwithstanding the provisions of paragraphs 1 and 2 but subject to the provisions of paragraph 6, where a person is acting in a contracting State on behalf of an enterprise and, in doing so, habitually concludes contracts, or plays the principal role leading to the conclusion of contracts that are routinely concluded without material modification by the enterprise, and these contracts are in the name of the enterprise, or for the transfer of the ownership of, or for the granting of the right to use, property owned by that enterprise or that the enterprise has the right to use, or for the provision of services by that enterprise, that enterprise shall be deemed to have a permanent establishment in that State in respect of any activities which that person undertakes for the enterprise, unless the activities of such person are limited to those mentioned in paragraph 4 which, if

	Old wording (as at July 2015)	New wording (as proposed in BEPS Action 7 work)
		exercised through a fixed place of business, would not make this fixed place of business a permanent establishment under the provisions of that paragraph.
Para 6	An enterprise shall not be deemed to have a permanent establishment in a Contracting State merely because it carries on business in that State through a broker, general commission agent or any other agent of an independent status, provided that such persons are acting in the ordinary course of their business.	Paragraph 5 shall not apply where the person acting in a Contracting State on behalf of an enterprise of the other Contracting State carries on business in the first-mentioned State as an independent agent and acts for the enterprise in the ordinary course of that business. Where, however, a person acts exclusively or almost exclusively on behalf of one or more enterprises to which it is closely related that person shall not be considered to be an independent agent within the meaning of this paragraph with respect to any such enterprise. *Subparagraph b) defines the term 'closely related'*

Dependent agents

9.20   The type of person whose existence can create a deemed PE without there being a fixed place of business as such is known as a dependent agent. Such a person might or might not be an employee of the enterprise. Employees, subsidiary companies, unrelated individuals and companies are all capable of being regarded as dependent agents. The rules for when a person is a dependent agent (and therefore creates a PE in respect of the non-resident enterprise) are found in paragraphs 5–6 of Article 5.

Independent agents

9.21   Only dependent agents can create a PE for a foreign enterprise. Paragraph 6 of the Commentary on Article 5 deals with the case where independent agents are used in the other state. Carrying on business through an independent agent will not give rise to a PE. Independence will be demonstrated by a combination of the following factors:

- an agent bearing a commercial degree of entrepreneurial risk;

- an agent being both legally and commercially independent of the enterprise (although this carries less weight under the proposals of BEPS Action 7);

- an agent not being required to comply with detailed instructions from the enterprise;

- an agent not being subject to comprehensive control by the enterprise;

- the agent having skill and knowledge on which the enterprise relies (eg a network of contacts, local market knowledge, expertise in local government rules and regulations, etc); and

- the agent working for a number of different clients.

Importantly, an independent agent must be shown to be acting in the ordinary course of the independent agent's business when concluding sales on behalf of the enterprise. A distinction is made between activities which are in the ordinary course of a commission agent's business, and those which are really part of the business of the enterprise for whom the agent acts. Thus, providing an aftersales service would really be part of the business activities of the enterprise itself, rather than the business activities of a commission agent. Any agent providing such services would be likely to bring into existence a PE for the enterprise.

Case law on agency permanent establishment

9.22   The question of whether a dependent agent existed was considered in the *Knights of Columbus* and the *American Income* cases (see above). Having established that the premises of the Canadian insurance agents did not constitute a PE of the US insurance companies, the judges in these cases then went on to consider if the Canadian agents were dependent agents. In other words, if there was no 'fixed place of business' type of PE, was there a 'dependent agent' PE? If so, then Canada would be able to tax all the profits arising from the business written by the agents for the US insurance companies. It was concluded that no dependent agent PE was created, and the judgments are instructive because of their careful analysis of the issues.

Commissionaire arrangements

9.23   A commissionaire company is usually either a sales or a manufacturing subsidiary which carries out a very limited range of business functions, bears very little risk and owns few assets. The idea is that, even using open market pricing on intra-group transactions, very little profit is earned by the commissionaire. It earns a commission on its sales or manufacturing services. Usually, it would be located in a relatively high tax country.

Two main tax issues arise from this type of planning: is the foreign subsidiary being rewarded on an arm's-length basis[1] (see Chapter 13); and has the foreign subsidiary been so stripped of business functions that it is now operating as no more than a dependent agent PE of another group company?

---

1   See *OECD Transfer Pricing Guidelines for Multinational Enterprises and Tax Administrations 2010*, Chapter IX 'Business Restructurings'.

Manufacturing commissionaire arrangements

9.24   Many MNEs have sought to limit their exposure to foreign taxes by making changes to their supply chains. Typically, the functions performed by a foreign subsidiary in a high tax jurisdiction will be radically reduced in order to reduce the attribution of group profits to that subsidiary. For instance, whereas before, the foreign subsidiary might have carried out manufacturing for the group, buying in materials, using its own intellectual property and employing its own sales force, the subsidiary could be converted to a 'contract manufacturer'. Typically, the intellectual property used in the manufacturing process and the materials processed would belong not to the manufacturing subsidiary, but to a group company in a low tax jurisdiction. The manufacturing subsidiary would then be paid only for its manufacturing activities, usually on a cost plus basis (see Chapter 13) which would result in a drop in taxable profits. The group has thus switched internal profits from a high tax jurisdiction to a low tax one.

Distributor (sales) commissionaire arrangements

9.25   Often, MNEs apply similar planning techniques to their distributor subsidiaries, stripping them of their assets, such as marketing intangibles, reducing the business risk borne by them, and limiting their functions to that of a commissionaire.

A sales commissionaire is an undisclosed agent of the principal which makes sales in its own name. This is a civil law concept; the question is whether it is acting as a dependent agent (PE) or an independent agent of the principal. Under a commissionaire arrangement, a firm enters into sales contracts in its own name, but on behalf of a principal. There is usually a back-to-back contract between the commissionaire and the supplier firm (the principal). Typically, a commissionaire resident in State A might sell goods to customers in State A. However, the commissionaire would then automatically enter into a contract with the supplier firm in State B to buy the goods for onward supply to the customer. The customer would only deal with the commissionaire firm and would have no recourse to the supplier firm. No authorization is required from the supplier firm before the commissionaire firm can enter into contracts with the customers.

Essential features of the sales commissionaire structure are that most of the business risk (eg inventory, credit risk, currency risk) is borne by the supplier company rather than the commissionaire. The functions of the commissionaire company are purely sales, and the turnover is normally presented as an amount of commission earned. This minimizes the amount of group profit which needs to be allocated to the commissionaire. Usually the income of the commissionaire will be shown as commission received minus expenses, rather than as profit from the purchase and onward sale of goods.

Sales commissionaires are sometimes referred to as 'low risk distributors'. Distributor companies which own the stock, bear risk and own substantial assets are usually referred to as 'fully-fledged distributors'.

Agency rules under common law and civil law

9.26   States often assert that a commissionaire company is acting as a dependent agent (and therefore as a PE) of another company in its group. If proven, this gives them the right to tax not only the profits of the resident commissionaire company, but also a portion of the profits of the non-resident group company. Commissionaire structures create problems in deciding whether there is an agency PE because the concept of agency is understood differently in different states, depending on whether the state has a common law or civil law system. Civil law recognizes that an agent can act either by direct or by indirect representation. Direct representation means that the agent acts in the name of the principal, and informs the other party that this is what the agent is doing.[1] In indirect representation, the agent acts in the agent's own name: personally binding in contract. There is then a further contract made between the agent and the principal, transferring the legal rights and obligations entered into by the agent to the principal.

Common law makes no such distinction between direct and indirect (or 'undisclosed') agency and the concept is somewhat simpler in that it does not make any difference whether the agent acts in the agent's own name or in the name of the principal. However, the broad effect of this difference in definition is that the civil law concept of agency is wider than the common law concept. As the term 'agency' is not defined in Article 3 of the OECD Model, each state uses its domestic law definition. Thus in a treaty between a civil law state and a common law state there can be a mismatch in interpretation of the term 'permanent establishment' where agents are involved. The differences between the two legal systems with respect to agents are illustrated in Figure 9.6.

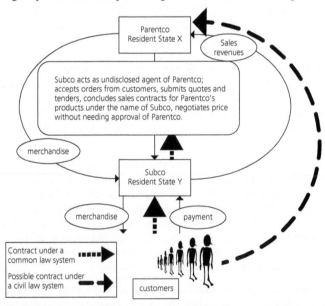

Figure 9.6: Based on an example intended for new Commentary on paragraph 4 (OECD, Final Report on Action 7)

Before the changes to paragraph 5 of Article 5 (set out in Table 9.1), paragraph 5 of Article 5 referred explicitly to 'an authority to conclude contracts in the name of the enterprise', indicating either the common law definition of agency, or direct representation in a civil law system. Prior to BEPS Action 7, the Commentary[1] attempted to clarify the position by stating that paragraph 5 applied to an agent who concludes contracts which are binding on the principal even if those contracts were not actually in the name of the principal. The example given was that of an agent who solicits and receives orders from customers of the principal, which the agent sent directly to a warehouse at which the order was routinely approved by the principal and fulfilled. The agent does not formally enter into any contract in the name of the principal, yet for the purposes of paragraph 5 of Article 5 would be considered to 'have authority to conclude contracts in the name of the enterprise'. In other words, the agent (probably a subsidiary) would be regarded as a PE of the principal (a non-resident company). This position has been confirmed in the OECD's Final Report on Action 7. New paragraph 32.8 of the Commentary on Article 5 explains that where an agent (typically, a commissionaire) acting on behalf of a principal, enters into contracts with customers in the name of the agent, but which result in the principal transferring goods or providing services to those customers directly, would result in that commissionaire being regarded as PE of the principal. This is so even though the contracts entered into by the commissionaire with the customer do not legally bind the principal in contract to deliver those goods or services. The usual exception for independent agents would still apply. Genuine distributor companies should not be caught by these rules.

---

1   At para 32.1 of the Commentary on Article 5 in the 2014 version of the OECD Model Tax Convention.

Changes for commissionaires: BEPS Action 7

9.27   The OECD acknowledges that states do not have a common view on whether an undisclosed agency, such as a commissionaire arrangement, can result in the foreign subsidiary (the commissionaire) being regarded as a PE of a foreign principal (the parent company). The 2015 Final Report on Action 7 sets out changes to paragraphs 5 and 6 of Article 5, reproduced in Table 9.1. Most of these changes are directed specifically at sales commissionaire arrangements. The wording or paragraph 5, current at July 2015, refers to a person concluding contracts in the name of the enterprise. However, a sales commissionaire company will often conclude contracts in its own name. Hence, the proposed new paragraphs 5(b)–(c):

'5.

.... where a person is acting in a contracting State on behalf of an enterprise and, in doing so, habitually concludes contracts, or plays the principal role leading to the conclusion of contracts that are routinely concluded without material modification by the enterprise, and these contracts are in the name of the enterprise, or for the transfer of the ownership of, or for the granting of the right to use, property owned by that enterprise or that the enterprise has the right to use, or for the provision of services by that enterprise, that enterprise shall be deemed to have a permanent establishment in that State in respect of any activities which that person undertakes for the enterprise…,'

These new subparagraphs widen the scope of paragraph 5 beyond the situation in which contracts are made 'in the name of the enterprise'. Under the new wording, a commissionaire company (White Co), selling to a customer (Black Co), under a contract in the names of Black Co and White Co, might still create a PE for another company (Red Co). This would happen if the parts of the contract between White Co and Black Co which relate to the transfer of ownership or use of property or provision of services will be performed by Red Co, rather than by White Co. Thus, the new wording catches 'undisclosed agents' where the customer (Black Co) does not necessarily know the identity of the company which will supply the product or services (Red Co). The key point is that goods sold under the contract between White Co and Black Co are never legally owned by White Co. Situations where a distributor company, even a low risk distributor, takes legal ownership of property before selling it on to a customer, would not create a PE for the supplier. Hence, if White Co took legal possession of the goods from Red Co before White Co contracted to sell them to Black Co, Red Co would not have a PE.

The Dell Products and the Zimmer commissionaire cases

9.28   The *Dell Products* and *Zimmer* cases prompted much of the proposed change to the rules affecting commissionaire structures just described. In the *Zimmer* case[1] the French Supreme Court gave great weight to the strict legalities of the arrangement between a UK parent company, its French commissionaire subsidiary and its customers. The UK parent company, Zimmer Limited, changed the nature of the business conducted by its French subsidiary (SAS) from that of a fully-fledged distributor company to a commissionaire. Although the legal form of the arrangement was that SAS made contracts with French customers and then with Zimmer Limited in the UK, the economic substance of the arrangement was that SAS acted as a dependent agent of Zimmer Limited. Although SAS made the contracts with the customers, Zimmer Limited was bound to honour the back-to-back contracts with SAS made, in turn, with Zimmer Limited. Any loss from the contracts with the customers would be ultimately borne by Zimmer Limited. SAS sold only Zimmer Limited's products. Zimmer Limited had a certain amount of control over SAS in the way the products (viz. walking frames for the elderly) were marketed.

The lower French court decided that this was a ploy to reduce the amount of Zimmer group profits liable to French taxation and argued successfully that SAS had become a PE of the UK company, Zimmer Limited. However, the French Supreme Administrative Court (the *Conseil d'Etat*) ruled that regardless of the degree of dependency of the French commissionaire company on the UK parent for its trade, a commissionaire does not have the power to legally bind the principal in contract. The eventual outcome of the case was that profits of Zimmer Limited from the sale of Zimmer products in France, made via SAS, were only taxable in the UK – there was no French PE. The French Supreme Administrative Court looked closely at the strict legal position between the two companies, rather than applying any 'substance over form' approach. The legal analysis was:

- the commissionaire is the only person engaged with customers because it acts in its own name;

- if the principal (in this case, the UK company) fails to deliver goods, the customer has no legal recourse against the principal;

- the principal is only engaged with the commissionaire: the principal has a commitment to deliver goods to the customer but this commitment is fulfilled by the commissionaire; and

- if the principal goes bankrupt, the customer does not run any risk – customers only bear the risk of the commissionaire becoming bankrupt.

Thus, the Court ignored the OECD's guidance that a PE may be found where the agent has *de facto* power to bind a principal, even if not in strict legal terms. The decision of the Supreme Court was something of a surprise, as the French Courts had previously ruled in a similar case[2] that there was a PE.

In *Dell Products (NUF) v Tax East*,[3] an Irish resident company (low tax jurisdiction) had a commissionaire subsidiary company in Norway (high tax jurisdiction) and the Irish company reported nil taxable profits in Norway. The Norwegian Court of Appeal decided, in November 2011, that the Irish parent did not have a PE in Norway.

This overturned the decision of the Norwegian lower court, which had ruled that the Irish company was operating in Norway through an agency PE in the shape of the Norwegian commissionaire company and levied Norwegian tax on 60 per cent of those profits of the Irish company which related to sales in Norway. In reaching its decision, the lower Norwegian Court of Appeal had noted that:

- All the sales were made under the Dell trademark, leading the customer to believe that he was transacting with the Dell group.

- The sales were made partly using the Dell group's standard conditions.

- In practice, the Irish company did not check or query sales agreements prepared by the Norwegian subsidiary and there was no evidence of any of these sales contracts being rejected by the Irish parent.

- Even if the Norwegian company had exceeded its authority it was unim-aginable that the Irish company would refuse to deliver the computer in question to the customer.

Although none of these features of the arrangements, by themselves, would make the Norwegian subsidiary a PE of the Irish parent, there was over-reliance by the Norwegian subsidiary on the assets and business functions of the rest of the Dell group. The lower court therefore considered that the Irish company had a PE. However, this decision was quickly overturned by the Norwegian

Supreme Court, who held that because the Norwegian commissionaire company did not have the strict legal power to bind the Irish company in contract, there was no Norwegian PE of the Irish company. Norway could not tax any of the profits of the Irish company after all. The Norwegian Supreme Court was heavily influenced by the decision in *Zimmer*.

A further French case confirming the strict legal approach resulted in profits from sales in France of a Swiss company with a French commissionaire subsidiary not being taxed anywhere.[4] The facts were similar to those in *Zimmer*. The French courts ruled that the Swiss company did not have a PE in France. The only profits that would be taxed in France were those of the Swiss company's French subsidiary, a commissionaire with very low profits. However, Switzerland exempts from Swiss tax the profits made by a PE of a Swiss company. The taxpayer claimed, for Swiss tax purposes that the Swiss company did have a PE in France and the Swiss tax authority agreed with this. Thus Switzerland exempted from tax the profits of the Swiss company with respect to the sales made through its French commissionaire company, even though France had decided there was no PE and thus had not taxed these profits.

In spite of the OECD's attempts in the Commentary to encourage countries to interpret Article 5, paragraph 5 as meaning that there is an agency PE even where the contracts are not actually concluded by the commissionaire or other agent, the pre-BEPS wording of Article 5 was so definite that courts have refused to extend the definition of agency PEs to commissionaire situations. As well as the *Dell Products* case, this has been exploited by the Google Group, that has consistently argued that because contracts for advertising services are not formally concluded in the UK, the Irish sales company within the Google Group does not have an agency PE in the UK. (See Chapter 19 for more discussion). The pre-BEPS wording of paragraph 5 of Article 5 is that the agent must habitually exercise an authority to conclude contracts 'in the name of the enterprise' (ie in the name of the foreign parent company). Commissionaire companies do not do this – they conclude contracts in their own names, earning a tiny profit, or else they do not formally conclude the contracts at all, but direct the customers to the non-resident supplier company when negotiations reach the point of signing a contract.

1   *Société Zimmer Ltd v Ministre de l'Economie, des Finances et de l'Industrie* (2010) 12 ITLR 739.
2   Supreme Administrative Court, 20 June 2003, No. 224407, sect., min. c/ Sté Interhome AG, RJF 10/03 No. 1147.
3   (2011) 14 ITLR 371.
4   *Pioneer Hi Bred Switzerland v South Pyrenees Tax Authority* (2014) Administrative Court of Toulouse (2014) 17 ITLR 431.

BEPS, Action 7: changes to Article 5

9.29   The changes to paragraphs 5–6 of Article 5 that result from BEPS Action 7 are designed to prevent the avoidance of tax in the customer country in two ways:

(1)   To deem that a PE exists even if a commissionaire does not actually enter into contracts with customers in its own name, but instead arranges for

the customer to enter into a contract with the principal company. This change is to the wording of paragraph 5.

(2)   To tighten up the rules on when an agent might be considered to be an independent agent within the meaning of paragraph 6, so that commissionaires entering into contracts in their own name, but working mainly for a 'closely related' company, eg the parent company, no longer enjoy the independent agent status.

The new wording of Article 5 is set out in Table 9.1 above. The changes are considered in detail in the sections that follow.

Changes to paragraph 5

9.30   The existing wording of paragraph 5 states that a person will be a dependent agent (and thus create a PE) if s/he/it has, and habitually exercises, authority to conclude contracts in the name of the enterprise. As we have seen, this has created opportunities for avoidance of PE status by multinational groups, notably Google, who have used this rule in order to avoid having PEs of their Irish subsidiaries in other countries such as the UK. When determining whether a person has authority to conclude contracts on behalf of an enterprise, the pre-BEPS guidance in the Commentary said that a state may look at the facts and ascertain the substance of arrangements rather than their strict legal form. For instance, if an agent routinely takes orders from customers and passes them to the enterprise's warehouse, where they are formally approved, the state will examine whether or not such approval is a mere formality ('rubber stamping') or whether each order is carefully examined. Routine approval would probably lead a state to decide that the agent in fact has power to bind the enterprise in contract. If a person is authorized to negotiate all details and elements of contracts in binding manner on an enterprise in a particular state, then he will almost certainly bring into existence a PE for the enterprise, even if the contracts have to be signed back at Head Office. However, in spite of this guidance, states have expressed concern that companies have been avoiding PE status by carefully controlling the powers and functions carried out by their staff or other persons who are based in states outside the state where the company is tax resident.

For this reason, the proposed new paragraph 5 refers not only to persons 'habitually concluding contracts', but also to persons who 'habitually play the principal role leading to the conclusion of contracts that are routinely concluded without material modification by the enterprise'. The definition of this is given in new paragraph 32.5 to the Commentary on Article 5.

Using an example, the new rule should be interpreted as meaning that there is someone in the customer country who is effectively acting as the sales force for a non-resident trader, even if that person does not have the authority in law to conclude contracts in the name of the non-resident. For example, suppose Enterprise X, resident in Country A wishes to sell to customers in Country B, without incurring any liability to taxation on its profits in Country B. It might ask Miss P, a resident of Country B, to make contact with potential custom-ers of Enterprise X in Country B. Miss P performs marketing activities for Enterprise X, contacts potential customers and tries to get orders for Enterprise X. When a Country B potential customer wishes to place an order, the order is not placed with Miss P but is, for instance, sent directly to a warehouse that Enterprise X maintains in Country B. The orders are identified as having been received as a result of Miss P's efforts and because of this, they are routinely approved without further checks. The goods are sent out to the Country B customers. This scenario happens repeatedly: it is not a one-off occurrence. Miss P has not accepted or signed the order on behalf of Enterprise X, but she has been instrumental in the making of the contract between Enterprise X and the Country B customers. She has habitually played a principal role leading to the conclusion of those contracts, that have been entered into, without material modification, by Enterprise X. Enterprise X has a PE in Country B and will be liable to tax on the net profits from the contracts with Country B customers. Miss P would have charged commission for her services and this would be a deductible expense in computing Enterprise X's country B tax liability.

Note that the contracts concerned must generally be with external customers rather than internally within the enterprise or being limited to the hiring of staff.

The OECD provides an example of a situation in which the new rules would apply. This is shown in Figure 9.7.

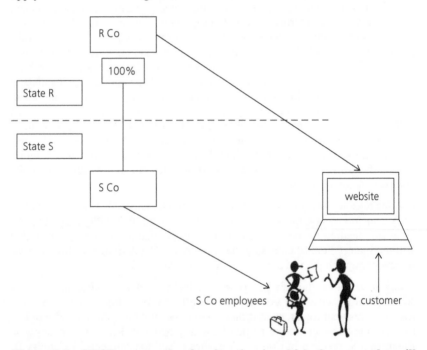

Figure 9.7: OECD – example of a situation in which the new rules will apply

S Co, resident in State S, is a wholly owned subsidiary of R Co, resident in State R. Employees of S Co promote the products and services of R Co to potential customers of R Co in State S. Whilst S Co's employees do not conclude contracts on behalf of R Co, they play an active role in negotiating these contracts:

- They are responsible for large client accounts in State S – they contact potential clients by email, telephone and personal visits.

- The remuneration of S Co employees is partially based on the revenues derived by R Co from these client accounts.

- When a client agrees to make a purchase of goods or services which have been promoted to the client by an S Co employee, the S Co employee indicates to the client the likely price and standard terms of R Co's contracts. This will include advising the client of R Co's fixed pricing structure, which the S Co employee cannot modify, and also advising the client of R Co's standard contract terms.

If the client wishes to proceed with the purchase, the client is advised by the S Co employee to go online to the R Co website, where a choice of payment options is offered.

In this example, S Co employees are considered to 'play the principal role leading to the conclusion of the contracts', even though the negotiation is limited to persuading the client to accept R Co's pricing structure and its other contractual terms.

Changes to paragraph 6

9.31   Following the BEPS Action 7 Final Report, the wording of paragraph 6 of Article 5 has been amended to try to prevent a person who acts solely for a foreign enterprise from being classed as an independent agent:

> 'Where, however, a person acts exclusively or almost exclusively on behalf of one or more enterprises to which it is closely related, that person shall not be considered to be an independent agent within the meaning of this paragraph with respect to any such enterprise.'

(Revised: Article 5 para 6(b), October 2015)

'Exclusively or almost exclusively' is not defined but guidance in new paragraphs to the Commentary suggests that it means that 90 per cent or more of sales are made by the agent to connected persons.

A 'closely related' person is defined in two ways:

- A *subjective test*: taking into account all relevant facts and circumstances, one person has control of the other or both are under the control of the same persons or enterprises. This subjective test would catch indirect shareholdings or shareholdings of less than 50 per cent but where the shares held carry special rights that put the shareholder into the same position as if more than 50 per cent of the shares were owned.

- *An objective legal test*: a person is considered to be connected to an enterprise if:

  — either one possesses more than 50 per cent of the beneficial interests in the other; or

  — a third person possesses, directly or indirectly, more than 50 per cent of the beneficial interests in both the person and the enterprise.

  In both these cases, if a company is involved, the test is >50 per cent of the aggregate vote and value of the company's shares or of the beneficial equity interest in the company.

  (Proposed new para 38.9 to the Commentary on Article 5.)

The subjective test has been heavily criticized by some commentators on the second Discussion Draft on BEPS Action 7 as introducing a high degree of uncertainty. New para 38.10 of the Commentary on Paragraph 6 suggests that 'closely related' would include situations where a person or enterprise controls an enterprise through special arrangements involving rights over the company similar to the rights that would be conferred by shareholdings.

Group companies as PEs – paragraph 7

9.32

'Paragraph 7 of Article 5

The fact that a company which is a resident of a Contracting State controls or is controlled by a company which is a resident of the other Contracting State, or which carries on business in that other State (whether through a PE or otherwise), shall not of itself constitute either company a PE of the other.'

Although normally a subsidiary company is considered to be independent of the parent company, and the presence of a subsidiary would not normally result in the parent company having a PE in the subsidiary's state, a PE of the parent can arise if the subsidiary acts as a dependent agent of the parent, or if the premises of the subsidiary are 'at the disposal of' the parent, so that they are a fixed place of business for the parent.

In the 2005 update to the Commentary provisions were added to the effect that if a parent company has space or premises belonging to the subsidiary at its disposal such that the space can constitute a fixed place of business through which the parent carries on its business, then the parent will have a PE. The key question is: whose trade is being carried on at the subsidiary's premises? Is it solely the trade of the subsidiary, or is the parent company also using them for core activities of the parent company's trade?

The 2005 update also clarified a point much debated – if a multinational group of companies has a subsidiary in a particular state which is deemed to be a PE of one of the other group companies, can the state in which the PE arises also automatically assume a PE exists in respect of all group companies? The 2005 update to the Commentary makes it clear that the relationship between each pair of companies must be separately considered. This clarification was made necessary by the decision of the Italian courts in the *Philip Morris* case.[1] In that case, the court decided that the activities of a single subsidiary company could be held to serve as a PE for several non-resident fellow subsidiaries.

---

1   *Ministry of Finance (Tax Office) v Philip Morris (GmbH)*, No 7682/02 (25 May 2002).

UK DOMESTIC LAW ON PE

9.33   The UK updated its domestic provisions on PEs in the Finance Act 2003, s 148. The UK legislation is now quite closely aligned with the OECD definition with a few important differences. The changes mean that businesses now have more certainty in setting up in the UK as they can rely, to some extent, on the Commentary on Article 5 in interpreting UK domestic law.

The definition of a PE refers, inter alia to 'a construction or installation project' without giving any minimum duration for such a project. This is because a DTT cannot impose a charge to tax where none exists under domestic law. If, say, the UK domestic legislation were to mirror the contents of many UK double tax treaties and provide that construction or installation projects are to be viewed as PE only if they have existed for at least 12 months, then the UK would not be able to tax the profits of any such projects until they had existed for at least 12 months, even if one of its double tax treaties provided for taxation after a period of six months. The definition of agent also differs slightly.

In UK domestic law, the concept of PE only applies for corporation tax purposes. Thus foreign partnerships and sole traders are dealt with differently and the test is not whether they have a PE in the UK but whether they are 'trading in the UK'. This test lacks the 'fixed place of business' and the 'six months presence' aspects of the PE test so that, in theory, non-corporates are more likely to find themselves liable to UK tax on their business profits than foreign companies. Summing up, the OECD Commentary can be used as a tool of interpretation of UK domestic law, but only with care. Remember that if there is an applicable tax treaty, then its provisions for PE will take precedence over UK domestic law for both foreign companies and foreign partnerships and sole traders.

UN MTC definition of a fixed place of business

9.34   The main differences from the OECD MTC are:

- A building site, construction or installation project need only exist for six months instead of 12 months. The six months will normally cover supervisory activities as well as the project itself.

- The list of activities which will not give rise to a PE is restricted in that delivery activities are omitted. Thus, for instance, the maintenance of a fixed place of business solely for the purposes of storage or display would not be a PE. However, a fixed place of business, such as a warehouse, might constitute a PE because it is used for the delivery of goods.

● There is provision for a services PE in the text of the UN MTC (rather than merely in the Commentary, as per the 2008 OECD Model).

Individual treaties will alter the Model in different ways. For example, Indian DTTs include fairly long lists of forms of business establishment that will be treated as a PE, notably a sales outlet or premises used for the soliciting of orders.

The 'services' permanent establishment

9.35   The UN MTC, unlike the OECD MTC, has always included an extra definition of PE: The Commentary on the OECD MTC provides wording for an optional services PE, which was introduced in 2008. Chapter 10 deals with the taxation of services in some detail.

Dependent agent under the UN Model

9.36   Under the OECD MTC, a dependent agent will constitute a PE if s/he has, and habitually exercises, an authority to conclude contracts in the name of the enterprise. The UN MTC extends the definition to persons who do not have this authority, but habitually maintain a stock of goods or merchandise from which they regularly make deliveries on behalf of the enterprise. Some treaties go further, with many Indian treaties deeming a PE to exist if the agent habitually secures orders for the enterprise. There is a further provision in the UN Model which deems an agent who would otherwise be regarded as an independent agent to constitute a PE if the agent's activities are devoted wholly, or almost wholly, on behalf of the foreign enterprise and dealings between the agent and the enterprise are not on wholly at arm's-length terms.

IMPORTANCE OF A STATE'S DOMESTIC LAW

9.37   Unless a state has the right to tax a non-resident under its domestic law, it cannot tax that non-resident by virtue of any DTT. Thus, before there can be any taxation of a non-resident's business profits, that non-resident must have a taxable business presence in the host state under the host state's domestic law. This follows the general principle that a DTT can only improve a taxpayer's position, not make it worse. For this reason, it is important to check whether there is a PE under a state's domestic law before going to the DTT. Many states have designed their domestic definition of a PE so as to reflect the OECD definition. This enables them to make use of the extensive Commentary on the OECD Model as a tool to interpret the PE concept for domestic law purposes as well as for treaty purposes. State practices in defining a taxable business presence (sometimes referred to as a PE but sometimes using a different name) are examined in this section. The material in Table 9.2 is largely taken from the 2009 Cahiers De Droit report *Is there a permanent establishment?* (IFA, 2009).

Table 9.2 Definition of PE under domestic laws

State	Summary of definition of PE under domestic law
Brazil	Brazil's domestic law does not contain any definition of a PE as such. Historically, Brazil has reserved the right to tax the gross profits of non-residents, applying a withholding tax. Thus under its domestic law, a non-resident might expect a heavy Brazilian tax liability. However Brazil has about 30 double tax treaties, all of which contain a PE provision which follows the OECD Model, so that residents of treaty states are taxed on business profits arising in Brazil far more lightly than residents of states with which Brazil has no treaty.
Japan	The definition of a PE in Japanese domestic law is wider than that found in the OECD Model. A fixed place of business would include a hotel room or a display area in which sales are also made. Supervisory work in connection with construction operations in Japan can give rise to a PE under domestic law, as can the presence of a Japanese agent who fulfils orders for a non-resident, even though he does not bind the non-resident in contract in Japan.
UK	The UK uses a definition of a PE for corporation tax purposes which is broadly consistent with the OECD Model, although it is a little wider. Non-corporate non-residents may be liable to UK tax if they are trading in the UK. In this case, it is not necessary for there to be any place of business in the UK. However, there is no requirement to self-assess and unless there is a UK agent of some sort, HMRC does not have the practical means of collecting any tax which is theoretically due.
Australia	The concept of PE in Australian domestic law broadly follows that of the OECD. However, The Australian definition will deem a PE to exist where a non-resident has substantial equipment located in Australia, even if there are no personnel there. This is carried through into most of Australia's double tax treaties. Note that, in January 2016, Australia enacted a Multinational Anti-Avoidance Law that includes PE issues.

State	Summary of definition of PE under domestic law
South Africa	The South African domestic definition follows the OECD definition. There is no need for premises used for carrying on a business to be owned. Nor does it matter if the activities carried on are illegal. In a private ruling in 2008 (BPR 2007), a non-resident labour broker with clients both in and outside South Africa who used the services of a South African management company to acquire work permits was considered not to have a PE in South Africa. The main reasoning was that the broker had no office and did not engage employees to act on its behalf in South Africa.
Italy	Italy broadly follows the OECD definition and there is case law on what is meant by a 'fixed place of business' both in terms of time and geography. A particularly interesting case concerned a non-resident doctor who conducted part of his private practice in an Italian hospital: although he had no legal interest in the hospital premises, he was deemed to have a PE in Italy because space in the hospital was 'at his disposal'.[1] Note that, in January 2017, official clarification has been issued.
India	Foreign enterprises are taxable in India on profits if they have a 'business connection' with India. This does not require a fixed place of business but refers to a real and continuing business relationship in India. This partly explains why India has been ready to argue that the mere presence of machinery or equipment in India can constitute a PE, for instance, an automated airline reservation system. India has also considered that a ship or other offshore vessel anchored in Indian waters is capable of being a PE. It is fair to say that although Indian courts do place reliance on the OECD Commentary, the concept of a PE under domestic law is considerably wider than that under the OECD Model.
Canada	Canada's domestic law broadly follows the OECD definitions. For a place of business to be regarded as a 'fixed place of business' there must be both physical control and either exclusive or unlimited access and right of use, so that customer premises are unlikely to count. However, the use of a booth at a fixed location for a period of three weeks in 15 consecutive years was found to constitute a PE.

State	Summary of definition of PE under domestic law
France	There has been some legal uncertainty as to whether a tax liability can arise in France through the carrying on of business there in the absence of a PE as defined under domestic law, if a tax treaty made appropriate provision for taxation of such income. This is due to a provision of the French tax code which allows France to tax income attributed to France by virtue of a tax treaty. In practice, so long as the tax treaty awards taxing rights to France, the lack of domestic provisions have not been seen as an obstacle in taxing non-residents from treaty partner states. Under domestic law, France will tax the profits of a non-resident if there is an 'installation d'affaires', which translates as premises and equipment which are at the disposal of the non-resident and the presence of employees.
Germany	The domestic law definition requires a fixed place of business but this is interpreted to mean any significant assets used for carrying on a business and in particular, a pipeline running through Germany. The domestic definition is wider than that in the OECD MTC: the fixed place of business merely has to serve the activity of the non-resident rather than be a place from which the business is wholly or partly carried on. An agency PE can arise under domestic law if the agent consistently carries out the business of the non-resident and is bound by instruction from the non-resident, but there is no requirement that the agent be a 'dependent agent'.
Netherlands	The domestic law definition is broadly consistent with the OECD MTC and the OECD Commentary is widely used in Netherlands case law on PEs.
Russia	The domestic law defines a PE as a place of business through which a foreign organization regularly conducts business activity in Russia. This domestic law is now interpreted as being generally consistent with the OECD definitions.
United States	The underlying concept governing PE is that foreign corporations engaging in trade or business within the US are taxable in the US on income effectively connected with the conduct of trade or business in the US. The OECD Commentary is relied upon for interpretation. The existence of mobile drilling rigs has given rise to US PEs, as has logging (forestry) equipment kept within the US for the purpose of demonstration.

---

1   See the Italian Report in *IFA Cahiers De Droit* 2009, at 'Further reading'.

EXPOSURE TO TAX WHERE THE PE IS LOCATED

9.38 *Note: in this section, the term 'company' is used, but the principles set out apply to any type of enterprise.*

If a company resident in State A has a PE located in State B, then State B is entitled to tax the profits attributable to the PE. This does not mean that State B can tax all of the profits of the company that arise from business which it carries on in State B but rather only so much as is attributable to the PE. For instance, the company may have a factory in State B which would clearly constitute a PE but it may also maintain a warehouse for products other than those produced by that factory which is operated by different personnel to those employed at the factory and at a different location. It may sell certain of its products (not the ones produced by the factory) in State B through independent agents who are resident in State B. Only the profits arising from the factory are attributable to a PE and thus these are the only profits of the company which State B may tax, even though they are not the only profits which the company is making in State B.

Some existing treaties, particularly those based on the UN Model contain limited provisions which extend the right of the host state to tax beyond the profits directly attributable to the PE. These are known as 'force of attraction' provisions, because the existence of the PE attracts other profits of the company into the host state's tax net and are discussed below under the paragraphs dealing with the UN Model.

The authorized OECD approach (AOA)

9.39 Before setting out the details of the methods advocated by the OECD to attribution of profits to a PE, readers should note that the OECD's methods (AOA) have been heavily criticized during the course of the BEPS Project work on PEs. The AOA is felt to be difficult to apply. There is a lack of detailed guidance on how to apply it, except for companies in the financial services sector. Also, because of its complexity, many countries have not implemented it, leading to many different methods used around the world in attributing profits to a PE.

9.40 The starting point for any attribution of profits to a PE is the branch accounts. However, in some cases the host state will wish to amend the profits shown in the branch accounts in accordance with the general principle for attribution of profits set out in the relevant DTT.

Article 7, para 2 of the Model current as at August 2011 states that the profits attributable to a PE are:

'the profits it might be expected to make, in particular in its dealings with other parts of the enterprise, if it were a separate and independent enterprise engaged in the same or similar activities under the same or similar conditions, taking into account the functions performed, assets used and risks assumed by the enterprise through the permanent establishment and through the other parts of the enterprise.'

This wording reflects a lengthy process of consultation and development and replaced the much simpler wording which existed until 2008:

'the profits which it might be expected to make if it were a distinct and separate enterprise engaged in the same or similar activities under the same or similar conditions and dealing wholly independently with the enterprise of which it is a PE.'

The reason for the change was that the OECD perceived that there was considerable uncertainty as to how it should be implemented. Some states believe that it is correct to look at the profits of the company as a whole and decide how much of them are to be attributed to the PE. Others believe that the PE should be viewed as a functionally separate enterprise and its profits determined without reference to the profits of the company as a whole. This uncertainty is evidenced by a whole series of consultations, draft reports, updates and reports issued by the OECD over the last couple of decades (see for example, the 1993 report Attribution of Income to PEs).[1]

In 2008 the OECD published its final report setting out a complete overhaul of the approach to the interpretation of Article 7 of the Model,[2] which sets out how profits of an enterprise are to be attributed to a PE (and thus taxable by the host state). The OECD had published landmark guidance on transfer pricing in 1995, and following that, the outcome of the OECD's work on the effect of e-commerce on the taxing rights of various states in which an enterprise operated. Many had expected that the work on attribution of profits to PEs would follow on directly after the publication of the transfer pricing guidelines, but the need to deal with the tax effects of e-commerce was found to be more pressing. In the event, the main outcome of the work on e-commerce was merely to confirm that what was really needed were better principles for dealing with the attribution of profits to any sort of PE, e-commerce related or otherwise. A Discussion Draft released by the OECD in 2001[3] went to some lengths to set out a 'working hypothesis' for the attribution of profits to a PE using the hypothesis that the PE is a 'distinct and separate enterprise' rather than any approach which merely attempts to apportion the total profits of the firm. Thus the approach to the attribution of profits to a PE places heavy reliance on the content of the OECD's transfer pricing principles (see Chapter 13). These principles are aimed at transactions between companies in the same corporate group. The OECD recognizes that dealings between different parts of the same company (eg head office and branch) are not the same as transactions between companies in the same corporate group but has stated that the transfer pricing principles apply by analogy. The July 2008 Report was the culmination of a series of discussion documents and draft reports produced from 2001 onwards. The OECD has declared that the question of attributing profits to PEs is to be determined without being constrained either by the original intent or any historical interpretation of Article 7.[4]

The new approach was introduced by the OECD in two stages: in 2008, new material was introduced into the Commentary, which did not conflict with previous material. In 2010, the new version of Article 7 itself was introduced, along with further changes to the Commentary.

The new approach involves two steps: a 'functional analysis' to determine the role of the PE in relation to the enterprise as a whole, and then the allocation of part of the profits of the enterprise to the PE.

The alternative choice to the 'distinct and separate enterprise' approach (now referred to as the 'functionally separate enterprise' approach) would have been to adopt a 'relative business activity' approach. This alternative would try to identify the profits generated by the enterprise by activities in which the PE was wholly or partly involved. Perhaps the key difference between the two approaches is that under the 'functionally separate enterprise' approach, it is possible for taxable profits to be attributed to a PE, whether or not the enterprise as a whole has made profits in the period in question. The 'relative business activity' approach would only permit an allocation of total profits of the enterprise to the PE so that if the enterprise as a whole had made a loss, there would be no question of any taxable profits being allocated to the PE. Part of the reason for the overhaul of Article 7 and its interpretation is to prevent situations where there is double taxation of profits, for example, where one state taxes the profits of a PE situated there on the functionally separate entity approach but the other state, using the relative business activity approach considers that the enterprise has made a loss and therefore fails to give double tax relief for the taxation suffered by the PE. Double non-taxation would also be possible.

---

1   *Attribution of Profits to Permanent Establishments*, OECD, Vol II of full version of OECD Model Tax Convention at R(13)-1.
2   *Report on the Attribution of Profits to Permanent Establishments*, OECD, 17 July 2008. (Note that this has been subsequently updated so that there is also a 2010 *Report* with the same title. The 2010 *Report* provides background to the 2010 changes to the OECD Model Tax Convention and Commentary on Article 7, whilst the 2008 version remains available as an aid to interpretation (in effect, an alternative source of OECD Commentary) to existing treaties which use the 2008 version of Article 7.)
3   *Discussion Draft on the Attribution of Profits to Permanent Establishments*, OECD, 8 February 2001.
4   See, for example, para 6 of the 2008 Commentary on Article 7.

Step 1 of the AOA: the functional and factual analysis

9.41   The PE must be viewed as a functionally separate entity. As a single legal entity cannot trade with itself, this is a fiction. The Commentary on Article 7 gives some guidance on the factors needed to form a view of the PE as a distinct and separate entity: A functional and factual analysis, along the lines set out in the OECD's transfer-pricing guidelines,[1] should be carried out to establish the economically significant activities and responsibilities undertaken by the PE. Broadly, this would involve:

● Establishing the rights and obligations arising out of transactions between the PE and separate enterprises: for instance, taking the relatively easy example of a PE which takes the form of a manufacturing and sales operation, the sales revenue from independent customers arising from the factory's output might properly be attributed to the PE rather than the head office. Similarly, the obligation to pay for the raw materials used by the factory might properly be attributed to the factory.

- Identifying the significant 'people functions' relevant to the attribution of economic ownership of assets, and the attribution of economic ownership of assets to the PE. Economic ownership is defined as the right to income attributable to the ownership of the assets, or the right to depreciate an asset and also the potential exposure to gains or losses from the appreciation or depreciation of an asset. The treatment of tangible and intangible assets will differ – tangible property should be attributed to the location where it is in use rather than to the place from which it is acquired and subsequently managed, if different. Thus, if a head office department in State A is in charge of procurement of fixed assets, keeping the fixed asset register and perhaps implementing a maintenance schedule, then this will not affect the attribution of the assets to the PE in which the assets are actually being used. Intangibles, on the other hand, having no physical location, are to be attributed to the business location where the work of developing, acquiring and management of them takes place. The idea of identifying 'people functions' is taken from the OECD's work on transfer pricing in the context of establishing arm's-length dealing terms between connected enterprises, rather than parts of the same enterprise. In essence, economic ownership of intangibles rests with the location in which the risks associated with the intangibles is borne. For instance, if an enterprise owns a patent for a particular drug which is sold by distributor companies in many states, the economic ownership would rest in that part of the enterprise responsible for commissioning the research to developing the drug, which would bear the losses if the medical trials failed or licences to manufacture were not obtainable, which brings legal actions to defend the patent against generic copies and whose profits would decrease should a competitor drug come on to the market.

- Identifying the significant 'people functions' relevant to the assumption of risks, and the attribution of risks to the PE. This separate requirement recognizes that one part of an enterprise may have economic ownership of an asset, but a different part of the enterprise may bear the risks associated with the use of that asset. For instance, road building equipment may be economically owned by a PE in State A, but the head office, located in State B, may have the power to determine on which road building projects the equipment is used. Hence the risk associated with profits or losses arising from the equipment lies with head office. Or a PE of an enterprise in one state may be relying on the successful development of a new drug for its future profits. If another part of the enterprise is developing that drug, then not only the developer of the drug but also the PE which hoped to market it would be adversely affected if the trials fail. If personnel at the PE take an active part in managing the development of the drug (possibly due to its effect on the profits of the PE) then both can be considered to be bearing risk in connection with the development of the drug. In practice, this part of the analysis is going to be difficult to carry out as the level of documentation of arrangements between PE and head office may not be the same as that between two separate (but related) companies. In essence, the more risks that are managed by the PE, the higher the share of the profit of the enterprise to be attributed to the PE. The 2008 Report looks for the place of active decision taking, rather than mere 'rubber stamping' of decisions taken elsewhere in the enterprise. For instance, for trade intangibles to be attributed to a PE, it would be expected that personnel based at the PE would be responsible for:[2]

— designing the test specifications and processes within which the research is conducted;

— reviewing and evaluating the data produced by the tests; and

— setting the 'stage posts' at which decisions to quit or proceed further with the project are taken. Note that there is a distinction made between enterprises in the financial sector and other enterprises. No separation of asset management and risk assumption functions is required for financial sector enterprises because it is considered highly likely that these functions would be carried out by the same people.

---

1 'Transfer Pricing Guidelines for Multinational Enterprises and Tax Administrations' (1994 1995 and 2010).
2 OECD 2008, para 119.

Step 2: allocating profits to the PE

9.42   Taking into account the picture built up in Step 1, the profits of the PE must then be established. This is relatively simple in respect of dealing between the PE and independent third parties, but the profits from dealings with other parts of the same enterprise will be determined by using the rules laid down in the OECD's Transfer Pricing Guidelines (see Chapter 13 for details of these).

Dealings between the PE and the rest of the enterprise are compared with transactions between independent enterprises. There is a difficulty in that there are unlikely to be any transactions between the PE (which is in essence a branch) and the rest of the enterprise in the same way that there are legally binding transactions between companies, even those in the same group. 'Dealings' include physical transfers of stock, the provision of services, use of intangible assets, use of capital assets, transfer of financial assets and so forth. The pricing of the 'dealings' is examined using the normal transfer pricing methods – preferably comparable uncontrolled price but if that is impossible, one of the other methods laid down in the OECD's Transfer Pricing Guidelines.

Two particular problems arise from the fact that the PE is not a separate legal entity: First, the PE has no sources of finance separate from the enterprise so it is difficult to determine the level of return on finance (eg interest payable) which ought to be deducted from the taxable profits of the PE. Second, the supporting documentation available to evidence the pricing policies between PE and head office/other parts of the enterprise will be less formal than that needed for transactions between separate legal entities (eg fellow subsidiaries).

What deductions are possible?

9.43   In legal terms, because the PE is part of the enterprise, it is not possible for the head office to make a profit on dealings with the PE or to make charges for interest and royalties to the PE. However, the AOA depends on the fiction that the PE is a separate and independent enterprise and so the traditional rules preventing many deductions from the profits attributable to the PE have been dropped in the 2008 and 2010 changes.

The main changes in the Commentary to deductions permissible when calculating profits attributable to PEs may be summarized as follows:

Table 9.3 Summary of the main changes in the Commentary to deductions permissible when calculating profits attributable to PEs

Expense	Before 2008/2010 changes	After 2008/2010 changes
Charges for the temporary transfer of assets to the PE	Amount equal to depreciation on the assets for the transfer period	Equivalent of arm's length rental payment
Services rendered (eg central functions of the head office)	Services rendered by the enterprise to third parties as well as to the PE: cost plus mark-up. If not rendered to third parties, recharge of costs only	Cost plus a mark-up
Interest	No deductions for internal interest charges, except banks	Deduction based on the amount of 'free capital' allocated to the PE – see section below
Royalties	Only to the extent that the PE is using IP on which the enterprise is paying royalties to a third party (ie cost sharing)	An allocation of the cost of creation or purchase of the IP is permitted and, in restricted circumstances, a notional royalty can be deducted by the PE

It must be remembered that not all OECD states agree with the changes and have stated their intention not to implement them (Chile, Greece, Mexico, New Zealand, Portugal and Turkey) and that the UN Group of Experts on Cooperation in International Tax Matters decided not to adopt the OECD changes at all.

Deductions for interest

9.44   With the exception of banking enterprises, 'internal' interest charges are not normally permitted except when interest is being paid in respect of specific treasury services. Hence a head office is not permitted to 'lend' money and charge interest to a PE for tax purposes. However, a portion of the interest paid by the enterprise to external lenders may be deducted in arriving at the taxable profits of the PE. To arrive at this figure, it is necessary to determine the amount of capital (both equity and debt) which the PE would require in order to carry out its functions were it a separate entity. What this amounts to is drawing up a balance sheet for the PE as if it were a separate legal entity, using the basic balance sheet equation familiar to accountants: assets minus liabilities = capital.

This figure for total capital attributable to the PE must then be divided up into equity capital and debt capital. The OECD Report refers to 'free capital' rather than equity capital, where free capital is capital, the return on which would not give rise to a tax deduction. Therefore, share capital would be 'free capital' because the return on share capital is in the form of dividends, which in most cases would not be tax deductible. Similarly, retained profits would constitute free capital. Once a figure for 'free capital' attributable to the PE is known, this is deducted from the total capital of the PE to leave the amount of debt capital, thus leading to a tax deduction for interest payable. There are four methods put forward by which the total capital of the PE can be split between free capital and debt capital but the common aim of each method is to arrive at a ratio of debt to equity capital which might be found in an independent entity similar to the PE (an application of the arm's-length principle which is analysed in Chapter 13). The 2008 Report noted that the ratio of free capital to debt capital will be influenced by the risk assumed by the PE – for instance, a food-producing PE which is part of a general non-food manufacturing enterprise might carry higher risks than other parts of the enterprise. The higher the risk, the greater the proportion of free capital (equity capital) to debt capital ought to be. The OECD Commentary on Article 7 has been revised to recommend that the method used to arrive at the split between free capital and debt capital should be the method used in the state where the PE is located, provided that the other state involved agrees that the proposed method is one of the four methods recommended by the OECD (Commentary on Article 7, para 48).

Then, having established the amount of debt capital attributable to the branch, it is necessary to decide what the interest and other terms ought to be, to give the amount of the tax deduction. Again, various methods are put forward: it might be possible to trace the funding provided by head office to the PE back to its original source and establish the amount of interest paid by head office to the bank (or other third-party lender). This is known as the 'tracing approach'. Alternatively, a formula approach could be used based on the cost of capital to the enterprise as a whole and the proportion of total debt capital attributed to the PE. This is known as the 'fungibility approach'. Whichever approach is used, the PE is assumed to have the same creditworthiness as the enterprise as a whole.

The question of whether internal interest charges can be made between head office and PE (as opposed to the allocation to the PE of part of the total external interest charges paid by the enterprise as a whole) depends on whether certain types of services are being provided to the PE. For banking enterprises, the OECD accepts that it will be appropriate for internal interest charges to be made but whether there are so-called 'treasury dealings' between parts of non-banking enterprises depends on the results of the functional and factual analysis. 'Treasury dealings', broadly speaking, are those by which the economic ownership of cash and financial assets changes hands. Again, the approach looks for 'significant people functions' in the management of cash and financial assets, and if the enterprise has no external borrowings then it is unlikely that such functions would be present. The general rule, that internal interest charges are not normally permitted within non-banking enterprises, is needed to prevent tax avoidance by manipulation of the allocation of profits between the PE and the rest of the enterprise.

Which transactions are recognized?

9.45   The fundamental premise in making the allocation of profits to a PE is that dealings between the PE and the rest of the enterprise are to be viewed in the same way as transactions between fellow group companies and the OECD's transfer pricing guidelines applied accordingly.

The problem addressed here is that an enterprise (eg a company) might well not insist on the same level of documentation for transactions between head office and branch (PE) as it would between the company and, say, external customers and suppliers or even between fellow group companies. A test is set: the 'threshold test' for the level of documentation needed in order for any particular transaction between head office and PE to affect the amount of profits allocated to the PE for tax purposes. So, before any transfer pricing tests can be applied to check whether the profit earned by the PE is akin to that which would have been earned were it an independent enterprise, we first have to decide if a particular transaction is even the kind of transaction that would be entered into between parties dealing with each other at arm's length. The type of internal transactions between a PE and the rest of the enterprise which can be recognized when determining the profits attributable to the PE are those relating to 'real and identifiable events'.[1] These would include the physical transfer of goods and materials, provision of services, use of intangibles, transfer of a financial asset and so on. The internal records (probably the management and branch accounts) would be the starting point for identifying these transactions but the true test is whether there has been an internal dealing of economic significance.

Because a company or other legal entity cannot make a contract with itself, it is not possible to apply the OECD's transfer-pricing guidelines exactly. That would require the scrutiny of the terms of the contract, and in legal terms, internal dealings cannot give rise to any contract. However, para 1.29 of the transfer pricing guidelines helpfully points out that certain materials may be used to supplement the review of any contract: internal correspondence, for example, or minutes of meetings or telephone conversations.

Generally, where there are notional charges for items which would normally attract withholding tax (such as interest or royalties) the principle used is that such charges are not really royalties or interest (because an enterprise cannot charge itself royalties or interest) and therefore no withholding tax can be imposed.

The profits allocated to a PE for tax purposes may be reduced by allocations of head office expenses (eg for strategic management or centrally managed support functions such as payroll). The OECD 2008 Report follows the position taken in the OECD transfer pricing guidelines – arm's-length pricing of these services is required, whether or not they are supplied to any external customers.

---

1   OECD (2008) at para 212.

What happens if the PE state increases the profits attributable to the PE?

9.46   If the transfer pricing principles embodied in the OECD's transfer pricing guidelines are to be used, then it is highly likely that, in some cases, a host state will contend that arm's-length principles have not been applied and will wish to increase the amount of profits attributed to the PE. This frequently happens with reference to transactions between companies in the same corporate group under Article 9. Article 9 of the Model contains a requirement for the other state to make a corresponding downwards adjustment in the profits taxed, to prevent double taxation of profits. Somewhat reluctantly and late in the proceedings leading up to the adoption of the revised Article 7, the OECD has included, at para 3 of Article 7, a requirement that the other state must make an appropriate adjustment:

> '3. Where, in accordance with paragraph 2, a Contracting State adjusts the profits that are attributable to a permanent establishment of an enterprise of one of the Contracting States and taxes accordingly, profits of the enterprise that have been charged to tax in the other State, the other State shall, to the extent necessary to eliminate double taxation on these profits, make an appropriate adjustment to the amount of the tax charged on those profits. In determining such adjustment, the competent authorities of the Contracting States shall if necessary consult each other.'

Allocation of profits to dependent agent PEs

9.47   In the case of dependent agents, the question arises, 'Are there two taxpayers involved, or just one?'. If the overseas enterprise pays the dependent agent an arm's-length remuneration for his services, then can the overseas enterprise be said to have made any profit out of the dependent agent PE?

If, in these circumstances, a state considers that the only taxpayer to have made any profit in that state is the dependent agent himself, rather than the over-seas enterprise, then it is said to take the 'single taxpayer' approach. In some circumstances, it will be obvious that the enterprise is making profits in the agency PE state over and above those profits reported by the agent himself. For instance, a dependent agent may be paid for the sales he procures on a com-mission basis. However, the selling enterprise may make a profit on those sales even after taking into account the commission paid to the agent. Thus both the dependent agent and also the foreign enterprise would be taxable in the state in which the dependent agent is resident.

The OECD 2008 Report considers that profits should be attributed to a depend-ent agent PE in the same way as for other types of PE. Thus even where an arm's-length remuneration is paid to the dependent agent for his services, the overseas enterprise may still be liable to tax in the PE state. Profits must be attributed to the dependent agent PE on the basis of assets, risks and capital attributed to the dependent agent PE. Again, it is necessary to look for 'signifi-cant people functions' which may be performed by the dependent agent and his staff, requiring an analysis of the skills and expertise of the employees of the agent. Mere sales agents are unlikely to be performing significant people func-tions. However, where a dependent agent (or an enterprise acting as a depend-ent agent) performs activities which lead to the development of marketing or trade intangibles, then the OECD considers that, whatever the strict legal posi-tion, the economic substance of the matter is that the dependent agent is at least partly the economic owner of that intangible and profits must be attributed to the PE accordingly. Ordinary transfer pricing principles could not be used to increase the profits reported by the enterprise acting as a dependent agent PE as it is not controlled by the foreign enterprise. The solution to this apparent underpayment (and hence, under-reporting of profits in the state where the dependent agent PE is located) is to attribute profit to the dependent agent PE based on the functional and factual analysis carried out on the PE, then raise a tax assessment on the foreign enterprise, allowing as a deduction the payments actually made to the dependent agent.

The 2010 OECD Profit Attribution Report observed that some jurisdictions adopt simplified approaches in the interests of administrative convenience, for example collecting tax only from the intermediary to reduce the reporting burden on the non-resident enterprise.

The UN Model – 'force of attraction' principle

9.48   The UN Committee of Experts did not adopt the OECD's complex approach to the allocation of profits to a PE which is set out earlier in this chapter. However, DTTs based on the UN MTC do sometimes contain addi-tional complexities in Article 7. Under Article 7 of the OECD MTC, the only profits of the foreign enterprise which may be taxed by the state where the PE is located are those attributable to the PE. A multinational enterprise might try to avoid host state taxation of profits of the PE by diverting some lucrative sales business away from the PE, say, via an independent agent in the same state as the PE. Tracking all business related to a foreign enterprise within its borders is likely to be more difficult for a developing country as it may not have the necessary manpower or information systems and could be outclassed in terms of professional expertise in this respect by the staff of the foreign multinational. Thus the UN MTC includes a limited 'force of attraction' provision. The effect of this is that any profits a multinational makes in the developing country through sales or other business activities there are taxable there if there is a PE and the activities are the same or similar to those conducted by the PE. Although this rule is permitted by the UN Model, not all treaties based on this Model include the rule. Some Indian tax treaties include a force of attraction rule. Under the UN Model rule, all the profits of a foreign enterprise having a PE in the state concerned will be taxable by the host state if they arise from the same or similar activities to those carried on by the PE. If the activities carried on in the state otherwise than by the PE are wholly different to those carried on by the PE then they are not caught by the rule:

> 'The profits of an enterprise of a Contracting State shall be taxable only in that State unless the enterprise carries on business in the other Contracting State through a permanent establishment situated therein. If the enterprise carries on business as aforesaid, the profits of the enterprise may be taxed in the other State but only so much of them as is attributable to (a) that permanent establishment; (b) sales in that other State of goods or merchandise of the same or similar kind as those sold through that permanent establishment; or (c) other business activities carried on in that other State of the same or similar kind as those effected through that permanent establishment.'

(Article 7(1), UN Model Tax Convention)

Deduction of expenses under the UN Model

9.49   The UN Model specifically forbids the deduction of internal interest and royalty charges by the head office to the PE. The profits of the PE may still be reduced by an allocation of the enterprise's external interest and royalty costs. Also forbidden are reductions in profits of the PE by way of management charges and commission. Thus the UN Model does not follow the OECD's Authorized Approach to the attribution of profits to a PE This is largely because of the UN's overriding concern for the constrained ability of developing country administrations to implement the OECD approach at a practical level.

PE – AN OUTDATED CONCEPT?

9.50   The concept of PE usually demands a physical presence and was developed in the 1930s at a time when foreign investment invariably consisted of setting up a foreign factory, shop or office. However, the bulk of overseas investment now consists of financial investments and other intangibles. Cross-border trade in services is now almost as important as cross-border trade in goods in many states. What this means is that in the twenty-first century it is far easier for a non-resident supplier to trade cross-border without the need for any physical presence in the customer state. Here are some examples of the way cross-border trade has changed since the 1930s, when the PE concept was developed:

- There has been a revolution in financial services, with most banks setting up Internet banking facilities and some banks emerging which only operate via the Internet.

- We routinely book our holidays and travel over the Internet rather than visiting the travel agent.

- The retail market for digital products such as music, computer software and games, videos and books continues to grow and customers can often purchase from a non-resident supplier as easily as from a resident supplier. Customer now routinely order physical items from non-resident suppliers as well as digital items.

- E-commerce has promoted an explosion in outsourcing of services and non-core processes due to the ease of data transfer and monitoring. A good example is the popularity of 'offshoring' of backroom services.

- Digital products have been an obvious focus in the discussions on taxation and e-commerce as practically all the operations in sourcing the product and supplying to the customer are capable of being carried out electronically.

- The supply chain has been affected by e-commerce in that improvements in communications and logistics processes has allowed the streamlining of ordering, selling and payment systems, and has allowed companies to access a far larger pool of both suppliers and customers through doing business on the Internet.

The OECD Article 5 concept of PE is outdated in a world where many business models do not require any physical presence in the customer's state. This results in the diminution of the tax base in many countries as they are unable to tax non-resident suppliers who have no physical presence within their borders.

The debate on the suitability of the PE concept in an era of e-commerce, which commenced in the late 1990s and has been led largely by the OECD, has traversed the full range of tax issues touched by the advent and proliferation of e-commerce. An initial flurry of academic interest polarized into two broad camps, those that suggested that e-commerce comprised a potential new tax base, ripe for exploitation, for example by means of a 'bit tax', a tax on streams of information. The opposite camp was of the view that e-commerce, as an emerging and innovative sector, should be completely free from tax. Neither view has made much headway, and the PE concept has emerged largely unchanged. What the debate has certainly done, however, is prompt a reconsideration of a number of embedded concepts, in particular in the case of direct taxation, that of the PE. It has also prompted consideration of the adequacy of tax-enforcement mechanisms in the face of the increasing invisibility or traceability of commercial transactions.

BEPS Action 1: Address the Challenges of the Digital Economy

9.51   Unlike the rest of the OECD's Base Erosion and Profit Shifting Project, which is concerned with tax avoidance, Action 1 addresses the fact that the traditional concept of the PE may no longer be a good basis for dividing taxing rights between states over the business profits of a firm. Thus Action 1 is not concerned directly with tax avoidance, but with the simple fact that a key concept in international tax is out of date because business models have changed significantly since the PE concept was developed.

Action 1 reads:

> 'Identify the main difficulties that the digital economy poses for the application of existing international tax rules and develop detailed options to address these difficulties, taking a holistic approach and considering both direct and indirect taxation. Issues to be examined include, but are not limited to, the ability of a company to have a significant digital presence in the economy of another country without being liable to taxation due to the lack of nexus under current international rules, the attribution of value created from the generation of marketable location relevant data through the use of digital products and services, the characterization of income derived from new business models, the application of related source rules, and how to ensure the effective collection of VAT/GST with respect to the cross-border supply of digital goods and services. Such work will require a thorough analysis of the various business models in this sector.'

There is some concern that without international cooperation, existing tax rules and procedures will lead to differences between the tax treatment of traditional business activities and e-commerce activities. Forgione (2003) for example, suggests that any proposals for reform should address practical and administrative issues, and any inclination to devise special procedures for e-commerce should be resisted. The OECD's October 2015 Final Report on Action 1 reflects this consensus. The public comments received on the OECD's discussion draft[1] on the Digital Economy urged the OECD not to try to 'ring-fence' the digital economy by developing a separate set of rules for e-commerce.

---

1   OECD Comments on Discussion Draft. Available at: www.oecd.org/tax/consumption/03_public-comments-oecd-international-vat-gst-guidelines.pdf.

Background – previous attempts at updating the PE concept

9.52 This is not the first time the OECD has attempted to update the PE concept to better deal with e-commerce: the final report of the OECD's Tax Advisory Group (TAG) on Monitoring the Application of Existing Treaty Norms for Taxing Business Profits was released in December 2005. This landmark report notes a significant consequence of the Internet has been its capacity to enable businesses to adopt new business models, streamlining processes including production, administration and customer services, and that business to business (B2B) e-commerce is much more prevalent than business to consumer (B2C).

A number of radical alternatives were examined by the TAG in the 2005 report:

- Modification of the PE definition to expressly exclude 'the maintenance of a fixed place of business used solely for carrying on of activities that do not involve human intervention'.

- A more limited option to exclude a fixed place of business which is used merely to carry on automated functions through equipment, data and software such as a server and website.

- Elimination of all of the preliminary or auxiliary exceptions to the definition of permanent establishment.

- Inclusion of a 'force of attraction' rule to deal specifically with e-commerce transactions.

- Adoption of a formulary apportionment rule to replace the separate entity and arm's-length principles. This proposal, of course, has much wider significance and has been debated elsewhere in the context of transfer pricing (see Chapter 13).

Having evaluated each of these alternatives, the TAG concluded, disappointingly, that it would not be appropriate at the present time to embark on any significant changes. Thus paragraphs 1–3 of Article 5 has remained virtually unchanged since the early 1960s, despite the huge changes in the way that international business is conducted since then. The only concessions have been the addition of sections of Commentary on Article 5 dealing with e-commerce and with trade in services (explored in Chapter 10).

Issues identified in BEPS Action 1

9.53 The issues may be broken down as follows:

- The ways in which the current definition of PE is inadequate in that it simply fails to award a reasonable share of the taxing rights over business profits of non-residents, even where there is no overt tax avoidance by the non-resident.

- Opportunities under the current rules for non-residents operating in the digital economy to deliberately avoid having a PE in a state where they have a significant customer base.

- The creation of value in the customer state via the collection of valuable customer and market data. Such data forms a valuable commercial asset which is then used to generate profits.

Digital economy business tax avoidance

9.54 A number of opportunities for tax avoidance by digital businesses are identified in the BEPS Action 1 Deliverable. These concern manipulation of PE status and also wider issues of tax avoidance. None of these are confined to digital economy businesses, but the OECD considers that such businesses have a greater opportunity to either avoid having a PE or to manipulate the amount of profits allocated to a PE. Strategies such as transfer of the legal owner-ship intangibles, without also transferring related staff functions and risks, and transfer pricing manipulation are also mentioned. The lack of import VAT on services in some countries and the centralized purchase of services by MNEs on behalf of multi-location subsidiaries, and PEs are also flagged as ways in which digital business might represent a tax loss to a country.

However, such practices are not confined to digital economy businesses, and the case for changing the definition of PE or replacing it with another concept entirely on these grounds is tenuous. In any case, other parts of the BEPS Project specifically deal with the types of problems mentioned in the previous paragraph:

- Some tightening up of the rules in Article 5, particularly those relating to agency Pes, is required and this is dealt with in BEPS Action 7 (Prevent the Artificial Avoidance of PE Status).

- The manipulation of PE status to avoid WHT is tackled by Action 6 (Prevent Treaty Abuse).

- Digital businesses often have high innovation and start-up costs which require significant financing. Locating the group company providing intercompany finance in a high tax country, and the operating subsidiar-ies or PEs in a low tax country provides a tax advantage. However, this is tackled by Action 4 (Limit Base Erosion via Interest Deductions) and Action 9 (Assure that transfer pricing outcomes are in line with value creation – risks and capital).

- Tax avoidance through manipulative transfer pricing between PE and Head Office is dealt with in Actions 8–10 (Assure that Transfer Pricing Outcomes are in Line with Value Creation).

Inadequacy of the current PE concept

9.55 Tax avoidance through artificially avoiding PE status or manipulating prices between PE and other parts of the corporate group is not the main prob-lem with Article 5. The main problem is that it no longer provides an adequate basis for splitting the profits of a firm between the different countries in which it operates. Put simply, it is now far easier to sell to foreign customers without needing any physical presence in the customer country than it was a century ago, when the Article 5 rules were being developed, and indeed than a decade ago, when the OECD last reported on the matter. The degree of physical presence in the customer country is no longer a good proxy for the extent of the business being done in that country. This is true for trade in goods and even truer for trade in services. These days, markets can be accessed without the need for a physical shop, and without the need for a dependent agent resident in the customer country. In some cases, contracts can be concluded remotely using computer programmes rather than a person.

Possible new PE rules

9.56 Several options are offered in the Action 1 Final Report ranging from relatively minor changes to an entirely new concept of a PE. However, it appears unlikely that any of the more radical options will be adopted.

Modify the paragraph 4 exemptions from PE status

9.57 Since the large scale export of goods to another country is often not feasible without maintaining a physical warehouse there; perhaps the exemption for having a physical presence only in the form of a warehouse should be abolished. This is justified by the fact that, for large-scale cross-border retailers, warehousing and delivery are key components of their business model, rather than being functions which are merely preparatory or auxiliary to core functions.

The justification for the exemptions from PE status in paragraph 4 of Article 5 are that the maintenance of a warehouse and the carrying out of other functions listed in paragraph 4 are preparatory and auxiliary to a firm's core functions. If this is no longer true, then the exemption should be withdrawn. There are two main problems with this suggestion:

- Withdrawing the exemption for all firms will affect all foreign suppliers, not merely those supplying on a large scale. Thus, the foreign supplier whose customer-country warehouse is truly preparatory or auxiliary to its trading there will, in future, have a PE. This could be a waste of everyone's time because the profits arising from the operation of that warehouse might well turn out to be minimal, and compliance costs will most likely be passed on to customers.

- The very large cross-border retailers do not use PE structures: for instance, Amazon has a UK subsidiary that owns and operates the warehouses from which contracts placed with the Amazon subsidiary in Luxembourg are fulfilled. The Luxembourg sales company has no warehouses in the UK, and would thus be unaffected by any change to paragraph 4 of Article 5.

Nevertheless, in the Final Report on Action 7, the OECD has introduced a proviso to the paragraph 4 exemptions: they will only apply if the activities in question are auxiliary or preparatory to the firm's core activities.

Add a digital presence test into Article 5

9.58   Under this proposal, which appeared in the BEPS Action 1 Discussion Draft and the 2014 BEPS Deliverable Report, the business profits of a non-resident could be taxed by a state if the non-resident trader has a 'significant digital presence' in that state. The state would then be entitled to tax the profits from 'fully dematerialized digital activities' which the non-resident trader carries on in the state. Effectively, this would be a parallel system to the current Article 5 'fixed place of business' and 'dependent agent' system of deciding whether a state has the right to tax business profits of a non-resident. Usable definitions of the new terms are crucial to the workability of this proposal:

Fully dematerialized digital activities

- The core business of the enterprise, accounting for all, or the vast majority of its profits, is wholly or mainly digital goods or services.

- These goods or services are both created and delivered by purely digital means: the only assets involved are IT and human resource.

- The use of the goods or services does not involve any physical products other than IT.

- Contracts and payment methods are paperless.

- Contact with the customer is solely via the website and no staff are located in the customer country.

- The customer is not concerned that residence or location of the vendor is overseas.

Significant digital presence

Would exist where:

- A non-resident carries on a significant amount of 'fully dematerialized digital activities' in a state.

- In that state, the non-resident has a large market for its digital products and services, resulting in substantial revenues for the non-resident trader.

- The non-resident has a conventional PE in the state that offers secondary functions such as marketing and consulting to customers, and these activities ae strongly related to the non-residents core functions which consist of fully dematerialized digital activities. (*Note: it is not clear whether this last example is standalone.*)

This proposal was dropped in the BEPS Final Report of 5 October 2015.

A new test of 'significant presence'?

9.59   Rather than adding a test into Article 5, one option would be to replace the current PE rules with a new test. The new rule would allow a source state to tax part of the business profits of a non-resident if that non-resident has a 'significant economic presence' there. Indications of whether there is a 'significant economic presence' might include:

- Revenue from customers in a country which exceeds a threshold – the OECD belatedly (not until the Action 1 Final Report) recognized that this is perhaps the clearest potential indication of the existence of a significant economic presence. However, significant customer revenues alone are not thought to be enough, and one or more of the following factors would also need to be present:

  — Relationships with customers or users extending over six months, together with a physical presence in the customer state. This could be either premises or the presence of a dependent agent.

  — Sale of goods or services to customers in the state where there is a close relationship with those customers. A close relationship might be identified as a website in the customer language, delivery to the customer from a warehouse in the customer state, use of banking facilities in the customer state or offering goods or services which originate in the customer state. A local domain name, local digital platform and local payment options would also be included.

  — Sales to customers in the state which result from or involve systematic data-gathering from persons in the customer state.

A withholding tax on digital transactions

9.60   It would be virtually impossible for the tax authority in the customer state to force the foreign supplier to pay tax to the customer state, due to purely practical concerns. However, if there are persons in the customer state who could be required to collect tax on behalf of the tax authority, that would be legally enforceable. It would not be practical to expect the customers to withhold part of the sale price of the digital goods or services: there would be too many customers involved and they would all have to be educated as to how to operate the withholding tax.

Most digital transactions are paid for using debit or credit cards or systems such as Paypal: the proposal in the BEPS Action 1 Deliverable was that the debit and credit card companies or Paypal should operate WHT on payments identified somehow as being subject to withholding tax.

This proposal to require financial and credit institutions to operate a withholding tax on payments made through them for digital good and services has received a particularly frosty reception:

> 'we emphatically reject the suggestion made in the Discussion Draft that withholding tax should be payable by financial institutions

involved in the making of outbound payments for digital goods or services. A financial institution providing payment services cannot be expected to determine whether a payment made under a contract to which the financial institution is not a party is being made for a digitized product or a physical product. A compliance requirement of this nature would be unreasonable and impractical.'[1]

The involvement of the credit institutions seems to have been dropped in the BEPS Final Report, which merely discusses a withholding tax as a back-up mechanism to enforce net-basis taxation, rather than a standalone method of collecting tax from non-residents. No practical aspects of enforcing the payment of any such withholding tax are offered.

---

1   OECD Ctr. for Tax Policy and Admin., *Comments Received on Public Discussion: Draft BEPS Action 1: Address the Tax challenges of the Digital Economy* (2014), Comments by the Banking and Finance Company Working Group on BEPS.

How likely is it that any of these proposals will be implemented in the OECD MTC?

9.61   It is highly unlikely that these proposals will be implemented in the OECD MTC in the short to medium term. The proposals, even in the OECD's Final Report on Action 1, are extremely vague and not well-developed. The only issue with respect to e-commerce that the OECD considers to merit urgent concern is the application of VAT to revenues from supplies of digital goods and service. This is dealt with in Chapter 21 of this book via the application of the OECD's VAT/GST Guidelines, an initiative that has been running parallel to BEPS. The hope appears to be that instances of deliberate avoidance of tax in connection with PEs will be dealt with by other parts of the BEPS Project. The OECD has promised to keep the position under review as the digital economy continues to develop.

There appears to be no appetite in the OECD member states for any fundamental change in the source rule for the taxation of business profits. The preferred option as at October 2015 is to concentrate on the collection of VAT on sales of electronic goods and services by non-residents. However, this shifts the burden of taxation directly, and completely (as opposed to indirectly and incompletely, which is likely to be the case with income or corporation tax on the profits of the non-resident) on to residents of the customer state. This leaves the customer state without any share of tax on the business profits of the non-resident at all.

The source rule will continue to be that business profits of a non-resident may only be taxed by a state if business is being carried on in that state through a permanent establishment: a fixed place of business or dependent agent. This is probably consistent with the position of OECD member states as net exporters of digital goods and services. It also avoids the problem inherent in the Action 1 proposals: that they would introduce rules specifically for the 'digital economy', making the assumption that it can be separately identified or 'ringfenced' from the rest of the economy. However, it leaves the fundamental rule in Article 5 – the fixed place of business rule – hopelessly out of date and unfit for application to modern business models. It is like having laws governing international travel applying only to voyages by sea and land without any mention of air transport. A decade after the OECD first examined the issue of application of the MTC to e-commerce, the OECD has once again avoided the issue.

Assessment of current OECD position on PE

9.62   The work on PE within the BEPS Project has eclipsed the basic difficulties with the PE concept that were being tackled by the OECD in its 2011 and 2012 Discussion Drafts on Article 5. The BEPS Action 7 proposals are aimed at preventing artificial avoidance of a PE rather than clarifying the definition as to what constitutes a basic, fixed place of business PE. The OECD still does not give any definite rule on how long a foreign enterprise must have a presence in a state for a PE to arise, although most states use a period of six months.

BEPS Action 7 brings some welcome clarification to the definition of an agency PE and the position regarding sales commissionaires. However, using a new definition of the group relationships in which the rules are to be applied ('closely related person') rather than any definition already in use may be an unnecessary complication. The restrictions on the applicability of the exemptions from PE status in paragraph 4 will only address situations where the paragraph 4 activities are carried out by the non-resident company itself, rather than by a fellow group company, unless the anti-fragmentation rule is utilized.

The OECD now recognizes (in the 2015 BEPS Action 7 Final Report) that its guidance on the allocation of profits to the PE has not met with universal acceptance and needs revisiting. The overriding aim of the guidance was to harmonize the approach taken by states to the attribution of profits to PEs, but this has not been achieved by the highly sophisticated system advocated by the OECD, either because it is too theoretical to be of use to states with limited capacity in their tax authorities, or because states have interpreted the OECD's guidance in different ways. There are many practical problems in adhering to the fiction of the PE as a separate enterprise and the OECD approach is not adopted in the UN Model.

Despite the Action 7 outcomes, the PE concept is still a concept developed for, and only really suitable for, traditional overseas manufacturing and sales business models. It fails altogether to recognize the twenty-first century scale of Internet trading in physical goods, digital goods and services. It belongs in an era when foreign profits were principally derived from foreign factories and sales offices. The greatly increased ease of access to foreign markets afforded by the Internet is not dealt with. Although the provision of a market ought not to give the customer's state the rights to tax all of the profits on sales there – because a proportion of the profit will be attributable to business functions carried out in the seller's state of residence – it is time for provision of the market to be specifically recognized as a factor affording the customer state the rights to tax over some of the non-resident suppliers' profits. The BEPS Final Report on Action 1 is a disappointment in this respect.

FURTHER READING

Basu, S (2007) *Global Perspectives on E-Commerce Taxation Law*, Ashgate.

Bird, R (2005) 'Taxing Electronic Commerce: The End of the Beginning?' *IBFD Bulletin*, April 2005, pp 130–140.

Cockfield, A J (2004) 'Reforming the Permanent Establishment Principle through a Quantitative Economic Presence Test', *Tax Notes International*, Vol 33, No 7, pp 643–54.

Cockfield, et al (2013) *'Taxing Global Digital Commerce'*, Wolters Kluwer Law and Business.

Doernberg, R L (2001) *Electronic Commerce and International Taxation*, Kluwer Law International.

Forgione, A (2003) 'Clicks and Mortar: Taxing Multinational Business Profits in the Digital Age', *Seattle University Law Review*, Vol 26, pp 719–779.

International Bureau for Fiscal Documentation, 'Interpretation and Application of Article 5 (Permanent Establishment) of the OECD Model Tax Convention. Response from IBFD Research Staff', IBFD, 2012. Available at: www.oecd.org/tax/taxtreaties/49782184.pdf, accessed 26 November 2015.

International Fiscal Association (2009) 'Is there a Permanent Establishment?' Cahiers de Droit fiscal international, 63rd Congress of the International Fiscal Association, Vancouver, ed J Sasseville.

Kersch, G A (2003) 'Comments on Definition of Permanent Establishment in the OECD Model Convention', *Tax Executive*, Nov/Dec 2003, 55, 6, p 489.

Krauze, M M (2015), 'Impact of Cloud Computing on Permanent Establishments Under the OECD Model Tax Convention', 44 *Tax Management International Journal*, Issue 3.

Langston, R (2011) 'Analysis – Practice guide: Handling Commissionaire Structures', *Tax Journal*, 21 October 2011.

Le Gall, J P (2007) 'The David R Tillinghast Lecture: Can a Subsidiary Be a Permanent Establishment of its Foreign Parent?', *Tax Law Review*, Vol 60, No 3.

Malherbe, J, Daenen, P (2010) 'Permanent Establishments Claim their Share of Profits: Does the Taxman Agree?', *Bulletin for International Taxation*, May 2010, Vol 64, No 7 (article on profit allocation under the new Article 7).

Nouel, L (2011) 'OECD – The New Article 7 of the OECD Model Tax Convention: The End of the Road?'.

OECD 'View', *Bulletin for International Taxation*, May 2008, p 174.

OECD (2005) Are the Current Treaty Rules for Taxing Business Profits Appropriate for E-Commerce? Final Report. Available at www.oecd.org/document/2 7/0,2340,en_2649_33741_35869083_1_1_1_1,00.html.

OECD (2008) Report on the Attribution of Profits to Permanent Establishments, OECD 17 July, 2008.

OECD (2010) Commentary on Articles 5 and 7 of the Model Convention on Income and Capital.

OECD (2012) OECD Model Tax Convention: Revised Proposals Concerning the Interpretation and Application of Article 5 (Permanent Establishment). Available at: www.oecd.org/ctp/treaties/PermanentEstablishment.pdf.

OECD (2013) Action plan on Base Erosion and Profit Shifting.

OECD (2014) Ctr., Public Discussion Draft: BEPS Action 7: Preventing the Artificial Avoidance of PE Status: 31 October 2014 to 9 January 2010.

OECD (2014) Comments Received on Public Discussion: Draft BEPS Action 1: Address the Tax challenges of the Digital Economy.

OECD (2014) Public Discussion Draft: BEPS Action 7: Preventing the Artificial Avoidance of PE Status: 31 October 2014 to 9 January 2015.

OECD (2015)(1) New discussion Draft on Action 7 (Prevent the Artificial Avoidance of PE Status), 15 May 2015.

OECD (2015)(2) Action 7: 2015 Final Report – Preventing the Artificial Avoidance of Permanent Establishment Status, 5 October 2015.

OECD (2015)(3) Action 1: 2015 Final Report – Addressing the Tax Challenges of the Digital Economy, 5 October 2015.

Pijl, H (2008) '*Morgan Stanley:* Issues regarding Permanent Establishments and Profit Attribution in Light of the OECD View', *Bulletin for International Taxation*, May 2008, p 174.

Pijl, H (2011) 'International/OECD/Netherlands – Interpretation of Article 7 of the OECD Model Permanent Establishment Financing and Other Dealings', *Bulletin for International Taxation*, May 2011, Vol 65, No 6.

Pleijsier, A (2015) 'Agency Permanent Establishment in BEPS Action 7: Treaty Abuse or Business Abuse', 43 *Intertax* 147.

Pollack, L A (1996) 'Tax Court's Taisei Case Sheds Light on the Definition of "permanent establishment"', *The Tax Adviser*, New York, January 1996, Vol 27, Issue 1, p 28.

Reimer, E, et al (2014) '*Permanent Establishments: a Domestic Taxation, Bilateral Tax Treaty and OECD Perspective*', Kluwer Law International.

Schwarz, J (2013) *Schwarz on Tax Treaties*, London, CCH.

Singh, M K (2014) 'Taxing E-Commerce on the Basis of permanent Establishment: Critical Evaluation', 42 *Intertax*, Issue 5.

Tanzi, V (2000) Globalization, Technological Developments and the Work of Fiscal Termites, Washington DC International Monetary Fund, WP/100/181.

Vincent, F (2005) 'Transfer Pricing and Attribution of Income to Permanent Establishments: The Case for Systematic Global Profit Splits (Just Don't Say Formulary Apportionment)', *Canadian Tax Journal*, Toronto, Vol 53, Issue 2, p 409.

Wustenberghs, T, Puncher, E (2011) 'Could a Commissionaire Arrangement Create an Agency Permanent Establishment in Belgium?' *Bulletin for International Taxation*, February 2011, Vol 65, No 4/5.

Yong, S 'Triangular Treaty Cases: Putting Permanent Establishments in their Proper Place', *Bulletin for International Taxation*, February 2010, Vol 64, No 3.

FURTHER STUDY

The UN Model and the use of the source principle by India

9.63   India is well known for its use of the source principle. In addition to the use of the UN Model for its DTTs, many of which include the concept of a service PE, there have been many cases where India has used its domestic law to interpret the provisions of its treaties so as to assert the existence of a PE. A variety of factors have resulted in India being regarded as a key location for inward investment by multinationals – huge population and potential market, a growing sector of the workforce that is relatively well educated and English speaking and a relatively stable political climate to name but a few. However, the multinationals have not had it all their own way – legacies of British rule included a well-developed legal system and a tax system which incorporated many aspects of the British tax system. India has continued to develop these and to use them effectively in insisting on its right to tax a portion of the profits of the multinational investors. In its double tax treaties, India has not only adopted most of the provisions suggested in the UN MTC but in many cases its treaties go further than the provisions of the UN MTC in allocating taxing rights to the state of source. In this section, the effect of India's domestic legislation on taxation of PEs, the effect of the provisions of its double tax treaties and some key decisions of the Indian courts are considered.

Section 9 of the Income Tax Act of India of 1961 provides that income from any business connections in India is deemed to arise in India. This is so irrespective of whether income actually arises in India. Where profits arise partly in India and partly abroad, India will tax an amount that is 'reasonably attributable' to the business operations carried out in India. There is no statutory definition of 'reasonably attributable'. Profits of a PE are determined by reference to the branch accounts. These must be kept as if the PE were an Indian company. The deduction for head office expenses is generally limited to 5 per cent of total income of the PE, by the ITA, s 44C.

If suitable branch accounts are not kept, then rule 10 of the Income Tax Rules 1962 provides that there are three methods of determining the profits of an Indian PE: a presumptive method, a proportionate method and a discretionary method. These methods give estimates of the profits attributable to the PE. There is little guidance as to the situations in which rule 10 might be invoked other than that it can be used either when branch accounts are not available or not considered a suitable basis for assessing the tax liability of the PE.

The presumptive method is used generally in Indian tax law and usually works by estimating taxable profits as a percentage of turnover, by reference to average margins achieved in the trade in question. The proportionate method is a unitary method which apportions profits of the whole entity by reference to the proportion of turnover achieved in India. Discretionary methods are not specified. Because of the use of the presumptive method in Indian domestic tax situations, this is likely to be the method chosen if, for some reason, the taxable profits of the PE cannot be ascertained by reference to Indian branch accounts.

In the case of *Rolls Royce Plc*,[1] Rolls Royce Private Ltd Company (RRPLC), a UK resident had a subsidiary tax resident in India (RRIL). The Indian company was paid for supplying marketing and support services, including organization of conferences and air shows, media relations, market research, press monitoring, identifying market opportunities for RRPLC, arranging discussions between RRPLC and current and potential customers and suppliers and various types of administrative and technical support. RRPLC argued that these services were merely preparatory or auxiliary and thus did not constitute a PE (see above for exemptions from the definition of PE on these heads). The Indian Air Force was the major customer and it was told to send requests for quotations to RRIL rather than directly to RRPLC. The requests were screened by RRIL and forwarded to RRPLC. Correspondence showed that RRIL took an active role in soliciting the orders and liaising with the customers. Senior staff at RRIL were functionally responsible to RRPLC for matters such as soliciting purchased orders and requests for quotations as well as being the principal point of contact for the Indian Ministry of Defence. The court held that under Indian domestic law, there was a 'business connection' (the Indian concept of PE) and also that there was a PE under para 2(f) of the India–UK Treaty (premises used as a sales outlet or for receiving or soliciting orders). As noted earlier, it is well established that 'premises' in the context of questions concerning s do not have to be owned by the entity to whom the PE is attributed. Thus the fact that the premises were owned by RRIL rather than RRPLC was not considered significant. The question of how much of the profits of RRPLC should be attributed to its Indian PE would normally be considered by reference to branch accounts.

The UK company, Rolls Royce Private Ltd Company had not considered that it had a PE in India and had therefore kept no branch accounts. Thus rule 10 was invoked. The goods (aero engines) were not manufactured in India and the court allocated 50 per cent of the profits on the sales attributed to the PE to manufacturing costs incurred outside India, 15 per cent to R&D costs incurred outside India, leaving 35 per cent of the profits to be attributed to the Indian PE.

The concept of a 'business connection' is key in establishing whether any of the profits of an enterprise are subject to tax in India. If a business connection exists, then part of the profits of a foreign enterprise may be deemed to arise in India. Explanation (a) to s 9(1) of the ITA states that income reasonably attributable to the operations carried out in India will be taxable there, if a business connection exists. However, exactly what type of business operation may give rise to a liability to Indian tax is not entirely clear. Particular problems have arisen with the precise manner in which foreign enterprises secure and conclude contracts with Indian customers. Generally, the Indian view of operations which, to use tax treaty terminology, are 'merely preparatory or auxiliary' is much narrower than that of most other states. A well-known quote from the case *CIT, Punjab v R.D. Aggarwal & Co* (56 ITR 20) provides some clues:

> 'The expression "business connection" postulates a real and intimate relation between the trading activity carried on outside the taxable territories and the trading activities within the territories, the relation between the two contributing to the earning of income by the non-resident in his trading activity.'

Some examples, taken from case law on the topic, of when a business connection might or might not be deemed to exist are given below:

- Such a connection exists when regular purchases are made in India through a regular agency. However, the mere procurement of orders on behalf of foreign principals does not establish a business connection.

- Where a company in India and a company outside India are both controlled by the same person and there is a flow of business between the two, there is a business connection even if the transaction between them is finalized outside India.

- A solitary loan transaction between a resident and a non-resident does not constitute a business connection between them, even if that loan and interest were to be paid over a period of, for example, five years.

- Where goods are sold by a non-resident through an agency for only one year, a business connection exists if a large number of orders are placed.

- A managing agent of a foreign company in India constitutes a business connection.

- In circumstances where there was regular correspondence between a firm of solicitors in India and a firm of solicitors in London regarding evidence to be adduced in certain suits and fixing hearings when a counsel from London would attend, a business connection was held to exist.

- In circumstances where technical information was provided by a German firm to an Indian firm in Germany, no business connection was held to exist.

- A business connection exists where a non-resident maintains a branch office in India for the purchase and sale of goods, or for transacting other business.

- Normally, when a non-resident deals with an Indian resident on the basis of principal-to-principal, such an arrangement *prima facie* negates the existence of any business connection.

- When an Indian broker is free to place the orders secured by him with any person he likes and he places his orders with a non-resident taxpayer, the relationship between them is not a business connection.

Agency PEs may be held to exist in circumstances not envisaged by the taxpayer. Section 185 of the ITA specifies the persons who may be treated as an agent, and it includes any person who has any business connection with the non-resident, or from or through whom the non-resident is in receipt of any income, whether directly or indirectly. If an Indian PE is to be avoided, the safest way to sell goods in India, or otherwise conclude contracts, is on a principal-to-principal basis. There are numerous Indian court cases on the subject of whether agency or service PEs exist and also numerous decisions of the AAR (Authority for Advance Rulings).

A recent major decision of the Indian Supreme Court on a disputed AAR ruling concerned Morgan Stanley,[2] the investment bank, which applied for a ruling as to whether or not it had a PE in India (AAR 661 of 2006). Very briefly, the facts were that Morgan Stanley Co seconded certain employees to an Indian subsidiary which provided it with support services for periods of up to two years in order to ensure the quality of the support services provided. They were employed and paid by the Indian subsidiary and their salaries were recharged to the parent company without any profit element. It was agreed that neither a 'fixed place of business' nor an agency PE arose, but that there was a services PE. The grounds for this decision were mainly that the salaries of the seconded employees were, in fact, paid by the Indian subsidiary, constituting around 50 per cent of the wages bill, their performance appraisals were conducted by the Indian subsidiary and they undertook part of the managerial activities of the Indian subsidiary. The fact that the value of their work was exclusively for the benefit of Morgan Stanley Co was, in the opinion of the AAR, not enough to prevent a PE being held to exist. Whilst this was confirmed in 2008 by the Indian Supreme Court, the Supreme Court ruled that the amount of the payments by Morgan Stanley Co to the Indian subsidiary was on an arm's-length basis and thus no further profits beyond those resulting from these payments could be taxed in India. This decision followed a close analysis of the transfer pricing principles used and concluded that in arriving at the arm's-length price the key concepts to be examined were the functions performed and risks assumed by the service PE.

The payment of an agent at an arm's-length amount may not be sufficient to prevent a PE being held to exist, as in *Dy Director of Income Tax v SET Satellite (Singapore) Pte Ltd*)[3] a 2007 Tribunal case. In this case, SET made arm's-length payments to a dependent agent in India but was faced with an

Indian tax assessment (under Rule 10) of 10 per cent of the advertising revenues generated by the agent. Although the question of whether payments to an agent representing an arm's-length amount had been explored in the Morgan Stanley ruling (separately from the salaries issue discussed above) and it had been held that such payments would extinguish any further liability in respect of the profits generated by the dependent agents' activities, the benefit of this ruling was not extended to SET. Rulings of the AAR are only applicable to the requesting party, not to taxpayers generally. Note that this decision indicates that India may agree with the OECD's 'two taxpayers' approach to the attribution of profits where there is a dependent agent PE. India is not an OECD member and can do what it likes in this respect.

Another interesting case on agents and PEs concerned a US company contracting with the Indian government. In *Re Sutron Corporation*[4] a US corporation entered into two contracts with an Indian state government to supply remote satellite weather reporting stations. The contracts were signed in India on behalf of Sutron by an Indian agent paid by Sutron, who was not an employee. This agent collected information about invitations to tender, submitted the bid on behalf of Sutron and eventually signed on behalf of Sutron. However, the goods in question were produced in the US, paid for in the US and the Indian customer took legal ownership of them on US soil. Sutron's only connection with India was the presence of this paid agent. It was held that the presence of the agent gave rise to a 'business connection' between Sutron and India, sufficient to evidence the existence of a PE in India. Part of Sutron Corporation's profits would therefore be liable to Indian taxation.

Agency PE was also considered in *Galileo International Inc*[5] in which an Indian company acted in a capacity as distributor, providing access to Galileo's comprehensive global reservation system for airline, hotel and taxi services to Indian travel agents. This case also considered some interesting e-commerce points. The Indian company was held to be a dependent agent partly because it acted exclusively for the US company and was economically dependent on it. Note that the attribution of profits to operations outsourced ('offshored') to Indian, typically call centres and back-office operations, is specifically addressed in two Circulars, Circular No 1 of 2004 and Circular No 5 of 2004. This analysis constitutes a superficial summary of the position regarding the existence of and the attribution of profits to an Indian PE. New cases are being brought all the time.

---

1   *Rolls-Royce Plc v Director of Income Tax* ITA Nos 1496–1501/DEL of 2007.
2   *DIT (International Taxation), Mumbai v Morgan Stanley & Co Inc; Morgan Stanley & Co Inc v DIT (International Taxation), Mumbai*, Civil Appeal Nos 2914 and 2915 of 2007, Supreme Court of India 9 July 2007.
3   ITA No 944/2007 Indian High Court, Mumbai.
4   AAR No 603 of 2002 Authority for Advance Rulings, India. Reported at 7 ITLR 185.
5   *Galileo International Inc v Deputy Commissioner of Income Tax, Non-Resident Circle, New Delhi*, 30 November 2007.

Chapter 10

Taxation of Cross-border Services

BASICS

10.1 Services represent, on average, 70 per cent of worldwide GDP yet the text of the OECD Model Tax Convention (MTC) does not deal specifically with income from services, although in 2008 wording was provided in the Commentary for those countries wishing to include a specific definition of a PE to cover trade in services. This recognizes that trade in services is very significant, in terms of total world cross-border trade, and is growing.

The OECD MTC permits a host state to tax profits earned by non-residents if there is a permanent establishment (PE) in the host state. As we have seen in Chapter 9, the OECD MTC recognizes two types of PE – the fixed place of business and the dependent agent. However, in the case of profits earned in a host state from the provision of services by a non-resident there is often no need for a fixed place of business. Under the OECD MTC, a company can send its employees overseas for short periods without incurring any liability to tax in the visited state. An independent professional can visit another state to provide client services. As we saw in Chapter 8, under the OECD MTC, so long as an employee is not present in the visited state for more than 183 days in the tax year, and no person or PE of his employer claims a tax deduction for his salary against taxable profits there, there is no host state tax on the salary earned from the visit. So long as an independent professional does not have a fixed base in the host state (or, as found in some treaties, is not present there for more than 183 days in the tax year), there is no liability to host-state tax.

By contrast, the UN MTC has always included a so-called 'services permanent establishment'. This is a deemed PE as it does not require that there be a fixed place of business in the host state. The usual rule is that there will be a deemed PE if services are provided in the host state for 183 days in any 365 days on the same or connected projects.

Some types of services are specifically dealt with in the OECD MTC. For example, income from services of sportspersons and entertainers may be taxed in the state in which the performances take place and profits of transport businesses are only taxed by the state in which the business is tax resident. However, there are no specific provisions dealing with the right of a host state to tax all other types of services, referred to as 'enterprise services'. These may be consultancy, technical assistance, equipment maintenance, training and education, to name but a few. The value of services performed in a state by non-residents may be very high, but under the OECD MTC, unless the non-resident has a PE in that state, the host state has no rights to tax the profits derived from them. More recently, in 2008, the OECD introduced wording for an optional 'services PE' in the Commentary on the OECD MTC. This optional provision contains two tests: a deemed services PE arises either where a single individual is present in the host state for more than 183 days in the year and accounts for more than 50 per cent of the business income of the enterprise; or if the test as set out in the UN MTC is met. A provision similar to this was adopted in the Fifth Protocol to the US–Canada treaty.

Some countries have dealt with the issue of taxation of non-resident foreign service providers (FSPs) by insisting upon the inclusion of special provisions in their double tax treaties (DTTs) that are not found in the OECD MTC, that give them the right to tax profits or gross income derived by non-residents from services. Where the tax takes the form of a final withholding tax this might inhibit the flow of cross-border services because the withholding tax charged may exceed the net profits. Despite this, developing countries often regard the payment of fees for services to non-resident FSPs as base-eroding, reducing their tax revenues because they have to grant tax deductions for these payments. The next version of the UN MTC will include an article dealing specifically with technical service fees, that permits withholding tax.

SCALE OF CROSS-BORDER TRADE IN SERVICES

10.2   The services sector represented 70 per cent of worldwide GDP in 2012.[1] According to Pascal Lamy, former Director-General of the WTO, more than half of annual world foreign direct investment flows are now in services and the growth in cross-border trade in services in recent years has been more rapid than that in world production and merchandise trade. Until the signing of the General Agreement on Trade in Services (GATS) in 1995, available data on the value and volume of cross-border trade in services was very patchy. The GATS may be viewed as the services equivalent of the General Agreement on Tariffs and Trade. Both were promulgated by the World Trade Organization (WTO). The GATS lays down a framework within which pairs or groups of countries can enter into trade-liberalization arrangements in respect of services, although it does not, of itself, liberalize trade. The GATS is important for two main reasons: First, it provides a major impetus for trade liberalization in services which should lead to further increases in the international trading of services. Second, it introduces a raft of definitions and reporting conventions covering trade in services and has brought about a vast improvement in the nature and scope of reporting of trade in services within the national accounts of many countries. One of the problems in ascertaining the importance of trade in services has long been the unreliable, heavily aggregated and incomplete nature of statistics on trade in services in the national accounts of individual countries. As part of the introduction of the GATS the IMF, in consultation with the bodies responsible for the contents of the internationally accepted blueprint for national accounts,[2] updated its requirements for the reporting of trade in services. Trade in services is now reported by most countries in some detail whereas prior to the GATS, very little was available.

The best way to appreciate the scale of cross-border trade in services is probably to compare it with total cross-border trade. This is illustrated in Figure 10.1 which illustrates the total value of services as a percentage of total exports and breaks this down into transport services, travel services and other commercial services.

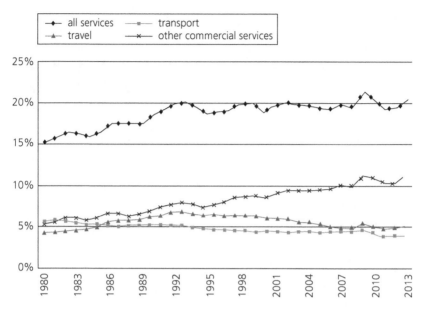

Source: constructed from WTO statistics

Figure 10.1: Exports of services (world) as a percentage of total world exports of goods and services

Notice that although services account for up to about 70 per cent of GDP in the EU and many other developed countries, services exports as a percentage of total exports is a much lower percentage: around 20 per cent in 2013. Liberalization of trade in services is proving difficult to achieve, although there are signs that negotiations are progressing (EU 2015). Taking into account the fact that world exports of goods have increased dramatically over the past few decades and are continuing to increase, trade in services represents an important element of global cross-border trade. If the liberalization of service trade progresses further, then, given that services output represents about 70 per cent of worldwide GDP, we may expect that cross-border trade in services will increase substantially. It is sometimes argued that the OECD MTC deals adequately with cross-border trade in services because the bulk of services provided to overseas customers are provided by forming or acquiring a subsidiary company (a foreign affiliate) in the customer's state. That foreign affiliate would be tax resident in the customer state and thus liable to tax there on the profits from services performed in the customer's state. It is certainly true that provision of cross-border services via foreign affiliates has grown significantly over the past few decades but so has the value of cross-border services provided other than through a foreign affiliate, eg by sending employees to the

293

customer state. The US is a major exporter of services and has maintained statistics on this type of trade for some years now. Figure 10.2 compares services provided in the customer state by foreign affiliates, tax resident in the customer state with services provided directly by a non-resident enterprise.

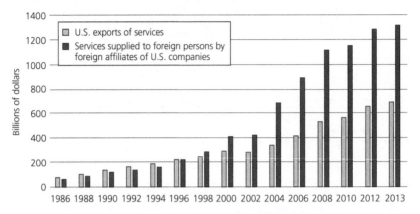

Figure 10.2: Total US exports of services and services supplied via foreign affiliates

The growth in trade in services looks set to continue. In developed countries, services account for more than 70 per cent of GDP, whereas in developing countries they only account for around 50 per cent. This suggests that as a state's economy develops, the balance between production of goods and services swings in favour of services.

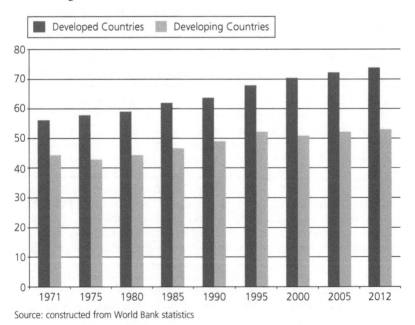

Source: constructed from World Bank statistics

Figure 10.3: Percentage of GDP accounted for by services

1   World Bank Development Indicators: Structure of Output Table 4.2. Available at http://wdi.
    worldbank.org/table/4.2#.
2   UN Commission of the European Communities, IMF, OECD, World Bank.

TYPES OF CROSS-BORDER SERVICES

10.3   The range of services which can be traded cross-border (ie between
a supplier in one state and a customer in another) has grown very significantly
over the past two decades due to improvements in electronic communications.
Before the use of the internet became widespread during the 1990s and before
international phone calls became cheap around the same time, due to the use of
optical fibre cabling, services were much less easily tradable cross-border

The GATS sets out an important framework which could be used to develop
policy on taxing profits from trade in services. Farrell (2013) examines the tax
regulation of services and FSPs under GATS. This framework not only sets
out the different types of services: transports, business and so on, but it defines
four main ways in which services can be delivered, the so-called four 'modes'.
They are set out below in Table 10.1.

Table 10.1 The GATS modes of supply of services

	Description	**Examples**
Mode 1	Cross-border supply: the service crosses the border but not the supplier	Telecoms Services supplied by post
Mode 2	Consumption abroad: the consumer crosses the border to the supplier's state	Tourism, repair of machinery
Mode 3	Commercial presence abroad	A foreign subsidiary or branch
Mode 4	Movement of natural persons, either: employees; or persons in business on own account.	Short-term consultancy involving the visit of an expert to the consumer's state

Possible tax treatment of cross-border services

GATS, Modes 1 and 2

10.4   The OECD MTC already deals adequately with this type – the
supplier is fully taxable in the state where resident. Because there is no PE in
the customer state, the supplier suffers no direct taxes there.

GATS, Mode 3

10.5   The OECD MTC usually deals adequately with this Mode, as either
there is a subsidiary company resident in the customer state or the supplier has

a PE in the customer state. However, if the commercial presence abroad does not breach the threshold for a PE, then there might not be any direct taxation in the customer's state – but see the comments on GATS Mode 4 below.

GATS, Mode 4

10.6 This is the Mode which presents the greatest number of problems in terms of international tax. The individual or the enterprise supplying the services visits the customer's state in the course of supplying the service. For instance, Mode 4 services would include a private consultant with customers in several countries who visits the customer and carries out consultancy services at the customer premises. Another example of Mode 4 services would be where an enterprise sends some of its employees abroad to provide technical assistance to its customers, perhaps as part of the installation of plant and machinery. Or employees could be sent to a customer site abroad to provide training for the customer's employees, say in the operation of new computer software. Another example would be where the head office company in State A temporarily transfers workers to a subsidiary company in State B. Although Mode 4 services so far appear to be the smallest category in terms of value, this is expected to change as more agreements are concluded under the GATS framework. To date progress has been slow due mainly to the fear amongst developed countries that permitting FSPs from developing countries to visit for the purposes of services provision constitutes a risk of uncontrolled migration. Nevertheless, Mode 4 services present a number of challenges in the international tax system.

Withholding tax on payments for services

10.7 A significant problem is that many countries, principally developing countries, charge a withholding tax on the gross amount of payments made to non-residents in respect of services. Often, these withholding taxes are final, so that there is no chance of repayment. (A non-final withholding tax gives the taxpayer the option of later filing a tax return, being taxed on the net profits rather than the gross amount and thus claiming a repayment.) This can render the provision of services to such a state unprofitable as illustrated in Example 10.1.

Example 10.1 Illustration of effect of withholding tax on a gross basis

Gross service fees	1,000
Withholding tax at 15%	−150
	850
Direct and indirect costs of providing the services	−900
Loss	−50
Profit before foreign taxes	100

Residence state tax	25
Deduct: double tax relief by normal credit	−25
Residence state taxation	0
Unrelieved foreign tax: 150–25	125

Were it not for the withholding tax, the provision of the services would be profitable. Even if host-state tax was levied on a net basis, say at 30%, it would be profitable, ie $(1000 - 900) = 100$. $100 \times 30\% = 30$. Profit after foreign tax: $100-30 = 70$.

There would still be a small amount of foreign tax unrelieved in the residence state, but overall, the activity would still be profitable. An unfortunate effect of the charging of withholding taxes on payments for services is that the FSP will routinely insist upon a 'gross up' charge so that the price payable for the services increases to take account of the withholding tax, leaving the FSP in the same net position as if there were no withholding tax. The burden of the withholding tax is shifted on to the customer; the services have become more expensive and may even have become unaffordable. Although there is not space to discuss this issue further here, for developing countries which require technology transfer from other states in order to develop their economies, withholding taxes can be counter-productive.

There are three types of treatment for income from services provided to a customer in another state:

1   Services income is treated as business profits within Article 7 and thus not taxable by the customer state (the host state), unless the FSP has a PE in the host state. The definition of PE contains no specific references to services, so that for the income to be taxable by the host state the FSP would either have to have a fixed place for business in the host state from which the business was wholly or partly carried on, or would have to have a dependent agent in the host state. In any case, the taxation would be computed on the net basis.

2   Services income is treated as business profits but the definition of PE includes the provision of services, without the need for a fixed place of business or a dependent agent. (See para **10.18**.) The definition would normally specify that services must be provided for periods totalling at least 183 days in any tax year, although there are many variations on this. Income from the provision of services which does not breach the threshold would not be taxable by the host state. Any taxation would be on the net basis in accordance with the provision of Article 7.

3   Services income is dealt with either as part of the royalties article or in a separate article and withholding tax on the gross amount is permitted up to a maximum specified rate. Again, many variations are found. Specific provision of this kind would take precedence over the provisions of Articles 5 and 7, usually by way of an express statement in Article 7 that Article 7 is not to apply to income specifically dealt with in other articles.

The first category of treatment is usually the most favourable for the FSP and the last is the least favourable.

SERVICES IN THE MODEL TAX CONVENTIONS

10.8   The following sections start by examining a new article that will be included in the next update to the UN MTC, permitting withholding tax on payments to non-residents for technical services. We then look at how the OECD and the UN MTCs deal with services through the concept of permanent establishment (PE).

UN's proposal for a tax on payments for technical services fees

10.9   The UN's Committee of Experts on International Cooperation in Tax Matters has been examining the question of the taxation of cross-border services in depth since 2009, and is introducing into the next version of the UN MTC an article specifically permitting source state tax (a withholding tax) on income of non-residents from fees for technical services. This is because:

- Payments for services made to non-residents are base-eroding in that they are tax deductible for the payer. This can be costly for developing countries that are usually net service importers.

- It is difficult for developing countries to challenge the transfer pricing practices of multinational groups with respect to intra-group service fees.

- Many developing countries already charge withholding tax on payments of royalties to non-residents, and dressing up royalties as fees for technical services is perceived to be a way in which non-residents can avoid the withholding tax on royalties.

- Without such an article, there is too much uncertainty about the taxation of service fees by the source country. Is there a services PE? Is the payment in respect of 'information concerning industrial, commercial or scientific experience' and thus a form of royalty? What about mixed contracts? Reducing uncertainty is cited in the draft Commentary on the UN MTC as a main reason for the introduction of the Article.

Such an article will require a detailed definition of what is meant by technical services fees. Essentially, these are fees closely connected with intellectual property, and in particular, know-how. In a note prepared for the 2013 meetings of the Committee of Experts, Brian Arnold (Arnold, 2013) summarized the key issues that need to be addressed in developing the new article:

- the definition of services to which the new article would apply;

- whether the tax should only apply to income from technical services physically performed in the host state or whether it should apply whenever a resident makes a payment to a non-resident in respect of technical service fees;

- whether any threshold should apply before the tax kicks in;

- whether the tax should be a pure withholding tax or whether it should attempt to tax the net profits made by the non-resident from provision of the technical services.

The text of the proposed new article reads as follows:

'UN MTC TAX CONVENTION

Article 12A – Payments for Technical Services

Fees for technical services arising in a Contracting State and paid to a resident of the other Contracting State may be taxed in that other State.

2. However, notwithstanding Article 14 and subject to the provisions of Articles 8, [17 and 20], fees for technical services arising in a Contracting State may also be taxed in the Contracting State in which they arise and according to the laws of that State, but if the beneficial owner of the fees is a resident of the other Contracting State, the tax so charged shall not exceed ___ percent of the gross amount of the fees (the percentage to be established through bilateral negotiations).

3. The term "fees for technical services" as used in this Article means any payment in consideration for any service of a managerial, technical or consultancy nature, unless the payment is made:

   (a) to an employee of the person making the payment;

   (b) to a director or top-level managerial official of a company that is a resident of the Contracting State in which the fees arise;

   (c) for teaching in or by educational institutions [as part of a degree granting program];

   (d) by an individual for services for the personal use of the individual; or

   [(e)] (f) or services that are ancillary and subsidiary, [as well as inextricably and essentially linked, to the sale of property].

4. The provisions of paragraphs 1 and 2 shall not apply if the beneficial owner of fees for technical services, being a resident of a Contracting State, carries on business in the other Contracting State in which the fees for technical services arise through a permanent establishment situated in that other State, or performs in the other Contracting State independent personal services from a fixed base situated in that other State, and the fees for technical services are effectively connected with

   (a) such permanent establishment or fixed base, or

   (b) business activities referred to in (c) of paragraph 1 of Article 7.

299

In such cases the provisions of Article 7 or Article 14, as the case may be, shall apply.

5. For the purposes of this Article, subject to paragraph 6, fees for technical services shall be deemed to arise in a Contracting State if the payer is a resident of that State or if the person paying the fees, whether that person is a resident of a Contracting State or not, has in a Contracting State a permanent establishment or a fixed base in connection with which the obligation to pay the fees was incurred, and such fees are borne by the permanent establishment or fixed base.

6. For the purposes of this Article, fees for technical services shall be deemed not to arise in a Contracting State if the payer is a resident of that State and carries on business in the other Contracting State or a third State through a permanent establishment situated in that other State or the third State, or performs independent personal services through a fixed base situated in that other State or the third State and such fees are borne by that permanent establishment or fixed base.

7. Where, by reason of a special relationship between the payer and the beneficial owner of the fees for technical services or between both of them and some other person, the amount of the fees, having regard to the services for which they are paid, exceeds the amount which would have been agreed upon by the payer and the beneficial owner in the absence of such relationship, the provisions of this Article shall apply only to the last-mentioned amount [the amount that would have been agreed upon in the absence of such relationship]. In such case, the excess part of the fees shall remain taxable according to the laws of each Contracting State, due regard being had to the other provisions of this Convention.'

Scope of the new Article

10.10 There is no threshold: even small-scale suppliers of services will suffer WHT under treaties that contain the new Article.

Only payments which are tax deductible are caught: payments for services intended for the personal use of individuals, as opposed to business use, are excepted from the Article.

If the foreign service-provider has a PE or a fixed base in the customer country through which the services are provided, then the profits from the services will be taxed in the customer country on the net profits basis, under the normal rules for PEs and fixed bases (Articles 5, 7 and 14 of the UN MTC). In the absence of a permanent establishment or fixed base, Articles 7 and 14 are amended so that even though fees for technical services give rise to business profits, these profits (not attributable to a PE or fixed base) are dealt with in the new Article rather than under Article 7 or 14. Without this amendment to Articles 7 and 14, countries would have no right to tax technical services fees unless there was a PE or fixed base.

A final withholding tax?

10.11   The new article closely follows the format of Articles 11 (interest) and 12 (royalties) and provides for WHT. Whether there could be any refund of tax to the non-resident if a tax return is submitting showing that the tax due on a net profits basis is less than that charged as withholding tax is uncertain. (In other words, whether it is to be a 'final' or 'non-final' withholding tax.) Also uncertain is whether the maximum withholding tax would be set at a level which approximates what the effective rate of tax on net profits would be. The draft Commentary warns against excessively high rates of withholding tax on the grounds that:

- Non-residents would probably insist on so-calling 'grossing-up' clauses in their contracts, which oblige the resident payer to pay to the non-resident the amount which would be due in the absence of any withholding tax. This means that the resident payer ends up suffering the withholding tax rather than the non-resident.

- A tax rate in excess of any foreign tax credit limit in the provider's country could be a deterrent to the provision of services.

- A high rate of withholding tax might wipe out profits of potential FSPs, again, deterring the provision of services.

Despite these caveats, the only practical way to enforce collection of the tax is by means of withholding. The requirement to withhold falls on the resident customer, who would normally be liable to remit the withholding tax to the tax authority, whether or not it had actually been withheld from the payment made to the foreign FSP.

A fundamental deficiency in the article is the failure to establish a source rule for the services income. Paragraph 1 merely refers to fees 'arising' in one contracting state and paid to a resident of the other. The draft commentary on Paragraph 1 does not attempt to define what is meant by fees 'arising'. Thus, the debate as to whether the source rule should be place of performance, place of utilization of the services or merely place of payment (base erosion) is not properly addressed. This undermines the level of certainty afforded to FSPs as to whether the withholding tax will be levied or not. Source rules for services are discussed at para **10.24** onwards below.

Definition of technical services

10.12   The Article defines technical service fees as 'any payment in consideration for any service of a managerial, technical or consultancy nature'. According to the draft Commentary, the services must involve:

- the application by the FSP of specialized knowledge, skill or expertise on behalf of a client; or

- the transfer of knowledge, skill or expertise to the client, other than a transfer of information covered by the definition of royalties in paragraph 3 of Article 12.

'Management' is defined to involve the application of knowledge, skill or expertise in the control or administration of the conduct of a commercial enterprise or organization. Thus, where an enterprise is managed by non-residents who are not directors, officers or employees of the enterprise, the payments to the non-residents will be technical service fees. Payments to consultants for advice concerning management of the enterprise would also be technical service fees.

'Technical' is defined to involve the application of specialized knowledge, skill or expertise with respect to a particular art, science, profession or occupation. Hence, technical services fees will include payments to lawyers, accountants, architects, medical professionals, engineers, dentists and other professionals.

'Consultancy' is defined to involve the provision of advice or services of a specialized nature, whether management or technical.

Countries adopting the new article must use these definitions. The Article deliberately makes no reference to domestic law definitions. This is so that all countries operating the new Article use a consistent set of definitions rather than their own. For instance, India has a particularly labyrinthine set of definitions of what might constitute technical services which it will no longer be able to apply to FSPs resident in countries with which India concludes or amends treaties containing the new Article. The new Article seeks to set out a common set of definitions which override the domestic definitions.

Application of knowledge, skill or expertise

10.13   This important part of the definition limits the definition of technical service fees to bespoke services, tailored to a particular client. For instance, a bank might use its knowledge, skill and expertise to develop general products and services that are made available to its clients in return for a fee, such as credit card services. A bundle of general credit card services would not involve research analysis or advice to a specific client, related to that client's particular services and hence payments to a foreign bank in return for the credit card services would not be technical service fees. However, advice given by the foreign bank on a proposed merger or acquisition by the customer would count as foreign service fees, because those services are particular to the needs of that particular client.

Treatment of expenses

10.14   Unfortunately, the question of whether expenses are technical service fees is not dealt with in the new Article. Even more unfortunately, in the draft Commentary, the matter is explicitly left to individual countries to decide. This is likely to result in continuing uncertainty for foreign FSPs as to the effective rate of tax they will suffer in the customer country. If expenses are not subject to the withholding tax, the effective rate suffered will be less than the headline rate of withholding tax. This will lead to FSPs skewing their charges to customers in that country away from pure fees and on to the reimbursement of expenses. The tax authority in the customer country will then be left with the task of auditing the split between fees and expenses, and it is likely that many expensive and time-consuming disputes will arise. The certainty of taxation, cited as a main reason for the adoption of the new Article, is severely undermined by this lacuna in the definition of technical service fees.

When will the new Article appear?

10.15 Inserting the new Article in to the text of the UN MTC does not change existing treaties. Countries which want to incorporate the new Article into their new treaties, or to renegotiate existing treaties so as to incorporate it face tough negotiations from their service-exporting treaty partners. Treaty partners are likely to want concessions in return and, at the very least, to insist on reciprocity in the matter of WHT on services. Such an Article could backfire on developing countries because their service sectors are, in general, growing and in time they might become net service exporters. In this case, a developing country's service exporters would be hit by WHT on payments received from treaty partner countries where the treaty contains the new Article.

DEEMED SERVICES PEs

10.16 In principle, there is no reason why profits from services performed in another state should not be taxable in that other state. However, in the absence of a fixed place of business or a dependent agent, profits from services could remain taxable only in the state where the enterprise is tax resident. Given the increasing importance of the services sector, denying the host state the opportunity to tax the substantial amounts of profits which are being made within its territory by foreign enterprises through the provision of services but with no fixed place of business or dependent agent, is inconsistent with the general approach taken by the OECD towards the division of tax revenues between states.

There are some good reasons for not extending the concept of a PE to the provision of services. The OECD Commentary points out (at para 42.12 to the Commentary on Article 5) that there would be no independent means of verifying the amounts of revenue earned by the services PE where the customers were principally retail (and so not preparing accounts which could be cross-checked with those of the PE), rather than business customers. Enterprises sending personnel to another state might not know at the outset exactly how long they would have to stay and thus any time limits for a services PE might be inadvertently breached, leading to the retrospective recognition of a services PE, for which no records had been kept. Even if a services PE was anticipated at the start of the overseas assignment, keeping appropriate books and records and attributing a share of the enterprise's profits to the activities of the personnel posted overseas is an inherently difficult task.

The OECD MTC was developed before cross-border trade in services had developed on the scale seen today. Hence most of the provisions in the MTC were designed to cope with trade in goods, rather than trade in services. Certain types of services are subject to specific provisions: transport services, services of entertainers and sports persons and, in most treaties in force at present, independent personal services of persons engaged in professional activities. The UN MTC has always included a deemed service PE. The OECD MTC does not mention services in Article 5 (permanent establishment), although since 2008 the Commentary has included wording that could be used to allow for the provision of services to be treated as if there was a PE.

The following sections examine first what happens if there is no mention of services in Article 5 and then go on to consider the services PE in the text of the UN MTC, and the optional wording for a services PE in the Commentary on the OECD MTC.

How Article 5 applies to services

10.17   If services are not explicitly mentioned in Article 5, then whether or not a PE can arise through the provision of services by a non-resident depends on the interpretation of Article 5. As discussed in Chapter 9 at para **9.5** if there is a fixed place which is 'at the disposal' of the FSP for a sufficiently long period of time, then there will be a PE. Thus, for instance, if the premises of a client are 'at the disposal' of a FSP, then that FSP could have a PE by virtue of its use of the client's premises.

The OECD interpretation of whether a PE arises in relation to FSPs, in cases where there is no explicit provision for services in Article 5, is contentious. The examples given in the Commentary, and particularly the 'painter' example at para 4.6 of the Commentary on Article 5, suggest that if the FSP carries out core functions of its business at the client premises for long enough, then a PE arises. This example reads:

> 'A fourth example is that of a painter who, for two years, spends three days a week in the large office building of its main client. In that case, the presence of the painter in that office building where he is performing the most important functions of his business (i.e. painting) constitute a permanent establishment of that painter.'

The example is contentious because it could be argued that although painting the offices is a core function of the business, it does not, by itself, constitution the carrying on of the business. If the painter does not issue invoices, advertise services, pursue possible new contracts, etc, then the painter would not have much of a business. So although the painter may be carrying out core business functions at the client premises, the painter cannot however, be said to be carrying on business from there. Of course, it is possible that if the painter has a sufficiently sophisticated smartphone, then the painter could possibly do so. Another argument sometimes made is that the client premises are merely the 'object' of business – the painter is doing something to them, rather than carrying on business within them.

Similar issues arise in the case of *R v Dudney* (see Chapter 9, para **9.9**).

The services PE and the independent personal services Article in the UN MTC

10.18   Treaties which follow the UN MTC offer an additional type of PE: the services PE. Like the agency PE, this is a deemed PE, because the non-resident does not need to have an actual establishment in the host state so that no premises are necessary. The justification for the inclusion of the provision in the UN MTC is baldly stated in the Commentary on Article 5 of the UN MTC:

> 'It is believed that management and consultancy services should be covered because the provision of such services in developing countries by corporations of industrialized countries often involves very large sums of money.'[1]

The UN MTC places greater emphasis on the source principle than the OECD MTC and Article 5 of the UN MTC includes the concept of a services PE:

'Article 5(b) UN MTC Tax Convention

(b)   The furnishing of services, including consultancy services, by an enterprise through employees or other personnel engaged by the enterprise for such purpose, but only while activities of that nature continue (for the same or a connected project) within the state for a period or periods aggregating more than 183 days within any 12-month period'.

This is broadly consistent with the temporal test for the source state taxation of employment remuneration under Article 15 which uses a test of 183 days' presence. The services PE test ignores the fact that not all the 183 days of presence in the host state will be working days.

An example of a treaty with an extended Article 5 along the lines of the UN MTC is the UK/India treaty:

'Article 5(k) UK/India double tax treaty

...   The term "permanent establishment" shall include especially:

> ...   the furnishing of services including managerial services, other than those taxable under Article 13 (Royalties and fees for technical services), within a Contracting State by an enterprise through employees or other personnel, but only if:

(i)   activities of that nature continue within that State for a period or periods aggregating more than 90 days within any twelve-month period; or

(ii)   services are performed within that State for an enterprise within the meaning of paragraph (1) of Article 10 (Associated Enterprises) and continue for a period or periods aggregating more than 30 days within any twelve-month period.'

The UN MTC also contains, at Article 14, provision for source state taxation of 'independent personal services' which reads:

'1. Income derived by a resident of a Contracting State in respect of professional services or other activities of an independent character shall be taxable only in that State except in the following circumstances, when such income may also be taxed in the other Contracting State:

    (a) If he has a fixed base regularly available to him in the other Contracting State for the purpose of performing his activities; in that case, only so much of the income as is attributable to that fixed base may be taxed in that other Contracting State; or

    (b) If his stay in the other Contracting State is for a period or periods amounting to or exceeding in the aggregate 183 days in any twelve-month period commencing or ending in the fiscal year concerned; in that case, only so much of the income as is derived from his activities performed in that other State may be taxed in that other State.

2. The term "professional services" includes especially independent scientific, literary, artistic, educational or teaching activities as well as the independent activities of physicians, lawyers, engineers, architects, dentists and accountants.'

This provision, with the omission of para 1(b) (the 183 days presence test) used to appear in the OECD MTC as well, but was deleted in 2000 on the grounds that it covered the same types of profits as those dealt with in Articles 5 and 7 and was therefore duplicating them, whilst causing confusion. Originally it had been thought that a distinction was needed between industrial and commercial profits (Articles 5 and 7) and the net income of professional persons (Article 14). However, because of the additional 183 days presence test which the UN MTC Article 14 provides and because of the lack of a services PE in the text of the OECD MTC itself, the UN MTC retains Article 14. Thus, if a state does not automatically tax an individual on the worldwide basis (on the grounds that he has become tax resident) after presence of 183 days in a tax year, then Article 14 enables the state the tax any profits from independent personal services supplied by that individual to its residents.

The 2011 version of the Commentary on the UN MTC offers wording so that the provisions of this Article can be included in Article 5 if states do not wish to have a separate article for independent personal services but wish to retain the 183-day test. There are many treaties in existence which do not include a general services provision in Article 5 but which do include an Article 14 with the 183-day test. In future negotiations, a developing state negotiating a tax treaty using the UN MTC will have a better chance of taxing at least some income from services provided by residents of the treaty partner state: even if the treaty partner will not agree to a services PE provision in Article 5, then because the UN MTC retains Article 14, the developing state may be able to put forward a stronger case for having that article included in the new treaty than if its provisions had been subsumed into Article 5 of the UN MTC.

Article 14 applies to 'a resident of a Contracting State' and this has caused difficulties in interpretation. Some treaties specify that Article 14 applies to individuals only, or to partnerships as well. In others, the term 'resident' is used and this can be interpreted applying to a partnership or even a company as well as to individuals. Different states have interpreted the Article differently. These kinds of arguments contributed to the OECD's decision to scrap Article 14.

The first test applied in Article 14 is whether or not the non-resident has a 'fixed base' in the other State. The concept of a 'fixed base' is not defined either by the OECD or the UN but is generally accepted as being equivalent to a fixed place of business. Some commentators think that the term denotes a more casual relationship between the FSP and the source state than the idea of a fixed place of business.

It seems likely that states which use the UN MTC in their treaty negotiations will continue either to keep Article 14 in their treaties or to incorporate its contents into Article 5.

---

1   Commentary on Article 5, para 9.

The services PE in the OECD Commentary

10.19   The text of the OECD MTC has never included any provision for a services PE and, as noted above, Article 14 was deleted in the year 2000. The Commentary to the 2008 version of the OECD MTC introduced new discussion of services, including wording for a services PE. This development is thought to have been controversial within the OECD, with some members keen to have such a provision within the MTC itself and others firmly opposed. Canada, stung by the decision in *R v Dudney*, is known to have been in favour of its inclusion.[1] In addition, some countries with strong dependencies in their domestic tax laws and treaty practices on services PEs have accepted observer status on the Committee on Fiscal Affairs within the OECD, which deals with tax treaty matters. In the period leading up to the 2008 update, Chile, India, China, Russia and South Africa had such status. India attained this status in 2006. These observer countries, in practice, are able to exert considerable pressure on the OECD.

The optional Article 5 provision provided by the OECD reads:

'Notwithstanding the provisions of paragraphs 1, 2 and 3, where an enterprise of a Contracting State performs services in the other Contracting State:

(a)   through an individual who is present in that other state for a period or periods exceeding in the aggregate 183 days in any twelve month period, and more than 50% of the gross revenues attributable to active business activities of the enterprise during this period or periods are derived from the services performed in that other state through that individual, or for a period or periods exceeding in the aggregate 183 days in any twelve month period, and these services are performed for the same project or for connected projects through one or more individuals who are present and performing such services in that other state

(b)   the activities carried on in that other state in performing these services shall be deemed to be carried on through a permanent establishment of the enterprise situated in that other state, unless these services are limited to those mentioned in paragraph 4 which, if performed through a fixed place of business, would not make this fixed place of business a permanent establishment under the provisions of that paragraph. For the purposes of this paragraph, services performed by an individual on behalf of one enterprise shall not be considered to be performed by another enterprise through that individual unless that other enterprise supervises, directs or controls the manner in which these services are performed by the individual.'[2]

The two tests set out in the Article are sometimes known as the 'key worker' and the 'large project' tests. Besides these tests which limit the right of the source state to assert the existence of a PE, the basic principles embodied in the provision are that:

1   For the source state to assert taxing rights, the services must be performed in that state; it is not enough that an enterprise happens to have a deemed services PE in that state. The location of the customer is irrelevant, such that even if the customer is in the state which wishes to assert the existence of a services PE, that state can only do so if the services are performed within its jurisdiction.[3]

2   By deeming a PE to exist, the source state is only permitted to tax the profits arising under Article 7 and hence on the net basis. Thus, final withholding taxes on payments for services will not be permitted where a treaty between the states includes the services PE provision. If withholding taxes are used, they must be refundable to the extent that they exceed the tax due under Article 7 principles. Failure to refund would give the FSP the right to invoke the non-discrimination article.

The two tests broadly equate to the provisions for the source state taxation of enterprise services contained in the UN MTC.

Where a PE arises due to a 'key worker', the individual concerned may be regarded as liable to taxation on his employment income in the source state under the employment article in the relevant treaty if present there for more than 183 days. The employer would be taxed on the net profits from the services contract with the customer. In arriving at the net profits, the salary paid to the key worker would be deductible so that there would be no double taxation in the source state.

Compliance and administration issues are expected to arise. Some authors have considered that tracking the number of days which employees spend in the other state will be problematic, although in the era of e-mail and computerized timesheets this ought not to be so. The main issue will be monitoring days spent in the other state on the requisite rolling 12-month basis and this appears to be a fairly straightforward add-on to the software which processes employee timesheets. Admittedly, the rolling 12-month monitoring will be more onerous for smaller enterprises and self-employed individuals.

---

1   5th Protocol (2007) to the United States–Canada Double Tax Treaty 1980.
2   Paragraph 42.23 of the Commentary.
3   This need for the services to be performed in the taxing state is also set out at greater length in para 42.31 of the Commentary.

Who is affected if a treaty contains an OECD-style services PE?

10.20   The provision deals with the taxation of 'an enterprise of a Contracting State'. The term 'enterprise' is not defined, but from the examples given in the OECD Commentary, it is clear that 'enterprise' in this context will include sole traders, partnerships and companies.

The position where a partnership is regarded as a transparent fiscal entity by one Contracting State but not the other is not dealt with. This could give rise to problems as illustrated in Example 10.2.

Example 10.2

A & B are in a partnership established in State X, which regards the partnership as opaque. B is present in State Y for 190 days, delivering services. State Y regards the partnership as fiscally transparent. The activities of B account for 60 per cent of the partnership's active business profits earned by B but only 40 per cent of the total active business profits of the partnership. If the DTT between X and Y does not deal specifically with entity recognition issues, then State Y could assert the existence of a services PE which would not be recognized by State X. At best, this might involve the partners in lengthy dispute-resolution procedures under the treaty; at worst it could result in double taxation. This could arise if State Y taxes B on his share of the profits of the partnership which were earned in State Y, but State X considers the profits to have been earned not by B but by the A& B partnership. State X, if it uses the credit method of double tax relief, would tax the entire profits of the partnership but might refuse to give double tax relief for the State Y tax on the grounds that State Y had not taxed the partnership.

'Key worker' test

10.21   Part (a) (the key worker test) identifies a services PE where more than 50 per cent of business revenues are accounted for by the provision of services by an individual present in the other Contracting State for more than 183 days. In applying the 50 per cent test, the OECD uses the term 'gross revenues attributable to active business activities' which it defines as being what the enterprise has charged or should charge for its active business activities, regardless of timing of the billing. Again, the term is defined by excluding what it is not – it excludes income from passive investment activities. The OECD Commentary offers some alternative formulations of the key worker test. Contracting States could use a limit of 50 per cent of business profits or simply apply the services PE provisions where services represent the most important part of the business activities of the enterprise. Several commentators have noted that the '50 per cent of gross revenues' part of the test may potentially disadvantage a smaller enterprise as illustrated in Example 10.3 below.

Example 10.3

Firm 1 has 300 employees and gross revenues attributable to active business of $4 million. It sends an employee to State X for 200 days to perform services on a series of unconnected projects, each lasting 50 days, with a total invoice value of $250,000.

Firm 2 has 5 employees and gross revenues attributable to active business of $480,000. It sends an employee to State X for 200 days to perform services on a series of unconnected projects, each lasting 50 days with a total invoice value of $250,000

Firm 2 has a deemed services PE under the 'key worker' test, whilst Firm 1 does not. Neither does Firm 1 have a deemed services PE under the 'large project' test, because the projects are not connected.

Paragraph 42.34 of the Commentary reveals that the OECD expects the 'key worker' test to apply primarily to enterprises carried on by a single individual. The test provides a measure of consistency in treatment of individuals in business on their own account and individuals who are employees and subject to the provision of Article 15, para 2(a). Nevertheless, the theoretical lack of equity demonstrated in Example 10.3 may assume greater importance as practical experience with the new provision is built up.

There is a requirement to compute the amount of the enterprise's gross active business revenues for the period for which the individual is providing services in the other Contracting State. Assuming the OECD proves correct in its belief that the key worker test will apply mainly to sole proprietors, this requirement may place a heavy accounting burden on small enterprises in that they are unlikely to have accounts drawn up for precisely the period(s) spent abroad providing services. Arguably, the accounting burden under the key worker test is heavier than that under the large project test, because under the large project test the only accounting requirement is to identify the profits attributable to the provision of the services.

Questions concerning the OECD services PE provision

10.22 Two interesting questions which arise in connection with the 2008 update of the Commentary are:

1   Why was the wording for a services PE only included in the Commentary and not in the MTC itself?

2   Why did the OECD not simply adopt the tried and tested wording used in the UN MTC since 1980?

The answer to the first question seems to be that the longer standing members of the OECD and in particular, the US, were strongly opposed to the inclusion of the provision in the MTC itself. To include such a provision in the text of the MTC would provide a strong bargaining position for developing countries, as service importers, in their treaty negotiations. Concluding a treaty with a services PE transfers part of the tax base of the developed state (the service exporter) to the developing state (the service importer). It is possible, if rather unlikely, that some more far-sighted participants in the development of the 2008 amendments to the OECD MTC might have realized that a services PE in the text of the MTC might, in the future, work to their disadvantage as they move from the status of service importer to service exporter as part of the development process, capitalizing on their comparative advantage in the provision of labour. Pijl (2008) believes that in addition to the desire to leave the rights to taxation of profits services in the MTC itself to the state of taxpayer residence, the location of the services PE provision in the Commentary reflects the OECD's view that the PE threshold has reached its limits. Pijl also sees the inclusion of the services PE in the OECD Commentary as a response to the deletion in 2000 of Article 14 (Independent Personal Services). States that particularly wish to have some provision in their treaties for independent personal services might, in the absence of any such provision in the OECD MTC, insist on the use of the UN MTC, which retains such a provision, albeit as an alternative formulation but also awards greater taxing rights to the source state in respect of royalties and 'other income'.

MEANING OF 'SAME OR CONNECTED PROJECTS'

10.23 Both the UN provision and the optional provision put forward by the OECD require an interpretation of what is meant by 'connected contracts'. All the MTC Tax Conventions have used this concept for many years in the context of construction PEs so that there has been relatively little debate on it in the context of the services PE. The Commentary, with respect to the deemed services provision, refers back to general material on the topic (at paras 5.3 and 5.4). In these paragraphs, the principle that to be connected, projects must constitute a coherent whole, commercially and geographically, is articulated. With respect to the services PE, the OECD Commentary notes that the term 'connected projects' refers to those which have a commercial coherence and that although any decision will rest on the facts and circumstances of the individual case, the following factors will normally be relevant:

1   whether the projects are covered by a single master contract;

2   where the projects are covered by different contracts, whether these were concluded with the same person or with related persons and whether the conclusion of the additional contracts would reasonably have been expected when concluding the first contract;

3   whether the nature of the work involved under the different projects is the same;

4   whether the same individuals are performing the services under the different projects.[1]

Example 10.4

The Technical Explanation to the US–Canada treaty (which contains a provision similar to the OECD services PE) gives the example of a technology consultant who is contracted to install a particular computer system for a client and also to provide training for that client's personnel on a different computer system. There would be geographic coherence but not commercial coherence, although this conclusion might be influenced by how closely the two computer systems in question were connected. For instance, a consultant could be retained to install a new suite of payroll software. Following immediately on from this, he could be required to train the same client's personnel on the use of that software. It is likely these would be viewed as 'same or connected'. On the other hand, if the training was on the use of software for controlling machines used in manufacture then there would likely be two separate projects.

---

1   OECD Commentary at para 42.41.

BASIS OF TAXATION

10.24   Assuming that a state decides to tax non-resident FSPs, it must decide on what basis. Will it tax the non-resident on profits from services performed within its borders, or will it tax on some other basis, eg profits from services sold to its residents, or used by its residents? In technical terms, we need to ask: what is the source rule?

Place of performance of the services

10.25   The OECD firmly believes that non-resident FSPs should only be taxed on profits from services provided in the host state. Paragraph 42.18 of the Commentary sets out that all member states agree that a state should not have source taxation rights on income from services which are performed by a non-resident outside that state. Income from services rendered outside a state for services rendered to that state's residents are considered analogous to income from sales to residents of that state by a non-resident supplier. The concept of economic allegiance upon which the source principle is founded requires more than the fact of a resident customer in order to permit taxation of the income of the non-resident.[1] Place of performance, as a test for whether or not profits from services are taxable by a particular state, has the merit of being easily proven. It is a simple question of fact as to whether a person was present in the customer state on a particular date or not. However, it is a rather crude test of the source of profits from services. It is quite possible that a FSP resident in State A could travel to State B for, say, one month. During that month, he could be providing services to a resident of State B. In order to provide those services, he might be relying heavily on back-up from colleagues still present in State A and on databases located at his firm's offices in State A. So a high proportion of the value of the services provided could be said to come from State A. If State B taxes services income on the net profits basis, this is not too much of a problem, because in computing the profits attributable to the services, deductions could be made for the cost of inputs from State A located staff and facilities. But if State B charges a simple withholding tax on the gross amount charged for the services, no deductions could be made and it could be argued that place of performance is not wholly satisfactory as a means of allocating the right to tax.

---

1   However, note India has sought to tax income from services on the basis of utilization of services in India in circumstances where services were not rendered in India.

Location where services are utilized

10.26   Some states, eg India, tax FSPs on profits from services they provide which are utilized in India, regardless of where those services are performed or of the location of the person paying for them. Thus, a UK FSP performing consultancy services in China on behalf of an Indian firm would technically be liable to tax in India. However, the Indian Government would find this tax virtually impossible to enforce: First, it has to know about the arrangements. Second, if the payment is not being made from India there is little it can do to physically collect the tax. However, if the payment is being made from India, eg by the Indian firm, then the Indian Government can, subject to the rules contained in the UK–India DTT, collect tax by imposing a withholding tax on the payment made to the UK FSP. Taxing services according to where they are utilized normally means that the customer deducts withholding tax on the payment to the FSP. This is sometimes known as a 'base erosion' approach. If the Indian customer pays the UK FSP, it will claim a tax deduction against its Indian taxable profits, reducing the tax revenues paid to the Indian Government. This causes the tax base upon which India can charge taxes (taxable profits of the Indian firm) to be reduces (or to erode). Imposing a withholding tax on the UK FSP compensates the Indian Government for the tax reduction enjoyed by the Indian customer and negates the base erosion.

A base erosion approach: the place of payment

10.27 This approach is the simplest to administer: if a resident pays a non-resident FSP then the customer state reserves the right to tax that non-resident FSP. The location of the customer is generally relatively easy to determine, although special rules may be needed if that customer has PEs in other countries that are involve in the purchase of the services.

Using the place of payment as the basis of taxation (ie as a 'source rule') gives symmetry in the tax treatment of the payment for the services: the payer is granted a tax deduction, whilst the recipient is taxed. In this way, the customer country's tax base is protected from the base erosion which would occur if a tax deduction had to be granted to the payer, but without the right to tax the foreign recipient.

Since the FSP might not have any physical or other type of presence in the customer country, the only practical way to enforce tax on the FSP is to oblige the customer to withhold tax from the payment.

SERVICES IN 'CONSTRUCTION' PEs

10.28 Article 5.3 of the OECD MTC reads:

> 'A building site or construction or installation project constitutes a permanent establishment only if it lasts more than twelve months.'

The UN MTC includes in the definition of a permanent establishment:

> 'a building site, a construction, assembly or installation project or supervisory activities in connection therewith, but only if such site, project or activities last more than six months.'

Installation or assembly projects consist largely of the provision of services. A construction project will usually consist of a contract to supply a bundle of goods and services. A typical contract might be for the supply of a building and would consist of the supply of the building materials and the labour to design and build. There is a category of contracts known as turnkey contracts. In these, the contract is to supply a commercial facility, for instance, a manufacturing or processing plant complete with all machinery and fitments such that all the customer needs to do to commence operations in the facility is to 'turn the key' to open the building and start using it. In such projects, it is often more difficult to identify the component parts than in a less comprehensive contract. Difficulties can arise if the host state levies a withholding tax on technical service fees and considers that part of the contract price is accounted for by such services.

The OECD MTC provides that a building site or construction or installation project will constitute a PE if it lasts for more than 12 months. Such projects normally contain a high proportion of services provision.

The rationale for the distinct time period required for a construction PE compared with the very general guidance on that required for a more general 'fixed place of business' PE is not made explicit. The OECD position seems to be that the construction PE is an exception to the rules governing a fixed place of business PE, in that it cannot come into existence until the specific time period has been breached. The UN position seems to be that it is a deeming provision: a PE can arise in connection with construction activities whether or not there is a fixed place of business if the time threshold is breached. The discussion in the Commentary on the OECD MTC (also adopted for the purposes of the UN MTC) on Article 5 (at para 6) as to the temporal requirements for the fixed place of business PE under para 5.2 suggests that to be regarded as fixed, a place of business should be at the disposal of an enterprise for six months. This time period is derived from a review of the practices of OECD members in asserting the existence of a PE. This part of the Commentary is by no means prescriptive as to the period of time required to attain the degree of permanence necessary to give rise to a taxable presence. The Commentary on the UN MTC on construction PEs does discuss the minimum time period adopted, which is six months in the UN MTC and which is consistent with the UN services PE time period. The UN Commentary states that:

> 'the idea behind the time limit is that business enterprises of one Contracting State should be encouraged to initiate preparatory or ancillary operations in the other Contracting State without becoming immediately subject to the tax of the latter state, so as to facilitate a more permanent and larger commitment at a later stage.'[1]

It is possible for a multinational group to split up a construction contract between several of its wholly-owned subsidiaries so that none of them breach the time limit for a construction (or services) PE. The OECD, in its Final Report on BEPS Action 6 (Prevent Treaty Abuse) identifies this practice as an abuse of the treaty concerned. If the two countries concerned have incorporated into their tax treaty with each other, general anti-abuse rules (the so-called 'principal purposes test', discussed in Chapter 15) then the customer country is within its rights to tax the net profits of all the subsidiaries amongst whom the contract has been split, even though none of them have breached the time limit that would bring a PE into existence.

Unlike the UN MTC, the OECD MTC does not include supervisory services in its definition of a construction PE in the text of the MTC. However, the Commentary, at para 17, indicates that states may wish to include them specifically, although according to the Commentary they are covered by para 3 anyway. The point of doing so is that they are definitely covered by the construction PE provisions, rather than by the general 'fixed place of business' provisions. Thus a subcontractor supplying supervisory services to a construction or installation site would not need a fixed place of business to have a PE but would need to be present in the other Contracting State for the minimum specified period of 12 months.

The question of what is to be defined as a 'building site or construction or installation project' PE and what must be defined as a PE on first principles is partially addressed by para 17. This brings renovations into the definition but provides that they must involve more than mere maintenance or redecoration. A further clarification was offered in the 2002 Report (para 81) which stated that it is the project as a whole that must be considered in the context of construction and installation. Thus constructing, say, an oil platform at different locations within a state and then installing one at a further location within that state would constitute a single project within that state.

It is possible for a PE to arise where an enterprise has no physical presence in the state where the construction or installation takes place. A main contractor might subcontract the whole of a project to another enterprise and have no employees or on-site presence of its own. Paragraph 19 of the Commentary states that the period spent by a subcontractor working on the building site must be considered as time spent by the main contractor on that project. Thus if the project exists beyond the time threshold stipulated in the treaty, the main contractor enterprise could find itself liable to taxation on the source principle on the net profits arising to it from the contract. The OECD 2011 Report on Article 5 recommends that the Commentary should make it clear that an enterprise which subcontracts an entire construction or installation project would have a construction PE in the same way as if the construction services had been supplied by its own staff. Hence it would be possible for an enterprise to have a construction PE without any of its own staff having been physically present in the host state, provided that the activities of the subcontractor were such that a PE arose according to the usual tests of fixed place of business and minimum time period. If the subcontractor firm itself is resident outside the state where the construction site is located, then the subcontractor firm could also have a PE in the construction site state. The main contractor would be taxable on the source principle on the profits made from the construction site, after deduction of expenses which would include amounts paid to the subcontractor. The subcontractor firm would be taxable on the source principle on the amounts received from the main contractor less deductible expenses.

Whether or not construction projects are connected, so that they should be amalgamated for the purpose of seeing if the time limit has been breached, is examined at para **10.23**. The same principle of 'same or connected project' applies both to construction PEs and services PEs.

---

1   It should be noted that the UN Commentary on the construction PE also records the reluctance of some members of the group of experts to include any time limit at all, on the grounds that such a limit would give rise to practices whereby tax could be evaded in the source state through manipulation of activities to stay within the limit.

INSURANCE SERVICES

10.29   The UN MTC includes a special PE provision in respect of insurance activities:

> '6. Notwithstanding the preceding provisions of this article, an insurance enterprise of a Contracting State shall, except in regard to re-insurance, be deemed to have a permanent establishment in the other Contracting State if it collects premiums in the territory of that other State or insures risks situated therein through a person other than an agent of an independent status to whom paragraph 7 applies.'

The reason for the inclusion of this provision is the ease with which a non-resident insurance company can establish a considerable client base in the source state through the activities of persons representing the foreign insurer on a part-time basis. The UN MTC Commentary on Article 5(6) records that it was thought that this could lead to difficulties in distinguishing between dependent and independent agents. Whilst the OECD MTC does not contain any specific provision for insurance services, para 39 of the Commentary acknowledges the potential problem with insurance business – that 'it is conceivable that these companies do large-scale business in a state without being taxed in that state on their profits arising from such business' (para 39). The Commentary goes on to suggest that a provision along the lines of that in the UN MTC could be adopted depending on the factual and legal situation prevailing in the Contracting States.

The reasoning expressed in the Commentary on the UN MTC on this point proved prescient in the light of major cases which later arose concerning the provision of insurance by US insurance enterprises to Canadian customers.[1] In one case,[2] although the court rejected the suggestion that the absence of a specific provision for insurance business along the lines of that in the UN MTC meant that the US and Canada must have been content with the fact that large-scale insurance business could be conducted in the other state without a PE arising, the judge stated that the only way for one state to tax the profits of insurance business conducted in that state by an enterprise of the other state via independent agents was for the treaty to be amended accordingly.[3]

---

1 *American Income Life Insurance Company v Canada* 2008 TCC 306 Tax Court of Canada, reported at (2008) 11 ITLR 52 and *Knights of Columbus v R* 2008 TCC 307 Tax Court of Canada, reported at (2008) 10 ITLR 827.
2 *American Income Life Insurance Company* (2008) 11 ITLR 52.
3 At 79.

ROYALTIES OR TECHNICAL SERVICE FEES?

10.30   The distinction between royalties and technical service fees is very important because, in many treaties, royalty payments may be subject to withholding tax on the gross amount. If services are included in the definition of royalties, then payments for services may attract the same withholding taxes as royalties. It is important to note that a state can only charge the withholding taxes specified in a DTT if their domestic tax laws also allow for them. For instance, the UK has entered into a number of tax treaties which permit withholding tax on the gross amount of service fees, but would not charge any withholding tax because there is no provision for this in UK domestic law. However, the treaty partner state probably does have provision in its domestic law. The general principle to remember is that a DTT can only improve the position of a taxpayer, not make it worse.

Although the recent versions of the OECD MTC do not permit any withholding tax on royalties, many treaties in existence do so. The UN MTC also still permits withholding tax on royalties. Article 12(2) of the OECD MTC Treaty defines royalties to mean:

> '... payments of any kind received as a consideration for the use of, or the right to use, any copyright of literary, artistic or scientific work including cinematograph films, any patent, trade mark, design or model, plan, secret formula or process, or for information concerning industrial, commercial or scientific experience.'

The last two legs of the definition ('any patent....') give rise to some boundary issues in the delineation of payments which are royalties and those which are payments in respect of services. Paragraph 10.2 of the Commentary on Article 12 explains that in order for a payment to be classed as a royalty, the intellectual property in question must exist prior to the making available of the design, model, etc, or to the imparting of the know-how. If a payment is in respect of the development or amendment of a model, plan, secret formula or process or for work which will result in the gaining of information concerning industrial, commercial or scientific experience, then there will be difficulties in asserting that such a payment constitutes royalties. This is so even if the developer contracts so as to retain all rights in the intellectual property once developed. The analysis presented in the Commentary is that the act of development constitutes a service.

Know-how presents particular problems as it constitutes intellectual property which has not been formally recognized, say, as a patent or trade mark and is a relatively amorphous asset.[1] The Commentary makes it clear[2] that Article 12 can only apply to the making available of prior knowledge, rather than the development of new knowledge. In practice, the dividing line may not be clear cut: Example 10.5 illustrates a possible scenario.

Example 10.5

If an enterprise sends an operative expert in the application of a certain piece of software to assist and provide training to a client, then it is reasonable to expect that the operative's store of knowledge might increase with each client visited. For instance, the enterprise might have developed the software for use in the overground railway sector but might send the operative to assist a client in its use in an integrated transport system. Technically, payments in respect of the operative' services ought to be apportioned between those relating to the imparting of knowledge already possessed and that gained as a result of advising a client in a slightly different business. The agreement between the enterprise and the client is that all knowledge imparted by the operative remains unrevealed to the public. This confidentiality clause would strengthen the case for all the payments to be regarded as being for know-how but it is quite possible that the client's state would not take this view. The enterprise providing the expertise faces tax uncertainty.

The distinction between a contract for use of know-how and a contract for the provision of services often rests on who carries out the work. In a contract for know-how, the client himself usually carries out the work, using secret information imparted to him by the know-how provider. In a services contract, it is the FSP who carries out the work for the client. However, this distinction[3] ignores the situation where know-how provider and client work together to apply a formula or to implement an industrial process. Paragraph 11.3 of the Commentary on Article 12 offers some criteria for use in distinguishing between services and know-how contracts:

1   To be know-how, the supply must be of information which already exists or which will exist, following its development. The Commentary does not explicitly state that payments which are in respect of the development of information cannot be know-how. In all cases, to be classed as know-how there must be specific provisions as to the confidentiality of the information supplied.

2   In contracts which are for services, rather than know-how, the supplier performs services using his special knowledge, skill and expertise, but does not transfer this knowledge, skill or expertise to the client.

3   The degree of involvement and contact with the client may be indicative of the type of contract: a contract for the making available of know-how would consist merely of the supply of existing information, necessitating little expenditure by the supplier in order to fulfil the contract. A supply of services, on the other hand, would require a much greater level of expenditure by the supplier: for instance, wages, payments to sub-contractors or value of his own time in research, design and testing.

Although these criteria are helpful they do not reflect the reality that know-how is likely to have to be adapted to the needs of each client, so that many contracts are mixed in terms of supply of know-how and services. The only example of mixed contracts considered in the Commentary is that of franchising and the advice offered is to split the contract, treating part of the consideration as payment for know-how and part as payment for services. The ancillary/subsidiary supply analysis is used in the case of payments which are mainly for one type of supply.

The Commentary gives some examples of payments which are to be considered as being made for services:

1   as consideration for after-sales service;

2   rendered by a seller to purchaser under a warranty;

3   for pure technical assistance;

4   for a list of potential customers, when developed specifically for the payer from generally available information (a list developed from confidential information would constitute a payment for know-how);

5   for an opinion given by an engineer, an advocate or an accountant; or

6   for advice provided electronically, for electronic communication with technicians or for accessing through computer networks, a troubleshooting database such as a database that provides users of software with non-confidential information in response to frequently asked questions or common problems that arise frequently.

Confidentiality is a recurring theme but cannot, of itself, characterize a payment as being for know-how. Perhaps a better characterization is that know how must be capable of being sold to multiple customers in the same or similar form. Even so, the position is unclear. Would a tax-planning scheme sold to multiple clients, each sworn to secrecy and with minimal tailoring to the needs of each client count as 'information concerning commercial experience'? The most objective criteria for making the distinction between payments for the use of know-how and payments for services is that know-how exists before anything is done for, or passed on to the client, ie it already exists. However, it is thought that India and some other important non-OECD states do not agree with this criteria, believing that know-how can be created during the provision of services.

Where the source state has levied a withholding tax on payments which it considers to be made for the use of intellectual property, double tax relief by credit will only be available to the recipient if his own tax authority also believes that the payment was made in respect of the use of intellectual property. The DTT between the two states will contain a definition of intellectual property but not in any detail. For example, under its domestic law, State A may consider that know-how includes a particular type of expert service supplied by P Ltd, a resident of State B to Q Ltd, a resident of State A. The DTT between State A and State B authorizes a withholding tax of 10 per cent on royalties. The problem comes when State B examines the receipt and determines that, under the domestic law of State B, the payment by Q Ltd was not made in respect of the use of intellectual property and is not therefore covered by the royalties article of the DTT. In these circumstances it might well refuse to give double tax relief for the withholding tax.

As well as the importance of the distinction between payments for intellectual property and payments for services for withholding tax purposes, the distinction is also important for transfer pricing purposes (see Chapter 13). In arriving at the price which an unconnected party would have been prepared to pay, the appropriate method for payments for services would usually be costs plus a profit margin. In contrast, the appropriate method in relation to payments for the use of intellectual property, ie a royalty, would usually be a method based on the extent of the use of the intellectual property, a so-called turnover method. In practice, this transfer pricing issue is often of more concern than the withholding tax issue.

---

1 Know-how is by no means the only type of intellectual property to lack formal recognition such as registration – marketing intangibles, for instance, are gaining widespread recognition.
2 At paragraph 11, Commentary on Article 12.
3 Paragraphs 11.1–11.2 of the Commentary on Article 12.

INTERACTION OF ARTICLES CONCERNING SERVICES

10.31 If the relevant DTT contains a services PE then the income and profits arising in respect of the services PE are dealt with under the business profits article, ie the host state can only tax the net profits from the services activity.

If the treaty does not contain a services PE provision then payments for services to non-residents are vulnerable to withholding taxes on the gross amount.

However, even where there is a deemed services PE provision in the relevant DTT, if a state's domestic law permits withholding tax on the gross basis on payment for service fees there is still a risk that this withholding tax will be applied. The starting point in the business profits article is that the host state may only tax business profits of an enterprise resident in the other state to the extent that they arise from a PE located in the host state. There are two sets of circumstances in which a deemed services PE will not necessarily result in taxation of service fees on the net basis by the host state. First, paragraph 4 of Article 7 in the OECD MTC states that where profits include items of income which are dealt with separately in other articles then the provisions of those articles take precedence over Article 7. Hence if there is provision for taxation of service fees on a gross basis, say, within the royalties article, then service fees will be dealt with under the royalties article, which may well allow withholding tax on the gross basis. Second, even in the absence of specific provision for the tax treatment of service fees elsewhere in the treaty, if the business profits article does not contain a definition of business profits (and most treaties do not) then it is open to the host state to assert that the service fees are not business profits.[1] If the fees are not 'business profits', then the rules of Article 7 do not apply to them and the rules of any other relevant article will apply. If no article deals specifically with service fees, then in these circumstances, they would fall into the residual 'other income' article. In the OECD MTC, 'other income' may only be taxed by the state in which the beneficial owner is a resident, but the UN MTC modifies this so that 'other income' arising in one of the Contracting States may be taxed by that state. This is the position historically taken by Brazil, whose treaties are based on the UN MTC, as justification for levying withholding tax at 25 per cent on outbound payments for services.[2] The Brazilian treatment is significant in that Brazil is a key market for international FSPs, but rather unusual in that Brazil, until recently, afforded treaty law equal status with domestic law and also, in its domestic law, did not consider technical service fees to constitute business profits.

---

1   The OECD MTC does not contain any definition of business profits: the Commentary on Article 7, at para 4, states that:
'Although it has not been found necessary in the Convention to define the term "profits", it should nevertheless be understood that the term when used in this Article and elsewhere in the Convention has a broad meaning including all income derived in carrying on an enterprise.'
2   *Ato Declaratório (Normativo)* COSIT No 1, January 5, 2000, which has been challenged in a succession of recent cases, including *Union (National Treasury) v Copesul – CIA/Petroquímica do Sul* No 2002.71.00.006530–5/RS.

FURTHER READING

Arnold, B J (2008) 'The new services permanent establishment rule in the Canada–United States tax convention', in Globalization and the Impact of Tax on International Investment: a Symposium in Honour of the Late Alex Easson, Queen's University, Kingston, Ontario.

Arnold, B J (2008) *The New Services Permanent Establishment Rule in the Canada-United States Tax Convention* (Queens University Ontario).

Arnold, B J (2010) 'The Taxation of Income from Services under Tax Treaties: Clearing up the Mess – Expanded Version', 65, *Bulletin for International Taxation*.

Arnold, B J (2013) Note on a New Article of the UN Model Convention Dealing With the Taxation of Fees for Technical and Other Services, E/C.18/2013/CRP.5. Available at: www.un.org/esa/ffd/tax/ninthsession/CRP5_Services.pdf.

Brown, C (2010), 'Strangers in a Strange Land: The Taxation of Services in a Global Economy', *Australian Tax Review*, 39 (2 May).

European Parliament (2015) Economic Significance of Trade in Services – Background to negotiations on a Trade in Services Agreement (TiSA). Available at: www.europarl.europa.eu/thinktank/en/document.html?reference= EPRS_IDA(2015)549000.

Farrell, J (2013) *The Interface of International Trade Law and Taxation*, IBFD Doctoral Series.

Hoekman, B and Mattoo, A (2007), 'International Trade: Trade in Services', in A T Guzman, and A O Sykes, eds *Research Handbook in International Economic Law*, Cheltenham: Edward Elgar.

International Fiscal Association (2012) *Taxation of Enterprise Services*, Cahiers De Droit, Vol 97a.

Kirsch, M S (2010) 'The Role of Physical Presence in the Taxation of Cross-border Personal Services', *Boston College Law Review*, 51.

OECD, '2002 Reports Related to the OECD Model Tax Convention' (Paris 2002).

OECD (2005) 'Are the Current Treaty Rules for Taxing Business Profits Appropriate for E-commerce?' Paris: OECD.

OECD, 8 December (2006), 'The Tax treatment of Services: Proposed Commentary Changes', Public Discussion Draft.

Pijl, H (2008) 'The OECD Services Permanent Establishment Alternative' *European Taxation*, September 2008.

United Nations (2001) 'Model Double Taxation Convention between Developed and Developing Countries', (Department of Economic and Social Affairs, New York).

United Nations (2015) 'Revised Draft Article XX and Commentary, United Nations Model Tax Convention, Article XX – Fees for Technical and Other Services' Paper E/C.18/2015/CRP.5. ('The United Nations Model Tax Convention Article XX – Fees for Technical and Other Services' © 2015 United Nations is reprinted with the permission of the United Nations.)

Chapter 11

Structuring a Foreign Expansion

BASICS

11.1 Before starting to study this topic, it is vital to recognize that if an enterprise has business operations in more than one country, it may make profits and pay tax in more than one country. The owners of the enterprise (assume these are the shareholders) are mainly concerned about the after-tax total global profits of the enterprise. The tax authorities of the countries in which the enterprise is operating will only be concerned with taxing the profits attributable to any branch or subsidiary which the enterprise has in that country. This is known as 'the entity principle'.

The entity principle provides opportunities for tax planning within multinational enterprises (MNEs), which usually take the form of a group of companies and possibly also other types of entities such as partnerships. In crude terms, the MNE will wish to maximize global profits, whilst minimizing global tax liabilities; although obviously other considerations come into play, such as long-term structural robustness and other legal and regulatory requirements. Tax planning may entail simply making use of beneficial tax rules, for example concessions, made available in many countries to attract investment. Another way of achieving this aim is to plan so that the MNE's profits for tax purposes are attributed, wherever possible within the bounds of the relevant legislation, to lower tax countries. Yet another way of achieving the same aim is to *exploit* differences in the tax systems of the countries in which the enterprise is operating. This is known as 'tax arbitrage'.

11.2 A company wishing to expand overseas must decide whether it wants to set up a separate subsidiary or whether the foreign operations will be a branch of the existing company. This choice can have an effect on the tax treatment of the business profits or losses from the overseas operations, in both the home country and the new country.

Branches are generally treated as an integral part of the head office entity and, as such, are not treated as separate taxpayers in the home country. This means that the country where the head office entity is located will seek to tax the branch profits as part of that entity's profits if it operates a worldwide approach to international tax. A subsidiary, on the other hand, is usually treated as a separate legal and taxpaying entity, and the country of residence of the parent company does not generally have the right to tax the profits of the subsidiary directly; only to tax dividends and other payments made from the subsidiary to the parent.

One important consideration is losses. If a branch makes a loss, it will generally be accounted for by the head office entity for the purposes of taxing the head office in its country of residence. If a subsidiary makes a loss, it usually cannot be utilised by the parent company, although some countries choose to allow for this.

The choice between branch and subsidiary is also important from a finance perspective. For a subsidiary, but not a branch, there is a choice between financing through equity (share capital) or debt (intra-group loans) as discussed in Chapter 12.

CHOOSING THE BUSINESS STRUCTURE

11.3   A key issue when deciding how to structure a new foreign venture is whether to set it up as a branch of the parent company, or as a separate subsidiary. These are by no means the only choices – foreign ventures can be structured as partnerships or joint ventures of various types as well. For simplicity, we will use the term 'parent and subsidiary' to denote two entities that have separate legal status and one of which (the subsidiary) is owned by the other (the parent). We will use the terms 'head office' and 'branch' to denote two entities in different jurisdictions that are not formally separate from one another, for example a company in one country with a permanent establishment (branch) in another.

The choice of vehicle is often influenced by the variety of rules found in different countries as to which types of legal entity are recognized there for tax purposes, and which are considered transparent. For instance, if a partnership arrangement is considered transparent, the effect will be that the foreign government will tax the partners (usually two or more companies) as if they each had separate PEs.

The alternative to transparent is 'opaque'. If a tax authority considers the partnership or joint venture to be a taxable entity in its own right, ie opaque, then it will levy tax on the partnership or joint venture rather than on the individual partners. Besides the choice of various types of partnership arrangement, firms operating within the EU may opt for the EU corporate vehicle, the Societas Europaea (see Chapter 20). However, for the purposes of this chapter the discussion will be limited to a choice between a branch structure and a subsidiary company structure.

Structuring: using a foreign branch

11.4   As we saw in Chapter 9, a branch is a PE that generally confers taxing rights on the country where the branch is located, according to the source principle. A branch is, in fact, the least controversial of the types of PE since it is universally accepted as being a physical presence sufficient to attract tax, and a company setting up a branch will usually do so with the clear understanding that the profits of the branch will fall to be taxed in the country of its location.

The most significant thing to note about a branch is that it is generally not a separate legal entity, and remains part of the head office company which establishes it. This has important consequences for tax purposes. If the country of residence of the company that establishes a branch operates a worldwide system, and therefore taxes all profits of the company wherever earned, the profits of the branch will fall to be taxed as part of the company's overall taxable income in the country of residence. The tax charge would be on an arising basis: the residence country of the head office would not wait for profits to be transferred from one country to another. In this situation, it will be usual for the country of residence to allow a credit for any tax paid in the host country in respect of the branch profits. On the other hand, if the head office residence country operates a territorial system so that foreign income is generally exempted, then this might also apply to branch profits. For instance, in 2011, the UK extended its exemption from corporation tax for foreign income to encompass the income of foreign branches as well as dividends received from foreign subsidiaries. The branch exemption is optional (see para **11.21**).

We must also consider how losses are dealt with in the context of a branch. Given that a branch is usually considered to be part of the same entity as the head office, if a branch makes a loss, relief will be given for the loss immediately in the course of aggregating the company's income and profits for the purpose of worldwide residence taxation. This is often considered to be the key advantage of setting up a foreign operation by way of a branch.

In addition, because there is no change of legal ownership, the transfer of assets to and from a branch will generally not attract any capital taxes in either the home or host jurisdictions. Remittance of profits from the branch to the head office company will often also not attract tax in the country of source, again because the branch is not a separate entity. Some countries, however, make a special charge on remittances of branch profits on the grounds that, had a subsidiary company been used instead, they would have charged a withholding tax on the remittance of company profits to the shareholders made in the form of a dividend.

In many countries, there are either prohibitions on the use of branches by foreign corporations, or else such branches do not enjoy the full range of investment incentives that are offered to subsidiary companies. Before thinking about what would suit the investing company best from a tax viewpoint, it is vital to check what is allowed in the foreign country. It may transpire that the host country will only grant incentives to a subsidiary rather than to a branch. The purpose of requiring foreign companies to invest in the form of subsidiaries rather than branches is usually so that the taxing rights of the host country are clear and also, in some cases, to provide for minimum levels of local participation in shareholdings. Indeed, some countries only permit 50/50 joint venture arrangements, to ensure that they share fully in the wealth that is being created. As an example, India does not automatically permit the use of branches for manufacturing activities, insisting instead that the foreign company subcontract the work to Indian resident companies. India also places restrictions on the percentage of ownership by non-residents in subsidiaries of foreign companies. These limits vary from industry to industry, and there is a plethora of rules to negotiate.

Structuring: using a foreign subsidiary

11.5   While establishing a separate legal entity in the form of a subsidiary company may be necessary in order to access tax incentives offered by the host country, one consequence is that any losses will probably not be available for offset against the profits of the parent company for tax purposes. They will often be trapped within the subsidiary, although the host country may well provide some mechanism for relieving the losses (eg carry forward to later periods).

If the subsidiary is profitable, it will be subject to tax in the host country (the country of residence of the subsidiary), but as a general rule those profits will not be subject to tax in the hands of the parent company until such time as they are remitted, either as dividends or some other form of payment such as interest. This is because the parent company and the subsidiary are separate legal entities for tax purposes. This deferral of parent company tax on the foreign profits provides an advantage compared to a branch operation, and if the subsidiary is located in a jurisdiction with a lower tax rate than the parent company, it represents a tax saving for the worldwide group of companies. It is this deferral advantage that leads to the adoption of controlled foreign company rules, as we see in Chapter 17. Many countries, including the UK, exempt the dividends received by holding companies from their subsidiaries, although the US does not, instead granting double tax relief under the credit method. However, interest and royalties received by holding companies from their subsidiaries are usually taxable in the hands of the holding company, subject to double tax relief by credit.

If the parent company's country determines company tax residence according to central management and control (or a similar rule), then it is important that any foreign subsidiary is not only incorporated abroad, but also managed and controlled abroad. Otherwise, it may be fully taxable in the parent company's country.

A further advantage to using a foreign subsidiary rather than a branch is that many countries grant exemption from tax on the capital gains made by parent companies on the gains on sale of shares in subsidiary companies. The UK, for example, would grant substantial shareholding relief, subject to the usual conditions attaching to this relief.[1]

Example 11.1 demonstrates the difference between a branch and subsidiary where the parent company is located in a country that operates a credit system of double tax relief. The example assumes that the parent company country, Unitia, permits the offset of foreign branch losses against other profits of the investing company.

Example 11.1 Branch versus subsidiary

- Growco Ltd is a retailer of garden furniture. It currently operates solely in Unitia but is considering opening a shop in the country of Inistania. It has prepared budgets as follows for the first few years of the Inistanian operation. The Unitian operations of Growco Ltd are expected to produce taxable profits of €500,000 per annum over the next five years.

- The effective rate of corporation tax in Inistania is 20 per cent and there is a withholding tax of 5 per cent on payments of dividends and interest to overseas residents.

- The effective rate of Unitian corporation tax faced by Growco Ltd is 30 per cent. Unitia operates a credit system of double tax relief, and gives relief for underlying tax as well as withholding tax.

- If a subsidiary is chosen, a dividend of 50 per cent of available profits will be paid to Growco Ltd each year.

- The Inistanian government permits the carry forward of losses in subsidiaries but not branches.

	Year 1	Year 2	Year 3	Year 4	Year 5
Budgeted results of Inistanian operation					
	€000	€000	€000	€000	€000
Turnover	200	300	400	600	800
Costs of Inistanian shop	300	350	400	400	350
Loss/profit	−100	−50	0	200	450
Tax position of an Inistanian branch					
Loss/profit	−100	−50	0	200	450
Inistanian tax	0	0	0	40	90
Tax position of Growco Ltd with Inistanian branch					
Unitian profits	500	500	500	500	500
Deduct branch losses	−100	−50	0	0	0
Add: branch profits	0	0	0	200	450
Taxable Unitian profits	400	450	500	700	950
Unitian tax at 30%	120	135	150	210	285
Double tax relief (Inistanian profits at 20%)	0	0	0	−40	−90
Unitian tax to pay	120	135	150	170	195
Inistanian tax	0	0	0	40	90
Total global tax liability with a branch	120	135	150	210	285
Tax position of an Inistanian subsidiary					
Loss/taxable profits	−100	−50	0	200	450
Losses from previous years				−150	0
	−100	−50	0	50	450

	Year 1	Year 2	Year 3	Year 4	Year 5
Inistanian tax	0	0	0	10	90
Profits after tax	0	0	0	40	360
Divided declared	0	0	0	20	180
Tax position of Growco with Inistanian subsidiary					
Unitian taxable profits	500	500	500	500	500
Inistanian dividend before all Inistanian taxes	0	0	0	25	225
Total taxable profits	500	500	500	525	725
Unitian tax at 30%	150	150	150	157.5	217.5
Double tax relief:					
Withholding tax 5%	0	0	0	–1	–9
Underlying tax (50% of Inistanian corporation tax)	0	0	0	–5	–45
Unitian tax payable	150	150	150	151.5	163.5
Inistanian taxes	0	0	0	11	99
Total global tax liability with a subsidiary	150	150	150	162.5	262.5

In this example, global tax liabilities are less in Year 1 and Year 2 with a branch, but greater in Year 4 and Year 5. If a subsidiary is used, the reverse is true. Growco Ltd could have the best of both worlds by starting with a branch and converting it to a subsidiary at the end of Year 3. If no dividend is paid, there would be no tax liability in Unitia on the subsidiary's profits.

The calculations depend on the way in which Unitia deals with foreign branch profits and losses. In this example, we have assumed that Unitia gives relief for foreign branch losses, and then taxes foreign branch profits. However, many countries have rules that seek to treat the profits or losses of foreign branches in the same way as profits or losses of foreign subsidiaries. These countries (which now include the UK) have rules which have the effect of not granting loss relief for foreign branch losses, but not taxing foreign branch profits. Thus their tax systems are neutral in their treatment of the foreign operations, however they are structured.

Complications can arise when both countries permit relief for the branch losses and the parent company's country operates a system of double tax relief by exemption. It is possible that Inistania may permit the losses to be carried forward and set against future branch profits. If, instead of the credit method, Unitia operates a system of double tax relief by exemption, then the branch losses may have been offset against head office (Unitian) profits in the early years, and then against Inistanian profits when the branch becomes profitable in Year 4. If this happens, then Unitia may wish to have a provision in its DTT with Inistania to the effect that branch profits will not be exempt to the extent that branch losses have reduced Unitian taxable profits in previous years (a so-called 'loss recapture' rule).

We have also assumed that Inistania does not levy a branch profits tax. Some countries charge a withholding tax when branch profits are remitted to the head office country, thus treating all profit repatriations in the same way, whether they are by way of branch profits or dividends. The UK rules on the taxation of foreign branch profits and losses are examined in the 'Further study' section of this chapter.

---

1   Taxation of Chargeable Gains Act 1992 (TCGA 1992), Sch 8.

Converting a branch to a subsidiary

11.6   As we have seen, operating a foreign business through a branch often means immediate relief for losses, which will not usually be available if the business is operated through a subsidiary. If there is an expectation that losses will be incurred, for example during the initial years of the new business's operations, it may make sense to establish it as a branch in the first instance, with a view to converting it to a subsidiary as and when it becomes profitable. The consequences of such a conversion will depend on the specific rules of the country where the branch is located, but may attract capital gains or other taxes as it effectively involves the sale of a business to a new legal entity. There may also be restrictions on the capacity to transfer any branch losses carried forward into the new subsidiary.

Corporate inversions

11.7   In recent years, we have seen a growth in numbers of 'inversions' from both the US and the UK. This is a process by which a MNE relocates its holding company to another jurisdiction, and is also referred to as 'migration', or 're-domiciliation'. The overall aim is to divert foreign income away from the current holding company location to a lower tax location. Typically, shares in foreign subsidiaries will be transferred into the ownership of the new holding company. The location chosen for the new holding company will not only be low tax – crucially, it will also lack 'controlled foreign company' (CFC) rules – see Chapter 17. Bermuda and the Cayman Islands have been popular choices, as they do not tax overseas income. Thus the tax authority in the current holding company location is no longer able to tax the MNE's foreign income, except that earned directly by the resident company, nor can it tax foreign income indirectly by means of CFC rules. The best it can do is to try to impose exit charges on the sale of the shares in foreign subsidiaries to the new holding company. The US Treasury defines corporate inversion as:

> 'a transaction through which the corporate structure of a U.S.-based [MNE] … is altered so that a new foreign corporation, typically located in a low- or no-tax country, replaces the existing U.S. parent corporation as the parent of the corporate group.'

Inversions have a long history in the US, but arise for the same reasons, the desire to escape the clutches of the worldwide taxation of US-resident companies. In 2002, the Office of Tax Policy in the US Department of the Treasury issued a document analysing the tax policy implications of corporate inversions, following a significant increase in these transactions. The announcement of measures in the US to combat inversions slowed the rush that had started in 1998, and the threat of retrospective legislation caused some companies to halt the process of inversion. Rules introduced in 2004 now, in some cases, treat the inversion corporation as a domestic corporation for US tax purposes: for example, where the new holding company is resident in a tax haven or where the shareholders in the original US holding company hold a certain percentage of the shares in the new holding company.

Cooklin (2008) describes this phenomenon from a UK perspective:

> 'An inversion involves the insertion of a non-UK incorporated and non-UK tax resident company (Topco) on top of an existing UK parent group company (PLC). The shareholders in PLC transfer their PLC shares to Topco (or more typically PLC shares are cancelled and reissued to Topco) and Topco issues shares to former PLC shareholders in return. The result therefore is that Topco is sandwiched between PLC and former PLC shareholders.'

Although such an inversion will not have immediate tax consequences as far as individual companies within a group are concerned, it does pave the way for future restructuring in order to mitigate exposure to, in this case, UK tax. A number of UK companies have moved to Bermuda, including Hiscox and Omega. Others have moved to Luxembourg or the Republic of Ireland. The repeated reductions in the rates of UK corporation tax, together with the introduction of exemption for foreign dividends received by UK companies and the well-received recasting of the UK's CFC regime (see Chapter 17, 'Further study' section) have all helped to reduce the attraction of such moves. Indeed, the UK has been chosen as the preferred location by Ensco, a US multinational inverting away from the US.[1] Ensco prefers to refer to the change as a 're-domiciliation' rather than a corporate inversion, on the grounds that the move was not tax driven but was done primarily to improve its management efficiency.

---

1   Stuart Webber, 'Escaping the U.S. Tax System: From Corporate Inversions to Re-Domiciling' (2011) 63 Tax Notes International 273.

Host country considerations

11.8   These sections set out some choices for host countries in taxing investment in their countries by foreign companies.

Taxing branches of foreign companies

11.9   This section sets out the way in which a host country may tax branches of foreign entities (the term 'branch' is used here to mean a PE):

- The branch is normally subject to tax on its net trading profits and on any income from real or intangible property that the branch holds. A tax return is required and the usual payment dates and other rules apply. The branch must be registered with the tax authority of the host country.

- The host country tax rules might permit the branch to offset tax profits or losses against the tax profits or losses of any fellow group companies which are resident in the same country as the branch. Following the decision in *Marks & Spencer*[1] it is likely that, in an EU Member State, a branch of a foreign company could offset losses of fellow subsidiaries resident anywhere in the EU, but only according to the limitations set out in that case, namely that there must be no possibility of obtaining relief for the losses in the other EU country.

- Some countries levy a withholding tax on branch profits repatriated in addition to charging corporation tax when the profits are earned. For instance, France, the US and Canada all charge a 'branch profits tax', although they waive the right to do so under many of their DTTs. This practice is to put the remittance of branch profits on the same footing as the remittance, via a dividend, of profits from a subsidiary company.

- If the head office is in a country which has no DTT with the branch country, the rates of tax charged by the host country need not be as favourable as those charged to residents. However, where the head office and the branch are both located in EU Member States, such unfavourable treatment would likely constitute an infringement of the rights of the foreign company under the EU Treaty (see Chapter 20 for more detail).

- A branch is normally entitled to double tax relief if it has any foreign income or gains.

- Transfer pricing provisions (see Chapter 13) would apply to transactions between the branch, other parts of the company and all other companies with which the company is connected.

- The head office part of the company might have immediate access to branch tax losses, as the branch is part of the same legal entity. This is an important practical point, as many new business ventures often make losses in their early years of operation. Of course, this point depends on whether the head office country taxes overseas branch profits or whether it operates a territorial tax system so that branch profits are exempted.

- The branch may be liable to tax on capital gains on chargeable assets (eg land and buildings) which are used for the purposes of the branch trade. This rule features in the OECD Model Tax Convention, as discussed in Chapter 7.

- Payments of service charges, interest and royalties by the branch to the head office are governed by the OECD Commentary on the OECD Model Tax Convention, as discussed in Chapter 7.

- If a branch capital asset leaves the host country or ceases to be used for the trade, the host country might levy tax on the deemed capital gain on exit of the asset.

---

1   Case C-446/03 *Marks & Spencer Plc v David Halsey (HM Inspector of Taxes)*, ECJ, 13 December 2005.

Taxing subsidiaries of foreign parent companies

11.10   The treatment of a subsidiary of a foreign parent is as follows:

- The residence of the subsidiary will be determined according to the rules used in the host country and also in the head office country. It is important to ensure that the subsidiary is resident in, and is *only* resident in, the host country. For instance, if the parent country determines company residence according to the place of central management and control, it will be important to ensure this is located in the host country. Otherwise, the subsidiary company might be considered resident in the head office country as well as the host country. In this case, any applicable DTT would have to be consulted to see if there is a tie-breaker rule.

- Thin capitalization rules and normal transfer pricing rules apply.

- Depending on the location of the shareholders, there may be withholding tax charged on dividends, interest and royalties paid, according to the terms of any relevant DTT or provision of host country domestic law if no treaty exists.

Converting a branch into a subsidiary

11.11   The conversion of a branch into a subsidiary is often done a few years into the new venture, when it starts to become profitable. Having a branch to start with, whilst the venture is loss making, can be advantageous because, as we noted earlier, the losses may be automatically used in the parent's country. However, once the branch starts to make a profit, this will be fully taxable in the host country as profits arise. Depending on the system of double tax relief in the head office country, these profits may also be taxable on an arising basis in the head office country. If this is the case, the foreign company may prefer to convert the branch into a subsidiary so that the profits are only taxable in the head office country when remitted there, in the form of interest, royalties or dividends.

There may be tax consequences of the conversion both in the host (branch) country and in the head office country. When a branch is converted into a subsidiary, what happens from a legal perspective is that the foreign company (the head office) sells the branch assets to a new company, the new subsidiary.

Consequences of conversion

11.12 Such a sale might give rise to tax in the host country (the branch country) on the gains made. However, reliefs are often available, for instance, if a foreign company transfers the trade of its UK branch into a newly formed UK subsidiary, then this is treated as the sale by the foreign company of its UK trading assets to a new company, and the foreign company has ceased to trade in the UK. The UK tax system contains various tax reliefs aimed at encouraging the conversion of UK branches into UK subsidiaries. The provisions of the Corporation Tax Act 2010 (CTA 2010), ss 944–945 apply to the incorporation of a branch into a UK subsidiary such that:

- any tax losses being carried forward can be transferred to the new subsidiary;

- the branch is not treated as selling all its capital assets at market value (that would give rise to the recapture of tax depreciation allowances: a so-called 'balancing charge'). For tax purposes, the new subsidiary takes on the assets at their cost minus tax depreciation to the date of transfer; and

- although the entire trading stock is being sold to a connected company, this sale is treated as taking place at cost. This avoids an immediate taxable profit on the sale of the branch's entire trading stock.

Head office country tax consequences of conversion

11.13 The head office country may also consider that the conversion of a foreign branch into a foreign subsidiary can give rise to a charge to corporation tax on a capital gain, calculated as if the branch assets had been sold at full market value. This is because the assets of a company are being sold to a foreign company (the new subsidiary), and any future growth in value will be outside the scope of tax in the head office country. That country may, therefore, seek to tax the growth in value from the date of acquisition of an asset until the date it leaves its tax jurisdiction. The tax analysis of the transaction is shown below in Figure 11.1.

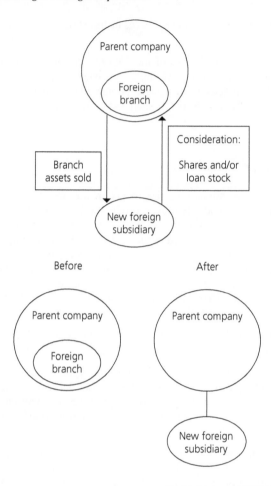

Figure 11.1

The exact treatment depends on the domestic law of the head office country, and also whether or not the head office and branch countries are EU Member States.

Entity characterization

11.14   Tax planning using entity characterization usually involves having a business unit (which we refer to as an 'entity') which is regarded as a corporation in one tax jurisdiction but in others it is regarded as something else (eg a branch or a partnership). The key point here is that a branch cannot pay, for example, interest to its head office, or vice versa, because a company cannot pay interest to itself. Having an interest payment made from an entity viewed as a company (a separate entity) in one country generally means that the payment will be regarded as valid for tax purposes and will thus be tax deductible.

If, however, the recipient's country views the payment as having come from within the same legal entity (eg from a branch to its head office), as opposed to coming from a separate legal entity, then the receipt may escape tax. This is because, in the same way that a company cannot pay interest to itself, it cannot receive interest from itself. Other planning involves the use of partnerships or quasi-partnerships and this type of planning is often set up to take advantage of the fact that some countries recognize partnerships as taxable entities in their own right, whilst others do not.

The characterization of an entity can affect the taxation of that entity under a double tax treaty (DTT). The low rates of withholding taxes on dividends are usually only extended to amounts paid by companies as dividends, not amounts paid by partnerships, which would have to pay the full domestic rate of withholding tax. Under domestic laws concerning foreign income, most countries will tax the profits of an interest in a foreign partnership or branch on an arising basis, whereas dividends will not be taxed until they are received by the investor. The type and extent of any foreign tax credit may also differ depending on whether the income is classified as business profits from a partnership, or a *quasi*-dividend. Many countries give double tax relief by exemption for foreign business profits, but only relief by credit for dividends.

Even when it has been established whether an enterprise should be regarded as a corporation or a partnership, there is an additional stage to consider. One of the most difficult aspects of entity characterization is determining whether the income of a partnership is to be taxed at the partnership level or whether the income is to be regarded as that of the individual partners. In other words, for tax purposes, will the partnership be regarded as opaque or transparent? Most countries regard partnerships as transparent, so that in practical terms they are disregarded for tax purposes. Some exceptions to this rule are:

- limited partnerships;

- the Japanese gomei-kaisha which is, in essence, a partnership, but which also has a separate legal personality and is taxed in Japan as a corporation;

- the Belgian société en nom collectif (SNC); and

- the Dutch venootschap onder firma (VOF) which has a capital divided into shares.

In deciding how to treat an entity for tax purposes, a country may apply its own specific rules, it may allow the taxpayer to choose (see remarks above on the US), or it may rely on the rules existing in the country under whose laws the entity is established. The UK adopts this last route: HMRC will compare the foreign entity with entities which exist under UK domestic law and assign the best match. This approach generally involves a consideration of general legal classification in the other country as well as looking at the tax treatment in the other country. The starting point for the UK analysis is to respect the characterization of the entity in the entity's home country. Difficulties arise when the form of the foreign entity simply has no parallel in the home country's laws, which is more likely to happen when one country has a system of civil law and the other, common law. German and Austrian entities (civil law) have always posed particular problems for the UK (common law), particularly German silent partnerships (Stille Gesellschaften). These were considered in the *Memec* case[1] which resulted in the development of formal guidance for taxpayers being provided by HMRC (see the 'Further study' section of this chapter).

---

1 *Memec Plc v CIR* [1998] STC 754.

11.15   There are many types of hybrid entity, including:

- *Silent partnerships*: a silent partner does not participate in the activities of the partnership but merely provides capital. They are popular in Germany, where they are known as 'Stille Gesellschaften'. The income is treated as investment income rather than trading income. The return is often treated as akin to interest rather than a share in the trading profits of the partnership.

- *Limited partnerships*: where the partner has no responsibility for the debts of the partnership beyond his investment. This differs from the normal joint and several nature of partnership liabilities. Again, common in Germany where it is known as the 'Kommanditgesellschaft'.

- *Atypical silent partnerships*: these have features of both the typical silent partnership and the limited partnership, but the partner is involved in the management of the enterprise and often commands a premium rate of return on his investment.

The US 'check the box' rules

11.16   A curiosity in the US Tax Code is the so-called 'check the box' rule.[1] This permits a US taxpayer to choose whether an entity is to be regarded as transparent or opaque for US tax purposes, regardless of the actuality. Taxpayers do not have this choice in the case of so-called 'per se' corporations. Per se corporations are, essentially, public limited companies such as the UK PLC, the French Société Anonyme, the Japanese Kabushiki Kaisha and the German Aktiengesellschaft. The IRS publishes a list of all per se corporations.

It is clear that the basis for many examples of cross-border tax arbitrage is the US 'check the box' rules. Offering MNEs the choice of tax characterization of various entities regardless of their legal form is an open invitation to arbitrage. The US 'check the box' rules and arbitrage are dealt with in more detail in Chapter 12.

---

1   US Internal Revenue Code section 7701. The actual box to be 'checked' (ie ticked) is found on Form 8832, *Entity Classification Election*.

Branch mismatches

11.17   So far, we have mainly focused on cases where both countries are in agreement about the status of the branch as a PE. This may not always be the case, however. From 2001, considerable OECD attention was focused on how the profits of a PE (and its definition will certainly include a branch) are to be arrived at. This culminated in the OECD's 2008 report.[1] General transfer pricing principles (arm's length, see Chapter 13) must be used to determine how a company's profits are to be split between a head office and a branch.

On 22 August 2016, the OECD released a discussion document dealing with branch mismatches, which are not 'hybrids' resulting from characterization of an instrument or entity, but rather result from differences in the way that head office and branch countries treat payments between them.

Five types of branch mismatch arrangements are identified:

1. Disregarded branch structure (ie not giving rise to a PE, so deduction with no matching income – D/NI).

2. Diverted branch payments – payments to the branch treated as attributable to the head office by the branch jurisdiction (also D/NI).

3. Deemed branch payments – the branch is treated as making a notional payment to the head office.

4. Duplication of deductible expenditure (DD).

5. Imported branch mismatches – the payee offsets the income from a deductible payment against a deduction arising under a branch mismatch arrangement.

Suggested rules to deal with these types of mismatch are:

- Limiting the scope of branch exemptions in the case of D/NI outcomes in types 1 and 2.

- Branch payee mismatch rule – similar to the reverse hybrid rule discussed at para **12.23**.

- Deemed payment mismatch rule – to restrict the deduction for the deemed payment to the amount of dual inclusion.

- Deductible hybrid payments rule – to deny the duplicated deduction in DD cases.

- An imported mismatch rule – to deny deduction for payment offset against a branch mismatch payment.

At the time of writing, final recommendations have not been made.

---

1 *Report on the Attribution of Profits to Permanent Establishments*, OECD, 17 July 2008.

BEPS Action 2: anti-arbitrage proposals

11.18 The Action 2 Report includes some recommendations for amendments to the OECD Model Tax Treaty (and thus, for actual current and future tax treaties). Many of the recommendations made in the report on BEPS Action

6 (Preventing Treaty Abuse) will also affect the scope for tax arbitrage. These include:

- limitation on benefits rules; and
- the 'main purpose' rule limiting treaty benefits where the main purpose of a transaction was to obtain a treaty benefit.

Dual resident entities

11.19   This section deals with the situation where the same entity is recognized as a taxpayer in two separate countries, ie they both treat the entity as opaque. This situation normally arises only with companies.

Unless the relevant DTT contains a tie-breaker clause for determining company residence (which many do) it is possible for a company to be considered tax resident in two countries. This will occur where a company is registered in Country A, which operates a strict legal rule for determining residency based on legal registration, but where the company is managed and controlled from a country that operates the economic test of company residence (central management and control). If the MNE has profitable group members in both of those countries then the tax advantage of having a dual-resident company is that the same losses could be offset twice. Many countries, including the US and the UK, have fairly sophisticated rules to prevent dual-resident companies from gaining this type of tax advantage. Some DTTs exclude dual-resident companies from most of the benefits available under that treaty, for instance:

> 'Where by reason of the provisions of paragraph 1, a company is a resident of both States, the competent authorities of the States shall endeavour to settle the question by mutual agreement, having regard to the company's place of effective management, the place where it is incorporated or otherwise constituted and any other relevant factors. In the absence of such agreement, such company shall not be entitled to claim any benefits under this Convention, except that such company may claim the benefits of paragraph 4 of Article 25 (Methods of elimination of double taxation) and of Articles 28 (Non-discrimination), 29 (Mutual agreement procedure) and 37 (Entry into force).'

> *(Paragraph 4 of Article 4 US Netherlands Income Tax Treaty of 18 December 1992.)*

Despite tie-breaker clauses in DTTs, the use of dual resident companies to gain tax advantages is thought to be quite widespread. In the BEPS Action 6 Final Report, the OECD has recommended that Article 4(3) of the OECD MTC should be amended to remove the general 'place of effective management' tiebreaker clause. The new Article 4(3) will read:

> 'Where by reason of the provisions of paragraph 1 a person other than an individual is a resident of both Contracting States, the competent

authorities of the Contracting States shall endeavour to determine by mutual agreement the Contracting State of which such person shall be deemed to be a resident for the purposes of the Convention, having regard to its place of effective management, the place where it is incorporated or otherwise constituted and any other relevant factors. In the absence of such agreement, such person shall not be entitled to any relief or exemption from tax provided by this Convention except to the extent and in such manner as may be agreed upon by the competent authorities of the Contracting States.'

The OECD has made recommendations in its Final Report on BEPS Action 2 with the aim of further limiting tax planning using dual resident companies. Even with the change to Article 4 as proposed, tax planning using dual residents to achieve multiple deductions for foreign losses is still possible, eg if an entity is a resident of Country A under Country A domestic law, but is also a resident of Country B, because of the wording of the tax treaty between Country A and Country B. A solution would be for countries to adopt a domestic law, similar to that found in the UK, which states that once a company or other entity is resident in a different country under a tax treaty, it will not be resident under the UK's domestic law.[1]

---

1   Corporation Tax Act 2009, s 18.

Transparent entities

11.20   The OECD produced a lengthy report in 1999 (*The Application of the OECD Model Tax Convention to Partnerships* – known as the Partnerships Report). The recommendations of this lengthy and complex report have found their way into the Commentary on the OECD MTC, mainly in the Commentary on Article 1 (Scope). However, the report only dealt with one type of transparent entity: a partnership. Also, the complexity of the issues dealt with have meant that not all countries have implemented its recommendations. BEPS Action 2 revisits the issue of whether transparent entities should be able to claim the benefits of tax treaties.

BEPS Action 2 aims to ensure that if a transparent entity is not taxed on its income in either Country A or Country B, then it should not be able to claim any benefits of the tax treaty between Countries A and B, such as reduced rates of withholding tax on interest payments received by it. Action 2 does this by proposing new wording for Article 1 of the OECD MTC. Currently, Article 1 reads: 'This Convention shall apply to persons who are residents of one or both of the Contracting States.'

A new paragraph 2 is proposed:

'For the purposes of this Convention, income derived by or through an entity or arrangement that is treated as wholly or partly fiscally transparent under the tax law of either Contracting State shall be considered to be income of a resident of a Contracting State but only to the extent that the income is treated, for purposes of taxation by that State, as the income of a resident of that State.'

In other words, income can only have the benefit of the treaty if it is subject to taxation in at least one of the Contracting States. To benefit from a treaty, not only must the person to whom the income accrues be a resident of one of the States, but also at least one of those States must tax the income concerned.

As an example, a partnership, XY, formed in Country A, has two equal partners. Mr X is tax resident in Country B and Mr Y, the other partner, is tax resident in Country A. Country A treats the partnership as an opaque entity, as if it was a company, ie as a full taxpayer. Country B does not recognize the partnership for tax purposes: it treats it as transparent and only taxes the individual partners in their personal capacity. Thus Country B would tax Mr X but not Mr Y. Under the new paragraph 2 of Article 1, Countries A and B would only apply the benefit of their tax treaty to half of XY partnership's income – the half attributable to Mr X. Thus, if a borrower in Country B pays interest to XY, then withholding tax will have to be applied at Country B's domestic rate to half of the interest payment, and the reduced treaty rate of withholding tax would apply only to the other half.

FURTHER READING

Barreix, A and Villela, L eds (2008) *Taxation and Latin American Integration*, Inter-American Development Bank/David Rockefeller Center for Latin American Studies, Harvard University, pp 173–195.

Cooke, D and Pennock, J (2014) 'Trading Overseas' in *Tolleys Tax Planning 2014*, Lexis.

Cooklin, J (2008) 'Corporate Exodus: when Irish Eyes are Smiling', *British Tax Review 2008*, 6, pp 613–623.

Cui, W (2010) 'Tax Classification of Foreign Entities in China: the Current State of Play', *Bulletin for International Taxation* 2010, Vol 64, No 11.

Lethaby, H (2014) 'Trading in the United Kingdom' in *Tolley's Tax Planning 2014*, Lexis

Lipp, M (2015) 'Germany – The German Silent Partnership', 55 *Bulletin for International Taxation* 7.

OECD (1999) 'The Application of the OECD Model Tax Convention to Partnerships'.

OECD (2009) 'Building Transparent Tax Compliance by Banks'.

Webber, S (2011) 'Escaping the U.S. Tax System: From Corporate Inversions to Re-Domiciling', 63, *Tax Notes International*, 273.

FURTHER STUDY

UK exemption for foreign branch profits

11.21   As part of its overhaul of the taxation of foreign profits of companies, the UK introduced in the Finance Act 2011 provisions intended to put the taxation of foreign profits earned through a branch on a par with that of foreign profits earned by foreign subsidiaries. Thus whether foreign profits are received as a foreign dividend or as a repatriation of branch profits exemption, is now available.

Companies must elect for the exemption of branch profits. The election must be made by the end of the accounting period preceding that from which the exemption is to take effect. Thus a UK company cannot 'wait and see' if it is worth making the exemption. The election is irrevocable and once made, no relief will be available against UK profits for losses incurred by the foreign branch. A company must make the election in respect of all its branches: it cannot cherry pick election for the profitable branches only. Once made, the election will cover any new branches as well.

If branches have made losses in the six years prior to the election taking effect, then the future branch profits will remain taxable up to the amount of loss relief granted in that six-year period, either to the company itself or to any group companies to which losses were surrendered.

It will still be necessary to carry out a proper apportionment of the results of the company between the UK head office and the foreign branches so that the correct amount of UK profits is charged to UK tax. The CFC rules are likely to apply to branches as well – once branch profits are exempt there will be a temptation to site branches in low-tax jurisdictions where there is a choice. The usual exceptions to the CFC charge will apply: the type of tax regime in which the branch is located will be considered, and the motive test as well as a *de minimis* test will apply. The branch will have to prepare accounts for UK tax purposes in the same currency as the functional currency chosen by the company. This may give rise to foreign exchange gains and losses, but as they are all likely to be of a trading nature they should be fully taxable/tax deductible.

Conversion of a branch into a subsidiary

11.22   For instance, there are two reasons why the incorporation of a foreign branch of a UK company into a foreign subsidiary rarely gives rise to a UK tax charge although the incorporation of the branch represents a disposal of assets:

●   First, the UK has a specific tax relief[1] that operates provided that, where the sale consideration given by the foreign subsidiary for the branch's assets consists wholly of shares or debt capital in the new subsidiary, any gain may be postponed. This relief operates until the UK parent company eventually sells the shares or loan stock in the subsidiary. The transfer must be for bona fide commercial reasons.

- Second, if the parent company and the foreign business are both in the EU, then any tax charge on the incorporation of the branch is eliminated by the EU Merger Directive as well. This operates rather differently, in that a deduction is available from the UK tax liability for any tax in the other EU country that would have been payable, were it not for the provisions of the Merger Directive. The Merger Directive is discussed further in Chapter 20. This is a permanent relief, not merely a postponement. Similar rules apply in all EU Member States.

The two reliefs are summarized in the table below:

Table 11.1

UK-specific relief (TCGA 1992, s 140)	*UK relief reflecting the requirements of the EU Merger Directive (TCGA 1992, s 140C)*
• Applies regardless of location of new subsidiary.	• Implements EU Merger Directive.
• Consideration may be shares or shares and loan stock.	• Applies to EU branches only.
• Tax on the gain is deferred if the UK company owns more than 25% of the ordinary shares in new subsidiary.	• Consideration may be shares or loan stock.
	• No minimum ownership of new subsidiary required.
• Recapture of relief when shares sold.	• No recapture of gain if shares subsequently sold.
• No clearance needed.	• Clearance required.

As well as a potential charge to tax on a capital gain, transferring a foreign branch to a foreign subsidiary may also have other tax consequences:

1. The sale of trading stock to the new subsidiary will be treated as taking place at open market value.

2. There may be balancing adjustments for capital allowances purposes.

3. If the foreign branch has incurred trading losses, then whether these may be carried forward and offset against future profits of the new subsidiary depends on the tax law of the host state.

---

1   TCGA 1992, s 140.

Classifying a foreign entity for UK tax purposes

11.23

'When considering the classification of a foreign entity (ie whether it is either opaque or transparent) for UK tax purposes, due regard is given to the approach of the Court of Appeal in the case of *Memec Plc v CIR* (70 TC 77) and the line of case law that precedes it.

In particular, the following matters should be considered:

a. Does the foreign entity have a legal existence separate from that of the persons who have an interest in it?

b. Does the entity issue share capital or something else, which serves the same function as share capital?

c. Is the business carried on by the entity itself or jointly by the persons who have an interest in it that is separate and distinct from the entity?

d. Are the persons who have an interest in the entity entitled to share in its profits as they arise; or does the amount of profits to which they are entitled depend on a decision of the entity or its members, after the period in which the profits have arisen, to make a distribution of its profits?

e. Who is responsible for debts incurred as a result of the carrying on of the business: the entity or the persons who have an interest in it?

f. Do the assets used for carrying on the business belong beneficially to the entity or to the persons who have an interest in it?

Some of those factors may point in one direction; others may point in another. An overall conclusion is reached from looking at all the factors together, though some have more significance than others. Particular attention is paid to factors c. and d.

In considering these factors we look at the foreign commercial law under which the entity is formed and at the internal constitution of the entity. How the entity is classified for tax purposes in any other country is not relevant. The conclusion that is reached is then used in considering the relevant piece of UK tax law.'

(Extract from HMRC International Manual at INTM180010.)

In addition to this general guidance, HMRC provides a list of how it classifies the most commonly encountered foreign entities (at INTM180030). More detail is provided on the UK approach to entity characterization below.

UK approach to entity characterization: some more detail

11.24 The UK defines a company in CTA 2010, s 1121 as: 'any body corporate or unincorporated association, but does not include a partnership, a local authority or a local authority association'.

The key tax case for the UK is *Memec*, following which the UK's approach was set out in some detail by HMRC (see main body of this chapter). *Memec* concerned the UK recognition of a German Stille Gesellschaft (a silent partnership). The court compared its attributes with those of a UK partnership. Was it carrying on business? Did it have rights over assets? Did the partners assume joint and several liability for partnership liabilities? The court concluded that there were few similarities with UK partnerships. The practical point at issue in *Memec* was whether or not the income of a UK company, a silent partner in the Stille Gesellschaft, should be treated as dividends received from a trading subsidiary, or whether the income should be treated as partnership profits.

The facts in Memec

11.25   The scheme was entered into to shield profits from high rates of German tax – instead of accruing to GmbH, being taxed and then the remainder going to Memec, they entered into a silent partnership in the business of GmbH so that 87 per cent of the profits made by GmbH automatically accrued to Memec, not GmbH. This had the effect of reducing German corporation tax payable. Memec argued that its receipts from the arrangement were shares paid by the subsidiaries, because this treatment would have allowed Memec to claim double tax credits in respect of certain local taxes paid by the subsidiaries in addition to German corporation tax. Without double tax credits for these local taxes, Memec was worse off than before.

Memec had no proprietary rights in the dividends coming up from the operating subs, only a contractual right against GmbH. The court held that the source of income was not shares in the German operating subsidiaries but its rights under the partnership agreement. The silent partnership was not a transparent entity. The UK partner had no automatic rights to enjoy the dividends paid by the subsidiaries, but had to wait until a payment to it was made by the silent partnership.

Before *Memec* and the ensuing HMRC guidance, the key cases on UK entity characterization were *Dreyfus v IRC*[1] and *Ryall v The Du Bois Company Ltd.*[2] In *Dreyfus* it was decided that a French société en nom collectif (SNC) was to be treated as a company for the purpose of deciding whether supertax should be levied on the members/shareholders. Corporate status protected them. Note that since then, HMRC have disregarded this decision and treat SNCs as flow-through entities, but the decision is still important for the principles it established: 'we must respect the foreign entity established, because it is not a mere matter for the lex fori; it is a matter of the status which an entity brings over here with it' (at p 577).

In other words, the starting point is the way in which the entity is characterized in its home country. In *Ryall*, it was held that a German GmbH was to be treated as a company for UK purposes. Although there are important differences between a GmbH and a UK company, for German purposes, a GmbH is treated as a company, and therefore this strongly suggested that, following *Dreyfus*, it should also be treated as a company for UK purposes. The capital of a GmbH is not divisible into small units. Members subscribe for Stammeinlage (original contribution/subscription). HMRC accepts

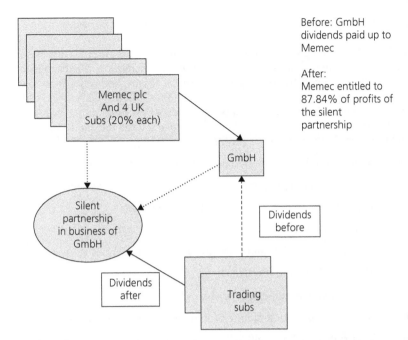

Before: GmbH
dividends paid up to
Memec

After:
Memec entitled to
87.84% of profits of
the silent
partnership

Figure 11.2

Stammeinlage as equivalent to issued share capital. The overriding considerations in characterization for UK tax purposes are:

● the specific terms of the UK taxation provision under which the matter requires to be considered;

● the provisions of any legislation, articles of association, by-laws, agreement or other document governing the entity's creation, continued existence and management; and

● the terms of any relevant Double Taxation Agreement (DTA).

The characterization for UK tax purposes of a Delaware limited liability company (LLC) was the subject of the 2011 case of *Revenue & Customs Commissioners v Anson*.[3] The question was whether a UK resident should be taxed as a partner, on a share of the LLC's trading profits, or as a company shareholder on dividends received. The UK Supreme Court reasoned that it was necessary to compare the profits taxed in the US and those in the UK and decide if they were the 'same' profits, bearing in mind the objects of the UK/US DTT. The court decided that the taxpayer should be permitted to claim double tax relief for tax paid in the US by the LLC.

1   [1929] 14 TC 560.
2   [1933] 16 TC 431.
3   [2015] UKSC 44, [2015] STC 1777.

Importance of having 'ordinary share capital' for UK tax purposes

11.26   Most of the key UK tax reliefs demand the existence of ordinary share capital, for instance, the substantial shareholding exemption, reliefs connected with company reconstructions, group relief for losses, and relief from tax on intragroup capital gains. The statutory definition is found in CTA 2010, s 1119: 'all the company's issued share capital, however described, other than capital the holders of which have a right to a dividend at a fixed rate but have no other right to share in the company's profits.'

Applying this definition to foreign entities we would first of all look for:

- a legal personality separate and distinct from that of the members;

- an ability to carry on business in its own right; and

- an ability to own assets.

HMRC Brief 87/09 applies and supplies further detailed questions:

- Is the member's interest like shares?

- Do the members subscribe for shares?

- Does the subscription money become the property of the company?

- What rights do the members have, in relation to profit shares, etc?

- What responsibilities do members bear?

- Can the interest be legally evidenced?

- Is the interest denominated in a stated fixed value?

- Does a member's interest form a fixed and certain amount of capital to which creditors can look as security?

- Does the foreign law require the amount subscribed to be allocated to fixed capital?

- Can the interest be transferred? Does a transfer consist of a transfer of proprietary rights?

Chapter 12

Finance, Treasury Management and Tax Arbitrage

BASICS

12.1   It is vital to remember that tax is only one factor amongst many in MNE financing decisions. Examples of non-tax factors include: cash flow needs of the firm, foreign exchange and interest exposure risks, and the stage in the business life cycle of the MNE member. The types of finance decisions typically facing MNEs include:

- Which companies should undertake borrowing from external lenders on behalf of other group companies?

- How should borrowings be structured – long/short term, convertible/ non-convertible (to equity)?

- How should currency risks and interest rate risks be managed?

- How should subsidiary companies be capitalized? What combination of debt and equity and in what forms?

- Should subsidiaries have local, external borrowings, or should their debt finance be provided by other companies within the MNE?

12.2   If a company wishes to invest in a new venture by forming a new subsidiary company, or buying an existing one, it can provide finance to that company either in the form of equity (by subscribing for shares in the company) or debt (by lending to the company). The consequences for the subsidiary company are that the investing company will require a return on the investment: disregarding capital growth for present purposes, in the case of share capital the return will take the form of dividends, in the case of loan capital (debt) it will take the form of interest.

Generally, in most countries:

- dividends payable are not tax deductible; and

- interest payable is deductible for tax purposes to some extent.

This means that profits used to pay interest are, in effect, tax free. Thus, if an investor requires a return of 10 per cent (before the investor's taxes) on capital, it is cheaper for the company in which the investment is made to have debt capital rather than equity. If the rate of corporation tax is 20 per cent, then paying interest of $100 only costs $80. However, paying a dividend of $100 costs $100 because it does not produce any tax saving for the payer – the dividend is not tax deductible.

The logic of disallowing a tax deduction for dividends is that dividends *are* the profit. Receipts of interest are almost always taxable, but in some countries dividends are not considered taxable income.

However, MNEs engage in much more sophisticated forms of tax arbitrage and other types of tax planning involving their financing. In some cases, arrangements are entered into solely for their tax benefits, rather than to satisfy the financing needs of the MNE. Such arrangements are targeted by the BEPS Project, specifically under BEPS Action 2.[1]

There are two main types of tax arbitrage:

1   Using hybrid financial instruments: at its simplest, the same legal arrangement is viewed as a loan in one of the two countries, but as share capital (equity) in the other country.

2   Using hybrid entities: an entity, often a partnership, is treated as a tax-payer in one of the two countries (and can thus claim tax deductions), but is not recognized as a separate taxpayer in the other country, ie the individual partners are the taxable unit.

MNEs make extensive use of arrangements involving hybrid instruments and hybrid entities to reduce their global effective tax rate. Most countries have detailed rules governing whether a financial arrangement is a loan or equity. They also have their own rules as to what sort of entity is recognized as a separate taxpayer. However, each country has its own rules on these matters and MNEs exploit these differences to save tax – ie they practise tax arbitrage.

Tax arbitrage reduces the amounts of profits which countries can tax, and so, unsurprisingly, it is a key aspect of the OECD's Base Erosion and Profit Shifting (BEPS Project) (see Chapter 2). Specifically, Action 2 aims to neutralize the effects of hybrid mismatch arrangements in two main ways:

1   By encouraging countries to adopt rules which eliminate the tax advantages of arrangements involving hybrids: for example, not granting a tax deduction for an interest payment if it seems likely that the payment will be treated as a tax exempt dividend by the recipient's country.

2   By changing the OECD Model Tax Convention so that payments under hybrid instruments do not benefit from reduced rates of withholding tax and that entities which are resident in both of the treaty countries cannot obtain any major treaty benefits.

---

1   OECD (2015a), 'Neutralising the Effects of Hybrid Mismatch Arrangements – Action 2: 2015 Final Report'.

12.3   As well as planning to optimize the MNE's tax position through the use of hybrid financing arrangements, groups also benefit from tax planning designed to maximize their interest deductions from taxable profits, without necessarily increasing the amount of interest paid to third party lenders. Such planning can involve maximizing the quantum of the interest deductions and also their value in terms of tax saved, eg by shifting interest expense into group companies with high effective tax rates.

Some countries have rules aimed specifically at limiting permissible deductions for interest where it appears that tax avoidance, as opposed to purely commercial financing of companies, is in play. BEPS Action 4 'Interest Deductions and Other Financial Payments' is concerned with developing a harmonized set of such rules and encouraging more countries to implement them. Currently, the types of rules limiting interest deductions used by various countries include:

- General application of the transfer pricing rules to examine whether the terms of a loan (interest rate, maturity date, security required, etc) are in accordance with the arm's length principle (see Chapter 13).

- Rules which look at the ratio of debt to equity capital and seek to disallow interest deductions on an amount of debt capital thought to be in excess of a commercial level of debt for the company concerned. These are known as 'thin capitalization' rules and may also apply the arm's-length principle.

- Rules which look at the ratio of the interest deduction claimed to other accounting figures, eg earnings before interest, tax, depreciation and amortization (EBITDA).

- Rules which look at the amount of external debt owed by the whole group and seek to restrict interest deductions in group companies which appear to have a disproportional amount of debt compared to the MNE's external debt. These rules tend to focus on internal lending within the MNE.

BEPS Action 4 develops a set of recommended rules that may be adopted by countries worldwide to discourage MNEs from inflating the deductions claimed for interest payments beyond those which represent interest incurred for non-tax driven purposes. The OECD recommends that countries adopt rules disallowing deductions for interest where interest deductions exceed a set percentage of earnings (known as the 'fixed ratio' approach to limiting interest deductions).

FINANCING MULTINATIONAL ENTERPRISES

12.4   At the heart of much cross-border tax planning involving arbitrage is the simple fact that some countries look at a financial arrangement and conclude that it is debt, whilst other countries look at the same financial arrangement and conclude that it is an equity investment – equivalent to an investment in share capital. Thus, the first group of countries think the return on the investment is interest, whilst the second group think the return is some form of a dividend. The factors commonly used by countries to decide whether a particular financial instrument is debt or equity are:

- The term of the instrument: the longer the term, the greater the indication towards equity status.

- The extent of assumption of the company's liabilities and the extent to which the holder of the instrument shares in any losses made by the company. The more protected the investor in this respect, the greater the probability that the instrument is a debt instrument.

- The basis on which the instrument earns its return: the more variable the return and the greater the link with the company's profitability, the more likely it is that the instrument is equity.

The use of hybrid financial instruments creates tax-planning possibilities in cross-border investment. The planner, when using hybrid instruments, will seek to achieve double non-taxation whereby the instrument is viewed as:

- debt capital in the country where it is issued, giving rise to tax deductible interest; and

- as an exempt dividend (eg under a dividend participation exemption) in the country where the return on the instrument is received.

Equity or debt? OECD guidance pre-BEPS

12.5   The classification of any particular financial instrument generally depends on the national laws of the country in which it originates. Tax treaties do not introduce rules to classify specific financial instruments. However, the standard definition of 'dividends' suggested in the OECD Model Convention refers users to national laws:

> 'The term "dividends" as used in this Article means income from shares, "jouissance" shares or "jouissance rights", mining shares, founders' shares or other rights, not being debt-claims, participating in profits, as well as income from other corporate rights which is subjected to the same taxation treatment as income from shares by the laws of the State of which the company making the distribution is a resident.'

(Article 10, para 3, OECD Model Convention.)

Although the OECD has, in the past, attempted to produce a definition of dividends that would remove the need to rely on each country's domestic laws, this has not proved possible due to the variety of financial instruments and approaches of national laws in dealing with them. The OECD Commentary on Article 10, para 3 observes that the definition permits a treaty partner to use its national rules on thin capitalization. These rules prevent excessive tax deduction for interest being generated by a holding company capitalizing its subsidiaries with levels of debt capital which are higher than those which would be found in a company operating independently (see para **11.35** for more on this). They usually operate by re-designating interest deductions as dividend payments, thus removing the tax deduction.

There is a potential problem in that the definition of interest in the OECD Model Tax Convention is such that certain instruments might be capable of being classified as both debt and equity. The definition of 'interest' is:

> 'income from debt-claims of every kind, whether or not secured by mortgage and whether or not carrying a right to participate in the debtor's profits, and in particular, income from government securities and income from bonds or debenture.'

(Article 11, para 3, OECD Model Convention.)

The OECD Commentary, at para 19 makes it clear that the term 'interest' as used in Article 11 does not include items of income which are dealt with under Article 10. Some tax treaties make this explicit. Thus, once an instrument has come under the definition of 'equity', it is excluded from being treated as debt for treaty purposes.

Loan instruments may have characteristics which mean that, in economic substance, they are more like equity. For instance, the rate of return may depend on the quantum of the company's profits, or the term of the loan may be such that it is virtually non-redeemable, or convertible into share capital. It may be subordinated debt, meaning that the holders of the instrument rank much closer to shareholders on a winding-up than to ordinary creditors. Equity instruments might have some of the economic characteristics of debt capital: for instance, they might carry a fixed dividend or be redeemable. Generally, debt instruments will bear less risk (eg of a return not being paid, or of the capital not being repaid) than equity. The greater the number of characteristics of equity which a debt instrument carries, the more likely it is that the tax authority in the issuing country will want to reclassify it as equity, thus denying any tax deduction as interest in respect of the periodic return on that instrument.

The adoption of International Financial Reporting Standards may well alleviate these difficulties of characterization of financial instruments, as IAS 32 (Financial Instruments: Presentation) and IAS 39 (Financial Instruments: Recognition and Measurement, to be replaced by IFRS9 effective from 2018) lay down detailed rules in this respect.

An Australian report identified some specific tests dealing with the debt/equity classification issue:[1]

> '*Equity:*
>
> — an interest in the company as a member or stockholder of the company;
>
> — an interest providing a right to a return,[1] where that right or the amount of the return is dependent upon the economic performance of the issuer or a connected entity;
>
> — an interest providing a right to a fixed or variable return, if either the right or the amount of the return is at the discretion of the issuer or a connected entity; or

— an interest that gives its holder the right to be issued with an equity interest, or will or may convert into such an equity interest in the company or a connected entity

Debt:

— there must be a 'scheme', which is very broadly defined as an arrangement or any scheme, plan, proposal, action, course of action or course of conduct, whether unilateral or otherwise;

— the scheme must be a 'financing arrangement';

— there must be a financial benefit that is received, or will be received by the issuing entity or a 'connected entity' of the issuing entity, under the scheme;

— the issuing entity, or its connected entity, must have an 'effectively non-contingent obligation' to provide a future financial benefit; and

— it must be substantially more likely than not that the value of the financial benefit to be provided will at least be equal to or exceed the financial benefit received, and the value provided and the value received must not both be nil.'

The Australian legislation provides that if a financial instrument satisfies both the equity and the debt test (eg redeemable preference shares) then it will be regarded as debt.

Denmark has introduced specific provisions aimed at curbing cross-border tax arbitrage by the use of hybrid instruments. The approach taken is that Denmark will classify a particular financial instrument by reference to its tax treatment in the other country concerned. Thus, if a return on a financial instrument is paid from Denmark to the UK and the UK classifies the return as a dividend, then Denmark will classify the financial instrument as an equity instrument, so that the return paid on it is also classed as a (non-tax deductible) dividend in Denmark.[2] This neat solution removes the asymmetry of tax treatment in two countries upon which much tax planning with hybrid instruments relies. It only applies within groups of companies, or where a foreign company has decisive influence over the Danish company. Decisive influence is defined as the ownership of voting rights by foreign corporations or individuals over more than 50 per cent of the capital or voting rights in a Danish company.[3]

The following example illustrates the point that countries only tax those parts of a MNE that are resident in or trading within their border and are not interested in the consolidated accounts of the MNE. However, shareholders in the enterprise hold shares in the ultimate parent company (the holding company) of the MNE. This is the company which will pay them dividends – the return on their investment in the shares. Because of this, they are only concerned about the consolidated post-tax results of the enterprise. They are not concerned as to which country the profits arise in. In the example, we assume that Country Y does not tax foreign dividends received by resident companies, but Country Y does tax foreign interest receipts. Country X permits a tax deduction for interest paid, but not for dividends paid.

Consider the position if the subsidiary is financed with equity (share) capital only. The return paid on this capital by the subsidiary will be a dividend.

Example 12.1

Subsidiary Company – resident in Country X
Country X effective rate of corporation tax = 25%

Trading profits before tax	50.00
Tax at 25%	−12.50
After tax profit	37.50
Dividend paid to Parent Company	−37.50
Retained profit	0.00

Parent Company – resident in Country Y
Country Y effective rate of corporation tax = 15%

Trading profits before tax	100.00
Tax at 15%	−15.00
After tax profit	85.00
Add: non-taxable dividend received from subsidiary	37.50
Maximum dividend for the MNE's shareholders	122.50

Now we assume that the subsidiary needs some additional capital and the parent company decides to make a loan of 1,000 to the subsidiary company at 3 per cent interest:

Subsidiary Company – resident in Country X
Country X effective rate of corporation tax = 25%

Trading profits before tax	50.00
Deduct: interest payable: 1,000 @ 3%	−30.00
	20.00
Tax at 25%	−5.00
After tax profit	15.00
Dividend paid to Parent Company	−15.00
Retained profit	0.00

Parent Company – resident in Country Y
Country Y effective rate of corporation tax = 15%

Trading profits before tax	100.00
Add; interest received from subsidiary company	30.00
	130.00
Tax at 15%	−19.50
After tax profit	110.50
Add: non-taxable dividend received from subsidiary	15.00
Maximum dividend for the MNE's shareholders	125.50

By arranging its financing in this way, the worldwide tax liability of the MNE has been reduced by 3. (Before the financing: 12.5 + 15 = 27.5; after the financing: 5 + 19.5 = 24.5.)

However, the net profits before tax of the MNE are exactly the same: before the financing, 50 + 100 = 150; after the financing, 20 + 130 = 150. The MNE has increased its post-tax profits without increasing its pre-tax profits. This is a very simple form of arbitrage, depending solely on the discrepancy in the rates of tax in Countries X and Y.

---

1   Australian Government Board of Taxation (2015) 'Review of the Debt and Equity Tax Rules'. Available at: www.taxboard.gov.au/files/2015/07/Debt_Equity_Final_Report.pdf.
2   Danish Corporation Tax Act, s 2B as discussed in Bundgaard (2008).
3   For a comparison of treatment in European member states, see Kahlenberg & Kopec (2016).

The Group treasury function

12.6   Most MNEs will have an international treasury function which typically operates somewhere along the continuum of highly centralized through to completely decentralized structures. Its principal functions include the management of group funds, financial risk, interest and foreign currency risks and input into the intra-group dividend payment strategy. It evaluates proposed financial decisions utilising various financial models, sensitivity analysis, and forecasting techniques.

12.7   The location of the MNE treasury company and the MNE's central bank account must be chosen carefully: ideally it will be located in a country with a good network of double tax treaties and/or which has a favourable tax regime for group finance companies. Some groups operate 'cash pooling' structures, and tax considerations, such as withholding taxes, can play a large part in the set up and management of these arrangements. Arm's-length transfer pricing methods (see Chapter 13) usually must be evidenced on interest charges and receipts to and from the individual companies.

Foreign exchange exposure

12.8   In most jurisdictions, losses or gains on foreign exchange transactions are dealt with as part of the normal taxable trading profits. In the UK, foreign exchange gains and losses are dealt with on the same basis as interest receipts and payments. However, there are certain tax planning points to watch out for:

• Currency transactions need to be planned so as to avoid currency gains arising in high-tax countries.

• In some jurisdictions, there may be differences in the tax treatment of gains and losses, particularly on hedging instruments.

Maximizing deductible interest: basic strategies

12.9   MNEs benefit from tax planning designed to maximize their interest deductions from taxable profits, without necessarily increasing the amount of interest paid to third party lenders. This includes shifting interest expense into group companies with high effective tax rates, for example:

● A group company, Company A, in a relatively high tax country is the company which borrows loan capital from external lenders. This generates interest deductions which save tax at a relatively high rate. Company A then uses the borrowings to invest in equity capital in other group companies, which are resident in lower tax countries. The return on this equity capital (usually dividends) is either tax-free or lightly taxed in the hands of Company A.

● A group company in a lower tax country making a loan to a company in a higher tax country. Loans can flow either up or down the MNE hierarchy. Where a subsidiary company makes a loan to a parent company, this is usually referred to as an 'upstream' loan.

● A subsidiary company is capitalized with a level of debt capital which is very high in relation to equity (share) capital, ie it is thinly capitalized, so that the return on the capital is tax-deductible interest rather than non-deductible dividends.

Respective tax rates

12.10   First, it should be remembered that interest paid within a MNE usually results in a tax deduction in the country of the payer and a taxable receipt in the country of the lender. Tax efficiency is achieved if the rate of tax faced by the payer is greater than the rate faced by the borrower. Effective rates of tax, rather than headline rates, are important here. This is illustrated in the following simple example:

Example 12.2

Assume that a parent company is resident in Ruritania which charges corporation tax at 40 per cent. Its subsidiary company is tax resident in Inistania where corporation tax is charged at 20 per cent. The parent company makes an interest charge of €10,000 on the subsidiary:

	Parent company Ruritania, tax 40%	Subsidiary company Inistania, tax 20%	tax
	€	€	€
Net profits before interest and taxation	120,000	100,000	
Interest paid by subsidiary company	10,000	–10,000	

355

	Parent company Ruritania, tax 40%	Subsidiary company Inistania, tax 20%	tax
	€	€	€
	130,000	90,000	
Tax at 40%	52,000		52,000
Tax at 20%		18,000	18,000
Total tax			70,000

If the interest charge was reduced to €5,000 there would be an overall tax saving of €1,000, as illustrated below.

	Parent company Ruritania, tax 40%	Subsidiary company Inistania, tax 20%	tax
	€	€	€
Net profits before interest and taxation	120,000	100,000	
Interest paid by subsidiary company	5,000	–5,000	
	125,000	95,000	
Tax at 40%	50,000		502,000
Tax at 20%		19,000	19,000
Total tax			69,000

Effect of tax incentives/special tax regimes

12.11 If the subsidiary paying the interest is entitled to tax incentives which lower its effective rate of tax (such as tax holidays, special investment allowances, special low rates, etc) then this will probably lower the effective rate of tax faced by the subsidiary below that faced by the lending company. In these circumstances, there is no point in trying to maximize the amount of the tax deduction in the subsidiary for interest payments, as the tax saved will be small and the tax liability generated in the lending company will be relatively large.

Effect of double tax relief by credit

12.12 This section considers the position of a group company with borrowings on which interest is payable. The company is resident in a country which operates double taxation under the credit method and the company has various sources and types of foreign income. The aim of the company is to maximize usage of foreign tax credits. Most countries have rules in their double tax relief systems which limit the foreign tax credits to the amount of residence country tax on the same income. If interest payments have to be set against the foreign income, this reduces residence country tax on that foreign income and thus restricts the amount of foreign tax which can be offset.

For instance, the US insists that lenders must offset interest payable against all categories of income pro rata with the relative values of all taxpayer's assets: thus, if the bulk of a company's assets are shares in foreign subsidiaries, then the bulk of interest payments must be set against dividends and other income from those subsidiaries. This has the effect of restricting the scope for offset of foreign withholding taxes relating to dividends and interest received from those subsidiaries. As the foreign tax credit attaching to receipts of interest will be just withholding tax, whereas the foreign tax credit relating to a dividend may consist of both withholding tax and underlying corporation tax, this is another reason why debt financing might be preferred: there might be insufficient scope for utilising the full double tax credit produced by the receipt of foreign dividends. Also, debt finance as opposed to equity finance will lower the value of the shareholding in the foreign subsidiary, thus reducing the allocation of interest payable by the US company which must be set against income from that subsidiary. The following example illustrates the effect of rules governing interest offset in the context of a system of double tax relief by credit.

Example 12.3

Elks Inc, a company resident in Ruritania, which has a corporation tax rate of 30 per cent, has the following income and interest expense:

Company assets by %

Land and buildings	10
Net current assets	10
Shares in foreign subsidiaries	80
	100

Income before deduction of interest payable:	$
Ruritanian trading income	400
Dividends from foreign subsidiaries (cash received)	400
	800
Interest payable	600
Foreign tax suffered on dividends from foreign companies	200

Elk Inc corporation tax computation	Trading income	Foreign dividends	Total
	$	$	
Income before interest (gross of foreign tax)	400	600	1000

357

interest deducted:

20% × 600 (land & buildings 10% + net current assets 10%)	−120		
80% × 600 (proportion of assets represented by shares in foreign subsidiaries)		−480	−600
	280	120	400
Ruritanian corporation tax at 30%	84	36	120
Double tax relief – restricted to Ruritanian corporation tax		−36	−36
Unrelieved foreign tax credit:		164	

Because of the rule requiring interest paid to be offset against income classes in proportion to the amounts of the underlying assets, the Ruritanian corporation tax allocated to the foreign dividends is severely restricted, which in turn has restricted the amount of double tax credits on the foreign dividends which can be offset. Without the rule governing offset of interest payments, the company could have allocated another $280 of interest against trading income. This would have left only $200 of interest to be offset against the foreign dividends so that the Ruritanian corporation tax applicable to the dividends (and hence the maximum offset of foreign tax credit) would have risen to $600 − $200 = $400 × 30% = $120k. The interest offset rule has restricted the offset of foreign tax credits on the dividends by $120 − $36 = $84k.

Even in countries which have no such interest allocation rules, it may be tax efficient to have a separate finance company which borrows externally on behalf of the MNE. Thus the interest deduction will be claimed in this company, whereas the dividends from the foreign subsidiaries will be received into a different company where there is greater capacity to utilize the available tax credits fully because there would be fewer interest payments to allocate against income.

CROSS-BORDER TAX ARBITRAGE

12.13   Proposals to limit opportunities for this type of tax planning are prominent in the OECD's BEPS Project: Action 2 seeks to neutralize the effects of hybrid mismatch arrangements. Before considering the Action 2 proposals we will attempt to define tax arbitrage using hybrid arrangements and consider some examples of this type of tax planning.

Most MNEs will use sophisticated techniques as legal means of reducing tax liabilities. Whilst the detail of such techniques is beyond the scope of this book, this section aims to give a flavour of what is possible. Tax arbitrage seeks to exploit differences in the tax systems in which the MNE operates. It exploits these differences through the use of hybrid arrangements: either hybrid entities, viewed as a separate taxpayer in one country but not the other, or hybrid instruments, regarded as debt instruments in one country but as equity instruments in another.

We might define tax arbitrage in very simple terms as the use of tax-avoidance techniques which involve more than one country. Rosambuj defines it as:

> 'the meeting point between fiscal planning and intentional tax avoidance in the local tax system or between tax systems of different countries through the use of structured financial transactions – circulated through special companies and institutions and opaque instruments aimed at minimizing the tax as a source of benefit'.[1]

It must be stressed again that tax arbitrage refers to tax planning that does not break any laws; in other words, it is not tax evasion. Tax arbitrage often involves the movement of large amounts of funds from one country to another. The use of tax arbitrage to achieve either double non-taxation or substantial reductions in taxation is one of the chief targets of the OECD's initiative to reduce base erosion and profit shifting (BEPS). This follows on from the publication in March 2012 of the OECD's report 'Hybrid Mismatch Arrangements'.

Differences in tax systems can give rise to either double taxation of the same income, non-taxation of income or a double tax deduction for expenditure. Whilst double taxation is usually eliminated by double tax treaties, governments have traditionally placed less emphasis on eliminating non-taxation of income or double deductions for expenses. There are no 'off the shelf' planning techniques in tax arbitrage: arbitrage schemes involve highly complex and bespoke tax-planning arrangements which are normally confidential. When a tax authority becomes aware that a particular technique is being used, it can develop legislation to render the technique ineffective for tax purposes (specific anti-avoidance regulation). Alternatively, a tax authority can use a more general form of legislation which identifies the types of planning regarded as tax arbitrage in more general terms and cancels the tax advantage (general anti-avoidance regulation). The UK is just one of the countries which has such legislation and this is examined in the 'Further study' section of this chapter.

Arbitrage opportunities arise in group financing arrangements due to differences in the policies adopted by the governments in the countries in which a MNE operates in relation to very fundamental matters, including:

- How to characterize a transaction: eg is it a loan or an outright sale?

- How to characterize a financial instrument: is it a loan or is it an equity instrument?

- Is the return on a particular instrument in the nature of interest or a dividend?

- How much income should be recognized and when?

- Is it income or is it a capital gain?

- Is related expenditure a deductible expense or an addition to the capital invested?

- Who are the taxpayers which are party to the transaction?

As mentioned earlier, many arbitrage schemes use hybrid financial instruments or hybrid entities.

1   Tuilio Rosembuj (2011) 'International Tax Arbitrage', *Intertax*, Vol 39, Issue 1.

Arbitrage: hybrid financial instruments

12.14   We start by looking at a basic example of this type of planning.

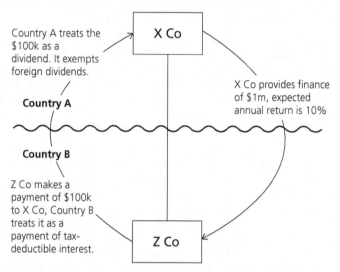

Figure 12.1: A basic arrangement using a hybrid instrument

This structure uses a hybrid financial instrument. It would be described as 'deduction/no inclusion' outcome (D/NI) because Z Co obtains a tax deduction for a payment, whilst X Co does not have to include the receipt in its taxable income.

12.15   Whilst it is possible to describe, in general terms, types of hybrid financial instruments, the details of each individual arrangement are complex. This is because the financial instrument must fulfil many criteria, including:

● It must produce a tax advantage, in global terms.

● It must be possible under the commercial laws of each of the countries involved (eg German law does not permit the issue of preference shares).

● The classification of the return on the instrument for tax purposes (essentially, interest or dividend) must be analysed under the domestic law of all the countries involved.

● The withholding tax (WHT) consequences must be analysed, both under domestic law of the countries involved and under their double tax treaties with each other. There is no point engineering the return on a financial instrument to look like interest if, under the relevant treaty, interest carries WHT at 20 per cent whilst dividends would be free of WHT.

● It must not fall foul of any general or specific anti-avoidance laws in the countries concerned or in their tax treaties with each other.

- The impact of the instrument on the financial statements in each country must be analysed in the light of national and international financial accounting standards. Financial institutions must also consider the hybrid instrument in the light of the Basel Accords which lay down regulations governing the capital base of financial institutions.

These complex forms of financial instruments are used not only to try to gain a tax advantage but also to improve the appearance of the borrower's balance sheet, where they will typically be shown as equity. One advantage is that whilst appearing as equity (and therefore strengthening the balance sheet of the subsidiary) the return on the finance is treated as interest and is tax deductible. Bonds which are convertible into equity, where there is a real possibility that conversion will occur, are one example of a hybrid instrument. Another example would be the transfer of rights to a stream of income or gains arising from a security. In general, the mark of a hybrid financial instrument is that the economic effects are inconsistent with its legal form. Hybrid financial instruments are also sometimes referred to as 'mezzanine' finance, because they fall somewhere between equity and debt capital.

Examples of hybrid financial instruments:

- *Certain types of preference shares*: eg redeemable, carrying a cumulative fixed rate of dividend and ranking before other classes of shares on a winding-up. Preference shares are sometimes convertible into equity capital. The income stream from preference shares is usually classed as a dividend because a return on the preference shares can only be paid out of distributable profits. If the company makes a loss in a particular year, no dividend can be paid on the preference shares. Where they take on a hybrid characteristic is in the terms of their redemption. The legal right to repayment of capital at a set date, or at the option of the lender, is indicative of debt finance. However, the longer the interval between issuing and repayment, the more likely it is that the finance will be classed as equity. A redemption payment other than the simple return of the capital amount, eg contingent upon the amount of profits retained by the company over the life of the shares, would again indicate equity rather than debt capital.

- *Jouissance rights*: jouissance shares or rights are financial instruments which grant rights of the types enjoyed by shareholders but which, in some jurisdictions, eg Germany, are viewed as debt rather than equity. However, the classification depends on the details of each individual arrangement.

- *Profit participating loans*: whilst the capital is repayable, the return and possibly also the amount repayable is linked to the profits of the borrower. Thus there are elements of equity participation which fall short of a formal shareholding. As with preference shares and jouissance rights, the return may be payable on a cumulative basis so that if the borrower cannot pay the return on the instrument in one year due to an insufficiency of profits, the return for the missed year is payable in the next year, alongside the normal return due for that year.

- *Convertible bonds*: the holder has the right to convert the bonds into share capital at some point in the future.

- *Subordinated loan*: usually this describes the situation where a bank will lend, often without security and will agree that its right to repayment ranks behind that of certain other investors. Thus this has some characteristics of equity capital. Banks charge high rates of interest on these loans to compensate for the increased risk.

The PepsiCo Puerto Rico *case*

12.16   In *PepsiCo Puerto Rico Inc*,[1] hybrid instruments referred to as 'advance arrangements' were entered into between a Dutch subsidiary and a US group company, with the intention that they should be treated as debt in the Netherlands and as equity in the US, which would give rise to a tax advantage for the MNE. Whilst the facts are complex, the case is notable because the Court considered 13 separate indicia in its attempt to determine whether, for US tax purposes, the instruments were debt or equity. These are summarized below. The material in italics did not form part of the case report but is intended to give a general idea of which way the various factors might point:

- the name given to the instruments;

- the presence or otherwise of a fixed maturity date and the term of the instrument *(short term with a fixed maturity date indicates debt)*;

- the source of the payments: were they out of profits or out of cash flow? *(if only out of cash flow, ie when funds available, suggests equity)*;

- the extent and nature of rights to enforce payments, the creditor safeguards and subordination of repayments *(extensive rights, safeguards and lack of subordination indicates debt)*;

- the participation in the management of the issuing company *(participation indicates equity)*;

- was the 'lender' under any obligation to ensure that the issuing company could fulfil its obligations to its regular corporate creditors? *(such obligation indicates debt)*;

- the intentions of the parties as to the characterization of the instruments in each of the countries;

- were the amounts 'lent' by the shareholders in proportion to their shareholdings? *('lending' in proportion to existing shareholdings indicates equity)*;

- the debt/equity ratio of the issuing company *(a very high debt to equity ratio would indicate equity)*;

- would a third party lender have loaned funds in the same amounts on the same terms as the instruments in question? *(if no, indicates equity)*;

- the use to which the funds were put *(if funds not spent on capital investment, may indicate debt)*;

- the consequences of failure to repay *(if legal consequences ensue, indicates debt)*; and

- the acceptance of risk by the 'lender' *(acceptance of risk indicates equity)*.

---

1   *PepsiCo Puerto Rico Inc v Commissioner of Internal Revenue* (2012) 15 ITLR 264. See also
    Korb et al (2013) for a discussion of the US position on debt-equity cases.

A more complex example: the use of a repo

12.17   Hybrid entities are frequently used for the purpose of 'double dip-ping'. Double dipping refers to the practice of obtaining a tax deduction twice for the same expenses or for the same tax loss. Usually, this means that tax relief is claimed for the same deduction or loss against taxable profits in two or more different jurisdictions. 'Repos': arrangements for the sale and repurchase of shares are a common way of achieving double dipping of interest deduction or credits for foreign taxes.

For the type of repo known as a 'foreign tax credit generator', allowing double dipping of foreign tax credits, typically, the arrangements would be as follows (see Figure 12.2):

Holding Co, in Country A, currently has foreign income of $500k, and associ-ated double tax credits of $40k. Holding Co wishes to borrow $1 million from an unconnected bank in Country B. Rather than take out a simple loan, Holding Co makes the following arrangements:

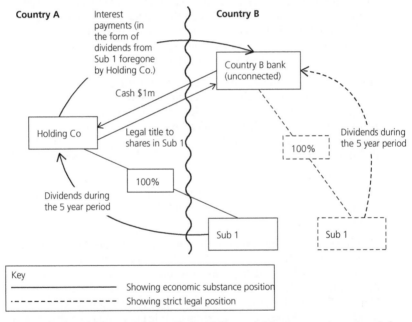

Figure 12.2: Arbitrage using a hybrid financial instrument – a tax-driven repo arrangement

1   Holding Co (resident in Country A) sells its 100 per cent shareholding in Sub 1 (resident in country B) to an unconnected bank in Country B for $1 million. We assume there is no tax on any capital gain on the sale

of shares due to participation exemptions such as the UK's 'substantial shareholding exemption'. The terms of the sale include an option for Holding Co to buy back the shares in Sub 1 in five years' time. Holding Co now has the £1m cash for use in its business.

2   Sub 1 makes of profit of $100k and pays corporation tax of $25k. It pays the maximum possible dividend of $75k to its new legal owner, the Country B bank. We assume that Country B does not tax Country B companies on the receipt of dividends from other Country B companies (to avoid economic double taxation). Therefore, the Country B bank has no tax liability in respect of the dividend received. Importantly though, Country B recognizes the Country B bank as the owner of the shares in Sub 1.

3   Country A treats the arrangements in line with their economic substance: it believes that what has really happened is that the bank in Country B has made a loan of $1 million to Holding Co, on which Holding Co will be paying interest. Country A does not recognize the Country B bank as the owner of the Sub 1 shares: Country A considers that Holding Co has merely provided the Country B bank with collateral (security) for the $1 million loan, in the form of some contingent rights over the shares in Sub 1.

4   Because Country A believes that Holding Co is still the owner of the shares in Sub Co, it taxes Holding Co as if Holding Co had received the dividend paid by Sub 1, even though this dividend was actually paid to the Country B bank. It grants a credit for underlying Country B corporation tax paid by Sub 1, so that Holding Co is taxed on gross dividend income of $100k, with an associated double tax credit of $25k.

5   Holding Co is also treated by Country A as if it had paid interest to the Country B bank. Although no actual interest payments have been made, Holding Co did not receive the dividend from Sub 1, even though Country A taxes Holding Co as if the dividend had been received by it. The dividend was paid to the Country B bank, and Country A treats this situation as if Holding Co had made interest payments of $75k to the Country B bank.

6   Holding Co's tax computation now shows gross dividend income of $100k minus deductible interest payment of $75k = $25k. Assuming a rate of tax in Country A of 20 per cent, Holding Co's corporation tax liability is $25k × 20% = $5k.

7   Holding Co can set the double tax credit of $25k against this tax liability. However, that still leaves $25k – $5k = $20k of tax credit unused. This is where the tax advantage happens. It is likely that Country A will permit this excess double tax credit to be used against other foreign income of Holding Co, on which there is still a Country A tax liability. This will be: $500k × 20% = $100k minus existing double tax credits of $40k, = $60k. The $20k of foreign tax credits generated by the repo arrangement can reduce this liability of $60k to only $40k.

In summary, Holding Co has borrowed $1 million, obtained a deduction for the interest liability on this amount but has also generated an extra $20k of double tax credits, which reduce Country A tax on other foreign income.

Double-dipping: lease payments

12.18 Besides repos, another type of transaction which can be treated differently for tax purposes in two different jurisdictions is the lease of plant and machinery. In some tax jurisdictions, the legal owner of the assets (the lessor) is entitled to tax depreciation allowances. In other jurisdictions, the economic owner (the lessee) is the person entitled to the allowances. Hence structuring leases of plant and machinery such that the lessor is tax resident in a country which gives the allowances to the lessor, and such that the lessee is tax resident in a country which gives the allowance to the lessee, will result in a double tax allowance for the same capital expenditure.

Tax arbitrage using hybrid entities

Interest deduction but no inclusion (D/NI)

12.19 A basic form of tax arbitrage using a hybrid entity is illustrated in Figure 12.3. X Co, resident in Country A, wishes to set up a business operation in Country B. It sets up Entity Z, which is a type of partnership recognized as a separate taxpayer from X Co by Country B, but not by Country A. Country A thinks that Entity Z is a branch of X Co. Entity Z trades in Country B, makes taxable profits and claims a deduction for the interest paid on the loan made to it by X Co. This reduces the tax payable in Country B. However, Country A thinks there is merely a branch of X Co in Country B, and that X Co is the head office. A branch and head office are the same person, legally speaking. A person cannot pay interest to himself/itself. Therefore, as far as Country A is concerned, there is no receipt of interest and thus no taxable income in respect of the amount of $100k received by X Co from Entity Z. This is generally known as a 'deduction/no inclusion' or D/NI form of tax arbitrage.

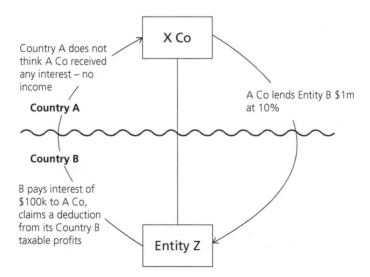

Figure 12.3: Arbitrage using a hybrid entity

A common variation on this would be for Entity Z not to have any trade or income, but to be grouped for tax purposes with another (non-hybrid) subsidiary in Country B, to which Entity Z would surrender the tax loss created by the interest payment.

Double deduction for interest (DD)

12.20   It is often commercially efficient for the overseas operation to borrow funds locally rather than borrowing from the parent company. The use of a hybrid entity, such as a partnership, might offer the opportunity to claim two deductions from taxable profits for the same interest payment. This is illustrated in Figure 12.4.

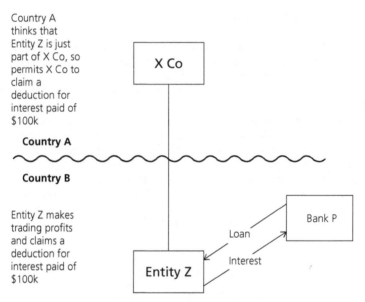

Figure 12.4: Arbitrage using a hybrid entity, local borrowing

As well as borrowing locally, it is often more commercially convenient for trading operations to be carried out by a separate subsidiary company rather by a hybrid entity such as a partnership. It is possible to obtain the same kind of tax advantage as illustrated in Figure 12.4 by taking advantage of the fact that most countries permit companies and other entities within their country which are in the same corporate group to pool tax profits and tax losses.

In Figure 12.5, X Co has a wholly owned subsidiary, Y Co, in Country B which requires an injection of capital of $1 million. Without any tax planning, this could be achieved by Y Co borrowing from a local bank, or by X Co either making a loan or subscribing for additional share capital. However, the MNE forms a hybrid entity, Entity Z. Entity Z could take many forms, but in this example, we assume it is a partnership in which X Co is the majority partner, with perhaps another group company resident in Country A being the other partner. Importantly, Country A does not recognize this type of partnership as a taxable entity, attributing all partnership transactions directly to the partners. In other words, it treats it as transparent for tax purposes. However, Country B treats this type of partnership as a taxable person (opaque). The partnership is formed under Country B law so that Country B recognizes it as a tax resident.

Entity Z borrows money externally and incurs interest. It uses the money to subscribe for shares in Y Co. Y Co does not pay dividends so that there is no income in Entity Z and the interest payments produce a tax loss of $100k.

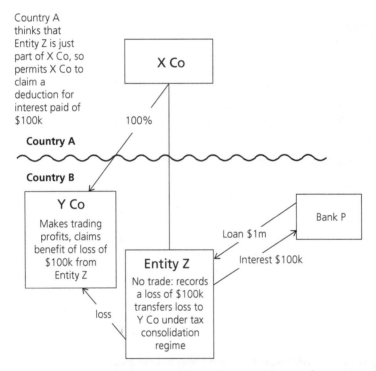

Figure 12.5: Arbitrage using a hybrid entity, local borrowing, surrender of loss to fellow group member

Since Entity Z is considered to be a tax resident in Country B, the loss caused by the interest payment is recognized for tax purposes in Country B. Entity Y pools this loss against tax profits of Y Co. However, because Entity Y is not recognized as a taxable person in Country A, Country A treats the interest as if paid by X Co and the other partner company. Hence, as in Figure 12.5, the interest payments also generate tax deductions in Country A.

Reverse hybrids

12.21   A reverse hybrid entity is one which is NOT recognized as a taxpayer in the country where it is set up, but IS recognized as a taxpayer in the country where its investors are tax resident. Thus, when the reverse hybrid entity, Entity B, resident in Country B, receives income (eg interest) from Country C, Country B does not charge any tax on Entity B, because it does not think it is a separate taxpayer. Country B thinks that the investors in Entity B, who are resident in Country A, are the true recipients of the income from Country C. However, Country A regards Entity B as a bone fide taxpayer and thinks the income from Country C properly belongs to Entity B rather than to the Country A investors. So Country A does not charge tax on the income from Country C either. This is illustrated in Figure 12.6.

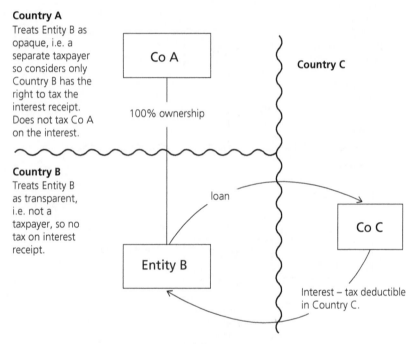

Figure 12.6: Arbitrage using a reverse hybrid entity

Shifting the benefit: 'imported mismatches'

12.22   Some countries already have rules which make it difficult for MNEs to undertake hybrid financial arrangements there. To get around this, MNEs can put in place hybrid financial arrangements in other countries and then simply transfer the tax benefit to the country which has the anti-hybrid rules under a transaction which is not caught by those rules. This is illustrated in Figure 12.7. In this example, X Co, Z Co and P Co are all members of the same MNE. X Co provides finance of $1m to Z Co, using a hybrid instrument. There is no tax advantage in Country B: the deduction for the payment to Co X is offset by the income received from P Co. However, the MNE still manages to obtain the tax advantage from the hybrid instrument by involving P Co, which is resident in a country which has not implemented the anti-hybrid rules. The position is:

● Country A; no income recognized;

● Country B: both a deduction and a receipt, which cancel out;

● Country C: a tax deduction is successfully claimed.

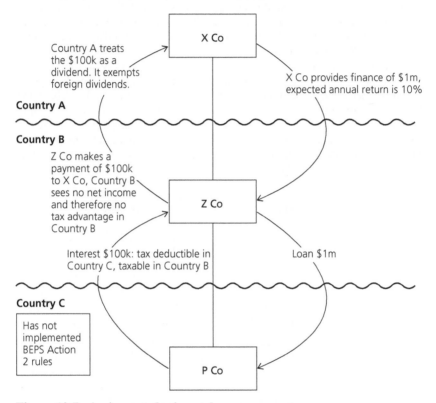

Figure 12.7: An imported mismatch arrangement

The US 'check the box' rules

12.23   This section examines an aspect of the US domestic tax rules which effectively invites MNEs to engage in tax arbitrage using hybrid entities.

A MNE wishing to engage in cross-border tax arbitrage involving the US tax system through the use of a special purpose vehicle (SPV – a company usually set up especially for a particular transaction) can do so with relative ease, having the right to choose how the SPV will be regarded for the purposes of US tax. The original purpose of the rules was to simplify questions of characterization as it was believed that in most disputes as to characterization of an entity, the taxpayer's view generally prevailed. However, the check the box facility has led to other countries having to enact anti-avoidance legislation to prevent large amounts of tax being avoided through arbitrage. For instance, in the UK, the Finance (No 2) Act 2005 contained a good deal of legislation aimed at curtailing cross-border tax arbitrage. (See the 'Further study' section of this chapter for more detail.)

Broadly, the UK legislation will operate so as to deny the UK tax deduction where the main purpose of the scheme is to obtain a UK tax advantage. There are corresponding rules aimed at taxing receipts in the UK where a deduction has been claimed in another country in circumstances where such a receipt would not normally be taxable under UK law. One strange effect of these rules is that the UK may be effectively penalizing multinationals for what amounts to avoiding tax in countries other than the UK, particularly in the US as a result of judicious use of the 'check the box' rules. A useful example is given by HMRC as to when the rules would apply – one aspect of the US 'check the box' rules is that taxpayers can choose to have certain entities (eg a UK holding company) treated as a division of a US company for US tax purposes. HMRC's example (see Figure 12.8) shows both the UK view and the foreign country's view of the transactions. In the version given below, it is assumed that the foreign country involved is the US.

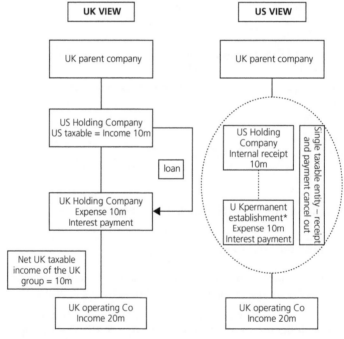

Figure 12.8

*The MNC elects for this treatment under the 'check the box' regulations even though the legal entity is in fact a UK limited liability company.

The UK tax consequences are that there is taxable income of 20 million and an interest expense of 10 million, giving net taxable income for the UK of 10 million. However, the US view would be that the loan is merely an internal transfer between the head office of the US Holding Co and its UK permanent establishment (the MNE will have opted for treatment of the UK Holding company as a division of the US holding company under the US 'check the box' rules). Thus for US tax purposes, there is neither a tax deduction nor a tax receipt in respect of the payment of interest of 10 million. A tax advantage has been obtained by the MNE in that income liable to UK tax has been reduced by 10 million without any corresponding increase in US taxable income. There is a tax deduction in the UK but no taxable receipt in the US. The effect of the UK's 2005 rules would be to disallow the deduction of 10 million by the UK holding company.

Danger: loss of treaty benefits

12.24 A key danger in the use of a hybrid entity is that when it seeks to access benefits under a DTT (eg favourable rates of withholding tax), it might not be classed as a tax resident. Only residents of either of the contracting states can benefit under a tax treaty. The most common example of this problem would be an entity classed as a partnership in one country and recognized as a taxable entity there, but not recognized as a taxable entity in the country from which the payment which is subject to withholding taxes is being made.

Illustration: problems with using hybrid entities (see Figure 12.9).

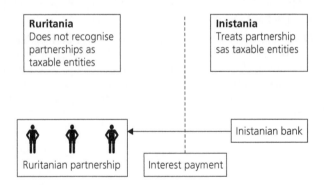

Figure 12.9

In this example, we will assume that the DTT between Inistania and Ruritania provides that withholding tax on interest payments is to be at a maximum rate of 5 per cent. Under its domestic law, Inistania charges a withholding tax of 30 per cent. Inistania treats partnerships as taxable entities but Ruritania does not. So Inistania regards the interest as being paid to a partnership, whilst Ruritania regards the interest as being paid to each of

371

the partners as individuals. The problem is that under Ruritanian domestic law, the partnership is not a tax resident. As far as Ruritania is concerned, the tax residents in this case are the individual partners. Because the partnership is not a resident of Ruritania, it cannot benefit under the DTT and might well suffer Inistanian withholding tax on the interest of 30 per cent. This is because Inistania regards the interest as being paid to an entity, the partnership, which is not recognized by Ruritania as a Ruritanian tax resident.

This type of problem was considered at length by the OECD in its 1999 report *The Application of the OECD Model Tax Convention to Partnerships*. The discrepancies in the extent to which a country recognizes partnerships, and the factors used by different countries in the recognition of partnerships are responsible for the infrequency with which partnerships are specifically dealt with in double tax treaties. The crucial question is whether or not the partnership itself is regarded as a resident of one of the contracting states to the treaty. Unless recognized as a resident, the partnership itself cannot take advantage of the tax treaty. To be a resident, the entity must be a 'person' as per the treaty definition of this term. That test is usually passed fairly easily, but then there is a further test – that to be considered a 'resident' a person must be fully subject to tax in that country. If a partnership is treated as transparent for tax purposes in its home state, then this leg of the residency test is failed. This applies where the partners' individual circumstances are taken into account in determining the tax liabilities and also where the tax is computed at the partnership level but the liability to pay the tax is allocated to the individual partners.[1] In these cases, it may or may not be possible for the individual partners to rely on the treaty in their capacity as resident individuals. For instance in the illustration above, Inistania might agree to treat the interest payment as being paid to three individuals (the individual partners) rather than to the partnership.

The OECD's guidance is now that the treatment of a partnership for treaty purposes is to be determined by its treatment in the country in which the partnership is organized. Where a country treats partnerships as transparent, this can have particular implications if the partnership has a permanent establishment in a third country and the partners are resident in different countries (see Figure 12.10).

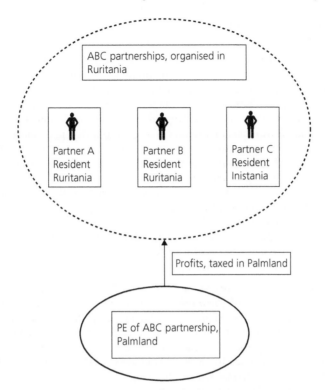

Figure 12.10: Hybrid entities and their permanent establishments

In this situation, the partnership itself is organized under Ruritanian law, which we will assume treats partnerships as transparent. If the partnership has a permanent establishment in Palmland, then each individual partner will have to claim treaty benefits in respect of profits of the permanent establishment under the appropriate DTT. In the case of Partners A and B, who are resident in Ruritania, this will be the Ruritania–Palmland Treaty, but in the case of Partner C, who is resident in Inistania, that partner will have to rely on the Inistania–Palmland Treaty. This type of situation is revisited in the provision in BEPS Action 2 dealing with transparent entities (see para **11.20**).

---

1   Note that France does not agree with this analysis, considering it to be a matter of tax collection only.

MOVES TO PREVENT INTERNATIONAL TAX ARBITRAGE

BEPS Action 2: anti-arbitrage proposals for domestic laws

12.25   Action 2[1] of the OECD's BEPS initiative sets out proposals for curbing the opportunities for tax arbitrage using hybrid arrangements, whether of hybrid entities or hybrid financial instruments. The OECD's proposals fall into two categories:

- *Recommended changes to domestic laws*: recommendations to governments as to rules which should be implemented in the domestic law of countries to remove the tax advantages from the use of hybrid financing arrangements. These recommendations are made with the aim of achieving harmonization of the laws regarding the categorization of entitles and financial instruments in different countries. If different countries classify the same financial instruments, and the same entities in the same way, then the differences in treatment on which planning with hybrids are based will disappear and, with them, the opportunities for tax planning with hybrids. For instance, if all countries change their domestic laws so that convertible debt is treated, for tax purposes, as equity, then no company in a MNE will be able to claim a tax deduction for the return paid on this debt. Because the convertible debt is classed as equity by all countries, all countries will treat the return paid on the convertible debt as a non-deductible dividend payment.

- *Recommended changes to the OECD MTC, to be adopted by countries in their treaties with each other*: recommendations designed to ensure that no entity is treated as a tax resident (ie opaque) for tax treaty purposes by one partner to the treaty but treated as transparent, and therefore disregarded, by the other partner to the treaty. There are also recommendations designed to restrict advantages sought by dual resident entities, ie those treated as resident by *both* treaty partner countries, and not adequately dealt with by any tie-breaker clause.

The recommendations on changes to domestic law, whilst good in theory, are open to criticism on the grounds that they are too ambitious. This is because:

- Every country has its own detailed laws on the tax classification and tax treatment of financial instruments, and the classification of business entities. It is most unlikely that harmonization of these laws could be achieved, even if all countries were willing and able to participate in the harmonization process. This is partly due to language and other interpretational difficulties, and partly due to the sheer complexity of the task.

- Countries are, in general, unwilling to amend their domestic laws in line with instructions from international agencies. To accept such instructions is seen as a loss of sovereignty by the governments. Even in a bloc such as the EU, where the Member States are committed to economic and political union, discrepancies in the transposition of EU Directives into the national laws of Member States (a harmonization process) is often fraught with political tensions and difficulties.

---

1   OECD (2015a), 'Neutralising the Effects of Hybrid Mismatch Arrangements – Action 2: 2015 Final Report'.

Types of hybrid arrangements tackled by BEPS Action 2

12.26   The Action 2 2014 Deliverables Report identifies the situations to be addressed by countries in their domestic laws in terms of the outcome of the tax planning using hybrids, and also in terms of the type of hybrid arrangement used.

Possible outcomes from the use of hybrids

12.27   *Deduction/no inclusion (D/NI)*: a deduction is claimed in respect of payments made by a taxpayer in Country A, but there is no tax on the receipt of the payment by the person receiving it in Country B. The income is not included in taxable income.

Double deduction (DD): Country A thinks a payment has been made by a tax-payer resident in Country A, and gives a tax deduction. However, Country B thinks a different taxpayer, resident in Country B, has made that very same payment so that Country B also gives a tax deduction.

Categories of hybrids identified by Action 2

12.28

- *Hybrid financial instruments*: see para **12.14** above.

- *Hybrid transfers*: such as transfer of share capital under a repo agreement – see para **12.17** above. The transfer of assets is recognized for tax purposes by one country, but not by the other.

- *Hybrid entity payments*: see para **12.19** above.

- *Payments by reverse hybrids*: see para **12.21** above.

- *Imported mismatches*: see para **12.22** above.

BEPS Action 2: summary of domestic proposals

12.29   The rules that BEPS Action 2 proposes for introduction into the domestic law of countries are broken down into:

- general improvements; and

- hybrid mismatch rules:

  primary – by the country being asked to grant a tax deduction for a payment under a hybrid arrangement; and

  defensive rule – by a country dealing with a receipt under a hybrid arrangement where the other country has not implemented any hybrid mismatch rule in respect of the corresponding payment.

Scope of the Action 2 proposed rules

12.30   Some of the proposed rules are limited to arrangements between defined types of connected persons: 'related parties' and 'controlled groups'. The OECD recommends that the term 'related party' is defined as persons in the same 'control group', or where one person has ≥25 per cent investment in the other, or a third person holds ≥25 per cent in them both.

A 'control group' consists of entities:

- whose results are consolidated for accounting purposes; or

- where one has effective control of the other, or a third person has effective control over them both; or

- where one has ≥50 per cent investment or effective control in the other or a third person has ≥50 per cent investment in, of effective control of them both; or

- where both are regarded as associated enterprises (for the purposes of Article 9 of the OECD Model Tax Treaty (transfer pricing)).

There are also 'acting together' rules to catch situations where there are less formal connections between entities, such as family ties or evidence that one entity acts in accordance with the wishes of the other, even in the absence of legal control.

Some of the rules also apply to 'structured arrangements'. A 'structured arrangement' is defined as 'any arrangement where the hybrid mismatch is priced into the terms of the arrangement or the facts and circumstances (including the terms) of the arrangement indicate that it has been designed to produce a hybrid mismatch'. This definition is designed to catch schemes promoted, and sold by banks and other financial advisors.

Examples of structured arrangements suggested by the OECD are:

- an arrangement that is designed, or is part of a plan, to create a hybrid mismatch;

- an arrangement that incorporates a term, step or transaction used in order to create a hybrid mismatch;

- an arrangement that is marketed, in whole or in part, as a tax-advantaged product where some or all of the tax advantage derives from the hybrid mismatch;

- an arrangement that is primarily marketed to taxpayers in a jurisdiction where the hybrid mismatch arises;

- an arrangement that contains features that alter the terms under the arrangement, including the return, in the event that the hybrid mismatch is no longer available; or

- an arrangement that would produce a negative return absent the hybrid mismatch.

However, if neither the taxpayer nor any member of the taxpayer's control group could reasonably have been expected to be aware of the hybrid mismatch, ie it was accidental, then provided that neither the taxpayer, nor any member of the control group enjoyed a tax benefit from the arrangement, the arrangement is not treated as a structured arrangement.

Rules for hybrid financial instruments

12.31   Most of the rules involve one country denying a tax deduction where hybrid arrangements exist. The rules take account of the fact that hybrid arrangements can, rarely, result in the same income being taxed in two different countries without any double tax relief. This type of income is called 'dual inclusion income', and the amount of disallowed payments under Action 2 rules can be reduced by the amount of any such 'dual inclusion income' suffered by the person whose tax deductions are being disallowed. Generally, countries are advised to deny tax exemptions for receipts of foreign dividends if the dividend is received from a related party that has claimed a tax deduction in respect of the payment. This prevents the taxpayers achieving a deduction but no taxable income (a D/NI outcome). If a country operates double tax relief by credit for foreign dividend income, then it should refuse to give double tax relief for any foreign withholding taxes suffered on the income to the extent that the dividend payment was tax deductible for the payer.

More specifically, the primary rule recommended in respect of payments under hybrid instruments is to deny a tax deduction. The defensive rules, where the payer's country has not implemented a primary rule, is for the recipient's country to tax the income, even if it would normally be considered tax exempt. These rules should only be applied where the hybrid financial instrument is made by related parties or as part of a structured arrangement. If the arrangements in question are so-called 'imported mismatch arrangements' (see Figure 12.7 above) then there is just a primary rule ('response'), but no defensive rule. The primary rule is for the payer to be denied a tax deduction. This rule is more limited in scope than the rule for other hybrid instruments – it should only be applied where the parties are members of the same 'control group', or where there are 'structured arrangements' in place.

In summary, the primary and secondary rules on hybrid financial instruments apply to two main types of financing arrangements:

- *Financial instruments*: arrangements which are recognized as either debt, equity, or derivative contracts under local laws.

- *Repo-type arrangements (hybrid transfers)*: where the same financial instrument, eg shares, is treated by two different countries as being held by more than one person.

The OECD's Final Report on Action 2 gives details of no less than 37 different types of arrangements involving hybrid instruments that are potentially within the scope of the Action 2 rules that are recommended for inclusion in the domestic laws of states.

Rules for hybrid financial entities

12.32 The rules vary depending on whether the hybrid entity is designed to produce a 'deduction/no income' (D/NI) outcome or a double deduction (DD).

For D/NI outcomes (eg as in Figure 12.3 above) the rule is known as the 'disregarded hybrid payments rule'. The 'primary rule' is for the country of the payer (the hybrid entity) to disallow the deduction, usually for interest paid either to a bank, or to the parent company. If the payer's country does not implement the 'primary rule', then the parent company's country should operate a 'defensive rule': effectively to recognize income from the hybrid entity in the parent company tax computation. This rule should be applied to entities in a 'control group' or where a 'structured arrangement' is used.

For D/NI hybrid arrangements involving reverse hybrids (see Figure 12.6 above), the primary rule is that the payer county (Country C in our example) should deny the borrower a deduction for interest paid. This rule should only be applied if the parties are in a 'control group' or the payments are made under a 'structured arrangement'.

There are also some recommendations that countries should ensure their controlled foreign company rules (see Chapter 17) cover reverse hybrid situations. Countries are also encouraged to treat hybrid entities as resident taxpayers in the country where they are established if it is known that the investors in the same 'control group' are not being taxed on the income of the entity.

For D/D outcomes from the use of hybrid entities (see Figures 12.5 and 12.6) the 'primary rule' is for the parent company country not to grant a deduction. There is no limit on the scope of this rule: there is no requirement that the parties to the arrangement are in the same 'control group' or that the arrangement must be a 'structured arrangement'. The 'defensive rule' is for the payer's country (where the hybrid entity is a taxpayer) to deny a deduction. The rules are limited to where the parties are in a 'control group' or where the arrangements are 'structured arrangements'.

D/D outcomes also arise where companies are dual resident and similar rules are recommended in these cases, even though the companies involved are not hybrid entities.

Table 12.1 Summary of the OECD BEPS Action 2 recommendations for changes to domestic laws

Type of mismatch	Type of arrangement	Specific recommendations on improvements to domestic law	Recommended hybrid mismatch rule		
			Response	*Defensive rule*	*Scope*
D/NI	Hybrid financial instrument	No dividend exemption for deductible payments Proportionate limitation of withholding tax credits	Deny payer deduction	Include as ordinary income	Related parties and structured arrangements
	Disregarded payment made by a hybrid		Deny payer deduction	Include as ordinary income	Control group and structured arrangements
	Payment made to a reverse hybrid	Improvements to offshore investment regime Restricting tax transparency of intermediate entities where non-resident investors treat the entity as opaque	Deny payer deduction	—	Control group and structured arrangements
DD	Deductible payment made by a hybrid		Deny parent deduction	Deny payer deduction	No limitation on response, defensive rules applies to control group and structured arrangements
	Deductible payment made by dual resident		Deny resident deduction	—	No limitation on response
Indirect D/NI	Imported mismatch arrangement		Deny payer deduction	—	Members of control group and structured arrangements

BEPS Action 2: prospects for success

12.33   The reason why tax planning using hybrid arrangements is ubiquitous within MNEs is because many countries have different definitions of what constitutes debt capital, what constitutes equity capital, and what kind of entitles should be recognized as taxpayers in their own right (ie they are opaque). Even if the OECD member countries are able to achieve harmonization of these definitions, there would still remain scope for arbitrage involving non-OECD countries. Countries choose or maintain policies on debt/equity, transparent entity/opaque entity as a matter of their sovereign legal and economic policy-making right. These choices have either been consciously made, or are bound up in a long history of economic and judicial development. Aiming for coherence in these definitions seems extremely ambitious.

As with any proposed changes aimed at harmonizing the laws of several countries, although there might be the will to harmonize at the supranational level, the fact remains that as long as taxpayers are complying with the laws of the countries in which they operate then the governments see no pressing need to change those laws. If a subsidiary, resident in Country A, of a MNE complies with the law and pays full taxes in Country A, then the motivation for Country A to change its laws because the MNE is achieving tax advantages through differences between Country A's laws and the laws of other countries in which the MNE operates, is weak. Matters of sovereignty cannot be ignored: if Country A and Country B define a taxable entity differently, then which country's definition should be adopted? If Country A adopts Country B's definition, then the government of Country A risks accusations of having ceded sovereignty in its law-making to another country. This is a difficult, perhaps intractable, issue.

Commentators on the BEPS Action 2 agenda have pointed out that the BEPS Action 2 rules are clearly aimed at situations where:

- there are hybrid financial arrangements;

- the arrangements involve members of the same MNE, so that the outcome of the arrangements is most probably intentional; and

- the arrangements result in deduction/no inclusion (D/NI) or double deduction (DD) outcomes.

Consequently, the arrangements are probably abusive and could probably be dealt with under general or specific anti-avoidance rules (GAARs and SAARs). The problem with this is that most domestic anti-avoidance laws of a particular country only operate where that country's tax is being avoided, not where the tax is being avoided somewhere else. There are also doubts as to whether GAARs and SAARs are robust enough to tackle hybrid financial arrangements, because it is relatively easy for a MNE to point to some commercial purpose in making the arrangement other than just saving tax.[1]

Importantly, if the aim of the BEPS project to achieve a coherent international tax system is to be achieved, not only do D/NI and DD situations need to be resolved but also double taxation situations, which are unresolved under the Action 2 recommendations.[2]

---

1   For instance, see Cooper G S (2015) 'Australia/OECD – Some Thoughts on the OECD's Recommendation on Hybrid Mismatches', *Bulletin for International Taxation*, Vol 69, No 6/7.
2   As observed by Kahlenberg & Kopec (2016) for example.

RESTRICTIONS ON INTEREST DEDUCTIONS

12.34   Some countries do not permit holding companies to deduct in full the interest paid by them in connection with money borrowed to invest in a subsidiary company, for instance, in the situation shown in Figure 12.11.

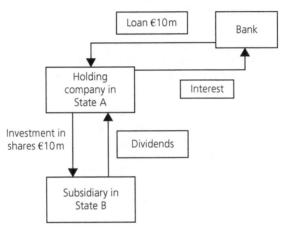

Figure 12.11

State A might operate a system of exemption for foreign dividends. Thus, if State A gives interest relief on the interest paid by the holding company on the €10 million borrowed from the bank it will reduce its tax revenues from the holding company. However, if State A also exempts foreign dividends from taxation, it will not receive any taxable income to compensate it for the tax deduction given in respect of the interest payments. Thus a country might decide not to give interest relief on borrowings used to fund overseas investments which do not result in taxable income. Note that this type of provision which was being operated in the Netherlands was held to be inconsistent with EC law where the overseas investments were in fellow EU Member States in the *Bosal Holding* case.[1] Hence, EU Member States have had to find alternative means of preserving their tax bases.

Many countries have specific rules aimed at preventing full tax deduction for interest paid to a connected company where either the rate of the interest or the terms of the loan are not such as would be found in a loan between unconnected companies. Following the *Bosal* case, the Netherlands adopted both thin capitalization rules and also more general rules which restrict the set-off of tax losses of holding companies resulting from interest payments and other financing costs to other income of the same year. Any losses not set off in the same year may only be relieved in past or future years against income from holding and financing activities. Germany also operates a set of rules limiting interest deductions, in addition to its thin capitalization rules. Introduced from 2008, there is a so-called 'interest barrier' (*Zinsschranke*) which limits deductions for interest paid. Interest payable which exceeds interest receivable may only be deducted from taxable profits up to an amount representing 30 per cent of earnings before interest, taxes, depreciation and amortization. Certain exceptions apply, principally for companies which are not part of a group.

The UK has, for some time, operated the so-called 'unallowable purpose' rules. Broadly, these rules can deny a tax deduction for interest payments where the interest payment is made as part of a scheme or arrangement which has an 'unallowable purpose' (ie UK tax avoidance). An unallowable purpose will be one which does not feature in the businesses or other commercial purposes of the company or is in respect of activities whose profits are not within the charge to UK corporation tax for the company (eg because the profits are made by a non-UK permanent establishment not subject to UK tax) or which have a tax-avoidance purpose.

The UK also has a set of rules designed to prevent excessive interest deductions by UK members of international groups. Broadly, there may be a disallowance of interest deduction if the borrowings of the UK group members exceed the aggregate worldwide borrowings of the MNE. This is only likely to occur where there have been 'upstream loans' – that is, loans made by subsidiaries to parent companies, which cancel out when the consolidated group accounts are prepared. These rules, known as the 'worldwide debt cap' are examined briefly below and in more detail in the 'Further study' section of this chapter.

The OECD considers that none of the approaches outlined so far are fully effective in preventing tax avoidance practices that involve the claiming of interest deductions. BEPS Action 4 is aimed at strengthening the ability of countries to combat excessive claims for interest deduction, and the proposals are examined in para **12.36** below.

---

1   C-168/01 *Bosal Holding BV v Staatssecretaris van Financien* [2003] STC 1483.

Thin capitalization rules

12.35   It is a well-established principle of international taxation that companies in the same group must apply open market pricing, or its equivalent, in their transactions with each other. This is known as the 'arm's length' principle. The pricing of intra-group transactions is usually referred to as 'transfer pricing'. Chapter 13 looks at this principle in detail, but there is one aspect of the rules, 'thin capitalization' which is directly concerned with the financing arrangements of MNEs and so is dealt with in this chapter. Transfer pricing principles can apply to financial transactions in the same way as they do to transactions involving goods and services. Rates of interest charged intragroup must be comparable, taking into account the terms of the intragroup loans, to the rates charged by and to lenders and borrowers outside the MNE. Discounts, commissions, and fees must also be computed using the arm's-length principle.

Thin capitalization is not concerned with the rates of interest charged, but with the amount of funds lent by a group company to a fellow group company, relative to the amount of equity share capital of the borrower. A company is said to be 'thinly capitalized' if its ratio of equity capital to debt capital is lower than would be expected if the company were an independent enterprise rather than a member of a group of companies. The temptation is for a MNE to finance subsidiaries in high-tax jurisdictions with a high ratio of debt to equity. Thus the return on debt capital is mainly tax deductible interest rather than non-deductible dividends. Although dividends are not tax-deductible, they are low risk because payment of dividends is optional: if no profits are paid, the company does not have to pay a dividend, nor does it ever have to repay the capital sum invested in its shares. High levels of debt capital create high levels of risk for the borrower, because the interest must be paid each year, and the capital repaid when the debt matures, regardless of whether the borrower has any cash or profits. If a company cannot pay its interest or repay its debt then, if the funds had been lent by an unconnected bank, that bank would be in a position to put the company out of business by seizing its assets. However, a group company lending to a fellow group company would be unlikely to follow such a harsh course of action. So, arrangements between the MNE lender, and the MNE borrower where the company in which investment is made has very high levels of debt capital relative to its equity capital are not arrangements that would be expected on the open market the borrower does not experience the same level of risk from having very large amounts of debt relative to its share (equity) capital.

Thin capitalization legislation reclassifies part of the interest deduction as a dividend, recognizing that at least part of the debt capital is, in effect, permanent capital. This is on the grounds that there is so much debt capital that the company which borrowed it could never hope to repay it and remain in business. Permanent capital is equity (share) capital and the return on equity capital is a dividend or other distribution out of profits, not interest. This is an application of the substance over form principle.

Example 12.4

Alder Ltd and Birch Ltd are both wholly-owned UK subsidiaries of Redwood Inc, a US company. A balance sheet extract showing the capital structure of the two subsidiaries is given below:

	Alder Ltd	Birch Ltd
	£	£
Issued share capital	10,000	100,000
Retained profits	40,000	30,000
Shareholder funds	50,000	130,000
Long-term 8% loan	50,000	400,000
Total capital	100,000	530,000
Debt to equity:	1:1	3.07:1

Extracts from the profit and loss accounts read as follows:

	Alder Ltd	Birch Ltd
	£	£
Profit before interest, tax and dividends	40,000	40,000
Loan interest	4,000	32,000
Taxable profits	36,000	8,000
Tax at 20%	7,200	1,600
Distributable profits	28,800	6,400
Dividend	10,000	0
	18,800	6,400

The two subsidiaries have identical profits before interest, tax and dividends. Due to the difference in financing structures, the taxable profit of Birch Ltd is much lower than that of Alder Ltd. The UK tax authority would be unlikely to challenge the capital structure of Alder Ltd, given the debt to equity ratio of 1:1. There may be a challenge regarding the interest payments by Birch Ltd. If the tax authority is successful, some part of the interest payment of £32,000 might be reclassified as a dividend, meaning that it would no longer reduce profits chargeable to corporation tax.

Every country with thin capitalization rules has its own version of them. Some are fairly general, whilst some are extremely prescriptive. As might be expected, the US rules are extremely prescriptive. No adjustment will be made to a US paying company's taxable profits under US thin capitalization legislation provided that interest amounts to less than 50 per cent of the corporation's tax-adjusted income, and provided that the ratio of debt to equity is 1.5 to 1 or less. This specification of an acceptable gearing ratio is an example of a 'safe harbour'. A ratio of 3 to 1 is more commonly used in this context by other countries, although not all countries employ this safe harbour concept. Italy introduced new thin capitalization rules in January 2004 for the first time. The legislation affects interest payments to shareholders owning directly or indirectly at least 25 per cent of the share capital of an Italian company whose debt to equity ratio is 4:1 or greater. As with most thin capitalization rules, interest paid on third-party loans guaranteed by other group companies is also caught.

BEPS Action 4 – proposals to limit deductions for interest

12.36 BEPS Action 4 is predicated on the belief that MNEs commonly arrange their external and internal borrowings so as to artificially inflate the tax deductions claimed by the MNE companies for interest payable. Whilst this might well be true in some cases, as mentioned earlier, a group's financing policies will have many drivers and tax is usually only one of these.

Is the OECD correct in its belief that MNEs routinely arrange their group financing so as to artificially inflate the tax deductions for interest claimable by the MNE as a whole? Certainly, in a MNE with a highly centralized finance function, it would be surprising if tax-efficiency was not a factor in decisions on whether and to what extent to finance group members with debt capital, whether through the MNE member borrowing externally or through the making of intragroup loans. There is a valid argument that, when it comes to financing decisions, it is the MNE as a whole which is important. The separate entity fiction, which deems each separate legal person in the MNE to be a separate economic entity is difficult to justify in the arena of group financing decisions.[1]

BEPS Action 4 aims to tackle the situation where a MNE claims worldwide deductions for interest that, due mainly to intragroup lending, amount to more than the interest paid by the MNE to third-party lenders. In other words, Action 4 is aimed at the situation where MNEs have manufactured interest deductions through intragroup lending, without incurring tax liabilities on interest receipts of an equivalent amount to the deductions claimed. Action 4 is not designed to restrict deductions for interest paid to third-party lenders (eg unconnected banks). However, it *is* also designed to discourage groups from causing group members that are resident in relatively high tax regimes from bearing a disproportionate share of the total external borrowing of the MNE. So, Action 4 has three principal aims:

1   to broadly limit the total net interest deduction in a group to the amount of net interest due to external (third party) lenders;

2   to prevent groups from maximizing the value of their interest deductions by funding group members which suffer high effective tax rates with disproportionate amounts of debt capital; and

3   to tackle tax avoidance whereby groups use third party or intragroup financing (claiming interest deductions on this) to generate tax free income.[2]

Many countries already have rules in their domestic law to tackle one or both of these issues, eg as noted above, at the time of writing the UK has the 'worldwide debt cap' to tackle the first and, in common with many other countries, has thin capitalization rules to tackle the second. Many countries also have rules which limit the deductions for interest to a specific percentage of profits. Notably, no country presently has rules which impose limitations on interest paid based on the position of the worldwide group. Many countries have no rules limiting interest deductions and amongst those which have, there is no international coordination of the rules.

---

1   This point is forcefully made in the Public Comments on the Article 4 Discussion Draft submitted by the BEPS Monitoring Group. This organization includes Sol Picciotto, a prominent author on the tax aspects of MNEs for many decades.
2   OECD (2015b), 'Limiting Base Erosion involving Interest Deductions and Other Financial Payments – Action 4: Final Report', 5 October 2015.

Why not just use arm's length rules?

12.37   Could the whole question of excessive interest deductions being claimed for by a group company be tackled by application of transfer pricing techniques: the arm's-length principle (discussed in Chapter 13)? In other words, is the interest deduction being claimed by a company which is a member of a MNE in line with the interest deduction which would be claimed by a similar company, in similar circumstances except that it is not part of a group? However, the OECD considers that this approach is too resource intensive, and too time-consuming to be of practical use to taxpayers and tax authorities.[1] In other words, the OECD considers that the arm's-length approach is simply too difficult to use in deciding whether interest deductions within a group of companies are justified. Given the huge resources which the OECD continues to pour into developing and updating the arm's-length principle, the decision to abandon it, as a means of determining whether interest deductions are being claimed in an acceptable amount, seems very surprising. Many commentators, for instance, the International Chamber of Commerce (ICC), have reacted with dismay to this abandonment of the arm's-length principle.

---

1   BEPS Action 4 2014 Discussion Draft, p 13.

Planning targeted by Action 4

12.38   The type of planning at which BEPS Action 4 is aimed is illustrated, in very broad terms, in Example 12.5.

Example 12.5

Company A owns 100 per cent of the share capital of Company B and Company C. Company A borrows $300K from an external bank at a rate of 6.667 per cent interest. Out of this borrowing, it on lends $90k to Company B and $120k to Company C at market rates of interest in the countries where Company B and Company C are resident.

Tax residence	Co. A Country X $k	Co. B Country Y $k	Co. C Country Z $k	Total $k
Net asset value	600	200	400	1200
Earnings before interest, taxes, depreciation and amortization (EBITDA)	100	60	40	200
External bank borrowings	300	0	0	300
Borrowings from Co. A	n/a	90	120	210
Interest payable	20	7	10	37
Interest receivable	12	0	0	12
Net tax deduction for interest	8	7	10	25

Although the total interest paid to external banks by the ABC group is only $20k, the total net tax deductions for interest within the global group are $25k. The deductions for interest paid by Company B and Company C have not been completely matched by taxable interest receipts in Company A. The most probable reason for this is that some of the financial instruments used between A and B, and A and C are hybrids, so that these financial instrument are viewed as debt by Countries Y and Z, but as equity by Country X (which does not tax returns on equity finance).

The Action 4 Discussion Draft published in December 2014 considers three broad approaches to limiting interest deductions: a so-called 'worldwide approach', a 'fixed ratio' approach, and an approach involving targeted rules. Combinations of approaches are also considered. The Final Report on Action 4[1] advocates the 'fixed ratio' approach, but both approaches are explained in the sections below. The public comments received on Action 4 run to more than 1000 pages and, overall, it seems that there is little appetite for a worldwide approach. There is a widespread belief apparent from the public comments that such an approach would be too draconian.[2]

---

1   OECD (2015b), 'Limiting Base Erosion involving Interest Deductions and Other Financial Payments – Action 4: 2015 Final Report', October 2015.
2   For a discussion of the BEPS Action 4 in the context of the Australian Chevron case, see Ting (2017).

The 'worldwide approach'

12.39   The worldwide approach has two main parts:

1   Find out how much interest the worldwide group of companies has paid to external borrowers during the period in question. The resulting figure is then reduced by the amount of interest receivable from third parties during the period.

2   Allocate a part of this net interest expense to each company in the worldwide group. The amount each company is allocated would depend on the level of economic activity carried out in that company relative to the total economic activity of the whole group.

How to decide each group member's allocation of deductible interest?

12.40   The choices are to allocate a portion of the worldwide group's total third-party net-interest expense to individual group companies based upon either:

● the earnings of the MNE company relative to the earnings of the MNE as a whole; or

● the value of assets owned by the MNE company relative to the total assets of the worldwide group.

The overriding criterion for allocation of interest deductions is that they should reflect the location of value creation within the MNE. The MNE companies which create the most value are those most in need of funding: to pay wages, buy new machinery and intellectual property, to carry out R&D activities, and so on. Therefore, they are the companies which we would naturally expect to have borrowings, on which they would need to pay interest. On the other hand, a relatively inactive group company would probably not need much funding as it would have relatively few expenses.

Profitability is probably the best measure of contribution to the value created by a group company. However, profits fluctuate from year to year and abnormal costs, such as the cost of purchasing new premises, can mask the true profitability of a group member. One of the key requirements of any system of allocation of interest deductions within a group of companies is that the result should be predictable. Basing the allocation on profits or earnings might not be predictable and so the OECD has recommended that the allocation be undertaken on the basis of net asset values instead.

Illustration – how the Action 4 proposals might operate

12.41

Example 12.6

	Co. A	Co. B	Co. C	Total
Tax residence	Country X	Country Y	Country Z	
	$k	$k	$k	$k
Net asset value	600	200	400	1200
Earnings before interest, taxes, depreciation and amortization (EBITDA)	100	80	20	200
External bank borrowings	300	0	0	300
Borrowings from Co. A	n/a	90	120	210
Interest payable	20	7	10	37
Worldwide approach: interest deduction permitted				
Using net earnings:	10*	8	2	20
Using net assets	10**	3.33	6.67	20

Notes: *100/200 × $20k; **600/1200 × $20k.

Note that the total interest deduction for the MNE is limited to $20k: the amount of the external borrowing.

This illustration shows how an interest allocation rule might work. In Example 12.6 we disregard the actual interest paid by any of the companies and substitute deemed interest expense. An alternative method, still using the worldwide approach, would be to have an 'interest cap'. For instance, using net earnings as the key, instead of Company B's interest deduction being deemed to be $8k, Company B could claim a deduction for interest actually payable (internal or external to the MNE) up to a cap of $8k. However, its actual interest payment was only $7k, so that would be the interest deduction claimable. However, using a cap would mean that the MNE would only obtain interest relief in total of $19k, rather than the total external interest paid of $20k.

Criticisms of the worldwide approach

12.42 Many commentators have criticized the OECD's proposals under Action 4. BIAC[1] raises the concern that MNEs will be encouraged to take on unnecessary levels of external debt. A more general observation is that the ratio of debt to equity chosen by a group and its component member companies is a product of internal and external pressures, by no means all of them driven by tax concerns. As referred to earlier, the split between debt and equity is influenced by other issues, such as minority interests, existing creditors, exchange controls, and other local regulatory constraints as well as foreign exchange issues (BIAC Public comments on Action 4).

A more fundamental criticism is that the worldwide approach is, in essence, a formulary apportionment of the MNE's interest expense. This sits uneasily with the OECD's longstanding refusal to base the allocation of taxable profits within a MNE to individual group members using a formula rather than strict application of the arm's-length principle. This departure from the arm's-length principle was noted with some alarm in the public comments received on the Action 4 Discussion Draft. Formulary apportionment was rejected in Action 1 and continues to be rejected in all the BEPS Actions in the area of transfer pricing. The idea of formulary apportionment is discussed in more detail in Chapter 13.

A major criticism of formulary apportionment is that it can only work if all the countries in which a MNE operates apply the same system and, in particular, the same formula. If any of the countries apply different rules, then this can result in double taxation or double non-taxation. For instance, if, in our example, Countries X and Z decide that they will use contribution to group EBITDA as their allocation key, but Country Y decides to use net asset values, the following results will appear:

Example 12.7

	Co. A	Co. B	Co. C	Total
Tax residence	Country X	Country Y	Country Z	
	$k	$k	$k	$k
Interest deduction if Countries X & Z use EBITDA, but Country Y uses net asset values:	10	3.33	2	15.33

389

The total of interest deductions for the MNE companies is now only $15.33k. Therefore $4.67k of interest is not relieved.

Overall, the principal criticism of this worldwide approach is a practical one: it would involve heavy compliance costs because every group company claiming an interest deduction would need to know the position of the entire group before it could establish the amount of interest deduction to which that company was entitled. These costs would be significant even if exemptions were granted for smaller companies within the MNE.

---

1   The Business and Industry Advisory Committee to the OECD. BIAC is an international network of 2800+ business experts, and is the officially recognized business voice to the OECD. See: www.biac.org.

The fixed ratio approach

12.43   This is the approach recommended by the OECD in its October 2015 BEPS Final Report on interest deductions. Under this approach, the allowable deduction for interest in any group company would be limited to a percentage of that company's earnings. In this way, the erosion of the tax base through interest deductions would be limited. The limitation need not be specifically by reference to earnings – it could be made by reference to assets or equity. Many countries already apply a version of such rules; so-called 'thin capitalization rules', which were discussed earlier in this chapter. Under thin capitalization rules, the interest deduction is limited to interest on the proposition of debt to equity within the claimant company which might be expected if the claimant company was an independent company and not part of a group. Although, strictly speaking, this uses the arm's-length approach, many countries have published ratios of debt to equity (commonly 3:1) below which they will not seek to apply these rules. The fixed ratio approach would be much simpler to apply and comply with than any 'worldwide approach'. This is because it relies solely on the tax position of a single entity – the MNE company and makes no reference to debt levels elsewhere in the MNE. The requirement for international cooperation is far lower, because each country could fix its own ratios.

EBITDA is recommended to be based on values determined under the tax rules of the country applying the rules, on the basis that using tax numbers reduces the risk that an entity with negative EBITDA becomes liable for taxes as a result of interest disallowance and also that linking interest deductions to taxable earnings makes it more difficult for a group to increase the limit on deductions without also increasing the level of taxable income in a country.

Applying the fixed ratio approach by reference to EBITDA to our example is shown in Example 12.8.

Example 12.8

	Co. A	Co. B	Co. C	Total
Tax residence	Country X	Country Y	Country Z	
	$k	$k	$k	$k
Net asset value	600	200	400	1200
Earnings before interest, taxes, depreciation and amortization (EBITDA)	100	80	20	200
15% EBITDA	15	12	3	30
External bank borrowings	300	0	0	300
Borrowings from Co. A	n/a	20	30	50
External interest payable	20	0	0	20
Net interest payable	12	7	10	37
Interest limited to higher of actual paid or 15% EBITDA	15	7	3	25

In this example, Countries X, Y and Z have all adopted 15 per cent of EBITDA as the limit on interest deductions. However, they could each choose different limits, although the OECD would prefer that each country used broadly the same limit. Each country is considered separately: for instance, even though Company B's interest payable is below 15 per cent of EBITDA, it cannot pass on its spare capacity for deducting interest ($12k – $7k = $5k) to fellow group companies in other countries. However, setting off within the MNE might be possible by companies that are resident in the same country.

At the time of the OECD discussion draft, some countries were identified as having such rules:[1]

1   Finland: 25 per cent of EBITDA calculated based on the taxable profit and loss account. The calculation is made by entity and adjusted by taking into account group contributions received or made.

2   Germany: 30 per cent of taxable EBITDA.

3   Greece: 30 per cent of EBITDA. Phased-in system according to which the percentage will reduce from 60 per cent in 2014 to 30 per cent in 2017.

4   Italy: 30 per cent of EBITDA, adjusted by adding rental payments under finance lease transactions.

5   Norway: 30 per cent of taxable EBITDA.

6   Portugal: 30 per cent of EBITDA, adjusted by excluding certain items such as income resulting from shares eligible for the participation exemption or attributable to a permanent establishment outside Portugal to which the option for exemption is applied. Phased-in system according to which the percentage will reduce from 70 per cent in 2013 to 30 per cent in 2017.

7   Spain: 30 per cent of operating profits adjusted by adding certain items such as depreciation and amortization and financial income from equity investments.

8   United States: 50 per cent of adjusted taxable income, ie EBITDA plus specific deductions taken into account when calculating the taxable income.

---

1   OECD Discussion Draft on Action 4.

Variation: a group ratio rule

12.44   A group ratio rule takes into account the fact that groups operating in certain commercial sectors have a higher debt to equity ratio than groups operating in other sectors. A two-stage test is recommended:

Stage 1: compute the 'group ratio': this would be:

$$\frac{\text{Net third party interest expense}}{\text{Group EBITDA}}$$

Stage 2: apply the 'group ratio' to the individual group company:

Group ratio = limit on net interest deduction

Individual company's EBITDA

$$\frac{\text{Group ratio}}{\text{Individual company's EBITDA}} = \text{limit on net interest deduction}$$

Such a group ratio rule could be used by a country in conjunction with a fixed ratio rule.

Advantages of the fixed ratio approach

12.45   The advantages of a fixed-ratio approach over a group wide approach are:

1   Consistency with the separate entity approach to taxing members of international groups of companies – the individual company only needs to know its own figures and the interest ratio limits applied by its own country – it does not need extra information about the MNE-wide position.

2   Flexibility for countries to set their own ratios, reflecting the local economic climate and taking account of other anti-avoidance measures which a particular country already has in place, such as anti-hybrid rules, CFC rules and so on. Countries can also use their own definitions of interest in accordance with their local laws.

3   Compliance and administration costs would be much lower than for a worldwide regime.

4   Countries can simplify the application of the rules, eg by having a *de minimis* threshold so that companies or entities with relatively small interest payments would not be caught.

5   The effects of any disallowances of interest can be ameliorated by permitting the carry forward of disallowed amounts of interest and also of excess capacity to offset interest to future years.

Criticism of the fixed ratio approach

12.46   In situations where relatively few group companies are in a position to secure external borrowing, disallowances of interest may occur if those companies are unable to push the debt down to the operating subsidiaries (via on-lending). For instance, in Example 12.8 we can see that although Company A had external interest payable of $20k, it would be unable to obtain a tax deduction for all of this.

The limit would have to be broadly agreed between OECD members: 30 per cent of EBITDA appears to be the limit most commonly used, but the OECD considers that this is too high.

Companies would not know their maximum permitted interest deductions in any period until they know the EBITDA for that period. This would make it difficult for companies to accurately budget for the costs of debt finance. This is because tax deductible interest has a lower net cost to the company than non-deductible interest. This problem could be lessened if companies were permitted to carry forward or back excess interest capacity.

There would need to be mechanisms to ensure that intragroup interest for which a deduction was disallowed was not taxed in the hands of the MNE lending company.

GENERAL TAX TREATY ISSUES AND EU DIRECTIVES

12.47   When the subsidiary company is tax resident in a different country to that of the investor, both the country where the investor is tax resident and the country where the subsidiary is tax resident may tax the investing company on the dividends and interest. The country where the subsidiary is tax resident usually taxes dividends and interest by means of a 'withholding tax'. A withholding tax is a payment by the payer of interest to the tax authority on behalf of the recipient, in satisfaction of the non-resident recipient's tax liability on that interest or dividend under the source principle (see Chapter 5 for more details). Article 11 of the OECD Model Tax convention deals with interest payments and permits withholding tax to be charged.

If no DTT exists between the countries of the payer and the recipient of the interest, then it is common for the payer's country to require the rate to be the standard rate of income tax under domestic law which is often at rates well in excess of the rate specified in any treaty. It is important to study the terms of the relevant treaty in detail. As an example, the impact of Article 11 of the UK & Ghana Treaty is considered below:

'Article 11 Interest

'(1) Interest arising in a Contracting State and paid to a resident of the other Contracting State may be taxed in that other State.

(2) However, such interest may also be taxed in the Contracting State in which it arises and according to the laws of that State, but if the recipient is the beneficial owner of the interest and is subject to tax in respect of the interest in that other Contracting State the tax so charged shall not exceed 12.5 per cent of the gross amount of the interest.

…

(6) Where, by reason of a special relationship between the payer and the beneficial owner or between both of them and some other person, the amount of the interest paid exceeds, for whatever reason, the amount which would have been agreed upon by the payer and the beneficial owner in the absence of such relationship, the provisions of this Article shall apply only to the last-mentioned amount of interest. In such case, the excess part of the payments shall remain taxable according to the laws of each Contracting State, due regard being had to the other provisions of this Convention.'

(Extract from the DTT between the UK and Ghana.)

Example 12.9

We can use this extract to answer the following questions:

1   A UK company, Nesbit Ltd, receives a cash payment of £10,000 in respect of interest due on a loan to a Ghanaian company. What are the UK and Ghanaian tax liabilities in connection with this interest, assuming a UK corporation tax of 20 per cent and a basic rate of Ghanaian income tax of 25 per cent?

Because Nesbit Ltd is the beneficial owner of the interest and is subject to UK tax on it, the rate of Ghanaian withholding tax will be 12.5 per cent:

	£
Cash payment received 10,000	
Ghanaian withholding tax at 12.5%	
10,000 × 12.5%/87.5%	1,429
Gross interest	11,429
UK corporation tax at 20% on $11,429	2,286
Double tax relief	−1,429
UK tax payable	857

2 How would the answer differ if the UK lender was a pension fund (UK tax exempt)? We will assume that the amount of interest paid by the Ghanaian borrower, before withholding tax, is the same, ie £11,429.

Ghana would not limit its withholding tax to 12.5 per cent because the pension fund would not be subject to UK tax on the interest received. However, note that the interpretation of these 'subject to tax' clauses varies from country to country, and here we are interpreting it to mean that Ghana would not consider a tax-exempt organization as being 'subject to tax' in the UK.

	£
Gross interest payable	11,429
Ghanaian withholding tax at 25%	
11,429 × 25%/75%	3,810
Net interest received by pension fund	7,619

3 What would be the result if the interest was received from a wholly-owned Ghanaian subsidiary and the £11,429 gross payment represented interest charged at a rate of at 20 per cent pa? In this case, we will assume that the open market rate of interest would only have been 5 per cent.

Paragraph (6) of Article 11 will apply as the fact that the Ghanaian subsidiary is wholly owned means that there is a 'special relationship'. In this case it is necessary to split the interest payment and apply two different rates of withholding tax. This type of anti-avoidance provision is considered in more detail in Chapter 15.

	£
Total interest payment before withholding tax	11,429
Withholding tax at 12.5% on interest representing the market rate: £11,429 × 5%/20% = £2,857 × 12.5%	357
Withholding tax on the 'excess' interest at 25%: £11,429 × 15%/20% = £8672 × 25%	2143
Total withholding tax	2500

Whatever the contents of the relevant DTTs, there is no withholding tax on interest payments between two companies within the EU under the terms of the Interest and Royalties Directive where one holds at least 10 per cent of the other, or the same person holds 10 per cent of both. Similarly, the Parent/Subsidiary Directive requires EU Member States to eliminate withholding taxes on payment of dividends between two EU companies subject to a 10 per cent shareholding.

Note that it is unusual for withholding taxes to result in double taxation. The rate of withholding tax is normally lower than the tax rate faced by the investing company in its country of residence. Depending on the double tax relief system used by the investor's country, the interest and dividends will either be exempt, or else the withholding tax will be creditable against the tax liability in the country of residence. However, if the recipient company has a low or non-existent domestic tax liability on the interest income (say, due to the offset of domestic losses) then the withholding tax may become an absolute tax liability which increases the total worldwide tax bill rather than merely redistributing it. The big disadvantage of suffering withholding tax is that the time for payment of tax is effectively brought forward to the time that the interest is paid, rather than when the recipient's tax liability falls due in the country of residence. It is usually a cash flow disadvantage.

A country will only give a double tax credit for withholding tax if it believes it has been correctly charged by the payer's country. A problem sometimes arises where one country classes a payment as a royalty and charges withholding tax, but the recipient's country classifies the payments as being for technical services. In such a case it is quite possible that withholding tax would be suffered without any corresponding double tax credit so that the payment suffers double taxation without any relief.

FURTHER READING

Barnes, P (2014) 'Limiting Interest Deductions' (Papers on Selected Topics in Protecting the Tax Base of Developing Countries) United Nations. Available at: http://www.un.org/esa/ffd/wp-content/uploads/2014/09/20140923_Paper_LimitingInterestDeductions.pdf.

Barreix, A and Villela, L eds (2008) *Taxation and Latin American Integration*, Inter-American Development Bank/David Rockefeller Center for Latin American Studies, Harvard University, pp 173–195.

Barsch, S-E, Olbert, M (2015) 'Germany – Tax Classification of Debt and Equity and Recent Jurisprudence in Germany', 69 *Bulletin for International Taxation*, 9.

Collier, R, Devereux, M and Lepoev, S (2017) 'Proposed UK Changes on the Tax Deductibility of Corporate Interest Expense' *British Tax Review* (2017) 1, 60–79.

Cooke, D and Pennock, J (2014) 'Trading Overseas' in *Tolleys Tax Planning 2014*, Lexis.

Harris, P (2014) 'Neutralizing Effects of Hybrid Mismatch Arrangements' (Papers on Selected Topics in Protecting the Tax Base of Developing Countries) United Nations. Available at: www.un.org/esa/ffd/tax/2014TBP2/Paper_%20HybridMismatchArrangements.pdf.

HM Treasury (2014) Consultation Document 'Tackling Aggressive Tax Planning: Implementing the Agreed G20-OECD Approach for Addressing Hybrid Mismatch Arrangements'.

Kahlenberg, C and Kopec, A (2016) 'Hybrid mismatch arrangements – a myth or a problem that still exists?' *World Tax Journal* February 2016, p 37.

Korb, D L, Wang, S E and Gadwood, J R (2013) 'Debt-equity litigation returns to US courts', *British Tax Review* [2013] No 5, p 597.

Janssens, P et al (2015) 'The End of Intra-Group Financing … Or not Just Yet? – Part 1', 55, *European Taxation* 7.

Janssens, P et al (2015) 'The End of Intra-Group Financing … Or not Just Yet? – Part 2', 55, *European Taxation* 343.

Lethaby, H (2014) 'Trading in the United Kingdom' in *Tolley's Tax Planning 2014*, Lexis.

OECD (2009) 'Building Transparent Tax Compliance by Banks'.

OECD (2012) 'Hybrid Mismatch Arrangements'.

OECD (2014) Public Discussion Draft, 'BEPS Action 2: Neutralise the Effects of Hybrid Mismatch Arrangements'.

OECD (2014) BEPS Action 2; 2014 Deliverable, 'Neutralising the Effects of Hybrid Mismatch Arrangements'.

OECD (2015a) BEPS Action 2 Final Report, 'Neutralising the Effects of Hybrid Mismatch Arrangements', 5 October 2015.

OECD (2015b) BEPS Action 4 Final Report, 'Limiting Base Erosion Involving Interest Deductions and Other Financial Payments', 5 October 2015.

Pijl, H (2011) 'The Netherlands – Interest from Hybrid Debts in Tax Treaties', *Bulletin for International Taxation* 2011, Vol 65, No 9.

Ring, D M (2002) 'One Nation among Many: Policy Implications of Cross-border Tax Arbitrage', *Boston College Law Review*, Vol 44, p 79.

Ruf, M and Schindler, D (2015) 'Debt Shifting and Thin-Capitalisation Rules' *Nordic Tax Journal*, 17.

Storke, A (2011) 'The Financing of Multinational Companies and Taxes: An Overview of the Issues and Suggestions for Solutions and Improvements', *Bulletin for International Taxation* 2011, Vol 65, No 1.

Ting, A (2017) 'Base Erosion by Intra-group Debt and BEPS Project Action 4's Best Practice Approach – A case study of Chevron' *British Tax Review* (2017) 1, 80–108.

Webber, S (2011) 'Escaping the U.S. Tax System: From Corporate Inversions to Re-Domiciling' 63, *Tax Notes International*, 273.

FURTHER STUDY

UK's anti-arbitrage rules

12.48   The UK's anti-arbitrage rules were introduced in the Finance (No 2) Act 2005, ss 24–31 and Schedule 3. They are now contained in the Taxation

(International and Other Provisions) Act 2010 (TIOPA 2010), s 231, et seq. The rules attempt to remove any tax advantage from the use of hybrid financial instruments to minimize UK tax liabilities by exploiting differences in treatment of the instrument in the UK and other countries. Six classes of instruments are covered:

- instruments whose character is capable of being altered;

- shares convertible into debt capital;

- securities convertible into shares;

- debt instruments treated as equity;

- shares issued to a connected company that are not ordinary shares fully paid up, and which confer a beneficial entitlement to share in profits and assets on winding-up at all times; and

- a transfer of rights to income or gains arising from a security to a connected person.

Tax deductions for interest payable will be limited if:

- the deduction arises from a scheme (as defined) involving the use of hybrids; and

- the scheme is designed to produce either a double deduction for the interest (ie in the UK and another country), or the deduction for the payer is not matched by a taxable receipt for the recipient (perhaps because it is treated as a dividend and is exempt from tax, eg under a dividend participation regime); and

- the main purpose, or one of the main purposes, is to achieve a UK tax advantage that is more than minimal.

To show that the main purpose was to achieve a UK tax advantage, it is necessary to demonstrate that in absence of the scheme, tax deductions arising from the scheme would not have arisen at all, or would have been of a lesser amount. Hence it will be relevant to draw a comparison in order to consider whether, in the absence of the hybrid entity or instrument:

- the transaction giving rise to the deduction would have taken place at all; and

- if so, whether it would have been of the same amount; and

- whether it would have been made under the same terms and conditions.

For example, if the scheme involves a loan and the deductions are for interest payments, it will be necessary to consider whether the size, nature, or very existence of the loan has been altered by the arbitrage scheme in a way that increases UK tax deductions. The comparison should be based on equivalent arrangements that did not make use of any hybrid entities or instruments. To take the example of a foreign parent lending an amount at interest to a

UK subsidiary company to finance the purchase of new equipment, if both the UK subsidiary and the foreign lender can claim a tax deduction for the same amount of interest paid then there is a risk that the rules would apply. However, if it can be shown that the UK company would have had to borrow the money from an unconnected lender in the absence of the parent company loan, and if the loan proceeds are applied to financing the equipment, then it is most unlikely that the main purpose of the transactions was to achieve a UK tax advantage.

- The rules are also designed to ensure that a receipt from a hybrid instrument will be taxable in the hands of the UK recipient if the foreign payer achieved a tax deduction for it and the two taxpayers expected this result. In either case, there must be deliberate avoidance of tax.

- A 'scheme' is defined under TIOPA 2010, s 258 as: '… any scheme, arrangements or understanding of any kind, whether or not legally enforceable, involving a single transaction or two or more transactions.'

The parties to the transactions need not be the same.

There is a UK tax advantage if, in consequence of the scheme, that company is in a position to obtain, or has obtained:

- a relief (including a tax credit) or increased relief from corporation tax;

- a repayment or increased repayment of corporation tax; or

- the avoidance or reduction of a charge to corporation tax.

In particular, avoidance or reduction of a charge to tax may be effected by receipts accruing in such a way that the recipient does not pay or bear tax on them, or by a deduction in computing profits or gains.

Schemes are dealt with under the headings of 'deduction schemes' and 'receipts schemes'. Deduction schemes may involve:

- hybrid entities – ie a limited partnership;

- hybrid effect – a characteristic of an instrument can be altered by election;

- hybrid effect – the scheme uses convertible shares or securities and it is reasonable to assume that conversion rights will be used;

- hybrid effect – debt instruments treated as equity under GAAP in the country of the issuing company;

- hybrid effect and connected persons – the scheme includes the issue of shares which do not confer a qualifying beneficial entitlement (ie rights to participate in profit in proportion to number of shares held); and

- hybrid effect and connected persons – the scheme includes transfer of rights under security. A person transfers rights to receive a payment under a security to a connected person.

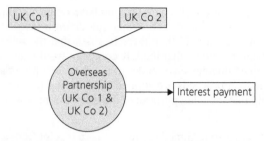

Figure 12.12:   Deduction scheme – the s 244 rule against double deduction

The UK sees the overseas partnership as transparent. Accordingly, the corporate partners (UK Sub 1 and UK Sub 2) are able to claim interest deductions in the UK for the payment of interest made by the overseas partnership. If the overseas partnership is resident in a country which recognizes it as a taxable entity, there will be a double deduction if the partnership is granted a deduction in that country.

Section 245 describes the deduction scheme which consists of a tax deduction but no corresponding taxable receipt.

Receipts schemes are dealt with under s 250. There is no need for HMRC to prove that a scheme exists. Section 250 will apply where there is provision between a company, and another person by means of a transaction or series of transactions, in circumstances where the payer makes a payment regarded as a contribution to capital of the payee, and the parties had an expectation that the receipt would not be chargeable to corporation tax. The benefit in receipts schemes is that a receipt is not subject to UK tax, whilst the payment is tax deductible for the payer overseas. Clearances are available from HMRC as to whether the anti-arbitrage rules will apply. There is no requirement for a company to self-assess under the anti-arbitrage rules.

2016 changes

Finance Act 2016 introduced new rules to address hybrid mismatches in accordance with the best practice recommendations of BEPS Action 2. The new rules take effect from 1 January 2017. The legislation is complex and comprises 14 chapters including 9 rules and targeted anti-avoidance rule (TAAR). On 31 March 2017, HMRC published an update to draft guidance,[1]

---

1   See: www.gov.uk/government/consultations/hybrid-and-other-mismatches-draft-guidance. following a consultation period that ran from 9 December 2016 to 10 March 2017.

UK restrictions on interest deductions

12.49   The UK has rules which restrict deductions for interest in cases where tax avoidance might be in point through the funding of UK subsidiaries with excessive amounts of intragroup debt. These rules are unilateral and only affect deductions from UK tax liabilities. However, they are of interest because they are the type of rules for limiting interest deductions which the OECD appears to favour, in that they take a worldwide approach. The UK's 'worldwide debt cap' rules limit interest deductibility for UK group members by reference to the overall interest costs of the worldwide group. The International Bar Association, in its public comments on the Action 4 2014 Discussion Draft, asserts that the UK's worldwide debt cap rules have not been a success.[1] This is because they have greatly increased compliance burdens by imposing complex additional tax calculations on many groups whilst raising little tax, and producing only marginal changes in tax planning behaviour of groups of companies.

The introduction of a cap on tax relief on interest payments made by UK companies in connection with the funding of foreign activities was proposed in HMRC's 2007 review of the taxation of companies' foreign profits.[2] The rationale is that if the returns on these foreign investments are made in the form of dividends, they will in future be exempt from UK taxation, and thus, to achieve symmetry, there should be a restriction on tax relief for interest paid to fund these investments. A more cynical view is that the loss of tax revenues from the move to an exemption system of double tax relief for foreign dividends had to be paid for somehow.

The legislation introduced a rule that effectively limits the amount of any interest deduction for a UK company to the amount of the worldwide third-party interest deductions claimed by the entire worldwide group. Hence the interest deduction claimed by the UK company cannot exceed the external interest costs of the MNE as a whole. This is known as the 'worldwide debt cap'. It applies to interest charges and other financing costs such as finance lease charges, debt factoring costs and hedging of related party debt. Broadly the rules are that UK deductions for interest and other financing costs paid to group members will be restricted to the lower of:

- where a group has net finance income on a worldwide basis: nil;

- the total net finance costs paid by UK members of the MNE to external lenders, provided the costs are not affected by any thin capitalization restrictions; and

- the total net finance costs of the worldwide group payable to external lenders.

Financing costs, for these purposes, are defined as interest, finance lease charges and exchange differences which related to foreign currency borrowings which are accounted for as adjustments to interest.

The restriction applies even if it can be shown that the interest was paid by the UK group member on wholly arm's-length terms. There are exceptions from the rules for banking and insurance businesses, and further exemptions are anticipated for certain other financial businesses. The rules apply only to large groups; therefore, groups with fewer than 250 employees and less than €50 million annual turnover, or less than €43 million group assets, are not affected. The calculations are complex and apply to wholly UK-based groups as well as multinationals. There is a preliminary test (the gateway test) which is used to eliminate groups who would clearly not exceed the cap. Special rules apply to companies in the oil extraction industry and to shipping profits (to allow for the effects of the UK's tonnage tax).

The worldwide debt cap is aimed mainly at preventing excessive tax relief to UK parent companies on interest paid by them on loans made to them by their foreign subsidiaries (so-called 'upstream loans'). However, if profits can be brought into the UK via dividends without UK tax liability then the need for upstream loans should be reduced. The debt cap also affects interest paid on 'downstream' loans – those made to a UK company by a foreign parent company. The reason for this is unclear, as the UK already has considerable protection against excessive interest deductions on such loans via its transfer pricing regime (see Chapter 13 for details) as well as the anti-arbitrage rules and the unallowable purpose rules. The debt cap rules are considered in more detail in the 'Further study' section of this chapter.

A further impetus for restrictions on tax relief for interest payable came from the ECJ judgment in the *Thin Capitalisation GLO*.[3] It had been thought that the UK's rules restricting tax relief on interest payments, where the UK company paying the interest was a subsidiary of a foreign company which had capitalized the UK company with an uncommercial level of debt (thin capitalization), were contrary to EU law, in particular the right to the freedom of establishment under Article 49 TFEU. However, the judgment in the *Thin Capitalisation GLO*, at para 74, permits the restriction of interest payments to a fellow group company in the EU if the rules are designed to:

> 'prevent conduct involving the creation of wholly artificial arrangements which do not reflect economic reality, with a view to escaping the tax normally due on the profits generated by activities carried out on national territory.'

---

1   OECD: *Comments received on public Discussion Draft BEPS Action 3: Interest Deductions and Other Financial Payments Part 1*, 11 February 2015, p 603.
2   Taxation of companies' foreign profits: discussion document, HMRC, June 2007.
3   C-524/04 *Test Claimants in the Thin Cap Group Litigation v IRC* Case [2007] STC 906.

The UK debt cap rules: some more detail

12.50   The UK debt cap rules, introduced in Finance Act 2009, limit the deduction for interest paid by UK holding companies, and were introduced to prevent the situation whereby:

● UK holding companies could borrow funds, incurring interest deductions, which would then be used to finance investments in foreign companies.

● Those UK holding companies could then receive a return on their investments in those foreign companies in the form of dividends, which would be exempt under the UK's post-1 July 2009 foreign dividend exemption.

In other words, in the absence of such a measure, the UK would be giving tax relief on an investment but would not be able to tax the return on that investment. The Netherlands had attempted to use similar rules until 2003, but as the Netherlands rules only prevented the deduction of interest used to finance foreign subsidiaries (as opposed to Netherlands subsidiaries) it was held to contravene the EU principle of freedom of establishment.[1]

The UK's legislation[2] is not quite as stringent as this simple explanation might suggest. The limit (or 'cap') on the deduction for interest paid will only apply where the borrowings of the UK company from other group companies exceeds the total amount that the MNE as a whole has borrowed from third parties (ie outside the MNE). The legislation is only likely to apply when UK group members have large borrowings from other group members, probably as a result of so-called 'upstream loans'. An upstream loan is a loan which travels up the MNE structure from subsidiary to parent, and might be made in lieu of a dividend payment. One consequence of setting the debt cap in this way is that the UK companies most likely to be affected are those whose groups have relatively little debt worldwide whilst groups with riskier, high worldwide debt to equity ratios will be less susceptible. The rules may thus operate to prevent a deduction for interest even where no tax avoidance is intended.

Where there is more than one UK company in the MNE, their borrowings from other group members will be aggregated. This is known as the 'tested amount'. This aggregated amount of debt is then compared with the amount of debt reported in the MNE's worldwide consolidated financial statements. This amount reported in the consolidated accounts will exclude any intragroup debt as the borrowers' and the lenders' amounts will have cancelled out when they were added together. Any interest payments relating to an excess of UK borrowings from the group companies over the MNE's total external borrowings will be disallowed for UK tax purposes. If there is more than one UK group member, they can decide how to share out the disallowance between themselves. Note that it is not necessary for there to be any non-UK companies involved for the debt cap provisions to apply. Even a group with solely UK group members might be affected.

Even if part of a company's interest paid is disallowed, this still might not increase the UK tax liability. If the company has interest income receivable from a payer who is resident in the EEA (but not the UK) then the disallowed interest payable can be used to reduce the amount of this interest receivable for UK tax purposes.

If a UK company bears a share of the MNE's disallowance of interest payable in excess of that relating to that particular company, other UK group companies are permitted to make payments to it in compensation. Such payments will be ignored for tax purposes.[3]

---

1   See C-168/01 *Bosal Holding BV v Staatssecretaris van Financien* [2003] STC 1483.
2   TIOPA 2010, s 260, et seq.
3   A similar system operates in connection with intra-group payments made in return for one group company permitting another group company to utilize its tax losses.

Which companies are affected?

12.51   Only groups which include at least one 'large' UK company are affected by the debt cap. Large means a company which both employs at least

250 people, and either has an annual turnover of more than £250 million or has a balance sheet which exceeds £43 million. A group company is one that is under the control of a parent company. Usually this will mean that the parent company owns more than 50 per cent of the voting rights in the other company, although exceptionally, control can be measured in other ways as well.

Even groups which include one or more large companies might not be affected by the debt cap: If the UK companies' combined net borrowing does not exceed 75 per cent of the worldwide group's debt, before offsetting intragroup lending and borrowing, the debt cap will not be applied. This is known as the 'gateway' test.

If a group is a 'qualifying financial services group', the debt cap provisions will not apply. To qualify, either all of the UK group's trading income or all of the MNE's worldwide income must be derived from lending, insurance, or dealing in financial instruments (other than as a broker). Small amounts of other types of activities are ignored.

The Finance Act 2012 introduced an anti-avoidance provision so that where companies are artificially excluded from the MNE for debt cap purposes, any scheme securing that result will be ineffective.[1]

In addition to these general exceptions, certain types of interest and other financing costs are excluded from the debt cap provisions: The exceptions are those relating to:

- oil extraction activities;

- profits dealt with under the tonnage tax regime;

- profits exempt from corporation tax under the REIT rules (broadly, relating to collective investments in real estate);

- short-term debt: the debt cap rules are aimed at limiting interest relief for long-term investment;

- group treasury companies; and

- the financing of charities, educational establishments, local authorities and health service bodies: because these are non-profit making bodies, there would be no income coming from them to escape UK tax under the dividend exemption regime.

UK companies must comply with the debt cap rules for accounting periods (ie tax periods) beginning on or after 1 January 2010. However, if other companies in the worldwide group draw up their financial statements to a different date, the start date could be earlier.[2]

---

1 TIOPA 2010, s 305A.
2 The rules apply to UK company accounting periods (for tax purposes) which start after 1 January 2010 but if that accounting period overlaps with a 'period of account' (for which financial statements are drawn up) of any member of the worldwide group, then the rules commence from the date on which the period of account of that other member of the worldwide group commences. There are anti-avoidance rules to prevent a company artificially deferring the commencement date by changing its accounting date.

Which companies constitute the MNEs?

12.52   Normally, the consolidated accounts will indicate the MNE companies relevant for the debt cap calculations. Sometimes, more complicated scenarios arise when it is not clear just how far the MNE extends. Section 339 of TIOPA 2010 sets out the concept of the 'ultimate parent' to determine the extent of a group where this is not otherwise obvious. An 'ultimate parent' is a corporate entity (as opposed to an individual or a trust) which is not a subsidiary of any other entity. Detailed definitions apply.

To be affected by the debt cap, a company must be a UK company which is either an 'ultimate parent' or a 'relevant subsidiary' of an ultimate parent. A 'relevant subsidiary' is one in which the ultimate parent owns, directly or indirectly, at least 75 per cent of the voting shares, and in which the ultimate parent has rights to at least 75 per cent of distributed profits or net assets on a winding-up.

If there is a 'relevant subsidiary' in the UK, then the debt cap provisions apply to that company and all its 75 per cent subsidiaries, since they would also be 'relevant subsidiaries'.

A UK PE of a foreign company could also be within the rules if the head office company is part of a 'large' group.

The Finance (No 3) Act 2010 changed the rules slightly so that limited liability partnerships and collective investment schemes can no longer be treated as ultimate parents. A limited liability partnership is commonly used as a consolidating entity in private equity arrangements.

Illustration: identifying a 'relevant subsidiary'

12.53

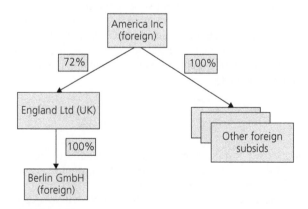

Figure 12.13

In this illustration (see Figure 12.13), England Ltd would not be a relevant subsidiary as it is not owned as to 75 per cent by an 'ultimate parent' and would not be subject to the debt cap rules.

Measuring the amount of the debt

12.54   The total worldwide debt is normally taken from the MNE's consolidated financial statements. To be acceptable to HMRC, those financial statements must have been drawn up according to International Financial Reporting Standards (IFRS) or under similar standards approved by HMRC for this purpose via regulations. Thus, for instance, financial statements drawn up under UK or US GAAP would be acceptable. Alternatively, if the results shown in the financial statements are essentially the same as those which would have resulted from using IFRS, that is also acceptable. However, because of the international nature of the debt cap provisions, it is likely that in some cases there will be no suitable set of consolidated financial statements. This might be because the MNE as defined for debt cap purposes, is different from the group for consolidated accounts purposes, or there simply may not be any consolidated accounts at all. In these cases, the taxpayer will have to construct a set of consolidated accounts for the worldwide group especially for the purposes of computing the debt cap. These consolidated accounts will have to follow IFRS principles.

Finance Act 2015 introduced minor changes following changes to IFRS rules. The amendments are designed to ensure that finance costs taken into account in the calculation of a UK company's net finance expenses or income, but not in the amount of gross finance costs of the MNE as a whole for the purposes of the debt cap calculations (due to the changes in both IFRS and GAAP) are included in the debt cap calculations.

Once an acceptable set of financial statements has been identified, the amount of debt within the worldwide group must be ascertained. If there are accounting mismatches, such that a debt is recorded differently for UK purposes to the way it is recorded in the consolidated accounts, the UK company is to adopt the value used in the consolidated accounts. For instance, a loan might be recorded at fair value in the consolidated accounts but at amortized cost in the UK company accounts.

Gateway test

12.55   The gateway test is designed to save companies the time and expense of running the full set of tests to see if the debt cap applies. It defines a relatively simple threshold for the UK debt which, if not exceeded, excuses the UK group from the necessity of complying with the detailed debt cap rules. If the threshold in the gateway test is not exceeded, there can be no liability under the debt cap provisions. If the threshold is exceeded, then there might be a liability, depending on the outcome of the further tests.

Besides being a 'large' group, as defined, for the debt cap provisions to apply, the so-called 'gateway test' must be failed. If the gateway test is passed, this is good news for the UK companies in the MNE as they will not be subject to the debt cap, and need not provide any further detailed calculations to prove this. In broad terms, the gateway test looks at whether the combined net debt of UK group members exceeds 75 per cent of worldwide gross debt of the MNE. The calculation is done separately for each UK group member which is a 'relevant group company', so that if a foreign 'ultimate parent' had a 100 per cent UK holding company which in turn had 10: 100 per cent-owned UK subsidiaries, there would be 11 calculations to be done.

Net debt is determined by examining the balance sheet for each company and is the amount of total debt minus the amount of total monetary assets.

Table 12.2

Debts ('relevant liabilities')	*Monetary assets ('relevant assets')*
Amounts borrowed	Amounts lent
Finance lease payables	Finance lease receivables
Any other amounts specified by HMRC in Regulations	Cash and cash equivalents
	Government bonds (any country)
	Any other amounts specified by HMRC in Regulations
Total debt	Total monetary assets

All these amounts are ascertained as at the first and last days of the period for which the worldwide group draws up its financial statements[1] (the 'period of account') and a simple average is taken. If the average is less than £3 million, this is treated as nil and does not count towards the total of UK net debt.[2] This also applies where a company has net receivables rather than net debt. Net receivables are effectively ignored in the gateway test.

'Gross worldwide debt' is arrived at by adding up the 'relevant liabilities' on the consolidated accounts at the start and end of the period and again, taking a simple average. Currency conversion is done by translating at the spot rates.

The amounts of net debt of each UK relevant subsidiary (where the amount came to more than £3 million) are combined and then compared to 'gross worldwide debt'. If this combined amount exceeds 75 per cent, the gateway test is passed, and the company concerned must then go on to comply with the detailed debt cap tests, although ultimately no charge to tax might result.

---

1   Where UK companies join or leave a group, part way through the year, the joining or leaving date amounts are substituted as appropriate.

2   Note that the debt of any UK dormant companies is regarded as nil, and does not count towards the combined UK net debt. This is so even if a dormant company has net debt in excess of £3 million.

Types of financing expense which might be disallowed (the 'tested' amount)

12.56 If a UK company is not excused from the debt cap provisions following the administration of the gateway test then the interest deduction claimed in the corporation tax computation must be examined to see whether the debt cap will act to limit it. The language of the UK tax rules for interest is used, the so-called 'loan relationships' regime. Under this regime, the term 'debits' includes interest payments, commissions, etc,[1] and 'credits' includes interest receivable plus commissions received, etc. The debt cap calculations expand the range of items included even further to include financing costs or income implicit in finance leases and in debt factoring arrangements and fees in respect of guarantees. The net of all these items is known as the 'net financing deduction'.

If the net financing amount of any company is less than £500K, that company's amount can be left out of the UK aggregate amount. However, companies who have net amounts receivable are also left out.

---

1   Although it will exclude debits which relate to impairment losses, exchange losses and 'related transactions' (broadly, debits relating to disposals or acquisition of debt, such as redemption premium).

Comparing the 'tested amount' with the 'available amount' to arrive at the debt cap disallowance

12.57 The amount of UK net finance costs (the 'tested amount') now has to be compared with worldwide financing costs (the 'available amount'). This amount is the gross finance expenses of the worldwide group and is based on the amount reported in the consolidated financial statements. The 'available amount' is the sum of:

- interest payable on borrowings;

- amortization of discounts, premiums and ancillary costs relating to borrowings;

- financing costs implicit in finance lease payments;

- finance costs of debt factoring; and

- any other amount specified in HMRC regulations.

Foreign exchange movements and preference share dividends are not included. To the extent that the amounts as defined here relate to any of the exempted activities (oil extraction, shipping under the tonnage tax regime, property investment under the REIT regime) the 'available amount' must be reduced. The disallowance under the debt cap is the amount by which the 'tested amount' exceeds the 'available amount'.

Mitigation of the debt cap disallowance where some companies have net financing income

12.58 The way the 'tested amount' is calculated is such that it ignores UK companies which have net finance income. If a group finds itself facing a disallowance under the debt cap, it may be able to mitigate the impact by taking advantage of provisions which allow it to have some of its finance income ignored for tax purposes. A calculation is done for each UK company which has net financial income under the 'tested amount' calculation. Note that the calculations to find net financial income are done for all UK subsidiaries,[1] not just those that are 75 per cent owned. If a company has net financing income of less than £500k it is ignored in the calculations, and thus must remain taxable. The net financing income of all UK group companies with net financing income of more than £500K is added up. The amount of this income which is exempt from UK tax is the lower of the total net financing incomes, and the amount disallowed under the debt cap computation.

---

1   Known as 'UK group companies'.

How the debt cap disallowance is shared out amongst UK companies in the multinational enterprises

12.59   Usually, the MNE will decide how the 'relevant UK companies' will share out the disallowed amount. If they do not, the legislation contains a formula to share it out on a pro rata basis. The reference period for each amount of disallowance is the period for which the financial statements of the worldwide group are drawn up. If this does not coincide with the UK company's tax period then it must be time-apportioned. The maximum disallowance which can be allocated to any company is the amount of its financing expenses before netting of any financing income. Thus companies which have net financing income can accept part of the disallowance even though they did not contribute to it.

The default formula is:

Net financing deduction × total disallowed amount

Tested expense amount

The MNE affected (the 'Reporting Group') must appoint one company to be its 'reporting body' and this must be notified to HMRC within nine months of the end of the worldwide period of account. In the notification, each of the companies in the Reporting Group must give their consent for the reporting body to act on its behalf (TIOPA 2010, s 276).

Where intragroup payments are made in return for bearing of the debt cap disallowance, these are not taken into account by either the payer or the recipient provided that the maximum payment is the lower of the exempt financing income in the payer, or the disallowed expenses in the recipient.

The exemptions

Group treasury companies

12.60   Group treasury companies exist to decentralize the supply and distribution of long- and short-term capital within a group. Their very business is borrowing and lending, although they are not banks in the conventional sense. The UK is keen not to dissuade such companies from being set up in the UK for several reasons:

- Having the treasury companies for major multinationals in the UK boosts the UK's standing as a major financial centre.

- Treasury is essentially a head-office function, even when devolved to a specialist subsidiary. A multinational with its treasury company outside the UK is less likely to have its ultimate holding company in the UK.

- Treasury companies deal with debt as an essential part of their trade, although they are not banks in the conventional sense.

A treasury company is defined for debt cap purposes as one which obtains 90 per cent of its income from group treasury revenue and, since the Finance Act 2013:[1]

- all or substantially all of the activities that those companies undertake throughout a period of account consist of treasury activities undertaken for the worldwide group of which they form part; and

- all or substantially all of the assets and liabilities of the companies relate to such activities.

The treasury company may elect for exemption under TIOPA 2010, s 316(2). The result is that its transactions are excluded from the MNE's total of tested expense and tested income amounts, although they are still taken in to account for the gateway test and if the treasury company has external borrowings, these will be included in the worldwide group's 'available amount'. If there is more than one UK group treasury company, they must each pass this or none of them can be exempt.[2]

---

1   Finance Act 2013, s 44.
2   Per the June 2010 Budget Announcement. Under FA 2009, the 90 per cent applied to the total income of any company carrying out treasury facilities, however minor, so that hardly any treasury companies would have qualified for exemption.

Short-term finance

12.61   The exemption applies to short-term internal financing and is subject to a number of conditions.

Both parties to the transaction must elect for exemption (so that if the expense is allowed, the related income is definitely taxable). The time limit is the usual 36 months from the end of the worldwide group's period of account. There are two conditions to be met:

- Both parties to the loan relationship in question are members of the same worldwide group.

- The financing arrangement must be a short-term loan relationship within the worldwide group. Short term is defined as a money debt or other loan relationship that either contractually exists for less than 12 months or in actual fact is in existence for no more than 12 months.

Proposed changes to UK interest deductibility rules

12.62 UK proposals to implement BEPS Action 4 recommendations are the result of a consultation[1] culminating in draft legislation[2] to restrict tax deductibility of corporate interest expense from 1 April 2017. Following the announcement of the general election, the legislation was removed from the Finance Bill and, at the time of writing, it is not clear when and if it will be reintroduced.[3]

---

1   HMT/HMRC (2015) Tax deductibility of corporate interest expense: consultation (updated in 2016); HMT/HMRC (2016) Tax deductibility of corporate interest expense: response to consultation.
2   See Finance Bill 2017 draft legislation overview documents available at: www.gov.uk/government/publications/spring-budget-2017-overview-of-tax-legislation-and-rates-ootlar.
3   For a discussion of the backdrop to the UK revised rules and alternatives, see Collier et al (2017).

Chapter 13

Transfer Pricing Practice

BASICS

13.1   The term 'transfer pricing' simply means pricing of business transactions between associated persons. Notice that the definition does not mention taxation. When discussing transfer pricing in an international tax context, however, the term is used to represent the artificial manipulation of internal transfer prices within a multinational group, with the intention of creating a tax advantage. For tax purposes, transfer pricing becomes a challenge because of the need to establish the amount of taxable profit for each taxable entity. This will usually be a single company, as most countries do not tax groups of companies as a single entity. It is also important when computing how much profit is attributable to a part of a company that is located in another tax jurisdiction (ie a PE).

Transfer pricing legislation provides a key tool by which governments protect their corporate tax base. To prevent the artificial shifting of profits within multinational groups of companies to countries that provide low effective tax rates, MNEs must be able to demonstrate that intragroup prices are 'arm's length'. This means the prices that would be charged in similar circumstances in a similar transaction between two unrelated parties. If the MNE cannot demonstrate the use of arm's-length pricing, then the tax authority may adjust the profits upwards to what they would have been if arm's-length pricing had been used. Depending on the tax treaty and other relations between the two parties to the transactions, there may or may not be a reciprocal adjustment to tax charged in the other country concerned.

The arm's length-principle is found in Article 9 of the OECD Model Double Tax Convention and is the method recommended in the OECD's influential *Transfer Pricing Guidelines for Multinational Enterprises and Tax Administrations*. It also forms the basis of the US s 482 rules, which tend to be far more detailed. There are two strands to ascertaining an arm's-length price – application of one of the approved methods, accompanied by a functional analysis of the multinational group as regards risk, asset allocation, head office functions assumed, and other factors not apparent at first glance. The approved methods generally consider individual transactions as opposed to a global split of the combined profits of the multinational group.

Because of the fundamental differences in dealings with group companies and those with independent parties, not just in prices charged but also in the types of transactions entered into, it can be extremely difficult to arrive at an arm's-length price. The OECD's BEPS Actions 8–10 deal with particularly problematic aspects of the application of arm's-length pricing rules.

Conceptually, the arm's-length principle is open to much criticism due to the fact that transactions between members of a multinational group are bound, by their very nature, to be considerably different from those between unconnected parties. Some commentators consider that the global profits of a multinational group would be better split between the relevant tax authorities using an agreed formula rather than trying to impose arm's-length principles.

Although there is a body of thought that transfer prices are not heavily influenced by tax at all, the increasing sophistication of multinational groups, and the potential for reduction of global tax liabilities through manipulation of transfer pricing polices means that tax is likely to be an important driver in the setting of cross-border intragroup prices.

INTRODUCTION AND KEY PRINCIPLES

13.2 There are two basic possibilities for allocating taxable profit to the individual entities within a MNE:

1   Top down – take the profit of the whole group and divide it between the individual entities ('unitary taxation').

2   Bottom up – look at each entity separately and calculate its profit as if it were an independent entity ('separate entity').

The 'separate entity' principle is currently the global norm for taxing MNEs. The separate entity principle allows each country to determine which entities within an MNE (eg subsidiaries or PEs) it is entitled to tax, usually by reference to residence and source principles as we saw in Chapter 2. Having identified entities which are chargeable to tax in a country, the next step is to devise a mechanism for determining how much profit belongs to each entity. Transfer pricing rules serve this purpose.

Most tax authorities will have legislation aimed at protecting their tax base from manipulative transfer pricing practices by deeming that intra-group transactions must be accounted for, for tax purposes, at market value using the 'arm's-length principle'. However, establishing open market value is not easy. Governments are anxious to ensure that the profits reported by members of multinational groups reflect a fair commercial level of profit. However, they do not want to be so draconian that they fail to attract investment from the multinational groups. This is a particular problem for developing countries.

Transfer pricing disputes between taxpayers and tax authorities are common and are usually settled by negotiation rather than litigation. Only a few cases ever make it to court (although transfer pricing litigation is relatively common in India). The mutual agreement procedure contained in Article 25 of the Model Tax Convention is widely used to resolve transfer pricing disputes. Ernst & Young[1] report that transfer pricing has entered an era of heightened tax risk and controversy. Transfer pricing practices are widely believed to be one of the key ways in which multinationals shift their taxable profits to lower tax countries. Curbing such practices is a key element of the OECD's BEPS Project.

BEPS Actions 8–10 deal with the difficult issue of aligning transfer prices with value creation, which is important because of concerns that the *Transfer Pricing Guidelines* (see paras **13.31–13.37** below) are open to manipulation – leading to outcomes that don't correspond to the underlying economic activity. Action 8 looks at intangibles, which are particularly difficult to value and ascribe a geographical location to. Action 9 is concerned with the contractual allocation of risks, and the potential for disconnect between the allocation of profits to those risks and the actually activities carried on. Action 10 is focussed on other high risk areas. BEPS Action 13 is concerned with transparency and provides for country-by-country reporting for transfer pricing to provide tax authorities with better information about the geographical location of activities.

Before looking more closely at the OECD BEPS actions relating to transfer pricing, we will first consider the nature of tax transfer pricing, and the way it is dealt with both unilaterally and under bilateral agreements.

---

1   Ernst & Young (2016) *Global Transfer Pricing Survey*. Available at: www.ey.com/gl/en/services/tax/ey-2016-transfer-pricing-survey-series.

Examples of transfer pricing

13.3   During 2004, the UK launched transfer pricing investigations into three major automobile manufacturers: Nissan, Honda and Toyota. The UK subsidiaries of these companies were carrying forward UK tax losses in 2004 in excess of £1 billion.[1] Nissan lost their case and paid an extra £37 million in UK tax.[2] In 2006, GlaxoSmithKline paid $3.4 billion extra tax as a result of a US transfer pricing enquiry. In 2008, Glaxo again lost a major transfer pricing case (discussed later in the chapter) which resulted in profits being increased by CAD $51 million.

A controversial study by Pak and Zdanowicz (2002) undertaken on behalf of Senator Byron Dorgan reported that the total estimated tax loss from manipulative transfer pricing practices by US-based multinationals during 2001 was $53.1 billion, of which $12 billion was accounted for by transactions with Japanese group member firms. This study, which was widely reported in the US press, gave examples of blatant price manipulations, such as pairs of tweezers imported from a Japanese member of a group at a price of $4,896 each and toilet tissue from Chinese group companies at $4,121 per kg. Briefs and panties were imported from Hungary by one US group member at $739 a dozen. Such extraordinary pricing within multinational groups also extended to exports; missile and rocket launchers went to Israel at the ridiculously low price of $52 each, whilst toilet bowls and cisterns went to Hong Kong for

$1.75 a set. Whilst the methods used by Pak and Zdanowicz to arrive at their overall estimate of tax lost have been subjected to considerable criticism,[3] their anecdotal evidence certainly attracted the public's attention.[4]

1 *Financial Times*, 22 July 2004.
2 *Daily Telegraph*, 12 November 2004.
3 See for example Fuest, C, and Riedel, N (2009) *Tax evasion, tax avoidance and tax expenditures in developing countries: A review of the literature*, Oxford University Centre for Business Taxation. Available at: www.dfid.gov.uk/r4d/SearchResearchDatabase.asp?OutPutId=181295.
4 For an interesting analysis of some of the misleading statistics that are used in the context of debates about transfer pricing, see Forstater (2015).

The basic problem illustrated

13.4

Example 13.1

Multinat Plc has two trading subsidiaries. One is tax resident in the country of Konganga where the effective rate of corporation tax is 10 per cent. This company extracts and exports greensand, the raw material used in the group's production processes. The open market price for greensand is $100 per tonne. The other subsidiary is resident in the country of Ruritania, where the effective tax rate is 40 per cent. The Ruritanian subsidiary buys its raw materials in bulk from the Konganga subsidiary. The quantity purchased each year is 80,000 tonnes.

Multinat Plc wishes to instruct the two subsidiaries to adopt a pricing policy that optimizes the after-tax profits for the group as a whole. Questions to be considered are:

● Should the price charged by Konganga for tax purposes be lower or higher than the price it might charge to an unrelated customer?

● Which government might object to the pricing policy and why?

	Tonnes	Intragroup price per 1000 tonnes ($000)		
	000s	100	70	130
Accounts of Konganga subsidiary:				
Sales to Ruritanian subsidiary	80	8,000	5,600	10,400
Sales to other customers $100 per tonne	200	20,000	20,000	20,000
	280	28,000	25,600	30,400
Deduct				
fixed and operating costs		15,000	15,000	15,000
Net profit before tax		13,000	10,600	15,400
Konganga tax at 10%		1,300	1,060	1,540
Profit after tax		11,700	9,540	13,860
Accounts of Ruritanian subsidiary				

	Tonnes	Intragroup price per 1000 tonnes ($000)		
	000s	100	70	130
Sales		20,000	20,000	20,000
Purchase of raw materials from Konganga		8,000	5,600	10,400
Other fixed and operating costs		5,000	5,000	5,000
Profit before tax		7,000	9,400	4,600
Ruritanian tax at 40%		2,800	3,760	1,840
Profit after tax		4,200	5,640	2,760
Tax in Konganga		1,300	1,060	1,540
Tax in Ruritania		2,800	3,760	1,840
Combined tax liabilities		4,100	4,820	3,380

Setting the price at $70 per tonne produces an increase in the global tax liability whereas setting it at $130 per tonne produces a reduction. Given that the combined profit before tax is $20,000,000 whatever the transfer price, the tax position is optimized if the transfer price is $130. The government which loses tax revenue as a result of this policy is Ruritania.

'ARM'S-LENGTH' PRINCIPLE

13.5   This principle states that the prices charged, for the purpose of calculating taxable profits, within MNEs must be comparable to those that would be charged between independent enterprises. The arm's-length principle is important in international tax and is contained in Article 9 of the OECD Model Tax Convention (MTC) which deals with associated enterprises, as we saw in Chapter 7. To recap, the text of the article is as follows:

> 'Where a) an enterprise of a Contracting State participates directly or indirectly in the management, control or capital of an enterprise of the other Contracting State ... and ... conditions are made or imposed between the two enterprises in their commercial or financial relations which differ from those which would be made between independent enterprises, then any profits which would, but for those conditions, have accrued to one of the enterprises, may be included in the profits of that enterprise and taxed accordingly.'

The purpose of Article 9 is to achieve a fair share of a multinational group's tax base for all the tax jurisdictions in which it operates by preventing the artificial manipulation of profits for tax purposes earned in various countries through uncommercial tax pricing practices.

The requirement to use arm's-length prices for intragroup tax transfer pricing is applied to a whole range of items, not merely goods sold from one subsidiary to another. Members of groups will supply technical and financial services to one another, will pay interest and patent royalties to one another as well as management and marketing fees, to name but a few.

In the example given above, the arm's-length price is $100 per tonne. As Multinat Plc controls both the Konganga and the Ruritanian subsidiaries it is open to the Ruritanian tax authority to argue that the transfer price of $130 per tonne represents a difference in commercial relations from those which would be expected between independent enterprises. The extra taxable profits which would have been included in the Ruritanian subsidiaries' accounts if arm's-length pricing had been used are $2,400,000 ($7,000,000 profit before tax minus $4,600,000 profit before tax). Ruritania will levy tax at 40 per cent on an additional $2,400,000 of profits.

Whether Konganga would grant a reciprocal reduction of $2,400,000 in profits to be taxed there depends on the wording of any DTT between the two countries. This is discussed further later in the chapter.

A VERY BRIEF HISTORY OF TRANSFER PRICING LEGISLATION

13.6   In 1928 the US Congress granted the Internal Revenue Service (IRS) the power to adjust the accounts of related companies. Here is a famous quote from that time: 'subsidiary corporations, particularly foreign subsidiaries are employed to "milk" the parent corporation or otherwise improperly manipulate the financial accounts of the parent company'.[1]

There was no requirement for consolidated accounts, but the IRS was given the power to adjust the accounts of individual companies. The League of Nations (the predecessor of the OECD) introduced in its 1935 Model Tax Treaty a requirement for the arm's-length method. Where arm's-length profits were difficult to determine, permitted profits were to be determined within groups of companies on the 'percentage of turnover' method. This alternative method forms the basis of *unitary taxation*, which is the main alternative to the arm's-length principle. This method is widely used in the US and Canada to allocate the taxable profits of a company or group of companies for the purposes of state/provincial (local) taxation. This method is also referred to as global formulary apportionment. For an interesting history of the development of the arm's-length principle in the US, see Avi Yonah (1995).

In the UK, temporary provisions were introduced during the First World War to prevent the avoidance of high wartime taxes by foreign companies trading in the UK. The problem was not properly addressed until in 1945 the League of Nations' Model Treaty was adopted as the basis for the agreement of bilateral treaties. To deal with enforcement of Article 9, the UK introduced transfer pricing provisions in the Finance Act 1951. These were updated in the Finance Act 1999[2] to more closely reflect the provisions of Article 9 and to take account of the growing variety and sophistication of transactions taking place within multinational groups. The UK also wanted its domestic legislation to follow Article 9 more closely as this makes it easier to resolve disputes. See the 'Further study' section at the end of this chapter for more detail about the UK transfer pricing provisions.

In the 1950s and 1960s the growth of the international tax-planning industry led to the introduction in the US of the s 482 Regulations in 1968.

'Section 482: Allocation of income and deductions among taxpayers

In any case of two or more organizations, trades, or businesses (whether or not incorporated, whether or not organized in the United States, and whether or not affiliated) owned or controlled directly or indirectly by the same interests, the Secretary may distribute, apportion, or allocate gross income, deductions, credits, or allowances between or among such organizations, trades, or businesses, if he determines that such distribution, apportionment, or allocation is necessary in order to prevent evasion of taxes or clearly to reflect the income of any of such organizations, trades, or businesses. In the case of any transfer (or license) of intangible property (within the meaning of section 936(h)(3)(B)), the income with respect to such transfer or license shall be commensurate with the income attributable to the intangible.'

The primary pricing test adopted was the comparable uncontrolled price (CUP) (see below). Relevant circumstances accounting for differences between actual prices and open market prices may be taken into account. The legislation contains the 'safe harbour' concept: for loans, services and leasing. This means that if firms stay within set limits, they can expect their policies to escape attack under s 482. Like most US legislation, s 482 is accompanied by copious detailed regulations,[3] which were substantially updated in 1994 to cover the transfer pricing of intangibles and the sharing of costs.

---

1   Report 350 67th Congress 1st Session p 14, cited in Picciotto (1992), p 174.
2   Taxation (International and Other Provisions) Act 2010, s 147.
3   Available at: www.irs.gov/pub/irs-apa/482_regs.pdf.

ROLE OF THE OECD

13.7   The OECD has been instrumental in promulgating best practice in relation to transfer pricing rules. In 1979, the OECD issued a landmark report, *Transfer Pricing Guidelines for Multinational Enterprises and Tax Administrations*. The OECD firmly rejected global methods of profit allocation (top down, or unitary taxation) or the use of predetermined formulae to allocate the profits of multinationals between the various host countries in which they operate. It is, and remains during the BEPS process, committed to the separate entity principle and its corollary, arm's length pricing.

In 1994 the OECD *Guidelines* were reissued, reconfirming opposition to global formulary methods: 'the global formulary apportionment approach would not be acceptable in theory, implementation or practice'. New chapters were added dealing with transfer pricing of intangibles and cost-sharing agreements (see below). A further revised set of guidelines was issued on 22 July 2010. In May 2016, the OECD announced that further changes would be made to the guidelines to accommodate the recommendation of the BEPS project, specifically Actions 8–10 and 13. These changes will be examined later in the chapter.

However, it should be noted that some commentators continue to prefer the US legislation to the OECD *Guidelines*, believing it to be superior in terms of the certainty that it affords to multinational groups. The US has always taken responsibility for developing its own rules rather than relying on the OECD *Guidelines* and the regulations accompanying s 482 of the Internal Revenue Code are a good deal more detailed than the OECD material. This higher level of detail is often preferred by taxpayers and tax administrations alike as it allegedly provides a higher level of certainty. A common criticism of the OECD materials is that they are too general.

OECD & US *GUIDELINES*

13.8 The OECD has historically recommended the use of bottom-up, transactions-based methods, rather than any other method of allocating the total profits of multinational groups to different countries. The methods recommended by the OECD are:

- comparable uncontrolled price;
- resale price minus;
- cost plus;
- profit split; and
- transactional net margin method.

This list closely resembles the methods permitted under s 482 of the US Internal Revenue Code. The individual methods are considered further below.

In 2010, the OECD *Transfer Pricing Guidelines* were re-issued with some substantial modifications. In relation to comparability and transactional profit methods, this was the culmination of a seven-year project. Draft notes on comparability and transactional profit methods were released in 2006 and 2008 respectively and both elicited considerable comment from the business community. The revised Chapters I–III of the *Guidelines* were released for comment in September 2009, and the response to those comments by the Committee of Fiscal Affairs was published on 22 July 2010.[1]

All the methods recommended by the OECD are based on establishing an arm's-length price for a transaction. The inherent problem with this requirement is that internal prices within companies and within groups of companies are invariably different to those which would be charged between independent enterprises. This is so, even where no tax-avoidance motive is present. Governments generally recognize this problem and have developed frameworks for adjusting actual prices to take account of justifiable differences. The IRS in its s 482 regulations[2] identifies five factors for determining comparability: these factors lead to adjustments being made to the actual and the independent price:

1   functions;

2   contractual terms;

3   risks;

4   economic conditions; and

5   property or services.

Each of these sources of adjustment between the internal transfer price and the prices charged between independent enterprises will be considered briefly.

---

1   Available at: www.oecd.org/dataoecd/23/10/45690455.pdf.
2   §1.482-1 available at: www.irs.gov/pub/irs-apa/482_regs.pdf.

Identifying the functions performed by individual companies

13.9   The functions carried out by different members of a multinational group must be considered, as they contribute towards internal price setting. The rationale behind this 'functional analysis' is that the more important the functions performed by a group company, the higher the proportion of the group's profit should be reflected in that company's taxable profit.

A good functional analysis must therefore:

● fully understand the economics of the particular business and its markets;

● aim to highlight the distinctiveness of the goods/services produced and the sensitivity of demand to price;

● recognize invisible factors not evident from the accounts; and

● identify the relative level of risk carried by the various group companies.

For an excellent case study on the application of functional analysis, see Lenz and Vogel (1999). According to the IRS, a comparison is required of the functions performed, and the resources employed, by the parties to the transaction. Such a functional analysis will consider:

● the type and scope of economically significant transactions undertaken;

● the resources that each party employs in connection with those activities – this could be tangible or intangible fixed assets;

● the type of value added by each party, which could include:

— research and development (R&D);

— product design and engineering;

— manufacturing, production and process engineering;

— product fabrication, extraction and assembly;

— purchasing and materials management;

— marketing and distribution functions, including inventory management, warranty administration, and advertising activities;

— transportation and warehousing; and

— managerial, legal, accounting and finance, credit and collection, training, and personnel management services.

Comparability of contractual terms

13.10   For transactions to be comparable, the contractual terms must be comparable. This is rarely the case when comparing an intragroup transaction with one between independent parties. Some common differences identified in the s 482 regulations, for example, are:

- the form of consideration charged or paid; intra-group transactions are normally settled via entries in the inter-company accounts (ie they are book entries rather than entries reflecting the receipt of currency). Payment is thus immediate, lessening the risk of exchange losses, and reducing administrative costs such as bank charges and debt collection;

- sales or purchase volume – group customers will often be repeat customers, purchasing in bulk;

- the scope and terms of warranties provided – purchasers buying from a fellow group company may require less extensive warranties than when buying from an unknown independent supplier;

- rights to updates, revisions or modifications;

- the duration of relevant licence, contract or other agreements, and termination or renegotiation rights; and

- collateral transactions or ongoing business relationships between the buyer and the seller, including arrangements for the provision of ancillary or subsidiary services.

Role of risk in price setting

13.11   A higher price could well be justified if the seller incurs a higher risk. Conversely, selling to a known, longstanding group member may well involve lower risk than when dealing with unconnected companies. The s 482 regulations identify relevant risks as:

- Market risks, including fluctuations in cost, demand, pricing, and inventory levels. For instance, say a wholly-owned UK subsidiary of a US washing machine manufacturer contracts with its parent company to take delivery of 10,000 washing machines per year for three years at a price of $300 per machine. The UK company must market the washing machines in the UK and there are no provisions for returning unsold stock to the US supplier. In year 1 only 8,000 washing machines are sold, at $350 each. In year 2 only 6,000 are sold at $300 each. However, in year 3 the marketing strategies adopted by the UK subsidiary finally begin to work and the remaining stocks are sold at $500 each. The UK subsidiary has had to bear the losses on the contract for the first two years without support from the parent and therefore this will assist the US supplier in convincing the IRS that the transfer price of £300 was not too low, notwithstanding the fact that much of the stock was sold by the UK subsidiary at a price well in excess of the transfer price.

- Risks associated with the success or failure of research and development activities – this type of risk is discussed further below in connection with transfer pricing in the pharmaceutical industry.

- Financial risks, including fluctuations in foreign currency rates of exchange and interest rates.

- Credit and collection risks.

- Product liability risks – if customers pursue claims for sub-standard goods, who bears the cost of meeting these claims? In the example discussed above, would it be the US supplier or the UK subsidiary who recompensed customers for faulty washing machines? The tax authority would look to see not just who makes payment to the customers, but whether there is any intragroup reimbursement.

- General business risks related to the ownership of property, plant, and equipment.

Economic conditions

13.12 Different profit margins are possible in different countries and at different times. For instance, profit margins in wartime transactions are often much higher than in peacetime due to scarcity and surges in demand caused by war. When comparing transactions, the types of adjustments for economic conditions could include:

- The similarity of geographic markets; for instance, similar profit margins should be achievable in most EU countries, whilst quite different profit margins might be expected when looking at a pair of transactions, one involving a customer in China and one involving a customer in Canada.

- The relative size of each market, and the extent of the overall economic development in each market. Super-profits might be available if a market is just opening up, say in a developing country.

- The level of the market (eg wholesale, retail, etc).

- The relevant market shares for the products, properties, or services transferred or provided; the higher the market share, the higher the expected profit margin.

- The location-specific costs of the factors of production and distribution; for instance, maintaining delicate machinery might be far more costly in a tropical climate than in a temperate one. Linking back to risk, security costs might be far higher for maintaining a production facility in a politically unstable country than in the US.

- The extent of competition in each market with regard to the property or services under review.

- The economic condition of the particular industry, including whether the market is in contraction or expansion.

- The alternatives realistically available to the buyer and seller. A monopoly supplier in a particular country can command a higher price than would otherwise be the case.

Property or services?

13.13   The point here is that it may not be possible to establish exactly what is being bought and sold from a simple observation of a transaction. This will be the case when the cost of services such as R&D, marketing, product development, supplier liaison and so on are embedded in a product price. Such a price may, on first examination, appear well in excess of an arm's-length price.

TRANSACTION-BASED METHODS

13.14   The OECD originally recommended the use of three methods: comparable uncontrolled price, resale price minus and cost-plus, although two additional transaction-based methods (transactional net margin, and profit split) were permitted as last resorts, eg in the absence of comparables. In the 2010 revised *Guidelines*, these five methods are now placed on an equal footing and it is stated that the process of selecting between them should take into account their respective strengths and weaknesses. Where, however, a traditional transaction method and a transactional profit method can be applied 'in an equally reliable manner', the traditional transactional method is preferred.

US s 482 Regulations require the use of the 'best method' rule. This means that a firm must consider the methods outlined below and use the one for which the most reliable comparables are available. For a distribution company, buying from a fellow group member and selling to unconnected customers without adding significant value, the best method is likely to be resale price minus. For a manufacturing company in a vertically integrated group, making sales only to group members where few comparable sales to unconnected parties are made, cost plus is likely to be the best method. This 'best method' rule generally means that complying with the US regulations is more difficult than complying with OECD *Guidelines*, which only require calculations under a single method.

It is important to be aware that transfer pricing is far from being an exact science. Provided intra-group prices are shown to be within an acceptable range of prices, an adjustment to taxable profits by the tax authority may be avoided. Determining the acceptable range is itself difficult and is essentially a qualitative matter requiring skill and judgement, considering all relevant factors. The US insists on a statistical approach: only values within the interquartile range (excluding the lowest 25 per cent and the highest 25 per cent of results) are considered acceptable. The IRS also favours the median point as the most appropriate point in the range for a comparable.

Comparable uncontrolled price

13.15   The rationale behind comparable uncontrolled price is to compare the actual transfer prices in controlled, or intragroup, transactions with comparable prices applying between unrelated parties (ie uncontrolled).

The main problem with this method is the difficulty in finding an exact match in terms of product, firms, market, risk, geographic location and so forth. A number of governments (eg Canadian) are known to be using 'secret' comparables, ie they do not disclose where they are getting their information from. This is a controversial practice.

According to the OECD *Guidelines*, the factors to consider in assessing how comparable two transactions really are may be stated as follows:

● the specific characteristics of the property or services in question;

● the functions that each enterprise performs, with specific reference to assets used and risk undertaken;

● the contractual terms;

● the economic circumstances: taking into account differences in market, country conditions and the position in the supply chain (eg wholesale, retail, etc); and

● any particular business strategies relevant to the transaction – eg is it a 'loss leader'?

The US s 482 regulations give a similar list, as seen at paras **13.10–13.11** above.

These factors should be taken into account when using *all* transactional methods of establishing an arm's-length price. Common adjustments when using CUP are adjustments to take account of differences in sales volumes, frequency of transactions and differences in contractual terms.

Example 13.2 Establishing an arm's-length price using CUP

Black Ltd, a UK wholly-owned subsidiary of Orange Plc, a UK company, supplies 1,000 Z-type widgets each month to its fellow subsidiary tax resident in Iceland, White Inc at a price of $700 per widget. The price charged by Black Ltd to unconnected customers is $1,000 per widget. These widgets are in common use in most of the countries to which Black Ltd sells, with many suppliers in the market. However, the Icelandic market is just opening up and Black is the first supplier in it. Because White Inc has detailed knowledge of the performance and reliability of the product it has agreed to forgo the usual product warranties.

Table 13.1

Price charged to unconnected customers per unit for an order of 1000 Z-type widgets	*1000*
Adjustments needed:	
Premium for first supplier in new market	+100
Adjustment for absence of warranties	−80
Absence of bad debt risk: discount	−50
Repeat/bulk order discount	−100
Immediate payment discount*	−50
Adjusted arm's-length price	820

Note: * Since settlement is by means of accounting (book) entries only, with no cash changing hands, payment is considered to be made as soon as the sale to White Inc is recorded in the books of Black Ltd. It would be normal to allow unconnected customers 30 days' credit.

The initial discrepancy in pricing appears to be $300 per widget. By making appropriate adjustments, the difference is narrowed to $120 ($820–$700). Any adjustment to profits of either company will be made based on $120 per widget, not $300.

Resale price minus

13.16   This method tends to be most appropriate where a group company (Company A) sells on to another group company (Company B) which makes the sale to the final (unconnected) consumer with a minimum of processing or otherwise adding value to the goods. It can be used to check the transfer price from the viewpoint of Company A or Company B although it would most likely be used to verify the price paid by Company B.

The method works by taking the price charged by Company B to the final consumer and deducting an appropriate gross margin – the resale price margin. This margin must be sufficient to cover the operating and selling expenses of Company B and to leave it with an appropriate net profit.

The difference between the price charged by Company B to its customers and the appropriate gross margin attributed to Company B should be the price charged by Company A to Company B. As with CUP, some adjustments may be appropriate to allow for differences in the characteristics of intragroup sales and sales to unconnected parties. In its crude form, an industry average gross profit percentage might be applied. A more accurate calculation would examine purchases by Company B from independent suppliers to establish an arm's-length gross profit margin.

Example 13.3

James Ltd is the UK distributor of Wasch brand televisions. It sources its stocks from its parent company in Germany. The only value added to the televisions by James Ltd is the provision of English language instruction manuals and delivery to wholesale customers. The margin earned by similar television distribution firms in the UK is 15 per cent. The price per television to the final customer is £3,000. The cost per television to James Ltd is £2,500. The cost of adding the instruction manuals is £10.

Price charged by German parent company	Costs incurred by James Ltd	Margin 15%	Price to UK customers
2,500+	10+	376.5	= 3,000?

The sums do not add up. If the 15 per cent margin is correct, the figures should read as below:

2,598+	10+	391.2*	= 3,000

Note: * 391.2 = 3000 × 15/115

The German tax authority may object to the transfer price of £2,500 which appears too low. The German parent company supplying James Ltd will have to defend the price by putting forward the types of adjustments referred to above: low risk of bad debt, immediate payment, market differences, bulk ordering, risk assumed, functions performed etc.

Cost plus

13.17 This is a popular method of establishing an arm's-length price, because it can be applied to transactions where there are no comparable sales of the commodity concerned to independent third parties (eg in the case of intermediate or partly finished goods).

This method takes cost of production plus an 'arm's-length' profit. It is most frequently used for group companies performing specific services or contract manufacturing.

This differs from resale minus in that it focuses on the seller and attempts to set a comparable gross margin between transactions with associates and transactions with unconnected third parties.

This method is of most use where two or more companies in the group add significant amounts of value to the product (eg by further processing). However, a frequent problem is the lack of an independent market in such intermediate goods.

Example 13.4

Browneyes Plc is a major chain of UK opticians. It has patented a new type of contact lens and contracts with a wholly-owned subsidiary in Guernsey for the manufacture of the lens. The raw materials have a negligible cost but the Guernsey factory has had to invest heavily in plant and machinery and staff training to utilize the manufacturing process patented by Browneyes Plc.

All other products sold by Browneyes are purchased from independent suppliers in the Far East. The Guernsey subsidiary is routinely engaged in manufacturing specialized optical equipment for a range of independent customers. The new plant and machinery purchased to fulfil the orders from Browneyes is capable of producing at approximately four times the current level of activity. This level of investment was made on the basis of the schedule of likely future orders from Browneyes Plc. The mark-up on cost added by the Guernsey subsidiary to other customers ranges from 40 per cent to 60 per cent. The mark-up on current sales to Browneyes Plc is 80 per cent.

This mark-up is well outside the normal range and so the group must expect the UK tax authority to object to the prices charged by the Guernsey subsidiary, particularly since corporate taxes in Guernsey on non-financial business is zero per cent.[1] It might be argued that the normal mark-up range of 40 per cent to 60 per cent requires adjustment to take account of:

● the risk assumed by the Guernsey company in investing in new plant, equipment and staff training;

● the fact that they have installed capacity well in excess of that currently required, presumably at the request of Browneyes Plc; and

● the market risk that the new contact lenses might not be a success and therefore resources will have been diverted to production of an unsuccessful product at the expense of servicing existing established markets.

Counter-adjustments which the UK tax authority might propose could include:

● lack of customer risk – dealing with the parent company;

● immediate payment via the inter-company account;

● lack of any apparent charge to the Guernsey subsidiary for the use of intangibles developed by Browneyes Plc (the patent and the production know-how); and

● bulk ordering with a healthy forward order book.

All these would suggest that a lower mark-up might have been applied.

---

1 Except for banking and certain other financial services companies.

TRANSACTIONAL PROFITS-BASED METHODS

13.18 Transactional profits-based methods were originally identified by the OECD as methods of last resort but are increasingly being used, particularly in the US, where as previously noted a 'best method' rule applies. A transactional profit method looks at the profits that arise from particular controlled (intragroup) transactions. The two principal transactional profits methods are the transactional net margin method and the profit split method. These methods differ from comparable uncontrolled price, resale price minus and cost plus (the transactional methods) in that they look at net profit on a transaction rather than the gross profit. The OECD now accepts that there are situations where the transactional profit methods are more appropriate than traditional transaction methods, but cautions against using transactional profit methods only because it might be difficult to obtain data concerning uncontrolled transactions.

Examples in the 2010 *Guidelines* of situations where a transactional profit method might be more appropriate include where each of the parties makes valuable and unique contributions, or where the parties are engaged in highly integrated activities. The OECD's *Discussion Document* on transactional profit methods contains some useful worked examples of the methods in various circumstances.

Transactional net margin method

13.19 The transactional net margin method (TNMM) is a variant of the comparable profits method and, despite its name, is not really transactional, as it involves a comparison of the earnings before interest and tax of a company suspected of having depressed profits due to manipulative transfer pricing practices with that of unrelated companies in the same industry.

Example 13.5

A Ltd wishes to defend its transfer pricing policies but cannot make use of the three transactional methods (CUP, retail price and cost plus) and no other method appears suitable. It decides to defend the level of its taxable profits by using the TNMM. A review of the financial ratios of comparable companies indicates that the arm's-length range of earnings before interest and tax (EBIT) compared to sales for a company such as A Ltd lies between 2 per cent and 4 per cent. A Ltd has an EBIT/sales ratio of only 1.5 per cent. However, A Ltd considered that there are significant differences in its working capital structure which have the effect of depressing its EBIT relative to comparable companies. A central feature of the TNMM is that any comparison using EBIT should adjust for differences in working capital structure.

First, a raw comparison of a suitable profits ratio would be made (eg EBIT/ sales):

	Year 1	*Year 2*
Company A	$k	$k
Sales	300.00	350.00
EBIT	4.56	5.15
EBIT/sales	1.52%	1.47%
Comparable Company 1		
Sales	260.00	280.00
EBIT	6.50	8.40
EBIT/sales	2.50%	3.00%

In practice, the comparison and all the adjustments would be done for at least five years and comparisons would be drawn between Company A and a number of comparable companies. On this raw comparison, the EBIT/ sales ratio of Company A appears very low by comparison to Comparable Company 1. However, at least part of the difference may be accounted for by differences in the working capital structures of the two companies. The working capital/sales ratio would next be computed as below:

	Year 1	*Year 2*
	$k	$k
Company A working capital		
Trade receivables (R)	57.00	65.00
Inventory (I)	55.00	58.00
Trade payables (P)	67.00	69.00
R + I − P	45.00	54.00
(R + I − P)/Sales	15.00%	15.43%
Comparable Company 1 working capital		
Trade receivables (R)	64.00	72.00
Inventory (I)	70.00	80.00
Trade payables (P)	47.00	55.00
R + I − P	87.00	97.00
(R + I − P)/Sales	33.46%	34.64%

Comparable Company 1 has a higher ratio of working capital to sales than Company A. Its EBIT/sales ratio needs to be adjusted to take into account the fact that it is using more working capital than Company A. This is done by applying an interest rate to the difference in working capital/sales ratios to account for the cost of the extra working capital. Thus the EBIT/sales ratio of Comparable Company 1 is reduced by the cost in notional interest of carrying more working capital than Company A.

	Year 1	Year 2
	$k	$k
Working capital adjustment		
Company A (R + I – P)/sales	15.00%	15.43%
Comparable Company 1 (R + I – P)/sales	33.46%	34.64%
Difference	–18.46%	–19.21%
Apply interest rate of	5.00%	5.00%
Interest rate applied to the difference	–0.92%	–0.96%
Comparable Company 1 EBIT/Sales	2.50%	3.00%
Working capital adjustment	–0.92%	–0.96%
Adjusted Comparable Company 1 EBIT/Sales	1.58%	2.04%
Company A EBIT/sales	1.52%	1.47%

For Year 1, after the working capital adjustment, the EBIT/sales ratios of the two companies appear on a par. However, there remains an unexplained difference in Year 2, which could be due to Company A being party to manipulative transfer pricing practices. TNMM has helped a little but there is still some work to be done by Company A in defending its transfer pricing. For instance, it might be able to argue that the Year 2 results are not typical for Comparable Company 1.

In a 2011 Australian case,[1] the Federal Court of Australia rejected the TNMM favoured by the Australian Taxation Office and accepted the taxpayer's evidence of the existence of comparable transactions. The case concerned the application of Australia's domestic transfer pricing legislation and it has been suggested that the outcome may have been different had Article 9 of a DTT been at issue.

---

1 *Commissioner of Taxation of the Commonwealth of Australia v SNF (Australia) Pty Ltd* [2011] FCAFC 74.

Profit split method

13.20 The profit split method aims to split the total profit earned on a transaction by all the group companies involved in it using an 'equitable' formula (eg by reference to capital employed). This formula is arrived at by studying comparable pairs of companies and the contribution made by each company to the overall profit achieved. There are two steps:

1   Identify the profit to be split for the associated enterprises from the controlled (comparable) transactions in which the associated enterprises are engaged.

2   Split those profits between the associated enterprises on an economically valid basis that approximates the division of profits that would have been anticipated and reflected in an agreement made at arm's length.

Note that strictly speaking, the computation should be done by reference to individual transactions, or groups of similar transactions. Unsurprisingly, the principal difficulty is the lack of publicly available information about the likely split of profits. This method is likely to be used in industries where there is a high degree of vertical integration. Under vertical integration, group entities supply everything from raw materials, through processing, right up to the finished product. Telecommunications, pharmaceuticals and automobile industries are good examples. One strength of this method is that it considers the profit position of all entities involved, meaning that it is more likely to arrive at a realistic result rather than allocating most of the profit to one entity, leaving the others in a theoretically loss-making position.

Example 13.6

Bells Ltd is a wholly-owned UK subsidiary of Whistles Inc, an Indonesian company. Bells Ltd imports unfinished traditional musical instruments from Whistles which it then completes, packages and markets to UK customers. The instruments are only otherwise available on a limited local scale in Indonesia. The UK tax authority is unhappy with the level of profitability of Bells Ltd and instigates a transfer pricing enquiry. Using the profits split method, the following results are obtained:

Profit split	Bells Ltd	Whistles Inc	Consolidated
	£	£	£
Sales	700	400	700
Cost of sales	400	50	50
Gross profit	300	350	650
Gross profit split	46.15%	53.85%	100%
Administration and payroll	200	50	250
Selling and marketing	90	10	100
Operating profit	10	290	300
Operating profit split	3.33%	96.67%	100%

This profit split is unlikely to be acceptable to the UK tax authority: at the gross profit level, profits are fairly evenly split, but at the operating profit level only 3 per cent of the profit on the transactions accrues to the UK company, Bells Ltd. The pricing arrangements do not appear to be arm's length. Ideally, the way profit is split on similar transactions between unconnected parties would be examined to provide comparables, but it is unlikely that such information would be available. In practice, a variant known as 'residual profit split' is more likely to be used. This would typically involve defending prices using comparable uncontrolled price as far as possible and then using the profit split method.

Comparable profits method

13.21   The comparable profits method (CPM) is a commonly used method in the US. Some commentators query whether it really represents a transactional method at all. Others think that the US is misunderstood and that the way in which the US uses the comparable profits method should produce a result very similar to the transactional net margin method. CPM is not recommended by the OECD, indeed the OECD's current review of transactional methods does not include CPM, although it is widely used in the US and increasingly so in Canada as well. The CPM examines the amount of operating profit that the company under investigation would have earned on controlled, related-party, transactions if its profit level indicators were equal to that of an uncontrolled comparable. In other words, the operating profit of the company is compared to the operating profit of comparable companies. It relies on being able clearly to identify the exact business activity in which the company and the comparable companies are involved. For instance, if Company A makes hats, but Company B makes hats and gloves, then only the operating profit of Company B with respect to hats should be considered.

This method applies various profit level indicators: broadly speaking, financial ratios such as rate of return on capital, operating profit to sales as well as other ratios examining the relationship between profits, costs and sales revenues. As with the other arm's-length methods, strenuous efforts must be made to adjust for differences between the company under consideration and other companies in the industry. For instance, the company under investigation may have a particularly skilled workforce, or own the know-how for an advanced form of manufacturing process compared to its competitor firms.

The CPM is popular for two main reasons. First, it is relatively easy for the IRS to apply. Under CUP, detailed transactional data is required which is probably only available to the taxpayer, who will use it selectively when presenting evidence to the IRS. It can take many months or years to gather sufficient evidence using the CUP method, with the IRS at an inherent disadvantage. However, when using CPM, industry statistical data is readily available in the public domain to which the financial ratio analysis can be applied. The IRS is thus far less reliant on evidence supplied directly by the taxpayer and less constrained by confidentiality. The method lends itself to statistical analyses of firms and as noted earlier the IRS generally only consider results within the inter-quartile range (ie they eliminate from consideration the top and bottom 25 per cent of results when applying ratio analysis to a selection of firms).

Second, as discussed below, because it takes a broader approach than a method such as CUP it is more suitable for use when negotiating an advance pricing agreement (see later in this chapter).

The method is criticized as not being overtly transactional and being applied retrospectively to the profit outcome of transactions rather than to the pricing policies governing those transactions. However, it should give the same results, broadly speaking, as transactional net margin method when that method is applied to a series of transactions.

The following Example 13.7 is adapted from the s 482 regulations.[1]

Example 13.7

1 Jones Plc, a UK company has a US subsidiary, USSub, that is under transfer pricing audit by the IRS for its XX06 taxable year. Jones Plc manufactures a consumer product for worldwide distribution. USSub imports the assembled product and distributes it within the United States at the wholesale level under the Jones Plc name.

2 Jones Plc does not allow uncontrolled taxpayers to distribute the product. Similar products are produced by other companies but none of them is sold to uncontrolled taxpayers or to uncontrolled distributors. The comparable uncontrolled price method is not appropriate here due to the lack of comparable transactions between independent enterprises. Neither is resale price minus, as there are no competitors selling similar products in similar markets under uncontrolled conditions. Cost plus is not appropriate as Jones Plc is not incurring significant additional costs, being merely a distributor.

3 Based on all the facts and circumstances, the IRS may determine that the comparable profits method will provide the most reliable measure of an arm's length result. USSub is selected as the tested party because it engages in activities that are less complex than those undertaken by Jones Plc.

There is data from a number of independent operators of wholesale distribution businesses. These potential comparables are further narrowed to select companies in the same industry segment that perform similar functions and bear similar risks to USSub. An analysis of the information available on these taxpayers shows that the ratio of operating profit to sales is the most appropriate profit level indicator, and this ratio is relatively stable where at least three years are included in the average. For the taxable years XX04 to XX06, USSub shows the following results:

	XX04	*XX05*	*XX06*	*Average*
	$	$	$	$
Sales	500,000	560,000	500,000	520,000
Cost of goods sold	393,000	412,000	400,000	401,800
Operating expenses	80,000	110,000	104,600	98,200
Operating profit	27,000	37,600	−4,600	20,000

4   After adjustments have been made to account for identified material dif-
     ferences between USSub and the uncontrolled distributor companies,
     A–J below, the average ratio of operating profit to sales is calculated
     for each of the uncontrolled distributors. Applying each ratio to USSub
     would lead to the following comparable operating profit (COP) for
     USSub:

Uncontrolled distributor company	Operating profit/ sales %	USSub Comparable Operating Profit ($520,000 × Op profit/sales ratio of competitor company) $
A	1.7	8,840
B	3.1	16,120
C	3.8	19,760
D	4.5	23,400
E	4.7	24,440
F	4.8	24,960
G	4.9	25,480
H	6.7	34,840
I	9.9	51,480
J	10.5	54,600

5   The data is not sufficiently complete to conclude that it is likely that all
     material differences between USSub and the uncontrolled distributors
     have been identified. The IRS will measure the arm's-length range in
     these circumstances by using the interquartile range of results, which
     consists of the results ranging from $19,760 to $34,840. In simple terms,
     the lowest 25 per cent and the highest 25 per cent of results will be dis-
     carded. Although USSub's operating income for 2006 shows a loss of
     $4,600, the IRS will determine that no transfer pricing adjustment should
     be made, because USSub's average reported operating profit of $20,000
     is within this range.

---

1   §1-482-5 Comparable profits method.

OTHER PROFIT-BASED METHODS

13.22   Where none of the methods considered so far produce an acceptable
result, other profit-based methods can be used. These might include the 'rate
of return' method or the use of the Berry ratio, sometimes used in cases where
there is a manufacturing company with complicated costs (eg high research
and development, and a company which simply acts as a selling and marketing
company).

The Canadian Glaxo case[1]

13.23   Major transfer pricing cases have not been common, although they are likely to increase in frequency in the post-BEPS era. The Canadian *Glaxo* case provides some evidence of the pre-BEPS attitude of the courts towards transfer pricing practices carried out by MNEs and towards the OECD *Guidelines*. The first point to note is that the transactions in question took place between 1990 and 1993, but the case was not finally decided until 2013, ending two decades of uncertainty for both the company and the tax authorities. The central issue concerned the prices paid by Glaxo Canada to a Swiss affiliate for supplies of a drug. Glaxo Canada entered into a licence agreement with Glaxo Group, the UK parent, for the right to produce, inter alia, the popular stomach ulcer drug, Zantac upon payment of royalties and it also entered into a supply agreement with the Swiss affiliate for the right to purchase the raw ingredient for Zantac from the Swiss affiliate. However, the Swiss affiliate was a middleman, with the ingredient being manufactured by a Glaxo group company in Singapore. The suspicion of the tax authorities was that the Swiss group company was 'creaming off' profits for tax purposes. As happens in the pharmaceutical industry, the exclusive licence to manufacture the ingredient (ranitidine) had expired and several generic versions were available in the years under examination, giving the tax authorities ample opportunity to make price comparisons. Glaxo Canada was paying around CAD$1,500 per kilo to the Swiss company, whilst the drug was available in generic form for between CAD$194 and CAD$304 per kilo. The Canadian tax authority took the price for the generic versions as being a comparable uncontrolled price, claimed that Glaxo Canada and the Swiss affiliate were not dealing at arm's length, and increased the taxable profits by CAD$51 million.

The defence was that the prices for the generic versions did not provide evidence of a comparable uncontrolled price nor evidence of dealing other than at arm's length. The quality of the generic ranitidine could not be assured and was not comparable to that manufactured by Glaxo in Singapore. Moreover, the licence agreement with the UK parent company (Glaxo Group) under which Glaxo Canada was permitted to market Zantac provided considerable advantages for Glaxo Canada. Glaxo Canada therefore claimed that the true comparable would be a company purchasing ranitidine under similar circumstances (ie one who was party to a similar licensing agreement to that between Glaxo Canada and the UK parent). Besides, after applying the resale pricing method to Glaxo Canada, it was making gross profits of between 45 per cent and 60 per cent which Glaxo claimed was reasonable. The Tax Court of Canada disagreed that the licence agreement with Glaxo Group should be taken alongside the purchasing agreement with the Swiss affiliate, as the two agreements were not interlinked. It further disagreed that the fact that Glaxo Canada appeared, on a resale minus basis, to be making reasonable profits meant that it should accept that the prices paid to the Swiss affiliate for supplies of ranitidine were at arm's length. In other words, the court took a narrow view of what was comparable and what should be taken into account in determining the arm's-length price. No explicit functional analysis of the role of Glaxo Canada within the worldwide group was considered. The court did not find that there were any significant differences between the position of Glaxo Canada and the companies buying generic versions of ranitidine and operating as secondary manufacturers (ie putting the ranitidine into pill form, packaging and marketing it) in much the same way as Glaxo Canada.

In the Federal Court, it was found that business realities should be taken into account when considering comparability, which includes the use of brand names resulting in higher prices. The Federal Court therefore found that the Tax Court erred in separating the licence and supply agreements and referred the case back for a determination on the reasonableness of the price.

In March 2011, the Crown was granted leave to appeal to the Supreme Court of Canada, and the taxpayer was granted leave for a cross appeal. The Crown's argument is that the bundling of the two agreements, licensing and supply, was contrary to the OECD *Guidelines* which require that the legal structure of the taxpayer be respected. It suggests that a new 'reasonable business person' test was being introduced. The taxpayer's cross appeal challenged the order of the Federal Court to remit the matter back to the Tax Court on the basis that this would allow the Minister to introduce new arguments. Very few transfer pricing cases reach this level of the judicial system and the fact that the Supreme Court granted leave to appeal is significant. While the Supreme Court found for the taxpayer, there remains considerable uncertainty about the 'reasonable business person' test and its relationship to the arm's length principal and OECD *Guidelines*.[2]

---

1 *GlaxoSmithKline Inc v HMQ* (Glaxo Canada) (2008 TCC 324).
2 For a discussion of this, see Pichhadze (2013).

Business restructuring

13.24   The 2010 OECD *Guidelines* contain a new chapter (IX) on 'Transfer Pricing Aspects of Business Restructuring', following extensive consultation culminating in a final paper released on 4 August 2010. The new chapter is concerned with internal business restructuring designed, for example, to shift risks or intangibles between members of a multinational group (ie it is concerned with associated enterprises in the context of Article 9 of the OECD MTC). The *Guidelines* note the following forms of restructuring:

- conversion of full-fledged distributors into limited-risk distributors or commissionaires for a foreign associated enterprise that may operate as a principal;

- conversion of full-fledged manufacturers into contract manufacturers or toll-manufacturers for a foreign associated enterprise that may operate as a principal; and

- transfers of intangible property rights to a central entity within the group.

Business restructurings are often the result of adopting integrated business models, usually for bona fide commercial reasons. Such integration, however, underscores the fundamental difficulty of applying the arm's-length principle as if all the parties were independent of one another. The OECD respects this conceptual difficulty in its development of practical approaches. The chapter addresses, inter alia, the allocation of risk among related parties, the treatment of compensation for the restructuring itself, how transfer pricing rules should apply subsequent to the restructuring and whether and when governments should be able to disregard a restructuring for the purposes of applying the transfer pricing rules.

Intangibles

13.25   In the process of revising the *Transfer Pricing Guidelines*, the OECD identified intangibles as an area of concern on which insufficient guidance exists. A number of issues relating to intangibles were left aside in the 2010 revision of the *Guidelines* and a Working Party (No 6) of the Committee on Fiscal Affairs was established to look at this aspect of transfer pricing more closely. Public comments were invited in July 2010 and 50 contributions received and fed into a consultation held in November 2010. A discussion draft was issued in September 2012[1] and a revised discussion draft in July 2013[2] following receipt of numerous comments and a public consultation. The revised discussion draft retains much of the content of the 2012 draft but contains a more refined analysis of factors affecting valuation and some explanatory changes to the definition of intangibles, which rejects traditional legal and accounting definitions of intellectual property in favour of a broad definition. Specifically:

> 'the word "intangible" is intended to address something which is not a physical asset or a financial asset, which is capable of being owned or controlled for use in commercial activities and whose use or transfer would be compensated had it occurred in a transaction between independent parties in comparable circumstances'.

The revised draft recognizes for the first time that funding the development of intangibles and bearing the risk are entitled to compensation, by reference to the degree of control over the use of contributed funds. A new section is included on the returns attributable to research and development and the use of company names. The OECD intangibles project is specifically listed as one of the base erosion and profit shifting action plan points, and work on intangibles carried on as part of the BEPS work. The BEPS proposals are considered at paras **13.31–13.32** below.

---

1   Available at: www.oecd.org/tax/transfer-pricing/50526258.pdf.
2   Available at: www.oecd.org/ctp/transfer-pricing/revised-discussion-draft-intangibles.pdf.

INDUSTRY FOCUS – THE PHARMACEUTICAL INDUSTRY

13.26   We have noted the need to take into account, inter alia, functions, risk, and economic conditions when trying to establish comparables in the use of the arm's-length principle. The issue of comparability of pricing is a particularly difficult one in relation to the pharmaceutical industry.

The pharmaceutical industry presents a number of challenges in applying the arm's-length principle. First, it consists of relatively few large firms which are vertically integrated (ie the multinational group owns the suppliers of raw materials through to the distribution companies supplying the group's customers). This means that there are many transactions between group members for which there are no comparable transactions between independent enterprises at all. Second, there is necessarily a very heavy investment in research and development, leading to the need for cost-sharing arrangements and detailed functional analysis of the transfer pricing policies. Third, it is heavily regulated by the governments of the countries in which it operates. No new drug can be tested or manufactured without a licence and each country has its own detailed regulations for the granting of these. This means that there is an additional crucial factor in the location decision for group members – besides taxation, the ease of obtaining licences and the burden of industry regulation in each country must be considered. Fourth, the government is often a major customer (eg the NHS in the UK). Therefore, governments act as regulators, tax collectors and customers, often sending out mixed and conflicting messages to the industry in the process. Then there are political and humanitarian pressures on firms; they are urged to allow developing countries to make generic copies of their painstakingly and expensively developed patented drugs (eg retro-virals for use in the treatment of AIDS patients).

Research and development

13.27   According to Wundisch (2003) up to a third of pharmaceutical groups' current costs are not directly attributable to the products currently sold but rather relate to R&D. The timeframe for development of new drugs is often between 12 and 14 years and even then the expenditure and time invested may not result in a successful product. For instance, in 2004 the pharmaceutical group Merck was forced to withdraw its ground-breaking anti-inflammatory drug, Vioxx, amidst claims of patient illness. For every successful new drug there are many more abortive programmes of research and development.

A successful programme of R&D may lead to the creation of an intangible asset; a patent on a new drug. Whilst it is reasonable that a group member should be compensated for making available the benefits of intangible assets which it owns to other group members, the problem in the pharmaceutical industry is that much R&D expenditure does not result in the creation of an intangible. The group member incurring R&D on unsuccessful ventures will have to recoup that expenditure from other group members either through a cost-sharing arrangement or by loading on to the cost of successful products the R&D expense of unsuccessful ventures. Supporting documentation is vital in protecting the group from an attack by the tax authorities on its transfer pricing policies with respect to R&D allocations. This is particularly relevant where the R&D centre does not invoice its costs to other group members at a margin, leaving the R&D costs to be included in the transfer pricing of the entities bearing the R&D costs. In practice this policy may lead to a demand for withholding taxes on part of the purchase price of the products as the tax authority could regard part of the purchase price as tantamount to the payment of a royalty.

Some tax authorities may argue that because R&D is carried out by Subsidiary A in Country X, the profits attributable to Company B, also located in Country X should be higher than actually reported, by virtue of the fact that R&D is carried out by the group in Country X. This is a false assumption, as the reward for carrying out R&D belongs to the company which is carrying it out, not the country as a whole.

Another question is whether the location of a group's R&D function in a particular country gives rise to a PE there, or whether the R&D functions can be viewed as merely 'preparatory or auxiliary' to the making of contracts. If a permanent establishment is held to exist then all the issues relating to attribution of profits to that establishment will have to be addressed in the very difficult context of R&D.

Marketing expenses

13.28   Because drug patents tend to have relatively short lives, heavy marketing expenditure is necessary to establish the brand so that it continues to be the market leader even after the patent has expired. Whilst much cheaper generic versions of the drugs may become available, the market must be persuaded to continue purchasing the original branded product. For instance, in the UK we can purchase paracetamol, aspirin and ibuprofen very cheaply indeed if we buy generic versions, but popular brands retain a large market share. This implies a heavy marketing campaign by the licensee of the drug, targeted at a specific country market. Another aspect of the pharmaceutical industry leading to exceptionally heavy marketing expenditure is that the primary market for many drugs is the body of prescribing practitioners. Most pharmaceutical companies employ a mini-army of highly trained drug representatives who visit doctors and other practitioners at their own premises and carefully explain the products in one-to-one meetings. In the run up to and immediately after the expiry of the patent there is normally a ballooning of marketing expenditure as firms seek to consolidate the position of their product in the market. Thus, even after the requirement to pay patent royalties has ceased to exist, the profitability of the licensee may deteriorate due to the need for increased marketing expenditure.

Cost-sharing arrangements

13.29   Cost-sharing arrangements are common in industries where there are heavy research and development costs associated with the development of intangibles such as patents. Rather than looking at whether a price is that which would be charged between parties operating at arm's length, a cost-sharing arrangement looks at the recharge made to other group companies for services carried out by one or more group members on behalf of the whole group. The OECD has given guidance on cost sharing in recent years and the US has recently updated its current regulations on cost sharing. Both the OECD and the US s 482 regulations insist that the costs contributed must be commensurate with the future benefits expected and with what would otherwise have to be paid to an unconnected partner. If a participant in a cost-sharing arrangement contributes intangible property to the arrangement, then the other participants must make an appropriate payment (a buy-in payment) to the contributor.

Under a typical cost-sharing agreement several companies in a multinational group will agree to share the costs of product development in return for being permitted to exploit the intangible assets (usually patents on the newly developed products) which result from the research and development. The parties to the arrangement contribute cash and often also intangible assets (eg know-how, patents) that they have acquired prior to or outside the cost-sharing arrangements. Normally the costs will be shared according to the anticipated benefit to each of the parties. These benefits will take the form of increased sales or increased operating profits. A typical example would be a company that updates the manufacturing processes used across its multinational group. The new processes are patented and each of the participants in the cost-sharing arrangement is permitted to use the new, improved manufacturing processes to increase profitability. However, the nature of research and development costs is that the eventual costs and the benefits from the work are uncertain. The US regulations governing cost sharing stipulate that if actual benefits differ significantly from the anticipated benefits then the cost-sharing arrangements must be revisited. New regulations effective as of 5 January 2009 specify that the ratio of:

$$\frac{\text{Present value of actually experienced operating profits}}{\text{Present value of cost contributions, in cash and in kind}}$$
(from exploiting cost shared intangibles)

should be within a set range, 0.5 to 2.0. If not, a retrospective revision of the cost sharing is required. The previous regulations merely required that the actual percentage of expected benefit should not deviate from the percentage used to determine cost-sharing payments by more than 20 per cent. This is illustrated below.

Example 13.8

Diet Inc (US company) is the parent company of Health Inc (US company) and Fizzy Ltd (UK company), US. They enter into a cost-sharing agreement to develop a new miracle diet drink, Lipozade. Taking into account the size of the relative markets for each company and the fit with existing product ranges, the anticipated split of benefits from the development of Lipozade is:

Diet Inc 45%

Health Inc 25%

Fizzy Ltd 30%

In the year ended 31.12.X001 Diet Inc incurs expenditure of $3 million on developing the product. It receives payments of $1 million from Health Inc and $500,000 from Fizzy Ltd. Comparing these contributions with the anticipated benefits gives:

	Share of anticipated benefits	Expected contribution towards costs of $3m	Actual contribution	Expected contribution +20%	Expected contribution −20%
Diet Inc	45%	1,350,000	1,500,000	1,620,000	1,080,000
Health Inc	25%	750,000	1,000,000	900,000	600,000
Fizzy Ltd	30%	900,000	500,000	1,080,000	720,000

The net contribution from Diet Inc is within the 20 per cent tolerance permitted by the s 482 regulations. However, contribution by Health Inc is above the upper limit of $900,000, whilst the contribution of Fizzy Ltd is below the lower limit of $720,000. The IRS would appear to have grounds for challenging the cost-sharing arrangement as the profits of Health Inc appear to have been depressed at the expense of the profits of Fizzy Ltd. In practice, all the circumstances of the arrangement would be closely examined and more than one year's data might be used. Even though this is the first year of the arrangement it is likely that by the time the IRS reach this stage in their investigations further data would be available.

The Xilinx case[1]

13.30 This 2005 US case concerned the scope of costs which ought to be dealt with under cost-sharing arrangements for R&D activities. The point at issue was whether or not the cost of employee stock options (defined here as the difference between the share price at which the options could be exercised and the market value at the date of exercise) should be included in cost-sharing arrangements. The taxpayer argued that it was impossible to predict with any accuracy what the spread between exercise and current market price would be, and partly for this reason cost-sharing agreements between unrelated parties would not include such future costs. Strangely, the IRS argued that there was no need for comparables in this instance, and the regulations governing cost sharing in the US for 2004 onwards specifically require the inclusion of such costs. This view appears to be rooted in the belief that unconnected parties do not enter into cost-sharing arrangements. Reichert and Wright (2006) dispute this view, likening cost-sharing arrangements to joint ventures, co-development and even to crop sharing as well as actual cost sharing. In all these examples, unconnected parties join together to contribute cash and intangibles. Certainly, the taxpayer, Xilinx, argued strongly as to the existence of cost sharing amongst unconnected parties, thus providing valid comparisons.

These are appropriate where two or more group companies work jointly to produce, develop or obtain products, services or rights. An example would be R&D in the pharmaceutical industry where two or more companies may collaborate to produce new drugs. A cost contribution arrangement would provide the framework for sharing in costs and profits.

The court decision in 2005 was that stock option costs need not be included in the R&D costs which were to be shared between the group companies in cases. This decision was overturned by the US Court of Appeals in 2009, but upon further appeal, the decision was again reversed back in 2010 to the 2005 position. The reason for the different decisions seems to lie in ambiguities present in US transfer pricing regulations.

Cost sharing or contribution arrangements form part of the OECD BEPS Project within Action 8, and are considered further at para **13.33** below.

---

1   *Xilinx Inc v Commissioner* 125 TC 4 (August 2005).

BEPS ACTIONS 8–10

13.31   The OECD 2013 Action plan identified that existing international standards for transfer pricing rules were deficient in that they could result in outcomes where the allocation of profits for tax purposes is out of alignment with the economic activity that produced those profits. Given the OECD's firm commitment to retain the arm's length principle, the Action Plan required the guidance on its application to be clarified and strengthened, and accepted that it was possible that special measures may be required either within or beyond the arm's length principle. The three key areas dealt with are intangibles (Action 8), risk and capital (Action 9) and other high risk transactions (Action 10). Each of these will be considered in turn.

BEPS ACTION 8: THE PROBLEM OF INTANGIBLES

13.32   The 2013 Action plan required the OECD to:

> 'Develop rules to prevent BEPS by moving intangibles among group members. This will involve (i) adopting a broad and clearly delineated definition of intangibles; (ii) ensuring that profits associated with the transfer and use of intangibles are appropriately allocated in accordance with (rather than divorced from) value creation; (iii) developing transfer pricing rules or special measures for transfer of hard to value intangibles; and (iv) updating the guidance on cost contribution arrangements.'

The 2014 Action 8 Deliverable 'Guidance on transfer pricing aspects of intangibles' contains revisions to Chapters I, II and VI of the OECD *Transfer Pricing Guidelines* to clarify the definition of intangibles, identification of transactions involving intangibles, supplemental guidance for determining arm's length conditions for transactions and guidance on the treatment of local market features and corporate synergies.

Chapters I–II of the OECD *Transfer Pricing Guidelines* are amended to provide additional explanations and examples to deal with the following:

- *Location savings* – these are defined as cost reductions arising due the operating in certain local markets. Determining the cost saving attributable to operating in a particular market is problematic and requires consideration of whether such savings exist, if so, whether they are retained or passed on, and if not fully passed on, the manner in which independent enterprises would allocate such retained savings. If comparables are available, this will be the most reliable indication of how any net location saving should be shared. In the absence of comparables, a functional analysis is needed along the lines of that applicable to business restructuring in Chapter 11.

- *Other local market features* – may have to be considered for the purposes of comparability adjustments even if they do not lead to location savings, for example, local infrastructure, regulatory requirements (eg licencing) and workforce capabilities.

- *Assembled workforce* – the existence of a 'uniquely qualified or experienced cadre of employees' should be taken into account in a comparability analysis.

- *Multinational enterprise group synergies* – can arise through pooling purchasing power, joint information and communication facilities, integrated management, etc. Where a group benefits from synergies through 'deliberate concerted action' which creates a material advantage, this must be analysed through a functional and risk analysis and the benefit allocated to group members according to their respective contribution to its creation.

Chapter VI of the *Transfer Pricing Guidelines* has been replaced completely and is now divided into four sections:

1 Identifying intangibles. The term intangible is defined as 'something which is not a physical asset or a financial asset, which is capable of being owned or controlled for use in commercial activities, and whose use or transfer would be compensated had it occurred in a transaction between independent parties in comparable circumstances'. The focus here is not on how intangibles are identified for other purposes such as financial accounting, but on the amount of compensation that would be agreed between independent parties in comparable transactions. There is no attempt to delineate separate categories of intangibles, however two commonly used terms are contained the glossary: marketing intangibles and trade intangibles. Illustrations are provided including patents, knowhow and trade secrets, trade marks, trade names and brands, rights under contracts or government licences, goodwill and ongoing concern value.

2 Ownership of intangibles and transactions involving the development, enhancement, maintenance, protection and exploitation of intangibles. The main point here is that the return on an intangible should be allocated to group members according to their functions, assets and risks,

which supersede contractual agreements. The 2014 deliverable builds on the 2013 draft but gives the control function a more prominent role.

3   Transactions involving the use or transfer of intangibles. It is necessary to identify and properly characterize the specific controlled transactions, which may be transfer of the intangible itself or rights therein, or transactions involving their use. Where a combination of intangibles is transferred, the individual components must be identified.

4   Supplemental guidance for determining arm's length conditions in cases involving intangibles. It is noted that in considering the options realistically available to each party as part of a comparability analysis, it is not appropriate to focus only on one side of a transaction and that the perspectives of each party must be considered. This section also provides a description of several important features relevant to a comparability analysis including exclusivity, extent and duration of legal protection, geographic scope, useful life and stage of development.

An Annexe to the 2014 deliverables provides a variety of new examples of specific fact patterns and recommended treatment.

In addition to the 2014 deliverables, two discussion drafts were published during 2015 in advance of the final report. One deals with cost contribution arrangements and the other with hard to value intangibles. These discussion drafts generated additional comment and discussion.

Cost contribution arrangements

13.33   The 2015 discussion draft on cost contribution arrangements (CCA) was released in April 2015 and defines a CCA as 'a contractual arrangement among business enterprises to share the contributions and risks involved in the joint development, production or the obtaining of intangibles, tangible assets or services with the understanding that such intangibles, tangible assets or services are expected to create direct benefits for the businesses of each of the participants'. The arm's-length principle requires that each participant's share of the overall contribution to the CCA be in proportion to the overall expected benefits to be received.

Two types of CCA are distinguished, development CCAs and services CCAs, the key difference being that in the case of the former benefits are ongoing into the future, whereas for the latter, only current benefits are created. In relation to intangibles, rights to the developed intangible often take the form of exploitation rights in a specific geographical location or for a specific purpose. CCAs can be distinguished from ordinary intragroup transfers by the expectation that mutual benefit will flow from pooling resources and skills.

Dealing with CCAs entails, identifying the participants and then measuring the value of their respective contribution by reference to the proportionate share of benefits, recognizing that this will need to entail projections and a choice of allocation method that may vary depending on the type of CCA. Under the arm's length principle, the value of each participant's contribution should be consistent with that of independent enterprise, which may not use cost as a basis. Balancing payments may be made in cases where proportionate contributions are lower than proportionate expected benefits.

The key point is that the rules on CCAs are now aligned with the other transfer pricing outcomes.

Hard to value intangibles

13.34 The discussion draft on hard to value intangibles (HTVIs) was released in June 2015. It is primarily concerned with situations where the valuation of intangibles is highly uncertain at the time of the transaction. Hard to value intangibles are defined as those: 'for which, at the time of their transfer in a transaction between associated enterprises, (i) no sufficiently reliable comparables exist, and (ii) there is a lack of reliable projections of future cashflows or income expected to be derived from the transferred intangible or the assumptions used in valuing the intangible are highly uncertain'. This may be because they are only partially developed at the time of transfer or not expected to be exploited commercially for some time.

The OECD recognizes that information asymmetry is particularly acute in these cases making it particularly difficult for tax administrations to verify the arm's length basis on which the pricing was determined, and so allows for the use of ex post evidence in determining *ex ante* pricing arrangement, with appropriate safe harbour provisions.

Final Report on Actions 8–10 in relation to intangibles

13.35 The October 2015 Actions 8–10 Final Report contains revisions to Chapter VI and, in respect of intangibles, is the final update to the OECD *Transfer Pricing Guidelines* from the BEPS Project, with the exception of the application of transactional profit split for intangibles which is likely to be revised in the 2017 guidance. One change from the 2014 guidance is the provision of a framework for the situation where an entity owns and funds intellectual property development but affiliates performs functions related to their enhancement, maintenance, protection and exploitation. The definition of intangibles is unchanged from the 2014 deliverable. The 2015 guidance confirms the approach that legal ownership of an intangible does not of itself confer rights to returns from its exploitation.

The 2015 *Guidance* also contains a new version of Chapter VIII covering cost contribution arrangements, based on the draft issued in April 2015, discussed at para **13.33** above, with some refinements developed following consultation.

BEPS ACTION 9

13.36 The 2013 OECD BEPS Action 9 is designed to:

'Develop rules to prevent BEPS by transferring risks among, or allocating excessive capital to, group members. This will involve adopting transfer pricing rules or special measures to ensure that in appropriate returns will not accrue to an entity solely because it has contractually assumed risks or has provided capital. The rules to be developed will also require alignment of returns with value creation.'

In December 2014, a *Discussion Draft* was published relating to Actions 8, 9 and 10; specifically revisions to Chapter 1 of the *Transfer Pricing Guidelines* including risk, re-characterization and special measures. The first part of the discussion draft deals with the arm's-length principle in relation to risk and so links most closely to Action 9, although the OECD concedes that the three Actions 8, 9 and 10 are interlinked, and also linked to other Actions.

The first step of a comparability analysis is the identification of commercial and financial relations between associated enterprises, and the 2014 *Discussion Draft* contains new guidance on this difficult issue. Written contractual arrangements provide a starting point, but in the absence of contractual arrangements or in the case of ambiguity, the delineation of a transaction can be deduced from the actual conduct of the parties. The discussion draft also contains new guidance on identifying risks in commercial and financial transactions, defining risk as 'the effect of uncertainty on the objectives of the business' and providing a framework for analysing risk as follows:

- 'Taking into account the nature and sources of risk, what are the specific risks included in the commercial or financial arrangements of the parties?

- How are those specific risks allocated in contractual arrangements? How are the risks assumed? Do the specific risks relate to operational activities from which the risks arise?

- What is the potential impact of those specific risks?

- How is each risk actually managed by members of the MNE group? How does risk management related to the risk – influence the occurrence or the impact of the risk?

- Does the party contractually assuming the risk either: (a) perform operational activities from which risk arises; (b) manage the risk; or (c) assess, monitor, and direct risk mitigation?

- What are the actual transactions undertaken? Are the contractual arrangements in relation to the risk allocation, the operational activities to which the risk relates and risk management aligned with the conduct of the parties?'

The 2014 draft observes that a number of issues can be grouped under the concepts of 'moral hazard' and 'risk return', and focuses specific attention on risks in the financial services sector. Action 9 also considers the case of a capital rich MNE group member whose returns are out of line with the level of activity of the funding company. The 2015 *Final Report* on Actions 8–10 requires that if an 'associated enterprise does not in fact control the financial risks associated with its funding ... then it will not be allocated the profits associated with the financial risks and will be entitled to no more than a risk free return'.

BEPS ACTION 10

13.37 The 2013 OECD BEPS Action 10 deals with other high risk transactions, and aims to:

'Develop rules to prevent BEPS by engaging in transactions which would not, or would only very rarely, occur between third parties. This will involve adopting transfer pricing rules or special measures to: (i) clarify the circumstances in which transactions can be recharacterised; (ii) clarify the application of transfer pricing methods, in particular profit splits, in the context of global value chains; and (iii) provide protection against common types of base eroding payments, such as management fees and head office expenses.'

Commodity transactions

13.38 Under the mandate of Action 10, cross-border commodity transactions are examined and an improved framework developed with the aim of achieving greater consistency in determining arm's length prices and also that pricing reflects value creation. The term 'commodities' refers to physical products for which a quoted price obtained in a commodity exchange market is used as a reference. The guidance on CUP has been enhanced for commodity transactions. In order to assess the comparability of the quoted price and the controlled transaction, 'economically relevant characteristics' such as quality of the commodity and volumes traded may result in material differences in which case 'reasonably accurate adjustments' can be made.

Transactional profit split method

13.39 A discussion draft dealing with the transactional profit split method was issued by the OECD in December 2014 which presented a variety of scenarios and invited comments, followed by a public consultation in March 2015. The overall view following consultation is that notwithstanding practical difficulties in its application, transactional profit split can offer a useful method in terms of aligning profits with value creation. The final report on Actions 8–10 published in October 2015 includes some clarification and strengthening of the guidance on transactional profit splits that will form the basis of subsequent work by WP6 leading to draft guidance being published in 2016, to be finalized in 2017.

The current guidance on transactional profit split is contained in Chapter II of the 2010 *Transfer Pricing Guidelines* as discussed at para **13.20** above. Comments received by the OECD on the 2014 *Discussion Draft* expressed concern about the potential for adoption of the method in inappropriate cases, merely because reliable comparables are not available. Difficulties arise not so much in the functional analysis of the contributions made by the various parties, but rather in valuing those contributions, ie the profit splitting factors.

Revisions to the guidance on the transactional profit split method are foreshadowed in relation to highly integrated business operations, unique and valuable contributions, synergistic benefits as well as the profit splitting factors. In addition, guidance is provided on when it is appropriate to use a transactional profit split method to support a TNMM range or royalty rates.

Low value-adding intragroup services

13.40   Intra-group services take several forms and may be those usually obtained from external parties, such as legal services, as well as those usually performed internally, such as staff training. A CUP method is recognized as being the most appropriate where there is a comparable service, otherwise cost plus. The 2014 *Discussion Draft* on low value adding services provides guidance developed by WP6 that 'seeks to achieve the necessary balance between appropriate charges for low value added services and head office expense and the need to protect the tax base of payer countries'. Low value intragroup services are defined as being of a supportive nature, not part of the core business of the group, not requiring the use of unique and valuable intangibles and not involving the assumption of substantial risk.

Where low value adding intra group services are provided, MNEs may adopt a simplified method, as an alternative to cost contribution arrangements (see para **13.33** above). The approach entails determining a pool of costs for services provided to multiple group members and using an 'allocation key', for example, for IT services this might be the share of total users. In determining the arm's-length price, a mark-up of between 2 per cent and 5 per cent can be used for all costs in the pool.

The use of this simplified approach is designed to remove the need for detailed testing and allow tax administrations to focus on higher risk transactions. The 2015 Final Report acknowledges that for a number of countries, excessive charges for intragroup management services and head office expenses is a major BEPS challenge, and that for the simplified approach to be effective, widespread adoption is required. Countries participating in BEPS have accordingly agreed a two-step process: First, is that a large group of countries will endorse the applicability of the method before 2018. Second, entails a follow up on design of the threshold and other implementation issues.

VALIDITY OF THE ARM'S-LENGTH PRINCIPLE

13.41 The main problems with the arm's-length principle are that, first, it is based on the separate entity principle and, secondly, that it tries to regulate the prices for every category of product, service or intangible which exists and is traded. In the case of intermediate products and vertically integrated industries, such as pharmaceuticals and automobiles, there often is no market at all in the intermediate goods from which to establish an arm's-length price. For instance, the *Bausch & Lomb*[1] case concerned royalties paid by an Irish subsidiary to the US parent for processes of manufacturing contact lenses. The IRS said they were too low, but no third-party price was available because no other manufacturer apart from the Irish subsidiary was permitted to use the patents.

The OECD BEPS process and the EU CCTB proposals (see Chapter 20) have broadened the debate about the validity of the arm's length principle. The push for an alternative comes largely from NGOs and activists who assert that transfer pricing as a tax avoidance practice is dysfunctional and deprives developing countries in particular of much-needed tax revenues. Proposals for formulary apportionment as an alternative (see para **13.42** below) are resisted by practitioners and also the OECD on the basis that, while it is recognized that the arm's length principle contains flaws, it is well understood and increasingly better managed by tax authorities. One of the problems with the current system is that MNEs have had a significant informational advantage over tax authorities. Arguably, Action 13 (discussed above) goes some way to correcting this asymmetry.

A switch to a completely new system would be, in some respects, a leap into the unknown not only for taxpayers but also tax authorities and it is unclear that the formula would be any more robust against manipulation than the current system. Devereux (2012)[2] considers it extremely difficult to say with any certainty where a MNE's profits are truly made. He considers that they are not necessarily made where the R&D is located, that they may possibly be made where the customers are, but that it is usually impossible to say where profits which arise from synergies within the MNE are made. This thinking is reflected in the discussions around BEPS Action 11 which deals with measuring the extent of base erosion and profit shifting; an extremely uncertain activity.

---

1   *Bausch & Lomb, Inc v Commissioner*, 92 TC 525.
2   Available at: http://eureka.bodleian.ox.ac.uk/4591/1/Michael_Devereux.pdf.

GLOBAL FORMULARY APPORTIONMENT

13.42 A weakness of the arm's length principle of testing transfer prices between group members is that it maintains the fiction that each individual company within a group is an independent economic entity. It could be argued that the arm's length principle is fundamentally unsuited to determining how the taxable profits of a multinational group should be shared out between the countries in which the group operates. Multinational groups of companies exist so that they can take advantage of synergies between the member companies. For instance, rather than having 20 separate companies all seeking technical advice from different external providers, if those 20 companies form a multinational group, they can appoint one of them to be the group's expert on technical matters, so that they no longer have to pay for expensive external advice. Moreover, the group company that is the technical expert can develop its expertise so that it is directly relevant to the needs of the group. In time, external providers would cease being able to provide the group with the technical expertise it requires because that expertise is specific to this one group and there are no other customers. So, when the price charged by the group technical expert comes under scrutiny, there is no comparable transaction to look at and the arm's length method cannot be properly applied. This type of situation is becoming more common as multinational groups continue to grow and become ever more integrated.

As noted in the previous section, a number of commentators have called for a complete rethink of transfer pricing methods. The main alternative to the arm's length principle is to take the group's worldwide profit and allocate it, for tax purposes, to each country in which the group operates by means of a formula. This would acknowledge the reality that the economic entity is the multinational group.

In a system of global formulary apportionment the share of profits of a multinational group that each country may tax is determined not by looking at the accounts of companies operating in each country but by dividing out the total global profits of the group according to a formula. The formula would typically incorporate factors such as sales and payroll.

It is important to realize that, in countries with a federal system of government such as the US, Canada and Switzerland, 'cross-border' has implications at the state, as well as the federal, level. In these countries, the local tax base of individual states is determined using a system of formulary apportionment. The combined income of the group is determined and allocated on a state by state (or country-by-country) basis using drivers such as property, payroll and sales. A few US states have gone further, insisting upon levying local taxation according to a share of a group's worldwide income rather than merely a share of total US-generated income. This extension of the principle has been very unpopular with multinational groups, leading Barclays Plc and Colgate-Palmolive Company to sue the state government of California. Multinational groups operating within the US now have the option to file a 'water's edge' election so that only their US operations are considered for the purposes of taxation at the state level.

Some argue that its main advantage is that it is simple and easy to enforce. The main disadvantage of formulary apportionment is that firms may manipulate the components of the formula.

The OECD has traditionally objected to the adoption of formulary apportionment on several grounds, most of which do not apply to the application of the system within a single country:

- There must be common agreement by all countries in which a multinational group operates as to the factors to be used and the weightings to be applied. However, inevitably, individual countries will attempt to construct their own formulae, to the advantage of each individual country. This would lead to overlaps and double taxation as the parts of the global profits of the group would be vulnerable to tax in multiple locations.

- The system would be open to manipulation by multinational groups: for instance, key factors of production influencing the profit allocation such as manufacturing facilities, could be shifted to low-tax jurisdictions to increase the allocation of global profits to those jurisdictions. Other possible methods of manipulation could include outsourcing of functions in high-tax jurisdictions to decrease payroll headcount and costs (and thus global profit allocation) in those jurisdictions.

- A pre-determined formula cannot properly take account of market conditions and efficiency differences, nor can it easily account for the degree of risk suffered by different entities within a multinational group.

- The use of different accounting policies in different countries leads to distortions of the true share of profits arising in each country when combined into a global profit figure. This objection may be watered down if the adoption of International Financial Reporting Standards (IFRS) proves widespread and successful. Although IFRS is increasingly widespread, its success is open to question.

Even if formulary apportionment could be proved to be a better system than the arm's-length principle, there is a further hurdle to be cleared. The arm's-length principle has been accepted as the worldwide standard for determining transfer pricing issues for the last 70 years or so. Any replacement principle must also be accepted worldwide in order to become the replacement international standard. In 2016, the EU produced a revised Draft Directive which, if implemented, would see a limited system of formula apportionment being operated by group companies resident in EU Member States. This is known as the Common Consolidated Corporation Tax Base (CCCTB). However, the plans have not been well-received. Member States appear reluctant to give up the right to set their own rules as to how companies should be taxed. Even advocates of formula apportionment have criticized the proposal, because it leaves intangibles out of the formula used to apportion the group taxable profits. The CCCTB plans are discussed in Chapter 20.

Despite the OECD's refusal to adopt formulary apportionment, some of the methods which it now approves of might be viewed as formula apportionment in all but name. In particular, the profit split method depends on looking at the functions performed, risks borne and assets used by the group companies between whom profits are being split. Comparing this approach with formula apportionment, there is not all that much difference. Profits are split according to which group company performs the most key functions in relation to a transaction, and which group companies bear the risk and own the assets which make the transaction in question possible. However, global formula apportionment must be distinguished from unitary taxation. Unitary taxation denotes a system where the multinational group is treated as a single (unitary) entity and all its profits are allocated via formulary apportionment. The profit split method is, essentially, a transactional method rather than one which attempts to split the entire profits of the whole group.

Rather than make a stark choice between the arm's length principle and formulary apportionment as methods of ensuring a fair split of a groups taxable profits between the countries in which it operates, some academics have suggested that a system could be adopted which combines them both. Under such a system, intra-group transactions for which there are suitable comparables would continue to be judged according to the arm's length principle. However, for the types of transactions which only occur internally within groups, for which there are no suitable comparables, a limited system of formula apportionment could be adopted. This would be based on the profit split method. Avi-Yonah and Benshalom[1] have advocated allocating a multinational taxable group's profits to the countries in which it operates using the arm's length method first. However, for group profits which result from internal transactions for which there are simply no usable comparable transactions, they suggest applying formulary apportionment to split these residual group taxable profits between the countries which are party to the transactions. Their idea is to use standard formulas to split the profits on certain types of transactions between group members. Governments would adopt standard formulas for particular types of transactions. By doing so, there would be no need to examine, say, royalty payments on a transaction by transaction basis, as a standard formula could be applied. This approach would not necessarily need all the countries involved to agree on a formula: for instance, if the royalty was being paid from a US subsidiary to a Bermudan subsidiary, a maximum tax-deductible rate of royalty could be set by the US. As the actual royalty might be higher, there would be a small tax deduction in the US and a large taxable amount in Bermuda. However, as Bermudan tax is practically non-existent, this would not matter.

One prominent supporter of unitary taxation is Professor Sol Picciotto, who has recently edited a compilation of essays from various proponents on aspects of global formulary apportionment.[2]

---

1   Avi-Yonah, R & Benshalom, I (2011) 'Formulary Apportionment – Myths and Prospects', *World Tax Journal*, October 2011, p 371.
2   Picciotto, S (2017) *Taxing Multinational Enterprises as Unitary Firms*. The book is available free of charge from: http://ictd.ac/publication/6-books-journal-articles/164-taxing-multinational-enterprises-as-unitary-firms.

FURTHER READING

Ahmadov, J (2011) 'The "Most Appropriate Method" as the New OECD Transfer Pricing Standard: Has the Hierarchy or Methods Been Completely Eliminated?', 18, *International Transfer Pricing Journal* 2011, 3.

Australian Taxation Office, *Applying the Arm's-length Principle.* Guide NAT 2726-04.2005.

Avi-Yonah, R (1995) 'The Rise and Fall of Arm's Length: A Study in the Evolution of US International Taxation', *Virginia Tax Review*, Vol 15, pp 89–159.

Avi-Yonah, R (2010) 'Between Formulary Apportionment and the OECD Guidelines: A Proposal for Reconciliation', 2, *World Tax Journal* 2010, 1.

Avi-Yonah, R and Benshalom, I (2011) 'Formulary Apportionment – Myths and Prospects', *World Tax Journal* October 2011, p 371.

Cooper, J and Agarwal, R (2011) 'The Transactional Profit Methods in Practice: A Survey of APA Reports', 18, *International Transfer Pricing Journal* 2011, 1.

Coronado, L, Cheung, P and Kyte, J (2010) 'An Overview of Arm's Length Approaches to Thin Capitalization', 17, *International Transfer Pricing Journal* 2010, 4.

Dujsic, M et al (2008) 'Digesting the *Glaxo* Decision: A Difficult Pill to Swallow for Transfer Pricing Practitioners', *International Transfer Pricing Journal*, Sept/Oct 2008.

Ernst & Young (2013) Global Transfer Pricing Survey: Navigating the Choppy Waters of International Tax.

Forstater, M (2015) Can Stopping 'Tax Dodging by Multinational Enterprises Close the Gap in Finance for Development? What do the big numbers really mean? Discussion paper draft, available at: http://www.cgdev.org/blog/how-much-do-we-really-know-about-multinational-tax-avoidance-and-how-much-it-really-worth.

Francescucci, D L P (2004) 'The Arm's Length Principle and Group Dynamics – Part 1: The Conceptual Shortcomings', *International Transfer Pricing Journal* Mar/Apr 2004, pp 55–75.

Francescucci, D L P (2004) 'The Arm's-Length Principle and Group Dynamics – Part 2: Solutions to Conceptual Shortcomings', *International Transfer Pricing Journal*, Nov/Dec 2004, pp 235–246.

Gill, S (2011) 'Intangibles and Transfer Pricing: The Perils Faced by Multinationals in India', 18, *International Transfer Pricing Journal* 2011, 1.

Gouthiere, B (2011) 'Key Practical Issues in Eliminating the Double Taxation of Business Income', 65, *Bulletin for International Taxation* 2011, 4/5.

Hamaekers, H (2005) 'Income Allocation in the 21st Century: The End of Transfer Pricing? Introductory Speech', *International Transfer Pricing Journal*, May/Jun 2005, pp 95–102.

Hammer R (1993), 'Will the Arm's Length Standard Stand the Test of Time? The Spectre of Apportionment', in Alpert and K Van Raad eds *Essays on International Taxation*, Kluwer Law International.

Hellerstein, W (2005) 'Income Allocation in the 21st Century: The End of Transfer Pricing? The Case for Formulary Apportionment', *International Transfer Pricing Journal*, May/Jun 2005, pp 103–111.

Joseph, A (2011) 'Australia – Increasing Role of Advance Pricing Agreements', 18, *International Transfer Pricing Journal* 2011, 4.

Mehafdi, M (2000) 'The Ethics of international Transfer Pricing', *The Journal of Business Ethics*, December 2000, 28: Pt 2.

Nias, P and Ivinson, J (2002) 'Back to Basics – Transfer Pricing Part 1 – The International Context', *Tax Journal*, 4 November 2002.

OECD (2005) *Are the Current Treaty Rules for Taxing Business Profits Appropriate for E-Commerce?*. Available at: www.oecd.org/topic/0,2686, en_2649_33741_1_1_1_1_37427,00.html.

OECD (2007) *Improving the Resolution of Tax Treaty Disputes*. Committee on Fiscal Affairs, February 2007. Available at www.oecd.org/dataoecd/17/59/38055311.pdf.

OECD (2008) *Transactional Profit Methods; Discussion Draft for Public Consultation*. OECD Centre for Tax Policy and Administration, 25 January 2008.

OECD (2010) *Transfer Pricing Guidelines for Multinational Enterprises and Tax Administrations* (with various updates since 1995).

Oosterhoff, D and Wingerter, B (2011) 'The New OECD Guidelines: The Good, the Bad and the Ugly', 18, *International Transfer Pricing Journal* 2011, 2.

Pak, S J and Zdanowica, J S (2002) *US Trade with the World: and Estimate of 2001 Lost US Federal Income Tax Revenues due to Over-invoiced Imports and Under-invoiced Exports*. Available at: http://dorgan.senate.gov/newsroom/extras/pak-zdan.pdf.

Patton, M F (2010) 'Xilinx v Comr: "I Think I Better Think it out Again"', 39 *Tax Management International Journal*, 499.

Pereira, M, Zambujal-Oliveira, J (2011) 'Transfer Pricing Analysis: The Case of a Manufacturing Company', 18, *International Transfer Pricing Journal* 2011, 1.

Picciotto, S (1992) Chapter 8, *International Business Taxation*, Butterworths.

Picciotto, S (2017) *Taxing Multinational Enterprises as Unitary Firms*. Institute of Development Studies.

Pichhadze, A (2013) 'Canada's Transfer Pricing Test in the Aftermath of GlaxoSmithKline Inc: A Critique of the Reasonable Business Person Test' *International Transfer Pricing Journal*, May/June 2013, pp 144–162.

Reichert, T A and Wright, D R (2006) 'Proposed Cost Sharing Regulations: A Departure from Arm's Length?' *International Transfer Pricing Journal*, Jan/Feb 2006, pp 2–7.

Stirling, M (2002) 'Global Attitudes Towards Transfer Pricing', *Tax Journal*, 3 June 2002.

United States Internal Revenue Service *Development of IRC Section 482 cases*, Ch 61 Internal Revenue Manual. Available at: www.irs.gov/irm/part4/ch46s03.html.

Vann, R J (2010) 'Taxing International Business Income: Hard-Boiled Wonderland and the End of the World', 2, *World Tax Journal* 2010, 3.

Wundisch, K (2003) 'Pharmaceutical Industry and Transfer Pricing: Anything Special?', *International Transfer Pricing Journal*, Nov/Dec 2003, pp 204–210.

FURTHER STUDY

The United Kingdom's transfer pricing legislation

13.43 As the nature of internal trading and the range of transactions undertaken between members of multinational groups widens, so tax authorities have had to move away from simple transfer pricing rules to more complex, open-ended legislation. Studying the UK legislation,[1] we can see that it is intended to cover a far wider range of transactions than the sale of tangible goods:

'Where:

- provision is made or imposed between any two persons by means of a transaction or a series of transactions; and

- the participation condition is met; and

- actual provision differs from arm's-length provision which would have been made as between independent enterprises; and

- actual provision confers a tax advantage in relation to UK tax, on one or both of the parties to the provision

then the profits of the potentially advantaged person(s) are to be computed for tax purposes as if the arm's-length provision had been made instead of the actual provision'.

This is known as the 'basic pricing rule'. In practice, it means that if UK-taxable profits are being depressed via intra-group transactions then there must be an adjustment to bring them back up to what they would have been if the arm's-length principle were applied.

The basic pricing rule is drafted very widely to include not just sales of goods or services but chains of transactions as well as single transactions. It includes transactions for which no price was set at all and those which would simply not have taken place at all between unrelated parties (eg loan guarantees).

A problem can arise if the adjustment is one sided. The UK company will be worse off, but the overseas group company no better off. Whilst many double tax treaties (per the OECD model) allow for a corresponding profit adjustment in the other country this is not guaranteed. Within the EU, the 1995 Arbitration Convention governs such adjustments.

Could the UK company be compensated by its group counterparts for the tax resulting from such an adjustment? It is considered that this would give rise to more tax in the UK, with no reduction elsewhere. Ideally in a multilateral situation there would be provision for compensating payments to be made to be ignored for tax purposes.

As with many other EU Member States, the UK applies its transfer pricing legislation not just to transactions involving a non-UK party but also to UK–UK transactions. This is to achieve compliance with the terms of the Treaty on the Functioning of the EU (the TFEU) following the decision in the case of *Lankhorst-Hohorst* which is discussed in Chapter 20.

Because HMRC are only really concerned with fairly large-scale tax avoidance through the use of manipulative transfer pricing practices, 'small' companies are not at risk of a tax charge under the UK transfer pricing regime. 'Medium-sized' companies are potentially exempt. Exemption is only given where transactions involve a non-UK company if the UK has a DTT with the other country which contains a non-discrimination provision similar to that in the OECD Model Treaty (Article 24). To be 'small', a company must have fewer than 50 employees, including owner-managers and partners and either the turnover or the value of net assets must not exceed €10,000. A 'medium-sized' company must have fewer than 250 employees and either the turnover must be less than €50 million, or the net assets must be less than €43 million. In both cases, if the company is part of a group of companies, the limits are applied to the figures for the whole group. Whilst small companies will definitely be exempt from transfer pricing adjustments, HMRC reserve the right to override the exemption in cases where the amount of tax at stake is significant. If a fellow group company has suffered an upwards adjustment in taxable profits and the party to the transactions involved is a small- or medium-sized UK company, then that company can waive the exemption in order to be eligible for a corresponding downwards adjustment in taxable profits.

---

1   The UK transfer pricing rules are found in the Taxation (International and Other Provisions) Act 2010 (TIOPA 2010), Pt 4.

The participation provision

13.44   The participation provision sets out the type of relationship between two parties which is needed before a transfer pricing adjustment can be made by HMRC. The participation provision is met if, at the time of making or imposing the actual provision (or, in the case of financing arrangements, in the preceding six months):

- one party directly or indirectly participates in management, control or capital of the other; or

- the same person(s) directly or indirectly participates in management, control or capital of each of other person involved.

'Direct participation' is where one person controls the other (eg where Company B owns more than 50 per cent or the ordinary share capital of Company B).

'Indirect participation' is present if a person would be a direct participant if certain rights and powers were taken into account besides the ownership of ordinary share capital (eg options to buy shares in Company A). Alternatively, if Company B owned at least 40 per cent of company B and another shareholder in Company B also owned at least 40 per cent then these two major shareholders would both fulfil the participation provision in relation to Company B. All transactions between A and B would be subject to the UK transfer pricing regime.

'Indirect participation' is also present if a number of parties are 'acting together' in relation to the financing arrangements of Company B, for example, if Companies X, Y and Z each hold one-third of Company B, and agree between themselves that they will each make loans to Company B on non-commercial terms, typically arranging loan finance which would mean that Company B would have a very high and non-commercial ratio of debt finance to equity finance. This 'acting together' rule is designed to prevent co-ordinated action by investors to thinly capitalize an investment in which they share.

DSG Retail and Others v HMRC[1]

13.45 This 2008 case was the first case heard concerning the UK's current transfer pricing rules. The case is important because it gives an insight into how HMRC interpret the UK rules and confirms the reliance placed by HMRC on the OECD Guidelines. It concerned the extended warranties sold to customers by DSG (Dixons, Currys and PC World). The precise arrangements altered throughout the period under examination, but the effect of the various arrangements in force was that the bulk of the profits from the extended warranties ended up in an Isle of Man subsidiary of DSG Retail, DISL. DISL was exempt from tax in the Isle of Man. Effectively, the profits from the warranty business were shifted from the UK to the Isle of Man. DSG Retail was not subject to a charge under the CFC legislation as it had planned around this, for instance, using affiliates in the Isle of Man who were not connected with DSG Retail under the definitions in the CFC legislation. Mainly to make the policies appear bona fide and respectable to customers, outside companies, such as the well-known Cornhill Insurance group were involved so that when a customer bought a warranty, it appeared to be underwritten by a household insurance name. However, in reality, Cornhill were reinsuring 95 per cent of the risk of having to pay out on the warranty with DISL, DSG's Isle of Man subsidiary, and were paying nearly all of the premium over to DISL. A key point for HMRC was that during the period of Cornhill's involvement, the amount of the customer premiums being retained by Cornhill was lowered so that Cornhill's profits were reduced. However, no such reduction was applied by the DSG group to the premiums going to DISL in the Isle of Man.

HMRC argued that the DSG Group had made a 'provision' within the meaning of the UK transfer pricing legislation with DISL. The 'provision' was that it had made available an attractive line of business to DISL (ie the reinsurance business). However, the provision was not at arm's length, because although it had reduced the amounts paid to Cornhill, an independent company, it had not made similar reductions to the amounts payable to DISL or required DISL to make any commission payment to DSG for the fact that DISL only got the reinsurance business from Cornhill because of DISL's connection to DSG. It had therefore favoured DISL, a connected company, in that it had caused DISL to earn more than the market rate from its reinsurance business. This situation had continued even after Cornhill had dropped out of the arrangements and different arrangements were in place, again involving a company not in the DSG Group and DISL (the main change was that extended warranties (a form of insurance) were replaced by extended service contracts following a substantial increase in UK insurance premium tax). The DSG Group had put much profitable business to DISL but had not required DISL to pay anything to the DSG group for the privilege. This demonstrates how wide the notion of a 'provision' is in the context of UK transfer pricing legislation. There were no direct dealings between DSG Retail and DISL and certainly no contractual relationship. It is a long way from a simple undercharge or overcharge on the sale of goods.

The pricing of this 'provision' between DSG and DISL was then examined by reference to the UK legislation which in turn relies heavily on the OECD Guidelines. DSG put forward a number of supposed comparables to make out a case that any provision made between it and DISL was justified by reference to the comparable uncontrolled price method. HMRC rejected the comparables offered; the first one dated back to 1982 and was considered too old and out of date. The second one related to satellite equipment; this was not similar enough to insurance arrangements and also the termination notice period under the supposedly comparable arrangements was far shorter than that under the DISL arrangements. An Office of Fair Trading Report produced by DSG showed commission on extended warranties by three unidentified retailers but DSG was unable to prove that these represented arm's-length rates. Instead, HMRC proposed a profit split approach – the DISL profit should be compared to a notional normal rate of return on investors' capital based on the capital asset pricing model, using the assumption that any profits in excess of capital needed for solvency requirements were paid out as a dividend each year. This was a novel approach, using finance theory and using one of the non-transactional profit methods recently approved in full by the OECD. The eventual adjustment to DSG's profits represented commission that should have been paid by DISL to DSG.

The DSG case tells us that a tax authority will be prepared to look beyond obvious forms of profit shifting and will be prepared to investigate sophisticated business arrangements to find out if there is any 'provision' between group companies in the context of transfer pricing legislation. It also tells us that a tax authority is prepared to argue that arm's-length profit should be computed using sophisticated methods.

1   *DSG Retail and Others v HMRC* [2009] STC (SCD) 397.

UK rules in relation to financial transactions

13.46   As we saw earlier, transfer pricing principles apply to financial transactions in much the same way as they do to transactions involving goods and services. There are some situations where transfer pricing issues arise which are a little difficult to identify, for example:

1 Sale of securities at less than market value

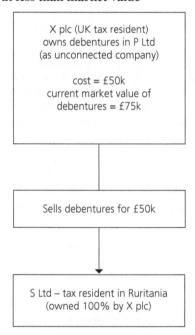

Figure 13.1

X Plc's taxable profits may be adjusted upwards by the UK tax authority. The debentures have been transferred to a connected company at less than arm's-length price.

2 Changes in the terms of a loan without compensation for the lender

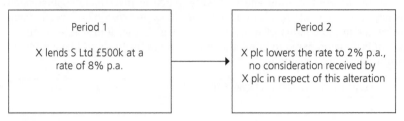

Figure 13.2

X Plc could be said to have given up a right to interest for nil proceeds. A value could be placed on the right to the interest foregone and a charge made on UK Plc.

3 Writing off debts due from overseas subsidiaries

In the UK, there is no relief for bad debts written off if they relate to connected companies (and no tax charge in relation to the debt forgiven in the borrower company).

However, if the debt is owed by a foreign subsidiary there is no guarantee that the foreign company will not be taxed on the amount of the debt forgiven. There is a danger that the foreign tax authority will impute a tax charge to the foreign subsidiary equal to the amount of the loan waived. This increases the global tax liability because there is no relief for the bad debt in the UK.

A possible solution to this is to issue convertible loan stock instead of simple loans. Then if debt goes bad or needs provision against it, it can be converted into equity. A loss on equity share capital would be tax deductible in the UK, although only against capital gains rather than trading profits.

4 Subsidiary unable to meet interest obligations to UK lender

If a UK company lends to an overseas company within its group and the over-seas company is unable to pay the interest, then the UK will continue to tax the UK lending company as if the interest *had* been paid. This applies to capital (long-term) funding loans, as opposed to short-term working capital loans.

The United Kingdom's thin capitalization legislation

13.47   Capitalization was dealt with in general terms in Chapter 12. Because it is an application of the arm's length principle, it is dealt with in the UK legislation within the UK transfer pricing regime. The UK's thin capitalization legislation was significantly amended in the Finance Act 2004[1] such that rather than relying on any prescriptive rules or formulae, all the circumstances of the loan must be taken into account. The UK thin capitalization rules come into play where there is a 'special relationship' between buyer and seller, broadly when one controls the other or both are under the control of the same person(s).

The borrowing capacity of a company is examined on a 'stand-alone' basis, as though it were not part of any group. The UK tax authority will then consider:

- whether the loan would have been made at all in the absence of the special relationship;

- the amount the loan would have been in the absence of the special relationship; and

- the rate of interest and other terms that would have been agreed in the absence of that relationship.

In Example 12.4, the fact that Birch has a debt-to-equity ratio in excess of 3:1 is not therefore conclusive of thin capitalization. Factors such as the trading history, future prospects, quality of security available to a lender will all be taken into account. Any guarantees given by the parent company or any other group company which might affect the borrowing capacity of Birch Ltd will be adjusted so that the borrowing capacity is considered as if the guarantees did not exist. If a group company guarantees third-party loans made to a fellow group company the interest payment on such loans could also be caught by the thin capitalization rules.

---

1   See Taxation (International and Other Provisions) Act 2010, s 152.

Chapter 14

Transfer Pricing Administration

BASICS

14.1 Because of the fundamental differences in dealings with group companies and those with independent parties, not just in prices charged but also in the types of transactions entered into, it can be extremely difficult to arrive at an arm's-length price. The OECD's BEPS Actions 8–10 deal with the particularly problematic aspects of the application of arm's-length pricing rules.

A key difficulty for any tax authority challenging the transfer prices used by a member of a multinational group is that most of the detailed evidence as to pricing lies with the taxpayer, putting the tax authority at a considerable disadvantage. Many countries have now introduced detailed requirements as to the transfer pricing documentation that must be produced by the taxpayer. In practice, compliance with these requirements can be onerous and can impose considerable costs on the taxpayer. The OECD BEPS Action 13 introduces new reporting requirements designed to standardize and improve the presentation of documentation to tax authorities.

Many countries also have facilities for taxpayers to enter into advance pricing agreements with tax authorities. These can involve the taxpayer and a single tax authority, or preferably all the tax authorities which have an interest in taxing the relevant transactions.

Transfer pricing disputes between taxpayer and tax authority are common and often remain unresolved for years. For this reason, the OECD introduced a provision for binding arbitration into Article 24 of the Model Tax Convention (MTC). Disputes within the EU can also be resolved under the provisions of the EU Arbitration Convention.

TRANSFER PRICING DOCUMENTATION REQUIREMENTS

14.2 Whilst in 1997 only five countries had transfer pricing documentation requirements, this had grown to 38 countries by the end of 2007. Naturally, each country has a somewhat different list of documentation requirements, so that MNEs can be faced with a plethora of varying requirements. To ease this situation, the EU adopted a Code of Conduct on transfer pricing documentation in 2006[1] which aims to standardize the documentation required within the EU. The documentation consists of a master file, generally available and country-specific files for each EU Member State in which the group operates. The country-specific files would only be available to the Member State concerned to prevent other Member States from using them as an excuse to initiate transfer pricing audits.

The adoption of this standardized documentation is optional for businesses but businesses are encouraged to be consistent throughout the EU and over time. The tax authorities of the Member States are urged to accept the standardized documentation rather than insisting on documentation prepared exactly to their national requirements. They are not to impose documentation-related penalties where taxpayers comply in good faith with these standardized requirements.

In promulgating this Code of Conduct, the EU is following in the footsteps of the Pacific Association of Tax Administrators (PATA) which introduced a standardized transfer pricing documentation package in 2003, which, like the EU measures, is optional. The US is a member of PATA and this list, which even the IRS describes as 'exhaustive', can be found on the IRS website.[2] There do not appear to be any provisions whereby country-specific information would only be made available to the country concerned. Again, the inducement to adopt the standardized documentation is the assurance of protection from penalties for failure to provide adequate documentation in any of the PATA countries.[3]

The latest wave of documentation requirements from African, Asian and Latin American countries have adopted more formal approaches, and as a result taxpayers who are used to relying on a master file to may need to reconsider their approach in relation to these new developments.[4]

In July 2013, the OECD released a White Paper on documentation,[5] bringing together work done by Working Party 6 in 2011 and 2012 reviewing documentation requirements of several individual countries. The White paper concludes that documentation requirements vary considerably and that attempts to achieve uniformity have not been very successful. In the interests of simplicity and efficiency, a two-tier structure is recommended comprising a master file and a local file. The aim of the master file is to provide a complete picture of the global business, financial reporting, debt structure and tax position of the MNE. The local file would provide assurance as to compliance with the arm's length principle for material transfer pricing positions.

---

1 2006/C176/01.
2 Available at: www.irs.gov/businesses/international/article/0,,id=156266,00.html.
3 Australia, Canada, Japan and the US.
4 Ernst & Young (2013) *Global Transfer Pricing Survey: Navigating the Choppy Waters of International Tax.*
5 Available at: www.oecd.org/ctp/transfer-pricing/white-paper-transfer-pricing-documentation. pdf.

Requirement that documentation be contemporaneous

14.3   It is a common requirement that documentation be contemporaneous, ie it must exist on or by a certain date. For instance, the IRS in the US and

HMRC in the UK require certain items of documentation to be in existence on the date the tax return is filed. Canada requires the documentation to exist by the theoretical, as opposed to the actual, filing date. Other countries impose strict deadlines from the date that documentation is requested and penalties follow if the documentation cannot be produced in time. For instance, Poland has operated a system requiring information within seven days of the request, although between one and two months is more common. Even if there is no cash penalty, there may be a procedural penalty whereby the taxpayer's rights to produce additional documentation evidencing their case are restricted as a result of failing to meet the initial documentation deadline.

TAX AUTHORITIES' RISK ASSESSMENT

14.4   In April 2013, the OECD released for public consultation, a draft *Handbook on Transfer Pricing Risk Assessment.*[1] This is the outcome of a project initiated in 2011 to produce a practical handbook that would be useful to both developed and developing countries. The draft acknowledges the difficulties faced by both taxpayers, who are recognized as being primarily compliant, or attempting to be so, especially in respect of large or complex transactions where reasonable people may differ over whether prices are arm's length. The handbook identifies when transfer risks exist, the processes for evaluating such risks and sources of information for conducting a risk assessment. The draft *Handbook* also contains a section on building productive relationships with taxpayers through enhanced engagement, drawing on the Netherlands, the UK and US as exemplars.

---

1   Available at: www.oecd.org/tax/transfer-pricing/Draft-Handbook-TP-Risk-Assessment-ENG. pdf.

OECD BEPS ACTION 13

14.5   Action 13 of the BEPS project is concerned with further developing rules for transfer pricing documentation 'to enhance transparency for tax administration, taking into consideration the compliance costs for business'. Getting this balance right is difficult and the aim is to produce a common template that will simplify the information reporting requirements for businesses globally but provide tax authorities with the information they need to be able to evaluate the allocation of economic activity and profits arising therefrom among the different countries involved.

Following a discussion draft in January 2014, the Action 13 Deliverable was published in September 2014[1] and proposes modifications to Chapter 5 of the *Transfer Pricing Guidelines* that deals with documentation requirements. Importantly it contained a template for country-by-country (CbC) reporting. The CbC template requires MNEs to report revenue, profits, income tax paid and taxes accrued, employees, stated capital and retained earnings, and tangible assets annually for each country in which they do business. Although many of the tax campaigners have been calling for this information to be made publicly available, the OECD has recommended that it only be provided to the relevant tax authorities.

The aim is to achieve standardization of documentation requirements across domestic laws. A three-tiered approach consists of a master file, a local file and a CbC report. The master file will provide an overview of the group's business and its overall transfer pricing policies to give a picture of the context in which the group operates. The local file provides more detailed information in relation to specific inter-company transactions. Both the master and local file guidance go further than the current documentation requirements. The CbC report is to be separate from the master file and is divided into three tables:

Table 1 – overview of allocation of income, taxes and business activities by tax jurisdiction;

Table 2 – list of constituent elements of the MNE group in each jurisdiction; and

Table 3 – additional information.

CbC reports are to be provided to tax administrations only, despite calls for them to be made public, and they aim to provide tax administrations with a high-level overview of the operations and tax risk profile of large MNEs. The ultimate parent entity of a MNE group will file its CbC report with the tax administration in its jurisdiction of residence for tax purposes. It is important to recognize that the information in a CbC report does not provide evidence of the efficacy of transfer prices, and tax administrations are specifically required not to use the reports as a substitute for detailed transfer pricing analyses, or for adjustments based on a global formulary apportionment of profit.

In February 2015, the OECD published the final Action 13 Report,[2] including an implementation package. The implementation package is designed to facilitate speedy implementation and includes model legislation as well as model competent authority agreements. On 22 March 2016,[3] the OECD released a standardized electronic format for the exchange of CbC reports between tax authorities requiring XML schema designed primarily for use by tax authorities. As of January 2017, there were 57 signatories to the Multilateral Competent Authority Agreement on the exchange of CbC reports. The guidance was updated in April 2017[4] to clarify such issues as the definitions of 'revenues' and 'related parties', as well as the determination of the relevant entities to be reported.

One important element of the CbC reporting is a process of peer review, designed to ensure effective and consistent implementation. The OECD released the terms of reference and methodology for peer reviews in February 2017.[5] The methodology requires that three key aspects be implemented and made operational: the domestic legal and administrative framework; the information exchange framework; and confidentiality/ appropriate use.

The take-up of CbC reporting in OECD countries and beyond has been remarkably rapid. The IRS, in early 2017, released for comment a draft form 8975 Country-by-Country Report, to be filed by the ultimate parent entity of a US MNE with annual revenue for the preceding period of US$850 million or more.

---

1   OECD Guidance on Transfer Pricing Documentation and Country by Country Reporting, available at www.oecd.org/ctp/guidance-on-transfer-pricing-documentation-and-country-by-country-reporting-9789264219236-en.htm.
2   OECD Action 13 Final Report, available at www.oecd.org/tax/transfer-pricing-documenta-tion-and-country-by-country-reporting-action-13-2015-final-report-9789264241480-en.htm.
3   OECD CbC Schema, available at www.oecd.org/tax/exchange-of-tax-information/country-by-country-reporting-xml-schema-user-guide-for-tax-administrations-and-taxpayers.htm.
4   OECD Guidance, available at www.oecd.org/tax/beps/guidance-on-the-implementation-of-country-by-country-reporting-beps-action-13.htm.
5   OECD Peer Review, available at www.oecd.org/tax/beps/beps-action-13-on-country-by-country-reporting-peer-review-documents.pdf.

RESOLUTION OF DISPUTES

14.6   In most cases, it is very difficult to find an obvious arm's-length price. Dealings within MNEs may be complex and are necessarily quite different to dealings with independent parties. In a cross-border transfer pricing adjustment, the arm's-length price has to be agreed between:

● the entity whose profits are to be increased and its home tax authority;

● the foreign entity which seeks a reciprocal decrease in its taxable profits and its home tax authority.

Example 14.1

For instance, the following situation could easily arise:

	Role in the dispute	*Amount of upwards adjustment considered acceptable*	*Amount of reduction in profits (reciprocal downwards adjustment) considered acceptable*
Company A, resident in Inistania	Company in the XYZ Group whose profits are to be increased following a transfer pricing dispute	$3 million	n/a
Tax authority of Inistania	Tax authority seeking the increase in taxable profits	$4 million	n/a

	Role in the dispute	*Amount of upwards adjustment considered acceptable*	*Amount of reduction in profits (reciprocal downwards adjustment) considered acceptable*
Company B, resident in Ruritania	Company in the XYZ Group which was party to the transactions with Company B and stands to have its profits reduced in a reciprocal adjustment	n/a	$3 million (the XYZ Group will have a common view so that this would be expected to match the upwards adjustment acceptable to Company A)
Tax authority of Ruritania	Tax authority which will have to give a reciprocal downwards adjustment in taxable profits	n/a	$2.5 million

The first dispute, between Company A and the Inistanian tax authority, is a purely domestic dispute and would have to be settled either by negotiation or through the Inistanian courts. Let us assume that they settle at $3.5 million. However, the second type of dispute: the mismatch between the amount of upwards adjustment sought by Inistania and the corresponding downwards adjustment which Ruritania is prepared to make would result in double taxation of $1 million worth of profits. Inistania taxes an additional $3.5 million of profits, whilst Ruritania only reduces the profits on which it charges tax by $2.5 million. $1 million of profits have been charged to tax in both Inistania and Ruritania.

Matters could be worse. At least Ruritania has agreed to make some sort of reciprocal adjustment (whether to the amount of profits taxed or just to the amount of tax payable in Ruritania). We will assume that Article 9 (Associated Enterprises) of the Inistania–Ruritania DTT requires such an adjustment.

Paragraph 2 of Article 9 of the OECD Model Convention is the paragraph which would require Ruritania to make a reciprocal adjustment and it reads:

'Where a Contracting State includes in the profits of an enterprise of that State – and taxes accordingly – profits on which an enterprise of the other Contracting State has been charged to tax in that other State and the profits so included are profits which would have accrued to the enterprise of the first-mentioned State if the conditions made between the two enterprises had been those which would have been made between independent enterprises, then that other State shall make an appropriate adjustment to the amount of the tax charged therein on those profits. In determining such adjustment, due regard shall be had to the other provisions of this Convention and the competent authorities of the Contracting States shall if necessary consult each other.'

Few double tax treaties deal with the position regarding 'secondary adjustments'. If one state makes an upwards adjustment of taxable profits and the other makes an exactly equal corresponding downwards adjustment, then the tax revenues of the two states might still be different to what they would have been had arm's-length pricing been applied in the first place. This is because higher profits in the state where the upwards adjustment took place might well have given rise to higher dividends or interest payments, on which withholding taxes might have been chargeable. So even though the state making the upwards adjustment has retrieved the tax deficit on the enterprise resident there, it has still not retrieved any deficit in withholding taxes. Whether it makes a secondary upwards adjustment to make good this deficit in withholding tax receipts depends on whether this is provided for in domestic law. If it does so, then double taxation will result which will not necessarily be relieved by the normal treaty article on elimination of double taxation and it may be necessary to invoke the mutual agreement procedure.

The XYZ Group can use two main tools to try to have the Inistanian and Ruritanian tax authorities reach an agreement as to the amount of the adjustment:

- the Mutual Agreement Article of the DTT; or

- assuming Inistania and Ruritania were Member States of the EU, the EU Arbitration Convention.

These will now be considered in turn below.

Mutual Agreement Procedure

14.7   Article 25 of the OECD Model Tax Treaty reads as follows:

'Where a person considers that the actions of one or both of the Contracting States result or will result for him in taxation not in accordance with the provisions of this Convention, he may, irrespective of the remedies provided by the domestic law of those States, present his case to the competent authority of the Contracting State of which he is a resident or, if his case comes under paragraph 1 of Article 24, to that of the Contracting State of which he is a national. The case must be presented within three years from the first notification of the action resulting in taxation not in accordance with the provisions of the Convention.'

Using Example 14.1 above, the fact that Company A is being taxed by Inistania on $1 million of profits that are also still being taxed by Ruritania (on Company B) means that there is double taxation of profits. That is not in accordance with the provisions of the treaty (the Convention). Assuming that the Inistania–Ruritania DTT has a provision similar to Article 25 of the OECD Model, Company A can present its case to the Inistanian tax authority and require it to try to reach a mutual agreement with the Inistanian tax authority as to what represents an arm's-length price, and therefore have a reciprocal downwards adjustment by Inistania which properly reflects the upwards adjustment made by Inistania.

Company A has three years to present its case. The three years would normally run from the date that a 'reasonably prudent person' would have realized he was being subjected to double taxation. In this case, it would probably be the date when it became apparent that Ruritania was not prepared to make a downwards adjustment as large as the upwards adjustment required by Inistania. It would not matter if time limits for appealing the relevant tax assessment under Inistanian law had already passed. Once Company A has invoked the mutual agreement procedure (MAP), the Inistanian tax authority has to contact the Ruritanian tax authority with a view to coming to an agreement as to the proper arm's-length price.

Weaknesses of the mutual agreement procedure

14.8   The tax authorities do not have to involve the taxpayer in their deliberations. In a transfer pricing dispute, the primary source of information on pricing policies and decisions will be the company itself. The company's knowledge of its markets and products will naturally be far more in-depth than that of the tax authorities. By not including the taxpayer in the MAP, the quality of decisions reached may be poor, as decisions may be based on incomplete information or inadequate understanding. When requesting a MAP, the taxpayer needs to co-operate fully with the tax authorities and make available all pertinent information, even though this may assist the tax authorities in future attacks on transfer pricing, either of the firm requesting the MAP or of its competitors. Although, in theory, information supplied to the tax authorities in the course of a MAP is confidential, in practice it would be unwise to assume that the tax authority will not make use of the information at some time in the future.

The MAP provision in the Inistania–Ruritania DTT may simply require that the two tax authorities 'shall endeavour to resolve' the problem. If they cannot come to an agreement, then the double taxation may remain. Since 2008, the OECD Model Tax Treaty introduced a taxpayer's right to demand binding arbitration, should the two tax authorities not be able to reach satisfactory agreement. Depending on its age and the positions taken by the two countries on the subject, the Inistania–Ruritania treaty may well not include this provision for arbitration. The introduction of a provision for the two contracting states to submit to binding arbitration in the 2008 update to the OECD Model Tax Treaty was intended to speed up the time taken to get a result under the MAP. Article 25, para 5, provides that if the tax authorities have still not reached agreement within two years of the taxpayer presenting his case, the taxpayer has the right to request binding arbitration. However, no arbitration is permitted if by that time, a court or tribunal in either of the states has given a decision on the issue in dispute. The provision regarding arbitration is not yet included in many treaties, a notable exception being the US–Canada Treaty 1980 via the 2007 Protocol (update) to that Treaty.

In the absence of binding arbitration, a MAP can take a very long time to be resolved. Ten years is not unheard of and although the average cycle time seems to be reducing, the growing popularity of the MAP means that it can still be a lengthy process. Current statistics from the OECD show that, at the end of 2015, the total number of open MAP cases reported by OECD member countries was 6,176, more than double the number of open cases at the end of 2007. The average time for completion of MAP cases with other OECD member countries was 20.47 months in 2015, down from the highest since 2006 of 27.30 months in 2010.

The EU Arbitration Convention and transfer pricing

14.9   The EU Arbitration Convention is a multilateral treaty which re-entered into force retroactively from 1 January 2000. Its main purpose is to assist the working of the European Single Market by achieving the elimination of double taxation which may result from one Member State making an upwards adjustment in taxable profits which is not matched by a broadly equivalent downwards adjustment in taxation in the other state(s) concerned, by reference to the transactions in question.

Member States of the EU are bound by the provisions of the EU Arbitration Convention (90/436/EEC of 23 July 1990). Member States are also expected to ratify the EU Code of Conduct[1] for the effective implementation of the Convention on the elimination of double taxation in connection with the adjustment of profits of associated enterprises. Under the Arbitration Convention and the Code of Conduct, a taxpayer company disagreeing with the amount of a transfer pricing agreement or suffering double taxation as a result of an upwards transfer pricing adjustment has three years in which to present its case to the tax administration of the state making the upwards adjustment. Under the Code of Conduct the three years runs from the date of first notification of the transfer pricing adjustment. The two Member States involved then have two years in which to reach an agreement which eliminates the double taxation resulting from the upwards transfer pricing adjustment. If they cannot reach agreement within this period then they must set up an advisory commission consisting of representatives of each tax authority and independent persons. This body then has six months to deliver its opinion. Although these time frames seem generous, as noted earlier, the other main alternative dispute resolution tool, the mutual agreement procedure provided for in tax treaties, often takes many years to produce a result.

Whilst the EU Arbitration Convention might appear to be a duplication of the MAP available under DTTs, it is useful to taxpayers for the following reasons:

- It fills any gaps which exist in the double tax network between EU Member States, ensuring that a form of MAP is available in all EU–EU tax disputes.

- It guarantees the elimination of double taxation (according to its own definition of such elimination).

- It is a specialist Convention which is only used in transfer pricing disputes, unlike the treaty MAP which is used for any kind of tax dispute involving the treaty partners.

- It uses OECD transfer pricing terminology so that the extensive OECD guidance on transfer pricing matters can be used.

- It includes a 'quick fix' provision where a reciprocal adjustment is sought and there is no dispute as to the actual arm's-length price acceptable to both Member States. This means that the reciprocal reduction in taxation can be put in place either in the same period or shortly after the period in which the upwards adjustment to profits falls to be taxed.

- The taxpayer can present his case to either of the tax authorities involved, not just to the one in which the company is resident. The authority which is notified of the case has to tell the other tax authority about it without any delay.

- There is a provision for binding arbitration if the two tax authorities are unable to reach agreement within two years of the presentation of the case by the taxpayer.

It is highly likely that a transfer pricing dispute in respect of which the taxpayer wishes to invoke the EU Arbitration Convention will be the subject of appeals under the taxpayer's domestic tax system. In practice, the taxpayer has a choice; either appeal tax assessments relating to the transfer pricing dispute under the domestic law or take his case under the Arbitration Convention. This is usually because domestic law does not allow the tax authority to derogate from (ie ignore) the decisions of the domestic courts. Also, if the case goes before the national courts, the two-year period for submitting a case under the Convention runs from the date final judgment is given. If no appeal is made, so that the case does not go before the national courts, the two-year time period runs from the date the time limit for appealing against the tax assessment under domestic law has expired. This is likely to be much sooner.

If no agreement can be reached by the tax authorities within two years from the taxpayer presenting his case, the arbitration process commences. An Advisory Commission is formed, consisting of representatives of the tax authorities and, importantly, the taxpayer, if the taxpayer so wishes. The Commission then has six months to come to a decision and the Member State tax authorities then have six months to act on the decision and eliminate the double taxation.

---

1   2006/C176/02.

BEPS ACTION 14: DISPUTE RESOLUTION

14.10   The aim of Action 14 of the OECD BEPS Project is to strengthen the efficiency and effectiveness of the MAP process. Countries signing up to BEPS agree to a minimum standard that will:

'Ensure that treaty obligations related to the mutual agreement procedures are fully implemented in good faith and that MAP cases are resolved in a timely manner; ensure the implementation of administrative processes that promote the prevention and timely resolution of treaty-related disputes; and ensure that taxpayers can access the MAP process when eligible.'

The OECD's final report on Action 14 was issued on 5 October 2015 and sets out a minimum standard with respect to the resolution of treaty-related disputes. The minimum standard is designed to ensure that:

- treaty obligations related to the MAP are fully implemented in good faith and that MAP cases are resolved in a timely manner;

- the implementation of administrative processes that promote the prevention and timely resolution of treaty-related disputes; and

- taxpayers can access the MAP when eligible.

In October 2016, the OECD released documents that will form the basis of MAP peer review and monitoring, which will be conducted by the Forum on Tax Administration. The terms of reference contain 21 elements that assess the member's legal and administrative framework and its practical implementation.

PENALTIES

14.11   Many countries operate specific penalties, which are applied on top of any transfer pricing adjustments.

The UK has no specific penalties for transfer pricing adjustments, except in the case of failure to keep proper records. The normal UK penalties for incorrect tax returns apply to transfer pricing adjustments.

In the US, penalties can be up to 40 per cent of the tax adjustment. If the offending transfer price was 200 per cent more or 50 per cent less than the arm's-length price the penalty will be 20 per cent (non-tax deductible). If the offending transfer price is 400 per cent more or up to 25 per cent less than the arm's-length price, the penalty is increased to 40 per cent of the tax underpaid. If the transfer pricing adjustment is large in relation to the company's total profits there is an additional penalty:

- 20 per cent of the adjustment if the adjustment exceeds $5 million or 10 per cent of gross receipts; and

- 40 per cent of the adjustment if the adjustment exceeds $20 million or 20 per cent of gross receipts.

ADVANCE PRICING AGREEMENTS

14.12   An advance pricing agreement (APA) is a binding written agreement between a company and the tax authority. Most countries have the facility for a group to obtain an advance ruling that pricing policies will be regarded as being at arm's length. This gives greater certainty than waiting for the tax authority to object to prices charged at a later date.

In some cases it is possible to obtain a bilateral APA – this means that both countries concerned agree that the prices used are arm's length. Alternatively, if this is not available it may be possible to use a unilateral agreement to protect against a transfer pricing adjustment in the home country only. The IRS Report for the calendar year 2016[1] shows the number of APAs filed between 1991 and 2016 is 2,245. Additional resources were provided to the new Advance Pricing and Mutual Agreement Program that superseded the old APA programme in the first quarter of 2012. The report also notes that the majority of transactions covered in APAs in 2016 involve the sale of tangible goods and the provision of services, although the IRS has successfully completed numerous APAs involving the use of intangible property. The term lengths of APAs executed in 2016 varied from 2 to 14 years, with the largest number (52) being for a duration of 5 years.

Given that APAs are negotiated for some years to come and that the precise nature of transactions over the period to be covered by the APA cannot be fully known, it is unsurprising that the comparable profits method has been more widely used than pure transactional methods in APA negotiations.

The availability of APAs is an important component of the effective operation of the arm's-length principle. The APA system enables transfer pricing issues to be identified in advance of the making of profits, giving greater certainty to multinational groups.

The transfer pricing methods most commonly used in US APAs appear to be CPM or TNMM.

---

1   *IRS Announcement and Report Concerning Advance Pricing Agreements.*

Contents of an advance pricing agreement request

14.13   The IRS Revenue Procedures[1] outlines the substantial amount of material that will need to be provided by the taxpayer before and APA can be agreed. In addition to providing supporting documents and explanations of the basis for transfer pricing methodologies adopted, the taxpayer may expect to have a series of meetings with the tax authority in order to reach agreement. Thus, although an APA may significantly reduce the likelihood of a lengthy and expensive transfer pricing enquiry, the list presented in the IRS Revenue Procedures should illustrate that obtaining an APA is time consuming and costly. The documentation requirements and the transfer pricing policy development that is required may not fall far short of that which would be required if no APA was sought but the group later faced a transfer pricing enquiry. The advantages of concluding an APA are principally to do with the reduction in tax risk through the relative certainty that the APA provides. The sheer discipline required to negotiate an APA successfully may well highlight shortcomings in a group's transfer pricing policies and should ensure that statutory documentation requirements are fulfilled. In certain cases, the IRS permits 'roll-back' of the APA which means that it can be applied to tax periods ending prior to the negotiation of the APA, providing added protection from costly transfer pricing audits. Supporters of APAs consider that their cost is well worth the effort not least due to the different relationship with the tax authority in the APA process compared to that in a transfer pricing audit/dispute. In the APA process, there is access to expert staff in the tax authority who are not driven by the size of the potential taxpayer settlement and penalties which transfer pricing audit staff would be seeking to impose. There is more time for considered development of the policies and, it is hoped, a supportive rather than a confrontational relationship with the tax authority.

---

1   IRS Revenue Procedures 2006–09.

Stages in the negotiation

14.14   The Canadian Revenue Agency helpfully sets out its practices in its annual report on its APA Program. These provide a good illustration of the APA process. It should be noted that this can typically take around three years to complete.[1]

- The taxpayer expresses an interest in negotiating an APA.

- A pre-filing meeting is held between taxpayer and tax authority to discuss suitability of the APA process.

- The taxpayer files a formal APA request, and the tax authority issues official acceptance.

- The tax authority reviews the request, performs due diligence and prepares a position paper which is sent to the taxpayer for a review of factual accuracy.

- The tax authority prepares a final position paper and, if a bilateral APA, resolves APA through the competent authority process.

- The proposed APA is then sent to the taxpayer for review, comments and acceptance.

- The taxpayer either accepts, or enters into further negotiation.

- If accepted, taxpayer files periodic compliance reports and at the end of the APA term, requests a renewal.

---

1   Canadian Revenue Agency APA Program Report 2014–2015. Available at: www.cra-arc.gc.ca/tx/nnrsdnts/cmp/p_rprt15-eng.html.

FURTHER READING

Drake, J, Rode, A and Wright, D R (2005) 'IRS APA Initiatives', *International Transfer Pricing Journal*, Sept/Oct 2005, pp 210–216.

Dujsic, M et al (2008) 'Digesting the *Glaxo* Decision: A Difficult Pill to Swallow for Transfer Pricing Practitioners', *International Transfer Pricing Journal*, Sept/Oct 2008.

Ernst & Young (2013) Global Transfer Pricing Survey: Navigating the Choppy Waters of International Tax.

Gill, S (2011) 'Intangibles and Transfer Pricing: The Perils Faced by Multinationals in India', 18, *International Transfer Pricing Journal* 2011, 1.

Joseph, A (2011) 'Australia – Increasing Role of Advance Pricing Agreements', 18, *International Transfer Pricing Journal* 2011, 4.

Lenz, M and Vogele, A (1999) 'A Case Study: What's in the Black Box', *International Tax Review*, February 1999.

Mehafdi, M (2000) 'The Ethics of international Transfer Pricing', *The Journal of Business Ethics*, December 2000, 28: Pt 2.

OECD (2007) *Improving the Resolution of Tax Treaty Disputes*. Committee on Fiscal Affairs, February 2007. Available at www.oecd.org/dataoecd/17/59/38055311.pdf.

OECD (2010) *Transfer Pricing Guidelines for Multinational Enterprises and Tax Administrations* (with various updates since 1995).

Patton, M F (2010) 'Xilinx v Comr: "I Think I Better Think it out Again"', 39 *Tax Management International Journal*, 499.

Picciotto, S (2017) *Taxing Multinational Enterprises as Unitary Firms*. Institute of Development Studies.

Pichhadze, A (2013) 'Canada's Transfer Pricing Test in the Aftermath of GlaxoSmithKline Inc: A Critique of the Reasonable Business Person Test' *International Transfer Pricing Journal*, May/June 2013, pp 144–162.

United States Internal Revenue Service *Development of IRC Section 482 cases*, Ch 61 Internal Revenue Manual. Available at: www.irs.gov/irm/part4/ch46s03.html.

Wundisch, K (2003) 'Pharmaceutical Industry and Transfer Pricing: Anything Special?', *International Transfer Pricing Journal*, Nov/Dec 2003, pp 204–210.

Chapter 15

Improper Use of Tax Treaties

INTRODUCTION

15.1 Most double tax treaties are bilateral. This means that they are made between a pair of countries and the tax concessions granted in the treaty, for instance, withholding tax rates below those which would be charged under domestic law in the absence of a treaty, are intended to benefit only persons who are resident in the two countries which have made the treaty. The term 'person' is usually defined to mean individuals, companies and other entities recognized as taxpayers separately from their members.

Several phrases are used to denote improper use of tax treaties. One of these is 'treaty abuse', which the OECD defines in the following terms:

'A guiding principle is that the benefits of a double taxation convention should not be available where a main purpose for entering into certain transactions or arrangements was to secure a more favourable tax position and obtaining that more favourable treatment in these circumstances would be contrary to the object and purpose of the relevant provisions.'[1]

One instance of the improper use of treaties is 'treaty shopping'. The OECD Glossary of Tax Terms defines 'treaty shopping' as an 'analysis of tax treaty provisions to structure an international transaction or operation so as to take advantage of a particular treaty'. The term is normally applied to a situation where a person not resident in either of the treaty countries establishes an entity in one of the treaty countries to obtain treaty benefits.

In this chapter, some of the more common corporate structures used for treaty shopping and treaty abuse purposes are examined and the common approaches to preventing the improper use of treaties are analysed.

Treaty shopping involves residents of countries other than those party to a double tax treaty (DTT) gaining access to reduced rates of tax on certain income types. It is viewed as being a form of tax avoidance which can be tackled through domestic anti-avoidance legislation, or increasingly through targeted provisions in DTTs. All treaty shopping consists, essentially, of a resident of a third state accessing benefits under a treaty of which she or he is not a resident. Treaty shopping practices can be challenged either under a state's domestic law on tax avoidance, using the concept of abuse or can be challenged under provisions written into the treaty itself. The three principal forms of provisions limiting treaty shopping that are found in tax treaties themselves are beneficial ownership clauses, specific anti-conduit clauses, and specific and detailed limitation of benefits provisions. Although the latter are primarily used in US treaties, they are starting to appear in other treaties as well (eg Japan). Developing countries may take a more lenient stance towards treaty shopping because if treaty benefits are readily granted, foreign investment flows may benefit. Review of treaty abuse is part of the OECD's Base Erosion and Profit Shifting Agenda (BEPS), specifically Action 6.

As well as treaty shopping, treaties can be abused when taxpayers, who are properly resident in one of the Contracting States to a treaty, attempt to circumvent the rules laid down in that treaty, eg structuring their activities so as to avoid falling within the definition of a permanent establishment (PE) through splitting up contracts between different companies in the same group, or by putting artificial ownership arrangements in place to obtain the lower of two treaty withholding tax rates on dividends.

Tackling international tax avoidance through treaty abuse is one of the central objectives of the OECD's BEPS Project. Action 6 is to:

> 'Develop model treaty provisions and recommendations regarding the design of domestic rules to prevent the granting of treaty benefits in inappropriate circumstances.'

Action 6 develops some major additions to the OECD MTC:

- A set of objective tests to identify persons who can qualify for treaty benefits (limitation of benefits tests).

- A more subjective, general anti-avoidance test: a so-called 'principal purposes test'. If one of the principal purposes of a transaction or set of transactions to obtain treaty benefits in circumstances where no benefits were intended to be given, then treaty benefits can be denied.

- Specimen wording for the titles of treaties and a preamble, stating clearly that one of the purposes of the treaty, besides the relief of double taxation, is the prevention of tax evasion and avoidance. The OECD recommends that this test is included in treaties either on a stand-alone basis, or together with the objective limitation of benefit tests.

- Removal of the residence tie-breaker test for companies and other entities: where a person other than an individual is resident under the domestic laws of both of the Contracting States to a treaty, the 'place of effective management' test is replaced by case-by-case examination of that person to decide if any treaty benefits should be granted beyond the basic benefit of non-discrimination. This is because dual resident entities are often set up with the aim of avoiding tax.

It is expected that, once these changes have been adopted into the text of the OECD MTC, countries will incorporate these changes into their treaties with each other via the operation of the multilateral instrument developed under Action 15 of BEPS. The multilateral instrument has the effect of automatically updating bilateral treaties in existence between signatories to the multilateral instrument to reflect changes to the OECD MTC.

---

1   OECD Model Convention, Commentary on Article 1, para 23.

TREATY SHOPPING

15.2   Treaty shopping is a common form of abuse of treaties. It means that a person tries to get the benefit of a treaty even though that person is not a resident of either of the Contracting States that made that treaty. Treaty shopping usually involves setting up a special purpose vehicle (typically, a 100 per cent-owned subsidiary) which is tax resident in one of the Contracting States. However, this special purpose vehicle will be used, typically, to receive income at reduced rates of withholding tax under the targeted treaty. This income will then be passed onto the owners of the special purpose vehicle.

Treaty shopping can be used to reduce exposure to withholding taxes where a taxpayer wants to invest in a country which does not have a treaty with his country of residence. For example, using back-to-back loans, treaty shopping could involve substituting a loan between entities in countries which have a treaty limiting withholding tax rates for a loan between entities in countries that do not have a treaty and which therefore would be subject to withholding tax on the interest payable. Typically, one of the entities would be located in a tax haven. By restructuring loan arrangements in an appropriate treaty country, the original parties can sidestep the absence of a treaty between their own countries. This, of course, involves 'shopping around' for treaties that fit the bill in terms of providing the appropriate shelter from withholding tax requirements – hence the term 'treaty shopping'.

Example 15.1

White Ltd is resident in a tax haven country (Baradas) that does not have a tax treaty with the country of Ruritania. Under its domestic law, Ruritania charges a withholding tax of 25 per cent on interest and royalty payments to non-residents. However, it charges no withholding tax on interest paid to residents of Inistania under the terms of the tax treaty between Ruritania and Inistania. If White Ltd invests $1 million in interest-bearing securities in Ruritania and earns $100,000 interest, it will be subject to a 25 per cent withholding tax when the interest is paid. It is unlikely that White Ltd could claim double tax relief for the withholding tax in Baradas, as Baradas, being a tax haven, would not charge White Ltd much, if any, tax. Thus:

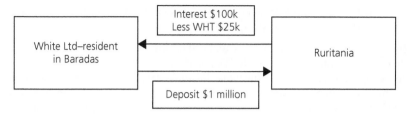

Figure 15.1

White Ltd could restructure its investment in Ruritania through a back-to-back loan by setting up an intermediary company in Inistania. This intermediary would be paid a small fee for its services. The intermediary company would make the investment in Ruritania. There would be no withholding tax on interest paid from Ruritania to the intermediary company in Inistania due to the terms of the tax treaty between the two countries. For this to work, it must be possible to make payments of interest from Inistania to Baradas free of withholding tax. This means that there must either be a DTT between these two countries (unlikely) or that Inistania's domestic law must not require the payment of withholding tax on interest paid to non-residents. The interest payments could then be paid to White Ltd without deduction of withholding tax. The intermediary company in Inistania would not be taxable in Inistania to any great extent, because it would deduct the interest payments to White Ltd from its interest income from Ruritania, leaving only its service fee liable to Inistanian tax. The financial flows would then look like this:

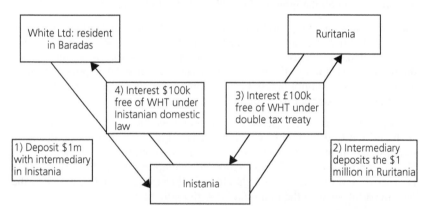

Figure 15.2: Financial flows: simple 'direct conduit' arrangement

This is a simple 'direct conduit' arrangement. By routing the interest via Inistania, White Ltd has eliminated its withholding tax liability which would have been 25 per cent if it had received the interest directly from Ruritania. Of course, White Ltd would have had to look carefully for a country which:

● did not charge withholding tax on payments of interest to non-residents under its domestic law; and

- had a DTT with Ruritania which provided for a low or zero rate of withholding tax on interest payments.

Inistania fits the bill perfectly, as under the terms of its treaty with Ruritania there is no withholding tax at all. We could say that White Ltd has been 'treaty shopping' and chosen the Ruritania–Inistania Treaty. However, if this treaty contains provisions to limit the benefits, either to cases where the beneficial ownership of the interest belongs to a person in Inistania or by setting tests as to which types of person in Inistania can benefit from the treaty, then it is highly likely that Ruritania will refuse to apply the zero rate of withholding tax on the interest and will charge the full rate which it applies under its domestic law.

Withholding taxes

15.3 Why is White Ltd Inc keen to reduce its liability to withholding tax? First, Baradas might be a tax haven, so that the only tax suffered at all on the interest is withholding tax. Second, White Ltd might be resident in a country which is not a tax haven, but which uses the exemption method of double tax relief, even for foreign interest. Again, in this case, the only tax suffered on the interest would be the Ruritanian withholding tax. Third, even if White Ltd can obtain full double tax relief in Baradas for the withholding tax, either under a system of double tax relief by exemption or by credit, the withholding tax creates a cash-flow disadvantage. It is effectively paid at the date the interest is paid to White Ltd, which may be many months earlier than the date tax would have to be paid on the interest if taxable only in Ruritania.

Similar treaty shopping arrangements can be made using equity funds to sidestep withholding tax requirements for dividend payments (ie by setting up controlled foreign companies in appropriate jurisdictions and routing dividend payments through these). In these cases, it would be important to pick a country which did not tax dividend income from subsidiaries (ie which had a participation exemption).

Common to most treaty abuse arrangements is the use of some form of 'conduit' entity in a country which has a favourable tax treaty. In order for a treaty shopping arrangement to be successful, two conditions must be satisfied: (1) the conduit entity itself must enjoy tax exemption in the country where it is created; and (2) the income should pass through the conduit entity to the beneficial owner with the minimum of withholding taxes.

Other forms of treaty abuse involve conduit companies and 'stepping stone' companies. The following example is a more complex form of treaty shopping using a conduit company.

Example 15.2

Taxsave Inc is tax resident in Country A (effective corporation tax rate 30 per cent), but wishes to set up a branch in Country B (where the effective corporation tax rate is 20 per cent). There is no DTT between Country A and

Country B so that Taxsave Inc will have to rely on the domestic measures giving double tax relief unilaterally to reduce its exposure to double taxation. These domestic provisions are not very generous as they only permit the deduction method. Country A *does* have a DTT with Country C. Under this treaty, between Countries A and C, Country A agrees that it will use the credit method to give double tax relief for tax suffered in Country C and will also give credit for corporation taxes (wherever paid) underlying dividends. To improve its global tax position, Taxsave Inc decides to form a subsidiary, Conduit Ltd, which is tax resident in Country C. The branch in Country B is set up as a branch of Conduit Co, rather than as a branch of Taxsave Inc. The treaty between Country B and Country C provides that Country C will exempt from tax any branch profits received from Country B, and Country B agrees that it will not charge any withholding tax on remittances of branch profits from Country B to Country C.

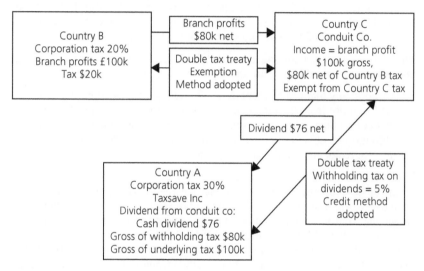

Figure 15.3

	Without Conduit Ltd	With Conduit Ltd
	$	$
Taxable profits of Taxsave Inc in Country A	100	100
Country A tax before double tax relief	30	30
Double tax relief:		
Deduction method: Country B tax ($20K) @ 30%	–6	
Credit method:		
Country C withholding tax ($80 @ 5%)		–4
Country B underlying corporation tax*		–20
Country A tax liability	24	6

481

	Without Conduit Ltd	With Conduit Ltd
Total tax liabilities:		
Country A	24	6
Country B	20	20
Country C	0	4
Total tax liabilities:	44	30

* Note that it would be crucial to the success of this structure to check that, under the terms of the tax treaty between Countries A and C, Country A would recognize corporation taxes underlying dividend payments where those corporation taxes had been paid in countries other than Country C.

Thus by setting up a subsidiary company in Country C, Conduit Ltd, Taxsave Inc has benefited from the double tax provisions of the treaties between B and C and between A and C, reducing the global tax liability by $14,000.

The type of provision envisaged by the OECD to prevent Taxsave Inc making this tax saving would be a 'look-through' provision (discussed later):

> 'A company that is a resident of a Contracting State shall not be entitled to relief from taxation under this Convention with respect to any item of income, gains or profits if it is owned or controlled directly or through one or more companies, wherever resident, by persons who are not residents of a Contracting State.'

Thus because Conduit Ltd is owned by Taxsave Inc, a resident of Country A, it may be denied benefits under the treaty between Country B and Country C. Country C would not be obliged to exempt the branch profits of Conduit Ltd earned in Country B from Country C tax. This would reduce, but not completely eliminate the benefits of establishing Conduit Ltd in Country C. If Country C's effective rate of corporation tax was 30 per cent, and its domestic law method of double tax relief was the credit method, then Country C would have charged an extra $10 tax. This in turn would have reduced the cash dividend payable from $80 to $70, reducing Country C withholding tax to $3.50. The increased tax liability in Country C would eliminate any tax liability in Country A, but the global tax liability would increase to $33.50 ($20 Country B + $10 Country C tax on Conduit Co + $3.50 withholding tax charged to Taxsave Inc).

Stepping-stone structures work in a broadly similar way. The objective is to route income from Country B to Country A in such a way that it passes through Country C. The tax savings are made by taking advantage of nil or low withholding tax rates on the journey from B to C and then from C to A, compared with a direct journey from B to A. In addition, Country C would generally be a high-tax jurisdiction, from which a high level of tax deductible expenses are paid. These expenses serve to reduce taxes in Country C on the income from Country B and thus to reduce the taxable receipt of income in Country A.

For instance, if Inistania in Example 15.1 was a high-tax country, then the arrangements in that example would be a simple stepping-stone structure.

Like most tax-avoidance activity, it is extremely difficult to estimate how much revenue is lost to governments in the form of withholding and other taxes through the use of treaty shopping arrangements. It is clearly a concern, however, as demonstrated by the increasing number of treaties which contain anti-treaty shopping, or limitation of benefits, provisions.

COUNTERING IMPROPER USE OF TAX TREATIES

15.4 One of the central themes of the OECD's BEPS Project is the prevention of granting of treaty benefits in inappropriate circumstances (Action 6). The following sections summarize the OECD's guidance on this matter.

The 2014 version of the OECD MTC does not directly deal with the question of treaty abuse, expecting that such issues will be dealt with through domestic anti-avoidance rules. Hence there is no specific anti-abuse rule in the wording of the MTC. Article 1 states simply that: 'this Convention shall apply to persons who are residents of one or both of the Contracting States'. However, the commentary Article 1 has long contained extensive guidance on countering treaty abuse. Some suggestions are for countering treaty abuse via domestic law provisions, whilst others suggest additional wording in the text certain articles of the treaty being concluded, or even a separate article dealing with the matter.

Paragraph 7 of the July 2010 Commentary on Article 1 states:

'The principal purpose of double taxation conventions is to promote, by eliminating international double taxation, exchanges of goods and services, and the movement of capital and persons. It is also a purpose of tax conventions to prevent tax avoidance and evasion. Taxpayers may be tempted to abuse the tax laws of a State by exploiting differences between various countries' laws. Such attempts may be countered by provisions or jurisprudential rules that are part of the domestic law of the State concerned. Such a State is then unlikely to agree to provisions of bilateral double taxation conventions that would have the effect of allowing abusive transactions that would otherwise be prevented by the provisions and rules of this kind contained in its domestic law. Also, it will not wish to apply its bilateral conventions in a way that would have that effect.'

Paragraph 8 goes on to note the risk of taxpayers using artificial legal constructions, such as companies set up specifically for the purpose of securing the benefits of a tax treaty.

In January 2013, the OECD issued extensive revisions to the Commentary dealing with the relationship between tax treaties and domestic anti-avoidance rules in the context of treaty abuse. It describes abuse as the, 'use of artificial legal constructions aimed at securing the benefits of both the tax advantages available under certain domestic laws and the reliefs from tax provided for in double tax conventions.'

Paragraph 8 goes on to note the risk of taxpayers using artificial legal constructions, such as companies set up specifically for the purpose of securing the benefits of a tax treaty (conduit companies).

A number of broad approaches are suggested in the Commentary on Article 1:

- reliance on a general interpretation of Article 1: as per para 7 to the Commentary, set out above;

- reliance on 'beneficial ownership requirements';

- reliance on anti-conduit clauses: 'look-through clauses', exclusion clauses, 'subject to tax' clauses, 'channel' approach;

- reliance on domestic anti-avoidance legislation, both specific and general;

- reliance on domestic legal doctrines which have been developed through the court system (so-called judicial doctrines, such as the 'Ramsay' doctrine); and

- inclusion of a specific, objective limitation of benefits article: the Commentary on Article 1 sets out at some length possible wordings for such an article at para 20. Such articles are usually adopted by the US in its treaties.

Additional approaches: BEPS Action 6

15.5 The October 2015 Final Report on Action 6 recommends three broad ways in which countries should counter the abuse of treaties:

1 Include in their treaties a clear statement that they intend to avoid creating opportunities for non-taxation or reduced taxation through tax evasion or avoidance including through treaty-shopping arrangements.

2 Include in their treaties a specific anti-abuse rule. This should take the form of a US-style limitation on benefits rules, specifying in detail the legal persons who may rely on the treaty. This is considered in more detail in para **15.21**. Note that wording for such a rule has long been included in the Commentary on Article 1 for countries which wanted to incorporate it into their treaties.

3 As a further protection, include in their treaties a general anti-treaty abuse rule. This rule, a so-called 'principal purposes' rules, would form a separate article and would deny treaty benefits in cases where one of the principal purposes of the transactions or arrangements in question was to obtain treaty benefits (eg a low treaty rate of WHT).

In the next sections we consider in turn each of the pre-BEPS and the BEPS recommendations for tackling treaty abuse.

Approach to treaty abuse: clear statement

15.6   The Final Report on BEPS Action 6 recommends that states, in their treaties, include the following title and preamble (opening statement):

'Title: Convention between State A and State B for the elimination of double taxation with respect to taxes on income and on capital and the prevention of tax evasion and avoidance.

Preamble: State A and State B

Desiring to further develop their economic relationship and to enhance their co-operation in tax matters,

Intending to conclude a Convention for the elimination of double taxation with respect to taxes on income and on capital without creating opportunities for non-taxation or reduced taxation through tax evasion or avoidance (including through treaty-shopping arrangements aimed at obtaining reliefs provided in this Convention for the indirect benefit of third States)

Have agreed as follows:' [Rest of the Treaty then follows.]

The importance of this preamble to the treaty is that it will affect the way in which the treaty is interpreted in the future, because it makes the intentions of the countries concluding the treaty very clear; in that it is not intended to be used for tax evasion or avoidance, and it is not intended to be used for treaty shopping.

The OECD has also updated the introduction to the OECD MTC to make it clear that the prevention of tax evasion and avoidance is one of the main purposes of the OECD MTC. The new recommended preamble is an explicit statement of the intentions of the countries concluding the treaty. The Vienna Convention on the Law of Treaties states that treaties should be interpreted according to their objects and purposes, and the new preamble is a clear statement of these.

Approach to treaty abuse: reliance on general interpretation

15.7   For many years, the leading case on treaty abuse was a US case from 1971, *Aiken Industries Inc v Commissioner.*[1] In a similar way to our first example of treaty shopping, this case effectively involved the use of back-to-back loans to sidestep a requirement to withhold tax on interest payments by using a then-existing DTT between the US and the Republic of Honduras, which provided for a zero withholding tax on interest received by a treaty country resident from sources within the other contracting state. A US company, MPI, borrowed funds from a Bahamian company, ECL. Interest payments from MPI to ECL were subjected to US withholding tax at the full rate of 30 per cent, as there was no DTT between the US and the Bahamas. In order to reduce this liability to US withholding tax, ECL assigned the debt to Industrias, a Honduran company and in turn the Honduran company borrowed an identical amount from ECL. Thus the Honduran company received the interest from the US borrower which was free of withholding tax under the US–Honduras Tax Treaty. The Honduran company then paid an identical amount of interest to ECL under the terms of the loan to it from ECL. All the entities involved complied with the formal incorporation requirements of the relevant countries – the US, Bahamas and Honduras – and all transactions (which were actually more complicated than we suggest here) were genuine (ie they were not shams). However, the companies involved were all members of the same group, and there was no valid economic or business purpose for the transactions; it was set up this way purely to avoid payment of withholding tax.

The case turned on the definition of the phrase 'received by', as interest was only exempt from withholding tax under the US–Honduras Tax Treaty if it was received by a resident of Honduras. As the term was not specifically defined in the treaty, the normal rule was followed, which is that the term had to be defined according to domestic law. The US defined 'received by' as meaning more than the mere physical possession on a temporary basis but rather having complete 'dominion and control' over the interest receipts. As Industrias (the Honduran company) had an obligation to pay on identical amounts of interest to ECL, it was not considered to have 'received' the interest at all. The US court decided that, in substance, the interest payments had been made to ECL in the Bahamas and therefore the US domestic rate of withholding tax of 30 per cent applied.

Hanna (2005) suggests that the case failed (for the taxpayer) before the Tax Court because the arrangement was 'too perfect' and no alternative explanations could be advanced for setting up the transactions in this way. The importance of this case is that it forms the basis for several US revenue rulings which negate the tax effectiveness of back-to-back arrangements such as the one described here.

By way of a contrast, consider a later case in 1995, *Northern Indiana Public Service Co v Commissioner.*[2] This was also a US treaty shopping case. Here, NIPSCO, a US corporation, formed a wholly-owned subsidiary, Finance, in 1981 in Curacao in the Netherlands Antilles under the Commercial Code of the Netherlands Antilles. Finance issued $70 million in Eurobonds to non-group investors in Europe at an interest rate of 17.25 per cent and loaned the proceeds to NIPSCO in the US at 18.25 per cent. NIPSCO paid the interest to Finance under the terms of the 1948 US–Netherlands DTT, which extended to the Netherlands Antilles as well. The treaty stated that interest payments were to be exempt from US withholding tax. In this way, Finance earned 1 per cent which, over the four years in which the arrangement ran, amounted to $2.8 million. This proved to be the key difference between this case and Aiken. The taxpayer in Northern Indiana won against the US government, which argued that Finance was merely a conduit and the NIPSCO itself should be viewed as having paid the interest directly to the Eurobond holders and should therefore have withheld tax on the interest payments at the US domestic rate of 30 per cent (unless there were any relevant tax treaties which applied to payments between NIPSCO and the European investors which permitted lower rates). The Tax Court, however, found that Finance carried on sufficient business activity in its own right so that its transactions could not be ignored and it could not be considered to be merely a conduit.[3]

---

1   56 TC 925 Case Docket No 292-67.
2   105 TC 341 Case Docket No 24468-91.
3   Hanna (2005) maintains that by deliberately falling short of being 'too perfect', the taxpayer in this case was able to convince the Tax Court that the transactions were legitimate.

Use of the 'general interpretation' approach in the UK

15.8   Prior to 2013 the UK did not have a general anti-avoidance rule (a GAAR) in its tax legislation and its treaties vary in the type and amount of anti-treaty shopping provisions they include. In August 2011, HMRC issued specific draft legislation aimed at preventing treaty shopping. This legislation has as its basis the OECD guidance in the Commentary on Article 1, that a country need not give the benefit of a treaty to a taxpayer who is involved in abusive practices aimed at benefiting from the treaty. The 17-page *Technical Note* entitled 'Tax Treaties Anti Avoidance'[1] explains the background to the proposed legislation. The creation of domestic rules is thought to be necessary because not all UK treaties are consistent in their treatment of treaty shopping. Rather than undergo a lengthy process of including limitation of benefits articles in each individual treaty, as the US has sought to do, the UK approach of introducing a domestic anti-avoidance rule will at least reduce some of the uncertainty that currently surrounds treaty protection from withholding tax on interest and royalties.

Subsequently, in the Finance Act 2013, the UK introduced a General Anti-Abuse Rule (GAAR), more limited in scope than anti-avoidance rules in other jurisdictions being focused in particular on abusive transactions and arrangements. The GAAR guidance notes[2] state that in relation to treaties 'where there are abusive arrangements which try to exploit particular provisions in a DTT, or the way in which such provisions interact with other provisions of the UK tax law, then the GAAR can be applied to counteract the abusive arrangements'.

---

1   Available at: www.hmrc.gov.uk/drafts/dta-avoidance-tech-note2.pdf.
2   Available at: www.hmrc.gov.uk/avoidance/gaar-part-abc.pdf.

Approach to treaty abuse: 'beneficial ownership' requirements

15.9   By far the most widely used tool for limiting treaty benefits to those for whom they were intended is the 'beneficial ownership' requirement which is commonly applied in tax treaties to payments of dividends, interest and royalties. Unfortunately, as we shall see, reaching agreement on what 'beneficial ownership' actually means has proved very difficult.

For example, the first part of Article 11 of the OECD Model Convention reads:

'1. Interest arising in a Contracting State and paid to a resident of the other Contracting State may be taxed in that other State.

2. However, such interest may also be taxed in the Contracting State in which it arises and according to the law of that State, but if the beneficial owner of the interest is a resident of the other Contracting State the tax so charged shall not exceed 10% of the gross amount of the interest.'

In practice, variations are found, with many older treaties requiring that the recipient of the interest be the beneficial owner of it. The current wording of the OECD MTC is that the beneficial owner should be resident in the state to which payment is made, not that the beneficial owner should be the direct recipient. The requirement for beneficial ownership is commonly used when granting the preferential treaty rates of withholding tax for dividends, interest and royalties, and sometimes 'other income' (ie income not specifically dealt with under any other Article as well). The OECD Commentary on Article 11 is relatively brief in its explanation of 'beneficial ownership'. It explains that mere receipt of the interest by a resident of the other state is not sufficient for the treaty rates of withholding tax to operate and that the term should be interpreted in context, in the light of the object and purposes of the treaty, rather than in a narrow technical sense. Thus a person receiving an interest payment in his capacity as nominee or agent would not have beneficial ownership of the interest and the domestic rates of withholding tax, rather than the treaty rates, would apply unless the nominee or agent had an obligation to pay the interest on to a beneficial owner who was resident in the same state as the agent. A longer report on the use of conduit companies[1] considered the meaning of 'beneficial ownership' only briefly, noting that:

'a conduit company can normally not be regarded as the beneficial owner if, though the formal owner of certain assets, it has very narrow powers which render it a mere fiduciary or an administrator acting on account of the interested parties (most likely the shareholders of the conduit company)' (At p R(6)–10.)

---

1   'Double Taxation Conventions and the Use of Conduit Companies' OECD 1986 (published in Volume II of the full version of the OECD Model Tax Convention at page R(6)–1).

Use of the beneficial ownership approach

15.10   The use of a beneficial ownership approach is achieved by including in the DTT rules which only require the low rates of withholding tax in the treaty to be applied by the paying state where the person who is ultimately entitled to spend the money in any way he sees fit is a resident of the other state. In other words, using our example in Figure 15.2, under the DTT between Ruritania and Inistania, Ruritania only has to reduce its withholding tax from 30 per cent to 10 per cent if the 'beneficial owner' of the interest is resident in Inistania. In our example, the subsidiary company in Inistania could not spend the interest itself but had to pass it on to White Ltd in Baradas. The beneficial owner is White Ltd which is not a resident of Inistania.

Most treaties will adopt the 'beneficial ownership' approach. Treaties which incorporate the 'qualifying persons' approach will normally use the beneficial ownership approach as well.

What is meant by 'beneficial ownership'?

15.11   Despite the widespread use of the requirement as to beneficial ownership by a resident in the other state and the lack of formal guidance on the issue from the OECD, the meaning of the term 'beneficial ownership' has only recently been examined by the courts.

The significance of the absence of a 'beneficial ownership' requirement was tested in the 2005 Swiss case of *A Holding ApS v Federal Tax Administration.*[1] The case concerned a dividend of CHF5.5 million paid to a Danish company by its Swiss subsidiary. The non-treaty rate of withholding tax applied by Switzerland is 35 per cent, whereas the rate under the Switzerland–Denmark DTT is nil. The treaty dates from 1973 and does not have a specific limitation of benefits clause. The only limitation is the reference to beneficial ownership in the dividend and interest articles. The Danish parent was 100 per cent owned by a Guernsey company, which in turn was 100 per cent owned by a Bermudan company. The dividend paid to the Danish company by the Swiss company was passed straight up the chain to the Guernsey company. The Danish company had no offices or any staff. Treaty shopping was obviously the prime motive behind the establishment of the Danish subsidiary, as there is no DTT between Switzerland and Guernsey as such. Despite the fact that the Danish company was a mere shell company, through which the dividend passed to the Guernsey company, Switzerland found that it could not refuse to exempt the dividend from withholding tax, because Article 10 of the treaty stipulates merely that dividends paid by a company resident in one state to a resident of the other state may only be taxed in that other state. There is no requirement as to beneficial ownership. However, the Swiss courts applied the doctrine of 'abuse of rights' so that the claim for repayment of the withholding tax by the Danish company was denied on the basis that the rights under the Swiss–Danish tax treaty were being abused. The courts relied on the OECD Commentary on Article 1 (scope of the treaty) which, at para 9.4 (Improper use of the Convention), notes that the states do not have to grant the benefits of a double taxation convention where arrangements that constitute an abuse of the provisions of the convention have been entered into. It is the first occasion on which the courts have used this doctrine in connection with DTTs and is thought to apply modern thinking in treaty shopping cases, even where the relevant double tax treaties contain no specific limitation of benefits clauses and no specific anti-abuse clauses.

At para 9.5 the OECD offers a word of warning on use of the 'abuse of rights' principle:

> 'It is important to note, however, that it should not be lightly assumed that a taxpayer is entering into the type of abusive transactions referred to above. A guiding principle is that the benefits of a double taxation convention should not be available where a main purpose for entering into certain transactions or arrangements was to secure a more favourable tax position and obtaining that more favourable treatment in these circumstances would be contrary to the object and purpose of the relevant provisions.'

None of these cases addressed the interpretation of 'beneficial ownership' and, somewhat oddly, the first case to do so was a UK case which was neither a tax case nor one involving UK taxpayers.

---

1 [2005] 8 ITLR 536.

Beneficial ownership – the Indofood case[1]

15.12 This case is particularly important because there is widespread accept-ance that it supplies an 'international fiscal meaning' of the term 'beneficial ownership'. This is despite the fact that the case was a civil case brought by bondholders who did not wish the issuer to repay their bonds, rather than being directly in connection with tax matters. The case was heard in the UK courts because the registered office of J P Morgan Chase Bank in London was the trustee of the bonds.

Indofood, an Indonesian company, wished to raise business finance through the issue of loan notes. Given the tax residence of the potential investors it would have been obliged to deduct withholding tax from interest payments at a rate of 20 per cent, which was unattractive to both lender and borrowers. Therefore, it set up a subsidiary company, a special purpose vehicle (Finance) which was tax resident in Mauritius. The terms of the Indonesia–Mauritius DTT in force at the time reduced the Indonesian withholding tax to 10 per cent. The loan notes were issued to the investors by Finance, who then passed the capital up to Indofood via a loan. Interest was thus paid by Indofood to Finance (at 10 per cent withholding tax) and then by Finance to the investors, without further withholding tax as Mauritius did not impose withholding tax on inter-est. This is shown in the following diagram, Figure 15.4:

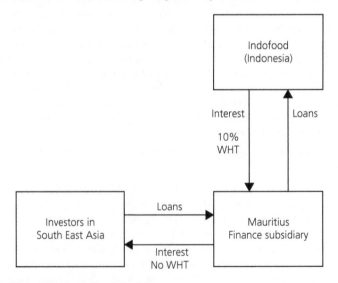

Figure 15.4: The Indofood decision

There were two relevant features of the loan notes:

- whatever happened to the rate of withholding tax on the interest imposed by Indonesia, the investors were to continue to receive the same amount of interest in net terms; and

- Indofood was only permitted to redeem the loan notes early if there was a change in the laws or double tax treaties of Indonesia or Mauritius which affected the tax position and, with respect to any increase in the withholding tax rate, the obligation to pay an increased rate could not be avoided by the issuer taking 'reasonable measures' to avoid it.

Although it is probable that Indonesia could have challenged the right to apply the 10 per cent treaty rate of withholding tax on the interest payments to Finance at any time, on the grounds that Finance was just a conduit company, it did not do so, for reasons unknown. All went well for Indofood, until Indonesia decided to terminate its DTT with Mauritius. This meant that the withholding tax rate increased to 20 per cent (the Indonesian domestic law rate) and the whole of the increase had to be borne by Indofood. At this point, interest rates generally were falling and Indofood decided it could replace the loan notes with cheaper finance elsewhere. For these two reasons, Indofood therefore gave notice of redemption of the loan notes on the grounds of a change in the Indonesian tax regime. However, the loan note holders (the investors) were keen to hold on to the loan notes as due to the changes in market rates, the interest rate they carried was by now very attractive and in any case they were shielded from increase in Indonesian withholding tax. They instructed the trustee, J P Morgan Chase Bank, to fight the decision by Indofood to redeem the notes on the basis that there were certain 'reasonable measures' which could be taken to avoid the obligation to pay the increased withholding tax. The 'reasonable measures' suggested on behalf of the loan note holders were that, effectively, Finance would assign its loan owed to it by Indofood to a new special purpose vehicle set up by Indofood, a Dutch finance subsidiary. This Dutch company would, in turn, lend on the finance to Indofood. Thus the interest payments would in future be routed to the loan note holders, first through the Dutch finance company, then Finance, and finally to the investors. Article 11 of the Indonesia–Netherlands DTT limits withholding tax on interest to 10 per cent of the gross amount if the beneficial owner is resident in the 'other State'. The Netherlands has no treaty with Mauritius but does not generally charge withholding tax on outbound interest payments. So if the new proposal worked, the withholding tax burden would be restored to the original 10 per cent and Indofood would have no legal grounds for insisting on redeeming the loan notes. The position would be as in the following diagram:

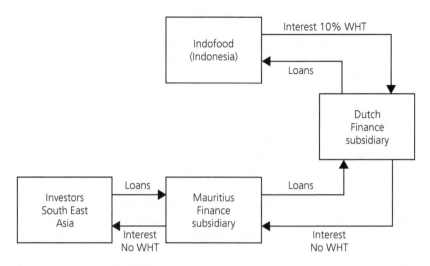

Figure 15.5

The UK Court of Appeal found itself in the curious position of having to ask the Indonesian tax authority to speculate as to whether, given these arrangements, it would permit the interest payments from Indofood to the Dutch finance company to carry withholding tax at the treaty rate of 10 per cent or whether it would insist on levying the full domestic rate of 20 per cent on the grounds that the Dutch finance company did not qualify for the benefit of the treaty with regard to the interest. Would the Indonesian tax authority be prepared to regard the Dutch finance company as the beneficial owner of the interest? If not, then Indofood could go ahead and redeem the loan notes. As party to the relevant DTT, the Dutch tax authority was also consulted, but as the paying state, it fell to the Indonesian tax authority to have the greater input. The matter was quite a sensitive one, as the principal reason for terminating the tax treaty with Mauritius had been the exasperation of the Indonesian tax authority with the willingness of Mauritius to condone the setting up of special purpose vehicles (eg Finance) there, for treaty shopping purposes.

The Indonesian tax authority advised the Court that the term 'beneficial owner' had been inserted into the tax treaty as an anti-abuse measure which was intended to limit the benefit of the reduced withholding tax only to those persons who were properly entitled to the benefit. It considered that the term meant: 'the actual owner of the interest income who truly has the full right to enjoy directly the benefits of that interest income' (Letter dated 24 June 2005).

It further advised the Court that in the circumstances outlined to it, the Indonesian tax authority would not permit the treaty rate of withholding tax to be applied but would charge the non-treaty rate of 20 per cent. Shortly after the date of this letter, the Indonesian tax authority issued a circular dated 7 July 2005 which expanded on this. An extract is given below:

'a. "Beneficial owner" refers to the actual owner of income such as Dividend, Interest, and or Royalty either individual taxpayer or business entity taxpayer that has the full privilege to directly benefit from the income.

b. Herewith, "Special purpose vehicle" in the form of "conduit company", "paper box company"', "pass-through company" and other similar are not included in "beneficial owner" definition as above.

c. If any other party that is not a "beneficial owner" as defined in a. and b. above receives payment of Dividend, Interest, and or Royalty originating from Indonesia, the party that paid for the Dividend, Interest and or Royalty is obligated to withhold income tax Art. 26 according to Indonesia Income Tax Law with 20% (twenty percent) tariff from the gross amount paid.'

The decision in the UK High Court was, put simply, that if the Indonesian tax authority had not objected to the arrangements between Indofood and Finance (which was a Mauritian SPV), then they had no grounds for complaining about the proposed replacement arrangements. However, this was overturned in the Court of Appeal, where the judges not only referred to the views of the Indonesian tax authority on beneficial ownership but set about construing their own definition of the term. As this was not a tax case, none of the judges were tax experts and the resulting interpretation of beneficial ownership is not as helpful as it might have been. The court noted a couple of factors in favour of the Dutch finance company being considered the beneficial owner of the income: for instance, it would not be a trustee, agent or nominee for the loan note holders. But the legal and commercial structuring of the proposed arrangements involving the Dutch company were simply inconsistent with the Dutch company having 'the full privilege to directly benefit from the income', as per the Indonesian circular letter, because it received the interest payments from Indofood two days before the loan note holders were due to receive their interest, and would be legally obliged to pay it on to the loan note holders the next business day. The Court of Appeal also considered that besides looking at these legal and technical matters, the substance of the arrangements should be considered, taking a 'substance over form' approach. Therefore, it would be most unlikely that the Dutch finance company would be treated by the Indonesian tax authority as the beneficial owner and, on those grounds, Indofood was permitted to redeem the loan notes.

This case has attracted criticism, not least for its slavish adherence to the rather vague definition of beneficial ownership given by the Indonesian tax authority: 'the full privilege to directly benefit from the income'. The enthusiasm of the Court of Appeal for the adoption of a substance over form approach is likely to be unhelpful given the appetite of international businesses for certainty in their tax planning.

---

1   *Indofood International Finance Ltd v JP Morgan Chase Bank NA* [2006] EWCA Civ 158, (2006) 8 ITLR 653, [2006] STC 1195.

Canada – Prévost Car and Velcro cases[1]

15.13   Beneficial ownership was also considered in two Canadian cases, *Prévost* and *Velcro*. In *Prévost*, decided in 2009, despite many indications to the contrary, the court decided that a company in receipt of dividends *was* the beneficial owner of them. This case is particularly interesting because it examines the meaning of the term 'beneficial ownership' in several different languages and attempts to fix comparable meanings in each. Also, the case was heard under the law of Quebec, which is a civil law territory. Unlike a common law jurisdiction such as the UK, where the concept of beneficial ownership is well developed in some areas of case law, say, with regard to trusts, the concept is not recognized in Quebec's law.

The facts were that shareholders in a Canadian bus manufacturer (Prévost) wanted to sell their shares to Volvo (Swedish) and Henlys (UK) who were both themselves bus manufacturers. A Dutch company, PH BV, was formed to which the Canadian shareholders sold their shares. PH BV was owned 51 per cent by Volvo and 49 per cent by Henlys. The joint venture was formed with the intention of the two manufacturers expanding operations into North America. A Dutch company was chosen partly because neither the UK nor Sweden was an acceptable choice to both parties and for reasons besides taxation. The joint venture agreement stated that 80 per cent of the profits of Prévost were to be paid up to PH BV as a dividend, and then on to Volvo and Henlys, provided that, taken together, Prévost and PH BV had sufficient financial resources to pay the dividends.

The issue was whether PH BV was the beneficial owner of the dividends paid to it by Prévost. Or was it merely a conduit? Things looked rather bleak: PH BV had never had any employees and had no other discernable activities other than holding the shares in Prévost. Unfortunately, PH BV had also told its bankers during the course of complying with the Netherlands's financial regulatory procedures that the beneficial owners of the shares in Prévost were in fact Volvo and Henlys. Canada therefore asserted that PH BV was not the beneficial owner and that the rate of withholding tax in the Netherlands–Canada DTT of 5 per cent did not apply, as it was only available where the recipient was also the beneficial owner and that therefore the full Canadian domestic law withholding tax of 25 per cent should be applied. As in Indofood, the term 'beneficial ownership' was not defined in the treaty and so the usual rule that any term not defined in the treaty should be defined according to domestic tax law was brought into play. Further, Canadian domestic law provided that the relevant domestic law was that in force at the time the definition was needed, rather than that in force at the time the treaty was concluded.

An OECD expert who gave evidence in the case stated that a holding company (such as PH BV) would normally be viewed as the beneficial owner of dividends received by it, rather than there being any presumption that the shareholders in the holding company were the true beneficial owners. He pointed out that in the 1987 OECD report referred to above, Double Tax Conventions and the Use of Conduit Companies, it was envisaged that conduit companies could, in some circumstances, still be beneficial owners of the income which they receive. All depends on the extent of the powers of the conduit company and the extent of the functions which it performs. It is necessary to ask whether the conduit company has ownership of its income and assets in name only (ie legal title, or whether it enjoys other economic, legal or practical attributes of ownership). According to this expert, the requirement for beneficial ownership was inserted into the OECD Model Convention explicitly to exclude intermediaries in third states, such as agents and nominees from treaty benefits. The OECD did not support any assumption that a holding company was a mere agent or nominee for its shareholders, so that the shareholders would automatically be considered the beneficial owners. He referred back to the OECD's 1987 report on conduit companies. According to this report, so long as a company is liable to tax in the country where it is resident and so long as the assets giving rise to the income have effectively been transferred to it, the conduit company cannot be considered to be a mere agent or nominee.

The court heard that under Dutch law, PH BV would definitely have been regarded as the beneficial owner of the shares in Prévost based on the result of an earlier Dutch case. However, if there was a legal obligation upon PH BV to pass on the dividends to its shareholders, PH BV would not be considered to be the beneficial owner of the dividends. The existence of an agreement between PH BV's shareholders (Volvo and Henlys) did not amount to an obligation on PH BV to pass on the dividends it received. Dividend payments had to be authorized by PH BV's directors in accordance with Dutch law. Actually, under Dutch law, payment of large and regular dividends is not considered unusual as the default scenario under the Netherlands civil code is that profits are to be distributed to shareholders in full, subject to capital maintenance requirements, but this practice can be avoided by a Dutch company opting to delegate to its shareholders the power to decide on the size of the dividends.

During the course of this case it became apparent that the term 'beneficial ownership' had been chosen in 1977 by the OECD experts for use in the Model Convention without much thought as to how the term might be interpreted. Partly this was because 18 out of the 24 OECD members who agreed on the 1977 changes to the Model Convention were civil law countries for whom the term carried far fewer connotations than for common law countries. In common law countries, the term has multiple meanings. So the OECD had adopted the term 'beneficial ownership':

• not really having thought about what it meant;

• which is not recognized in the law of most OECD members; therefore the fallback position in the definitions Article of double tax treaties, which states that terms not specifically defined in the treaty are to be given the meaning which they have in domestic tax law is of no use, because it does not necessarily appear in domestic tax law; and

• which has multiple meanings in those OECD members which do recognize the term in law, but none of those meanings quite fits the bill as far as tax treaties are concerned.

The court resorted to looking up the phrase in several languages in dictionaries, which did not help much either. In the end, the court settled on the following definition:

> 'the "beneficial owner" of dividends is the person who receives the dividends for his or her own use and enjoyment and assumes the risk and control of the dividend he or she received. The person who is beneficial owner of the dividend is the person who enjoys and assumes all the attributes of ownership. In short the dividend is for the owner's own benefit and this person is not accountable to anyone for how he or she deals with the dividend income' (at para 100).

Thus shareholders of a holding company would not necessarily be treated as the beneficial owners of income received by a company unless the company was a conduit with absolutely no discretion as to the use or application of that income. Because the dividends received by PH BV were that company's and it could do what it wanted with the income until the directors authorized the payment of a dividend to Volvo and Henlys it was not regarded as a mere conduit, but as the beneficial owner of the dividends it received from Prévost.

The Canadian Federal Court subsequently upheld the decision of the Tax Court of Canada finding that Prévost was the beneficial owner of the dividends.

The notion of beneficial owner was also argued by the Canadian government in *Velcro Canada* in 2012.[2] Velcro Canada, resident in the Netherlands Antilles, incorporated an intermediary company in the Netherlands to which it assigned the right to receive royalties from a Canadian Company, with a sublicencing agreement between the Dutch intermediary and the Netherlands Antilles company: a 'stepping stone structure'. The court followed the *Prévost* case in finding that the Dutch intermediary was not the beneficial owner of the royalties.

In 2013, the Canadian government issued an invitation for public comment on possible measures to prevent treaty shopping. A consultation document outlines Canada's position on and experience with treaty shopping together with some suggested possible approaches to the prevention of treaty shopping.[3]

---

1 *Prévost Car Inc v The Queen* (2009) FCA 57TCC 231, *Velcro Canada* 2012 DTC 1100.
2 TCC 231, *Velcro Canada* 2012 DTC 1100.
3 Available at: www.fin.gc.ca/activty/consult/ts-cf-eng.asp#a1.

OECD stance on beneficial ownership

15.14 On 29 April 2011, the OECD's Centre for Tax Policy and Administration issued a public discussion draft[1] of proposed changes to Articles 10, 11 and 12 of the Model Convention to clarify the meaning of 'beneficial owner'. This has resulted in updates to the Commentary on Articles 10, 11 and 12 in 2014.

The OECD stance is that the term should be understood in the treaty context, although the meaning of 'beneficial ownership' under domestic law is not automatically irrelevant. The 2014 Commentary adopts the view that 'beneficial owner' refers to the full right to enjoy the dividend, interest or royalty without being contractually or otherwise required to pass it on to another party. Thus the use and enjoyment refers to the payment itself, not to the ownership of the underlying property that generates the payment.

The aim is to move towards an international consensus, in some ways endorsing the *Indofoods* decision that as a global concept, 'beneficial ownership' needs a fiscal meaning that stands outside of domestic legislation.

Not all commentators agree with the OECD stance. The City of London Law Society, for example, in its response to the OECD discussion draft dated 12 July 2011,[2] suggests that tackling the problem of treaty shopping through a definition of beneficial owner is problematic, and further that there is no international consensus that the 'full right' is the correct test to use to determine beneficial ownership.

---

1   Available at: www.oecd.org/dataoecd/49/35/47643872.pdf.
2   Available at: www.oecd.org/dataoecd/34/52/48391035.pdf.

Approach to treaty abuse: anti-conduit clauses

15.15   Conduit arrangements, even where the conduit vehicle can be shown to have beneficial ownership of its income, are disliked by governments as they are usually artificial arrangements entered into with the principal purpose of accessing the benefits of a tax treaty to which the underlying parties would not be entitled in the absence of the conduit vehicle. The 1987 OECD report on conduit companies identified two main types of conduit vehicle:

- *Direct conduit*: this is illustrated in the diagram at para **15.2** above. The country in which the conduit company is set up does not tax the conduit company on its income to any significant extent (eg under a participation arrangement whereby dividends received from subsidiary companies are exempted from corporation tax).

- *'Stepping stone' conduit*: the distinguishing feature of this type of arrangement is that the country whose tax treaties are being taken advantage of is a relatively high-tax country, but the conduit company set up there has low net profits due to a high level of tax deductible payments to a third country.

In both cases, the conduit company itself is not liable to tax to any significant extent in the country in which it is resident and the income passing through it ends up with a person who would not have been eligible to benefit from the tax treaties which are used as the income makes its journey through the conduit structure.

The OECD identified five approaches to tackling the use of conduit companies in double tax treaties: where possible, examples from actual treaties are shown.

Anti-conduit rules: the 'look-through' approach

15.16   Under this approach, treaty benefits are denied to a company if it is owned directly or indirectly by persons who are not residents of one of the contracting states (ie the countries which are parties to the treaty). This is a rather drastic approach as it entails disregarding the legal status of the company. Up-to-date information on the identity of the shareholders would be needed. This approach is only really appropriate when a treaty is being made with a low-tax country, where the risk of conduit activity would be high.

> 'Notwithstanding the provisions of the Articles mentioned above, tax reductions or exemptions which would otherwise apply to dividends, interest, royalties and capital gains, shall not apply if these items of income from a Contracting State are derived by a company which is a resident of the other Contracting State, where persons who are not residents of that other State hold, directly or indirectly, more than 50% of the capital of that company. This provision shall not apply if the company shows that it performs in the Contracting State of which it is a resident substantial trade or business activities, not being activities consisting principally of holding or managing shares or other business property.'

> (Protocol, para 2, Belgium–Spain 1995 Treaty, applying to Articles 10, 11, 12 and 13 (dividends, interest, royalties and gains).)

Notice that this example includes an 'active business' clause. This is discussed below under 'bone fide' provisions.

Anti-conduit rules: the exclusion approach

15.17   The successful conduit operation requires that the conduit company itself does not pay much, if any, tax in the country where it is resident. This low-tax status can be achieved by taking advantage of a dividend participation exemption (simple conduit), by paying out most of the income in the form of tax deductible expenses (stepping stone) or by setting up the conduit as a particular type of legal entity which is exempt from tax. States could simply exclude certain types of legal entity from all, or a selection of treaty benefits.

Anti-conduit rules: the subject-to-tax approach

15.18   Under this approach, a conduit company would only be eligible for treaty benefits (which is the whole point of the conduit) if it was actually subject to tax in the state where resident. However, this would not catch stepping-stone structures where perfectly legitimate expenses are paid out to a low-tax country, thus reducing the tax bill in the conduit state to virtually nil. Such a company would be subject to tax, but might not actually have paid any. There would be complications if a state wanted to attract foreign companies by offering tax exemptions, tax holidays, etc, and tax-exempt bodies, such as charities would have to be specially catered for.

'Article 20

Investment or holding companies

A corporation of one of the Contracting States deriving dividends, interest, royalties, or capital gains from sources within the other Contracting State shall not be entitled to the benefits of Articles 8 (Dividends), 9 (Interest), 10 (Royalties), or 12 (Capital gains) if:

(a) by reason of special measures the tax imposed on such corporation by the first-mentioned Contracting State with respect to such dividends, interest, royalties, or capital gain is substantially less than the tax generally imposed by such Contracting State on corporate profits, and

(b) 25 percent or more of the capital of such corporation is held off record or is otherwise determined, after consultation between the competent authorities of the Contracting States, to be owned directly or indirectly, by one or more persons who are not individual residents of the first-mentioned Contracting State (or, in the case of a Norwegian corporation, who are citizens of the United States).'

(Norway–US 1971 Treaty. (Note this type of clause is sometimes referred to as a 'British Virgin Islands' clause.))

Anti-conduit rules: the channel approach

15.19 This is the approach favoured by the OECD. Where a conduit company is owned or controlled by non-residents, the state in which the conduit company is resident refuses to grant treaty benefits if more than, say, 50 per cent of the conduit company's income is paid out to the non-resident owners in tax deductible form. However, such an approach, whilst catching conduit arrangements, might also catch perfectly innocent commercial arrangements, so that a motive test (eg a 'bone fide' clause) would also be needed.

'1. A legal entity which is a resident of a Contracting State, and in which persons who are not residents of that State have, directly or indirectly, a substantial interest in the form of a participation, or otherwise, may only claim the tax reductions provided for in Articles 10, 11 and 12 with respect to dividends, interest, and royalties, derived from sources in the other Contracting State, where:

(a) the interest-bearing debts to persons who are not residents of the first-mentioned State are not higher than six times the equity capital and reserves; this condition shall not apply to banks of both Contracting States;

(b)   the interest paid on loans contracted with such persons is not paid at a higher rate than the normal interest rate; the normal interest rate means:

    a.   in Belgium: the legal rate of interest permitted as professional charges;

    b.   in Switzerland: the average interest rate on debentures issued by the Swiss Confederation plus two percentage points;

(c)   not more than 50 per cent of the relevant income from sources in the other Contracting State is used to satisfy claims (interest, royalties, development, advertising, initial and travel expenses, depreciation on any kind of business asset including intangible assets, processes, etc) by persons not resident in the first-mentioned State;

(d)   expenses connected with the relevant income derived from sources in the other Contracting State are met exclusively from such income; and

(e)   the corporation distributes at least 25 per cent of the relevant income derived from sources in the other Contracting State.'

(Article 22, para 1, Belgium–Switzerland Treaty 1978.)

Approach to treaty abuse: general anti-avoidance legislation

15.20   The Commentary on Article 1 makes it clear that the use by a state of its domestic anti-avoidance provisions are consistent with its treaty obligations. This material was added to the Commentary in 2003 and there is some debate as to whether a state can apply its domestic anti-avoidance legislation (such as a general anti-avoidance rule – GAAR) in deciding whether to grant treaty benefits under treaties concluded prior to 2003. Perhaps the key point is made in Paragraph 9.5 of the commentary on Article 1:

'A guiding principle is that the benefits of a double tax convention should not be available where a main purpose for entering into certain transactions or arrangements was to secure a more favourable tax position and obtaining that more favourable treatment in these circumstances would be contrary to the object and purpose of the relevant provisions.'

A good example of the use of a domestic law general anti-avoidance rule to combat treaty abuse seems to be the recent developments concerning the application by India of its GAAR to combat abuse of the 1982 India–Mauritius Treaty (see para **15.38**).

Reliance on domestic anti-avoidance provisions to tackle what is perceived as an abusive practice, however, is uncertain and arguably a better way of dealing with treaty shopping is by tightening up the operation of the DTTs themselves by introducing anti-abuse clauses into the text of the treaties. This is certainly the view taken by the US, and increasingly adopted in other countries also.

As well as relying on any general anti-avoidance rules in a country's domestic law, it is possible for countries to enact specific legislation to tackle treaty abuse. For instance, a country could deny the nil rate of withholding tax on royalties available under its treaties if it appears that a foreign resident has set up a special purpose vehicle in that country in order to benefit from the nil rate, in circumstances where the IP involved was technically registered in the country but managed from abroad. However, this would constitute treaty override.

OBJECTIVE LIMITATION OF BENEFITS TEST: US MODEL AND BEPS ACTION 6

15.21   The US strongly believes that the best way to tackle treaty shopping is through specific provisions in bilateral treaties to preclude the misuse of beneficial treaty treatment by residents of countries not party to the treaty (ie third-country residents). The longstanding US approach is to say exactly which *persons* qualify for benefits rather than to try to identify specific situations in which conduit arrangements might be being used. Most current US treaties include such limitation of benefits provisions. This is the 'channel approach' as discussed above, in that only those persons who could not conceivably be acting as a conduit for channelling income or gains to a person not resident in either contracting state will qualify for benefits under the treaty. However, the distinguishing feature of the US approach is the degree of detail which has been developed in the channel approach to countering treaty abuse.

The OECD's Final Report on BEPS Action 6 recommends that countries incorporate an objective limitation of benefits test into their treaties and elevates (with some amendments) the current optional wording for such a test from the Commentary on Article 1 into the text of the OECD MTC. The 2016 US Model was released on 17 February 2016.

The 'qualifying person' approach – general considerations

15.22   The 'qualifying person' approach can be used to counter treaty shopping. By stating exactly which types of person will qualify for the reduced rates of tax and any tax exemptions available under the treaty. Typically, a country will state that individuals will definitely qualify but will set a series of tests to be passed before the rates of tax set out in the treaty will be applied to companies and other legal persons. If a company fails the tests, then the full domestic rates of withholding tax are applied unless the company can persuade the tax authorities that its transactions are not specifically designed to take advantage of the tax treaty. This 'qualifying persons' approach is usually adopted by the US in its treaties.

These 'qualifying person tests' appear in other treaties, such as the 1995 France–Japan Treaty. The exact detail of the 'qualifying person' tests varies from treaty to treaty, and the complexity of the rules relates mainly to the way in which the minimum connection requirement is framed. It is usually a requirement that a certain percentage of the shares of the entity have to be owned, directly or indirectly, by certain qualified persons, which generally includes individuals resident in either the US or the other Contracting State, publicly traded companies, charitable organizations, and maybe even the Contracting State itself (eg through local authorities). The limitation of benefits provision may also include some form of active business test, to preserve benefits for third-country residents who have a good reason for establishing the structure unrelated to obtaining benefits under the treaty. Generally speaking, the tests have become progressively more detailed over time, although one interesting development has been the 2004 Protocol to the US–Netherlands Treaty which removed much of the quantitative detail from the limitation of benefits article, arguably simplifying it.

The structure of the limitation of benefits articles in the US MTC and BEPS Action 6

15.23   Unless indicated otherwise, the analysis of the content of the limitation of benefits article containing the objective 'qualifying person' tests set out below apply equally to the tests in use in US treaties and the test as recommended in the Final Report on BEPS Action 6. Note that the BEPS Action 6 test is given in two versions – a simplified version and a detailed version, although the simplified version is no easier to understand and apply than the detailed version.

Most benefits of a treaty, with the usual exceptions of the non-discrimination and mutual agreement articles, may only be claimed by:

- individuals (this category can sometimes include a collective investment vehicle);

- the contracting state itself: where the taxpayer is the government, a local authority or a governmental agency; and

- a 'qualifying person'.

An individual, or a government itself is considered unlikely to be acting as part of a conduit arrangement. However, all other legal persons must pass at least one of a series of tests to establish whether or not they are a 'qualifying person'. The tests broadly follow the OECD guidance. The list of tests in any given treaty will comprise some or all of the following:

- publicly traded corporations (and their subsidiaries);

- not-for-profits organizations/pension funds;

- ownership/base erosion;

- derivative benefits;

- active trade or business;

- multinational corporate group headquarters;

- triangular provision; and

- competent authority/motive test.

The 'publicly traded' test

15.24   The broad rationale behind this test is that persons wishing to set up a conduit arrangement are hardly likely to go to the trouble and expense of establishing and maintaining a company with a stock exchange listing for this purpose. If a company meets the requirements for a stock exchange listing it will be a company with substantial business activities and will be subject to a heavy degree of regulation by the stock exchange authorities. Only certain stock exchanges are recognized and these are specified in the treaty. Normally the stock exchanges of the two contracting states will be recognized, sometimes along with a list of further stock exchanges. In the case of recent US limitation of benefits articles in treaties with Member States of the EU, qualifying stock exchanges are those not just in the treaty states, but in the case of the EU taxpayer, any stock exchange in the European Economic Area (EEA) and in the case of the US taxpayer, any state party to the North American Free Trade Agreement (NAFTA).

If the stock exchange on which the company's shares are traded is not in the same country as that in which the company is resident then there is a requirement that the primary place of management and control be in the country in which the company is tax resident.

It is not enough that a company's shares are traded on a recognized stock exchange and further tests must be passed before a listed company can be considered a 'qualifying person' for treaty benefits. These tests are that the following classes of shares must be traded on a recognized (as listed in the treaty) stock exchange:

- the principal class of the company's shares; and

- classes of shares carry disproportionate benefits (eg with respect to rights to a share of the profits or to the assets on a winding up).

In addition, the shares must be regularly traded. This means that a significant proportion of the company's shares must be traded on a significant number of days during the tax year.

Subsidiaries of companies which pass the 'publicly traded' test will normally also qualify for treaty benefits, provided that both the subsidiary and the parent are resident in a Contracting State. The usual rule is that a subsidiary company will be entitled to the benefits of the treaty if five or fewer direct and indirect owners of at least 50 per cent of the aggregate vote and value of the company's shares are 'publicly traded' companies.

If the publicly-traded companies are indirect owners, however, there may be a requirement that each of the intermediate companies must be a resident of one of the contracting states. This requirement appears in the detailed version of the Action 6 recommendation.

Not-for-profit organizations and pension funds

15.25 Certain types of organizations: pension funds, or religious, charitable, educational, scientific, artistic, cultural or other organizations fulfilling public purposes may qualify for treaty benefits regardless of the residence of the beneficiaries or members.

The Action 6 recommended test for pension schemes specifies that at least 50 per cent of the beneficial interests in the fund must be owned by individuals resident in either of the Contracting States, or else a set percentage is owned by individuals resident in another State who could benefit in an individual capacity from a treaty with the pension fund's state. A Discussion Draft on potential changes to the OECD MTC concerning the treaty residence of pension funds was issued on 29 February 2016,[1] and the draft update to the MTC was issued in July 2017.[2]

In more recent US treaties, the test as to whether a pension fund is a 'qualifying person' may be passed either by reference to the tax residence of the scheme members or by reference to the organization whose pension fund it is. Typically, a pension fund will qualify for treaty benefits if at least 50 per cent of the beneficiaries, members or participants are individuals resident in one of the contracting states, or if the organization (eg the company whose pension scheme it is) sponsoring the pension fund is a 'qualifying person' (ie the company itself qualifies for treaty benefits).

---

1 Available at: www.oecd.org/tax/treaties/discussion-draft-treaty-residence-pension-funds.pdf.
2 Available at www.oecd.org/ctp/beps/oecd-releases-draft-contents-2017-update-model-tax-convention.htm.

The 'ownership/base erosion' test

15.26 Any legal person: a company, a trust, a partnership (if recognized as a taxable entity) can qualify under this test. The test confers 'qualifying person' status on a legal person which is:

- owned as to more than 50 per cent by persons entitled to treaty benefits (ie by persons who are themselves 'qualifying persons'); and

- a person which pays out less than 50 per cent of its pre-tax income in the form of, broadly speaking, payments which represent a tax-deductible return on investment (ie interest and royalties) to persons not resident in either of the Contracting States.

Both of these requirements must be met. The first test is a test of ownership, the second looks at whether the tax base of the country to which a payment enjoying treaty benefits is made is being eroded. This could happen if, say, a company in Country A pays interest at a reduced rate of withholding tax under the Country A–Country B treaty to a corporate shareholder, X Ltd, resident in Country B, but Company X pays little tax on the interest receipt in Country B due to the fact that it pays large amounts of tax deductible interest and royalties to persons resident in Country C. To be a qualifying person, Company X needs to be owned as to at least 50 per cent by residents of either Country A or Country B and also, no more than 50 per cent of its pre-tax income can be paid out in tax-deductible form (eg interest and royalties) to persons not resident in either Country A or Country B. In other words, if Country A is to permit the payment to Company X to be made at treaty rates of withholding tax, it wants to be sure that the resulting receipt is taxable within Countries A and B.

The required percentages can vary. Often, there is a requirement that the ownership requirements are fulfilled for at least 183 days in the tax year. Sometimes there is an exclusion from the second test (the 'base erosion') test for bank interest.

The 2016 US Model tightens the base erosion test found in the previous Model by applying the test to both the person claiming the benefits and the tested group and treating deductible payments benefiting from a special tax regime (see para **15.32** below) as base eroding.

The 'derivative benefits' test

15.27   Again, the broad aim of this test is to establish that a legal person is not being used as part of a conduit arrangement. The logic of this test is that if a person would themselves be entitled to perfectly good treaty benefits under one treaty, say, the US–Netherlands Treaty, then that person is unlikely to go to the bother of setting up treaty shopping arrangements under, say, the US–Belgium Treaty, in order to extract income or gains from the US at treaty rates of withholding tax.

There are normally two parts to this test: ownership and base erosion. For a company to pass this test, it would typically have to show that at least 95 per cent of its voting power and value is owned by persons who are themselves entitled to broadly equivalent treaty benefits, not under this treaty but under another treaty ('equivalent beneficiaries'). For instance, a Belgian company might qualify for benefits under the 2006 US–Belgium Treaty if:

- 95 per cent of its shares are owned by persons resident in a country which has a treaty with the US (eg suppose they are resident in the Netherlands); and

- under which those owners are considered to be 'qualifying persons'; and

- the benefits under the US–Netherlands Treaty are at least as good as those offered by the US–Belgium Treaty; and

- no more than 50 per cent of the company's income is paid out in the form of tax-deductible interest and royalties or similar types of payment to persons who are not 'equivalent beneficiaries'.

If the treaty between the state in which the company's owners are resident (in our example, the Netherlands) and does not contain a limitation of benefits article which sets out 'qualifying person' tests, then it is necessary to show that the company owners would qualify under, in our example, the US–Belgium Treaty, were they in fact residents of Belgium. (Note that the Netherlands–US Treaty includes highly detailed 'qualifying person' tests, so that in our example there would be no need for the company owners to demonstrate that they would be capable of passing the tests in the US–Belgium Treaty; they will just have to show that they are 'qualifying persons' under the US–Netherlands Treaty.)

Some US treaties acknowledge that a taxpayer resident in the EU might enjoy benefits under, say, the EU Interest and Royalties Directive which are better than those under, say, the US–Netherlands Treaty and thus permit comparisons by reference to rates of withholding tax laid down in the Directive rather than the bilateral tax treaty in question.

A derivate benefits test appears in many US treaties and is included by the OECD in the proposed detailed limitation of benefits article developed in Action 6 of BEPS. The 2016 US Model includes a derivative benefits test that provides that a company that is resident in a contracting state may qualify for treaty benefits if, at the time the benefit would be accorded, the company satisfies an ownership and a base erosion test, both of which differ slightly from existing tests in current US DTTs. The derivative benefits test is more restrictive than the OECD's recommendation in that the ownership requirement is more stringent, intermediate owners are accounted for and the OECD recommendation does not include a base erosion test.

The 'active business' test

15.28 A feature of many conduit arrangements is that the conduit company does very little apart from channel dividends, interest or royalties from one country to another. Persons wishing to take advantage of a tax treaty to which they are not properly entitled are unlikely to go to the trouble of setting up a fully active trading company in a foreign state just to save a bit of withholding tax. Thus, companies with an active trade or business will not normally be considered to be conduit companies and even if the ownership-type tests set out above are failed, ie they are not 'qualifying persons', they may still qualify for treaty benefits.

The rule is usually worded so that a taxpayer resident in State A will be entitled to treaty benefits under the treaty between States A and B if the taxpayer is receiving income from State B which is in connection with an active trade or business which the taxpayer runs in State A. However, it is very important that the income received from State B is connected to the trade being carried on in State A. The income arising in State B must be from an activity which forms a part of, or is complementary to, the business being carried out in State A. For instance, the activities in States A and B could involve the same products or services, they could both be manufacturing these products, or alternatively, they could be manufactured in State A but distributed in State B. Investment activities in State A such as making or managing of investments would not count unless the taxpayer was a bank or a specified type of financing institution.

Alternatively, the income arising in State B would normally enjoy treaty benefits if it is incidental to an active business carried on in State A. The US Technical Explanations to US treaties generally cite an example of incidental income as being interest earned on the temporary investment of working capital by the company resident in State A in securities issued by persons in State B.

To prevent a taxpayer resident in State A, who would not otherwise qualify for treaty benefits from passing the active business test by setting up a 'shell' operation in State A purely in order to pass the active business test, there is normally a requirement that the activity in State A be 'substantial' in relation to the activity which is producing the income in State B. In some treaties (eg US–France) 'substantial' is defined in terms of specific accounting ratios.

The active business test will generally be applied to corporate groups, rather than rigidly to individual companies. Thus, if the company in State A did not own the shares in a company paying income to it from State B directly but perhaps owned the paying entity indirectly, or if both payer and recipient were members of the same corporate group. The BEPS Action 5 recommendation is that a company will be connected to another company if there is 50 per cent control.

This test contains elements of subjectivity: for instance, when will activity be considered to be 'substantial' or when will an activity be considered to be 'complementary to' another activity?

The 2016 US Model contains an active business test, but is now more restrictive than the previous model as it applies only in relation to activities that are between related persons in the same line of business.

The 'group headquarters' test

15.29   Most countries are keen to attract the headquarters of multinational companies to their tax jurisdictions. However, excluding them from benefiting under a country's tax treaties would severely reduce the appeal of a country as a headquarters location. Hence, there is sometimes a special test by which headquarters companies can be counted as 'qualifying persons' when they might otherwise not pass any of the other tests.

Typically, a headquarters company of a multinational corporate group will be a 'qualifying person' if it supervises a number of companies in other countries. Note that it is supervision rather than ownership which is the key. The 2006 US–Belgium Treaty contains the following list of requirements which must be met in order for a legal person (ie not necessarily a company) to pass the 'multinational corporate group headquarters' test:

- it must provide a substantial portion of the overall supervision and administration of the group;

- it must consist of corporations resident, and engaged in active trades or businesses, in at least five countries which in turn contribute substantially (at least 10 per cent) to the income generated by the group;

- the business activities carried on in any one country other than the headquarters company's state of residence must generate less than 50 per cent of the gross income of the group;

- no more than 25 per cent of the headquarters company's gross income may be derived from the other contracting state;

- it must have and exercise independent discretionary authority to carry out the overall supervision and administration functions;

- it must be subject to the generally applicable income taxation rules in its country of residence; and

- the income derived in the other contracting state must be derived in connection with or be incidental to the active business activities referred to above.

The 2016 US Model includes a headquarters test that, unlike current treaties, requires a headquarters to exercise primary management and control functions.

A rule covering collective investment schemes

15.30   This is included in the BEPS Action 6 proposals for use where a treaty recognizes collective investment schemes (CIVs) as residents – ie where it treats them as opaque rather than transparent. If CIVs are regarded as tax residents, then this specific rule may be needed because it is likely that a CIV will not pass any of the other tests: it does not have shares or beneficial interests which are traded on a stock exchange, the interests in the scheme will probably be held by persons not resident in either of the Contracting States, the distributions made by the CIV are tax deductible (fails ownership/base erosion test) and is not engaged in the active conduct of a business. Probable wording of the CIV rule would be that a CIV is a qualifying person:

> 'but only to the extent that, at that time, the beneficial interests in the CIV are owned by residents of the Contracting State in which the collective investment vehicle is established or by equivalent beneficiaries' (BEPS Action 6 Final Report at p 33).

A 'triangular' test concerning permanent establishments

15.31   Treaty benefits with respect to interest, royalties or insurance premiums may be limited so that withholding tax is charged on these at 15 per cent. For this to apply, the interest, royalties or insurance premiums paid out of the

US would have to be exempt from tax in Germany on the grounds that they form part of the income attributable to a PE which the German recipient enterprise has in a third State. Unless the tax suffered on the interest, royalties or premiums in the state where the PE is situated is at least 60 per cent of what the tax would have been in Germany if taxable there, the US will apply WHT of 15 per cent. The US will apply its domestic rate to insurance premiums in these circumstances. This test may be needed in situations similar to the following scenario:

A PE is simply a part of a company. If Y Co, resident in Country B earns, say, interest from X Co, resident in Country A, but the assets giving rise to that interest form part of Y Co's assets which are, for internal accounting purposes, the assets of its PE, which happens to be located in Country C, then this test examines whether the interest can still enjoy the lower rate of withholding tax provided for under the treaty between Countries A and B. This is illustrated below:

Example 15.3

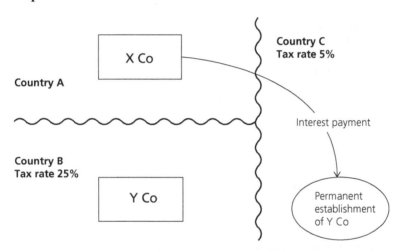

Figure 15.6: Interest received by a PE in a low tax country

Assume that there is a treaty between Countries A and B providing for a rate of withholding tax on interest of 3 per cent, but that there is no treaty between Countries A and C. The rate of withholding tax on interest under the domestic law of Country A is 30 per cent. Also assume that Country B uses the exemption method of double tax relief, so that the income attributed to the PE in Country C is not taxed by Country B.

The proposed test in the OECD MTC: if the tax in Country C is less than 60 per cent of the tax that would be payable if the interest had been paid directly to Y Co in Country B, then Country A does not have to use the treaty rate of withholding tax of 3 per cent and can charge a higher rate (to be agreed upon in the treaty, or simply set to be Country A's domestic law withholding tax rate of 30 per cent).

This rule would not apply if the interest was received by the PE in Country C in connection with, or if it was incidental to, an active trade carried on by the PE in Country C. Neither will it apply if the payments received from Country A are royalties derived from intellectual property (IP) that was actually produced or developed by the PE itself (as opposed to anyone in the head office in Country B or elsewhere). In other words, if it can be shown that the PE is not set up principally to extract payments from Country A under the favourable terms of the treaty between Countries A and B, then the rule will not apply. It is a tax avoidance rule.

A similar rule has been used in some US treaties for some time. The 2016 US Model takes into account the terms of any tax treaty between the US and the country where the PE is located (Countries A and C in Example 15.3 above).

The US Model goes further than the PE triangular test proposed by the OECD in that it also applies to payments between a US resident company and a PE which that company might have. This is illustrated below:

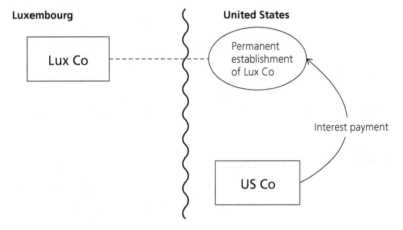

Figure 15.7: Application of US triangular PE test

In Figure 15.7 above, the PE of the Luxembourg company is located in the US. However, it is exempt from Luxembourg tax on its income because the Lux Co itself enjoys a statutory exemption from Luxembourg tax, which also covers any income of its foreign PEs. The PE does not pay corporation tax on its income in the US because it is set up so as not to be within the scope of US corporation tax: it would be treated as not being engaged in a US trade or business, and therefore not subject to US tax. The income of the PE is therefore not taxed anywhere. The treaty between the US and Luxembourg provides for zero withholding tax on interest payments.

The new limitation of benefits article in the 2016 US MTC has the effect of denying the benefit of the treaty in this situation: US domestic rate of withholding tax on interest of 30 per cent would apply to the payment of interest to the US PE of Lux Co.

This rule differs from the rules proposed by the OECD in that the OECD rule requires the use of a PE in a third country, whereas the US rule also applies even where all the parties are located in the two Contracting States to the treaty. It is thought that this tightening up of the US limitation of benefits rules stems from the so-called 'Lux Leaks' files, published by a group of journalists in 2014. These files provided evidence of some tax avoidance strategies used by multinational groups of companies.[1] This evidence of the granting of advantageous tax rulings by Luxembourg on a large scale has led to the action being taken by the EU to force EU Member States to disclose tax rulings granted (see Chapter 20).

---

1   Available at: www.icij.org/project/luxembourg-leaks/new-leak-reveals-luxembourg-tax-deals-disney-koch-brothers-empire for reporting of the 'Lux Leaks'. The reporting alleges that up to 340 groups of companies have secured secret tax rulings from the Luxembourg Government.

A 'special tax regime' test

15.32   A 'special tax regime' test has been used in some US treaties and is now included in the 2016 version of the US MTC. It is aimed at preventing the granting of treaty benefits (essentially, low treaty rates of WHT) in situations where the payment is made to a beneficial owner resident in a country with a normal (as opposed to low tax) regime, but the payment is not taxed on in line with the countries normal rules. Instead, it enjoys a special, low tax regime which the recipient's country offers alongside its normal tax regime. In the past, this type of test has been known as the 'BVI test' (the reference being to the British Virgin Islands).

The US model special tax regime (STR) clause considers an STR to be one providing preferential treatment and that results in an effective tax rate less than 15%, or 60% of the general corporation tax rate in the source country, whichever is lower. It is limited in scope to specified income types: interest, royalties and certain guarantee fees falling under Article 21 ('other income').[1] The May 2015 Technical Explanation includes rulings practices as a form of 'administrative practices' STR. At the time of writing, the Technical Explanation for the final 2016 model has not been published and it is not clear whether rulings are still within scope.

While there are no plans to adopt a general exclusion clause for preferential tax regimes, the OECD does plan to include a separate 'special tax regime' test in each of Articles 11, 12 and 21 of the OECD MTC, rather than to include such a test in the detailed limitation of benefits article. Such a test (for Article 11) would read:

> 'Interest arising in a Contracting State and beneficially owned by a resident of the other Contracting State may be taxed in the first-mentioned Contracting State in accordance with domestic law if such resident is subject to a special tax regime with respect to interest in its Contracting State of residence at any time during the taxable period in which the interest is paid.'

(BEPS Final Report on Action 6, p 98)

A 'special tax regime' does not just refer to the rates of tax charge, but also to special tax deductions that might be granted, eg for notional interest as opposed to interest actually incurred. The OECD's definition, to be included in Article 3 in the OECD MTC, is:

> 'the term "special tax regime" with respect to an item of income or profit means any legislation, regulation or administrative practice that provides a preferential effective rate of taxation to such income or profit, including through reductions in the tax rate or the tax base. With regard to financing income, the term special tax regime includes notional interest deductions that are allowed without regard to liabilities for such interest'.

> [A number of exceptions follow, including regimes which do not disproportionately benefit interest, royalties or other income and regimes which are subject to a substantial activity requirement although financing income is excluded from this exception.]

At the time of writing, there are no plans to introduce a special tax regime clause into the Multilateral Instrument.

---

1   For a detailed discussion of the 2016 US Model STR clause, see Borrego (2017).

A discretionary test

15.33   If all these tests are failed, both the US MTC and the Action 6 recommendation include a final 'motive' test so that treaty benefits can still be claimed by a person even though it is not a qualifying person. The tax authority in question would have to be convinced that:

- the establishment, acquisition or maintenance of the resident; and

- the conduct of its operations did not have as one of their principal purposes the obtaining of benefits under the treaty.

As with the 'active business' test, this test is subjective.

Limitation of benefits in the UK–US Treaty – link to the dividends article

15.34   The most recent DTT between the US and the UK entered into force on 24 July 2001 and for the first time included a limitation of benefits clause. Following the experience of the Netherlands after the treaty with the US introduced in 1992 resulted in the loss of business from the Netherlands, the limitation of benefits article in the US–Netherlands Treaty was subsequently toned down considerably. During the negotiations, the UK negotiators apparently ought a more favourable limitation of benefits clause which allowed benefits to be preserved for EU companies. According to Dodwell (2001):[1]

> 'for the first time in any US treaty, there is a complete exemption from withholding tax on certain dividends. In general the exemption applies to dividends paid to UK resident shareholders that have owned shares

representing at least 80% of the voting power of the payer for the 12 months period ending on the date on which the dividend is declared and which satisfy one of the following:

- the 80% ownership test has been met (directly or indirectly) since before 1 October 1998; or

- certain condition[s] of the LOB clause are met.'

Note that 80 per cent ownership is the standard generally adopted in US treaties for exemption from withholding tax. The treaty contains detailed provisions for defining ownership percentages for determining qualified persons and also contains a 'conduit route' rule. As Dodwell further notes:

'This sort of treaty could probably only have been entered into by the UK and the US, reflecting the close working relationship between the two authorities, who meet frequently and exchange considerable amounts of information. This treaty will no doubt help the revenue authorities of both countries in reducing the number of one-sided tax deductions available. Tax planners are now firmly on notice that in some cases it is more effective to shut down tax planning through treaties rather than through amendments to domestic laws.'

Even so, the UK–US Treaty limitation of benefits clause goes much further than such clauses in the UK's other tax treaties, in that it applies to benefits under the treaty generally. Normally, the limitation of benefits clauses apply only to specific articles such as those dealing with dividends, interest and royalties and are targeted at specific abuses.

---

1   Dodwell B, 'Significant UK-US Treaty Agreed', *Tax Adviser*, October 2001.

BEPS ACTION 6: PRINCIPAL PURPOSES TEST

15.35   Despite the seemingly exhaustive nature of the objective limitation on benefits test just analysed, the OECD is of the opinion that countries might like to further strengthen their defences against treaty abuse by including a general anti-treaty article in their treaties. Some countries might prefer just to incorporate the much simpler-looking general anti-abuse rule in their treaties rather than a series of complex objective tests. The recommended wording for such a test in the Final Report on BEPS Action 6 is:

'Notwithstanding the other provisions of this Convention, a benefit under this Convention shall not be granted in respect of an item of income or capital if it is reasonable to conclude, having regard to all relevant facts and circumstances, that obtaining that benefit was one of the principal purposes of any arrangement or transaction that resulted directly or indirectly in that benefit, unless it is established that granting that benefit in these circumstances would be in accordance with the object and purpose of the relevant provisions of this Convention.'

This test could be used to deny treaty benefits even where the same treaty contains an objective limitation on benefits test and the taxpayer in question is a 'qualified person'. For instance, it could be applied where a public company, resident in Country X, whose shares are regularly traded on a recognized stock exchange applies for treaty benefits – eg a reduced rate of withholding tax – under the treaty between Countries X and Y. If that company was a bank which had entered into financial arrangements intended to help a resident, Mr P, of a third country, Country Z (ie not one of the Contracting States party to the treaty concerned) to obtain a reduced rate of withholding tax on payments to Mr P from Country Y, then this general anti-abuse provision would enable Country Y to deny the treaty benefit and charge its full domestic rate of withholding tax.[1]

A 'principal purpose' is defined in the negative sense. A purpose will not be a principal purpose where it is reasonable to conclude, taking into account all the relevant facts and circumstances that obtaining the treaty benefit:

- was not a principal consideration; and

- would not have justified entering into any arrangement or transaction that has resulted in, or contributed towards, the benefit.

It is not possible to sidestep the principal purposes test by saying that you were trying to obtain benefits to which you were not really entitled under a large number of treaties, so that obtaining a benefit under one particular treaty, say between Countries X and Y, was not a principal purpose.

The Final Report on Action 6 presents a number of examples on when the principal purposes test might or might not be failed. These include the following:

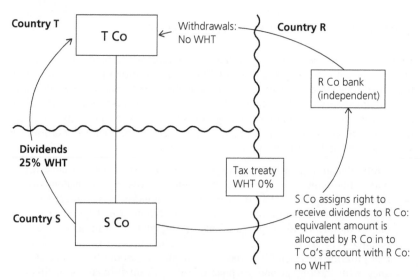

Figure 15.8: Final Report on Action 6 derived diagrammatic examples: on when the 'principal purposes test' might or might not be failed

In this scenario, there is no tax treaty between Countries T and S. Country S charges 25 per cent WHT on the payment of dividends to non-residents under its domestic law. T Co wishes to avoid this tax. Country S has a DTT with Country R, under which there is no WHT on the payment of dividends. T Co arranges with R Co, an unconnected bank, for the dividends due to T Co to be assigned to R Co. In return, T Co's account with R Co is credit with an amount equivalent to the dividends. The arrangements have somehow been made so that R Co is regarded as the beneficial owner of the dividends. Result:

- No WHT when the dividends are paid by S Co to R Co.

- No WHT when T Co withdraws the cash equivalent of the dividends from its account with R Co – this is regarded as a withdrawal of funds from a bank account, not income.

- Note that the Action 6 Final Report also supplies a more detailed example along these lines which better explains how this type of arrangement might be set up so that R Co is the beneficial owner of the dividends.

In this scenario, the principal purpose of the arrangements is for T Co to abuse the treaty between Country R and Country S. If the treaty includes the new 'principal purposes' test, then S Co would be justified in refusing to allow the dividends to be paid to R Co without WHT and could charge its normal domestic rate of WHT of 25 per cent.

Figure 15.9 illustrates a different kind of treaty abuse: rather than treaty shopping, abuse of rules within the treaty itself, in this case, the PE definition.

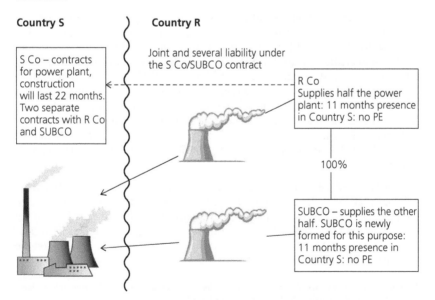

Figure 15.9: Joint and several liability under the S Co/SUBCO contract

In this scenario, all the parties involved are residents in either Country S or country R and can therefore rely on the treaty between Country S and Country R. This Treaty states, in Article 5, that a resident of the other Contracting State will be treated as having a PE in that State if it has a construction site there for a period longer than 12 months. Under Country S domestic law, it would normally treat a foreign construction firm as having a PE in Country S if it is present there for more than six months. Let us assume that the effective rate of tax in Country S is higher than in Country R, so that R Co does not want to have a PE in Country S.

S Co wishes to enter into a contract with R Co for the supply of a power station. This will take 22 months to build, so that R Co would have a PE in Country S. It would have to pay Country S tax on the profits it makes from this venture and even allowing for double tax relief in Country R, its worldwide effective rate of tax would be increased. To avoid having a PE in Country S, R Co incorporates a new subsidiary company, SUBCO, also resident in Country R. R Co and SUBCO each contract separately with S Co to supply half the power plant each, which means that R Co will have a construction site in Country S for only 11 months. SUBCO will also have a construction site in Country S for 11 months. Neither of them will have a PE there, as neither of them would have a construction site in Country S lasting more than 12 months. An added element of artificiality is present: S Co insists that R Co take full responsibility for the whole project and so R Co accepts joint and several liability for the contract between SUBCO and S Co. This means that if anything goes wrong between SUBCO and S Co, R Co will have to step in and put it right, bearing any costs.

Since there are elements of artificiality in the arrangements – the fact that SUBCO is newly formed for this purpose, and the joint and several liability assumed by R Co, it is likely that the principal purpose of splitting up the contract was to artificially avoid a PE in Country S, Country S can use the 'principal purposes' test to ignore the promise made in the Treaty only to recognize a construction if it exists for more than 12 months. Instead, Country S can use whatever rules on PEs it has in its domestic law. In this case, because Country S domestic law is that foreign construction firms will be treated as having PEs in Country S if they are present for more than six months, Country S can tax the whole of the net profits of both R Co and SUBCO from their contracts with S Co.

The Germany–Australia DTT, signed on 12 November 2015 and effective from 1 January 2017, includes in both the title and preamble express reference to the prevention of tax avoidance as a purpose of the treaty and clarifies that the treaty will not create opportunities for treaty shopping. The limitation of benefits provision in Article 23 includes a principal purpose test.[2] The US, on the other hand, remains opposed to the concept of a principal purpose test.

---

1   For a discussion of whether the principal purpose test conforms with the principle of legal certainty under EU law and elsewhere, see Cunha (2016).
2   See Maurer et al (2017) for more detail.

The UN Model Tax Convention

15.36   In the 2011 update, the Commentary on Article 1 of the UN MTC was significantly expanded to deal with the improper use of treaties, following a programme of work on the topic which began around 2005. As well as discussing the various approaches to combating improper use of treaties in theory, as per the OECD MTC, the Commentary helpfully sets out a number of examples. Baker (2012) criticizes the content of the examples for not tackling some of the known practices of wide scale tax avoidance being used by multinational groups, such as hybrid entities and hybrid instruments. However, it does offer the following example of the use of derivatives to circumvent withholding taxes:

> 'Derivative transactions can allow taxpayers to obtain the economic effects of certain financial transactions under a different legal form. For instance, depending on the treaty provisions and domestic law of each country, a taxpayer may obtain treaty benefits such as no or reduced source taxation when it is in fact in the same economic position as a foreign investor in shares of a local company. Assume, for instance, that company X, a resident of State A, wants to make a large portfolio investment in the shares of a company resident in State B, while company Y, a resident in State B, wants to acquire bonds issued by the government of State A. In order to avoid the cross-border payments of dividends and interest, which would attract withholding taxes, company X may instead acquire the bonds issued in its country and company Y may acquire the shares of the company resident in its country that company X wanted to acquire. Companies X and Y would then enter into a swap arrangement under which they would agree to make swap payments to each other based on the difference between the dividends and interest flows that they receive each year; they would also enter into future contracts to buy from each other the shares and bonds at some future time. Through these transactions, the taxpayers would have mirrored the economic position of cross-border investments in the shares and bonds without incurring the liability to source withholding taxes (except to the extent that the swap payments, which would only represent the difference between the flows of dividends and interest, would be subject to such taxes under Article 21 and the domestic law of each country).'[1]

---

1   Commentary on Article 1 of the UN Model Tax Convention at para 93.

CHANGE TO THE TIE-BREAKER RULE FOR COMPANY RESIDENCE

15.37   As discussed in Chapter 4, for many years the test used to allocate a company that is resident under the domestic law of both of the Contracting States to a treaty to just one of those Contracting States has been to look for the place of effective management. This tie-breaker test can also be applied to any other type of entity, but not to individuals. However, it has been found that cases of dual resident companies, and other entities are more common than was the case when the 'place of effective management' tie-breaker test was introduced. According to the OECD, the view of many countries is that where companies are dual-resident (ie resident under the domestic law of more than one country) this is likely to be a deliberate state of affairs, and to be linked to tax avoidance arrangements, such as offsetting the same tax loss against taxable profits twice, in each of the countries.

Under the new rules, in paragraph 3 of Article 4, the application of a tax treaty to a company or other entity which is resident in both of the Contracting States will be dealt with on a case-by-case basis. Thus, if State A and State B enter into a treaty and subsequently a dual resident company applies for benefits, such as a low rate of withholding tax, under the treaty, then the tax authorities in State A and State B will have to consult together to decide whether this should be allowed or not. If they think that the reason for the company's dual residence is to avoid tax in either or both of their countries, they can refuse to give the benefit of the treaty to it.

The precise wording of the new test and the accompanying Commentary is analysed in more detail in Chapter 4.

THE INDIA–MAURITIUS DOUBLE TAX TREATY

15.38   For many years, this treaty has facilitated the flow of investment into India (apparently accounting for 36 per cent of such investment in 2014).[1] To put this into context, the Mauritian economy, measured by GDP is about 150th the size of India's, which renders the flow of FID from Mauritius rather extraordinary at first glance. This treaty permits only the country of residence to tax capital gains. Mauritius domestic law does not tax capital gains, so a foreign investor (say, resident in Ruritania, a country that we assume to tax capital gains) who wishes to make an investment into India simply sets up a company in Mauritius, and invests via that company. When the Mauritius company sells the Indian investment, there is no tax on the capital gain either in India or Mauritius. This gives investors valuable protection from the rather draconian source taxation regime which applies under Indian domestic tax law and under many of India's other tax treaties. Indian domestic law provides that non-residents making gains on the sale of shares in Indian companies are taxed at rates of up to 40 per cent. This is enforced partly by a requirement that the buyer must withhold the tax due from the sales proceeds and pay it over to the Indian Tax Office. However, if a Mauritian company sells shares in an Indian company, there is no tax on the capital gain in either country.

India appeared to accept treaty shopping under the India–Mauritius Treaty as a price to be paid for a continuing flow of foreign investment. In the *Azadi Bachao Andolan*[2] case this was clearly acknowledged by the Indian court which quoted from a leading author on international taxation:

'Overall, countries need to take, and do take, a holistic view. The developing countries allow treaty shopping to encourage capital and technology inflows, which developed countries are keen to provide to them. The loss of tax revenues could be insignificant compared to the other non-tax benefits to their economy. Many of them do not appear to be too concerned unless the revenue losses are significant compared to the other tax and non-tax benefits from the treaty, or the treaty shopping leads to other tax abuses.'

(Roy Rohtagi, *Basic International Taxation*, pp 373–74, Kluwer Law International.)

The judge went on to give this famous quote:

'There are many principles in fiscal economy which, though at first blush might appear to be evil, are tolerated in a developing economy, in the interest of long-term development. Deficit financing, for example, is one; treaty shopping, in our view, is another. Despite the sound and fury of the respondents over the so-called "abuse" of "treaty shopping", perhaps, it may have been intended at the time when the Indo–Mauritius DTAC was entered into. Whether it should continue, and, if so, for how long, is a matter which is best left to the discretion of the executive as it is dependent upon several economic and political considerations. This court cannot judge the legality of treaty shopping merely because one section of thought considers it improper. A holistic view has to be taken to adjudge what is perhaps regarded in contemporary thinking as a necessary evil in a developing economy.'

Treaty shopping via the India–Mauritius Treaty was again under threat in a ruling given in 2009 by the Indian Authority for Advance Rulings, *E*Trade Mauritius*.[3] In this case, a US company had sold shares in an Indian company to HSBC. The sale had been effected indirectly, through Mauritian companies, as shown in the diagram below. E*Trade Mauritius had requested a ruling from the Indian tax authority that the India–Mauritius treaty would apply so that it would not suffer Indian tax on the gain and also so that the purchaser (the Mauritian subsidiary of HSBC) could pay over the sales proceeds to E*Trade Mauritius without having to withhold tax on account of any tax liability on the gain and pay the tax withheld to the Indian tax authority. The only requirement that E*Trade Mauritius had to fulfil was to hold a certificate of residency in Mauritius. The Indian tax authority had previously stated that such a certificate would be accepted as proof that a company was resident in Mauritius and was the beneficial owner of income or sales proceeds paid to it.

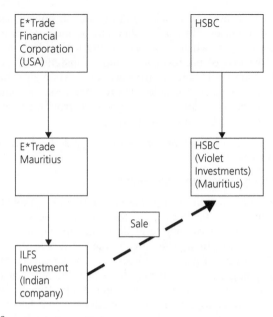

Figure 15.10

Possibly because of the amount of the tax at stake (over US$5 million) the Indian Tax Authority decided to 'have a go' and directed the purchaser to deposit about US$5 million with the court. The Indian Tax Authority argued that E*Trade Mauritius was not the beneficial owner of the sales proceeds. The evidence for this was that the sale had been negotiated by the US parent, the share sale agreement was not signed by any employee or director of E*Trade Mauritius and the dividends received on the shareholding by E*Trade Mauritius had been effectively paid on to the US parent, which had provided the funds for the purchase of the shares by E*Trade Mauritius in the first place. However, the Indian Authority for Advance Rulings found in favour of the taxpayers and ruled that E*Trade Mauritius should be given the benefit of the treaty so that the gains were not taxable in India (and, of course, not taxed by Mauritius). The Authority for Advance Rules declined to question whether a certificate of residency in Mauritius really signified beneficial ownership of the sales proceeds by E*Trade and dismissed any notion that the fact that E*Trade Mauritius had received funds from the US parent to buy the shares and had remitted amounts representing the dividends back to the US parent signified any lack of beneficial ownership. Thus the stance of the Indian courts towards treaty shopping in *Azadi Bachao Andolan* was preserved.

Although the rulings in these cases suggest that the Indian courts believe that treaty abuse should be accepted by India as the price for the flow of inward foreign investment, the India GAAR, enacted in 2012, is now being used to deny treaty benefits under the India–Mauritius Treaty on the grounds that the arrangements concerning the Mauritius SPV lack economic substance. There is evidence that the GAAR is having a deterrent effect, apart from successes of the Indian Tax Authority in actual cases involving the GAAR and the India–Mauritius Tax Treaty. Interestingly, it appears that the 1994 India–Singapore Treaty may be taking the place of the India–Mauritius Treaty in facilitating foreign direct investment (FDI) into India, through giving a similar protection from tax on capital gains. Sharma (2012) explains that a limitation of benefits clause inserted into this Treaty in 2005, surprisingly, protects the Singapore SPV from tax on capital gains provided the annual expenditure in India exceeds a monetary limit in the two years preceding the date that the capital gains arise. India can only tax the capital gains of the Singapore SPV, using the limitation of benefits clause, if inward investment in the two years prior to the gain falls short of the limit. This limitation of benefits clause effectively protects large inward investors using a Singapore SPV from the application of India's GAAR.

---

1   Department of Industrial Policy & Promotion, *Fact Sheet on Foreign Direct Investment (FDI) From April, 2000 to May, 2014.* Available at dipp.nic.in/English/Publications/FDI.../india_FDI_March2014.pdf.
2   *Union of India v Azadi Bachao Andolan* 263 ITR 607 (SC).
3   *E*Trade Mauritius Ltd* (AAR No. 826 of 2009).

Future of the India–Mauritius Treaty as a conduit for investment into India

15.39   India has recently enacted general anti-avoidance legislation which would, in theory, enable it to deny the benefits of the treaty in cases of treaty abuse. However, the use of Mauritian holding companies (or, indeed, holding companies in any tax haven) was held not to be impermissible tax avoidance so that treaty benefits would not be denied in *Vodafone International Holdings BV* (2012).[1]

In May 2016, however, the Indian and Mauritian governments signed a protocol to modify their DTT.[2] With effect from the 2017/18 financial year, capital gains arising from the transfer or shares will be taxed at the full domestic rate, subject to a transition phase during which 50 per cent of the domestic rate will apply. The new limitation of benefits clause contains a 'main purpose' and a 'bona fide business' test.[3]

---

1   *Vodafone International Holdings v Union of India* (2012) 341 ITR 1.
2   For the press release announcing the Protocol, see www.incometaxindia.gov.in/Lists/Press%20Releases/Attachments/468/Press-release-Indo-Mauritius-10-05-2016.pdf.
3   For a discussion, see Bose (2017).

Targeted anti-abuse provisions found in existing treaties

15.40   As all of the suggested methods could potentially affect innocent taxpayers not involved in conduit operations at all, some supplementary test is desirable. Examples of supplementary tests are given below.

A 'general motive' test:

> '10. The provisions of this Article shall not apply, with the exception of paragraph 9, if it was the main purpose or one of the main purposes of any person concerned with the creation or the transfer of the debt-claim for which interest is paid to take advantage of this Article by means of that creation or that transfer.'

> (Article 11, France–Japan Treaty as amended by 2007 Protocol para 10.)

A 'business activity' test:

Alternatively, it could take the form of a test that looks at the business activity of the suspected conduit to see whether it is really a genuine and active business:

> 'Article 27

> Limitation on benefits

> Notwithstanding any other provisions of this Convention, where:

> a company that is a resident of a Contracting State derives its income primarily from other States

> (a)   from activities such as banking, shipping, financing or insurance; or

> (b)   from being the headquarters, co-ordination centre or similar entity providing administrative services or other support to a group of companies which carry on business primarily in other States; and

> (c)   except for the application of the method of elimination of double taxation normally applied by that State, such income would bear a significantly lower tax under the laws of that State than income from similar activities carried out within that State or from being the headquarters, co-ordination centre or similar entity providing administrative services or other support to a group of companies which carry on business in that State, as the case may be

> any provisions of this Convention conferring an exemption or a reduction of tax shall not apply to the income of such company and to the dividends paid by such company.'

> (Poland–Sweden Treaty 2004.)

A detailed 'subject to tax' test. A test which looks at the relative amounts of tax saved under the treaty benefits and the tax bill paid by the suspected conduit company in the state where it is resident:

> 'The exemption provided under subparagraph (b) of paragraph 3 of Article 12 (*exemption from withholding tax on royalties*) shall not apply where the enterprise benefiting from the royalties has, in a State which is not a Contracting State, a permanent establishment to which

the royalties are attributable and where the royalties are subject, in the State of residence of the enterprise and in the State where the permanent establishment is situated, to a tax the total of which is less than 60 per cent of the tax that would be imposed in the State of residence of the enterprise if the royalties were attributable to the enterprise and not to the permanent establishment. The provisions of this paragraph shall not apply:

(a) if the royalties are derived in connection with or incidental to the active conduct of a trade or business carried on in the state which is not a Contracting State; or

(b) when Belgium is the State of residence of the enterprise, to royalties taxed by Canada according to section 91 of the Income Tax Act, as it may be amended without changing the general principle hereof.

(Article 27, para 5, Canada–Belgium Treaty 2002.)

An 'equivalent benefits' test within the dividends, interest or royalties articles:

An 'equivalent benefits' provision so that the anti-conduit clause will not apply if the person ultimately benefiting from payments from the suspected conduit could have claimed benefits equally as good had he dealt directly with the state in which the suspected conduit is resident:

'5. A resident of a Contracting State shall not be considered the actual beneficial owner of royalties collected for the use of intangible assets, when the payment of such royalties to the resident was subject to the payment of royalties by the latter, for the same intangible assets, to a person:

(a) not entitled, in connection with the royalties originating from the other Contracting State, to benefits at least equivalent to those granted by this Convention to a resident of the first Contracting State; and

(b) that is not a resident of either Contracting State.'

(Article 12, France–Japan Treaty as amended by the 2007 Protocol, para 5.)

FURTHER READING

Arnold & MacIntyre (2002) *International Tax Primer*, Kluwer Law International.

Baker, P (2013) 'Improper Use of Tax Treaties, Tax Avoidance and Tax Evasion' Paper No. 9-A, United Nations Papers on Selected Topics in Administration of Tax Treaties for Developing Countries. Available at www.un.org/esa/ffd/tax/2013TMTTAN/Paper9A_Baker.pdf.

Baker, P (2015) 'The BEPS Action Plan in the Light of EU Law: Treaty Abuse', *British Tax Review* 3, pp 408–16.

Baker, P and Liao, T (2012) 'Improper Use of Tax Treaties: The New Commentary on Article 1 and the amended Article 13(5)', 66 *Bulletin for International Taxation* 598.

Borrego, F A V (2017) 'The Special Tax Regimes Clause in the 2016 U.S. Model Income Tax Convention' *Intertax*, 45(4), 296.

Bose, D (2017) 'From Lax to Tax: India's changing policy on overseas taxation' *Intertax*, 45(4), 341.

Cunha, R C (2016) 'BEPS Action 6: Uncertainty in the Principal Purpose Test Rule' *Global Taxation* Volume 1, 186.

De Broe, L, Bammens, N (2010) 'Treaty Shopping and Avoidance of Abuse' in *Tax Treaties: Building Bridges Between Law and Economics*, pp 52–72, eds M Lang et al, IBFD 2010.

De Broe et al (2011) 'Tax Treaties and Tax Avoidance: Application of Anti-Avoidance Provisions', *Bulletin for International Taxation* 2011, Vol 65, No 7.

Dodwell, B (2001) 'Significant UK-US Treaty Agreed', *Tax Adviser*, October 2001.

Elliffe, C (2011) 'International Tax Avoidance – the Tension Between Protecting the Tax Base and Certainty of Law', *Journal of Business Law* 7, pp 647–65.

Hanna, C (2005) 'From Enron to Gregory: The Too Perfect Theory and Tax Law', *Virginia Tax Review*, 24(4), pp 737–96.

Kandev, M N (2008) 'Treaty Shopping in Canada: The Door is (Still) Open', *Bulletin for International Taxation*, October 2008, p 463.

Malik, G, Singhania, S (2010) 'India Casenote – The E*Trade Decision', *Asia-Pacific Tax Bulletin*, 2010, Vol 16, No 4.

Maurer, L, Port, C, Roth, T & Walker, J (2017) 'A Brave New Post BEPS world: New Double Tax Treaty between Germany and Australia Implements BEPS Measures' *Intertax*, 45(4), 301.

OECD (2014) Model Tax Convention on Income and Capital, July 2014 Condensed Version.

OECD (2015) 'Preventing the Granting of Treaty Benefits in Inappropriate Circumstances, Action 6 2015 Final Report'.

Palao Taboada, C (2015) 'OECD Base Erosion and Profit Shifting Action 6: The General Anti-Abuse Rule', 69, *Bulletin for International Taxation*, 10.

Schwarz, J (2013) *Schwarz on Tax Treaties*, 3rd edn, CCH: London.

Sharma, P (2012) 'The Intentional Use of the India–Mauritius (1982) and India–Singapore (1994) Tax Treaties to Promote Foreign Direct Investment in India', 66, *Bulletin for International Taxation*, 12.

US Department of the Treasury (2015) '2015 Proposed Revisions to US Model Tax Convention'. Available at: www.treasury.gov/resource-center/tax-policy/treaties/Pages/international.aspx.

Van Weeghel, S (1998) *The Improper Use of Tax Treaties*, Kluwer Law International, London.

Wheeler, J (2011) 'The Missing Keystone of Income Tax Treaties', *World Tax Journal* 2011, Vol 3, No 2 (NB: in this extensive article, the author proposes an entirely new approach to establishing entitlement to treaty benefits).

Chapter 16

Introduction to Tax Havens

BASICS

16.1   This chapter attempts to give the reader some background to the nature of tax havens and how and to what extent they are used. Broadly speaking, multinational groups tend to use tax havens to reduce and defer the payment of tax on their profits by legal means, whilst individuals are more likely to attempt to illegally evade taxes by concealing their assets and income in tax havens.

The existence of tax havens offers tax-planning opportunities for multinational groups of companies to reduce their average worldwide tax rate. Whilst tax havens can be used as a base for manufacturing operations they are more usually used as a locations for bank deposits and intellectual property (IP), insurance business and other business involving mobile capital. Many tax havens are found in the Caribbean, and several have historical connections with the UK.

Due to of the ease of transfer of money and documentation, tax havens are often heavily involved in banking business. However, not all major banking centres are tax havens. The largest offshore banking centre, the Cayman Islands, is a well-known tax haven but, along with many other traditional tax havens, has come under increased scrutiny from supra-national bodies such as the OECD, and has been forced to relax its banking secrecy to some extent.

The 1981 Gordon Report named the key characteristics of tax havens. There are three main types of tax havens – the traditional or 'base' tax havens, charging little or no tax, treaty havens, and concession havens. Since the tax regimes of nearly every country contain concessions which could be considered to be a means of competing for international business most countries are, to some degree or other, tax havens.

When providing its tax residents with relief from double taxation, a country will want to ensure that they are not avoiding tax entirely. If a country chooses the exemption method in its simple form, this could lead to no tax at all being paid on income arising outside the country of residence, in a tax haven. Thus, most systems of double tax relief will contain provisions limiting relief when overseas income arises in tax havens. However, most countries also go further than this and have legislation which treats income arising in a tax haven as if it arose in the country of residence of the shareholder. This form of anti-haven legislation, controlled foreign companies legislation, is examined in some detail in Chapter 15.

The growth of tax haven usage in the latter quarter of the twentieth century is the subject of considerable debate. KPMG noted that in a 2006 poll of senior tax executives from 120 multinational corporations, 62 per cent reported that they were planning to move assets or operations to low-tax regimes. Further, 14 per cent said they had already moved part of their operations to a lower tax regime in response to more aggressive tax-planning challenges from tax authorities, the US being the most aggressive, followed by the UK and Germany. A report from the US Government Accountability Office in December 2008[1] found that 83 of the 100 largest corporations in the US had subsidiaries in offshore tax havens in 2007. Although there was some dissent as to how the list of tax havens was compiled, the report provides one of the more trustworthy sources of information regarding the use of tax havens by multinational companies. One corporation was reported as having 427 subsidiaries in tax havens.

This raises interesting questions about the way in which governments of developed nations manage the use and alleged abuse of tax havens. In this chapter we will clarify the nature and prevalence of tax havens and briefly examine the extent of their use. Chapter 17 will then examine forms of legislation adopted by many countries to combat the use of tax havens for tax avoidance. In Chapter 18 we will then continue the analysis of tax havens by examining measures to curb the use of tax havens for illegitimate purposes (eg tax evasion).

---

1 Large US Corporations and Federal Contractors with Subsidiaries in Jurisdictions Listed as Tax Havens or Financial Privacy Jurisdictions, GAO-09-157 December 2008. Available at: www.gao.gov/new.items/d09157.pdf.

RATIONALE FOR THE USE OF TAX HAVENS

16.2 A multinational enterprise (MNE) setting up abroad using a 100 per cent-owned subsidiary has considerable influence over the amount of profits declared by that subsidiary: transfer prices, royalties, and interest charged, and management charges can all be manipulated to some extent without causing the subsidiary to be considered tax resident in the parent company's country.

Generally, an MNE will aim to minimize the worldwide tax burden of the group by:

● seeking to limit the amount of taxable income arising in high-tax jurisdictions;

● preventing or delaying earnings and/or investment income from entering high-tax jurisdictions by 'parking' them in a very low-tax country until needed elsewhere within the group; and

- siting operations (especially financial operations) in low-tax countries wherever possible to reduce the MNE's average tax rate on its worldwide profits.

The result is that the 'foreign tax credit' mechanism is no longer efficient as a means of ensuring equity between the taxation of earnings abroad and at home. If profits are not repatriated from low-tax countries then MNEs have a tax advantage over firms operating solely in the domestic market. Put another way, firms may bear low tax rates abroad, but never bring the money back to their home (and high tax) countries. The result is that overseas investment is financed mainly out of retained earnings or foreign borrowings as the MNE recycles the foreign profits outside its home country.

Tax havens are used mainly to shelter portfolio income and gains as opposed to profits and gains from foreign direct investment. This is mainly because portfolio income is more mobile and because most tax havens do not have the infrastructure to support or attract foreign direct investment such as manufacturing plants. The factors influencing the location decisions of firms were briefly considered in Chapter 2.

What is a tax haven?

16.3 When asked to identify tax havens, most people automatically think of small islands, possibly in the Caribbean. However, whilst many Caribbean islands do operate to some extent as tax havens, we must examine the properties of tax havens to make a more considered judgement. We should note that by acting as a tax haven, in whatever shape or form, a country is competing for business. Countries use their tax systems to attract business and particularly to attract mobile capital. In some cases tax havens charge hardly any tax, in others they charge a rate which they judge to be lower than that charged by competitor countries.

Countries generally recognized as tax havens often prefer to be described as offshore financial centres. The distinction between a tax haven and an offshore financial centre can be difficult but it is probably true to say that whilst all tax havens are offshore financial centres, not all offshore financial centres are tax havens. For instance, London is an important offshore financial centre but one would not normally think of the UK as a tax haven. Offshore financial centres are jurisdictions in which transactions with non-residents far outweigh transactions related to the domestic economy (Dixon 2001). They have some or all of the following attractions: favourable tax regime, favourable legal environment, and a favourable regulatory system. Although the tax system will inevitably play some part in their popularity, those offshore financial centres which are not primarily tax havens use these other attractions to bring in business. For instance, a favourable legal environment may permit MNEs to adopt new financial products quickly and flexibly.

The Gordon Report, prepared for the US Treasury in 1981, listed certain characteristics of a tax haven:

- Low or nil tax on some or all types of income and capital.

- Secrecy: banking and/or commercial. This provides opportunities not only for tax avoidance but for tax evasion. The OECD term that includes banking secrecy is 'lack of effective exchange of information' and/or 'lack of transparency'.

- Absence of exchange controls.

- Provision of offshore banking facilities.

- Good communication facilities. ?

- Political stability: offshore investors in Panama had a nasty shock in 1988 where there was a crisis involving the president being indicted of narcotics offences. This prompted sanctions by the US government and, eventually, invasion.

- Opportunity for multilateral tax planning.

- Favourable disposition to foreign capital.

- Availability of professional advisers.

- Convenient location, good climate for communications and to attract staff. (Hence the traditional attraction of the Caribbean for US taxpayers.)

In addition, freedom from excessive regulation is an important factor, particularly for the offshore insurance sector. Jersey is well known for this type of business. On a general definition, Gordon had this to say:

> 'The term "tax haven" has been loosely defined to include any country having a low or zero rate of tax on all or certain categories of income, and offering a certain level of banking or commercial secrecy .... The term "tax haven" may also be defined by a "smell" or reputation test: a country is a tax haven if it looks like one and if it is considered to be one by those who care.'

One study (Dharmapala and Hines 2009) indicates that tax havens actually tend to have stronger governance institutions than comparable non-haven countries (ie better legal and political systems). Many of them are small islands, on average more affluent than non-havens and have relatively sophisticated communications facilities.

Zielke (2011) considers that the role of tax havens has altered over the past decade due to the activities of the OECD and the G20 and that the defining characteristic of a tax haven nowadays is that it enables an MNE to enjoy a low effective rate of taxation.

Types of tax havens

16.4   According to Kudrle (2003) tax havens perform three types of functions. They may:

1   *produce* goods and services;

2   *shift* tax claims among jurisdictions; and

3   *hide* tax claims.

Frequently, however, they combine these functions. There are many ways of classifying tax havens, and again, tax havens often fall into more than one classification. Within each classification, there are subcategories but the four main types are outlined below.

Production havens

16.5   A production haven is where real activity is transferred to the tax haven: things are made there and there is tangible value added. Ireland, with its 12.5 per cent corporation tax rate is a good example. Ireland has attracted a great deal of foreign investment in manufacturing through its tax policy (see Killian (2006) and Tobin and Walsh (2013)).

Base havens

16.6   Base havens are those with no/very low taxes on all business income – these are usually colonies or former colonies of onshore jurisdictions. For instance, the EU 'Code of Conduct' on tax competition, discussed in Chapter 18, identified no fewer than 17 tax havens associated with the UK which mostly fall under this heading. These are sometimes referred to as *sham havens*. More often than not, base havens are small islands with few natural resources and limited labour. Most of the Caribbean and Pacific tax havens fall into this category. The lack of labour, land and infrastructure generally rules out the location of manufacturing or large-scale distribution operations although there are notable exceptions, such as Specsaver Plc's extensive operations on Guernsey. US companies also carry out substantial manufacturing operations on the island of Puerto Rico, which, although technically a part of the US, is not subject to US federal taxes.

These havens do not usually have many double tax treaties (DTT) so they are unsuitable for intermediate holding companies because payments to the tax haven would incur high withholding taxes. Most base havens are also *secrecy havens* although some countries with substantive tax systems, such as Switzerland and Luxembourg, also act to some extent as secrecy havens. Due to inevitable links with money laundering, base havens, and particularly those also widely recognized to be acting as secrecy havens, are coming under increasing pressure to conform to international standards of disclosure and co-operation, as discussed in Chapter 18.

Treaty havens

16.7   These are countries, such as the Netherlands, with very favourable networks of DTTs. They are particularly suitable for intermediate holding companies. The benefits of treaty havens are low withholding taxes on money flowing into and out of the haven, often no tax while it remains there and no withholding tax when it flows back out again.

Concession havens

16.8   This term applies to countries offering particular tax incentives or benefits (eg Swiss branch of a Netherlands company, Belgian co-ordination centres). These have increased in popularity in recent years and now present a real problem for the major trading nations in their attempts to curb the use of tax havens. There are many types of concession haven and in fact the Belgian example might come under a subset of concession havens, would-be *'headquarters'* havens.

Thus a country may have a traditional tax system but still act as a haven. Most countries operate as concession havens to some extent, even the UK and the US. However, some countries offer more concessions than others. It might be argued that the Netherlands is a good example of a concessions haven.

GROWTH OF THE OFFSHORE FINANCIAL SECTOR

Early history[1]

16.9   Historically, tax havens were used primarily by wealthy individuals. However, in the latter half of the twentieth century, their use by MNEs became widespread. One of the first offshore financial centres was the Netherlands Antilles which from 1953 onwards has benefited from an excellent range of tax treaties extended to it by the Netherlands. It also announced low tax rates specifically designed to attract intermediate holding companies of MNEs. Such activities are seen as a good way of attracting financial business and boosting the economy.

A strong explanation for the growth in the sector is over-regulation and over-taxation in OECD economies in the post-war years (Kurdle, 2003). In the early 1960s there was a balance of payments crisis in the US and this was viewed by some as being at least partly due to the investment by US multinationals in foreign subsidiaries, which made it necessary for the government to limit the amount of investment capital which could leave the country. The Interest Equalization Tax, introduced in 1963, was designed to halt outflow of US portfolio investments towards the higher interest rates available in Europe. The US introduced a number of sets of rules in the mid-1960s, in particular the Voluntary Foreign Credit Restraint Program and the Offices of Foreign Direct Investment regulations. The thrust of these regulations was a requirement for

US persons investing abroad to do their borrowing to finance overseas expansion abroad in order to maintain positive payments balances.

Added to this, the US banking sector was heavily regulated in its domestic market. For instance, banks were unable to charge interest on deposits made for under 30 days. This pattern of archaic and distortionary regulation was also found in the major European economies but often working in the opposite direction, such that foreign lenders were constrained as to the amounts they could lend or deposit in European countries. The result was that a large tranche of US money and capital markets moved offshore. The use of offshore financial centres was also being facilitated by a general relaxation in regulations governing the holding of deposits and other investments in foreign currencies.

In the 1950s only a few US banks had offshore branches and, until the mid-1960s, London was the principal location for US funds held overseas and for overseas branches of US banks. However, the combined effects of measures designed by the US to discourage US corporate investors from investing in Europe, and measures designed by European governments to discourage foreign investors from investing in Europe[2] opened the way for alternative locations to establish themselves as offshore financial centres.

By 1975, according to the 1981 Gordon Report, 125 US banks had 732 foreign branches in total, mainly in the Caribbean. The Gordon Report showed that in 1968 assets of banking, financial and insurance companies in tax havens amounted to $3.7 billion whilst in 1976 this had grown to $20.9 billion. Although US foreign investment was growing fast in most sectors, growth in the offshore banking and finance outstripped overseas growth in other sectors by a large margin. In 1968 bank deposits held in offshore financial centres amounted to $10.6 billion. By 1978 this figure had grown to $384.9 billion.

Many of the Caribbean countries had enacted secrecy laws similar to the Swiss ones, a fact noted in the Gordon Report:

> 'Lack of meaningful exchange of information is the real problem and that lack encourages abuse. The IRS does not have available the process of the courts to command the production of records that are in the hands of third parties in the tax havens. Even if information is obtained it is rarely in a form admissible in the United States courts.'

Apart from this history of financial regulation and the covert encouragement of the development of former dependencies into self-supporting offshore financial centres, there are a number of other theories concerning the growth in tax havens. One, certainly correct, is that banking and financial secrecy encouraged the growth in secrecy havens as a home of dirty money (ie to facilitate money laundering). However, over-regulation of the financial sector and criminal activity are not sufficient to explain the growth of tax havens. The growth has also been fuelled by the rise of the multinational corporation, which in its turn was fuelled by rapid advances in communications technologies and transport links.

Partly due to the Republican (US) and Conservative (UK) political policies of the 1980s, the concerns about the growing popularity of tax havens were not acted upon to any great extent for a long time. Although the US had introduced anti-haven measures in the early 1960s these were not particularly effective, and UK anti-haven legislation (see Chapter 17) was not introduced until 1984. Towards the end of the 1980s, concern grew over the perceived abuse of tax havens when it was becoming apparent that they were not just being used to defer taxation, but to avoid it altogether.

---

1   For an informative history of tax havens, on which much of this section is based, see Picciotto (1992).
2   For example, Germany imposed a 25 per cent withholding tax in 1965 on interest paid by residents to non-residents.

Scale of tax haven usage today

16.10   Because many tax havens operate a policy of secrecy it is not possible to estimate the scale of tax haven usage with any accuracy. The table below gives a collection of various estimates:

Table 16.1

How much/ how many?	*What and where?*	*Source*
About 350	Major multinational corporate groups implicated in the 2014 so-called 'Luxleaks' reporting – taking advantage of favourable secret Luxembourg tax rulings to avoid taxes in Luxembourg and elsewhere	See: http:// uk.businessinsider. com/full-list-every-company-named-in-the-luxembourg-secret-tax-deal-database-2014-11
27	Average number of company directorships held by each of the 31,000 inhabitants of the British Virgin Islands in 2012	Schjelderup (2015)
285,000	The number of companies whose legal address is: 1209 North Orange Street, Wilmington, Delaware, United States	*New York Times*, 2012 See: http://www.nytimes. com/2012/07/01/ business/how-delaware-thrives-as-a-corporate-tax-haven.html?_r=0
$100 billion	US taxes evaded by the use of offshore tax abuses	US Senate (2008)
2065%	Percentage of Cayman Islands GDP in 2010 represented by profits of subsidiaries of US multinationals based there	Congressional Research Service. See: https://www.fas.org/sgp/ crs/misc/R40623.pdf

How much/ how many?	*What and where?*	*Source*
$100 billion	Estimate of annual loss of US tax revenues through use of tax havens	Statement of Senator Carl Levin on introducing the Stop Tax Haven Abuse Act, Part 1, March 2009 at: http://levin.senate.gov/newsroom/press/release/?id=680c7457-9c8d-4be7-b4ca-2e918f9935b9
59%	Percentage of overseas profits of US MNCs reported as arising in 2010 as a % of the combined GDP of the following countries: Bahamas, Barbados, Bermuda, British Virgin Islands, Cayman Islands, Guernsey, Jersey, Liberia, Marshall Islands, Mauritius, Netherlands, Netherlands Antilles.	Congressional Research Service See: https://www.fas.org/sgp/crs/misc/R40623.pdf
4%	Percentage total overseas workforce in Bermuda, Ireland, Luxembourg, the Netherlands and Switzerland	Congressional Research Service 2013 See: www.fas.org/sgp/crs/misc/R42927.pdf
One third	Of international profits of French banks are declared in tax havens	Oxfam (2016)
$7.6 trillion	Worldwide wealth hidden in offshore accounts	Zucman (2015)

Estimates of the scale of cross-border banking activity can be obtained by looking at figures supplied by the Bank for International Settlements (BIS) which facilitates cross-border banking transactions.

The banking sector

16.11   Tax havens usually offer a selection of the following benefits that are of particular interest to the banking sector:

- no reserve requirements in respect of banking activities for non-residents;

- exemption from exchange controls;

- legal protection of confidentiality of bank records and customer information (not only that held by banks but also by accountants and lawyers); and

- company laws giving wide protection of the confidentiality of both financial and commercial transactions, eg the right to issue bearer shares, minimum annual reporting obligations.

Three types of offshore banking centres

16.12   There are basically three types of offshore banking centres:

- *Fully operational*: London, New York, Singapore and Hong Kong are the principal ones. People meet face to face and put deals together; securitization deals are struck. The attraction of these centres is partly the concentration of firms and clients in one place, but also tax concessions: for instance, the London Eurobond market is dependent on the fact that the UK allows interest on Eurobonds to be paid without withholding tax being levied.

- *Offshore/onshore centres*: where onshore banks are allowed to set up subsidiaries with the same privileges as offshore centres (eg American banks' 'international banking facilities'). These are freed from the usual US banking regulations and exempted from state taxes, so that they are on a par with the offshore subsidiaries of US banks.

- *Booking centres*: these are characterized by low tax and light regulation – 'brassplate' operations. However, there have been problems with them being used for money laundering in the past. Money was being deposited offshore with no questions asked, but then transferred via 'correspondent' accounts into the banks' main onshore branches. This led to 400 shell banks in Nauru and 50 in Vanuatu being closed in 2003/04 in response to pressure from the Financial Action Task Force, a supranational sister-organization to the OECD whose main objective is to reduce opportunities for money laundering.

The Cayman Islands is in the world's top 10 banking centres. A 2009 IMF report[1] states that total banking assets held in the Cayman Islands in 2009 amounted to ES$1.8 trillion and insurance assets stood at $35 billion. Only a fraction of the banks registered there have physical premises there apart from a nameplate – most of the work is done by staff in the main onshore offices. The IMF report states that over $1 trillion of the banking assets consist of accounts in Cayman branches of US banks. The funds from these branches are transferred to the US each night in so-called 'sweep' accounts, and transferred back the following morning. A total of 208 of the 278 licensed banks had no physical presence in the Cayman Islands.

---

1   IMF (2009) Cayman Islands: Off-Shore Financial Center Assessment Update – Assessment of Financial Sector Supervision and Regulation. Available at: www.imf.org/external/pubs/ft/scr/2009/cr09323.pdf.

The case of Switzerland

16.13   Switzerland is probably the oldest and one of the best-known tax havens. This is partly because tax evasion was considered a civil rather than a criminal offence, meaning that Switzerland was not in a position to co-operate with other countries in the matter of exchanging information on tax matters. In 1934, the Swiss Banking Law of 1934 was passed which made it a criminal offence for bank officials to divulge any information concerning a customer's identity, even to the Swiss government (see Palan, 1998).

Tax havens and the UK government

16.14   The Channel Islands, the Isle of Man and Gibraltar were all under Bank of England supervision from 1960 onwards, and continued to co-operate with the Bank of England even after the end of exchange control in 1979. They are Crown Dependencies, with their own system of law and fiscal sovereignty (but note that the Isle of Man is within the EU customs union).

Although it can be argued that the UK could do more to limit the use of these islands as offshore financial centres, they are tolerated in order to make the City of London more attractive. There is also the political difficulty in that according to a Special Report in the *Financial Times*[1] about 60 per cent of these islands' GDP relates to the financial sector. Any moves by the UK to curtail the income from this source would have severe implications for the economies of the Crown Dependencies.

Although there has been a growing trend for co-operation with the UK in the matter of information exchange, this has normally not extended to the tax authorities. The more recent developments on information exchange are considered in Chapter 18.

There have been occasional scandals where many investors have lost their money, notably those involving the Savings and Investment Bank in the Isle of Man in 1982 and Barlow Clowes in 1988. Barlow Clowes was refused permission to buy banks in the Isle of Man (following a tightening up after the Savings and Investment Bank affair) but was able to do so in Gibraltar. As banking and other financial regulation has increased, there has been a shift towards using these places for avoiding taxes. The dilemma of the UK government is that, if it closes down all financial attractions of the Channel Islands and the Isle of Man, it may create political and economic instability in those places.

---

1   *Financial Times*, 6 October 2004.

Tax havens and the US government

16.15   US corporations currently face the highest rates of corporate tax in the world: about 39 per cent when federal, state and local taxes are taken into account, although proposals are under discussion to reduce this considerably. The US only operates the credit method of double tax relief. Thus, if a foreign subsidiary pays a dividend to its US parent company, there will probably be US tax to pay, after giving double tax relief. For this reason, it has become the practice of US MNEs not to send dividends or interest back to the US if they can help it. Although the US has certain laws designed to tax profits of overseas subsidiaries whether or not a dividend is paid, these are not terribly effective. (These are the 'controlled foreign company' rules, discussed in Chapter 17.)

Stewart (2007) calculates the effective tax rate borne by subsidiaries of US corporations in a selection of countries for 2008.

Table 16.2

Location of subsidiary company	Net income (US$ millions)	Effective rate of tax in that country*
Netherlands	2,971	4.1%
Luxembourg	382	0.4%
Ireland	3,386	4.2%
Bermuda	400	0.6%
Switzerland	1,882	3.5%
UK Islands and Caribbean	486	1%
France	3.326	26.8%
Germany	4.387	21.6%

Note: *This is defined as tax actually paid divided by accounting profits before tax.

Tax havens and tax evasion

16.16 It is very important to consider the difference between the use of tax havens for ex ante tax planning and tax avoidance, ie channelling profit through tax havens in order to reduce worldwide tax liabilities, and the use of tax havens for ex post tax evasion. Tax evasion, as we saw in Chapter 1, is quite a different phenomenon and requires very different regulatory responses. Many commentators fail to distinguish the two activities, which has led to a very negative view of tax havens. The use of tax havens for tax planning and avoidance requires a regulatory response that seeks to curb such activities only where they are viewed as exploiting domestic legislation in an unacceptable way. Two instances of this are controlled foreign company rules (Chapter 17) and transfer pricing regulations (Chapter 13).

The use of tax havens for tax evasion is quite different, involving fraudulent activity, and requires the use of criminal sanctions, for which information about tax haven investments is required. In considering this aspect of tax haven abuse, we return to the issue of information exchange. In recent years there has been a significant increase in the use of information exchange agreements, both as part of DTTs and also as separate agreements: Taxation Information

Exchange Agreements (TIEAs). TIEAs were first used by the US in the early 1980s with certain countries in the Caribbean and Central America. The steady increase in the number of these agreements being entered into world-wide, flows largely from the work of the OECD on harmful tax competition which commenced with a report in 1998 and is covered in more detail in Chapter 18. The OECD's Global Forum on Taxation has worked with a variety of jurisdictions to develop standards for transparency and effective informa-tion exchange, with some degree of success.

Another achievement of the OECD in the context of tax evasion, is a common definition of 'tax fraud' as 'an act, attempted act or failure to act by any person that is intended to violate a legal duty concerning the accurate reporting, deter-mination or collection of tax' (OECD 2003). This definition has been endorsed by all OECD members with the exception of Luxembourg and Switzerland. Tax evasion is now high on the agenda of many governments and the G8 Heads of State in July 2008 called for the OECD to strengthen its work in this area (see OECD 2008b). Pressure from the G8 and G20 groups of countries has increased and has resulted in further OECD work. The increased focus on tax evasion through the abuse of tax havens was given impetus as a result of the Liechtenstein scandal, discussed below.

Sharman and Rawlings (2006) discuss the way in which many jurisdic-tions create 'blacklists' of tax havens. They note that these lists are not for-mulated scientifically, but by trial and error, copying from other countries and bodies such as the OECD, and tend not to be updated to reflect chang-ing circumstances. They note the example of Christmas Island and Cocos (Keeling) Islands, which are in the Indian Ocean off the west coast of Australia and were used as part of unacceptable tax-avoidance arrangements in the 1970s. These islands were blacklisted by Argentina, Mexico, Portugal and Venezuela – despite the fact that from 1994 they have been fully integrated legally into Australia and are fiscally indistinguishable. The use of blacklists to identify and target tax havens is more prevalent in South America and Southern Europe.

The Liechtenstein scandal

16.17   In February 2008, a former employee of a Liechtenstein trust company made public information on approximately 1,400 persons with bank accounts at LGT Bank in Liechtenstein. The German authorities subsequently arrested a prominent businessman for allegedly using Liechtenstein bank accounts to evade €1 million in tax. Other countries followed suit; the US embarked on enforcement action against over 100 taxpayers and the UK, Italy, France, Spain and Australia also announced intentions to investigate taxpayers with Liechtenstein accounts. The global breadth of the scandal was shocking and galvanized the international community to increase its attack on tax evasion facilitated by tax haven banks. The US Senate (2008) investigation details this, and other cases of tax evasion, with reference to specific taxpayers, document-ing evidence from a number of participants and advisers. In the UK, a BBC news report[1] quoted the head of LGT, His Serene Highness Prince Max von und zu Liechtenstein as saying that Liechtenstein was being treated unfairly and that Britain, which at the time, stated that it expected to recover around £100 million in tax from the affair, is, in fact a keen player in offshore finance markets. Subsequently, the UK introduced a special facility for UK residents to own up about their funds hidden in Liechtenstein (the so-called 'Liechtenstein Disclosure Facility'). This is discussed in Chapter 18.

---

1 Available at: http://news.bbc.co.uk/1/hi/business/727911.stm.

WHICH COUNTRIES MIGHT BE CLASSED AS TAX HAVENS?

16.18   There is no universal list of tax havens. Table 16.3 gives a selection of listings.

Column 1 is derived from reports from the Global Forum, an organization set up by the OECD to assess compliance against an agreed 'international standard' of tax transparency by means of a series of peer reviews of countries. This is discussed further in Chapter 18. The countries listed are those which have not been able to facilitate full reviews of their tax compliance due to deficiencies in their reporting ability, and their continuing adherence to banking secrecy, as well as those which have been fully assessed against the OECD's agreed international standard, but which have been found to be only partially compliant.[1]

The December 2008 report by the US Governmental Accountability Office (GAO) referred to at the beginning of this chapter provided an interesting listing, which encompasses three possible reasons for including a country on a list of tax havens. First, there are those which were identified as possible tax havens by the OECD. This is not used in Table 16.3 as it is now somewhat out of date. The second source used by the GAO is based on a NBER working paper based on academic research.[2] The third GAO source is derived from US District Court Orders granting leave for the IRS to serve a 'John Doe' summons.[3] The list is not exhaustive and nor does it prove that any of the countries listed is, in fact, a tax haven. Nevertheless, the list provides some grounds for reaching conclusions as to the status of certain countries.

The final column is rather controversial: it is a compilation made in 2014 of the 30 countries most likely to appear on lists of countries regarded as tax havens by some of the EU Member States.[4] However, some Member States, such as the UK and Sweden, do not have any such lists and therefore do not contribute to this list. The OECD and even the Tax Justice Network have expressed concerns about this list, but nevertheless it provides an insight into the views of certain governments as to which countries around the world might be tax havens.

---

1   Global forum on Transparency and Exchange of Information for Tax purposes (2015) 'Phase 1 and Phase 2 Reviews as of August 2015'. Available at: www.oecd.org/tax/transparency/GFratings.pdf.

2   Dharmapala and Hines (2009), which was based on Hines and Rice (1994).

3   This Order included a list of jurisdictions recognized as offshore tax havens or financial privacy jurisdictions by industry analysts and which are believed to be actively promoted as such by promoters of offshore schemes. A 'John Doe' summons is a legal device which permits the IRS to obtain information about persons whose identities are currently unknown to the IRS, for instance, from credit card companies on individuals using their cards in countries considered to be tax havens.

4   'Tax good governance in the world as seen by EU countries'. Available at: http://ec.europa.eu/taxation_customs/taxation/gen_info/good_governance_matters/lists_of_countries/index_en.htm.

The EU Haven Blacklist

16.19   The EU is currently compiling a blacklist of tax havens with a view to publishing it in 2017. In November 2016, EU Finance Ministers agreed the criteria and process for this list, which was proposed by the Commission in its External Strategy for Effective Taxation in January 2016. The Commission seeks to develop 'clear, coherent and objective' criteria and the process will entail a neutral scoreboard of indicators, screening of third (non-EU) countries and listing of those that refuse to engage with the EU regarding its vision of 'good governance'.

The Commission initially considered 213 third countries, but decided not to include the 48 least developed countries. The scoreboard comprises 165 indicators grouped into the following dimensions:[1]

- economic ties with the EU;

- financial activity;

- stability factors; and

- risk factors.

---

1   Details of the scoreboard can be found at: https://ec.europa.eu/taxation_customs/sites/taxation/files/2016-09-15_scoreboard-indicators.pdf.

Table 16.3 Jurisdictions listed as tax havens or financial privacy jurisdictions and the sources of those jurisdictions[1]

Jurisdiction	OECD Global Forum results	NBER	US District Court order granting leave for IRS to serve a 'John Doe' summons	Countries treated as tax havens in ActionAid report on FTSE 100 tax haven usage	Top 30 countries listed as tax havens by certain EU Member States 2014
Andorra	×	×	×	×	×
Anguilla	×	×	×	×	×
Antigua and Barbuda	×	×	×[a]	×	×
Aruba			×[a]	×	
Bahamas		×	×[a]	×	×
Bahrain		×		×	
Barbados	×	×	×[a]	×	×
Belize		×	×		×
Bermuda		×	×[a,b]	×	×
British Virgin Islands	×	×	×[c]	×	×
Brunei					×
Cayman Islands		×	×[a]	×	×
Cook Islands		×	×	×	×
Costa Rica			×[a]	×	
Cyprus	×	×	×[b]	×	
Dominica	×	×	×[a]		
Gibraltar		×	×	×	
Grenada		×	×[a]		×
Guernsey	×[d]		×[a,d]	×	×
Hong Kong		×	×	×	×
Ireland		×			
Isle of Man		×	×[a]	×	
Jersey	×[d]		×[a]	×	
Jordan		×		×	
Latvia			×[b]	×	
Lebanon	×	×		×	
Liberia	×	×		×	×
Liechtenstein		×	×	×	×
Luxembourg	×	×	×[b]	×	
Macao		×		×	
Maldives		×		×	×
Malta		×	×	×	

Jurisdiction	OECD Global Forum results	NBER	US District Court order granting leave for IRS to serve a 'John Doe' summons	Countries treated as tax havens in ActionAid report on FTSE 100 tax haven usage	Top 30 countries listed as tax havens by certain EU Member States 2014
Marshall Islands		×			×
Mauritius				×	×
Monaco		×		×	×
Montserrat		×			×
Nauru	×		×		×
Netherlands				×	
Netherlands Antilles		×	×[a]	×	
Panama	×	×	×	×	×
Samoa			×	×	
Seychelles	×			×	×
Singapore		×	×	×	
St Kitts and Nevis		×	×	×	×
St Lucia	×	×	×[e]	×	
St Vincent and the Grenadines	×	×	×		×
Switzerland		×	×[b]	×	
Trinidad and Tobago	×				
Turks and Caicos Islands	×	×	×		×
United States: State of Delaware				×	
US Virgin Islands	×			×	×
Vanuatu	×	×	×		×

Sources: OECD, NBER, and US Governmental Accountability Office and 'John Doe' summons.

Notes:

(a) A Tax Information Exchange Agreement (TIEA) is in force between the US and this jurisdiction.

(b) A DTT is in force with an exchange of information provision. For Switzerland, the treaty provides that the competent authorities of the contracting states shall exchange such information as is necessary 'for the prevention of tax fraud or the like'.

(c)   NBER's list included the Channel Islands. Jersey and Guernsey are part of the Channel Islands. The two other sources used to identify tax havens listed Jersey and Guernsey as two separate tax havens and did not include the Channel Islands on their lists of tax havens. To be consistent, we are including Jersey and Guernsey as tax havens on the bureau's list rather than the Channel Islands.

(d)   The John Doe summons lists Guernsey/Sark/Alderney. OECD only included Guernsey. Since Sark and Alderney are part of the Bailiwick of Guernsey, to be consistent, we are only including Guernsey on our list of tax havens.

(e)   The TIEA signed by the United States and St Lucia on 30 January 1987, is not fully in effect within the meaning of s 274(h)(6)(A)(i) of the Internal Revenue Code because the government of St Lucia has not enacted legislation to implement the agreement.

---

1   Adapted from Large US Corporations and Federal Contractors with Subsidiaries in Jurisdictions Listed as Tax Havens or Financial Privacy Jurisdictions, GAO-09-157 December 2008. Available at: www.gao.gov/new.items/d09157.pdf.

Extent of the use of tax havens by MNEs

16.20   Although now dated, a report by the US Government Accountability Office in 2008 examined the use of tax haven subsidiaries by US publicly traded corporations and produced some interesting insights into the extent of tax haven usage. A few highlights are reproduced in the following table.

Table 16.4 Tax haven usage by US publicly traded corporations

Company	Total tax haven subsidiaries	Bermuda	Cayman Islands	Hong Kong	Luxembourg	Switzerland
Bank of America Corporation	115	2	59	8	15	0
Chevron	23	16	0	0	0	0
Citigroup	427	19	90	40	91	8
ConocoPhillips	44	17	9	0	2	2
General Motors	11	2	4	0	0	2
Proctor and Gamble	83	5	2	10	6	24
Pepsico	70	13	2	10	7	6
News Corporation	152	1	33	21	4	2
Morgan Stanley	273	3	158	15	29	4

In September 2012, the UK arm of ActionAid, a charity devoted to combatting poverty in the developing world, released a report analysing the extent to which the UK's top 100 companies use tax havens, with a total of 8311 subsidiaries in countries classed by ActionAid as tax havens.[1] They include the US state of Delaware and the Netherlands as tax havens, although these locations are often used for their company law regime rather than just to take advantage of their tax regimes. It found that all used tax havens, with the banking sector making the heaviest use with the big four banks owning 1,619 tax haven companies. The report notes that operation in a tax haven does not prove tax avoidance. Figure 16.1 shows the popularity with the FTSE 100 groups of each country classed by ActionAid as a tax haven, excluding Delaware and Netherlands subsidiaries. Ireland appears to be the most popular location, with the FTSE 100 companies, taken together, having a total of 736 subsidiaries located there. The bald number of subsidiaries in a particular location does not tell us all that much: a single Jersey subsidiary could be responsible for as much business as 50 other subsidiaries in the same group. However, the ActionAid data does provide an insight into the locations chosen by major groups of companies.[2]

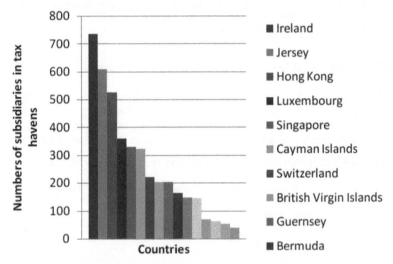

Figure 16.1: Popular locations for FTSE 100 subsidiaries in countries classed by ActionAid as tax havens

An earlier report by Publish What You Pay (Norway) studied the world's large extractive industry countries, which reportedly together have some 6,038 subsidiaries of which 2,083 are incorporated in 'secrecy jurisdictions'. The report acknowledges that there is nothing to suggest that the companies studied either use controversial techniques to reduce profits, and thereby tax liabilities, or illegally evade tax.

---

1   Full data is available at: www.theguardian.com/news/datablog/2013/may/12/ftse-100-use-tax-havens-full-list#data.
2   For a robust defence against the classification of Ireland as a tax haven, see Tobin and Walsh (2013).

The 'Luxleaks' – evidence of use of Luxembourg as a tax haven by MNEs

16.21 In 2014, Luxembourg attracted a good deal of adverse publicity when a group of journalists published online a cache of documents running to 28,000 pages which detailed the contents of about 550 secret rulings issued to about 350 Luxembourg-based subsidiaries or branches of multinational groups. These had been leaked to the press by an auditor employed by one of the large accounting firms.[1] Whilst some are relatively innocuous, seeking to confirm matters such as whether a non-interest bearing loan should be considered as equity capital, others provide evidence of the overt avoidance of tax using Luxembourg entities. A common strategy appears to have been to interpose a Luxembourg-resident subsidiary in the group structure so that deductions for interest on intragroup loans could be generated in operating companies around the world that were not mirrored by taxable interest receipts. This is illustrated in Figure 16.2.

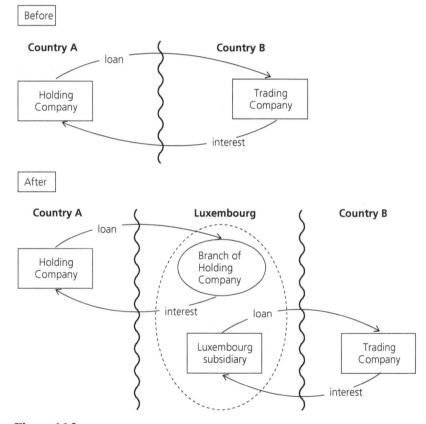

Figure 16.2

Before any tax planning takes place, Holding Company, tax resident in Country A, makes a loan to a trading subsidiary in Country B. There is a tax deduction for the payment in Country B and a taxable receipt in Country A. Luxembourg is then used to obtain the result that the group still gets the interest deduction, but the taxable receipt disappears. This works as follows:

1   Holding company sets up a branch in Luxembourg. It makes a 'loan' to the branch and receives 'interest' from the branch. However, as there is still only one legal entity (the Holding Company) these transactions are ignored for tax purposes.

2   A Luxembourg subsidiary is formed, owned 100 per cent by Holding Company. The subsidiary is put in funds and makes a loan to Trading Company which replaces the original loan from Holding Company. Trading company still gets an interest deduction.

3   The group obtains a ruling from the Luxembourg tax authority that the Luxembourg branch of Holding company and the Luxembourg subsidiary of Holding Company can be regarded as a tax group or a single entity.

4   The Luxembourg Tax authority then agrees to treat the loan made to the Luxembourg branch as if it was, in essence, the same loan as the one made by the Luxembourg Subsidiary to Trading Company.

5   The Luxembourg combined branch/subsidiary entity thus has interest receivable (from Trading Company) and interest payable (to Holding Company). These more or less cancel out so that there is no net interest to be taxed in Luxembourg.

6   Holding Company receives interest from Luxembourg Branch: but this is ignored for Country A purposes because a company cannot receive interest from itself.

---

1   A database of Luxembourg leaks documents has been made available by the International Consortium of Investigative Journalists, available at: www.icij.org/project/luxembourg-leaks/ explore-documents-luxembourg-leaks-database.

FURTHER READING

ActionAid (2011) Addicted to tax havens: The secret life of the FTSE 100. Available at: www.actionaid.org.uk/doc_lib/addicted_to_tax_havens.pdf.

ActionAid (2013) Tax haven Tracker. Available at: www.actionaid.org.uk/ tax-justice/ftse-100-tax-haven-tracker.

Christian Aid (2007) *Haemorrhaging Money: A Christian Aid Briefing on the Problem of Illicit Capital Flight.*

Dibout, A (2001) *General Report in Limits on the Use of Low-tax Regimes by Multinational Businesses: Current Measures and Emerging Trends,* Vol LXXXVlb of Cahiers de Droit fiscal international, International Fiscal Association, San Francisco Congress.

Dharmapala, D and Hines, J R, Jr (2009) 'Which Countries Become Tax Havens?', NBER Working Paper. Available at: http://ssrn.com/abstract=952721.

The Guardian (2013) 'FTSE 100's Use of Tax Havens – Get the Full List'. Available at: www.theguardian.com/news/datablog/2013/may/12/ftse-100-use-tax-havens-full-list.

Gordon, R A (1981) *Tax Havens and their Use by US Taxpayers – An Overview*, IRS Publication 1150 (4–18) 1981 Washington DC. Available at: www.archive.org/details/taxhavenstheirus01gord.

Government Accountability Office (2008) *Large US Corporations and Federal Contractors with Subsidiaries in Jurisdictions Listed as Tax Havens or Financial Privacy Jurisdictions*, GAO-09-157 December 2008. Available at: www.gao.gov/new.items/d09157.pdf.

Gravelle, J G (2015) 'Tax Havens; International Tax Avoidance and Evasion', Congressional Research Service 7-57. Available at: www.fas.org/sgp/crs/misc/R40623.pdf.

IMF (2000) 'Offshore Financial Centres' Background Paper, available at: www.imf.org/external/np/mae/oshore/2000/eng/back.htm, IMF Monetary & Exchange Affairs Dept, June.

Killian, S (2006) 'Where's the Harm in Tax Competition? Lessons from US Multinationals in Ireland', *Critical Perspectives on Accounting*, Vol 17, pp 1067–1087.

Kurdle, R T (2003) 'The Campaign Against Tax Havens: Will it Last? Will it Work?', *Stanford Journal of Law, Business & Finance 9 Stan JL Bus & Fin* (2003–2004).

Morgan, C (2003) 'Full of Eastern Promise – Not Quite!', Article re exempt activities test for CFCs *Tax Journal*, 22 February 2003.

OECD (2008a) Tax Co-operation: Towards a Level Playing Field – 2008 Assessment by the Global Forum on Taxation.

OECD (2008b) Overview of the OECD's Work on International Tax Evasion.

Oxfam (2000) 'Tax Havens: Releasing the Hidden Billions for Poverty Eradication', Oxfam Policy Department 3, 2000.

Oxfam (2016) French Banks in Tax Havens.

Palan, R (1998) 'Trying to Have Your Cake and Eating It: How and Why the State System has Created Offshore', *International Studies Quarterly* 42, pp 625–644.

Picciotto, S (1992) *International Business Taxation*, London, Butterworths.

Publish What You Pay (Norway) 2011 *Piping Profits*. Available at: www.publishwhatyoupay.org/sites/publishwhatyoupay.org/files/FINAL%20pp%20norway.pdf.

Rohagi, R (2007) Chapter 5, 'International Offshore Financial Centres' in *Basic International Taxation*, Vol 1, 2nd edn, E,. Kluwer Law International.

Sanders, B (2015) 'Legalized Tax Fraud: How Top UK Corporations Continue to Profit Through Offshore Tax Havens'. Report by Budget Committee Ranking Member Bernie Sanders, US Senate. Available at: www.budget.senate. gov/democratic/public/_cache/files/3eaf7d6c-a87e-49cc-aa1a-be496f6c213e/ legalized-tax-fraud.pdf.

Schjelderup, G (2015) 'Secrecy Jurisdictions'. Available at SSRN: http:// papers.ssrn.com/sol3/papers.cfm?abstract_id=2576228.

Sharman, J C and Rawlings, G (2006) 'National Tax; A Comparative Analysis', *Journal of International Taxation*, Vol 17, No 9, pp 38–48.

Shaxson, N (2011) *Treasure Islands: Tax Havens and the Men Who Stole the World*, Bodley Head, London.

Sikka, P (2003) 'The Role of Offshore Financial Centres in Globalization', *Accounting Forum*, Vol 22, No 4, pp 365–399.

Stewart, J (2011) 'Corporation Tax: How Important is the 12.5% Corporation Tax Rate in Ireland?' IIS Discussion Paper No 375. Available at: www.tcd.ie/ iiis/documents/discussion/pdfs/iiisdp375.pdf.

Sullivan, M (2004) 'Data Show Dramatic Shift of Profits to Tax Havens', *Tax Notes*, 13 September 2004, Tax Analysts.

Tobin, G and Walsh, K (2013) 'What makes a country a tax haven? An assessment of International standards shows why Ireland is not a tax haven', *The Economic and Social Review*, Vol 44, No 3, pp 401–424.

US Senate Permanent Subcommittee on Investigations (2008) 'Tax Haven Banks and US Tax Compliance'.

US Senate Permanent Subcommittee on Investigations (2014) 'Onshore Tax Evasion: The Effort to Collect Unpaid Taxes on Billions in Hidden Onshore Accounts'. Available at: www.hsgac.senate.gov/subcommittees/investigations.

Zielke, R (2011) 'The Changing Role of Tax Havens – An Empirical Analysis of the Tax Havens Worldwide', *Bulletin for International Taxation*, Vol 65, No 1.

Zucman, G (2015) *The Hidden Wealth of Nations: The Scourge of Tax Havens*, University of Chicago Press.

Chapter 17

Controlled Foreign Companies

BASICS

17.1   As noted in the previous chapter, the use of tax havens in international tax planning increased considerably in the latter part of the twentieth century and became the focus of government tax policy initiatives. Tax haven abuse can potentially be controlled by a number of means:

- *Pressure from supranational bodies such as the OECD and EU, and non-governmental organizations such as the Tax Justice Network*: members of these bodies can collectively threaten tax havens with economic and reputational sanctions.

- *Use of information-gathering powers*: against a country's own residents (eg a bank resident in Country A may be forced by the government of Country A to disclose details of accounts held by Country A residents with overseas branches or fellow group companies of the Country A bank).

- *Amnesties to persuade residents to 'own up' to using tax havens and cease doing so in future*: this effectively tries to put the tax havens out of business by depriving them of customers.

- *Exchange controls*: to prevent residents investing or transferring funds overseas. Exchange controls may prevent direct transfer to havens, but cannot adequately control indirect transfers. With deregulation of the financial and foreign exchange markets, exchange controls are no longer an appropriate tool for dealing with tax havens.

- *Transfer pricing rules*: can be used to limit tax haven abuse, however they only apply to non-arm's-length transactions, and therefore do not cover all types of haven abuse (eg a substantial equity investment in a tax haven company will not necessarily involve a non-arm's-length transfer). Transfer pricing rules also do not adequately address indirect transfers. Transfer pricing rules are considered in more detail in Chapter 13.

- *Company residence rules*: it is arguable that tax haven abuse is largely the result of a failure by governments to adequately define company residence for tax purposes. If a definition of residence looking to the residence of the shareholders were used, some of the problems of tax haven abuse could be overcome. There are practical difficulties, however, in that beneficial ownership can be difficult to trace and further, that even if residence of a company could be determined by shareholder control, the collection of tax remains problematic.

- *Controlled foreign companies (CFC) legislation*: the most effective method of eliminating deferral is through CFC legislation. The domestic shareholders of foreign companies must pay tax currently on their pro rata share of the income of the foreign company. The effect of these rules is to bring forward the timing of the liability for domestic tax from the time of distribution of the foreign company's profits to its shareholders to the time at which it is derived by the foreign company.

The first three will be considered in Chapter 18, but it is this last form of control of tax haven usage on which we focus in this chapter.

Most developed countries and some developing countries have introduced CFC legislation to protect their domestic tax base. This legislation usually operates so as to tax the resident shareholders on the income derived by the subsidiary located in the tax haven, regardless of whether such income has been remitted to the shareholder's country of residence. In this way, a country breaks the usual tax rule of treating a group of multinational companies (MNEs) as being a collection of independent companies.

Such legislation may consider the location of the foreign subsidiary, or the nature of the transactions carried out in the tax haven, or may take a mixed approach. All systems of CFC legislation must consider which types of shareholders will be caught, how to define a foreign company as a CFC, the importance of the rate of tax suffered in the CFC's country, the type of income which will be the subject of the CFC charge, and whether location of a subsidiary in certain countries will lead to them automatically being regarded as CFCs.

The CFC legislation usually aims to tax the resident shareholder on the passive income of the foreign subsidiary, rather than on any trading or other actively derived profits. This is because it is far more likely that financial investments, giving rise to passive income, will be transferred to the subsidiary to take advantage of a low rate of tax than it is that a physical trade or business would be transferred merely to take advantage of low tax rates. It is far cheaper and much easier to relocate financial investments than it is to relocate factories and employees, although the digital economy requires special consideration.

Most countries insist upon self-assessment because it is not practicable to expect the tax authority to be able to uncover the use of tax haven subsidiaries to shelter passive income.

As part of the BEPS Project, the OECD has urged countries that do not currently have CFC legislation to adopt it, and recommends that countries with weak CFC regimes improve their legislation. BEPS Action 3 does not prescribe a particular system of CFC legislation but the Final Report on Action 3 sets out the various elements which such a regime ought to include, and discusses various options for rules within a CFC regime such as who and what should be taxed.

There is an argument that CFC rules override tax treaties and are thus illegal. The OECD supports the use of CFC legislation and considers that it can be defended in legal terms. Whether or not it is legal, most developed countries have CFC legislation so that they are not in any position to complain about other countries having it. EU Member States need to take particular care that their CFC rules are not in contravention of their obligations under the EU treaties, eg the right to freedom of establishment (see Chapter 20). Their CFC rules must not favour their own businesses over businesses resident elsewhere in the EU. In other words, unless there is clear evidence of avoidance of tax, such as where a subsidiary in another (low tax) EU Member State lacks all economic substance, the governments of the EU Member States cannot use their CFC legislation in respect of subsidiaries resident elsewhere in the EU.

When we look at other measures to tackle the use of tax havens in Chapter 18, we may ask ourselves why domestic anti-haven legislation appears insufficient to cope with the threat from tax havens, such that the OECD, and other supranational bodies have sought to introduce co-ordinated measures to limit the operations of tax havens.

CFC LEGISLATION – INTRODUCTION

17.2   It is usual for countries to treat a multinational group of companies for tax purposes as a collection of separate companies rather than a single economic entity. Thus if Company A, resident in the country of Ruritania, has a profitable subsidiary company, Company B, in the country Inistania, the Ruritanian tax authority will not be able to tax the profits earned by the Company B, because it is neither tax resident in Ruritania nor has any source of income there. The Ruritanian tax authority will have to wait until the profits of the Company B are paid to its Ruritanian parent company, Company A, usually by way of a dividend. Assuming that any such dividend would result in tax becoming payable in Ruritania, then by instructing Company B not to pay dividends, Company A achieves deferral of Ruritanian tax on the profits earned in Inistania.

Most of the major capital-exporting nations have anti-avoidance legislation aimed at preventing the loss or postponement of tax revenues through the failure of their residents to repatriate (send home) income and profits earned abroad by subsidiary companies, particularly with regard to portfolio income, ie income from passive investments. Under most tax systems, income from foreign sources only becomes taxable when it is remitted to the country of the taxpayer's residence. Even where a country operates an exemption system of double tax relief, there is often a parallel system of credit relief in operation for portfolio income. In the case of MNEs, CFC legislation attempts to prevent the deferral or outright avoidance of tax in the country where the parent company is resident. It usually does this by deeming the income and profits of the tax haven subsidiary to have been earned by the resident parent company or other major shareholders. Governments must walk a tightrope when designing CFC legislation: too restrictive and their firms will not be able to compete in international markets, too flexible and firms will find ways around the legislation. No government wants to dissuade its firms from expanding abroad. Essentially,

CFC legislation is intended to be a deterrent to the use of tax havens, rather than as a revenue-raising measure.

CFC legislation is sometimes considered as a failsafe mechanism to bolster the effectiveness of transfer pricing legislation. If, despite transfer pricing rules, profits have been successfully shifted to a low tax member of a group through the use of non-arm's length transactions, then although the transfer pricing rules have failed, the country from which profits have been shifted can still retrieve some tax on those profits by invoking its CFC rules. However, this result tends to be serendipitous rather than as a result of careful legislative drafting. Also the coverage of transfer pricing rules and CFC rules is not an exact match: the scope of income caught by the CFC rules of a country is unlikely to be exactly the same as the income targeted by its transfer pricing rules. For instance, the UK's CFC rules do not cover capital gains made by foreign subsidiaries, whereas these would be within the scope of UK transfer pricing rules.

Although the description 'controlled foreign company', or 'controlled foreign corporation' in US nomenclature, could equally apply to subsidiaries in high-tax countries, the phrase 'controlled foreign company' is generally only used to describe a subsidiary resident in a country where it pays little or no tax. In the US, it forms Subpart F of the United States Tax Code and is thus known there as 'Subpart F'.

How CFC legislation works

17.3   If a government applies its CFC legislation to a resident taxpayer, it charges tax on the resident taxpayer as if the income of the CFC had been earned by that taxpayer.

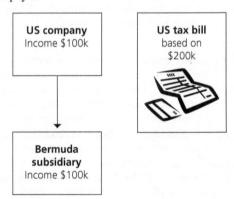

Figure 17.1: US company with a wholly owned Bermudan subsidiary

In Figure 17.1 a US company has a wholly owned Bermudan subsidiary. Some years ago, the US company created some intellectual property (IP), eg an innovative computer program. Before the commercial value of the program became apparent, the US company transferred ownership of the program to the Bermudan subsidiary for a small sum. The program is now licensed to customers around the word, bringing in large sums of royalties. The US cannot tax the Bermuda subsidiary on these royalties because it is not resident in the US and has no source of income in the US. However, the US company *is* resident in the US. The US can apply whatever tax rules it likes to this US company, and so it can tax the US company as if the US company had received the royalties which were received by the Bermudan company. So, although the US company has not received any dividend, interest or any other form of payment from the Bermudan subsidiary, it is taxed on all the income of that subsidiary.

The CFC legislation prevents the US company from deferring tax on the Bermudan income until a dividend or other payment is made by the Bermudan subsidiary. Such deferral could otherwise be very long term, or indefinite: income received by the Bermudan subsidiary could be 'recycled' without ever being paid to the US company (see Figure 17.2):

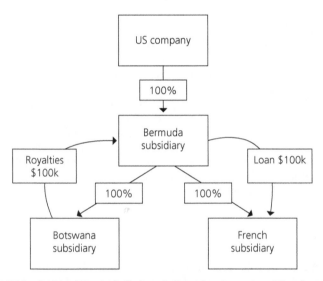

Figure 17.2: Achieving indefinite deferral of tax on foreign income through recycling

In this example, the Bermudan subsidiary holds 100 per cent of the shares in trading subsidiaries in Botswana and France. The Botswana subsidiary pays royalties on the computer software of $100,000 and the Bermudan subsidiary reinvests this by making a loan to the French subsidiary. This has two advantages for the group: First, the $100,000 of royalties are not paid to the US, where they would suffer some US tax, after double tax relief. Second, the French subsidiary will pay interest, which is tax deductible, to the Bermudan company in future, reducing French taxable profits and increasing the income in Bermuda which is free of tax.

Parent company 'base-stripping' v foreign to foreign 'base-stripping'

17.4   In Figure 17.1, the country that lost tax revenues due to the use of the Bermuda subsidiary was the US, the country where the CFC's parent company was resident. In the absence of CFC legislation, the US is unable to tax the royalty income. Without CFC legislation, the tax base (the income which the US is permitted to tax) is reduced, or 'stripped', by the use of the Bermudan company. However, in Figure 17.2, not only is the US losing tax revenues, but so are Botswana and France. This is because they will have to grant tax deductions for royalty and interest payments made to the Bermudan company, which reduces the amount of profits they can tax. This is known as 'foreign to foreign base stripping': in this case, we are thinking about US CFC legislation, but taxes have been avoided in countries outside the US as well as in the US. Should the US CFC legislation be concerned with the position of Botswana and France, or should the US CFC legislation be only concerned with reductions in US tax revenues?

It might be thought that once the royalties and interest arrive in Bermuda, they become income of the Bermudan company and are thus vulnerable to US CFC legislation. However, we must remember that the US has a very generous set of rules which allow US taxpayers to choose how their foreign investments should be characterized for US tax purposes – the 'check the box' rules (see Chapter 11). If the US company 'checks the box' so that the Botswana company is regarded, for US tax purposes, as merely a branch of the Bermudan subsidiary, then the royalty income of the Bermudan subsidiary disappears. This is because a company cannot pay royalties to itself: royalties between branches and their head offices are disregarded for tax purposes. The Botswana government continues to give a tax deduction for the royalty payments, because, as far as the Botswana government is concerned, there is still a separate Botswana company, regarded as a separate taxpayer for Botswana tax purposes. This is discussed further below.

Comparative CFC legislation

17.5   As is often the case in international tax matters, the first country to attempt to deal with the problem of deferral was the US. In 1962 the Kennedy administration proposed the complete elimination of the deferral of US tax by using foreign companies. There was considerable debate in Congress and ultimately the rules enacted were confined to passive income and certain sales and services income from related-party transactions. Avi Yonah (2005)notes:

> 'it is common to assert that Subpart F as enacted represented a compromise between capital export neutrality and competitiveness. While that is true, in practice the Administration got over 90% of what it wanted because in the early 1960s the vast majority of active US investment abroad went to high tax countries in Europe and Canada. Given that state of affairs, the Administration could give up on taxing

active business income of CFCs without diminishing capital export neutrality, since the taxes foregone by the US were in fact collected by other countries.'

In other words, the foreign tax credits on active business income would have wiped out any US tax liability anyway. No major changes have taken place since the legislation was introduced, although it has regularly been reviewed. Other countries followed suit during the 1970s and 1980s. In the UK, CFC legislation was introduced in 1984 and several refinements have been made subsequently (see the 'Further study' section of this chapter).

The broad approach is to deem residents who are shareholders of a tax haven company to be liable to tax on the income of that company, even if the income is not paid to the shareholders.

Countries which act as tax havens, either by being base havens, such as Bermuda, or which have particular features of their tax regimes which make them attractive as locations for financial investments, such as the Netherlands or Switzerland, tend not to have CFC legislation.

The OECD's Final Report on BEPS Action 3 sets out a number of building blocks for effective CFC legislation and these are considered throughout this chapter.

GENERAL APPROACH TO ANTI-HAVEN (CFC) LEGISLATION

17.6   Any system of CFC legislation must consider:

- Which type of shareholders (companies or individuals) and what level of shareholding is required? Does it include foreign investments other than shareholdings, such as foreign branches, or interests in foreign partnerships?

- What type of, and what level of, control over the foreign company by residents is required before a foreign company can be considered to be a CFC?

- Is the level of foreign tax suffered important in identifying a CFC, and if so, what level of foreign tax indicates that the foreign country might be used as a tax haven? Should a minimum statutory rate of tax apply, below which the foreign subsidiary will be considered a CFC? Should the effective rate suffered by the foreign subsidiary be used? Should the rate of foreign tax relative to the rate in the investing company's country be used?

- Should certain countries be named as either definitely considered to be tax havens, so that any company resident there is automatically considered a CFC, regardless of the tax rate suffered or the type of income in question? Should there be a list of countries which are definitely *not* considered to be tax havens? This is a locational approach.

- What type of income does CFC legislation apply to? Should trading income be excluded from the CFC charge on residents? How are dividends received by the CFC to be treated – is it necessary to find out what type of income was used to pay them (ie passive income or trading income)? This is a transactional approach.

A further choice to be made in designing CFC legislation is whether there should be an 'all or nothing' application of the legislation in respect of a foreign subsidiary. If the legislation is structured so that a parent company is taxed either on an amount equal to its entire share of the subsidiary's profit or none of it, this is known as the 'entity approach'. On the other hand, if all of a certain type of income or profits earned by a subsidiary results in a tax charge for the parent, regardless of the location of the subsidiary, this is known as the 'streaming approach'.

If a country exempts foreign branches of resident companies from its taxation, then it might be expected to extend its CFC rules to the passive income of foreign branches.

CFC LEGISLATION IN PRACTICE

BEPS Action 3 recommendations

17.7   This section presents some key features of the CFC legislation of a number of countries which have been selected in order to illustrate the differences in approach to CFC legislation.[1] Under each heading, the recommendations contained in the OECD's BEPS Action 3 Final Report are summarized and discussed.

---

1   The taxation of foreign passive income was one of the two main subjects studied at the 2013 Congress of the International Fiscal Association: 38 countries submitted length written reports which included details of their CFC legislation and the material in this section is primarily based on those reports. Other useful sources are Deloitte (2015), *Guide to Controlled Foreign Company Regimes*. Available at: http://www2.deloitte.com/global/en/pages/tax/articles/guide-to-controlled-foreign-company-regimes.html, and Arnold (2012).

Types of shareholders covered

17.8   Some countries recognize that the use of CFCs to achieve deferral of tax on foreign income is most likely to be practiced within multinational groups of companies via wholly owned foreign subsidiaries. Other countries apply their CFC legislation to impose tax on any shareholder in a foreign company classed as a CFC. Some countries limit the application of their rules to corporations, whilst others apply them to any type of shareholder. The problem which can arise in a system which applies a CFC charge to small minority shareholders is that those shareholders will not have any control over the foreign company, may not even know who the other shareholders are and may have no way of knowing that they are exposed to a charge under their country's CFC legislation. This is a particular problem in those countries which require residents to self-assess their liability to tax, including any charge under CFC legislation.

Table 17.1 Which types of shareholders are covered?

Argentina   Any shareholder in a foreign entity classed as a CFC, no matter how small the shareholding.

Australia   An Australian company whose interest in the CFC, together with those of its associates, amount to at least 10% of either shares, voting rights, rights to profits or rights to assets on a winding up. This is known as the 'associate inclusive control interest' and is the sum of the shareholdings in the CFC held by the Australian shareholder company, held by any of its subsidiaries or co-subsidiaries.

Brazil   A Brazilian corporation which has either:

- a 'relevant influence' over a foreign corporation. This is a very wide definition, catching Brazilian corporations which have the power to participate in financial or operational decisions, even if they do not control the foreign company; or

- shareholding of at least 20%.

Indirect holdings are taken into account.

China   Chinese resident shareholders owning 10% or more of the shares, directly or indirectly are able to exert substantial control with respect to key business decisions.

Germany   Any shareholder in a foreign entity classed as a CFC, no matter how small the shareholding.

South Korea   Korean corporations or individuals 'specially related' to the CFC and owning, directly or indirectly, at least 10% of its capital at the end of the fiscal year. 'Specially related' means one company owns >50% of another or a third party owns 50% of each of two companies or there are common interests through certain investments and transactions or ability to exercise certain powers or a third party has such common interests.

Family interests are amalgamated for individuals. Indirect shareholdings count.

UK   Any UK resident company having an 'interest' of 25% or more. An interest is defined as share capital or voting rights, options over these, entitlement to distributions of profit, entitlement to secure that income or assets of the CFC, current or future, will be applied directly or indirectly to the UK resident company's benefit. Alternatively, a resident UK company who has control of the CFC, defined as power to secure that the affairs of the CFC are conducted in accordance with their wishes.

US   A citizen, resident or domestic entity (which includes, but is not limited to, companies) owning 10% or more of the total voting power in a CFC on the last day of the taxable year. Direct and indirect, as well as constructive ownership counts. Even persons not normally classed as shareholders can be caught in this definition of 'US shareholder'.

When is a foreign company a CFC?

17.9   This question looks at the level of participation in a foreign company required before a foreign company can be classed as a CFC. The level of control must be set, either in terms of legal or economic ownership. The types of shareholders or other participators in the foreign company must be set out. The Final Report on BEPS Action 3 recommends that both a legal and an economic test of ownership is used. As a legal test, the recommendation is that residents should, as a minimum, own more than 50 per cent control. Indirect control should be taken into account as well as direct control. Consideration should be given to treating a permanent establishment (PE) located in a low tax country as a CFC if the residence country exempts the profits of foreign branches. Countries should ensure their CFC rules do not let hybrid entities slip through the tax net. If a hybrid entity is not recognized for tax purposes in the parent tax jurisdiction but is recognized as a separate taxpayer in the (lower tax) country in which the entity is based, then the parent tax jurisdiction ought to apply its CFC legislation in respect of the entity.

Table 17.2 summarizes the main rules used by our group of countries to decide when a foreign company is a CFC.

Table 17.2 Which foreign companies are regarded as CFCs?

Argentina	Any company resident in a blacklisted country whose income is more than 50% passive is a CFC, regardless of the level of control exercised over it by Argentine residents.
Australia	If controlled by Australian residents, either:

- five or fewer Australian individuals, companies, partnerships or trustees control at least 50% of the shares;
- five or fewer Australian individuals, companies, partnerships or trustees control less than 50% of the shares, but between them, have *de facto* control of the company, eg by being able to determine the composition of the board of directors or the dividend policy because the other shareholders are not interested in doing so;
- the foreign company is controlled by a single Australian shareholder who owns at least 40% and no other shareholder, or group of shareholders acting together control the company; or
- in all these tests, the percentage shareholding is measured as the 'associate inclusive control' amount, as defined in the previous section.

Brazil	If a Brazilian resident corporation has either:

- a shareholding of at least 20%;

- 'relevant influence' over a foreign corporation. This is defined as the power to participate in policy decisions.

Thus Brazil's CFC rules catch the profits of foreign companies which might not be under the control of Brazilian residents.

Indirect holdings are taken into account.

China	If:

- more than 50% shares are owned by Chinese residents; or

- the foreign company is substantially controlled by Chinese residents with respect to financing, business, purchasing and sales decisions;

direct and indirect holdings count.

Germany Any overseas entity that is a company for the purposes of German tax law; this could include a partnership, which is controlled by German taxpayers. Indirect holdings count. Whether or not a company is a CFC is determined according to the position on the last day of the fiscal year.

It is quite possible that shareholders could cause a foreign company to be a CFC unintentionally: holders of small amounts of shares would not necessarily know the proportion of shares in the foreign company held by other German taxpayers

Foreign companies whose income consists as to more than 90% of financial investment income are treated as CFC regardless of whether or not they are controlled by German taxpayers, unless their shares are publicly traded. Thus a German shareholder with only a tiny interest in such a company could have a liability under the CFC regime.

South Korea If there is a 'special relationship' between a Korean resident and the foreign company. 'Special relationship' means one company owns >50% of another or a third party owns 50% of each of two companies or there are common interests through certain investments and transactions or ability to exercise certain powers or a third party has such common interests.

UK	A company controlled by UK residents (companies or individuals). Control is defined as either legal or economic. Legal control denotes control via ownership of shares and/or voting rights. Economic control denotes entitlement to rights to more than half of the company's income or assets on a winding up. A UK company might also control a foreign company for CFC purposes if it is the parent undertaking for the purposes of FRS2 (UK GAAP).
	Cells within protected cell companies are also subject to the CFC rules. Overseas partnerships are not covered by the UK's CFC rules.
US	If >50% of both vote and value owned by 'US shareholders' as defined above. Note that only voting power is relevant when deciding which US shareholders actually get charged under the CFC legislation.
	Alternatively, a company is a CFC if US shareholders can elect a majority board of directors (or equivalent body).
	It must be a CFC for at least a 30-day continuous period in its taxable year. If not, there is no charge on the shareholders.

Notice that some countries use an economic test of control. The OECD also recommends a rule to deal with potential situations where two or more minority shareholders, each resident in a different country 'act in concert' to control the company. However, if the rules already provide that shareholdings in the potential CFC of related companies are to be amalgamated, most 'acting in concert' situations would already be covered by the legislation. It would be relatively unusual for two unrelated shareholders, in separate countries, to 'act in concert' to control a third company.

BEPS Action 3: application of CFC rules to hybrid entities

17.10   The OECD has considered whether CFC rules should apply only to foreign subsidiaries or whether they should also apply to partnerships, trusts and PEs. In many countries, CFC rules apply to all these types of entity, not just to foreign subsidiaries. More problematic are entities which are recognized for tax purposes in one country (ie opaque) but not in the other (ie transparent). In particular, the OECD has considered the question of hybrid entities owned by a company which is itself a CFC. If these are treated as transparent in the CFC jurisdiction, then the total income of the CFC will be the sum of the CFC income plus that of the transparent entity.

Blending of tax rates

17.11   The CFC rules are also less effective if the CFC receives interest pay-ments which are technically taxable in the CFC's (low tax) country, but not recognized for tax purposes in the holding company's country.

Country A

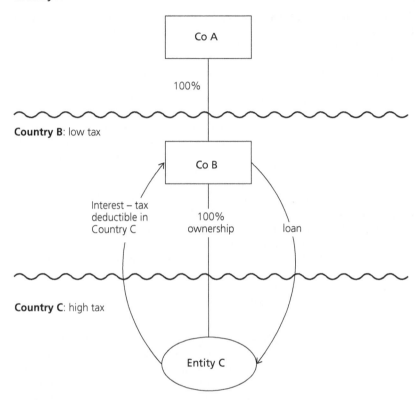

Figure 17.3: Blending of tax rates

This can happen if the entity paying the interest is considered opaque by the countries in which both the payer and the recipient are resident but not by the country trying to impose a charge under its CFC legislation. In Figure 17.3 the interest payment creates a tax deduction in Country C, saving tax at a high rate. The receipt is taxable in Country B, but that is a low tax country. Country A then tries to impose a CFC charge on Company A in respect of Company B's profits. Country A does not recognize Entity C as a separate taxpayer from Company B and therefore, as far as Country A is concerned, the interest receipt does not exist. This situation could arise from differ-ences in the ways that Entity C is classified under the laws of Country A and Country B.[1] However, it could also arise if Country A has 'check the box' rules similar to those in the US, and Company A has 'checked the box' in respect of

Entity C to have it regarded as a transparent entity (eg a branch of Company B) for US tax purposes, including US CFC legislation. This is an example of how 'check the box' rules on entity classifications can weaken a CFC regime. A criticism made by several commentators on the Action 3 Discussion Draft is that this serious weakness in the US CFC regime, allows US-based multi-national groups to sidestep a CFC charge in the US, effectively undermining the US CFC regime.[2]

The 'check-the-box' regulations – which permit lower-tier foreign group members which are subsidiaries of CFCs to be regarded as branches of the CFC, thus eliminating any passive income receipts between them for US tax purposes. The subsidiary of the CFC is then known, for US tax purposes, as a 'hybrid branch'. This is considered in Figure 17.2 above.

The CFC 'look-through' rule[3] was enacted in 2006, when there were strong pressures on the US Treasury to repeal the check-the-box regulations.[4] This rule was enacted to preserve the advantage of the check-the-box rules for US shareholders in CFCs even if the check-the-box regulations are repealed. Note that repeal of Treasury regulations such as check-the-box can be effected by the US Treasury without having to be considered by Congress. The 'look-through' rule eliminates related party passive income for most passive income payments made from a related CFC to a CFC of US shareholders. Thus, as illustrated in Figure 17.2, a US shareholder might own a company resident in Bermuda. If the Bermudan company receives passive income from its subsidiaries, generating tax deductions in the countries where those subsidiaries are tax resident, the 'look-through' rule would exclude this income from the income of the Bermudan company which would form the basis of any CFC charge on the US shareholder. The 'look-through' was a temporary measure when it was introduced in 2006 but it has been extended several times and is still in existence.

The Obama Administration's Budget proposals for 2016[5] resurrect the idea of closing these loopholes in the US CFC regime. In particular, they propose that branches will be treated as CFCs, thus negating the advantage of 'checking-the-box' to have a foreign subsidiary of a CFC treated as a branch. In our example in Figure 15.2, even if the Botswana subsidiary were to be treated as a branch for US tax purposes, the royalty income paid by the Botswana 'branch' to the Bermudan subsidiary would still be vulnerable to a US CFC charge on the US shareholder in the Bermudan company. However, another Budget 2016 proposal is to extend the 'look-through' rules permanently, albeit with the imposition of a minimum tax at 19 per cent (part of a wider Budget proposal).

At the time of writing, it seems unlikely that these Budget proposals will be implemented, rather, President Trump has announced 'outline' plans for changes to the US Tax code, with very little details supplied and no specific reference to CFC legislation to date.

A solution put forward in the Action 3 Discussion Draft is to introduce a 'modified hybrid mismatch rule'. This would operate so as to include the interest payment from Entity C in the CFC charge by Country A if the interest (or other type of payment) would have been included in CFC income if the parent jurisdiction (Country A) had classified the entities (eg Entity C) in the same way as the payer or payee jurisdictions (ie the same as Countries B and C). However, this is only a suggestion made by the OECD rather than a firm recommendation.

1 Note that the Action 2 hybrid mismatch rule would not come into play because the payment and receipt are between Countries B and C. Country B cannot disallow the interest deduction under an Action 2-style rule because the interest payment is taxable in the country where it is received: Country B, albeit at a low rate.
2 As one commentator notes: 'Irish-Dutch sandwiches and Luxembourg hybrids work, because the US subpart F rules (*the US CFC rules*) do not: comments of Johann H. Müller on Action 3 Discussion Draft. Available at: http://www.oecd.org/tax/aggressive/public-comments-beps-action-3-strengthening-cfc-rules.htm, at p 424.
3 S954(c)(6) of the US Tax Code.
4 See US Congress, Memorandum to Members of the Permanent Subcommittee on Investigations, 'Offshore Profit shifting and the U.S. Tax Code – Part 2 (Apple Inc.) Mary 21 2013. Available at: graphics8.nytimes.com/.../MemoOnOffshoreProfitShiftingAndApple.pdf.
5 United States Department of the Treasury, 'General Explanations of the Administration's Fiscal Year 2016 Revenue Proposals. Available at: http://www.treasury.gov/resource-center/tax-policy/Documents/General-Explanations-FY2016.pdf.

Level of foreign tax

17.12   In deciding what level of foreign tax implies that the foreign country is used as a tax haven, the choice is whether to look at the headline rate or the effective rate. If the effective rate is chosen, the question then is should that be decisive, or should it be examined as a percentage of the effective rate that would have applied, had the CFC been tax resident in the shareholder's country? Alternatively, a country might just publish a list of those countries which it considers to be tax havens and apply CFC rules irrespective of the actual rates of tax charged in the countries listed.

The Final Report on BEPS Action 3 discusses whether a tax rate exemption from CFC legislation is desirable. Targeting CFC legislation at situations where the CFC enjoys a low level of taxation concentrates government efforts on those arrangements where there is most risk of tax avoidance through the use of CFCs. Two types of tax rate exemptions are identified:

- A *fixed benchmark approach*: the tax rate in the CFC country is compared to a chosen minimum tax rate.

- A *relative approach*: a benchmark is set in terms of the effective tax rate suffered by the CFC as a percentage of the effective tax rate which would be charged on the CFC's income in the shareholder country.

Table 17.3 illustrates the approaches taken on this point by our group of countries.

Table 17.3 Rules on foreign tax rates – when is a CFC liable to a 'low rate' of tax?

Argentina	Not relevant: Argentina relies solely on a black list.
Australia	Any tax rate.
Brazil	Any tax rate.
China	If tax rate 'obviously lower': effective rate is less than 50% of the Chinese headline rate.
Germany	An effective rate of less than 25% applied to passive income. Tax credits accompanying dividends must also be taken into account in calculating the effective rate. This is to counter a device whereby Malta applies a high effective rate to passive income of German-owned Maltese companies, so that they appear not to be CFCs, but then negates the effect of this high taxation by refunding the tax charged to shareholders by way of tax credits.
South Korea	If the effective rate of tax is 15% or less.
UK	Level of tax is unimportant for defining a company as a CFC in the first instance. However, there is an exemption from the CFC charge based on whether or not the effective rate of tax in the foreign country is at least 75% of what the UK tax on the same income would be.
US	Income subject to foreign tax at 90% or more of the US rate is exempted – known as the 'high-tax kickout'.

Use of white lists and black lists

17.13   Countries may have good reason to suppose that some other countries are either frequently used for the deferral of income and that in the case of some other countries, it is actually quite unlikely that they would be used for tax avoidance or deferral. Hence the use of black lists and white lists is common. White lists are perhaps more politically acceptable: naming a country on a blacklist inevitably makes political and diplomatic relations with that country more difficult.

Table 17.4 Use of white lists and black lists

Argentina	Extensive use of blacklisting.
Australia	White list of seven 'comparable tax' countries, but income in these countries not exempt if it has enjoyed tax concessions there.
Brazil	None.
China	White list of 12 countries.
Germany	None, although there is an informal black list.
South Korea	None (abolished in 2010).

UK	A white list is used. If a foreign company is on the white list, none of its income is apportioned to UK shareholders. However, certain conditions must be met before this exemption is applied.
US	Blacklist: countries where the US is required to participate in an international boycott and countries with which the US has severed diplomatic relations.

In the BEPS Action 3 Final Report, the OECD observes that lists of countries, black or white, can make it easier to decide when CFC rules do and do not apply and they provide a measure of certainly for taxpayers. The use of white lists is recommended.

Types of income

17.14   Most CFC legislation seeks to tax passive income of CFCs. If a foreign subsidiary has a trade, then the location of that trade has almost certainly been chosen according to commercial factors, rather than simply because there is a low tax rate on offer there. Thus 'active income' is commonly excluded from the CFC charge on resident shareholders. A point of difference is whether capital gains are covered by the CFC legislation: some countries take the view that a capital gain may have been accrued over a period of some years, which may include periods when the foreign company was not a CFC. Also, it is not always possible to determine if the value of an asset has increased due to investment or to trading activity.

As well as income from investing, CFC legislation also commonly covers so-called 'base company' income. This is the income of distribution companies set up in low tax regimes. Such companies do not usually take delivery of the goods or services in question, but they buy them from fellow group companies at a low price and sell them, usually to external customers, for a higher price. Some of the group's profit on the sale to the external customer is booked to the low tax country, reducing the group's tax liabilities. There is an overlap here between CFC legislation and transfer pricing legislation, because the prices charged between the group companies ought to be examined under the transfer pricing regime of the group company which is selling to the base company in the low tax country. However, not all countries have effective transfer pricing legislation. In some cases, the CFC rules will state that transfer pricing adjustments must be taken into account when determining the position under CFC legislation.

Deciding what is income for CFC purposes

17.15   The BEPS Action 3 Final Report states that, although there are a number of approaches to identify income caught under CFC rules, a general principle is that CFC rules should be applied to income that has been separated from the underlying value creation, in order to obtain a reduction in tax. A typical example would be where a company resident in a high tax country develops IP, but then transfers the IP asset to a group company in a low tax country. The transferee company is then the one which receives the royalty income, although it was not involved in the value creation, ie the development of the IP. Countries might then either base their rules on categories of income or analysis of CFC.

Entity or transactional approach?

17.16   Once a foreign company has been identified as a CFC, countries need to decide if the resident shareholders will suffer a CFC charge based on all of the income of the CFC, or whether the CFC's income will be divided into active and passive income. In the latter case, the resident shareholder's CFC charge would be based on passive income of the CFC only. The approach to deciding this overarching question influences the way in which the CFC system is developed.

Legal classification approach

17.17   Income is categorized, eg as either dividends, interest, royalties, sales and services income, and the CFC rules are applied to income in specified categories. The underlying assumption is that certain classes of income are passive (and thus vulnerable to the CFC charge) and others are active (and so not vulnerable). This creates some difficulties: are dividends received by the CFC automatically vulnerable to a CFC charge, or is a rule needed to examine whether or not the dividends were paid out of trading income – in which case the dividends would *not* be vulnerable to a CFC charge on the shareholder. Rules would be needed to deal with in-house invoicing companies ('base companies') so that pure sales commission income is not disguised as trading income.

'Source of income' approach

17.18   A 'source of income' approach looks at where the income was really derived. Such an approach is best suited where the CFC regime focusses on parent company base stripping: where income which is really the income of the resident parent company is artificially shifted to the foreign subsidiary.

Substance approach

17.19 The substance approach is very similar to the 'source of income' approach. The UK includes this approach in its CFC regime. Substance analysis rules fall into three categories:

- *Substantial contribution analyses*: Where was value created? Where are the employees who created it?

- *Viable independent entity analysis*: Is it likely that the CFC would be owning the assets it owns and bearing the level of risk it bears if it was an independent entity rather than a group member?

- *An employees and establishment analysis*: Are the CFC's core functions performed by its own employees at its own premises? Or is it the case that its core functions are really carried on by employees of the shareholder company, at the shareholder's premises, in the shareholder's country?

These approaches all bear some resemblance to the approaches to verifying group transfer prices under BEPS Actions 8, 9 and 10: they rely on the concept of 'significant people functions'. This reinforces the fact that CFC and transfer pricing rules overlap.

An 'excess profits' approach

17.20 This is an approach not used anywhere at present, but suggested by the OECD in the Action 3 Final Report. Instead of categorizing the income of a CFC into passive and active income, and targeting the passive income only, the excess profits approach seeks to identify the income of the CFC which is in excess of a 'normal return' from the CFC's activities. Critics, such as the Tax Executives Institute (a US-based association of tax professionals), consider that this type of approach is aimed at a narrow range of tax avoidance using CFCs, and that the categorization approach, in universal use at present, should be retained. The types of tax avoidance activity which would be caught by an excess profits approach are instances where the CFC is located in a low tax jurisdiction and receives 'excessive' IP income.

A fundamental criticism of the excess profits approach is that it would be applied after transfer pricing rules had been applied. If transfer pricing rules operate efficiently, then such excess profits ought to have been reallocated to other group companies and brought into tax. If a group company still has profits in excess of a normal return, then it is likely that the transfer pricing rules have been only partially effective. BEPS Actions 8, 9 and 10 are all aimed at improving the transfer pricing rules and they include new rules covering the pricing of difficult to value transactions, such as royalties charge on unique IP between companies in the same group.

What exemptions should there be?

17.21   In the BEPS Action 3 Final Report, the OECD recommends that there should be a number of exemptions from the CFC charge:

- *A de minimis threshold*: there should be no CFC charge on the shareholders if the income of the CFC is below a certain threshold. CFC legislation is very expensive to use and if there is hardly any income in the CFC there is little point in going to the expense of imposing a CFC charge on the resident shareholders. Anti-fragmentation rules might be necessary to prevent the *de minimis* threshold being circumvented, although this would add considerable complexity to the rules.

- *An anti-avoidance requirement*: so that CFC rules apply mainly where there is a tax avoidance motive for the existence of the CFC.

- *A tax rate exemption*: so that the CFC rules are only applied where the CFC is resident in a country with a low tax rate.

Table 17.5 summarizes the types of income subject to CFC legislation in our group of countries and indicates the principal exemptions.

Table 17.5 What income is the subject of a CFC charge?

Argentina	Passive income where this represents at least 50% of the CFC's income. Includes dividends, interest, royalties and rent. Also includes capital gains on sale of financial investments.
Australia	Passive income: dividends, interest, annuities, some rental income, royalties. If a CFC has a high level of active income (at least 95%), all its income may be exempt from the CFC rules (entity approach). Base company income (ie of a group distributor company) but only to the extent that the group's practices are not caught under the transfer pricing rules. Dividends where the CFC owns at least 10% of the paying company are exempt. This means that passive income of non-CFCs can be paid to a CFC as a dividend and thus escape the CFC charge. Rents and royalties from active development and management of the underlying assets are exempt Capital gains on sale of shares are exempt in some circumstances
Brazil	All income, not just passive income. Brazil is unique in this respect.
China	All income, unless the company's income is mainly active income.

Germany	Passive income. This is negatively defined as not being active income. Royalties where the underlying IP results from research & development (R&D) carried out by the CFC itself is active income. Rental income from properties actively managed by the CFC is active income. The test is whether it would be active income under the normal foreign income rules, were the income to be received directly by the shareholder, rather than indirectly via the CFC. Dividends received by the CFC from its own subsidiaries are treated as active income. However, the charge on the German shareholder extends not only to passive income of the foreign CFC, but also to passive income of the CFC's subsidiaries.
	Base company sales and services income is also caught. Germany has a *de minimis* threshold but operates an anti-fragmentation rule: if a single German shareholder has shareholdings in several CFCS and, taken together, their combined income exceeds the *de minimis* threshold, then the shareholder is still liable to a charge under German CFC legislation even though no single one of the CFCs has income which exceeds the *de minimis* threshold.
South Korea	All profits are attributed but if the CFC conducts active business through a fixed facility in the foreign country, there is no liability for Korean shareholders. However, this exception does not apply if the company carries on wholesaling, financing, insurance, real property rental or certain services business where the totals of revenues and purchases from those classes of business exceeds the total of all its revenues plus purchases.
	Neither does it apply if more than 50% of the company's revenues are generated from the holding of financial investments, leasing IP rights, ships or aircraft or investing in trust funds.
UK	Non-trading income, subject to a *de minimis* exemption where such income is less than 5% of the trading profits. The rules are particularly aimed at catching income which derives from the use of UK based assets or personnel. Certain trading income: there are complex rules for determining whether trading income is apportionable on UK residents. Note that there is a special exemption for 75% of the income of non-resident group finance companies. Profits of group distributor companies.

US   Dividends, interest, rents, royalties and annuities, gains
             from certain property transactions. In general, the nature of
             the income must be passive.
             Profits of group distributor companies.
             Profits from intra-group services, where the services are
             performed outside the CFC's country of residence.
             Exemptions for:

- same country income received from a related company;

- dividends, interest, rents or royalties received from a
  related company and paid out of active income earned
  by the paying company, eg a dividend paid out of
  trading profits. This is the 'look-through; rule.

             Rent and royalties derived from an active trade are also
             exempt.

APPLYING CFC LEGISLATION

17.22

Example 17.1

Example 17.1 demonstrates how CFC legislation works, using an imaginary
CFC regime. Tinpan Inc is a company that is resident for tax purposes in the
(imaginary) country of Palumbia. It is owned by the following persons:

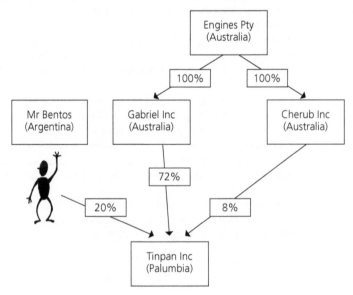

**Figure 17.4: Example illustrating how controlled foreign companies
legislation operates**

Tinpan Inc has the following income for the year ended 31 December 200X:

	Palumbia ($)
Royalties receivable	50,000
Interest receivable	100,000
Trading income	80,000
Dividends receivable	60,000
Capital gain on sale of shares in a non-trading subsidiary (one of the Hong Kong subsidiaries)	20,000
Total	310,000
Palumbian corporation tax	31,000

Tinpan Inc's trade consists of the manufacture and sale of specialist radios. The IP for their manufacture was mainly developed by Mr Bentos, although Tinpan Inc's own staff also developed some of it. It is estimated that the royalties receivable in respect of the IP developed by Tinpan Inc's own staff in the year amounted to P$10,000.

Because of the favourable rate of tax in Palumbia, Engines Pty transferred its 100 per cent shareholdings in its Hong Kong subsidiaries to Tinpan Inc. These Hong Kong subsidiaries do not trade, but hold certain financial investments of the Engines group. Hong Kong does not charge withholding tax on the payment of dividends to Palumbia. All the dividends receivable of P$50,000 are from the Hong Kong subsidiaries. The interest receivable of P$100,000 arises from the investment over the years of royalty and dividend income and also from the retention of net profits from trading. Tinpan Inc had sold the shares in one of these subsidiaries during the year.

Question: how will Australia apply its CFC legislation?

Step 1: is Tinpan Inc a CFC?

Tinpan Inc is a CFC, because five or fewer Australian individuals, companies, partnerships or trustees control at least 50 per cent of the shares. The rate of tax suffered in Palumbia is irrelevant for Australian CFC purposes. Although Australia has a 'white list' of countries which it does not consider to be tax havens, we can safely assume that Palumbia is not on this list.

Step 2: which income of Tinpan Inc can be apportioned to Australian residents?

Royalties:	Yes
Interest:	Yes
Trading income:	No
Dividends:	No – because Tinpan Inc owns more than 10% of the shares in the companies. The fact that the dividends are paid out of passive income by the Hong Kong companies is ignored.

Capital Gain:	Yes, but if the Hong Kong company disposed of had had any active business income, the amount of the gain attributed to Australian shareholders would be reduced. In our case, the Hong Kong companies have no active business income.

The total income which can be attributed to shareholders is thus:

50,000 + 100,000 + 20,000 = P$170,000

Step 3: which of the Australian shareholders will suffer a CFC charge and how much?

Australia only applies its CFC legislation to Australian companies, not individuals. The Australian shareholders are all companies.

Only the companies that are the front-line shareholders in Tinpan Inc are at risk. Thus, Engines Pty will not suffer a charge.

Gabriel Inc holds more than 10 per cent of the shares, so is liable.

Cherub Inc holds only 8 per cent. However, under Australia's 'associate inclusive control interest' rules, because the total of the holdings in Tinpan Inc of Gabriel and Cherub, taken together, exceed 10 per cent, Cherub is also liable.

	Gabriel Inc	Cherub Inc
	72%	8%
Apportionment of CFC income and gain:		
170,000 × 72%/8%	122,400	13,600
Australian corporation tax at 30%	36,720	4,080
Double tax relief for Palumbia tax at 10% effective rate*	–12,240	–1,360
Australian tax liability under CFC rules	24,480	2,720

*It is assumed that the tax paid in Palumbia is apportioned pro-rata across all categories of income. However, in reality, detailed rules might apply if different categories of income have suffered different effective rates of Palumbia tax.

Question: Could Mr Bentos (resident in Argentina) have a CFC liability?

Step 1: is Tinpan Inc a CFC?

If we assume that Palumbia is on Argentina's black list, then it would be a CFC. More than 50 per cent of its income is passive income. The level of control exercised over it by Argentinian residents is not taken into account, so the fact that only 20 per cent of its shares are held by Argentine residents does not prevent it from being regarded as a CFC. The rate of tax suffered in Palumbia is not taken into account under Argentinian CFC legislation.

Step 2: which income of Tinpan Inc can be apportioned to Argentinian residents?

Royalties:	Yes
Dividends:	Yes
Interest:	Yes
Trading income:	No
Capital gains:	Yes

The total income which can be attributed to shareholders is thus:

50,000 + 100,000 + 60,000 + 20,000 = P\$230,000

Step 3: is Mr Bentos in the class of persons vulnerable to Argentinian CFC liability?

Yes: all shareholders are caught, regardless of whether they are individuals or corporations and regardless of the size of their shareholding.

Apportionment of CFC income and gains: 230,000 × 20%	46,000
Argentinian income tax at, say, 35%	16,100
Argentinian double tax relief at 10% effective tax rate	–4,600
Argentinian liability under CFC rules	11,500

LEGALITY OF CFC LEGISLATION

17.23   The rules of international taxation generally provide that a country has the right to tax income and gains if:

- the income or gains arise within its jurisdiction (the physical territory in which it has the right to levy taxation); or

- the income or gains accrue to a person resident in that country.

CFC legislation taxes income which arises to a person not resident in the country and which is not earned in that country. It taxes income that is neither the income of a resident nor has a source in the country. Commentators on the topic have argued for some time now that CFC legislation is simply illegal.[1] Several cases have been brought by French taxpayers who have been subject to CFC charges in France in respect of Swiss subsidiaries. In the *Schneider* case[2] it was held that assessing the French company to tax on profits of a Swiss subsidiary was incompatible with Article 7 (business profits) of the France–Switzerland DTT. As the Swiss subsidiary was not a PE of the French company, France had no right to tax any of its profits, even if the assessment was made on the parent company. This decision has been followed in later cases. However, in a Finnish case concerning a Finnish company with a subsidiary that took the form of a Belgian co-ordination centre (paying very little Belgian tax), the Finnish authorities held that neither the Finland–Belgium Tax Treaty, nor EC law prevented the application of the CFC legislation.[3]

The OECD addresses the issue of legality of CFC legislation in its Commentary on Article 1 of the Model Tax Convention. The OECD considers that CFC legislation is not in conflict with double tax treaties although Belgium, the Netherlands and Ireland disagree. The Commentary (at para 23 of the Commentary on Article 1) notes that CFC rules are internationally recognized as a legitimate instrument to protect the domestic tax base. Paragraph 13 of the Commentary on Article 7 specifically states that Article 7 does not limit the right of a state to tax its own residents under CFC legislation.

In the UK, the key case on this issue has been *Bricom v IRC*.[4] In this case, the taxpayer argued that the terms of the UK–Netherlands DTT prevented the UK from applying its CFC legislation. The case concerned interest earned by the Netherlands subsidiary on an upstream loan made by the Netherlands subsidiary to the UK parent company (Bricom). Bricom relied on the wording of Article 11 of the UK–Netherlands Treaty: 'Interest arising in one of the States which is derived and beneficially owned by a resident of the other State shall be taxable only in that other State.' It was agreed that the treaty exempted from UK tax the interest, rather than any particular taxpayer. However, HMRC argued that the assessment was not an assessment to tax on the exempted interest, but rather on an amount of corporation tax merely calculated by reference to the interest received by the Netherlands company. As such the assessment under the CFC legislation was not prohibited by the treaty, as it was not the interest itself which the UK was taxing. Thus the precise wording of the UK's CFC legislation renders it compatible with most UK tax treaties.

Countries can prevent this type of attack on the legality of their CFC legislation by reserving the right to apply it in their double tax treaties. Canada commonly insists on this and France has started to insert it into its treaties as they come up for renegotiation.[5] However, Switzerland is naturally reluctant to renegotiate its treaty with France in this respect.

---

1   See, for instance, Sandler, D *Tax Treaties and Controlled Foreign Company Legislation: Pushing the Boundaries*, 2nd edn, Aspen Publishers, 1998. Note that when the first edition of this work appeared in 1994 there were only 10 countries which had adopted CFC legislation, but by the publication of the second edition this had risen to 16.
2   French Supreme Tax Court, 28 June 2002, *Schneider Electric*, No 232276.
3   Case *A Oyi Abp*, 20 March 2002, ITLR 2002, 1009.
4   *Bricom Holdings Limited v Commissioners of Inland Revenue* [1997] STC 1179.
5   See, for example, Article 28 of the treaty between Canada and Austria.

Compatibility of CFC legislation with EU treaty obligations

17.24   As discussed above, the CFC regimes of EU Member States need to be compatible with their obligations under EU treaty freedoms. However, if the Member States of the EU exempt all EU-resident subsidiaries of EU parent companies from CFC rules, then multinational groups operating mainly within the EU have a competitive advantage compared with multinational groups operating outside the EU. The Action 3 Final Report suggests that this problem could be tackled either by:

- Including an 'economic substance' rule: CFC rules could be applied in respect of a subsidiary which was resident in a fellow EU Member State only if that subsidiary was engaged in genuine economic activities. However, whether this goes further than the *Cadbury Schweppes* requirements that the arrangements concerning the subsidiary must not be 'wholly artificial' is debatable. The Discussion Draft appears to equate 'genuine economic activities' with 'arrangements which are not wholly artificial'.

- Applying CFC rules equally to both domestic subsidiaries and subsidiaries resident abroad, thus avoiding discrimination and accusations of limitations upon treaty freedoms. This is an unsatisfactory suggestion as it implies a large compliance burden which, in many cases, will not result in any tax being collected.

- Applying CFC rules to transactions that are 'partly or wholly artificial'. In other words, apply the rules even if only part of the arrangements concerning the subsidiary are wholly artificial.

Over the past decade or so, CFC legislation has been challenged under the terms of the TFEU (the Treaty on the Functioning of the European Union). This provides that residents of Member States should have the freedom to establish their businesses anywhere in the EU without any hindrance. These challenges have led to a major reform of CFC legislation in many EU Member States. The EU challenge to CFC legislation and the response of the UK and some other Member States are considered further in Chapter 20.

CAPTIVE INSURANCE COMPANIES

17.25   Captive insurance companies are used as tools of international tax planning to allow some profits to arise in low-tax jurisdictions. The companies are part of a multinational group, usually a subsidiary which is either licensed to operate as a direct insurance company for the group, or acting as a reinsurance company mediating between a commercial insurance company and the insured (ie the parent and the other subsidiaries). The British Crown Dependencies are active in this field – the 1998 Edwards Report[1] stated that Guernsey had 344 companies with assets of £5.2 billion and gross annual premium income of some £1.6BN. The Isle of Man had 177 companies, assets of £4.7 billion and gross premium income of £1 billion. The principal owners of captives in the Crown Dependencies are large companies, mostly UK companies or multinationals. The leader in the field by a long way though, is Bermuda, with a reported 1,405 captives (see Carmichael 2002).

The functions performed by a captive insurance company include assuming risk from the insured parties and establishing a reinsurance policy. The typical founder of a captive is an industrial multinational group with many subsidiaries, but many other types of organizations have formed them, including the Roman Catholic Church and the City of Oslo (Skaar (1998) p 12). Captives are used to avoid having to accept the prices and terms of commercial insurance as well as to achieve a reduction in administrative costs and to obtain terms which reflect the good record of the group untainted by higher risk companies as may occur with commercial insurance companies. Another advantage is that the premium paid to the captive is available for investment by that company adding to the overall profits of the group.

Most countries will not allow a tax deduction for provisions for self-funded insurance within the same taxpayer. For payments to be deductible, a separate legal entity is required for the premium to be paid to. While the group's motivation for establishing a captive may not be tax driven, revenue authorities are suspicious and seek to examine the transactions closely for a tax avoidance motive, especially if the captive is located in a tax haven.

There are a number of ways in which the revenue authorities can 'attack' transactions with captive insurance companies for tax purposes:

- the validity of the payment for tax deduction purposes can be challenged as not being for genuine 'insurance services';

- the amount of the premium can be examined using arm's-length criteria (ie invoking the transfer pricing rules); and

- the CFC rules can be used, a tactic commonly used by the capital exporting countries, by taxing shareholders on the profits of the captive.

---

1   Review of Financial Regulation in the Crown Dependencies 1998 (the Edwards report) at para 9.2. Available at http://www.archive.official-documents.co.uk/document/cm41/4109/4109-i.htm.

Protected cell companies

17.26   One way in which firms have been able to plan so as to avoid a charge under the CFC legislation, particularly with respect to captive insurance companies, is by using protected cell companies. Also known as segregated portfolio companies, protected cell companies originated in Guernsey under the Protected Cell Companies Ordinance 1997, and have been copied by other jurisdictions, partly in response to the problems arising through the use of 'rent a captive' schemes. These schemes emerged to meet the needs of companies not able to self-insure through traditional captive insurance companies, allowing them to share the services of a captive with other similarly placed companies. The problem that arises with 'rent a captive' schemes is that to third parties, the captive appears as a single entity, and a company participating in a 'rent a captive' scheme may find itself exposed to third party claims unrelated to the risks it wanted to insure. In order to provide some element of ring fencing of risk for participating companies, a protected cell company (PCC) contains separate cells that can be used to prevent the aggregation of funds and assets of the participants. So although the PCC has its own separate legal existence, its assets and liabilities are compartmentalized into different cells, with a residual portion of unallocated non-cellular assets to be used as last resort. Whereas, if a firm had its own 100 per cent owned foreign captive insurance company it might be vulnerable to CFC legislation, by using a PCC structure the percentage of the PCC owned can be managed so as to fall short of the CFC ownership thresholds. Some countries, including the UK, specifically state that their CFC legislation treats each cell in a PCC as if it was a separate company.

The use of a PCC to manipulate ownership thresholds is useful to tax planners in other areas as well, notably transfer pricing. PCCs are also used as collective investment vehicles, as the structures rely on contractual arrangements between the various participants. In 2008, the IRS released Revenue Ruling 2008–8 dealing with cell captives; providing several examples and an explanation of their treatment in terms of deductibility of insurance premiums paid.

FURTHER READING

Arnold, B J (2012) 'A Comparative Perspective on the U.S. Controlled Foreign Company Rules', 65, *Tax Law Review*, 473.

Deloitte *Controlled Foreign Company Regime Essentials 2012*. Available at: www.deloitte.com/assets/Dcom-Global/Local%20Assets/Documents/Tax/Taxation%20and%20Investment%20Guides/matrices/dttl_tax_cfc_regimes_essentials.pdf.

International Fiscal Association (2013) *The Taxation of Foreign Passive Income for Groups of Companies*, Cahiers De Droit Fiscal International, Vol 98a.

Lang, M, Aigner, H J, Scheuerle, U, Stefaner, M (2004) *CFC Legislation, Tax Treaties and EC Law*, EUCOTAX Series, Kluwer Law, The Hague 2004.

OECD (2015) *Designing Effective Controlled Foreign Company Rules Action 3 2015: Final Report*.

Sandler, D (1996) 'Tax Treaties and Controlled Foreign Company Legislation – a World Premier in the United Kingdom: *Bricom Holdings v IRC*', *British Tax Review* 1996, p 544.

Sandler, D (1999) *Tax Treaties and Controlled Foreign Company Legislation: Pushing the Boundaries*, 2nd edn, Kluwer Law International, 1999.

Skaar (1998) *Captive Insurance Companies*, IBFD.

Taylor, D, and Sykes, L (2007) 'Controlled Foreign Companies and Foreign Profits', 2007 *British Tax Review*, No 5. Available at: www.taxbar.com/LS_taxation_foreign_profits.pdf.

FURTHER STUDY

United Kingdom's CFC rules

17.27 The UK's system of CFC legislation was reformed following the adoption in 2009 of the exemption method of double tax relief for foreign dividends. Originally, it was intended that the change to the exemption method for dividends would be accompanied by a considerable tightening of the CFC rules. It was proposed that a 'streaming' approach be adopted, such that all passive income of foreign companies would be apportioned to their UK corporate shareholders, subject to minimum shareholding requirements. However, this proposal proved unacceptable to UK businesses and instead of the CFC reforms being implemented at the same time as the change to double tax relief for foreign dividends, there was a lengthy period of debate and consultation on CFC legislation. As well as the link to the introduction of exemption for foreign dividends, the UK Government was conscious that some MNEs were moving their head office companies out of the UK (Informal, Henderson, UBM to name a few) and that the uncertainty inherent in the previous system of CFC legislation was one of the causes. Thus improving the competitiveness of the UK as a location for multinational business was a further reason behind the reforms.

The focus of the new rules is on income from IP and monetary assets, these being highly mobile. A particular sticking point was that the UK Government wanted to treat all foreign royalty income as passive income. However, businesses argued that income from IP is not necessarily passive, in that firms devote a huge amount of resources to developing their IP and then managing it. This is especially true for non-registrable IP such as marketing intangibles, and other so-called 'soft' intangibles. The Government walks a tightrope in the taxation of income from IP: on the one hand, it wishes to attract innovation and the development and holding of IP to the UK, via the Patent Box regime, which subjects IP income to an exceptionally low rate of UK tax. On the other hand, it has been aware that IP developed in the UK has been transferred to low-tax jurisdictions, for instance, Cyprus. Not only is it very difficult to establish the arm's length price on such transfers, they are also often made at an early stage in the life of the IP before its true value has become apparent. Also, the UK Government recognizes that there are situations where IP is located in a low-tax country, but the maintenance and management of the assets is still carried out in the UK to a significant extent, so that income from the IP derives from UK activity. Using this argument, royalties derived from the IP have their source at least partly in the UK, despite what any DTT might state to the contrary.

Although income from monetary assets earned by group companies is a clear target of the new regime, the UK Government is keen to ensure that the UK remains an attractive location for MNEs to locate their head offices and thus there is a generous exemption from the CFC rules for the income of group finance companies located outside the UK. This acknowledges that MNEs commonly have dedicated group finance companies not merely to take advantage of low tax regimes for their mobile investment income, but also for valid commercial purposes. Of such income 75 per cent can be exempt.

A further impetus for reform came from adverse decisions of the Court of Justice of the EU, to the effect that the UK's previous system of CFC legislation, under which EU subsidiaries could be treated as CFCs, infringed the UK's obligations under the Treaty on the Functioning of the EU. This is discussed further in Chapter 20.

The reforms have been the subject of extensive consultation by HMRC. The main Consultation Document set out the aims of the new CFC regime:

- to target and impose a CFC charge on artificially diverted UK profits, so that UK activity and profits are fairly taxed;

- to exempt foreign profits where there is no artificial diversion of UK profits; and

- not to tax profits arising from genuine economic activities undertaken offshore.

As it is now possible to elect for foreign branch income to be exempt from UK tax, the new CFC regime is extended to cover foreign branches where a company has made the relevant election for exemption.

The rules[1] are complex and what follows is a brief summary. HMRC has published extensive and very detailed guidance notes on each aspect of the new system.[2] The new system was not implemented until 1 January 2013 and applies to accounting periods commencing after that date.

Although developed before the OECD's work on CFC legislation as part of the BEPS Project, the UK's CFC regime is generally considered to be consistent with the principles for a good system of CFC legislation, embodying most of the features highlighted by the OECD in the BEPS Action 3 Final Report.

---

1 Taxation (International and Other Provisions) Act 2010 (TIOPA 2010), Pt 9A and were mainly introduced by the Finance Act 2012, Sch 20.
2 Available at: www.gov.uk/hmrc-internal-manuals/international-manual/intm190000.

The language of the system – 'gateways'

17.28 The new system uses a so-called 'entity approach'. This means that, if certain initial tests are passed, none of the foreign company's income will be apportioned to UK shareholders, even if some of it is passive income. If these initial 'entity-level' tests are failed, then some or all of the foreign company's income *might* be apportioned, depending on the results of further tests.

The CFC legislation does not refer to 'tests' as such, but rather to 'gateways'. Profits which do not pass through the gateways do not result in any tax charge for the UK shareholders. Thus, profits passing through a gateway are potentially subject to the CFC charge.

In outline, to decide whether any UK shareholders might suffer a charge to tax under the CFC legislation, it is first necessary to see whether any of the 'entity-level exemptions' apply. If they do not, then it is necessary to see if any of the foreign company's profits pass through any of the 'gateways'. If they do, there will be a charge to tax on UK corporate shareholders who own more than a certain percentage of the foreign company.

Which UK shareholders might be charged?

17.29   Only UK companies are within the CFC charge. Broadly, a company owning 25 per cent of the CFC is caught by the CFC legislation, although the rules are detailed and take into account different types of rights in the CFC and also holdings of related companies.

If there are several tiers of UK companies in a group that includes a CFC, then only the UK company which directly holds the interest in the CFC is caught. The interests of a UK person which count as relevant interests are:

- owning shares or voting rights such that the UK person has control of the company, either alone or with other persons;

- entitlement to receive distributions of profits from the CFC; and

- entitlement to direct how the income or assets of the CFC are to be applied, and to have them applied for the UK person's own.

The relevant interests of UK companies which are related are taken together. Thus if Company A and Company B are UK co-subsidiaries in the same group and Company A has a relevant interest in a CFC of 15 per cent and Company B has a relevant interest in the same CFC of 10 per cent, then they will both face an apportionment of the CFC's profits, even though neither of them, considered alone, has 25 per cent.

There are special rules for CFCs which are offshore funds and for UK companies which hold shares in CFCs as trading assets.

Total amount charged to tax

17.30   The total potential amount of profits which might be charged to tax in the hands of UK residents is known as 'assumed total profits'. To arrive at this figure, a notional computation is performed as if the CFC was a UK company: the profits per the accounts are adjusted for tax purposes in the same way as if the CFC had been a UK resident company. All elections are assumed to be made (except for group relief) and all anti-avoidance provisions are applied. (Capital gains are excluded.)

Definition of a controlled foreign company

17.31   A CFC is a non-resident company controlled by UK resident persons. Although only companies can be charged under the CFC legislation, the interests in a foreign company of UK resident individuals are taken into account in deciding whether a company is a CFC.

There are three ways in which control can be defined – legal control, economic control and accounting control – which are examined in three tests:

- A test looking at powers exercised over the non-resident company: do UK persons have the power to secure that the affairs of the company are conducted in accordance with their wishes, either by means of their shareholding or voting powers or by any powers conferred by the articles of association or other document regulating the company.

- A test looking at the rights to income and assets of the company: do UK residents hold more than 50 per cent of rights to:

  — distribution of the company's income; or

  — the proceeds from the sale of the company's shares; or;

  — the assets on a winding up.

- A test looking at the financial accounting position and whether or not the foreign company's results would be consolidated with those of a UK company:

  — is a UK company the foreign company's 'parent undertaking' within the meaning of Financial Reporting Standard 2 (UK GAAP); and

  — if the foreign company is defined as a CFC, would that UK parent company be apportioned at least 50 per cent of the profits of the CFC?

There are special rules to prevent the CFC charge being avoided through the use of joint ventures, typically where two companies, one UK and one non-UK, each hold exactly 50 per cent in a foreign company so that neither of them can be said to control it and thus they both hope to escape the CFC legislation in their respective countries. The UK's rules for joint ventures will apply where:

- there are two persons who, taken together, control a non-UK company;

- at least one of them is a UK resident holding at least 40 per cent; and

- the other person holds at least 40 per cent but not more than 55 per cent.

For instance, Company A (UK resident) and Company B (Australian resident) each own 40 per cent and 53 per cent respectively of X Inc, a Bermudan company. The remaining shares are held by Bermudan residents. Although it could be said that Company B controls X Inc, for the purposes of the UK CFC legislation, the large interest of Company A Inc is taken to mean that Company A has joint control over X Inc. Company A is at risk of a charge under UK CFC legislation. Notice that X Inc is not controlled by UK shareholders in this case.

There are detailed rules to determine in which country a CFC is considered to be resident. The basic rule is that the CFC is resident in the territory where it is liable to pay tax by reason of its domicile, residence or place of management. If this rule cannot be made to work, eg because the CFC is located in a base haven which does not charge tax, then it will be considered resident in the territory which it is incorporated. Notice that for this purpose, we consider 'territories' rather than countries. This is because some places are not countries as such, but nevertheless are independent states for tax purposes, such as Jersey and Guernsey.

The CFC definition is also applied to cells within non-UK resident companies as if those cells were separate companies.

The 'entity level' exemptions

17.32   If any of these exemptions apply, then there will be no charge on any of the UK shareholders of the CFC. There is no need to apply any of the 'gateway' tests.

EXCLUDED TERRITORIES EXEMPTION

17.33   This forms the locational aspect of the UK CFC regime. It consists of a white list[1] of about 100 territories but with several conditions attached. Even if a CFC is resident in a white list territory, this exemption will not apply unless several other conditions are satisfied:

- The CFC must be resident in and carry on business in, the excluded territory.

- No more than 10 per cent of the CFC's accounting profits, or £50,000, whichever is greater, consists of 'relevant income'. 'Relevant income' can be any of the following four types:

  - *Category A*: income exempt from tax or which enjoys a reduced tax rate in the CFC's territory (eg a special rate for certain types of income, or special investment incentives such as a tax holiday). Dividends received are not included in this category, because they are not tax deductible for the paying company;

  - *Category B*: non-trading income against which the CFC is permitted to set a notional interest deduction;

  - *Category C*: income from a settlement of which the CFC is either a settler or a beneficiary. Partnership income also falls into Category C; and

  - *Category D*: income which has been reduced under a transfer pricing adjustment, but where there has been no corresponding upwards adjustment in profits in any other company.

The way in which the limitations are framed is of interest because there is a longstop of £50,000. In the past, MNEs have practiced so-called 'swamping' whereby financial income has been shielded from CFC apportionment by having it arise in a company which has a very large proportion of trading income. A CFC which had, say, £10 million of total accounting profits, would, in the absence of the £50,000 limit, be able to shield up to £1 million of financial income.

- No significant amounts of IP must have been transferred to the CFC from UK-resident related parties within the previous six years. Significance is measured by the amount of income produced by the IP relative to the total income of the CFC, and the value of the IP relative to the total IP assets of the CFC and of the transferring party. Where only part of the IP is transferred (eg rights to income but not the legal ownership), then the excluded territories will only apply if the IP rights so transferred do not form a significant part of the IP assets of the CFC or if the CFC's 'assumed profits' are significantly increased by the rights transferred.

- Finally, there is a motive test: the CFC must not be involved in any arrangement whose main purposes, or one of whose main purposes, is to obtain a UK tax advantage during the period, whether for the CFC itself or for any other person.

There is a more generous version of this exemption for CFCs resident in Australia, Canada, France, Germany, Japan or the US. The rules regarding the percentage of relevant income are not applied so that any level of relevant income is allowed. Also, and importantly, the exemption will still apply even if IP has been transferred to the CFC within the previous six years.

---

1   The Controlled Foreign Companies (Excluded Territories) Regulations 2012, SI 2012/3024.

LOW PROFITS EXEMPTION

17.34   As is fairly common in systems of CFC legislation, the UK is only interested in pursuing a CFC charge where significant amounts of tax are at stake. Hence, if the CFC has low profits, there is exemption. 'Low profits' means:

- the CFC's accounting profits or total taxable profits are no more than £50,000; or

- the CFC's accounting profits or total taxable profits are no more than £500,000, but of these profits, no more than £50,000 are non-trading income.

Accounting profits must be computed in line with generally accepted accounting practice. Any foreign dividends that would be exempt from UK tax if the CFC was a UK company may be excluded. Profits from real property and capital gains or losses are also excluded. If the UK would have subjected the CFC to a transfer pricing adjustment, this must be included, unless it would alter the profits by no more than £50,000.

This exemption is disapplied if special arrangements have been entered into with the objective of achieving a profit level in the CFC that falls below the limits. It does not apply to the profits of personal service companies.

LOW PROFIT MARGIN EXEMPTION

17.35   Besides the low profits exemption, there is also an exemption where profits of the CFC are low in relation to its 'relevant operating expenditure'. This is because a low profit margin indicates that the principal reasons for establishing and running the CFC was unlikely to have been to save tax. Relevant operating expenditure is operating expenditure per the accounts minus the cost of any goods purchased which are not actually used in the CFCs residence territory (such as goods bought from a fellow subsidiary and sold at a profit to a third party, without actually taking delivery of the goods). Again, if arrangements have been entered into especially to secure this exemption, the exemption will be denied.

HIGH RATE OF TAX EXEMPTION

17.36   This is commonly referred to just as the 'tax exemption' and looks at the effective rate of tax suffered by the CFC in the territory where it is resident. A relatively high rate indicates the CFC was not established to avoid tax.

To apply this test, the tax paid in the CFC's territory on its profits for the period is expressed as a percentage of what the UK tax would have been, had the CFC been a UK resident company. If the foreign tax is at least 75 per cent of this notional UK liability, there is an entity level exemption so that none of the CFC's profits are apportioned to UK residents.

Because, in the past, some territories have colluded with groups of companies so as to charge subsidiaries an amount of tax just in excess of the 75 per cent limit, this test cannot be applied to CFCs resident in Jersey, Guernsey, the Isle of Man or Gibraltar. No matter how high the rate of tax paid to these governments, this particular exemption will not apply.

TEMPORARY PERIOD EXEMPTION

17.37   To allow UK groups to get their house in order once they invest in a non-resident company there is a period of grace following the date on which the foreign company becomes a CFC before the UK shareholders will be liable to tax. This is normally 12 months from the date of acquisition, although this may be extended by agreement with HMRC. Certain conditions apply, including a requirement that, following the 12-month period of grace, there is at least one accounting period during which the company is a CFC. If it is restructured so as to avoid this, the temporary exemption will not apply.

If none of these entity level exemption apply: continue to the 'gateway' tests

17.38   At this stage, it is necessary to see if any of the CFC's profits fall into categories of profits which are potentially apportionable to the UK-resident shareholders. These categories of profit are known as 'gateways'. If profits fall into a designated category, they are said to pass through that gateway. However, this still does not mean that the UK shareholders will definitely have a charge to tax under the CFC legislation. Within each 'gateway', there are a further series of possible exemptions. We have just been looking at the 'entity level' exemptions: now we move on to the 'gateways' and their associated exemptions.

FIRST GATEWAY: PROFITS ATTRIBUTABLE TO UK ACTIVITIES

17.39   The idea behind this category of profits is quite novel: often, foreign subsidiaries located in tax havens exist mainly on paper. They might, in legal terms, own assets, have a registered office and receive or earn income, but in reality the work is often done, and the risks are still borne, by people in the parent company's country. So, although the profits appear to arise in a tax haven, in reality they are being generated by persons resident in the UK. These 'profits attributable to UK activities' so generated might be apportioned to UK shareholders. This test seeks to identify profits which have been artificially diverted from the UK.

To start with, it is assumed that all of a CFC's profits are attributable to UK activities, and it is for the taxpayers to show that they are not. This can be done by convincing HMRC that:

● the CFC is not established with the main purpose of saving UK tax, through the transfer of assets and/or risks to the CFC; or

● none of the CFC's assets or risks are managed from the UK; or

● even if they were managed from the UK, the CFC has the capability (for instance, enough suitably qualified staff and suitable premises and equipment) to carry on being commercially effective, were the UK management to cease. In other words, even though assets or risks are being managed from the UK, the CFC could do this for itself; or

● the CFC only has non-trading finance profits or property business profits. (Separate rules apply to these categories.)

HMRC provides guidance to help ascertain whether profits of the CFC derive from management of assets and/or risks from the UK. The UK shareholder at risk of a charge under the CFC legislation must identify the assets owned and risks borne by the CFC which are responsible for most of its profits. It must then identify the staff who manage the assets and are responsible for causing the assets to generate profits. This is referred to as the 'significant people function' concept, developed by the OECD, that is also used in deciding on the arm's length allocation to branches and in certain other transfer pricing scenarios. If all the staff responsible for generating the profits (ie the significant people functions) are in the UK, then all of the CFC's profits will be at risk of being apportioned to UK shareholders, unless a different exemption can be claimed under one of the other gateways.

Any loss-producing assets and liabilities are excluded from the computations.

Only the profits which derive from management of assets or risks from the UK are caught under this gateway. If this applies to only part of the CFC's profits, then some of the CFC's profits will be exempted from the CFC charge. These exempted profits are those which:

- are due to activities carried on by the CFC or risks borne by the CFC;

- arise from arrangements which are similar to those which independent parties (rather than the CFC and its group companies) would have entered into;

- are trading profits. This is an important component of the exemption and only applies where at least one of the following conditions, known as 'safe harbours' are met:

  - the CFC has its own premises which it occupies with a reasonable degree of permanence for carrying on its activities (similar to the concept of a 'fixed place of business' for PE purposes);

  - no more than 20 per cent of the 'relevant trading income' derives from UK residents or UK PEs of foreign residents. This excludes income from the sale of goods in the UK which were produced by the CFC in the CFC's territory. Such income is not the type of income at which the CFC legislation is aimed;

  - management expenses of the CFC must not contain more than 20 per cent relating to the cost of staff who carry out management functions for the CFC in the UK. If all the other four safe harbour conditions are met, then the limit is raised to 50 per cent;

  - no IP must have been transferred to the CFC within the previous six years where this IP significantly boosted the CFC's profits, represented a significant increase in the amount of IP held by the CFC or represented a significant drop in the value of IP held by the transferor; and

  - no more than 20 per cent of the total trading income of the CFC is due to sale of goods exported to customers from the UK, disregarding any such exports made to customers in the CFCs own territory.

As with the entity level exemptions, there is a general anti-avoidance rule so that the exemptions will not apply if arrangements are entered into with the sole or main purpose of securing the exemption.

SECOND GATEWAY: NON-TRADING FINANCE PROFITS

17.40   This is the next category of profits that will be apportioned to UK shareholders unless specific exemptions can be claimed. It deals with profits derived from lending by CFCs, which does not amount to financial trading. Non-trading finance profits are defined as profits from loan relationships: interest receivable, commissions, fees, etc, profits from finance leases and non-exempt distributions.

Non-trading finance income will not be apportioned to UK shareholders if it is only incidental to the foreign company's main sources of income. Non-trading finance profits are considered incidental if they are no more than 5 per cent of:

- the total of trading profits and/or property business profits;

- the total of the exempt distribution income, providing it is a holding company with one or more 51 per cent subsidiaries; or

- the sum of these.

Finance company exemption

17.41 Before moving on to the next gateway, notably, there is an important exemption that can apply to profits passing through this, and the next gateway. If profits pass through this gateway, such that they can be apportioned to a UK chargeable company, that company can take advantage of a major concession in the UK CFC regime, known as the 'finance company exemption'. UK companies facing a CFC charge can claim exemption so that they are only taxed on 25 per cent of the non-trading finance profits of the CFC. The exemption of 75 per cent of the profits is available providing the profits arise from qualifying loan relationships. These are loan relationships where the CFC is the creditor and the ultimate debtor is a company connected with the CFC, outside the charge to UK tax in respect of the debt payments.

There is the possibility of a 100 per cent exemption if it can be shown that the funds lent come out of 'qualifying resources', which are, broadly, the CFC's own assets located in the country in which the loan giving rise to the income is made. The loan must be made to members of the same group and be used for the CFC's own business. Detailed rules set out other possible types of 'qualifying resources'.

Group treasury companies, who will generally be carrying on a financial trade, and thus have their profits dealt with under the next gateway, the trading finance gateway, can also benefit from this exemption if a claim is made. Technically, the claim is for their trading finance profits to be treated as non-trading finance profits so that they can take advantage of the exemption.

The rationale for this exemption is that it recognizes the fact that much of the profits of a group finance company stem from transactions with non-UK group members, rather than representing the diversion of taxable profits from the UK. A source of great dissatisfaction with the early proposals for the reform of the UK's CFC legislation was the assumption by the UK Government that groups of companies set up non-UK group treasury companies not as a matter of commercial convenience and efficiency, but merely to divert taxable profits from the UK. The exemptions from the CFC charge in respect of profits falling in this gateway represent a climb-down by the UK Government in this respect.

There are some other exclusions from the amount of such profits that can be apportioned to UK shareholders:

- profits which arise from the investment of funds held for the purposes of the CFC's own trade (eg interest on the investment of spare cash), providing all the assets concerned are managed by the CFC and not from the UK;

- investment income from funds held for the purposes of a UK or overseas property business of the CFC.

There are some detailed limitations on these exclusions.

The non-trading finance profits which pass through the gateway (and therefore might be apportioned to UK shareholders unless any other exemption applies to them) are:

- profits attributable to UK activities (as per the previous exemption);

- profits resulting from the investment of UK monetary or non-monetary assets, unless received by the CFC in return for goods and services provided, or by way of a loan;

- non-trading finance profits which result from an arrangement with a UK resident company connected with the CFC. The types of arrangements caught are upstream loans (or other alternatives to paying dividends to the UK), and other arrangements aimed at reducing tax liabilities in the UK;

- non-trading finance profits arising from finance leases of assets to UK companies, where the lease is made as an alternative to purchase of the asset by the UK company and the reason for the lease was to save UK tax.

THIRD GATEWAY: TRADING FINANCE PROFITS

17.42   Where there is a CFC which has a financial trade, the profits will only be apportioned to UK shareholders if it appears that UK surplus funds have been shifted into the group treasury company so that it can invest them at lower rates of tax than could be achieved if invested in the UK. Without CFC legislation, this could be done by investing surplus funds in equity capital in a foreign group treasury company. That company would invest the funds and, due to being located in a low tax regime, suffer little tax on the income generated. It could then pay this income back to the UK investor as a dividend, which would be exempt, because the UK now exempts most foreign dividends from tax.

Two factors are examined:

- the extent to which the CFC is capitalized other than with loans – usually by looking at the amount of equity capital on which no interest obligations arise. This would include share capital, share premium and the retained profits and is termed 'free capital'; and

- the extent to which the CFC has been funded with capital contributions from the UK.

If it appears that the CFC is over-capitalized and that capital contributions have been made to it from the UK, then some or all of the CFC's income may be apportioned to the UK shareholders.

Whether the CFC is over-capitalized or not is decided upon by comparing the capital structure of the CFC with the hypothetical structure which the CFC might be expected to have if no company owned more than 50 per cent of its capital, ie if it were not a subsidiary. It is early days yet, but it seems the intention is that this comparison will involve looking at comparable financial companies outside the CFC's group. If it appears that the CFC has excess free capital, the test then looks at how much capital was contributed from the UK.

There are complex detailed rules governing this gateway, including special rules for banking and insurance businesses.

An important point is that companies with trading finance income can elect to have it treated as non-trading finance income. The big advantage of doing this is that the income then qualifies for the 'finance company exemption' (see below) whereby 75 per cent of it is exempt from the CFC apportionment to the shareholders.

CAPTIVE INSURANCE AND 'SOLO CONSOLIDATION' GATEWAYS

17.43 These categories of potentially apportionable CFC income apply to specialist group insurance subsidiaries and to banking subsidiaries. Solo consolidation refers to the practice whereby a UK bank is permitted to treat an unregulated (for banking purposes) CFC as if it was a division rather than a subsidiary. These are specialist rules and are not considered further in this brief overview.

HOW MUCH OF THE CONTROLLED FOREIGN COMPANIES PROFIT IS APPORTIONED TO EACH SHAREHOLDER?

17.44 Only corporate shareholders with an interest (variously defined) of at least 25 per cent is at risk from a charge to UK tax based on the profits of the CFC.

The chargeable profits are apportioned in proportion to the interests held in the CFC. If the CFC has paid tax, then this is creditable against the UK tax liability.

ADMINISTRATION ISSUES

17.45   UK companies must declare their liability under the CFC regime and self-assess the tax due on their self-assessment tax returns.

Clearances are available to assist companies in deciding whether or not they have a liability under the CFC regime. However, no further assistance is available on the matter of how to compute the liability.

Chapter 18

Tax Evasion

BASICS

18.1 This chapter considers how the illegal use of tax havens to evade tax on income by locating investments in tax havens and non-declaration of the capital or income to the country of residence might be tackled. Having considered the use of anti-haven legislation in the previous chapter, this chapter now considers in more detail the other forms of action that can be taken in relation to tax havens, in particular to curb their use for illegal evasion of tax by individuals. The OECD, encouraged by the G20 group of finance ministers, has a long history of developing initiatives in this respect:

Tax havens are used both legitimately and illegitimately. A legitimate use is to invest funds or carry out certain activities, usually financial, in the tax haven with full disclosure made of income, profits and gains arising to the tax authority in which the taxpayer is resident. This may well result in a tax saving, if the taxpayer can benefit from a system of double tax relief by exemption in the country of residence. As noted in Chapter 7, though, most systems of double tax relief by exemption apply only to active, as opposed to passive income, with credit relief applying to passive income. Countries also often restrict the exemption method to corporate taxpayers rather than individuals and trusts, who must still use the credit method.

Discouraging the legitimate use of tax havens is very difficult, but preventing the illegitimate use of them is impossible. Illegitimate use depends on non-disclosure of income, profits and gains arising in the tax haven to the country of the taxpayer's residence. A combination of a dishonest taxpayer and a tax haven which operates a policy of secrecy makes it unlikely that the country of residence will be able to tax the income arising in the tax haven, as it will be unable to find out about it. Anti-haven legislation is ineffective against the illegitimate use of tax havens and, in any case, often only applies to corporate taxpayers.

The main initiatives promoted by the OECD and used by governments around the world to reduce the illegal evasion of tax by hiding assets and income in tax havens are:

- The establishment of the OECD Global Forum on Transparency and Exchange of Information (Global Forum) in the early 2000s and later restructured in 2009. The inclusiveness of its membership (currently 140 members) and system of peer reviews may reduce the availability of secrecy for would-be tax evaders, and may improve the ability of small tax havens to comply with information exchange procedures. The first round (2010–2016) of peer reviews of exchange of information on request (EIOR) have assigned ratings to 116 jurisdictions with the vast majority rated 'compliant' or 'largely compliant'. For 2016–2020 a second round of peer reviews will evaluate progress under a more challenging EOIR standard.

- Article 26 of the OECD Model Tax Treaty (Exchange of Information) was strengthened and extended considerably in 2005 and 2014. A major change in 2005 was that information to be exchanged no longer had to be 'necessary', merely 'foreseeably relevant'. Information can be requested under a double tax treaty (DTT) even if the requested state does not need that information for its own tax purposes. States are not permitted to decline to supply information on the grounds of banking secrecy.

- The OECD model tax information exchange agreement has been largely adopted in hundreds of bilateral tax information exchange agreements (TIEAs). The effectiveness of these agreements is not yet proven, although they have undoubtedly been useful in certain cases.

- The Mutual Convention on Administrative Assistance in Taxation is a multilateral treaty for the exchange of information and, optionally, assistance in collection of taxes. It is widely regarded as a laudable advance in the fight against the illegal use of tax havens although it is still too early to assess just how effective it is likely to be.

- The OECD introduced, in 2014, a Common Reporting Standard (CRS) for the automatic exchange of information (AEOI) for tax purposes, accompanied by a multilateral treaty which enables tax authorities to communicate directly with each other, the Multilateral Competent Authority Agreement. Many countries have signed up to this as early adopters.

All these measures are voluntary – no country can be forced to join in – although by participating in these initiatives, countries signal their intention to abandon banking secrecy and engage in exchange of information, which will make it harder for citizens of non-tax haven countries to hide their offshore income.

The US has introduced its FATCA legislation (The Foreign Account Tax Compliance Act) that forces banks and financial institutions around the word to report accounts held with them by US citizens, so that the IRS can check whether those citizens have been declaring their offshore assets and income on their US tax returns. FATCA is legislation designed to prevent evasion of US tax by US citizens. FATCA is a powerful piece of legislation, with worldwide reach, due to the sanctions it contains which will be applied against financial institutions which do not report to the IRS on the financial assets and income of their US account holders. Most non-US financial institutions hold financial assets in the US, and the sanctions consist of a 30 per cent withholding tax applied to US-source income paid to any foreign financial institution not complying with FATCA.

Besides bilateral and multilateral measures (and FATCA) many countries offer offshore voluntary disclosure facilities (OVDPs) which usually consist of partial amnesties with respect to the penalties charged for failure to disclose offshore income. These appear to have been reasonably successful and may have a deterrent effect beyond the taxpayers actually making use of them.

The measures that can be applied against tax havens are summarized in Table 18.1.

Table 18.1 Possible measures against tax havens

Measure	*Use of tax havens*		*Level of application*	
	Legitimate	*Illegitimate*	*National*	*Supranational*
CFC legislation (as discussed in Chapter 17)	✓		✓	
Economic and political sanctions	✓	✓		✓
Information exchange and better cooperation between tax authorities	✓	✓		✓
Taxpayer amnesties		✓	✓	
Legal action against intermediaries facilitating investment into tax havens	✓	✓	✓	

ECONOMIC AND POLITICAL SANCTIONS

18.2   The threat of sanctions is at the heart of any supranational initiative against tax havens. The OECD has been actively pursuing measures to limit the use of tax havens since the late 1990s. At first, the OECD focused on the fact that low tax rates were being used by countries as a form of competition in attracting foreign investment. A campaign against so-called 'harmful tax competition' was pursued which is discussed below. This campaign foundered due to two main factors:

● The non-OECD countries targeted by the OECD responded to OECD pressures by making the case that many OECD members acted as tax havens, usually by offering favourable tax regimes in limited circumstance. For instance, many OECD countries were offering special tax regimes aimed at persuading multinational groups to locate their finance companies within their territory.

● Terrorist activity, and in particular the 2001 attack in New York, prompted the supranational bodies to be more vigilant in monitoring the ownership of financial investments in tax havens. Cutting off funding to terrorist and other illegal organizations was seen as a vital part of the strategy to clamp down on terrorism around the world. Anti-money laundering (AML) initiatives, and initiatives to force tax havens to hand over information about the ownership of assets and income became more important than persuading tax havens to give up their low tax rates.

Nevertheless, the initiative to eliminate harmful tax competition was an important step towards the current position of countries which either still are, or used to be regarded as tax havens and the concept of tax competition is now examined.

Concept of tax competition

18.3   Tax competition generally refers to competition between different tax jurisdictions to encourage businesses to locate their operations there. It may take the form of overall lowering of tax rates or more specific measures such as tax holidays where enterprises meeting certain specified criteria are granted favourable tax treatment for a limited period following their move into a new country.

If the reason is to attract foreign investment then many commentators and organizations are of the opinion that it is harmful and there has been considerable debate in recent years as to what constitutes harmful tax competition and how it should be dealt with at a global level.

Countries may use their tax systems to compete with each other to attract both portfolio investment and foreign direct investment. Portfolio investment is essentially investment which does not involve running a business. It includes bank deposits, holding of government securities and minority holdings in company shares. Bank deposits and bond holdings (eg Eurobonds) are highly mobile and can easily be switched from one country to another. Foreign direct investment on the other hand involves setting up a subsidiary company or branch in another country.

Arguably tax competition results in fiscal degradation. This means essentially that there is a loss of revenue to the countries engaged in the lowering of their taxes on income derived from capital investments and ultimately the erosion of their tax base. As competition intensifies, tax rates have to be reduced even further meaning that less and less revenue is derived from foreign investment. On one view, the only winners are the multinational firms and their shareholders. One potential loser from intensified tax competition tends to be labour, as most countries get the majority of their tax revenues from taxes upon earnings. This is where any shortfall in corporation taxes usually has to be made up.

On the other hand, fiscal sovereignty is illusory in a tax-competitive world – although countries may perceive that they have freedom to set their rates as they wish, in reality they are forced to set their rates according to what their rivals are doing. To a large extent, tax policies are dictated by internationally mobile taxpayers rather than by the correct aim of imposing a reasonable part of the cost of public expenditure on every production factor, industrial, domestic, fixed and mobile. So countries competing for foreign direct investment will want to offer competitive corporation tax rates and tax breaks for capital investment. Countries competing for portfolio investment will want to offer low or zero rates of tax and the opportunity to invest 'discreetly', so that investments are not brought to the attention of the investor's home country tax authority.

Tax competition: portfolio investment and evasion

18.4 Competition in relation to portfolio investment can take the form of imposing low or non-existent withholding taxes on outbound payments of interest, dividends and royalties, combined with low or non-existent tax on income earned on those investments. Where this is combined with banking secrecy, there is a great temptation for the taxpayer not to declare the income to the home tax authority.

This is an issue that is not confined to traditional tax havens. Some countries have preferential regimes for certain types of income payments: eg the London Eurobond market enjoys an exemption from withholding tax. This represents a huge amount of tax foregone by the UK as in the year to November 2010, funds raised through Eurobonds issued on the main UK market amounted to £393 billion.[1]

---

1 Office of Tax Simplification: 'Review of tax reliefs: Final Report' March 2011. Available at: www.hm-treasury.gov.uk/d/ots_review_tax_reliefs_final_report.pdf.

INFORMATION EXCHANGE AND GREATER TRANSPARENCY

18.5 During the ten-year period ending in 2009, the OECD had pursued an initiative aimed at preventing what it termed 'harmful tax competition' – see the 'Further study' section of this chapter. This was an attempt to pressure tax havens into ceasing to offer favourable tax terms to foreign investors and to give up banking secrecy. However, it applied to both foreign direct investment and to portfolio investment and there was some controversy as to whether there was anything wrong with countries offering favourable tax rates to attract foreign direct investment. A further problem was that, under the OECD's definition of harmful tax competition, many OECD members were themselves involved in such practices, so that the non-OECD tax havens largely refused to succumb to the OECD's demands. These demands were accompanied by plans for OECD members to apply sanctions against countries deemed to be acting as tax havens.

The nature of the sanctions which might be used against countries which declined to co-operate with the OECD in its new approach was made more explicit at the G20 Summit meeting in London in April 2009. On the subject of non-cooperative jurisdictions acting as tax havens, the summit communiqué stated, 'We stand ready to deploy sanctions to protect our public finances and financial systems. The era of banking secrecy is over'.[1]

Since then, four main strands of activity aimed at lifting banking secrecy and making it easier for countries to find out what income their residents are earning abroad have been pursued by the OECD, both centrally and by its individual member states:

- encouraging countries (OECD and non-OECD) to enter into bilateral tax information exchange agreements (TIEAs) if no bilateral DTT exists between the two countries concerned;

- encouraging countries to participate in the Global Tax Forum, which seeks to promote minimum standards of tax transparency via a system of peer reviews;

- encouraging countries (OECD and non-OECD) to sign up to the OECD/Council of Europe Convention on Mutual Administrative Assistance in Tax Matters; and

- encouraging all countries to adopt the OECD's Common Reporting Standard for the automatic exchange of information for tax purposes.

All four strands are aimed mainly at preventing tax evasion by wealthy individuals and trusts through illegally hiding income in tax havens and not declaring it in the country where they are tax resident.

---

1 Declaration on Strengthening the Financial System, G-20, April 2 2009. Available at: www. g20.org/Documents/Fin_Deps_Fin_Reg_Annex_020409_-_1615_final.pdf.

Bilateral tax information exchange agreements

18.6 Many countries, including many small island tax havens have been persuaded to enter into bilateral TIEAs with OECD member states. The OECD has developed a model tax information exchange agreement.[1] By May 2011, about 1,300 such agreements had been made. The question remains as to why a non-OECD member country would agree to any form of co-operation with OECD countries on the matter of tax competition or information exchange. The answer lies in the nature of informal sanctions, which could easily be enforced against such countries. For instance, if the IRS in the US were to make it known that all US taxpayers thought to have bank accounts in Jersey could expect to have their US tax returns closely scrutinized and could expect to pay the full amount of any tax penalties due without mitigation, then this would be bad for business for Jersey. Another reason is concerned with the fragile constitutional position of some of the Caribbean tax havens and the US, and also the relationship of the British Crown Dependencies and Overseas Territories (which include the Channel Islands, Gibraltar, the Turks and Caicos Islands to name but a few) with the UK. Whilst these territories have traditionally been permitted self-governance, increased participation in their affairs by the US and the UK is by no means impossible.

The effect of the combined G20/OECD pressures resulted in a flurry of signing of TIEAs. Besides the signing of TIEAs, many countries, notably Switzerland, also amended their DTTs to reflect the standards of exchange of information set in the OECD Model Convention.

Loosely speaking, countries were expected to have signed at least 12 TIEAs or have at least 12 DTTs containing a full exchange of information article. The danger with setting numerical targets for the signing of information exchange agreements runs the risk that tax havens will simply sign agreements with one another – agreements that will never be used in practice.

Figure 18.1 shows the breakdown of partner countries to exchange information agreements by agreements made with OECD/G20 countries and those with other countries.

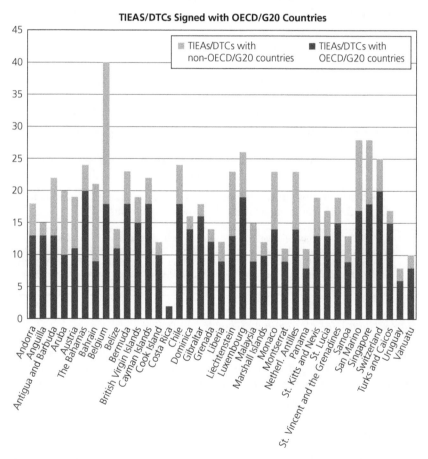

Source: OECD 2011

Figure 18.1

The OECD stated that fewer than 10 per cent of the 600 or so TIEAs/ amendments to existing DTTs signed as at 2011 were between jurisdictions which had not implemented the required standard of information exchange as at April 2009 (see para **18.9** below) and insisted that its initiative is 'not just a numbers game' (OECD 2011, p 24). However, as having a total of 12 TIEAs represents 'substantial implementation of the standard' it is probable that there are many targeted countries whose requisite 12 TIEAs are not all likely to be used. Even where the partner country is not considered to be a tax haven, there are situations where the agreement is quite unlikely to be used very much. For instance, the Faroe Islands have helpfully entered into agreements with:

Table 18.2 The Faroe Islands Agreements (as at October 2013)

Macao	Monaco	Andorra	San Marino
The Seychelles	Grenada	Cook Islands	British Virgin Islands
Liechtenstein	Saint Lucia	Samoa	Bermuda
Montserrat	Dominica	Turks and Caicos	Guernsey
Liberia	Antigua and Barbuda	Gibraltar	Jersey
Vanuatu	St Kitts and Nevis	Aruba	Isle of Man
Marshall Islands	St Vincent and the Grenadines	Netherlands Antilles	Anguilla
Belize	Bahamas	The Marshall Islands	The Cayman Islands

This was the entire list of agreements entered into by the Faroe Islands as at October 2013 and readers must draw their own conclusions.

---

1   OECD 2011 The Global Forum on Transparency and Exchange of Information for Tax Purposes: a background Information Brief, 2 May 2011 at p 4. Available at: http://www.oecd. org/dataoecd/32/45/43757434.pdf As at May 2011, Botswana, Trinidad, the Former Yugoslav Republic of Macedonia and Lebanon have been deemed to require such special attention. Macedonia and Botswana have now joined the Global Forum.

How useful are tax information exchange agreements?

18.7   TIEAs are an imperfect tool in combating international tax evasion and money laundering through the use of tax havens. For instance, para 5 of the tax information agreement between Jersey and the US reads as follows:

'Any request for information made by a party shall be framed with the greatest degree of specificity possible. In all cases, the request shall specify in writing the following:

(a) The identity of the taxpayer under examination

(b) The period of time with respect to which information is requested

(c) The nature of the information requested

(d) The matter under the requesting party's tax law with respect to which the information is sought

(e) The reasons for believing that the information requested is foreseeably relevant or material to tax administration and enforcement of the requesting party ...

(f) A statement that the requesting party has pursued all reasonable means available in its own territory to obtain the information ...'.

If the request does not meet these (and other subsidiary) criteria, Jersey may decline the request. Realistically, the US will be the party making requests. The US must already know the: who, when, what and why of any information it requires from Jersey. Viewed like this, the US can do little more than seek confirmation of what it already knows in many cases. Note the requirement for the information to be 'foreseeably relevant' which mirrors the standard set for exchange of information in pre-2005 versions of Article 26 of the OECD MTC. Another limitation with information exchange is, however, that it will only be effective if the information that is exchanged is reliable and so an important feature of agreements to enhance information exchange is appropriate standards with respect to accounting records.

Coupled with the criticism noted above regarding the fact that many agreements are made with other countries that might reasonably be regarded as tax havens, or, as with the Faroe Islands, countries of convenience, the usefulness of TIEAs is, in the authors' opinion, highly questionable. It is unclear whether information will ever be made public to substantiate their usefulness, such as statistics on the numbers of requests made and met and between which countries. In the meantime, what is evident is that OECD member countries are not relying solely on information exchange agreements to counter tax evasion. As is discussed in the next section, many OECD members are acting independently with initiatives aimed at countering the use of tax havens.

Although it is still too early to reach any firm conclusions on the usefulness of TIEAs, it seems likely that history will judge them to have been a costly diversion of effort away from strategies with more chance of success of reducing the opportunities for tax evasion through concealing investments in countries acting as tax haven. In particular, it might have been better for the OECD to push for countries to sign up to a multilateral automatic exchange of information treaty rather than encouraging a proliferation of TIEAs. Possibly the degree of pressure being exerted on the OECD in 2009 by the G20, following the 2008 Financial Crash, caused the OECD to concentrate on the TIEA strategy because it would produce quick results in terms of agreements signed, giving at least the appearance of progress.

The Global Forum

18.8   The initiatives against tax havens, which include but are not limited to TIEAs had been promulgated under the auspices of the 'Global Forum on Taxation' whose members, until 2009, were chiefly the OECD countries.

In 2009, co-ordinating with the G20 pronouncements, the Global Forum on Taxation was renamed the Global Forum on Transparency and Exchange of Information for Tax Purposes and its membership was expanded considerably and now includes approximately 140 member countries, all of whom, it is claimed, participate on the same footing. The Global Forum, although remaining connected the OECD, has established a degree of independence form the OECD, which is important in persuading non-OECD members to join and fully participate. All major financial centres are now members.

The Global Forum categorized countries into black, grey and white lists. A country was at risk of being placed on the black list, and therefore at risk of the sanctions outlined above unless it entered into a minimum of 12 tax information exchange agreements. Grey list countries are those which have committed to the Global Forum/OECD's internationally agreed standard of having tax information exchange agreements with at least 12 other countries but have not yet achieved this goal. White list countries are those which have achieved the minimum number of 12 agreements.

The 'internationally agreed standard'

18.9   The definition of the Global Forum's 'internationally agreed standard' is somewhat vague. According to the OECD:[1]

> 'The internationally agreed tax standard on exchange of information, as developed by the OECD and endorsed by the UN and the G20, provides for full exchange of information on request in all tax matters without regard to a domestic tax interest requirement or bank secrecy for tax purposes. It also provides for extensive safeguards to protect the confidentiality of the information exchanged.'

The standard is set to be roughly equivalent to that in Article 26 (Exchange of Information) in the OECD Model Tax Convention and to that in the OECD's 2002 Model Agreement on Exchange of Information. They require:

- exchange of information on request where it is 'foreseeably relevant' to the administration and enforcement of the domestic laws of the treaty partner;

- no restrictions on exchange caused by bank secrecy or domestic tax interest requirements;

- availability of reliable information and powers to obtain it;

- respect for taxpayers' rights; and

- strict confidentiality of information exchanged.

As to whether a country has met the standard:

> 'a good indicator of progress is whether a jurisdiction has signed 12 agreements on exchange of information that meet the OECD standard. This threshold will be reviewed to take account of (i) the jurisdictions

with which the agreements have been signed (a tax haven which has 12 agreements with other tax havens would not pass the threshold), (ii) the willingness of a jurisdiction to continue to sign agreements even after it has reached this threshold and (iii) the effectiveness of implementation.'

The OECD's 2012 Progress Report indicated that as at December 2012 only Nauru and Niue had not yet met the standard, although they made commitments to work towards it.

Besides insisting on the signing of tax information exchange agreements, the Global Forum organizes peer reviews of all its members and other jurisdictions which may require special attention. The peer reviews examine each country's legal and regulatory standards and in a further phase, its standards on transparency and exchange of information for tax purposes. The standards of transparency and exchange of information which the peer reviews look for are essentially those contained in Article 26 of the OECD Model Convention and the 2002 Model Agreement on Exchange of Information on Tax Matters:

- exchange of information on request where it is 'foreseeably relevant' to the administration and enforcement of the domestic laws of the treaty partner;

- no restrictions on exchange caused by bank secrecy or domestic tax interest requirements;

- availability of reliable information and powers to obtain it;

- respect for taxpayers' rights;

- strict confidentiality of information exchanged.

Countries are reviewed by reference to ten essential elements:

A   AVAILABILITY OF INFORMATION

    A.1. Jurisdictions should ensure that ownership and identity information for all relevant entities and arrangements is available to their competent authorities.

    A.2. Jurisdictions should ensure that reliable accounting records are kept for all relevant entities and arrangements.

    A.3. Banking information should be available for all account-holders.

B   ACCESS TO INFORMATION

    B.1. Competent authorities should have the power to obtain and provide information that is the subject of a request under an EOI agreement from any person within their territorial jurisdiction who is in possession or control of such information.

    B.2. The rights and safeguards that apply to persons in the requested jurisdiction should be compatible with effective exchange of information.

C EXCHANGING INFORMATION

C.1. EOI mechanisms should provide for effective exchange of information.

C.2. The jurisdictions' network of information exchange mechanisms should cover all relevant partners.

C.3. The jurisdictions' mechanisms for exchange of information should have adequate provisions to ensure the confidentiality of information received.

C.4. The exchange of information mechanisms should respect the rights and safeguards of taxpayers and third parties.

C.5. The jurisdiction should provide information under its network of agreements in a timely manner.

Over time, it appears that this list has come to be the principal measure used to assess whether countries have met the 'internationally agreed standard'.

---

1   OECD (2009) Countering Offshore Tax Evasion: Some Questions and Answers on the Project. Available at: www.oecd.org/ctp/harmful/42469606.pdf.

Review process and outcomes to date

18.10   There are currently two types of review:

● *Phase 1* reviews examine the legal and regulatory framework for transparency and exchange of information;

● *Phase 2* reviews report on the practical implementation of the framework.

Countries which are known to have well developed legal and regulatory frameworks are subject to combined reviews. The reports can be lengthy: the Phase 2 report on Bermuda runs to some 115 pages.

Countries are classified in the first phase of the review according to whether these elements are in place, in place but need improvement, or not in place. In the second phase, countries are classified according to whether they are compliant, largely compliant, partially compliant or not compliant, and given an overall rating. The Global Forum is sensitive to the fact that developing countries might not have the infrastructure and resources to fully meet its 'internationally acceptable standard' and it has made available certain resources to assist them and organizes periodic seminars for their tax staff.

The peer reviews are conducted by assessment teams consisting of two expert assessors drawn from the Peer Review Group, a subgroup of the Global Forum. Assessors are matched to countries in terms of languages, their familiarity with the type of legal system in the assessee country, size and location of the countries and the need to avoid conflicts of interest.

The findings of the Phase 1 peer review reports for some countries were so dire that they are unable to proceed to Phase 2 reviews, specifically, Botswana,

Brunei, Costa Rica, Guatemala, Lebanon, Liberia, Panama, Trinidad and Tobago, United Arab Emirates, Uruguay and Vanuatu.

As of March 2017, the Global Forum had completed 116 Phase 1 reviews and assigned compliance ratings to 113 jurisdictions that have undergone Phase 2 reviews. The ratings are as follows: 99 jurisdictions were rated 'compliant' or 'largely compliant'; 12 were 'partially compliant; and 5 were rated as 'non-compliant'. Details can be found in the Global Forum's report to the G20 meeting of March 2017.[1]

A total of 21 second-round reviews have been launched and the first evaluation results are expected in August 2017, with another 20 peer reviews to be launched before the end of 2017.

---

1   See www.oecd.org/tax/oecd-secretary-general-tax-report-g20-finance-ministers-march-2017. pdf.

Effectiveness of the threats: the case of Niue

18.11   Niue is a tiny island in the Pacific Ocean. It has no beaches and a population of about 1,300. Its citizens also have New Zealand nationality. It was devastated by a cyclone in 2005. However, it reportedly had a thriving industry as a tax haven, having passed secrecy laws for international business corporations in 1994. The key features of this regime, which reportedly attracted 3,000 companies to Niue, were:

●   complete tax exemption for profits arising outside Niue;

●   no stamp duty;

●   bearer shares permitted (so that the beneficial owner is anonymous);

●   details of shareholders and directors is kept secret;

●   no need to make any tax return; and

●   no requirement for the directors to meet in Niue.

The only charge made by the Niue government, and the key source of its income from the regime was an annual licence fee.

However, under pressure from the Global Forum, the International Business Companies Registry legislation was repealed in 2006. Thus, even though Niue remains on the Grey List, having failed to make the requisite 12 information exchange agreements, it is difficult to see how sanctions against it could be justified. Indications are that Niue is now turning to eco-tourism to replace the financial revenues, although it is still reliant on foreign aid.

Niue signed the Multilateral Convention on Mutual Administrative Assistance in Tax Matters (see para **18.14**) on 27 November 2015 and was rated 'largely compliant' in the Phase 2 review published on 14 March 2016.[1]

---

1   See www.eoi-tax.org/jurisdictions/NU#latest.

The OECD Common Reporting Standard

18.12   At the G20 leaders' meeting in St Petersburg in September 2013, the G20 endorsed the development of a new global standard on the automatic exchange of information. Normally, such a standard would take many years to develop, but because the US brought in its FATCA legislation (see the next section) in 2014, the OECD was forced to produce something quickly. The Common Reporting Standard (CRS) is a set of standards which countries should adhere to regarding the provision of information for tax purposes to other countries. The OECD describes this as a 'shift to a new era in tax transparency'.[1]

Under this system, rather than waiting to receive piecemeal information on particular taxpayers, countries will upload tax information in bulk on a multilateral basis. The information to be reported is financial information with respect to reportable accounts representing all types of investment income: interest, dividends, income from some insurance contracts, the account balances, and details of the sales proceeds of financial assets. The financial institutions which must report to their governments under the CRS include banks, custodians, brokers, some collective investment vehicles, and some insurance companies. Reportable accounts are those held by individuals and entities (broadly, trusts and foundations). Importantly, the CRS requires that the reporting institutions 'look-through' passive entities such as trusts to report on the individuals who ultimately control the assets held by the entities. The checks which the financial institutions must make in order to identify reportable accounts are also set out in some detail. These checks are known as due diligence procedures.

As the OECD cannot make law, in order for countries to put the CRS into practice, they must adopt its requirements into their domestic laws. Then, they must ensure there is a proper legal basis for the exchange of the information with the countries to whom information will be automatically provided. This is generally either a bilateral DTT which contains a full exchange of information article (usually Article 26) or a multilateral treaty to which all the countries involved are signatories. This could be the OECD/Council of Europe's Multilateral Convention on Mutual Administrative Assistance in Tax Matters (see above) or it could be the Multilateral Competent Authority Agreement (MCAA) (see below).

A practical model for automatic exchange of information has existed since 2006, that deals with matters such as the use of XML and encryption methods. It even provides chunks of code that could be used.[2] The basic process is described by the OECD as follows:

1   Payer or paying agent collects information from the taxpayer and/or generates information itself.

2   Payer or paying agent reports information to the tax authorities.

3   Tax authorities consolidate information by country of residence.

4   Information is encrypted and bundles are sent to residence country tax authorities.

5   Information is received and decrypted.

6   Residence country feeds relevant information into an automatic or manual matching process.

7   Residence country analyses the results and takes compliance action as appropriate.

Countries exchanging information must ensure that taxpayer confidentiality is protected. As at 5 May 2017, 50 jurisdictions have agreed to participate in the first exchanges by 2017, with another 50 in 2018.[3]

Domestic data collection and reporting laws are now in place in the majority of participating jurisdictions. The OECD is keen that developing countries should participate in the CRS and has involved the Global Forum (see above) which has established an AEOI Group. This AEOI Group is expected to use the 'roadmap' developed by the Global Forum on developing country participation.[4] The roadmap deals with the various stages a country needs to progress through before it can implement the CRS. Government officials must gain a sound understanding of what the CRS is all about. Next, the governments need to consult with their financial industries to understand what changes to customer due diligence procedures will be required, and how the information needed can best be gathered from the financial institutions. The countries then need to make the necessary additions and amendments to their domestic laws in order to implement the CRS reporting requirements into law. The countries must ensure they have adequate data handling capacity and expertise, and the ability to ensure confidentiality of taxpayer information.

Four benefits of adopting the CRS are advertised to developing countries:

• detection of tax evasion and offshore wealth;

• deterrence from future tax evasion;

• better domestic tax compliance due to availability of taxpayer information, better anti-money laundering capability; and

• enhancement of the country's international reputation.

The EU effectively adopted the CRS via the amended EU Directive on Administrative Cooperation (DAC) in December 2014. The parallel EU initiative is discussed in more detail in Chapter 20.

---

1   Report to the G20, available at: www.oecd.org/tax/oecd-secretary-general-tax-report-g20-finance-ministers-march-2017.pdf.
2   OECD (2012) Manual on the Implementation of Exchange of Information Provisions for Tax Purposes: Model 3 on Automatic (or Routine) Exchange of Information. Available at: www.oecd.org/tax/eoi/toolkit.
3   For a list of jurisdictions, see: www.oecd.org/tax/transparency/AEOI-commitments.pdf.
4   Global Forum on Transparency and Exchange of information for Tax Purposes 'Automatic Exchange of Information: a Roadmap for Developing Country Participation', 5 August 2014.

Multilateral Competent Authority Agreement

18.13   Recognizing that domestic regulation by itself is insufficient, and to achieve uniformity and agreement as to how the CRS will operate, the

OECD has promoted a separate Multilateral Competent Authority Agreement (MCAA) alongside the CRS. The initial agreement was signed on 29 October 2014 by 51 jurisdictions and, as of April 2017, the MCAA has been signed by 88 countries. It specifies the details of what information will be exchanged and when, which will govern the bilateral exchanges of information which will be made under the CRS.

According to the OECD website:[1]

'the notifications filed by each jurisdiction include (i) confirmation that domestic CRS legislation is in place and whether the jurisdiction will exchange on a reciprocal or non-reciprocal basis, (ii) a specification of the transmission and encryption methods, (iii) a specification of the data protection requirements to be met in relation to information exchange by the jurisdiction (iv) a confirmation that the jurisdiction has appropriate confidentiality and data safeguards in place and (v) a list of its intended exchange partner jurisdictions under the CRS MCAA.'

The 'International Tax Compliance Regulations' give effect to the MCAA that implements the CRS in the UK.[2] In the 2015 Budget, the UK recognized the importance of the CRS by implementing a higher band of penalties for taxpayers found to be evading UK tax by hiding assets in countries that are not committed to the CRS.

The OECD is keen to involve developing countries in the CRS, and has published a CRS implementation handbook, a list of FAQs as well as providing workshops for government officials, and implementation assistance to specific countries. The Global Forum is closely involved in this work.

The advantages of automatic exchange of information over exchange of information on request are mostly obvious. Less obviously, it may have an important deterrent effect on would-be tax evaders.

There is some debate as to whether this initiative of the OECD's duplicates the US 'FATCA' rules, or whether it is being promulgated in order to prevent the spread of multiple sets of FATCA-type rules as other countries emulate the US in its information gathering powers. The OECD acknowledges that FATCA has been a key driver in its activities regarding automatic exchange of information. In time, the mechanisms developed to enable FATCA compliance may well form the basis of a multilateral system of automatic information exchange. FATCA is covered in more detail at para **18.15** below.

---

1   See: www.oecd.org/tax/automatic-exchange/international-framework-for-the-crs/.
2   The same Regulations (SI 2015/878) also implement the DAC, and the UK's IGA with the US under FATCA.

The OECD/Council of Europe Multilateral Convention on Mutual Administrative Assistance in Tax Matters

18.14   In November 2015, Niue became the 92nd country to sign the above Convention and, as at May 2017, 110 jurisdictions participate. All the G20 countries are signatories. The Mutual Assistance Convention is of interest because:

- it is open to all states, not just OECD members;

- it has been signed by a wide range of states, not all of whom have extensive DTT networks, and it contains provisions which, whilst similar to those in Article 26 of the OECD's MTC, go further than the MTC;[1]

- reservations on the Convention are limited to those detailed on a short menu so that, if a state wishes to make further reservations, it will not be able to become a signatory;

- it provides a template for the management of a multilateral instrument: there is a coordinating body whose members are the competent authorities of the Parties to the Convention and who finance it. States which have, so far, merely signed the Convention may be represented on the Coordinating Body as observers;

- it covers a wider range of taxes than DTTs, such as VAT; and

- it can be used to exchange information on all types of taxpayers: individuals, partnerships, trusts and companies, to name a few.

By becoming a signatory to the Convention (and, importantly, ratifying it, so that its provisions actually take effect) a country simultaneously agrees with all other signatories to exchange information. It is thus a far more powerful tool than an individual TIEA. Signing the Convention has a 'signalling' effect: by doing so, a country is telling the world that it does not want to be perceived as a tax haven, is a good place to do business, has a government for whom transparency in public dealings is important, and so on.

The main commitments which a country makes under the Convention are to:

- exchange information which is 'foreseeably relevant' for the administration of a country's laws (not specifically limited to tax laws) upon request;

- spontaneously exchange information where it appears there will be a loss of tax to another signatory country in the absence of the supply of the information – eg if one country becomes aware that a resident of a co-signatory country has investments there and is not declaring the income on them to the tax authority in the country of tax residence;

- automatically exchange information with specific countries if they wish to, the exchange being limited to categories of information agreed with the other countries concerned. This is an optional part of the Convention and is effectively superseded by the OECD's Common Reporting Standard (see para **18.12** above);

- take part in simultaneous tax examinations: where the tax affairs of a person are examined at the same time in two different countries, which will pool the information which comes to light;

- permit other tax authorities to visit their country to conduct tax examinations: eg the UK, as a signatory to the Convention, must permit members of staff of the tax authorities of other signatory countries to visit the UK and be allowed access to UK tax records, subject to confidentiality requirements. This can be a much more effective way of investigating a taxpayer than conducting the enquiries with a foreign tax authority by email or phone; and

● help to collect tax liabilities from non-residents who are present in their country, where that person is resident in a co-signatory country. So, if a person is tax resident in France and owes tax there, but is currently living in the UK, the UK undertakes to try to get the money from that person to hand it over to the French tax authority.

The Convention, by including provisions whereby countries promise to help collect tax debts due to other governments, is of great importance. It marks a change from the established doctrine that one country will not help another country in the collection of its taxes – the so-called 'revenue rule'. By doing so, it potentially opens up the way for fundamental changes in the international tax system. For instance, if Country A has undertaken to help Country B collect its taxes from Country B residents, then a resident of Country B, Company X, which has a source of income (say, interest) in Country A could be taxed by Country A. However, at present, the main way in which Country A collects its tax, on the source principle, is by imposing withholding tax. This is a crude mechanism which is unpopular with taxpayers. In future, it might be possible for Country A to inform the tax authority in Country B that Company X has a liability to pay tax to Country A and to request that the tax authority in Country B collect the tax from Company X and send it to Country A. Country B would also want to tax the interest, on the grounds that Company X is tax resident there, and would have to give double tax relief for the Country A tax.

Countries can limit their obligations under the Convention by entering 'reservations'. There is a limited menu of these, for instance, a country may state that it will not provide assistance in the collection of another country's taxes. Otherwise, it is an 'all or nothing' commitment.

By signing the Mutual Assistance Convention, countries go beyond any bilateral tax treaty obligations they may already have to each other. How effective the Mutual Assistance Convention will be remains to be seen. Certainly, the commitments entered into by ratifying it are not onerous, given that the more radical provisions, such as automatic exchange of information, require further agreement between two states, and given the menu of possible reservations.

---

1   For instance, the Mutual Assistance Convention contains requirements to permit simultaneous tax examinations. It also covers a wide range of taxes and contains provisions for mutual assistance in collection. Whilst these features are present in the 2010 version of the MTC, they are absent in many DTTs.

THE US FOREIGN ACCOUNT TAX COMPLIANCE ACT

18.15   The US Foreign Account Tax Compliance Act (FATCA), which came into effect in 2014, is widely viewed as a response by the US to the perceived ineffectuality of the OECD initiatives described so far in this chapter. The imposition by the US of the regime could be viewed as a vote of no-confidence in the Mutual Assistance Convention and, indeed, the whole of the OECD's exchange of information programme. FATCA is the unilateral imposition by the US of demands for financial intermediaries, such as banks, broker-dealers, insurance companies, hedge funds and investment fund managers, in other countries to supply the US with details of accounts held with them by US residents. If the financial intermediaries fail to supply the right information at the right time, in the right format and in the right amount of detail, they face a heavy penalty. This penalty is that the US will impose a 30 per cent withholding tax on any payments made to the foreign financial intermediary from the US, whether income, or the proceeds of sales of US securities. If the withholding tax were to be used, this could put the financial intermediaries out of business, damaging the economies of the countries in which they are resident.

In brief, the main type of information to be provided to the US tax authority, from January 2014, is:

- the name, address and tax identification number of the account holder;
- the account number;
- the account balance or value;
- payments made during the year with respect to the account. This includes the aggregate gross amount paid or credited to the account with respect to:
  — dividends;
  — interest;
  — the sale or redemption of property;
- transfers and closings of deposit, custodial, insurance, annuity financial accounts.'

FATCA reporting is required for accounts where the balance exceeds US$1 million.[1]

As well as reporting to the US on specific customer accounts, financial intermediaries are expected to carry out due diligence procedures to find out which of their customers might be US taxpayers. Technically, they are required to determine whether an account holder has 'US indicia'. Such indicia would be a US place of birth, per the person's passport, or a US mailing address, or US telephone number. There might be a standing instruction to transfer funds to a US account. If the signs are that an account holder has a US connection, then the financial intermediary must take further steps to check this. If it turns out that the account holder probably is a US tax resident, then the account holder must be formally asked for their US tax identification number (TIN) and for a waiver of the account holder's rights under any financial secrecy laws which might otherwise apply. If the account holder refuses, then the financial intermediary must report the account holder as a recalcitrant account holder. In this case, the financial intermediary will be expected to apply 30 per cent withholding on payments to the account holder on behalf of the US.

The US National Taxpayer Advocate has expressed concern about the impact of FATCA on compliant taxpayers, and especially US expatriates. In the conclusion to its 2016 report to Congress, it is stated:[2]

> 'The IRS has gradually shifted to an enforcement-based regime with respect to international taxpayers. The underlying assumption is that all such taxpayers should be suspected of fraudulent activity until they can prove otherwise, an outlook that causes the IRS to mistrust stakeholders, dismiss useful comments and suggestions, and misallocate resources.'

---

1 See de Clermont-Tonnerre, J and Ruchelman, S (2013) 'A Layman's Guide to FATCA Due Diligence and Reporting Obligations', 42, *Tax Management International Journal*, 75. Available at: www.ruchelaw.com/pdfs/A%20Laymans%20Guide%20to%20FATCA%20Due%20 Diligence%20and%20Reporting%20Obligations.pdf.
2 Taxpayer Advocate Service 2016 Annual Report to Congress, Volume 1, Most Serious Problems, No 16, p 220 ff. Available at: https://taxpayeradvocate.irs.gov/Media/Default/ Documents/2016-ARC/ARC16_Volume1_MostSeriousProblems.pdf.

Intergovernmental Agreements

18.16   Many countries where financial intermediaries are resident have negotiated with the US to agree upon how their financial intermediaries will comply with FATCA. France, Germany, Italy, Spain, and the UK have negotiated with the US to produce so-called inter-governmental agreements (IGAs) under which the financial institutions will report their FATCA information to their own tax authorities, who in turn will relay it to the US. These are known as Model 1 IGAs. There are two versions, Model 1A that provides for a limited amount of reciprocity by the US and Model 1B, that does not.

Japan and Switzerland have negotiated slightly different arrangements, under which their financial institutions would report directly to the US: Model 2 IGAs. Many more countries are expected to negotiate IGAs with the US. There are reciprocal and non-reciprocal versions of Model 1, meaning that, in theory, a country such as the UK, could place equivalent demands on US financial intermediaries as the US is placing on UK financial intermediaries. Rather than present the signing of the IGA with the US as capitulating to US extraterritorial tax practices, HMRC presented it as a groundbreaking move, forming part of a new standard in international tax transparency (HMRC, 2013).

IGA Model 1A – some detail

18.17   As can be seen from Table 18.3, although this is advertised as a reciprocal model, reciprocity is rather limited.[1]

Table 18.3

Information to be supplied by IGA partner country to the US	*Information to be supplied by the US to the FATCA partner country*
Name	Name
Address	Address
US TIN	FATCA Partner Country TIN of account holders in the US who are residents of FATCA Partner Country. *Note the absence of any 'look-through' provisions for entities controlled by a Partner Country resident.*
Name, address and US TIN of any entity which has one or more US 'Controlling Persons' that are 'Specified US Persons'. Same information for the 'Specified US Persons'.	
The account number.	The account number.
The name and identifying number of the Reporting FATCA Partner Institution.	The name and identifying number of the Reporting US Financial Institution.
The account balance (including the cash value or surrender value of insurance or annuity contracts).	No requirement to report the account balance.
For custodial accounts: The gross amount of interest, dividends or other income and: The total gross sales or redemption proceeds credited to the account where the FATCA partner country institution acted as a custodian, broker, nominee or otherwise as agent for the account holder.	No requirements to report on custodial accounts.
Depository accounts: Total gross interest paid or credited to the account.	Depository accounts: Total gross interest paid Gross amount of other US source income paid or credit to the account.
Other accounts: Total gross amount paid or credited with respect to which the FATCA Partner financial institution was the debtor, including redemption payments.	No other accounts covered.

Only countries which have DTTs with a full exchange of information article, or a separate tax information exchange agreement (TIEA) can enter into a Model 1A IGA. Even then, the US will only agree to enter into a Model 1A IGA where it is satisfied that the candidate country has satisfactory legal and practical protections to ensure the confidentiality of the US-supplied information and the restriction of its use to tax purposes only.

---

1   Full texts of the IGAs are available at: www.treasury.gov/resource-center/tax-policy/treaties/Pages/FATCA.aspx.

The spread of FATCA-style legislation

18.18   Several commentators have expressed concern over the potentially significant compliance costs associated with FATCA.[1] Christians (2013) has expressed concern about the legal efficacy of IGAs, which raises questions about enforcement. The big question is to what extent other countries will follow the lead of the US and also adopt their own FATCA-style legislation. The UK has imposed FATCA-style requirements on Jersey, Guernsey, Gibraltar and the Isle of Man, complete with FATCA-style IGAs.[2] These all provide for reciprocal exchange of information on an automatic basis. Further arrangements have been put in place between the UK and a number of its Overseas Territories. The IGAs with these Territories are non-reciprocal.

---

1   Available at: www.gov.uk/government/publications/automatic-exchange-of-information-agreements-other-uk-agreements/automatic-exchange-of-information-agreements-other-uk-agreements.
2   See for example Coder (2013).

Comparing FATCA with the OECD's Common Reporting Standard and the DAC

18.19

Table 18.4

Point of comparison	FATCA	OECD CRS/EU DAC
Reciprocity	Not automatic. There is partial reciprocal exchange of information under Type 1 IGAs, but not under Type 2.	Full reciprocity
Enforcement of reporting requirement on financial institutions	Threat of 30% withholding tax on income paid to the financial institutions from US investments held by them.	General system of penalties as set out under the domestic law of individual countries.
Date effective from	January 2014	No set date – countries can choose.
Confidentiality of information	Specific confidentiality assurances	Specific confidentiality requirements
Sanctions	Threat of 30% withholding tax on income received by the financial institutions on investments in the US. Very effective as nearly all financial institutions around the world have US investments.	None beyond domestic law penalties.

Point of comparison	FATCA	OECD CRS/EU DAC
Thresholds	Different due diligence procedures for 'lower-value' pre-existing accounts) between USD$ 50k and USD$1 million) – electronic search only. Depository Accounts: no reporting needed if total of connected accounts <USD$ 50k; (applies to pre-existing and new accounts). Account balance >USD $1 million: additional due diligence requirements apply in identifying pre-existing accounts – search paper as well as electronic records.	No threshold as such but different reporting requirements for pre-existing high value accounts (>USD$1 million) no threshold for new accounts. Threshold for pre-existing entity accounts is > USD$250k.
Nationality of account holders who must be reported on.	US account holders only.	All account holders in all the countries participating in the CRS.
Registration requirements on financial institutions.	FIs must register the the IRS and obtain an ID number (GIIN).	No registration requirements, although under DAC a list of non-reporting (non-compliant) FIs will be published by the EU.

Automatic exchange of information

18.20   FATCA represents a unilaterally imposed system of automatic supply of information for tax purposes, although not necessarily an exchange. It is a far more powerful system than anything devised to date by the OECD, because it is coercive rather than voluntary. The penalty for non-compliance with FATCA is clear: the 30 per cent withholding tax. In addition, it is clear exactly which taxpayers will suffer the penalty: the non-compliant financial intermediary. In contrast, it is not clear exactly what 'bad things' might happen to a country which does not get around to complying with the OECD's initiatives, eg by not responding to criticisms made in a Peer Review or by signing the Mutual Assistance Convention but not getting around to ratifying it. Penalties for non-compliance with the OECD initiatives are indirect, in that a country's reputation may be damaged which might, in turn, lead to a decline in the business prospects for some of its residents.

The drawbacks of the current agreements for information exchange, be they in the form of DTTs containing a full Article 26 (Exchange of Information) or a TIEA, are that these methods of information exchange depend on requests being made. As we have just seen, requests can only be made when the requesting country has already established grounds to suspect one of its residents of tax evasion.

The position of the OECD as the primary instigator of world tax policy is being threatened by the US and whilst FATCA may be superior to anything so far offered by the OECD, it is a unilateral measure, so far imposed by a single jurisdiction. This contrasts with the consensual, multilateral approach of the OECD, and appears to have prompted the OECD to pursue work on the automatic exchange of information more keenly.

EXCHANGE OF INFORMATION AND TAX TRANSPARENCY WITHIN THE EU

18.21   The European Union has its own parallel set of initiatives to promote exchange of information between the Member States of the EU. Several EU Directives deal with both exchange of information and mutual assistance in the collection of each other's taxes. These contain many of the same rules as the OECD's Common Reporting Standard, although due to the political and economic commitments owed by the Member States to each other, the requirements tend to go further. Directive 2014/107/EU, on Administrative Cooperation in the Field of Taxation (known as the DAC) extends the previous version (Directive 2011/16/EU) but requiring mandatory automatic exchange of information along the lines of the CRS. This supersedes the EU Saving Tax Directive (Directive 2003/48/EC).

The latest initiative is the European Union's Tax Transparency Package.[1] This is different from the OECD Common Reporting Standard and from FATCA in that it is directed at increasing the exchange of tax information between Member States on the tax affairs of multinational groups of companies, rather than of individuals. Every three months, national tax authorities within the EU will have to send a report to all other Member States on all cross-border tax rulings issued. This is aimed at promoting 'healthier' tax competition within the EU, aid the detection of abusive tax planning by multinational groups through playing-off one country against another, and will make it more difficult for a Member State to offer multinationals secret sweetheart' (preferential) deals which bypass normal tax rules.[2]

The EU measures on information exchange and tax transparency are discussed in more detail in Chapter 20.

---

1   European Commission COM (2015) 136 final, 'On Tax Transparency to Fight Tax Evasion and Avoidance' 18.3.2015. See also: http://europa.eu/rapid/press-release_IP-15-4610_en.htm.
2   As an example, see FT Com, 'EU tax: Tough love for multinationals' sweetheart deals' 13 July 2015. Available at: www.ft.com/cms/s/0/32e6a5c4-1a80-11e5-a130-2e7db721f996.html#axzz3ociJOLSV.

THE 'RUBIK' AGREEMENTS

18.22   These agreements take their name from the Rubik's Cube because of the complexity of negotiating information exchange with Switzerland and

Austria. They are agreements made by a small group of countries for whom banking secrecy continues to be of huge importance. The central feature of any Rubik agreement is that banking secrecy is upheld, but the anonymous account holder suffers heavy withholding taxes. Switzerland is the country with most Rubik agreements, although there are others.[1] The Tax Cooperation Agreement between the UK and Switzerland came into force on 1 January 2013. It permits Switzerland to retain banking secrecy with regard to accounts held there by UK residents, but the price is heavy: there is a one-off charge of between 21 per cent and 41 per cent of the account balance, which is intended to cover previous UK taxes evaded by the account holder. Thereafter, there is withholding tax of 48 per cent on interest, 40 per cent on dividends and 27 per cent on capital gains. As well as all this, there is a 40 per cent withholding tax on assets which would be subject to inheritance tax, assuming the UK knew about them. The account holder can avoid these charges if he/she agrees to full disclosure of the account to HMRC. Switzerland, as is the case with other Rubik agreements, hands over 75 per cent of the tax collected to residence country of the account holder, in this case, the UK.

As well as these payments to the UK, the UK will be entitled to request information on individuals suspected of holding Swiss bank accounts, but subject to a limit of up to 500 requests a year for the first three years. The information which must accompany such requests is similar to that required when making a request under a Tax Exchange Information Agreement (TIEA). However, if the account in question is one which suffered the initial charge, and has subsequently been subject to withholding taxes under the Rubik agreement, the Swiss do not have to supply information concerning the account.

The Rubik agreements are controversial, not just because they permit Switzerland to maintain a degree of banking secrecy, but also because it is highly likely that even with the apparently high charges involved for the account holders, account holders are probably still paying less than they would, if they had made full and timely disclosure of the account to the country where they are tax resident, and had paid all taxes due at the correct time. To this extent, Baker (2012) considers that the Rubik agreements amount to tax amnesties.

---

1   EU–Switzerland (2004), EU–Andorra (2004), EU–Liechtenstein (2004), EU–San Marino (2004), EU-Monaco (2004), Switzerland–UK (2011), Austria–Switzerland (2012).

EU–Switzerland Tax Transparency Agreement

18.23   This agreement, signed on 27 May 2015, represents a step away from banking secrecy by Switzerland. It provides for OECD CRS-style reciprocal exchange of information between Switzerland and the Member States of the EU. Information to be exchanged is the name, address, tax identification number and date of birth of account holders and details of the account balance and receipts. It will take effect in 2018. It replaces the Swiss–EU Agreement of 2003.[1] In all likelihood it will also replace the Rubik agreements.

---

1   Agreement between the European Community and the Swiss Confederation providing for measures equivalent to those laid down in Council Directive 2003/48/EC on taxation of savings income in the form of interest payments (known as the EU Savings Directive).

TOO MANY REGIMES?

18.24 Financial institutions in some countries face a multiplicity of reporting requirements under a variety of information exchange arrangements: in the UK, a financial institution must report on its clients under:

- FATCA;

- the Crown Dependencies and Gibraltar Regulations (ie UK versions of FATCA);

- the OECD CRS; and

- the EU Directive on Administrative Cooperation in Tax Matters.

The same level of reporting requirements exists for financial institutions in many OECD member states. These multiple reporting regimes not only place a heavy compliance burden on financial institutions, they also present an administrative challenge for the governments concerned, who must monitor the working of each regime, and process the information supplied under each of them.

A summary of the introduction of the various regimes is given below:

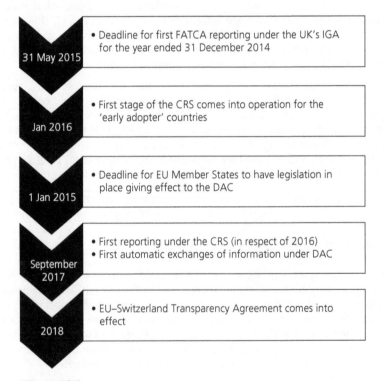

Figure 18.2

OFFSHORE VOLUNTARY DISCLOSURE PROGRAMMES

18.25 If an individual taxpayer resident in a non-haven country has unde-clared income from overseas investments then that taxpayer is potentially evading tax. Assuming the residence country grants double tax relief using the credit method and assuming that the overseas investments are in a low-tax jurisdiction, the amount of tax evaded can mount up over the years and when taken together with penalties incurred for non-payment, the amount at stake can quickly escalate to the point where the taxpayer either cannot afford to, or simply cannot face making a confession of the evasion. Penalties for this type of evasion can be very high indeed. For instance, the UK introduced a special penalty regime to tackle offshore tax evasion in the Finance Act 2010. This penalty regime is structured so that the rate of penalty depends on the category of jurisdiction on which the income has arisen, with a minimum penalty rate of 100 per cent of the tax evaded. Penalties in connection with undisclosed income in the 57 jurisdictions regarded by the UK as the worst type of tax havens can be levied at 200 per cent of the tax evaded.[1]

Information on investments held in tax havens and collection of residence-country tax due can be achieved in several ways:

1   Conduct in-depth investigations into the financial affairs of wealthy indi-viduals. This is rather hit and miss and conducting such investigations is very expensive for the tax authority. The tax authority would only have the resources to investigate a small minority of potential tax evaders. TIEAs could be used, but as noted above they may not prove very helpful.

2   Use legal powers against resident entities to force them to disclose details of accounts held by resident taxpayers in foreign affiliate organi-zations. This strategy has been employed by the UK with some success against banks with UK holding companies or subsidiaries, to force them to reveal names of accounts held by UK residents with their Channel Islands affiliate companies. In the US, attacks are being made on tax haven banks and a Senate Permanent Subcommittee on Investigations embarked on a hearing entitled 'Tax Haven Banks and US Compliance – Obtaining the Names of US Clients with Swiss Accounts'. This hearing follows a demand from the US Justice Department that the Swiss Bank, UBS, disclose names and account details of US investors.

3   Introduce FATCA-style legislation to compel non-resident financial intermediaries to disclose information on the offshore capital and income of residents.

4   Tempt taxpayers to make voluntary disclosure of undeclared income by offering either a complete or partial amnesty with respect to penalties. Such amnesties are referred to as offshore voluntary disclosure pro-grammes or facilities – OVDPs.

Governments usually implement penalty amnesties or partial amnesties (OVDPs) when they become aware that there is probably a large number of their residents concealing foreign income in a certain way or in a certain coun-try. Such a situation often comes to light through the actions of whistleblowers, such as happened in the UBS case, where an employee told the IRS about certain practices that UBS was engaged in which were designed to help wealthy US citizens evade US tax (see para **18.32** below). In the case of the US 2003 OVDP, it had come to the attention of the IRS that there was widespread use by US residents of credit cards issued in tax haven countries, suggesting that there were substantial funds concealed in those countries. Although the specific information supplied to a tax authority by a whistleblower might only concern a finite number of residents, it may be apparent that there are probably many more residents who are evading tax in a similar manner, but whose identities are unknown.

The OECD has produced guidance for countries wishing to introduce OVDPs (OECD, 2010; OECD, 2015). This suggests that to encourage take-up by taxpayers, clear guidance must be made available to taxpayers as to:

- the process to be followed, in terms of who to contact and paperwork;

- what to do if the taxpayer only has incomplete information about the assets in the tax haven;

- the confidentiality of any disclosures made;

- the extent to which making a disclosure will mean the taxpayer is subject to increased monitoring by the tax authorities in future (ie what is the risk of being selected for investigation in future?);

- the extent to which third parties will be contacted by the tax authority to gather information (ie how likely is it that the tax authority will discover the undisclosed income anyway?);

- the risk of criminal prosecution; and

- the willingness of the tax authority to enter into initial discussions on a 'no names' basis.

More generally, to be effective, an OVDP must be widely publicized and the fear factor is important: taxpayers who have been evading tax need to be convinced that if they do not make voluntary disclosures under the OVDP then they will be found out anyway and, as a result, suffer worse penalties than if they had come clean.

The OECD considers that a successful OVDP will:

- be clear about its aims and terms;

- deliver demonstrable and cost-effective increases in current revenues;

- be consistent with the generally applicable compliance and enforcement regimes;

- help to deter non-compliance;

- improve levels of compliance among the population eligible for the programme; and

- complement the immediate yield from disclosures with measures that improve compliance in the longer term (OECD 2015 at p 7).

OVDPs in practice

18.26   OVDPs are widely used: the past, or have programmes which are currently open for disclosures. Most OVDPs do not excuse disclosers from paying the tax due or from paying interest on late payment. What most OVDPs do is to reduce the penalties which taxpayers would otherwise suffer if they disclosed their offshore accounts outside an OVDP. The OECD produced a report in 2015 summarizing the OVDP regimes in the 47 OECD member countries (OECD, 2015). The following sections looks at just a few of the OVDPs.

The US Offshore Voluntary Disclosure Programs

18.27   The US has offered voluntary disclosure programmes since 1925 aimed at persuading its residents to disclose their offshore income. US residents are required to file a so-called 'FBAR' (Report of Foreign Bank and Financial Accounts, Form TD F 90-22).[1] If they have a financial interest in, or signature authority over, offshore accounts with an aggregate value exceeding $10,000. The normal penalties for failing to file the FBAR are civil penalties up to the greater of $100,000 or 50 per cent of the highest balance in an unreported foreign account for each year since 2004 in which there was a failure to file. There is also a risk of criminal penalties. The US appears to have an ongoing policy of offering an Offshore Voluntary Disclosure Program (OVDP). The 2012 OVDP has been extended through 2013 and was renewed in June 2014.

As well as disclosing sources and amounts of income, participants in the OVDPs also have to provide details of the creation and maintenance of their foreign accounts, identifying the foreign financial institutions involved, dates of opening and closing of accounts, names of contacts at the foreign institutions and also details of meetings and communications with independent advisors and managers in relation to the accounts.

Although the OVDP offer reductions in penalties, taxpayers can still be faced with a substantial bill. For instance, taking the 2014 US OVDP: a US taxpayer with £1 million on deposit, say in Switzerland, earning interest of $50 million pa from 2005 to 2012, which was not declared on the US tax return would have resulted in payment of tax and penalties of $553k (plus interest on tax paid late) under the 2014 OVDP. However although this is a large bill, had the taxpayer NOT disclosed under the 2014 OVDP and had the taxpayer's Swiss income been discovered by the IRS, the bill would have been about $4 million.[2]

The Governmental Audit Office (GAO) reported on the outcomes of the 2009 OVDP. This report revealed that through scrutiny of the disclosures made, the IRS was able to identify other Swiss banks and financial advisors who had advised on ways of hiding foreign income. As a result, other Swiss banks faced legal action to make them name their US customers, so that they, too, could be investigated. As well as Swiss banks, banks in Israel, Liechtenstein and India were also implicated.

The GAO estimates that more than half of these 'large penalty' taxpayers had accounts with the Swiss bank, UBS. There was also evidence that in the run-up to the 2009 OVDP, some of these had transferred funds away from UBS to other, smaller, Swiss banks which had no presence in the US when it became apparent that UBS was going to have to give details of its account holders to the IRS. Presumably this was to try to keep them hidden.

Nearly all taxpayers incurred the main rate of OVDP penalty of 20 per cent rather than any reduced rate, meaning that nearly all accounts had capital of at least $75,000 and nearly all were being actively used by the US citizens.

The GAO report also provides an interesting breakdown of which countries were being used to try to hide offshore income: Figure 18.3 shows that Switzerland was by far the most popular choice, although it appears that a high proportion of US citizens with accounts in the UK only disclosed these to the IRS under the OVDP.

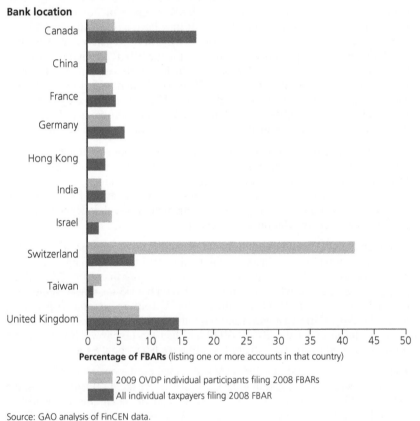

Figure 18.3

1 Most of this penalty is for failure to file complete and correct FBARs (the Foreign Bank Account Report). Available at: www.irs.gov/Individuals/International-Taxpayers/Offshore-Voluntary-Disclosure-Program-Frequently-Asked-Questions-and-Answers-2012-Revised.
2 United States Government Accountability Office (GAP) March 2013 *Report to Congressional Requesters: Offshore Tax evasion – IRS Has Collected Billions of Dollars, but May be Missing Continued Evasion* GA)-13-318, available at: www.gao.gov/assets/660/653369.pdf.

Voluntary disclosure programmes in the UK

18.28 Following on from the success of an initiative involving Liechtenstein (see below), HMRC opened up an offshore disclosure facility, for a limited period (until 22 June 2007) and invited taxpayers with offshore accounts to get their tax affairs up to date. According to the HMRC website:

> 'HMRC is now pursuing those with offshore accounts and tax liabilities who did not notify their intention to disclose under the scheme by 22 June 2007 as well as those who notified but decided not to disclose. In some cases penalties could amount to 100 per cent of the tax due and in exceptional circumstances criminal investigation may be considered.'

The offshore disclosure facility resulted in around 45,000 disclosures and generated approximately £512 million. In the Pre-Budget Report in November 2008, the UK government launched a further offshore disclosure facility in 2009, this time known as the 'New Disclosure Opportunity'. Under this programme taxpayers had to make full disclosure of undeclared income and gains by a deadline, going back 20 years. The Treasury estimated that the disclosure programme would raise £500 million over a period of four years. However, the UK Government reports that only about £157 million was raised to January 2015.[1] The incentives offered to taxpayers were that penalties would be limited to 10 per cent of taxes underpaid (but 20 per cent if a taxpayer now making disclosure had been contacted during the 2007 campaign and had then failed to respond). The tax and relevant interest on tax paid late also had to be paid over. This compared with penalties of between 30 per cent and 100 per cent of tax underpaid if discovery was made by HMRC outside the disclosure facility.

Besides the Liechtenstein OVDP discussed below disclosure schemes were also put in place for the Isle of Man, Jersey and Guernsey which ran from April 2013 to December 2015.

1 United States Government Accountability Office (GAP) March 2013 *Report to Congressional Requesters: Offshore Tax evasion – IRS Has Collected Billions of Dollars, but May be Missing Continued Evasion* GA)-13-318. Available at: www.gao.gov/assets/660/653369.pdf. And see: www.gov.uk/government/publications/2010-to-2015-government-policy-tax-evasion-and-avoidance/2010-to-2015-government-policy-tax-evasion-and-avoidance.

UK's Liechtenstein disclosure facility

18.29 It became apparent in 2008 that many residents of other countries had funds invested in banks in Liechtenstein and that many investors were not declaring the existence of these accounts to their tax authorities and were thus evading tax on the income earned. Liechtenstein banks appeared popular with Germans, no doubt due to the physical proximity. Two features made Liechtenstein an attractive location: very low tax rates, and trust laws which permitted trusts to be revoked at any time. Famously, a bank employee sold a CD containing details of German investors to the German Ministry of Finance for €1.4 million. The same employee apparently sold data to a number of other governments as well, including the US and the UK, before going into hiding.

The UK, along with some of the other countries, took action. It introduced the 'Liechtenstein Disclosure Facility', which is an OVDP. It was announced on 11 August 2009, following the conclusion of the UK–Liechtenstein Tax Information Exchange Agreement. The terms were: tax plus interest, plus penalties of 10 per cent of the tax, but penalties applied only to tax evaded in the previous 10 years. This compared with the 20-year period and potential penalty of 20 per cent under a pre-existing UK OVDP, the 'New Disclosure Opportunity' which had only just been announced. Controversially, taxpayers are able to opt for a simple composite rate of tax of 40 per cent to cover all taxable income, gains and inheritance tax liabilities, at a cost of giving up the right to claim any tax reliefs. Moreover, the time period for making disclosure was far longer than under the 'New Disclosure Opportunity', running until March 2015 (but later extended to 31 December 2015). The Liechtenstein Disclosure Facility was expected to be taken up by up to 5,000 taxpayers and to reveal the existence of up to £3 billion of assets of UK taxpayers in Liechtenstein. As at August 2013, HMRC has reported about 3,710 disclosures. The yield in terms of taxes, penalties and interest to March 2015 was more than £1bn. The average settlement figure to March 2013 was £174,000 and the total amount paid £523 million.[1]

A feature of this facility is that it also targets financial intermediaries. These are defined as persons subject to supervision by Liechtenstein's Financial Markets Authority who provide a service to those holding investments in Liechtenstein. Intermediaries must review all clients, to identify those who need to 'confirm' their position with HMRC and advise them to take up the facility. If the client fails to confirm to the intermediary that he/she is co-operating with HMRC, then the intermediary must cease to act for the client or face sanctions. Liechtenstein is required to introduce new laws to audit this process.

To prevent taxpayers arranging their affairs to take advantage of the Liechtenstein Disclosure Facility rather than the New Disclosure Opportunity, a rule was introduced to limit the application of the Liechtenstein facility to funds already in Liechtenstein at the date the Liechtenstein Facility was announced. Otherwise taxpayers might have been tempted first to move their undisclosed funds to Liechtenstein and then make their disclosure under the more favourable terms of the Liechtenstein Facility. By May 2011, 1,351 taxpayers had registered under the Liechtenstein facility and £140 million had been received by HMRC. HMRC has stated that it hopes to raise about £3 billion by 2015.[2]

---

1   Available at: www.hmrc.gov.uk/disclosure/liechtenstein-disclosure.htm.
2   *Daily Telegraph*, 13 May 2011.

The problem with voluntary disclosure programmes

18.30 Disclosure programmes will only be truly effective if taxpayers truly believe that they really will be their last opportunity to come clean. But governments seemingly cannot resist having another try. Italy, for example, has granted partial amnesties in 1982, 1984, 2001, and 2009, 2010 and 2011, all on very generous terms compared with the OVDPs offered by the US and the UK. Repeated disclosure programmes engender a lack of urgency in taxpayers and the tendency to put off making a disclosure this time around because in economic terms, they may be better off waiting for a later programme. In the meantime, they continue to enjoy their overseas income and gains tax free and potentially stand to benefit from a later disclosure programme offering more generous terms than the current one.

Alm and Back (1993) studied the long-run effects of the 1985 Colorado State Tax amnesty, which offered taxpayers the opportunity to pay taxes on undeclared income without penalty. The amnesty was well advertised, user-friendly and portrayed as the taxpayer's last chance to come clean. Alm and Beck, using a range of sophisticated time series analyses to detect any longer term improvement in tax collections concluded that the amnesty had no long-run effect. Torgler and Schaltegger (2005)[1] went further, concluding that tax amnesties might actually make matters worse. Not only would taxpayers continue to evade, counting on a future amnesty, but the granting of amnesties represented a violation of the principle of equity amongst taxpayers. To be effective, an amnesty, or partial amnesty as represented by the UK and US programmes, needs to be accompanied by a perceived step-up in the enforcement powers of the tax authority granting the amnesty.

Despite these reservations on the effectiveness of OVDPs, there is some evidence from the US that they can be effective in increasing compliance. Figure 18.4 shows the numbers of US taxpayers declaring offshore accounts to the IRS. The Government Audi Office report from which this is taken, questions whether US taxpayers would really have been busy opening foreign bank accounts during 2010 and 2011, years during which the US was in a deep recession. A more likely explanation is that the continuing US OVDP programme prompted not just disclosure of hidden accounts but a greater rate of compliance with normal reporting requirements. It is quite possible that offshore accounts which have existed for many years were reported as new accounts in 2010 and 2011.

The 2014 extension to the 2012 OVDP carries no closure date: the IRS appear to have made this an open-ended arrangement. In the UK, HMRC announced in 2015 that there will be a 'last chance' disclosure facility. Penalties are to be 30 per cent with no guarantee of immunity from prosecution (as opposed to 10 per cent in the Liechtenstein Disclosure Facility). Whether anyone will believe the UK Government when it says that this is the 'last chance' appears doubtful.

In the UK, HMRC published an interesting study[2] to identify the important factors in persuading individuals to take up the offer of voluntary disclosure programmes (VDPs) in general. Whilst the study focussed on in-country VDPs (eg for e-traders) the findings are relevant to OVDPs. Three factors were identified as contributing to a successful take-up of VDPs:

- Demonstrate preventative work has been undertaken with 'at risk' groups – ie make it clear to evaders that the tax authority has already warned them of their responsibility to report offshore income and assets on their tax returns, so that evaders cannot claim ignorance of the law.

- Promote awareness of the VDP through multiple channels; direct letters are very effective, particularly when combine with previous notification of the VDP through other channels, eg newspapers and financial press.

- Give tailored messages to would-be respondents, setting out the future consequences of non-response. This information is considered crucial in persuading deliberate tax evaders to respond.

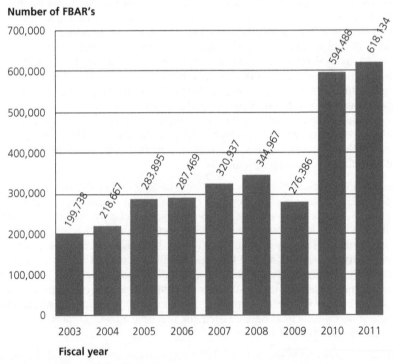

Number of FBAR's

Source: GAO analysis of FinCEN annual reports.

Figure 18.4

---

1   Torgler, B and Schaltegger, C A, 'Tax Amnesties and Political Participation' *Public Finance Review*, May 2005, Vol 33, No 3 pp 403–431.
2   HMRC (2015) 'Understanding the Motivators and Incentives for Voluntary Disclosure' HMRC Research Report 397. Available at: www.gov.uk/government/publications/motivators-and-incentives-for-voluntary-disclosure.

Legal action against intermediaries

18.31 As well as relying on the incentive of reduced penalties to encourage voluntary disclosure, there have been several notable instances of governments taking direct action against the providers and facilitators of offshore investments. In the UK, HMRC consulted in 2015 on the possible introduction of a new corporate criminal offence of 'failure to prevent the facilitation of evasion'.[1] This is an interesting development in which the new criminal offence would be levied against the directors and employees of corporations judged to have facilitated offshore evasion of UK taxes by UK resident individuals. Some difficult legal technicalities will have to be overcome in order to attribute the offences of the corporation to specific individuals. This is necessary because only individuals can be sent to jail. This proposal is thought to be partly a reaction to the revelation of alleged facilitation of tax evasion in the UK by HSBC's Swiss arm.[2] Although HSBC directors were questioned by the UK Government about these allegations, they denied knowledge of the activities of their Swiss arm. Alongside this proposal for a new criminal offence, HMRC is also consulting on a new civil penalty for facilitating tax evasion, under which advisers found to be facilitating tax evasion will face the same penalties as the taxpayer.

---

1   HMRC (2015) 'Tackling offshore tax evasion: a new corporate criminal offence of failure to prevent the facilitation of evasion', Consultation Document 16 July 2015. See: www.gov.uk/government/consultations/tackling-offshore-evasion.
2   The information on HSBC came to light when the International Consortium of Investigative Journalists released information on nearly 60,000 files from HSBC's Swiss private banking branch. See: www.icij.org/project/swiss-leaks/new-law-new-loophole-new-business-giant-global-bank-hsbc; see also Matthew Allen, HSBC and Falciani: How it happened, see: www.swissinfo.ch, 9 February 2015.

US action against the Union Bank of Switzerland

18.32 In 2008, UBS (the Union Bank of Switzerland) admitted inciting investors to evade US tax liabilities and agreed to provide the names of 4,450 UBS account holders and to pay fines of $780 million including $380 million to the IRS. The action against UBS resulted from information supplied by a whistleblower, an employee of UBS who went to the US tax authorities with information about the scale of the use of UBS facilities by US taxpayers. This employee, a Mr Bradley Birkenfeld, was then given a 40-month prison sentence in the US for his part in assisting his client to evade US taxes. Birkenfeld had apparently tried to cover up his own part in the tax schemes. However, he was also paid an enormous reward from the US government for supplying them with the information, reportedly $104 million.[1] Under US law, informants can collect up to 30 per cent of the fines, penalties and interest ultimately collected by the IRS. Alongside the civil action, a criminal prosecution against UBS was launched, which resulted in the disclosure by UBS of the names and details of 250 US investors. To complicate the issue, the Swiss government had brought a legal action against the US government, accusing it of violating the terms of the US–Switzerland double tax agreement by filing a summons on a Swiss national (UBS), which was insufficiently supported by evidence.

The wider outcome of the case was that the IRS were able to force UBS to enter into a settlement, made publicly available,[2] which requires UBS not only to pay the fine and hand over client details as just described, but also to comply with specific information exchange requirements going forward. Whilst these information exchange arrangements are set out in the US–Switzerland DTT (as amended in 2009), the requirements imposed by the IRS on UBS under the treaty are now very specific:

UBS had 270 days to produce the information on the 4,450 accounts already referred to. UBS was obliged to notify all those account holders within 90 days warning them of the disclosure, telling them to designate an agent in Switzerland and encouraging them to execute a written instruction directing that the relevant account information be transmitted to the IRS by UBS. The account holders were at liberty to take advantage of the voluntary disclosure scheme, although they would have to make their voluntary disclosures very quickly, because a disclosure made after UBS had supplied the account holder's details to the IRS would not be recognized as a voluntary disclosure.

UBS was to be subject to accelerated and expanded audit procedures with respect to its designation as a Qualified Intermediary.

However, the UBS action has not been an unmitigated success for the IRS. In January 2010, in a test case, the Swiss courts ruled in favour of a UBS account holder, ordering the Swiss Federal Tax Administration not to disclose account information to the IRS. The reasoning seems to have been that Switzerland will not lift its bank secrecy laws unless there is evidence of tax fraud and, intriguingly, stated that tax fraud was not the same as tax evasion, so that failure to disclose income from Swiss investments to the IRS was not tax fraud. Crucially, the US–Switzerland DTT only allows for the exchange of information in the case of tax fraud.

As noted above, the UBS action was the principal driver for the 2009 US OVDP.

In February 2015, it was reported that UBS is once again being investigated in the US on the matter of helping clients evade US taxation, this time in connection with the use of bearer securities. These are a means of holding securities anonymously.[3]

---

1   Reported by the *New York Times*, 26 November 2009 at: www.nytimes.com/2009/11/27/business/27whistle.html. Bradley Birkenfeld also has a Wikipedia page devoted to him: http://en.wikipedia.org/wiki/Brad_Birkenfeld.
2   Available at: www.irs.gov/pub/irs-drop/bank_agreement.pdf.
3   FT Com, 5 February 2015 'UBS Faces Fresh US Tax Evasion Inquiry', Available at: www.gov.uk/government/publications/2010-to-2015-government-policy-tax-evasion-and-avoidance/2010-to-2015-government-policy-tax-evasion-and-avoidance.

The Panama papers

18.33   In May 2016, the International Consortium of Investigative Journalists (ICIJ) released a database of leaked data obtained from the Panamanian law firm, Mossack Fonseca, consisting of over 11 million records spanning a period of some 40 years.[1] The data revealed ownership of offshore entities and caused significant fallout following media pressure on governments, including tax authorities, to investigate the data with a view to detecting tax evasion. The leak gave additional impetus for the already existing movement demanding transparency around beneficial ownership.

For a discussion of this and other data leaks and the implications for tax law, see Oie & Ring (2017).

---

1 See https://panamapapers.icij.org.

FURTHER READING

Alm, J and Beck, W (1993) 'Tax Amnesties and Compliance in the Long Run: a Time Series Analysis', *National Tax Journal*, Vol 46, No 1, pp 53–60.

Ashford, G (2011) 'Was it worth the wait?' (article on the UK Swiss Agreement) *Tax Adviser*, November 2011.

Avi-Yonah, R S (2009) The OECD Harmful Tax Competition Report: A Retrospective After a Decade, 34, *Brooklyn Journal of International Law*, 783 (2008–2009).

Baker, P (2012) 'Legislative Comment – Finance Act nots: section 218 and Schedule 36: the UK--Switzerland Rubik Agreement', 2012, *British Tax Review*, 4.

Christians, A (2013) 'The Dubious Pedegree of IGAs (and Why it Matters)', 69, *Tax Notes International*, pp 565–568.

Coder, J (2013) 'FATCA's Practical Efforts Limit Good Intentions' 69 *Tax Notes International* pp 718–719.

Davies, R B and Voget, J (2008) Tax Competition in an Expanding European Union, Oxford University Centre for Business Taxation Working Paper WP08/30.

De Clermont-Tonnerre, J-F and Ruchelman, S C (2013) 'A Layman's Guide to FATCA Due Diligence and Reporting Obligations', 42 *Tax Management International Journal* 1.

Eccleston, R (2012) *The Dynamics of Global Economic Governance: the Financial Crisis, the OECD and the Politics of International Tax Cooperation*, Edward Elgar, Cheltenham.

European Union (2008) Commission Staff Working Document presenting an Evaluation of the Effects of Council Directive 2003/48/EC, SEC (2008) 2420.

Global Forum on Transparency and Exchange of Information for Tax Purposes: Information Brief, November 2013. Available at www.oecd.org/tax/transparency/global_forum_background%20brief.pdf.

Griffith, R and Klemm, A (2005) *What has been the Tax Competition Experience of the last 20 years?*, Institute for Fiscal Studies, London.

Griffith, R, Hines, J and Sorensen, P (2008) International Capital Taxation. Available at: www.ifs.org.uk/mirrleesreview/press_docs/international.pdf.

HMRC (2013) *No Safe Havens – Our Offshore Evasion Strategy 2013 and Beyond*. Available at: www.gov.uk/government/uploads/system/uploads/attachment_data/file/193112/offshore-strategy_1_.pdf.

HMRC (2014) 'Implementing Agreements under the Global Standard on Automatic Exchange of Information to Improve International Tax Compliance', Discussion Document 31 July 2014. See: www.gov.uk/government/consultations/implementing-agreements-under-the-global-standard-on-automatic-exchange-of-information.

Horton, R (2010) 'The UBS/IRS Settlement Agreement and Cayman Island Hedge Funds', Spring 2010, 41 *University of Miami Inter-American Law Review*, 357.

Jackson, James K (2010) The OECD Initiative on Tax Havens, Congressional Research Paper 7-5700, 11 March 2010. Available at: http://assets.opencrs.com/rpts/R40114_20100311.pdf.

Janeba, E and Schjelderup, G (2004) *Why Europe should Love Tax Competition – and the US even more so*, National Bureau of Economic Research Discussion Paper 23/04.

Killian, S (2006) 'Where's the Harm in Tax Competition? Lessons from US Multinationals in Ireland', *Critical Perspectives on Accounting*, Vol 17, pp 1067–1087.

Kudrle, R T (2003) 'The Campaign Against Tax Havens: Will it Last? Will it Work?', 9, *Stanford Journal of Law, Business & Finance* (2003–2004).

Oberson, X (2015) *International Exchange of Information in Tax Matters*, Edward Elgar Publishing Ltd.

OECD/Council of Europe (2008, as amended 2011) Multilateral Convention for Mutual Assistance in Tax Matters.

OECD (2000) Improving Access to Bank Information for Tax Purposes.

OECD (2001) The 2001 Progress Report, OECD Project on Harmful Tax Practices.

OECD (2010) Offshore Voluntary Disclosure – Comparative Analysis, Guidance and Policy Advice.

OECD (2013) The Global Forum on Transparency and Exchange of Information for Tax Purposes: Information Brief. Available at: www.oecd.org/tax/transparency/GF%20Brief%20Background%20presseoifinal_2.pdf.

OECD (2013) Global Forum on Transparency and Exchange of Information for Tax Purposes; Progress Report to the G20 Leaders: Global Forum Update on Effectiveness and On-going Monitoring.

OECD (2013) Automatic Exchange of Information: The Next Step (Information Brief). Available at: www.oecd.org/ctp/exchange-of-tax-information/Background_Brief_AEOI_27082013.pdf.

OECD (2015) Automatic Exchange of Financial Account Information – Background Information Brief, 4.6.2015. Available at: www.oecd.org/tax/automatic-exchange/about-automatic-exchange.

OECD (2015) *Update on Voluntary Disclosure Programmes: A pathway to Tax Compliance*, August 2015. Available at: www.oecd.org/ctp/exchange-of-tax-information/update-on-voluntary-disclosure-programmes-a-pathwaypto-tax-compliance.htm.

Oei, S and Ring, D (2017) 'Leak-Driven Law' *UCLA Law Review* Vol 65, 2018; Tulane Public Law Research Paper No. 17-1; Boston College Law School Legal Studies Research Paper No. 442. Available at SSRN: https://ssrn.com/abstract=2918550 or http://dx.doi.org/10.2139/ssrn.2918550.

Parada, L (2015) 'Intergovernmental Agreements and the Implementation of FATCA in Europe', 7, *World Tax Journal*, 2

Pross, A and Russo, R (2012) 'The Amended Convention on Mutual Administrative Assistance in Tax Matters: A Powerful Tool to Counter Tax Avoidance and Evasion', 68, *Bulletin for International Taxation*, 361–365.

Rawlings, G (2005) 'Responsive Regulation, Multilateralism, Bilateral Treaties and the Continuing Appeal of Offshore Financial Centres', Working Paper No 41, Centre of Tax System Integrity, Australian National University, June 2005.

Rettig, C P and Keneally, K (2011) 'The Last, Best Chance to Disclose Foreign Financial Accounts and Assets – The 2011 Offshore Voluntary Disclosure Program and Beyond!', *Journal of Tax Practice and Procedure*, 1 February, 2011.

Sawyer, A (2014) 'Comparing the Swiss and United Kingdom Cooperation Agreements with their respective agreements under the Foreign Account Tax Compliance Act', *eJournal of Tax Research*, 12(2), p 285.

Teather, R (2005) *The Benefits of Tax Competition*, The Institute of Economic Affairs, London.

United Nations (2003) 'Report on Panel Discussion on International Co-operation in Tax Matters', 10 November 2003.

Urinov, V (2015) 'The Rubik Model: An Alternative for Automatic Tax Information Exchange Regimes?', 69, *Bulletin for International Taxation* 2.

Zagaris, B (2015) 'The Death of Tax and Secrecy Havens? FATCA, GATCA and What's Next in Global Financial Transparency', Paper presented at the Financial Crime Conference, 20 April 2015, New York.

FURTHER STUDY

Harmful tax competition

18.34   In 1998, the OECD established a Forum on Harmful Tax Practices as a subsidiary body of its Committee on Fiscal Affairs. From the start, this initiative had its critics who questioned whether tax competition was necessarily harmful. The OECD was criticized for making this assumption and also for failing to develop any acceptable definition of harmful tax competition. The Forum produced a report which identified so-called harmful tax practices and guidelines which asked member countries to identify, by self-review, and then followed by peer review, preferential tax regimes and practices. In 2000, the Committee on Fiscal Affairs identified 47 preferential tax regimes in 35 countries in nine categories of 'potentially harmful': specifically insurance, financing and lending, fund managers, banking, headquarter regimes, distribution centre regimes, service centre regimes and miscellaneous activities.

In the view of the OECD, preferential regime criteria were:

● zero or nominal taxes on foreign-owned investments;

● no effective information exchange with other countries;

● lack of transparency in legislative, administrative or legal issues connected with foreign investment; and

● little substantive activity.

The OECD threatened to place these 35 countries on a 'blacklist' of uncooperative tax havens unless they signed letters committing to removing the preferential tax regimes listed by April 2003, with benefits to users eliminated by December 2005. By 2002, 28 of the 35 countries had signed letters of commitment to effective information exchange. By 2008, only Liechtenstein, Andorra and Monaco remained on the list of uncooperative tax havens.

OECD members performed a further self-review in 2000, and identified regimes within OECD member countries with reference to these criteria, following which 18 regimes were abolished, 14 amended to remove their harmful features and 13 were found not to be harmful. Some of the changes made to remove harmful features, particularly in the case of Belgian co-ordination centres, appeared rather cosmetic. The revelation of the extent of overt tax competition within the OECD itself combined with the extent of tax competition either engaged in or covertly approved of by EU Member States led to the OECD work being somewhat discredited. For instance, during the UK presidency of the EU Code of Conduct, it emerged that the UK, along with most other EU Member States, engaged in tax competition and/or sanctioned tax competition in non-EU dependent territories.[1]

One of the obvious problems with OECD action in this regard is that a large number of jurisdictions were not OECD members. A number of non-OECD countries nevertheless committed themselves to greater fiscal transparency and information exchange. Many of these countries included a reciprocity clause in their letters of commitment, to the effect that their commitments would only be fulfilled if the OECD members themselves ceased to engage in harmful tax competition. A small number of jurisdictions initially chose not to participate and were identified as 'uncooperative tax havens': viz. Andorra, Liechtenstein, Liberia, Marshall Islands and Monaco. The original proposals of the OECD included plans for member countries to instigate sanctions against non-cooperative states, such as the disallowance for tax purposes of deductions, exemption, credits or allowances relating to transactions with uncooperative tax havens, heavy withholding taxes on payments into such countries, threat of termination of existing tax treaties with them, and so on. The intrinsic problem with the sanctions proposals is that to implement them would be an uncompetitive measure. The first country to impose sanctions would be placing itself at a disadvantage as its residents with interests in uncooperative tax havens migrated to other countries.

The OECD continued to publish reports updating the harmful tax competition initiative but by 2002 the emphasis had shifted firmly towards securing exchange of information on tax matters and abolishing banking secrecy rather than clamping down on countries which wished to charge little or no tax to non-residents.

The nail in the coffin for 'defensive measures', as sanctions were known, was the arrival of the Republican administration which took office in the US in 2001. Whilst the former Democrat administration had been broadly sympathetic to the OECD's position, the new Treasury Secretary Paul O'Neill was less keen, possibly viewing the initiatives as favouring the European arm of the OECD. He announced[2] that the US would not oppose practices designed to encourage foreign investment and unconnected with the enforcement of any other country's tax law. The US wished to focus on what it considered to be the core issues of transparency and information exchange, which are key to countering money laundering activities and other illegal uses of tax havens. Money laundering, in turn, is key to financing crime and terrorism. The 'no substantive activities test' would henceforth be dropped.

This change of direction was also influenced from within the OECD itself, with the publication of the 2000 report 'Improving Access to Bank Information for Tax Purposes' (OECD, 2000). In that report, the OECD noted that globalization, technology and the lifting of exchange controls had made it easier for taxpayers to escape taxes by using banking services in jurisdictions which practised banking secrecy. The potential for tax evasion using banking secrecy had increased exponentially at a time when the main traditional source of information for tax authorities on capital movements, namely exchange controls, had been removed.

---

1   See House of Commons, Select Committee on Treasury, Minutes of Evidence, 22 July 1999 at para 165, 'About one in five of these 47 possible tax havens are, in fact, Crown Dependencies or British overseas territories ...'. Available at: www.publications.parliament.uk/pa/cm199899/cmselect/cmtreasy/425/9072209.htm.
2   See www.treasury.gov/press-center/press-releases/Pages/po366.aspx.

Is tax competition really harmful?

18.35   One study by Desai, Foley and Hines (2004) points out that there are no reliable estimates of the magnitude of diversion of investment to low-tax jurisdictions (see Chapter 15). Their study, which analyses the use of tax havens by American multinationals, reaches three conclusions:

> 'First, tax haven affiliates serve to facilitate the relocation of taxable income from high-tax jurisdictions and to facilitate deferral of repatriation taxes, suggesting that multinational parents with differing foreign tax rate exposures can benefit from havens. Second, affiliates located in larger tax haven countries are the most useful for reallocating taxable income from high jurisdictions and their effects are most pronounced within regions .... Third, there is no evidence that havens divert activity from non-havens within the same region, and in fact the opposite seems to be the case.'

Thus, it seems that tax haven operations can actually serve to enhance regional activities in adjacent non-haven countries.

Killian (2006) suggests that the presumption that tax competition to attract MNEs is harmful is not beyond doubt, indeed she says 'the nature of the harm is rarely analysed'. Using the case of Ireland she considers the various stakeholders, benefits and hazards of tax competition and points out that 'the flow of capital to less developed tax-bidding countries can be a good thing, creating employment and spreading the benefits of prosperity'. It should be said, though, that Killian also expresses concern at the potential negative aspects of tax competition.

Teather (2005), in a study produced for the Institute of Economic Affairs, suggests there are allocation inefficiencies in public spending that can be checked by tax competition, which would force governments to seek maximum benefits from their spending. The view that tax competition is likely to be beneficial is shared by Janeba and Schjelderup (2004).

Teather (2005) further points out that much of the opposition to tax competition is part of a wider concern about global free markets (ie protectionism). Yet low-tax jurisdictions arguably make global capital markets more efficient 'as lower tax rates increase the available pool of investment capital, low-tax jurisdictions allow it to flow smoothly to the places where it will be most valuable'. He further suggests that tax competition brings opportunities for the UK specifically:

> 'Our moves in the 1980s towards simplified tax structures with low rates ... put us in a good position to benefit from tax competition when compared with other European countries that combine high tax rates on successful businesses with handouts for failures.
>
> Our international outlook, geographical position and the legacy of relatively low regulation (in an EU context) business economy mean that in an efficient global capital market the UK would be a natural recipient of capital investment. If tax competition and low-tax jurisdictions increase the pool of available investment capital and make global capital markets more efficient ... then the UK is ... in an ideal position to benefit from this.

The close historical and constitutional ties, and the common legal framework, that the UK shares with many low-tax jurisdictions are also valuable. They make the UK a natural home for investment capital that flows through these countries, but also provide wealth through valuable ancillary finance and legal jobs in London. In a time of increasing globalisation the UK should be strengthening these ties, not weakening them by siding with European competitors in attacking our friends.'

Griffith, Hines and Sorensen (2008), in a study produced for the UK Mirrlees Review, observe that economic models that predict welfare gains flowing from co-ordination of tax policy tend to assume that governments act in the best interest of their citizens. Some advocates of tax competition take the view that voter resistance to higher tax rates is exacerbated by distortionary effects of tax resulting from tax-base mobility, and forces politicians to pay more attention to the greater good, rather than being distracted by lobby groups, and further that tax competition can lead to improved public sector efficiency. Looking at it from the other perspective, tax co-ordination can have negative effects in light of the failure to accommodate particular national needs; that is, it potentially constrains policy choices (Griffith et al, 2008: 27–28).

In early 2009, KPMG released a report based on a study of UK tax competitiveness, which ranked the UK fourth, behind Ireland, the Netherlands and Luxembourg, but ahead of key competitors such as Germany, France and the US. The study was based on interview data collected from 50 senior finance or tax professionals from large UK corporations (FTSE 100 and FTSE 250). The survey notes the recent exodus of a number of high-profile companies from the UK and finds that complexity of the tax system is the most important issue impeding expansion in the UK. There is some evidence, however, to suggest that recent government attempts to consult more widely on significant changes is appreciated by business.

At an EU level, a number of studies[1] show some evidence that as the Union expands, Member States respond more to other Member States' taxes. This issue is addressed, in some part, by the proposals for the common consolidated corporate tax base, discussed in more detail in Chapter 20.

Another KPMG study, published in 2008, examined changes in rates of corporate taxes across 106 countries and concludes as follows:

'governments are increasingly exchanging information and revising their tax structures to meet the demands of a commercial world where country borders matter less and less. At the same time, they are looking for new ways to encourage companies to repatriate earnings, as evidenced by the discussions now under way in the UK, Japan and elsewhere over appropriate tax treatment of dividends earned abroad and profits from controlled foreign companies. There is an obvious tension here between the undoubted economic benefits to all of more efficient supply chains and freer trade, and the need for governments to secure their revenues'

There is clear evidence that tax competition for foreign investment has led to a decline in corporation tax revenues in developing countries (see Avi-Yonah, 2009). Whilst high income countries have compensated for the international trend of declining corporation tax rates by broadening their tax bases, developing countries have both reduced their tax rates and narrowed their tax bases. In high income countries, tax reliefs have been curtailed (for instance, in the UK, the generosity of tax allowances for fixed assets has declined dramatically over the past decade), but in developing countries, tax reliefs and even tax holidays have increased. Corporation tax accounts for a higher proportion of the tax take in developing countries than in high income countries and so a decline in corporation tax is more serious in developing countries.

It certainly is not clear whether tax competition is entirely detrimental to global welfare; empirical evidence is weak, although there is plenty of anecdotal evidence. Counter arguments concerning the benefits of tax competition indicate that the debate will run for some time to come.

---

1   See, for example, Davies and Voget (2008).

Chapter 19

Tax Planning Strategies of Multinational Groups

BASICS

19.1   A combination of governmental and public concerns over the tax practices of multinational enterprises (MNEs) led to the publication by the OECD during 2013 of its report: *Base Erosion and Profit Shifting* (BEPS) and its associated Action Plan. MNEs are organized as global entities whilst the tax authorities which attempt to tax their profits are not global entities. They are fragmented, with each tax authority being limited to taxing those members of the MNE that are tax resident within its territory. Base erosion and profit shifting refer to practices of the MNEs that reduce the amounts of profits *taxable* in certain countries, usually those with relatively high taxes, and allocate their profits to group members located in lower tax countries.

Details of the tax practices of a number of large MNEs came to light during 2012 and 2013; through the questioning of these groups by governmental committees in the US, the UK, and Australia. In particular, many details of the tax planning practices of the Starbucks, Apple, Google and Amazon Groups have become public. These practices vary from group to group. They take account of the different definitions of company tax residence in various countries to create 'stateless' companies, they exploit the definitions of permanent establishment (PE), they make use of hybrid entities, and hybrid financial instruments, and they take advantage of the fact that it is difficult to apply the arm's-length principle to situations in which no external comparables exist, making their pricing practices difficult to challenge.

As we have seen in earlier chapters, many of the final BEPS reports from the OECD were published on 5 October 2015, although in some areas further work will be needed to refine the proposals. The aims of the BEPS agenda can only be achieved, however, if countries are willing to cooperate in setting their tax laws. In particular, harmonization of national laws concerning the characterization of certain business entities and of certain financial instruments will be needed. Due to the nature of the problems that it addresses – ie stemming from the 'international nature' of the MNEs – it is likely that some of the BEPS Action Plan will be achieved through the development of one or more multilateral instruments. The BEPS initiative sits alongside developments in information exchange across borders as part of the growing internationalization of tax administrations.

The planning strategies of Apple, Google and Amazon at the time of the public hearings are examined in this chapter, so that the background context to the BEPS project can be better understood. The 'Further study' section of this chapter explains a new tax introduced in the UK to counteract some of these strategies; the Diverted Profits Tax (DPT).

INTRODUCTION

19.2 Google, Apple, Starbucks, Amazon, General Electric ... all global groups of companies, highly profitable and all much in the news during 2012 and 2013 because of a perception that they manage to avoid tax in the countries in which they operate. Indeed, it is reported that they plan so that under the current international tax rules, most of their profits are taxable in countries which charge very little tax. These groups in particular have been singled out for scrutiny by governmental committees in the UK, US and Australia. Governments of a number of countries have become openly critical of the strategies used by MNEs.

Besides criticism of MNEs at governmental level, there is a populist movement against tax avoidance by big businesses. For example, 'UK Uncut' has been involved in direct protest action on the grounds that the UK Government should not be cutting welfare but should be stopping tax avoidance.

Root causes of tax avoidance by MNEs

19.3 MNEs exist primarily to make profits. What matters most is after-tax profits, as only these can be used to reward the shareholders. Directors and senior personnel of the group are also likely to receive much of their remuneration in the form of shares and share options, which means that they have a direct interest in the group's ability to pay dividends. Even where dividends are not paid, retained profits, whether in the holding company or further down the group, cause the assets of the group to increase, driving up the share price. So, whether post-tax profits are paid out as dividends, or whether they are retained within the group, shareholders in the holding company prosper.

Some commentators argue that MNEs have a moral, as well as a legal, duty to pay tax to the countries in which they operate. In theoretical terms, if a company is legally registered or otherwise tax resident in a country, then it owes a debt of political allegiance to that country. Less theoretically, if a company carries on business in a country, using personnel which that country has paid to educate, using the roads, the legal system and deriving sales revenues from its residents, then the company may also owe a debt of economic allegiance to the country. However, it is for the country's government to enforce this debt through taxation and insist that taxes are paid. There is considerable tension, therefore between the MNE's social responsibility towards the country in which it operates and its economic imperative to create value for shareholders, which may or may not include maximizing profits.

Origins of the source and residence principles

19.4   The question of allocation of taxing rights over profits is dealt with in Chapter 7 at para **7.17**. The key principles were developed early in the twentieth century by the League of Nations with a view to preventing two countries from taxing the same income. Although it was known at the time that the rules were imperfect and could possibly result in a source of income not being taxable anywhere (double 'non-taxation' as opposed to double taxation), the ability of MNEs to implement complex cross-border planning to take advantages of mismatches between domestic tax laws was limited. International trade consisted mainly of trading in goods, so that it was usually relatively clear where the profits were made. International communications were slow and cumbersome: the only way of communicating instantaneously was by telegraph. Written letters could take weeks to arrive by sea. Later in the twentieth century, it became possible to make international telephone calls, but connections were unreliable and expensive. Because it was difficult to communicate regularly and in detail with overseas branches and subsidiaries, their holding companies had far less control over them than is the case today. Obviously, recent technological advances in communications and provision of services have transformed global business, with implications for tax residence (as referred to in earlier chapters) and tax incidence.

Concern that MNEs are not paying 'enough' tax

19.5   Tax theorists sometimes argue that corporation tax is, by its nature, double taxation (so-called 'economic double taxation'). Some even recommend that corporation tax be abolished altogether. This is because all the profit a company makes will eventually be taxable in the hands of its shareholders, either in the form of dividends or capital gains. Whilst companies are frequently exempted from paying tax on dividends or capital gains, individual shareholders are not. So, as we saw in Chapter 1 at para **1.12**, in the absence of any relief, profits which a company makes are taxed first in the hands of the company – corporate income tax – and then, when those profits are distributed to the shareholders as dividends, the shareholders pay income tax on them. Alternatively, if the company does not pay dividends, it keeps the cash generated by its profits, spends it on other assets, thus boosting the asset base of the company and thus making the company's shares worth more. So when the shareholder eventually sells his or her shares, the capital gain is larger than it would have been if the company had paid all its pre-tax profits out as dividends. So, dividends or no dividends, the company's profits are effectively taxed twice.

The main problem with the arguments for eliminating corporation tax is that the shareholder may live in a tax haven and thus escape tax on dividends and gains (although dividends being sent to a known tax haven usually suffer withholding tax). Also, shareholders who are resident in non-haven countries might be exempt from tax: for instance, pension funds, who are very large holders of shares in quoted companies. Even where the shareholders do have to pay tax, if no dividends are paid by the company, in most cases the tax authority will have to wait until the shares are sold by the taxpayer and a capital gain becomes taxable. This might be many years after the profits were earned. So corporation tax, which is charged annually, means that a tax authority receives tax revenue more quickly than if it had to wait for a shareholder to sell shares. On a very practical note, if corporation tax was removed, the revenues from it would have to be replaced, possibly by an increase in VAT or income tax, both of which are likely to be unpopular with the voting public.

Case studies on MNE tax planning

19.6   The following case studies are designed to give an insight into the types of tax planning which was much in the news in 2012 and 2013. They are based on what is publicly known and reflect the structures as discussed in various public hearings at the time. It is likely that the actual tax planning strategies are far more sophisticated and complex than described below and may have subsequently changed following the various government investigations that brought these structures into the public arena. The aim is to provide a flavour of the types of arrangement and their consequences rather than forensically analyse them.

Apple Inc

19.7   An extraordinary amount of detail emerged concerning the way the Apple Group is structured and its effect on the group's US tax liabilities during the course of a US Senate investigation held in May 2013.[1] Between 2009 and 2012, this investigation reported that the group's primary offshore (ie non-US) holding company, Apple Operations International, reported net income of $30 billion, yet paid no corporate income tax anywhere. Note, however, it may have paid some local taxes and employment taxes. What is remarkable about Apple's tax planning is how simple, yet how highly effective it is. Global tax bills are minimized without necessarily using sophisticated financial instruments and highly artificial schemes.

Much of Apple's international tax planning appears to be directed at avoiding paying US taxes on profits earned abroad. The US uses the credit method of double tax relief and does not provide tax exemption for foreign dividends. Dividends received by a US parent from a foreign subsidiary are initially taxed at the US corporation tax rate of 35 per cent which is then reduced by a credit for foreign taxes suffered. Because the US tax rate is one of the highest in the world, paying dividends to a US parent company usually results in a liability to US tax, even after double tax relief. Along with many other US-based MNEs, Apple appears to go to some lengths to avoid bringing foreign profits back to the US (repatriation), so as to avoid US taxes on foreign income.

---

1   Available at: www.hsgac.senate.gov/subcommittees/investigations/hearings/offshore-profit-shifting-and-the-us-tax-code_-part-2.

Tax planning using the rules on company tax residence

19.8   A key feature of this group's planning has been to take advantage of the rules on company tax residence and establish entities that are not tax resident in any jurisdiction. As mentioned in Chapter 4, Ireland has come under criticism in recent years arising from its corporate tax regime, which saw it in particular being a party to arrangements whereby some companies were deemed 'stateless', thereby avoiding a tax liability in any country. This arose due to a mismatch between different countries' residence rules. Consequently, Ireland amended its residency rules such that, with effect from January 2015, a company incorporated in Ireland is considered to be tax resident in Ireland if it is not considered to be resident elsewhere. This change effectively put an end to this type of tax planning which the Apple Group (and other US MNEs) had in place. The details of the Apple case, provided below, refer to the position vis-à-vis Ireland's legislation prior to the above change.

In Chapter 4, we noted that a country may consider a company to be tax resident using two main rules: either the company is legally registered in the country, or its central management and control, or effective management, are found there. Although Ireland uses both the tests, so that companies incorporated in Ireland are tax resident in Ireland, there are a number of important exceptions of which Apple Inc had taken advantage. For instance, if a company, incorporated in Ireland, is ultimately controlled by persons resident in a country with which Ireland has a double tax treaty (DTT) (ie the US) and also either carries on a trade in Ireland, or is related to a company which does so, then it will not be considered tax resident in Ireland. The US, on the other hand, only considers companies incorporated in the US as tax residents. The US–Ireland DTT only deals with cases where a company is considered resident in both states, rather than the situation where a company is not resident, under the domestic laws, in either of them. Several important Apple subsidiaries were incorporated in Ireland and took advantage of these rules so that they were not tax resident anywhere.

One of these, Apple Operations International (AOI) ultimately owns most of Apple's non-US companies, so that its holdings include Apple Retail Europe Holdings, the company that effectively owns Apple's European retail stores. Over a four-year period from 2009 to 2012, the Senate Subcommittee heard that this Irish company received $29.9 billion in dividends from other Apple Group companies. During 2009 to 2011, AOI's income represented 30 per cent of the total worldwide net income of the Apple Group, yet during that period AOI paid no corporate income tax at all.

The Senate Subcommittee was told that AOI had no physical presence in Ireland: of its directors and sole officer, two lived and worked in California and also worked for other Apple Group companies. Only one resided in Ireland and the company had apparently never had any employees. Board meetings took place in California, with the Irish director participating in only 7 out of 33 meetings held between May 2006 and December 2012, and of those 7, her attendance was by telephone. Thus AOI was not managed and controlled in Ireland. Although it was registered there, it was able to take advantage of the exceptions from resident status for Irish incorporated companies.

What is the effect of these (for tax purposes) stateless companies? Any subsidiary companies owned by them and resident in other countries, will probably be paying some corporation tax to the tax authorities of the countries where they are resident. When they pay dividends, those dividends are ultimately received by, say, AOI, one of the stateless companies. So the profits accruing in AOI have not necessarily escaped tax altogether. However, the vital point is that they are not liable to tax in the US.

The type of arrangements which Apple has put in place may be illustrated as follows (see Figure 19.1):

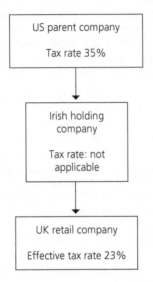

Figure 19.1

In this structure, the only tax payable would be UK tax, assuming no dividends are paid by the Irish company to the US company. Because the Irish company had no tax residence anywhere, it could receive dividends or interest from the UK company without incurring any Irish tax. However, if the UK company made payments of interest to the Irish company, then because the Irish company is not tax resident in Ireland, it would not benefit from the UK–Ireland DTT and the interest payments would be subject to UK withholding tax at a rate of 20 per cent. If the UK company paid dividends to the Irish company, this would not reduce taxable profits in the UK but there would be no withholding tax under UK law.

Why the US CFC regime is ineffective

19.9   Apple Operations International is reported to have gathered in the profits from the subsidiaries which it owned, in the form of dividends. It then recirculated some of this cash to its subsidiaries as and when they needed it (presumably in the form of loans or subscriptions for new shares). A key question is why the US parent was not taxed on this dividend income as a result of the US's controlled foreign company legislation (the 'Subpart F' rules). The answer seems to be that by judicious use of the US's 'check the box' rules, the subsidiaries owned by AOI could be artificially designated, for US tax purposes, as transparent entities: effectively, they were treated as branches of AOI. Thus, for US tax purposes, the trading profits earned by AOI's subsidiaries were treated as being earned by AOI and the dividends were disregarded. The US tax system viewed AOI's income as being trading profits (from the activities of its subsidiaries) rather than passive dividend income. Trading income is not caught by the Subpart F rules. More surprisingly, since 2006, MNEs have not even had to rely on this use of the 'check the box' rules to avoid a charge under Subpart F. This is because Congress enacted temporary legislation in 2006[1] which eliminated from the charge on the US parent any passive income (such as dividends) received by one CFC from another, provided the income can be identified as having originated through active trading. Thus Apple Inc would not have any Subpart F liability in respect of dividends received by AOI from its subsidiaries. This temporary legislation has been repeatedly extended.[2]

---

1   Section 954 (c)(6) United States Tax Code, known as the 'look-through rule'.
2   Most recently, by the Tax Increase Prevention Act on 19 December 2014.

Other anti-avoidance rules which the US could employ

19.10   It could be argued that AOI was merely a shell company: it reportedly had no employees, no physical presence and it did not produce anything. The US has laws which enable it to 'pierce the corporate veil' so as to disregard a shell company and attribute its income to the parent company. This legislation can only be used if 'one entity so controls the affairs of a subsidiary that it 'is merely an instrumentality of the parent'.[1] This is a common law concept and there are no hard and fast rules and each case must be looked at on its merits. The IRS has been extremely reluctant to make use of this power, except in cases where it is clear that the subsidiary is a sham. However, it is difficult to prove that a subsidiary is a sham if the corporate housekeeping, such as holding of board meetings and filing annual reports, has been maintained.

---

1   IRS Priv. Ltr. Rul. 2002-25-046 (Mar. 28, 2002), citing *Moline Properties*, 319 U.S. at 438; *Britt v United States*, 431 F. 2d 227, 234 (5th Cir. 1970); and *Krivo Indus. Supply Co v National Distillers and Chem. Corp*, 483 F.2d 1098, 1106 (5th Cir. 1973).

The Irish subsidiaries that are tax resident in Ireland

19.11   For the Apple companies which are considered tax resident in Ireland and which do pay Irish corporation tax, the effective rate of tax in Ireland is very low. Although the headline rate of corporation tax in Ireland has been 12.5 per cent in respect of trading profit for many years, evidence provided to the Senate Subcommittee showed that Apple subsidiaries which were tax resident in Ireland had been provided, by special arrangements with the Irish tax authority, with tax rates of 2 per cent or even less.

'Since the early 1990s, the Government of Ireland has calculated Apple's taxable income in such a way as to produce an effective rate in the low single digits .... The rate has varied from year to year, but since 2003 has been 2% or less.'[1]

It is often suspected that, as a condition of making an investment in the country, MNEs negotiate special tax rates with the relevant country's government. In the case of Apple, this practice was confirmed in the evidence given by Apple to the Senate Subcommittee.

---

1   Reported in the US Senate Subcommittee Hearings, p 20.

The use of distribution agreements

19.12   Apple Sales International (ASI) was another subsidiary incorporated in Ireland, but not tax resident in Ireland or anywhere else. It bought Apple products from a Chinese manufacturer (independent of the Apple Group) and resold them at a substantial profit to other Apple companies, which sold them on to customers in Europe, the Middle East, Africa, India, Asia and the Pacific countries. Usually, this was done without ASI physically taking possession of the goods, so that they were shipped by the Chinese manufacturer directly to the country where they were to be sold. ASI paid very little corporation tax on the profits from this activity, which amounted to $74 billion over the four years from 2009 to 2012. ASI filed corporate tax returns in Ireland, presumably on the basis that, although not tax resident in Ireland, it had a permanent establishment there. However, the tax paid in 2011 was reportedly only $10 million on income of $22 billion. 'Locating the entities in Ireland seemed primarily designed to facilitate the concentration of offshore profits in a low tax jurisdiction'.[1]

---

1   Reported in the US Senate Subcommittee Hearings, p 28.

Why Subpart F appears to be ineffective

19.13   Whilst the Subpart F rules contain provisions to catch the profits of distributor companies (the so-called foreign base company sales (FBCS) rules) set up in low tax regimes (which extract profits by buying goods from a fellow subsidiary and selling them on, at a profit, to another fellow subsidiary or to the final customer), these rules can be circumvented by using the 'check the box' facility. By using 'check the box', distributor company profits, which are, essentially, passive income, can be transformed for tax purposes into active trading income which is not caught by Subpart F. Effectively, the distribution companies are viewed not as separate entities but as branches of ASI. Therefore ASI's income is viewed, for US tax purposes, as being the income from sales to the final customers. This is active income, rather than passive FBSC (distributor company) income.

This is illustrated below (Figure 19.2) using a hypothetical scenario. In this scenario, because 'check the box' elections have been made for both the Irish distributor company and the Ruritanian distributor company to be treated as transparent entities, the sale from the Irish distributor company to the Ruritanian distributor is disregarded for US tax purposes. As far as the US is concerned, the only transactions that have taken place are in the Irish holding company: the purchase from the Chinese assembly company and the sale to the end consumer. No dividend is paid to the US parent. In spite of this, the US parent remains shielded from any assessment to US tax under Subpart F. This is because, rather than viewing the Irish holding company as having received passive income (the dividend), it views it as having earned trading income (the overall profit on buying from the Chinese assembly company and selling to the Ruritanian consumer). Trading profit is excluded from the Subpart F rules.

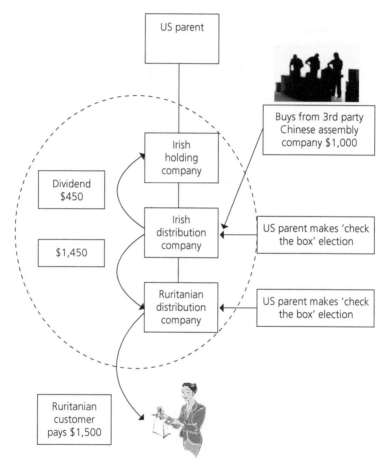

Figure 19.2

Figure 19.2 is a simplified illustration of the type of arrangements entered into by the Apple Group. If the price charged to the Ruritanian company by the Irish distribution company is set too high, it is likely that the Ruritanian tax authority would invoke its transfer pricing legislation to try to establish what the arm's-length price ought to have been. However, as discussed in Chapter 13, in transfer pricing disputes, the taxpayer holds a substantial informational advantage such that even the adjusted price may not be an arm's-length price. Transfer pricing legislation can thus limit this tax planning but not eliminate it completely. The evidence to the Subcommittee indicated that in 2011, Apple's UK group members recorded only $155 million in pre-tax profits, whilst in France and Germany its group companies paid no corporation tax at all. This is despite all three countries having well-developed transfer pricing legislation.

Besides this use of the 'check the box' facility, attribution of distributor company profits to the US parent under Subpart F can also be avoided where the distributor company itself performs some activity in relation to the goods. However, rather than require that, say, an Irish distributor company performs physical manufacturing activities in relation to the goods in question, the US rules merely require that the distributor company makes a 'substantial contribution'. The lack of definition of 'substantial contribution' makes it relatively easy for profits of distributor companies to escape the Subpart F rules. The concept appears to have been designed to extend the exemption from Subpart F not only where income derives from manufacturing activity abroad, but also to the mere supervision of contract manufacturing by another party.

Another exception to the Subpart F rules is of use to Apple: the 'same country' exception.[1] The US parent has no liability under Subpart F in relation to income received by a foreign subsidiary incorporated in Country A received from a fellow foreign subsidiary in Country A. Thus income received by one Irish subsidiary from another would not be subject to the Subpart F rules. This affords additional protection from Subpart F to the dividends received by AOI from ASI and other Irish-incorporated subsidiaries. Especially helpful to Apple is the fact that this exception to Subpart F looks at the place of incorporation of foreign subsidiaries rather than the place of tax residence.

---

1   Section 954(c)(3) United States Tax Code.

The use of a cost-sharing agreement

19.14   Although legal rights to all of the Apple Group's intellectual property (IP) were reportedly owned by Apple Inc in the US, the group had devolved the economic rights to the income from IP relating to non-Americas sales to two Irish subsidiaries, ASI and AOE. Like its parent company, AOI, ASI was not considered tax resident in any country. These subsidiaries contributed towards the worldwide research and development costs in proportion to the share of sales in the Americas (Apple Inc) and the rest of the world (AOR and ASI). The evidence to the Senate Subcommittee showed that, in 2011, these proportions were 40 per cent /60 per cent so that research and development (R&D) costs of $2.4 billion were split $1 billion/$1.4 billion. This suggests that around 60 per cent of the sales revenues arose outside the US. There is an apparent incompatibility with the location of sales revenues and the location of the group's profit-earning ability: the Committee heard that, in 2011, 95 per cent of Apple's R&D was conducted in the US. Why would Apple want to cause this flow of funds from the two Irish subsidiaries into the US, where it would be taxable?

The answer seems to be that, by presenting the two Irish subsidiaries as substantial contributors to the R&D effort, it was possible to justify their earnings as what are referred to as 'entrepreneurial investment' profits, on the grounds that they were, in economic terms at least, co-owners of the IP. In other words, the arrangement made it possible to justify the large profits which the two Irish subsidiaries were making. (During the four-year period 2009–2012, payments under the cost-sharing arrangement of $5 billion were made, whereas the two subsidiaries earned income of $74 billion in the same period, most of which was earned by ASI.) During this same period, Apple Inc contributed $4 billion under the cost sharing arrangement but only reported pre-tax earnings of $38.7 billion. The Irish companies made nearly twice as much pre-tax earnings as Apple Inc but paid only about 20 per cent more in terms of R&D contribution. The companies contributed only a tiny part to the R&D effort but appeared to benefit far more in terms of profits than the company (Apple Inc) which carried out nearly all the R&D. The evidence presented to the Subcommittee suggested that the cost-sharing arrangement was not a commercial arrangement but merely a device to direct revenues away from the US and into Ireland. This suspicion is deepened by the fact that the Apple Group had transferred IP into the ownership of these Irish companies only and not to any subsidiaries in any other countries.

Apple's international tax policy in perspective

19.15   Although the descriptions and explanations given above deal with the ways in which the Apple Group managed its global tax liabilities at the time of the Senate investigation, it is important to recognize that it has not attempted to avoid every dollar of US tax:

- Profits from sales to customers in the Americas are, by and large, taxable in the US: it pays a great deal of US corporation tax. In the financial year 2012, it paid nearly $6 billion, which it claims is $1 in every $40 of corporate income taxes collected by the US in 2012.[1] Apple's tax planning activities appear to have been mainly directed at shielding profits from sales to the rest of the world from US taxes.

- Apple Inc pays a significant amount of other taxes in the US besides corporation taxes: employment taxes and local taxes such as local corporation tax, sales and use taxes, amounted to some $1.627 billion in 2012.[2] However, such taxes are paid by all US companies, whether or not they plan to shield foreign income from US corporation tax.

- Apple does not appear to use 'small island' tax havens but rather has made open use of opportunities offered to it by Ireland. Relatedly, the European Commission has accused Ireland of providing state aid in a controversial case which is discussed further in Chapter 20.

- Apple Inc claims it has paid all US taxes which are legally due.

Lessons which other US-based MNEs could learn from the Apple Group in terms of minimizing the US tax bill were usefully summarized by J Richard Harvey, Jr, in his testimony to the Senate Subcommittee:

- Contribute equity to a foreign subsidiary.

- Transfer valuable intangible assets to it, but minimize the compensation paid, bearing in mind that the valuation of a unique intangible asset is extraordinarily difficult to prove or disprove.

- Isolate substantial non-US income in the tax haven entity.

- Avoid Subpart F (CFC) income for US tax purposes, eg via the 'check the box' facility or the manufacturing (effectively the 'substantial contribution') or same country exemptions.

- Adopt 'indefinite reinvestment' assumption for financial accounting purposes: in other words, never pay the foreign income to the US parent but recirculate it within the non-US part of the MNE. This prevents having to disclose details of what US taxes would be, were the foreign income to be repatriated to the US.

---

1   Available at: www.apple.com/pr/pdf/Apple_Testimony_to_PSI.pdf, p 2.
2   Reported in the Senate Subcommittee Hearings, p 7.

Google Inc

19.16   The Google Group also makes use of Ireland to minimize its global tax liabilities, but not in the same way as the Apple Group. The effect is the same, however: around 90 per cent of Google Group sales outside the US are made from Ireland[1] and thus subjected to low rates of corporation tax.[2] Details of the Google Group's tax planning came to light when it was questioned by the UK Parliamentary Committee of Public Accounts (PAC) in November 2012 and May 2013.[3] The Committee's main interest was in the extent to which it could be shown that the Google Group planned its tax affairs so as to minimize the amount of corporation tax paid in the UK. The Committee's work was hampered in that it failed to call the correct witnesses: rather than call any of Google Group's tax experts, it instead, inexplicably, asked specifically for Google to be represented by Matt Brittin, the Vice President for Sales and Operations in Northern and Central Europe. Thus Google was unable to answer many of the Committee's questions.

---

1   House of Commons Public Accounts Committee Hearing 12 November 2012, at Q448 (see 'Further reading').
2   Although note that Apple makes all its sales throughout the Americas, not merely the US, via its US subsidiaries.
3   The Public Accounts Committee is appointed by the House of Commons to examine 'the accounts showing the appropriation of the sums granted by Parliament to meet the public expenditure, and of such other accounts laid before Parliament as the committee may think fit' (House of Commons Standing Order No 148). Note that the Committee has no powers to levy taxes or to make any determinations concerning taxes. Its members are MPs and are not required to be tax experts.

Avoiding a UK permanent establishment

19.17   The planning undertaken by the Google Group is of interest not just because of the adverse publicity it generated in the popular press, but because of the type of aggressive planning to avoid PE status which is the target of some of the main proposals in BEPS Action 7: Prevent Artificial Avoidance of PE Status, and which is also partly the target of the UK's recently enacted Diverted Profits Tax (DPT).

Essentially, the Google Group minimizes the taxes it pays in the UK by not having any substantial taxable presence in the UK. Sales of advertising (Google's main revenue stream) to UK customers are concluded in Ireland. Whilst UK customers may well be contacted by Google staff working from within the UK, their involvement in making contracts for advertising does not necessarily amount to an agency PE under paragraph 4 of Article 5 of the UK–Ireland DTT, which reads:

> 'A person acting in a Contracting State on behalf of an enterprise of the other Contracting State – other than an agent of independent status to whom the provisions of paragraph 6 of this Article apply – shall be deemed to be a permanent establishment in the first-mentioned State if he has, and habitually exercises in that State, an authority to conclude contracts in the name of the enterprise, unless his activities are limited to the purchase of goods or merchandise for the enterprise.'

This type of PE is discussed in Chapter 9, at para **9.20**. Thus, as the Irish subsidiary had neither a fixed place of business in the UK nor any dependent agents, it had no liability to tax in the UK on its activities there. It has been reported[1] that in the period from 2006–2011, the Google Group earned $18 billion in revenue from UK customers but because so little of this was attributed to the UK company, and because there was no UK PE of the Irish company, it paid only $16 million in UK taxes over the same period. Following assurances in the hearing of the PAC in November 2012 to the effect that Google Ireland did not conclude contracts in the UK and therefore had no UK dependent agent, PE, a Reuters investigation looked at Google's UK job adverts, spoke to former Google UK employees and customers and studied the LinkedIn profiles of around 150 London-based Google employees. On the evidence gathered, it was claimed that Google had misled the PAC and that contracts were, indeed, being effectively concluded in the UK, so that the UK subsidiary was acting as a permanent establishment of the Irish subsidiary. As a result, the PAC re-called Mr Brittin and a further hearing was held in May 2013 but he maintained the position that the country where the contracts were made was Ireland.[2] The PAC, in its report, disagreed with this position, summarizing its findings as:

> 'To avoid UK corporation tax, Google relies on the deeply unconvincing argument that its sales to UK clients take place in Ireland, despite clear evidence that the vast majority of sales activity takes place in the UK. The big accountancy firms sell tax advice which promotes artificial tax structures, such as that used by Google and other multinationals, which serve to avoid UK taxes rather than to reflect

the substance of the way business is actually conducted. HM Revenue & Customs (HMRC) is hampered by the complexity of existing laws, which leave so much scope for aggressive exploitation of loopholes, but it has not been sufficiently challenging of the manifestly artificial tax arrangements of multinationals. HM Treasury needs to take a leading role in driving international action to update tax laws and combat tax avoidance.'[3]

If the PAC was so convinced that Google Ireland had a PE in the UK, the question is: why had HMRC not reached the same conclusion? HMRC must have had a far better understanding of the Google position than the PAC members who are, in terms of tax knowledge, not experts. The answer is that Google are operating in one of the many unclear areas in the international tax regime. The OECD Commentary (pre-BEPS Action 7) on the agency permanent establishment rule (para 5 of Article 5 in the OECD MTC) explains what level of involvement is necessary before a person negotiating contracts on behalf of a foreign enterprise can be said to create a dependent agent PE. First, only persons having the authority to conclude contracts will count. Then, paragraph 33 of the Commentary on Article 5 goes on to say:

'A person who is authorised to negotiate all elements and details of a contract in a way binding on the enterprise can be said to exercise this authority "in that State", even if the contract is signed by another person in the State in which the enterprise is situated or if the first person has not been formally given a power of representation. The mere fact however that a person has attended, or even participated in such negotiations in a State between an enterprise and a client will not be sufficient, by itself, to conclude that the person has exercised in that State an authority to conclude contracts in the name of the enterprise. The fact that a person has attended or even participated in such negotiations could however, be a relevant factor in determining the exact functions performed by that person on behalf of the enterprise.'

The OECD, in its 2012 Discussion Document on Article 5,[4] addressed the issue of the meaning of 'to conclude contracts in the name of the enterprise', but only in the context of undisclosed agents, such as are often found in commissionaire arrangements.

At the November 2012 hearing, Google's representative, Mr Brittin had maintained that the UK staff employed in the UK by Google Ireland were engaged in promotion and explaining Google's products to potential customers. Because they did not close the sales, they did not make the contract and were therefore not dependent agents of the Irish subsidiary. However, during the second hearing in May 2013, Mr Brittin, further maintained that although there may have been some inconsistency between the tax explanations of the arrangements and the view of the arrangements afforded by the job advertisements, the facts were as set out in the previous hearing.

In 2016, further investigations into Google in the UK arose as a result of a large dispute settlement with HMRC of £130m, which several commentators believe falls short of Google's actual liability.

It is believed that the new rules analysed in Chapter 9, rewriting paragraphs 5 and 6 of Article 5, of the OECD MTC, with respect to agents, was prompted by PE avoidance strategies such as Google's. The UK's Diverted Profits Tax, introduced in 2015 (see the 'Further study' section of this chapter) is a direct response to Google's tax planning, but it remains to be seen if the new wording of Article 5 is sufficient to prevent this type of planning to avoid PE status. The Diverted Profits Tax rules could apply to Google with immediate effect, but the BEPS Action 7 proposals will have no effect unless and until the DTT between the UK and Ireland is updated to incorporate those proposals. This could happen relatively soon given that both the UK and Ireland have signalled that they will enter in to the multilateral instrument proposed under BEPS Action 15 for the automatic updating of bilateral treaties in accordance with changes to the OECD MTC.

1 Tom Bergin, 'How Google Clouds its Tax Liabilities' *Reuters* (London, 1 May 2013). Available at: http://uk.reuters.com/article/2013/05/01/uk-tax-uk-google-specialreport-idUKBRE94005 R20130501.
2 16 May 2013.
3 House of Commons Committee of Public Accounts, *Tax Avoidance – Google* (Ninth Report of Session 2013–14, 2013).
4 *OECD Model Tax Convention: Revised Proposals Concerning the Interpretation and Application of Article 5 (Permanent Establishment)* (2012). Available at: www.oecd.org/ctp/treaties/48836726.pdf.

The 'Dutch Sandwich'

19.18 This is another tax planning strategy that the Google Group is known to have used. By making large royalty payments, even the relatively modest rate of Irish corporation tax could be largely avoided. Until recently, if royalties were paid by an Irish company to a Bermudan tax resident, then because there is no DTT between Ireland and Bermuda, withholding tax would be payable according to Irish domestic law. To avoid Irish withholding tax on the payment of royalties to the holding company resident in Bermuda, a Dutch holding company was interposed and the IP is sub-licensed to it. Under the Ireland–Netherland DTT, there is no withholding tax. Neither is there any withholding tax under Netherlands domestic law, so that the funds can be paid on to the Bermudan holding company free of withholding tax. There is nothing to prevent the company, which is tax resident in Bermuda from being incorporated in Ireland. The Irish Government, in 2010, relaxed the rules on charging withholding tax on royalties paid to non-residents so that it is now possible for royalties to be paid to any country without withholding tax.[1]

Because the US parent might be taxed on the royalty income of the Irish incorporated company which is tax resident in Bermuda under the US CFC rules, it 'checks the box' to have the Irish operating company and the Dutch companies treated as transparent. In this way, the royalty payments do not exist for the purposes of US taxation.

1 Corporation Tax Statement of Practice SP-CT/01/10, 'Treatment of Certain Patent Royalties Paid to Companies Resident Outside the State'.

Amazon Inc

19.19   Amazon was also called before the November 2012 hearing of the UK PAC. The concern in this case was that, whilst Amazon has a large physical presence and workforce in the UK in the form of major distribution centres, most of the profit from sales to UK customers was being reported as profits of the Luxembourg subsidiary rather than the UK subsidiary. Similar concerns have been expressed in relation to Amazon's activities in Germany. Unfortunately, as with Google, the PAC did not call the most appropriate witness from Amazon. Amazon was represented by Andrew Cecil, the Director of public policy for Amazon across Europe, who repeatedly professed ignorance of the group's tax affairs.

Amazon maintained that it operates a single European business, based in Luxembourg. The strategic (ie profit-generating) functions are, according to Amazon, based in Luxembourg, whilst the other European subsidiaries are merely service companies, undertaking low level tasks such as running the warehouses and despatching the goods – so-called 'fulfilment' operations. When a UK customer places an order via the internet, he contracts with the Luxembourg subsidiary, Amazon EU SARL. In the UK, this company trades under the name, and uses the internet address 'amazon.co.uk'. In this way, sales to UK customers are made by the Luxembourg company. Similar arrangements exist in other European countries. Thus all sales revenues are earned by the Luxembourg company. According to the evidence given to the November 2012 hearing of the PAC by Andrew Cecil, there are around 500 employees in Luxembourg and around 15,000 in the UK. In 2011, the UK subsidiary recorded revenues of £207 million and a UK tax liability of £1.8 million.[1] Amazon EU SARL, the Luxembourg subsidiary, recorded revenues of €9.1 billion but an after tax profit of only €20 million Under repeated questioning, Cecil failed to give a breakdown of the €9.1 billion by country sales, although in later written evidence from Amazon, a breakdown of sales was supplied:

Amazon Group: net sales 12 months ended 31 December 2011 (US$ millions).[2]

Table 19.1

Germany	7,230
UK	5,348
France	1,225
Italy	212
Spain	107
Other international	7,250
Total net sales international	21,272
Total net sales North America	26,705
Total net sales worldwide	48,077

The Amazon Group argues that it is the Luxembourg company which generates profits, having the IT (there are two Luxembourg companies: one holding IT, and one holding the inventory and making the sales). However, even in Luxembourg, hardly any tax has been paid due to favourable tax rulings granted to Amazon by the Luxembourg Government.

Amazon's planning to avoid paying substantial amounts of UK corporation tax on its business with UK customers will not be affected by the changes to Article 5 proposed by BEPS Action 7. This is because the UK operations are undertaken by a separate subsidiary company, and not by a UK PE of the Luxembourg companies.

However, Amazon's arrangements in Luxembourg have run into other serious problems. In January 2015, the EC published preliminary conclusions from an investigation into the arrangements entered into by the Luxembourg Government with Amazon to the effect that the tax rulings granted to Amazon by Luxembourg amount to state aid, and are thus incompatible with the single market. The state aid rules ensure that no EU government can unfairly favour its own companies over companies resident in other EU Member States. Full details of the arrangements between Amazon and the Luxembourg Government which resulted in very little tax being paid in Luxembourg are available in the decision of the EU Commission in the Amazon state aid case (see Chapter 20).[3]

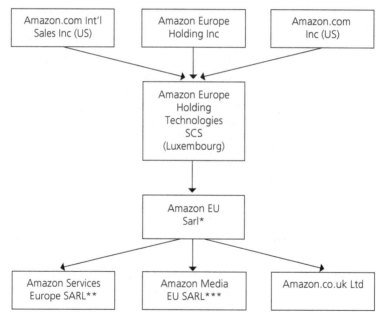

Figure 19.3

* This is the company that trades, inter alia, under the name: amazon.co.uk.
** This company supports sellers on Amazon marketplace.
*** This company sells the digital products to EU customers.

The precise ownership of amazon.co.uk Ltd is unclear.

1   Available at: www.publications.parliament.uk/pa/cm201213/cmselect/cmpubacc/716/121112.
   htm Question 349.
2   Available   at: www.publications.parliament.uk/pa/cm201213/cmselect/cmpubacc/716/
   716we06.htm.
3   State aid SA.38944 (2014/C) – Luxembourg, 'Alleged aid to Amazon by way of a tax ruling',
   Brussels 01.10.2014 C(2014) 7156 final.

The VAT angle

19.20   In addition to taking advantage of lower corporation tax in Luxembourg than in many other countries, Amazon also made use of a weakness in the EU VAT laws that enabled it to retain a much greater proportion of the sales price of e-books than would have been possible if its European operations were based in, say, France or the UK. VAT is covered in more detail in Chapter 21, but for the purposes of this chapter it is sufficient to know that, whenever a VAT-registered trader makes a sale to a customer in the same country of goods liable to VAT, the trader must charge the price of the goods plus the appropriate percentage of VAT. The VAT is then paid over by the trader to the trader's tax authority. Suppliers do not normally have to charge VAT on exports (VAT is paid direct to the tax authority of the customer country by the customer, rather than to the supplier). However, exports of digital products to private (non-VAT registered) customers within the EU are an exception to this rule. Prior to 1 January 2015, the rule was that the VAT rate to be charged was the VAT rate in the supplier's country, rather than the customer's country.[1]

If the same customer bought the same e-book for a VAT-inclusive price of £12 from a Luxembourg supplier prior to 1 January 2015, the VAT element would only be 35 pence (£12 × 3/103) and the Luxembourg supplier would retain £11.65. This is because Luxembourg only charged 3 per cent VAT on e-books as at 2013. The Luxembourg supplier could increase his market share by undercutting the German supplier, say, by charging the UK customer only £10.50. The Luxembourg VAT on this would be about 32 pence, so the Luxembourg supplier would retain £10.18. Thus the Luxembourg supplier was, at the same time, undercutting the German supplier on price, but getting a better ex-VAT price for the e-book, so making more profits. The same principle applied to all the other items sold by Amazon to which the standard 15 per cent rate of Luxembourg VAT applies. Wherever it sold to a non-VAT registered customer in an EU country with a VAT rate higher than 15 per cent, Amazon was at an advantage.

Since 1 January 2015, a UK private customer is charged 20 per cent VAT by Amazon, and the VAT advantage enjoyed by Amazon from being based in Luxembourg has largely disappeared.

1   From 1 January 2015, the EU supplier of such products must charge the customer the price of
   the products plus the rate of VAT applicable in the customer's country. Thus, if a German supplier sells an e-book to a private customer in the UK, the rate of VAT would be 20 per cent. If
   the ex-VAT price of the book was £10, the customer would be charged the VAT-inclusive price
   of £12. The supplier would keep the £10 and pay the £2 VAT to the German tax authority.

Australian investigations

19.21 In August 2015, the first part of a report on *Corporate Tax Avoidance* by the Australian Senate Economics References Committee was published.[1] The report is titled 'You cannot tax what you cannot see', and is an interim report based on an inquiry comprising 6 public hearings, and over 100 submissions. The final report was published in April 2016.[2] The Senate Inquiry was prompted by the publication of a report by the Tax Justice Network Australia and United Voice in September 2014: *Who Pays for our Common Wealth?*[3] Technology companies such as Apple, Google and Microsoft appeared before the Committee. The report makes 17 recommendations over the following 4 areas:

- evidence of tax avoidance and aggressive minimization;

- multilateral efforts to combat tax avoidance and aggressive minimization;

- potential areas of unilateral action to protect Australia's revenue base; and

- the capacity of Australian government agencies to collect corporate taxes.

Several of the specific recommendations relate to transparency for both MNCs and the Australian Taxation Office (ATO), with the latter to produce an annual report on aggressive tax minimization and avoidance activities to be tabled in Parliament along with details of audits and settlements with MNCs. The report also recommends an independent audit of ATO resourcing funding and staffing.

---

1 Available at: www.aph.gov.au/Parliamentary_Business/Committees/Senate/Economics/ Corporate_Tax_Avoidance/Report_part_1.
2 Available at: www.aph.gov.au/Parliamentary_Business/Committees/Senate/Economics/ Corporate_Tax_Avoidance/Report_part_2.
3 Available at: www.unitedvoice.org.au/news/who-pays-our-common-wealth.

Unilateral measures against MNEs

19.22 In January 2013, France proposed dealing with the perceived tax avoidance by Internet firms such as Google, by imposing a special tax on the purchase price of online advertising services. This followed the publication of a key report on tax reform of the digital economy.[1] It called for a redefinition of the concept of PE to allow for the allocation of tax revenues where there is no conventional form of PE. In particular, where customers enter data which is then sold by companies such as Google, the location of those customers might constitute a PE of Google, even though Google itself might have no conventional PE in the customer's country. However, these proposals have been put aside following the publication of the 2013 OECD Report and Action Plan on BEPS.

Other countries have taken unilateral action, for example, the UK has introduced a Diverted Profits Tax (DPT, and popularly referred to as the 'Google tax') in the Finance Act 2015 to take effect from 1 April 2016. In May 2016, the Australian government announced the introduction of a diverted profits tax with effect from 1 July 2017. The tax allows the tax authority to impose a penalty DPT rate of 40% on significant global entities, ie global groups with global revenue of AU$1 million or more. France has proposed a diverted profits tax, but it has been struck down by the French Constitutional Court. The 'Further study' section of this chapter provides more detail on the UK's Diverted Profits Tax.

In addition to new taxes, some countries, including the UK, are introducing new measures requiring companies to publish their tax strategies. Australia has also introduced a Multinational Anti-Avoidance Law (MAAL) and the Australian Taxation Office is pursuing several audits of MNEs from which it expects to raise AU$2.9 billion in tax.

---

1   The Collin & Colin Report, 18 January 2013, 'Mission d'expertise sur la fiscalité de l'économie numérique'. Available at: www.redressement-productif.gouv.fr/files/rapport-fiscalite-du-numerique_2013.pdf (in French).

The requirement for a multilateral solution to BEPS

19.23   Action 15 of the BEPS Action Plan calls for the development of a multilateral instrument to implement some of the other Actions contained in the Plan. This recognizes the fact that the types of tax avoidance behaviour in which MNEs are engaged are only possible because they operate in a multilateral environment. In other words, they are international economic entities. Unless the tax authorities of the world begin to cooperate not just bilaterally, but multilaterally, any attempt to curb the tax avoidance practices described in the BEPS report seems futile. In other words, to tackle the tax avoidance practices of multinational organizations, the tax authorities of the world must themselves start to operate as a multinational organization.

A multilateral approach to curbing BEPS practices can achieve two principal aims:

●   Bilateral double tax treaties could be updated and expanded far more quickly if countries sign a multilateral agreement that they will implement into their double tax treaties any changes to the OECD Model Tax Convention, without alteration and in their entirety. Currently, it takes between 5 and 15 years for changes to the OECD Model Tax Convention to work their way into the network of 2500 or so bilateral treaties. This means that tackling BEPS practices through changes to individual tax treaties is currently ineffective.

●   Countries could agree on a harmonized subset of domestic laws. For instance, if all countries agreed on a common set of rules for categorizing payments as either interest or dividends then the scope for tax avoidance using arbitrage techniques would be much reduced.

If only a small group of countries begin to cooperate in this way, then those countries may find that MNEs relocate away from them. Thus there is a risk associated with being the first to implement measures to counter BEPS practices. Ideally, a large group of countries would act together, for instance, the OECD Members. It would be awkward for MNEs to continue practices of tax arbitrage and manipulative transfer pricing practices if they were effectively forced out of the economically powerful OECD Member countries. However, the chances of all the OECD Members reaching any agreement appear slim when Members such as Luxembourg and the Netherlands are active in providing the tax facilities which enables BEPS practices.

The development of the multilateral instrument, which is due to be signed in June 2017, is considered in some detail in Chapter 7.

New ways of allocating tax revenues?

19.24   Often, the possibilities for changing the international tax system are presented in very bleak terms: replace profit allocation by reference to source and residence with profits according to where the customers are (a consumption tax). Replace the arm's-length principle with global formulary apportionment. Remove corporation tax altogether and tax the shareholders and employees more. Realistically, none of these suggestions are likely to be widely adopted.

One proposal being developed by Devereux and colleagues[1] is to replace corporation tax with a simple tax which is calculated purely by reference to sales revenues in the relevant country minus purchase and minus labour costs incurred – but nothing else. So there would be no deductions for provisions for bad debts, future expenses, capital allowances/depreciation, deductions for interest and royalties and so on. The tax would be applied on a cash flow basis: the business is taxed when the customer pays for the goods or services sold, and the deductions for purchase and labour are only claimable when suppliers and employees are paid. This is referred to as a destination-based cash flow tax. No physical presence of the foreign company would be necessary before it could be taxed.

Under this system, the amount of tax paid would be unaffected by the type of financing used (debt or equity). If most countries adopted this system, and if they all used the same rate of tax, then there would be no tax advantage to a MNE in moving its head office or any of its subsidiaries to any particular country. However, it is unlikely that countries would harmonize their tax rates to the degree needed to eliminate tax competition or the manipulation of internal prices charged for goods and services. Given the length and complexity of supply chains within MNEs, identifying the purchase costs to be offset against the sales revenues could be far more complicated than it first appears.

The concept of the destination-based cash flow tax has been taken up by the US government and is under intense scrutiny at the time of writing.

---

1   See Auerbach et al (2017).

A new era in the taxation of multinational enterprises?

19.25   An optimist might view the publication of the BEPS Action Plan as the point in history where countries changed from competing with each other to secure the greatest slice of the tax pie from MNEs, to cooperating with each other so as to maximize the size of that tax pie in global terms.

The fact remains, that whilst there are countries in the world which are prepared to act as tax havens by welcoming subsidiaries of MNEs as tax residents without charging them very much tax, MNEs are going to take advantage of this offer. The information exchange initiatives may well curb some of the worst tax evasion practices, particularly those of wealthy individuals. However, it is hard to see how mere information exchange can stem the tax leakage from MNEs. In many cases, it will be a simple matter of economics. Countries without natural resources, which are small in geographical terms and particularly those in remote locations, may currently have few alternatives for revenue raising other than to act as tax havens. They may not charge taxes, but the annual company registration fees, commission, and the employment generated by tax haven activity is what keeps their economies afloat. It is probably unreasonable to expect them to give up their principal source of revenues without offering alternatives.

Both the BEPS initiative and the push toward widespread exchange of information on taxpayers (discussed in Chapter 18) are aimed at increasing the global pool of taxable profits from the MNEs. Taken together, the measures attempt to make it harder for MNEs to shelter profits in tax havens, to reduce the scope for slipping through the tax net altogether through the use of hybrid instruments and hybrid entities and to strengthen the systems used to evaluate the transfer pricing policies of the MNEs.

Two criticisms may be directed at this work. First, it assumes that revenues from corporation tax can be increased without a corresponding decrease in revenues from employee and shareholder taxation. Is it realistic to assume that the holding companies of the MNEs will maintain current levels of dividend payments if corporation tax liabilities increase? There is also the issue that the country where these increased corporation tax revenues are collected may not be the country which suffers a decrease in tax collections from the shareholders and the employees. Second, developing countries have pointed out that there is likely to be little benefit for them from either the exchange of information or the BEPS initiatives. Such countries do not generally have the capacity to develop or administer the type of sophisticated anti-avoidance legislation required to counter BEPS practices. It could be argued that the corporation tax base of a developing country is even more important than for a developed country, because it is generally easier for a developing country to collect tax from a few large corporations than from thousands of small businesses and from individuals.

There is a danger that if the OECD countries tighten up their rules for taxing corporations, MNEs may turn their focus to tax avoidance in developing countries. The developing countries are keen to ensure that if MNEs extract their natural resources, use their infrastructure and labour, and base manufacturing activity within their borders, then they should pay corporation tax there. They would like more freedom to protect themselves against profit shifting through the application of withholding taxes: although an unpopular suggestion with most of the OECD countries, such a move would favour the developing countries, as payments of dividends, interest, management fees and royalties flow mainly out of developing countries and into developed countries rather than vice versa. The position of developing countries is covered in Chapter 22.

FURTHER READING

Actionaid (2013) *A Level Playing Field? The Need for non-G20 Participation in the BEPS Process*. Available at: http://www.actionaid.org.uk/sites/default/files/doc_lib/beps_level_playing_field_.pdf.

Auerbach, A, Devereux, M P, Keen, M and Vella, J (2017) 'Destination-based cash flow taxation', Oxford University Centre for Business Taxation, Working Paper 17/01, available at: www.sbs.ox.ac.uk/sites/default/files/Business_Taxation/Docs/Publications/Working_Papers/Series_17/WP1701b.pdf.

Australian Senate Economic References Committee (2015) *Corporate Tax Avoidance*. Available at: http://www.aph.gov.au/Parliamentary_Business/Committees/Senate/Economics/Corporate_Tax_Avoidance/Report_part_1.

Avi Yonah, R S (2016) 'Three steps forward, one step back? Reflections on "google taxes" and the destination-based corporate tax' *Nordic Tax Journal*, 2, 69–76.

Bank, S A (2013) 'The Globalization of Corporate Tax Reform', 40 *Pepperdine Law Review* 1307.

Bergin, T (2013) 'How Google Clouds its Tax Liabilities', *Reuters* (London, 1 May 2013). Available at: http://uk.reuters.com/article/2013/05/01/uk-tax-uk-google-specialreport-idUKBRE94005R20130501.

Boghal, S (2015) 'FA 2015 analysis – Diverted Profits Tax: An Overview' 10 *Tax Journal* 1259, 24 April 2015.

Christians, A (2015) 'Friends with Benefits: Apple's Cautionary Tale' *Tax Notes International*, 15 June 2015, p 1031.

Cockfield, A J (2002) 'The Law and Economics of Digital Taxation: Challenges to Traditional Tax Laws and Principles', (2002) *Bulletin for International Taxation* 606.

Congressional Budget Office (2013) *Options for Taxing U.S. Multinational Corporations* (Pub No 4150).

Devereux, M (2012) 'Issues in the Design of Taxes on Corporate Profit', Oxford Working Papers, Apr. Available at: www.sbs.ox.ac.uk/sites/default/files/SBS_working_papers/issuesDesign_complete.pdf.

Fleming, J C (2017) 'The EU Apple Case: Who has a Dog in the Fight?' *Tax Notes* 154, 251.

Harvey, J Richard (Dick) (2013) 'Apple Hearing: Observations from an Expert Witness' (3 June 2013) *Tax Notes*, p 1171; Villanova Law/Public Policy Research Paper No. 2013-3050. Available at SSRN: https://ssrn.com/abstract=2273634.

House of Commons Public Accounts Committee (12 November 2012) 'Minutes of Evidence HC716'. Available at: www.publications.parliament.uk/pa/cm201213/cmselect/cmpubacc/716/121112.htm.

House of Commons Committee of Public Accounts (2013) *Tax Avoidance – Google* (Ninth Report of Session 2013–14). Available at: www.publications.parliament.uk/pa/cm201314/cmselect/cmpubacc/112/11202.htm.

International Fiscal Association (2009) *Taxation by Design (Mirlees Review)*, Chapter 18 'Corporation Taxation in an International Context'. Available at: www.ifs.org.uk/mirrleesReview/design.

Kleinbard, E D (2013) 'Through a Latte, Darkly: Starbucks's Stateless Income Planning', Tax Notes 24 June 2013, pp 1515–35. Available at: http://papers.ssrn.com/sol3/papers.cfm?abstract_id=2264384.

Loomis, S C (2012) 'The Double Irish Sandwich: Reforming Overseas Tax Havens' *St Mary's Law Journal*, v 43, p 825.

McIntyre, M J (2009) 'A Program for International Tax Reform', 122, *Tax Notes International* 1021.

Miller, D S (2017) 'Tax Planning under the Destination-Based Cash Flow Tax: A guide for policymakers and practitioners' *Columbia Journal of Tax Law*, 8, p 295.

Muller, J (2014) 'BEPS Case Study', 24, *International Tax Review*, 29, 2013–2014.

OECD (2011) *Corporate Loss Utilisation through Aggressive Tax Planning*.

OECD (2012) *Hybrid Mismatch Arrangmenes: Tax Policy and Compliance Issues*.

OECD (2013) *Addressing Base Erosion and Profit Shifting*.

OECD (2013) *Action Plan on Base Erosion and Profit Shifting*.

Robertson, D and Taylor, I (2016) 'Ten Questions on the Apple state aid decision' *Tax Journal*, 6 September 2016.

Rosenzweig, A H (2012) 'Thinking Outside the (Tax) Treaty', [2012] *Wisconsin Law Review*, 717.

Sanchirico, C W (2015) 'As American as Apple Inc.: International Tax and Ownership Nationality' *Tax Law Review*, 68, 207 (pointing out, inter alia, that the vast majority of 'unrepatriated' foreign earnings of Apple and others already reside in US investments, they are only 'unrepatriated' from a legal/tax point of view).

Smyth, J (2013) 'Q&A: How multinationals use Ireland to lower their tax bills', *Financial Times* (London, 21 May 2013).

Tax Justice Network Australia & United Voice (2014) *Who Pays for our Common Wealth?* Available at: www.unitedvoice.org.au/news/who-pays-our-common-wealth.

Ting, A (2014) 'iTax – Apple's International Tax Structure and the Double Non-Taxation Issue' *British Tax Review* 1, p 40.

Ting, A (2015) 'The Politics of BEPS – Apple's International Tax Structure and the US attitude towards BEPS' *Bulletin for International Taxation* June/July 2015, p 410.

United States Senate Permanent Subcommittee on Investigations (2013) *Offshore Profit Shifting and the U.S. Tax Code Part 2 (Apple Inc.)*, Committee on Homeland Security and Governmental Affairs.

FURTHER STUDY

The United Kingdom's Diverted Profits Tax

19.26   In the run up to the 2015 government election in the UK, the 'Google tax', properly known as the Diverted Profits Tax (DPT), was announced at the Conservative Party Conference, and then included in the Autumn Statement to target multinationals who use artifical arrangements to divert profits overseas in order to avoid UK tax.

The new tax was included in the Finance (No 2) Bill 2015 published in March and subsequently came into force from 1 March 2015. It imposes a 25 per cent tax in certain circumstances, which is higher than the current rate of corporation tax in the UK, currently 20 per cent and set to reduce to 18 per cent. This penalty rate is apparently designed to encourage multinationals to adopt different business models. The DPT can be viewed as radical in that it departs from the long-standing principle that the UK will not tax foreign companies doing business with UK clients unless they have established a PE in the UK. In light of the BEPS Project, however, it can be seen rather as a measure introduced in anticipation of the outcome of BEPS, and consistent with the gradual move away from a narrow interpretation of PE.

The DPT applies in two distinct situations:

- where a foreign company structures its affairs so as to avoid having a taxable presence (a PE) in the UK; and

- where a company that is otherwise taxable in the UK, creates a tax advantage by involving entities, or using transactions that lack economic substance.

Avoided permanent establishment

19.27   For the first situation to apply, leading to a potential tax charge under the DPT, the following conditions must be met:

- a 'foreign' company carries on a trade;

- an 'avoided PE' carries on activity in the UK supplying services, goods or other property of the foreign company;

- it is reasonble to assume that the activities of the avoided PE are designed to ensure that it is not classifed as a PE; and

- either a 'mismatch' condition or a 'tax avoidance' condition is met'. The former is met where a material provision is made between parties meeting the participation condition, resulting in an 'effective tax mismatch outcome' (see below). The latter is more familiar, ie have the arrangements been put in place wholly or mainly for the purposes of avoiding or reducing UK corporation tax?

The avoided PE provision will not apply if sales or expenses related to the UK activity by the foreign company and connected persons do not exceed £10 million, or £1 million respectively.

Insufficient economic substance

19.28   The 'insufficient economic substance' condition is met when the following occurs:

- a company is UK resident or non-UK resident, but trading through a UK PE;

- there is a material provision made between the company and another person by means of a transaction or series of transactions;

- the parties meet a participation condition; and

- the material provision causes an 'effective tax mismatch outcome' between the company and the person.

Key concepts

19.29   A **participation condition** is met if one party directly or indirectly participates in the management, control or capital of the other, or a third person directly or indirectly participates in the management, control or capital of both parties.

An **effective tax mismatch outcome** arises if in relation to supplies, the reduction in UK tax by one party exceeds the tax payable by the other relevant party, and the tax payable by that other party is less than 80 per cent of the reduction achieved by the first party.

For the condition of **insufficient economic substance** there are two tests: the first test is transaction-based ie was the transaction designed to secure a tax reduction, and are the non-tax benefits less than the financial benefits arising from the tax reduction. The second test is entity-based ie is a person party to a transaction in order to secure a tax reduction, and is the non-tax benefit of that person's contribution less than the financial benefit of the tax reduction?

Exclusions: For both the avoided PE and the insufficient economic substance condition, there is an exception where the company and transacting person are both SMEs.

In order to exclude financing arrangements from the scope of DPT, there is an exclusion for 'excepted loan relationship outcomes' which is applied if the increase in expenses or reduction in income arises from something that would produce debits or credits under the loan relationship rules or derivative contract rules.

Calculating Diverted Profits Tax

19.30 DPT is at the rate of 25 per cent and applied to the company's taxable diverted profits, which are essentially calculated using transfer-pricing principles, although in some cases re-characterization may be required.

Avoided permanent establishment cases

19.31 In the case of an avoided PE, notional PE profits must be ascertained. These are the profits that would have been chargeable and attributable to the avoided PE if it had been an actual PE. Where there is a material provision that meets the mismatch condition, a 'relevant alternative provision' must be calculated which entails assuming a counterfactual set of arrangements, ie a hypothetical provision, which is bound to be controversial in practice. If it is found that the arrangement does not erode the UK tax base, the actual provision condition is satisfied. The profit to which DPT is applied depends on the reason for the avoided PE situation.

If it is because of the tax avoidance condition, the taxable diverted profits are the notional PE profits.

If it is because of the mismatch condition, but the actual provision condition is met, then the taxable diverted profits are the notional PE profits. If the mismatch condition is met, but the relevant alternative provision (the hypothetical provision) would have resulted in UK taxable income for a connected party, then the taxable diverted profits will be the sum of the notional PE profits, and that UK taxable income.

Lack of economic substance cases

19.32   The same concepts of relevant alternative provisions and actual provision condition apply in the cases where there is an absence of economic substance. There is no DPT charge if the actual provision condition is met and the material provision is at arm's length. In other cases where the actual provision condition is met, then the DPT taxable profits are the result of applying a transfer-pricing adjustment to the material provision. As with the avoided PE case, if the actual provision condition would have been met but the relevant alternative provision would have resulted in UK taxable income for a connected party, then the taxable diverted profits will be the sum of the notional PE profits and that UK taxable income. We should note here that the UK Government intends to use the arm's-length principle in arriving at the amount of the profits to be charged. There is potential for DPT to give rise to double taxation, in which case, credit will be allowed for home country taxation to the extent that it is just and reasonable.

Notification procedures

19.33   Importantly, the DPT is not self-assessed. Instead, companies are required to notify HMRC if they are potentially within its scope within three months of the end of the relevant accounting period. Where a designated HMRC officer determines a company has a DPT liability, a preliminary notice will be issued that includes an estimate of the taxable diverted profits.

There are three exclusions to the notification requirements:

1   It is reasonable for the company to conclude that no DPT charge will arise.

2   Where an officer of HMRC has confirmed that the company is not required to notify.

3   Where it is reasonable to assume that HMRC have been provided with the information sufficient to determine whether to give a preliminary notice.

There is a short period following issue of a preliminary notice during which representations can be made. Payment must then be made within 30 days and interest will be charged from 6 months after the end of the accounting period to the date of the charging notice. A 12-month review period is available to challenge the level of the charge, with right of appeal to the First Tier Tribunal thereafter.

Conclusion

19.34   There is a lot of uncertainty about the application of the DPT rules. It is not clear how widely cast the net is and it is possible that it will include structures that are commonly used for investment into the UK. The government expects to raise approximately £300 million from the measures. Some commentators suggest that it is possible that other countries will introduce retaliatory measures. There is also considerable uncertainty about how aggressively HMRC will enforce the new tax, which leads to fears that some multinationals may choose to abandon their UK presence altogether. Other questions arise such as how the tax will be treated under the UK's DTTs: the HMRC view is that it is not 'corporation tax', and therefore falls outside of the treaties, but this is by no means assured. There are also questions about the compatibility of the tax with EU law, for example, whether it is discriminatory.

Chapter 20

European Corporation Tax Issues

BASICS

20.1   Direct tax harmonization is not possible within the EU without the agreement of all Member States, although a subset of Member States may agree to co-operate on certain initiatives. It is considered that the objectives of the EU, principally to operate as a single trading bloc, cannot be fully met without a degree of harmonization of direct taxation. The fundamental freedoms contained in the Treaty on the Functioning of the European Union (TFEU) mean that taxpayers can expect to work in, invest in and operate within the EU without a tax disadvantage compared to the position that would apply if they operated merely within their home country, and without being treated worse than nationals or resident companies in the host State.

The EU has been working towards achieving the harmonization of the direct tax systems of its Member States through the introduction of a number of Directives governing the tax treatment of pan-EU groups of companies – the Merger Directive, the Parent/Subsidiary Directive, the Interest and Royalties Directive and, more recently, the Anti-Tax Avoidance Directive and the draft Common Consolidated Corporate Tax Base (CCCTB) Directive. Whilst far from perfect, these Directives represent significant progress towards achievement of EU goals.

The need to achieve a measure of harmonization at EU level is more urgent due to the increasing numbers of tax cases brought by EU taxpayers, usually alleging discrimination, and the denial of freedom of establishment. These cases tend to be decided in favour of the taxpayer.

INTRODUCTION

20.2   The European Union is a group of countries in geographic proximity to each other that have entered into economic and political co-operation. Originally, the purpose of the union was to create a unified coal and steel industry and also, by engendering close industrial and economic co-operation, to lessen the risk of future wars between the members. The founding members: Germany, France, Italy, the Netherlands, Belgium and Luxembourg signed the first treaty in 1951. The Treaty of Rome established a common market (a trading bloc) in 1957, abolishing customs duties on movements of goods between its Member States. In 1993, when there were ten Member States, the 'single market' was introduced so that many more trade barriers were removed, such as payment of value added tax at the point of import. Non-tax improvements included the harmonization of technical norms and health and safety standards and the abolition of exchange controls. The objective of the 1993 reforms was to stimulate industrial and commercial growth in the Member States to enable the EU to compete with the US economy. The US economy is far larger than that of any of the single Member States. Since the 1950s, the role of the EU has grown beyond trade to include social and political issues such as human rights.

As far back as 1985, the EU has sought to abolish tax-related barriers to free trade within the EU. However, these early aspirations to achieve harmonization of direct taxation within the EU have yet to be realized. Member States must adopt the Value Added Tax (VAT) as their principal indirect tax as a condition of membership but there is no requirement for Member States to adopt a common system of direct taxation. However, the enthusiasm of EU residents for upholding their EU rights in the courts has meant that direct tax systems need to converge to some extent. This convergence is being achieved both through centrally managed initiatives such as the Parent/Subsidiary Directive and the draft common consolidated corporate tax base (CCCTB) and in a more ad hoc manner by taxpayers having their cases referred to the Court of Justice of the European Union (CJEU).

EU PRINCIPLES AFFECTING TAX ISSUES

The 'fundamental freedoms'

20.3   The founding treaty of the EU, originally known as the Treaty of Rome, laid down a number of 'fundamental freedoms' to which residents of EU Member States are entitled in respect of commercial matters, which includes taxation. The Treaty of Lisbon (2009) amended the two treaties (the Treaty of Rome (1957) and the Maastricht Treaty (1992)) which comprised the constitution of the EU and changed the name of the Treaty of Rome to the Treaty on the Functioning of the European Union (TFEU). The 'fundamental freedoms' are part of the TFEU:

Article 45(39)

Freedom of movement for workers.

Article 49(43)

Freedom of establishment of nationals of a Member State in the territory of another Member State. Article 49(43) reads as follows:

'... restrictions on the freedom of establishment of nationals of a Member State in the territory of another Member State shall be prohibited. Such prohibition shall also apply to restrictions on the setting-up of agencies, branches or subsidiaries by nationals of any Member State established in the territory of any Member State.

Freedom of establishment shall include the right to take up and pursue activities as self-employed persons and to set up and manage undertakings, in particular companies or firms within the meaning of the second paragraph of Article 54, under the conditions laid down for its own nationals by the law of the country where such establishment is effected, subject to the provisions of the Chapter relating to capital.'

Article 56(49)

Freedom for a national of one Member State to provide services to a person in another Member State.

Article 63(56)

Freedom of movement of capital between Member States, and between Member States and third countries.

(*Note*: the numbers in parentheses are the Article numbers in the pre-2009 Treaty.)

Constitutional issues in the EU

20.4   The four 'fundamental freedoms' summarized above apply to companies as well as to individuals. They are crucial in the taxation of pan-EU corporate groups. Taxpayers who consider that they have been denied any of these fundamental freedoms can have their case referred to the CJEU. The underlying principle is that a business should not suffer any discrimination in tax matters as a result of operation in one EU Member State rather than another (eg its home State). In particular, a company should not be disadvantaged from a tax viewpoint by expanding operations into another EU country. The fundamental freedoms, particularly the right to freedom of establishment, imply that a taxpayer can expect capital export neutrality and capital import neutrality (see Chapter 2) when operating within the EU. For example, if a company sets up a branch in another Member State, it should not expect that branch to be taxed more harshly than residents of the State where it is located, and neither should it expect any kind of tax penalty in its home State.

There is no common system of direct taxation within the EU. Each Member State has the right to have its own laws regarding income tax and corporation tax, as well as other direct taxes (tax sovereignty). The powers of the Council of the EU with respect to direct taxation are limited to the issuing of Directives, which must be approved by all the Member States (Article 94, TFEU) before they can be adopted by the EU. EU Directives are templates for national laws; they lay down the end results which the legislation of each

Member State should achieve, without giving precise wording. This contrasts with the position regarding VAT and customs and excise duties, where Article 113 TFEU gives the Council of the EU the power to adopt provisions for the harmonization of taxes. Thus, all Member States must adopt, in their national laws, the measures prescribed by the Council of the EU in the field of indirect taxation, although they do not have to use the EU wording.

Hence, agreement of all Member States would be needed to impose harmonization of corporate taxation on all the EU Member States. However, the Treaties of Amsterdam (1997) and Nice (2003) established the mechanism of 'enhanced co-operation' as a last resort in the absence of unanimity, which makes it possible for a group of at least eight Member States to enter into agreements for the harmonization of direct taxes. This has opened the door for moves towards harmonization not previously thought possible when agreement of all 28 member States was the only option. The road to harmonization for direct taxation is not smooth and in the following section we review some of the earlier developments and recommendations before considering current proposals for change.

In 1960, the EU set up a committee of tax and financial experts under the chairmanship of Professor Fritz Neumark to examine, inter alia, taxation and in particular those aspects that might distort the achievement of a common market. The report recommended harmonization, of turnover taxes in the first instance, together with withholding taxes on dividends and interest, then personal income tax and corporate taxation and finally implementation of a system of common information and a Community tax court. More than 40 years later, many of these recommendations have not yet been implemented. In 1966, the Segre committee reported on the establishment of an integrated capital market and considered fiscal obstacles to the free movement of capital. The committee recommended replacing bilateral double taxation treaties with a multilateral community convention, which has yet to be achieved and possibly never will be.

In 1975, the EU proposed that the corporation tax rate should be set in the range 45 per cent to 55 per cent, that each Member State should have a dividend imputation system (see Chapter 1 for a brief explanation of dividend imputation) and a common system of withholding tax on dividends at a rate of 25 per cent. These recommendations were not, however, implemented and the next review occurred in 1992 with the Ruding Committee recommendations that the band of tax rates be 30 per cent to 40 per cent, relief from double taxation of dividends be extended to non-residents and a set of standards established for determining the corporation tax base (in other words, a standard corporation tax computation). These recommendations, like those of the preceding committees, have not been implemented. In 1999, a new study on company taxation (European Commission, 2002) was set up to consider the differences in effective levels of corporation tax and identify the main taxation provisions that hamper cross-border activity. Devereux (2004) analyses this report and concludes that neither a source-based nor residence system of international corporation tax is attractive or efficient and that it is sensible to explore other alternatives.

Further discussions were initiated in 2001 when the EU published plans for company taxation in the coming years. The stated long-term aim was to move towards a single consolidated base for calculating tax on EU-wide profits.

Benshalom (2008) identifies two political impediments to the harmonization of corporation tax within the EU:

- The pressure for harmonization comes from the EU itself – the Commission and the decisions of the Court of Justice, rather than directly from the business community. However, it could be said that by invoking principles of EU law, businesses are, de facto, pressuring for harmonization.

- The Commission's plans are not sufficiently detailed or clearly formulated to permit Member States to determine if they will be able to implement the plans.

Multinational enterprises have mixed views regarding the desirability of a fully harmonized EU corporation tax system. On the one hand, they have to cope with wide variations in the corporation tax systems in each EU Member State. This is not just a matter of varying tax rates. The computation of taxable profits and gains also varies widely from State to State. Losses incurred by a subsidiary in one State may, or may not be capable of being offset against profits in other Member States. Transfer pricing rules vary from State to State. Such variations create a heavy compliance burden, both in terms of the sheer cost of paying external advisers in the relevant States and in the retention of the internal expertise required to cope with this multi-jurisdictional taxation. On the other hand, the variations in taxation provide endless opportunities for optimization of the tax liability at the EU level.

Before examining the more ambitious proposals for corporation tax harmonization, we first consider three measures that have already been put in place, specifically the Merger Directive, the Parent/Subsidiary Directive and the Interest and Royalty Directive. We also briefly discuss the Directives relating to administrative cooperation and anti-avoidance.

THE DIRECTIVES

20.5   While movement towards harmonization of the direct tax base for corporation tax has been slow, a number of Directives have been implemented to deal with specific problematic areas. These are designed to help enterprises operate in more than one EU Member State without suffering taxation in more than one State and to help enterprises move from one Member State to another without incurring tax charges.

Merger Directive[1]

20.6   The Merger Directive was adopted in 1990 and amended in 1994, 2003 and 2006 to accommodate new Member States, and in 2005 to expand the scope of the Directive. The Directive was codified in 2009 (2009/133/EC). The broad aim of the Directive is to permit enterprises to set up in a different Member State without incurring tax charges in the Member State which assets are leaving. In other words, the aim is to level the playing field between purely domestic expansion and restructuring and that involving another EU Member State. It applies to:

- mergers: where all the trade of one or more companies is transferred to a new or to an existing company;

- divisions of a company into several other companies, including partial division where the original company continues to trade;

- transfers of assets to another company where only part of the trade is transferred;

- exchanges of shares; and

- the transfer of the registered office of a Societas Europaea (see below).

This Directive seeks to alleviate tax liabilities incurred as a result of mergers or setting up new subsidiaries and branches. In 2005, the list of entities to which it applies was extended and several other improvements were made.[2] Examples of the type of tax liabilities that can arise on cross-border restructuring and expansion are a charge on a capital gain on sale of assets to a new foreign subsidiary in return for shares, tax charges on any reserves previously treated as tax exempt or the forfeiture of losses where these cannot be carried forward in the company which is now to carry on the trade.

A principal effect of the Directive is that taxation on capital gains arising from non-cash cross-border company restructurings is deferred.[3] Deferral usually extends until the disposal of shares or securities. This is achieved by the provisions of the Merger Directive:

- A merger, division or transfer of assets should not give rise to any taxation of capital gains on the assets transferred that are effectively connected with a permanent establishment of the receiving company in the Member State of the transferring company.[4]

- The allotment of the shares representing the capital of the receiving or acquiring company to a shareholder of the transferred or acquired company in exchange for shares representing the capital of the latter company should not, of itself give rise to taxation in the hands of the shareholders.[5] The UK's legislation implementing the Merger Directive is found in TCGA 1992, s 140A et seq.

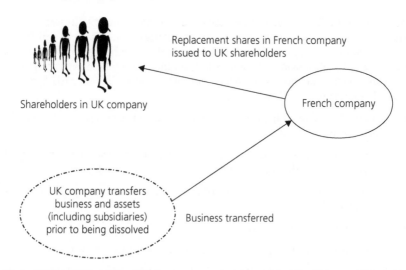

Replacement shares in French company
issued to UK shareholders

Shareholders in UK company

French company

UK company transfers
business and assets
(including subsidiaries)
prior to being dissolved

Business transferred

Figure 20.1: Example of merger as contemplated by the Merger Directive

1   Council Directive 90/434/EEC, 23 July 1990.
2   Council Directive 2005/19/EC which must be implemented into the domestic laws of Member
    States by December 2007.
3   For example, UK TCGA 1992, s 140. Note that the Directive permits a cash payment of up to
    10 per cent of the nominal value of the value of any securities taken in partial consideration or
    as part of an exchange of shares.
4   Article 4(1).
5   Article 8(1).

Ongoing problems with the Merger Directive

20.7   One particular problem with the Merger Directive is that it applies
only to the *tax* consequence of mergers but the legal systems of some EU States
do not contemplate some of the transactions covered, especially mergers and
demergers. For instance, in the UK a merger cannot be achieved without liqui-
dating the two companies, whereas the Directive contemplates dissolution of
the original companies forming the merger without a liquidation.

In January 2009, the EU published a survey, carried out by Ernst and Young,
on the implementation of the Merger Directive across the (then) 27 Member
States.[1]

The report by Ernst and Young found that 37 items were identified in the
27 Member States and evaluated as possibly being non-compliant with either
the Merger Directive or EU primary law. Indeed 476 out of a total of 1,675
evaluations were found to be doubtful as to their compliance, and the survey
concludes that:

> 'many of the items raised in the Survey will continue to be subject
> to controversy discussion between EU tax experts. The uncertainty
> on these tax issues might underline the practical experience that in

planned EU cross-border reorganisations companies often do not take advantage of the Merger Directive.'

Apart from the uncertainty arising from the failure of the Directive, and the CJEU, to define important terms (such as 'provisions and reserves', and 'head office' which leads to the adoption of local interpretations and potential confusion), loss of taxation rights and exit charges were flagged up as being a contentious issue. The Merger Directive is silent on the subject of exit charges, which may arise when assets leave a taxing jurisdiction, and according to the survey almost all of the Member States assume from this that exit charges are compliant with EU law.

The Merger Directive contains a provision to deny the benefits of the Directive where tax avoidance is present. If there is a 'valid commercial reason' then no tax avoidance is present and vice versa. The survey notes that the Merger Directive fails to 'mark the borderline between these concepts clearly'. Some guidance as to the interpretation of these phrases can however be found in CJEU decisions. According to the survey:

'The "Leur Bloem" case suggests that tax avoidance will be present where a taxpayer intends to obtain a purely fiscal advantage. Other [CJEU] cases suggest that tax avoidance will be present where, along with the subjective intention to obtain a purely fiscal advantage, the objective circumstances of the operation confirm that the arrangement is "wholly artificial". It can be concluded from the case law that Member States may refuse to apply the benefits of the Merger Directive where both the subjective intention and objective circumstances confirm that the arrangement does not have any economic purpose.'

---

1 Available at: http://ec.europa.eu/taxation_customs/resources/documents/taxation/company_ tax/mergers_directive/study_impl_direct.pdf.

Parent/Subsidiary Directive[1]

20.8 The original Parent/Subsidiary Directive which was adopted in 1990 abolished withholding taxes on payments of dividends between associated companies of different Member States and prevented the double taxation of parent companies on the profits of their subsidiaries by insisting on a full credit for underlying tax.

The Directive was expanded in 2003 to encompass a greater range of entities. The 2003 Directive also relaxed the conditions for exempting dividends from withholding tax by reducing the participation threshold from 25 per cent to 10 per cent, the reduction to take place in stages, reducing to 20 per cent in January 2005, 15 per cent in January 2007 and then to 10 per cent in January 2009.

The Directive eliminates double taxation of subsidiary companies by insisting that double tax relief is to be given for underlying taxes all the way down a chain of shareholdings without tier restrictions. A 2009 survey[2] noted that significant differences exist in the way in which Member States have implemented the provisions of the Directive. In particular, many Member States have adopted provisions which permit payment of dividends without withholding tax in circumstances where the percentage shareholding and the period of ownership are lower than specified in the Directive.

In July 2014, the Council of the EU adopted provisions (2014/86/EU) preventing corporate groups from using hybrid loan arrangements. Instead of a blanket ban on the taxation of dividends covered by the Directive in the Member State of the recipient, the exemption from taxation now only applies to the extent that no tax deduction was obtained for the payment. If the paying company obtained a tax deduction in respect of the 'dividend', then the Member State of the recipient is bound to tax the recipient on it. This is the first time that a direct tax Directive has imposed an obligation to tax on member States, requiring them to collect a tax they may otherwise not collect.

In December 2014, the Council approved an amendment to the Directive aimed at preventing tax avoidance and aggressive tax planning by corporate groups, which became Council Directive 2015/121/EU. Member States were given until 31 December 2015 to transpose the anti-abuse rule into domestic law. The common minimum anti-abuse standard is as follows:

> 'Article 1(2) Member States shall not grant the benefits of this Directive to an arrangement or series of arrangements which, having been put into place for the main purpose or one of the main purposes of obtaining a tax advantage that defeats the object or purpose of this Directive, are not genuine having regard to all relevant facts and circumstances. An arrangement may comprise more than one step or part.'

---

1   90/435/EC, updated by 2003/123/EC.
2   'Implementation of the amended Parent-Subsidiary Directive' Ernst & Young 2009. Available at: http://tax.uk.ey.com/NR/rdonlyres/er362o7ruta53lf2r6nmm2g6m636iamtkcjyelawjbu-z7ou6nre2duowtcaflynpf3qyjem3xmwd66ixeim2whep7td/EU+Study_11SEP09.pdf.

Interest and Royalties Directive

20.9   The Interest and Royalties Directive requires Member States to remove withholding taxes on cross-border payments of interest or royalties between associated companies. Again, the minimum shareholding was set at 25 per cent although Member States are permitted to set a lower level. The Directive applies from 1 January 2004. It took about 14 years since its inception for this Directive to be fully adopted.

The Directive applies to:

- companies and other bodies as listed in the Directive; and

- companies that are subject to the taxes listed in the Directives, or ones which are similar if a Member State makes changes to its taxes after adoption of the Directive.

The Directive may be criticized for insisting upon a set list of legal entities rather than taking a more inclusive approach. Both the Parent/Subsidiary and the Interest and Royalties Directives originally suffered from uncertainty as to the application of the 'subject to tax' clause. This now stipulates that the Directives only apply if the funds used to make the payments have arisen from income or profits which have already been taxed, rather than from income or profits which are theoretically subject to tax but which are, in fact, exempt.

Because interest can be payable between any two parties (as opposed to dividends, where there needs to be a shareholding), rules are needed to govern the relationship between payer and recipient which must exist before the terms of the Directive can be relied upon. The Directive has been criticized for insisting upon direct, rather than indirect, shareholdings although individual Member States can extend the scope of the exemption from withholding tax to indirect shareholdings if they wish. A further criticism is that the scope of the Directive is considered uncertain as regards some fiscally transparent entities.

Some commentators (eg Aussilloux et al, 2017) suggest that differences in the way Member States tax royalties, for example, leads to the unintended effect that royalties charged to subsidiaries in high tax States are untaxed therein, but not necessarily taxed in another State. In this regard, the authors recommend that the Directive be modified so as to allow for more extended use of source taxes on interest and royalties.

Mutual Assistance for the Recovery of Tax Claims Directive (2010/24/EU)

20.10   The EU Mutual Assistance for the Recovery of Tax Claims Directive (2010/24/EU) updated several earlier Directives and has, as one of its objects, the provision of clearer and more precise rules for information exchange. The previous Directive[1] had been criticized for being ineffective due to the inefficiencies of the procedures employed and to differences in the way in which it had been implemented by the different Member States. Only a small fraction of the taxes at stake in claims made under the former Directive resulted in any recovery of tax revenue for the requesting State. States are to provide any information which is 'foreseeably relevant' to the requesting State in the recovery of its taxes. There is a bar on declining requests solely on the grounds of banking secrecy, which mirrors the requirements in the latest version of Article 26 of the OECD MTC. A particular type of information that would need to be exchanged under the terms of this Directive is information to support the belief that the taxpayer has assets in the requested State (so that there is evidence that the taxpayer could actually pay the tax if pursued). Technically, all that is required is a statement that the requesting State has such information, but in practice it is likely that the requested State would prefer to have the details. Under this Directive, the requested State cannot claim its costs of recovering the debt except where the action for recovery proves to be unfounded, eg where it turns out there is no liability to the tax after all) from the requesting State. Therefore, it is in the interests of the requesting State to supply as much information relating to the claim as possible.

This Directive represents a deliberate erosion of the so-called international 'revenue rule' whereby one country will not assist in the collection of another's taxes. The need for better assistance within the EU was highlighted in the 1999 UK case of *QRS 1 ApS and Others v Frandsen*.[2] In this case, the Danish tax authorities tried to collect unpaid Danish taxes in England. The taxpayer (Mr Frandsen) was resident in the UK, domiciled in England and within jurisdiction of the English courts. Some business occurred involving companies owned by Mr Frandsen, and his companies went into liquidation owing Danish tax. The Danish tax authorities funded an action against Mr Frandsen based on Danish law which prohibits companies from the provision of financial assistance for the purchase of their own shares. The companies were asking him to give back the money they had used to purchase his shares from him. Mr Frandsen contended that the English courts could not rule on this matter as it was the enforcement of a foreign revenue law. Although Mr Frandsen was resident in the UK under the Brussels Convention on Jurisdiction and Enforcement of Judgments in Civil and Commercial Matters, this Convention does not extend to revenue, customs or administrative matters. The point at issue was held to be a revenue matter using the principles of treaty interpretation. The test applied was to ask what would be understood by all Member States as a revenue matter, per Article 1 of the Brussels Convention. The court held that despite being a possible restriction on the liquidator's rights under the TFEU, the revenue rule should apply.

As one of the principal aims of the EU is to encourage cross-border trading and movement of enterprises between one Member State and another, the lack of any formal mechanism to help another Member State in the collection of its taxes was clearly highly unsatisfactory, hence the need for a better Directive on mutual assistance. With internationalization of business increasing it is vital that countries have the facility to exchange information on taxpayers. Tax authorities are at a distinct disadvantage when dealing with the affairs of a multinational group, in that the group forms an economic whole, with administrative co-operation and free flow of information between group entities in different countries a given. Without effective procedures for exchange of information between tax authorities, multinationals in particular are always going to have an unfair advantage over the tax authorities in the countries in which they do business.

Some, but by no means all, of the bilateral double tax treaties concluded between EU Member States contain the equivalent of Article 27 of the OECD MTC (assistance in the collection of taxes, see Chapter 7). The Mutual Assistance Directive is designed to help plug the gaps.

---

1   Council Directive 2008/55/EC.
2   [1999] BTC 8023, [1999] STC 616, CA.

Directive on Administrative Cooperation in the Field of Taxation (2014/107/EU)

20.11   The need for exchange of tax information is well understood by the EU. The legal basis for information exchange within the EU was established in 1977 with the Exchange of Information Directive 77/799/EC, updated in 2006 which applied to direct taxes. It was replaced by the EU Directive on Administrative Cooperation in the Field of Taxation (2011/16/EU) which entered into force on 11 March 2011, and this Directive has been, in turn, replaced by Directive 2014/107/EU. This Directive, like its predecessor, is often referred to as the 'DAC'. The foreword to this Directive acknowledges that Member States cannot manage their internal tax systems without receiving information from other States, due to the number of cross-border transactions taking place and the internationalization of financial instruments. Deep weaknesses in the former Directive have been acknowledged which have, in part, made missing trader fraud possible on such a large scale over the last decade. The DAC contains some simple but effective measures such as requiring each Member State to publish the contact details within its tax authority for the purpose of the Directive and to designate a central single liaison office to be the point of contact between other Member States requesting information and other parts of that tax authority. There is a time limit of six months for the supply of the information, reduced to two months where the tax authority already holds the requested information. The requested authority has only one month in which to inform the requesting State of any deficiency in the request.

Under the DAC, information can be exchanged:

- Automatically: lists of interest payments, etc are automatically transmitted to the other country. The DAC provides for the automatic exchange of information in the following categories:

  - income from employment;
  - directors' fees;
  - certain life insurance products not already covered by exchange of information provisions;
  - pensions; and
  - ownership of and income from immoveable property.

  This automatic exchange of information is mandatory and is intended to embody the principles of the OECD's Common Reporting Standard.

- Upon request: either via a provision in a DTT based upon Article 26 of the OECD MTC or in accordance with a special Tax Information Exchange Agreement.

- Spontaneously: without a request being made, for instance, where a country discovers matters which would be of considerable interest to a tax authority in a treaty partner country, for instance, during the course of a tax or criminal investigation. The DAC elaborates on the types of information which could be exchanged in this way:

'The competent authority of a Member State shall without prior request forward the information referred to in Article 1 (1) of which it has knowledge, to the competent authority of any other Member State concerned, in the following circumstances:

(a) the competent authority of the one Member State has grounds for supposing that there may be a loss of tax in the other Member State;

(b) a person liable to tax obtains a reduction in or an exemption from tax in the one Member State which would give rise to an increase in tax or to liability to tax in the other Member State;

(c) business dealings between a person liable to tax in a Member State and a person liable to tax in another Member State are conducted through one or more countries in such a way that a saving in tax may result in one or the other Member State or in both:

(d) the competent authority of a Member State has grounds for supposing that a saving of tax may result from artificial transfers of profits within groups of enterprises;

(e) information forwarded to the one Member State by the competent authority of the other Member State has enabled information to be obtained which may be relevant in assessing liability to tax in the latter Member State.'

Other forms of information exchange include simultaneous investigation of the same taxpayer in two or more countries and granting the facility for a foreign tax authority to visit and conduct a tax investigation into the affairs of a taxpayer on foreign soil. Whilst not, strictly speaking, exchange of information, countries can also assist each other by sharing best practice and experience in tax administration.

In March 2015, the Commission published a tax transparency package (COM(2015) 136) following which the DAC was further amended to provide for the automatic exchange of information on cross-border rulings and advance pricing arrangements (Directive 2015/2376/EU). The DAC was later amended in May 2016 (Directive 2016/881/EU) to enable country-by-country reporting, and in June 2016 to provide access to money laundering information (COM (2016) 452 final).

As was seen in Chapter 18, the DAC is one of several reporting requirements being introduced creating heavy compliance burdens on financial institutions.

European Union Savings Directive[1]

20.12 The 2005 Savings Directive has been largely replaced by Directive 2014/107/EU on Administrative Cooperation in the field of Taxation (the DAC, as discussed in para **20.11** above), and with respect to Switzerland by the European Union–Swiss Tax Transparency Agreement (see para **20.16** below). It was repealed on 10 November 2015. The following paragraphs briefly summarize the history of the Savings Directive.

The aim of this Directive was to enable savings income in the form of interest payments paid in Member State A to beneficial owners who are individuals resident for tax purposes in Member State B to be made subject to effective taxation in accordance with the laws of Member State B. Some Member States, notably the UK, objected vehemently to the requirement to withhold tax at source. In particular, the UK feared that the London Eurobond market, which pays interest gross, would be severely disadvantaged with respect to non-EU competitor markets such as Tokyo if a requirement to withhold tax at source on interest payments was introduced.

The Directive required Member States to either withhold tax at source or exchange information on the interest paid with other relevant tax authorities, in effect either giving up banking secrecy or starting charging tax. Tax withheld was paid over to the tax authority of the investor. The Directive extended to certain non-EU countries[2] and territories with which EU Member States have constitutional links.[3] Switzerland agreed to participate in return for being granted the principal benefits of certain other EU Directives such as the Parent/Subsidiary Directive and the Interest and Royalties Directive. Crucially, a country opting for withholding tax rather than information exchange does not disclose details of individual investors. Austria, Luxembourg and Belgium opted for withholding tax rather than information exchange, along with non-Member States, Liechtenstein and the Channel Islands. These States started with a rate of 15 per cent, which rose to 35 per cent by 2011. The option of levying withholding tax was a compromise for the EU. The problem was to ensure that the Member States operating withholding tax were doing so in a comprehensive manner in strict accordance with their commitments to the EU. Otherwise, those Member States continued to have a distinct tax advantage over the Member States which opted for information exchange. To some extent, this explains the apparent openness with which Switzerland disclosed its figures on withholding publicly.

The original Directive was criticized for containing so many loopholes that even moderately determined individuals were able to plan their way around it. A review of the Directive in 2012[4] found widespread use of offshore jurisdictions for intermediary entities, but also increased compliance with reporting obligations and improved data quality, although with some variability.[5] As noted at the beginning of this section, the reporting requirements under the Savings Directive have been replaced by reporting requirements under the DAC.

---

1   Council Directive 2003/48/EC.
2   Andorra, Liechtenstein, Monaco, San Marino, Switzerland.

3   British Virgin Islands, Turks and Caicos, Guernsey, Jersey, Isle of Man, Netherlands Antilles (but note that Netherlands Antilles no longer exists as such).

4   Available at: http://ec.europa.eu/taxation_customs/resources/documents/taxation/personal_tax/savings_tax/savings_directive_review/com_2012_65_en.pdf.

5   A Commission Staff Working Paper on the application of the Directive can be found here: available at: http://ec.europa.eu/taxation_customs/resources/documents/taxation/personal_tax/savings_tax/savings_directive_review/sec_20111_775_en.pdf.

Anti-Tax Avoidance Directive[1]

20.13   Following the publication of the Commission's 'Action Plan for a Fair and Efficient Corporate Tax System in the European Union' (COM (2015) 302 final), the Commission tabled a proposal for an Anti-Tax Avoidance Directive (ATAD) on 28 January 2016,[2] together with a staff working document.[3] The ECOFIN Council agreed to the Directive on 20 June 2016. The ATAD is novel in that it goes beyond the existing Directives by requiring Member States to implement substantive law that is more far reaching and potentially applies to purely domestic issues that do not have a cross-border element.

The Directive contains several legally binding anti-abuse measures designed to combat practices that affect the functioning of the internal market and which Member States are to apply with effect from 1 January 2019. The measures are as follows:

- **Controlled Foreign Company** (CFC) rule. Not all member States have CFC rules and so the ATAD requires implementation of a rule, with some options as to the detail.

- **Exit taxation**, to discourage transfer of residence or assets for aggressive tax planning purposes. The rule takes into account CJEU decisions in relation to exit taxation.

- **Interest limitation rule**, which provides for a ceiling on deductibility for the amount by which the deductible borrowing costs exceed taxable interest revenue received. The restriction is 30% of EBITDA. There is some flexibility in the detail of implementation for Member States in terms of de minimis threshold and carry forward/back, for example.

- **General anti-abuse rule**. This rule allows tax authorities to disregard structures or arrangements where one of its main purposes is to obtain a tax advantage not in accordance with the purpose of the relevant law.

As part of the final June 2016 political compromise on the ATAD, the Council issued a statement on **hybrid mismatches**, which was followed by a proposed amendment to the ATAD in October, accompanied by a staff working document. The proposal carefully follows the OECD BEPS recommendations but is limited to intra-EU situations. ECOFIN agreed the new rules (ATAD 2) on 21 February 2017 and they will come into force on 1 January 2020.

Member States are required to apply the provisions of the ATAD from 1 January 2019. The ATAD does not seek to achieve harmonization of anti-avoidance rules across Europe, but offers a suite of options subject to a minimum level, and in some cases existing domestic provisions may already be robust enough to meet the standard.

---

1   Council Directive 2016/1164/EU.
2   COM (2016) 26.
3   COM (2016) 23 final.

The European Union's Code of Conduct

20.14   In 1997 the European Council adopted a Code of Conduct on business taxation with a view to identifying and countering harmful tax practices that threaten the integrity of the single market.

The EU Code of Conduct is not legally binding, rather it comprises a set of principles accompanied by a political commitment to freeze the introduction of new tax incentives aimed at attracting business and eliminating existing harmful measures by January 2003.

Each country is required to outline its plan to achieve transparency in its tax regime and effective exchange of information for all tax matters. Also Member States are to eliminate any regimes that attract business without substantial business activity. Although the Code of Conduct applies formally to EU Member States only, it has enabled the EU to put neighbouring non-EU States such as Switzerland and the Channel Islands under considerable pressure to amend their tax and/or banking secrecy regimes.

More recently, the Code of Conduct Group has extended its remit to hybrid mismatch arrangements and intellectual property regimes, mirroring the work of the BEPS project. The Council has given the Group the mandate to monitor the implementation of BEPS.

State Aid

20.15   The Code of Conduct principles, whilst voluntary in name, exist within the EU alongside the legally enforceable ban on the provision of State aid by a Member State to businesses without prior approval of the European Commission. In particular, Article 107(1) of the TFEU states:

> 'Save as otherwise provided in the Treaties, any aid granted by a member state or through state resources in any form whatsoever which distorts or threatens to distort competition by favouring certain undertakings or the production of certain goods shall, in so far as it affects trade between member states, be incompatible with the internal market.'

The CJEU has consistently held that aid in this context includes not only overt subsidies but also mitigation of charges that would otherwise apply and it has long been known that tax reliefs are included.

In 2013, the Commission began to step up its activities in relation to tax, in particular the tax ruling practices of several Member States.[1] An important element of the State aid rules is that, in order to be prohibited, the aid must be selective (ie give preference to a particular category of goods, companies, economic sectors or even geographical regions).

In late 2013, the Commission began an investigation into the Belgian excess profit exemption. The scheme allows Belgian entities that are part of a multi-national group to deduct an 'excess profit' from their taxable profit calculated by reference to a hypothetical standalone company carrying out comparable activities. The Commission's decision, that Belgium unlawfully implemented the scheme in contravention of Article 108(3) of the TFEU, was handed down in January 2016.[2]

In the meantime, in 2014, the Commission opened three high-profile State aid investigations into Ireland, the Netherlands and Luxembourg. The companies involved are Apple, Starbucks, Amazon, Fiat Finance and Trade (hereafter 'Fiat') and McDonalds. In relation to Fiat, the Commission decided in October 2015 that the Netherlands had granted selective tax advantages. At the same time, a similar finding was made in respect of Starbucks in the Netherlands. The McDonalds case related to two tax rulings issued in 2009 by Luxembourg, in relation to royalties received and the existence of a permanent establishment respectively. The Commission's decision was handed down in June 2016.

The Commission does not always require recovery of the 'underpaid' tax but it has done so in recent cases including Apple, Starbucks and Fiat. This raises questions about the legitimate expectations of the companies involved.[3]

In August 2016, the decision in the Irish case was announced and Apple was held to have been in receipt of tax benefits valued at €13 billion. The Commission's decision was released in redacted form on 9 December 2016[4] and has caused considerable controversy in light of the large sum involved.

There is some suggestion that, in respect of the advance pricing agreement cases, the Commission is setting a higher standard than is required under arm's length pricing.[5]

On 19 May 2016, the Commission published a Notice on the notion of State aid[6] to clarify the scope of the rules in light of CJEU cases. In relation to tax rulings, the notice confirms that, where rulings are designed to provide legal certainty and predictability on the application of the ordinary tax regime, they will not constitute State aid. In relation to advance pricing agreements, the Notice states that an arrangement is unlikely to be considered selective if it complies with the OECD guidelines and leads to a reliable approximation of a market-based outcome. Settlements may constitute State aid when they reduce the tax liability disproportionately.

A number of these cases are likely to be appealed and the final outcome will not be known for some time. Specifically, in the Apple/Ireland case, both the Irish Government and Apple have appealed. The Irish government has claimed it did not give favourable tax treatment to Apple, the full amount of tax was paid and no State aid was provided. The outcome of the appeal is still awaited at this time.

1   See Mason (2017a) for an overview of tax rulings as State aid.
2   http://ec.europa.eu/competition/state_aid/cases/256735/256735_1748545_185_2.pdf.
3   For a detailed discussion of the Apple decision, see Mason (2017c). See also Fleming (2017).
4   See, for example, Cachia (2017) who discusses these cases and observes the adoption of a new 'prudent independent market operator' (PIMO) standard emerging.
5   See Mason (2017b) for a discussion of this point from a US perspective.
6   See http://ec.europa.eu/competition/state_aid/modernisation/notice_aid_en.html for the text of the notice.

EU TAX TRANSPARENCY PACKAGE

20.16   In March 2015 the EC presented a package of tax transparency measures ('the Package'). This will include the introduction of automatic exchange of information between Member States in relation to their tax rulings.

In relation to corporate taxation, the package also contains initiatives for assessing new transparency requirements for MNEs, and a review of the Code of Conduct on Business Taxation (see para **20.14** above). The Commission views the launch of the Action Plan as part of the general fight against tax evasion and avoidance. It defines corporate tax avoidance as:

> 'a situation where certain companies use aggressive tax planning in order to minimise their tax bills. It often entails companies exploiting legal loopholes in tax systems and mismatches between national rules, to artificially split profits to low or no tax jurisdictions. As such, it goes against the principle that taxation should reflect where the economic activity occurs.'[1]

Note that the language used here mirrors that used in the OECD BEPS Project.

In relation to transparency on tax rulings, the Commission proposal is that national tax authorities will be required to regularly report to all other Member States all advance cross-border tax rulings and APAs that they have issued.

In addition to the State aid investigations, the European Parliament's Special Committee on Tax Rulings and Other Measures Similar in Nature or Effect (known as the 'TAXE Committee') was constituted in February 2015, and heard evidence from a wide range of sources as well as visiting several Member States as part of a fact-finding mission. In July 2015, the TAXE Committee published an interim report following investigations into the practices of Member States in relation to rulings. The report observes that tax rulings are not intrinsically problematic but covers a wide scope extending beyond the granting of rulings.

In the meantime, the European Parliament issued a paper in October 2015 on tax ruling practices as part of a series of analytical papers dealing with key tax issues.[2] The results of this research will feed into the TAXE Committee in its work. The paper covers the context in which tax rulings are issued, the various types of ruling, and the prospects for harmonizing the various rulings systems in the EU.

1 Available at: http://ec.europa.eu/taxation_customs/taxation/company_tax/transparency/index_
   en.htm.
2 Available at: www.europarl.europa.eu/RegData/etudes/STUD/2015/563451/IPOL_STU
   (2015)563451_EN.pdf.

AGREEMENTS BETWEEN THE EU AND NEIGHBOURING COUNTRIES

EU–Swiss Tax Transparency Agreement[1]

20.17   This agreement, signed on 27 May 2015, represents a step away from banking secrecy by Switzerland. It provides for OECD CRS-style reciprocal exchange of information between Switzerland, and the Member States of the EU. Information to be exchanged is the name, address, tax identification number, and date of birth of account holders, and details of the account balance and receipts. It will take effect in 2018. It replaces the Swiss–EU Agreement of 2004.[2] In all likelihood it will also replace the Rubik agreements (see para **18.22**).

1 See www.consilium.europa.eu/en/press/press-releases/2015/05/27-eu-switzerland-taxation-
   agreement.
2 Council Decision of 2 June 2004 (2004/911/EC) on the signing and conclusion of the Agreement between the European Community and Swiss Confederation providing for measures
   equivalent to those laid down in Council Directive 2003/48/EC on taxation of savings income
   in the form of interest payments and the accompanying Memorandum of Understanding.

European Economic Area Agreement

20.18   The European Economic Area (EEA) consists of the EU plus Liechtenstein, Norway and Iceland. The EEA Agreement extends the free trade area of the EU to these three countries and also the terms of the Parent Subsidiary Directive. Their taxpayers also enjoy the four fundamental freedoms and their governments have to adopt some of the EU's legal framework. However, the three non-EU members do not participate financially in the EU to the same extent as EU Member States and neither do they play a significant role in EU policy making.

Brexit

20.19   On 23 June 2016, the UK voted to leave the EU in a referendum, and on 29 March 2017 the UK Prime Minister gave formal notice under Article 50, thereby triggering a two-year period during which the nature of the exit process will be determined. There will be many issues to be resolved, including the UK's relationship with the single market beyond 2019. One interesting question will be the status of CJEU case law following the UK's exit.[1]

1 For an overview of the tax implications of Brexit, see Freedman (2017).

ACTION PLAN FOR FAIR AND EFFICIENT CORPORATE TAX IN THE EU

20.20   On 17 June 2015, the EC launched an action plan to fundamentally reform corporate taxation in the EU. Pierre Moscovici, Commissioner for Economic and Financial Affairs, Taxation and Customs, has said:

> 'Corporate taxation in the EU needs radical reform. In the interests of growth, competitiveness and fairness, Member States need to pull together and everyone must pay their fair share. The Commission has today laid the foundation for a new approach to corporate taxation in the EU. Member States must now build on it.'[1]

One of the key actions includes the re-launch of the Common Consolidated Corporate Tax Base (CCCTB) proposals (see below).

In addition to re-launching the CCCTB (or CCTB) the somewhat ambitious Action Plan proposes closing legislative loopholes, improving transfer pricing system, and implementing stricter rules for preferential tax regimes. It also sets out plans for improved transparency and a uniform approach to non-cooperative jurisdictions.

---

1   Available at: http://europa.eu/rapid/press-release_IP-15-5188_en.htm.

CURRENT EU PROPOSALS FOR HARMONIZATION OF DIRECT TAXATION

Common consolidated corporate tax base

20.21   The tax unit for corporation tax in most EU Member States is the individual company. Within the EU and also in the wider world, this presents problems because although the individual company is a legal unit it is often not the economic unit. The economic unit is usually the corporate group. To the world at large, the only set of published accounts that matters is the consolidated accounts of the group, but tax systems ignore the consolidated accounts and base tax liabilities on the individual group members' accounts. This state of affairs is at odds with the goal of a single market within the EU. A single economic unit (a pan-European group of companies) could potentially have to produce 28 tax computations produced according to 28 different sets of national tax laws and based on 28 different sets of accounts, albeit with some commonality following the adoption of International Financial Reporting Standards (IFRS).

It is considered impossible for EU companies to take full advantage of the Single Market in the absence of a CCCTB. Besides the administrative burden of dealing with 28 different tax regimes, there are all the problems of dealing with the interaction of those 28 tax regimes. Companies operating in more than one Member State need to cope with different transfer pricing regimes, the issue of obtaining relief for losses arising in different Member States and difficult tax issues thrown up by cross-border mergers and acquisitions. Companies with branches in other Member States need to cope with complex rules for allocating an acceptable share of profits to that branch, taking into account not only complex overhead allocations but also theoretical notions of branch capitalization and head office/branch interest payments. An early proposal was for so-called 'home-state taxation' (see para **20.34** below).

The idea of a CCCTB was first floated in 2001 and has been the subject of considerable debate and speculation. Since the Commission presented plans in late 2001, it has been engaged in follow-up work on the various individual measures as well as the longer-term objective of a common base which culminated in the 2011 Draft Directive. In 2002, a speech by Benedetto Della Vedova MEP, at the European Company Tax Conference in Brussels, concluded with the following comments on future developments in company taxation within the EU:

'(1)   We should welcome the dual strategy of the Commission in the field of company taxation: a long-term strategy for the creation of a consolidated corporate tax base must not lead to any relaxation with respect to the need to identify the targeted measures ... aimed to the rapid removal of some of the main obstacles to cross-border activity by European firms ...

(2)   The objective of the long-term strategy must necessarily be that of the creation of a consolidated corporate tax base; among the possible solutions, however, we must choose those which allow virtuous tax competition among Member States ...

(3)   home state taxation and optional consolidated corporate tax base appear to be the most feasible solutions ...

(4)   In no event, (and by no means, not even through the introduction of minimum tax levels) must we call into question the principle that the level of company taxation must be set by the individual Member States.'

In essence, the CCCTB proposal is that a corporate group operating in more than one EU Member State should be given the choice to calculate its taxable profits on its consolidated accounting profits, applying a uniform set of tax adjustments. Rather than applying national rules, such as the UK rule that no deduction is permitted for entertaining expenditure, the CCCTB would allow corporate groups to complete one tax computation for all their companies within the EU and deal with one EU tax authority, thus reducing compliance costs. An evaluation of the CCCTB by Deutsche Bank, published in 2007, indicated muted support for the proposal, noting that the benefits of reduced compliance costs could only be realized if the administrative framework is right (ie that companies only have to deal with one revenue authority). Importantly, there is no harmonization of corporation tax rates under the CCCTB. Groups of companies could adopt the CCCTB irrespective of size.

If the system were to be optional, only those companies that will benefit from it will participate. Devereux and Loretz (2007) estimate a decline in revenue in the order of 1 per cent if companies are given a choice as to whether to participate in the regime. A mandatory regime, on the other hand, is estimated to increase revenue by as much as 8 per cent.

The apportionment formula is an important issue, as it is this that dictates the manner in which company tax revenues will be shared among participating States. A Report published by the Commission in 2005[1] outlines the issues involved in the apportionment of the tax base (for an earlier study, see Sorenson (2003)). The ultimate specification of the formula will inevitably see winners and losers among Member States.

---

1   Available at: http://ec.europa.eu/taxation_customs/sites/taxation/files/resources/documents/ taxation/gen_info/economic_analysis/tax_papers/2004_2073_en_web_final_version.pdf.

Loss Offset

20.22   The main benefit of consolidation for groups of companies would be the automatic offset of losses against profits across the EU. However, groups would be disadvantaged, in that traditional methods of tax planning and tax avoidance would be less effective. Strategies in current use which depend on shifting profits from a higher tax EU Member State to a lower tax one would no longer be as effective. Such strategies include artificial manipulation of intra-group transfer prices, use of hybrid investment vehicles (which produce a tax deduction in one Member State without a corresponding taxable receipt in another) and use of low-tax Member States such as Ireland or Cyprus for the holding of group intellectual property. Consolidated accounts eliminate all profits and losses on intra-group dealings, not merely those which would be the subject of transfer pricing adjustments.

Gammie and Lodin (2001) cite a survey carried out by the Federation of Swedish Industries in which it was reported that 81 per cent of companies surveyed had suffered tax losses in one or more Member States but that 96 per cent of companies which had suffered cross-border losses had not been able to obtain full tax relief for them. However, some countries (Belgium, Greece, Italy) do not permit offset of losses within groups in their domestic legislation and they would be unlikely to participate in the CCCTB for this reason. The other side of this coin is that countries in which the profitable parts of the group are resident will find that, once intra-group profits have been excluded, their corporate tax base will have shrunk somewhat.

The Base

20.23   Many groups operate not only within the EU but also in other countries. Consolidated accounts are prepared for the worldwide group and not for the EU part of the group. Thus adoption of the CCCTB may place an additional burden on groups which would have to prepare a set of consolidated accounts just for the EU members of the corporate group.

The CCCTB proposal does envisage that Member States would run two separate tax bases side by side: the national tax base, applied to groups not operating within other EU countries and the CCCTB for groups operating in other EU countries. This necessarily constitutes an added layer of complexity within the tax administration.

A fundamental problem in the design of the CCCTB is that the 28 Member States have different accounting standards. Would Member State A be prepared to accept an apportionment of consolidated profits where the bulk of the consolidated profits had been based on accounting standards not approved of by Member State A? It has been suggested that this problem could be solved if the accounts on which the CCCTB taxable profits were based were prepared in accordance with International Financial Reporting Standards (IFRS).

The reasoning behind this apparent weakness in the CCCTB Draft Directive bears examination. In its 2003 report,[1] the EU Commission considered that a tax specific method of consolidation might be more workable than insisting on the use of accounts consolidated according to the IFRS principles. The initial proposal was that IFRSs could be used as a common base for arriving at accounting profits. The CCCTB would then agree on the necessary adjustments, using IFRSs as a neutral starting point. Although this appears to be a logical proposition, there are objections. The International Accounting Standards Board is a private sector body and has its own agendas to follow and the accounting methods required by it, in particular the IFRSs' consolidation principles, may not be suitable for tax purposes. Additionally, IFRSs place a greater emphasis on the principle of materiality than might be acceptable for tax purposes where a greater level of detailed accuracy may be required. IFRSs' principles include 'fair value' accounting, which results in unrealized gains being included in accounting profits. The accepted norm in taxation is only to tax gains on a realization basis.

IFRSs have been developed with the needs of a range of user groups in mind, especially shareholders of large corporations, and these needs are not the same as the needs of a tax authority. (Note that this is the usual argument against using accounting profits for computing tax liabilities.)

The EU Commission put forward a public consultation on the use of IFRSs for tax purposes in February 2003 to elicit opinion on the use of IFRSs as a starting point for arriving at a common tax base. Responses to the consultation displayed support for the idea of the CCCTB but mixed opinion as to the appropriateness of IFRSs. The Commission has explicitly stated that it is not possible to make a formal link between IFRSs and the common base, not least because not all accounting standards are appropriate for tax purposes.[2] At one stage, there was a proposal[3] that most companies would start with the different national GAAP and adjust key elements to satisfy the CCCTB rules.

1   IFRSs must be complied with by about 7,000 holding companies (EU 2003 Report) but in fact the number of companies is much greater in practice, as the subsidiaries of those companies will also have to observe the IFRSs. This still leaves a very large number of companies who are not required to use IFRSs and for whom they are likely to be inappropriate in many respects. About 99% of EU companies are SMEs.

2   An Internal Market without Obstacles: Achievements, Ongoing initiatives and Remaining Challenges' COM (2003) 726 EU Commission, at para 4.3.

3   CCCTB/WP/057.

Elimination of transfer pricing issues

20.24   Theoretically, because intragroup transactions will be cancelled out on consolidation of the group's profits, scope for shifting taxable profits from one EU State to another through non-arm's length pricing policies will be vastly reduced. Following *Lankhorst-Hohorst* (see para **20.53** below), many Member States extended their transfer pricing regimes to include transactions between resident connected companies as well as cross-border transactions, in order to avoid discrimination between home-country transactions and cross-border transactions which had been held to be a restriction on the freedom of establishment. Whether the CCCTB will simplify tax administration for EU corporate groups depends on the extent to which Member States are willing to dismantle or relax their current transfer pricing regimes. If they continue to insist on use of the arm's-length principle for intra-EU transactions, with associated documentation requirements, then the CCCTB is unlikely to produce savings in connection with transfer pricing administration for corporate groups.

Rather than dismantling their transfer pricing regimes for intra-EU trade, tax administrations are likely to have to amend them to cope with different kinds of tax avoidance behaviour. If the CCCTB is adopted, it is more than likely that taxpayer groups would attempt to optimize their tax liabilities under the formula adopted by using transfer pricing strategies to manipulate the profits attributable to each State according to the formula adopted. There may be physical movement of employees so that the formula allocates more of the consolidated taxable profits to low tax Member States. As this would entail actual movement of people, or hiring and firing of certain employees, it would be difficult for the corporate group to justify such a strategy on the grounds of mere tax saving and difficult for the tax authorities to argue that the arrangements were artificial. Thus detailed transfer pricing rules will still be needed although their application will be rarer. There may be greater scope for manipulation in other areas though, for instance, in having sales appear to take place in low tax Member States.

In any case, there will still be the need for detailed transfer pricing policies in connection with transactions outside the CCCTB group.

Anti-abuse rules

20.25   A working document[1] issued by the Commission on 26 March 2008 dealt with the question of anti-abuse rules. It was generally accepted that anti-abuse rules are required to prevent abusive tax planning. The working document considered specific and general anti-abuse provisions, with a view to including such provisions in the CCCTB Directive.

Consistent with CJEU decisions, a general anti-abuse provision would be directed to wholly artificial transactions, which leaves it open for the taxpayer to establish a commercial rationale. On its own, however, such a provision would inevitably lead to interpretive difficulties and it is more likely that it would be combined with specific provisions. The specific provisions considered in the working document included:

- interest deductibility restrictions based on a proportion of EBIT or EBITA;

- a switch from exemption to credit method in relation to dividends from major shareholdings in third-country companies;

- some form of CFC rules to deal with undistributed profits of third-country companies; and

- rules to prevent manipulation of the factors in the formulary apportionment mechanism, which potentially affect the distribution of the tax base between participating Member States.

At the 13th meeting of the CCCTB Working Group in Brussels in April 2008, the Commission confirmed that the intention was that anti-abuse measures would apply to both cross-border and domestic transactions and would be in line with the EU Treaty. In relation to the manipulation of the apportionment formula, the Commission confirmed that it would take account of the actual place of use of assets rather than the balance sheet in which they are recognized, although one expert at the meeting pointed out that treatment in the balance sheet recognizes where the risk is located.

---

1 CCCTB/WP065/doc/en: see: http://ec.europa.eu/taxation_customs/resources/documents/taxation/ company_tax/common_tax_base/CCCTBWP065_antiabuse_en.pdf).

The 2011 draft Directive

20.26 The EU Commission proposal for a CCCTB was issued as a Draft Directive in March 2011.[1] The debates about CCCTB became muted for a time until June 2013, when ECOFIN (the council comprised of EU Member State finance ministers) reported to the European Council on progress with the CCCTB proposal.[2] This noted that the work should progress on a step-by-step basis, starting with the definition of the tax base, and that the proposal was not yet ready for political discussion. The Irish Presidency (commenced 1 January 2013) issued a compromise text on 24 November 2014. On 8 October 2015, the EC launched a public consultation to help identify the key measures to be considered for a re-launch of the CCCTB proposals.

---

1 Available at: http://ec.europa.eu/taxation_customs/sites/taxation/files/resources/documents/ taxation/company_tax/common_tax_base/com_2011_121_en.pdf.
2 Ecofin report to the European Council on Tax issues, Brussels, 25 June 2013, no. 11507/13, par. 40.

Allocation of the consolidated tax base

20.27 The 2011 Draft Directive adopted formulary apportionment as the basis for allocating the tax base to the Member States under the CCCTB. The method adopted is similar to that used in the US where a US corporation has a liability to state taxes in more than one state.

The requirements for allocation of the profits calculated for the purposes of corporation tax under the CCCTB to individual countries are that it should be equitable, transparent, administratively simple, based on sound economic principles and it must meet with political approval from all Member States involved in it. Agreement on the method of allocation is thus a crucial issue. The options considered were:

- Sharing at the macro level: taking the aggregate corporation tax base from all participating companies and apportioning this aggregate figure. This is the chosen route.

- Sharing at the micro level: performing a separate apportionment of each company's tax base. This was the preferred method in early discussions.

The ultimate choice of apportionment mechanism had to take into account a conflict between the tax principles of equity (fairness) and efficiency.[1] The chosen method of formulary apportionment appears to have favoured efficiency.

Going forward, agreement on the precise formula is likely to be a significant obstacle to the adoption of the CCCTB. Member States which are host to companies with substantial financial assets are likely to object on the grounds that the current formula, which excludes such assets, disadvantages them in that they will be allocated a share of the corporation tax base which does not properly reflect the corporate assets held within their territory.

---

1 See Working Paper No 9/2006 for a review of issues and options.

Reaction of EU Member States to the 2011 Draft Directive

20.28 Several Member States (Ireland, the Netherlands, Malta, Poland, Germany and Sweden) announced their rejection of the Draft Directive. The German rejection was particularly serious as Germany had been a champion of the proposal for a long time. The grounds for doing so vary, but include:

- Subsidiarity: Violation of the principle of subsidiarity – under Article 5(2) of the Treaty of the European Union, the EU is to act only if, and in so far as, the objectives of proposed actions cannot be sufficiently achieved by the Member States, but can be better achieved at EU level. There should be clear benefits compared with action at the level of the individual Member State. The UK considers that it is better left to the individual Member States.

- Inaccurate estimates of cost savings: The estimates of the cost savings put forward by the EU Commission are considered to be over-optimistic. The 'Impact Assessment' (IA) which accompanied the 2011 Draft

Directive estimated the reduction in compliance costs for companies at about 7 per cent. Apart from doubts as to the accuracy of this figure, the savings for companies would have to be considered in the light of an increase in costs for the tax administrations: if the CCCTB is adopted on an optional basis, then each EU Member State would have to run two parallel corporation tax systems. The EU response to this criticism is that such increased costs should be outweighed by increases in tax revenues arising from the fact that the CCCTB effectively negates a whole raft of tax-avoidance strategies currently being employed.

Ireland has been particularly vociferous in its objections, fearing pressure on its corporation tax rate of 12.5 per cent, approximately 10 percentage points lower than the 2011 EU average.[1]

---

1   The Taoiseach, Enda Kenny, was quoted as complaining that the CCCTB was 'another method of tax harmonisation by the back door', *Irish Examiner*, 19 May 2011, 'Taoiseach steps up fight against EU tax plans'.

The 2016 proposed Directives

20.29   The EC eventually withdrew the 2011 Draft Directive in light of difficulties achieving consensus and, in October 2016, two new draft Directives were issued,[1] effectively separating two aspects of the CCCTB: the definition of the base (CCTB), and the process of consolidation/allocation (CCCTB). The rationale for the separation of the two issues is that it allows more time to resolve the allegedly more problematic issue of consolidation and apportionment.

A public consultation elicited responses from some 175 companies as well as various non-governmental organizations and public bodies. An impact assessment, including studies by the Joint Research Centre of the European Commission and the Centre for European Economic Research (ZEW), suggests that expected economic benefits of the proposal are positive, with reduction in the costs of compliance as well as the cost of setting up a subsidiary.

---

1   See   https://ec.europa.eu/taxation_customs/business/company-tax/common-consolidated-corporate-tax-base-ccctb_en.

CCTB: The proposed base

20.30   The proposed new base does not make reference to accounting profits; rather it adopts the system of an independently defined tax base which is broadly designed. All revenues are taxable unless expressly exempted, and profits and losses are only recognized when realized. Business expenses and certain other deductions will be allowed, and the list of non-deductible expenses from the 2011 proposal has been replicated.

There are several differences between the 2016 and 2011 proposals in terms of the definition of the tax base:

- While the 2011 proposal was to be optional, the 2016 CCTB will be mandatory for groups incorporated in a Member State with consolidated revenue of more than €750 million. The common rules will be optional for companies not meeting these criteria.

- A new interest limitation rule, consistent with the ATAD (see para **20.13** above), restricts interest costs in excess of financial revenues to 20 per cent of taxable earnings before interest, tax, depreciation and amortization (EBITDA).

- To address the bias to debt financing, the 2016 proposed base provides for a new allowance for growth and investment (AGI) with a deemed deduction at the EU government bond rate plus 2 per cent.

- To make research and development (R&D) more beneficial for EU companies, the proposal provides for a new super-deduction for R&D. For expenditure up to €20 million, an annual deduction of 50 per cent will be available, reducing to 25 per cent for expenditure in excess of this threshold. An enhanced super-deduction of 100 per cent will be available for small start-up companies.

- In the absence of consolidation, arm's length pricing adjustments will be required in relation to transactions between a taxpayer and its associated enterprise(s).

Base issues that are consistent between the 2016 and 2011 proposals are:

- Clear rules for fixed asset depreciation, which in some cases will accelerate, and in others slow down, the write-off of assets compared with national rules.

- Carry-forward of losses indefinitely, reinforced by an anti-abuse rule. In the absence of consolidation in this first stage of CCCTB implementation, temporary loss relief is provided for subject to subsequent recapture as the relevant subsidiary or permanent establishment generates profits.[1]

---

1   Proposed Council Directive on a Common Corporate Tax Base: (38210), 13730/16 + ADDs 1–3, COM(16) 685; (b) Proposed Council Directive on a Common Consolidated Corporate Tax Base (CCCTB): (38211), 13731/16 + ADDs 1–3, COM(16) 683.

Anti-abuse rules in the CCCTB

20.31   Chapter XIV of the Draft Directive contains the anti-abuse rules. There is a general anti-abuse rule, Article 58, which states:

> '[A] Member State may disregard an arrangement or series of arrangements which, having been put in place for the essential purpose of obtaining a tax advantage that defeats the object or purpose of this Directive, are not genuine, having regard to all relevant facts and circumstances.'

Articles 59 and 60 contain the controlled foreign company rules that subject passive income to tax unless the CFC is resident or situated in a Member State or in an EEA country and has been 'set up for valid commercial reasons that reflect economic reality', ie 'supported by commensurate staff, equipment, assets and premises'.

Hybrid mismatches are dealt with in Article 61 dealing with double deductions, deductions without inclusion and non-taxation without inclusion. Article 61a deals with tax residency mismatches.

Consolidation and apportionment

20.32   The definition of 'group' remains unchanged from the 2011 proposal. Qualifying subsidiaries are those with more than 50 per cent voting rights and more than 75 per cent capital stake. The consolidation process includes permanent establishments, defined by reference to the OECD definition.

The entry into or leaving of a group creates issues in relation to both trading losses and capital gains. The rules for these are also unchanged from the 2011 proposal.

The apportionment formula is unchanged from the 2011 proposal. There are three equally weighted factors: labour, assets and sales by destination. The labour component is split equally between the number of employees and payroll costs in an attempt to take into account the skills and experience of the labour force. Intangibles and financial assets are excluded. In the event that the outcome of the apportionment does not fairly represent the extent of business activity, an alternative allocation method is available.

There are no specific rules to prevent the manipulation of the formula factors. Article 29 of the Draft Directive does, however, contain a 'safeguard clause', under which, if either the taxpayer or the tax authority thinks that the formula has not produced a result which fairly represents the business activity of a group member, use of an alternative method of apportionment can be requested. An alternative method can only be used when all competent authorities agree.

From an administrative point of view, groups will deal with a single tax administration – a 'one stop shop' – where the parent entity is resident. The principal tax authority will deal with audits and disputes.

Reaction to the 2016 proposed Directives

20.33   The UK government[1] maintains its position that direct taxation is a matter for which individual Member States have sovereignty and which affects not only revenue but also social and other policy choices. In Ireland, the Joint Committee on Finance, Public Expenditure and Reform and Taoiseach discussed the proposals and states that the EC has not adequately met the requirement to provide sufficient quantitative and qualitative indicators to allow Member States to fully assess the implications, observing that the impact assessment is silent on the impact of the CCCTB on individual States, focusing only on aggregate impact. There are also concerns that the proposals will effectively narrow the tax base in Ireland, and increase complexity through the need to operate two systems in parallel, and further that the proposals are counter to the ongoing BEPS initiatives. The three allocation factors are criticized as being 'arbitrary' and will not remove the ability for tax planning.

The Netherlands has also objected to the proposals on a number of grounds including subsidiarity and proportionality, stating that the proposal goes beyond the BEPS package unnecessarily. In addition, it is noted that it is better to wait for the new US government to implement policy changes in respect of corporate income tax.

---

1   House of Commons European Scrutiny Committee, Twenty-third Report of Session, 2016–17.

Home State Taxation

20.34   This proposal, which pre-dates the CCCTB proposal, is for a system similar to the CCCTB in many respects, but intended to be of more limited application. Although it now appears unlikely that this proposal will ever be developed into policy, it is extremely well-researched and many of the issues in home state taxation (HST) are identical to those which arise with the CCCTB. The proposal for home state taxation is designed to simplify cross-border trading within the EU for SMEs. The home state taxation proposal originated in academic research by Gammie and Lodin (2001). As with the CCCTB, it has been in the background for a number of years, but may well resurface as a variant of the CCCTB. Home state taxation was first proposed as a possible way forward in 2001 and a public consultation held in 2003. In June 2004 a questionnaire and detailed proposal were issued and the following month a non-paper[1] on the pilot scheme was submitted. Despite the enthusiasm of the Commission for the home state taxation measures to tackle the problems that hamper small- and medium-sized enterprises expanding across borders, no substantial discussion of the non-paper has taken place, and the proposed trial to take place in 2007 did not happen. Certainly, attention has now shifted to the CCCTB, which has a much larger potential impact on Member States.

---

1   Available at: http://ec.europa.eu/taxation_customs/business/company-tax/initiatives-small-business/home-state-taxation_en.

PATENT BOXES

20.35   The European Commission reported in October 2013 that the UK patent box regime amounted to harmful tax competition. Subsequently the EU Economic and Financial Affairs Council initiated an examination of all EU patent boxes for the potential breach of State aid rules. Following this investigation, the EC has announced that it won't pursue it further.

In June 2015, the European Commission published a working paper entitled *Patent Boxes Design, Patents Location and Local R&D.*[1] The paper presents the findings of an economic study of the use and effect of patent box use. It covers not only EU Member States but also some third countries, and shows that the number of patent boxes in the EU increased from 2 in 1995 to 11 in 2015, and also that the existence of a patent box regime incentivizes MNEs to shift the location of their patents without a necessary concurrent shift in research activities.

The issue is one that is dealt with by the OECD BEPS Project, specifically Action 5. The proposed modified nexus approach effectively overtakes the European level review of this issue, and we are now beginning to see Member States adapting their patent box rules in line with Action 5.

---

1   Available at: http://ec.europa.eu/taxation_customs/resources/documents/taxation/gen_info/ economic_analysis/tax_papers/taxation_paper_57.pdf.

FINANCIAL TRANSACTIONS TAX

20.36   An ongoing problem with the EU system of VAT is that there are many financial transactions to which VAT does not apply. Whilst this was not such a big problem back in the early 1970s when VAT was first introduced, it is now considered a major shortcoming, given the huge growth in the financial sector within the EU since the 1970s. The EU Commission, in late 2011, issued a Draft Directive for a financial transaction tax (FTT).[1] The tax would be payable by EU financial institutions: banks, pension funds, charities, mutual funds and any other entities where financial transactions are a significant proportion of their activities. It would be payable, as the name suggests, on financial transactions: broadly transactions in securities and derivatives. The rate would be 0.1 per cent of the consideration (or market value of the transaction, if higher).

However, many EU Member States made it clear they would not agree to adopt the Directive. Those Member States which wanted to implement the tax, principally France, Germany, Italy and Spain, are planning to adopt the Directive under the EU's 'enhanced cooperation' rules, which mean that the usual requirement of unanimous approval of a Draft Directive is waived so that providing at least 11 Member States are in favour of the Directive, they can adopt it on their own. Eleven Member States have invoked the enhance cooperation procedure and the Commission has published a further Draft Directive, which limits the application of the FTT to the 11 participating Member States.

Whether this Draft Directive will be ever adopted is uncertain; if it can only be adopted under the 'enhanced cooperation' rules, whereby a subset of Member States go ahead without the others, then problems ensue. The EU legal department has issued an opinion to the effect that the FTT proposal is discriminatory and infringes upon the taxing competences of the non-participating Member States. The problems arise due to the territorial scope of the tax; it would apply to financial institutions 'established' in the 11 Member States. This means institutions which are resident, authorized, incorporated or acting via a branch in one of the 11 Member States. However, it would also apply to any transactions where the *clients* are 'established' in one or more of the 11 Member States and hence the objections from the non-participating Member States. For instance, a UK bank selling shares to a German client would have to pay the FTT. Not only that, but if the UK bank did not pay up, then the German tax authority would have the right, under the EU Mutual Assistance Directive, to require HMRC to collect the tax on behalf of Germany.

In February 2014, both Angela Merkel and François Hollande announced continued support for the FTT and hinted at preference for a phased introduction. The UK has argued before the CJEU that the use of enhanced cooperation would be contrary to European law, however the Court found that the UK's challenge was premature and therefore rejected it.[2]

Progress towards agreement between the 11 Member States has been slow, but in March 2015 the finance ministers issued a joint statement that renewed their commitment to the FTT. On 19 January 2017, the European Parliament issued a press release stating that the draft text for the European FTT could be ready by the middle of 2017, although there is still some opposition to the measure.

---

1   COM (2011) 594final.
2   Available at: http://curia.europa.eu/juris/documents.jsf?num=C-209/13.

SOCIETAS EUROPAEA – THE EUROPEAN COMPANY

20.37   The principal aim of the development of the Societas Europaea is to permit a company to be formed which can operate throughout the EU according to a single set of company laws. The intention is that it can replace the traditional structure of parent company and subsidiaries scattered throughout the EU, each subject to a different company law regime with a divisionalized company governed principally by EU Regulation. Thus a Societas Europaea (SE) is a company organized under European law rather than the law of an individual Member State. It is envisaged that the SE will result in substantial administrative and legal costs savings: estimated at up to €30 billion per year.[1]

The use of the SE is designed to facilitate quick and easy restructuring without the need to dissolve and wind up a company in one Member State, then form a new company in another. Thus it will maximize freedom of movement. As discussed above, the Merger Directive is not wholly effective in facilitating cross-border restructuring due to differences in company law in individual Member States. The SE may be established by the merger of two or more existing companies (publicly listed) from at least two Member States, the formation of a holding company promoted by such a group of companies, the formation of subsidiary companies from at least two public limited companies in two different Member States, or by the transformation of a public limited company which has, for at least two years, had a subsidiary in another Member State.

---

1   See European Commission Press Release MEMO/04/235.

Tax treatment of the Societas Europaea

20.38 Unfortunately, the Regulations governing the SE do not contain any directions as to the tax effects of a SE. The SE will therefore be taxed according to the laws in the country of tax residence and the countries where it has PEs. An important feature of the SE is that it can transfer its registered office between Member States, raising the possibility of migration to the Member State perceived to have the most favourable tax regime.

However, questions are being asked about the extent to which any special treatment for the SE will lead to yet more tax cases alleging discriminatory treatment (in favour of the SE). Gammie (2001) considers that the freedom to transfer the seat of the company with minimal company law or tax impediment will hasten the transformation of the tax systems of Member States so that they all feature uniform models for the relief of economic double taxation of dividends and source- rather than residence-based taxation, with the consequent adoption of the exemption method of double tax relief. There is also speculation that Member States will move towards formulaic rather than arm's-length methods of allocating profits between fixed establishments. However, if this degree of harmonization is achieved it would only be a relatively short step to move to a CCCTB. Unless the SE can be subject to a single tax regime, the advantages of being subject to a single company law regime are decidedly diminished. The SE may never truly be adopted until this happens.

THE EU AND BEPS

20.39 The relationship between EU law and the OECD's BEPS proposals is interesting, in that there is a possibility that EU law will restrict the implementation of the BEPS outcomes. One example relates to the BEPS transfer pricing Actions 8, 9 and 10 that moves towards pricing based on value creation and real economic activity as discussed in Chapter 13. This is potentially incompatible with the EU stance that transfer pricing adjustments can be disregarded only where they are wholly artificial arrangements. This question is discussed in Schön (2015).

There are also potential inconsistencies in the context of Action 5 in terms of State aid (as discussed above) and the Code of Conduct (see Luja (2015) and Taversa & Flamini (2015) respectively).

FURTHER READING

Aussilloux, V, Bénassy-Quéré, A, Fuest, C and Wolff, G (2017) 'Making the Best of the European Single Market', Policy Contribution Issue No 3, available at http://bruegel.org/2017/02/making-the-best-of-the-european-single-market/.

Baker, P et al (2011) 'International Assistance in the Collection of Taxes', *Bulletin for International Taxation*, April/May 2011.

Baker, P (2015) 'The BEPS Action plan in the light of EU Law: Treaty Abuse', *British Tax Review* [2015] No 3, p 408.

Benshalom, H (2008) 'A Comprehensive Solution for a Targeted Problem: A Critique of the European Union's Home State Taxation Initiative', *European Taxation*, December 2008.

Cachia, F (2017) 'Analysing the European Commission's Final Decisions on Apple, Starbucks, Amazon and Fiat Finance and Trade', *EC Tax Review* 2017/1 pp 23–35.

Cerioni, L (2006) 'The Possible Introduction of Common Consolidated Base Taxation via Enhanced Cooperation: Some Open Issues', *European Taxation*, May 2006, pp 187–196.

Danish, M (2015) 'What Remains of the *Marks and Spencer* Exception for Final Losses – Examining the Impact of *Commission v United Kingdom* (Case C0172/13)', *European Taxation*, September 2015, p 417.

Deutsche Bank Research (2007) *One Europe One Tax? Plans for a Common Consolidated Tax Base*.

Devereux, M (2004) 'Debating Proposed Reforms of the Taxation of Corporate Income in the European Union', *International Tax and Public Finance*, Vol 11, pp 71–89.

Devereux, M and Loretz, S (2007) *The Effects of EU Formula Apportionment on Corporate Tax Revenues*, Oxford Centre for Business Taxation, Working Paper No 07/06.

Douma, S (2015) 'Limitations on Interest Deductions: an EU Law Perspective', *British Tax Review* [2015], No 3, p 364.

Dourado, A (2015) 'The Role of CFC Rules in the BEPS Initiative and in the EU', *British Tax Review* [2015], No 3, p 340.

Englisch, J (2015) 'BEPS Action 1: Digital Economy – EU Law Implications', *British Tax Review* [2015], No 3, p 280.

EU Commission (2001) Communication from the Commission to the Council, the European Parliament and the European Economic and Social Committee: 'Tax policy in the European Union – Priorities for the years ahead' 23.5.2001 COM (2001) final. Available at: http://europa.eu.int/prelex/detail_dossier_real.cfm?CL=en&DosId=164839.

EU Commission (2005) Annex to the Communication from the Commission to the Council, the European Parliament and the Economic and Social Committee. 'Tackling the Corporation Tax Obstacles of Small and Medium-Sized Enterprises in the Internal Market – Outline of a Possible Home State Taxation Pilot Scheme', SEC (2005) 1785.

EU Commission (2006) *Implementing the Community Lisbon Programme: Progress to date and next steps towards a Common Consolidated Corporate Tax Base*, COM (2006) 157 final.

EU Commission (2011) *Proposal for a Council Directive on a Common Consolidated Corporate Tax Base* (CCCTB) COM (2011) 121/4.

Fleming, J C (2017) 'The EU Apple Case: Who has a Dog in the Fight?' *Tax Notes*, January 9, 2017.

Freedman, J (2017) 'Tax and Brexit', *Oxford Review of Economic Policy* 33(S1), S79–S90.

Gammie, M (2001) 'Corporate Tax in Europe – Paths to a Solution', *British Tax Review* 4, pp 233–249.

Helminen, M (2015) 'EU Law Compatibility of BEPS Action 2: Neutralising the Effects of Hybrid Mismatch Arrangements', *British Tax Review* [2015], No 3, p 325.

Lang, M (2015) 'Tax Rulings and State Aid Law', *British Tax Review* [2015], No 3, p 391.

Lodin, S O and Gammie, M (2001) *Home State Taxation*, IBFD.

Luja, R (2015) 'Will the EU's State Aid Regime Survive BEPS?', *British Tax Review* [2015], No 3, p 379.

Mason, R (2017a) 'Tax Rulings as State Aid FAQ', *Tax Notes*, January 23, 2017.

Mason, R (2017b) 'State Aid Special Report – Part 2: Legitimate Expectations', *Tax Notes*, January 30, 2017.

Mason, R (2017c) 'State Aid Special Report – Part 3: Apple', *Tax Notes*, February 6, 2017.

Meussen, G T K (2004) 'Bosal Holding Case and the Freedom of Establishment: a Dutch Perspective', *European Taxation*, February/March 2004, 59–64.

Mintz, J (2004) 'Corporate Tax Harmonization in Europe: It's All about Compliance', *International Tax and Public Finance* 11, pp 221–234.

Neidle, D (2013) 'Analysis – The EU Council Legal Service's Opinion on the FTT', *Tax Journal* 1185, 9, 20 September 2013.

O'Shea, T (2008) *EU Tax Law and Double Tax Conventions*, Avoir Fiscal Limited, London, 2008.

O'Shea, T (2011) 'Tax Avoidance and Abuse of EU Law', *EC Tax Journal* Vol 11, 2010–11, pp 77–115.

O'Shea, T (2012) 'Dutch Exit Tax Rules Challenged in National Grid Indus', *Tax Notes International* Jan 16, 2012, pp 201–205.

O'Shea, T (2013) 'Finnish Tax Rules on Cross-Border Mergers Challenged', *Tax Notes International* 71(13).

Osterweil, E (2002) 'Reform of Company Taxation in the EU Internal Market', *European Taxation*, August 2002, pp 271–275.

Rust, A (2015) 'BEPS Action 2: 2014 Deliverable – Neutralising the Effects of Hybrid Mismatch Arrangements and its Compatibility with the Non-Discrimination Provisions in Tax Treaties and the Treaty on the Functioning of the European Union', *British Tax Review* [2015], No 3, p 308.

Schön, W (2015) 'Transfer Pricing Issues of BEPS in Light of EU Law', *British Tax Review* [2015], No 3, p 417.

Schonfeld, J (2004) 'The *Cadbury Schweppes* Case: Are the Days of the United Kingdom's CFC Legislation Numbered?', *European Taxation*, October 2004, pp 441–452.

Streinz, R (2015) 'Multilateral Instruments and EU Competence', *British Tax Review* [2015], No 3, p 429.

Taussig, A (2011) 'Analysis – European Cross-border Mergers', *Tax Journal*, 24 January 2011.

Terra, B J M and Wattel, P J (2012) *European Tax Law*, 6th edn, Kluwer.

Traversa, E & Flamini, A (2015) 'The Impact of BEPS on the Fight Against Harmful Tax Practices: Risks … and Opportunities for the EU', *British Tax Review* [2015], No 3, p 396.

Zalasiński, A (2015) 'Conclusion of the BEPS Multilateral Instrument and Distribution of Competences between the EU and its Member States'. *British Tax Review* [2015], No 3, p 44.

FURTHER STUDY

Recent and important cases

20.40   Tax harmonization is happening whether Member States like it or not, via the decisions of the Court of Justice of the European Union (CJEU). The CJEU does not make decisions about the tax liabilities of individual taxpayers. When tax disputes are being decided upon in national courts and questions of interpretation of the TFEU arise, the national courts may refer questions of interpretation to the CJEU. The CJEU answers the questions of interpretation put to it and these answers are then used in the national courts in settling the tax disputes. Although Member States have the right to set their own direct tax laws, they must exercise that right in a way which is consistent with EU law. This principle was itself decided in a number of tax cases.[1]

A series of cases has been heard involving taxpayers who consider that various aspects of their national tax systems infringe their rights under the TFEU. The tests used by the courts follow three stages:

- Whether a discrimination or restriction applied by a Member State infringes the rights of taxpayers to at least one of the fundamental freedoms to which taxpayers are entitled under the EC Treaty.

- Whether the Member State can produce an acceptable justification – a national measure which restricts a taxpayer's rights under the EC Treaty is generally only permissible if it pursues a legitimate objective compatible with the EC Treaty and it is justified by imperative reasons in the public interest.

- Whether the principle of proportionality is complied with – the national measure must not go beyond what is necessary to attain that legitimate objective.[2]

The justifications put forward by the Member States where a restriction on one or more of the fundamental freedoms is held to exist are usually:

- the non-resident's situation is not comparable with that of the State's own nationals and therefore different tax treatment is appropriate;

- the treatment is necessary for the balanced allocation of taxing rights between the Member State concerned and the Member State in which the taxpayer is resident;

- the treatment is necessary for the prevention of tax avoidance; and

- fiscal cohesion: for example, if a State permits a tax deduction for a particular type of expense, then it should be able to tax the corresponding receipts. Another example would be that if a State does not tax the profits of a non-resident, then it should not be obliged to permit the losses of that non-resident to be used to reduce the taxable profits of its residents. This defence is rarely accepted.

The CJEU has now heard hundreds of tax cases. These can be grouped in several ways: according to the tax point at issue (eg offset of losses), according to the point of EU law at issue (eg the circumstances in which a Member State is entitled to discriminate), whether the case involves tax treatment accorded by a host State or a residence State and so on. Because this book is not aimed exclusively at legal scholars, the cases are grouped according to the tax issue at stake. EU direct tax law is now an established area of jurisprudence in its own right. Readers requiring an in-depth analysis of the general legal principles to be drawn from the cases and the development of those principles are directed to legal texts such as Terra (2012).

Following a decision of the CJEU, every Member State needs to examine its tax rules to see if they are in accordance with the interpretation of the TFEU as set out in the court's judgment. If not, they can expect numerous claims from their own taxpayers for refunds of tax and will have to set about amending their national tax laws to comply with the judgment. Thus every tax case heard by the CJEU has the potential to result in changes to the national tax laws of every Member State, not merely the Member State directly involved in the case.

---

1   See Case C-250/95 *Futura Participations and Singer* [1997] and Case C-9/02 *De Lasteyrie du Saillant* [2004].

2   See Case C-80/94 *Wielockx* [1995] ECR I-24933, para 16, Case C-264/96 *ICI* [1998] ECR I-4695, para 19 and Case C-311/97 *Royal Bank of Scotland* [1999] ECR I-2651, para 19.

Entitlement to certain types of payments or deductions from the tax authority

Avoir Fiscal[1]

20.41 This is one of the earliest tax cases to invoke the right to freedom of establishment. It concerned the failure of France to grant to branches of companies resident in other Member States the tax credit (the 'avoir fiscal') granted to French taxpayers. The taxpayers argued that they were at a disadvantage in comparison with French taxpayers. They were taxed in the same way as French companies, but not accorded the same tax advantages. The court held that this was a restriction on the right to freedom of establishment of foreign companies in France.

---

1 Case C-270/83 *Commission v France* [1986] ECR 273, ECJ, 28 January 1986.

Commerzbank[1]

20.42 This early case is important for two reasons. In it, the UK courts set out an excellent summary of the UK approach to the interpretation of double tax treaties. In the EU context, the case established that discrimination on the grounds of nationality is not permissible under EU law. Commerzbank had a UK branch which found itself in a position to make a claim for tax overpaid in the UK. The UK tax authority made the tax refund but refused a claim for repayment supplement (essentially, interest on tax overpaid) on the grounds that the company was not resident in the UK. The Court of Justice ruled that a national provision which entails unequal treatment of residents and entities resident in another EU Member State is discriminatory. This firmly established the principle that a Member State must afford so-called 'national treatment' to enterprises resident in another Member State.

---

1 Case C-330/91 *The Queen v Inland Revenue Commissioners, ex parte Commerzbank AG*, ECJ, 13 July 1993.

Metallgesellschaft/Hoechst[1]

20.43 These joined cases are important because they deal with the consequences of a ruling in favour of the taxpayer by the CJEU. The judgment considers matter such as the form of remedy available to taxpayers where tax has been found to have been charged contrary to EU law and also considers administrative and procedural matters such as payment of interest on tax repaid.

At the time the case was brought, the UK required an advance payment of corporation tax by a company whenever that company paid a dividend. This requirement was waived where the recipient of the dividend was a UK company owning more than 50 per cent of the equity in the paying company, provided an election was made. Advance corporation tax paid by UK companies could be offset against their final corporation tax liability for the period. Groups of companies therefore enjoyed a cash-flow benefit from making the election. In this case, the taxpayers, German parent companies, argued that these rules were a restriction on their freedom of establishment, as no such election was possible because the recipient companies were not UK resident companies, although the paying companies were UK resident. The paying companies (the UK subsidiaries) had to make payments of advance corporation tax whenever dividends were paid to their foreign parents. The German parent claimed that this amounted to indirect discrimination on grounds of nationality, contrary to the TFEU. They claimed that, to put them in the same position as UK parent companies, HMRC should make payments of interest to the UK subsidiaries to cancel out their cash-flow disadvantage. The case was complicated by the fact that, at the time, some of the UK's tax treaties contained provisions for the repayment of part of the advance corporation tax to the foreign parent. This case was distinctive as the taxpayers' claims were not for repayment of overpaid tax, but were claims for compensation or reparation for having paid tax too early.

The Court of Justice ruled in favour of the taxpayers and also ruled on the consequences for the UK tax authority (HMRC). It held that it is for national law to deal with the procedures for and the applicability of interest on tax overpaid. In particular, it is for the national court to deal with matters such as the rate of interest and whether interest should be computed as simple interest or compound interest. Importantly, the principle of effectiveness must be observed in that the national rules must not render it theoretically possible but, in practical terms, impossible to obtain to make claims for restitution or compensation. HMRC had argued that, in order for damages to be claimed by the taxpayers, they would have had to have made an election for group treatment which had been rejected by HMRC. The taxpayers had made no such elections. Regarding the precise way in which the taxpayers were to be compensated, the court held that it was for the national courts to determine the procedures and the appropriate remedies, but this case imposed a code of constraints upon how the national courts compensate taxpayers to ensure that, in practice, the requirements for claiming compensation are not so onerous as themselves to constitute a restriction on freedom of establishment.

---

1 Joined cases C-397/98 and C410/98 *Metallgesellschaft Ltd and Others, Hoechst AG, Hoechst UK Ltd v Commissioners of Inland Revenue, HM Attorney General*, ECJ, 8 March 2001.

Bosal Holding[1]

20.44 The Netherlands tax system is particularly famous for two features:

- the participation exemption regime for dividends received from foreign shareholdings; and

- the refusal to allow a deduction for interest paid in connection with the financing of foreign subsidiaries.[2]

The reasoning behind the disallowance of interest on funding for foreign subsidiaries is that the profits of those subsidiaries are not themselves subject to Netherlands taxation. Also, when a Netherlands holding company disposes of shares in a subsidiary, there is no tax on the capital gain. So the interest deduction would be a 'one-way' matter in favour of the taxpayer. Bosal Holding challenged this refusal to grant a deduction for interest paid on the grounds that it contravened the freedom of establishment principle. The question was put to the CJEU who replied that it did so. In the judgment delivered by the CJEU on 18 September 2003, the questions put to the CJEU were phrased as follows:

> 'whether Community law precludes a national provision which, when determining the tax on the profits of a parent company established in one Member State, makes the deductibility of costs in connection with that company's holding in the capital of a subsidiary established in another Member State subject to the condition that such costs are indirectly instrumental in making profits which are taxable in the Member State where the parent company is established?'

The CJEU decided that the Netherlands law *was* an impediment to freedom of establishment. It could not justify the Netherlands law on the basis of the principle of fiscal cohesion. This principle can be used by Member States to defend apparently discriminatory practices where there would be a 'one-way street' as regards tax deductions. The reason in this case is that the Netherlands does not permit Netherlands subsidiaries of parent companies in other Member States to deduct from Netherlands profits any costs in relation to parent company expenses. In other words, the system already lacks fiscal cohesion, to the benefit of the Netherlands. Neither could it justify the denial of the interest deduction on the principle of territoriality, as the parent and subsidiaries were separate companies. The Netherlands could not reasonably expect to have tax jurisdiction over the foreign subsidiaries.

The Netherlands estimated the loss from the Bosal Holding decision at €1.6 billion immediately and €1 billion annually. Given that the annual corporation tax revenues are only around €16 billion, this was a substantial blow. The Netherlands government reacted to the decision by removing the interest deduction for funding in respect of domestic subsidiaries, thereby removing the discrimination. It also introduced thin capitalization rules and placed additional restrictions on the use of tax losses of holding companies.

1   Case C-168/0-1 *Bosal Holding BV v Staatssecretaris van Financien*, ECJ, 18 September 2003.
2   Article 13(1) Vbp 1969.

Denkavit[1]

20.45   This case concerned the levying of a 5 per cent withholding tax on French dividends paid to a Netherlands holding company, before the Parent/Subsidiary Directive entered into force. No such withholding tax was levied on a dividend paid to a French shareholder. The Netherlands shareholder objected because in the Netherlands the dividends were subject to the participation exemption so that no Netherlands tax was payable on them. Thus the French

5 per cent withholding tax constituted a real tax burden. In addition the French and the Netherlands shareholders were treated differently. The reason for the near-exemption from tax in the hands of the French corporate shareholders was to alleviate economic double taxation (where the same profits are subjected to tax twice within the same country, in the hands of both the company that earns them and in the hands of shareholders who receive those profits in the form of dividends). The CJEU held that if a State relieves economic double taxation for its residents, it must also extend this relief to non-residents if economic double taxation would arise. As the Netherlands shareholder could not obtain relief for the French tax, the profits used to pay the dividends had suffered economic double taxation – French corporation tax when the profits were earned by the French company and then French withholding tax when the profits were paid to the Netherlands company as a dividend. France had therefore relieved economic double taxation in the case of French shareholders but not in the case of the Netherlands shareholders. The withholding tax was held to be discriminatory and a restriction of the rights of the Netherlands shareholder to freedom of establishment under Article 43 of the EC Treaty (now Article 49 TFEU).

1   C-170/05 *Denkavit Internationaal BV and Another v Ministre de l'Economie, des Finances et de l'Industrie*, [2007] STC 452, ECJ, 13 March 2001.

Manninen[1]

20.46   Question: if shareholders are entitled to a credit for corporation tax paid on profits used to pay a dividend against shareholding tax liabilities on that dividend, should the credit be given on dividends received from companies resident in any EU Member State and not just on those received from companies within the State in which the shareholder is tax resident?

The Finnish tax system aimed to eliminate economic double taxation by granting shareholders a tax credit in respect of the corporation tax suffered by the paying company on profits used to pay dividends. Both companies and individuals paid tax at 29 per cent and individuals were granted a tax credit equal to 29/71ths of the amount of dividends received from Finnish companies. Thus the tax liability of individuals on dividends received from Finnish companies is cancelled out by the tax credit. If the actual corporation tax paid by the company paying the dividends was less than the tax credits granted to shareholders on dividends, then the company suffered a special tax charge equal to the difference. Thus the tax credits enjoyed by the shareholders could never exceed the corporation tax paid by the company.

Mr Manninen held shares in a Swedish company and argued that the refusal of the Finnish tax authorities to grant him a tax credit equivalent to that on a Finnish dividend amounted to a restriction of his freedom of movement of capital (Article 63 TFEU). Article 65 of the TFEU permits Member States to apply different tax rules to taxpayers who are not in the same situation with regard to their place of residence or with regard to the place where their capital is invested. The Finnish tax authority argued that because of the arrangements whereby Finnish companies paid tax at least equal to the tax credits granted to

Finnish shareholders, it was entitled to refuse a tax credit on a dividend from a Swedish company. Article 65 permits differential treatment only where different taxpayers are in situations which are not objectively comparable. It does not permit arbitrary discrimination.

The Court of Justice considered that this situation deterred fully taxable persons in Finland from investing their capital in companies established in other EU member States and also constituted an obstacle to companies established in other EU Member States raising capital in Finland. The court held that the principle of territoriality did not justify the restriction on freedom of movement of capital. Neither did the court consider that Finland's fiscal cohesion would be lost. If Finland wished to grant shareholders a tax credit based on the corporation tax suffered on the profits used to pay the dividends, then it could take into account the corporation tax paid by the Swedish company. The fact that this would mean that tax receipts in Finland would fall (because it would not have received any corporation tax from the Swedish company) did not assist the Finnish tax authority. The Court of Justice has consistently held that a reduction in tax revenues is not an overriding reason, in the public interest, for allowing tax rules which restrict the fundamental freedoms.

Result: Finland was not permitted to grant tax credits only to taxpayers in receipt of dividends from Finnish companies.

An important point which was decided in this case is that although Member States have the freedom to set their own direct taxes, they must do so in a manner consistent with EU Law (para 19).

---

1   Case C-319/02 *Petri Manninen*, ECJ, 7 September 2004.

Truck Center[1]

20.47   Belgian-sourced interest paid to non-Belgian residents is charged with withholding tax which discharges the final tax liability. Interest paid to Belgian-resident companies is exempt from the withholding tax since it is taxed in the hands of the Belgian recipient. In this case, the CJEU held in a decision handed down on 22 December 2008, that this arrangement is not precluded by freedom of establishment or free movement of capital. The court noted that resident and non-resident companies are not in an objectively comparable situation because:

1   In relation to the payments to the Luxembourg company, Belgium acted as the source State. However, in respect of payments of interest made by a Belgian company to a fellow Belgian company, Belgium would be acting as the State of residence.

2   The tax liability suffered by the Luxembourg company was a withholding tax made under a specific power accorded to Belgium in its DTT with Luxembourg, whereas a payment to a Belgian company would be charged to Belgian corporation tax. These are entirely different tax charges.

3   The different arrangements reflect the difference in the situations in which the recipient companies find themselves. Belgium could enforce the tax liability of a Belgian recipient but might need the assistance of the Luxembourg tax authority to recover the withholding tax.

The court also observed that the exemption does not necessarily provide an advantage to resident companies who are subject to Belgian corporation tax as they suffered the 15 per cent withholding tax on a gross basis rather than on a net profit basis as enjoyed by Belgian recipients.

The Interest and Royalties Directive did not apply as the interest payments in question were made in the three years ending 1996, before the Directive had entered into force. Had the Directive been in force, the problem would not have arisen. However, the significance of the case is that a taxpayer who does not enjoy the protection from withholding tax under the Interest and Royalties Directive cannot claim that they have received discriminatory treatment and therefore that their right to freedom of establishment under Article 43 has been restricted. The rules established in the case of *Schumacker*[2] that the situation of residents and non-residents are not, as a rule, comparable, and that discrimination can arise only through the application of different rules to comparable situations or the application of the same rule to different situations were upheld.

Note that *Truck Center* is distinguished from *Denkavit* (above) because the problem in *Denkavit* was two shareholders in the same circumstances, one enjoying relief from economic double taxation and the other not. Economic double taxation does not arise in the case of interest, as the interest is tax deductible in arriving at the payer's taxable profits.

1   C-282/07 *Truck Center SA v Belgium*, ECJ, 22 December 2008.
2   Case-279/93 *Finanzamt Köln-Altstadt v Roland Schumacker*, [1996] QB 28, ECJ, 14 February 1995.

Tate & Lyle[1]

20.48   The Tate & Lyle Investments case concerns the compatibility of Belgian withholding tax on dividends paid to non-resident shareholders imposed in respect of a deemed distribution arising on a partial demerger. Belgian resident companies subjected to this tax are able to offset it against corporate tax liabilities and receive a refund for any excess. The CJEU ordered in July 2012, that by not allowing non-resident companies to benefit from the same rules, a restriction on the freedom of movement of capital arises. The Belgian government argued that the UK/Belgium double tax agreement would provide credit for the withholding tax, however the Court stated that was a matter for the National Court to consider.

1   C-384/11 *Tate & Lyle Investments Ltd*, ECJ, 12 July 2012.

Exit taxes

National Grid[1]

20.49   Questions of freedom of establishment and the balance of allocation of taxing rights among Member States also arise in the case of exit taxes
imposed when an entity or part of an entity move from one jurisdiction to
another. In the *National Grid* case, the company moved its place of central
management and control from the Netherlands to the UK. Dutch legislation
charged tax on the exchange gains accrued up to the time of relocation. The
CJEU was asked for a ruling as to whether the exit tax breached freedom of
establishment, in which case the court would have to consider whether such a
breach is justified.

The CJEU held that National Grid Indus could rely on its rights under
Article 49 of the TFEU. O'Shea (2012)[2] suggests the decision leaves open
the question of whether the host State must then grant a step-up in value for
the assets subjected to the exit tax. In the absence of such a step-up, double
taxation remains possible.

1   Case C-371/10 *National Grid Indus BV* [2012] All ER (EC) 883, ECJ, 29 November 2011.
2   At p 205.

Commission v Spain[1]

20.50   In a judgement handed down in April 2013, it was held that freedom
of establishment does not preclude exit taxes in the form of a tax on unrealized capital gains when a permanent establishment ceases to operate in Spain.
However where the place of residence or of the assets of a company established
in Spain is transferred to another Member State, it does constitute a discriminatory measure in that it puts companies at a cash flow disadvantage. The Court
takes the view that the measures go beyond what is necessary to achieve the
objective of safeguarding Spain's taxing powers.

It is therefore not the act of taxing capital gains generated in a territory but not
yet realized that breaches freedom of establishment, but rather the fact that that
tax is required to be paid immediately.

This decision follows the criteria of *National Grid Indus*, and will require
Spain to amend its exit tax rules accordingly.

1   Case C-64/11 *Commission v Spain*, ECJ, 25 April 2013.

Interaction between EU law and bilateral double tax treaties

Gilly[1]

20.51   In this case it was established that Member States have the freedom to
choose the connecting factors by which they will determine their jurisdiction

to tax: source, residence and so on, and to decide on their own double tax relief mechanisms in their bilateral double tax treaties. Mrs Gilly, a German national, was a teacher resident in France, but employed in Germany. Because of the different definitions of residence in the France–Germany DTT and the rules therein for determining residence, she found herself taxable in Germany and France, with Germany having the primary taxing right so that she had to claim double tax relief for the German tax in France. She objected to this because German tax was higher than French tax, so that her overall tax bill was higher than if she had been taxed only in France.

---

1 Case C-336/96 *Gilly v Directeur des Services Fiscaux du Bas-Rhin* [1998] ECR I-2793, [1998] All ER (EC) 826, ECJ, 12 May 1998.

Saint-Gobain[1]

20.52 This case illustrates the principle that bilateral tax treaty obligations and practices cannot be used to defend infringements of the fundamental freedoms. The case concerned the taxation of a German branch of a French company. The branch was only taxed in Germany on its income arising in and capital located in Germany. Part of the branch capital assets included some US and Swiss shareholdings on which dividends were received. Some benefits of the Germany–US and Germany–Switzerland DTTs were denied to the branch. Although Germany permitted a double tax credit for the withholding taxes suffered by the branch in the US and Switzerland it refused to exempt the dividends from German tax altogether. The refusal was on the grounds that the treaty benefit of exemption applied only to German companies and, in the case of the Swiss treaty, only to German companies subject to unlimited tax liability in Germany.

There was no question of the US or Switzerland having to give up any of their rights under the treaties. However, Germany found itself in the position where, because it taxed branches of French companies in the same way as German companies, it had to ensure that such branches found themselves in the same position as would a German company in similar circumstances. In effect, this meant that Germany had to compensate the German branch of the French company to restore it to the position it would have been in had it been granted benefits under the two tax treaties. The rationale for such compensation was that the French company's rights, with respect to its German branch, had been infringed under the TFEU freedom of establishment.

The Court of Justice affirmed its earlier statement in *Gilly*[2] that Member States are competent to determine the criteria for the taxation of income and capital in cross-border situations by the used of bilateral tax treaties concluded to prevent double taxation. In particular, they are free to decide the connecting facts for the allocation of powers of taxation between the contracting States. However, the overriding rule remains – Member States, in exercising their powers of taxation may not override EU rules and although direct taxation is a matter for the Member States, they must exercise this power consistently with EU law.

1 Case C-307/97 *Compagnie de Saint-Gobain, Zweigniederlassung Deutschland v Finanzamt Aachen-Innenstadt* [2000] STC 854, ECJ, 21 September 1999.
2 Case C-336/96 *Mr and Mrs Robert Gilly v Directeur fiscaux du Bas-Rhin* [1998] ECR I-2793, [1998] All ER (EC) 826, ECJ, 12 May 1998.

Tax avoidance

Lankhorst[1]

20.53   This case concerned a German company, Lankhorst-Hohorst GmbH, which was a subsidiary of a Dutch company, Lankhorst-Hohorst BV. The German subsidiary had a debt outstanding to a third-party bank which was refinanced by way of a loan from the Dutch parent. The loan from the Dutch parent was interest-bearing and interest was paid to the Dutch company. German domestic law permitted the interest payable on the loan to the parent to be treated as a distribution on the grounds that the German company was thinly capitalized. The ECJ ruled that German law in this instance was contrary to Article 43 of the EC Treaty which prohibits restrictions on the freedom of establishment in another Member State, which would include disadvantages arising from setting up subsidiaries in other Member States. The court ruled that the German thin capitalization rules did involve a difference of treatment of German-resident subsidiary companies according to whether or not their parent company was resident in Germany.

As a result of this case, the UK HMRC and other Member States have revised their transfer pricing rules so that not only prices on cross-border transactions, but also prices on same-country transactions between associated enterprises must be at arm's length (see Chapter 13). This might be termed 'harmonization downwards' because although the discrimination is removed, taxpayers are worse off than before. However, we have probably not heard the last of this. It is considered unlikely that tax inspectors will dispute transfer prices between two UK parties to the same extent as between a UK party and a party resident in another Member State. Thus it is likely that more cases will be heard on discrimination in practice, even though it no longer exists on paper.

1   C-324/00 *Lankhorst-Hohorst GmbH v Finanzamt Steinfurt*, ECR, 12 December 2002.

Cadbury Schweppes[1]

20.54   Although this case was primarily concerned with the legality of controlled foreign companies legislation within the EU, there was an extensive discussion on tax avoidance. The facts of the case are discussed earlier in this book but, briefly stated, were that Cadbury Schweppes had established two subsidiary companies in Ireland where they enjoyed a low rate of corporation tax. HMRC assessed Cadbury Schweppes to UK corporation tax on an amount of profits equal to that on which the subsidiaries would have been taxed, had they been established in the UK. One of the questions considered was whether the UK's CFC legislation could be justified on the grounds of prevention of tax avoidance. HMRC, supported by several other EU governments, argued that CFC legislation is intended to counter a specific type of tax avoidance: the artificial transfer by a resident company of profits to a low-tax State by establishing a subsidiary in that State and entering into transactions which resulted in a transfer of profits to that subsidiary.

The court considered that the fact that the subsidiaries enjoyed a low rate of tax in a different Member State did not permit the home state to offset that advantage by tax treatment designed to recoup the advantage. Neither could there be any general presumption of tax evasion because a resident company sets up a subsidiary in a Member State where taxes are lower. The court observed that the UK CFC legislation already contained provisions aimed at excluding profits from the charge where there had evidently been no attempt to avoid UK tax (such as the 'acceptable distribution' exemption, whereby if most of the foreign subsidiary's profits had been remitted back to the UK, there would be no CFC charge). The court considered that in addition to the subjective element of an intention to obtain a tax advantage, there must also be objective circumstances showing that the objective pursued by the concept of freedom of establishment had not been achieved. The objectives of freedom of establishment are to allow a national of a Member State to set up a secondary establishment in another Member State to carry on activities there and assist economic and social interpenetration and to participate on a stable and continuing basis in the economic life of the other Member State, making a profit there. There needs to be an actual establishment intended to carry on genuine economic activities. This must be evidenced by objective factors, ascertainable by third parties, and will definitely include the extent to which the CFC physically exists in terms of premises, staff and equipment. So even if a tax authority considers that there was a definite intention to avoid tax by setting up in a low-tax Member State, so long as the objective factors are present, CFC charges are not permitted.

---

1   C-196/04 *Cadbury Schweppes Plc, Cadbury Schweppes Overseas Ltd v Commissioners of Inland Revenue*, ECR, 12 September 2006.

Masco Denmark ApS, Damixa ApS[1]

20.55   This thin capitalization case sought clarification as to whether an exemption from the Danish rules, which are designed to prevent shifting of tax revenues, is compatible with freedom of establishment. It was held that the prohibition of deduction of interest expenses does not constitute a restriction on freedom of establishment. Article 43 does not preclude a Member State from denying a resident company a tax exemption for interest income where the affiliated company established in another Member State is not entitled to a tax deduction for the corresponding interest expenditure due to thin capitalization rules.

---

1   C-593/14 *Masco Denmark ApS, Damixa ApS v Skatteministeriet*, Opinion of the Advocate General delivered 12 May 2016.

Set-off of losses cross-border

Futura Participations[1]

20.56   This case concerned the losses of a Luxembourg branch of a French company. The Luxembourg domestic law denied carry forward of losses except against income economically earned in Luxembourg (and thus the profit of the French head office establishment did not count) and also the branch had to keep branch accounts complying with Luxembourg rules.

Luxembourg demanded that there must be an economic link between the losses carried forward and the income earned in the Member State in which tax is charged, so that only losses arising from the non-resident taxpayer's activities in that State can be carried forward. However, a Luxembourg resident company would have been able to carry forward losses against income from sources other than the trade which produced the loss. The Court of Justice ruled that this system was in accordance with the principle of territoriality and thus did not give rise to any discrimination. Resident taxpayers were, in theory, taxable on their worldwide income and this fact justified the Luxembourg loss set-off regime, which allowed resident companies to offset losses brought forward which arose from sources other than that giving rise to the profits.

However, the rule that, in order to be permitted to offset losses brought forward, branch accounts should have been kept at the Luxembourg premises and in accordance with Luxembourg laws was held to go beyond the stated object of that rule. The object was to ascertain clearly and precisely the amount of losses. An apportionment of total company losses would probably not be sufficiently accurate, but it was open to the Luxembourg tax authorities to request the necessary information from the taxpayer's residence in order to make an accurate calculation of the branch tax losses. The taxpayer won this case on the grounds that a denial of loss relief amounted to an infringement of the right of establishment: establishing in Luxembourg had produced a tax disadvantage.

The case is notable for the overt approval shown by the Court of Justice for the principle of territoriality.

---

1   Case C-250/95 *Futura Participations and Singer*, ECJ, 15 May 1997.

Marks & Spencer[1]

20.57   The question in this case was whether the losses of subsidiary companies in other Member States could be offset against the UK profits of the parent company. Marks & Spencer suffered heavy losses in connection with their French, Belgian and German subsidiaries. Despite street protests in Paris from devotees of the Marks & Spencer prawn sandwich and sensible underwear, the subsidiaries ceased to trade. Marks & Spencer argued that their right to freedom of establishment was infringed, as they were worse off by having subsidiaries tax resident in France, Belgium and Germany than if those subsidiaries had been tax resident in the UK. UK tax-resident members of the same corporate group (as specifically defined for this purpose by ICTA 1988) have the right to offset tax losses and profits within the group. The loss relief claim was for some £100 million.

The CJEU concluded that provisions which generally prevent a resident parent company from deducting from its taxable profits losses incurred in another Member State by a subsidiary do *not* constitute an infringement of Article 43 (freedom of establishment). However, in cases where the non-resident subsidiary has exhausted the possibilities for utilising the losses in its own Member State, denial of offset against the parent company's profits would constitute an infringement of the right to freedom of establishment. Thus, because the Marks & Spencer subsidiaries in France, Belgium and Germany had ceased to trade, with no possibility for loss offset in those countries either now or in the future, the UK HMRC is obliged to permit offset of the losses against the UK taxable profits of the UK parent company.

This is a partial victory for the UK HMRC in that the verdict does not give an automatic right of offset of taxable profits and losses within groups with members in more than one Member State.

The UK offered three arguments as to why losses of a non-resident subsidiary should not be offset against profits of a resident company.

First, there was a need to protect the balanced allocation of the power to impose tax between the UK and the subsidiaries' countries. Profits and losses are two sides of the same coin and must be treated symmetrically in the same tax system. A general right to cross-border offset of losses could damage the tax base of certain Member States. A group would be able to choose where to allocate losses, thus gaining the ability to reduce tax liabilities in Member States having high effective rates of tax. At the same time, the tax base of the Member State in which the loss-making subsidiary was resident would increase. This would result in an unbalanced allocation of power to impose taxes between Member States. This assumes that a loss cannot be used in more than one Member State. The UK tax authority argued that the principle of territoriality applies – the foreign subsidiaries were beyond the UK's tax jurisdiction. The argument of fiscal cohesion has also been advanced, as there is a direct link between the group relief granted for losses incurred by a surrendering company and the taxation of profits by the claimant company. However, the fiscal cohesion argument is weak where, as in this case, the plus and the minus occur in different legal entities.

Secondly, if losses were taken into consideration in the parent company's Member State they might well be taken into account twice. The CJEU had some sympathy with this view and agreed that the danger is avoided by a rule which precludes relief in respect of losses of non-resident subsidiaries. However, a general restriction on such loss offset was considered disproportionate in preventing such double relief, hence the decision that the losses of subsidiaries resident in other Member States could only be offset against the parent company's profits in circumstances where there was no possibility of offset in the subsidiaries' Member States.

Thirdly, if the losses were not taken into account in the Member State in which the subsidiary was established there would be a risk of tax avoidance. The CJEU accepted that groups would naturally attempt to utilise losses in those countries where they would save the greatest amount of tax, but again the principle of proportionality was used to overrule this argument. A general ban on the cross-border offset of losses is a disproportionate response to this threat.

As in the *Bosal* case, a reduction in tax revenue was not regarded as being an overriding reason in the public interest which may be relied on to justify a Member State adopting rules which infringe a fundamental freedom. Similar reasoning was given in this case.

Although not a universally popular outcome, the limited victory for the taxpayer means that at least the danger that the UK HMRC would follow the reasoning adopted after the *Lankhorst* case and dispose of the alleged discrimination by abolishing group relief for domestic groups has also been averted. It appears that the only hope now for a general scheme of cross-border loss relief between group companies in different Member States is the adoption of home state taxation or common consolidated tax base.

---

1   Case C-446/03 *Marks & Spencer Plc v David Halsey (HM Inspector of Taxes)*, ECJ, 13 December 2005.

Oy AA[1]

20.58   This Finnish case also concerned the cross-border offset of losses. The hearing took place the day after the delivery of the court's judgment in *Marks & Spencer.*

Under Finnish national law, group loss relief is effected by a process of transferring profits to loss-making companies rather than the other way around. A UK parent company, AA Ltd made losses and a Finnish subsidiary, Oy AA, had profits. Oy AA proposed to make a transfer of its profits to AA Ltd and claimed a deduction from profits liable to tax in Finland. Finland argued that both the transferor and transferee of the profits had to be Finnish companies. The taxpayer (Oy AA) argued that this was a restriction on freedom of establishment and freedom of movement of capital.

The Court of Justice held that a difference in treatment between resident subsidiary companies according to whether the seat of their parent company was in Finland or another Member State constituted an obstacle to the freedom of establishment so that they are discouraged from acquiring, creating or maintaining a subsidiary in Finland. The fact that the UK parent could have set up a branch in Finland and thus obtained UK tax relief for the UK losses against the profits of the Swedish branch was not an acceptable argument – freedom of establishment includes the freedom to decide upon the legal form in which they do business in another Member State. HMRC also argued that AA Ltd could carry forward its losses without time limit so that real effect was a delay in giving relief for the UK losses rather than an outright denial of relief. This was not accepted by the Court of Justice, which decided, at para 42:

> 'for legislation to be regarded as a restriction on the freedom of establishment, it is sufficient that it be capable of restricting the exercise of that freedom in a Member State by companies established in another Member State, without there being any need to establish that the legislation in question has actually had the effect of leading some of those companies to refrain from acquiring, creating or maintaining a subsidiary in the first Member State.'

The court proceeded, as usual, to consider whether there were any acceptable justifications for the restriction on the fundamental freedom of establishment. The requirement that only overriding reasons in the public interest constitute acceptable justifications was reiterated, as was the requirement that any national measures restricting fundamental freedoms must be proportionate and not go beyond what is required.

Justifications offered were:

- the coherence of the Finnish tax system;

- the need to maintain a balanced allocation of taxation powers between the UK and Finland;

- discouragement of tax avoidance;

- adherence to the principle of territoriality.

In other words, the usual list. Fundamentally, allowing taxpayers to choose the Member State of taxation would limit the taxation powers of Member States by undermining a balanced allocation of those powers (at para 48).

The need to maintain a balanced allocation of taxation powers did not justify the systematic refusal to grant a tax advantage to a resident subsidiary (the deduction from Finnish taxable profits of the profits transferred to AA Ltd), on the ground that the income of the parent company (Oy AA Ltd) was not capable of being taxed in Finland. However the automatic right to loss relief in any EU Member State rather than only in the State where the losses were generated would seriously undermine a balanced allocation of powers to tax. That had been the decision in *Marks & Spencer*.

As in *Marks & Spencer*, the justifications put forward by the Finnish tax authorities were that to allow the effective offset of the losses against the profits would undermine the balance of taxing rights between Finland and the UK, and there would be a risk of tax avoidance, as groups sought to utilise losses in the Member States in which they suffered the highest effective rates of tax. Allowing companies the choice of Member State in which to claim loss relief would undermine the balance of power to tax amongst the Member States. The Court of Justice also considered the likelihood of groups entering into tax-avoidance schemes based on choice of State in which to use the losses.

The Court of Justice therefore considered the Finnish law to be justified. The next question was whether the Swedish restrictions were proportionate to the mischief they sought to discourage. Because of the wide choice that might be afforded to companies in choosing the company to which the profits would be transferred, it was considered that the Swedish rules were proportionate.

This case therefore resulted in a rare outright win for the tax authorities.

---

1   Case C-231/05 *Proceedings brought by OY AA*, ECJ, 18 July 2007.

Papillon[1]

20.59   Under the French tax legislation, restrictions apply to the participation in a tax group where lower-tier subsidiaries are held indirectly by a subsidiary resident in another Member State. This restriction does not apply where the lower-tier subsidiary is held by a French subsidiary. The CJEU held, in November 2008, that the restriction is not compatible with Article 43, freedom of establishment. There are alternative measures that could be used to prevent double deduction of losses, including application of the Mutual Assistance Directive to obtain information regarding the intermediate subsidiary. The decision opens the way for possible claims in France going back to 2005.

---

1   C-418/07 *Société Papillon v Ministry of Finance (France)*, ECJ, 27 November 2008.

Deutsche Shell[1]

20.60   This case concerned events that occurred before Germany and Italy adopted the Euro as their common currency. Deutsche Shell incurred a currency loss on the capital invested in its Italian branch (in Italian Lira). The branch was subsequently closed down. The German tax system exempts Italian profits from German tax and does not recognize Italian losses. The Italian tax system could not give relief for the exchange loss because Italy accounted for the branch profits and charged tax on them in Lira, and thus as far as the Italians were concerned, there was no exchange loss. Deutsche Shell claimed that this failure to afford tax relief for the exchange losses on the repatriation of the branch capital to Germany was a restriction on its freedom of establishment under Article 43 of the EC Treaty. The CJEU agreed, holding the failure of Germany to give relief for the losses was an unjustifiable restriction which could not be excused on the ground of fiscal coherence, or by arguing that Italy ought to have relieved the loss.

---

1   C-293/06 *Deutsche Shell GmbH v FA Fur Grossunternehmen Hamburg* [2008] STC 1721, ECJ, 28 February 2008.

Lidl Belgium[1]

20.61   In May 2008, the CJEU passed a ruling in relation to the offset of losses of a PE located in another Member's State holding that a prohibition on deduction of losses by Germany was not contrary to EC law. The DTT between Germany and Luxembourg meant that the profits of the Luxembourg PE were exempt from tax in Germany and Germany argued that the losses of the PE should not be relievable against German profits. Here the ECJ confirmed that a permanent establishment falls within the scope of Article 43, and that the possibility of loss offset in relation to a domestic permanent establishment is a tax advantage denied to permanent establishments located in other Member States, therefore there is a restriction of freedom of establishment. The principles established in the *Marks & Spencer* case were held to be potentially applicable, however because the Member State in which the permanent establishment was located, in this case Luxembourg, allowed for the carry forward of the loss, it could be distinguished from the *Marks & Spencer* case. Accordingly, the German regime was held to be proportionate in that Lidl was likely to be granted tax relief for the losses in Luxembourg in future (which actually happened about four years after the losses were incurred). Lidl had, however, suffered a cash-flow disadvantage by having to wait until the Luxembourg PE made taxable profits before it could obtain relief for the loss. This cash-flow disadvantage was not held to constitute a restriction of rights under Article 43, or if it was, that restriction was proportionate and therefore permitted.

---

1   C-414/06 *Lidl Belgium GmbH & Co KG v FA Dusseldorf Mettmann*, ECJ, 20 May 2008.

Philips Electronics UK Ltd[1]

20.62   This case also concerns the cross-border offset of losses, but this time involving a UK branch of a EU company. The group sought to offset the losses incurred by a UK branch of a Netherlands group company against the taxable profits of a UK group company. The Netherlands group company was part of a Netherlands subgroup, which all went into liquidation. Arguments have centred on whether there was any possibility of utilising the losses in the Netherlands. A simplified diagram is given below:

There were two reasons why HMRC denied the group relief claim

1   Under UK law as it stood in 2009, Electronics UK could only make a claim for the losses of a company held as to less than 75 per cent by the common parent company if the common parent company, known as the link company (K), would itself have been entitled to make a claim. As K was not resident in the UK, HMRC argued that in this consortium situation, K would not have been entitled to make a claim.

2   The UK has rules to try to ensure that losses of UK branches of foreign companies are set off against profits of the foreign company rather than against any UK taxable profits, thus reducing taxation in the foreign country rather than in the UK. These rules are strictly interpreted and state that the losses cannot be utilised in the UK if any part of the loss could be offset against non-UK profits of the head office company or any other non-UK company. In this case, the question was whether the loss could have been used anywhere in the Netherlands subgroup.

Philips Electronics UK Ltd argued that denial of the loss relief claim constituted a restriction on the freedom of establishment in that there was a disadvantage in LG.PD Sub 2 having a UK branch rather than a UK subsidiary.
Had LG.PD Sub 2 had a UK subsidiary which had made the losses, a loss
relief claim would have been possible in the UK with no questions asked. The
judgment in *Papillon* had made it clear that discrimination on the grounds of
the Member State in which an intermediate group member was resident was a
restriction on the freedom of establishment.

The First-tier Tribunal agreed that the consortium point constituted a restriction on freedom of establishment, because if K and Philips GmbH had been
UK companies, loss relief would have been available.

The second point regarding the rules on the use of losses by UK branches of
foreign countries was more difficult. The taxpayer argued that the rules constituted discrimination against UK branches of EU companies compared with
UK subsidiaries of EU companies. It was noted that, unlike the position in
Marks & Spencer, the UK did not exercise any tax jurisdiction over the loss-
making European subsidiaries, whereas in this case, the UK branch was fully
within the jurisdiction to UK tax so that if profitable it would be liable to UK
tax. It was not good enough to say that the Philips group could have obtained
loss relief if a UK subsidiary, rather than a branch had been formed, as the
TFEU expressly leaves traders free to choose in which legal form they wish
to operate. Referring to the judgment in *Lidl*, the tribunal held that it was for
the Netherlands, as the country of residence of the head office of the company,
LG.PD Sub 2, to worry about the double use of any losses, not the country
where the permanent establishment was situated.

Hence, both reasons for denying the group relief claim in the UK constituted
restrictions on the freedom of establishment.

Timeline:

July 2001	UK branch set up. LG.PD Sub 2 not in the Netherlands fiscal unity (group for purposes of surrendering losses)
1 January 2002	LG.PD Sub 2 joins Netherlands fiscal unity
February 2003	Agreement to surrender losses to Electronics UK (total losses £197 million). Electronics UK to pay half the UK corporation tax saving to LG.PD Sub 2.
March 2005	UK branch of LG.PD Sub 2 closed
January 26 2006	Business and assets of branch transferred to another Netherlands subsidiary (a UK company, but loss-making throughout)
January 27 2006	LG.PD Sub 2 and other Netherlands companies (including LG.PD) go into bankruptcy proceedings, although not immediately dissolved
January 9 2009	LG.PD Sub 3 enters bankruptcy

The UK's First-tier Tribunal ruled in favour of the taxpayer without making a referral to the Court of Justice.

A restriction may be justified by overriding reasons in the public interest, such as the fiscal coherence of the tax system and it must be a proportionate response to a potential or actual problem. The three justifications put forward by the UK for the restrictions were the same as those in the *Marks & Spencer* case (above).

None of the justifications were accepted by the tribunal as being overriding reasons in the public interest. As to proportionality, it was argued for HMRC that the test for branch losses echoed the 'no possibilities' of use of the losses abroad test in *Marks & Spencer*, and therefore acceptable under EU law. The taxpayer argued that the requirement that no part of the loss had been used abroad (which in this case, it had), went too far. The tribunal agreed but favoured the only slightly less restrictive 'no possibilities' test in *Marks & Spencer.*

The UK's rules for permitting consortium relief were subsequently relaxed in the Finance (No 2) Act 2010 so that the company linking the loss-making company with the profitable company (the 'link company') may now be an EU/EEA-resident company rather than a UK company.

The CJEU decided in September 2012[2] that Philips Electronics UK, could use the losses sustained by the UK branch of LG Philips, finding that HMRC was restricting LG Philips' freedom to establish a PE in the UK and further the UK could not argue that its taxing rights were being undermined.

---

1   *Philips Electronics UK Ltd v HMRC* [2009] UKFTT 226 (TC), [2009] SFTD 629.
2   Case C-18/11 *The Commissioners for Her Majesty's Revenue & Customs v Philips Electronics UK Ltd*, ECJ, 6 September 2012.

A Oy[1]

20.63   Here the CJEU considered Finnish rules which denied loss relief when a Finnish company merged with a Swedish company, yet granted relief for a merger of two Finnish companies. A Oy, a Finnish business, owned 100 per cent of a Swedish subsidiary that had incurred losses and ceased trading but retained two long-term leases. A Oy merged with it so as to transfer the leases and simplify the group structure.

O'Shea (2013) observes that the judgement of the CJEU in favour of the taxpayer 'demonstrates how EU law continues to evolve in the eyes of the' CJEU and notes:

'The Court gives further guidance on the scope of freedom of establishment, develops the need to ensure balance in the allocation of taxing rights between member states as a general interest justification, and clarifies the so-called "no possibilities" test, first formulated in the *Marks and Spencer* judgement.'

An important point is that the Finnish loss relief legislation attaches a condition to domestic mergers, ie that the merger not have to be carried out for the purpose of obtaining a tax advantage. O'Shea suggests this may change the result of the case in the national court if the same rule is applied to the cross border merger.

The *A Oy* case clarifies the 'no possibilities test' by acknowledging cross border relief can be denied when relief is available in the State of residence of the subsidiary; but when the test is met, there can be no threat to the allocation of taxing rights. The CJEU, in upholding the Marks & Spencer doctrine, went against the opinion of the AG in July 2012.

---

1   C-123/11, ECJ, 21 February 2013.

Commission v United Kingdom[1]

20.64   The Grand Chamber of the CJEU issued its decision in *Commission v United Kingdom* on 3 February 2015. The case follows on from the *Marks & Spencer* decision (see para **20.57** above) the Court found in favour of the UK, finding that the Marks & Spencer exception for losses that cannot be relieved elsewhere still has application. Advocate General Kokott found that the UK's restrictive conditions for loss relief are justified by the principle of symmetry of taxing powers, given that the non-resident subsidiaries are not taxed in the UK. For a discussion of the implications of this decision, see Danish (2015).

---

1   C-172/13 3 February 2015.

Mutual assistance

ELISA[1]

20.65   This case concerned the application of the original Mutual Assistance Directive (Directive 77/799) and the annual French tax levied on French immovable property at 3 per cent of its value. France sought to levy the tax on a Luxembourg resident when it would have exempted a French resident, even though the double tax treaty (DTT) between the two countries contained a non-discrimination clause and a clause facilitating exchange of information. However, the treaty did not apply to certain types of holding company, such as ELISA which was a Luxembourg '1929 holding company'. '1929 holding companies' hardly paid any tax in Luxembourg and were very lightly regulated. France granted exemption from the annual tax only to French residents, or foreign residents of a country with which France had a treaty on administrative assistance to combat tax evasion and avoidance, or with which France had a DTT containing a non-discrimination clause. To obtain the exemption, certain information had to be disclosed to the French tax authority – details of the property and the identity and address of the company's shareholders or other members, with details of their shareholdings and their tax residence. Luxembourg was not permitted, under its domestic laws, to disclose information about shareholders of 1929 holding companies and exchange of information on such companies was, as noted, excluded from the ambit of the DTT. However, the information could, in theory, have been obtained under the Mutual Assistance Directive.

The French tax authority requested a ruling from the Court of Justice as to whether its requirements for granting the exemption to non-residents were in accordance with the TFEU (freedom to provide services and freedom of movement of capital). Freedom of establishment was not in point as in order to benefit from that freedom, a taxpayer must have a permanent presence in the host Member State. If that permanent presence consists of immovable property, that property must be actively managed, not merely held as an investment.

The denial of exemption was held to be a restriction on the freedom of movement of capital. For non-residents, the exemption would only be granted conditional upon a requirement additional to that imposed on French residents (ie the application of a treaty). The foreign taxpayer had no control over whether such a treaty existed or was applicable or not. The court then moved on to consider whether the restriction was justified. The French justified the restriction on the grounds that it was aimed at the prevention of tax evasion, which is an overriding requirement of general interest. It had been held in a previous case[2] that this was an acceptable justification for a restriction of the fundamental freedoms.

The next question was whether or not the restriction (ie the denial of the exemption) was proportionate or whether some lesser measure might have been appropriate. Prevention of tax evasion is only a justification for denying the fundamental freedoms if the legislation in question is directed at wholly artificial arrangements, the objective of which is to circumvent tax laws. Measures which are enacted on the presumption that those affected by them are engaged in tax evasion are not acceptable as grounds for denying the fundamental freedoms. The court held that France could have framed the denial of the exemption differently. Instead of a blanket denial where the required treaties were not in existence or not applicable, it could have restricted the denial of the exemption to cases where the taxpayer company failed to supply the required information. France had failed to provide foreign companies with an opportunity to supply the information voluntarily, without recourse to their tax authorities.

The denial of the exemption to the Luxembourg company was therefore a restriction on the freedom of movement of capital and unlawful.

---

1   Case C-451/05 *Européenne et Luxembourgoise d'investissements SA (ELISA) v Directeur général des impôts, Ministère public* [2008] STC 1762, ECJ, 11 October 2007.
2   *Centro di Musicologia Walter Stauffer* [2006] ECR I-8203.

Établissements Rimbaud[1]

20.66   This case also concerned the French tax on French immoveable property (ie land and buildings) but in this case, it was charged to a Liechtenstein resident. Liechtenstein is a member of the EEA and thus its residents enjoy the four fundamental freedoms, including the freedom of movement of capital. The freedom of movement of capital includes a bar on discrimination based on nationality or residence or on the place where the capital is invested. France does not have a DTT with Liechtenstein so that there was no non-discrimination article to protect the Liechtenstein taxpayer. The taxpayer would also have been protected if there had been a treaty on mutual assistance between France and Liechtenstein. France exempted French companies from the tax on immovable property but charged the Liechtenstein company. Following *ELISA*, France had altered its domestic legislation to afford foreign companies not benefiting from a tax treaty with France the opportunity to claim the exemption by supplying the necessary information concerning their shareholders themselves.

In this case, France justified its practice on the grounds that countries generally have the right to tax income and gains from, and capital represented by, immovable property situated within their borders. In the absence of a mutual assistance treaty it would have no assurance that the foreign owners of French property would pay up. In the absence of a DTT it did not have to treat foreign owners as favourably as French owners. Even though the foreign company could supply the necessary shareholding information itself, France would have no way of checking it with the Liechtenstein tax authority. Distinguishing *ELISA*, the court noted that the Mutual Assistance Directive did not apply because Liechtenstein was not a member of the EU. In *ELISA*, there was a slight chance that France could have obtained the information from Luxembourg, whereas in *Rimbaud*, there was no chance of obtaining the information from Liechtenstein.

The court decided that France was entitled to deny the Liechtenstein company exemption from the immovable property tax.

The importance of this case is that the Court of Justice has stated clearly that transactions between taxpayers in EU Member States and members of the EEA who are not members of the EU take place in a different legal context. The EU case law concerning restrictions on the exercise of the fundamental freedoms cannot be automatically applied.

---

1   C-72/09 *Établissements Rimbaud SA v Directeur général des impôts and Directeur des services fiscaux d'Aix-en-Provence* [2010] STC 2757, ECJ, 28 October 2010.

GROUP LITIGATION

20.67   Once a taxpayer has won a case in the Court of Justice so that a certain tax practice by the tax authority has been held to constitute a restriction on one of the fundamental freedoms, it is usually the case that the taxpayer is in a position to claim a tax refund. Because the practice of the tax authority has been held in contravention of the TFEU and therefore unlawful, many other taxpayers also find themselves in a position to claim refunds, either for income wrongly charged to tax or for deductions wrongly denied. Such claims often result in further litigation and this is often brought on a group basis, where a number of aggrieved taxpayers band together to bring an action against the tax authority, seeking compensation. Neither is the original case settled – all the Court of Justice has done is rule on questions put to it by the national court. The national court then has to use those answers to reach a decision. The verdict of the Court of Justice in the original case is therefore better viewed as a beginning rather than a conclusion.

The rights of taxpayers to repayments of tax held to have been charged unlawfully under EU law was first examined in the *San Georgio* case.[1] In this case, a taxpayer had paid health inspection charges which were found to have been unlawful by the EU. The Court of Justice held that entitlement to the repayment of charges levied by a Member State contrary to the rule of EU law was a consequence of, and an adjunct to, the rights conferred upon individuals by the EU provisions prohibiting charges which had an effect equal to that of customs duties. National conditions as to repayment may not be less favourable than those relating to similar claims regarding national charges – this is the principle of 'equivalence'. Member States are not allowed to make the conditions for obtaining repayment so onerous that, in reality, no one would be likely ever to get their money back – an application of the principle of 'effectiveness'. However, if it was not the taxpayer who paid the tax who was made worse off by the unlawful tax; for instance, if a trader had passed on the unlawful tax burden to his customers in the form of higher prices, then repayment might not be made. The principle of unjust enrichment – obtaining refunds of tax which you had passed on to your customers – would be relevant here.

Group litigation orders (GLOs) are an administrative and cost-saving facility which enables many similar cases to be heard at once. Representative cases are selected from the group for examination in court. Although commonly thought of as tax cases, they are technically claims for restitution or damages, for having complied with tax laws now held to be incompatible with EU law. A claim for damages is possible if there is a sufficiently serious breach of EU law[2] and there is a direct causal link between the unlawful tax and the loss or damage sustained by the taxpayer. A damages claim has been made in one of the UK cases seeking tax refunds, the *Thin Cap GLO*.[3]

Paying tax which was not due is the simplest example of why a claim might be brought, but taxpayers also look beyond the immediate effects of the unlawful provisions. For instance, believing Group Company A to be facing a high effective rate of tax, a group might have directed that losses be surrendered to that company, whereas in the absence of the unlawful tax provision, they might well have been surrendered to Group Company B. So the company whose taxable profits were affected by the unlawful provision (Group Company A) is not necessarily the one which ended up paying more tax – that would have been the company which had to do without the loss surrender (ie Group Company B).[4] In 2011, there were GLOs resulting from Court of Justice verdicts in the direct tax areas of ACT (advance corporation tax, following the decision in *Metallgesellschaft*), loss relief, franked investment income, thin capitalization and CFCs and dividends. All are extremely complex.

1   C-199/82 *Amministrazione delle Finanze dello Stato v SpA San Giorgio*, ECJ, 9 November 1983.
2   C-48/93 *Brasserie du Pêcheur* and *Factortame Ltd and Others* [1996] QB 404, ECJ, 5 March 1996.
3   C-524/04 *Thin Cap Group Litigation v Commissioners of Inland Revenue*, ECJ, 13 March 2007.
4   For an excellent analysis of UK tax group litigation issues, see Whitehead, S 'Group Litigation and the European Court of Justice', *The EC Tax Journal* Vol 8, Issue 3, 2006.

Example: UK litigation following a decision of the CJEU

20.68   Taking as an example, the verdict in *Marks & Spencer* regarding the offset of group losses incurred in a different Member State, a large amount of litigation has ensued in the UK and in other Member States. The original case was remitted back to the UK courts where the case is still not finalized. The UK courts have struggled to apply the test handed down by the Court of Justice – the 'no possibilities' test (ie that cross-border loss relief is only available where there is no possibility of a claim for loss relief in the Member State in which the loss arose). The manner of making the claims and whether the claims were made within the applicable time limits has also been in dispute. At the time of writing, the case was expected to be heard in the Court of Appeal in June 2011 but had not been reported.

Autologic Holdings Plc v HMRC[1] is a test case in the loss relief GLO and examined whether basic claims for group relief wrongly denied should be made via the normal procedures (ie a claim under self-assessment) or whether such claims could be part of the GLO. It was not in dispute that claims for consequential (indirect) repayments of tax should be made via the GLO. The *Autologic* decision is controversial because claims pursued via the GLO are made directly to the High Court, whereas claims made under normal administrative procedures (such as self-assessment) are not. If a claim pursued in the High Court is successful this has several advantages for the taxpayer over success with a normal claim – the rate of interest on overpaid tax may be higher, the costs of the claim may be recoverable from HMRC and longer time limits might be available. Thus the decision in *Autologic* is disadvantageous for taxpayers and highly controversial. In the UK, the normal time limit for companies for making a claim for a repayment of tax is four years from the end of the accounting period.

The *Autologic* case also offers an insight into the type of losses for which claims have been made:

'(1)   A claim for group relief. This comprises loss of profits of the UK profit-making company which should have been relieved by the losses of a non-UK resident company.

(2)   A claim in respect of utilised reliefs. Profit-making companies used other reliefs (eg capital allowances or surplus ACT) they would not have used had basic group relief been available.

(3)   A claim for recovery of surrendered reliefs. Other UK members of the group surrendered their own reliefs to the UK profit-making company.

(4)   A claim for payments. Companies which would have surrendered losses, possibly for payment, had the group relief rules not been confined to UK resident companies seek compensation for the loss of those payments'.[2]

The *Autologic* case report reveals that six groups of companies were selected as test cases, including such well-known names as Heinz, British Telecommunications and BNP Paribas. This GLO involves 95 claimants, representing 70 corporate groups and over 1,000 individual companies.

---

1   *Autologic Holdings Ltd v IR Commrs (Loss Relief Group Litigation)* [2005] BTC 402, UKHL 54.
2   *Autologic*, at para 8.

Chapter 21

VAT, Customs, and Excise Duties

BASICS

21.1   In Chapter 1, we considered several possible models of consumption tax. VAT is the most commonly used broad-based indirect tax on consumption. VAT systems normally allow for export without VAT charge and for VAT to be payable by importers. This ensures that the VAT is due to the country where consumption takes place. This is known as a destination system. Importers must account for VAT on their purchases directly to their own tax authority, rather than paying VAT to the foreign supplier. Usually they can also make a claim for input tax of the equivalent amount, provided they do not make exempt supplies. Thus VAT is neutral as to whether a trader purchases imported goods and services, or makes purchases in the domestic market. VAT is the indirect tax adopted by the EU, and the ethos of the Single Market dictates that the normal ways of dealing with imports and exports are not suitable for intra-EU trade. The Single Market requires that goods can pass freely between Member States without tax being paid at the border.

The EU has given up the goal of implementing a definitive system of all registered traders charging VAT to EU customers regardless of the Member State in which they are based and has been concentrating on making pragmatic improvements to the transitional system. These improvements consist of measures designed to lessen the need for multiple registrations and to simplify VAT administration, particularly for small- and medium-sized enterprises (SMEs). The need to reduce the costs of complying with VAT rules for SMEs, and the systemic and serious nature of missing trader intra-community (MITC) fraud, made possible by the transitional regime, has prompted a wide-ranging review of VAT in the EU.

The other principal indirect taxes encountered in international trade are customs and excise duties. Unlike VAT these are not recoverable by businesses and so represent a real cost. The EU has a customs union, meaning that customs duty is paid according to a single EU system at the point at which goods enter the EU, but not on movements of goods within the EU. Excise duties, on the other hand, are levied separately by each state in the EU and, although there has been some attempt at harmonization, the rates and scope of excise duty vary widely, leading to problems with excessive cross-border shopping and smuggling. Customs and excise duties are particularly important in developing countries due to the relative ease with which they can be collected.

In this chapter we start with a review of how VAT works and the issues which arise in VAT customs duties in international trade. We then go on to examine the VAT and customs duty system as operated within the EU and in particular, the VAT issues which arise from intra-EU trade. Most countries in the world operate a system of VAT as a major consumption tax, although in developing countries, customs duties are sometimes of greater importance. The US alone amongst the member countries of the OECD does not have a federal (national) system of VAT, as most of the individual states collect their tax revenues via indirect taxes such as sales taxes and other forms of consumption tax some of which resemble VAT. A federal VAT would thus duplicate the individual state tax systems. Note that many commentators believe that the US ought to have a federal consumption tax, and current proposals under the new Trump administration include a border adjustment that would fill this gap.

VAT is an important factor in planning to minimize taxes on international trade although this is often a matter of optimizing the cash flow, as VAT is merely collected by most businesses on behalf of the government rather than being borne by the business. Customs duties though, are levied on the import of goods and are a real cost to the importing firm in that they are not refundable. VAT is not usually levied on exports but is usually payable to the taxpayer's home country on imports. Unlike direct taxes such as corporation tax and income tax, VAT systems are generally self-contained in that a country will only charge VAT to its own residents rather than to anyone buying goods or services within its territory.

HOW VALUE ADDED TAX WORKS

21.2   Value added tax (VAT) is an indirect consumption tax. This means that the tax is paid as a result of the purchase of goods or services rather than as a result of earning income. A business registered for VAT will charge VAT to its customers. It will pay this VAT to the tax authority after deducting the VAT it has been charged by its suppliers. There are several types of VAT system: the simplest systems are subtraction VAT systems and addition VAT systems, where VAT is computed by reference to the taxpayer's periodic accounts. For instance, a subtraction VAT will calculate VAT due by applying the VAT rate to sales minus purchases. Addition methods of VAT take the sum of an enterprise's profits, wage bill, depreciation, interest and rent paid, and apply the VAT rate to the total. Under addition methods, VAT is effectively charged on the factors of production employed by a business. However, most countries use the 'credit-invoice' method of VAT. Under this method, VAT is charged on each individual sales invoice. To obtain a credit for VAT on purchases which is set against VAT collected from customers, the firm must be able to produce a valid purchase invoice evidencing the VAT paid.

All VAT systems have categories of sales that are exempt from VAT. This should not be confused with 'zero-rating' which applies widely in the UK, but which is technically a VAT charge at a rate of 0 per cent. Exemptions normally apply to categories of goods and services which are socially desirable and not necessarily run to make a profit, such as health care and education. Some systems also exempt financial services and some categories of transactions in land, on the grounds that it is difficult to compute value added in transactions of this nature. The problem with exemptions is that where a firm makes sales of exempt items, no VAT may be reclaimed (credited) on the associated purchases. Hence, where VAT is charged on imports of goods and services made in order to make sales of exempt items, that import VAT will not be reclaimable.

To avoid the need for very small businesses having to comply with the VAT system, each country will set a turnover threshold which determines whether a firm must register for VAT and hence charge VAT on sales. Turnover thresholds vary widely around the world. Once registered, a firm must charge VAT on sales and may reclaim VAT suffered on purchases.

The credit-invoice method of operating a value added tax

21.3   There are several methods of operating a VAT. Some, such as the 'subtraction' and 'addition' methods compute the tax due from a business according to global figures, often taken from the profit and loss account. These are harder for a tax authority to enforce, although Japan uses a subtraction method. They are appropriate where the standard of bookkeeping in a country is poor, or where a government is keen to keep the costs to businesses of complying with the VAT system to the bare minimum. The credit invoice method, unlike the subtraction or addition methods, requires registered businesses to keep records of every transaction on which they either charge VAT, or are charged VAT by their suppliers. This system is self-auditing to an extent, because no credit can be claimed for VAT paid unless the supplier gives the purchaser business a proper invoice. Thus customers demand proper invoices, making it much harder for sellers to either sell without charging VAT, or appearing to charge VAT but not paying it over to the tax authority. The basic credit-invoice system of VAT may be illustrated as follows: assume that Business 1 makes a sale to Business 2 on which VAT is chargeable at 10 per cent. Both Business 1 and Business 2 are VAT registered.

Example 21.1

Business 1

Net selling price	200
+ VAT	20
Gross selling price	220

On its VAT return, Business 1 must declare VAT charged of 20 and pay this over to the tax authority

Business 2

Gross cost	220
– VAT refund	(20)
+ required profit	100
Net selling price	300
+ VAT	30
Gross selling price	330

On its VAT return, Business 2 must declare VAT charged of 30 and may reclaim VAT paid of 20, making a net payment to the tax authority of 10.

If the supplies which Business 2 makes are exempt from VAT, then the position is:

Business 1

Net selling price	200
+ VAT	20
Gross selling price	220

On its VAT return, Business 1 must declare VAT charged of 20 and pay this over to the tax authority

Business 2

Gross cost	220
– VAT refund	–
+ required profit	100
Net selling price	320
+ VAT	–
Gross selling price	320

On its VAT return, Business 2 makes no entries with respect to these transactions. Thus it suffers the 20 VAT charged to it by Business 1 as an additional cost.

Notice that VAT is collected at each stage in the supply chain, not merely when there is a sale to the final consumer. This is known as the 'staged collection' process (or sometimes referred to as the 'fractionated nature' of VAT). In the first example, the burden of the VAT falls only on the final consumer. The second example, involving exempt supplies, illustrates the imperfect nature of most VAT systems. Ideally VAT should flow through the business, but exemptions interfere with this.

VAT is commonly charged on classes of transactions which include, but are not limited to, sales for consideration. VAT can also be charged on gifts and in instances where the business takes goods for its own use (self-supply). For this reason, when dealing with VAT it is usual to refer to 'supplies' rather than 'sales'. The associated VAT is known as 'output VAT'. Purchases are usually referred to as 'inputs' and the associated VAT is known as 'input VAT'.

Partial exemption

21.4 Many businesses make a mixture of supplies, on some of which VAT is chargeable ('taxable') and some which are exempt from VAT. Such businesses are known as 'partially exempt'. To determine whether input VAT may be reclaimed, inputs must be matched with related outputs (supplies). Some input VAT may not relate directly to any particular supply (eg VAT on overheads[1]). In the UK, the usual way this is dealt with is for partial reclaim to be allowed: the proportion of VAT on overheads which can be reclaimed is determined by the proportion of taxable supplies made, compared to total supplies.[2] Thus a business in which 60 per cent of supplies made are taxable may normally reclaim 60 per cent of VAT suffered on overheads.

---

1 Other categories of input on which partial reclaim of VAT may be appropriate are certain land transactions and expenditure on computer systems. In the UK, special anti-avoidance rules apply to prevent the manipulation of the percentage of recoverable VAT on these large transactions.
2 But note that alternative calculations are possible, for instance, based on numbers of transactions of various types.

CROSS-BORDER TRADE AND VALUE ADDED TAX

21.5 The basic issue in international VAT is to decide the place of taxation – which country is permitted to tax a transaction? 'Place of taxation' rules are used to determine this. Broadly, the place of taxation should be the same as the place of consumption: probably the customer's country. Determining the place of taxation is more difficult when the customer is a VAT-registered business because that business might not be the final consumer. Rather, the destination of the goods is the place of business use of them. Different rules tend to be applied to business-to-business (B2B) transactions and business-to-consumer (B2C) transactions.

There are effectively two alternative ways of treating international supplies for VAT:

- *Destination system*: the exporting supplier charges no VAT but VAT is charged to the customer on the import by the tax authority in the country in which the customer is located.

- *Origin system*: VAT is charged by the exporting supplier in the country where the supplier is based.

There is no real international consensus on which method should be used, so some countries use one method and some another (some countries use different methods for different kinds of supply) although destination systems are the most common and considered to align the place of taxation with the place of consumption better than the origin system. There are also countries (including the US and many tax havens) who do not charge VAT at all. This variety of treatment means that cross-border transactions might suffer a double charge to VAT (on export and on import) or they might suffer no VAT at all. This is considered in Figure 21.1. The ability to rebate VAT on export is an important factor in a country's international competitiveness. GATT (see below) only permits the rebate of indirect taxes on export if these can be properly quantified. This was a key factor behind the adoption of the Goods and Services Tax (GST, effectively a VAT) in Australia in place of the previous wholesale sales tax.

Customer's country uses: Supplier's Country uses	Origin system	Destination system	No VAT
Origin system	Single charge	Double charge	Single charge
Destination system	No charge	Single charge	No charge
No VAT	No charge	Single charge	No charge

Figure 21.1: Effect of different treatments of cross-border transactions

An international framework: the OECD's Guidelines

21.6   The OECD has been active in developing guidelines for dealing with the cross-border aspects of VAT since the late 1990s, starting with its *Consumption Tax Guidance* series of reports in 2003. There has been a particular focus on trade in services and intangibles, which are harder to deal with for VAT purposes than transactions involving goods. The OECD's *International VAT/GST Guidelines* were finally issued in 2014 with the aim of promoting international trade via reducing uncertainty in the matter of VAT treatment of cross-border transactions. A further aim is to ensure that transactions are not either taxed twice, or not taxed at all, for VAT purposes. The *Guidelines* are purely advisory in nature and are expected to continue to be developed and added to, in line with changes in the conduct of international trade. Although the focus of the guidelines is on cross-border supplies of services and intangibles they deal with cross-border trade generally.

Destination system

21.7   Theoretically, VAT should use the destination system; VAT is supposed to be a tax on consumption, and so ideally it should be charged by the country in which the consumption takes place (ie in the country where the consumer is resident). Using the destination system in cross-border trade means that the supplier does not charge VAT. Instead, the VAT is collected directly by the consumer's tax authority from purchasers. Where the purchasers are VAT registered, this is relatively easy, but more difficulty if the purchasers are not VAT-registered, because it is impractical to try to keep track of many small purchases by many individuals. Even where the purchasers are VAT-registered, the system is imperfect because the general principle of VAT, that it is an indirect tax, paid as part of the purchase price, is compromised if VAT is collected directly by the government from the purchaser.

Ideally, foreign suppliers would charge VAT as part of the purchase price and then transfer the VAT collected to the government of the purchaser's country. This is known as using the origin system as a proxy for the destination system. The OECD unreservedly advocates the destination principle in the International VAT/GST Guidelines (the OECD Guidelines).

Why the origin system is little used

21.8   A pure origin system removes the enforcement problems inherent in the destination system. If the supplier firm is charging VAT on exports under its domestic law (ie in our example above, under the law of the Far Eastern country rather than UK law), then the supplier country's tax authority has the jurisdiction it needs to enforce collection of the VAT by the supplier. A major point in favour of the origin system is that it taxes the value created within the country's borders. However, the overarching principle of VAT is that it is a tax on consumption, rather than purely on value-added, despite the name. In its favour, the origin system eliminates a major weakness of the destination system of VAT which is the break in the VAT chain resulting from cross-border supplies being made VAT free. The destination system, whilst theoretically pure, permits large-scale fraud within the EU due to the non-imposition of VAT on exports and the EU's system of cashless accounting for import VAT. However, if a country adopts a pure origin VAT system it may put its business at a competitive disadvantage, in two ways:

- *Imports*: It will be cheaper for its citizens to buy imports from countries which rebate VAT on exports or which have lower or no VAT, rather than to buy home-produced goods or services.

- *Exports*: If a country's businesses have to charge VAT on exports then they will be at a disadvantage if they are trying to sell to customers in a country with lower or no VAT, or which will not give credit for the foreign VAT.

This competition issue is very serious for governments. Under an origin system, if its residents buy imports instead of home-produced products, the government will not collect any VAT, but more importantly that country's businesses will have less profits to tax, and will provide less employment. In extreme situations, businesses may even relocate to another country to avoid high rates of VAT, taking their profits, investment and employment with them. This is not just a theoretical problem; in 2001 a large part of the UK's online betting industry moved offshore to Gibraltar in order to avoid tax (betting duty rather than VAT, but the issues are similar). In response the UK government drastically reduced the tax on betting in order to persuade the industry to remain in the UK, but this is not really an option with VAT, as the revenues raised by VAT account for such a large proportion of total tax revenues.

Despite these drawbacks, the New Zealand Goods and Services Tax (GST) might be classified as an origin system. This is because VAT is imposed according to the residence of the supplier. Supplies of goods by non-residents are considered to take place in New Zealand if the goods are in New Zealand at the time of supply. Supplies of services by non-residents are deemed to be taxable in New Zealand if the services are rendered in New Zealand. New Zealand protects itself against buyers preferring imports to home supplies by imposing its VAT on imports of goods and services.

The Chinese system

21.9 China actively uses its VAT system to influence the activity of Chinese firms with respect to exports. Since 2006, exports of certain highly polluting products not only have to carry VAT as if they were domestic sales, but exporters are prevented from reclaiming input VAT. China also attempts to discourage the export of high volume, low value added items such as clothes and shoes by restricting the amount of input VAT which may be reclaimed by exporters. On the other hand, China rewards exporters of high technology products by permitting both the zero rating of export sales and the full reclaim of input VAT.

Exports of goods in a destination system – 'place of supply'?

21.10 If a destination system is used, then rules are needed to govern when a sale is a domestic sale (on which VAT must be charged) and when it is not a domestic sale. This is because the VAT should be paid to the government of the consumer (the customer), not the government of the supplier. In other words, it is necessary to determine the territory in which the supply is made. If a taxpayer who is resident in Country A sells goods to a customer in Country B and at the time the sale is made, those goods are located in Country C, then Country C might consider that the sale is made within its territory. Thus VAT would have to be charged under Country C rules and accounted for to the tax authority in Country C. country where the supplier is resident, the country where the services are carried out, or perhaps the country These kinds of rules are known as 'place of supply' rules. The concept of the 'place of supply' determines where a supply is made for VAT purposes, and therefore determines which country is allowed to charge VAT on the supply. The usual rules are:

- If the goods are to be transported from the supplier's country to the customer's country, then if the customer is in a different country, the place of supply will be the supplier's country: where the transport begins. However, VAT will not normally be payable on the supply in the supplier's country because most countries zero rate supplies which are exports. The zero rating enables the supplier to reclaim the input tax on purchases associated with the export sale. Most countries use a procedure so that the VAT on the export sale must be accounted for by the purchaser, to the purchaser's government. In this way, the place of supply can differ from the place of taxation.

- Goods that do not leave the supplier's country: the place of taxation is the supplier's country, regardless of the location of the customer.

- Goods which are not in the supplier's country at the date of sale: the place of supply is not the supplier's country, but the location of the goods at the time of sale.

Although the rules themselves may be fairly simple to understand, the administrative consequences for the firm which is resident in Country A of having to register in Country C are considerable and expensive. Staff in the selling company will have to familiarize themselves with the VAT system in Country C, register for VAT there and make VAT returns there, in addition to continuing to be registered for VAT in Country A. Most countries only require non-resident suppliers to register for VAT in their country if they are making supplies there through the VAT equivalent of a PE. Some countries (eg Canada and the UK) require non-residents who organize concerts or sporting events or similar within their territory to account for VAT on the admission fees. Thus if an entertainment promoter who is resident in the US arranges for, say, Rihanna, to appear at Wembley Arena then the US promoter would be liable to charge VAT on the ticket price and pass this on to HMRC. Other countries such as South Africa require non-residents who are involved in installing equipment they have supplied in that country to register for VAT, and charge VAT on the contract price, even though the installation contract might not constitute a PE for corporation tax purposes

Imports of goods in a destination system – the 'reverse charge' system

21.11   Under the destination system, instead of paying VAT on imported goods and services to the foreign supplier as part of the purchase price, the customer pays the VAT directly to his/her own tax authority. The rate of VAT and all applicable VAT rules are those of the customer's country, not the supplier's. On the VAT return, the import VAT is treated as if it were VAT on outputs. In effect, the importing firm must charge itself VAT, leading to this procedure being commonly known as the 'reverse charge'. Thus, there are two reasons why a firm might owe VAT to its government:

- The firm has made taxable sales to in-country customers and has collected VAT on those sales from the customers. It must pay over this VAT to its government.

- The firm has made purchases from a foreign supplier. The supplier has not charged VAT. VAT is still due on these purchases but must be paid directly by the purchaser to the purchaser's own government.

If the import VAT relates to inputs used by the firm to make taxable supplies, this import VAT may be reclaimed on the next VAT return. If this is the case, there is no net payment by the importer – the same amount of VAT is treated as both input VAT and output VAT. However, a firm which makes exempt or partially exempt supplies may not be able to reclaim the import VAT in full.

Example 21.2 Reverse charge mechanism

A UK VAT-registered company, Black Ltd, buys goods for £20,000 from Noir Pty Ltd, an Australian company, during its VAT return period. Black Ltd is a clothing retailer, making fully taxable supplies. The term 'reverse charge' simply means that Black Ltd must charge itself VAT on the import by recording it along with other outputs. The rate of VAT is 20 per cent.

Black Ltd's VAT return	ex VAT	VAT 20%
	£	£
Supplies made	100,000	20,000
Imports from Noir SA – treated as an output	20,000	4,000
Total outputs	120,000	24,000
UK inputs (purchases)	30,000	6,000
Input: goods purchased from Noir SA – treated as supplied to self	20,000	4,000
Total creditable inputs	50,000	10,000
Net VAT due (output VAT minus input VAT)		14,000

Now assume that Black Ltd has expanded its operations to include the provision of loan finance (assumed to be VAT exempt) and, of the £20,000 goods imported from Noir Pty Ltd, £3,000 is attributable to new uniforms for its financial services staff. Financial services are, broadly, exempt from VAT. Thus the input VAT attributable to the clothes purchased for the financial services staff will not be creditable.

Black Ltd's VAT return	ex VAT	VAT
	£	£
Taxable supplies made (excluding the new supplies of financial services)	100,000	20,000
Imports from Noir Pty Ltd – treated as an output	20,000	4,000
Total outputs	120,000	24,000
UK inputs (purchases)	30,000	6,000
Input: goods purchased from Noir Pty Ltd – treated as supplied to self – portion attributable to clothing retailer trade only	17,000	3,400
Total creditable inputs	47,000	9,400
Net VAT due (output VAT minus input VAT)		14,600

Whilst output VAT is due on the full £3,000 paid to the foreign supplier for clothes for the financial services staff, it is not creditable as input tax as it is attributable to exempt supplies. Whether the business buys the uniforms from a UK supplier or a foreign supplier, it will still have to pay VAT on them that will not be recoverable.

One effect of the reverse charge mechanism on imports of goods and services is that a business which makes wholly exempt supplies may nevertheless find that the output VAT for which it has to account on imports exceeds the turnover threshold for VAT registration. In these circumstances the business may have to register for VAT despite making no taxable supplies to customers. Sometimes this is avoided by having the importing done via an agent, who will account for the output (import) VAT on his own VAT return. Other shortcut measures where the importer is not the end consumer of the goods include arranging for the VAT on import to be accounted for by the ultimate customer, provided he is VAT registered.

Imports of goods by non-value added tax-registered customers

21.12   In the UK, import VAT on sales to non-VAT registered customers is collected on behalf of HMRC in the UK by the delivery company at the time of delivery. Thus the account system for regular importers and the collection of VAT from non-registered customers by the delivery companies avoids having to hold up vast quantities of goods at the port of entry until the import VAT is paid. There are two circumstances where the treatment of imports of goods by non-registered persons might differ from this. First, some countries operate a 'low value parcel' exemption from VAT and other import duties. Under these rules, a country would set a monetary limit, below which no import VAT or duties need be paid. The foreign supplier would need to indicate on the parcel the value of the contents. Second, some countries insist that foreign suppliers with a large non-registered customer base must register for VAT in the customer country, and charge the customer country's VAT. These are known as 'distance selling' rules, and would commonly apply to foreign firms which sell consumer goods (not services) via the Internet, or via printed catalogues to non-VAT-registered customers. Again, a monetary limit for sales value would be set, but this time the limit is applied to the annual aggregate value of sales made in the country concerned. Many EU Member States operate such a limit and set it at €100,000.

Temporary imports

21.13   There are various reliefs for VAT-registered businesses from the charge to VAT (and other import taxes) on imports such as:

● *Temporary importations*: where it is intended that goods will be re-exported in a certain time period, up to a maximum of two years, no VAT or duty is payable at the time of importation although security may be required. The types of goods qualifying for this relief can include means of transport, travellers' personal effects, and professional equipment such as broadcasting equipment, medical equipment, mobile inspection units owned by foreign persons.

● *Inward processing relief*: where goods are imported, processed and then re-exported. Processing is widely defined and can encompass anything from simple repackaging to complex manufacturing processes.

Postponement of import value added tax on goods

21.14 VAT planning for imports usually revolves around achieving the post-ponement of payment of import VAT for as long as possible. If payment has to be made at the port, this creates an extra layer of administration and has the potential for long delays in the delivery of goods. In some countries, goods are not permitted to proceed beyond the port until the VAT and other import duties have been paid. However, in many countries it is possible to make arrange-ments for the VAT and import duties to be paid at a later date. In the UK, trad-ers can delay payment of import VAT and duties for about 30 days provided they put in place arrangements to pay the taxes by direct debit, and provide a suitable bank guarantee.[1] In some parts of the world, particularly those devel-oping countries which rely heavily on border taxes and where the customs staff are poorly paid, knowledge of local practices of taking bribes is needed.

Apart from these general issues, postponement from import VAT is often possible in two main instances:

● *When goods are imported into free zones*: goods may be imported into a free zone and processed there. Import VAT only becomes payable when the goods leave the free zone.

● *Fiscal warehousing*: goods are subject to a fiscal warehousing regime: this can be either a physical 'customs warehouse' or in some instances fiscal warehousing is achieved through bookkeeping measures. Process-ing might not be allowed. This is commonly used for a wide range of goods besides the traditional use for postponement of excise duty on alcohol and tobacco products. Import VAT and other duties become pay-able when the goods leave the warehouse or the warehousing system.

---

1 Known as the 'deferment approval system' and detailed in UK VAT Notice 101 'Deferring duty, VAT and other charges'. The import VAT and other charges are deducted from the importer by direct debit on the 15th of the month following import. The business must give an appropriate bank guarantee.

CROSS-BORDER SUPPLIES OF GOODS WITHIN THE EU

21.15 So far in this chapter we have considered VAT concepts in general terms. VAT in the EU is of huge importance because the EU aims to oper-ate as a single trading bloc with minimal barriers to trade, so as to be able to compete better with the world's biggest economies such as the US and Brazil. The US has an enormous internal market for its goods and services because it is a country with a big population. A US corporation has a very large inter-nal market into which it can sell without needing to worry about import and export taxes which reduce profits and increase the administrative burden. One of the principal aims of the EU is to operate as a single market so that goods and services can be freely traded anywhere in the EU with no greater tax or administrative burden to the supplier than if the customer were resident in the supplier's own country. In this way, the internal market for EU suppliers is effectively expanded to be the whole of the EU. The EU VAT system tries to facilitate the EU Single Market by:

●   having a common system of VAT, rather than many different VAT systems – thus traders need only know one set of rules – note that in practice there are some variations and each Member State is allowed, within limits, to decide its own rates of VAT; and

●   allowing imports and exports within the EU to take place without payment at the border of VAT.

In addition to the VAT rules aimed at encouraging the Single Market, no customs duties are charged on sales of goods from one EU Member State to another.

VAT was adopted by the EU as the common system of indirect tax in 1967 and since that date its importance has continually increased. VAT now accounts for around 18 per cent of national tax and social security revenues within the EU.[1]

---

1   Taxation Trends in the European Union (2014) Table 7: Indirect Taxes as % of Total Taxation.

21.16   At first sight the issues surrounding VAT in the EU (or any other customs union – the CIS[1] has experimented with similar systems) may be seen to be the same as the general cross-border issues discussed above, but magnified due to the greater volume of trade between the member countries. However, as noted above, a principal objective of the EU is establishment of the Single Market. This means that the EU aims to adopt common policies on product regulation and freedom of movement of all the factors of production (goods, services, capital and labour). The development of the Single Market raises some additional issues:

●   There are not supposed to be any internal border controls, so the 'stop and charge VAT at the port of entry' method normally used to charge VAT on imported goods in a destination system is not possible.

●   Member States will enforce each other's VAT laws, because it is seen as being an EU-level tax rather than a national tax. This means that the jurisdiction problems that are at the heart of the international VAT system discussed above are not relevant. The usual rule that one country will not assist in the enforcement of another country's tax system is waived. This is the theory – how well it works in practice is debatable.

●   There is an active desire to promote inter-state trade and free movement of labour and capital within the EU that is not really present in the full international scene. This will be discussed further below.

A note on terminology: as the EU is supposed to be a single trading bloc, supplies within it are not referred to as 'imports' or 'exports'. Instead supplies from one EU country (a 'Member State') to another are called 'intra-Community' supplies. The term 'dispatches' is used for supplies to customers in fellow EU Member States and 'acquisitions' for purchases from EU Member States.

---

1   The Commonwealth of Independent States, whose customs union, EurAsEc consists broadly, of Russia and some of the former Soviet bloc countries.

Intra-Community supplies of goods: the 'transitional' regime

21.17   In principle, the Commission has always supported the origin system, used as a proxy for the destination system; under the origin system, wherever a business sells in the EU, it would just charge its own national VAT. At a later date, the VAT collected would be paid over to the government of the customer's country, in line with the destination principle. This would make trade with other Member States much easier, because suppliers would charge all their customers VAT, according to the VAT system in the supplier's country. It would also fulfil the Commission's desire to facilitate inter-state trade. However, it has proved impossible to implement an origin system and in 2012, the Commission declared that it was abandoning the goal of implementing the 'definitive regime' of VAT – one where all registered businesses charge VAT to all their customers, and the resulting VAT is then paid over to the government of the consumer's country. The rates of VAT charged by the various Member States are too different and no satisfactory method has been worked out for getting the VAT charged to customers in other member States to the customers' governments. For these reasons, the EU for many years has used a version of the destination system known as the 'transitional regime'. It appears unlikely that the origin system can ever be adopted and that the transitional regime, with amendments, will become permanent.

Current EU regime

21.18   Under the current regime, most intra-Community supplies of supplies are taxed under the destination system, but the origin system is used in some cases, depending on the VAT status of customer and the type of supply. The terms B2B and B2C are used as shorthand for 'business to business' (transactions between two VAT-registered businesses) and 'business to consumer' (supplies by a VAT-registered business to a non-VAT registered business or individual). There are two sets of rules within the EU: one for transactions involving a party outside the EU and another for transactions where both parties are located in the EU, in different Member States. The rules where the customer is outside the EU are as outlined for VAT destinations systems generally. The specific rules on intra-Community supplies of goods are:

●   B2B: these are known as 'intra-Community'. Where the goods are transported to a customer in a different Member State the customer is responsible for accounting for the VAT under the 'reverse charge' procedure. Thus the destination principle is used. There is an exception: where the customer is present in the supplier's country and makes the purchases whilst there, eg foreign hotel bills. Special rules apply to goods which are the subject of installation or assembly operations.

- B2C: the supplier must charge VAT at the rate in the supplier's country. In other words, for this limited class of transactions, the origin principle is used. The main exception to this rule is where the customer visits the supplier's country personally, makes the purchase there and then transports the goods back home personally, eg if a French person goes on a shopping trip to Dublin. There are special rules for particular means of transport (eg cars, planes and boats).

As noted earlier, any destination system needs to have rules to determine the place of supply of goods and services. These are needed to identify the country which has the right to tax any particular supply. In the EU, the supply of goods which are delivered to the customer is deemed to take place at the place where the goods are located when the transport begins.

Multiple registration problem

21.19   It frequently happens that a business registered for VAT in one EU country nevertheless finds itself making supplies in excess of the VAT registration threshold in another country. For instance, in complex supply chain scenarios, the invoicing chain may not mirror the physical journey of the goods with the result that a firm is deemed to be supplying goods in a Member State which is not its home state. This then leads to a requirement to register for VAT in that other country, leading to two VAT returns, two separate sets of VAT rules to understand and so on. This aspect of the present regime is a severe hindrance to the operation of the EU as a single market because it inhibits cross-border trade within the EU particularly for small- and medium-sized businesses.

Specifically, multiple country registrations arise where:

- There is a delivery of goods from a supplier in one country to an end customer in another, but the invoicing chain involves an intermediary in a third country. The intermediary is deemed to make the supply in the country in which the goods are first allocated to the customer, usually in the customer's country.

- A firm makes sales to non-business customers in another country and those sales are caught by the 'distance selling rules'. The limit on the value of goods sold under these rules into another EU country must be set either at €35k or €100k (or its local equivalent, for instance, the UK limit is £70k). Rather than collecting VAT from individual customers, the UK government requires the overseas supplier to register for VAT in the UK if supplies to non-registered customers in the UK exceed £70k per annum. In this way HMRC only need to deal with one company rather than potentially thousands of individuals.

The EU has attempted to put a 'patch' on the first problem by allowing the customer to account for the VAT on the goods, effectively operating the reverse charge procedure. This is the idea behind the First Simplification Directive[1] but it is an imperfect solution in that it does not cover more complex supply chains.

---

1 Directive 92/111/EEC of December 1992.

VAT ON CROSS-BORDER SUPPLIES OF SERVICES

21.20 Under a destination system, it is much harder to identify and tax imports of services than it is to identify and tax imports of goods. Services cannot be stopped at the port until VAT is paid. Services are commonly provided electronically without the supplier ever visiting the customer's country. To operate the destination system of VAT on services, either the importing customer needs to pay the VAT directly to the customer's government (under the reverse-charge mechanism) or there needs to be a system whereby the supplier charges VAT to the foreign customer, and then that VAT is handed over to the customer's government. In recent years, VAT on cross-border services has become controversial due to the proliferation of services available for download over the Internet. As there are different rules governing VAT on cross-border supplies of goods and cross-border supplies of services, we need to define what we mean by 'services'. The EU definition is that anything which is not 'goods' is, by default, services.[1] The detailed guidance in the OECD's *VAT/GST Guidelines* concentrates on cross-border services and these Guidelines are considered now. Following this, we proceed to consider the rules adopted by the EU for VAT on cross-border services. The OECD *Guidelines* broadly mirror the system already in place within the EU.

---

1 OECD (2014) 'Guidelines on Place of Taxation for Business-to-Consumer Supplies of Services ad Intangibles/Provisions on Supporting the Guidelines in Practice' Discussion Draft, 18 December 2014.

OECD's VAT Guidelines

21.21 The OECD's Guidelines on International VAT/GST were published on 12 April 2017[1] in conjunction with the fourth meeting of the OECD Global Forum on VAT attended by some 300 delegates including non-OECD countries. The OECD's Guidelines closely follow the systems already adopted by the EU. The aim of the Guidelines is to minimize inconsistencies in the application of VAT in a cross-border context, and the overriding principle is that VAT revenues from these types of supplies should accrue to the country where consumption takes place – usually the country of the end-consumer. The Guidelines include recommendations in relation to cross-border sales of digital products, addressing the challenges identified in BEPS Action 1. Theoretically, the country where the end-consumer is resident might not be the same as the country where the services or intangibles are used. For instance, an e-book might be downloaded by a consumer to be read on a foreign holiday. The EU has some detailed rules in these circumstances, but the OECD Guidelines consider that it would be too difficult for a business to track the place where its services were actually consumed.

The Guidelines have been developed in a staged process with regular interim drafts released for public consultation. Chapter 1 describes the core features of VAT and Chapter 2 deals the fundamental principles in the context of international trade, specifically the need for neutrality. Chapters 3 and 4 deal with the supply of services and intangibles and mechanisms for supporting the Guidelines respectively.

1 OECD Guidelines on International VAT/GST. Available at: www.keepeek.com/Digital-Asset-Management/oecd/taxation/international-vat-gst-guidelines_9789264271401-en#. WR6_rcaZMUE#page5.

B2B supplies of services and intangibles – OECD's main rule

21.22   This rule is the centrepiece of Chapter 3 of the *Guidelines* which endorses the destination principle, ie supplies should be charged to VAT in the country of the customer's location: where it has its permanent business presence. Customer location is used as a proxy for the place of business use. Where a customer has multiple establishments (branches) in different countries, the country of taxation is the country where the establishment using the service or intangible is located. This is similar to the EU's 'fixed establishment' rules. The problem is that the establishment paying for the services might not be the same as the establishment actually using the services, eg where the head office of a company in Country A buys services from a foreign supplier in Country B, and these services are used by other establishments of the purchasing company in Countries C and D. Can Countries C and D charge VAT in these circumstances? To help answer this question, the OECD identified the approaches to this problem in current use around the world. They are:

●   *The direct use approach*: find the establishment actually using the services or intangibles. This approach can be used where it is obvious to all the countries involved which is the country where use occurs.

●   *The direct delivery approach*: to which establishment are the services or intangibles delivered? This approach is of most use in the case of services delivered face-to-face, such as training or catering, where the place of use is obviously the same as the place of delivery.

●   *The recharge method*: find the establishment(s) which actually use the services or intangibles in question by looking at the company's internal recharge arrangements. This method is useful where, say, the head office pays for the services or intangibles, but they are for the benefit of all or parts of the company and recharged to the company's foreign establishments in accordance with their use. This approach acknowledges that it is common for many services to be centrally purchased as a matter of business efficiency and to achieve economies of scale. The OECD also recognizes that in some cases it might not be possible to apportion the cost of services around the different parts of the company according to actual usage. With some services, such as legal services which benefit the company as a whole, cost allocation or apportionment methods involving estimation can be used. However, the allocation keys should be fair and reasonable.

The OECD envisages that in some cases, customer location might not be the best proxy for the place of business use. Different proxies are approved if the main rule (customer location) leads to an inappropriate result. For instance, location of immovable property could be used to determine the country that can charge VAT on services related to that property.

Global purchasing agreements for services and intangibles within multinational groups of companies

21.23   In its International VAT/GST Guidelines,[1] the OECD presents a number of examples of global purchasing structures and analysis of the VAT consequences. One of these is given below.

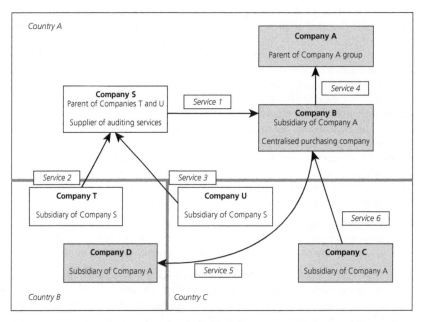

Figure 21.2: OECD Diagram (reproduced with the kind permission of the OECD)

Company B, the group's centralized purchasing company, purchases from Company S a global auditing service to cover the group companies resident in Countries A, B&C. However, Company S, for legal and operational reasons, is unable to supply the required services directly in Countries B&C. Therefore, it subcontracts the Country B work to its subsidiary resident in Country B, Company T, and also its Country C work to its subsidiary resident in Country C, Company U. There are six business agreements (ie contracts) to consider in this example, between:

•   B&S: the centralized purchasing agreement – the place of taxation will be Country A because that is the location of Company B, the customer.

- T&S: for the supply of auditing services by T in Country B to S – the place of taxation will be Country A because that is the location of Company S, the customer.

- U&S: for the supply of auditing services by U in Country C to S – the place of taxation will be Country A because that is the location of Company S, the customer.

- B&A: B recharges part of the price of the centralized purchasing agreement to A – the place of taxation will be Country A: a domestic supply.

- B&C: B recharges part of the price of the centralized purchasing agreement to C – the place of taxation will be Country B, because Company D is the customer for this transaction and is located in Country B.

- B&D: B recharges part of the price of the centralized purchasing agreement to D – the place of taxation will be Country C, because Company D is the customer for this transaction and is located in Country C.

All the VAT due on the centralized purchasing agreement thus accrues to Country A. This may seem puzzling, when the services supplied to B by S are actually being provided in Countries B&C as well as Country A. The OECD justifies this treatment on the grounds that all the services will eventually be subject to VAT in the countries where they are provided: eg the VAT on the audit in Country B will accrue to the government of Country B via the contract between A&D. There is no double taxation: although it might appear that there are two layers of VAT present, it must be remembered that Company B will be able to claim the VAT charged to it by Company S under the central purchasing agreement as input VAT because this is attributable to its supplies to A, C&D. Similarly, Company S will claim the VAT on its purchases from T&U (in these cases, payable under the reverse charge procedure on Country A) as input tax, because this is attributable to its supply to Company B.

---

1   The diagram is presented in the OECD (2015) *International VAT/GST Guidelines*, Annexe 1, Example 3.

B2C supplies of services and intangibles – OECD proposed guidelines

21.24   Most services imported by non-registered persons – private customers rather than businesses – are ones which are delivered electronically, such as downloads of music and software. There is no problem if such services are supplied to VAT-registered businesses: the business simply has to report the purchase of the service on its next VAT return and account for the import VAT on them. The position is much more complicated when the customer is not VAT registered. How does a government know what private individuals are buying from non-resident suppliers of electronically delivered services? Would your government know what you had downloaded from iTunes this week?

Broadly, the 2014 draft guidelines echo the system which has been in place within the EU since 2003 for B2C supplies by non-EU suppliers to EU customers (see the next section). As with B2B supplies, the guidelines attempt to

743

identify workable proxies for the place of consumption, and ensure that the VAT due ends up with the country of consumption. These differ according to the type of services provided:

- *On the spot services*: if a rock star resident in Country A but appearing in concert in Country B insists on flying out a particular hairdresser who is normally resident in Country C to do his hair for the forthcoming concert, then the place of performance, and the country which is entitled to collect and retain the VAT on the services, is Country C. The proxy for place of consumption in this case is the place of performance of the services. This will apply where the services are consumed 'on the spot' at the place in which they are performed and where the supplier and consumer are physically present at the same time. Place of performance is not recommended as a good proxy for place of consumption where services are provided remotely.

- *All other services*: the country permitted to charge and retain the VAT on the services is the country in which the customer is usually resident. This will cover the vast majority of cross-border services. It will include online supplies of digital content (eg films, music, etc), software, telecoms and broadcasting services. Also covered are other types of services if they are provided from the supplier's country rather than the customer's country: eg consultancy, accountancy, legal services, financial services, long-term equipment leasing, and insurance. The overriding Guideline is Guideline 3.1: 'for consumption tax purposes internationally traded services and intangibles should be taxed according to the rules of the jurisdiction of consumption'.

The relative lack of reliance on place of performance of the services as an indicator of which country has the right to charge VAT presents an interesting contrast with the heavy reliance on place of performance in determining which country can levy direct taxation on profits from cross-border services.

Determining the customer's country of residence for the 'all other services' category presents some practical difficulties given that the supplier will probably have no ongoing relationship with the customer. To ascertain the customer's country of residence, it is recommended that, normally, suppliers simply rely on the address information supplied by the customers at the time of ordering. Countries could, if they wished, insist upon additional address checks, such as checking the Internet Protocol address of the device being used to download digital content.

How VAT would be collected from non-resident suppliers

21.25   The mechanics of collecting VAT from non-resident suppliers supplying services to resident, non-VAT registered customers which are recommended by the OECD are very similar to those in use in the EU in the case of non-EU suppliers of B2C services, which are discussed in the next sections. The non-resident supplier should be required to register for VAT in the customer's country. However, compliance is problematic. No country can enforce its laws against a non-resident. The OECD recommends that countries make it as easy as possible for non-resident suppliers to register for VAT, in order to encourage voluntary compliance. Full registration and VAT compliance procedures need to be cut down for these suppliers, to keep their administrative costs of compliance to a minimum. Even though less VAT might be collected this way than if the non-resident supplier could be successfully subjected to the full VAT rules, it should actually result in more VAT because fewer non-resident suppliers will refuse to register at all. Simplifications might include fewer checks on the supplier as part of the registration process and, importantly, no refund of any VAT on inputs for the supplier. Payment should be electronic. Invoice requirements for VAT purposes could be waived. Everything should be done online, or else the use of VAT agents to deal with the VAT compliance should be permitted.

Although the lack of legal jurisdiction over non-resident suppliers might seem to be an insurmountable problem, the OECD expects that the increased level of information exchange and assistance in collection of taxes between countries which is facilitated by the OECD's Common Reporting Standard for tax information and the OECD/Council of Europe Mutual Assistance Convention (see Chapter 18) will solve it. In other words, the OECD hopes that countries will help each other to collect VAT on B2C supplies of cross-border services. If Company X, resident in Country A is supplying such services to customers in Country B, then the Company X should register in Country A for VAT. If it does not, the hope is that Country A (which has legal jurisdiction over Company X) will step in and help Country B in some way, eg by collecting the VAT from Company X and passing it on to Country B. A major practical problem here is that many countries have great difficulty collecting taxes from their own residents, and simply do not have the ability or the resources to collect taxes on behalf of other governments. Even if a country has signed up to the Mutual Assistance Convention, and is enthusiastic about exchange of information and mutual assistance between countries in collection of taxes this does not mean that it has the resources to collect the VAT revenues of other countries on a day-to-day basis.

Which country has the right to tax particular services?

21.26   The two proxies for place of consumption of services considered so far are:

• place of performance of the services; and

• usual residence country of the customer.

The OECD recognizes that, as with B2B supplies of cross-border services, there will be instances where neither of these two proxies give the right answer. In other words, the services might be consumed somewhere other than in the country where the customer is usually resident. For instance, customers might be consuming services whilst on a foreign holiday. If these are 'on the spot' services such as restaurant meals or sporting events, then the 'on the spot' proxy can be used. Other types of services consumed other than in the country of residence might not involve the supplier being present there, such as accessing TV channels in a foreign hotel room, or downloading the newspapers or e-books onto a tablet whilst travelling abroad. In these cases, other proxies can be used, such as the actual location of the customer at the time of the download. So if Miss X, usually resident in Australia, holidays in Indonesia and whilst there, downloads books from Amazon onto her electronic reading device to read by the swimming pool, then the country entitled to collect the VAT on her purchase from Amazon would be Indonesia. Policing this requirement though, would be even more difficult than policing the collection of VAT where the rule used is the normal residence of the customer.

Special rules would also be applied to services in connection with immovable property. If Mr and Mrs X have a holiday flat in Morocco and a Spanish company is engaged to carry out regular maintenance, then irrespective of where Mr and Mrs X are normally resident, or where they are at the time the maintenance is carried out, the country entitled to collect the VAT would be Morocco.

SUPPLIES OF SERVICES WITHIN THE EU

21.27   As with the OECD's VAT/GST Guidelines, the EU has always treated cross-border services differently for VAT purposes depending on the VAT status of the customer.

EU rules on supply of B2B services

21.28   The usual rule is that B2B services are deemed to be supplied in the Member State where the customer is based (ie using the destination system). VAT is collected from the VAT-registered customer using the 'reverse charge' system. The EU adopted a new Directive on the supply of services[1] which took effect for most businesses from 1 January 2010, with the exception of telecoms services, where the implementation date is not until 2015. Before 2010, many types of B2B services were deemed to be supplied where the supplier (rather than the customer) was 'established'. The word 'established' broadly equates to the concept of tax residence for corporation tax, although with some important differences.

---

1   Council Directive 2008/8/EC of 12 February 2008 amending Directive 2006/112/EC as regards the place of supply of services.

21.29   The basic rule is that the place of supply of services is the customer's country and if supplied to a fixed establishment of the customer, the country where that fixed establishment is located. This rule applies to all services, including electronically supplied services, unless they are specifically excepted from the rule.

The principles established in *Berkholz*[1] are used to determine the place where the customer is established, so that provided a fixed establishment of a business has sufficient human and technical resources to be capable of receiving the services in question, the location of that establishment, rather than the business's head office, will determine in which country the VAT is due. The rules are a little different to the permanent establishment rules under Article 5 of the OECD Model Tax Treaty (see Chapter 9).

In the *Berkholz* case the arguments centred on whether gaming machines on board North Sea ferries could be said to constitute a fixed establishment of the German company which owned them. The general rule in EU law, set out in *Berkholz*, was that the place where the supplier has established his business (the head office) is the primary point of reference in establishing the place of supply. Other possible places (fixed establishments) could only be considered if taking as the place of supply the head office location did not lead to a rational result, or created a conflict with another Member State. In this case, the ECJ held that the ferries on which the gaming machines were located could not be said to be fixed establishments unless both the human and technical resources necessary for the provision of the services were permanently present. If *Berkholz* had won their case, much of the machines' takings would have escaped VAT altogether as the ships spent a fair amount of time in international waters. The principles established in *Berkholz* were further developed in *Faaborg-Gelting Linien*[2] in which the place of supply of catering services on-board ships was considered. The need for human personnel 'mind and management' was emphasized. The mere location of equipment is insufficient for the creation of a fixed establishment, a key point of difference between 'establishment' for VAT purposes and 'tax residence' for corporation tax and income tax purposes.

Suppliers of services must check the VAT status of their customers (ie whether or not they are registered for VAT) using the EU's VAT Information Exchange System (VIES). They must also record the services supplied on the EU services sales listing.

---

1 *G Berkholz v Finanzamt Hambury-Mitte-Altstadt* (1985) ECR 2251 C168-84.
2 C-231/94 *Faaborg-Gelting Linien A/S v Finanzamt Flensburg* [1996] All ER (EC) 656.

B2B services connected with land

21.30 Article 45 of the VAT Directive provides that the place of supply of services connected with immovable property, such as services of architects, estate agents and the supervision of construction works, are treated as supplied in the place where the property is situated. Thus if a UK firm incurred estate agents' and architects' fees in connection with a property located in the US there would be no VAT liability, because the US has no VAT system. The VAT Package leaves these rules unchanged.

Place of supply: B2B transport services

21.31   The basic rule will apply that the services are supplied in the place where the customer is established, provided the customer is registered for VAT.

For supplies of transport of goods to non-registered persons, the rules vary according to whether the transport takes place wholly within the EU, or not. Transport wholly within the EU is deemed to be supplied at the place of departure. Otherwise the rule is that the supply is where the transport takes place, proportionate to the distances covered.

Passenger transport services are deemed to be supplied at the place where the transport takes place, in proportion to the distances covered. Special rules apply to tour operators.

EU rules on supply of B2C services

21.32   Over the past few decades, the EU has tried to find a way of imposing VAT on these types of services.

The rules applicable since January 2015 are as follows:

- Any supplier, whether resident inside or outside the EU, has to charge VAT to non-VAT-registered EU customers at the rate applicable in the customer's country.

- If the supplier is resident outside the EU, then it should register for VAT in a single EU country of its choice. Note that this rule has been in existence since 2003.

- The supplier hands over the VAT collected from non-registered customers to the government of the country where the supplier is registered.

- The supplier's government then distributes the VAT revenues to the customer countries, minus a deduction for administration costs. (However, note this is to be phased out.)

These rules are designed to bring the VAT treatment of imports of electronic services by individuals into line with the destination principle: the VAT revenues go to the country where consumption takes place. There are some problems: The system of registration in a single EU country for these purposes is referred to as the 'mini one-stop shop' (MOSS). There are two MOSS systems, one for companies resident outside the EU (the 'Non-Union MOSS') and the one for EU-resident companies, who would normally register under the Union MOSS in their own country.

- Registration by non-EU suppliers is, in effect, optional. If a US supplier of music downloads decided that it did not want to register for VAT anywhere in the EU, the EU has no way of making it do so. However, this particular part of the system has been in place since 2003, and the evidence seems to be that all the big suppliers are complying with the registration rules.

- Small suppliers who would not otherwise need to register for VAT (because their annual supplies fall below the registration threshold) must, since January 2015, register for VAT. This creates a heavy administrative burden for such firms. If they decide not to register, they have to charge their customers in other EU countries the rate of VAT applicable in the customer country and pay it directly to that country's VAT authority. This would be even worse for them in administrative terms. Small businesses have complained bitterly about the new registration rules, many claiming that they have effectively been forced to stop selling to customers in other EU Member States. This is exactly the opposite of what the EU Single Market is supposed to achieve in terms of expanding potential markets for suppliers in the EU.

On 1 December 2016, the European Commission announced[1] a series of measures to improve VAT for e-commerce as part of a Digital Single Market strategy. Key actions include an annual threshold of €10,000 for online sales (making compliance simpler for some 430,000 companies) and a new annual threshold of €100,000 for simplified rules for identifying where customers are located.

---

1   See: http://europa.eu/rapid/press-release_IP-16-4010_en.htm.

EU CROSS-BORDER VAT REGIME – MISSING TRADER INTRA-COMMUNITY FRAUD

21.33   Since 1 January 1993, registered businesses have been able to acquire goods from other EU countries without paying VAT at the point of import or under a deferral system. This is entirely consistent with the EU's long-term aim to establish a Single Market where goods and services can be freely traded within the EU. Under the reverse charge procedure for intra-Community acquisitions, registered traders who are not exempt or partly exempt, on the same VAT return, both report the VAT on the acquisitions as output VAT and claim it back as input VAT. The entries cancel out, meaning that goods are effectively acquired from other EU countries free of VAT. The trader then sells the goods on in the domestic market, charging VAT and pays this over to his home tax authority. Because no VAT was paid upon acquisition of the goods, there is no input tax to claim at this point.

At its crudest, there is the simple 'acquisition fraud'. In this version, Missing Trader Intra-Community (MTIC) fraud is committed where a trader sells on the goods in his home country, charges the customer (who may be wholly innocent) VAT and fails to pay this over to the tax authority. The fraud only comes to light when a trader, perhaps somewhat further down the chain, re-exports the goods. This trader will have paid input VAT but will not be charging output VAT, because the sale is an export. Thus this trader claims a refund of the input VAT rather than merely offsetting the input VAT against output VAT. The tax authority is thus asked to make a large refund of VAT which has not been matched by a large receipt of VAT, when the goods were first sold on by the fraudulent trader. True MTIC fraud occurs if the importing and exporting traders are conspirators. Then, it is possible that the very same goods might then re-enter the country, be sold on to yet another trader, unsuspecting or otherwise, and then re-exported a further time. In this case, the fraud might be referred to as 'carousel fraud' because the same goods keep on going around.

Typically, the goods involved are high value, low-bulk technology items such as mobile phone handsets and computer chips. Importantly, there is a thriving 'grey market' for these goods, as lead times for new products tend to be long, so that by the time the products are despatched by the manufacturer, they may already have been overtaken by new technology. Hence the purchaser has to find a way to dispose of them. Typically, consignments of these goods can change hands without written contracts, usually over the telephone, without sight of the goods and the same consignment might change hands several times a day.[1] More recently, carbon trading permits were targeted by the fraudsters, with the result that they are now exempt from VAT because there did not seem to be any other satisfactory way of protecting against the fraud.

---

1   For a good description of a typical simple acquisition fraud, see *Deluni Mobile Limited*, VAT Tribunal 19201, Case ref MAN/04/0465 (2005).

Missing Trader Intra-Community fraud: simple acquisition fraud

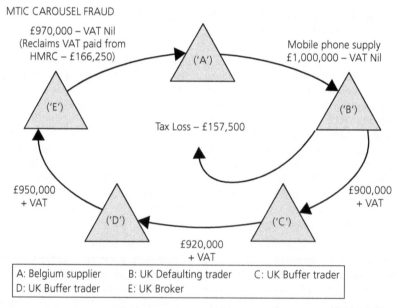

MTIC CAROUSEL FRAUD

£970,000 – VAT Nil
(Reclaims VAT paid from
HMRC – £166,250)

Mobile phone supply
£1,000,000 – VAT Nil

('A')

('E')

('B')

Tax Loss – £157,500

£950,000
+ VAT

£900,000
+ VAT

('D')

('C')

£920,000
+ VAT

| A: Belgium supplier | B: UK Defaulting trader | C: UK Buffer trader |
| D: UK Buffer trader | E: UK Broker | |

SOURCE: HMRC

Figure 21.3

21.34   Measuring the extent of the fraud has proved extremely difficult. In the UK alone, the revenue loss was estimated at between £2.5 billion and £3.5 billion (note the degree of imprecision!) in 2005–06.[1] It remained between £0.5 billion and £1.5 billion a year from 2007–08, and from 2012–13 is thought to have reduced to between £0.5 billion and £1 billion.[2] Recent figures for the whole of the EU put the revenue loss at between €45 billion and €53 billion annually.[3]

---

1 'A tax net full of holes', The Economist, 13 May 2006.
2 HMRC (2014) *Measuring Tax Gaps*, 2014 Edition. Available at: www.google.co.uk/#q=%22 MTIC+fraud%22+2015+HMRC.
3 European Commission: VAT Gap Study.

Missing Trader Intra-Community fraud: involving a non-EU country

21.35 Around 2003–2004 the fraud mutated so that, typically, the goods would be routed out of the EU and into Dubai, thus making it difficult for tax authorities to detect. By 2006, Dubai, which has a population of only 900,000, had officially appeared to become the UK's tenth largest trading partner. The intra-Community transit rules meant that Dubai traders can export to the EU, say to a trader in Country A in the diagram below. Country A will not insist on the VAT being paid at the point of entry or under deferral arrangements, as would be normal for imports from outside the EU because the intra-Community transit procedures permit Country A to allow the goods into Country A without VAT on the understanding that they are destined for customers in Country B. Once inside Country A, the consignments are split up to disguise their origins and fraudulently exported to Country B where they are held out as having originated in Country A, rather than in Dubai. The sole reason for involving Dubai in the arrangements was to disguise the true nature of the transactions. The choice of Dubai (and to some extent, Switzerland) may reflect the attitude of the authorities in those countries towards the regulation of imports.

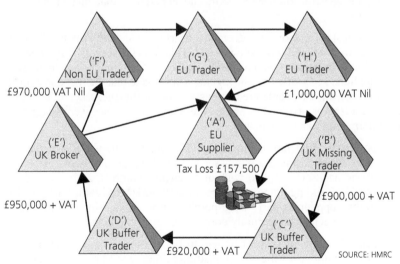

Figure 21.4

Approaches to tackling Missing Trader Intra-Community fraud

21.36 The first approach adopted by HMRC and several other countries was to try to deny the input tax credit to the trader who exported the goods and claimed the input tax refund. Unfortunately, in many cases, the exporter is an innocent party and in the case of *Bond House*[1] the CJEU ruled that the exporter must have had the 'means of knowing' that the goods being exported had been the subject of a missing trader fraud before the claim for the refund of input tax could be denied. (Theoretically, this was achieved by making the purchaser jointly and severally liable for the output tax which had gone unpaid further down the chain.) This approach requires the innocent trader to engage in an onerous and expensive programme of checks on the supply chain. In *Olympia Technology*[2] the VAT refund at stake was some £1.6 million and the VAT Tribunal ruled that the tests which ought to have been used were similar to those used in the Insolvency Act 1986, s 214(4):

> 'For the purposes of subsections (2) and (3) [which includes that that person knew or ought to have concluded that there was no reasonable prospect that the company would avoid going into insolvent liquidation], the facts which a director of a company ought to know or ascertain, the conclusions which he ought to reach and the steps which he ought to take are those which would be known or ascertained, or reached or taken, by a reasonably diligent person having both
>
> (a) the general knowledge, skill and experience that may reasonably be expected of a person carrying out the same functions as are carried out by that director in relation to the company, and
>
> (b) the general knowledge, skill and experience that that director has.'

In fact, the test at (a) above was deemed too stringent and the Tribunal favoured a 'they knew or should have known' test. This falls far short of the range and thoroughness of the tests which HMRC wished to force purchasers to apply to their suppliers. In *Mobilx Ltd*[3] the argument was made that the fact that a trader had not taken all reasonable precautions was not sufficient reason to conclude that the trader was involved in fraud. Alternative approaches were sought and the preferred approach is now to:

• prevent the VAT falling into the hands of the fraudulent trader in the first place by requiring the purchaser to send VAT on purchases of mobile phone handsets supplied without an airtime contract, and certain other goods, including computer chips, directly to HMRC rather than paying to the supplier as part of the purchase price (extension of the reverse charge mechanism to purely domestic transactions); and

• deny the right of suspect traders to be registered for VAT in the first place. Without a valid VAT registration, they would be treated as non-registered customers and would have to pay VAT at the point of entry to the UK of the goods or show that they had been charged VAT by the foreign supplier.

Neither of these two strategies is without risk. The first strategy runs the risk that the fraudsters will merely turn their attentions from goods on the blacklist to other goods, and there has been some evidence of MTIC fraud involving diamonds, soft drinks and confectionery. Also, there is a *de minimis* limit of £5,000 per invoice below which the rules do not apply, allowing fraudsters to fragment large contracts into many small ones, each below the limit. Unsurprisingly, the reverse charge procedure is accompanied by a considerable increase in VAT administration for the traders concerned.

The tightening up on the issue of VAT registrations has led to considerable hardship for genuine businesses that are not legally permitted to trade without registration, once over the registration threshold. The extended checking procedures have resulted in long delays in the issue of VAT registrations.

The EU has considered the extension of the reverse charge procedure to all purchases, not just imports, which would represent a considerable alteration of the basic system of VAT. More interestingly, it has finally been forced to return to the difficult subject of the adoption of the origin system so that traders must charge VAT on goods which are being sold to any customer anywhere in the EU (see European Commission, 2008). This is the 'definitive system' which was always intended to follow on from the current transitional system. However, in the shorter term, it has opted to try to improve the information flows between Member States so that the country of import knows that a potentially fraudulent consignment of goods is either on its way or has recently arrived. The goal was for the time lag to be cut from six months to two months. Various specific solutions to the problem of missing trader fraud have been examined over the years. A 2010 study (European Commission, 2010(2)) considered four alternative proposals for reducing missing trader fraud:

1   a split payment model: the VAT is paid by the purchaser into a 'blocked' bank account held in the supplier's name;

2   a central VAT monitoring database which gives tax authorities faster and better access to information on sales transactions but does not ring-fence the VAT;

3   a data warehouse system whereby all VAT data is sent automatically to the tax authority at the time the trader enters it on to his accounting system; and

4   certified taxable person status for those with 'approved' VAT accounting systems.

---

1   Joined Cases C-354/03, C-355/03 and C-484/03 *Optigen and Others*.
2   *Olympia Technology Ltd* VAT Tribunal 20570.
3   *Mobilx Ltd (in administration) v HMRC; HMRC v Blue Sphere Global Ltd and Calltel Telecom Ltd v HMRC* [2010] EWCA Civ 517.

CUSTOMS AND EXCISE DUTIES

21.37   Customs duty is a tax levied on the importation of goods by a country. Most goods are subject to customs duty. Excise duties are levied on both importation and domestic manufacture of a limited range of goods. According to Cnossen (1978), excise duties may be defined as: 'a tax which is selective in coverage, discriminatory in intent and which uses some form of quantitative measurement in determining the tax liability'.

Some tax issues are relevant to both taxes and these common issues will be dealt with after the two taxes have been examined separately.

Customs duties

21.38 Customs duties are widely levied on imports of goods. Unlike VAT on import, they cannot be recovered by the importing firm and constitute a real cost to the business. Categorization is a crucial issue: different goods will be subject to different rates of duties and much tax planning revolves around ensuring that goods are classified in the most advantageous manner. Categorization is also what turns this relatively simple tax into a more complex one as countries often have many different categories of goods. The Indian Customs Tariff has 21 sections and 99 chapters. The EU Common Customs Tariff ran to three large volumes until it was taken out of print format. Whilst having imports classified in a favourable manner might constitute good tax planning, in some countries, tax evasion through fraudulent misclassification of goods is rife. Fisman (2004) reports that some importers and customs officials have been executed in China for this misdemeanour.

The value on which duty is payable is generally the price actually paid with certain adjustments to include commissions and brokerage, the cost of containers and packing costs.

EU's Customs Union

21.39 One of the terms of the EU Treaty is that Member States will eliminate customs duties and quantitative restrictions on the import and export of goods between themselves. The EU customs union is effectively extended to countries in the European Economic Area – Norway, Iceland and Liechtenstein as well as to Turkey and Switzerland. All Member States charge customs duty on goods entering the customs union by reference to the Common Customs Tariff (CCT) of the EU. This lays down common rates of duty for all goods. Goods must be presented to Customs (ie notified to the customs authorities) within three hours of their arrival or, if the customs office is closed, then within one hour of its reopening.

Excise duties

21.40 Excise duties can be either 'specific' (so much per quantity, eg per packet of 20 cigarettes) or 'ad valorem', a percentage of the value of the goods. The main items on which the UK levies excise duties are tobacco products, alcohol, hydrocarbon fuels (eg petrol) and perfume. Excise duty systems are usually 'limited' in that the duties are confined to a small range of goods; usually no more than 10–15 or so. However, it is possible to have extended systems covering a far wider range of goods. Although charging on a specific basis is simple, the rates need to be kept under review to take account of inflation and other market factors. Specific taxes tend to be more regressive than ad valorem, due to luxury and economy brands bearing the same tax. Thus those who can afford the luxury brand pay no more in excise duty.

Imposing excise duty at the retail level is preferable in theoretical terms as it avoids questions as to the point at which tax should become chargeable and avoids distortion in production decisions. It also accords better with the nature of excise duty as a tax on consumption. However, charging at the manufacturer level means fewer taxpayers and thus the tax is simpler to collect. If tax is being charged on an ad valorem basis at the manufacturer level, then detailed rules are needed as to how the ex-tax value should be computed. Should it include transport and warehousing costs or merely manufacturing costs? Detailed valuation rules are thus needed. For this reason, where taxes are charged at manufacturer level it is far easier to charge on a specific basis rather than on an ad valorem basis.

There is no standardization of excise duty rates within the EU generally, although Member States are required to charge certain minimum limits on tobacco products.

Issues common to both customs and excise duties

21.41   The General Agreement on Tariffs and Trade (GATT) governs the extent to which countries may discriminate against imports by way of customs and excise duties as well as by the use of import quotas (see Farrell 2013). Countries which are contracting parties to GATT may impose import taxes (such as excises) providing they are merely compensatory. This means that they amount to no more than would be paid on goods sourced from the domestic market. Contracting parties may also remit taxes on exports, a prime example being the zero rating of exports under VAT.

The EU issued COM (2008) 169 final in April 2008 in which the intention to move to a paperless system for customs duties was announced along with the 'Modernised Customs Code' but implementation of this initiative is not expected before 2014 at the earliest.

When is duty payable?

21.42   The law in this area must specify a chargeable event – a trigger which makes a person liable to pay the tax. This is usually manufacture (for excise duty) or importation (for both customs and excise duties). Most excise duty systems will set the payment date for the tax according to the principle of 'release for consumption'. This assumes that there will be a gap between the date of manufacture and the date duty is payable. During this period, the tax authority must be able to keep track of the goods, usually by requiring them to be kept in an authorized warehouse. This postponement of payment of duty is known as a 'suspension arrangement'. Suspension arrangements also apply to importations for customs and excise duties and the most common provisions are for suspension of payment until:

- departure of goods from an authorized warehouse (duty suspension arrangement);

- manufacture, where goods are not subject to a suspension arrangement.

Transit procedures and suspension arrangements

21.43   This section considers arrangements that exist in EU countries, although other countries will have similar rules. Procedures for temporary import reliefs from duties apply to goods entering the EU on a temporary basis, for instance, goods for use in an exhibition, disaster relief materials, professional equipment, as well as various means of transport.

Customs and excise duties may be postponed by storing goods in a customs warehouse on their arrival in the EU. A certain limited range of activities is permitted in an EU customs warehouse, for instance, processing the goods under the 'inward processing procedure'. A certain amount of maintenance (or 'handling' work) is permitted to keep the goods in a suitable condition or prepare them for sale, but retail sales are not permitted within the warehouse. The warehouse may be a traditional dockside or airport warehouse, or it may be at another approved location. For some businesses, the tax authorities will approve a system of 'fiscal warehousing' where the duty is suspended according to bookkeeping entries evidencing movement of the goods, rather than according to the physical location of the goods. In this case, a separate customs warehouse is not needed.

Issues arising from customs warehousing

21.44   To prevent fraud, it is important that customs and excise duties should be payable when the amount of goods held in the warehouse reduces for reasons other than sale to customers. For instance, if there is no duty payable on common theft of goods, then there is less incentive for the firm to put in place anti-theft measures. Some shortfalls unaccounted for by customer sales should be exempt from duty – for instance, from natural disasters or events beyond the control of the taxpayer. There must be clear procedures for documentation; no goods should leave the warehouse without appropriate documentation and all movements of excise goods must be accompanied by documentation in the prescribed form. Preferably, the owner of the warehouse, if separate from the manufacturer, should be required to give guarantees for the payments of excise duties on goods stored in the warehouse.

Smuggling

21.45 Because of the high impact of excise duties and the fact that neither customs nor excise duties are recoverable by businesses (contrast with VAT), these taxes encourage smuggling of goods cross border. The general causes of smuggling may be summarized as follows:

- avoiding very high levels of tax (eg up to 83 per cent of final price on tobacco in the UK);

- avoiding having to comply with extremely complex rules and regulations; and

- avoiding having to supply only those products that meet minimum quality requirements.

In addition, the geographical location of a country is obviously important. The longer and less well manned the border, the more scope for smuggling. Also, if a country has less-developed neighbours, then there may be a willing stream of 'carriers' to bring goods in. In the EU, the issue is one of avoiding excise duties. VAT and customs duties do not make much difference on intra-EU movements of goods, but excise duties are still levied separately by each state, subject to the minimum requirements of Directive 2011/64/EU which requires each state to levy an overall minimum 60 per cent excise duty of the weighted average retail selling price of cigarettes. The prevalence of UK citizens shopping for tobacco in France is thought to have decreased significantly since the rates of excise duty were increased in France. The problem is by no means confined to the EU: according to the World Bank (2000), approximately one-third of internationally traded cigarettes (some 355 billion per year) were eventually sold illegally. In 2010, the World Health Organization (WHO) estimated that, based on the discrepancy between reported exports and reported imports of cigarettes, 90 billion cigarettes were smuggled in that year.[1] The main attraction of smuggling is not so much to pay a lower excise tax in one country rather than a higher tax in another, but to avoid such taxes altogether. Large-scale container fraud is thought to account for around 80 per cent of smuggled cigarettes.

A more difficult problem with smuggling occurs if manufacturers are complicit in the process: a major tobacco producer might sell infeasible quantities of cigarettes to a small nation in the certain knowledge that those cigarettes will be smuggled back into the manufacturer's country. This increases the tobacco company's profits through increased sales.

---

1 COM (2001) 260 final, updated by COM (2003) 0614.

FURTHER READING

Chandra, P & Long, C (2013) 'VAT Rebates and Export Performance in China: Firm Level Evidence', 102 *Journal of Public Economics*, 13.

Chappello, G (2010) 'VAT Focus – 2010 Changes on Global Financial Services', *Tax Journal*, Issue 1046, 20, 27 September 2010.

Cnossen, S (1978) *Excise Systems: A Global Study of the Selective Taxation of Goods and Services*, Johns Hopkins University Press.

Ebrill, L and Keen, R (2001) *The Modern VAT*, IMF.

European Commission (2008) Communication from the Commission to the Council and the European Parliament on measures to change the VAT system to fight fraud, COM(2008) 109 final.

European Commission (2010)(1) Green Paper of 1 December 2010 on the future of VAT – Towards a simpler, more robust and efficient VAT system, COM(2010) 695 final.

European Commission (2010)(2) 'Study on the feasibility of alternative methods for improving and simplifying the collection of VAT through the means of modern technologies and/or financial intermediaries'. Available at: http://ec.europa.eu/taxation_customs/resources/documents/common/consultations/tax/future_vat/vat-study_summ_en.pdf

European Commission (2015) 'Implementing the "Destination Principle" to Intra-EU B2B Supplies of Goods', Final Report TAXUD/2013/DE/319.

European Union (1992) Council Directive 92/12/EEC of 25 February 1992 on the general arrangements for products subject to excise duty and on the holding, movement and monitoring of such products.

Farrell, J (2013) *The Interface of International Trade Law and Taxation*, IBFD Doctoral Series.

Fisman, R and Wei, S J (2004) 'Tax Rates and Tax Evasion: Evidence from "Missing Imports" in China', *Journal of Political Economy* 112(2) pp 471–496.

Hall, K (2013) 'VAT Focus – Back to Basics: Cross-border VAT Issues', *Tax Journal*, Issue 1159, 24, 1 March 2013.

House of Lords (2007) Stopping the Carousel: Missing Trader Fraud in the EU, European Union Committee 20th Report of Session 2006–07. Report with Evidence.

Lyons, A (2010) 'VAT Focus: VAT Case Study: International Services: B2B & Reverse Charge', *Tax Journal*, Issue 1043, 19, 6 September 2010.

Millar, R et al (2014) 'VAT on B2B Supplies by Non-Resident Sellers', 68, *Bulletin for International Taxation*, 10.

OECD (2014) 'Guidelines on Place of Taxation for Business-to-Consumer Supplies of Services and Intangibles/Provisions on Supporting the Guidelines in Practice' Discussion Draft, 18 December 2014

OECD (2015) *International VAT/GST Guidelines*. Available at: www.oecd.org/ctp/consumption/international-vat-gst-guidelines.htm.

PwC (2013) Study on the feasibility and impact of a common EU standard VAT return ('Study on a common VAT return'), 2013 – as published by the European Commission. Available at: http://ec.europa.eu.libezproxy.bourne-mouth.ac.uk/taxation_customs/common/publications/studies/index_en.ht

Schenk, A, Thuronyi, V and Cui, W O (2015) *Value Added Tax A Comparative Approach*, second edn, Cambridge University Press.

Terra, B J M (1998) Chapter 8 – 'Excises', in Thuronyi, V ed, *Tax Law, Design and Drafting*, IMF 1998: www.imf.org/external/pubs/nft/1998/tlaw/eng/ch8.pdf.

Vynke, K, Cordewener, A and De Broe, L (2011) 'Towards a Simpler, More Robust and Efficient VAT System by Levying VAT at EU Level', *International VAT Monitor*, Vol 22, No 4.

Woolwich, R (2013) 'VAT Focus – Telecoms, Broadcasting and Electronic Services and the One Stop Shop', *Tax Journal*, Issue 1194, 18, 22 November 2013.

FURTHER STUDY

EU: fundamental reform

21.46   The current 'transitional regime' for dealing with cross-border VAT issues within the EU suffers from two major drawbacks. One is the endemic nature of missing trader and carousel fraud. The other is the heavy burden of VAT compliance costs suffered by SMEs when they trade cross-border within the EU. Various studies and reports have been produced in recent years to address these problems. This section considers the studies and reports on the future of VAT which have appeared over the last few years, starting with the most recent.

Ernst & Young 2013 study: value added tax on trade in goods

21.47   A major study was commissioned by the EU Commission in 2013 to deal with two fundamental issues with the current EU regime for B2B trade in goods:

- The VAT compliance cost burden created by cross-border trade – which is thought to dissuade many SMEs from international expansion. The increase in compliance costs burden is estimated at 11 per cent compared with the VAT compliance costs of just trading in the domestic market. This is entirely inconsistent with the ethos of the EU Single Market. It is an important issue because SMEs generate 58 per cent of value added within the EU outside the financial sector, and are therefore crucial to the health of the EU economy.

- The ongoing high level of missing trader and carousel fraud.

The study, produced by Ernst & Young, is aimed at improving the working of the destination system within the context of the EU Single Market.[1] It identified five options, two of which would reduce the scope for MTIC fraud, if adopted, to around €8 billion per year. These two options are:

- *'Taxation following the flow of the goods'* – meaning that the supplier would charge the VAT of the destination State. The supplier would use a one-stop shop arrangement similar to that already in use (since January 2015) for supplies of electronic services to non-registered persons within the EU. Under this system it would not be possible for a business to purchase goods from a supplier in another Member State without the supplier charging VAT. This would remove the possibility of MTIC fraud, which relies on the fact that a registered customer can purchase goods without paying VAT either to the supplier or to its own government before it takes possession of the goods. To combat new types of fraud, purchases would have to report all purchases from suppliers resident in other EU Member States, together with the supplier's VAT number.

- *'Taxation following the contractual flow'* – meaning that the supplier would charge the VAT of the State in which the customer is established. This would often give the same result as 'taxation following the flow of goods' but would be different if the customer required the goods to be delivered to a Member State other than the one in which the customer is established for VAT purposes. Again, this would remove the possibility of being able to acquire goods without paying VAT to the supplier. For VAT purposes, a customer is 'established' in the place where the functions of the business's central administration are carried out.[2]

Both these options would effectively limit MTIC fraud to the VAT on the margin – the difference between the VAT paid to the EU supplier and the VAT charged fraudulently to the same-country customer. This is because the supplier would charge VAT, even though the customer was established in a different Member State. Either option might thus reduce the revenue lost through MITC fraud to around €8 billion. There could be exceptions for customers with a good VAT compliance record, who could continue to buy goods cross-border within the EU without paying VAT to the supplier, instead continuing to use the reverse charge procedure. These could be known as 'Certified Taxable Persons'. Further exceptions might be made in the case of supplies between two companies the same pan-European corporate group. In these cases, full lists of purchases from non-resident suppliers would have to be kept by the certified customers.

Both options could only be implemented if the Member States all adopted standardized lists of products eligible for reduced rates of VAT (to avoid damaging competition) or, alternatively, application of the standard rate of VAT to all B2B supplies. Whilst there would be differences in the standard rate of VAT, these would not create 'shopping around' behaviour in the same way as if some countries applied only a reduced rate of VAT on certain goods and other countries charged their standard rate on the same goods. If implemented, either of these option could be extended to non-EU suppliers of goods, via a 'one-stop shop' registration similar to that already used for supply of B2C services.

The report also proposes measures which would reduce compliance costs and improve the working of the EU VAT system generally. Other options being considered are:

• Limited improvement of the current rules, eg requiring the customer to sign a document declaring receipt of the goods in the Member State of delivery. This option would not reduce MTIC fraud significantly.

• A reverse charge following the flow of goods – this would have no effect on MTIC fraud.

• Alignment of VAT with the place of supply of services – this proposal would harmonize the place of supply rules for services and goods.

---

1 European Commission (2013) 'Implementing the "Destination principle" to Intra-EU B2B supplies of Goods', Final Report TAXUD/2013/DE/319. Available at: http://ec.europa.eu/taxation_customs/taxation/vat/key_documents/reports_published/index_en.htm.
2 Implementing Regulations for Directive 2006/112/EC. If the goods are purchased by a branch of the customer, then the VAT charged should be the VAT of the customer's branch – the 'fixed establishment'. To count, this branch must be an establishment characterized by a sufficient degree of permanence, and a suitable structure in terms of human and technical resources to enable it to receive and use the services supplied to it for its own needs.

The 2011 EU report on the future of VAT

21.48   This report, entitled 'Towards a simpler, more robust and efficient VAT system tailored to the single market'[1] (the '2011 Report') took into account responses to a public consultation carried out following the publication of the EU's 2010 Green Paper (see below). This had generated many responses and the flavour of these was that change was needed. The principal problem identified was the fragmentation of the EU's VAT system into 27 national VAT systems, making it very difficult for SMEs to take advantage of the EU single market due to the additional VAT compliance costs of trading outside their home country. In fact, in some cases it was reported as being easier to trade with non-EU customers and suppliers than with customers and suppliers within the EU.

---

1 COM (2011) 851 final, 6 December 2011.

A landmark decision – abandonment of the ideal of the 'definitive regime'

21.49   It was in the 2011 Report that the European Commission officially abandoned the goal of having a definitive VAT regime: one where a supplier would charge and account for VAT on intra-EU supplies in the same way as for domestic supplies. This goal was acknowledged to be politically unachievable. Resources would be better spent in future on developing alternative concepts for a properly functioning destination-based EU system of VAT. This paved the way for the 2013 EY study, discussed above. With this out of the way, the 2011 Report outlined the following main goals:

- Examine ways to better implement the destination system: this resulted in the 2013 EY study just discussed.

- Reduce the complexity of VAT compliance for businesses trading intra-EU by the introduction of 'one-stop shop' VAT registration and charging arrangements. This has now been done with respect to broadcasting, telecoms and electronic services (BTE), starting in 2015. However, the goal is to broaden this concept over time so that it extends to trade in goods as well. If this is done, the distance selling regimes, which required businesses to be registered with and comply with VAT in multiple EU Member States, could be dismantled.

- Make it easier for businesses to find out what the VAT rules are in other EU Member States: by providing the information on a central web portal in several languages.

- Standardizing the VAT return form across the EU, to be adopted optionally by businesses. Further standardization, eg in registration formalities, might follow. Following the 2011 Report, the EU Commission requested PricewaterhouseCoopers (PwC) to carry out a study into the introduction of a common set of VAT return procedures for use in all Member States (PwC, 2013). The recommendations are for a monthly VAT return with quarterly returns for smaller businesses (annual turnover <€2 million). There would be an option for making the return on paper, although most would be made electronically. PwC estimated that, on average, it costs a firm €265 to submit each VAT return under current systems. The proposal is merely for harmonization of the VAT return, deadlines and associated procedures, rather than for harmonization of the underlying VAT rules and rates in use in all the Member States.

- Review the rate structure of VAT with a view to simplification, especially by reducing the number of different VAT rates within the same country.

- Address the problems caused by having VAT exemptions for the public sector and for health, social security, etc, in terms of distortion of competition and complexity. These problems are acute where there is a high degree of private sector involvement in the exempt class of transactions.

- Develop a quick reaction mechanism to deal with sudden fraud, such as the missing trader fraud which became endemic in the energy trading markets. Also to improve the data warehousing arrangements already in place and to give further consideration to a split-payment system.

The 2010 Green Paper

21.50　The background to the 2011 Report is found in a series of papers issued by the EU Commission since 2000. Acceptance that the definitive regime – the origin system – is likely to remain theoretical was at the core of the report issued by the EU in 2000, 'Tax Policy in the European Union: Priorities for the Years Ahead'.[1] The Commission reluctantly accepted that its efforts would be better directed towards improving the transitional regime rather than concentrating on achieving implementation of a definitive regime. The focus was to be on simplification, modernization, a more uniform application of current arrangements and closer administrative co-operation.

The European Commission published a Green Paper at the end of 2010, 'The Future of VAT in the EU', to stimulate public debate on the future of the EU VAT system. According to the Green Paper, the system required rethinking not just because of missing trader fraud, but also because:

- The current VAT rules and administrative requirements are extremely burdensome for businesses, particularly small businesses. Non-EU firms are thought to be discouraged from setting up in the EU due to the administrative burden represented by VAT. Businesses have to treat transactions with domestic customers and customers in other EU Member States differently.

- The world has changed since VAT was introduced in the 1970s, both in terms of technology available to run and police the system and in terms of the types of business undertaken. For instance, the financial services sector is now many times more important than in the 1970s but is not adequately catered for in VAT terms. In fact, services generally now account for about 70 per cent of total economic activity within the EU, but the EU VAT system was designed primarily to deal with trade in goods.

- VAT has become far more important as a source of government revenues since its introduction. As populations age and non-earning pensioners form a higher proportion of the population, income taxes are not so effective as a revenue-raising tool. Pensioners may not be earning but they still have to spend. Also, VAT is a more stable source of government revenue, as the level of revenues is not directly dependent on the economic health of a country to the extent of, say, corporation tax.

- The original aim of having a common system of VAT is not being achieved. Despite the requirement for Member States to have a VAT system which conforms to the VAT Directive, the VAT systems operated by the 26 Member States tend to be very different, so that businesses wishing to operate cross border in the EU need knowledge of several VAT systems. This discourages firms from expanding into Europe.

- The Green Paper notes that VAT revenues represent only about 55 per cent of the VAT that could be collected if VAT was charged at a standard rate on everything. There are many items which are either exempt from VAT or taxed at a reduced rate. Some non-EU countries do much better in this respect.

- The EU VAT system is leaky – the 'VAT gap' (ie the difference between the amount of VAT collected under the current rules and that which ought to be collected is around 12 per cent on average and in some EU Member States it is as high as 20 per cent). Much of the VAT gap can be attributed to missing trader fraud but, even so, the amount of VAT uncollected due to other causes is considered unacceptable.

---

1   COM (2001) 260 final, updated by COM (2003) 0614.

Dealing with cross-border trade within the EU – the 2010 Green Paper proposals

21.51   Two of the more important of these proposals are considered below. However, the reality of MTIC fraud and the ineffectiveness of the short-term informational measures and limited extension of the reverse charge to combat it mean that the adopting of the origin system at some time in the future cannot be ruled out. Whilst these more radical proposals contained in the 2010 Green Paper are not been developed further at present (see discussion of the 2011 Report above for details of the proposals being taken forward by the EU), they are nevertheless of interest.

Green Paper proposal 1 – a general reverse charge

21.52   The Green Paper controversially suggested that the reverse charge mechanism could be applied to all transactions, both domestic and cross border. Whilst this would put an end to missing trader fraud, it would radically alter VAT. The key feature of VAT – that it is paid to the supplier as part of the purchase transaction – would be lost and VAT would arguably change from being an indirect tax to a direct tax on consumption. Under a general reverse charge, every VAT-registered business would have to pay VAT on purchases not to the supplier but to the government. VAT would no longer have the concept of the 'fractionated payment'. Suppliers would no longer charge VAT to other registered traders but only to non-registered customers. This would present governments with a cash-flow problem as, in practice, little VAT would be paid over to the government until there was a sale to a non-registered customer. This is because VAT due to be paid to the government when a purchase is made (output tax) is cancelled out by a claim for an input tax deduction of the identical amount, because the purchase is attributable to taxable supplies. Table 21.1 below compares the current system with this proposed system. The example assumes that traders are fully taxable, make VAT returns on a quarterly basis on 31 March, 30 June, 30 September and 31 December, and that VAT due is payable one month after the end of the quarter.

Table 21.1 Current system and a general reverse charge system: a comparison

Current system ('*fractionated payment*')		*Proposal (general reverse charge)*	
Business 1		Business 1	
Net selling price Feb XX01	200	Net selling price Feb XX01	200
+ VAT	20		
Gross selling price	220		200
On its VAT return, Business 1 must declare VAT charged of 20 and pay this over to the tax authority by 30 April XX01		Business 1 merely reports the sale	
Business 2 (VAT registered)		Business 2 (VAT registered)	
Gross cost	220	Gross cost	200
		Add: tax payable to HMRC under the reverse charge	20
− tax refund	(20)	− tax refund	(20)
+ required profit	100	+ required profit	100
Net selling price (to a non-registered customer) 10 May XX01	300	Net selling price (to a non-registered customer) 10 May XX01	300
+ VAT	30	+ VAT	30
Gross selling price	330	Gross selling price	330
On its VAT return, Business 2 must declare VAT charged of 30 and may reclaim VAT paid of 20, making a net payment to the tax authority of 10. This payment would be due 31 July XX01		On its VAT return, Business 2 declares VAT charged of 30 and pays this over to HMRC. This payment would be due 31 July XX01	

Although, in both cases, the total amount of VAT paid to the government is 30, the result of the change to a general reverse charge system is that the government has to wait until 31 July XX01 before it receives any VAT revenue.

Green Paper proposal 2 – an origin system

21.53   An alternative proposal is for the supplier to charge VAT to a customer in a different Member State at the rate of VAT and according to the VAT system in the customer's country. However, this would be inordinately burdensome for the supplier unless the VAT charged could be paid over to the supplier's tax authority rather than that in the particular customer's Member State. This would presuppose some kind of clearing house with all the pitfalls and complications that entails. This appears to have been carried forward into the options proposed in the 2013 EY study, discussed above.

Review of VAT exemptions

21.54   The Green Paper contains a review of VAT exemptions, noting that these are contrary to the principle of VAT as a broad-based consumption tax. In particular, the exemptions for financial services and for postal services are no longer deemed appropriate.

Types of purchase on which VAT is deductible

21.55   At present, the UK denies the recovery of input tax on a small range of items, notably entertainment and motor cars. Other countries have different lists, and so the proposal is to harmonize the list, to put businesses in each Member State on an equal footing. A proposed list is:

- amusements and entertainment;

- motorized road vehicles, boats and aircraft;

- travel, accommodation, food and drink; and

- luxuries (however these might be defined).

The Green Paper does not give a list as such.

The need for greater harmonization of VAT systems

21.56   This aspect of the Green Paper covers not just the actual VAT rate, but the extent to which individual VAT systems properly reflect the VAT Directive. At present, if a Member State is seen to be flouting the requirements of the VAT Directive, action can be taken by the EU – so-called 'infringement proceedings' – but these are cumbersome, costly and time consuming, often adding to the overall complexity of the system.

Some commentators (eg Vyncke et al, 2011), have called for an end to separate VAT systems and for VAT to be paid directly to the EU under a single EU VAT regime. The main problem with this proposal is that there would need to be a mechanism acceptable to all the Member States for sharing out the VAT revenues.

Chapter 22

Tax and Development

BASICS

22.1   Developing countries as a group, although varying considerably in their levels of development, face similar problems in terms of their capacity to use their tax systems for both raising much needed revenue, and for attracting foreign investment.

Domestic tax policy design is problematic for developing countries and the role of foreign experts, and the international dimension is increasingly important as the pace of globalization changes. Many developing countries use tax incentives commonly used to attract foreign direct investment (FDI) despite evidence that suggests that tax incentives are not efficient in this regard.

Developing countries are vulnerable on a number of levels, not only in terms of their capacity to administer their tax systems effectively, including the provision of tax incentives, but also in their relationships with developed countries in the context of treaty negotiations, and their relationships with transnational companies who are looking for tax-efficient locations in which to place their investments. The OECD BEPS Project has attempted to take into account the needs of developing countries, although some claim that more should be done in this regard, for example, the BEPS Monitoring Group.

Throughout this book, we have from time to time referred to specific issues that affect developing countries. The purpose of this chapter is to review, and in some cases expand upon, some of these issues and bring them together in a policy-based overview of the relationship between taxation and development.

INTRODUCTION

22.2   The United Nations Conference on Trade and Development (UNCTAD) classifies countries as developed, transitional and developing, as follows:

- Developed economies are the member countries of the OECD (other than Mexico, the Republic of Korea and Turkey), plus the new European Union (EU) member countries that are not OECD members (Bulgaria, Cyprus, Estonia, Latvia, Lithuania, Malta, Romania and Slovenia), plus Andorra, Israel, Liechtenstein, Monaco and San Marino.

- Transitional economies are South-East Europe and the Commonwealth of Independent States.

- Developing economies are, in general, all economies not classified as developed or transitional.

In the political literature, there is a growing tendency to use the terms 'north' and 'south', in place of 'developed' and 'developing' to describe essentially the OECD countries (the north) and the rest (the south). Unfortunately, both sets of distinctions fail to capture the rich diversity of what were once also known as less developed countries which demonstrate considerable variance in terms of their economic and infrastructure development as well as political stability. Moore (2004) suggests that given the variations, particularly within the category of 'south', rather than a dichotomy, it should be thought of as a continuum. For the purposes of this chapter, the term 'developing' countries will be used.

Disregarding the variations in conditions for the moment, it is fair to say that developing countries face similar constraints with respect to their extractive capacity, that is, their ability to extract tax revenue from their residents or non-resident investors. For example most developing countries have a larger informal economy that is difficult to tax and have low levels of voluntary compliance. Many developing countries also have a large agricultural sector that may be similarly difficult to tax. At a broader level, developing countries generally are not as well equipped to use the tax system for distributive purposes, and also frequently lack administrative capacity. Despite the difficulties in designing and administering tax systems adequate to the task of raising revenue to support public expenditure, international funding bodies, such as the IMF, frequently impose tax design requirements as conditions for loans. Developing countries have traditionally relied very heavily on taxes on imports and exports, as these provide convenient tax 'handles' in that they are relatively easy to administer and collect. Traditional reliance on taxes on international trade is now also constrained by trade liberalization movements.[1]

---

1 For a discussion of these issues together with some fascinating case studies, see Bräutigam et al (2008). Bird and Zolt (2008) also provide a good overview of a variety of tax policy issues affecting what they refer to as 'emerging' economies.

TAX POLICY IN DEVELOPING COUNTRIES

22.3 Growing attention is being given to the particular difficulties faced by developing countries in terms of design and delivery of tax systems. It is now clear that effective taxation is essential for state building and is clearly linked to citizenship. Yet many developing countries have tax systems that don't deliver expected levels of revenue for a variety of reasons. In 2010, the European Commission published a report entitled *Tax and Development*[1] in which difficulties encountered by developing countries were outlined, including:

- *Domestic factors* – structure and competitiveness of economies (eg large informal sectors, predominance of agriculture), political and macro-economic instability, narrow tax bases, inappropriate balance between direct and indirect taxes, weak link between tax policy and tax administration, and lack of administrative capacity; and

- *International factors* – resulting from increasing integration of international markets and economic globalization.

The European Commission (EC) acknowledges the importance of assistance in designing developing countries' tax systems as well as implementing good tax governance.

Developing countries historically, however, have been vulnerable to interference from well-meaning experts. Richard Bird[2] describes three phases of tax model recommendations for developing countries. Development Model 1.0 emerged in the 1960s, and embraced the view that comprehensive personal income tax was the ideal tax for developing countries, with indirect consumption tax viewed as a 'necessary evil'. The outcome of implementation of version 1.0 was disappointing and relatively few developing countries increased their tax to GDP ratios. From the 1980s, Development Tax Model 2.0 switched the emphasis to VAT in preference to personal income tax as the mainstay of tax policy, along with general broad base/low rate thinking. Bird argues that not enough attention was given to the administrative and political economy aspects of taxation, which counteracted the effectiveness of version 2.0. He recommends a move toward Development Tax Model 3.0, which would see closer attention being paid to distributional aspects of tax systems, understanding that simple is not always either achievable or the best course of action, and that a longer term perspective is needed. Development Tax Model 3.0 would see custom built systems with the following features taken into account:

- non-tax revenues;

- administrative aspects;

- linked spending (social security, earmarking, decentralization);

- transfers;

- regulations;

- macroeconomic environment;

- international aspects; and

- decentralization policy.

There is also considerable unrest about the extent of capital flight from developing countries, although in this regard empirical evidence is patchy at best. In order to tackle capital flight through tax evasion in particular, developing country tax authorities need to develop capacity to obtain information about offshore activities of its citizens. The UK Department for International Development provides technical assistance to development countries and has achieved success, eg in Rwanda and Zambia.

Research to help developing countries in the design and management of their tax systems includes work done by the International Centre for Tax and

Development.[3] A recent report by the International Bar Association[4] explores the important connections between tax and human rights, with particular reference to developing countries. A wide range of stakeholders was consulted to consider how developing countries could be assisted in tackling tax evasion so as secure revenue to diminish reliance on foreign aid.

In a *World Bank Note* published in February 2013,[5] Moore reflects on the wide range of political actors that influence tax policy reform in developing countries. He observes that, historically, tax policy in developing countries has been captured by closed policy making by lobbyists or transnational experts. On a more optimistic note, he predicts more open tax policy debate going forward, incorporating a wider range of political actors, including business associations, for example, the National Association of Garment Exporters, professional associations such as the Inter-American Center of Tax Administrations (CIAT), the Big 4 accounting firms, and last but by no means least, civil society organizations, eg Action Aid, Christian Aid, Oxfam and the Tax Justice Network.

The OECD in 2013 released a study that seeks to assess the role of 'aid modalities' in supporting tax system. By this is meant the various instruments that can be mobilized to improve tax systems in developing countries. Seven aid modalities are examined by reference to case studies and a survey of aid agency officials. Some of the principal findings are as follows:[6]

- Host country ownership and leadership is of paramount importance. Aid can effectively support government programmes to improve the tax system, but it generally cannot 'buy' effective and lasting reforms that are not aligned with domestic political objectives.

- Although basic principles of taxation are applicable everywhere, and common themes are widely applicable, there is no 'best' approach to tax reform. Donor programmes should be customized to fit country conditions.

- The objective of tax reform is not just to boost the ratio of tax revenue to GDP, but also to establish a tax system that is efficient, growth oriented, and equitable. How revenue gets collected is as important as how much gets collected.

- There are broad areas of synergy between the governance agenda and the standard technical agenda for tax reform. Aid programmes should give special weight to activities that address these synergies.

- The quality of the tax system is itself a central pillar of state building and good governance. But linkages between taxation and governance also involve supporting institutions and organizations outside the revenue system, which include the justice system, Parliament and civil society.

- Efforts to widen the tax net and mobilize revenue depend not only on tax reforms but also on broader reforms that influence citizens' attitudes to the quality of governance.

The IMF, in its April 2017 *Fiscal Monitor Report*[7] which is entitled 'Achieving more with less', notes that fiscal policy has a greater role to play in encouraging sustainable and inclusive growth, but that it faces challenges in achieving more within a resource-constrained environment. Chapter 1 sets out three main objectives to guide fiscal policy: it should be countercyclical, growth friendly and promote inclusion. Chapter 2 makes a case for upgrading tax systems in order to reduce distortions and therefore boost productivity.

---

1   COM (2010) 163 final, *Tax and Development: Cooperating with Developing Countries on Promoting Good Governance in Tax Matters*, SEC(2010)426.
2   Bird, R (2013). See also Stewart (2009).
3   Available at: www.ictd.ac.
4   Available at: www.ibanet.org/Article/Detail.aspx?ArticleUid=4A0CF930-A0D1-4784-8D09-F588DCDDFEA4.
5   Available at: http://siteresources.worldbank.org/PUBLICSECTORANDGOVERNANCE/Resources/285741-1361973400317/GPSM2_v2.pdf.
6   OECD (2013) p 17.
7   Available at: www.imf.org/en/Publications/FM/Issues/2017/04/06/fiscal-monitor-april-2017.

Tax expenditures in developing countries

22.4   As we saw in Chapter 1, tax expenditures are reductions in tax otherwise collectable and are created for a variety of reasons. They effectively provide a subsidy to specific categories of taxpayers or activities, and can be delivered as exemptions from the tax base, variations in tax rate, or direct reductions in tax liability through tax credits. There has been considerable debate recently about the efficacy of tax expenditures, which run counter to the idea of optimal tax systems and economic efficiency, as well as the question of transparency.

In a 2011 report prepared for the International Budget Partnership, Burton and Stewart[1] discuss the way in which tax expenditure management can be improved for developing countries, by reference to case studies of tax expenditure reporting in India, South Africa, Chile and Brazil. The authors identify some 'best practices', but acknowledge that tax expenditure reporting should be tailored to the individual needs of each country.

One interesting form of tax expenditure, broadly defined, is that of presumptive income taxation. In many developing countries, presumptive taxation is used to counter the problems arising from the large small business and informal sectors. A presumptive income tax calculates tax based on turnover rather than net income, in an attempt to reduce compliance costs.

Developing countries frequently use tax expenditures to attract foreign direct investment. This issue is covered in more detail below.

---

1   Burton, M. and Stewart, M (2011) 'Promoting Transparency through Tax Expenditure Management: A Report on Country Experience for Civil Society Advocates'.

INTERNATIONAL TAX AND DEVELOPING COUNTRIES

22.5   As noted in the previous section, developing countries face particular difficulties not only in relation to their domestic tax system design and operation, but also in relation to international developments. While the OECD's BEPS project is expected to bring improvements to the international tax regime more broadly, it acknowledges that it will only partially address the challenges faced by developing countries. The OECD Secretariat estimates that capacity to deal with international tax matters is lagging behind in as many as 54 countries. A more structured approach to supporting developing countries is needed alongside capacity building and improved data acquisition.

The extent to which developing countries lose revenue as a result of the behaviour of MNEs is not entirely clear, despite numerous attempts to quantify this. One problem is that many of the debates on this question conflate various types of activity as well as fail to distinguish different types of developing country. Forstater (2015)[1] documents some of the studies, by both economists and non-governmental organizations (NGOs) that attempt to bring some order to discussions by clarifying categories of behaviour, and also calls for the debate to move beyond the 'big numbers' that have been successful in raising awareness, but now need closer analysis if recommendations for improvement are to be made effective.

---

1 Forstater, M (2015) *Can stopping 'tax dodging' by multinational enterprises close the gap in finance for development?* Discussion paper available at: www.cgdev.org/sites/default/files/ Can-stopping-tax-dodging-by-MNEs-close-the-gap-in%20FFD-Consultation-Draft.pdf.

Transfer pricing

22.6 Increasing integration has led, among other things, to the increased focus on transfer pricing practices of multinational groups of companies. In the past two years a number of reports have been produced which specifically address the difficulties faced by developing countries in relation to the design and operation of transfer pricing rules, most of which are consistent with the OECD *Transfer Pricing Guidelines*.

In evidence to the UK House of Commons International Development Committee[1] in 2012, the Centre for Trade Policy and Development (Zambia) for example, notes that transfer pricing legislation is extremely complex to enforce given the lack of access to necessary information. A report by PwC Zambia is quoted as saying: 'In Zambia transfer pricing legislation exists … The enforcement of the legislation by ZRA has however, not been as aggressive as expected'.[2]

In recent years there has been an explosion of transfer pricing regulations around the world, including many developing countries. The lack of administrative capacity in developing countries is particularly problematic in the context of enforcing arms-length pricing using comparability analysis. Substantial commercial data is needed to evaluate the efficacy of transfer prices adopted by multinationals. In addition, there is considerable space for interpretation and negotiation in the OECD guidelines, as we saw in Chapter 13, which makes tax administrations in developing countries vulnerable and increases the possibilities for corruption.

The experience of India is instructive in this regard, where following the introduction of transfer pricing regulations in 2001, a 'boom area of professional practice, controversy and litigation' developed.[3]

In 2017, the United Nations released a second edition of the *Practical Manual on Transfer Pricing for Developing Countries*.[4] The updated version is divided into four parts: (1) transfer pricing in a global environment, (2) design principles and policy considerations, (3) practical implementation, and (4) country practices. New chapters are includes on intra-group services, cost contribution arrangements and intangibles. The revised manual takes into account BEPS transfer pricing actions.

As part of the Platform for Collaboration, which brings together the IMF, OECD, UN and World Bank Group, in January 2017 a draft toolkit in relation to access to comparables was published[5] for comment. The toolkit recognizes that many developing country tax administrations struggle to obtain information they need to undertake comparability analysis and discusses some practical possibilities, while acknowledging that a comprehensive solution is not possible. At the time of writing (May 2017) the toolkit has not been finalized.

---

1 House of Commons, International Development Committee (2012) *Tax in Developing Countries: Increasing Resources for Development*, HC130.
2 Ibid at Ev81.
3 Picciotto (2013) at p 23.
4 Available at: www.un.org/esa/ffd/publications/united-nations-practical-manual-on-transfer-pricing-for-developing-countries-2017.html.
5 Available at: www.oecd.org/tax/discussion-draft-a-toolkit-for-addressing-difficulties-in-accessing-comparables-data-for-transfer-pricing-analyses.pdf.

Double tax treaties

22.7   It has long been recognized that the OECD MTC does not suit the circumstances of developing countries, and the UN MTC is designed to provide alternative approaches that better protect their interests. Michael Lennard explains the key differences between the UN and OECD Models (as they stood before the 2011 update) in a 2009 article.[1]

The UN MTC was updated in 2011.[2] The introduction to the 2011 update acknowledges that the UN Model generally favours retention of greater so-called 'source country' taxing rights under a tax treaty, which is of special significance to developing countries. This revision is noted as being the beginning of an ongoing process of review with more frequent updates and revisions anticipated in the future.

Not everyone agrees that the work of the UN in this area is appropriate. India's view is expressed in a letter to the UN in August 2012[3] which suggests that the UN 'should be independently developing global standards in international taxation, treaty policies and transfer pricing etc. after proper appreciation of the concerns of the developing countries.' The letter further states that 'UN work should focus on addressing challenges faced by tax administrations and policy makers in developing countries and give guidance rather than merely recognizing the OECD work and reacting thereto', and lists the following areas requiring further work:

- developing international standards and guidance for transfer pricing under Article 9;

- formulating a separate Article for taxing the 'Fees for Technical services' on a gross basis;

- providing guiding principles for tax treatment of 'electronic commerce' transactions, which in the interests of developing countries should move away from the concept of fixed place of business;

- vesting taxation rights with the source country for 'Re-insurance businesses through a separate provision under Article 5;

- studying and creating standards and guidance on treaty issues regarding 'Environment-related Taxes' from the perspective of developing countries;

- formulating processes and procedures to be adopted by countries for giving foreign tax credit in order to bring consistency of approach among various countries; and

- establishing a robust system of exchange of information under Article 26 to bring true transparency as mandated by G20 and various other international bodies.

In October 2016, the Committee of Experts on International Cooperation in Tax Matters released new draft provisions for the treatment of payments made through hybrid entities.[4] At the same time, the Committee released a report on the taxation of services.[5]

The following section of this chapter considers in more detail the use of tax incentives by developing countries to attract foreign direct investment (FDI).

---

1   Lennard, M (2009) 'The UN Model Tax Convention as Compared with the OECD Model Tax Convention – Current Points of Difference and Recent Developments', *Asia Pacific Tax Bulletin*, January/February, pp 3–11.
2   Available at: www.un.org/esa/ffd/documents/UN_Model_2011_Update.pdf.
3   Available at: www.un.org/esa/ffd/tax/LetterIndia_13aug12.pdf.
4   Available at: www.un.org/esa/ffd/wp-content/uploads/2016/10/12STM_CRP7_Hybrids.pdf.
5   Available at: www.un.org/esa/ffd/wp-content/uploads/2016/10/12STM_CRP1_Services.pdf.

ATTRACTING FOREIGN DIRECT INVESTMENT THROUGH THE USE OF TAX INCENTIVES

22.8   In Chapter 16, it was noted that countries adopt a range of measures to attract investment, giving rise to tax competition, the harm of which is subject to considerable debate. The focus of Chapter 16 was incentives offered by developed countries, and the problem that tax havens present in terms of harmful competition. Here we extend this discussion, but in the specific context of developing countries, rather than tax havens per se, although the two may coexist in the same jurisdiction, of course.

According to the most recent report from UNCTAD,[1] a number of trends are emerging. Global FDI fell by 18 per cent to $1.35 trillion in 2012 and is forecast to remain relatively static, with the recovery taking longer than expected. For the first time, developing countries have taken the lead in absorbing more FDI than developed countries. FDI outflows from developed countries fell back to almost 2009 levels. Importantly, FDI is increasing in economies that are structurally weak and inflows to least developed countries have hit a record high. In the context of global value chains (GVCs), the report notes:

> 'In developing countries, value added trade contributes nearly 30 per cent to countries' GDP on average ... and there is a positive correlation between participation in GVCs and growth rates of GDP per capita. GVCs have a direct economic impact on value added, jobs and income. They can also be an important avenue for developing countries to build productive capacity, including through technology dissemination and skill building, thus opening up opportunities for longer-term industrial upgrading.'

Incentives designed to attract FDI, typically manufacturing, assembly, service centres and R&D centres, take a variety of forms including:

- low tax rates for foreign investors;

- tax holidays;

- tax-free zones;

- reduction/elimination of withholding taxes;

- special investment allowances;

- accumulation of tax-free reserves; and

- accelerated depreciation deductions for foreign investors.

This chapter considers the use of some of these incentives by developing countries in more detail, and draws on a report issued by UNCTAD in 2000 *Tax Incentives and Foreign Direct Investment: A Global Survey*. Despite numerous studies that attempt to establish the role of tax incentives in promoting FDI, no consistent direct relationship has been established, and it is reasonably clear that the availability of tax incentives is a secondary consideration in FDI decisions following more commercial considerations such as market size and access to raw materials and skilled labour. The importance of tax incentives is heightened when countries in close geographical proximity share similar infrastructure capabilities. The UNCTAD (2000) report defines tax incentives as 'any incentives that reduce the tax burden of enterprises in order to induce them to invest in particular projects or sectors'. As a general rule they will be exceptions to the normal tax regime and their availability is usually subject to conditions, for example relating to requirements to employ certain numbers of local staff, for transfer of technology or establishing operations in particular regions.

Asian governments were initially the most proactive in providing tax incentives to attract FDI and have put considerable energy into designing incentives to attract investment capable of generating technology transfer. Singapore and Malaysia, for example, introduced pioneer industry incentives to attract research and development activities and technology projects.

In October 2015, a report to the G20 development working group was published.[2] The report was prepared by the IMF, OECD, UN and World Bank and is entitled 'Options for Low Income Countries' Effective and Efficient Use of Tax Incentives for Investment'. It offers guidance on the design, governance and reform of tax incentives.

---

1   UNCTAD (2013) World Investment Report 2013.
2   Available at: www.oecd.org/tax/tax-global/options-for-low-income-countries-effective-and-efficient-use-of-tax-incentives-for-investment.pdf.

Reduced corporate tax rates and tax holidays

22.9   Reduced corporate tax rates and tax holidays are the most widely used forms of tax incentives to attract FDI. A reduction in the standard rate of corporation tax may be offered in order to attract FDI into certain industry sectors or geographical regions. Tax holidays are used similarly and provide an exemption from payment of corporate income tax for a specified period, often five years. Both forms of tax incentive are generally considered to be 'blunt instruments', in that it is difficult to constrain their application to specific target recipients, but they have the advantage of relative simplicity with a relatively low compliance burden for recipient enterprises.

Malaysia, for example, uses two main forms of tax incentives: Pioneer Status (tax holiday for five to ten years) and Investment Tax Allowance (deductibility of capital expenditure). There are no requirements as to minimum levels of investment or employment, but the incentives apply to particular activities, and more attractive packages of incentives are available for technology and knowledge-based activities. In addition, the corporate tax rate has been reduced from 27 per cent in 2007, to 26 per cent in 2008 and to 25 per cent in 2009. India's tax holiday for IT developers ended in 2011, amid concerns that this would dent India's attractiveness as an investment destination. Developers that enjoyed the tax holiday for locating in Special Economic Zones will now have to pay a minimum alternate tax.

A number of problems arise in respect of both these forms of tax incentives. In the case of reduced corporate tax rates, the reduction needs to be to a level well below the prevailing global average in order to be effective. In addition, it is of no benefit to loss-making enterprises. Where the reduced rate is applied only to specified activities or sectors, it may also result in market distortions. It should be remembered that in making investment decisions, headline corporate tax rates are not decisive; rather firms look at effective rates which, calculated by dividing total tax by taxable income, can differ significantly from headline rates depending on progressive bands and special reductions, and also may vary as a result of different enterprise characteristics such as financing profile.

Tax holidays may also result in market distortions if they are aimed at specific industries, and there is an argument that they are attractive to highly mobile, 'footloose' industries that potentially avail themselves of the holiday then move on to another jurisdiction once the holiday period expires. Tax holidays, therefore, may have limited potential to attract long-term investment.

Investment allowances and credits

22.10   Investment allowances and credits are more targeted forms of tax incentive designed to encourage specific forms of investment. Investment allowances are deductions from taxable income based on some percentage of capital investment, and come in two main forms, accelerated depreciation and enhanced deductions. Accelerated depreciation entails providing for faster write off, for tax purposes, of the cost of capital acquisitions than would normally be available, that is, over a shorter period of time than that indicated by the asset's useful economic life. Enhanced deductions entail granting tax deductions for an amount in excess of the expenditure actually incurred, for example 150 per cent or 200 per cent of qualifying expenditure will be treated as deductible. The former creates a timing and cash-flow advantage to the taxpayer, but the overall cost to the government providing the incentive is the same as if normal depreciation provisions provide. The latter, however, entails some loss of potential revenue to the government. In both cases, the value of the incentive to the firm will vary depending on the applicable corporate income tax rate. Where an investment project involves high levels of capital expenditure in the early stages, investment allowances may only be of benefit if there are provisions for excess deductions to be carried forward to future periods to offset future tax liabilities.

Investment tax credits are similar to investment allowances in that they are allowed as a fixed percentage of qualifying investment expenditure. They may be flat, that is the relevant percentage is applied to the expenditure incurred each year, or they may be incremental, such that the percentage is applied to expenditure in excess of some defined base, for example a moving average of expenditure of a specified number of preceding years. In some countries, unused investment tax credits may be refundable, which makes the scheme considerably more attractive than the alternative of carry forward, but can be expensive for the government.

ADMINISTRATION OF TAX INCENTIVES

22.11   There is an important difference between attracting short-term and long-term investment; for the latter, stability and predictability of the tax system become important considerations for investing firms. Administrative capacity in developing countries varies considerably, and can be constrained by cultural and social as well as economic and political conditions.[1]

Several administrative factors impact particularly on the effectiveness of tax incentive systems, including transparency, discretion and follow up (UNCTAD 2000). Arguably, the more transparent the incentive system, the easier it will be for investors to understand. This includes clarity about conditions attached to the incentives, for example, specifying which regions qualify by name, rather than by some form of generic description such as 'less developed regions'. The question of discretion relates to the extent to which government officials are able to use their own discretion in making decisions about the granting of incentives. Allowing too much discretion may pave the way for corruption; on the other hand, a certain degree of discretion facilitates greater flexibility in tailoring incentives to the needs of particular investors. The follow up of firms that have benefited from the incentives is also important, ensuring that, where conditions have been attached to the incentive, those conditions have been fulfilled, such as completion within a particular time frame. If FDI projects are not properly monitored, it becomes impossible to ensure that the expected investment actually materializes.

A recent report by the OECD (2010) includes the following example of the potential for abuse of tax incentives, demonstrating how political interference can significantly reduce the beneficial effects of tax incentives with ramifications beyond loss of tax revenue:

> 'Ghana appears to have a relatively well-administered incentives scheme – incentives are quite clearly defined in law and require parliamentary approval. However, the fact that there is still strong evidence of significant abuse indicates the widespread abuse of tax incentives in the developing world. The most glaring example was the registration of major timber companies in tax-free Export Processing Zones (EPZs) during the 1990s. These timber companies were granted EPZ status despite the fact that they secure most of their inputs, and conduct most of their operations (ie logging) within the domestic economy. This means that there is little need for incentives because the resource (timber) is a fixed asset. As a result the country received only a fraction of the potential tax revenue, while logging was leading to widespread deforestation. It is widely believed that the economically unjustifiable granting of EPZ status was driven by political patronage. In 2008, the government passed a law forbidding logging firms from acquiring EPZ status, and while the new law is good news for Ghana, it is also an implicit acknowledgement of the scope of earlier abuses. The same law forbade EPZ status for plastics firms, apparently in response to evidence that they were illegally trading within the domestic economy without paying appropriate taxes).'

---

1   See Bird (2004) for a discussion of administrative capacity in developing countries.

WHAT DO HOST GOVERNMENTS HOPE TO ACHIEVE?

22.12   At the most general level, the host government hopes to achieve an increase in national welfare by increasing the degree of economic integration of its economy with those of other countries. However, the use of tax incentives achieves this goal by expanding foreign control of productive assets rather than by other available means, such as an increase in trade in goods, more international licensing of technology or by encouraging larger cross-border flows of portfolio capital (Hanson 2001). The host government typically anticipates that there will be 'spill-over effects' from the FDI. Such effects may include the adoption by domestic firms of superior management and production techniques brought in by the foreign MNEs, the increase in demand for local goods and services brought about by the increased wealth of the workforce employed by the MNEs and the possibility that the MNEs will source at least some of their raw materials from local suppliers. The host government may be able to share in economic rents with the MNE, although if it has granted a tax holiday or similar incentive, this advantage is foregone. Against these spill-over effects must be weighed the loss to the host economy through the 'crowding out' by the MNEs of domestic firms. Measuring the net gains from FDI is notoriously difficult. The political kudos that accrues from successfully attracting a large MNE to build a substantial production facility should not be overlooked.

HOME COUNTRY DILUTION OF TAX INCENTIVES

22.13   The way in which home countries recognize tax incentives offered by host countries – if at all – will impact on the attractiveness of those incentives to investors. Home countries that use a worldwide system that is taxing all foreign income with a subsequent credit for foreign taxes paid, will effectively claw back the benefit of any incentive to the extent that the home country tax rate exceeds the effective (ie post-incentive) rate in the host country. It is for this reason that tax-sparing provisions are included in DTTs, as first discussed in Chapter 7. The UNCTAD 2000 Report suggests that home countries are beginning to question the efficacy of tax sparing, arguing that 'it may offer a windfall gain to the investor with no impact on net additional investment'.

The precise terms of tax-sparing provisions depend on the preferences of the particular countries involved, and the relative bargaining power of each. Developing countries will obviously try to have tax-sparing provisions included in treaty negotiations and secure as much credit as possible. The potential for variation is illustrated by Van der Bruggen's (2002) study of treaties negotiated by Thailand between 1988 and 1998:

> 'Treaties with Israel and the Czech Republic provide a mutual tax sparing credit. In the treaty with Spain, it is simply mentioned that tax exempt or reduced (under the Investment Promotion Act) is deemed paid. Treaties with Japan, Australia and New Zealand all include a minimum shareholding percentage to qualify for a foreign tax credit on dividends from Thai companies. Certain treaties provide a "deemed paid rate" (Switzerland, Luxembourg) and for Sweden, it is higher than the current Thai withholding tax on interest, dividend or royalty.'

A recent study[1] of the impact of tax-sparing provisions on Japanese outbound FDI between 1989 and 2000 confirmed a link and concludes that the evidence suggests that Japanese FDI flows in tax-sparing countries were almost three times bigger than in non-tax sparing countries, indicating at a broader level that tax-sparing provisions influence investors' location choices. The US does not normally enter into tax-sparing arrangements. Even those countries that do offer tax sparing often place a time limit on the life of the arrangements, typically ten years from the day the treaty was made. Whilst provision is sometimes made so that the arrangements can be extended, extensions are by no means always made.

Another potential source of distortion in the context of tax incentives, is the use of transfer pricing by investors to artificially inflate the profit attributable to the host country and concurrently deflate the profits in the home jurisdiction. The extent to which this occurs, however is extremely difficult to detect, let alone quantify. Interestingly, some countries which used special tax incentives to attract foreign investment are now paying much closer attention to transfer pricing. China, for example, is adopting a more intensive approach to transfer pricing amid concerns that it is being used to shift profits *out* of China to avoid Chinese taxes. In January 2009, China introduced a system of special tax adjustments, to tackle tax-avoidance practices, including transfer pricing. These measures include requirements for contemporaneous documentation and a narrow interpretation of the range of acceptable arm's-length prices. One interpretation of these changes is that China is seeking to signal that it is ready to join developed countries in terms of the sophistication of its tax policies.[2]

---

1   Azemar et al (2007).
2   DeSouza (2009).

TAX COMPETITION AND DEVELOPMENT

22.14   Empirical evidence of the impact of tax competition in attracting FDI remains mixed, but importantly, as noted by Gurtner and Christensen (2008), 'it is notable that empirical studies have not supported the notion that tax incentives play a significant part in attracting' FDI. They make reference to a study by McKinsey & Co of fiscal inducements in China, Brazil, Mexico and India which concluded that they may indeed have had negative and unintended consequences in that the incentives may have reduced the value of investments that would have been undertaken in the absence of the tax incentives.

The persistence of the introduction of tax incentives by developing countries in an attempt to attract FDI reflects in part the enormous bargaining power of the transnational companies that offer their investment capacity. Gurtner and Christensen (2008) go so far as to suggest that the extent to which transnational enterprises put pressure on developing countries to offer preferential tax treatment potentially leads to corruption. There is no doubt that tax incentives distort markets, arguably to the detriment of the revenue-raising capacity of the world's poorer nations, which in turn results in increased dependency on foreign aid.

The relationship between capital flight, tax evasion and development is complex and not well understood. The Tax Justice Network is unequivocal in its assertion that 'capital flight and tax evasion represent significant barriers to the process of enabling developing countries to finance their development from domestic resources'. They call for international support in tackling abusive international practices in order to allow developing countries space to undertake necessary reforms to their domestic tax systems so as to strengthen their extractive capacity.

BEPS AND DEVELOPING COUNTRIES

22.15   The UN Committee of Experts on International Cooperation in Tax Matters established a subcommittee in October 2013 to monitor BEPS issues, and ensure views of officials in developing countries were fed into the OECD BEPS Project.[1] The initial report of the subcommittee notes that there is not one single cause of BEPS, and that in some cases it 'reflects gaps and inadequacies in the design of domestic laws'.

A short questionnaire elicited submissions from twelve countries as well as two responses from NGOs,[2] all of which said that BEPS had a concerning impact on tax revenues, with transfer pricing raised as the most problematic issue.

The OECD reports[3] that over 80 developing countries and other non-OECD/ G20 countries have participated in the technical working groups. In addition, in November 2014, the OECD launched a new strategy for deepening the engagement of developing countries. The OECD's task force on tax and development will assume responsibility for publishing toolkits to assist developing countries with the implementation of BEPS action items, including model legislation and real-life cases.

Wagenaar (2015) identifies a number of BEPS issues of particular relevance to developing countries. For example, Actions 11, 12, 14 and 15 all deal with administrative aspects of BEPS, and in aggregate can be expected to make more information available to developing countries, although the capacity of developing country tax administrations to digest and analyse such data may remain a problem.

The response to the OECD BEPS recommendations from NGOs has been critical, for example an ActionAid publication[4] released immediately after the BEPS final reports were published says the BEPS process comes up short in many respects, for example, the failure of country-by-country reports to be made public, and to apply to large companies only, and the failure to deal with harmful tax practices. The publication calls for a UN tax body to be established with universal membership to overcome the lack of representation of developing countries in the debates on global tax rules.

In 2015, UNCTAD produced a working paper[5] on FDI, Tax and Development which attempts to rebalance the debate about the impact of tax avoidance by MNEs on developing countries. It provides estimates of the contributions by MNEs to government revenues in developing countries, and importantly reminds us that there is an investment perspective to international tax avoidance, providing new insights on the relationship between investment, and tax.

In June 2016, an inaugural meeting of the inclusive framework for BEPS implementation took place in Kyoto and brought together more than 80 countries and jurisdictions, including a broad group of developing countries. Regional meetings have been held throughout the BEPS process to allow the OECD secretariat to update on latest developments and seek feedback. These meeting provide a focal point for capacity building in the various regions.

---

1   Available at: www.un.org/esa/ffd/tax/BEPS_note.pdf.
2   Available at: www.un.org/esa/ffd/wp-content/uploads/2014/10/10STM_CRP12_BEPS1.pdf.
3   Available at: www.oecd.org/tax/developing-countries-and-beps.htm.
4   Available   at: www.actionaid.org.uk/sites/default/files/publications/beps_-_patching_up_a_broken_tax_system_0.pdf.
5   Available at: http://investmentpolicyhub.unctad.org/News/Hub/Archive/286.

TAX ADMINISTRATION: INDIAN CASE STUDY

22.16   In 2014 India embarked on a major review of tax administration, setting up a Tax Administration Review Committee (TARC).[1] The terms of reference of the Committee included reviewing the organizational structure, and business processes of the tax administration, reviewing dispute resolution mechanisms, and measures for improving taxpayer services and education. The Committee produced a series of chapters in four volumes.[2] In 2015 a final *Feedback Report* was published that outlines the recommendations of TARC, and the outcomes of discussions with field officers and staff associations about the recommendations.

The introduction to the *Feedback Report* observes that:

'[a] tax administration is a litmus test of how good or bad the rest of public administration is. Its problems are a microcosm of those affecting the rest. Hence, successfully reorganising a tax administration should point to how the rest should be organised'.

Recommendations from TARC include a customer focus with training for staff at all levels, and a centralized taxpayer service and delivery for large taxpayers, improved research and benchmarking, and greater functional autonomy from other government structures, as well as a functionally separate dispute management structure. The need for improved data collection and analysis was clearly noted, together with the need for ongoing research in tax governance 'so that there is sufficient and modern thinking available to improve processes, structures and people functions in the tax administration'.

---

1   Available at: www.finmin.nic.in/the_ministry/dept_revenue/tarc_report.asp.
2   For a review of the four volumes of recommendations, see Akhand (2015).

FURTHER READING

Akhand, Z (2015) 'Review of the Tax Administration Reform in India – Spirit, purpose and empowerment', *Journal of Tax Administration*, Vol 1(1). Available at: http://jota.website/article/view/12.

Azemar, C, Desbordes, R and Mucchielli, J L (2007) 'Do Tax Sparing Agreements Contribute to the Attraction of FDI in Developing Countries?', *Journal of International Tax and Public Finance*, Vol 14, pp 543–562.

Bird, R M (2004) 'Administrative Dimensions of Tax Reform', *Asia Pacific Tax Bulletin*, March 2004, pp 134–150.

Bird, R M and Zolt, E M (2008) 'Tax Policy in Emerging Countries', *Environment and Planning C: Government and Policy*, Vol 26, pp 73–86.

Bird R (2013) 'Foreign Advice and Tax Policy in Developing Countries' International Center for Public Policy, Working Paper, 13-07.

Bräutigam, D, Fjeldstad, O and Moore, M, eds (2008) *Taxation and State Building in Developing Countries*, Cambridge University Press.

Burton, M and Stewart, M (2011) 'Promoting Transparency through Tax Expenditure Management: A Report on Country Experience for Civil Society Advocates', University of Melbourne Legal Studies Research Paper No 544. Available at: http://ssrn.com/abstract=1864324.

DeSouza, G (2009) 'China Unveils Special Tax Adjustments', *International Tax Review*, February 2009.

Gurtner, B and Christensen, J (2008) 'The Race to the Bottom: Incentives for New Investment?', *Tax Justice Network*. Available at: www.taxjustice.net/cms/upload/pdf/Bruno-John_0810_Tax_Comp.pdf.

Klemm, A (2009) *Causes, Benefits and Risks of Business Tax Incentives*. IMF Working Paper WP/09/21. Available at: www.imf.org/external/pubs/ft/wp/2009/wp0921.pdf.

Lennard, M (2009) 'The UN Model Tax Convention as Compared with the OECD Model Tax Convention – Current Points of Difference and Recent Developments', *Asia Pacific Tax Bulletin*, January/February, pp 3–11.

Moore, M (2004) 'Taxation and the Political Agenda, North and South', *Forum for Development Studies*, No 1 – 2004.

OECD (2010) *Citizen–State Relations: Improving Governance Through Tax Reform*, OECD Paris.

OECD (2013) *Tax and Development: Aid Modalities for Strengthening Tax Systems*, OECD Publishing, Paris.

Picciotto, S (2013) 'Is the International Tax System Fit for Purpose, Especially for Developing Countries?', ICTD Working Paper 13.

Stewart, M (2009) 'Tax Policy Transfer to Developing Countries: Politics, Institutions and Experts', in *Global Debates about Taxation*, Palgrave Macmillan.

United Nations (2015) 'Report by the Coordinator: Subcommittee on Base Erosion and Profit Shifting for Developing Countries', Committee of Experts on International Cooperation in Tax Matters Eleventh Session, Paper No E/C.18/2015/CRP.11

UNCTAD (2000) Tax Incentives and Foreign Direct Investment: A Global Survey. Available at: www.unctad.org/en/docs/iteipcmisc3_en.pdf.

UNCTAD (2009) World Investment Report 2008: Transnational Corporations and the Infrastructure Challenge, overview. Available at: www.unctad.org/en/docs/wir2008overview_en.pdf.

Van der Bruggen, E (2002) 'Tax Treaty Renegotiations by Developing Countries: A Case Study Using a Comparative Analysis to Assess the Feasibility of Achieving Policy Objectives', *Asia Pacific Tax Bulletin*, July/August 2002, pp 255–272.

Wagenaar, L (2015) 'The Effect of the OECD Base Erosion and Profit Shifting Action Plan on Developing Countries', *Bulletin for International Taxation* February 2015, p 84.

Appendix

ARTICLES OF THE OECD MODEL TAX CONVENTION ON INCOME AND CAPITAL

OECD (2014), *Model Tax Convention on Income and on Capital: Condensed Version 2014*, OECD Publishing, DOI:10.1787/mtc_cond-2014-en

[as they read on 9 December 2015]

SUMMARY OF THE CONVENTION

TITLE OF THE CONVENTION

Convention between (State A) and (State B)

with respect to taxes on income and on capital[1]

PREAMBLE TO THE CONVENTION[2]

---

1 States wishing to do so may follow the widespread practice of including in the title a reference to either the avoidance of double taxation or to both the avoidance of double taxation and the prevention of fiscal evasion.
2 The Preamble of the Convention shall be drafted in accordance with the constitutional procedure of both Contracting States.

Chapter I

SCOPE OF THE CONVENTION

ARTICLE 1

PERSONS COVERED

This Convention shall apply to persons who are residents of one or both of the Contracting States.

ARTICLE 2

TAXES COVERED

1. This Convention shall apply to taxes on income and on capital imposed on behalf of a Contracting State or of its political subdivisions or local authorities, irrespective of the manner in which they are levied.

2. There shall be regarded as taxes on income and on capital all taxes imposed on total income, on total capital, or on elements of income or of capital, including taxes on gains from the alienation of movable or immovable property, taxes on the total amounts of wages or salaries paid by enterprises, as well as taxes on capital appreciation.

3. The existing taxes to which the Convention shall apply are in particular:

a)   (in State A): ....

b)   (in State B): ....

4. The Convention shall apply also to any identical or substantially similar taxes that are imposed after the date of signature of the Convention in addition to, or in place of, the existing taxes. The competent authorities of the Contracting States shall notify each other of any significant changes that have been made in their taxation laws.

Chapter II

DEFINITIONS

ARTICLE 3

GENERAL DEFINITIONS

1. For the purposes of this Convention, unless the context otherwise requires:

a)   the term "person" includes an individual, a company and any other body of persons;

b)   the term "company" means any body corporate or any entity that is treated as a body corporate for tax purposes;

c)   the term "enterprise" applies to the carrying on of any business;

d)   the terms "enterprise of a Contracting State" and "enterprise of the other Contracting State" mean respectively an enterprise carried on by a resident of a Contracting State and an enterprise carried on by a resident of the other Contracting State;

e)   the term "international traffic" means any transport by a ship or aircraft operated by an enterprise that has its place of effective management in a Contracting State, except when the ship or aircraft is operated solely between places in the other Contracting State;

f)   the term "competent authority" means:

     (i)   (in State A): ....

     (ii)   (in State B): ....

g)   the term "national", in relation to a Contracting State, means:

     (i)   any individual possessing the nationality or citizenship of that Contracting State; and

     (ii)   any legal person, partnership or association deriving its status as such from the laws in force in that Contracting State;

h)   the term "business" includes the performance of professional services and of other activities of an independent character.

2. As regards the application of the Convention at any time by a Contracting State, any term not defined therein shall, unless the context otherwise requires, have the meaning that it has at that time under the law of that State for the purposes of the taxes to which the Convention applies, any meaning under the applicable tax laws of that State prevailing over a meaning given to the term under other laws of that State.

ARTICLE 4

RESIDENT

1. For the purposes of this Convention, the term "resident of a Contracting State" means any person who, under the laws of that State, is liable to tax therein by reason of his domicile, residence, place of management or any other criterion of a similar nature, and also includes that State and any political sub-division or local authority thereof. This term, however, does not include any person who is liable to tax in that State in respect only of income from sources in that State or capital situated therein.

2. Where by reason of the provisions of paragraph 1 an individual is a resident of both Contracting States, then his status shall be determined as follows:

a)   he shall be deemed to be a resident only of the State in which he has a permanent home available to him; if he has a permanent home available to him in both States, he shall be deemed to be a resident only of the State with which his personal and economic relations are closer (centre of vital interests);

b)   if the State in which he has his centre of vital interests cannot be determined, or if he has not a permanent home available to him in either State, he shall be deemed to be a resident only of the State in which he has an habitual abode;

c)   if he has an habitual abode in both States or in neither of them, he shall be deemed to be a resident only of the State of which he is a national;

d)   if he is a national of both States or of neither of them, the competent authorities of the Contracting States shall settle the question by mutual agreement.

3. Where by reason of the provisions of paragraph 1 a person other than an individual is a resident of both Contracting States, then it shall be deemed to be a resident only of the State in which its place of effective management is situated.

ARTICLE 5

PERMANENT ESTABLISHMENT

1. For the purposes of this Convention, the term "permanent establishment" means a fixed place of business through which the business of an enterprise is wholly or partly carried on.

2. The term "permanent establishment" includes especially:

a)   a place of management;

b)   a branch;

c)   an office;

d)   a factory;

e)   a workshop, and

f)   a mine, an oil or gas well, a quarry or any other place of extraction of natural resources.

3. A building site or construction or installation project constitutes a permanent establishment only if it lasts more than twelve months.

4. Notwithstanding the preceding provisions of this Article, the term "permanent establishment" shall be deemed not to include:

a)   the use of facilities solely for the purpose of storage, display or delivery of goods or merchandise belonging to the enterprise;

b)   the maintenance of a stock of goods or merchandise belonging to the enterprise solely for the purpose of storage, display or delivery;

c)   the maintenance of a stock of goods or merchandise belonging to the enterprise solely for the purpose of processing by another enterprise;

d)   the maintenance of a fixed place of business solely for the purpose of purchasing goods or merchandise or of collecting information, for the enterprise;

e)   the maintenance of a fixed place of business solely for the purpose of carrying on, for the enterprise, any other activity of a preparatory or auxiliary character;

f)   the maintenance of a fixed place of business solely for any combination of activities mentioned in subparagraphs *a)* to *e)*, provided that the overall activity of the fixed place of business resulting from this combination is of a preparatory or auxiliary character.

5. Notwithstanding the provisions of paragraphs 1 and 2, where a person – other than an agent of an independent status to whom paragraph 6 applies – is acting on behalf of an enterprise and has, and habitually exercises, in a Contracting State an authority to conclude contracts in the name of the enterprise, that enterprise shall be deemed to have a permanent establishment in that State in respect of any activities which that person undertakes for the enterprise, unless the activities of such person are limited to those mentioned in paragraph 4 which, if exercised through a fixed place of business, would not make this fixed place of business a permanent establishment under the provisions of that paragraph.

6. An enterprise shall not be deemed to have a permanent establishment in a Contracting State merely because it carries on business in that State through a broker, general commission agent or any other agent of an independent status, provided that such persons are acting in the ordinary course of their business.

7. The fact that a company which is a resident of a Contracting State controls or is controlled by a company which is a resident of the other Contracting State, or which carries on business in that other State (whether through a permanent establishment or otherwise), shall not of itself constitute either company a permanent establishment of the other.

Chapter III

TAXATION OF INCOME

ARTICLE 6

INCOME FROM IMMOVABLE PROPERTY

1. Income derived by a resident of a Contracting State from immovable property (including income from agriculture or forestry) situated in the other Contracting State may be taxed in that other State.

2. The term "immovable property" shall have the meaning which it has under the law of the Contracting State in which the property in question is situated. The term shall in any case include property accessory to immovable property, livestock and equipment used in agriculture and forestry, rights to which the provisions of general law respecting landed property apply, usufruct of immovable property and rights to variable or fixed payments as consideration for the working of, or the right to work, mineral deposits, sources and other natural resources; ships, boats and aircraft shall not be regarded as immovable property.

3. The provisions of paragraph 1 shall apply to income derived from the direct use, letting, or use in any other form of immovable property.

4. The provisions of paragraphs 1 and 3 shall also apply to the income from immovable property of an enterprise.

ARTICLE 7

BUSINESS PROFITS

1. Profits of an enterprise of a Contracting State shall be taxable only in that State unless the enterprise carries on business in the other Contracting State through a permanent establishment situated therein. If the enterprise carries on business as aforesaid, the profits that are attributable to the permanent establishment in accordance with the provisions of paragraph 2 may be taxed in that other State.

2. For the purposes of this Article and Article [23 A] [23B], the profits that are attributable in each Contracting State to the permanent establishment referred to in paragraph 1 are the profits it might be expected to make, in particular in its dealings with other parts of the enterprise, if it were a separate and independent enterprise engaged in the same or similar activities under the same or similar conditions, taking into account the functions performed, assets used and risks assumed by the enterprise through the permanent establishment and through the other parts of the enterprise.

3. Where, in accordance with paragraph 2, a Contracting State adjusts the profits that are attributable to a permanent establishment of an enterprise of one of the Contracting States and taxes accordingly profits of the enterprise that have been charged to tax in the other State, the other State shall, to the extent necessary to eliminate double taxation on these profits, make an appropriate adjustment to the amount of the tax charged on those profits. In determining such adjustment, the competent authorities of the Contracting States shall if necessary consult each other.

4. Where profits include items of income which are dealt with separately in other Articles of this Convention, then the provisions of those Articles shall not be affected by the provisions of this Article.

ARTICLE 8

SHIPPING, INLAND WATERWAYS TRANSPORT AND AIR TRANSPORT

1. Profits from the operation of ships or aircraft in international traffic shall be taxable only in the Contracting State in which the place of effective management of the enterprise is situated.

2. Profits from the operation of boats engaged in inland waterways transport shall be taxable only in the Contracting State in which the place of effective management of the enterprise is situated.

3. If the place of effective management of a shipping enterprise or of an inland waterways transport enterprise is aboard a ship or boat, then it shall be deemed to be situated in the Contracting State in which the home harbour of the ship or boat is situated, or, if there is no such home harbour, in the Contracting State of which the operator of the ship or boat is a resident.

4. The provisions of paragraph 1 shall also apply to profits from the participation in a pool, a joint business or an international operating agency.

ARTICLE 9

ASSOCIATED ENTERPRISES

1. Where

a)   an enterprise of a Contracting State participates directly or indirectly in the management, control or capital of an enterprise of the other Contracting State, or

b)   the same persons participate directly or indirectly in the management, control or capital of an enterprise of a Contracting State and an enterprise of the other Contracting State,

and in either case conditions are made or imposed between the two enterprises in their commercial or financial relations which differ from those which would be made between independent enterprises, then any profits which would, but for those conditions, have accrued to one of the enterprises, but, by reason of those conditions,

have not so accrued, may be included in the profits of that enterprise and taxed accordingly.

2. Where a Contracting State includes in the profits of an enterprise of that State – and taxes accordingly – profits on which an enterprise of the other Contracting State has been charged to tax in that other State and the profits so included are profits which would have accrued to the enterprise of the first-mentioned State if the conditions made between the two enterprises had been those which would have been made between independent enterprises, then that other State shall make an appropriate adjustment to the amount of the tax charged therein on those profits. In determining such adjustment, due regard shall be had to the other provisions of this Convention and the competent authorities of the Contracting States shall if necessary consult each other.

ARTICLE 10

DIVIDENDS

1. Dividends paid by a company which is a resident of a Contracting State to a resident of the other Contracting State may be taxed in that other State.

2. However, dividends paid by a company which is a resident of a Contracting State may also be taxed in that State according to the laws of that State, but if the beneficial owner of the dividends is a resident of the other Contracting State, the tax so charged shall not exceed:

a)   5 per cent of the gross amount of the dividends if the beneficial owner is a company (other than a partnership) which holds directly at least 25 per cent of the capital of the company paying the dividends;

b)   15 per cent of the gross amount of the dividends in all other cases.

The competent authorities of the Contracting States shall by mutual agreement settle the mode of application of these limitations. This paragraph shall not affect the taxation of the company in respect of the profits out of which the dividends are paid.

3. The term "dividends" as used in this Article means income from shares, "jouissance" shares or "jouissance" rights, mining shares, founders' shares or other rights, not being debt-claims, participating in profits, as well as income from other corporate rights which is subjected to the same taxation treatment as income from shares by the laws of the State of which the company making the distribution is a resident.

4. The provisions of paragraphs 1 and 2 shall not apply if the beneficial owner of the dividends, being a resident of a Contracting State, carries on business in the other Contracting State of which the company paying the dividends is a resident through a permanent establishment situated therein and the holding in respect of which the dividends are paid is effectively connected with such permanent establishment. In such case the provisions of Article 7 shall apply.

5. Where a company which is a resident of a Contracting State derives profits or income from the other Contracting State, that other State may not impose any tax on the dividends paid by the company, except insofar as such dividends are paid to a resident of that other State or insofar as the holding in respect of which the dividends are paid is effectively connected with a permanent establishment situated in that other State, nor subject the company's undistributed profits to a tax on the company's undistributed profits, even if the dividends paid or the undistributed profits consist wholly or partly of profits or income arising in such other State.

ARTICLE 11

INTEREST

1. Interest arising in a Contracting State and paid to a resident of the other Contracting State may be taxed in that other State.

2. However, interest arising in a Contracting State may also be taxed in that State according to the laws of that State, but if the beneficial owner of the interest is a resident of the other Contracting State, the tax so charged shall not exceed 10 per cent of the gross amount of the interest. The competent authorities of the Contracting States shall by mutual agreement settle the mode of application of this limitation.

3. The term "interest" as used in this Article means income from debt-claims of every kind, whether or not secured by mortgage and whether or not carrying a right to participate in the debtor's profits, and in particular, income from government securities and income from bonds or debentures, including premiums and prizes attaching to such securities, bonds or debentures. Penalty charges for late payment shall not be regarded as interest for the purpose of this Article.

4. The provisions of paragraphs 1 and 2 shall not apply if the beneficial owner of the interest, being a resident of a Contracting State, carries on business in the other Contracting State in which the interest arises through a permanent establishment situated therein and the debt-claim in respect of which the interest is paid is effectively connected with such permanent establishment. In such case the provisions of Article 7 shall apply.

5. Interest shall be deemed to arise in a Contracting State when the payer is a resident of that State. Where, however, the person paying the interest, whether he is a resident of a Contracting State or not, has in a Contracting State a permanent establishment in connection with which the indebtedness on which the interest is paid was incurred, and such interest is borne by such permanent establishment, then such interest shall be deemed to arise in the State in which the permanent establishment is situated.

6. Where, by reason of a special relationship between the payer and the beneficial owner or between both of them and some other person, the amount of the interest, having regard to the debt-claim for which it is paid, exceeds the amount which would have been agreed upon by the payer and the beneficial owner in the absence of such relationship, the provisions of this Article shall apply only to the last-mentioned amount. In such case, the excess part of the payments shall remain taxable according to the laws of each Contracting State, due regard being had to the other provisions of this Convention.

ARTICLE 12

ROYALTIES

1. Royalties arising in a Contracting State and beneficially owned by a resident of the other Contracting State shall be taxable only in that other State.

2. The term "royalties" as used in this Article means payments of any kind received as a consideration for the use of, or the right to use, any copyright of literary, artistic or scientific work including cinematograph films, any patent, trade mark, design or model, plan, secret formula or process, or for information concerning industrial, commercial or scientific experience.

3. The provisions of paragraph 1 shall not apply if the beneficial owner of the royalties, being a resident of a Contracting State, carries on business in the other Contracting State in which the royalties arise through a permanent establishment situated therein and the right or property in respect of which the royalties are paid is effectively connected with such permanent establishment. In such case the provisions of Article 7 shall apply.

4. Where, by reason of a special relationship between the payer and the beneficial owner or between both of them and some other person, the amount of the royalties, having regard to the use, right or information for which they are paid, exceeds the amount which would have been agreed upon by the payer and the beneficial owner in the absence of such relationship, the provisions of this Article shall apply only to the last-mentioned amount. In such case, the excess part of the payments shall remain taxable according to the laws of each Contracting State, due regard being had to the other provisions of this Convention.

ARTICLE 13

CAPITAL GAINS

1. Gains derived by a resident of a Contracting State from the alienation of immovable property referred to in Article 6 and situated in the other Contracting State may be taxed in that other State.

2. Gains from the alienation of movable property forming part of the business property of a permanent establishment which an enterprise of a Contracting State has in the other Contracting State, including such gains from the alienation of such a permanent establishment (alone or with the whole enterprise), may be taxed in that other State.

3. Gains from the alienation of ships or aircraft operated in international traffic, boats engaged in inland waterways transport or movable property pertaining to the operation of such ships, aircraft or boats, shall be taxable only in the Contracting State in which the place of effective management of the enterprise is situated.

4. Gains derived by a resident of a Contracting State from the alienation of shares deriving more than 50 per cent of their value directly or indirectly from immovable property situated in the other Contracting State may be taxed in that other State.

5. Gains from the alienation of any property, other than that referred to in paragraphs 1, 2, 3 and 4, shall be taxable only in the Contracting State of which the alienator is a resident.

[ARTICLE 14 – INDEPENDENT PERSONAL SERVICES]

[Deleted]

ARTICLE 15

INCOME FROM EMPLOYMENT

1. Subject to the provisions of Articles 16, 18 and 19, salaries, wages and other similar remuneration derived by a resident of a Contracting State in respect of an employment shall be taxable only in that State unless the employment is exercised in the other Contracting State. If the employment is so exercised, such remuneration as is derived therefrom may be taxed in that other State.

2. Notwithstanding the provisions of paragraph 1, remuneration derived by a resident of a Contracting State in respect of an employment exercised in the other Contracting State shall be taxable only in the first-mentioned State if:

a)　the recipient is present in the other State for a period or periods not exceeding in the aggregate 183 days in any twelve month period commencing or ending in the fiscal year concerned, and

b)　the remuneration is paid by, or on behalf of, an employer who is not a resident of the other State, and *c)* the remuneration is not borne by a permanent establishment which the employer has in the other State.

3. Notwithstanding the preceding provisions of this Article, remuneration derived in respect of an employment exercised aboard a ship or aircraft operated in international traffic, or aboard a boat engaged in inland waterways transport, may be taxed in the Contracting State in which the place of effective management of the enterprise is situated.

ARTICLE 16

DIRECTORS' FEES

Directors' fees and other similar payments derived by a resident of a Contracting State in his capacity as a member of the board of directors of a company which is a resident of the other Contracting State may be taxed in that other State.

ARTICLE 17

ENTERTAINERS AND SPORTSMEN

1. Notwithstanding the provisions of Article 15, income derived by a resident of a Contracting State as an entertainer, such as a theatre, motion picture, radio or television artiste, or a musician, or as a sportsperson, from that resident's personal activities as such exercised in the other Contracting State, may be taxed in that other State.

2. Where income in respect of personal activities exercised by an entertainer or a sportsperson acting as such accrues not to the entertainer or sportsperson but to another person, that income may, notwithstanding the provisions of Article 15, be taxed in the Contracting State in which the activities of the entertainer or sportsperson are exercised.

ARTICLE 18

PENSIONS

Subject to the provisions of paragraph 2 of Article 19, pensions and other similar remuneration paid to a resident of a Contracting State in consideration of past employment shall be taxable only in that State.

ARTICLE 19

GOVERNMENT SERVICE

1. *a)* Salaries, wages and other similar remuneration paid by a Contracting State or a political subdivision or a local authority thereof to an individual in respect of services rendered to that State or subdivision or authority shall be taxable only in that State.

b) However, such salaries, wages and other similar remuneration shall be taxable only in the other Contracting State if the services are rendered in that State and the individual is a resident of that State who:

(i) is a national of that State; or

(ii) did not become a resident of that State solely for the purpose of rendering the services.

2. *a)* Notwithstanding the provisions of paragraph 1, pensions and other similar remuneration paid by, or out of funds created by, a Contracting State or a political subdivision or a local authority thereof to an individual in respect of services rendered to that State or subdivision or authority shall be taxable only in that State.

b) However, such pensions and other similar remuneration shall be taxable only in the other Contracting State if the individual is a resident of, and a national of, that State.

3. The provisions of Articles 15, 16, 17, and 18 shall apply to salaries, wages, pensions, and other similar remuneration in respect of services rendered in connection with a business carried on by a Contracting State or a political subdivision or a local authority thereof.

ARTICLE 20

STUDENTS

Payments which a student or business apprentice who is or was immediately before visiting a Contracting State a resident of the other Contracting State and who is present in the first-mentioned State solely for the purpose of his education or training receives for the purpose of his maintenance, education or training shall not be taxed in that State, provided that such payments arise from sources outside that State.

ARTICLE 21

OTHER INCOME

1. Items of income of a resident of a Contracting State, wherever arising, not dealt with in the foregoing Articles of this Convention shall be taxable only in that State.

2. The provisions of paragraph 1 shall not apply to income, other than income from immovable property as defined in paragraph 2 of Article 6, if the recipient of such income, being a resident of a Contracting State, carries on business in the other Contracting State through a permanent establishment situated therein and the right or property in respect of which the income is paid is effectively connected with such permanent establishment. In such case the provisions of Article 7 shall apply.

Appendix

Chapter IV

TAXATION OF CAPITAL

ARTICLE 22

CAPITAL

1. Capital represented by immovable property referred to in Article 6, owned by a resident of a Contracting State and situated in the other Contracting State, may be taxed in that other State.

2. Capital represented by movable property forming part of the business property of a permanent establishment which an enterprise of a Contracting State has in the other Contracting State may be taxed in that other State.

3. Capital represented by ships and aircraft operated in international traffic and by boats engaged in inland waterways transport, and by movable property pertaining to the operation of such ships, aircraft and boats, shall be taxable only in the Contracting State in which the place of effective management of the enterprise is situated.

4. All other elements of capital of a resident of a Contracting State shall be taxable only in that State.

Chapter V

METHODS FOR ELIMINATION OF DOUBLE TAXATION

ARTICLE 23 A

EXEMPTION METHOD

1. Where a resident of a Contracting State derives income or owns capital which, in accordance with the provisions of this Convention, may be taxed in the other Contracting State, the first-mentioned State shall, subject to the provisions of paragraphs 2 and 3, exempt such income or capital from tax.

2. Where a resident of a Contracting State derives items of income which, in accordance with the provisions of Articles 10 and 11, may be taxed in the other Contracting State, the first-mentioned State shall allow as a deduction from the tax on the income of that resident an amount equal to the tax paid in that other State. Such deduction shall not, however, exceed that part of the tax, as computed before the deduction is given, which is attributable to such items of income derived from that other State.

3. Where in accordance with any provision of the Convention income derived or capital owned by a resident of a Contracting State is exempt from tax in that State, such State may nevertheless, in calculating the amount of tax on the remaining income or capital of such resident, take into account the exempted income or capital.

4. The provisions of paragraph 1 shall not apply to income derived or capital owned by a resident of a Contracting State where the other Contracting State applies the provisions of this Convention to exempt such income or capital from tax or applies the provisions of paragraph 2 of Article 10 or 11 to such income.

ARTICLE 23

B CREDIT METHOD

1. Where a resident of a Contracting State derives income or owns capital which, in accordance with the provisions of this Convention, may be taxed in the other Contracting State, the first-mentioned State shall allow:

a)   as a deduction from the tax on the income of that resident, an amount equal to the income tax paid in that other State;

b)   as a deduction from the tax on the capital of that resident, an amount equal to the capital tax paid in that other State.

Such deduction in either case shall not, however, exceed that part of the income tax or capital tax, as computed before the deduction is given, which is attributable, as the case may be, to the income or the capital which may be taxed in that other State.

2. Where in accordance with any provision of the Convention income derived or capital owned by a resident of a Contracting State is exempt from tax in that State, such State may nevertheless, in calculating the amount of tax on the remaining income or capital of such resident, take into account the exempted income or capital.

Chapter VI

SPECIAL PROVISIONS

ARTICLE 24

NON-DISCRIMINATION

1. Nationals of a Contracting State shall not be subjected in the other Contracting State to any taxation or any requirement connected therewith, which is other or more burdensome than the taxation and connected requirements to which nationals of that other State in the same circumstances, in particular with respect to residence, are or may be subjected. This provision shall, notwithstanding the provisions of Article 1, also apply to persons who are not residents of one or both of the Contracting States.

2. Stateless persons who are residents of a Contracting State shall not be subjected in either Contracting State to any taxation or any requirement connected therewith, which is other or more burdensome than the taxation and connected

requirements to which nationals of the State concerned in the same circumstances, in particular with respect to residence, are or may be subjected.

3. The taxation on a permanent establishment which an enterprise of a Contracting State has in the other Contracting State shall not be less favourably levied in that other State than the taxation levied on enterprises of that other State carrying on the same activities. This provision shall not be construed as obliging a Contracting State to grant to residents of the other Contracting State any personal allowances, reliefs and reductions for taxation purposes on account of civil status or family responsibilities which it grants to its own residents.

4. Except where the provisions of paragraph 1 of Article 9, paragraph 6 of Article 11, or paragraph 4 of Article 12, apply, interest, royalties and other disbursements paid by an enterprise of a Contracting State to a resident of the other Contracting State shall, for the purpose of determining the taxable profits of such enterprise, be deductible under the same conditions as if they had been paid to a resident of the first-mentioned State. Similarly, any debts of an enterprise of a Contracting State to a resident of the other Contracting State shall, for the purpose of determining the taxable capital of such enterprise, be deductible under the same conditions as if they had been contracted to a resident of the first-mentioned State.

5. Enterprises of a Contracting State, the capital of which is wholly or partly owned or controlled, directly or indirectly, by one or more residents of the other Contracting State, shall not be subjected in the first-mentioned State to any taxation or any requirement connected therewith which is other or more burdensome than the taxation and connected requirements to which other similar enterprises of the first- mentioned State are or may be subjected.

6. The provisions of this Article shall, notwithstanding the provisions of Article 2, apply to taxes of every kind and description.

ARTICLE 25

MUTUAL AGREEMENT PROCEDURE

1. Where a person considers that the actions of one or both of the Contracting States result or will result for him in taxation not in accordance with the provisions of this Convention, he may, irrespective of the remedies provided by the domestic law of those States, present his case to the competent authority of the Contracting State of which he is a resident or, if his case comes under paragraph 1 of Article 24, to that of the Contracting State of which he is a national. The case must be presented within three years from the first notification of the action resulting in taxation not in accordance with the provisions of the Convention.

2. The competent authority shall endeavour, if the objection appears to it to be justified and if it is not itself able to arrive at a satisfactory solution, to resolve the case by mutual agreement with the competent authority of the other Contracting State, with a view to the avoidance of taxation which is not in

accordance with the Convention. Any agreement reached shall be implemented notwithstanding any time limits in the domestic law of the Contracting States.

3. The competent authorities of the Contracting States shall endeavour to resolve by mutual agreement any difficulties or doubts arising as to the interpretation or application of the Convention. They may also consult together for the elimination of double taxation in cases not provided for in the Convention.

4. The competent authorities of the Contracting States may communicate with each other directly, including through a joint commission consisting of themselves or their representatives, for the purpose of reaching an agreement in the sense of the preceding paragraphs.

5. Where,

a)   under paragraph 1, a person has presented a case to the competent authority of a Contracting State on the basis that the actions of one or both of the Contracting States have resulted for that person in taxation not in accordance with the provisions of this Convention, and

b)   the competent authorities are unable to reach an agreement to resolve that case pursuant to paragraph 2 within two years from the presentation of the case to the competent authority of the other Contracting State,

any unresolved issues arising from the case shall be submitted to arbitration if the person so requests. These unresolved issues shall not, however, be submitted to arbitration if a decision on these issues has already been rendered by a court or administrative tribunal of either State. Unless a person directly affected by the case does not accept the mutual agreement that implements the arbitration decision, that decision shall be binding on both Contracting States and shall be implemented notwithstanding any time limits in the domestic laws of these States. The competent authorities of the Contracting States shall by mutual agreement settle the mode of application of this paragraph.[1]

---

1   In some States, national law, policy or administrative considerations may not allow or justify the type of dispute resolution envisaged under this paragraph. In addition, some States may only wish to include this paragraph in treaties with certain States. For these reasons, the paragraph should only be included in the Convention where each State concludes that it would be appropriate to do so based on the factors described in paragraph 65 of the Commentary on the paragraph. As mentioned in paragraph 74 of that Commentary, however, other States may be able to agree to remove from the paragraph the condition that issues may not be submitted to arbitration if a decision on these issues has already been rendered by one of their courts or administrative tribunals.

ARTICLE 26

EXCHANGE OF INFORMATION

1. The competent authorities of the Contracting States shall exchange such information as is foreseeably relevant for carrying out the provisions of this Convention or to the administration or enforcement of the domestic laws concerning taxes of every kind and description imposed on behalf of the Contracting States, or of their political subdivisions or local authorities, insofar as the

taxation thereunder is not contrary to the Convention. The exchange of information is not restricted by Articles 1 and 2.

2. Any information received under paragraph 1 by a Contracting State shall be treated as secret in the same manner as information obtained under the domestic laws of that State and shall be disclosed only to persons or authorities (including courts and administrative bodies) concerned with the assessment or collection of, the enforcement or prosecution in respect of, the determination of appeals in relation to the taxes referred to in paragraph 1, or the oversight of the above. Such persons or authorities shall use the information only for such purposes. They may disclose the information in public court proceedings or in judicial decisions. Notwithstanding the foregoing, information received by a Contracting State may be used for other purposes when such information may be used for such other purposes under the laws of both States and the competent authority of the supplying State authorises such use.

3. In no case shall the provisions of paragraphs 1 and 2 be construed so as to impose on a Contracting State the obligation:

a)　　to carry out administrative measures at variance with the laws and administrative practice of that or of the other Contracting State;

b)　　to supply information which is not obtainable under the laws or in the normal course of the administration of that or of the other Contracting State;

c)　　to supply information which would disclose any trade, business, industrial, commercial or professional secret or trade process, or information the disclosure of which would be contrary to public policy (*ordre public*).

4. If information is requested by a Contracting State in accordance with this Article, the other Contracting State shall use its information gathering measures to obtain the requested information, even though that other State may not need such information for its own tax purposes. The obligation contained in the preceding sentence is subject to the limitations of paragraph 3 but in no case shall such limitations be construed to permit a Contracting State to decline to supply information solely because it has no domestic interest in such information.

5. In no case shall the provisions of paragraph 3 be construed to permit a Contracting State to decline to supply information solely because the information is held by a bank, other financial institution, nominee or person acting in an agency or a fiduciary capacity or because it relates to ownership interests in a person.

ARTICLE 27

ASSISTANCE IN THE COLLECTION OF TAXES[1]

1. The Contracting States shall lend assistance to each other in the collection of revenue claims. This assistance is not restricted by Articles 1 and 2.

The competent authorities of the Contracting States may by mutual agreement settle the mode of application of this Article.

2. The term "revenue claim" as used in this Article means an amount owed in respect of taxes of every kind and description imposed on behalf of the Contracting States, or of their political subdivisions or local authorities, insofar as the taxation thereunder is not contrary to this Convention or any other instrument to which the Contracting States are parties, as well as interest, administrative penalties and costs of collection or conservancy related to such amount.

3. When a revenue claim of a Contracting State is enforceable under the laws of that State and is owed by a person who, at that time, cannot, under the laws of that State, prevent its collection, that revenue claim shall, at the request of the competent authority of that State, be accepted for purposes of collection by the competent authority of the other Contracting State. That revenue claim shall be collected by that other State in accordance with the provisions of its laws applicable to the enforcement and collection of its own taxes as if the revenue claim were a revenue claim of that other State.

4. When a revenue claim of a Contracting State is a claim in respect of which that State may, under its law, take measures of conservancy with a view to ensure its collection, that revenue claim shall, at the request of the competent authority of that State, be accepted for purposes of taking measures of conservancy by the competent authority of the other Contracting State. That other State shall take measures of conservancy in respect of that revenue claim in accordance with the provisions of its laws as if the revenue claim were a revenue claim of that other State even if, at the time when such measures are applied, the revenue claim is not enforceable in the first-mentioned State or is owed by a person who has a right to prevent its collection.

---

1 In some countries, national law, policy or administrative considerations may not allow or justify the type of assistance envisaged under this Article or may require that this type of assistance be restricted, *e.g.* to countries that have similar tax systems or tax administrations or as to the taxes covered. For that reason, the Article should only be included in the Convention where each State concludes that, based on the factors described in paragraph 1 of the Commentary on the Article, they can agree to provide assistance in the collection of taxes levied by the other State.

---

5. Notwithstanding the provisions of paragraphs 3 and 4, a revenue claim accepted by a Contracting State for purposes of paragraph 3 or 4 shall not, in that State, be subject to the time limits or accorded any priority applicable to a revenue claim under the laws of that State by reason of its nature as such. In addition, a revenue claim accepted by a Contracting State for the purposes of paragraph 3 or 4 shall not, in that State, have any priority applicable to that revenue claim under the laws of the other Contracting State.

6. Proceedings with respect to the existence, validity or the amount of a revenue claim of a Contracting State shall not be brought before the courts or administrative bodies of the other Contracting State.

7. Where, at any time after a request has been made by a Contracting State under paragraph 3 or 4 and before the other Contracting State has collected and

remitted the relevant revenue claim to the first-mentioned State, the relevant revenue claim ceases to be

a)   in the case of a request under paragraph 3, a revenue claim of the first-mentioned State that is enforceable under the laws of that State and is owed by a person who, at that time, cannot, under the laws of that State, prevent its collection, or

b)   in the case of a request under paragraph 4, a revenue claim of the first-mentioned State in respect of which that State may, under its laws, take measures of conservancy with a view to ensure its collection

the competent authority of the first-mentioned State shall promptly notify the competent authority of the other State of that fact and, at the option of the other State, the first-mentioned State shall either suspend or withdraw its request.

8. In no case shall the provisions of this Article be construed so as to impose on a Contracting State the obligation:

a)   to carry out administrative measures at variance with the laws and administrative practice of that or of the other Contracting State;

b)   to carry out measures which would be contrary to public policy (*ordre public*);

c)   to provide assistance if the other Contracting State has not pursued all reasonable measures of collection or conservancy, as the case may be, available under its laws or administrative practice;

d)   to provide assistance in those cases where the administrative burden for that State is clearly disproportionate to the benefit to be derived by the other Contracting State.

ARTICLE 28

MEMBERS OF DIPLOMATIC MISSIONS AND CONSULAR POSTS

Nothing in this Convention shall affect the fiscal privileges of members of diplomatic missions or consular posts under the general rules of international law or under the provisions of special agreements.

ARTICLE 29

TERRITORIAL EXTENSION[1]

1. This Convention may be extended, either in its entirety or with any necessary modifications [to any part of the territory of (State A) or of (State B) which is specifically excluded from the application of the Convention or], to any State or territory for whose international relations (State A) or (State B) is responsible, which imposes taxes substantially similar in character to those to which the Convention applies. Any such extension shall take effect from such

date and subject to such modifications and conditions, including conditions as to termination, as may be specified and agreed between the Contracting States in notes to be exchanged through diplomatic channels or in any other manner in accordance with their constitutional procedures.

2. Unless otherwise agreed by both Contracting States, the termination of the Convention by one of them under Article 30 shall also terminate, in the manner provided for in that Article, the application of the Convention [to any part of the territory of (State A) or of (State B) or] to any State or territory to which it has been extended under this Article.

---

1 The words between brackets are of relevance when, by special provision, a part of the territory of a Contracting State is excluded from the application of the Convention.

Chapter VII

FINAL PROVISIONS

ARTICLE 30

ENTRY INTO FORCE

1.   This Convention shall be ratified and the instruments of ratification shall be exchanged at .... as soon as possible.

2.   The Convention shall enter into force upon the exchange of instruments of ratification and its provisions shall have effect:

a)   (in State A): ....

b)   (in State B): ....

ARTICLE 31

TERMINATION

This Convention shall remain in force until terminated by a Contracting State. Either Contracting State may terminate the Convention, through diplomatic channels, by giving notice of termination at least six months before the end of any calendar year after the year ...... In such event, the Convention shall cease to have effect:

a)   (in State A): ....

b)   (in State B): ....

TERMINAL CLAUSE[1]

---

1 The terminal clause concerning the signing shall be drafted in accordance with the constitutional procedure of both Contracting States.

Index

[all references are to paragraph number]